Principles of Forensic Medicine and Toxicology

Principles of Forensic Medicine and Toxicology

Rajesh Bardale MD

Department of Forensic Medicine
Government Medical College and Hospital
Nagpur (Maharashtra), India

JAYPEE BROTHERS MEDICAL PUBLISHERS (P) LTD

New Delhi • Panama City • London

Jaypee Brothers Medical Publishers (P) Ltd.

Headquarter

Jaypee Brothers Medical Publishers (P) Ltd
4838/24, Ansari Road, Daryaganj
New Delhi 110 002, India
Phone: +91-11-43574357
Fax: +91-11-43574314
Email: jaypee@jaypeebrothers.com

Overseas Offices

J.P. Medical Ltd.,
83 Victoria Street London
SW1H 0HW (UK)
Phone: +44-2031708910
Fax: +02-03-0086180
Email: info@jpmedpub.com

Jaypee-Highlights Medical Publishers Inc.
City of Knowledge, Bld. 237, Clayton
Panama City, Panama
Phone: 507-317-0160
Fax: +50-73-010499
Email: cservice@jphmedical.com

Website: www.jaypeebrothers.com
Website: www.jaypeedigital.com

Inquiries for bulk sales may be solicited at: jaypee@jaypeebrothers.com

Publisher: Jitendar P Vij
Publishing Director: Tarun Duneja
Editor: Richa Saxena
Cover Design: Seema Dogra

Principles of Forensic Medicine and Toxicology
First Edition: **2011**

ISBN 978-93-5025-493-6

Printed at: Replika Press Pvt. Ltd.

Dedicated to

My Wife Sheetal and
Daughter Tanaya

Preface

It is with great pleasure that I am presenting the book, *Principles of Forensic Medicine and Toxicology*. The book is primarily designed for undergraduates and presented in a simple and lucid language. For ease of students, conventional pattern has been modified whenever feasible and the contents are presented in point-wise manner. About 337 tables and about 638 photographs and flow charts are added for easy understanding and learning. Keeping with contemporary period, recent advances are included. A new chapter, Forensic Osteology, is added and aimed to cater theoretical and practical need of students. Latest trends in management of poisoned patients have been included.

While preparing this textbook, I have consulted various textbooks and journals and I am indebted to these authors.

I hope this book will serve the purpose and help students to learn the subject in easy way. The suggestions and healthy criticism will be of immense help for future improvement of this book.

Rajesh Bardale
E-mail: bardalerv@yahoo.co.in

Acknowledgments

It is not possible to accomplish such enduring job without the help of innumerable people; indeed many give the indispensable impulsion to proceed with the task. This is small way to express a deep sense of gratitude towards them.

- I gratefully acknowledge Prof Dr VV Pillay MD, DCL (Professor, Department of Forensic Medicine and Toxicology and Chief, Department of Analytical Toxicology, Amrita Institute of Medical Sciences and Research, Cochin, Kerala) since he has been great source of inspiration to undertake this task. Probably without such inspiration, I would not have undertaken such work.
- I am indebted to my revered teacher and guide, Prof Dr AP Dongre MD, LLB (former Professor and Head, Department of Forensic Medicine and Toxicology, Indira Gandhi Government Medical College, Nagpur), Dean, IGGMC, Nagpur for his valuable support.
- I am obliged to Prof Dr PG Dixit MD (FMT), MD (Path), PGDMLS (Professor and Head, Department of Forensic Medicine and Toxicology, Government Medical College, Nagpur) for his valuable support, constant encouragement and providing photographs.
- I am indebted to Prof Dr SS Gupta MD (Professor and Head, Department of Forensic Medicine and Toxicology, SBH Government Medical College, Dhule) for nurturing me while learning. He always remains helpful whenever I was in need.
- I am indebted to Prof Dr HT Katade MD (FMT), MD (Path) (formerly Professor and Head, Department of Forensic Medicine and Toxicology, Government Medical College, Akola) Dean, GMC, Akola for his unrelenting help and constant encouragement.
- I am grateful to Dr Shailendra Dhawane MD, DNB (Associate Professor, Department of Forensic Medicine and Toxicology, VN Government Medical College, Yavatmal) and Dr AA Mukherjee, MD (Associate Professor, Department of Forensic Medicine and Toxicology, Government Medical College, Akola), the duo, without whom the endeavor have never seen the light of day.
- I am indebted to Dr Manish Shrigiriwar MD (Associate Professor, Department of Forensic Medicine and Toxicology, Indira Gandhi Government Medical College, Nagpur) for his help, support and providing photographs.
- I am indebted to Dr Vipul Ambade MD, LLB (Associate Professor, Department of Forensic Medicine and Toxicology, Government Medical College, Nagpur) for his help and providing photographs.
- I am thankful to Dr Vaibhav Sonar MD (Lecturer, Department of Forensic Medicine and Toxicology, GMC, Miraj) for his constant help and providing photographs.
- I am thankful to Shri Jitendar P Vij, Chairman and Managing Director, M/s Jaypee Brothers Medical Publishers (P) Ltd., New Delhi for believing me and encouraging me to go ahead with the project. I am thankful to Mr Tarun Duneja (Director-Publishing) and his entire editorial team for kind co-operation and nice printing of the book. I am also thankful to Mr Prasun Bhattacharjee and his team members of Nagpur branch for rendering help.
- I express my sincere gratitude to the authors/writers/editors of the various textbooks and journals whose references have been cited in the text.
- Finally, I express my deep sense of gratitude and acknowledgment to my wife Sheetal and daughter Tanaya in accomplishing the task. They have been very enduring, cooperative and stood by me through all the odds.

Contents

Section A: Forensic Medicine

Section B: Toxicology

Section A
Forensic Medicine

CHAPTER 1

Legal Procedure

If the law has made you a witness, remain a man of science. You have no victim to avenge, no guilty man to convict, and no innocent man to save. You must bear testimony within the limits of science.

—Paul H Bouardel

Forensic Medicine and Medical Jurisprudence are not synonymous terms. Though they are related to each other, however, carry different meaning. *Forensic Medicine deals with application of medical knowledge in the administration of law and justice*. In fact the word 'Forensic' is derived from the Latin word *forensis*–meaning forum that was the meeting place where civic and legal matters were discussed by people with public responsibility. Here doctor is expected to use his medical knowledge, which is helpful in solving civil and criminal matters. For example if a person is brought to doctor by police with alleged history of consumption of alcohol and causing public nuisance then doctor is expected to examine the person and opine whether he has consumed the alcohol and if yes then whether he is under its influence or not? Then doctor have to issue a certificate to police and also have to collect necessary samples (e.g. blood, urine) and forward to forensic science laboratory for further analysis. Other examples include application of medical knowledge in injuries, alleged murder, alleged sexual offenses, cases, pregnancy and delivery etc. Thus this branch of medicine deals with medical aspects of law.

The term *Medical Jurisprudence (juris = law, prudentia = knowledge) deals with legal aspect of medical practice*. This branch deals with legal responsibilities of doctor while practicing medicine. For example doctor is expected to have knowledge regarding disposal of hospital waste as per the Biomedical Waste (Management and Handling) Rules 1998. Other examples include – having knowledge of the Medical Termination of Pregnancy Act, medical negligence, consent, medical ethics, professional misconduct, doctor-patient relationship, rights of doctor, etc. In other words this branch deals with legal aspects while practicing medicine.

Medical men have to appear in Court of law to give evidence in matters related with medicolegal cases. Therefore it will be helpful if doctors are acquainted with legal procedure, legal terms and court procedures.

INQUEST (IN = IN, QUEST = TO SEEK)

Definition

An inquest is a legal inquiry or investigation to ascertain the circumstances and cause of death.

- It is conducted in sudden, suspicious or unnatural deaths.
- There are four types of inquests:
  - Police inquest
  - Magistrate inquest
  - Coroner inquest
  - Medical Examiner's system
- Only Police and Magistrate's inquest are held in India.

Police Inquest

- The inquest is held under section 174 of CrPC.
- It is conducted by the police officer, usually not below the rank of police subinspector.
- The officer conducting the inquest is called as "Investigating Officer" (IO).
- On receipt of information about any sudden, suspicious or unnatural death of any person, the IO forwards the information to the nearest Magistrate and proceeds to the place where the dead body is lying. At that place, the IO in presence of two or more responsible persons of the area (called as Panchas) makes an investigation and prepares a report called as Panchnama.

- The Panchnama (inquest report) includes the description of scene of crime, apparent cause of death and presence of any injuries over body. The IO and the panchas then sign the report. The IO then forwards the dead body to the nearest government doctor with the requisition and a copy of inquest report (Panchnama).

Magistrate Inquest

- Magistrate inquest is held under section 176 CrPC.
- The Magistrate empowered to hold inquests are: District magistrate, Sub-divisional Magistrate or any other Executive Magistrate specially empowered in this on behalf of the State Government or the District Magistrate.
- It is considered to be superior to police inquest.
- Magistrate inquest is done in following circumstances:
  - Death in prison/jail
  - Death in police custody
  - Death due to police firing
  - Exhumation
  - Dowry death (Under section 304 B of IPC)
  - Death in mental hospital
- Similarly in any case of death, the Magistrate can conduct an inquest instead of police inquest or in addition to the police inquest.
- Difference between police and Magistrate inquest are summarized in Table 1.1.

Coroner's Inquest

- Under Coroner's Act 1871, previously it was held at Kolkata (Calcutta) and Mumbai (Bombay). However it was abolished in Kolkata way back and was discontinued on 29 July 1999 in Mumbai.
- A Coroner was an Officer of the rank of First Class Magistrate, appointed by State Government. The Coroner may be a doctor or a lawyer or both. Under Coroner's Act, the Coroner was empowered to inquire all unnatural or suspicious deaths and death occurring in jail. After examining a body he then decide whether an autopsy is required and if necessary he holds an inquiry and forward the body to government doctor for postmortem examination. He had also power to order for exhumation.
- Coroner's court is only court of inquiry into the cause of death. In pursuance of investigation, the Coroner examines witnesses on oath and records their evidence. After completion of an inquiry, the Coroner finds a *verdict* as to the cause of death. If the coroner founds a verdict of foul play, he issues warrant to the concerned accused and then handed over the case to the concerned Metropolitan Magistrate. When the accused was not found, the Coroner returns an open verdict. *Open verdict means an announcement of the commission of crime without information regarding the accused.*

Table 1.1: Difference between police and magistrate inquest

Police inquest	*Magistrate inquest*
1. Conducted by police	1. Conducted by District Magistrate, Sub-divisional Magistrate or Executive Magistrate
2. Cannot hold inquest in death in jail, police custody, due to police firing or dowry death	2. Can hold inquest in death in jail, police custody, due to police firing or dowry death
3. Investigation is considered inferior to Magistrate investigation	3. Investigation is considered superior to police investigation
4. Cannot order for exhumation	4. Can order for exhumation

Medical Examiner System

- Medical examiner system is a type of inquest prevalent in most states of USA.
- This type of inquest is done by a Medical Examiner who is a Forensic Pathologist. All sorts of sudden, unnatural or suspicious deaths are analyzed by Medical Examiner.
- This type of investigation is considered to be superior to all other type of investigations. In India this system is not followed.

COURTS

There are two types of Courts of law in India and they are:
1. Civil Courts
2. Criminal Courts

The criminal courts deal with criminal cases and are of four types and they are (Fig. 1.1):
i. The Supreme Court
ii. The High Court
iii. The Sessions Court
iv. The Magistrate Court

Powers of different Criminal courts are summarized in Table 1.2

Table 1.2: Powers of different criminal courts

Court	Imprisonment and fine
1. The Supreme Court	Can award any punishment provided in law
2. The High Court	Can award any punishment provided in law
3. The Sessions Judge	Can award any punishment provided in law*
4. The Additional Sessions Judge	Can award any punishment provided in law*
5. The Assistant Sessions Judge	Imprisonment up to 10 years
6. Chief Judicial Magistrate *Or* Chief Metropolitan Magistrate	• Imprisonment up to 7 years • Unlimited fine
7. First class Judicial Magistrate *Or* Metropolitan Magistrate	• Imprisonment up to 3 years • Fine not exceeding 5000 rupees
8. Second class Judicial Magistrate	• Imprisonment up to 1 year • Fine not exceeding 1000 rupees

*Death sentence passed by Sessions Court must be confirmed by the high court

The Supreme Court

- Located at Delhi and is the highest judicial tribunal in the country.
- It supervises all the courts in India and the rulings of Supreme Court are binding on all courts.
- For criminal cases, it acts as appeal court. No criminal case can be initiated in the Supreme Court.

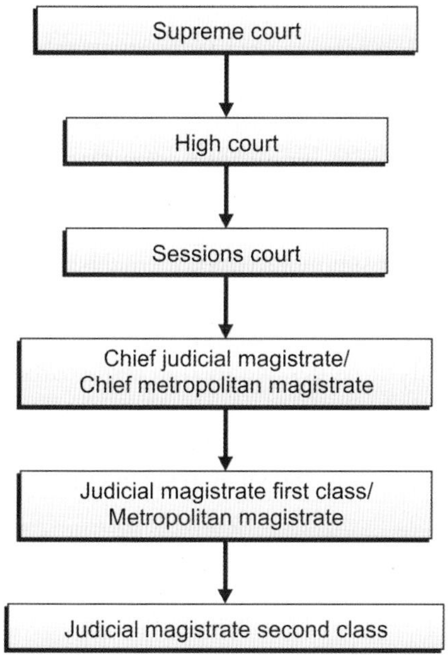

FIG. 1.1: Structure of courts in India

- It can sustain or alter the punishment awarded by lower courts.

The High Court

- Generally they are located in the capital of state and are the highest tribunal in that state.
- It deals with appeal criminal cases.
- Confirms the death sentence passed in a Sessions court.

The Sessions Court

- Usually located at district headquarters.
- The court of sessions is presided by a senior judge known as Principal courts of sessions and other courts of sessions are called as Additional Courts of Sessions.
- The Sessions court can pass any sentence authorized by law; however, death sentence passed by it must be confirmed by the high court.

Assistant Sessions Court

- Usually located at sub-division in a district.
- Presiding officer is called as Assistant Sessions Judge.
- An Assistant Sessions court can pass a sentence of imprisonment up to 10 years and unlimited fine.

Magistrate's Court

They are of three types namely:

1. Chief Judicial Magistrate
2. First Class Judicial Magistrate
3. Second Class Judicial Magistrate
   - In metropolitan cities, the Chief Judicial Magistrate is designated as Chief Metropolitan Magistrate and

First Class Judicial Magistrate as Metropolitan Magistrate.
- In every district, the High court appoints a judicial magistrate of first class to be the Chief Judicial Magistrate for the purpose of general control.

Special Courts[1]

- In some districts, Mahila courts have been established to try offenses against women. The Mahila courts are Additional court of Sessions presided by women judge.
- Special courts of sessions are also established to try offenses under Scheduled caste (SC), Scheduled tribe (ST), Prevention of Atrocities Act, Essential Commodities Act, Narcotic Drugs and Psychotropic Substance Act (NDPS), Terrorists and Disruptive Activities Act (TADA). Prevention of Terrorism Act (POTA), Maharashtra Control of Organized Crime Act (MCOOCA) and cases of economic offenses and corruption.

Juvenile Courts[2]

- The Juvenile Justice (Care and protection of children) Act 2000 has provided that a "**juvenile**" (or child) is a person who has not completed eighteen year of age. It is uniform for both sexes i.e. for boys and girls.
- 'Juvenile in conflict with law' means a juvenile who is alleged to have committed an offense. The juvenile offenders are produced before the Juvenile Justice Board. The Juvenile Justice boards are constituted to make juvenile system meant for juvenile and are more appreciative for the developmental needs of children in comparison to criminal justice system as applicable to adults.
- The Juvenile Justice Board consists of three persons comprising of:
  1. One the Metropolitan Magistrate or a Judicial Magistrate of the first class as the case may be.
  2. Two social workers, of whom at least one shall be a woman.
- Every such Bench shall have the powers conferred by the code of Criminal Procedure.
- The Metropolitan Magistrate or a Judicial Magistrate of the first class, as the case may be, shall be designated as the Principal Magistrate.
- Where an inquiry into a juvenile offender ceases to be a juvenile, the inquiry shall continue in the same bench.

Punishments

As per section 53 of IPC, the various punishments that can be awarded are:

1. Death sentence
2. Imprisonment for life (regarded as equal to 20 years in prison)
3. Imprisonment- either- rigorous (with hard labour) or simple
4. Forfeiture of property
5. Fine
   - Fine and imprisonment may be awarded one along with or without the other.
   - Capital punishment refers to death sentence and in India it is carried out by hanging.

Offenses

The offenses may be:

1. Cognizable
2. Non-cognizable
   - Cognizable offense refers to an offense in which a police officer can arrest a person without warrant from the Magistrate. Examples are – rape, murder, dowry death, ragging etc.
   - In non-cognizable offense, for arrest of a person, a warrant from the Magistrate is necessary without which a police officer cannot arrest a person.

Different Types of Cases

The cases may be:

1. Criminal cases
2. Civil cases

Criminal cases: are related with commission of crimes and are tried in criminal courts. The cases may be of following types:

- **Cognizable cases**: related with cognizable offenses
- **Non-cognizable cases**: related with non-cognizable offenses
- **Warrant cases**: the offenses punishable with death, imprisonment for life or for a term exceeding two years are treated as warrant case.
- **Summons cases**: these are the cases, which are not warrant cases. In summons cases, the punishment for offense does not exceed more than two years.

Civil cases: These are the cases related with disputes between two individuals or parties and tried in civil courts. These cases are not related to offense or crimes. The individual who lodges the complaint is called as **complainant** and the other individual (the opposite party) is known as **respondent**.

SUMMONS OR SUBPOENA

Definition

A summons is a writ compelling the attendance of the witness in a court of law, at a specified place and time, and for a specified purpose under penalty (Subpoena, sub = under, poena = penalty).

Types

These are of two types and are:
1. Subpoena adtestificandum
2. Subpoena duces tecum.

Subpoena adtestificandum *is a type of summons where a person is directed to appear personally before court to give evidence.*

Subpoena duces tecum *is a type of summons served to witness only to submit a document.*

Procedure

A summons is issued by the Court in writing, in duplicate, signed by the presiding officer (Judge) and bears the seal of the court. It is served to witness by a police officer or an officer of the court or other government servant specifically authorized for the purpose. After receiving a summons, the witness should sign the other copy of summons and one copy is to be kept with him.

- A summons must be obeyed and the court must be attended on specified date and time. If the witness has a valid and urgent reason, he should communicate to the court.
- In spite of summons served on a person and if the witness remains absent without any sufficient reason, the court may issue bailable or non-bailable warrant or may order to attach the property of that person.
- In criminal cases, if court issues notice to witness under section 350 of CrPC and if court finds that witness has neglected or refused to attend, the court may sentence him to fine not exceeding one hundred rupees.
- Disobedience of summons issued by court is also an offense punishable under section 172 of IPC and the punishment may extend to simple imprisonment for six months or fine of Rs 100 or both.
- If a witness receives two summonses from different courts, say for example civil and criminal court, on same day, then the doctor should give priority to criminal court and accordingly inform to civil court. If two courts (criminal or civil) summons doctor (Witness) on the same day then, the witness should first attend the higher court. However, if a witness received summons from two different courts (civil or criminal) of same status, then the doctor should attend the court from where he received the summons first and inform the other court accordingly and can attend the second court after finishing his evidence in the first court.

Conduct Money

- It is the money given or paid to a witness in civil cases to meet the expenses towards attending the court.
- In civil cases, conduct money is paid to the doctor at the time of serving the summons. If the money is not paid or the doctor feels that the sum paid is inadequate, he can inform the court accordingly. Then the judge will decide regarding the amount to be paid.
- In criminal cases, no such money is paid to the witness at the time of serving the summons. The witness must attend the court because every citizen is duty bound to attend the court whenever summoned. However, conveyance charges and daily allowance is paid to the doctor according to the prevailing government rules.

MEDICAL EVIDENCE

Definition

Evidence means and includes

1. *All statements which the court permits or requires to be made before it by a witness in relation to matters of fact under inquiry (such statements are called as oral evidence).*
2. *All documents produced for the inspection of the court (such documents are called as documentary evidence).*

Types

Medical evidence is of following types:
1. Documentary evidence
2. Oral evidence

Documentary Evidence

It comprises of documents produced before the court and includes:
1. Medical certificate
2. Medico-legal report
3. Dying declaration etc.

Medical Certificates

- These are the certificates issued by the doctor regarding ill-health (sickness certificate), unsoundness of mind, death certificate, birth certificate, fitness certificate etc.
- These certificates are the simplest forms of documentary evidence.
- Only certificates given by registered medical practitioners (RMP) registered with state medical council are accepted in the court of law as evidence.

- Doctors should exercise due care while issuing such certificates. Issuing a false certificate is an offense.

Medico-legal Reports

- Medicolegal reports are the documents prepared and issued by doctors on the request of the investigating officer (Police or Magistrate), usually in criminal cases such as assault, rape, murder etc.
- Examples of such reports are: Injury certificate, age report, postmortem reports, reports regarding examination of exhibits such as weapons, clothes etc.
- Generally these reports are made of three parts *viz.*:
  1. Part I – Introduction (Preamble): Comprising of preliminary data such as name of person, age, sex, address, identification marks, date and time of examination etc.
  2. Part II – Examination (Observation): Consisting of the findings observed and recorded by doctor and entered in the report.
  3. Part II – Opinion (Inference): Consisting of opinion or inference drawn by the doctor from the medical examination.
- The report should be written with great care and should bear the signature and name of the examining doctor.
- Any exhibits, e.g. clothes or weapons etc. sent for medical examination should be described in detail with appropriate diagram/sketches whenever applicable then these articles should be properly sealed, labeled and returned to the investigating officer.

Dying Declaration

Definition: *A dying declaration is a statement, verbal or written, made by a person as to the cause of his death, or as to any of the circumstances of the transaction which resulted in his death (Section 32 IEA).*

Whenever such patients are admitted and who are going to die, the doctor should call the Magistrate to record dying declaration. Before recording the statement, doctor should certify that the person is conscious and have sound mind (compos mentis). If the dying person is serious and there is no time to call the Magistrate, then doctor should record the dying declaration. When doctor or Magistrate is not available, dying declaration recorded by investigating officer is also admissible under section 32 of IEA. No oath is administered while recording a dying declaration since it is believed that the dying person tells the truth only.

Procedure of Recording

- The dying declaration, if possible, should be written by the person who is recording it. The statement should be recorded in the man's (dying man's) own words and in the language in which the person prefers to speak. It must be recorded in the presence of two or more witnesses. No addition of words or phrases should be made or altered. No prompting or suggestions should be made and no undue influence must be placed on the person.
- No information must be sought by asking leading questions.
- After recording a declaration, it should then be read over to the declarant who should affix his signature or thumb impression. The doctor and witness should also sign the declaration.
- While recording a statement if the person becomes unconscious, the doctor recording it must record as much information as he has to obtained and sign it.
- If the person prefers to write the statement himself then the statement should be signed and attested by witness,
- If the person is unable to speak and can only make signs in answer to questions put to him then the questions and signs can be recorded as verbal statement.
- The dying declaration should be forwarded to the Magistrate in a sealed envelope.
- A dying declaration can also be written in ink on hand also.
- A dying declaration is accepted in court as evidence after the death of a person who made it. However, if the declarant (person who make the statement) survives, the declaration is not admitted as dying declaration but the declaration has corroborative value.

Dying Deposition

- *It is a statement or deposition made by a dying person on oath.* The Magistrate in the presence of accused or his lawyer records it.
- The procedure of dying deposition is not followed in India.
- Dying deposition has more value then dying declaration in the court as it is recorded by the Magistrate in presence of accused.
- Difference between dying declaration and dying deposition are summarized in Table 1.3.

Oral Evidence

- It means statement made by the witness verbally in the court.
- As per Section 60 of IEA, the oral evidence should be direct i.e. it is to say:[3]
  1. If it refers to a fact which could be seen, it must be the evidence of a witness who says he saw it;

Table 1.3: Difference between dying declaration and dying deposition	
Dying declaration	*Dying deposition*
1. Recorded by magistrate or doctor or investigating officer	1. Always recorded by magistrate
2. No oath is administered	2. Oath is administered
3. Inferior to dying deposition	3. Superior to dying declaration
4. Accused or his lawyer is not necessary while recording a statement	4. Statement is always recorded in presence of accused or his lawyer
5. No cross examination	5. Cross examination is allowed
6. Has corroborative value if patient survives	6. Retains full legal value even if the person survives

2. If it refers to a fact which could be heard, it must be the evidence of a witness who says he heard it;
3. If it refers to a fact which could be perceived by any other sense or in any other manner, it must be the evidence of a witness who says he perceived it by that sense or in that manner;
4. If it refers to an opinion or the grounds on which that opinion is held, it must be the evidence of the person who holds that opinion on those grounds.

- In other words, oral evidence is direct evidence of a witness regarding what he had seen, heard or perceived.
- Oral evidence is more important and superior than documentary evidence because:
  1. It has to be proved on oath or affirmation and
  2. It can be subjected to cross-examination.

Exceptions to Oral Evidence

Following are the exception to oral evidence:
1. Dying declaration
2. Expert opinion expressed in a treatise (for example opinion expressed by author in book) when the author is dead or cannot be found or is otherwise incapable of giving evidence.
3. Deposition of medical witness taken in lower court.
4. Chemical examiner's report.
5. Evidence given by a witness in a previous judicial proceeding or in lower court.
6. When the certificate or document is acceptable to the counsels (lawyer of accused) without cross-examination.

Other Types of Evidences are

1. Hearsay evidence
2. Circumstantial evidence
3. Corroborative evidence

Hearsay evidence: It is type of indirect evidence in which the witness has no personal knowledge about the facts but he has only heard what others had said regarding the matter. For example witness "X" gives evidence in court that "Y" had told him (i.e. X) that he (i.e. Y) had seen "Z" beating to "W" with iron rod.

Circumstantial evidence: It is indirect type of evidence, which was obtained from the suspicious circumstances for example finding of blood stained shirt over body of accused, recovery of bullet shells at the spot of crime or recovery of weapon from the accused etc.

WITNESSES

Definition

- *Witness is a person who gives sworn testimony or evidence in the court of law in relation to matters of fact under inquiry.*
- Any person can testify as witness or give evidence in the court if the said witness is able to understand the nature of questions put to him or is able to give rational answers to the questions asked. Such difficulty may arise in witnesses who are of tender age (say for example boy of 6 years) or of extreme old age or affecting from any disease of body or mind.

Types

There are two types of witnesses and they are:
1. Common
2. Expert

Common Witness

- Common witness is one who testifies or gives evidence to the facts observed or heard or perceived by him.
- The common witness cannot draw inferences or form opinions.

Expert Witness

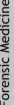

- *An expert witness is a person who, by virtue of his professional training, is capable of forming opinions or*

draws conclusions from the facts observed by him or noticed by others.

- Examples are doctor, handwriting expert, fingers print expert, ballistic expert, and chemical analyzer.
- A doctor is both common and expert witness. For example, if a doctor is giving evidence in relation to injuries, when he mentions size, shape or position of injury he is acting as common witness. When the doctor says that the injury is antemortem or postmortem, caused by such type of weapon etc. then he is acting as expert witness.
- The Indian Medical Council Act 1956 in section 15 (2) (C) states that no person other than a medical practitioner enrolled on a state medical register shall be entitled to give evidence at any inquest or in any court of law as an expert under section 45 of IEA on any matter relating to medicine.

Hostile Witness

- *A hostile witness is one who purposely makes statements contrary to facts or does not give his evidence fairly and with a desire to tell the truth to the court.*
- The common or expert witness may turn hostile.
- While examining a hostile witness, **leading questions** are permitted even during examination-in-chief.

Perjury

- *Perjury means willful utterance of falsehood by a witness under oath.*
- It is false evidence tendered by witness and he fails to tell what he knows or believes to be true (Section 191 of IPC).
- A witness is liable to be prosecuted for perjury under section 193 of IPC.

PROCEDURE IN COURT

When a doctor is called in the court of law as a witness, he has to take oath before tendering his evidence. The evidence is recorded in the following sequence (Section 138 of IEA) (Fig. 1.2):

1. Oath
2. Examination-in-chief
3. Cross-examination
4. Re-examination
5. Questions put by the court (Judge).

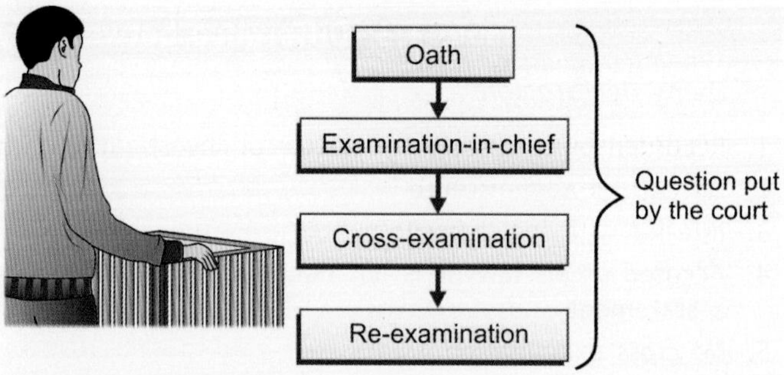

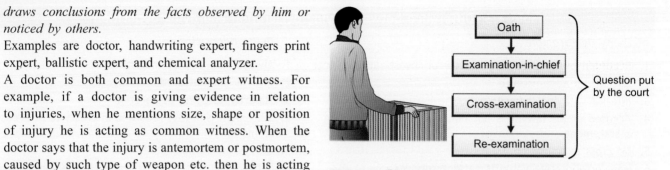

FIG. 1.2: Diagrammatic representation of procedure of recording evidence

Examination-in-Chief

- It is carried out by the council (Lawyer) of the party who called the witness (Section 137 of IEA). In government prosecution cases say for example in murder case, the public prosecutor (Government lawyer) first examines the doctor to elicit the findings of case under inquiry.
- Objective of this examination is to put all the facts before the court.
- **No leading questions are allowed in this part of examination**. Leading questions are the question that suggests the answer (Section 141 of IEA). For example "doctor, was the injury caused by sharp cutting weapon?" is a leading question and the suggested answer may be "yes" or "no". The proper way to put the question is "doctor, what weapon would cause this injury?"

Cross-Examination

- In this part of examination, the lawyer for the opposite party (Lawyer for accused or Defense council) questions the witness.
- Objectives of this examination are:
  1. To elicit facts favorable to his case.
  2. To test the accuracy of the statements made by the witness.
  3. To modify or explain what has been said.
  4. To discredit the witness.
- Leading questions are permitted during cross-examination (section 143 of IEA).
- There is no time limit for cross-examination. Well-known author and eminent medicolegal expert, Prof. Dr B. V. Subrahmanyam was crossed-examined for two complete days.[4]

Re-Examination

- The lawyer who has started the examination-in-chief has the right to re-examine a witness.

- Objectives of re-examination are to explain any ambiguities or correct any mistake or add details to the statements the witness has made in cross-examination.
- **Leading questions are not allowed in re-examination.**
- **No new things or new subject may be introduced** by the witness without the consent of the judge or the Defense counsel. If new subject have been introduced in re-examination, the lawyer of opposing party has the right to re-cross-examine a witness on the new matter.
- Under section 311 CrPC, the court is empowered to recall, re-examine any witness already examined if his evidence appears to be essential to the just decision of the court.

Court Questions

The judge or the presiding officer of the court may put the question to witness during any stage of examination to clear up any doubtful points.

CONDUCT OF DOCTOR IN THE COURT[5,6]

- Doctor giving evidence in the court of law should be modest. He should well dressed and have appropriate personal appearance.
- Doctor should be honest, impartial in his evidence. He should maintain the dignity and should show respect for the court.
- He should address the judges by their titles. A High Court Judge is addressed as 'My Lord' and a District Court/ Sessions Judge as 'Your Honour'.[1]
- Refresh memory: a witness may, while under examination, refresh his memory by referring to any writing made by himself at the time of the transaction concerning which he is questioned or soon afterwards that the court considers it likely that the transaction was at that time fresh in his memory (Section 159 of IEA).
- He should be modest in stating his qualifications and experience
- He should be attentive towards each question and should answer honestly. His speech should be clear, easily audible, confident and polite. Speak slowly so that the judge, recorder, who is recording/typing the evidence and defense council, may hear clearly.
- Use plain and simple language; avoid technical terms as far as possible. He should avoid using superlatives and exaggerations for example enormous bruise, ghastly injury, savage blow, most agonizing pain etc.
- He should state the facts observed by him. Avoid discrepancies between your earlier statements and your testimony in court.
- Do not evade any question. If question is unclear or ambiguous or not heard properly, request for repeating the question. If you do not know the answer to a particular question, be frank and admit it.
- Keep going cool; do not lose your temper. Always remain calm, composed and courteous. Do not argue over any point. If you want to disagree with any point, be firm but don't leave impression of being dogmatic. At times, defense council may put irritating questions to you or may take doubt over your honesty and creditability. Be cool; don't get irritated with such questions. The court may forbid any questions or inquiries which it regards indecent or scandalous (Section 151 of IEA). The court shall forbid any question which appears to it to be intended to insult or annoy, or which, though proper in it, appears to the court needlessly offensive in form (Section 152 of IEA).
- As far as possible do not volunteer any statement. If you feel that by not making any statement or clarification, injustice may be caused, do mention it.
- Always remember to be honest and impartial. You are a man of science and remain a man of science. Please keep in mind, you have to help the court for admitting justice, you are not judge!

REFERENCES

1. Mathiharan K, Patnaik AK. Legal procedure in criminal courts and medical evidence and medical witness. In: Modi's Medical Jurisprudence and Toxicology, 23rd edn. 2005. LexisNexis Butterworths, New Delhi. 19–76.
2. The Juvenile Justice (care and protection of children) Act 2000 (56 of 2000). Published in Gazette of India.
3. Satyanarayana, Krishna Rao. In: The Law relating to medical profession in India, 1st edn. 1962. Bestseller Publications, Hyderabad.
4. Subrahmanyam BV. Legal procedure in criminal courts. In: Modi's Medical Jurisprudence and Toxicology, 22nd edn. 2001. Butterworths India, New Delhi. 1–24.
5. Pillay VV. Legal procedure. In: Textbook of Forensic Medicine and Toxicology, 14th edn. 2004. Paras Publishing, Hydrabad. 2–15.
6. Rudra A. Medical expert in court and general guidelines on court appearances. In: Dogra TD, Rudra A (ed) Lyon's Medical Jurisprudence and Toxicology, 11th edn. 2007. Delhi Law House, Delhi. 20–7.

CHAPTER 2

Medical Jurisprudence

My old and much-respected teacher of forensic medicine used to tell his class that provided they retained that knowledge which they possessed at the time of qualification and acted upon it, they were safe from any action in negligence.

—**J Leahy Taylor**

Medical Practitioner means an individual who practices the art of medicine. Registered Medical Practitioner (RMP) means Medical Practitioner whose name appear on the official register kept for the purpose in accordance with the law of the land to which one belongs.[1]

Medical profession is governed by

1. Medical ethics
2. Law of the land

Thus the practice of medicine includes ethical practice and within legal framework of the State (Country).

MEDICAL COUNCIL OF INDIA

In the year 1933, the Indian Legislative Assembly passed an Act known as the Indian Medical Council Act 1933 (Act No XX VII of 1933). Now this Act stands repealed and in its place, the **Indian Medical Council Act 1956** is enacted with following particulars.

1. To give recognition for representation of the licentiate medical practitioners.
2. To provide registration of foreign medical qualifications.
3. To provide for formation of a committee to help in reorganizing postgraduate medical education in the country.
4. To maintain an "All India Medical Register" containing names of Registered Medical Practitioner all over India.

However, the Act was amended in 1964 to reconstitute Medical Council of India and reorganize medical education of the country.

Composition of Medical Council of India[2]

Section 3 of the Act states that the medical Council of India (MCI) shall consist of:

1. One member from each State, other than Union territory to be nominated by the Central Government in consultation with the State government concerned.
2. One member from each University to be elected from amongst the members of medical faculty of the University by members of the senate of the University or members of the court if there is no senate.
3. One member from each state, in which a state medical register is maintained, to be elected from amongst themselves by persons enrolled on such register, who possess the medical qualifications included in the first or second schedule or part II of the third schedule.
4. Seven members to be elected from amongst themselves by persons enrolled on any of the state medical register and who possess the medical qualifications included in part I of the third schedule.
5. Eight members to be nominated by the Central government
   - The President and the Vice-President of the Council shall be elected by the members of the council from amongst themselves.
   - The President and the Vice-President shall hold office for a term not exceeding five years and not exceeding beyond the expiry of term as a member of the council.
   - The members of the council shall hold office for five years.
   - The council appoints a Registrar who acts as a Secretary for day to day work of the council.
   - Dr B C Roy was the first Indian to be President of MCI in 1939.

– The MCI carries out the purpose of Indian Medical council Act through an Executive Committee and through such other committees, as the council may deem necessary. These committees are constituted from amongst the members of the council.

Functions of MCI

Following are the functions of Medical Council of India
1. Recognition of medical qualification
2. Recognition of foreign medical qualifications
3. Maintenance of Register
4. Medical education
5. Disciplinary control
6. Appellate tribunal
7. Maintenance of Indian Pharmacopoeia

Recognition of Medical Qualification

The MCI recognizes medical qualification granted by universities/institutions. The MCI maintains three schedules for recognition of medical qualification. The schedules are as follows.
1. As per **First** schedule of the Act, medical qualifications granted by recognized universities in India are recognized by council.
2. As per **Second** schedule, the medical qualifications granted by institutions outside India are recognized by council.
3. **Third** schedule has two parts
   – Part I: As per part I of third schedule, the medical qualification granted by institution of India but not included in first schedule
   – Part II: Part II of third schedule recognizes those medical qualifications granted by institutions outside India but not included in second schedule.

Recognition of Foreign Medical Qualifications

The MCI as per Act may permit registration of Indian Citizens who have obtained foreign medical qualifications, which are not recognizable under the existing Act.

Maintenance of Register

- The MCI maintains a register of medical practitioners practicing medicine in India and this register is called as "**Indian Medical Register**"
- The register contains names of medical practitioners
- The registered is considered as a public document within the meaning of Indian Evidence Act 1872.

Medical Education

- MCI regulates the standard of undergraduate and postgraduate medical education. The council prescribes minimum standards for teaching medicine to undergraduate and postgraduate level. The MCI appoints a committee for undergraduate and postgraduate medical education.
- The MCI sends Inspector to various institutions imparting medical education. The inspectors assess the facilities provided by the institute and find out whether institutes are maintaining the stipulated specifications prescribed by MCI. Under Sec 17, MCI is authorized to inspect the institute during examination period to assess the standard of such examinations.

Disciplinary Control

- The MCI prescribes minimum standards for Registered Medical Practitioner with reference to professional conduct, ethics and etiquette. The MCI exercises disciplinary control over RMP.
- The MCI can issue warning notices to its members for involvement in unethical practices falling under the meaning of the term 'infamous conduct in a professional sense'.

Appellate Tribunal

The MCI act as an appellate tribunal. If any State medical Council has taken an action against a RMP, then such RMP can make a representation to Central Government. The Central Government will consult MCI and MCI then examines the facts under inquiry and furnish its recommendations to Central Government. The recommendations made by MCI are binding on the appealing person.

Functions Related with Maintenance of Indian Pharmacopoeia

The MCI advises and assists the Government of India to maintain and revise the Indian Pharmacopoeia from time to time.

ETHICAL ASPECTS OF MEDICAL PRACTICE

Medical Ethics

The word "ethics" is derived from Greek word "ethikos" which means manner and habit of man. *Medical ethics deals with the moral principles, values and guidelines that govern the conduct and relationship of doctor with his patients, fellow doctors and the State.*[3] In other words, medical ethics are the code of behaviour accepted voluntarily within the profession.[4]

Medical etiquette: *Refers to the conventional laws of courtesy observed between members of the medical profession.*[5]

Medical profession is considered as a noble profession. From ancient times, attempts have been made to regulate the conduct of medical practitioners. Such regulations are also called as 'Code for Medical Practitioner'. The **Hippocratic oath** is earliest known code. The modern version of Hippocratic oath is the **"International Code of Medical Ethics"**.[6] In keeping with the spirit and to maintain the dignity of medical profession, the Medical Council of India brought out regulations relating to the professional conduct, etiquette and ethics for Registered Medical Practitioners. In 2002, the MCI had brought revised regulations replacing the older ones. These regulations are binding on all doctors registered with the Medical Council of India/State Medical Council. Medical ethics differ from law as the ethics are governed by the Medical Council of India and do not govern by any legislation. Violation of the code of conduct prescribed by the Medical Council of India by any RMP would be liable to the charges of professional misconduct and if proved, he/she may either temporarily or permanently debarred from practicing medicine. The regulations prescribed by the Medical Council of India are given below and contain eight chapters. (*Code of medical ethics prescribed by MCI – new guidelines vide infra*)

Chapter 1: Code of medical ethics
Chapter 2: Duties of Physician to their patients
Chapter 3: Duties of Physician in consultation
Chapter 4: Responsibilities of physician to each other
Chapter 5: Duties of Physician to the public and to the paramedical profession
Chapter 6: Unethical acts
Chapter 7: Misconduct
Chapter 8: Punishment and disciplinary action

Professional Misconduct

- Also called as infamous conduct
- It is defined as *conduct or behaviour of a doctor, which is considered as disgraceful or dishonorable by his professional colleagues of good repute and competence.*
- The MCI's 2002 regulations state misconduct in chapter number 7 as – acts of commission or omission on part of a doctor constitute professional misconduct (*vide infra new MCI guidelines*).

Following are the acts that are considered as misconduct (Fig. 2.1):

1. Violation of regulations prescribed by the Medical Council of India.
2. Adultery – doctor should not engage in adultery. Adultery is voluntary sexual intercourse with other married female other than his wife.
3. Improper association – doctor should not associate or employ unqualified person to perform operation, treatment etc.
4. Conviction by Court of law – conviction by a Court of Law for offenses involving moral turpitude/Criminal acts shall be considered as professional misconduct.
5. Involved in sex determination test – on no account sex determination test shall be undertaken with the intent to terminate the life of a female fetus developing in her mother's womb.
6. Issuing false certificates – any registered practitioner who is shown to have signed or given under his name and authority any certificate, notification, report or document of a similar character which is untrue, misleading or improper, is liable to have his name deleted from the Register.
7. Contravene the provisions of Drugs and Cosmetic Act and regulations.
8. Involved in criminal abortion.
9. Dichotomy or fee splitting – doctor should not engage himself in receiving or giving commission or other benefits to a fellow doctor. Taking or giving such commission is referred as dichotomy.
10. If doctor issues certificate of efficiency in modern medicine to unqualified or non-medical person.
11. Advertising – it is improper for a physician to use an unusually large sign board and write on it anything other than his name, qualifications obtained from a University or a statutory body, titles and name of his specialty, registration number including the name of the State Medical Council under which registered. The same should be the contents of his prescription papers. It is improper to affix a signboard on a chemist's shop or in places where he does not reside or work.
12. Medical record – if doctor does not maintain the medical records of his/her indoor patients for a period of three years or refuses to provide the same within 72 hours when the patient or his/her authorized representative makes a request for it shall be considered as professional misconduct.
13. Registration number – If doctor does not display the registration number accorded to him/her by the State Medical Council or the Medical Council of India in his clinic, prescriptions and certificates etc shall be considered as professional misconduct.

14. Employing agents or touts – a Physician shall not use touts or agents for procuring patients.
15. Specialist – a Physician shall not claim to be specialist unless he has a special qualification in that branch.
16. Artificial reproductive technique – no act of *in vitro* fertilization or artificial insemination shall be undertaken without the informed consent of the female patient and her spouse as well as the donor. Such consent shall be obtained in writing only after the patient is provided, at her own level of comprehension, with sufficient information about the purpose, methods, risks, inconveniences, disappointments of the procedure and possible risks and hazards.
17. Research – clinical drug trials or other research involving patients or volunteers as per the guidelines of ICMR can be undertaken, provided ethical considerations are borne in mind. Violation of existing ICMR guidelines in this regard shall constitute misconduct. Consent taken from the patient for trial of drug or therapy, which is not as per the guidelines, shall also be construed as misconduct.

The acts may be remembered as 6 A's

1. Adultery
2. Association
3. Abortion
4. Associated with unqualified persons
5. Alcohol
6. Addiction.

Unethical Acts

A physician shall not aid or abet or commit any of the following acts, which shall be considered as unethical (*vide infra, under new MCI guidelines*):

- Advertising
- Running an open shop
- Rebates and commission
- Prescribing or dispensing secret remedies
- Violating human rights
- Practicing euthanasia.

Duties of Medical Practitioners

Following are the duties of RMP towards his patient, his colleagues and the State.

Duties of RMP Towards Patients

1. Duty to exercise reasonable degree of skill and knowledge
2. Duty to attend the patient and examine him
3. Duty to furnish or prescribe proper medicines
4. Duty to give proper instructions
5. Duty to inform risks
6. Duty to third parties
7. Duty in relation to operation
8. Duty in relation to poisoning cases
9. Duty of professional secrecy
10. Duty in relation to X-ray examination.

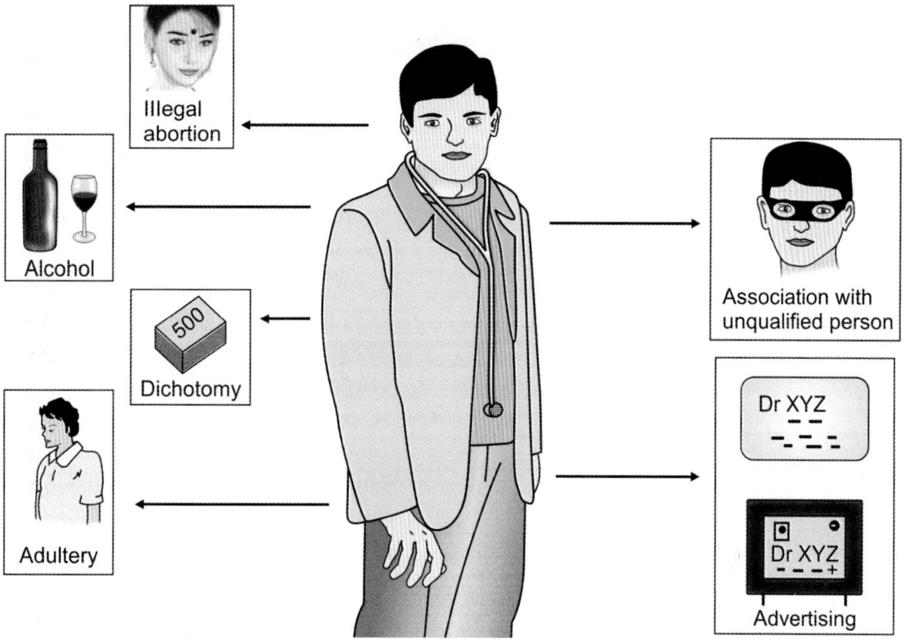

FIG. 2.1: Diagrammatic representation of professional misconduct

Duties of RMP Towards Professional Colleague

1. Not to criticize colleague
2. Never take fees
3. Always help
4. Duties with regard to consultation.

Duties of RMP Towards State

1. Duty to notify certain diseases
2. Duties to inform vital events
3. Duties under Geneva Conventions
4. Duties regarding medicolegal cases

Duties of Patients

1. Duty of patient to furnish all information related with health to doctor
2. Duty of patient to follow the instructions/advice given by doctor
3. Duty to pay fees to the doctor
4. If the patient wishes to take second consultation or second opinion, the patient should inform the first doctor
5. The patient should have faith in the doctor chosen for treatment
6. The patient should not contribute to medical negligence
7. The patient should co-operate with the Medical Practitioner for the necessary laboratory investigations such as X-rays, ECG etc. because these tests may be necessary for the diagnosis and proper treatment.

Rights and Privileges of Registered Medical Practitioner

1. Right to practice medicine
2. Right to choose patient
3. Right to prescribe/dispense medicines
4. Right to possess, dispense or prescribe drugs listed in the Dangerous Drug Act
5. Right to add professional titles to his name
6. Right to perform surgical operations
7. Right to issue certificate
8. Rights for appointment to public (government) hospital
9. Right to give evidence as an expert witness in the Court of law
10. Right to claim payments of fees for professional services given.

Rights and Privileges of Patients

1. Right to choose doctor
2. Right to access health care facilities available regardless of age, sex, caste, religion, and economic or social status.
3. Right to be treated with dignity, with care, respect and without any discrimination
4. Right to have privacy during consultation or treatment
5. Right to have confidentiality of all his information furnished to doctor
6. Right to receive full information about the diagnosis, investigations and available methods of treatment.
7. Right to know the procedure of operation, risk involved therein, available alternatives, the type of procedure, and the safety of procedure, results and prognosis.
8. Right to seek second opinion from another doctor
9. Right to demand for the medical record
10. Right to complain and rectification of grievances
11. Right to obtain compensation for medical injuries or negligence.

Professional Secrets and Confidentiality

Professional secret is one, which a doctor comes to know in his professional capacity. Professional secrets should not be divulged to any one except under following circumstances:

1. In a court of law under orders of the Presiding Judge
2. Privileged communication or
3. In cases of notifiable diseases

Except for the circumstances mentioned above, the Medical Practitioner is duty bound (ethical, moral and legal) not to divulge any information pertaining to his patients. A Medical Practitioner may be sued in court of law and liable to damages if divulge any information without excuse.

- "*And whatsoever I shall see or hear in the course of my profession, as well as outside my profession in my intercourse with men, if it be what should not be published abroad, I will never divulge, holding such things to be holy secrets….*" Extract from the Hippocratic Oath.
- "*I will respect the secrets which are confided in me, even after the patient has died…*" Extract from the Declaration of Geneva, World Medical Association, 1948 restated in 1983.
- "*A physician shall preserve confidentiality on all he knows about his patient even after the patient has died*". Extract from the International Code of Medical Ethics, World Medical Association, Geneva, Switzerland, 1983.
- MCI guidelines state that the registered medical practitioner shall not disclose the secrets of a patient that have been learnt in the exercise of his/her profession except –
  1. In a court of law under orders of the Presiding Judge;

2. In circumstances where there is a serious and identified risk to a specific person and/or community; and
3. Notifiable diseases. In case of communicable/notifiable diseases, concerned public health authorities should be informed immediately.

Privileged Communication

Usually a Medical Practitioner is not supposed to divulge information of his patients learned while discharging his duties. However, at times under certain circumstances, a doctor may be justified in disclosing information regarding his patients and at times indeed it may be his duty to do so. Under such circumstances communication made by Medical Practitioner is regarded as privileged communication. Therefore a privileged communication may be defined as "*a bonafide statement made by doctor upon any subject matter to the appropriate authority to protect the interests of the community or of the State*". In other words it is a statement made by a doctor, under legal, social, ethical or moral obligation to protect the interest of society to other concerned authority though such communication may, under normal conditions, amount to defamation or slander. Remember, while making a privileged communication, the communication should be made to:

1. Proper authority
2. The communication should be bonafide
3. The communication should be without malice
4. The communication should contain the facts alone regarding the issue.

Example – A Medical Practitioner has a privilege to inform the railway authorities if he finds that a particular engine driver is colour blind.

Therapeutic Privilege

If the Medical Practitioner, while exercising his duties, believes that the patient is so anxious or anxiety prone or the information may cause psychological harm or may disturbed him (patient), then the physician may not told the disease process and information related to the disease to the patient. *Here the non-disclosure of such information is referred to as therapeutic privilege.* Under such circumstances, the Medical Practitioner treating the patient should consult the family doctor of the patient and the issue may be discussed with close relative or attendant of the patient.

LEGAL ASPECTS OF MEDICAL PRACTICE

Medical Practitioner, practicing the art of medicine, is under legal obligation to follow the law of land – various Acts, rules and regulation made from time to time.

Acts, Rules and Regulations

Registered Medical Practitioner has to follow Acts, rules and regulations made by government from time to time. Following are the Acts, rules and regulations.

1. The Bio-medical Waste (Management and Handling) Rules 1998
2. The Consumer Protection Act 1986
3. The Children Act 1960
4. The Code of criminal procedure, 1973
5. The Drugs and Cosmetics Act 1940
6. The Dentists Act 1948
7. The Dock workers (safety, health and welfare) Act 1986
8. The Drugs and Magic Remedies (objectionable advertisement) Act 1954
9. The Drug (control) Act 1950
10. The Epidemic Disease Act 1897
11. The Employees' State Insurance Act 1948
12. The Environment protection Act 1986
13. The Factories Act 1948
14. The Fatal Accidents Act 1855
15. The Indian Evidence Act 1872
16. The Insecticides Act 1968
17. The Indian Majority Act 1875
18. The Indian Penal Code 1860
19. The Leprosy Act 1898
20. The Indian Medical Degrees Act 1916
21. The Indian Medical Council Act 1956
22. The Maternity Benefit Act 1961
23. The Mental Health Act 1987
24. The Minimum Wages Act 1948
25. The Medical Termination of Pregnancy Act 1971
26. The Mines Act 1952
27. The Motor Vehicles Act 1988
28. The Personal Injuries (emergency provisions) Act 1962
29. The Personal Injuries (compensation, insurance) Act 1963
30. The Pharmacy Act 1948
31. The Poisons Act 1919
32. The Pre-natal diagnostic Technique (regulations and prevention of misuse) Act 1994
33. The Protection of Human Right Act 1993
34. The Registration of Birth and Death Act 1969
35. The Transplantation of Human Organs Act 1994
36. The Vaccination Act 1880
37. The Workman's compensation Act 1923.

Law and Doctor

Section 176 of IPC – omission to give notice or information to public servant by person legally bound to give it.

Section 177 of IPC – furnishing false information
Section 191 of IPC – giving false evidence
Section 192 of IPC – fabricating false evidence
Section 193 of IPC – punishment for false evidence
Section 194 of IPC – giving or fabricating false evidence with intent to procure conviction of capital offense.
Section 195 of IPC – giving or fabricating false evidence with intent to procure conviction of offense punishable with imprisonment for life or imprisonment.
Section 197 of IPC – issuing or signing false certificate
Section 201 of IPC – causing disappearance of evidence of offense, or giving false information to screen offender.
Section 203 of IPC – giving false information respecting an offense committed
Section 204 of IPC – destruction of documents to prevent its production as evidence
Section 269 of IPC – negligent act likely to spread infection of disease dangerous to life
Section 270 of IPC – malignant act likely to spread infection of disease dangerous to life
Section 271 of IPC – disobedience to quarantine rules
Section 272 of IPC – adulteration of food or drink intended for sale
Section 273 of IPC – sale of noxious food or drink
Section 274 of IPC – adulteration of drugs
Section 275 of IPC – sale of adulterated drugs
Section 276 of IPC – sale of drugs as a different drug or preparation
Section 277 of IPC – fouling water of public spring or reservoir
Section 278 of IPC – making atmosphere noxious to health
Section 284 of IPC – negligent conduct with respect to poisonous substance
Section 304 A of IPC – causing death by negligence
Section 312 of IPC – causing miscarriage
Section 39 of Cr PC – public to give information of certain offenses
Section 53 of Cr PC – examination of accused by Medical Practitioner at the request of police officer
Section 54 of Cr PC – examination of arrested person by Medical Practitioner at the request of the arrested person.

Legal Protection to RMP

Following sections of law provide protection from liability to doctors who may not be at fault while discharging their duties with utmost care and acted in the best interest for the patients.

Section 88 of IPC:
- This section deals with act not intended to cause death done by consent in good faith for the person's benefit.
- Example: Suppose a surgeon "X" performs an operation on patient "Y" who was suffering from disease. The intention of X is to relieve Y from pain and suffering by performing operation and not to cause of death of Y. Thus X has not committed any offense.

Section 89 of IPC
- Act done in good faith for benefit of child or insane person by consent of guardian
- In both of above sections i.e. 88 and 89 of IPC, the law does not provide sanction for mercy killing or euthanasia. The important features are that:
  1. The intention is not to kill the patient but to cure his disease
  2. Consent of the particular patient or guardian has been obtained for the procedure.

Section 90 of IPC
- Consent taken under fear or misconception is not considered as valid consent

Section 92 of IPC
- Act done in good faith for benefit of a person without consent
- For example – suppose a surgeon "X" performs an operation on patient "Y" because it is necessary to save the life. Now consider that the patient Y is unconscious and there is no time to call his family members and take consent or person appears to be unidentified (unknown) one. Then question arises from whom the consent should be obtained? In such situation, if surgeon X operates Y without consent with good faith to save the life of patient, then the act of surgeon is not an offense.
- This section highlights important principles that
  1. The act is done in good faith for the benefit of patient.
  2. The intention of doctor is to save the life and not to kill the person.

Section 93 of IPC
- Communication made in good faith
- No communication made in good faith is an offense by reason of any harm to the person to whom it is made, if it is made for the benefit for that person.

Responsibility of RMP in Criminal Matters

Communication to Police
- Under section 39 of CrPC, RMP should communicate to the police any information about a criminal act that has come to his knowledge
- Offense of attempt to commit suicide (section 309 of IPC) is not included in section 39 of CrPC. It is therefore not mandatory for RMP, doing private practice, to

supply such information of his own accord to police or magistrate. However, he is duty bound to inform police if the person happens to die.[6, 7]

- Under section of 175 of CrPC, the doctor has to provide all the information if asked by police or magistrate
- Not providing such information or concealing of such information is punishable under section 202 of IPC. Also a doctor may be charged under section 201 of IPC for destruction of evidences and/or if doctor fails to discharge his duties to inform police in time.[8]
- Similarly giving false information by doctors to police on such matters is punishable under law.
- Preservation of trace evidences and samples (e.g. gastric lavage, blood etc.), clothes, foreign bodies such as weapon, bullet/pellets etc. in an injured or poisoning patient or sexual offenses cases should be done by doctor and handed over to the police/investigating officer.
- Preservation of record: The indoor patient's record should be made and preserved.

Emergency Services and Doctors

Medical emergency is not defined in India. Therefore what constitute emergency largely depends on the perception of patient or doctor. From patient's point of view, an emergency is anything that bothers him at any time of the day or night and for that matter the patient expect doctor should examine him and treat accordingly. Doctor's perception regarding emergency is somewhat different. For doctor a patient who is very near to death and needs urgent attention constitutes an emergency.[6]

1. It is responsibility of a doctor to attend the patient in an emergency and treat him accordingly.
2. The MCI regulations of 2002 provides that a doctor should attend the patient in an emergency.
3. It would be contrary to medical ethics on part of doctor to deny services to patient who is in need.
4. Section 92 of IPC offers legal immunity for doctors to proceed with treatment even without consent of the patient in an emergency condition.
5. **Triage** is a French word used in military medicine to refer to the process of sorting of sick and wounded patients on the basis of urgency and type of condition presented. Accordingly the cases are sorted into following three groups
   - Those who cannot be expected to survive even with treatment
   - Those who will recover without treatment
   - The highest priority group of patients who need treatment in order to survive.

DOCTORS AND MEDICAL RECORDS[9-11]

Medical records means and includes the record pertaining to the admission, diagnosis, treatment, investigation, daily progress, operations, consultations etc.

Importance of Medical Record

Medical record is required for patients or hospitals.

Medical Record is Required for Patients for:

1. Medical negligence cases
2. For life insurance policy purpose
3. For third party claims under health and accident insurance
4. As a proof of disability
5. Workman's compensation cases
6. Traffic accidents cases
7. Follow-up cases or taking treatment from another doctor
8. Medico-legal cases

Medical Record is Required for Doctors/ Hospitals for

1. For medical research
2. For cost accounting
3. Hospital audit
4. Evaluation of drug therapy
5. Planning
6. Legal purpose
7. Administration
8. Follow-up cases
9. Insurance claims

What Constitute Medical Record?

1. OPD cards
2. IPD cards
3. Details of provisional and final diagnosis
4. Treatment record
5. X-ray films/USG report/CT scan/MRI films
6. Laboratory reports

Features

- The medical record should be adequate, appropriate and complete
- The patient or the representatives have got the right of access to their medical record.
- Well-maintained medical records will help the doctors and the hospitals to defend in medical negligence cases.

MCI and Medical Record

Indian Medical Council (professional conduct, etiquette and ethics) Regulations, 2002 (chapter 1, Section 1.3, subsection 1.3.1 and 1.3.2) states that:

- Every physician shall maintain the medical records pertaining to his/her indoor patients for a period of 3 years from the date of commencement of the treatment in a standard proforma lay down by the Medical Council of India and attached as Appendix 3.
- If any request is made for medical records either by the patients/authorized attendant or legal authorities involved, the same may be duly acknowledged and documents shall be issued within the period of 72 hours.
- Failure to maintain medical records for a period of three years or refuses to provide the same within 72 hours to the patient or his authorized representative will amount to misconduct.

CONSENT

Definition

- *Consent is defined as free and voluntary agreement, compliance or permission given for a specified act or purpose.*
- It is based upon the Latin maxim "*volenti non fit injuria*" means '*he who consents cannot complain*'. This is founded on two straightforward factors, firstly every patient is best judge of his own interest and secondly no man will consent to what he think is harmful to him.
- There is no official or codified definition of consent. Section 90 of IPC defines consent in negative terms.[12] As per this section, any consent given under the following five circumstances will not be a true consent. The consent becomes invalid if given:
    1. By a person under fear of injury or
    2. By a person who is under misconception of the facts and person who obtains consent knows or has a reason to believe this or
    3. By an intoxicated person or
    4. By a person who is of unsound mind or
    5. By a person who is below the age of 12 years of age.
- Section 13 of Indian Contract Act states consent as "*two or more persons are said to consent when they agree upon the same thing in the same sense*".
- As per Section 14 of Indian Contract Act, consent is said to be free and voluntarily when:[13]
    1. It is not obtained by coercion/force
    2. It is not obtained by fraud
    3. It is not obtained under influence
    4. It is not obtained under influence of intoxication
    5. It is not obtained by misrepresentation
    6. It is not obtained from mistaken subjects
    7. It is not obtained from mentally unsound persons.

Importance of Consent

Following are the importance of consent

1. Consent is obtained by a doctor to examine, treat or operate a patient. Treating/examining a patient without consent is considered as an assault on patient. Every person has the right to determine what shall be done to his body. Self-defense of body (IPC 96 to 102, 104, 106) provides right to the protection of bodily integrity of a patient or person by other. Medical procedure like examination, treatment, operation, diagnostic procedure or research on patient trespass the right of person (a tort – civil wrong) and can be considered as assault (IPC 351) in absence of valid consent.[14]
2. Thus an adult who is conscious and have sound mind is at liberty to decline the consent for treatment even if the results of his act doing so will result in his death.[15]
3. Consent and submission are not the same things. Consent involves submission but it is not said that mere submission amounts to consent. The maxim that is not observed is "*scienti non fit injuria*" but "*volenti, non fit injuria*". This clearly indicates that submission without full disclosure of the concerned act on the person does not cause him to loose his right to complain against injury caused by that particular act.[12] Therefore it can be added that, while taking consent of a patient, if doctor fails to provide the patient the required information regarding the disease or operation or treatment modality, the doctor may be charged for negligence. Moreover, not taking consent is considered as a deficiency in medical services under the Section 2(1) of the Consumer Protection Act.
4. For operations, which are illegal or unlawful, there cannot be any valid consent for example procuring criminal abortion.

Types of Consent

Consent may be

1. Implied

2. Expressed – it may be
   a. Oral or verbal
   b. Written.

Implied Consent

- Implied consent is common type of consent observed in medical practice
- Here the consent is presumed (i.e. implied). For example if a patient enter in clinic, it is presumed that the patient has came for examination and consultation. Thus the conduct of patient suggests the willingness to undergo for medical examination.
- The consent is not written but legally it is effective
- The consent is provided for medical examination such as inspection, palpation and auscultation. It does not cover the consent for examination of:
  - Private parts
  - Vein puncture or injection
  - Major intervention or operation.

Expressed Consent

Anything other than implied consent is expressed consent. In other words, *an expressed consent is one, which is stated, in distinct and explicit language*. The expressed consent may be of following types

A. Oral (verbal) consent
   - It is consent, which is given verbally. This method is employed for minor procedures. However, such consent should be obtained in the presence of a disinterested third party for example nurse or receptionist
   - Oral consent, when properly witnessed, is of equal validity that of written consent.[16]
   - Whenever oral consent is taken, it is appropriate to make an entry in the patient's clinical record. Such precautions taken may be of use in future if any action is brought on the doctor by patient.[14]

B. Written Consent
   - Here the consent is obtained in a written format. The doctor should explain the type of therapeutic procedure or surgical operation properly to the patient.
   - Written consent afford documentary evidence
   - When such consent is obtained after explaining the nature and consequences of the treatment procedure being contemplated, is called as informed consent.[5]

Doctrine of Informed Consent

Every person has the right to know, in non-professional terms, regarding the disease, its status and treatment options. Informed consent is a step that will maintain transparency between doctor-patient relationships. The doctrine of informed consent is related to the rule of full disclosure and includes:

1. Right of patient to know about disease
2. Right of patient to know diagnostic tests
3. Right of patient to know proposed treatment plan and alternative methods available
4. Right of patient to know risk involved in the procedure
5. Right of patient to know benefits from procedure
6. Right of patient to know the prognosis.

Exception to Informed Consent

There are few exceptions to informed consent and are:

1. Emergency
2. Incompetence
3. Therapeutic privilege
4. Waiver

Components of Consent

In medical practice, consent becomes valid when it involves voluntary-ness, capacity and knowledge.[14,16]

1. Voluntariness – It suggest willingness of a patient to undergo treatment
2. Capacity – it means degree or ability of a patient to understand the nature and consequences of treatment offered
3. Knowledge – it means, sufficient amount of information about the nature and consequences of disease and/or treatment has been disclosed to patient.

Thus, consent should be always:

1. Free
2. Voluntary
3. Informed
4. Clear
5. Direct
6. Without undue influence/fear
7. Without fraud
8. Without misinterpretation of facts
9. Without threat or compulsion.

Criteria for Consent

Following are the criteria for persons who can give valid consent (sec 90 IPC)

1. The person should be mentally sound
2. The person should be above 12 years of age
3. The person should be not under any fear of injury or threat
4. The person should be not under misconception or false conception of facts
5. The person should be not intoxicated

Other Types of Consent

1. Blanket consent: Consent not taken for specific purpose or procedure but is broad and vague.
2. Surrogate consent – It is a proxy consent.
3. Proxy consent – Consent not given by patient himself but given by some other person on his behalf is called as proxy consent.[17]

Consent is Not Required[18]

Consent of the patient or relatives is not required under following circumstances
1. Emergency
2. Notifiable disease
3. Public interest
4. Public health
5. The court order
6. Prisoner
7. Immigrants
8. Medicolegal postmortem examinations
9. Armed forces, if medical examination is statutory requirement.

Invalid Consent

Consent is not valid when given by
1. Mentally unsound person
2. Blanket consent
3. Consent obtained by fraud, misconception, threat or by force
4. Consent obtained for criminal activity such as for procuring criminal abortion, euthanasia etc.
5. When consent is not voluntary and free.

Consent of Spouse

Preferably consent of spouse should be taken in following conditions
1. Termination of pregnancy
2. Sterilization
3. Artificial insemination
4. Donation of sperm/semen
5. Any operation that hampers sexual right of the spouse.

Doctrine of Locoparentis

- In an emergency situation involving children, when parents are not available or legal guardians are not available, consent from the person-in-charge of that child can be taken.
- For example, if a child is ill and needs operation, the school teacher can give consent in absence of parents of child
- As per this doctrine, here the teacher of child is acting as a local guardian of child i.e. local parent (locoparentis).

Law and Consent

Indian Penal Code (IPC)

1. Section 87 of IPC – Act not intended and not known to be likely to cause death or grievous hurt, done by consent.
2. Section 88 of IPC – Act not intended to cause death, done by consent in good faith for person's benefit
3. Section 89 of IPC – Act done in good faith for benefit of child or insane person, by consent of guardian
4. Section 90 of IPC – Consent known to be given under fear or misconception
5. Section 92 of IPC – Act done in good faith for benefit if a person without consent
6. Section 53 (1) of CrPC – When a person is arrested on a charge of committing an offense of such a nature and alleged to have been committed under such circumstances that there are reasonable ground for believing that an examination of his person will afford evidence as to the commission of an offense, it shall be lawful for a Registered Medical Practitioner, acting at the request of a police officer not below the rank of subinspector, and for any person acting in good faith in his aid and under his direction, to make such an examination of the person arrested as is reasonably necessary in order to ascertain the facts which may afford such evidence, and to use such force as is reasonable necessary for that purpose.

Consent and Medicolegal Cases

1. For medicolegal autopsies no consent is required
2. For clinical or pathological autopsy, consent is must
3. For examination of a victim for medicolegal purpose, consent is required
4. For examination of accused for medicolegal purpose, consent can be obtained. But if the accused is not giving consent then examination can be done without his consent.

Right to Refuse Consent

A competent person has a right to refuse treatment and refuse to consent for medical treatment or procedure.

Advance Directives

- These directives are also known as living Will
- Issuing or execution of advance directives entitles the patient to refuse treatment at any time in future.

- The advance directive is rather new concept and not prevailing in India.

MEDICAL NEGLIGENCE

Medical negligence was previously called as malpractice. Still medical negligence and medical malpractice (or malpraxis) are used as synonymous terms but the terms are not same. Medical malpractice includes other forms of irregular medical practices including unethical acts i.e. the medical practice, which is not fair or is a wrong practice.[4,19]

Definition and Explanation

- Medical negligence is defined as *want of reasonable degree of care and skill or willful negligence on the part of Medical Practitioner while treating a patient resulting in bodily injury, ill health or death.*
- Thus in the above definition, there are two important components and for negligence either one condition has to be proved i.e.
  - **Firstly** – either there is lack of reasonable degree of care and skill applied by doctor while treating a patient. The want of care and skill results in the bodily injury or ill health of a patient or patient has died due to non-application of reasonable degree of care and skill.
  - **Secondly** – willful negligence on part of doctor while treating a patient.
- Now the question arises, what is reasonable degree of care and skill? How this is to be judged? The law presumes that a person who enters in medical profession is competent and can use a reasonable degree of skill, care, knowledge and prudence in the treatment of his patient to the best of his judgment. Reasonable degree of care and skill is not defined but it is assumed that the doctor should possess such skill and knowledge as possessed by ordinary competent men practicing medicine at that time under similar circumstances and conditions. Thus a doctor may not be the best in the community of doctors but he should possess average degree of knowledge and his expertise should be at least average in his peer group.[5,8,20] Let us take an example – a doctor having MBBS degree is expected to treat patient within his competence and the MBBS graduate is not expected to do coronary by-pass surgery or renal transplantation procedure.
- The next question is what is willful negligence? It is neglect or carelessness exhibited towards the patients and doctor fails to take care of patient as circumstances demand. The act is said to be performed without due diligence.
- Before the application of Consumer Protection Act, medical negligence was governed by the law of torts. Tort means civil wrong. It can also be defined as a failure to respect the general rights of others, independent of a contract. Law of torts is the law of compensation for accidents that involve the damage to the person or property for which a court may provide a remedy in form of an action for damages.[18] The classical judicial definition of negligence as defined by **Justice Baron Alderson** in 1856 is "negligence is omission to do something which a reasonable man could do or doing something which a prudent and a reasonable man would not do".
- Thus, in simple words, negligence can be put as
  1. Failure to do something (omitting to do) which an ordinary man is supposed to do i.e. act of omission or
  2. Doing something (committing something) which an ordinary man is not supposed to do i.e. act of commission.

Classification

Negligence is a legal concept, not a medical concept. Negligence is actionable and an action for negligence may be brought against doctor in a civil or criminal court. Thus, negligence can be classified as

1. Civil negligence
2. Criminal negligence.

Civil Negligence

- Negligence is a tort i.e. civil wrong
- In civil negligence a patient brings charges of negligence against doctor for monetary compensation for the damages suffered by him.
- For civil negligence cases, a patient has to approach civil court or consumer redressal forum (Consumer court).
- To be valid, the suit for negligence must be filed in a civil court within three years from the date of alleged negligence. If the court has taken decision on a particular case, the same case cannot be reopened in any other court (**res judicata**).
- The burden of proving negligence lies on the plaintiff (i.e. patient).
- In civil action, the plaintiff (patient) has to prove that:
  1. The recognized legal right of patient had been infringed.
  2. There was existence of a **duty of care** by the doctor.
  3. Failure of doctor to exercise such duty of care and skill i.e. **dereliction of duty** by doctor or breach of duty by doctor.
  4. This breach of duty (dereliction of duty) was the cause of injury or harm to patient (i.e. **direct causation**).

5. As a result of injury or harm, the patient had suffered **damage**. (Here damage refers to harm suffered by patient, which had causes loss of income, extra expenses for treatment for harm and had mental and physical suffering. These damage/damages should be compensated by money). Thus, there are **four D's** i.e. duty, dereliction of that duty, direct causation and damage suffered.

Duty of Care

- In case of negligence, it is important for patient to prove that the doctor was duty bound to treat the patient. In other words, **doctor-patient relationship** was already existed and thus the doctor owes to care the patient. If it is shown that doctor was not under a duty of care to the patient, then the doctor cannot be charged for negligence (i.e. doctor-patient relationship does not exist).
- Doctor-patient relationship develops once the doctor accepts the patient. It is of no importance that the patient being treated free of charge or doctor has treated a patient in an emergency.
- However, when doctor examines a patient for some other purpose other than providing treatment for example doctor examining the person for medicolegal purpose or doing medicolegal autopsy, no patient-doctor relationship exists and thus under such circumstances a doctor cannot be charged for negligence.

Dereliction of Duty

- Dereliction or breach of duty means failure on part of doctor to exercise his duty and treat the patient with due care and skill.
- Such breech of duty may be an act of commission or an act of omission.
- Example of act of omission – failure on part of doctor to provide proper post-operative services that resulted in death due to sudden fall of blood pressure or cardiac arrest. Another example – failure of doctor to give anti-tetanus prophylaxis in an injured.
- Example of act of commission – operating a patient under influence of alcohol. Another example – ligation of ureter during hysterectomy operation instead of artery.

Direct Causation (Damage)

- The plaintiff (patient) has to prove that due to breach of duty of doctor, the patient had suffered the harm or negligence of doctor was the proximate cause of injury or harm sustained by the patient. Thus, the dereliction of duty of doctor is directly responsible for the damage occurred to patient.
- Damage is the injury or harm or disability suffered by patient. The damage caused is due to breach of duty of doctor and is directly responsible. The damage has to be foreseeable.
- Thus, in medical negligence cases, the burden of proof lies with the plaintiff (patient) who has to prove the presence of duty of doctor to care → breach of duty of care → causes damages → patient suffer harm → the damages should be compensated in terms of money (Fig. 2.2).

Criminal Negligence

- Here the patient or relatives of patient brings allegation of criminal negligence against a doctor. In criminal negligence, the doctor is prosecuted by the police and charged in a criminal court.
- Criminal negligence is gross negligent acts that had caused death or severe harm to the patient. The doctor showed a gross carelessness or gross neglect for the life and safety of the patient.[3]
- Criminal negligence is a serious than civil negligence. The negligence amounts to a criminal offense and goes beyond a mere matter of compensation.[21] The doctor is liable to be punished under the Indian Penal Code (IPC), example, Section 304-A, 304, 336, 337, 338 etc.

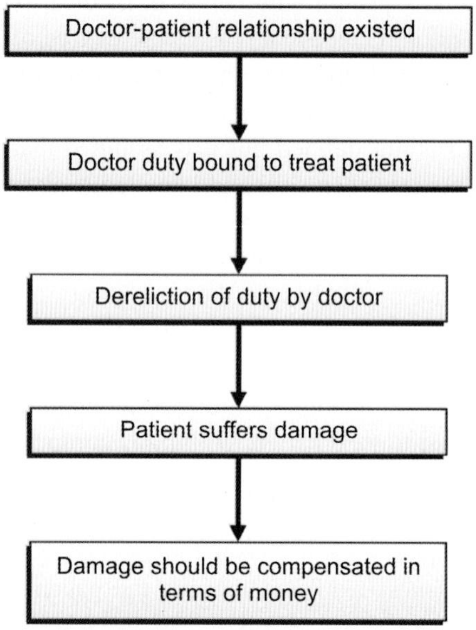

FIG. 2.2: Flowchart showing civil negligence

- In criminal law, the criminal negligence must be proved beyond reasonable doubt unlike civil negligence. In criminal negligence, the negligence that is justified for convection must be of a gross degree or culpable (also called as wicked, criminal) and not the negligence founded on a mere error of judgment or inherent risks. It is something more than mere omission or neglect of duty. Thus, in criminal negligence, there is rashness on part of doctor.[6]
- In criminal negligence, the prosecution has to prove all the facts to establish civil negligence (except monetary loss) and gross negligence by doctor and have to show that doctor has disregard for the life and safety of the patient.[22] The Supreme Court in one case held that "the negligence or rashness of such a higher degree as to indicate a mental state which can be described as totally apathetic towards the patient is punishable under law.[23] Thus, in criminal negligence, **mens rea** (guilty mind) i.e. rashness or guilty mind of degree (criminal negligence) is required and mere carelessness is not enough.
- As per Section 357 of CrPC, there is provision for award of compensation. In addition to imprisonment or other penalty prescribed by the IPC, compensation may also have to be paid to the victim in criminal negligence.
- On August 2005, the Supreme Court of India gave a landmark judgment regarding the interpretation of medical negligence. As per the judgment, no doctor can be arrested simply on filling the complaint against him by any patient or relative of the patient. His arrest can only be there if needed for furthering the investigation or for collecting evidence or investigating officer think that doctor may run away to evade arrest. The judgment has given direction for the investigating officer how to proceed in such cases. Before proceeding against doctor, the investigating officer should obtain an independent and competent opinion preferably from a doctor in government service qualified in that branch of medical practice.[24]

Examples of Criminal Negligence

1. Operation on wrong limb
2. Removal of wrong organ
3. Wrong blood transfusion
4. Leaving instruments in abdomen
5. Performing criminal abortion

Differences between civil and criminal negligence are mentioned in Table 2.1. Differences between negligence and infamous conduct are mentioned in Table 2.2.

Doctrine of Res Ipsa Loquitar[25]

- Cicero had quoted *"Res loquitur ipsa, judices, quae simper valet plurimum"* (Judges, the case speaks for itself, than there is no more powerful advocacy)
- Literally translated, res ipsa loquitar means *"the things or facts speaks for itself"*.
- The doctrine, legally, is a rule of circumstantial evidence that gives rise to an inference of responsibility for an injury or damage. In a negligence case where patient is unable to prove the breach of duty of care by doctor, the doctrine of Res ipsa loquitar may provide help. The doctrine is not an arbitrary rule, but rather, a common-sense appraisal of the probative value of circumstantial evidence.
- In doctrine of Res ipsa loquitar, the facts of case are sufficient to justify the conclusion that doctor was negligent and negligence of doctor is responsible for the harm suffered by the plaintiff (patient). The legal and procedural effect of the Court's acceptance of res ipsa loquitar in a negligence action is to shift the burden of proof from the plaintiff (patient) to one of disproof by the defendant (Doctor).
- The doctrine is not applicable – if the factors involved are so technical that ordinary layman are not competent to reach a proper conclusion unaided by expert testimony. Similarly, if the injuries/damages are an inherent risk of treatment and where the result, although rare, could have ensued even with the exercise of reasonable medical skill and care.
- Examples of Res ipsa loquitar are as follows:
  1. Amputation of wrong digit or limb
  2. Leaving a swab or instrument in abdomen of patient after operation.
  3. Giving medicine carelessly or prescribing overdose of medicines producing ill effect.
- This doctrine is applied to both civil and criminal negligence.[13, 22]
- However, this doctrine cannot be applied against several defendants (i.e. doctors).
- To prove Doctrine of Res ipsa loquitar, the following conditions should be satisfied:
  1. That in absence of negligence, the injury would not have occurred.
  2. Patient has not contributed to negligence.
  3. Doctor had exclusive control of the circumstances or injury producing instruments or treatment.

Doctrine of Calculated Risk

- In certain treatment procedures or operations, there is inherent risk or unavoidable risk. For example – a female brought at term for delivery has to undergo Caesarian

Table 2.1: Differences between civil and criminal negligence

Features	*Civil negligence*	*Criminal negligence*
Negligence	Absence of care and skill	Gross carelessness and disregard for patient's life or welfare
Offense	No violation of law	Violation of criminal law
Conduct of doctor	Compared with peer group	Not compared to single test
Consent for act	Good defense in court	Not a defense
Trail	Civil or consumer court	Criminal court
Evidence	Strong evidence is sufficient	Guilt should be proved beyond reasonable doubt
Punishment	Liable to pay damages	Imprisonment

Table 2.2: Differences between professional negligence and infamous conduct

Features	*Professional negligence*	*Infamous conduct*
Nature of offense	Absence of care and skill or willful negligence	Violation of code of medical ethics prescribed by MCI
Duty of care	Should be present	Need not be present
Damages to patient	Should be present	Need not be present
Trail by	Courts - Civil or criminal or Consumer redressal forum	State Medical Council
Punishment	Fine or pay damages or imprisonment	Warning or erasure of name from Register
Appeal	To higher courts	To MCI/Central government

Section. Now the operation (i.e. Caesarian Section) may carry risk to mother or fetus or both. At times, mother or fetus may die. In spite of all adequate care and skill, there is risk that in 0.1% of cases the mother may die.

- This inherent risk or danger is basis for doctrine of calculated risk.
- In such cases, the charge of negligence cannot be proved or stand against doctor.

Doctrine of Common Knowledge

- A doctor may be charged for negligence in a particular case, not for his technical or medical knowledge, but for act involving application of common sense or common knowledge only.
- For example – if a patient with gastroenteritis with dehydration comes to doctor; it is a matter of common sense that the patient requires fluid replacement. If doctor fails to do the needful then the doctor can be charged for negligence.
- Here the plaintiff (patient) need not to show that doctor did not show reasonable degree of care and skill but it is common knowledge that such patient requires fluid therapy.[23]

Novas Actus Interveniens

- It means an unrelated action intervening
- At times, it occurred that patient might suffer damage or harm due to new action, which intervene or intercede the treatment. For example – suppose an operated patient is shifted to recovery room and suddenly, due to earthquake, ceiling falls over the patient and the patient dies in the accident. Here the falling of ceiling is a new intervention that has occurred.
- A doctor may not be held responsible if damage occurred to patient due to new action, which intervenes in the treatment.

Medical Maloccurrence

- Also called as inevitable accidents or act of God
- Human beings show biological variation. It is often said that diversity in biology is a rule rather than exception. Thus, an individual may show varying biological variation. In some individuals, despite giving good medical care and skill, the patient may suffer or does not respond properly to treatment. This is known as medical maloccurrence.

- If the doctor had exercised reasonable degree of care and skill and in spite of this the patient do not respond or medical maloccurence develops; the doctor would not be held responsible.

Therapeutic Misadventure

- Therapeutic misadventure is a mis-chance or accident or disaster, in which an individual may be injured or die due to some unintentional act of doctor or hospital.[16]
- Therapeutic misadventure is of three types
  1. Therapeutic – when treatment is being given
  2. Diagnostic – when diagnosis is being done or diagnostic test is being done.
  3. Experimental – where the patient had agreed to serve as subject in an experimental study.
- It is known that many of the therapeutic drugs or procedures may cause death. A doctor would not be held responsible for harm caused to the patient by adverse reaction by drug provided that doctor had exercised due care.
- Examples:
  1. Anaphylaxis to drug like penicillin, provided that doctor had exercised due care.
  2. Radiological procedure may prove fatal due to adverse reaction to dye used for contrast, provided that doctor had exercised due care.

Doctrine of Error of Judgment

- A doctor is not held responsible for negligence caused due to error of judgment
- In medical practice, the decision regarding the diagnosis and/or management of particular disease or condition is made based on the judgment of a treating doctor. It is expected from a doctor to apply reasonable skill and care while diagnosing/treating a patient. A mistake or error in judgment made by a doctor does not constitute negligent conduct.

Captain of the Ship Doctrine

- This sort of doctrine is applicable where team works with one of the senior doctor being the leader i.e. the captain.
- For example, in operation theatre, the surgeon is the leader of team. For any negligence occurred during operation, the surgeon will be held responsible as per this doctrine because it becomes difficult to singled out any person as a negligent. The surgeon being leader of the team heads responsibility for every action occurring within the operation theatre.
- The captain of ship doctrine has been largely replaced by the "**barrowed servant doctrine**". According to this doctrine, a surgeon may be held responsible for the negligence of nurse or any other junior doctor.

Doctrine of Respondent Superior

- This is one of the oldest axioms of common law. According to this doctrine, a superior person can be legally saddled for another's liability (vicarious liability). It is founded on the principle that a duty rests on every man in managing his affairs, whether by himself or by his agents or servants to conduct them so as not to injure/damage others. If he or his subordinate does not conduct the assignment smoothly due to which another is suffering injury/damages, then he shall answer for the damage. Literally respondent superior means "*let the master answer*". The concept is best summarized by the ancient Latin phrase "*qui facet peralium, facet per se*" i.e. *he who acts through another, acts himself.*[25]
- In other words, for any negligent act of subordinate, the master or superior authority can be held responsible (vicarious responsibility).

Contributory Negligence

- In this condition, patient is also responsible and contributed to the injury/damage suffered by him. Thus, it is a combination form of negligence where patient has also contributed.
- Example – such as – not giving correct history to doctor, not following the instruction and advise of doctor, failure to attend treatment at prescribed time, tampering with wound dressing/plaster etc.
- Here the defendant (doctor) has to prove that plaintiff (patient) has contributed for the injury because of want of care or wrong act. Here plaintiff fails to take reasonable care and causes harm.
- If this plea is accepted by court, the doctor is not held responsible for the damage caused to the patient.

Corporate Negligence[27]

- Under the doctrine of corporate liability, a corporate house or hospital may have a duty to properly select the persons of professional competence.
- The hospitals may even be duty bound to intervene actively where a physician is negligent and prevent errant staff from endangering hospitalized patients.
- To prove a charge of corporate negligence, the plaintiff would have to show that the hospital was aware that

the physician associated with the hospital was providing sub-standard care.

To Avoid Negligence

The following points, certainly not exhaustive, could, it is thought, lead to reasonable reduction in number of allegations of negligence being brought against doctors.[28]

1. Verbal communication – be sure, time spent securing and maintaining rapport with one's patient is not time wasted. Many allegations are made due to breakdown or improper communication or relationship. Be enduring, hear the grievances of patient and encourage communication.
2. Always obtain complete history because inadequate history leads to an inadequate diagnosis and inadequate treatment. Remember – every clinical teacher has said to every student, **the history is all-important**.
3. Examine the patient completely.
4. Seek appropriate investigations and laboratory support.
5. If the patient does not progress, as expected, re-examine him.
6. The doctor, being professional man, is expected to maintain his standard of professional knowledge and skill.
7. Apply reasonable degree of skill and knowledge, it is dangerous to trespass one's specialty or treat beyond one's competence.
8. Many complaints allege that another doctor expressed or implied criticism. Such criticism on fellow doctor is invariably unfair and seldom required.
9. Do not guarantee treatment; especially while practicing in India, people equate doctor to God and expect miracle. Explain the facts and condition of patient to relatives in plain and honest words.
10. The law does not require a doctor to guarantee results; care should be taken to see that the patient has no grounds for considering that a guarantee has been implied.
11. Record and notes – adequate, legible and signed notes recorded in patient sheet are the doctor's main defense in negligence cases.

In conclusion, Medical Practitioner may draw consolation and courage from the observations of Lord Denning in a case (Whitehouse Vs. Jordan) "the worrying number of medical malpractice cases, juries having sympathy for the patient, the insurance premiums getting higher, scare in the mind of experienced practitioner and prospective medical graduates as is presently happening in USA, is a matter of concern and we must avoid such consequences. We must say and say firmly that in a professional man; an error of judgment is not negligence".[29]

CONSUMER PROTECTION ACT

Consumer Protection Act (CPA) was enacted by Parliament in 1986 to provide better protection of the interests of consumers in the background of guidelines contained in the Consumer Protection Resolution passed by U.N. General Assembly on 9th April 1985. The aims of CPA are:

1. Protection of consumer from hazards to their health and safety.
2. Availability of effective consumer redressal forum.
3. Cheap and speedy remedy.

The National Commission in 1993, in a ruling, includes medical services under the provisions of Consumer Protection Act (CPA). In 1995, the Supreme Court of India (Indian Medical Association versus V.P. Shantha) includes medical services under the ambit of CPA.

Structure and Functioning of Consumer Redressal Agencies

Under CPA, the consumer dispute redressal agencies have been set up at three levels i.e. at district level, state level and at national level to provide speedy and inexpensive judicial remedies to the consumers. The composition is given in Table 2.3 and Figure 2.3.

1. Consumer Dispute Redressal Forum – District forum
2. Consumer Dispute Redressal Forum – State commission
3. Consumer Dispute Redressal Forum – National commission

Features[29]

- A complaint can be filled in forum or commission by either consumer, any voluntary consumer association (registered under the companies Act 1956 or under any

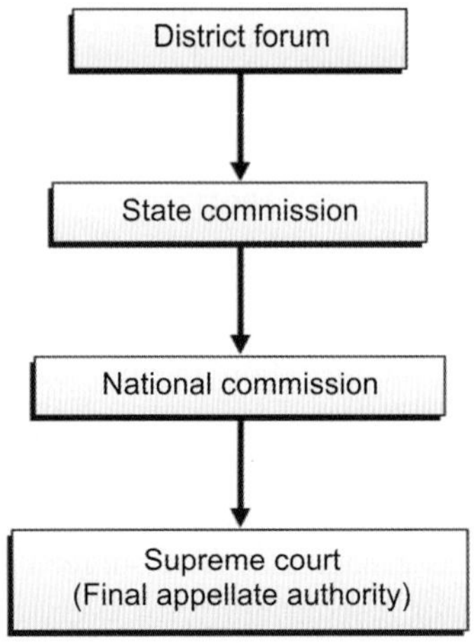

FIG. 2.3: Showing consumer redressal agencies

Table 2.3: Composition of consumer redressal forum

Forum/Commission	*Composition*	*Jurisdiction*
District	District forum has three members. 1. One chairman – a sitting or retired Sessions and District Judge 2. Others two members are eminent citizens and amongst them one should be female. The age of the members should not be less than 35 years and they should possess at least some bachelor's degree. The appointments are made by State government for a period of 5 years or up to age of 65 years whichever is earlier.	- Original jurisdiction - Entertain complains that does not exceed Rs. 20 lakhs
State	State Commission has three members. 1. Presided by sitting or retired High Court Judge 2. Other two members are eminent citizens and amongst them one should be female.	- Original jurisdiction - Appellate jurisdiction - Revision jurisdiction - Entertain complains that does not exceed 1 crore but over 20 lakhs
National	It is located at New Delhi and consists of 5 members. 1. Presided by sitting or retired Supreme Court Judge 2. Other four members are eminent citizens and amongst them one should be female.	- Original jurisdiction - Appellate jurisdiction - Revision jurisdiction - Entertain complains that exceed Rs. 1 crore.

other law for the time being in force) or State Govt./Central Govt./Union Territory or more than one consumers having same interest, or in case of death of consumer by his legal heir or representative.

- A complaint is to be filled within two years from the date on which a cause of action has arisen.
- The Act has prescribed time limit for deciding complaint by Forum or Commission – as far as possible within 3 months from the date of receipt of notice by the opposite party where the complaint does not require any analysis or testing. In case, some analysis or testing is required, the time limit prescribed is 5 months.
- Any appeal should be filled within 30 days of the order. Any person, who is aggrieved by an order made by the District Forum, the State Commission or the National Commission, can file an appeal to the Appellate Court (Supreme Court) within a period of 30 days from the date of the order.
- *Consumer means any person who buys any goods or hires any services for a consideration.*
- *Service means service of any description, which is made available to* potential users. Service by a Medical Practitioner is under a contract for personal service.
- Deficiency means any fault, imperfection, shortcoming or inadequacy in the quality, nature and manner of performance, which is required to be maintained as per law, in section 2(1) (g) of CPA.
- The opinion of the majority of members is the order of Consumer Forum/Commission
- The consumer redressal agencies are conferred with the powers of the First Class Judicial Magistrate
- The consumer redressal agencies can issue interim orders
- A complainant can represent his case on his own without the help of lawyer. Every complaint filled shall be accompanied with the prescribed amount of fee
- It was believed that government and public sector hospitals are immune to litigations under CPA as the services are rendered free-of charge. However, the Supreme Court of India, in the year 2000 (State of Harayana versus Smt. Santra) in its decision clearly stated that the immunity is applicable to those hospitals, which are treating all patients/consumers free-of charge.[30]

BIOMEDICAL WASTE MANAGEMENT

Biomedical waste is an important source of health hazard. *Biomedical waste refers to any waste generated from health care industry such as hospitals, clinics and medical laboratories.*

Importance

1. Health hazard to patient and relatives.
2. Microbiological and chemical contamination of soil and ground water.

3. Increased risk of HIV infection and HBV infection among the workers engaged in hospital waste disposal.
4. Causes air pollution.

Types of Medical Waste

1. General waste – it is non-risk or uncontaminated waste similar to domestic waste.
2. Hazardous waste.
3. Highly hazardous waste.

Hazardous Waste

- Usual infectious waste
- Anatomical or pathological waste
- Waste contaminated with human blood or body fluids, excreta or vomitus
- Chemical and pharmaceutical residues
- Discarded containers.

Highly Hazardous Waste

- Sharps – includes hypodermic needles, scalpels, blades, glass etc.
- Highly infectious non-sharp waste – includes microbial cultures, carcasses of inoculated laboratory animals, body fluid, blood etc.
- Genotoxic waste – such as radioactive and cytotoxic waste

According to Biomedical waste (management and handling) Rules 1995, the waste is categorized into 10 types and is mentioned in Table 2.4.

Principles of Waste Management

1. Collection of waste and segregation
2. Transportation of waste to disposal unit
3. Treatment of waste

Collection and segregation should be done at source.

Table 2.4: Categories of biomedical waste

Category	*Waste*
1	Human anatomical waste, blood and body fluids
2	Animal and slaughter house waste
3	Microbiology and biotechnology waste
4	Waste sharps
5	Discarded medicines
6	Solid wastes
7	Disposables
8	Liquid wastes
9	Incinerator ash
10	Chemical waste

Transport and Disposal of Waste

- General waste – can join the municipal waste stream
- For others – following methods may be employed
  1. Incineration
  2. Deep burial
  3. Autoclave and microwave
  4. Chemical disinfection
  5. Shredding/ mutilation/cutting
- All biomedical waste except chlorinated plastics and radioactive waste may be subjected to incineration.

ETHICS AND MEDICAL RESEARCH (HUMAN EXPERIMENTATION)

Biomedical research involving human beings is aimed to:

1. Improve diagnostic procedure
2. Improve therapeutic procedure
3. Improve prophylactic procedure
4. Understanding the etiology and pathogenesis of disease.

Medical advancement is based on medical research and for conducting research human subjects are necessary. At times, medical research may prove hazardous to the human subjects involved therein. In India, all research involving human subjects should be conducted in accordance with the guidelines prescribed by Indian Council of Medical Research (ICMR). The ICMR guidelines are based on following four basic ethical principles:

1. Autonomy – respect for the human subject
2. Beneficence
3. Non-malfeasance – do not involve harm to patient
4. Justice.

Ethical Aspects

- A physician should act for the benefit of his patient
- In 1984, World Medical Association (WMA) drew up code of ethics on human experimentation, known as "**Declaration of Helsinki**". As per the declaration:
  - ⇨ Biomedical research involving human subjects should be done after adequate laboratory and animal experiments and should be conducted by scientifically qualified persons
  - ⇨ Health of human subject involved in research should be paramount and responsibility rest with medical person
- In India research should be conducted in accordance with ICMR guidelines for human research 1995.

ICMR Guidelines[31]

General principles are given below

1. Principles of essentiality – it should be clear that the research is absolutely essential to have human subjects.
2. Principles of voluntariness – research subject should be told regarding the research, the risk involved. Informed consent should be obtained. The person has right to abstain or withdraw from future or further participation in research.
3. Principles of non-exploitation – the research subjects should be remunerated for their involvement. The subjects are entitled for compensation either through insurance or other means for all foreseeable or unforeseeable risks.
4. Principles of privacy and confidentiality.
5. Principles of precaution and risk minimization.
6. Principles of professional competence – research should be conducted by competent and qualified persons.
7. Principles of accountability and transparency.
8. Principles of maximization of the public interest and distributive justice.
9. Principles of public domain.
10. Principles of totality and responsibility.
11. Principles of compliance.

INDIAN MEDICAL COUNCIL (PROFESSIONAL CONDUCT, ETIQUETTE AND ETHICS) REGULATIONS, 2002

MCI notification of April 6, 2002, the Indian Medical Council (professional conduct, etiquette and ethics) Regulations, 2002

(Published in Part III, Section 4 of the Gazette of India, dated 6th April 2002)

MEDICAL COUNCIL OF INDIA

NOTIFICATION

New Delhi, dated 11th March, 2002

No. MCI-211 (2)/2001/Registration. In exercise of the powers conferred under section 20A read with section 33(m) of the Indian Medical Council Act, 1956 (102 of 1956), the Medical Council of India, with the previous approval of the Central Government, hereby makes the following regulations relating to the Professional Conduct, Etiquette and Ethics for registered medical practitioners, namely:-

Short Title and Commencement: (1) These Regulations may be called the Indian Medical Council (Professional conduct, Etiquette and Ethics) Regulations, 2002. (2) They shall come into force on the date of their publication in the Official Gazette.

CHAPTER I

1. Code of Medical Ethics

A. Declaration: Each applicant, at the time of making an application for registration under the provisions of the Act, shall be provided a copy of the declaration and shall submit a duly signed Declaration as provided in Appendix 1. The applicant shall also certify that he/she had read and agreed to abide by the same.

B. Duties and responsibilities of the Physician in general:

1.1 Character of Physician

(Doctors with qualification of MBBS or MBBS with postgraduate degree/diploma or with equivalent qualification in any medical discipline):

1.1.1 A physician shall uphold the dignity and honour of his profession.

1.1.2 The prime object of the medical profession is to render service to humanity; reward or financial gain is a subordinate consideration.

Who-so-ever chooses his profession, assumes the obligation to conduct himself in accordance with its ideals. A physician should be an upright man, instructed in the art of healings. He shall keep himself pure in character and be diligent in caring for the sick; he should be modest, sober, patient, prompt in discharging his duty without anxiety; conducting himself with propriety in his profession and in all the actions of his life.

1.1.3 No person other than a doctor having qualification recognized by Medical Council of India and registered with Medical Council of India/State Medical Council(s) is allowed to practice Modern system of Medicine or Surgery. A person obtaining qualification in any other system of Medicine is not allowed to practice Modern system of Medicine in any form.

1.2 Maintaining good medical practice

1.2.1 The Principal objective of the medical profession is to render service to humanity with full respect for the dignity of profession and man.

Physicians should merit the confidence of patients entrusted to their care, rendering to each a full measure of service and devotion. Physicians should try continuously to improve medical knowledge and skills and should make available to their patients and colleagues the benefits of their professional attainments. The physician should practice methods of healing founded on scientific basis and should not associate professionally with anyone who violates this principle. The honoured ideals of the medical profession imply that the responsibilities of the physician extend not only to individuals but also to society.

1.2.2 Membership in Medical Society: For the advancement of his profession, a physician should affiliate with associations and societies of allopathic medical professions and involve actively in the functioning of such bodies.

1.2.3 A Physician should participate in professional meetings as part of Continuing Medical Education programmes, for at least 30 hours every five years, organized by reputed professional academic bodies or any other authorized organizations. The compliance of this requirement shall be informed regularly to Medical Council of India or the State Medical Councils as the case may be.

1.3 Maintenance of medical records:

1.3.1 Every physician shall maintain the medical records pertaining to his/her indoor patients for a period of 3 years from the date of commencement of the treatment in a standard proforma laid down by the Medical Council of India and attached as Appendix 3.

1.3.2. If any request is made for medical records either by the patients/authorized attendant or legal authorities involved, the same may be duly acknowledged and documents shall be issued within the period of 72 hours. 1.3.3 A Registered medical practitioner shall maintain a Register of Medical Certificates giving full details of certificates issued. When issuing a medical certificate he/she shall always enter the identification marks of the patient and keep a copy of the certificate. He/She shall not omit to record the signature and/or thumb mark, address and at least one identification mark of the patient on the medical certificates or report. The medical certificate shall be prepared as in Appendix 2.

1.3.4 Efforts shall be made to computerize medical records for quick retrieval.

1.4 Display of registration numbers:

1.4.1 Every physician shall display the registration number accorded to him by the State Medical Council/Medical Council of India in his clinic and in all his prescriptions, certificates, money receipts given to his patients.

1.4.2 Physicians shall display as suffix to their names only recognized medical degrees or such certificates/diplomas and memberships/honors which confer professional knowledge or recognizes any exemplary qualification/achievements.

1.5 Use of generic names of drugs:

Every physician should, as far as possible, prescribe drugs with generic names and he/she shall ensure that there is a rational prescription and use of drugs.

1.6 Highest Quality Assurance in patient care:

Every physician should aid in safeguarding the profession against admission to it of those who are deficient in moral character or education. Physician shall not employ in connection with his professional practice any attendant who is neither registered nor enlisted under the Medical Acts in force and shall not permit such persons to attend, treat or perform operations upon patients wherever professional discretion or skill is required.

1.7 Exposure of Unethical Conduct:

A Physician should expose, without fear or favour, incompetent or corrupt, dishonest or unethical conduct on the part of members of the profession.

1.8 Payment of Professional Services:

The physician, engaged in the practice of medicine shall give priority to the interests of patients. The personal financial interests of a physician should not conflict with the medical interests of patients. A physician should announce his fees before rendering service and not after the operation or treatment is under way. Remuneration received for such services should be in the form and amount specifically announced to the patient at the time the service is rendered. It is unethical to enter into a contract of "no cure no payment". Physician rendering service on behalf of the state shall refrain from anticipating or accepting any consideration.

1.9 Evasion of Legal Restrictions:

The physician shall observe the laws of the country in regulating the practice of medicine and shall also not assist others to evade such laws. He should be cooperative in observance and enforcement of sanitary laws and regulations in the interest of public health. A physician should observe the provisions of the State Acts like Drugs and Cosmetics Act, 1940; Pharmacy Act, 1948; Narcotic Drugs and Psychotropic substances Act, 1985; Medical Termination of Pregnancy Act, 1971; Transplantation of Human Organ Act, 1994; Mental Health Act, 1987; Environmental Protection Act, 1986; Pre-natal Sex Determination Test Act, 1994; Drugs and Magic Remedies (Objectionable Advertisement) Act, 1954; Persons with Disabilities (Equal Opportunities and Full Participation) Act, 1995 and Bio-Medical Waste (Management and Handling) Rules, 1998 and such other Acts, Rules, Regulations made by the Central/State Governments or local Administrative Bodies or any other relevant Act relating to the protection and promotion of public health.

CHAPTER 2

2. Duties of Physicians to their Patients

2.1 Obligations to the Sick:

2.1.1 Though a physician is not bound to treat each and every person asking his services, he should not only be ever ready to respond to the calls of the sick and the injured, but should be mindful of the high character of his mission and the responsibility he discharges in the course of his professional duties. In his treatment, he should never forget that the health and the lives of those entrusted to his care depend on his skill and attention. A physician should endeavor to add to the comfort of the sick by making his visits at the hour indicated to the patients. A physician advising a patient to seek service of another physician is acceptable, however, in case of emergency a physician must treat the patient. No physician shall arbitrarily refuse treatment to a patient. However for good reason, when a patient is suffering from an ailment, which is not within the range of experience of the treating physician, the physician may refuse treatment and refer the patient to another physician.

2.1.2 Medical practitioner having any incapacity detrimental to the patient or which can affect his performance vis-à-vis the patient is not permitted to practice his profession.

2.2 Patience, Delicacy and Secrecy:

Patience and delicacy should characterize the physician. Confidences concerning individual or domestic life entrusted by patients to a physician and defects in the disposition or character of patients observed during medical attendance should never be revealed unless their revelation is required by the laws of the State. Sometimes, however, a physician must determine whether his duty to society requires him to employ knowledge, obtained through confidence as a physician, to protect a healthy person against a communicable disease to which he is about to be exposed. In such instance, the physician should act as he would wish another to act toward one of his own family in like circumstances.

2.3 Prognosis:

The physician should neither exaggerate nor minimize the gravity of a patient's condition. He should ensure himself that the patient, his relatives or his responsible friends have such knowledge of the patient's condition as will serve the best interests of the patient and the family.

2.4 The Patient must not be neglected:

A physician is free to choose whom he will serve. He should, however, respond to any request for his assistance in an emergency. Once having undertaken a case, the physician should not neglect the patient, nor should he withdraw from the case without giving adequate notice to the patient and his family. Provisionally or fully registered medical practitioner shall not willfully commit an act of negligence that may deprive his patient or patients from necessary medical care.

2.5 Engagement for an Obstetric case:

When a physician who has been engaged to attend an obstetric case is absent and another is sent for and delivery accomplished, the acting physician is entitled to his professional fees, but should secure the patient's consent to resign on the arrival of the physician engaged.

CHAPTER 3

3. Duties of Physician in Consultation

3.1 Unnecessary consultations should be avoided:

3.1.1. However in case of serious illness and in doubtful or difficult conditions, the physician should request consultation, but under any circumstances such consultation should be justifiable and in the interest of the patient only and not for any other consideration.

3.1.2 Consulting pathologists/radiologists or asking for any other diagnostic Lab investigation should be done judiciously and not in a routine manner.

3.2 Consultation for Patient's Benefit: In every consultation, the benefit to the patient is of foremost importance. All physicians engaged in the case should be frank with the patient and his attendants.

3.3 Punctuality in Consultation: Utmost punctuality should be observed by a physician in making themselves available for consultations.

3.4 Statement to Patient after Consultation:

3.4.1 All statements to the patient or his representatives should take place in the presence of the consulting physicians, except as otherwise agreed. The disclosure of the opinion to the patient or his relatives or friends shall rest with the medical attendant.

3.4.2 Differences of opinion should not be divulged unnecessarily but when there is irreconcilable difference of opinion the circumstances should be frankly and impartially explained to the patient or his relatives or friends. It would be open to them to seek further advice, as they so desire.

3.5 Treatment after Consultation: No decision should restrain the attending physician from making such subsequent variations in the treatment if any unexpected change occurs, but at the next consultation, reasons for the variations should be discussed/explained. The same privilege, with its obligations, belongs to the consultant when sent for in an emergency during the absence of attending physician. The attending physician may prescribe medicine at any time for the patient, whereas the consultant may prescribe only in case of emergency or as an expert when called for.

3.6 Patients Referred to Specialists: When a patient is referred to a specialist by the attending physician, a case summary of the patient should be given to the specialist, who should communicate his opinion in writing to the attending physician.

3.7 Fees and other charges:

3.7.1 A physician shall clearly display his fees and other charges on the board of his chamber and/or the hospitals he is visiting. Prescription should also make clear if the Physician himself dispensed any medicine.

3.7.2 A physician shall write his name and designation in full along with registration particulars in his prescription letter head.

Note: In Government hospital where the patient-load is heavy, the name of the prescribing doctor must be written below his/her signature.

CHAPTER 4

4. Responsibilities of Physicians to Each Other

4.1 Dependence of Physicians on each other:

A physician should consider it as a pleasure and privilege to render gratuitous service to all physicians and their immediate family dependants.

4.2 Conduct in consultation:

In consultations, no insincerity, rivalry or envy should be indulged in. All due respect should be observed towards the physician in-charge of the case and no statement or remark be made, which would impair the confidence reposed in him. For this purpose no discussion should be carried on in the presence of the patient or his representatives.

4.3 Consultant not to take charge of the case:

When a physician has been called for consultation, the Consultant should normally not take charge of the case, especially on the solicitation of the patient or friends. The Consultant shall not criticize the referring physician. He/she shall discuss the diagnosis treatment plan with the referring physician.

4.4 Appointment of Substitute: Whenever a physician requests another physician to attend his patients during his temporary absence from his practice, professional courtesy requires the acceptance of such appointment only when he has the capacity to discharge the additional responsibility along with his/her other duties. The physician acting under such an appointment should give the utmost consideration to the interests and reputation of the absent physician and all such patients should be restored to the care of the latter upon his/her return.

4.5 Visiting another Physician's Case: When it becomes the duty of a physician occupying an official position to see and report upon an illness or injury, he should communicate to the physician in attendance so as to give him an option of being present. The medical officer/ physician occupying an official position should avoid remarks upon the diagnosis or the treatment that has been adopted.

CHAPTER 5

5. Duties of Physician to the Public and to the Paramedical Profession

5.1 Physicians as Citizens: Physicians, as good citizens, possessed of special training should disseminate advice on public health issues. They should play their part in enforcing the laws of the community and in sustaining the institutions that advance the interests of humanity. They should particularly co-operate with the authorities in the administration of sanitary/public health laws and regulations.

5.2 Public and Community Health: Physicians, especially those engaged in public health work, should enlighten the public concerning quarantine regulations and measures for the prevention of epidemic and communicable diseases. At all times the physician should notify the constituted public health authorities of every case of communicable disease under his care, in accordance with the laws, rules and regulations of the health authorities. When an epidemic occurs a physician should not abandon his duty for fear of contracting the disease himself.

5.3 Pharmacists/Nurses: Physicians should recognize and promote the practice of different paramedical services such as, pharmacy and nursing as professions and should seek their cooperation wherever required.

CHAPTER 6

6. Unethical Acts

A physician shall not aid or abet or commit any of the following acts, which shall be construed as unethical -

6.1 Advertising:

6.1.1 Soliciting of patients directly or indirectly, by a physician, by a group of physicians or by institutions or organizations is unethical. A physician shall not make use of him/her (or his/her name) as subject of any form or manner of advertising or publicity through any mode either alone or in conjunction with others which is of such a character as to invite attention to him or to his professional position, skill, qualification, achievements, attainments, specialties, appointments, associations, affiliations or honors and/or of such character as would ordinarily result in his self-aggrandizement. A physician shall not give to any person, whether for compensation or otherwise, any approval, recommendation, endorsement, certificate, report or statement with respect of any drug, medicine, nostrum remedy, surgical, or therapeutic article, apparatus or appliance or any commercial product or article with respect of any property, quality or use thereof or any test, demonstration or trial thereof, for use in connection with his name, signature, or photograph in any form or manner of advertising through any mode nor shall he boast of cases, operations, cures or remedies or permit the publication of report thereof through any mode. A medical practitioner is however permitted to make a formal announcement in press regarding the following:

- On starting practice
- On change of type of practice
- On changing address
- On temporary absence from duty
- On resumption of another practice
- On succeeding to another practice
- Public declaration of charges.

6.1.2 Printing of self photograph, or any such material of publicity in the letter head or on sign board of the consulting room or any such clinical establishment shall be regarded as acts of self advertisement and unethical conduct on the part of the physician. However, printing of sketches, diagrams, picture of human system shall not be treated as unethical.

6.2 Patent and Copyrights:

A physician may patent surgical instruments, appliances and medicine or Copyright applications, methods and procedures. However, it shall be unethical if the benefits of such patents or copyrights are not made available in situations where the interest of large population is involved.

6.3 Running an open shop (Dispensing of Drugs and Appliances by Physicians):

A physician should not run an open shop for sale of medicine for dispensing prescriptions prescribed by doctors other than himself or for sale of medical or surgical appliances. It is not unethical for a physician to prescribe or supply drugs, remedies or appliances as long as there is no exploitation of the patient. Drugs prescribed by a physician or brought from the market for a patient should explicitly state the proprietary formulae as well as generic name of the drug.

6.4 Rebates and Commission:

6.4.1 A physician shall not give, solicit, or receive nor shall he offer to give solicit or receive, any gift, gratuity, commission or bonus in consideration of or return for the referring, recommending or procuring of any patient for medical, surgical or other treatment. A physician shall not directly or indirectly, participate in or be a party to act of division, transference, assignment, subordination, rebating, splitting or refunding of any fee for medical, surgical or other treatment.

6.4.2 Provisions of Para 6.4.1 shall apply with equal force to the referring, recommending or procuring by a physician or any person, specimen or material for diagnostic purposes or other study/work. Nothing in this section, however, shall prohibit payment of salaries by a qualified physician to other duly qualified person rendering medical care under his supervision.

6.5 Secret Remedies:

The prescribing or dispensing by a physician of secret remedial agents of which he does not know the composition, or the manufacture or promotion of their use is unethical and as such prohibited. All the drugs prescribed by a physician should always carry a proprietary formula and clear name.

6.6 Human Rights:

The physician shall not aid or abet torture nor shall he be a party to either infliction of mental or physical trauma or concealment of torture inflicted by some other person or agency in clear violation of human rights.

6.7 Euthanasia:

Practicing euthanasia shall constitute unethical conduct. However on specific occasion, the question of withdrawing supporting devices to sustain cardio-pulmonary function even after brain death, shall be decided only by a team of doctors and not merely by the treating physician alone. A team of doctors shall declare withdrawal of support system. Such team shall consist of the doctor incharge of the patient, Chief Medical Officer/ Medical Officer incharge of the hospital and a doctor nominated by the incharge of the hospital from the hospital staff or in accordance with the provisions of the Transplantation of Human Organ Act, 1994.

CHAPTER 7

7. Misconduct:

The following acts of commission or omission on the part of a physician shall constitute professional misconduct rendering him/her liable for disciplinary action -

7.1 Violation of the Regulations: If he/she commits any violation of these Regulations.

7.2 If he/she does not maintain the medical records of his/her indoor patients for a period of three years as per regulation 1.3 and refuses to provide the same within 72 hours when the patient or his/her authorized representative makes a request for it as per the regulation 1.3.2.

7.3 If he/she does not display the registration number accorded to him/her by the State Medical Council or the Medical Council of India in his clinic, prescriptions and certificates etc. issued by him or violates the provisions of regulation 1.4.2.

7.4 Adultery or Improper Conduct: Abuse of professional position by committing adultery or improper conduct with a patient or by maintaining an improper association with a patient will render a Physician liable for disciplinary action as provided under the Indian Medical Council Act, 1956 or the concerned State Medical Council Act.

7.5 Conviction by Court of Law: Conviction by a Court of Law for offences involving moral turpitude/Criminal acts.

7.6 Sex Determination Tests: On no account sex determination test shall be undertaken with the intent to terminate the life of a female foetus developing in her mother's womb, unless there are other absolute indications for termination of pregnancy as specified in the Medical Termination of Pregnancy Act, 1971. Any act of termination of pregnancy of normal female foetus amounting to female foeticide shall be regarded as professional misconduct on the part of the physician leading to penal erasure besides rendering him liable to criminal proceedings as per the provisions of this Act.

7.7 Signing Professional Certificates, Reports and other Documents: Registered medical practitioners are in certain cases bound by law to give, or may from time to time be called upon or requested to give certificates, notification, reports and other documents of similar character signed by them in their professional capacity for subsequent use in the courts or for administrative purposes etc. Such documents, among others, include the ones given at Appendix -4. Any registered practitioner who is shown to have signed or given under his name and authority any such certificate, notification, report or document of a similar character which is untrue, misleading or improper, is liable to have his name deleted from the Register.

7.8 A registered medical practitioner shall not contravene the provisions of the Drugs and Cosmetics Act and regulations made there under. Accordingly, - a) Prescribing steroids/psychotropic drugs when there is no absolute medical indication; selling Schedule 'H' and 'L' drugs and poisons to the public except to his patient; in contravention of the above provisions shall constitute gross professional misconduct on the part of the physician.

7.9 Performing or enabling unqualified person to perform an abortion or any illegal operation for which there is no medical, surgical or psychological indication.

7.10 A registered medical practitioner shall not issue certificates of efficiency in modern medicine to unqualified or non-medical person. (Note: The foregoing does not restrict the proper training and instruction of bonafide students, midwives, dispensers, surgical attendants, or skilled mechanical and technical assistants and therapy assistants under the personal supervision of physicians.)

7.11 A physician should not contribute to the lay press articles and give interviews regarding diseases and treatments which may have the effect of advertising himself or soliciting practices; but is open to write to the lay press under his own name on matters of public health, hygienic living or to deliver public lectures, give talks on the radio/TV/internet chat for the same purpose and send announcement of the same to lay press.

7.12 An institution run by a physician for a particular purpose such as a maternity home, nursing home, private hospital, rehabilitation center or any type of training institution etc. may be advertised in the lay press, but such advertisements should not contain anything more than the name of the institution, type of patients admitted, type of training and other facilities offered and the fees.

7.13 It is improper for a physician to use an unusually large sign board and write on it anything other than his name, qualifications obtained from a University or a statutory body, titles and name of his specialty, registration number including the name of the State Medical Council under which registered. The same should be the contents of his prescription papers. It is improper to affix a signboard on a chemist's shop or in places where he does not reside or work.

7.14 The registered medical practitioner shall not disclose the secrets of a patient that have been learnt in the exercise of his/her profession except -

i) In a court of law under orders of the Presiding Judge;
ii) In circumstances where there is a serious and identified risk to a specific person and/or community; and
iii) Notifiable diseases. In case of communicable / notifiable diseases, concerned public health authorities should be informed immediately.

7.15 The registered medical practitioner shall not refuse on religious grounds alone to give assistance in or conduct of sterility, birth control, circumcision and medical termination of Pregnancy when there is medical indication, unless the medical practitioner feels himself/herself incompetent to do so.

7.16 Before performing an operation the physician should obtain in writing the consent from the husband or wife, parent or guardian in the case of minor, or the patient himself as the case may be. In an operation, which may result in sterility, the consent of both husband and wife is needed.

7.17 A registered medical practitioner shall not publish photographs or case reports of his/her patients without their permission, in any medical or other journal in a manner by which their identity could be made out. If the identity is not to be disclosed, the consent is not needed.

7.18 In the case of running of a nursing home by a physician and employing assistants to help him/her, the ultimate responsibility rests on the physician.

7.19 A Physician shall not use touts or agents for procuring patients.

7.20 A Physician shall not claim to be specialist unless he has a special qualification in that branch.

7.21 No act of *in vitro* fertilization or artificial insemination shall be undertaken without the informed consent of the female patient and her spouse as well as the donor. Such consent shall be obtained in writing only after the patient is provided, at her own level of comprehension, with sufficient information about the purpose, methods, risks, inconveniences, disappointments of the procedure and possible risks and hazards.

7.22 Research: Clinical drug trials or other research involving patients or volunteers as per the guidelines of ICMR can be undertaken, provided ethical considerations are borne in mind. Violation of existing ICMR guidelines in this regard shall constitute misconduct. Consent taken from the patient for trial of drug or therapy, which is not as per the guidelines, shall also be construed as misconduct.

7.23 If a physician posted in rural area is found absent on more than two occasions during inspection by the Head of the District Health Authority or the Chairman, Zila Parishad, the same shall be construed as a misconduct if it is recommended to the Medical Council of India/State Medical Council by the State Government for action under these Regulations.

7.24 If a physician posted in a medical college/institution both as teaching faculty or otherwise shall remain in hospital/college during the assigned duty hours. If they are found absent on more than two occasions during this period, the same shall be construed as misconduct if it is certified by the Principal/Medical Superintendent and forwarded through the State Government to Medical Council of India/State Medical Council for action under these Regulations.

CHAPTER 8

8. Punishment and Disciplinary Action

8.1 It must be clearly understood that the instances of offences and of Professional misconduct which are given above do not constitute and are not intended to constitute a complete list of the infamous acts which calls for disciplinary action, and that by issuing this notice the Medical Council of India and or State Medical Councils are in no way precluded from considering and dealing with any other form of professional misconduct on the part of a registered practitioner. Circumstances may and do arise from time to time in relation to which there may occur questions of professional misconduct which do not come within any of these categories. Every care should be taken that the code is not violated in letter or spirit. In such instances as in all others, the Medical Council of India and/or State Medical Councils have to consider and decide upon the facts brought before the Medical Council of India and/or State Medical Councils.

8.2 It is made clear that any complaint with regard to professional misconduct can be brought before the appropriate Medical Council for Disciplinary action. Upon receipt of any complaint of professional misconduct, the appropriate Medical Council would hold an enquiry and give opportunity to the registered medical practitioner to be heard in person or by pleader. If the medical practitioner is found to be guilty of committing professional misconduct, the appropriate Medical Council may award such punishment as deemed necessary or may direct the removal altogether or for a specified period, from the register of the name of the delinquent registered practitioner. Deletion from the Register shall be widely publicized in local pres as well as in the publications of different Medical Associations/ Societies/Bodies.

8.3 In case the punishment of removal from the register is for a limited period, the appropriate Council may also direct that the name so removed shall be restored in the register after the expiry of the period for which the name was ordered to be removed.

8.4 Decision on complaint against delinquent physician shall be taken within a time limit of 6 months.

8.5 During the pendency of the complaint the appropriate Council may restrain the physician from performing the procedure or practice, which is under scrutiny.

8.6 Professional incompetence shall be judged by peer group as per guidelines prescribed by Medical Council of India.

REFERENCES

1. Satyanarayana, Krishna Rao. In: The Law relating to medical profession in India, 1st edn, 1962. Bestseller Publications, Hyderabad.
2. Mukherjee JB. In: Forensic Medicine and Toxicology Vol. I, 2nd edn, 1994. Arnold Associates, New Delhi.
3. Koley TK. In: Medical negligence and Medicolegal aspects of patient care, 1st edn, 2004. Mehta Publishers, New Delhi.
4. Knight B. Medical negligence. In: Legal aspects of medical practice, 5th edn, 1992. Churchill Livingstone, Edinburgh. 59-76.
5. Pillay VV. Medical law and ethics. In: Textbook of Forensic Medicine and Toxicology, 14th edn, 2004. Paras Publishing, Hyderabad. 16-43.
6. Mathiharan K, Patnaik AK. Legal and ethical aspects of medical practice, medical negligence and Consumer Protection Act. In: Modi's Medical Jurisprudence and Toxicology, 23rd edn, 2005. LexisNexis Butterworths, New Delhi. 77-201.
7. Parikh CK. Law in relation to medical men. In: Parikh's Textbook of Medical Jurisprudence and Toxicology, 5th edn, 1995. CBS Publishers and Distributors, Bombay. 548-88.
8. Sharma RK. Law in relation to medical practice: Part I and II. In: Concise Textbook of Forensic medicine and Toxicology, 1st edn, 2005. Reed Elsevier India Pvt. Limited, New Delhi. 157-200.
9. The Indian Medical Council (professional conduct, etiquette and ethics) Regulations, 2002. Published in Part III, Section 4 of the Gazette of India, dated 6th April, 2002.
10. Dabla S, Pal V, Yadav DR. Medical Records – a vital link in doctor-patient relationship. Int J Medical Toxicol Legal Med 2001; 4:18-20.
11. Mathiharan K. Medical records. Indian J Med Ethics 2004; 1:59.
12. Patil DT, Franklin CA. Consent in Indian medical practice. J Medicolegal Assoc Maharashtra 2000; 12: 9 – 14.
13. Dikshit PC. Laws in relation to medical practice. In: Textbook of Forensic Medicine and Toxicology, 1st edn, 2007. Peepee Publishers and Distributors (P) Ltd., New Delhi. 16-34.
14. Murkey PN, Khandekar IL, Tirpude BH, Ninave SV. Consent – Medicolegal aspects. Medicolegal Update 2006; 6:91-7.
15. Palmer RN. Fundamental principles. In: Stark MM (ed) Clinical Forensic Medicine – a physician's guide, 2nd edn, 2005. Humana Press, New Jersey. 37-59.
16. Rao NG. Ethics of medical practice. In: Textbook of Forensic Medicine and Toxicology, 1st edn, 2006. Jaypee Brothers Medical Publishers (P) Ltd., New Delhi. 31-76.
17. Kulkarni JV, Joshi AS. Consent in medical practice. Milestone 2005; 4: 5 – 7.
18. Sunila Sharma. In: Law and the Doctor, 1st edn, 2055. Paras Publishing, Hyderabad.
19. Subrahmanyam BV. Medical jurisprudence. In: Forensic medicine, Toxicology and Medical Jurisprudence, 1st edn, 2004. Modern Publishers, New Delhi. 233-66.
20. Subrahmanyam BV. Law in relation to medical men. In: Modi's Medical Jurisprudence and Toxicology, 22nd edn, 2001. Butterworths India, New Delhi. 683-740.
21. Vij K. Legal and ethical aspects of medical practice, medical negligence, consent to and refusal of treatment. In: Textbook of Forensic Medicine and Toxicology, 3rd edn, 2005. Reed Elsevier India Pvt. Limited, New Delhi. 501-34.
22. Reddy KSN. Medical law and ethics. In: The Essentials of Forensic Medicine and Toxicology, 22nd edn, 2003. K. Suguna Devi, Hyderabad. 19-46.
23. Shinde SK. Medical negligence. J Medicolegal Assoc Maharashtra 2004; 16:7-9.
24. Sharma RK. Current status of medical negligence in India in view of Supreme Court judgment. Medicolegal Update 2005; 5:71-86.
25. Sagall EL, Reed BC. In: The law and clinical medicine, 1st edn, 1970. JB Lippincott Company, Philadelphia.
26. Nandy A. Legal and ethical aspects of practice of medicine. In: Principles of Forensic Medicine, 2nd edn, 2005. New Central Book Agency (P) Ltd., Calcutta. 14-47.
27. Dogra TD, Rudra A (ed). Medical jurisprudence. In: Lyon's Medical Jurisprudence and Toxicology, 11th edn, 2007. Delhi Law House, Delhi. 93-364.
28. Taylor JL. In: The Doctor and Negligence, 1st edn, 1971. Pitman Medical, London.
29. Sapare DP, Karmarkar MD. C.P.A. with amendments in reference to medical negligence. J Medicolegal Assoc Maharashtra 2002; 14:1-4.
30. Yadav JU, Joshi JK. Overview of medical negligence cases at D.C.F. Sangli. J Medicolegal Assoc Maharashtra 2004; 16:10-12.
31. Sharma RK. Ethical guidelines for biomedical research on human subject – ICMR code. In: Legal aspects of patient care, 2nd edn, 2003. Modern Publishers, New Delhi. 99-138.

CHAPTER 3

Identification

Everyone has the right to recognition everywhere as a person before the law.

-Universal Declaration of Human Right

Definition

Identification means determination of individuality of a person. Thus identification deals with the recognition of person. It is done in living person or dead by recognizing certain features or characteristics that are unique to that person.

Types

Identification may be:
1. Complete
2. Partial

- Complete identification is also called as **absolute identification** and refers to the perfect fixation of individuality of a person.
- Partial identification is also called as **incomplete identification** and implies ascertainment of only some traits or characteristics regarding the identity.

Medicolegal Importance

I) **In Living Persons**:

A) **Civil cases**:

1. In impersonation or false personification cases in relation with:
   - Inheritance of property
   - Pension
   - Life insurance
   - Voting rights
   - Passport
2. Disputed identity in cases of divorce or nullity of marriage
3. Disputed sex
4. Missing person
5. Lost memory patients.

B) **Criminal cases**:

1. Identification of accused in criminal offenses of assault, murder, dacoity, sexual offenses etc.
2. Absconding soldiers
3. Interchange of new born babies in hospital
4. Criminal abortion
5. To fix-up age of criminal responsibility and majority
6. Impersonation in criminal cases.

II) **In Dead Persons**:

Identification is important to identify the individuals who died in mass disaster, air-crash accidents, fire victims, exhumation, explosion and bomb-blast injuries, mutilated and decomposed bodies and in skeletal remains.

- In India police have to establish the identity of a person. However, doctor may provide help by supplying certain facts or data to police, which might be helpful in identification of a person.
- During medicolegal examination, doctor should record at least two identification marks and the marks should be described in all certificates issued by him.

Corpus delicti

Accurate identification is necessary for the establishment of corpus delicti in homicide cases. The term corpus delicti means **the body of offence** or **the body of crime** or the essence of crime. In homicide cases, it is done by:

- Identification of dead body i.e. the identity of victim (i.e. the person who had died).
- Conclusive evidence that the death was caused by the criminal act.

- Corpus delicti is important since after establishment of identity of victim, a trail for murder can take place in court and the sentence can be awarded. *However, cases had occurred in which commission of crime had been established even in absence of corpus delicti*[1].

Data

Data for identification consist of:
1. Religion
2. Race
3. Sex
4. Age
5. Stature
6. Dactylography
7. Foot prints
8. Cheiloscopy
9. Tattoo marks
10. Scars
11. Deformities
12. Anthropometry
13. Teeth
14. DNA typing – *refer chapter 5*
15. Blood group and HLA typing
16. Miscellaneous data
    - Complexion and features
    - Hair
    - Personal effects: clothes, pocket contents, jewelry etc.
    - Handwriting and signature
    - Speech and voice
    - Occupation marks
    - Gait
    - Ticks, manner and habit
    - Mental power, memory and education
    - Ear morphology[2]
    - Palate prints[3-5]
    - Frontal sinuses[6]
    - ECG (Sreenivas method) [7]
    - Namaste technique (Subrahmanyam method) [8]
    - X-ray[9]

RACE

Definition

race is defined as *"biological grouping within the human species distinguished or classified according to genetically transmitted differences"*.

Thus, race is a population concept. Races are populations, which differ in the frequency of some genes.

The population of world is divided into three types of race namely:
1. Caucasians or Caucasoid
2. Mongolians or mongoloids
3. Negro or Negroid

The race can be determined by:
1. Clothes
2. Complexion
3. Eyes
4. Hairs
5. Physical features
6. Teeth
7. Skeletal characteristics and indices

The differentiating points are summarized in Tables 3.1 and 3.2. (*For skeletal features and different indices please refer chapters - Forensic Osteology*).

SEX

Determination of Sex is Important for:

1. For the purpose of identification in living or dead.
2. For determination of sex of a person when:
    - Sex appears ambiguous (doubtful)
    - Sex is concealed
    - A person appears to posses' sex organs of both sexes.
3. For deducing whether an individual can exercise certain Civil Rights reserved to one particular sex only.
4. For deciding questions related to legitimacy, divorce, paternity, affiliation, heir-ship and also some criminal offences.
5. In case of national or international sports meet or games.

Evidence of Sex

The evidence of sex is divided into:
1. Presumptive evidence of sex
2. Probable evidence of sex
3. Positive evidence of sex

Presumptive Evidence of Sex

- It is based on external appearance of an individual considering the general body features and appearance, clothing, body contour, distribution of hairs, habits, voice, inclinations etc.
- Difficulty arises when some one tries to conceal the sex and behave like a person of the opposite sex.

Probable Evidence of Sex

- It is based on assessment of secondary sexual characteristics such as development of breasts and genitals,

Table 3.1: Differentiating points between races

Features	*Caucasians*	*Mongolian*	*Negro*
Complexion	Fair	Yellowish	Black
Eyes (Iris colour)	Gray or blue	Black	Black
Forehead	Raised	Inclined backward	Small and compressed
Nasal aperture	Narrow and elongated	Rounded	Broad
Nose	Sharp	Flattened	Blunt
Face	Small	Large and flattened	Jaw projecting, malar bone prominent, teeth set obliquely
Hard palate	Triangular	Large and flattened	Rectangular
Upper extremity	Normal	Small	• Large in proportion to body • Forearm large in proportion to arms • Hand small
Lower extremity	Normal	Small	• Leg large in proportion to thigh • Feet wide and flat • Heel bone projecting backward

Table 3.2: Differentiating features of hairs in different races

Characters	*Caucasians*	*Mongolian*	*Negro*
Features	Straight or wavy, blondes brown or fair.	Coarse, straight or wavy, black or brown	Thick, woolly, curly and self spiraled
Diameter	70–100 μm	90–120 μm	60–90 μm
Cross-section	Oval	Round	Flattened
Pigmentation	Uniform distribution	Dense abundant through the cross-section	Dense and clumped towards the periphery
Cuticle	Medium	Thick	--
Undulation	Uncommon	Rare	Prevalent

presence of vagina in females and penis in males, distribution of subcutaneous fat, muscular development etc.
- Difficulty arises in intersex conditions or ambiguous conditions when there is mixing of features of both sexes.

Positive Evidence of Sex

This can be done by confirming
1. Presence of ovaries in females and testis in males OR
2. Presence of Barr bodies and Davidson bodies.

Sex of a Person has to be Established in:

1. Living person
2. Dead person
3. Skeletal remains

This chapter deals with determination of sex in living and dead person. *For determination of sex in skeletal remains (bones) please refer chapter no. 4 - Forensic osteology.*

Sex of a person can be determined by:
1. Physical/morphological examination
2. Microscopic examination
3. Hormone assay
4. Gonadal biopsy
5. DNA profiling
6. Radiological examination
7. Metric system

Physical Examination

Sex can be differentiated on physical examination by noting the morphological features of a person. Differences are summarized in Table 3.3.

Microscopic Examination

It can be done by determination of:
1. **Barr body or sex chromatin** (Fig. 3.1)

- Barr bodies or sex chromatins are basophilic intranuclear condensed structure located near the inner surface of nuclear membrane of somatic cells in females.
- These bodies are absent in males. Thus the females are called as chromatin positive.
- These bodies are appreciated in the cells of buccal mucosa, skin, cartilage, nerve, amniotic fluid etc. Buccal smears are routinely used.

2. **Davidson body** (Fig. 3.1):
   - Some neutrophils in female demonstrate an additional lobe (drumstick), which is rarely found in males. Davidson described these neutrophilic drumsticks as dense chromatins head 1.5 μ in diameter and are attached to nucleus by a thread like connecting piece.
   - Davidson bodies can be demonstrated in the peripheral smears with Leishman or Giemsa stains.
   - To diagnose female sex by this method, the peripheral smear must show minimum of six percent counts.
3. **Karyotyping** (Fig. 3.2): In this method human chromosomes are studied in detail. Human cells are grown in tissue culture; treated with the drug colchicine that arrests mitosis at the metaphase of developing cell. The cells are exposed to hypotonic solution that makes the chromosomes swell and disperse and then they are put on slides. Fluorescent or staining technique allows studying the chromosome in detail. The individual chromosomes are usually arranged in an arbitrary pattern (karyotype). The individual chromosomes are identified based on their morphological features.[10]
4. **Demonstration of Y-chromosome**: Y-chromosome present in cells can be demonstrated by quinacrine or acridine stain under fluorescent microscope. The cells from buccal mucosa, hair follicle, leukocyte or dental pulp can be used.[11, 12]
5. Tissues from kidneys offered a reliable sex determination when detecting fluorescent Y-bodies. Counts higher then 10 percent in tissue from kidneys indicate male sex of the examining material.[13]

Table 3.3: Differentiating features between male and female

Features	*Male*	*Female*
Built	Muscular and strong	Less muscular, delicate
Height	More	Less
Weight	More	Less
Scalp hairs	Short and coarse	Long and fine
Eyebrow	Coarse and thick	Fine and thin
Voice	Hoarse after puberty	Soft
Moustache	Present	Absent/rudimentary
Beard	Present	Absent/rudimentary
Hair on pinna	Present	Absent
Body hairs	Grow over chest, Abdomen, limb	No significant growth of hairs
Pubic hairs	Thicker, coarse, extend upwards towards navel	Horizontal, covering only mons pubis, triangular distribution
Breast	Rudimentary	Well developed
Thyroid cartilage angle	Prominent and angle less than 90°	Less prominent, angle more than 120°
Shoulder and hip	Broader than hip	Hip broader than shoulder
Chest and abdomen	Chest dimensions more	Abdomen dimensions more
Waist	Not well defined	Well defined
Gluteal region	Flat	Full and roundish
Forearm	Antero-posteriorly flat	Roundish
Thigh	Cylindrical	Conical
Wrist and ankle	Coarse and rough	Smooth and delicate
External genitalia	Scrotum, testis and penis	Labia, clitoris, and vagina
Internal genitalia	Vas deferens, prostate, seminal vesicle, ejaculatory ducts	Ovaries, uterine tube, and uterus

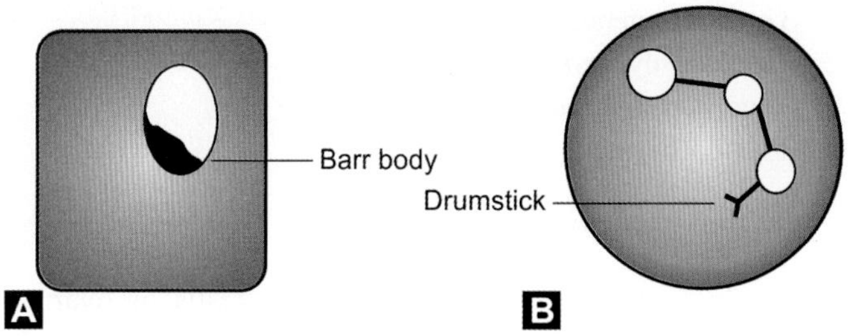

FIGS 3.1A and B: Microscopic determination of sex. **A:** Barr body in buccal cells and **B:** Davidson body (drumstick appearance) in neutrophil

Hormone Assays

The androgens are the steroid sex hormones and have musculinizing effect whereas estrogens are having feminizing action. Both types of hormones are secreted in both sexes but testes secretes large amount of androgens – chiefly testosterone. The ovaries secretes large amount of estrogen. Estimation of hormonal level can give idea regarding the sex, however, the method is not reliable.

Gonadal Biopsy

This is a confirmatory method of determining sex. Biopsy from primary gonads i.e. testis in male or ovary in female can indicate definitive sex of an individual. Figures 3.3 and 3.4 give normal histological appearance of testis and ovary.

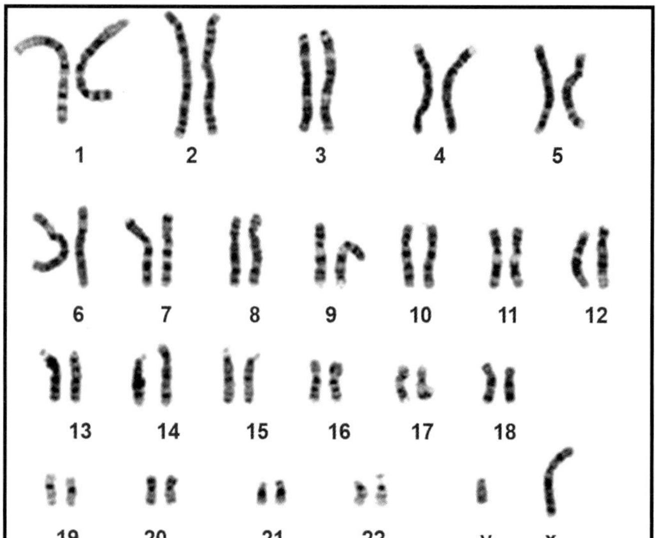

FIG. 3.2: Karyotyping

DNA Profiling

DNA profiling: Can determine the sex of person from bloodstains or even from fragmentary remains.[14] (*Refer Chapter 5 – DNA Profiling for detail*).

Radiological Examination

Following are the radiological methods used in identification:

1. Rao and Pai's classification: Radiological sex determination is based on the calcification pattern of costal cartilage. Three patterns are described in Indian population. The costal cartilage calcification pattern (2-12th rib) is presented and is considered helpful in determining the sex in the age group of 16-20 years and the stated accuracy is > 92.3%. The patterns are presented below.[15]

- Costal cartilage calcification pattern – square bracket type – found in male
- Costal cartilage calcification pattern – linear type – found in male
- Costal cartilage calcification pattern – central tongue shaped type – found in female

2. Mandibular canine index can determine the sex of a person and the accuracy of this method is reported[16] to be 85 percent.

Metric System

Footprint dimensions and footprint ratios are utilized to determine sex of a person[17, 18] – *vide infra*

Difficulty in Sex Determination

Difficulty in determination of sex arises in following conditions:

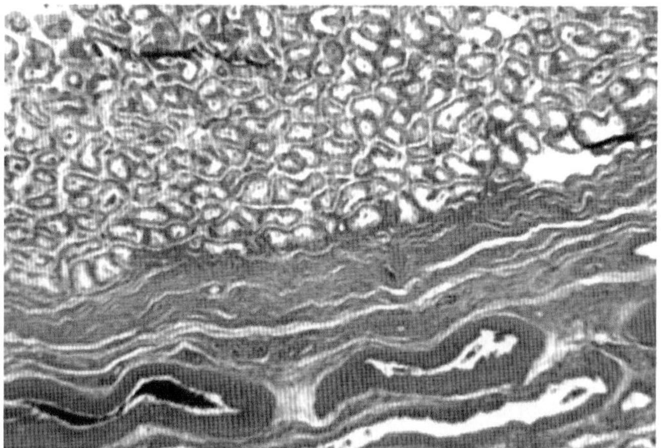

FIG. 3.3: Normal histology of testis

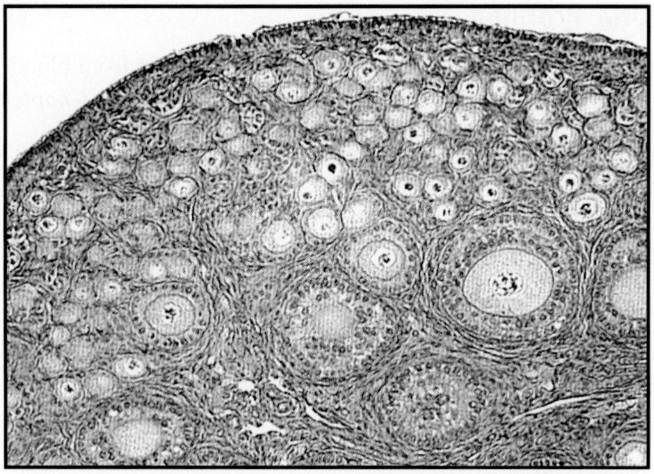

FIG. 3.4: Normal histology of ovary

1. Concealed sex
2. Decomposed or mutilated bodies
3. Skeleton
4. Hermaphroditism or intersex state

Concealed Sex

Criminals or some persons may hide their sex to avoid detection by changing their clothes or by other means. These cases do not posses difficulty in identifying sex because physical examination of individual will reveal the true sex.

Decomposed Bodies

- In decomposed bodies determination of sex may cause difficulty. In such cases, identifying the presence of uterus or prostate will be of help. Prostate or uterus resists decomposition for considerable long time.
- In mutilated bodies or when body is cut into many pieces, determination of sex can be possible by identifying the distribution of body hairs, subcutaneous fat, presence of secondary sexual features and organs, examination of chest etc.

Skeleton

Refer Chapter 4: Forensic Osteology

Intersex State

- Intersex is an intermingling of sexual characters of both sexes in varying degrees in one individual. The intermingling of features may be of physical form, reproductive organs or sexual behaviour.
- It results from embryonic development.
- Davidson had divided the intersex state into following four types:[19]

1. Gonadal agenesis
2. Gonadal dysgenesis
3. True hermaphroditism
4. Pseudo hermaphroditism

Gonadal Agenesis

- In this condition, the sexual organs (testis or ovaries) have never developed and the abnormality occurs early in foetal life.
- Nuclear sex is negative
- Physical characters may contain features of both sexes or may have dominance of one particular sex.

Gonadal Dysgenesis

- In this condition the external sexual features are present but at puberty, the testis or ovaries fail to develop.
- The following are the examples of clinical syndromes due to gonadal dysgenesis:
  A. Turner's syndrome
  B. Klinfelter syndrome

Turner's Syndrome (Fig. 3.5)

- It is a female type of gonadal dysgenesis (hypogonadism).
- In Turner's syndrome, the anatomical structure is of female but nuclear sexing is male.
- It results from complete or partial monosomy of the X-chromosome due to which there is hypogonadism.
- It is a common type of sex chromosome abnormality in females and karyotype is 45XO (45 chromosome).
- Physical features include short stature (height), low posterior line, webbing of neck, broad chest with widely spaced nipples, congenital defects like cubitus valgus, lymphedema, coarctation of aorta and primary ammenorrhea.
- Ovaries are infantile and streak like.

Klinefelter Syndrome

- It is male type of gonadal dysgenesis (hypogonadism).
- The anatomical structure is male but nuclear sex is female.
- The sex pattern is XXY (47 chromosomes).
- It is characterized by eunuchoid tall appearance with thin, abnormally long legs. There are small atrophic testes (histologically testicular dysgenesis with hyalinisation of seminiferous tubules) with small penis and gynecomastia, Axillary and pubic hairs are absent.

Hermaphroditism

Hermaphroditism implies a discrepancy between the morphology of the gonads and that of external gentiles[20]. Thus, hermaphroditism means presence of both ovaries and testis in a person. It may be true hermaphroditism or pseudo hermaphroditism.

True Hermaphroditism

- It is rare condition in which an individual may have gonads of both sexes. The person may have testis on one side and ovary on the other side or testis and ovaries on both side combined together called as **ovotestes**. An external feature may pose characters of both sexes with phallus penile or clitorial; the labia may be bifid as in females or fused resembling scrotum of male.
- The chromosomal pattern will be of either male (XY) or that of female (XX).

Pseudo Hermaphroditism

In this condition the gonads of one sex is present internally but external appearance is that of opposite sex. They are of two types:

1. Male Pseudo Hermaphroditism:
2. Female Pseudo Hermaphroditism

Male Pseudo Hermaphroditism

In this condition the gonads are testes internally with chromosomal pattern of 46XY but external features are of female type because of underdeveloped penis and testicular feminization (Fig. 3.6). In this situation, there is inability to convert testosterone into active form dihydro-testosterone hence the external genitals showing feminization. It results from:

1. Defective androgen synthesis
2. Defective androgen action
3. Defective Müllerian duct regression or
4. Uncertain causes

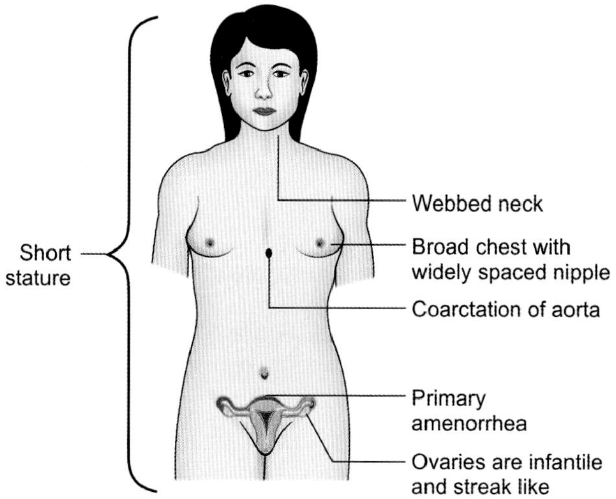

FIG. 3.5: Turner's syndrome

Female Pseudo Hermaphroditism

In this condition, the gonads are ovaries internally with chromosomal pattern of 46XX. The external genitals are ambiguous or doubtful with enlarged clitoris (Fig. 3.7). This defect is due to excessive and inappropriate exposure to androgens. The causes are summarized below.[21]

1. Congenital adrenal hyperplasia
2. Placental aromatase deficiency
3. Arrhenoblastomas of mother
4. Luteomas of mother
5. Developmental disorders of Müllerian ducts

AGE

Age has to be determined in:

1) Foetus
2) Children
3) Adults
4) Dead person
5) Decomposed or mutilated bodies
6) Skeletal remains

Determination of Age in Fetus

Growth and development begins with fertilization. Gestational age or intrauterine age is the period that stretches from conception to delivery at term. The various terms are used to designate this period as:

Prenatal Period

1. Ovum (zygote) – 0 to 14 days
2. Embryo – 14 days to 8 weeks
3. Fetus – 9 weeks to birth

Perinatal period – 28 weeks of gestation to 7 days after birth

Postnatal period

1. New born (neonate)– first 4 weeks after birth
2. Infant – up to one year
3. Toddler – 1 to 3 years

The age of foetus can be assessed by

1) Length (crown-heel length)
2) Crown-rump length

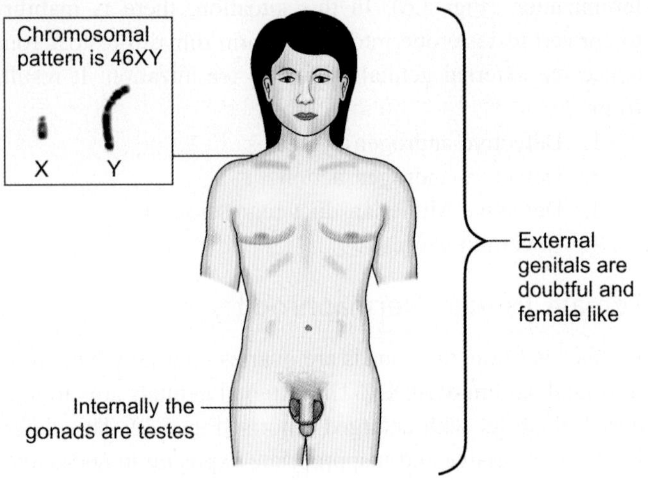

FIG. 3.6: Male pseudo hermaphroditism

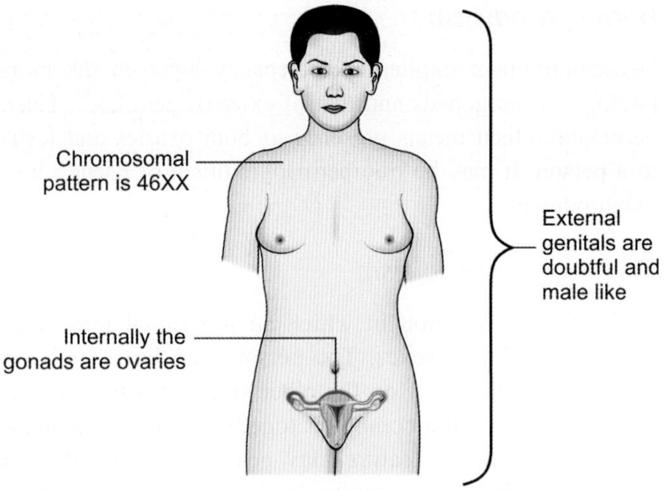

FIG. 3.7: Female pseudo hermaphroditism

3) Weight
4) Physical features and morphology
5) Appearance of ossification centers
6) Appearance of germination centers
7) Length of hand and foot
8) Miscellaneous methods
   - Assessment of serum placental lactogen[22]
   - Microscopic examination of body tissue[23]

Length and Weight

- Embryologically speaking, ideally age during initial period (*i.e. up to 30 days or 4 weeks*) is estimated by calculating somites because they are the main external features. Therefore, during third to fourth week period of development, the age of embryo is expressed in number of somites. Table 3.4 displays the approximate age of embryo correlated with number of somites.[24]
- As the embryo grows (*i.e. after 30 days*), the counting of somites become difficult and during this period usually crown-rump length (CRL) in millimeters is taken to estimate the age of embryo. Table 3.5 displays the fetal age and CRL. CRL is taken from vertex of the skull to midpoint between the apices of buttock. It is said that in early period of pregnancy (*i.e. up to 2 months or 8 weeks*), crown-rump length (CRL) is the most accurate method to estimate fetal age.[25]
- From the beginning of ninth week to the end of intrauterine life, the period is known as fetal period. This fetal period is characterized by growth of body with maturation of tissue and organs. The length of fetus can be taken as **crown-rump or crown-heel length**. In forensic practice, usually **crown-heel length** is taken. Table 3.6 displays the crown-heel length (CHL) in centimeters and weight correlated with age of fetus in months (lunar months).
- Haase's Rule: Age of foetus in lunar months is determined by Haase's rule. In this, the length of foetus is taken from crown to heel. The rule is as follows:

Table 3.4: Developmental age of embryo

Age in days	*No. of somites*
20	1-4
21	4-7
22	7-10
23	10-13
24	13-17
25	17-20
26	20-23
27	23-26
28	26-29
30	34-35

Table 3.5: Fetal age estimation by crown-rump length

CRL in mm	*Age in weeks*
5-8	5
10-14	6
17-22	7
28-30	8

Table 3.6: Crown-heel length (CHL) in centimeters and weight correlated with age of fetus in months (lunar months)

Age in months	*Length in cm*	*Weight in grams*
1	1	2.75
2	3-4	10
3	9	30–35
4	16	120–130
5	25	400
6	30	700
7	35	1000
8	40	1500
9	45	2000–2500
10	50	3000

- Up to 5th month: Square root of length of foetus will give the age in lunar months (*for example if length of fetus is 16 cm then square root of 16 would be √16 = 4 – age would be 4 months*).
- After 5th month: Length divided by 5 will give the age in lunar months (*in other words age multiplied by 5 will give the length of fetus*).

Morphological Features

The age of fetus is also assessed by studying the developing morphological features. Table 3.7 gives developing morphological appearance (Figs 3.8 to 3.17).

Ossification Centers

The age of fetus is also assessed by studying the appearance of ossification centers (Fig. 3.18). Table 3.8 gives the appearance of ossification centers.[26]

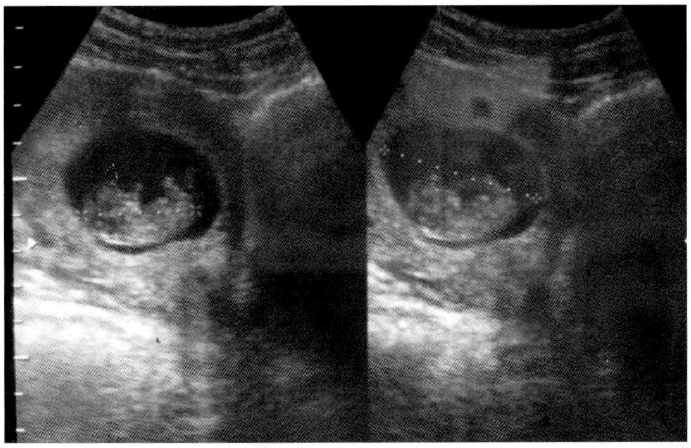

FIG. 3.8: USG appearance of fetus of gestational age about 9 weeks (CRL = 3.02 cm)

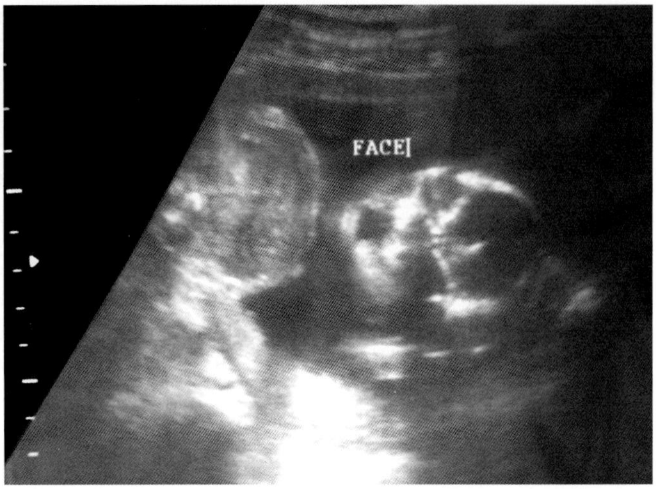

FIG. 3.9: USG appearance of developing fetus having more human looking face—gestational age about 11 weeks

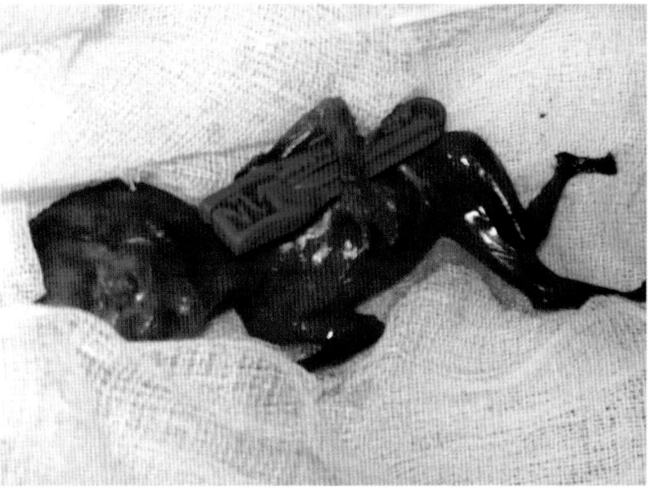

FIG. 3.10: Fetus of gestational age about three months

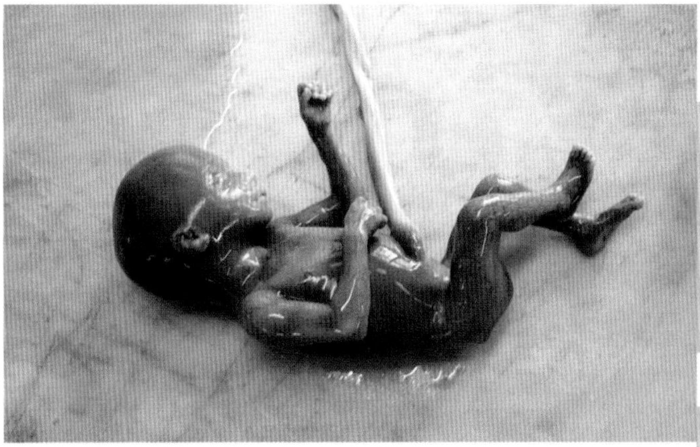

FIG. 3.11: Fetus of gestational age about 4 months

Table 3.7: Developing morphological features in fetus

Age in months	Morphological features
1	Eyes are indicated by two dark spots, mouth as cleft, beginning of limb bud like process
2	Mouth and nose are separated, anus appears as dark spot, placenta commenced to form, feet and hand webbed
3	Placenta is developed, head is rounded, larger than trunk (head constitutes approximately half of the crown-rump length of fetus), becomes more human looking, separated by appearance of neck, heart four chambered, limbs, fingers and toes well developed but nail remains in membranous form. The alimentary tract is situated in abdominal cavity
4	The sex can be differentiated, skin covered by appearing downy lanugo hairs. Skin is rosy and firmer; the head is one-fourth of the length of body. Umbilicus is situated near the pubic symphysis. Brain convolutions begin to appear. Gall bladder is formed and meconium is found in duodenum. Pupillary membrane appears. The fetus can be detected on X-ray.
5	Light hairs appear at scalp, the head is larger and about 1/3rd of crown-rump length of fetus. Lanugo distinct, nails are distinct and soft, the position of umbilicus recedes upwards, skin covered with vernix caseosa. Bile begins to form, meconium found in beginning of colon (ascending colon).
6	The skin has wrinkled appearance due to less fat in body, reddish in colour. Eyelash and eyebrow appears, eyelids are adherent. The umbilicus os situated farther from pubic symphysis. Brain - cerebral hemispheres cover the cerebellum, Sylvian fissure formed. Meconium present in transverse colon and testis near kidneys (on psoas muscle).
7	Skin is dusky red, thick and fibrous and covered with vernix. The eyelids are separated, Pupillary membrane disappeared, scalp hairs are about 1 cm long, and nails thick and up to fingertip. Meconium in descending colon, testes near the inguinal ring.
8	The skin is rosy, not wrinkled, covered with soft hairs, lanugo has disappeared from face, and the hairs of scalp are denser and longer. The nails reached up to tip of fingers but not up to tip of toes. Left testis is in scrotum, right in canal. Scrotum corrugated. Meconium reaches up to rectum.
9	Scalp hairs longer and is about 2-4 cm, lanugo has disappeared from body except on shoulder, vernix found in flexures of joints. Nail grows beyond the tips of fingers and up to tip of toes. Both testes in scrotum. Meconium found in rectum. Posterior fontanelle closed.
10	Scalp covered with 3-5 cm hairs, lanugo absent from body except at shoulders, face not wrinkled, skin pale and covered with vernix caseosa. Umbilicus is mid-way between pubis symphysis and xipisternum. Nails projected beyond tips. The rectum contains meconium. Vulva closed; labia majora cover labia minora and clitoris.

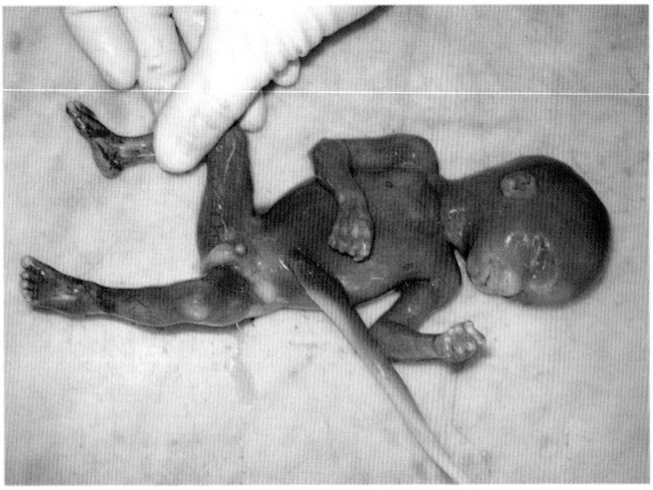

FIG. 3.12: Sex of fetus can be differentiated at four months of intrauterine life

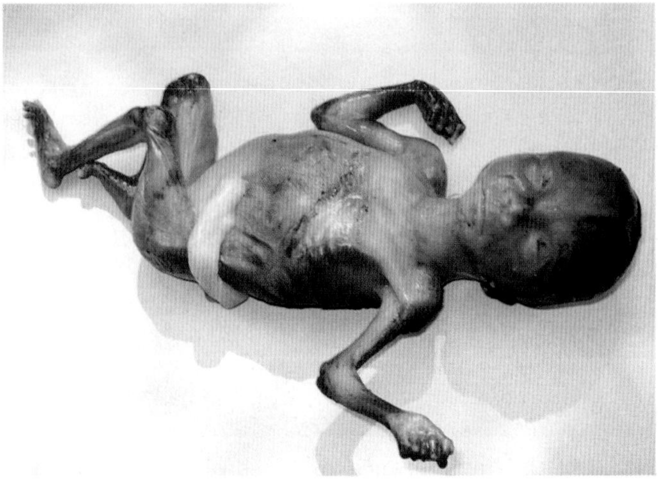

FIG. 3.13: Fetus of gestational age about five months

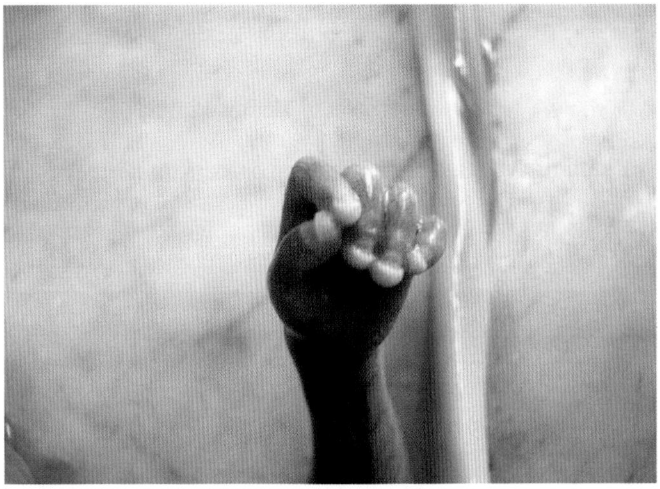

FIG. 3.14: Fetus with five months of gestational age, note that nails of hand is distinct and soft

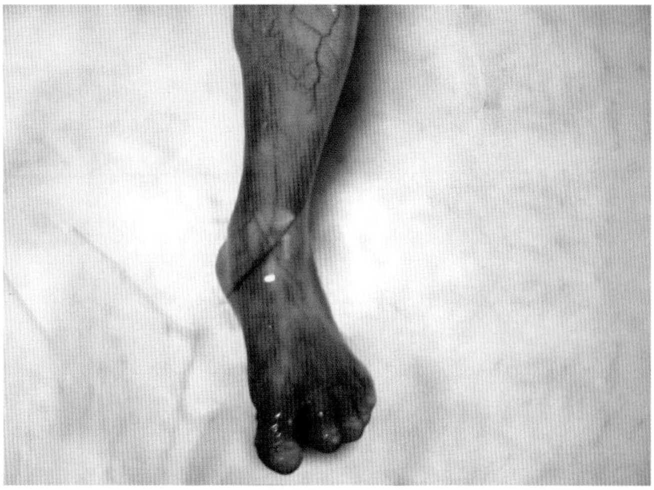

FIG. 3.15: Fetus with five months of gestational age, note the development of foot

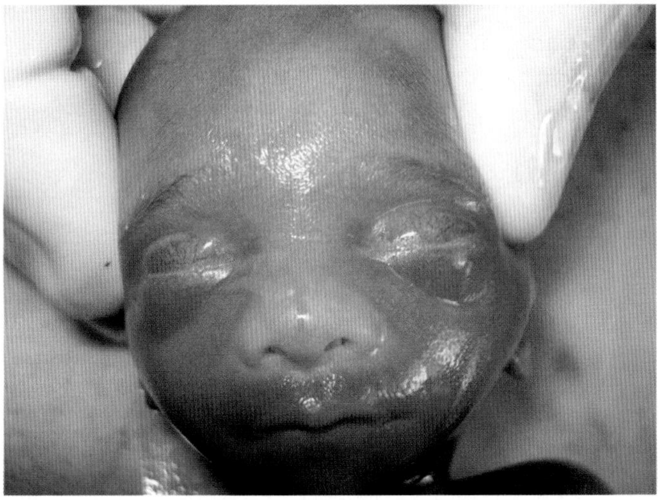

FIG. 3.16: Eyebrow begins to appear, eyelids are adherent

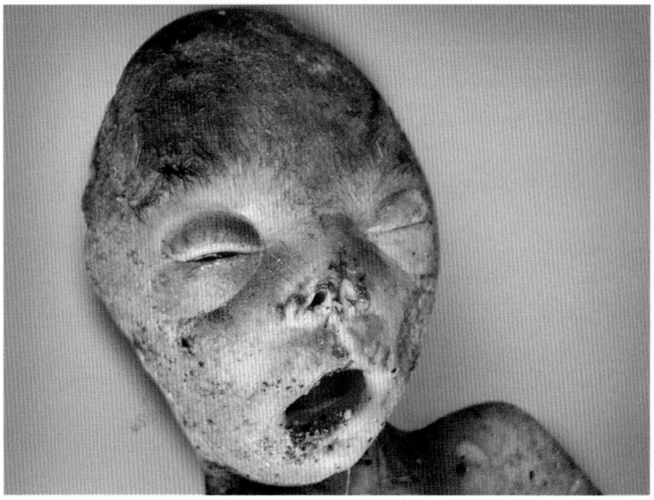

FIG. 3.17: Fetus of gestational age about 7 months (note eyelids are separated)

Table 3.8: Appearance of ossification centers

Appearance	*Ossification centers*
5-6 weeks	Two primary centers for clavicle and fuse together at about 45 days
6 weeks	- Center for mandible appears - Center for maxilla appears
7 weeks	- Primary center for shaft of femur - Primary center for shaft of tibia
8 weeks	- Primary center for body of scapula - Primary center for shaft of Humerus - Primary center for shaft of radius - Primary center for shaft of ulna - Primary center for ilium - Primary center for shaft of fibula - Center for squamous part of temporal bone appears - Center for frontal bone appears - Center for greater wing of sphenoid bone appears

Count...

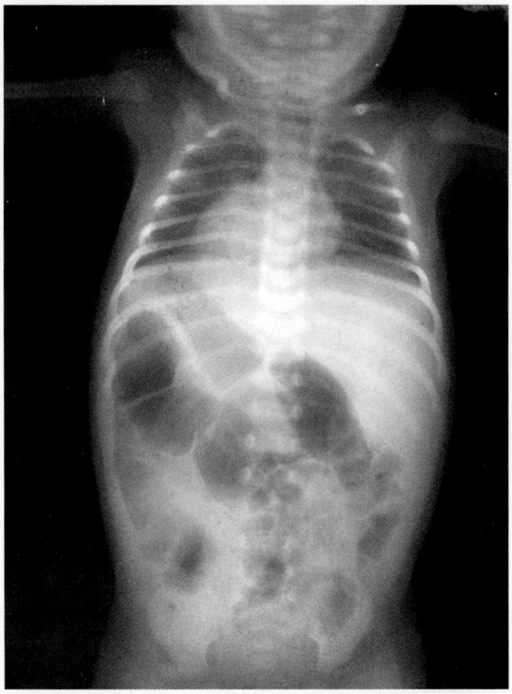

FIG. 3.18: X-ray of fetus showing various ossification centers

9 weeks	Center for lesser wing of sphenoid bone appears
11 weeks	Center for sphenoid body appears (pre-sphenoidal part)
12 weeks	Center for tympanic part of temporal bone appears
16 weeks	- Primary center for pubis appears - Centers for ischium appears - 2 Primary centers for sphenoid body (post-sphenoidal part) - Centers for lower segment of sacrum - Ear ossicles ossified
20 weeks	- Center for petrous part of temporal bone appears - Center for manubrium and first and second segment of sternum - Center for calcanium appears
16-20 weeks	Center for ethmiod bone appears
28 weeks	Center for talus appears
36 weeks	- Center for lower end of femur - Center for cuboid appears

Germination and Calcification of Teeth

Germination of teeth may also give information for assessing fetal age. Table 3.9 displays the dental feature helpful for fetal age estimation.[24]

Table 3.9: Dental feature

Age	*Features*
6 weeks	Development of dental lamina
8 weeks	Dental papilla forms
3 months	Bud or germination centers for permanent teeth appears
4-5 months	Calcification of temporary teeth occurs

Table 3.10: Determination of age from hand and foot length

Formula for fetal age
Using foot-length
PG = 8.8649 + 3.4863 × FL
Standard error = 0.75 of the estimate
Using hand-length
PG = 8.0514 + 4.8824 × HL
Standard error = 1.04 of the estimate
PG = period of gestation in weeks
FL = foot length in cm
HL = hand length in cm

Length of Hand and Foot

It is said that the length of hand and foot correlates with the gestational age of fetus. The regression formula is derived which is given in Table 3.10. The respective length of hand and/or foot is recorded and put in formula to obtain the age of fetus.[27]

AGE ESTIMATION IN INFANTS, CHILDREN AND ADULTS LESS THAN 25 YEARS

It is based on

- Physical examination
- Secondary sexual characteristics
- Teeth
- Radiological examination- consist of:
  - ⇨ Appearance and fusion of ossification centers
  - ⇨ Assessment of teeth.

Physical Features

Height/Length

Measurement of height gives idea regarding the development of an individual. Average height is term employed *which means height of a person within range of permissible limits i.e. in other words; it lies between third and ninety-seventh percentiles of height or within two standard deviations above or below the mean height of the age.* The length of child at birth is about 50 cm, 60 cm at 3 months, 70 cm at 9 month and 73 to 75 cm at 1 year of extrauterine life. At age of 2 years, the height is about 90 cm and at 4.5 years, the height is about 100 cm. After that the child gains about 5 cm in height every year up to 10 years of age. During the onset of puberty, there occurs growth spurt and add about 20 cm in height of a person. Thus, there is about 20 cm net increment in height of a person at puberty.

Disorder affecting height may result either in short stature or long stature. The causes are given in Table 3.11.

Weight

Measurement of weight gives idea regarding the development of an individual. Average weight is term employed *which means weight of a person within range of permissible limits i.e. in other words; it lies between third and ninety-seventh percentiles of weight or within two standard deviations above or below the mean weight of the age.* After birth, for few days, the newborn lose about 10 percent of weight due to loss of extracellular fluid but regains the weight by the age of 10 day. Subsequently, the child gains weight at a rate of approximately 25 to 30 gm per day for the first 3 months of life and after that about 400 gm of weight every month for the rest period of first year of life. The infant double his birth weight by the age of 5th month, trebles at 1 year of age and is four times at 2 year of age. At three years the weight of child is about 5 times that of birth weight. At 5th year of life, the expected weight is calculated by multiplying the birth weight by 6 and at 10 years by 10. A child gains about 2 kg of weight every year between 3 to 7 years and thereafter 3 kg per year up to puberty.[28] During the onset of puberty, there occurs growth spurt and add about 20 kg in weight of a person. Thus there are about 20 kg net increments in weight of a person at puberty.

Disorder affecting growth may result either in under weight or over weight for age. The causes are given in Table 3.12.

Chest Circumference and Abdominal Girth

- The chest circumference is measured at the level of nipples, midway between inspiration and expiration. Abdominal girth is taken at the level of umbilicus.
- In male – measurements at chest level are more than at abdominal level, unless the person happen to be obese
- At birth of a child, the circumference of chest is about 3 cm less than the head circumference. The circumference of head and chest are almost equal by the age of 1 year and thereafter the chest circumference surpasses the head circumference.

Table 3.11: Causes of abnormal stature

Short stature
1. Familial
2. Intrauterine growth retardation
3. Intrauterine infections
4. Genetic disorders
5. Nutritional deficiencies
6. Acondroplasia
7. Hypochondroplasia
8. Osteogenesis imperfecta
9. Spondylo-epiphyseal dysplasia
10. Mucopolysaccharidosis

Long stature
1. Constitutional
2. Familial
3. Marfan syndrome

Table 3.12: Causes of under or overweight

Causes of abnormal weight

Underweight
1. Malnutrition
2. Hyperthyroidism
3. Pheochromocytoma
4. Malabsorption syndrome
5. Infection (viz. HIV etc)
6. Malignancy
7. Anorexia nervosa
8. Pulmonary tuberculosis

Overweight
1. Hypothyroidism
2. Overeating
3. Cushing's syndrome
4. Hypothalamic disorder

Table 3.13: Head circumference at different age

Age	*Head circumference*
Birth	35 cm
3 month	40 cm
1 year	45 cm
2 year	48 cm
7 year	50 cm
10 year	52 cm

Head Circumference

- The maximum circumference of head from the occipital protuberance to forehead is recorded.
- This parameter is useful in children. The head circumference at different age is provided in Table 3.13. The

crown-rump length is always less than head circumference during the first year of life.

Secondary Sexual Characteristics

Secondary sexual characteristics develop in a person at puberty. *Puberty is the period where the endocrine and gametogenic functions of gonads have developed to the point that reproduction is possible.* Adolescence is the period of final sexual maturation. In other words, puberty is a period for girl or boy for his or her sexual maturity whereas adolescence is the period between puberty and maturity.

At puberty, the events in **girls** are

- Telerche – development of breasts
- Pubarche – development of axillary and pubic hairs
- Menarche – onset of menstrual periods.

The puberty period is divided into three phases and is described in Table 3.14. There is gradual enlargement of labia majora, labia minora and clitoris. The vaginal mucosa becomes dull in appearance. Few months before, clear whitish fluid is secreted from Bartholin's gland. Acne and comedones formation begins. Axillary hair appears few months before the onset of feminine type of body contour. Size of uterus and ovaries increases and Graffin follicles begins to mature with ovulation occurs. The phase in which these development occurs is – breast development → development of pubic hairs → menarche. **The first sign of puberty in girls is the development of breast bud and in boys is testicular enlargement**.

Table 3.14: Describing various stages in puberty

Period	*Female*	*Male*
Pre-pubescent	10-12 years	12-14 years
Pubescent	12-14 years	14-16 years
Post-pubescent	14-18 years	16-20 years

Sexual Maturation and Correlation with Age

Sexual maturation in an individual, usually, follows a pattern and Tanner divides the stages. These stages are commonly known as **Tanner grading** or **sexual maturity rating** (SMR). The SMR for male and female are given[29] in Tables 3.15 to 3.17 (also see Figs 3.19 and 3.20).

The puberty may occur early or may be delayed. Early occurrence of puberty is called as **precocious puberty**. In gynecological sense, precocious puberty means sexual maturity and/or menarche before 9 years[30] and the causes are given in Table 3.18. Delayed puberty is considered when the menarche has failed to occur by the age of 17 years or testicular development by the age of 20 years and the causes are given in Table 3.19.

Table 3.15: Tanner staging for pubic hairs in male and female (also see Fig 3.19)

SMR stage	*Age*	*Male (pubic hairs)*	*Female (pubic hairs)*
1	< 12 years	Pre-adolescent stage. No pubic hairs	Pre-adolescent stage. No pubic hairs
2	12-13 years	Scanty, sparse, long, lightly pigmented, at base of penis	Sparse, lightly pigmented, straight, not extending on to mons pubis
3	13-14 years	Darker, starts to curl, small amount, begins to spread laterally	Pigmentation in hair increases and becomes darker, increase in amount, begins to curl, grows over mons pubis
4	14-15 years	Resembles adult type but less in quantity, coarse, curly, covering most part but not going up to thighs	Coarse in texture, curly, abundant, covering most part but not going up to thighs
5	> 15 years	Adult distribution, spared to medial part of thighs	Adult distribution. Triangular spread, mature pubic hairs, spreads to medial part of thighs

Table 3.16: Tanner staging for genital development in male (also see Fig 3.19)

SMR stage	*Age*	*Penis*	*Scrotum & testis*
1	< 12 years	Pre-adolescent, small size penis	Pre-adolescent, small size testis and scrotum
2	12-13 years	Slight enlargement	Testis enlarge, enlarged scrotum, pink texture altered
3	13-14 years	Longer	Testis and scrotum enlarge further
4	14-15 years	Larger, thicker (breadth increase in size), glans penis is developed	Testis and scrotum larger, scrotum becomes darker
5	> 15 years	Adult size	Adult size, mature testis and scrotum

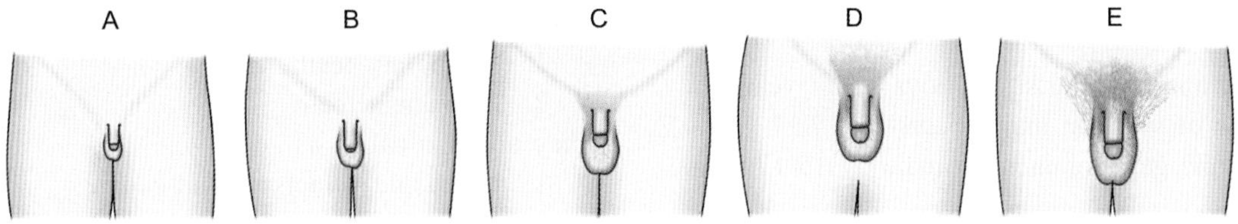

FIGS 3.19A to E: Diagrammatic representation of sexual maturity in male (pubic hair appearance as well as development of testis and penis). **A** = stage 1, **B** = stage 2, **C** = stage 3, **D** = stage 4 and **E** = stage 5.

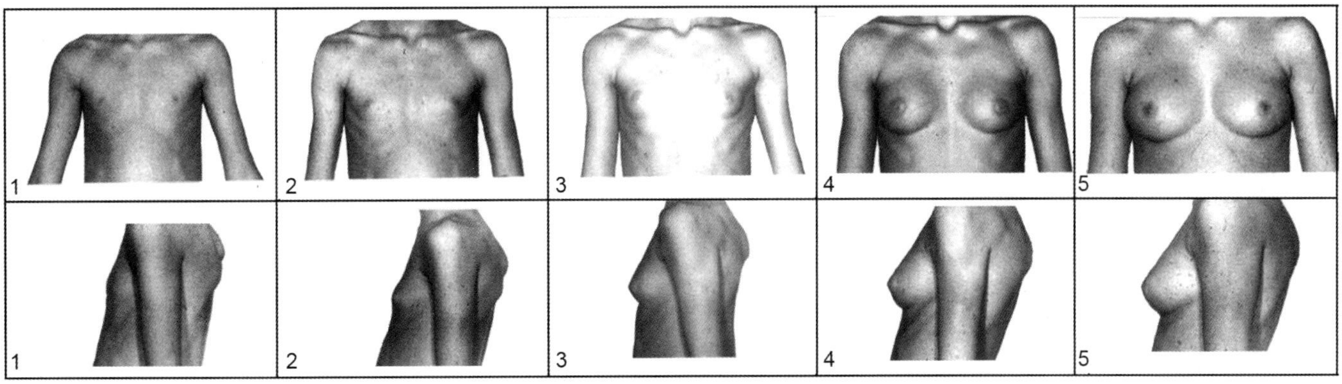

FIG. 3.20: Diagrammatic representation of breast development in female anterior and lateral view. Figures 1, 2, 3, 4, and 5 indicate stages of breast maturation

Table 3.17: Tanner staging for breast development in female (also see Fig 3.20)

SMR stage	*Age*	*Breast development*
1	9-10 years	Pre-pubertal. Elevated papilla, small fat areola
2	10-11 years	Papilla forms a palpable nodule (breast bud)
3	13 years	Breast and areola enlarged, contour of breast not defined
4	13-14 years	Contour of breast well defined, more breast development with elevation of the areola and papilla forming second mound
5	15-16 years	Mature breast - papilla projects as nipple, areola part of general breast contour

Table 3.18: Causes of precocious puberty

Constitutional
Disorders of posterior hypothalamus
Congenital virilizing syndrome
Androgen-secreting tumors
Leydig cell tumors
Granulosa cell tumors
Albright syndrome

Table 3.19: Causes of delayed puberty

Panhypopitutarism
Congenital absence of organs
Rokitansky-Kuster-Hauser syndrome
Turner's syndrome
Polycystic ovarian disorder
Hypogonadism

Other Features at Puberty

- Moustache and beard arises in boys 15-17 years
- Hoarseness of voice in male occurs by 15-17 years
- Adam's apple get prominent in male by 15-17 years.

Teeth

Teeth represent the exoskeleton in human body. In human beings, the teeth are replaced by only one time i.e. after falling of temporary teeth permanent teeth erupts and are known as **diphyodont** whereas in some other vertebrates, the teeth are constantly replaced throughout life and are called as polyphodont.

A tooth consists of three parts (Fig. 3.21):

1. Crown – projecting above the gum
2. Root – embedded in the jaw
3. Neck – connecting crown and root, surrounded by gum

Structurally each tooth is composed of (Fig. 3.22):

1. Pulp
2. Dentine
3. Enamel
4. Cementum
5. Periodontal membrane

Types

Teeth are of following types:

- Incisors
- Canine
- Premolars
- Molars

They are also classified as

1. Temporary teeth
2. Permanent teeth

They are also called as

1. Unicuspid – incisors and canine
2. Bicuspid – premolar
3. Tricuspid – molars

They are also called as

1. Anterior teeth – includes Unicuspid (incisors and canines)
2. Posterior teeth – includes all bicuspid and molars

Tooth Surface Nomenclature

Each tooth presents five surfaces. The surfaces are named in following way

- Occlusal surface – the surface in contact with opposite tooth or can be called as chewing surface
- Mesial surface – is the surface directed towards midline
- Distal surface – is the surface faces away from the midline
- Buccal or labial surface – is the surface facing cheek or lips
- Lingual surface – is the surface facing towards tongue

Age from teeth can be determined by noting

- Nature of teeth – temporary or permanent
- Number of teeth – whether 20, 24, 28 or 32
- Eruption of teeth
- Laboratory methods – like Boyde's method, Stack method etc

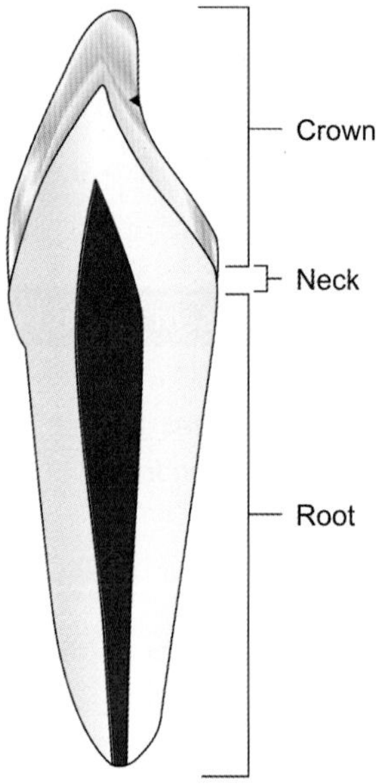

FIG. 3.21: Parts of tooth

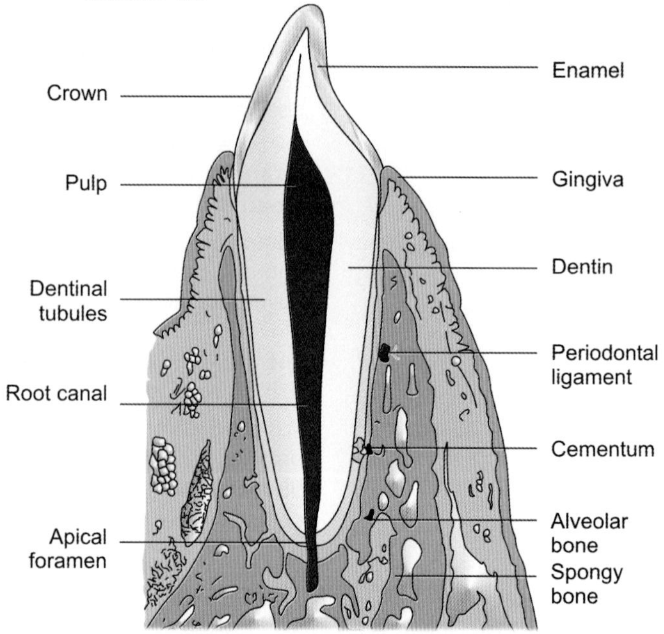

FIG. 3.22: Morphology of tooth

Nature of Teeth

Human being poses two types of teeth, temporary and permanent.

Temporary Teeth

These are also called as **deciduous teeth** or **milk teeth** or **primary dentition**. They are 20 in numbers and present in childhood. The teeth consist of (note that no premolars are present in childhood):

- 8 incisors
- 4 canines
- 8 molars

Each jaw contains 10 teeth consisting of 4 incisors, 2 canine and 4 molars (Fig. 3.23). Thus in each half of jaw, we will have 5 teeth consisting of 2 incisors, 1 canine and 2 molars. They are placed from midline to backwards as – medial incisor → lateral incisor → canine → first molar → second molar. Difference between temporary and permanent teeth are given in Table 3.20.

Eruption of Temporary Teeth

The deciduous teeth begin to develop during the 6th week of intra-uterine life. Mineralization of these teeth begins at 14 ± 2 weeks and continues after birth.[31] After birth, teeth start erupting by the age of 6 months. Student can easily remember by going with this rough formula. First tooth erupt in childhood is lower medial (central) incisors at 6 month of age → upper medial incisor at 7 month → upper later incisor at 8 month → lower lateral incisor at 9 month. Thereafter first molar erupts at 1 year (12 months) of age → canine at 1.5 years (18 months) → second molar erupt at 2 year of age. Remember half-year formula; add 6 months to each type of tooth and get the period of eruption (for example incisor erupt at 6 month, add 6 month you will get 1 year, the period of eruption of first molar tooth). The age of eruption of temporary teeth and their calcification of root is given in Table 3.21.

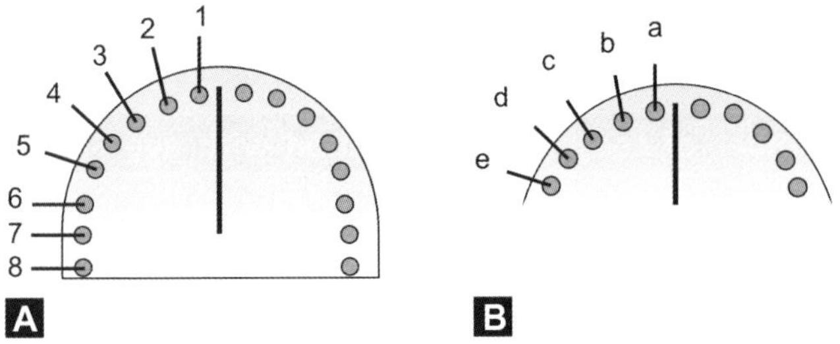

FIGS 3.23A and B: Diagram showing permanent teeth (**A**) and temporary teeth (**B**). **A:** 1 = medial incisor, 2 = lateral incisor, 3 = canine, 4= 1st premolars, 5 = 2nd premolars, 6 = 1st molar, 7 = 2nd molar and 8 = 3rd molar. In **B:** a = medial incisor, b = lateral incisor, c = canine, d = 1st molar, e = 2nd molar

Table 3.20: Difference between temporary and permanent teeth

Features	*Temporary teeth*	*Permanent teeth*
Number	20 (8 incisor, 4 canine, 8 molars)	32 (8 incisors, 4 canine, 8 premolars, 12 molars)
Premolars	Absent	Present
Size & weight	Smaller and lighter, more delicate	Larger and heavier, stronger
Colour	China white	Ivory white
Placement	Anterior teeth are vertically placed	Anterior teeth are inclined or projected forwardly
Neck	More constricted	Less constricted
Presence of ridge	Present between neck and body	No ridge
Root of molars	Smaller and more divergent	Longer and less divergent
Replaced by	Permanent teeth	Not replaced
X-ray	Reveals bud or germination center of permanent teeth	No such features noted

Table 3.21: Eruption and calcification of root of temporary teeth

Teeth	*Eruption*	*Calcification of root*
Medial incisor lower	6-8 months	1.5-2 years
Medial incisor upper	7-9 months	1.5-2 years
Lateral incisor lower	10-12 months	1.5-2 years
Lateral incisor upper	7-9 months	1.5-2 years
First molar	12-14 months	2-2.5 years
Canine	17-18 months	2.5-3 years
Second molar	20-30 months	3 years

Permanent Teeth

They are 32 in numbers and consist of:

- 8 incisors
- 4 canines
- 8 premolars
- 12 molars

Thus, each jaw contains 16 teeth consisting of 4 incisors, 2 canine, 4 premolars and 6 molars (Fig. 3.23). Thus in each half of jaw, we will have eight teeth consisting of 2 incisors, 1 canine, 2 premolars and 3 molars. They are placed from midline to backwards as – medial incisor → lateral incisor → canine → fist premolar → second premolar → first molar → second molar → third molar.

Eruption of Permanent Teeth

Eruption of permanent teeth can be remembered by mnemonic "**m**other **i**s **i**n **b**ed **b**aby **c**ome **m**onday **m**orning". The first alphabet of each word denotes the name of tooth. Therefore eruption of teeth will be (first) **m**olar → (medial) **i**ncisor → (lateral) **i**ncisor → (first premolar) **b**icuspid → (second premolar) **b**icuspid → **c**anine → (second) **m**olar → (third) **m**olar. The age of eruption of permanent teeth and their calcification of root is given in Table 3.22.

Features of Erupting of Teeth

- Age estimation of teeth is based on their regular eruption pattern
- Mixed dentition is a period when both the temporary and permanent teeth are present in the oral cavity. It is the period starting from 6 year of life (because first permanent molar erupt at 6th year) till 11 years of age (because the temporary canine is replaced by permanent canine). Table 3.23 displays the salient features of period of dentition (Fig. 3.24).

Table 3.22: Eruption and calcification of root of permanent teeth

Teeth	*Eruption*	*Calcification of root*
First molar	6-7 years	9-10 years
Medial incisor	7-8 years	10-11 years
Lateral incisor	8-9 years	11-12 years
First premolar	9-10 years	12-13 years
Second premolar	10-11 years	13-14 years
Canine	11-12 years	14-15 years
Second molar	12-14 years	14-16 years
Third molar	17-25 years	20-23 years

- Remember that temporary incisors and canines are replaced by permanent incisors and canines whereas temporary molars are replaced by permanent premolars. The erupting permanent molars do not replace any temporary tooth that is the reason why these permanent molars are called as **superadded teeth**. These permanent molar erupt behind the temporary teeth.
- Successional teeth – these are the permanent teeth replacing the temporary teeth. Incisors and canine replaces temporary canine whereas premolar replaces temporary molars. Since temporary teeth are succeeded by permanent teeth therefore they are called as **sucessional teeth** or **succedaneous teeth**.
- Eruption of third molar occurs between 17 to 25 years. After eruption of second molar, the mandibular ramus extends backward to make space for eruption of third molar. This developing space is known as **spacing for third molar**. Initially, the space is small and known as half space and with complete formation, it is known as full space. Half space usually develops by the age of 14 to 15 years and full space by the age of 15 to 17 years.
- The eruption of third molar is not regular. In some individuals it may erupt at time, in some it may be delayed or in some it may not erupt at all! It was mentioned in Modi's textbook of medical jurisprudence that – *Dr. Modi had noted the erupted third left lower molar at 14 and 15 years. Similarly Dr. Modi had seen a man of 40 without third molar tooth.* Therefore due precaution should be exercised while interpreting the third molar tooth. The teeth may remain impacted or may not erupt at all and the reasons are given in Tables 3.24 and 3.25. The causes for early eruption of teeth are given in Table 3.26. In non-erupted third molar with spacing, X-ray examination is warranted to access the condition of tooth. In case of impacted third molar, complete calcification of root without eruption, age can be presumed to be more than 25 years. **Impacted tooth** means tooth that do not develop in oral cavity but trapped in jawbone (Figs 3.25 and 3.26).

Table 3.23: Showing period of dentition with number of teeth and correlation with age

Age	*Number of teeth*	*Period of dentition*	*Comment*
2-5 years	20	Temporary	-
6	21-24	Mixed dentition	Due to eruption of first permanent molar
7-11 years	24	Mixed dentition	Due to eruption of permanent teeth replacing temporary teeth.
12-14 years	25-28	Permanent	Due to eruption of second molars
14-17 years	28	Permanent	There is no eruption of other teeth in this period
17-25 years	29-32	Permanent	Due to eruption of third molars
> 25 years	32	Permanent	Eruption of teeth completed

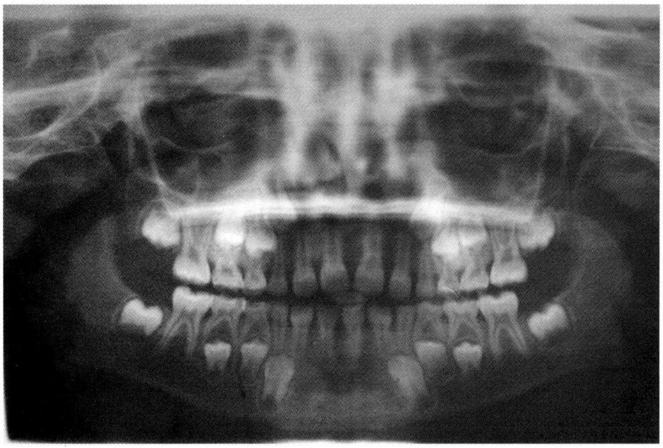

FIG. 3.24: OPG showing mixed dentition

- The X-ray or more preferably **orthopentogram** (OPG) (see Fig. 3.24) of the jaw would show developmental status of un-erupted teeth and degree of root calcification. A tooth erupts in an oral cavity only when there is a half root formation inside the jaw.
- Teeth develop earlier in females in comparison to males.
- Tooth eruption can be described as "just appearing", "half appeared" (i.e. below occlusal surface) or "fully appeared" (i.e. when the tooth is near or in the occlusal surface).[29]
- The germination center of third molar appears between 7 to 9 years. The development of crown and root in third molar is given in Table 3.27.

Abnormalities of Number and Size

- One or more teeth may fail to develop. The most common absent tooth is third molar followed by upper lateral incisors
- Many teeth may be missing from both the primary and secondary dentition in partial anodontia or all teeth may fail to develop in total anodontia.
- Supernumerary teeth – eruption of additional tooth in oral cavity are **supernumerary tooth** or **supplemental tooth** and often resemble adjacent tooth.

Laboratory Methods

1. **Boyde's method** – Boyde has suggested a method to determine the age of child up to few months after birth. He studied the cross-striations developed in the enamel of teeth. The cross-striations are thought to be daily increments of growth that are deposited in the enamel. These are called as incremental lines. After birth one major incremental line develops known as neonatal line. After this neonatal line, subsequent incremental lines are calculated and the age is deduced. It is stated that by this method, the age can be estimated in terms of days.
2. **Stack's method** – Stack had developed this method where he had taken the weight and height of tooth. From the height and weight of tooth, he deduced the age of child.

Table 3.24: Causes of delay in eruption of teeth

Delay in eruption
Malnutrition
Recurrent illness
Mental insufficiency
Rickets
Mongolism
Cretinism
Acondroplasia

Table 3.25: Causes of impacted teeth

Causes of impacted third molar
Evolutionary reduction of jaw bone
Overcrowding of teeth
Presence of supernumerary teeth
Failure of growth of alveolar bone
Hypoparathyroidism
Cleidocraniodysostosis

Table 3.26: Causes of early eruption of teeth

Early eruption of teeth
Well nourished baby
Congenital syphilis
Eosinophil cell tumor
Hyperpituitarism
Macro-somia praecox

Table 3.27: Crown and root development of third molar

Features	*Girls*	*Boys*
Complete crown formation	15 years	16-17 years
Crown with 1/3rd root formation	16 years	17-19 years
Crown with 2/3rd root formation	17 years	17-19 years
Crown with complete root formation	18-19 years	19-21 years
Apical closure of root	20-23 years	20-23 years

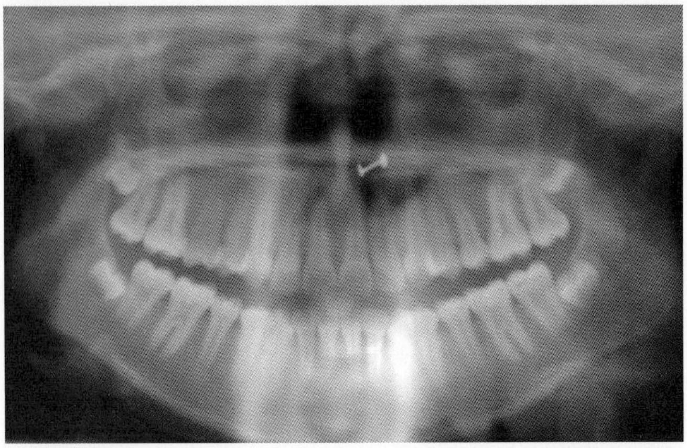

FIG. 3.25: OPG showing erupting third molar

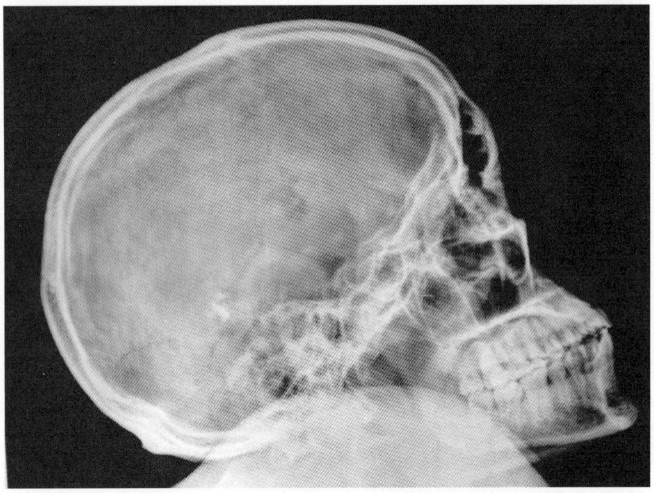

FIG. 3.26: X-ray lateral view of skull showing complete eruption of third molar

Table 3.28: Factors affecting appearance and fusion of ossification centers

Factors
Climate
Dietary habits
Geographical variation
Hereditary factors
Association with diseases
Growth and development

Radiological Examination

This method is useful in
- Studying the appearance and fusion of ossification centers
- Radiographic study of diaphyseal length
- Calcification of root of teeth

A. Appearance and Fusion of Ossification Centers

Radiological survey of ossification centers may provide considerable help in estimating age of a person. However, we cannot place too much reliance over such method as many factors affect the process of appearance and fusion of bone. Roughly this method provides one parameter in conjugation with others to deduce age of a person and it cannot be superior criteria when considered in isolation (Figs 3.27A to E and 3.28A to F). Similarly it has to be remembered that the progression of fusion of bone is a process and not an event, so it may be liable for variation. The factors affecting the appearance and fusion of these centers are provided in Table 3.28. Galstaun while studying Bengali population had provided the data, which are given in Table 3.29.

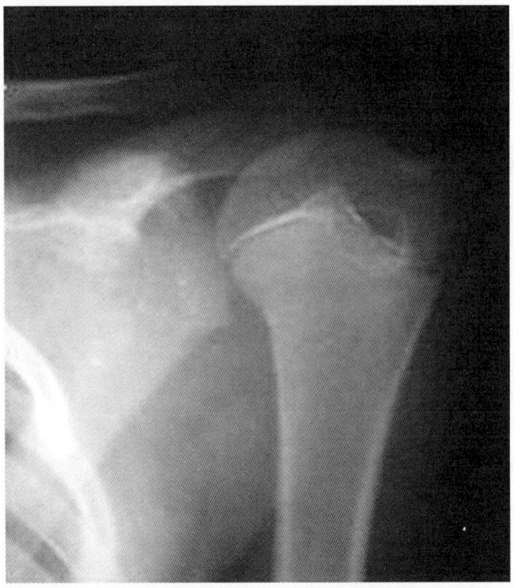

FIG. 3.27A: X-ray AP view of shoulder showing non-fusion of head with shaft

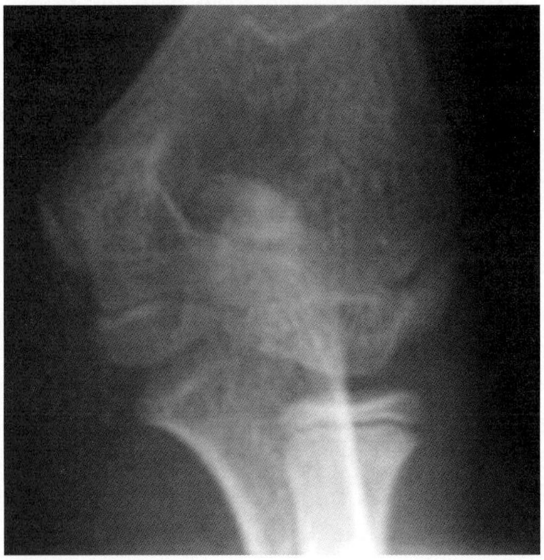

FIG. 3.27B: X-ray AP view of elbow showing non-fusion of lower end of humerus and upper end of radius and ulna

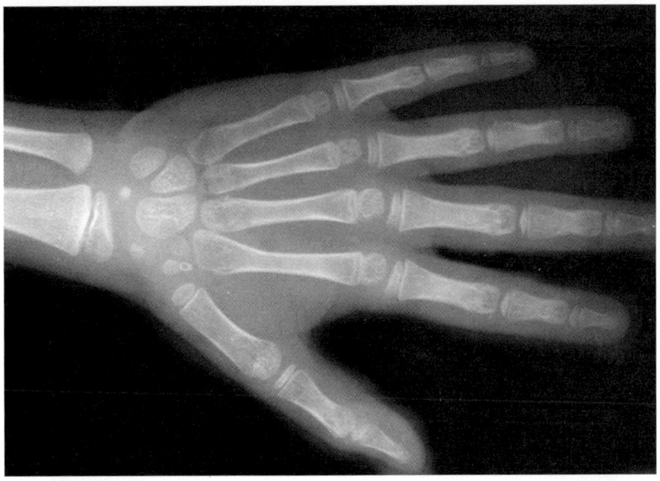

FIG. 3.27C: X-ray wrist with hand AP view showing non-fusion of lower end of radius and ulna

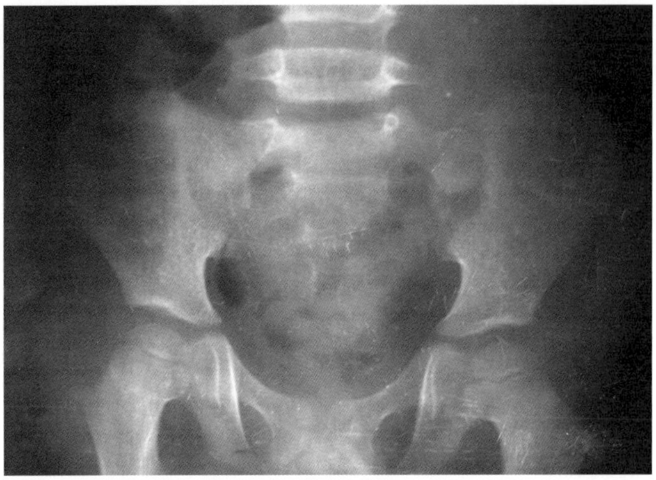

FIG. 3.28A: X-ray AP view - upper end of femur - not fused

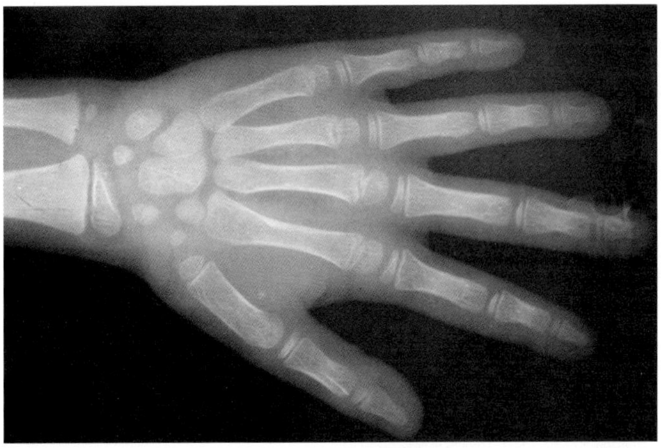

FIG. 3.27D: X-ray wrist with hand AP view showing non-fusion of lower end of radius and ulna

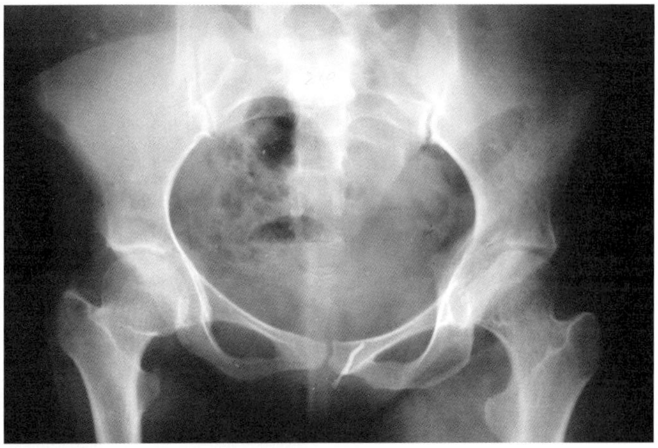

FIG. 3.28B: X-ray AP view - upper end of femur - fused

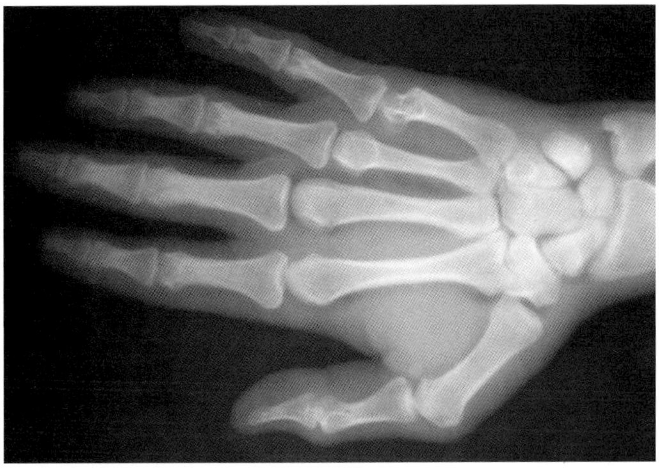

FIG. 3.27E: X-ray wrist with hand AP view showing fusion of lower end of radius and ulna

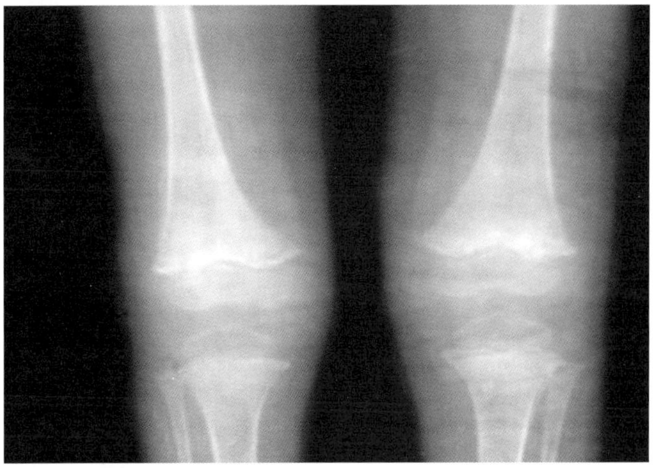

FIG. 3.28C: X-ray AP view - lower end of femur and upper end of tibia and fibula not fused

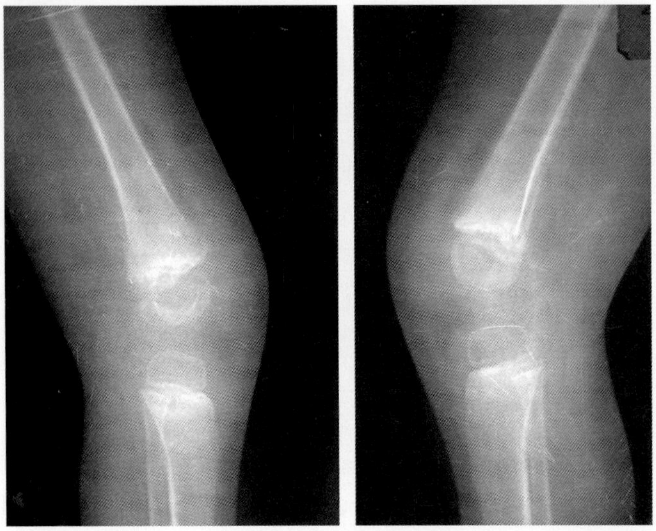

FIG. 3.28D: X-ray lateral view - lower end of femur and upper end of tibia not fused

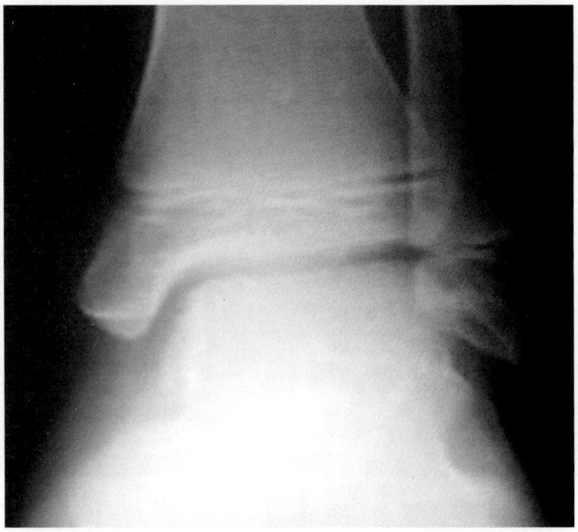

FIG. 3.28F: X-ray AP view of ankle showing non-fusion of lower end of tibia and fibula

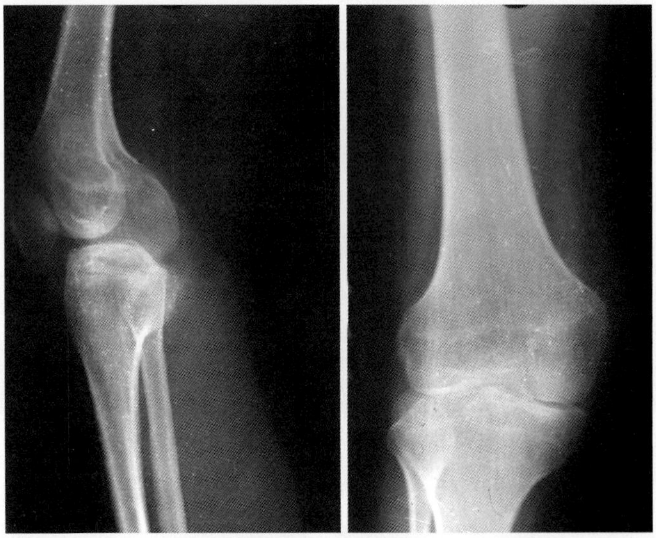

FIG. 3.28E: X-ray AP and lateral view - lower end of femur and upper end of tibia are fused

Table 3.29: Ossification centers as observed in Indian subjects[32] (after Galstaun G. 1937)

Bone	*Female*	*Male*
Humerus		
Head	A† – 1 year F# – 14-16 years	A – 1 year F – 14- 18 years
Greater tubercle	A – 7 month F – (with head) 2–4 years F – (with lesser tubercle) 5–7 years	A – 7 month F – (with head) 2–4 years F – (with lesser tubercle) 5–7 years
Trochlea	A – 7-10 years F – (with capitellum) 9–13 years	A – 9-11 years F – (with capitellum) 11–15 years

Count...

Bone	Female	Male
Lateral epicondyle	A - 10 years F - (with capitellum) 10-12 years	A - 12 years F - (with capitellum) 11-16 years
Medial epicondyle	A - 5 years F - 14 years	A - 7 years F - 16 years
Radius		
Head	A - 6 years F - 14 years	A - 8 years F - 16 years
Distal end	A - 1 years F - 16.5 years	A - 1 years F - 18 years
Ulna		
Olecranon	A - 9-12 years F - 15 years	A - 11-13 years F - 17 years
Distal end	A - 8-10 years F - 17 years	A - 10-11 years F - 18 years
Carpal bones		
Capitate	A - 6 months	A - 6 months
Hamate	A - 8-14 months	A - 8-14 months
Triquetrum	A - 2-3 years	A - 3-4 years
Lunate	A - 5 years	A - 5 years
Trapezium	A - 5-6 years	A - 7 years
Trapezoid	A - 5-6 years	A - 4-7 years
Scaphoid	A - 6 years	A - 7-11 years
Pisiform	A - 9-12 years	A - 12-17 years
Metacarpals		
1st metacarpal	A - 3 years F - 14-16 years	A - 4 years F - 16-18 years
2,3,4 and 5th metacarpal	A - 2-3 years F - 14-15 years	A - 3-4 years F - 16-18 years
Phalanges (hand)		
Proximal row	A - 1.5 years F - 14-15 years	A - 2-4 years F - 17-18 years
Middle row	A - 2-3 years F - 14-16 years	A - 3 years F - 16-18 years
Terminal row	A - 3 years F - 15 years	A - 3-5 years F - 17-18 years
Hip bone Crest of ilium	A - 14 years F - 17-19 years	A - 17 years F - 19-20 years
Disappearance of Triradiate cartilage	13-14 years	15-16 years
Ischium and pubis	F - 8.5 years	F - 8.5 years
Ischial tuberosity	A - 14-16 years F - 20 years	A - 16-18 years F - 20 years

Count...

Count...

Bone	*Female*	*Male*
Femur Head	A - 1 years F - 14-15 years	A - 1 years F - 16-17 years
Greater trochanter	A - 3 years F - 14 years	A - 3 years F - 17 years
Lesser trochanter	A - 1 years F - 15-17 years	A - 1 years F - 15-17 years
Distal end	A - before birth F - 14-17 years	A - before birth F - 14-17 years
Tibia Proximal end	A - shortly before birth F - 14-15 years	A - shortly before birth F - 16-17 years
Distal end	A - 1 year F - 14.1-14.4 years	A - 1 year F - 16 years
Fibula Proximal end	A - 2 year F - 14-16 years	A - 4 year F - 14-16 years
Distal end	A - 1 year F - 13-15 years	A - 1 year F - 14-16 years
Patella	4 years	3-7 years
Tarsal bones		
Calcaneum	At birth	At birth
Talus	At birth	At birth
Cuboid	At birth	At birth
Internal cuneiform	A - 1-3 years	A - 1-4 years
External cuneiform	A - 1-3 years	A - 1-4 years
Middle cuneiform	A - 1-3 years	A - 1-4 years
Navicular	A - 1-3 years	A - 1-4 years
Metatarsals		
1st metatarsal	A - 3 year F - 14-15 years	A - 4-5 year F - 16-18 years
2,3,4 and 5th metatarsal	A - 3 year F - 14-15 years	A - 4-5 year F - 16-18 years
Phalanges (foot)		
Proximal row	A - 1-3 year F - 14-15 years	A - 3-4 year F - 16-18 years
Middle row	A - 3-4 year F - 14-15 years	A - 3-4 year F - 16-18 years
Distal row	A - 4-6 year F - 13-14 years	A - 4-6 year F - 15-17 years

Count...

Count...

Bone	Female	Male
Clavicle	A - 14-16 year F - 20 years	A - 15-19 year F - 22 years
Scapula		
Base of coracoid	A - 2.5 months F - 2.5 years	A - 2.5 months F - 2.5 years
Coracoid tip	A - 10-11 years F - 16 years	A - 10-11 years F - 16 years
Angle of coracoid	A - 8-10 years F - 16 years	A - 10-14 years F - 17-18 years
Acromion*	A - 12-14 years F - 16 years	A - 15-16 years F - 19 years

* Majority of cases exhibited appearance and fusion as mentioned by Galstaun, page no. 280 of reference.
† A = denotes appearance of ossification center
# F = denotes fusion of center

B. Radiographic Study of Diaphyseal Length[33]

Hunt and Hatch had developed a method whereby they studied the diaphyseal length of either femur or tibia to estimate age. Hoffmann is of the opinion that diaphyseal length is reasonable means of age estimation for individuals below 12 years especially when skeletons are devoid of epiphysial ends or if dental data is missing.

Age Estimation in Adults Over 25 Years

It is based on
1) Physical examination
2) Secondary changes in teeth
3) Changes in skeleton
4) Radiology

Physical Examination

Depends upon the age, some changes initiates early at about 40 years and some appear late.

- Graying of hairs: Graying of scalp hairs usually starts from 40 years onwards but this is not reliable means since it is observed even in young boys (Fig. 3.29). Graying of body hairs and pubic hairs occur in old age.

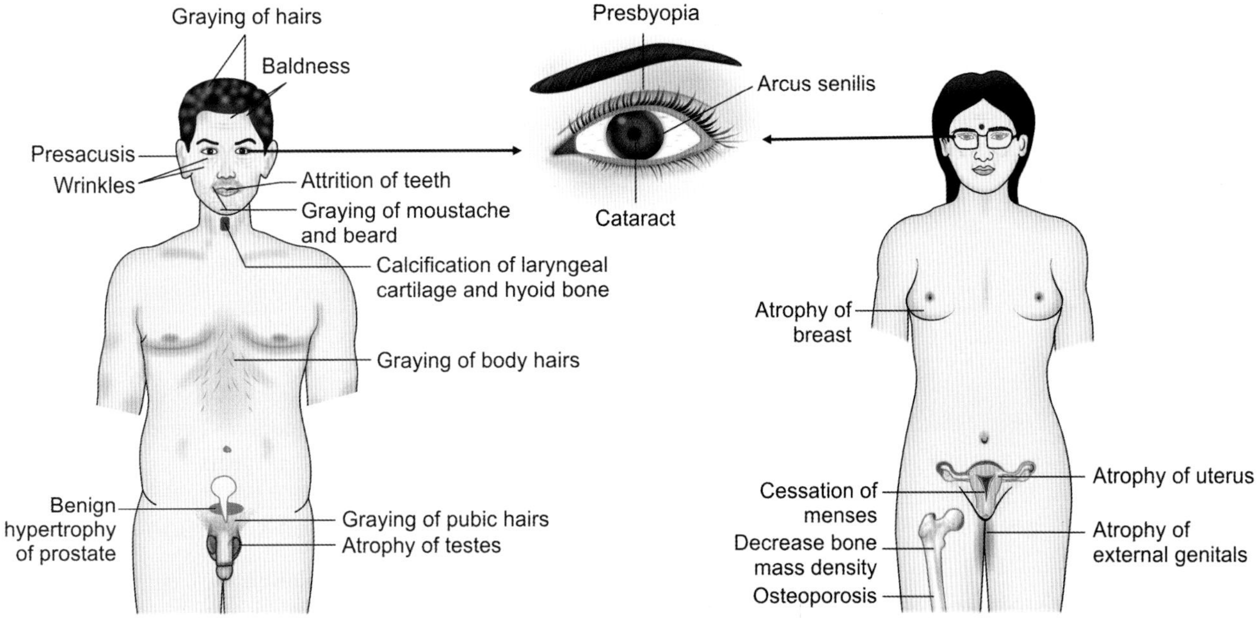

FIG. 3.29A: Physical changes as age advances

- Baldness: As the age advances, baldness may appear in men however it has to consider with other criteria (Fig. 3.29).
- Changes in skin: As the age advances, the skin becomes lax with appearance of creases and wrinkles over face (Fig. 3.29). The skin becomes dry and thin. In advance age, ecchymoses may be observed in skin due to brittle and hardened vessels.
- Changes in eye: Following are the changes (Fig. 3.29)
  - ⇨ Presbyopia – causes difficulty with reading, accommodation
  - ⇨ Cataract – there is opacification of lens
  - ⇨ Arcus senilis – appearance of whitish ring at the periphery of the cornea due to degenerative changes.
- Presacusis – decreased hearing acuity, may be deafness (Fig. 3.29)
- Vestibular dysfunction
- Decreased lean body mass, muscle
- Decrease bone density
- Prostate enlargement
- Vaginal/urethral mucosal atrophy
- Musculoskeletal disorders
- Postural hypotension
- Anemia
- Brain atrophy – results in benign senescent forgetfulness
- Decreased righting reflexes – results in sway of body
- Stiffer gait
- Increased body fat resulting in obesity
- Systemic examination - CVS – decreased arterial compliance and increase systolic blood pressure may cause left ventricular hypertrophy

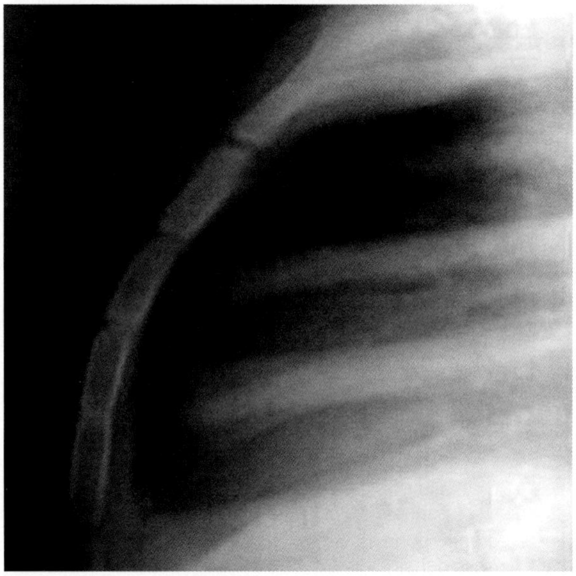

FIG. 3.29B: X-ray sternum oblique view showing non-fusion of sternal segments

- Respiratory system – decrease lung elasticity and increase chest wall stiffness may cause ventilation/perfusion mismatch and decrease Po_2 leads to dyspnea, hypoxia
- Decrease colonic motility → constipation → fecal impaction.

Changes in Teeth

The eruption third molar teeth occur at 25 years (maximum), and after this no further eruption of any tooth occur. The estimation of age after the age of 25 years is based on the secondary changes occurring in teeth. Following are methods for estimation of age.

A. Examination of Oral Cavity

Eduntulous jaw suggests advancing age. After loss of teeth, there is general atrophy of the alveolar margins.

B. Gustafson's Method

In this method, age estimation is done by noting the changes occurring in teeth. Gustafson had included six parameters to record these changes –

1. Attrition: These are the changes caused on masticating surface due to wearing and tearing.
2. Periodontosis: If oral hygiene is bad, the tooth root may be exposed with deposition of debris.
3. Secondary dentine: With advance age there may be deposition of secondary dentine tissue in the pulp cavity.
4. Root resorption: It is a decaying process with resorption of root.
5. Cementum apposition: In this condition, Cementum deposition increases.
6. Transparency of root: It occurs due to rarefaction of dentine tissue.

The parameters are included in Table 3.30. Of all the above criteria, transparency of root alone is the single most important one to determine age. For the purpose of estimation of age, a standard regression line was made and a formula provided to estimate age. The formula is:

$A_n + P_n + S_n + R_n + C_n + T_n$ = points → age in years

Here "n" denotes number of points recorded. The points are to be added as shown in equation. The derived points are compared and age is derived in years.

Advantages of Gustafson's Method

1. Useful in adult population
2. Fairly reliable method

Table 3.30: Gustafson's method of estimating age

Degrees	Features
	Attrition
A-0	No attrition
A-1	Attrition within enamel
A-2	Attrition within dentine
A-3	Attrition exposes the soft pulp of tooth
	Periodontosis
P-0	No Periodontosis
P-1	Exposure less than 1/3 of root near crown
P-2	Exposure of root more than 1/3 but less than 2/3
P-3	Exposure more than 2/3 of root
	Secondary dentine
S-0	No deposition
S-1	Deposition in upper part
S-2	Deposition in upper half of pulp cavity
S-3	Deposition in almost whole pulp cavity
	Root resorption
R-0	No resorption
R-1	Resorption in some spots
R-2	Resorption noticed over larger area
R-3	Involve Cementum and dentine
	Cementum apposition
C-0	Only normal layer of Cementum is noticed
C-1	Slightly greater than normal
C-2	Thick layer has occurred
C-3	Heavy layer has occurred
	Root transparency
R-0	No transparency
R-1	Noted at apical region
R-2	In upper 1/3rd from apical region
R-3	Noticeable up to 2/3rd

Disadvantage of Gustafson's Method

1. The method is applicable in only dead subjects, as tooth has to be extracted so application is limited in living persons.
2. If oral hygiene is not maintained properly, erratic results may be obtained.
3. Practically difficult procedure.

C. Miles Method

The method suggested by Miles is adaptation of Gustafson's method. Miles used translucency of root as a sole criteria to estimate age. In this method, the tooth is grounded up to thickness of 1 mm. The translucency is assessed by placing the grounded tooth on dotted paper and outline of tooth is drawn. Thereafter, dots visible through tooth are calculated and then the tooth is removed and the dots in tooth outline are calculated. From the percentage of dots visible through tooth and actual number, the age of a person is estimated.

D. Biochemical Method

Biochemical examination of tooth can provide age of a person. The amino acids are present in teeth. When the amino acids are incorporated into teeth, they are of the Levo or left handed variety. Once these amino acids have been fixed in dentine they undergo a slow and irreversible change to dextro or right-handed variety. The ration of levo and dextro amino acids will give the age. Aspartic acid shows a high racemization rate and used as useful indicator for estimation of age.[34]

E. Fluorescence Method

A method using intensity of fluorescence in dentine and Cementum was proposed by Kvaal et al in 1989. It shows strong correlation between ages and as age increases there is deepening of tooth colour with proportionate increase in intensity of fluorescence.[35]

Changes in Skeleton

Bone exhibit changes and these changes are useful to estimate the age of person. *The changes are dealt with chapter on forensic osteology.*

Radiological Changes

- Calcification of thyroid cartilage and cricoid cartilage may be evident at about 40 years onwards
- Calcification of hyoid bone may be evident at about 40 years onwards
- Calcification of laryngeal cartilage and epiglottis may be noted from 40 years onwards
- Lipping of body of lumbar vertebral body may start at around 40 to 50 years of age
- Atrophic changes in the intervertebral discs is observed in 50 to 60 years
- Fusion of xipiod with sternum occurs at about 40 years and fusion of sternum with manubrium occurs at about 60 years (Fig. 3.29A)
- Changes occurring in sternal end of rib with reference to calcification and shape had been studied and complex criteria presented for age estimation.[36]
- Deposition of secondary dentin can be assessed using periapical radiograph to estimate age in adults. Pulp diameter to crown diameter ratio and pulp/root length and pulp/root width is measured.[37]

Table 3.31: Medicolegal importance of different age

Age	*Importance*
4 months IUL	Quickening
7 month IUL	Viability
1 year	Killing a infant under one year of age is infanticide
3 years	Half fare in bus/public transport
5 years	- Half fare in railway - Eligible for admission in first standard - Child is held responsible for any wreckage caused to train (as per Railway Act)
7 year	Under this age a child is not held criminally responsible for his criminal act and not punished (Section 82 of IPC)
7-12 years	A child can be held responsible for his act if that child posses sufficient maturity and understands the nature and consequences of the act (Section 83 of IPC)
12 years	- Above this age, a child is held responsible for his act - If less than 12 years the child cannot give consent for medical examination (Section 89 of IPC) - If less than 12 years, Oath not necessary in Court of law - Entitle for full ticket (fare) in public transport
14 years	If a child is less than 14 years, he cannot be employed in factories (Indian Factories Act 1948)
14-15 years	Can be employed in non-hazardous job in factory in day time
< 15 years	Sexual intercourse with wife less than 15 years with or without consent is punishable
> 15 years	Can be employed in factory if a fitness certificate is given
< 16 years	- Sexual intercourse with a girl less than 16 years with or without consent amounts to rape (Section 375 of IPC) - Taking away a boy from legal guardianship amounts to kidnapping
> 16 years	A girl can give consent for sexual intercourse
18 years	- Attainment of majority except when the person is under the guardianship of a court - Minimal permissible limit for marriage for girls - Can give consent to suffer any harm not indented or known to cause death/grievous hurt (Section 87 of IPC) - Below 18 years - taking away a female from legal guardianship amounts to kidnapping - Eligible for casting vote in Assembly/Loksabha/local bodies - Below 18 years - boys and girls are considered as juvenile and tried in juvenile court (Juvenile Justice Act 2000) - A person above this age can be employed - Usual age to enter into government service - Kidnapping a boy or girl below this age for the purpose of begging is punishable
21 years	- Attainment of majority for the person who are under the guardianship of courts - A male can make a valid marriage above this age - If a girl below this age is imported from foreign country or from the state of Jammu & Kashmir for the purpose of forcing her or seducing her to illicit sexual intercourse, the act amounts to kidnapping
25 years	A person can contest State Assembly elections
30 years	A person can contest Parliamentary elections
35 years	Minimum age for appointment as the President or the Vice-President of India or the Governor of a state
58 years	Age of retirement for government employee in some states

Count...

Count...

Age	Importance
60 years	Age of retirement for government employee working with Central Government
65 years	- Age of retirement for all government employee - A person gets concession in fare if traveling in public transport such as bus, railway etc as he is considered as senior citizen

Medicolegal Importance of Age

The medicolegal importance of different age is given in Table 3.31.

STATURE

Stature means body height of a person. Estimation of stature is major forensic anthropological concern used in identification of unknown and commingled human remains.[38] The procedure to estimate stature is to use its components. From intrauterine life, stature increases up to 20 to 21 years of age of a person. According to Roche, generally stature at 18 years is accepted as adults; although there are small increment occurs in stature after this age. The sex difference in reaching adult height is considerable; the median age for attaining adult height in males is 21.2 years and in females 17.3 years with growth continuing in 10 percent of male until 23.5 years and in 10 percent of females until 21.1 years[39].

Recording height

- Length is recorded in babies less than two years of age. The child is placed in supine position on infantometer. The head is held against reference point of infantometer and legs are straightened keeping feet at right angles to legs with toes pointing upward. A free footboard is brought in contact with the child's heels and length is recorded.
- Height is recorded in persons who are more than two years. Standing height is recorded with person standing in upright position. Heels are slightly separated and weight is borne evenly on both feet. Heels, buttock and back are brought in contact with vertical surface of height measuring rod (stadiometer). The head is maintained in Frankfurt plane and bi-auricular plane being horizontal. The headpiece of stadiometer is kept firmly over the vertex to compress the hairs. Thus, the height is recorded from vertex to heel.
- In dead body – the height of dead body may differ from height of person during life, either it may be longer or shorter though lengthening is more common. In addition, the measured height may change with different period in postmortem state for example the body may lengthen in primary phase of muscular relaxation by 2 to 3 cm whereas it may shorten in rigor mortis phase and again it increases during decomposition.[40]

Stature is more in:

1. Stature is maximum between 20 to 25 years of age of a person.
2. It is more during morning hours.
3. It is more in recumbent position.
4. It is more in dead bodies in stage of primary relaxation.

Stature is less in:

1. After the age of 25 years, stature decreases about 1 mm per year.
2. It is less in evening hours than morning hours because of decreased elasticity and increased tonicity of the vertebral muscles.
3. It is less in standing posture than recumbent position.
4. In dead bodies, stature is less during the stage of rigor mortis.

Stature is estimated from

1. Body parts
2. Skeleton or bones - *refer chapter on forensic osteology*

Estimation of Stature from Body Parts

1. When both upper limbs are overstretched in a straight line then distance between the tips of two middle fingers of both hands is approximately equal to the living stature of a person.
2. Twice the length from vertex to symphysis pubis is equal to the stature of a person or twice the length from symphysis pubis to heel is equal to the stature of a person.
3. Stature of a person is equal to the length of one upper limb (from tip of middle finger to the acromial process) × 2 + 34 cm. (34 cm is taken as = 30 cm length of two clavicle + 4 cm for the breadth of manubrium).
4. Stature = length from sternal notch to symphysis pubis × 3.3.
5. Stature = Length of forearm (length from tip of finger to tip of olecranon) × 3.7.
6. Stature[41] = length of head (from top of head to tip of chin as vertical length) × 7.
7. From hand[42] – stature had been estimated from the length and breadth of hand by Bhatnagar et al (1984) and the regression equations are given as follows:
   - Stature = 127.97 + 2.06 × hand length
   - Stature = 141.67 + 3.13 × hand breadth.
8. Stature from foot *vide infra* (footprints)

9. Stature[43] = length of vertebral column × 35/100.
10. From lower limb[44] – stature = trochanteric height × 1.10 + 737.03 (trochanteric height is measured from the lateral bulging of the greater trochanteric protrusion to the heel).

Anthropometry

It is also called as Bertillon system. It is based on the principle that:

1. After 21 years of age, the measurement of various body parts of adult do not alter and
2. The ratio in size of different parts to one another varies considerably in different individuals.

- This system is used mainly for the identification of habitual criminals.
- This system includes recording of:
  1. **Descriptive data**: such as colour of iris, hair, complexion, shape of nose, chin and ears. Photograph of full face and the right profile are also taken.
  2. **Recording of body marks**: such as moles, birthmark, tattoo mark, scars etc.
  3. **Body measurements**:
     - ⇨ Standing and sitting height
     - ⇨ Length and width of head
     - ⇨ Length and width of right ear
     - ⇨ Span of outstretched arms
     - ⇨ Length of left middle and left little finger
     - ⇨ Length of left forearm and hand
     - ⇨ Length of left foot.
- The information is recorded on cards and is kept in specially arranged cabinets. This system is now replaced by fingerprint system.

Drawbacks of this system:

- Applicable only to adults
- Subjective error occurs while measurements
- Requires trained man power and instruments

Deformities

Presence of deformity in person is useful to identify that person. The deformities may be congenital or acquired.

A. Congenital deformities: Such as cleft palate, haire lip. polydactylism, supplementary mammae, web-fingers, claw hand, birth mark (naevi), moles, kyphosis (hump back), port wine stain, Mongolians spots, Hutchinson teeth etc. (Figs 3.30 to 3.32).

B. Acquired deformities: Such as poliomyelitis, mal-united or non-united fracture bone of extremity, old amputations etc. (Figs 3.33 and 3.34).

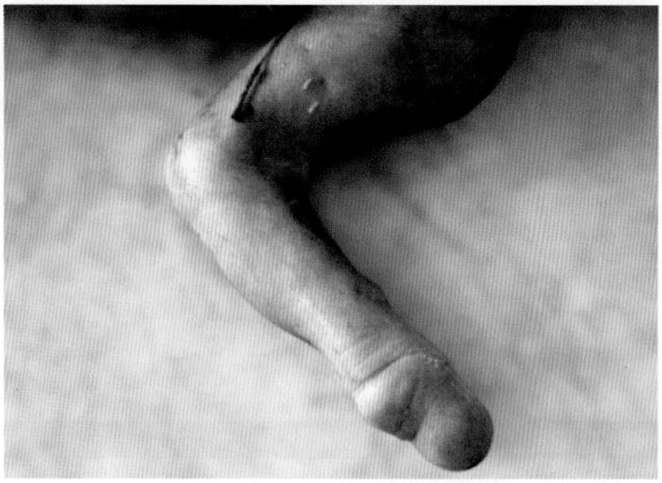

FIG. 3.30: Congenital deformity

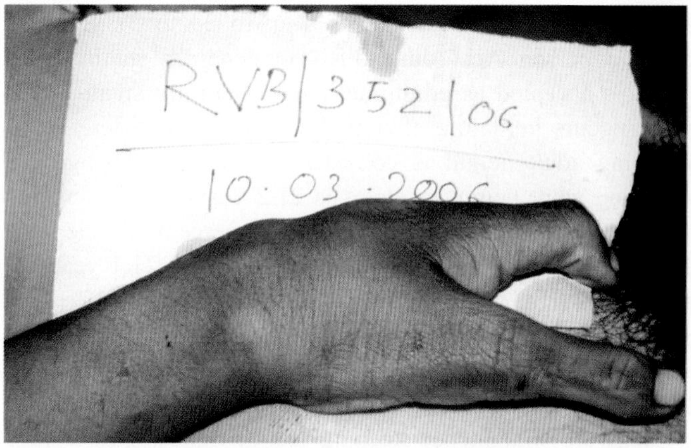

FIG. 3.31: Claw hand deformity

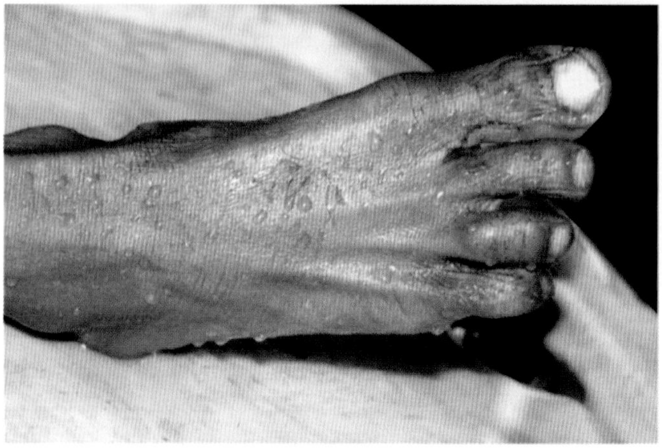

FIG. 3.32: Foot with four digits

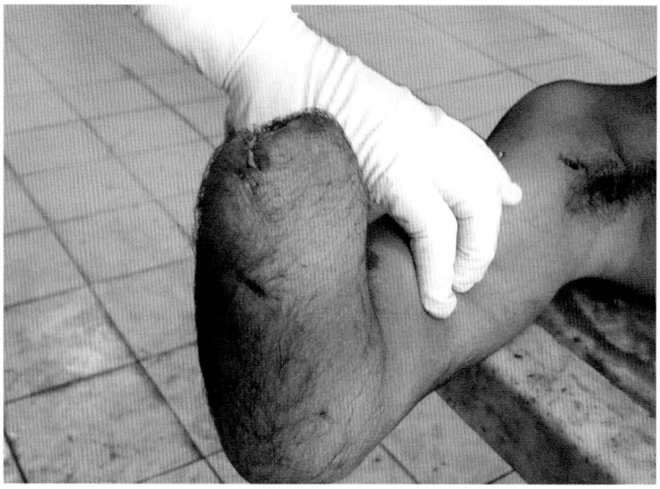

FIG. 3.33: Acquired deformity—amputation

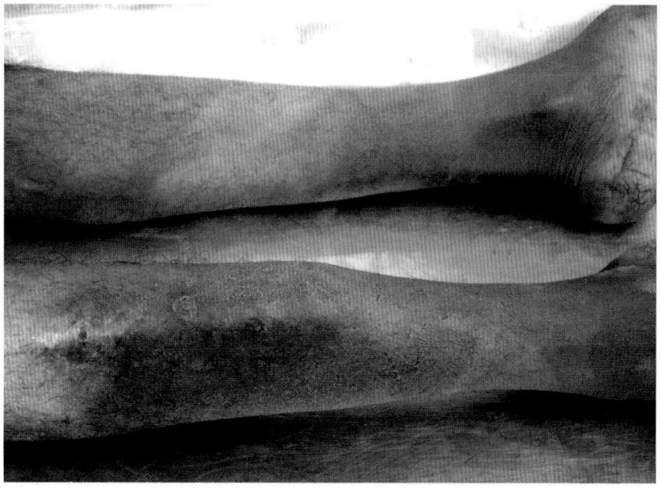

FIG. 3.34: Acquired deformity—malunion of fracture

Scars

Definition

A scar is a fibrous tissue produced as a result of healing of wound and it is covered by epithelium devoid of hair follicles, sweat glands or pigment.

Features

- Scars are permanent.
- Damage to epidermis does not produce scar. Injury to dermis is necessary to form a scar.
- Scars usually assumes the shape of wound causing them for example:
  1. Scar resulting from incised wound would be linear (Fig. 3.35).
  2. Lacerated wound produces broad and irregular scar.
  3. If healing of wound were by secondary intention, the resultant scar would be wider and thicker in the center than periphery (Fig. 3.36).
  4. Scars from scalds are spotted in appearance and appears running downwards.
  5. Stab wound produces oval, elliptical or triangular scar depending on the shape of weapon.
  6. Scars due to burns or corrosive chemicals are irregular and coarse scars,
  7. Vaccination scars are circular, oval, flat or slightly elevated (Fig. 3.37).
  8. Diseases such as small pox may cause multiple scars.
  9. Scar from bullet wounds would be circular and depressed one.
  10. Striae gravidarum scars are multiple and usually over abdomen in females who are pregnant or who were pregnant (Fig. 3.38).
  11. Drug addicts may have scar marks at cubital fossa due to repeated injections.

Appearance of Scars[1, 45]

- Time required for formation of scar depends on the nature of injury, size and site of wound over body and presence of absence of infection.
- Roughly a clean wound (healing by first intention) heals in 5 to 6 days and a definite reddish scar will be apparent in less than two weeks.
- If scar is large and edges cannot be approximated or infection is present the granulation tissue forms within few days and scar appears within 2 weeks to 3 months.

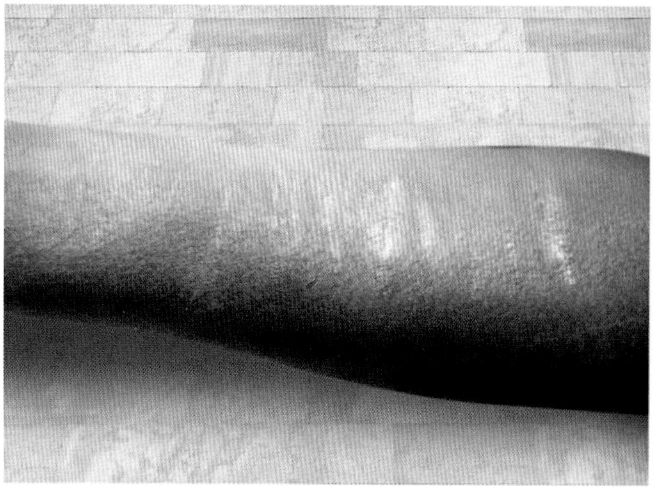

FIG. 3.35: Scars due to tentative cuts

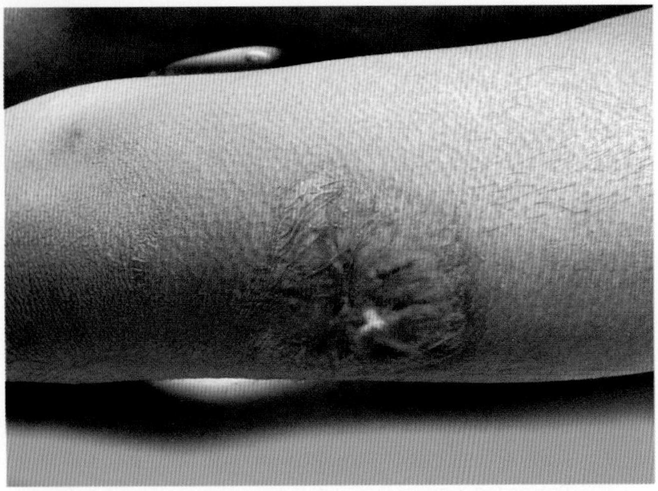

FIG. 3.36: Wider scar

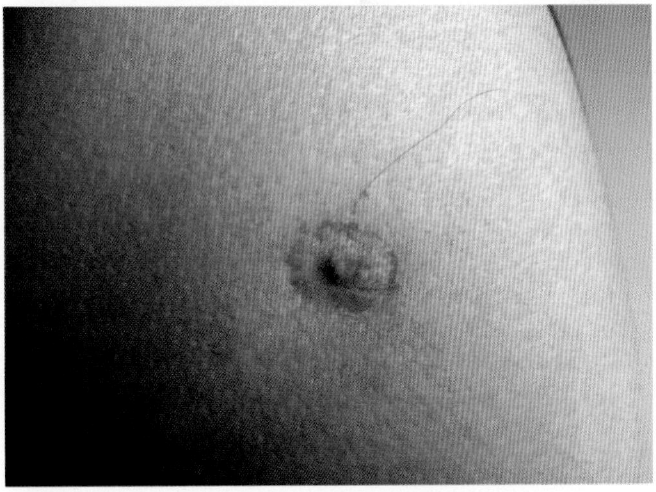

FIG. 3.37: Vaccination scar

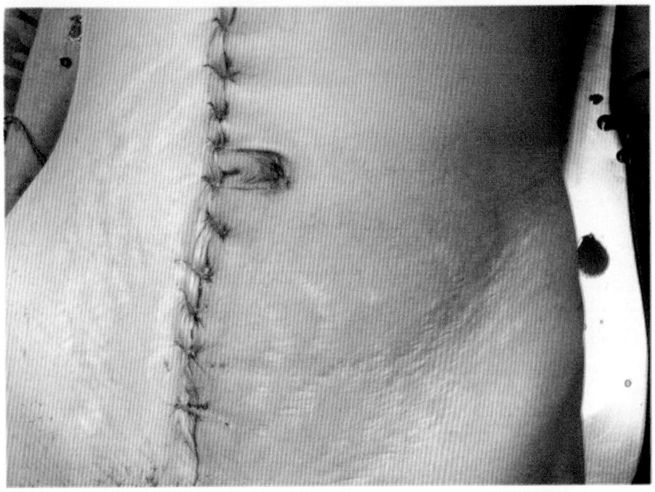

FIG. 3.38: Scar marks due to pregnancy

Growth of Scar

Scars produced in childhood will grow in size with the development of the person, especially if the scars are located on chest or limbs.

Age of scar

- When first formed, the scar is red, tender and covered by scab (< 2 weeks).
- Then it becomes denser and brown (2 week - 2 month).
- Then it becomes whit and glistening, tough and may be wrinkled (2-3 month).
- After this no further change occurs and it becomes difficult to date the scar.

Scar erasure

Scars cannot be erased or removed completely however, the size and shape can be altered by operative procedure such as excision and skin grafting.

Recording scars for identification

- While recording scars for identification, the number of scars, shape, size and situation over body should be recorded. Whether the scar is fixed or mobile, the consistency of scar and colour of overlying skin should be noted.
- Faint scars can be made visible by filtered ultraviolet light or by magnifying lens.

Medicolegal importance of scar

1) Important for identification.
2) Indicate type of weapon used for causing injury.
3) Age of scar can be determined.
4) Type of injury can be commented for example lacerated wound, stab wound etc.
5) Striae gravidarum indicate present or past pregnancy.
6) Scars causing following injuries amounts to grievous hurt (section 320 of IPC):
   A. Permanent disfiguration of face
   B. Causing contracture and/or joint restriction or hamper function of joint
   C. Over cornea causing permanent total or partial loss of vision.

Tattoo Marks

Definition

Tattoo marks are designs effected by multiple small puncture wounds made through the skin with needles or similar penetrating tools dipped in colouring material.

Dye Used

The different dyes used for tattooing are mentioned in Table 3.32. The technique and dye varies from country to country.

Table 3.32: Different dyes used to impart different colors	
Dye	**Color**
Carbon (India ink)	Black
China ink	
Soot	
Cinnabar	Red
Vermilion	
Ochre	Brown
Chromic oxide	Green
Prussian blue	Blue
(Ferric ferrocyanide)	
Indigo	
Cobalt	
Ultramarine	

Features

- The permanency of tattoo marks depends on the depth of deposition of dye and the type of dye used.
- If the pigments of dye are deposited below the epidermis, the tattoo marks stay longer. The type of pigment used affect the duration of tattoo marks. Dyes such as vermilion or ultramarine disappear earlier than India ink.
- The situation of tattoo marks over body is also important. Parts protected by clothes retain dye for longer period than exposed parts. For example, tattoos on hands or forearm disappear early due to exposure and constant friction.
- Tattoo marks may present on any part of the body however, commonly they are found on arm or forearms.
- Usually the tattoo marks are distinct up to 10 years.

Revealing Latent Tattoo Marks

Latent tattoo marks are faded marks and they can be visualized by:

1) Use of ultraviolet light.
2) Infrared photography.
3) Rubbing the part and examining under magnifying glass.
4) If tattoo marks are obscured by decomposition, they can be visualized[46] by treating the area with three percent H_2O_2.
5) Tattoo marks can also be developed by treating the skin with 0.5% caustic potash.[45]
6) Faint or faded tattoo marks can be made out on histological examination of regional lymph nodes. The lymph nodes near a tattoo mark show deposit of pigment used for tattooing.

Complications

Following are the complications, which may develop by tattooing.

1) Infection:
   - ⇨ Septic inflammation
   - ⇨ Abscess
   - ⇨ Spread of infectious disease such as AIDS
2) Scar or keloid may be formed.

Erasure or Artificial Removal of Tattoo Mark:

There are various methods to erase the tattoo mark and they are:

1) Surgical method:
   - ⇨ Complete excision of tattoo mark followed by skin grafting
   - ⇨ Application of carbon dioxide snow
2) Electrolysis: By utilizing 2-5 milliampeare of current with needle to remove mark.
3) Laser beams: Particles of dye get vaporized.
4) Application of caustic substance: Crude method.

Medicolegal Importance:

1) Identification of person (Fig. 3.39).
2) Religion can be known from the pattern or design of tattoo mark (Fig. 3.40).
3) Country can be known.
4) God of worship can be known.
5) Social status can be known.
6) Mental makeup of person can be known (Fig. 3.41).
7) Language of the person can be known (Figs 3.42 and 3.43)

Occupation Marks

These marks offer help in identification as certain occupation or trade may leave marks. These marks may be temporary or permanent.

1) Temporary marks: Paints, dyes or chemical or grease etc. at fingertips in case of painters, dyers, engineers or mechanic respectively. Microscopic examination of the dust or debris under nail beds or in clothes or in earwax may also aid in identification.
2) Permanent: Heavy and rough hands are seen in manual labourer. Tailors may have needle puncture marks on their left index fingers. Thickening of palmer skin of fingers is seen on hands of butcher. Certain occupation may impart colour changes to hairs for example copper smelters have greenish hair, indigo and cobalt miners have bluish hairs.

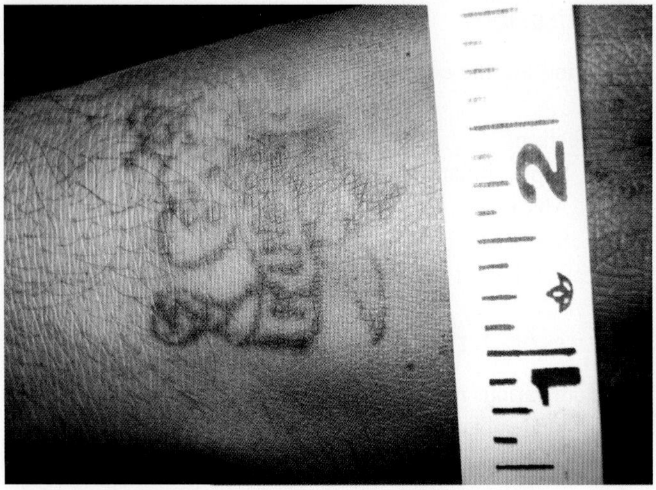

FIG. 3.39: Tattoo showing design

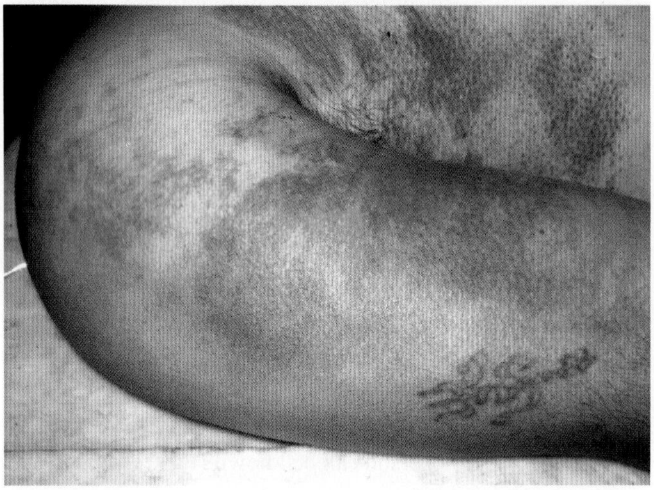

FIG. 3.40: From tattoo marks religion can be known

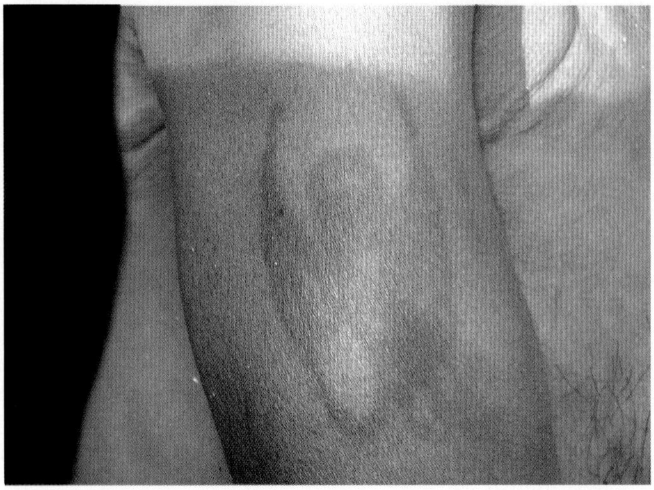

FIG. 3.41: Tattoo showing design - mental makeup can be known

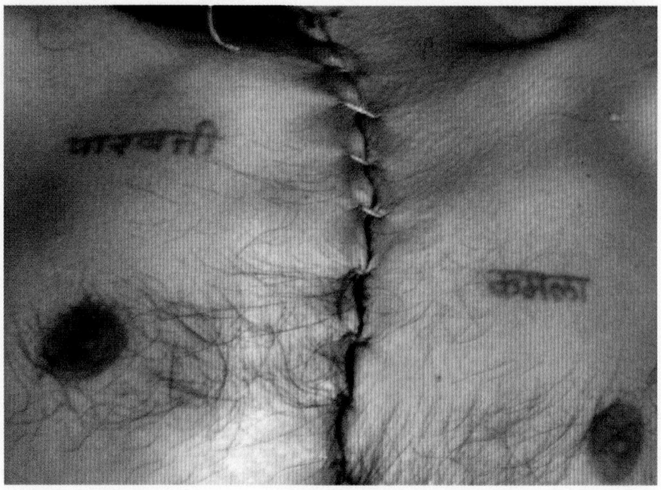

FIG. 3.42: Tattoo showing name—note language can also be known

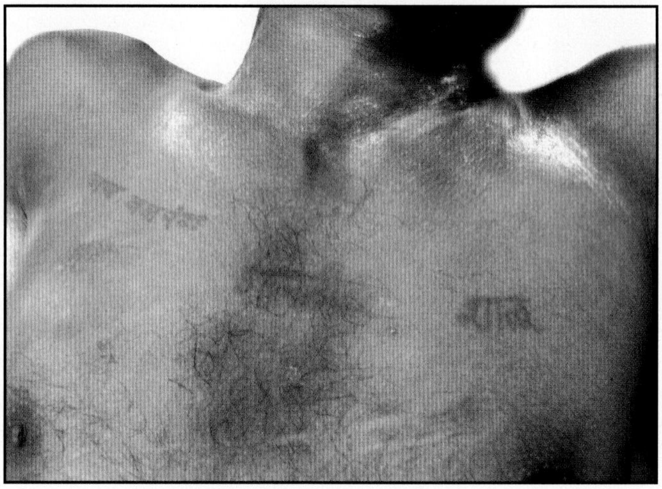

FIG. 3.43: Tattoo marks with name

Fingerprint System

Synonyms: Also known as Dactylography or dermatoglyphics or Galton system of identification.

Definition: *Fingerprints are impressions of pattern formed by the papillary or epidermal ridges of the fingertips.*

Principle: It is based on principle that the individual peculiarities of the patterns formed by the arrangement of the papillary or epidermal ridges on the fingertips are absolutely constant and persists throughout life from infancy to old age and that the patterns of no two hands resemble each other.

Features

- Identification by this system is absolute.
- Fingerprints are highly individualistic even in monozygotic twins.

- Fingerprints are formed during intra-uterine life. The epidermal ridges are regularly spaced small down-growths of epidermal cells, which appear in finger and toe pads during the second and third months. They are known as primary epidermal ridges separated by corresponding dermal ridges. Secondary ridges develop by fifth month.[47]
- It has been estimated that the chances of two persons having identical fingerprints is about one in sixty four thousand millions.[48] The fingerprints follow Quetelet's rule, "all nature made things have unlimited and infinite variations of forms.[49]

Classification

Fingerprints are classified into four types as mentioned in Table 3.33 (also see Figs 3.44 to 3.47).

Table 3.33: Classification of fingerprints

Type	%
Arch	07
Loops	65
Whorl	25
Composite	2-3

They are further sub-classified as (Fig. 3.45):

1. Loop:
   - ⇨ Ulnar loop-loop opens on ulnar side
   - ⇨ Radial loop-loop opens on radial side
2. Whorl:
   - ⇨ Concentric
   - ⇨ Spiral–clockwise
   - ⇨ Spiral – anticlockwise
   - ⇨ Double spiral
   - ⇨ Almond shape
3. Arch:
   - ⇨ Plain
   - ⇨ Tented
   - ⇨ Exceptional
4. Composite:
   - ⇨ Central pocket loop
   - ⇨ Twined loop
   - ⇨ Accidental.

Recording of Fingerprints

The fingerprints are taken over unglazed white paper using printer's ink. Before taking prints, hands are washed and dried. The fingerprints are taken in two ways.

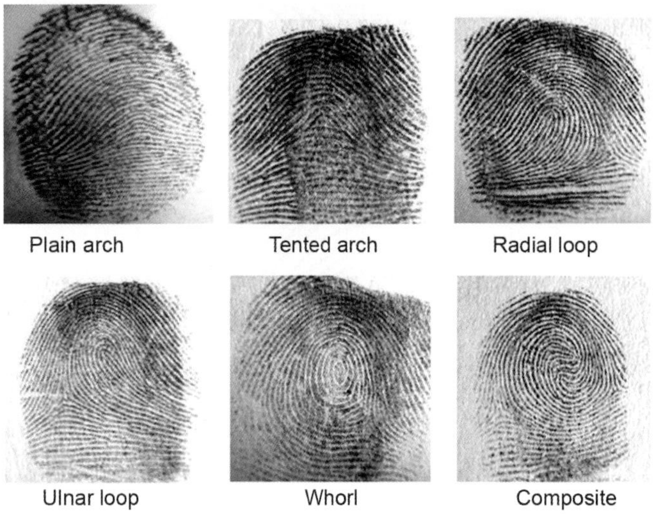

FIG. 3.44: Different fingerprint patterns (*Courtesy* Dr Vipul Ambade, Associate Professor, Forensic Medicine, GMCH, Nagpur)

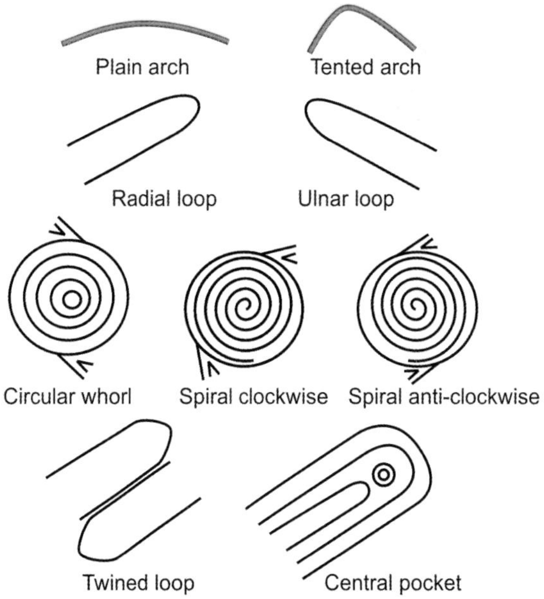

FIG. 3.45: Diagrammatic representation of different types of fingerprints

FIG. 3.46: Fingerprint showing delta and core

1) Plain impression or plain method.
2) Rolled impression or rolled method.

Plain Method:

- In this method, inked fingers are brought in contact with unglazed paper and impressions are taken (Fig. 3.48).
- Advantage of plain method is that it is quicker and easy to do. Disadvantage of this method is that larger surface area is not obtained for comparison.

Rolled Method:

- In this method, the fingerprints are taken by rolling the fingers on paper from outward to inward direction without lifting fingers in such a way that an impression of whole tip is obtained (Fig. 3.49).

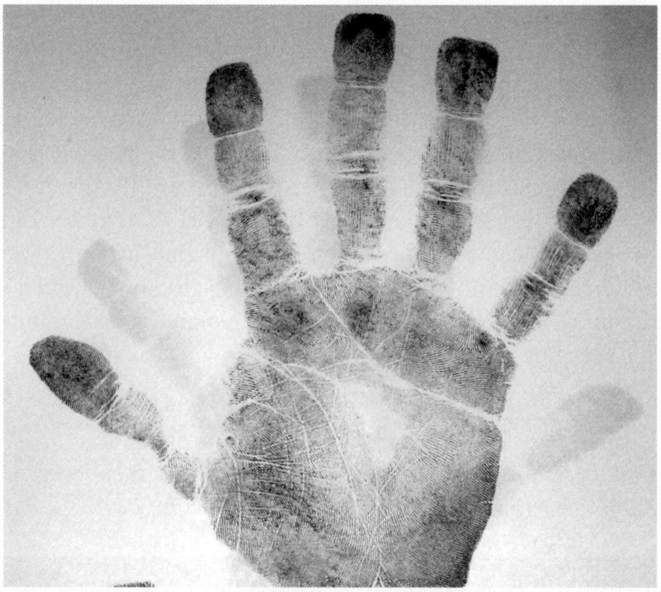

FIG. 3.47: Hand impression (courtesy Dr Vipul Ambade, Associate Professor, Forensic Medicine, GMCH, Nagpur)

- Advantage of this method is that it gives impression of a large area than plain method. Disadvantage is that it is somewhat difficult procedure and may blur the prints at places.

Comparison of Fingerprints

The obtained fingerprints are compared with reference print at the fingerprint bureau and about 16 to 20 points

FIG. 3.48: Fingerprints taken by plain method (*Courtesy*: Dr Vipul Ambade, Associate Professor, Forensic Medicine, GMCH, Nagpur)

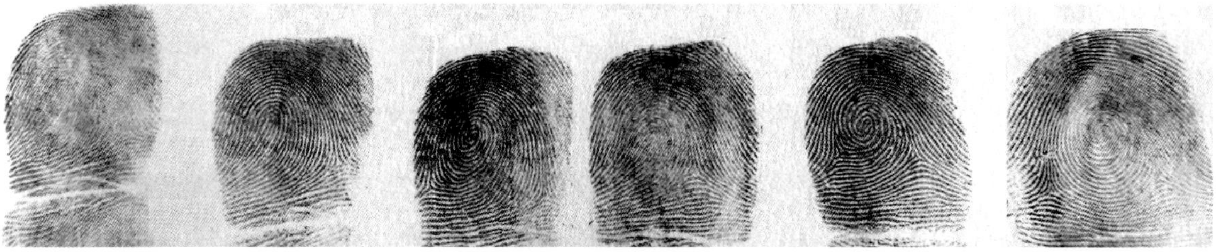

FIG. 3.49: Fingerprints taken by rolled method (*Courtesy*: Dr Vipul Ambade, Associate Professor, Forensic Medicine, GMCH, Nagpur)

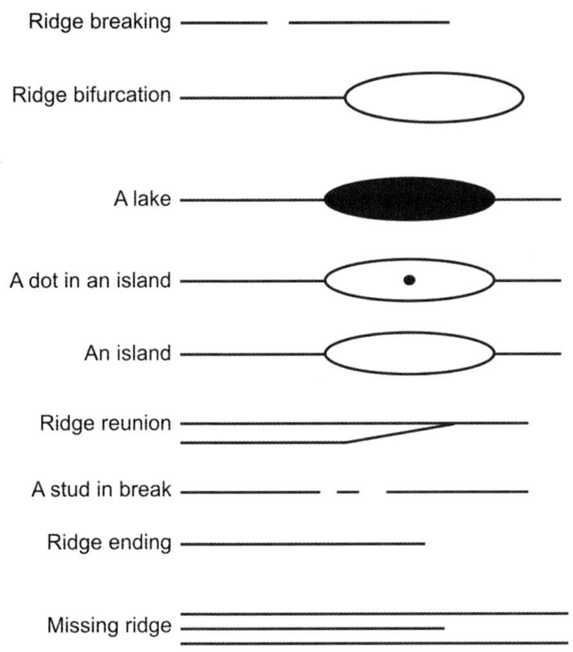

FIG. 3.50: Various ridge patterns

of similarities are matched. For the purpose of matching, pattern of ridge, ridge ending, missing ridge, counting of ridge, ridge breakage, fork formation, delta, island etc. are compared (Fig. 3.50).

Fingerprints at Scene of Crime

Fingerprints encountered at a scene of crime are classified as:
1) Visible print
2) Plastic print
3) Latent print

Visible prints: These are the fingerprints left at scene when the fingers are smeared with or contaminated with blood, paint, oil, grease, dust, secretions etc. These prints are visible prints.

Plastic prints: These are the prints left over soft surface or articles such as soap, wax, clay, cheese etc.

Latent prints:
- These prints are either invisible or barely visible that were left at scene of crime.
- These impressions are left over surface or articles due to sebaceous and sweat gland secretions.
- These prints have to be made visible by developing with reagents.
- If such prints are obtained by chance, then they are called as **chance fingerprints**.
- Different methods used to develop fingerprints are given in Table 3.34.

Mode of Fingerprint Production

The finger and fingertips of person is usually smeared by sebaceous secretion and sweat. Whenever a person touches any article or material, due to presence of sebaceous secretion, he leaves the impression of fingers over that article or material. These impressions can be visualized, developed and lifted by fingerprint experts.

Fingerprints in Dead Bodies

- Fingerprints are present over dermis and epidermis. If the skin is degloved as in advance decomposition, the skin should be removed, preserved in formalin and impressions can be taken from that degloved skin.

Table 3.34: Methods used to develop fingerprints

Developing agent	*Surface*	*Method*	*Principle*
Aluminium dust (gray powder)	Dark coloured surface	Spread over with camel brush	Powder adhere to the sebaceous secretion of the print and makes prominent the ridges
Charcoal powder (black powder)	Light or white colour surface	Spread over with camel brush	Same as above
Iodine vapour	Such surface that can be hold over iodine vapour such as paper etc	Exposed to iodine vapour	Ridges takes yellowish brown colour
Ninhydrin solution	Over articles or surface	Spread over prints	Amino acids present in sebaceous secretion react with ninhydrin and imparts black or reddish brown colour to the ridges.

Table 3.35: Allotment of scores to fingers

Presence of whorl pattern in finger	*Score allotted*
Right thumb or right index finger	16 scores
Right middle or right ring finger	8 scores
Right little or left thumb	4 scores
Left index or left middle finger	2 scores
Left ring or left little finger	1 score
Fingers with no whorl	No scores

- If the degloved skin is lost, still prints can be taken from dermis.
- In mummified bodies, the fingers are dry and shriveled and therefore prints are not possible. In such condition, the fingertips or skin is immersed in weak alkali solution to make them swell-up and then prints are taken.[49]

Maintenance of Fingerprints

- The prints are maintained in a systematic way. There are eight successive classifications of fingerprints.
- In primary classification, scores are allocated for presence of whorl pattern in different fingers of hand. No scores are allotted for fingers with no whorl type of print present. The allotted scores are presented in Table 3.35. The arrangement of scores are as follow:

$$\frac{RI + RR + LT + LM + LL + 1}{RT + RM + RL + LI + LR + 1}$$

- Here RI indicates right index finger, RR = right ring finger and so on.
- At, both numerator and denominator, score 1 is added for convenience of calculation
- Example: suppose in a person, in all fingers he have whorl pattern, then the score will be as mentioned in Table 3.36. The total score at the numerator and denominator will be 32 × 32 = 1024 score. If no whorl is present in any finger, then the score will be as per Table 3.36. The total score at the numerator and denominator will be 1 × 1 = 1 score. Thus by presence or absence of whorl in finger we have score from 1 to 1024. Therefore, on basis of this primary classification, 1024 boxes are made and these boxes are called as **pigeon holes**.

Mutilation or Alteration of Fingerprints

- Criminals may at times, tries to hide the identity by destroying the fingerprints by applying burns or corrosive agents. But the prints are not destroyed unless the skin is destroyed completely.
- Ridge alteration occurs in eczema, acanthosis nigricans, scleroderma, dry and atrophic skin.
- Permanent impairment of fingerprint pattern occurs in leprosy, electric injury, and radiation injury.
- In derm-abrasion, identification by fingerprints can be circumvented (evade).
- In coeliac disease, fingerprints may temporarily modify.
- Distance between ridges may change but pattern not change in rickets and acromegaly.

Fallacy of using fingerprint[50]
If there is no reference available, even though fingerprints are available, they will have no use.

Advantages of fingerprints
1) Recognition of chance prints at scene of crime.
2) Absolute identification is possible.
3) Data can be stored and can be transferred telegraphically.
4) Can be obtained from decomposed bodies.

Medicolegal importance
1) Absolute method of identification.
2) Identification in case of exchange of new born babies.
3) Identification in case of impersonation.
4) Used in lieu of signature.
5) To maintain identity records.
6) Identification of criminals, weapons etc.

Poroscopy

- Edmund Locard developed this method of identification. *Poroscopy means study of pores present on ridges of fingers and hand.*

Table 3.36: Example of scoring system in primary classification of fingerprints

If whorls are present in fingers, then the score will be as	*If no whorl is present in fingers, then the score will be as*
$\frac{16+8+4+2+1+1}{16+8+4+2+1+1} = \frac{32}{32}$	$\frac{0+0+0+0+0+1}{0+0+0+0+0+1} = \frac{01}{01}$
Therefore 32 X 32 = 1024	Therefore 1 X 1 = 1

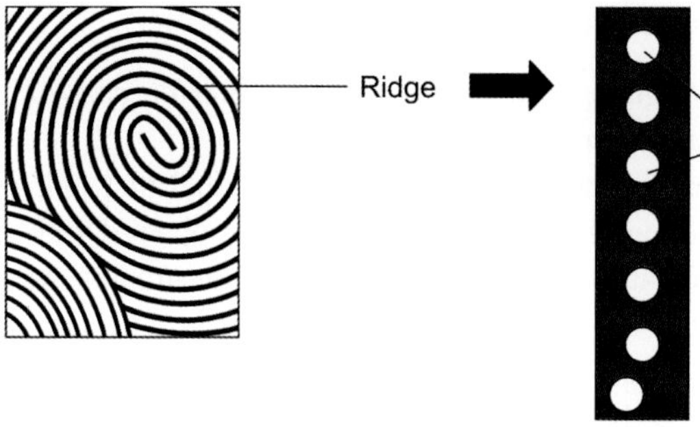

FIG. 3.51: Poroscopy

- It is noted that ridges on fingers and hand have microscopic pores through which sweat exudes (secrete) (see Fig. 3.51). These pores are opening of the ducts of sweat glands located in sub-epidermal region.
- It is seen that each millimeter of a ridge contains 9 to 18 pores.
- These pores are permanent and unchanged during life of a person
- These pores vary in size, shape, position, extent and number over a given length of ridge in each person.
- This method is reliable as fingerprints and useful for positive identification
- This method is particularly useful when only fragment of fingerprint or partial fingerprints are available.

Footprints

These are the foot patterns left by person at the scene of crime. They are of two types:

1. **Bare footprint**: These are prints left by barefoot
2. **Shoe prints**: These are prints left with shoe or chappal (footwear) worn by person.

- These prints are also individualistic like fingerprints.
- Footprints produced while walking is usually larger than that produced while a person is standing.
- Footprints can be recorded by photography or by making plaster cast.

Bare footprints

- Bare footprint of a suspected person can be compared with the reference print and peculiarities such as ridge pattern, flat foot, supernumerary toes, scars, callosities etc. found are compared.
- Latent footprints are also developed in a same way as fingerprints
- If there is absence of ridge pattern, the measurements such as length and width of foot, length and width of toe, toe pad, angle of declination from each toe and from ball to its juncture with the arch help in identification (Fig. 3.52).

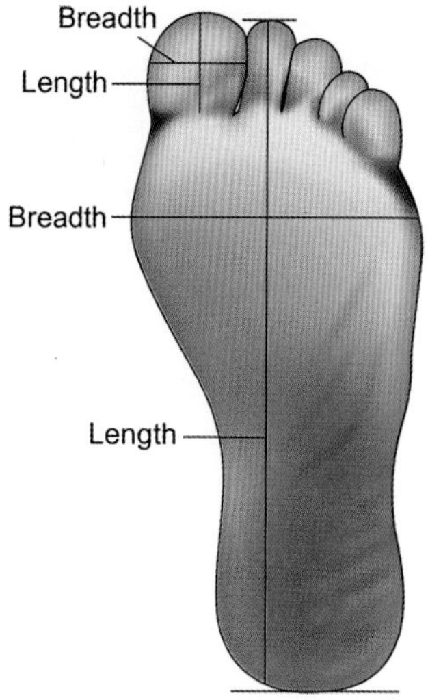

FIG. 3.52: Footprint and its measurement

Shoe Prints

Shoe prints are also helpful in identification. In case of shoe prints, there are two type of markings[51]

Primary markings: These refer to markings about the make of shoes or soles of shoe (Fig. 3.53).

Secondary markings: These are the markings that are imparted over sole of shoe by the user and these markings are individualistic (Fig. 3.53).

Features

1) Helps in identification.
2) Stature can be estimated from footprints – stature of the individual constitutes 15 percent ratio of foot length. Thus, Stature = Maximum foot length ÷ 0.15
3) Weight of person can also be estimated[33]
   - In male above 14 years: Weight of a person is about 60.5% ratio of foot outline width. Thus weight = Maximum foot outline width ÷ 0.60
   - In female above 14 years: Weight of a person is about 67 percent ratio of foot outline width. Thus weight = Maximum foot outline width ÷ 0.67
4) Sex[18] can also be determined – see Table 3.37.
5) Shoe print or boot print also helps to estimate height.[52, 53]

Table 3.37: Sex determination from footprint

Measurements	*Male*	*Female*
Footprint length (in CM)	24.67	22.43
Standard deviation	1.15	1.17

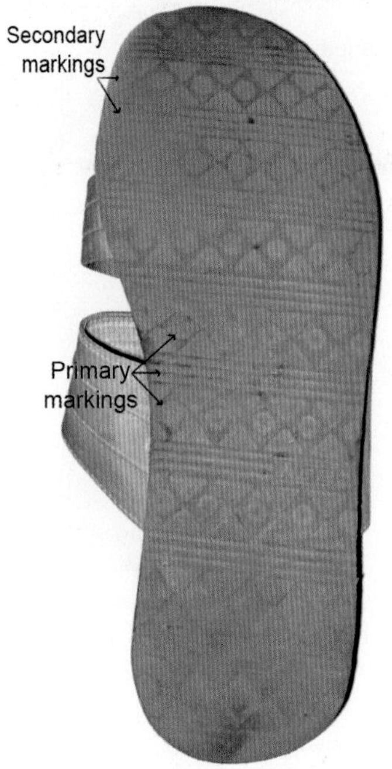

FIG. 3.53: Shoe print with primary and secondary markings

Lip Prints (Cheiloscopy)

Definition

Lip prints or Cheiloscopy is the study of furrows or grooves present in the human lips. Suzuki[54] classified the lip prints and the classification is given in Table 3.38 (Fig. 3.54).

Features

- It is held that lip prints pattern are unique to individual and help in identification.
- The patterns remain unchanged over person's lifetime. However, twins' children possessed similar lip patterns.[55]
- Sex of a person can also be determined by lip prints.[56]

Table 3.38: Classification of lip prints

Type	*Features*
Type I	Vertical, complete longitudinal fissures
Type I'	Incomplete longitudinal fissures
Type II	Branching Y shaped patterns of fissure
Type III	Criss-cross pattern of fissures
Type IV	Reticular, typical chequered pattern, fence like
Type V	Non-classified

Palatal Rugae (Rugoscopy) [3-5]

- *Palatal rugae are the ridges on the anterior part of the palatal mucosa on each side.*
- Palatal rugae are unique to each individual and helps in identification. The rugae patterns do not change with the development of a person and reappears after trauma. Males have better developed rugae in comparison with females.
- Thomas and Kotze have classified them and are mentioned in Table 3.39.
- The shape of rugae may be curved, wavy, straight or circular.

Radiological Methods

Outline of the frontal sinuses seen in X-rays can be used in identification of individuals. Antemortem radiographs of head can provide the objective data required for comparison.[57]

Superimposition

This is a method of comparative identification. In this method, skull of a person is compared with the photograph of the deceased person by way of superimposition. Thus, superimposition is a technique applied to determine whether the skull is that of a person in the said photograph or not. Superimposition techniques fall into three categories:[58]

1. Photographic
2. Video-graphic
3. Computer aided

Features

- This is a comparative method of identification
- If features of skull and photographs are in tally then it can be stated that the skull could be that of a person in photograph. However, it is 100 percent not sure.
- The test has more negative value (exclusion value) than confirmatory value (inclusion value). In other words, by comparison, it can be stated definitely that the stated skull is not that of a person in photograph i.e. the skull and photographs are not matching and thus may be of different persons.

Table 3.39: Thomas and Kotze's classification of palatal rugae

Type of rugae	*Size*
Primary rugae	5-10 mm 10 mm or more
Secondary rugae	3-5 mm
Fragmented rugae	< 3 mm

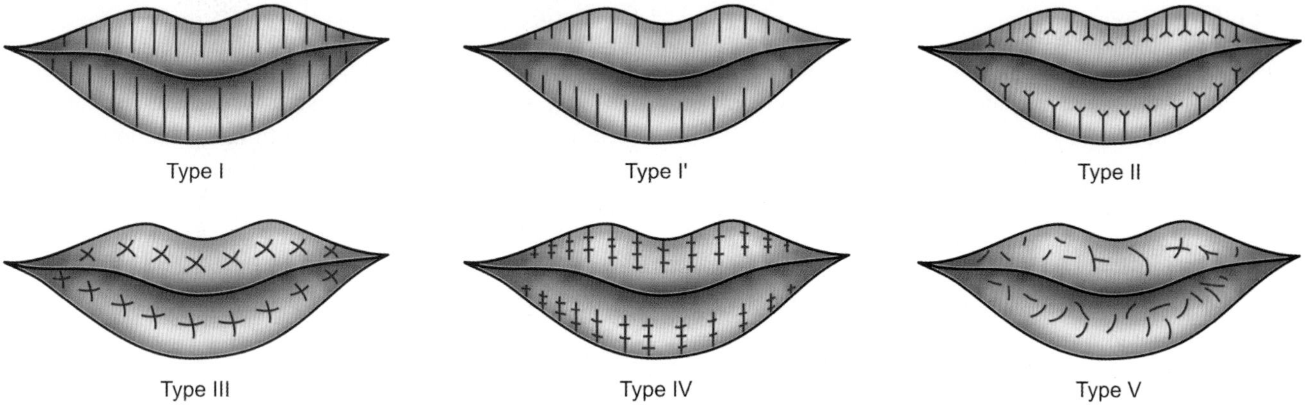

FIG. 3.54: Lip prints

Photographic Superimposition

Photographic superimposition technique was introduced by Glaister & Brash (1937) for the identification of questioned skull from victim's photograph. In this method the photograph of person is taken and the negative is prepared of it. The skull photograph's negative film is taken. The both negatives i.e. the skull and that of photograph are superimposed by aligning and the photograph is developed. The resulting superimposed photograph brings out the details revealing the similarity or dissimilarity.

Video-Graphic Superimposition

In India, video-graphic superimposition technique was first tried by Chandra Shekharan[59] in 1988. In this method the skull is mounted on support that allows moving the skull in three directions. A photograph to be tested is also mounted similarly. Video cameras are placed to record the photograph and skull separately on each side. The individual video signals from each camera are fed into a vision mixer.

Computer Aided Video Skull/Face Superimposition

Delfino et al in 1986 had introduced computer aided superimposition technique.[60] This is new technique for personal identification. In this method, facial photographs are taken and a radiograph (X-ray) of the skull in question is taken. The skull radiograph is then photographed. Both photographs (i.e. the face and skull) are stored in computer database. The photographic images of the faces and radiographs of the skull are then drafted with common photographic software such as Adobe photo Deluxe, Microsoft PhotoDraw etc. The images are displayed over monitor and the anatomical landmarks are compared.[61] With advancement in science, instead of skull radiograph photograph, the skull is fixed over craniophore and was recorded in video camera. With the development of CASS (computer aided superimposition software, written in C language and developed at Forensic Science Laboratory, Ahmedabad, Gujarat) the accuracy has increased further.[62]

Miscellaneous Methods of Identification

- Tricks of manner and habit: Like left-handedness or jerky movements of shoulder or face may be individualistic for a particular individual.
- Speech and voice: Certain features of voice like stammering, nasal twang, husky etc. may be important in identification
- Handwriting and signature of an individual are characteristic to a particular individual.
- Clothes, ornaments and belonging like valet contents, driving licensee etc. may reveal identity.
- Complexion and features: For example black colour or fair colour of individual or typical features of face, nose, ears, lips, chin etc. may help in identity.
- Eyes: Colour of iris, presence of disease like cataract, corneal opacity, scar marks, squint, nystagmus etc. or presence of artificial eye or lens implantation may offer help in identification.

Forensic Odontology

Forensic odontology is a branch of dental science that deals with application of dental knowledge in the administration of law and justice. Forensic odontology is also called as forensic dentistry or forensic odontostomatology.

Dental Charting

There are many methods of identifying, numbering and charting of teeth. Some common methods used in practice are described below.

A. Universal system

The method is commonly used in America. Separate numbering system is existed for temporary and permanent teeth.

- For permanent teeth – in this method, tooth is allotted number and the number ranged from 1 to 32. It starts from the upper right third molar (given as number 1) to the upper left third molar (given as number 16) and then continuing with the lower left third molar (given as number 17) and ends at lower right third molar (given as number 32) (Fig. 3.55).
- For temporary teeth – instead of using numbers, alphabets (from A to T) are used in this method. The alphabet "A" ranged from the upper right second molar (given as alphabet "A") to the upper left second molar (given as alphabet "J") and then continuing with the lower left second molar (given as alphabet "K") and ends at lower right second molar (given as alphabet "T") (Fig. 3.56).

B. Palmer's Notation

In this method each tooth of jaw is given number from 1 to 8. The teeth are placed in four quadrants and each quadrant bears the number from 1 to 8. Therefore, for medical incisor the number is 1, for lateral incisor – 2, canine – 3, first premolar – 4, second premolar – 5, first molar – 6, second molar – 7, and third molar number 8 is given. This method is simple to use. It is described in Figure 3.57.

C. Haderup System

The method is similar to Palmer's system except that in Haderup system, a plus (+) sign is used to indicate upper teeth and minus (–) sign is used to designate lower teeth. It is illustrated in Figure 3.58.

D. FDI (Federation Dentaire Internationale) Two Digit System or International System of Numbering of Teeth

In this system, the teeth are placed in four quadrants. Each quadrant bears a number and each tooth in that particular quadrant has its number that's why this system is called as two-digit system. The right upper quadrant, of permanent tooth, has number 1, left upper quadrant has 2, left lower quadrant has 3 and right lower quadrant has number 4. The teeth are designated as per Palmer's system. For temporary teeth, each quadrant has different number. For right upper quadrant has number 5, left upper quadrant has 6, left lower quadrant has 7 and right lower quadrant has number 8. The system is displayed in Figure 3.59. Let us take example, if we want to locate lower right canine, the number of permanent dentition will be 43 whereas the number of same canine in temporary system will be 83.

E. Diagrammatic or Anatomical Charting

In this method, each tooth is represented by pictorial symbol.

Scope and Importance of Forensic Odontology

Forensic odontology has importance in:

Upper	*Right*	1	2	3	4	5	6	7	8	9	10	11	12	13	14	15	16	*Left*
Lower	*Right*	32	31	30	29	28	27	26	25	24	23	22	21	20	19	18	17	*Left*

FIG. 3.55: Universal dental charting for permanent teeth

Upper	*Right*	A	B	C	D	E	F	G	H	I	J	*Left*
Lower	*Right*	T	S	R	Q	P	O	N	M	L	K	*Left*

FIG. 3.56: Universal dental charting for temporary teeth

Upper teeth - Right								*Upper teeth - Left*							
8	7	6	5	4	3	2	1	1	2	3	4	5	6	7	8
8	7	6	5	4	3	2	1	1	2	3	4	5	6	7	8
Lower teeth - Right								*Lower teeth - Left*							

FIG. 3.57: Showing Palmer's notation

Upper teeth - Right								Upper teeth - Left							
+8	+7	+6	+5	+4	+3	+2	+1	+1	+2	+3	+4	+5	+6	+7	+8
-8	-7	-6	-5	-4	-3	-2	-1	-1	-2	-3	-4	-5	-6	-7	-8
Lower teeth - Right								Lower teeth - Left							

FIG. 3.58: Showing Haderup system of dental charting

Upper teeth - Right									Upper teeth - Left									
P*	18	17	16	15	14	13	12	11	21	22	23	24	25	26	27	28	P*
Temporary teeth				55	54	53	52	51	61	62	63	64	65	Temporary teeth			
Temporary teeth				85	84	83	82	81	71	72	73	74	75	Temporary teeth			
P*	48	47	46	45	44	43	42	41	31	32	33	34	35	36	37	38	P*
Lower teeth - Right									Lower teeth - Left									

FIG. 3.59: Displaying international system of dental charting. *indicate permanent teeth

1. Identification
2. Estimation of age of a person – *vide supra*
3. Determination of sex
4. Determination of race
5. DNA evidence
6. Bite mark evidence
7. Injury
8. Occupation
9. Habit
10. Time since death
11. Detection of poison

Identification

Dental identification is a method of comparative identification. It is known that teeth are usually protected from fire or decomposition or mutilation. Dental identification is sought in following conditions.

- Decomposed remains
- Mutilated/dismembered body
- Skeletal remains
- Charred body
- Mass disaster

Method of Identification

Sassouni (1963) has classified the identification technique into two groups as:[34]

- Comparative identification
- Reconstructive identification

Comparative Identification

Here, the antemortem record of a person is matched with the postmortem status of teeth in order to make positive identification. The technique used is based on the principle of comparison and includes

1. Number of teeth.
2. Type of teeth – temporary/permanent.
3. Condition of teeth – erosion, cleanliness, hygiene, conservation such as filling or presence of caries etc.
4. Peculiarities of teeth – such as crowded, Malposition, deformities, rotation, supernumerary tooth, additional tooth, incinerated tooth[63] etc.
5. Presence of denture – such as full, partial,[64] type, shape, restorative material used etc. (Fig. 3.60).
6. Mesodiatal width of teeth.
7. Old injury or disease.
8. Root canal therapy.
9. Pattern on X-ray examination.

Reconstructive Identification

Here absolute identification is not possible but age, sex, race, occupation etc. can be known leading to probable identification.

Determination of Sex

- Tooth measurements – in permanent teeth, roots are larger in male than female
- Specific gravity of tooth
- Mandibular cuspid show greatest sexual dimorphism. According to Anderson, in 74 percent of cases, if mesiodistal diameter is less than 6.7 mm then it is female and if the diameter is more than 7 mm then it is male.[65]
- In maxillary cuspid, the average root length is 3 mm longer than females
- Mandibular canine index[16]

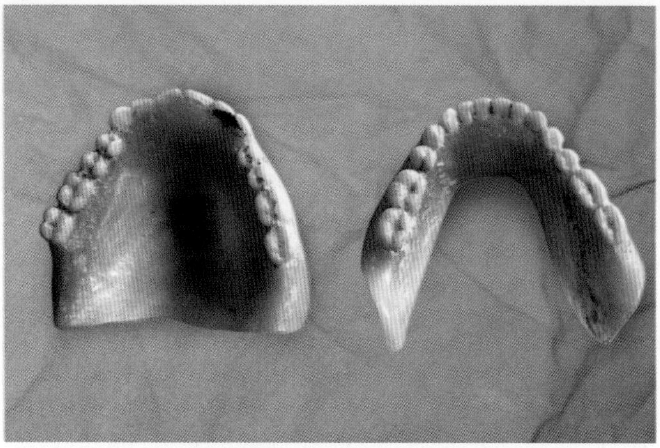

FIG. 3.60: Artificial dentures

- Demonstration of Y-chromosome on fluorescence microscopy in the nucleated cell of dental pulp
- DNA profiling.

Race from Teeth

- Sizes of tooth – variation in size of different populations of different regions have been noted. Indians have smaller teeth whereas Australian aborigines have larger teeth. Similarly in civilized societies, first permanent molar is larger than third molar whereas in primitive races, it is just the reverse.
- Cusp – extra cusps may be present in molar tooth, as Americans have higher frequency in comparison to Indians. The cusp may be present up to six and even up to seven in number.
- Shape – shovel shaped incisors are present in Mongoloid. The trait of shovel shaped incisors appears in the primary as well as in the permanent teeth. Peg shaped lateral incisors are common in Europeans.
- Surface – it was noted that almost 100% of the European population has a flat lingual surface of incisor teeth.
- Ridges – in Japanese and certain other Mongoloid people have ridges on the lingual surface of teeth.
- Root – in Mongolians lower molars have three roots
- Appearance – the occlusal surface of the first molar in Caucasoid is larger and more tapered; in Negro it is small and square shaped whereas in Mongoloid, it is larger and rounded.

Bite Mark Evidence

Definition: MacDonald[66] has defined bite mark as "*a mark by the teeth either alone or in combination with other mouth parts*".

Bite marks are important for identification. Each human dentition is unique, differing even in identical twins. Its imprint in skin can show this individualization due to which identification of perpetrator is possible. For this reason, bite marks have been referred[31] to as "**dental fingerprints**".

Classification

According to type of injury[67]
- Erythema
- Laceration
- Bruising
- Avulsion of tissue
- Abrasion
- Combination

According to agents producing the bite marks
- Human bite marks – either children or adult
- Animal bite marks – produced by biting of animals such as dog, cat, fish, fox etc.
- Mechanical bite marks – produced by dentures

According to materials used for biting
- Skin and body parts
- Food substances for example apple
- Others – such as pen, pencil, pipe stems, bottle lids etc.

According to McDonald
- Tooth pressure marks
- Tongue pressure marks
- Tooth scrape marks
- Complex marks

Recording of bite marks

Description of bite marks includes location over body, shape, size, colour, type of injury, and surface of bite site. If facilities are available, forensic odontologist should be asked for help. The mark should be preferably photographed. Salivary swabbing should be done and impression of the marks may be taken to make cast. Human bite marks are circular or oval whereas animal bite marks are narrow U-shaped.[68] Examination and evaluation of bite marks with any obtained templates or known marks are done in relation with following parameters:[69]
- The relationship of the jaws
- The form and size of arches
- Missing teeth
- Spacing between teeth
- Presence of supernumerary teeth
- Observed rotation of teeth
- Presence of special features such as fractures and ridges.

Toothless bite mark – a simple ring of homogenous contusions approximating the size and shape of human arches but not showing individual tooth marks should be regarded as possible toothless bite mark.[69]

Differential diagnosis of bite mark

Bite marks have to be differentiated from other conditions that may resemble bite marks. The conditions are mentioned below.

1. Heel mark.
2. Dermatological (skin) disease.
3. Marks made by ECG electrode.
4. Patterned door knobs.
5. Burns.

REFERENCES

1. Mathiharan K, Patnaik AK. Personal Identity. In: Modi's Medical Jurisprudence and Toxicology, 23rd edn, 2005. LexisNexis Butterworths, New Delhi. 218-34.
2. Singh P, Purkit R. Anthropological study of human auricle. J Indian Acad Forensic Med 2006;28: 46-8.
3. English WR, Robinson SF, Summit JB, Osterle LJ, Brannon RB, Morlang WM. Individuality of human palatal rugae. J Forensic Sci 1988;33:718-26.
4. Thomas CJ, Kotze TJVW. The palatal rugal pattern in six South African population part I. J Dent Assoc South Africa 1983; 38:66-72.
5. Thomas CJ, Kotze TJVW. The palatal rugal pattern in six South African population part II. J Dent Assoc South Africa 1983; 38:547-53.
6. Marlin DC, Clark MA, Standish SM. Identification of human remains by comparison of frontal sinus radiographs: a series of four cases. J Forensic Sci 1991; 36: 7165-72.
7. Sreenivas. Indian Heart J 1956; 227-45. Cited in Franklin CA. In Modi's Medical Jurisprudence and Toxicology, 21st edn. 1988. Tripathi Private Ltd., Bombay. 448–500.
8. Subrahmanyam BV. Identity (Biometric profiling). In: Forensic medicine, Toxicology and Medical Jurisprudence, 1st edn. 2004. Modern Publishers, New Delhi. 9-27.
9. Healey T. Identification from radiographs. Clin Radiol 1983; 34:589-92.
10. Ganong WF. The gonads: Development and function of the reproductive system. In: Review of Medical Physiology, 19th edn. 1999. Prentice-Hall International, London. 393-432.
11. Pearson PL, Bobrow M, Vosa CG. Technique for identifying Y-chromosome in human interphase nuclei. Nature 1970; 226:78-80.
12. Kringsholm B, Thomsen JL, Henningsen K. Fluorescent Y-chromosomes in hair and blood. Forensic Sci 1977; 9:117-26.
13. Thomsen JL. Sex determination of severely burned bodies. Forensic Sci 1977;10:235-42.
14. Fukushima H, Hasekura H, Nagai K. Identification of male bloodstains by dot hybridization of human Y chromosome-specific deoxyribonucleic acid (DNA) probe. J Forensic Sci 1988;33:621-7.
15. Rao NG, Pai ML. Costal cartilage calcification pattern – a clue for establishing sex identity. Forensic Sci Int 1988; 38:193-209.
16. Rao NG, Rao NN. Mandibular canine index – a clue for establishing sex identity. Forensic Sci Int 1989;42:249-54.
17. Rao NG, Kotian S. Footprint ratio (FPR) – a clue for establishing sex identity. J Indian Acad Forensic Med 1990;12:51-6.
18. Oberoi DV, Kuruvilla A, Saralaya KM, Rajeev A, Ashok B, Nagesh KR, Rao NG. Estimation of stature and sex from foot print length using regression formulae and standard foot-print length formula respectively. J Punjab Acad Forensic Med Toxicol 2006;6:5-8.
19. Davidson WM. Sex determination: diagnostic methods. BMJ 1960;4:1901-7.
20. Gupta S, Roychowdhury UB, Deb PK, Roy D, Chhetri D, Moitra R. Testicular feminization syndrome – a case report. Medicolegal Update; 6:29-30.
21. Wilson JD, Grif JE. Disorders of sexual differentiation. In: Fauci AS, Braunwald E, Isselbacher KJ, Wilson JD, Martin JB, Kasper DL, Hauser SL, Longo DL (Eds): Harrison's Principles of Internal Medicine, Vol.2, 14th edn, 1998. McGraw-Hill, New York. 2119-31.
22. Whittaker PG, Lind T, Lawson JY. A prospective study to compare serum human placental lactogen and menstrual dates for determining gestational age. Am J Obst Gynecol 1987; 156:178-82.
23. Kellet RJ. Infanticide and child destruction – the historical, legal and pathological aspects. Forensic Sci Int 1992; 53:12
24. Sadler TW. Head and neck. In: Langman's Medical Embryology, 8th edn. 2000. Lippincott Williams and Wilkins, Philadelphia. 345-81.
25. Hadlock FP. Sonographic estimation of fetal age and weight. Radiol Clin North Am 1990; 28:39-50.
26. Sahana SN. The Osteology. In: Human Anatomy, Special edn. 1988. KK Publishers, Howrah. 302-527.
27. Kumar GP, Kumar UK. Estimation of gestational age from hand and foot length. Med Sci Law 1993; 33:48-50.
28. Ghai OP. In: Essential Pediatrics, 4th edn. 1996. Interprint Publisher, New Delhi.
29. Murty OP. Manual for medical officers dealing with medicolegal cases of victims of trafficking for commercial sexual exploitation and child sexual abuse. An initiative of Department of Women and Child Development, Government of India and UNICEF. 2005.
30. Dawn CS. In: Textbook of Gynecology and Contraception, 13th edn. 2001. Dawn Books, Kolkata.
31. Bernstein M. Forensic odontology. In: Eckert WG (ed) Introduction to Forensic Sciences, 2nd edn. 1997. CRC Press, Florida. 295-342.
32. Galstaun G. A study of ossification as observed in Indian subjects. Indian J Med Research 1937; 25:267-323.
33. Pillay VV. Identification. In: Textbook of Forensic Medicine and Toxicology, 14th edn. 2004. Paras Publishing, Hyderabad. 49-81.
34. Dayal PK, Srinivasan SV, Paravatty RP. In: Textbook of Forensic Odontology, 1st edn. 1998. Paras Medical Publisher, Hyderabad.

35. Shamim T, Ipe VV, Shameena PM, Sudha S. Forensic odontology – a new perspective. Medicolegal Update 2006; 6:1-4.
36. Iscan MY, Loth SR. Determination of age from the sternal rib in white males: a test of the phase method. J Forensic Sci 1986;31:122-32.
37. Kvaal SI, Kolltveit KM. Thomsen I. Age estimation of adults from dental radiographs. Forensic Sci Int 1995; 74:175-85.
38. Bardale R, Dixit PG. Estimation of stature from somatometry of skull. J Medicolegal Assoc Maharashtra 2006;18:22-6.
39. Roche AF, Davila GH. Late adolescent growth in stature. Pediatrics 1972; 50: 874–80.
40. Saukko P, Knight B. The establishment of identity of human remains. In: Knight's Forensic Pathology, 3rd edn. 2004. Arnold, London. 98-135.
41. Parikh CK. Personal identity. In: Parikh's Textbook of Medical Jurisprudence and Toxicology, 5th edn. 1995. CBS Publishers and Distributors, Bombay. 29-64.
42. Bhatnagar DP, Thapar SP, Batish MK. Identification of personal height from the somatometry of the hand in Punjabi males. Forensic Sci Int 1984; 24: 137 – 41.
43. Dikshit PC. Identification. In: Textbook of Forensic Medicine and Toxicology, 1st edn. 2007. Peepee Publishers and Distributors (P) Ltd., New Delhi. 47-88.
44. Özaslan A, İşcan MY, Özaslan İ, Tuğcu H, Koç S. Estimation of stature from body parts. Forensic Sci Int 2003; 132: 40 – 5.
45. Mant AK. Identification of the living and dead. In: Mant AK (ed). Taylor's Principles and Practice of Medical Jurisprudence, 13th edn., 2000. B I Churchill Livingstone, New Delhi. 156-82.
46. Haglund WD, Sperry K. The use of hydrogen peroxide to visualize tattoos obscured by decomposition and mummification. J Forensic Sci 1993; 38:147-50.
47. Collins P. Embryology and development. In: Williams PL, Berry MM, Collins P, Dyson M, Dussek JE, Ferguson MWJ (ed) Gray's Anatomy, 38th edn., 1995. Churchill Livingstone, Edinburgh. 296.
48. Vij K. Identification. In: Textbook of Forensic Medicine and Toxicology, 3rd edn., 2005. Reed Elsevier India Pvt. Limited, New Delhi. 20-148.
49. Subrahmanyam BV. Personal identity. In: Modi's Medical Jurisprudence and Toxicology, 22nd edn., 2001. Butterworths India, New Delhi. 37-90.
50. Basu R. Identification. In: Fundamentals of Forensic Medicine and Toxicology, revised reprint 2004. Books and Allied (P) Ltd., Kolkata. 15-54.
51. Nandy A. Identification of an individual. In: Principles of Forensic Medicine, 2nd edn. 2005. New Central Book Agency (P) Ltd., Kolkata. 48-111.
52. Giles E, Vallandigham JD. Height estimation from foot and shoe print length. J Forensic Sci 1991; 36:1134-51.
53. Gordon CC, Buikstra JE. Linear models for the prediction of stature from foot and boot dimensions. J Forensic Sci1992; 37:771-81.
54. Suzuki K, Tsuchihashi Y. Personal identification by means of lip prints. J Forensic Med 1970; 17:52-7.
55. Vahanwala Sonal, Nayak CD, Pagare SS. Study of lip-prints as aid for sex determination. Medicolegal Update 2005; 5:93-8.
56. Vahanwala S, Parekh BK. Study of lip prints as an aid to forensic methodology. J Forensic Med Toxicol 2000; 17:12-8.
57. Marlin DC, Clark MA, Standish SM. Identification of human remains by comparison of frontal sinus radiographs: a series of four cases. J Forensic Sci 1991; 36:1765-72.
58. Pathak AK, Mangal HM. Role of superimposition technique in practice of forensic medicine. J Punjab Acad Forensic Med Toxicol 2006; 6:45-7.
59. Chandra Shekaran P. The video superimposition technique practiced in India. Indian J Forensic Sci 1988; 2:45-50.
60. Delfino VP, Colona M, Vacca E, Potente F, Introna F. Computer sided skull/face superimposition. Am J Forensic Med Pathol 1986; 7:201-12.
61. Ricci A, Marella GL, Apostol MA. A new experimental approach to computer-aided face/skull identification in forensic anthropology. Am J Forensic Med Pathol 2006; 27: 46-9.
62. Nandy AD, Mazumdar HS, Mehta AK, Rawal LP, Vyas JM. A skull/face superimposition using computer graphics. J Forensic Med Toxicol 2001;18:30-4.
63. Fairgrieve SI. SEM analysis of incinerated tooth as an aid to positive identification. J Forensic Sci 1994; 39:557-65.
64. Shamim T, Ipe VV, Shameena PM, Mehul RM. Forensic odontology to the rescue – a case report. Medicolegal Update 2006; 6:115-8.
65. Anderson JL. Thompson GW. Interrelationships and sex differences of dental and skeletal measurements. J Dent Res 1973; 52:431-3.
66. MacDonald DG. Bite mark recognition and interpretation. J Forensic Sci 1979;14: 229-33.
67. Payne-James J, Crane J, Hinchliffe JA. Injury assessment, documentation and interpretation. In: Stark MM (ed) Clinical Forensic Medicine – a physician's guide, 2nd edn., 2005. Humana Press, New Jersey. 127-58.
68. Gorea RK, Jha M, Jasuja OP, Vasudeva K, Aggarwal AD. Marvelous tools of identification – bite marks. Medicolegal Update 2005;5:61-4.
69. Wagner GN. Scientific methods of identification. In: Stimson PG, Mertz CA (ed) Forensic Dentistry, 1st edn. 1997. CRC Press, Florida. 1-36.

CHAPTER 4

Forensic Osteology

Bones make good witness – although they speak softly, they never lie and they never forget. Each bone has its own tale about the past life and death of the person whose living fleshes once clothed it like people. Some bones impart their secrets more readily than others; some are laconic others are positively garrulous.

- Clyde Collinis Show and John Fitzpatrick

Introduction

Forensic osteology is a sub-specialty of forensic medicine and deals with examination and assessment of human skeleton. The assessment includes both — the identification of the victim's characteristics and cause and manner of death from skeleton.[1] This chapter deals with examination of bones and skeletal remains. Whenever whole or partial skeleton or bundle of bones are submitted by legal authorities for medical examination then medical examiner should be able to answer following questions (Fig. 4.1):

1. Are they bones?
2. Are they human bones?
3. What is the sex?
4. What would be age at the time of death?
5. What is the stature?
6. What is the race?
7. How identity could be established?
8. What would be time since death?
9. What was the cause of death?
10. What is the manner of separation?

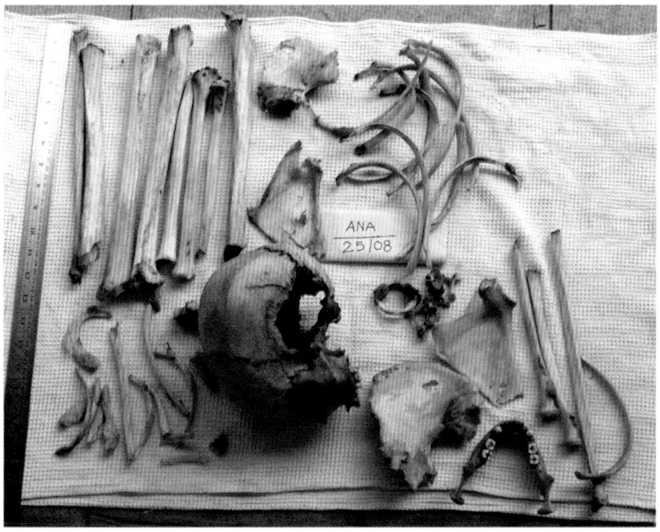

FIG. 4.1: Bones for forensic examination (*Courtesy*: Dr Vaibhav Sonar, Lecturer, Forensic Medicine, GMC, Miraj)

While examining the bones, it is customary to begin with what is called as "the big four" – i.e. stature, the age at time of death, sex and race. This chapter will deal individual bones with assessment of the big fours! Other part of examination — such as bones or not, time since death etc. shall be dealt in integrated form.

Bone or Not

It is necessary to examine a given article and opine whether the stated article is bone or not. The following description will help in evolving the answer.

- **Gross examination of bone**: Examination of bone in respect to shape, size, texture, weight and morphology with established anatomical landmark will reveal true nature (Fig. 4.2).
- **Microscopic examination**: Microscopic examination of bone will reveal true Haversian system and presence of osteons (Fig. 4.3).

Human or Animal

Usually identification of human remains does not pose difficulty. However, at times it may become difficult to opine especially dealing with small bones or when taxonomically close related species bones are available such as great apes and humans. Differentiation is done by:

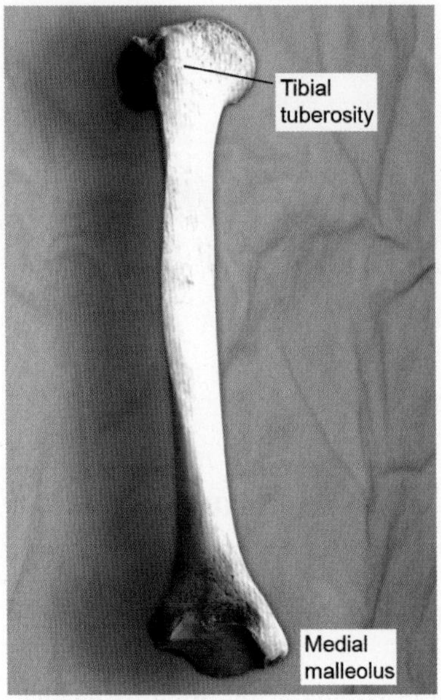

FIG. 4.2: Tibia with gross features and typical anatomical landmarks

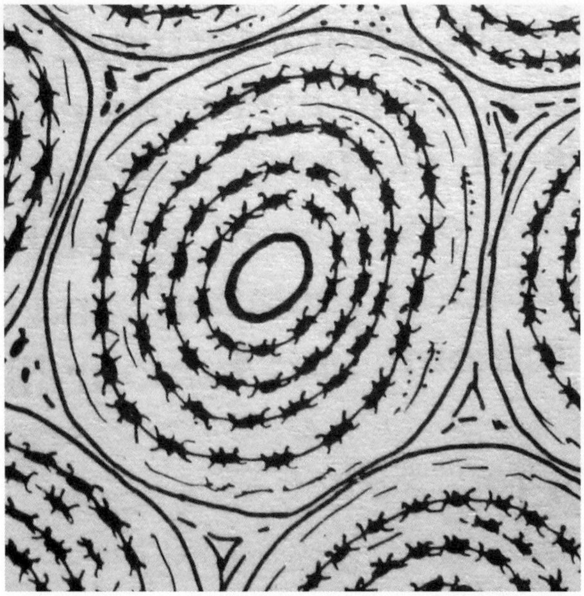

FIG. 4.3: Microscopy of cortical bone

- Gross examination
- Microscopic examination: Microscopic examination may provide differentiation feature or at least helps to exclude a human origin. The Haversian system is different in animals than human. Haversian systems and canals are of larger diameter in humans than animals.[2]
- Serological examination: Precipitin test can be done by extracting species-specific protein from bone into solution and tested against specific antisera of human. The techniques such as electrophoresis or gel diffusion can now identify human tissue.

Sex of Bone

Sex from bone is determined by:
- Morphological examination
- Morphometry or osteometry i.e. by taking various measurements of bone
- Multivariate discrimination function analysis

According to Krogman, the sexing from skeleton and individual bones are given in Table 4.1. General sex difference of skeleton is provided in Table 4.2. Sex can also be determined from soft parts available with bones by:
- Demonstration of Y-chromosome
- DNA profiling

Table 4.1: Sexing from bones

Sexing from bones
Entire skeleton - 100%
Pelvis alone - 95%
Skull alone - 92%
Pelvis + skull - 98%
Long bones - 80%

Table 4.2: General sex difference in skeleton

Feature	*Male*	*Female*
Size	Large, massive	Small, slender
Weight	4.5 kg	2.75 kg

Age

Age at the time of death from bone/skeleton is determined by noting the:

- Dental status
- Ossification data – the appearance and fusion of ossification centers
- Age related changes occurring in individual bones
- Radiographic method
- Histological method – it is observed that size and shape of osteons increases with age.[3] The relation between osteons and age is presented in table 4.3. Rai et al had derived a regression equation for estimation of age.[3] The equation is – Age = number of osteons + 8.3.

Stature

Determination of stature from bone means estimation of body height of that person. For estimation of stature, long

Table 4.3: Showing number of osteons and age

No. of osteons	Age (in year)
12	20
15	23
30	38
40	48
50	58

bones are widely preferred and are more reliable than flat or irregular bones. The length of bone is taken with the help of Hepburn osteometric board (Fig. 4.4).

When stature is estimated from a bone, an allowance of 2.5 to 4 cm is added to the calculated stature in order to compensate the loss of soft tissues. (The total thickness of the soft tissues in between the bones at different joint from heel to vertex is about 2.5 to 4 cm).

Different formulae are used to estimate stature and includes

- Karl Pearson
- Trotter and Glesser
- Dupertuis and Haden
- Pan
- Nat
- Shah and Siddiqui

If fragmented long bones are submitted for medical examination, stature can be estimated by following formulae:

- Muller
- Steele
- Steele and McKern

Race

- Determination of race is difficult from bones, partly because racial traits are not so marked and partly because so much ethnic mixing has taken place.[4]
- Amongst bones, skull offers better evidence regarding race and according to Krogman and Iscan, race can be determined in 90 to 95% of cases.

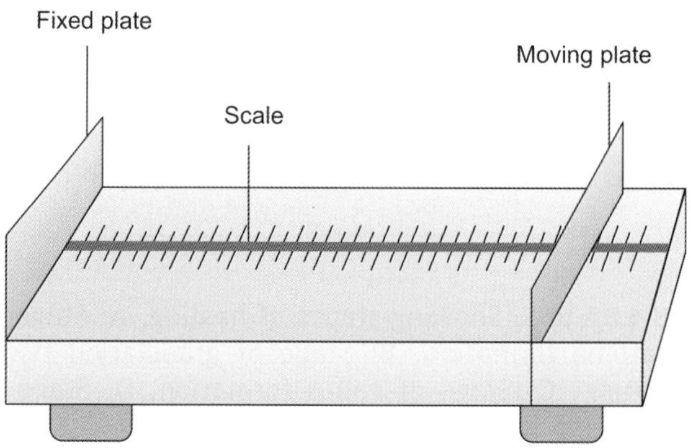

FIG. 4.4: Osteometric board

- There are racial differences in the pelvis, but specialized measurements as described by Todd and Lindala (1928) must be made in order to detect these.
- Amongst long bones, femur is better indicator for determination of race.
- Genetic DNA identification will offer help and revolutionize this aspect in near future.
- For determination of race, morphological features and various indices are used
- Apart from this, presence of teeth and hairs provide additional benefit for race determination.

Personal Identity

Determination of personal identity can be done by following methods:

- Presence of congenital or acquired peculiarities, malformations, deformities, injuries, fracture, healing etc.
- Presence of nail, implant, plate etc. in bone
- From dental examination and presence of prosthesis, filling material, root canal treatment etc.
- Radiological methods
- Determination of blood group from marrow/teeth
- DNA profiling.

Time Since Death

Time since death is determined by analyzing:

- Gross examination of bones and/with state of soft tissue available
- Stage of healing in case of fracture
- Physical tests
- Chemical tests.

Gross Examining

- Recent bones will have soft tissue attached in form of ligaments and/or tendons, especially at or near joints. Periosteum may be visible so do the cartilage especially over articular surface. Such bones may emit putrid smell. The bones will be soft, moist and greasy to touch (Fig. 4.5).
- It is estimated that within 3 to 10 years all sot tissues will be removed when the bodies are lying in coffins. But this period may be much shorter in India where the climate conditions are often hostile and bodies are buried without much protection.[5]
- The recent bones, on sawing, will be hard and uniform through the whole thickness. In old bones, the bones become lighter due to loss of organic matter and collagenous stroma. On sawing, the outer cortex and to a lesser extent, the zone around marrow cavity will loose stroma

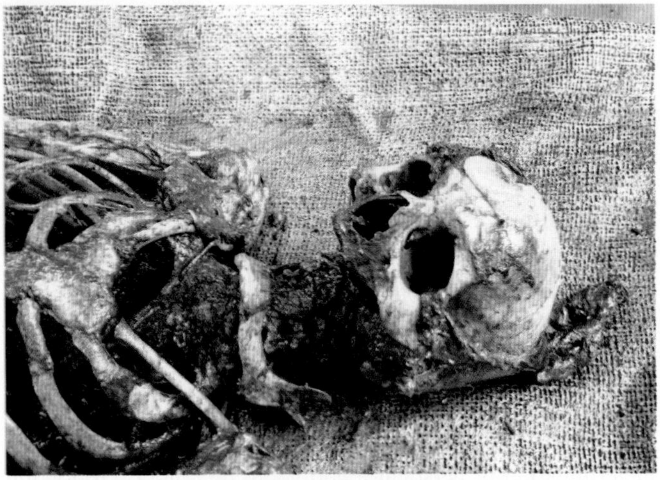

FIG. 4.5: Bones with soft tissues attached

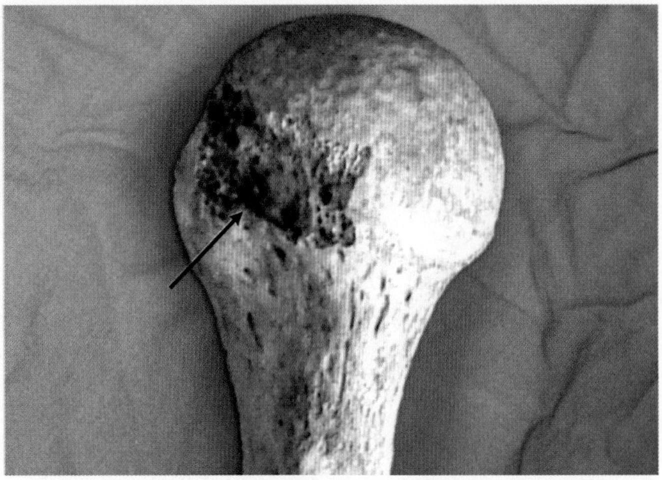

FIG. 4.7: Humerus head showing wear and tear effect (black arrow)

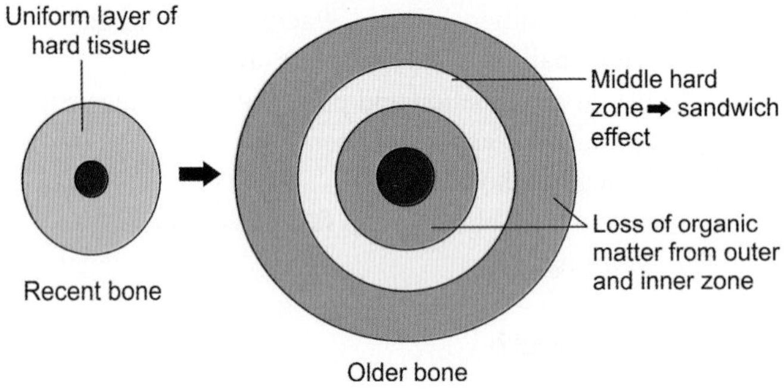

FIG. 4.6: Recent and old bone

first so a "sandwich" effect may be seen in which a central ring of hard collagenous bone is layered on each side by a zone of more porous crumbling material[4] (see Fig. 4.6).

- Due to wear and tear, the ends of long bone may be fragile and brittle (Fig. 4.7).

Stage of Fracture Healing (Fig. 4.8)

Examination of stage of fracture healing offers help in dating time since death. Stages of healing of fracture (cortical bone) are described as follows:

- Stage of hematoma formation – at the fracture ends hematoma forms due to bleeding from torn blood vessels. This hematoma fills the area surrounding fracture site. Loose meshwork is formed by blood and fibrin clot that act as a framework for subsequent granulation tissue formation. This stage lasts up to seven days. The osteocyte differentiates into daughter cells.
- Stage of granulation tissue formation – the daughter cells produce cells which differentiate and organize to provide blood vessels, fibroblasts, and osteoblasts. Collectively they

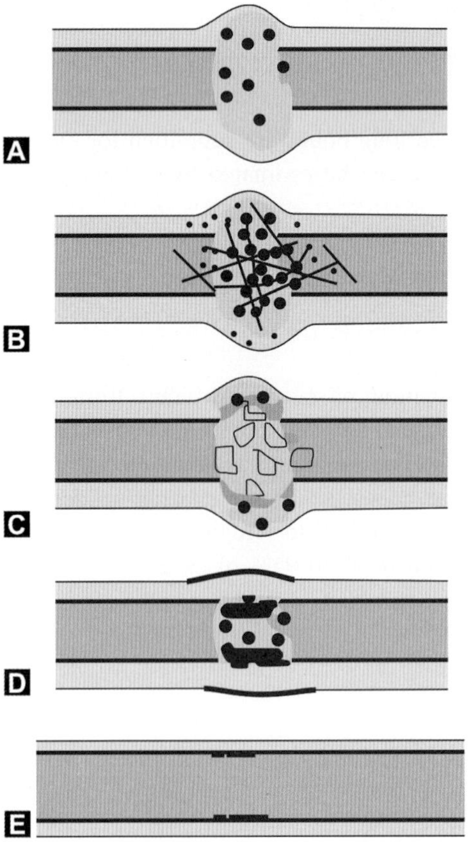

FIGS 4.8A to E: Showing stages of healing. **A:** Stage of hematoma formation, **B:** Stage of granulation tissue formation, **C:** Stage of callus formation, **D:** Stage of remodelling **E:** Stage of modelling

form a soft granulation tissue in the space between the fracture fragments. This stage lasts for about 2 to 3 weeks.

- Stage of callus formation – the granulation tissue differentiates further and creates osteoblasts. The osteoblasts lay down an intercellular matrix that gets impregnated with calcium salts. This results in formation of the callus (also called as woven bone). This callus is the first sign of union visible on X-ray, usually 3 weeks after fracture. This stage lasts for 4 to 12 weeks.
- Stage of remodelling – here the woven bone is replaced by mature bone with typical lamellar pattern. This is a slow process.
- Stage of modeling – here the bone is gradually strengthened with shaping of bone occurs at the endosteal and periosteal surfaces.

Physical Test

- After sawing, if the cut surface of bone is examined under ultraviolet light, recent bone will be fluorescence (shine) with a silvery-blue tint across the whole cut surface. With advancing age, the outer rim and rim around the marrow cavity will cease to fluorescence (due to loss of organic matter) and this progressively deepens towards center. In older bones, the surface will be non-fluorescent (Fig. 4.9). The total time taken for loss of complete fluorescence was estimated somewhere at 100 to 150 years.[6]
- Specific gravity and density test – the specific gravity of bone is two. As the bones become older, it becomes less dense and loses specific gravity. The specific gravity of 1.2 indicates fossil bone whereas a value of 1.7 is forensically significant and it distinguishes from fossils.

Chemical and Serological Test

- Benzidine test or Kastel-Mayer test may be positive up to 100 years. These test detects presence of blood (Fig. 4.10).
- Serological test such as precipitation test, gel diffusion or Coombs reagent may be positive for 5 to 10 years (Fig. 4.11).
- Presence of nitrogen – fresh bones have 4.5% nitrogen. With bone become older, it progressively loses nitrogen. If the nitrogen content is about 4% then the death interval may be up to 100 years. At about 350 years, the nitrogen content falls to 2.5% or less (Fig. 4.12).
- Presence of amino acids – fresh bone contains 15 amino acids mostly derived from collagen. Glycine and alanine are predominant but proline and hydroxyproline are more specific markers for collagen. The proline and hydroxyproline will vanish in about 50 years.[4]

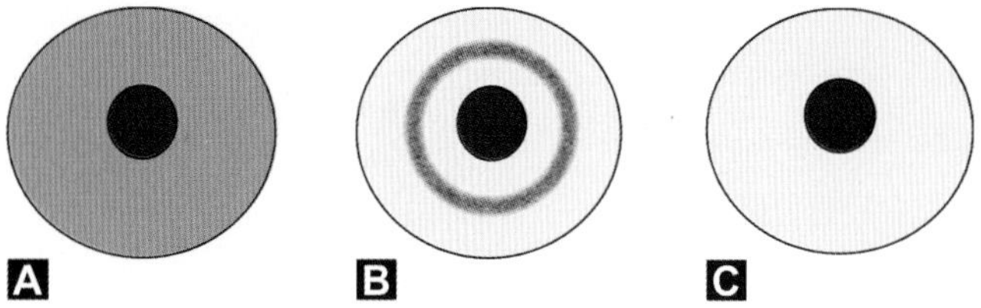

FIGS 4.9A to C: Cut surface of bone, if examined under ultraviolet light then **A:** Recent bone surface will fluorescence across whole cut surface area, as bone becomes older, the outer zone and zone of bone adjacent to marrow cavity ceases to fluorescence as shown in **B:** **C:** No fluorescence across the whole surface of bone and denote much older bone

Cause of Death

Up to some extent, cause of death can be offered based on following features:

- Any injury/fracture incompatible with life
- Presence of foreign body – bullet, pellets or any piece of weapon
- Chemical analysis for poison
- Radiological examination for any pathology/disease/malignancy/secondaries.

Manner of Separation

The manner in which the bones are separated should be noted. Absence of any cut marks with presence of complete bone with intact articular cartilage suggests natural separation. The state of soft tissues, if available, should be examined for any cut mark/bite mark etc.

SKULL

Sex

Sex from the skull is determined by morphological examination and by doing craniometry. Table 4.4 provides differences between male and females (Fig. 4.13).

Stature

Stature from skull can be estimated by performing somatometry. Following are the various formulas for estimating stature from skull.

1. Height of skull × 8 = stature

- Eight times the height of skull will give approximate height of the individual
- Height of skull is measured from basion to the bregma

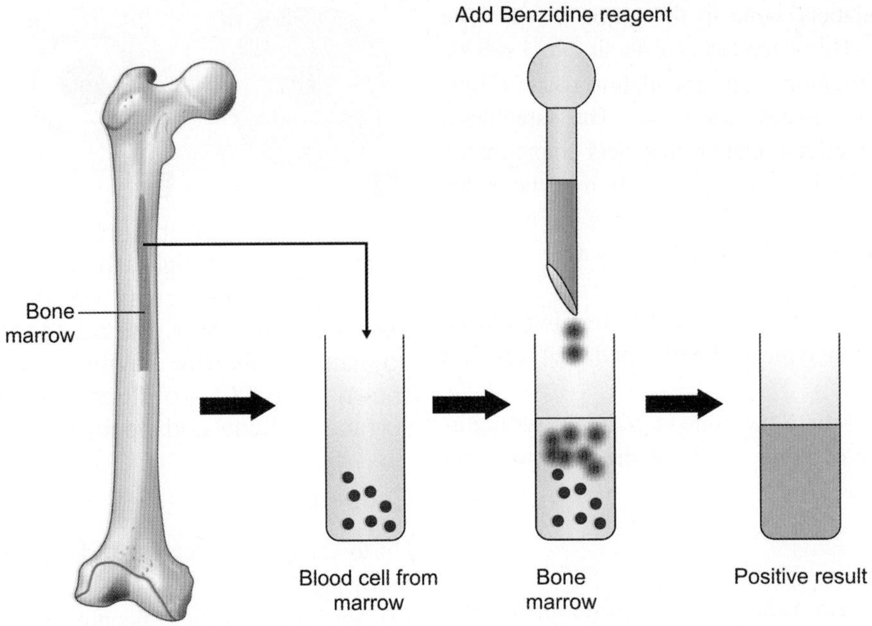

FIG. 4.10: Diagrammatic representation of benzidine test

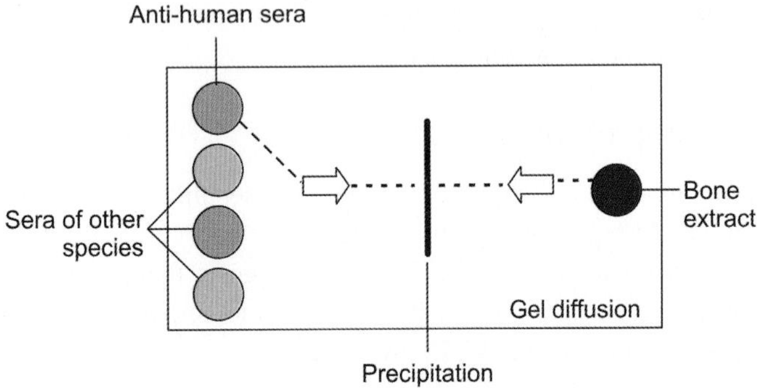

FIG. 4.11: Diagrammatic representation of precipitation test

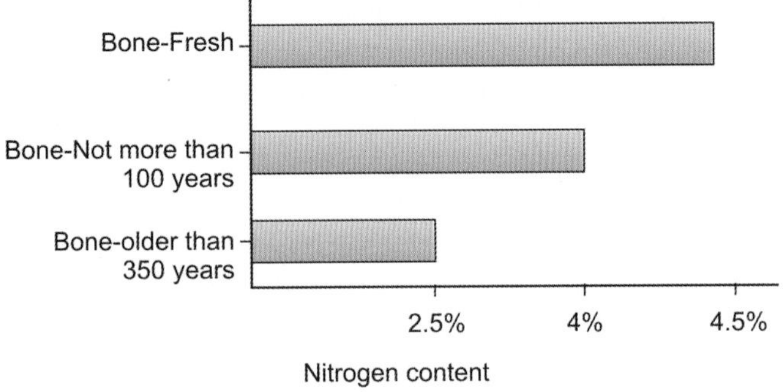

FIG. 4.12: Diagrammatic representation showing diminishing bone nitrogen content with time

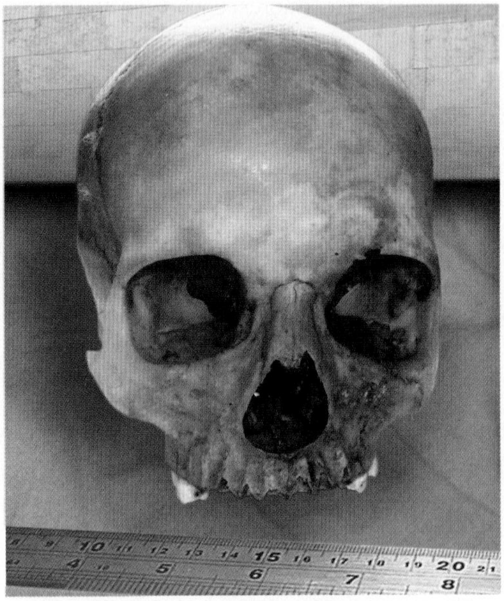

FIG. 4.13: Male skull (*Courtesy*: Dr Vaibhav Sonar, Lecturer, Forensic Medicine, GMC, Miraj)

- Basion is the point where the anterior margin of foramen magnum meets the mid-sagittal plane.

2. From regression equation[7]

- Stature in male = (diameter + circumference of skull) × 1.35 + 70.6 (S.E. = 6.96 cm)
- Stature in female = Circumference of skull × 1.28 + 87.8 (S.E. = 6.59 cm)

Table 4.4: Showing male and female differences

Features	*Male*	*Female*
General		
Size	Large, longer	Small
Architecture	Ragged	Smooth
Anterior surface		
Forehead	Steep and less rounded	Vertical, rounded, full and infantile
Glabella	Prominent	Less prominent
Supra-orbital ridge	Prominent	Less prominent
Supra-orbital margin	Rounded	Sharp
Orbit	Placed lower on the face	Higher on the face
	Rectangular	Rounded
Zygoma	Prominent	Less prominent
Fronto-nasal angle	Distinct angulation	Smoothly curved
Nasal aperture	Higher placed	Lower placed
	Narrower	Broad
	Margins sharp	Margins rounded
Malar bone	Prominent	Less prominent
Superior surface		
Frontal eminence	Less prominent	More prominent
Parietal eminence	Less prominent	More prominent
Inferior surface		
Palate	U - shaped	Parabola
Articular facets	More prominent	Less prominent
Foramen magnum	Large and longer	Small and rounded
Maxillary teeth	Larger	Smaller
Dental arc	Larger	Smaller
Lateral surface		
Mastoid	More prominent, large, round and blunt	Less pointed and smooth
External auditory meatus (suprameatal crest)	Bony ridge along upper border prominent	Often absent
Digastric groove	More deep	Shallow
Posterior surface		
Occipital protuberance	More prominent	Smooth
Nuchal lines	More prominent	Not prominent
Cranial capacity	1500 to 1550 cc	1350-1400 cc
Foramen magnum	Surface area of foramen magnum is 963 sq. mm or larger	Surface area is 805 sq. mm or less
Mid-sagittal arc	Is shorter and thus the neurocranium is less arched	Is highly arched and threrfore neurocranium is more arched
Breath index of face	Higher	Lower
Relative weight of skull compared to rest of skeleton	Smaller (1:8)	Larger (1:6)

Table 4.5: Showing differences in skull for determination of race

Features	Caucasoid	Negroid	Mongoloid
Skull shape	Rounded	Narrow and elongated	Square
Skull length	Long to short	Long	Long
Skull breadth	Narrow to broad	Narrow	Broad
Skull height	High	Low	Middle
Sagittal contour	Rounded	Flat	Arched
Face breadth	Narrow to wide	Narrow	Very wide
Face height	High	Low	High
Orbital opening	Angular to rounded	Rectangular	Rounded
Nasal opening	Narrow	Wide	Narrow
Lower nasal margin	Sharp	Trough or guttered	Sharp
Nasal profile	Straight	Downward slant	Straight
Palate shape	Narrow	Wide	Medium

3. From regression equation[8]
- Stature (in cm) in male = 103.14 + 3.38 × Length of skull
- Stature (in cm) in male = 92.15 + 1.36 × Circumference of skull
- Stature (in cm) in female = 116.64 + 2.09 × Length of skull
- Stature (in cm) in female = 91.72 + 1.19 × Circumference of skull

Race

Race can be determined from morphological features and cephalic index. Table 4.5 presents differences found in skull, which are useful for determination of race. Table 4.6 present cephalic indices found in various race.

Cephalic Index

Cephalic index (CI) is measured as follows.
C.I. = Maximum breadth of skull × 100 ÷ Maximum length of skull.

Age

Age from the skull can be determined by studying the:
- Closure of fontanelle
- Fusion of bone
- Suture closure
- Secondary changes occurred in skull.

Closure of Fontanelles (Fig. 4.14)

- Lateral and occipital fontanelle closed within two months
- Posterior fontanelle closes at 6–8 months after birth
- Anterior fontanelle closes at 1.5–2 years after birth

Table 4.6: Showing cephalic index

Type of skull	Cephalic index	Race
Dolichocephalic (Long headed)	70-75	Pure Aryans, Aborigines, Negroes
Mesaticephalic (Medium headed)	75-80	European, Chinese
Brachycephalic (Short headed)	80-85	Mongolian

Fusion of Bone

- At the end of second year of life, squamous part of occipital bone unites with condylar part
- Squamous portion of occipital bone fuses with the basilar part at 6th year

Suture Closure

Skull bones are united by sutures and the union is analogous with the epiphseal-diaphyseal union. Epiphseal-diaphyseal union begins centrally and proceeds peripherally; similarly suture closure begins endocranially and precedes ectocranially. In other words, union begins first endocranially and then ectocranially. Before proceeding further, some terminology needs attention
- Lapsed union is the incomplete union in the sense that the process of fusion has begun but has not gone to completion
- Precocious closure is the closure of suture before the age of seven years. At this age the cranial growth is about 95 percent complete

- Premature closure is closure after the age of 7 years but considerably before the usual or normal age of closure
- Vault sutures are – sagittal, coronal and lambdoid suture
- Circummeatal sutures are – sphenotemporal, parietomastoid, masto-occipital and squamous suture
- Basal suture is spheno-occipital.

Pattern of Closure

- Sagittal suture unites evenly from front to back
- Coronal suture fuses from medial to lateral end
- Lambdoid suture fuses from medial to lateral end
- No difference exist between right and left sides of skull
- No sex difference in fusion of suture
- According to Krogman, vault suture fuses between 17 to 50 years whereas circummeatal suture closes above 50 years.

Age of Fusion

Here it is important to note that aging an individual solely on suture closure will be unsafe exercise because the method is not reliable. McKern and Stewart had concluded that suture closure has only a general relationship with age. So erratic is the onset and progress of closure that an adequate series will provide just about any pattern at any age level.[1] The age provided by this method is in range of decade. Due to phenomenon of lapsed union, which is found frequently ectocranially, therefore more reliance should be placed on endocranial closure. Following are the approximate age of fusion of skull suture (after McKern and Stewart) (Fig. 4.15).

- Metopic suture closes at 2 to 4 years
- Sagittal – 30 to 40 years
- Coronal – 40 to 50 years
- Lambdoid – 40 to 50 years
- Sphenotemporal – 50 to 60 years
- Parietomastoid – 80 to 90 years
- Masto-occipital – 80 to 90 years
- Squamous – above 80 years
- Basal suture fuses by 18 to 20 years (Fig. 4.16). Yadav and Suri (1971), based on 200-skull examination of Uttar Pradesh have concluded that commencement of union at junction of basisphenoid and basiocciput occurs at the age of 18 years in male and 17 to 18 years in female and complete obliteration occurs at 23 years in male and 22 to 23 year in female.[9]

Secondary Changes in Skull

- Texture – (after Todd 1939 and Cobb 1952) the texture of a young adult skull is smooth and ivorine on both surfaces. At about 40 ± 5 years, the skull surface begins to assume "matted, granular and rough appearance".
- Markings on skull – after the age of 25 year onwards the muscular markings become increasingly evident. The markings are – temporal line, nuchal lines, and masseteric attachment on side of mandible.
- After 50 years, the diploe becomes less vascular with increasing replacement by bone.
- The grooves for middle meningeal artery becomes deeper
- Thickness of skull – (after Todd 1924) the thickness of skull increases with age. The increase in thickness is more after 50 years up to 60 years with no decrease thereafter.
- Increase in skull size – (after Israel 1967 and 1968) on lateral skull radiograph, Israel noted increase in skull size with increase in skull thickness and skull diameter with advancing age.

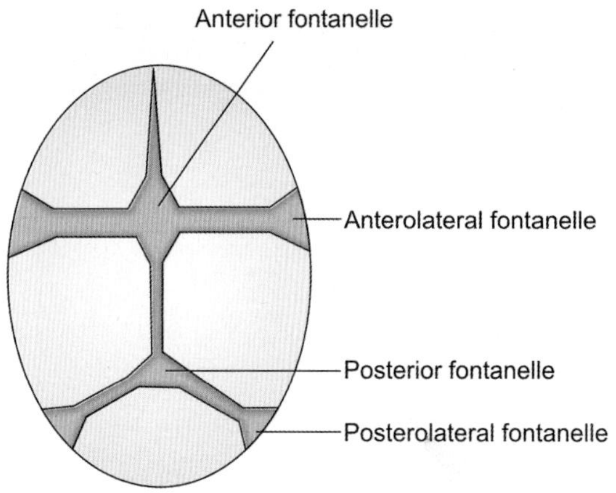

FIG. 4.14: Closure of fontanelle

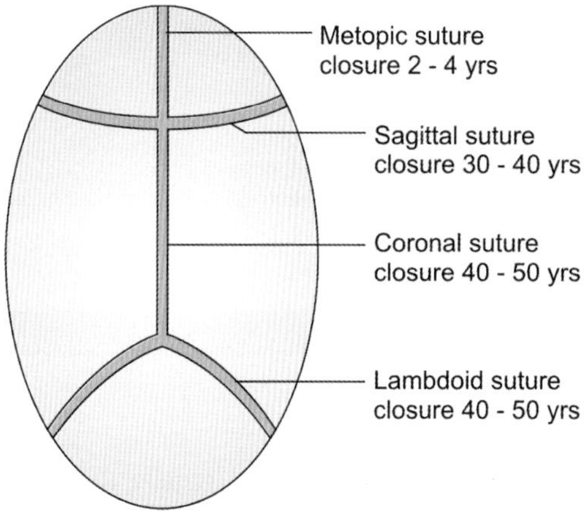

FIG. 4.15: Diagrammatic representation of suture closure of vault of skull

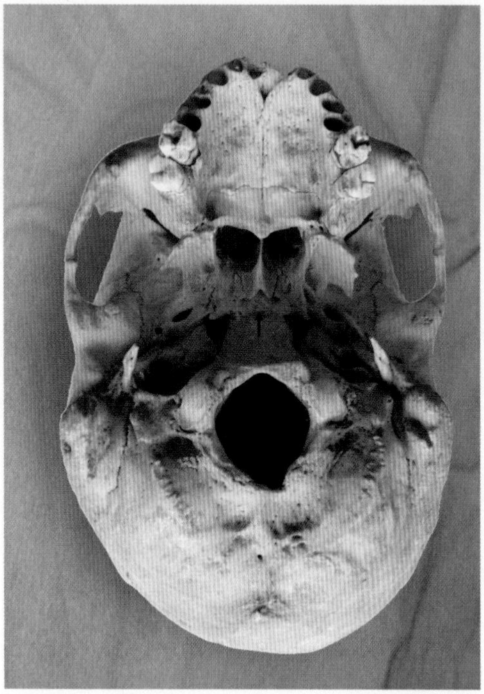

FIG. 4.16: Showing fused basal suture (black arrow)

MANDIBLE

Sex

The differences between male and female in mandible are described in Table 4.7 (Figs 4.17A and B).

Table 4.7: Showing male and female difference in mandible

Features	*Male*	*Female*
Size	Large	Small
Architecture	Ragged	Smooth
Muscular impression	Prominent	Not prominent
Mandibular angle	Everted	Inverted
Chin	Square shaped	Round
Shape of bone	"V" shaped	"U" shaped
Mental tubercle	Large and prominent	Insignificant
Myelohyoid line	Prominent and deep	Shallow
Height at symphysis menti	More	Less
Ascending ramus	Broad	Narrow
Condylar process	Larger	Smaller

Stature

The distance between symphysis menti and angle of mandible is taken and is multiplied by 16, which will give stature. Stature = length from mandibulr angle to symphysis menti × 16.

Race

According to Schultz (1933) mandible in white people have

- Larger breadth,
- Higher and narrower ramus
- Greater gonial angle
- Ramal surface more parallel to the median sagittal plane
- Protrusive chin
- Mental tubercles placed more lateral in position

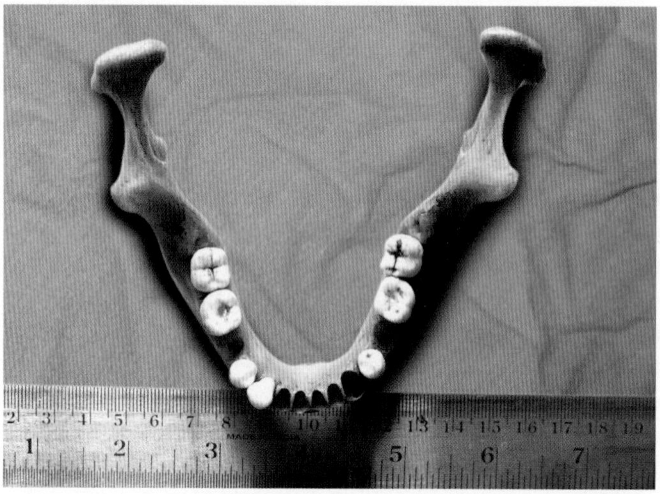

FIG. 4.17A: Male mandible - superior view (*Courtesy*: Dr Vaibhav Sonar, Lecturer, Forensic Medicine, GMC, Miraj)

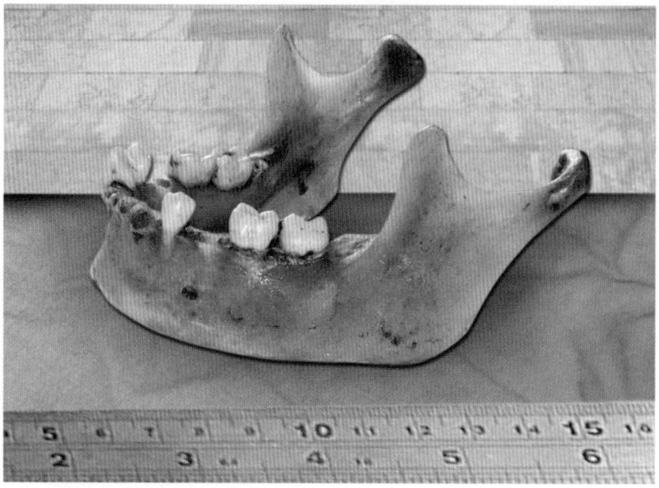

FIG. 4.17B: Male mandible - lateral view (*Courtesy*: Dr Vaibhav Sonar, Lecturer, Forensic Medicine, GMC, Miraj)

According to Schultz (1933) mandible in black people have
- Lower, wider and more vertical ramus
- Greater dental arch length i.e. a long "U" shaped dental arch
- Small breadth
- Less prominent chin
- Mental tubercles are placed more medial in position and are smaller.

Age[10]

The mandible shows remarkable changes with age. Following are the age related changes in mandible (Fig. 4.18).

At Birth

- Two halves of mandible are united by fibrous symphysis menti
- Body is shell like with imperfectly separated sockets of deciduous teeth
- Mandibular canal is near the lower border
- Mental foramen opens below the first deciduous molar
- Mental foramen is directed forwards
- Coronoid process projects above the condyle.

At 1-3 Years

- At first year, two halves joins at symphysis from below upwards with separation at alveolar margin – may persist into second year
- Body elongates behind mental foramen
- During first and second years, chin develops
- Condylar cartilage is covered on articular aspect by fibrous tissue
- Body height increases, alveolar growth make place for root of teeth
- The sub-alveolar region (area) becomes thicker and deeper.

At 6 Years

- Mandible increase in size
- Remodelling continuous with bone added at posterior border of ramus.

Adults

- Alveolar and sub-alveolar areas are about equal in depth (size)
- Mental foramen midway between upper and lower border
- Mandibular canal nearly parallels the mylohyoid line
- Ramal height increase
- The condyloid process is at a higher level than the coronoid process.

Old Age

- Bone is reduced in size
- Alveolar region is absorbed. Absorption affects mainly the thinner alveolar part and after completion of absorption, a linear alveolar ridge is left at the superior border of mandible
- Mandibular canal near to superior border
- Mental foramen near to superior border
- Ramus become oblique, the angle is about 140 degree
- Neck is inclined backwards

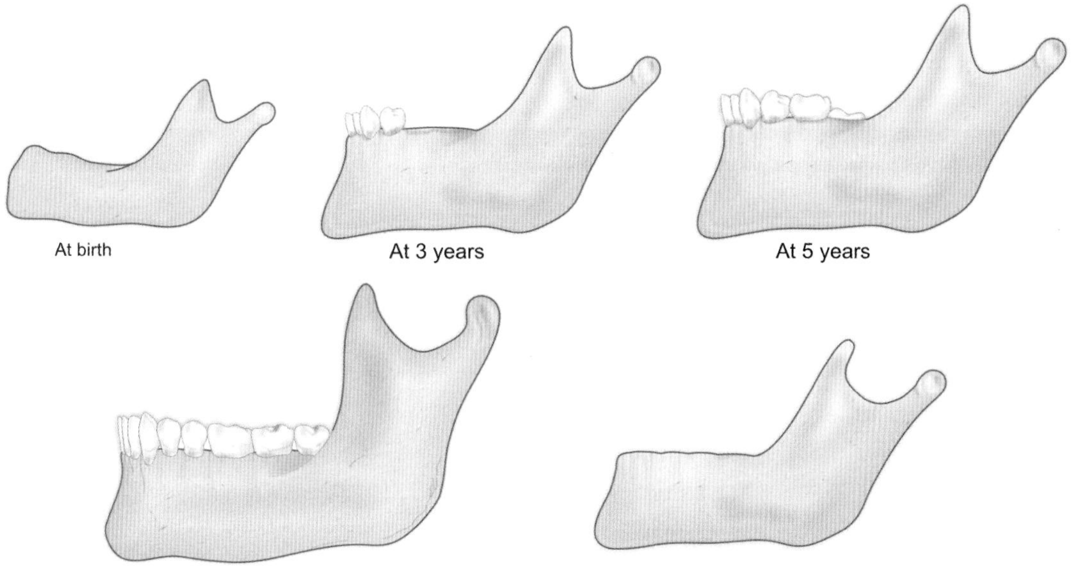

FIG. 4.18: Diagrammatic representation of age related changes in mandible

- The coronoid process again projects higher than condyloid process.

FEMUR

Sex

Table 4.8 presents sex differences between male and female femur bone (Fig. 4.19).

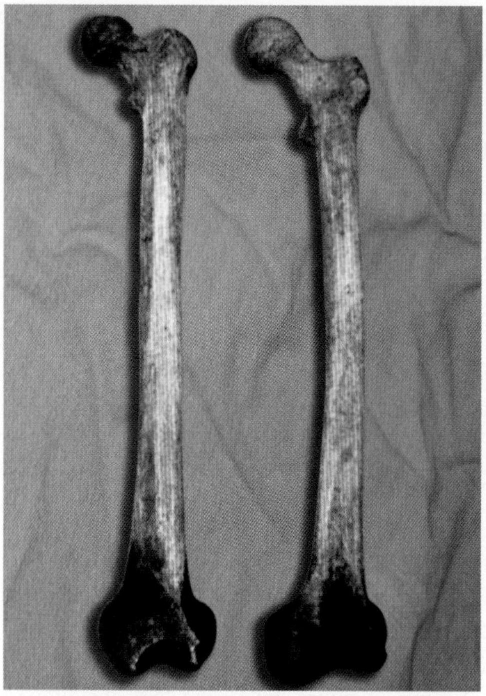

FIG. 4.19: Male and female femur bones

Age

Age estimation from femur can be done by noting following changes.

- Ossification events
- Radiographic changes

Ossification Event

Table 4.9 provides ossification centers with their appearance and fusion in male and female[12] (Fig. 4.20).

From Radiographic Changes

Radiographic age determination from the proximal epiphyses of femur – radiographs of the proximal end of femur show the progressive proximal-ward extension of medullary cavity as age advances and the features are more obvious in age ranges of 31.4 to 67.8 year. Acsadi and Nemeskeri (1970) divided the changes into five phases. The phases are described below and the correlation with age is presented in Table 4.10.

- Phase 1: Apex of the medullary cavity below the lesser trochanter. Texture of trabeculae is thick.
- Phase 2: Apex of medullary cavity reaches or surpasses the lower limit of lesser trochanter
- Phase 3: Apex of medullary cavity reaches the upper limit of the lesser trochanter
- Phase 4: Apex of the medullary cavity extends above the upper limit of lesser trochanter
- Phase 5: Apex of medullary cavity extends beyond the upper limit of lesser trochanter. A cavity of 3 mm diameter is formed in the greater trochanter. Cavity appears in the head beneath fovea capitis and at the medial and later border
- Phase 6: Cavities in medial part of neck merges with medullary cavity. Cavities formed in neck and greater trochanter gets enlarged.

Table 4.8: Showing male and female difference in femur

Features	*Male*	*Female*
General	Heavier, rough with prominent muscle impressions	Light, smooth
Head	Articular surface is more than 2/3rd of a sphere	Articular surface is less than 2/3rd of a sphere
Collodiaphyseal angle	45° (low angle)	46° (high angle)
Angulation of shaft with condyles	Around 80°	Around 76°
Length[11]	438.4 mm	400.2 mm
Head diameter, horizontal[11]	44.1 mm	39.8 mm
Head diameter, vertical[11]	> 48 mm	44 mm
Bicondylar breadth	77.9 mm	71.1 mm
Popliteal length	135–145 mm	106–114 mm

Table 4.9: Ossification of femur (after Galstaun)		
Ossification centers	***Female***	***Male***
Head		
- Appearance	1 year	1 year
- Fusion	14–15 years	16–19 years
Greater trochanter		
- Appearance	5 years	5 years
- Fusion	14 years	17 years
Lesser trochanter		
- Appearance	12–14 years	12–14 years
- Fusion	15 years	15–17 years
Lower end of femur		
- Appearance	36 weeks	36 weeks
- Fusion	14–17 years	14–17 years

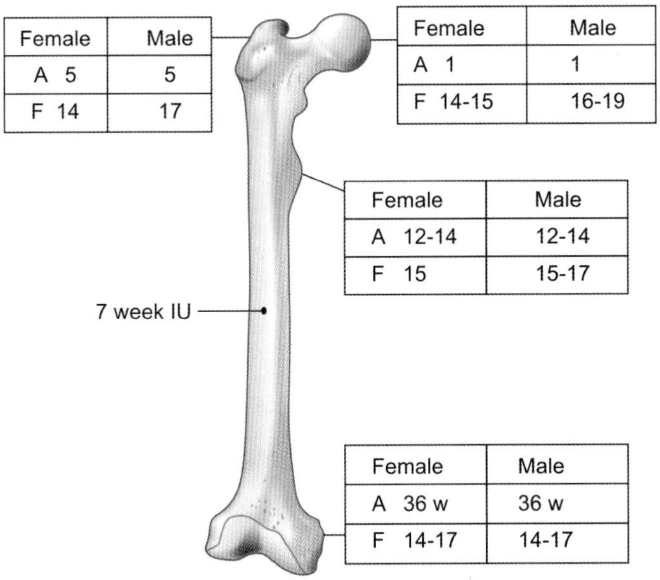

FIG. 4.20: Diagrammatic representation of appearance and fusion of ossification centers of femur (A = appearance, F = fusion)

Race

Race from femur can be determined from
- Morphological features
- Bone length
- Index

Table 4.10: Correlation of various phases and age (in years)	
Phase	***Mean age***
1	31.4
2	44
3	52.6
4	56
5	63
6	67.8

Morphological Features

Stewart (1962) and Walensky (1965) studied the femur in respect with the anterior curvature and they have noted that:
- In Black people the femur are much straighter
- In White people the femur are bowed forward
- In American Indians, the femur has greater anterior curvature and a more distal positioning of the point of maximum curvature.

Bone Length

Table 4.11 shows racial variation in femur bone length in American blacks and whites (after Krogman 1955). Male bones are longer than female bones and slightly longer in Blacks than in Whites.

Index

Following are the indices frequently used to determine race. Table 4.12 provides information regarding indices and Table 4.13 provides value of indices in various races.
- Crural index
- Intermembral index
- Humoro-femoral index

Stature

Stature of an individual can be estimated from femur. The length of bone is taken and is multiplied with multiplication factor i.e. length of femur × multiplication factor = stature. Different formulas and multiplication factors are available

Table 4.11: Racial variation in femur bone length (in mm)

Variable	***White***		***Black***	
	Male	***Female***	***Male***	***Female***
Maximum femoral length	434	399	449	416
Femur length (in range)	377-480	338-455	379-480	355-473

Table 4.12: Showing various indices	
Index	*Measurements*
Crural index	Length of tibia × 100 ÷ Length of femur
Intermembral index	Length of humerus + length of radius × 100 ÷ length of femur + length of tibia
Humoro-femoral index	Length of humerus × 100 ÷ length of femur

Table 4.13: Indices in various races			
Index	*Indian*	*European*	*Black*
Crural	86.49	89.3	86.2
Intermembral	67.27	70.4	70.3
Humero-femoral	71.11	69	72.4

such as Karl Pearson formula for Europeans, Trotter and Glesser formula for American persons. In India, various researchers of different states have evolved multiplication factor to estimate stature. Table 4.14 presents multiplication factor. Following account shows the authors and study states.

- Pan – for residents of Bengal, Bihar and Orissa
- Nat – for residents of Uttar Pradesh
- Shah and Siddiqui – for residents of Punjab
- Singh and Shoha – for residents of East Punjab
- Mehta and Thomas – for residents of Mysore

TIBIA

Sex

Table 4.15 presents sex differences between male and female tibia bone (Fig. 4.21).

Stature

Stature can be estimated from the multiplication factors mentioned in Table 4.16.

Race

Race is determined from Crural and Intermembral index.

Age

Table 4.17 provides ossification centers with their appearance and fusion in male and female[12] (Fig. 4.22).

FIBULA

Sex

Table 4.18 presents sex differences between male and female fibula bone (Fig. 4.23).

Stature

Stature can be estimated from the multiplication factors mentioned in Table 4.19.

Table 4.14: Showing multiplication factors for estimating stature (femur)							
Femur	*Shah and Siddiqui*	*PAN*		*NAT*	*Singh and Shoha*	*Mehta and Thomas*	
Sex	*Male*	*Male*	*Female*	*Male*	*Male*	*Male*	*Female*
Multiplication factor	3.6	3.82	3.8	3.7	3.57	3.6	3.75

Table 4.15: Showing male and female difference in tibia		
Features	*Male*	*Female*
General	Heavier, rough with prominent muscle impressions	Light, smooth
Length[13]	373 mm	341.5 mm
Mid-shaft circumference[13]	76.4 mm	65.7 mm
Proximal breadth[13] (Bicondylar breadth)	73.3 mm	64.4 mm
Distal breadth[13]	47.7 mm	42.6 mm

Table 4.16: Showing multiplication factors for estimating stature (tibia)

Tibia	*Shah and Siddiqui*	*PAN*		*NAT*	*Singh and Shoha*	*Mehta and Thomas*	
Sex	*Male*	*Male*	*Female*	*Male*	*Male*	*Male*	*Female*
Multiplication factor	4.2	4.49	4.46	4.48	4.18	4.2	4.39

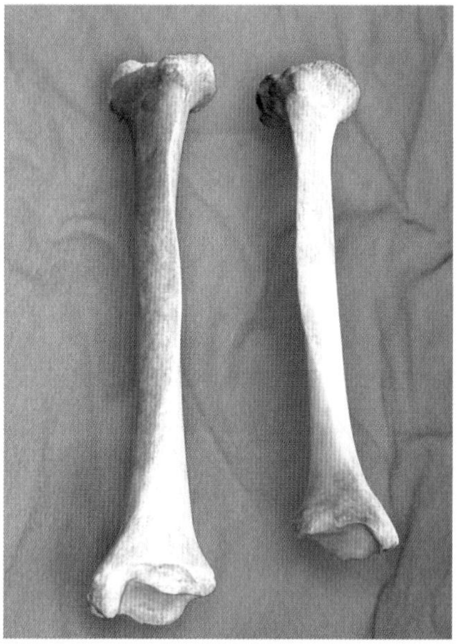

FIG. 4.21: Male and female tibia bones

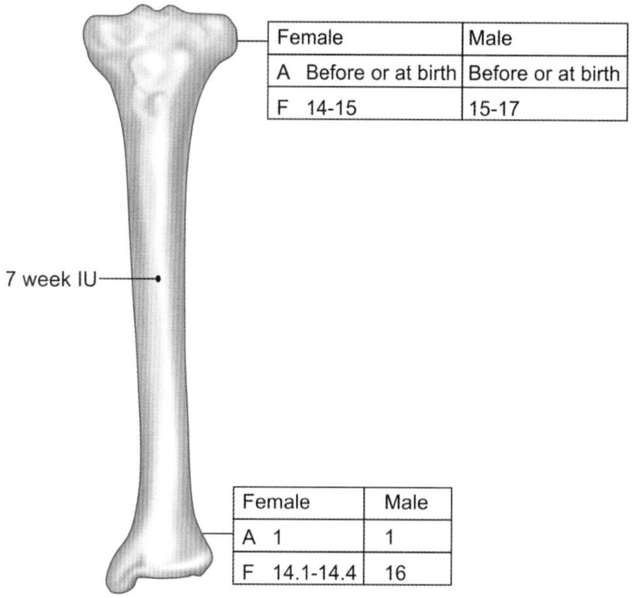

Female
Male
A Before or at birth
Before or at birth
F 14-15
15-17
7 week IU
Female
Male
A 1
1
F 14.1-14.4
16

FIG. 4.22: Diagrammatic representation of appearance and fusion of ossification centers (A=appearance, F=fusion)

Table 4.17: Ossification of tibia (after Galstaun)

Ossification centers	*Female*	*Male*
Upper end		
- Appearance	Before birth	Before birth
- Fusion	14-15 years	15-17 years
Lower end		
- Appearance	1 year	1 year
- Fusion	14.1-14.4 years	16 year

Age

Table 4.20 provides ossification centers with their appearance and fusion in male and female[12] (Fig. 4.24).

HUMERUS

Sex

Table 4.21 presents sex differences between male and female humerus bone (Figs 4.25A and B).

Table 4.18: Showing male and female difference in fibula

Features	*Male*	*Female*
General	Heavier, rough with prominent muscle impressions	Light, smooth
Length[14]	> 362 mm	< 236 mm
Mid-shaft circumference[14]	40.3 mm	34.9 mm
Distal end breadth[14]	24.5 mm	21.8 mm

Age

Age estimation from femur can be done by studying following changes.

- Ossification events
- Radiographic changes

Table 4.19: Showing multiplication factors for estimating stature (fibula)

Fibula	*Shah and Siddiqui*	*PAN*		*NAT*	*Singh and Shoha*	*Mehta and Thomas*	
Sex	*Male*	*Male*	*Female*	*Male*	*Male*	*Male*	*Female*
Multiplication factor	4.4	4.46	4.43	4.48	4.35	4.44	4.55

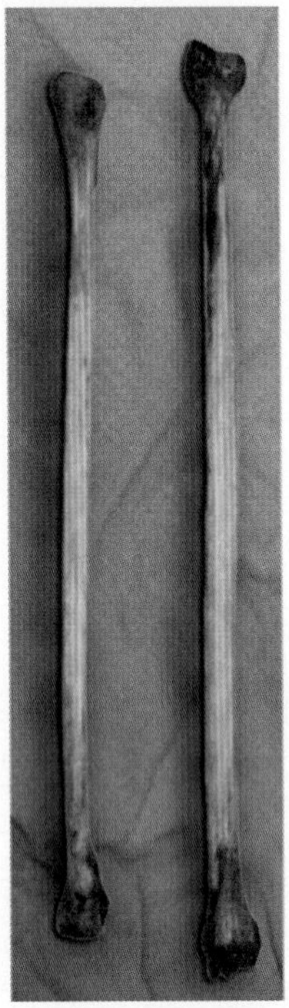

FIG. 4.23: Male and female fibula

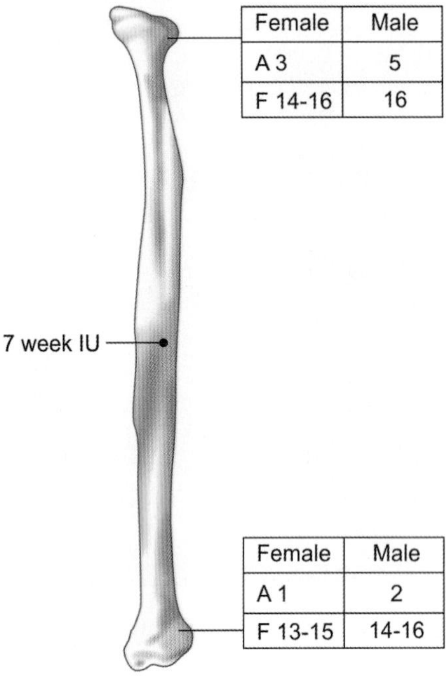

FIG. 4.24: Diagrammatic representation of appearance and fusion of ossification centers (A=appearance, F=fusion)

Table 4.20: Ossification of fibula (after Galstaun)

Ossification centers	*Female*	*Male*
Upper end		
- Appearance	3 years	5 years
- Fusion	14-16 years	16 years
Lower end		
- Appearance	1 year	2 year
- Fusion	13-15 years	14-16 year

Ossification Events

Table 4.22 provides ossification centers with their appearance and fusion in male and female[12] (Fig. 4.26).

Radiographic Changes

Radiographic age determination from the proximal epiphyses of humerus – radiographs of the proximal end of humerus show the progressive proximal-ward extension of medullary cavity. Age ranges from 41 to 61.1 year. Acsadi and Nemeskeri (1970) divided the changes into five phases similar to femur.

Stature

Stature can be estimated from the multiplication factors mentioned in Table 4.23.

Race

Race from humerus can be determined from

- Bone length
- Index

Bone Length

Table 4.24 shows racial variation in humerus bone length in American blacks and whites (after Krogman 1955). Male bones are longer than female bones and slightly longer in Blacks than in Whites.

Table 4.21: Showing male and female difference in humerus		
Features	***Male***	***Female***
General	Heavier, rough with prominent muscle impressions	Light, smooth, muscle impression less prominent
Length[15]	31.1 cm	27.9 cm
Vertical diameter of head	48 mm	40.5 mm
Transverse diameter of head	44.6 mm	38.9 mm
Mid-shaft circumference[15]	58.5 mm	49.1 mm
Epicondylar breadth[15]	60.4 mm	52.4 mm

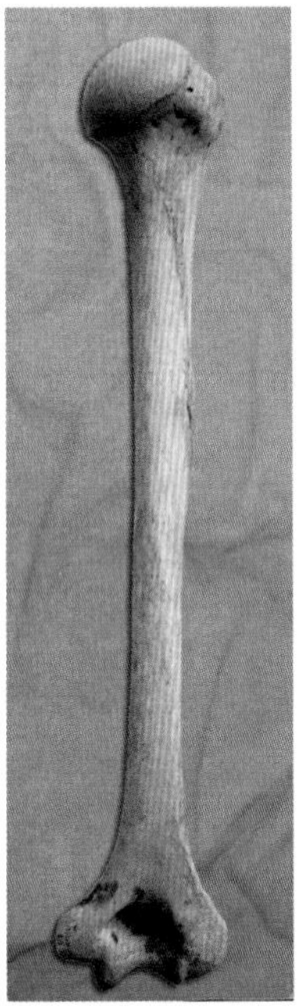

FIG. 4.25A: Male humerus

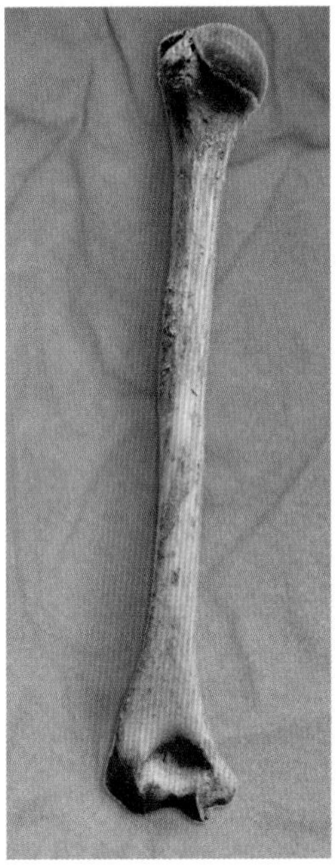

FIG. 4.25B: Female humerus

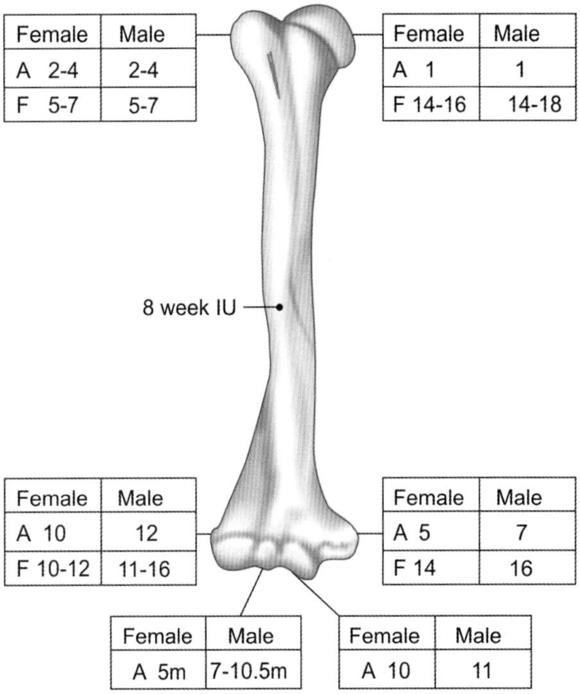

FIG. 4.26: Diagrammatic representation of appearance and fusion of ossification centers (A=appearance, F=fusion)

Index

Following are the indices frequently used to determine race. Table 4.25 provides information regarding indices and Table 4.26 provides value of indices in various races.

- Brachial index
- Intermembral index
- Humoro-femoral index

RADIUS

Sex

Table 4.27 presents sex differences between male and female radius bone (Fig. 4.27).

Age

Table 4.28 provides ossification centers with their appearance and fusion in male and female[12] (Fig. 4.28).

Stature

Stature can be estimated from the multiplication factors mentioned in Table 4.29.

Race

Race can be determined from

- Brachial index
- Intermembral index

Table 4.22: Ossification of humerus (after Galstaun)

Ossification centers	*Male*	*Female*
Head		
- Appearance	1 year	1 year
- Fusion	14-18 year	14-16 year
Greater tubercle		
- Appearance	2-4 year	2-4 year
- Fusion with head	5-7 year	5-7 year
Medial epicondyle ∞		
- Appearance	7 year	5 year
- Fusion with shaft	16 year	14 year
Lateral epicondyle ∞		
- Appearance	12 year	10 year
- Fusion with capitulum	11-16 year	10-12 year
Capitellum ∞		
- Appearance	5 months	7-10 ½ months
Trochlea ∞		
- Appearance	11 year	10 year
- Fusion with capitulum	11-15 year	9-13 year

∞ The lateral epicondyle, capitulum and trochlea fuse together to form larger lower epiphysis that unites with shaft at 14 years in female and 14 to 16 years in male. According to Galstaun[12], the unions of three components are not always found. Pillai MJS[16] noted fusion of lateral epicondyle with shaft at 13 years in female and 14 years in male. The medial epicondyle forms a separate small epiphysis at lower end and unites with shaft separately.

Table 4.25: Showing various indices

Index	*Measurements*
Brachial index	Length of radius × 100 ÷ Length of humerus
Intermembral index	Length of humerus + length of radius × 100 ÷ length of femur + length of tibia
Humoro-femoral index	Length of humerus × 100 ÷ length of femur

Table 4.26: Indices in various races

Index	*Indians*	*European*	*Black*
Brachial	76.49	75.5	78.5
Intermembral	67.27	70.4	70.3
Humero-femoral	71.11	69	72.4

Table 4.27: Showing male and female difference in radius

Features	*Male*	*Female*
General	Heavier, rough with prominent muscle impressions	Light, smooth, muscle impre-ssion less prominent
Diameter of head	22.50 mm	21.50 mm
Head circumference[17]	67.8 mm	59.5 mm
Tuberosity circumference[17]	48.5 mm	42.2 mm
Mid-shaft circumference[17]	67.8 mm	59.5 mm
Distal end breadth[17]	32.7 mm	28.5 mm

Table 4.23: Showing multiplication factors for estimating stature (humerus)

Humerus	*Shah and Siddiqui*	*PAN*		*NAT*	*Singh and Shoha*	*Mehta and Thomas*	
Sex	*Male*	*Male*	*Female*	*Male*	*Male*	*Male*	*Female*
Multiplication factor	5	5.31	5.31	5.3	4.97	5.08	5.31

Table 4.24: Racial variation in humerus bone length (in mm)

Variable	*White*		*Black*	
	Male	*Female*	*Male*	*Female*
Maximum humerus length	321	292	329	303
Humerus length (in range)	276-371	240-328	278-364	265-348

Table 4.28: Ossification of radius (after Galstaun)

Ossification centers	*Female*	*Male*
Upper end		
- Appearance	6 year	8 year
- Fusion	14 year	16 year
Lower end		
- Appearance	1 year	1 year
- Fusion	16.5 year	16-17 year

ULNA

Sex

Table 4.30 presents sex differences between male and female ulna bone (Figs 4.29A and B).

Age

Table 4.31 provides ossification centers with their appearance and fusion in male and female[12] (Fig. 4.30).

Stature

Stature can be estimated from the multiplication factors mentioned in Table 4.32.

STERNUM

Sex

Table 4.33 presents sex differences between male and female sternum bone.

Age

Sternum ossifies from 6 centers; 5 are primary centers and 1 secondary center. One each primary center is for manubrium and sternal segments respectively.

- Primary center for manubrium appears by 5 months of intrauterine life
- Primary center for 1st segment of sternum appears by 5 months of intrauterine life
- Primary center for 2nd segment of sternum appears by 5 months of intrauterine life
- Primary center for 3rd segment of sternum appears by 5 months of intrauterine life
- Primary center for 4th segment of sternum appears by 6 months of intrauterine life
- Secondary center for xiphoid appears by 3rd year of life
- Xiphoid unites with body (sternum) by 40 years
- Manubrium unites with sternum by 60 years
- Union between different sternal segments begins at puberty from lower segment to upper segment and they all are united during 25th year.

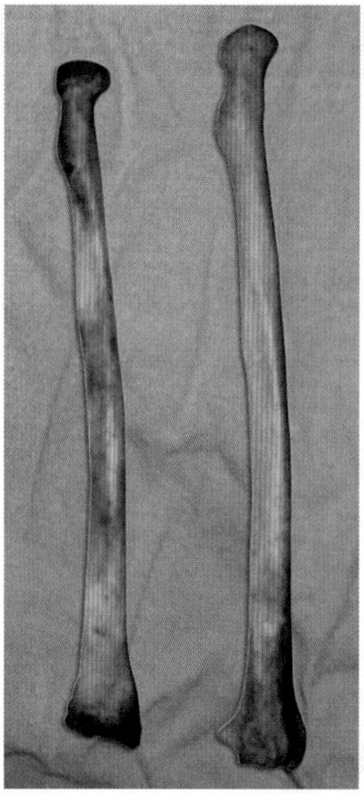

FIG. 4.27: Male and female radius

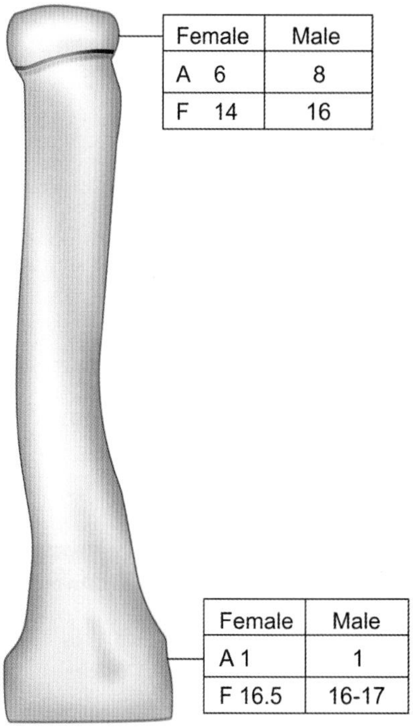

FIG. 4.28: Diagrammatic representation of appearance and fusion of ossification centers (A=appearance, F=fusion)

Table 4.29: Showing multiplication factors for estimating stature (radius)							
Radius	*Shah and Siddiqui*	*PAN*		*NAT*	*Singh and Shoha*	*Mehta and Thomas*	
Sex	*Male*	*Male*	*Female*	*Male*	*Male*	*Male*	*Female*
Multiplication factor	6.3	6.78	6.7	6.9	6.63	6.01	6.24

Table 4.30: Showing male and female difference in ulna		
Features	*Male*	*Female*
General	Heavier, rough with prominent muscle impressions	Light, smooth, muscle impression less prominent
Mid-shaft circumference[18]	43 mm	37.1 mm
Distal end breadth[18]	19 mm	16.7 mm

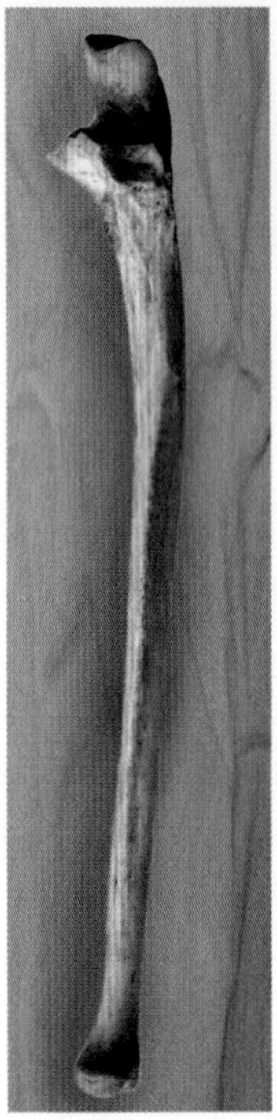

FIG. 4.29A: Male ulna

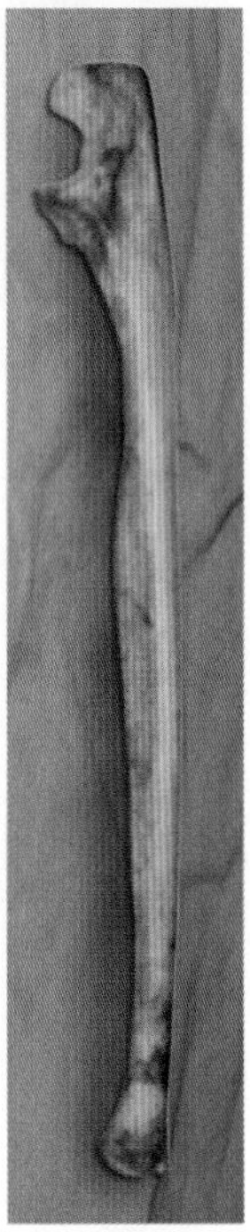

FIG. 4.29B: Female ulna

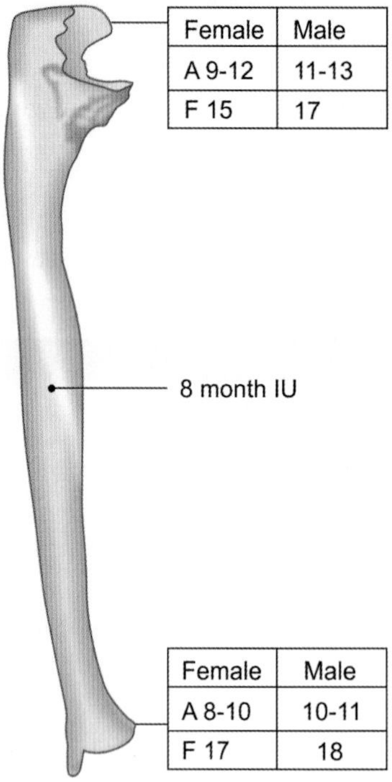

FIG. 4.30: Diagrammatic representation of appearance and fusion of ossification centers (A=appearance, F=fusion)

Table 4.31: Ossification of ulna (after Galstaun)		
Ossification centers	*Female*	*Male*
Upper end olecran		
- Appearance	9-12 year	11-13 year
- Fusion	15 year	17 year
Lower end		
- Appearance	8-10 year	10-11 year
- Fusion	17 year	18 year

SCAPULA

Sex

Table 4.34 presents differences between male and female scapula bone (Fig. 4.31).

Age

Age from scapula can be determined from:

Table 4.32: Showing multiplication factors for estimating stature (ulna)

Ulna	Shah and Siddiqui	PAN		NAT	Singh and Shoha	Mehta and Thomas	
Sex	Male	Male	Female	Male	Male	Male	Female
Multiplication factor	6	6	6	6.3	5.93	6.4	6.85

Table 4.33: Showing male and female difference in sternum

Features	Male	Female
General	Body longer and more than twice the length of manubrium	Body shorter and less than twice the length of the manubrium
Manubrial length[19]	51.7 mm	48.4 mm
Body length[19]	95.4 mm	78.6 mm
Length	> 149 mm	<149 mm
Width of first segment of sternum (sternebra) [19]	27.5 mm	24.3 mm
Width of third segment of sternum (sternebra) [19]	32.6 mm	29.2 mm
Sternal index (Manubrium-corpus index)	46.2	54.3
Relative width index[19]	85.2	84.3

- Sternal index = Length of manubrium X 100 ÷ length of mesosternum
- Asley's rule = the total midline length of manubrium and mesosternum male in > 149 mm and in female it is < 149 mm.
- Relative width index = width of first sternebra X 100 ÷ mesosternal breadth
- Hyrtl's law index is basically manubrium-corpus index. According to this law index, the value of index to be grater than 50 in female and less than 50 in male

- Ossification data – given below
- Secondary changes in scapula – given in Table 4.35
- Post-maturity atrophic process – given in Table 4.36.

Ossification Data

Scapula ossifies from two primary and seven secondary centers.

- One primary center appears for body of scapula by 8th week of intrauterine life
- Second primary center for coracoid process appears by 1st year of life
- 2 secondary centers for acromial cartilage appear at puberty and fuses soon. It joins with spine at 20th year
- 2 secondary centers for coracoid appear at puberty and fuses at 14 to 17 year
- 1 secondary center for vertebral border appear by 17th year and fuses at 20th year
- 1 secondary center for inferior angle appear by 16th year and fuses at 20th year
- 1 secondary center for glenoid cavity appears at puberty and fuses at 20th year
- Union is completed by 20th year.

Table 4.34: Showing male and female difference in scapula ($^{\Psi}$ after Iordanidis 1961)

Features	Male	Female
General	Heavier, rough with prominent muscle impressions	Light, smooth, muscle impre-ssion less prominent
Scapular height$^{\Psi}$	> 157 mm	<144 mm
Scapular breadth$^{\Psi}$	>106 mm	<93 mm
Total length of spinous process$^{\Psi}$	> 141 mm	<128 mm
Width of glenoid cavity$^{\Psi}$	> 29 mm	< 26 mm

Secondary Changes

Secondary changes occurring in scapula that are helpful in estimating of age are given in Table 4.35.

Post-Maturity Atrophic Process

Post-maturity atrophic process occurring in scapula that is helpful in estimating of age is given in Table 4.36.

Table 4.35: Secondary changes in scapula

Features (Secondary changes in scapula)	*Age*
Lipping of circumferential margin of glenoid fossa begins as notch at junction of upper and middle third of ventral margin ⇨ order of progression is ventral ⇨ Inferior ⇨ dorsal ⇨ superior margin, begins at	30-35 years
Lipping of clavicular facet begins	35-40 years
Appearance of a plaque or facet on the undersurface of acromial process	40-45 years
Increasing demarcation of the triangular area at base (vertebral margin) of scapular spine	50 years
Appearance of cristae scapulae	> 50 year

Table 4.36: Postmaturity atrophic process

Features (Post-maturity atrophic process)	*Age*
Surface vascularity - seen as number of delicate fine lines - diminishes in visibility and finally disappear as age advances	< 25 year
Deep vascularity - seen as similar lines, but now by transillumination - tend to diminish with age	25 - 30 years
Atrophic spots - localized, discrete or coalescing areas of bone atrophy noted by transillumination, especially in infraspinous fossa - begins at	45 years

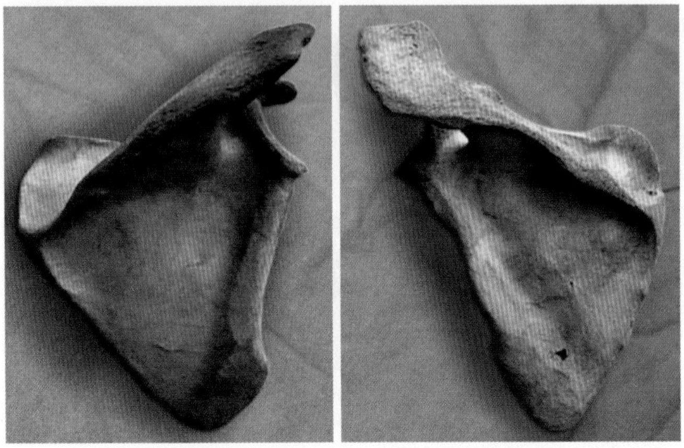

FIG. 4.31: Male and female scapula

Age

Table 4.38 provides ossification centers with their appearance and fusion in male and female.[12]

PELVIS AND HIPBONE

Sex

The differences between male and female in articulated pelvis are given in Table 4.39 and differences in hip bones are given in Table 4.40.

CLAVICLE

Sex

Table 4.37 presents sex differences between male and female clavicle bone (Fig. 4.32).

Stature

Stature is estimated by formula proposed by Singh and Sohel (1954)[21] as

- Stature = Length of clavicle X Multiplication factor
- Here multiplication factor is 11.1 , thus it can be stated as
- Stature = Length of clavicle X 11.1.

Table 4.37: Showing male and female difference in clavicle

Features	*Male*	*Female*
General	Heavier, longer, rough with prominent muscle impressions, more curved	Light, shorter, smooth, muscle impression less prominent, less curved
Length (mean)[20]	147.6 mm	129.8 mm
Weight	> 20.10 gm	< 7.82 gm
Mid-clavicular circumference[20]	35.7 mm	29.5 mm

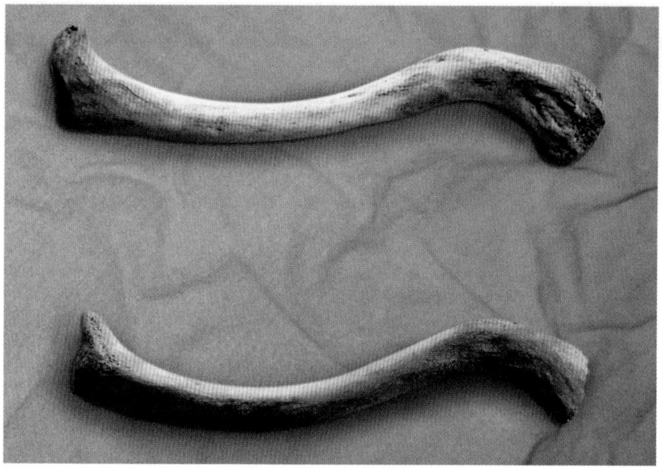

FIG. 4.32: Male and female clavicle

Age

Age from the hipbone is estimated by
- Ossification events
- Pubic symphysis: phase analysis
- Pubic symphysis: component analysis

Ossification Events

- Hipbone occifies from 3 primary centers and 5 to 6 secondary centers.
- Primary center for ilium appears at 8th week of intrauterine life
- Primary center for body of ischium appears at 4th month of intrauterine life
- Primary center for ilium appears at 4-5th month of intrauterine life
- Appearance and fusion of secondary centers[12] are given in Table 4.41.

Table 4.38: Ossification of clavicle (after Galstaun)

Ossification centers	*Female*	*Male*
Sternal end		
- Appearance	14-16 year	15-19 year
- Fusion	20 year	22 year

Pubic symphysis: phase analysis
In 1920, Todd had proposed this method for age estimation from hipbone. According to Todd, each pubic symphysis has more or less oval outline and had five main features as:
1. Surface
2. Ventral border or rampart
3. Dorsal border or plateau
4. Superior extremity
5. Inferior extremity

Todd analyzed these features and divided them into 10 phases for estimation of age ranging from 18 years to 50 and above years. These phases are presented in Table 4.42.
Pubic symphysis: component analysis
McKern and Stewart in 1957 made revision in the method described by Todd. Accordingly, McKern and Stewart had divided surface of pubic symphysis into three components by a vertical grove into dorsal and ventral halves. These components are termed accordingly as – dorsal demi-face and ventral demi-face. The third component consists of whole surface. Each component had allotted scores ranging from 0 to 5. The scores and the features are mentioned in Table 4.43 and the age at particular score in male and female is given in Table 4.44. It is important to note that there is a developmental sequence from component I to component III. The three components are as follows:
- Component I: dorsal plateau (dorsal demi-face)

Table 4.39: Showing male and female difference in articulated pelvis

Features	*Male*	*Female*
General	Heavier, rough with prominent muscle impressions	Light, smooth, muscle impression less prominent
Pelvic inlet	Heart shaped	Circular/oval shaped
Pelvic cavity	Conical and funnel shaped	Broad and round
Sub-pubic angle	Narrow ("V" shaped) 70° to 75°	Wide ("U" shaped) 90° to 100°
Pelvic outlet	Smaller	Larger
Symphysis	Higher	Lower
Chilotic line pelvic part[22]	63 mm	67.3 mm
Chilotic line sacral part	65.5 mm	55.6 mm

Table 4.40: Showing male and female difference in hipbone

Features	*Male*	*Female*
General	Heavier, rough with prominent muscle impressions	Light, smooth, muscle impression less prominent
Obturator foramen	Large, oval	Small, triangular
Acetabulum	Large, directed laterally,	Small, directed antero-laterally,
Acetabulum[22]		
- Vertical diameter	51.8 mm	43.6 mm
- Transverse diameter	51 mm	42.9 mm
Greater sciatic notch	Smaller, narrower, deeper	Larger, wider, shallower
Ischiopubic rami	Slightly everted	Strongly everted
Pre-auricular sulcus	Not frequent	More frequent, better developed
Post-auricular sulcus[23]	Not frequent	More frequent, sharper auricular surface edge
Post-auricular space[23]	Narrow	Wide
Ilium	High, tends to be vertical	Lower, laterally divergent
Iliac crest[24]	Steeper anterior and posterior slope	Not so
Ischial tuberosity	Inverted	Everted
Body of pubis	Narrow, triangular	Broad, square
Ventral arc on ventral surface of pubis as a slightly elevated bony ridge extending from pubic crest down to pubic ramus[25]	Absent	Present
Sub-pubic concavity is a deep concave structure located immediately below the symphysis in the ramus[25]	Absent	Present
Medial aspect of Ischiopubic ramus[25]	Broad & flat	Narrow and crest like
Innominate length (mean)[26]	197.2 mm	182.1 mm
Iliac breadth (mean)[26]	143.5 mm	137.8
Ischial length (mean)[26]	83 mm	76 mm
Pubic length (mean)[26]	72.1 mm	79.6 mm
Acetabulo-symphysis distance[22]	56.1 mm	61.4 mm
Auricular facet[22]	51.1 mm	42.9 mm
- Antero-posterior diameter		
- Vertical diameter	36.8 mm	32.6 mm
Ischio-pubic index	73 to 94	91 to 115
Sciatic notch index	4 to 5	5 to 6
Coxal index[26]	72.6	75.8
Pubo-acetabular index[22]	110.5	143.3

- Ischio-pubic index = length of pubis × 100 ÷ length of ischium
- Sciatic notch index = width of sciatic notch × 100 ÷ depth of sciatic notch
- Coxal index = iliac breadth × 100 ÷ Innominate height
- Pubo-acetabular index = acetabulo-symphyseal distance × 100 ÷ acetabular transverse diameter

Table 4.41: Ossification of hipbone (after Galstaun)

Ossification centers	*Female*	*Male*
Crest of ilium		
- Appearance	14 year	17 years
- Fusion	17-19 year	19-20 years
Triradiate cartilage		
- Fusion	13-14 year	15-16 years
Ischial tuberosity		
- Appearance	14-16 year	16-18 years
- Fusion	20 year	20 years
Ischio-pubic rami		
- Fusion	81/2 years	81/2 years

- Component II: ventral rampart (ventral demi-face)
- Component III: symphyseal rim (symphyseal surface)

Race

Race can be known from
- Morphology
- Interspinous diameter (see Table 4.45)
- Bi-iliac diameter (see Table 4.45)

Morphology

In White people
- Ilium flare outward and upward
- Pelvis is broader
- Symphysis is placed low

Table 4.42: Showing pubic symphysis: Phase analysis (after Todd 1920)

Phase	*Age in Years*	*Symphyseal surface*	*Ossific nodules*	*Ventral margin*	*Dorsal margin*	*Extremities*
First	18-19	Rugged horizontal grooves, furrows and ridges	None	None	None	No definition
Second	20-21	Grooves filling dorsally and behind	May appear on Symphyseal surface	Ventral bevel begins	Begins	No definition
Third	22-24	Ridges and furrows going progressively	Present almost constantly	Beveling more pronounced	More definite dorsal plateau	No definition
Fourth	25-26	Rapidly going	Present	Beveling greatly increased	Complete dorsal plateau present	Lower commencing definition
Fifth	27-30	Little change	May be present	Sporadic attempt at ventral rampart	Completely defined	Lower clearer; upper extremity forming
Sixth	30-35	Granular appearance retained	May be present	Ventral rampart complete	Defined	Increasing definition of both extremities
Seventh	35-39	Texture finer; diminishing activity	May be present	Complete	Defined	Carry on
Eighth	40-44	Smooth and inactive; no rim	May be present	No lipping	No lipping	Oval outline complete, extremities clearly outlined
Ninth	44-50	Rim present	May be present	Irregularly lipped	Uniformly lipped	Carry on
Tenth	50 +	Erosion and erratic ossification	Broken down	Broken down	Broken down	Broken down

Table 4.43: Showing pubic symphysis: Component analysis (after McKern and Stewart 1957)

Score	Dorsal plateau	Ventral rampart	Symphyseal rim
0	No margin on dorsal border	Ventral beveling is absent	Symphyseal rim is absent
1	Margin formation begins in middle one-third of dorsal border	Ventral beveling is present only at superior extremity of ventral border	A partial dorsal rim is present usually at superior end of the dorsal margin
2	Margin formed all along dorsal border	Bevel extends inferiorly along ventral border	Dorsal rim is complete and ventral rim is beginning to form
3	Filling of grooves and resorption of ridges to form a beginning plateau in the middle one-third part	Ventral rampart begins by means of bony extensions from either or both of the extremities	Symphyseal rim is complete. The enclosed symphyseal surface is finely grained in texture and irregular or undulating in appearance
4	The plateau extends over most of the dorsal demi-face	Rampart is extensive but gaps are still evident along the ventral border; most evident in the upper two-third	The rim begins to break down. The face becomes smooth and flat and the rim is no longer round but sharply defined. There is some evidence of lipping on the ventral edge
5	Surface becomes entirely flat and slightly granulated in texture	The rampart is complete	Further breakdown of rim and rarefaction of the symphyseal face. There is also disintegration and erratic calcification along the ventral edge

Table 4.44: The total score in male and female for pubic symphysis: component analysis

Total score Male	Male (mean age in years)	Total score Female	Female (mean age in years)
0	17.3	0	16
1-2	19	1	19.8
3	19.8	2	20.2
4-5	20.8	3	21.5
6-7	22.4	4-5	26
8-9	24.1	6	29.6
10	26.1	7-8	32
11-13	29.2	9	33
14	35.8	10-11	36.9
15	41	12	39
		13	47.8
		14-15	55.7

In Black people
- Ilium is more vertical
- Pelvis is not broader
- Symphysis is placed high

Table 4.45: Racial variation in Interspinous and bi-iliac diameter (after Adair 1921)

Population	Interspinous diameter	Bi-iliac diameter
American Indian	226 mm	257 mm
Chinese	205-226 mm	220-252 mm
European	222 mm	266 mm
Aryan	260 mm	270 mm
Bengalese (Indian)	179 mm	216 mm

SACRUM

Sex

The sex difference between sacrum is presented in Table 4.46.

Age

Sacrum ossifies from 35 centers consisting of 21 primary centers and 14 secondary centers. The centers are as:
- 15 primary centers – 3 primary centers for each vertebra and includes one for body and two for vertebral arches (3 × 5 = 15)

- 6 primary centers – for costal elements
- Primary centers for first, second and third segment appears at three-month intrauterine life whereas centers for fourth and fifth segments appear between 5 to 8 months intrauterine life. Primary centers for costal elements appear between 5 to 6 months of intrauterine life.
- Secondary centers appear at puberty. Two centers are for upper and lower surface of body of each vertebra (5 × 2 = 10). Amongst two secondary centers, one appears for articular surface and other for narrow edge below it.
- Fusion between vertebras commences from below upwards at 18th year and by 21st year all the vertebrae are fused except the first. The first vertebra fuses with rest of bone at about 30th year. (Therefore the sequence is 18 years → 21 years → 30 years).

Race

Some authors had presented work related with determination of race from sacrum. Kimura in 1982 had evolved base-wing index for determination of race. The features are mentioned in Table 4.47.

Table 4.47: Determination of sex and race variation in sacrum (after Kimura 1982)

Dimensions	*Japanese*	*White*	*Black*
Width of base (mean)			
- Male	50 mm	48.9 mm	48.8 mm
- Female	45.1 mm	43.6 mm	43.6 mm
Width of wing (mean)			
- Male	32.7 mm	37 mm	32.3 mm
- Female	35.7 mm	40 mm	37.5 mm
Base-wing index (mean)			
- Male	65.8	76.2	66.7
- Female	79.7	92.2	86.4

- Width of base is transverse length of sacral vertebra
- Width of wing refers to transverse width of wing (ala)
- Base-wing index = width of wing × 100 ÷ width of base

REFERENCES

1. Krogman WM, Iscan MY. In: The human skeleton in forensic medicine, 2nd edn. 1986. Charles C Thomas, Illinois.
2. Hillier ML, Bell LS. Differentiating human bone from animal bone: a review of histological methods. J Forensic Sci 2007; 52: 249 – 63.
3. Rai B, Anand SC, Dhattarwal SK. Osteons as an age determinant. Medicolegal Update 2005; 5:99-100.
4. Saukko P, Knight B. The establishment of identity of human remains. In: Knight's Forensic Pathology, 3rd edn. 2004. Arnold, London. 98-135.
5. Mathiharan K, Patnaik AK. Postmortem examination. In: Modi's Medical Jurisprudence and Toxicology, 23rd edn. 2005. LexisNexis Butterworths, New Delhi. 357-416.
6. Knight B, Lauder I. Methods of dating human skeletal remains. Human Biol 1969; 41:322-41.
7. Chiba M, Terazawa K. Estimation of stature from somatometry of skull. Forensic Sci Int 1998; 97:87-92.
8. Bardale R, Dixit PG. Estimation of stature from somatometry of skull. J Medicolegal Assos Maharashtra 2006; 18:22-6.

Table 4.46: Showing male and female difference in sacrum

Features	*Male*	*Female*
General	Heavier, rough with prominent muscle impressions, larger	Light, smooth, muscle impression less prominent, smaller
Breadth of body of first sacral vertebra	More than breadth of one side ala	Less than breadth of one side ala
Sacral promontory	More projected ventrally	Less prominent and less projected
Inner curvature	Uniformly curved anteriorly	Abruptly curved at last two segments
Sacro-iliac articulation	Extends up to 3rd segment	Extends up to 2 and 1/2 to 3rd segment
Number of sacral segments	May be 5 or 6	Always 5
Corporo-basal index	> 42	< 42
Sacral index	< 114	> 114

- Corporo-basal index = breadth of body of 1st sacral vertebra X 100 ÷ transverse diameter of base of sacrum
- Sacral index = transverse diameter of base of sacrum X 100 ÷ anterior length of sacrum

9. Yadav SS, Suri PR. J Indian Acad Forensic Sci 1971, cited in Franklin CA, personal identity, in Modi's Medical Jurisprudence and Toxicology, 21st edn. 1988. N.M. Tripathi Private Ltd. Bombay. 28-68.
10. Soames RW. Skeletal system. In: Williams PL, Berry MM, Collins P, Dyson M, Dussek JE, Ferguson MWJ (ed) Gray's Anatomy, 38th edn. 1995. Churchill Livingstone, Edinburgh. 425-736.
11. Singh SP, Singh S. The sexing of adult femora – demarking points for Varanasi Zone. J Indian Acad Forensic Sci 1972; 11: 1-6.
12. Galstaun G. A study of ossification as observed in Indian subjects. Indian J Med Res 1937; 25:267-323.
13. Singh G, Singh S, Singh SP. Identification of sex from tibia. J Anat Soc India 1975; 24:20-24.
14. Singh G, Singh SP. Identification of sex from the fibula. J Indian Acad Forensic Sci 1976; 15:29-34.
15. Singh S, Singh SP. Identification of sex from the humerus. Indian J Med Res 1972; 60:1061-7.
16. Pillai MJS. The study of epiphyseal union for determining the age of South Indians – a study of one hundred cases chiefly from the Madras schools and colleges, ages ranging from 10 to 23. Indian J Med Res 1936; 23:1015-17.
17. Singh G, Singh SP, Singh S. Identification of sex from the radius. J Indian Acad Forensic Sci 1974; 13:10-6.
18. Singh S, Singh G, Singh SP. Identification of sex from ulna. Indian J Med Res 1974; 62:731-5.
19. Jit I, Jhingan V, Kulkarni M. Sexing the human sternum. Am J Phys Anthropol 1980; 53:217-24.
20. Jit I, Singh S. The sexing of adult clavicle. Indian J Med Res 1966; 54:551-71.
21. Singh and Sohel. Indian J Med Res 1952; 40:67. Cited in Mathiharan K, Patnaik AK. Postmortem examination. In: Modi's Medical Jurisprudence and Toxicology, 23rd edn. 2005. LexisNexis Butterworths, New Delhi. 357-416.
22. Raju PB, Singh S. Sexual diamorphism in hip bone. Indian J Med Res 1979; 65:846-52.
23. Iscan MY and Derrick K. Determination of sex from the sacro-iliac: A visual assessment technique. Florida Sci 1984; 47:94-8.
24. Straus WL. The human ilium: sex and stock. Am J Phys Anthropol 1927; 11:1-28.
25. Phenice TW. A newly developed visual method of sexing the Os pubis. Am J Phys Anthropol 1969; 30:297-301.
26. Singh S and Raju PB. Identification of sex from hip bone – Demarking point. J Anat Soc India 1977; 26:111-7.

CHAPTER 5

DNA Profiling

Some techniques are poor in most cases, some good in many cases and some are good in most cases, but none are reliable in every case.

- William R Maples

Introduction

- DNA profiling is also called as DNA fingerprinting, DNA typing
- The application of DNA technology to forensic medicine is the most remarkable recent advances in forensic identification.
- In DNA profiling, DNA extracted from the sample is analyzed. DNA profiles are unique to each individual except in monozygotic twins.
- Alec Jeffreys in 1984 discovered unique application of RFLP technology to personal identification and labeled it as DNA fingerprinting akin to fingerprinting[1] (See Box 5.1).
- The chances that DNA profiles in two individuals are similar are about 1 in 30 billion to 300 billion i.e. half the population of world.

Box 5.1

Alec Jeffreys is called as father of DNA fingerprinting. He was working at Leicester University where he discovered a variance in the DNA of human sample. By 1984, he discovered that with the help of restriction enzymes, DNA could be fragmented and obtained bands akin to bar-code employed for articles in supermarket. His discovery has revolutionized the forensic field.

BASIC CONSIDERATION

- Nucleus is present in all eukaryotic cells. The nucleus is made up of in large part of the chromosomes. Each chromosome is made up of two complementary strands of deoxyribonucleic acid (DNA) (Fig. 5.1).
- DNA is a long polymer of nucleotides. Each nucleotide consists of phosphate, doxyribose and one of the four bases that consist of adenine (A), thymine (T), guanine (G), and cytosine (C). The complementary bases are joined by hydrogen bonds: A – T, C – G (Fig. 5.2).
- Types of DNA
  1. Nuclear DNA
  2. Mitochondrial DNA

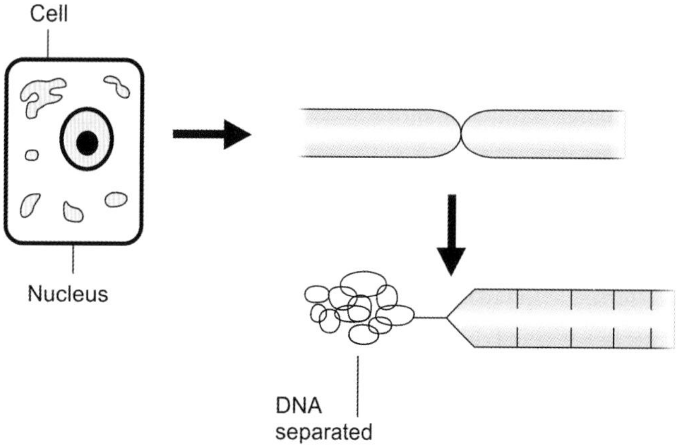

FIG. 5.1: Cell with DNA

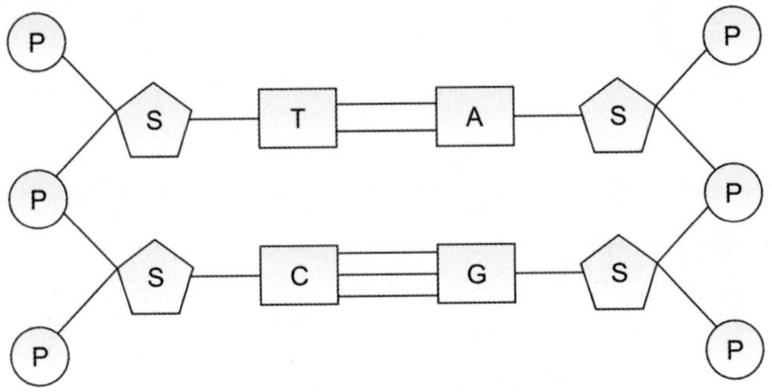

FIG. 5.2: Structure of DNA

TYPING

There are four methods of analysis as:

1. RFLP technique – called as **R**estriction **F**ragment **L**ength **P**olymorphism
2. PCR technique – called as **P**olymerase **C**hain **R**eaction
3. STR method – **S**hort **T**andem **R**epeats
4. Mitochondrial DNA analysis

A) RFLP DNA Typing[2] (Fig. 5.3)

- The DNA is extracted from sample
- DNA is subjected to restriction enzymes (called as endonucleases). The restriction enzymes cut the DNA into pieces.
- The restriction enzymes are of different types for example Eco-R-1, PsT-1, Hin-F-I etc. These enzymes recognized a particular sequence.
- When DNA is subjected to the enzymes, the enzyme recognizes a particular sequence and cut these sequences in one or two or more fragments.
- These restriction fragments are then separated by gel electrophoresis. The gel electrophoresis separate the pieces of DNA based on their size. These fragments migrate towards the positive electrode and in this, the smaller fragments move faster than larger fragments thus separating the DNA samples into bands.
- These double stranded fragments are then denatured by high alkali treatment into single strands.
- These single stranded separated fragments are then transferred (blotted) to nitrocellulose filter or nylon membrane. This transfer technique (blotting) is called as **Southern Blot** (the name is given after E.M. Southern who first described the technique).
- Next step is to make these single stranded fragments into double stranded fragments. This process of making single stranded into double stranded is known as **hybridization**. This is done by addition of probe to the nylon membrane (or nitrocellulose filter).
- A probe is single stranded DNA segment (or synthetic DNA) and is tagged with radioactive marker such as P_{32}.
- When the probe DNA mixes with single stranded fragments on nylon membrane, the probe will attach to particular segments (i.e. complementary sequence). Thus the attached fragment will be radioactive.
- The nylon membrane is then washed with 0.05% SDS and in this process, the loose probe are removed.
- Then the nylon membrane is put in contact with X-ray film and the X-ray film is exposed.
- The X-ray film is then developed. The X-ray film shows gray to black bands. These bands represent hybridized radioactive probe with complementary sequences.

Advantages of RFLP Method[3]

1. It can differentiate two samples originating from different sources, using fewer loci than other systems.

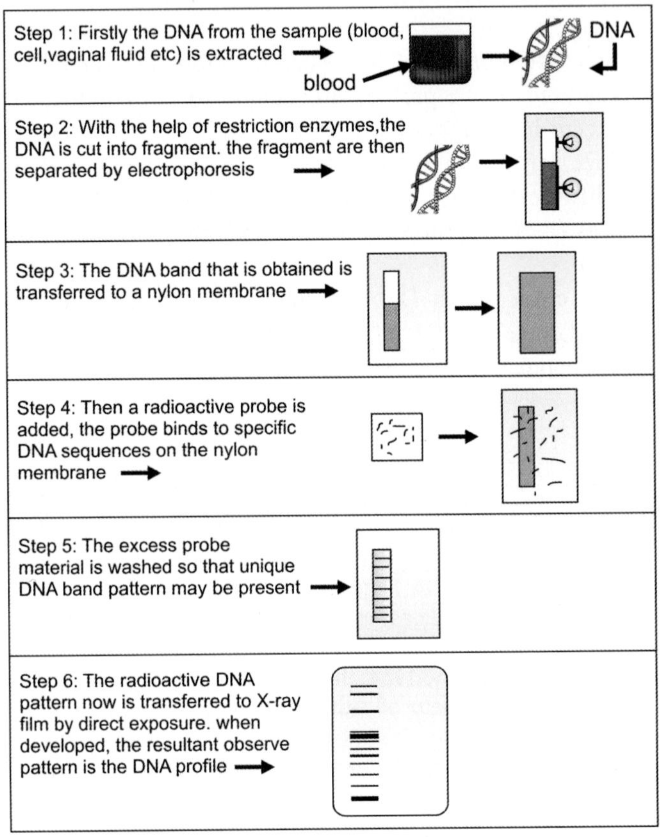

FIG. 5.3: RFLP method of DNA typing

2. Determine more readily whether single sample contains DNA from more than one person.
3. Power of discrimination is more due to hyper-variability at each locus and ability to look at many loci.

Disadvantages of RFLP Method

1. Requires high-molecular weight, high-quality DNA.
2. Require large sample.

B) PCR Method

- When very small sample is available, this method is convenient and used.
- In this method, DNA is extracted from sample and the extracted DNA is mixed with short fragments of known DNA called **primers**. It is three step procedure:
  1. First step – extract DNA, denatured the DNA to form single strand DNA.
  2. Second step – mix this single strand DNA with single strand primer DNA
  3. Third step – DNA is synthesized by primer extension from 3' end, in a 5' to 3' direction.
- At the end of third cycle, identical double strands DNA appear.

Advantages of PCR Technique

1. Require only trace amount of DNA
2. Procedure is fast and requires less time
3. Highly sensitive method.

Disadvantages of PCR Technique

1. Susceptible to contamination
2. PCR amplification is difficult from degraded DNA sample.

C) STR Method (Fig. 5.4)

- Tandem repeated DNA sequences are present in human genome and they show variability in different individuals.
- These tandemly repeated regions of DNA are classified into several groups depending on the size of the repeat region such as:
  1. Minisatellites – variable number of tandem repeats – VNTRs
  2. Microsatellites – short tandem repeats – STR – have repeats with 2-5 bp (Fig. 5.5).
- STR is a PCR technique that may replace RFLP. This technique is rapid and can be performed on small quantities of DNA.

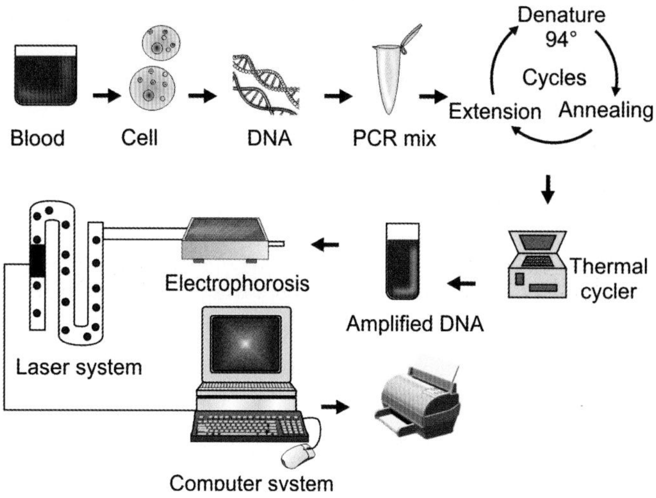

FIG. 5.4: STR method of DNA typing

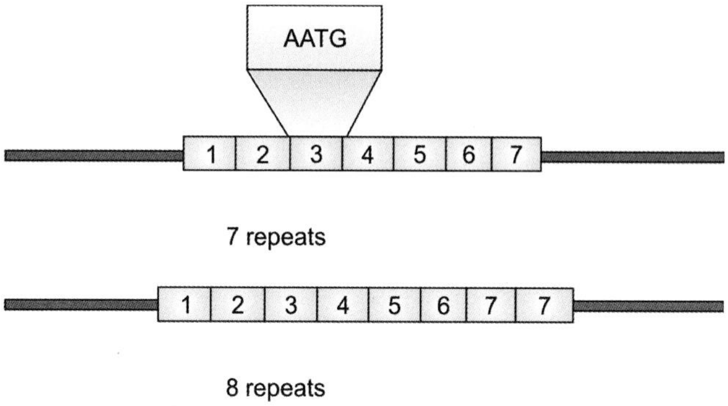

FIG. 5.5: Short tandem repeats

- STR is done by:
  1. Isolating the DNA
  2. Replicating the STR fragments by PCR
  3. Performing gel electrophoresis
  4. Identifying the fragments using stains or laser technique.

Advantages of STR Technique

1. Rapid
2. Small sample required
3. Degraded DNA may be typed using STR.

Advantages of DNA Fingerprinting

1. Conclusive method of identification of an individual
2. Method can be applied to old stains or biological material
3. Small quantity of sample is required.

Disadvantages of DNA Fingerprinting

1. DNA profiling cannot differentiate between monozygotic twins
2. Expensive
3. Interpretation requires trained manpower
4. Susceptible for contamination.

APPLICATION OF DNA PROFILING

1. To establish identity of a person in
   - Sexual crimes – rape/sodomy/buccal coitus
   - Violent crimes – murder
   - Accidents/ mass disaster
   - Missing person
   - War fighters
   - Baby mix-ups
   - Amnesia/disabled person
   - Mistaken identity.[4]
2. To acquit a falsely implicated person from such similar crime.
3. Identification in postmortem practice
   - Accidents
   - Disasters
   - Decomposition[5]
   - Mutilated remains
   - Skeleton
   - Exhumation
   - In embalmed tissues.[6]
4. Disputed paternity.[7]
5. Disputed maternity.
6. To resolve disputes of:
   - Adultery
   - Incest
   - Child born out of rape cases
   - Custody of a child born out of wedlock
   - False implication on a person being father of a certain child.
7. Extortion cases.
8. Immigration cases.
9. Determination of twin zygosity.
10. To identify sex.

Factors Influencing the Applicability of DNA Technique

1. Non-human DNA
2. Degradation of sample
3. Contamination of sample
4. Multiple contributors to sample.

Sources of DNA Contamination[8]

1. Sample contamination with genomic DNA from environment
2. Contamination between samples during preparation
3. Contamination of a sample with amplified DNA from previous reaction.

DNA EVIDENCE

- Few cells are sufficient to obtain DNA information to help in the investigation.
- DNA evidence (sample) can be obtained from the scene of crime, from clinical examination of person or from dead bodies.
- Common objects or items that can be helpful to obtain DNA material,[9] found at scene of crime or during autopsy, are mentioned in Table 5.1.

Table 5.1: Common evidentiary material and sources found at scene of crime

Evidence/material	*Sources of DNA*
Weapons	Blood, hair, tissue
Bullet	Blood, tissue
Clothes	Blood, semen, sweat
Toothbrush	Saliva
Used cigarette/butts	Saliva
Used condom	Semen, vaginal cell, penile cell, hairs
Bite mark	Saliva
Finger scrapings/content	Tissue, blood

COLLECTION, PRESERVATION AND FORWARDING OF SAMPLE

Collection, preservation and forwarding of sample for DNA analysis are equally important. Unless the samples are properly collected and preserved, it will not be useful for investigation. The consequences of improper collection and preservation of samples are:

1. If not properly collected, the biological activity of sample may be lost.
2. If improperly packed, cross contamination may occur.
3. If improperly preserved, decomposition and degradation may occur. DNA extraction from degraded sample is difficult and challenging.[10]

Collection and Preservation of Sample

1. Dried blood stains/samples can be lifted from non-porous surface with conventional adhesive tape.
2. Liquid blood: Collect 2–5 ml intravenous blood, place it in clean and sterile test tube. Add four per-cent EDTA as preservative.[11]
3. Semen/vaginal swabs should be preserved in clean and sterile container. In gang rape case, more than two vaginal samples/swabs should be collected and send in separate tubes. In case of delay, vaginal swabs should be stored[12] at 4°C.
4. Whenever swabs from saliva are taken, they should be air-dried. Preferably double swab technique should be used. In this method, initially first wet cotton swab should be taken followed by dry cotton swab.[13]
5. Clothes should be air dried at and packed in paper, never use polythene bag or plastic sheet to wrap. Store at room temperature.
6. In exhumation cases – dry tissues are placed in a sterile container without adding any preservative and sent to laboratory at room temperature.
7. It is possible to use fetal tissue for DNA typing. The optimal sample consists of fetal blood obtained by heart puncture. But this is possible in older fetus. In young fetus, analysis of chorionic villi may provide the fetal pattern without maternal contamination. Other tissue suitable for DNA analysis is – quadriceps muscle or ribs.[14]
8. Alternatively, as such fetus can be sent in normal saline or DMSO (dimethyl sulphoxide) saturated with sodium chloride (NaCl). The jar-containing fetus should be placed in ice box.[12]
9. If fetus is macerated, fetal lungs and brain tissues are more suitable for DNA typing.[14]
10. The samples and preservatives used are summarized in Table 5.2.

Care to be Taken

- Short-term storage (2 weeks) at 25°C – 37°C temperature can cause degradation of DNA extracted from seminal stains. PCR amplification is difficult in such cases.
- While storing and transporting clean paper packets are ideal for trace evidences whereas airtight containers are suitable for soft tissue sample.
- Samples should never be packed in plastic bag (polythene bag) as it retains moisture and moisture may contribute for DNA degradation or at times may help to grow bacteria. Bacterial growth may pose difficulty in DNA analysis.
- Blood for DNA should not be collected immediately from person who has received blood transfusion. The blood can be collected after 4 to 6 month after receiving transfusion.

Table 5.2: Samples and preservatives used

Sample	*Method for collection/packing*	*Preservative*
Blood	- Use clean sterile container - Add recommended preservative - Bring the sample on ice	4% EDTA
Tissue, muscle, skin, organs	Place sample in clean sterile container	Normal saline or Keep tissue as it is in -20°C
Teeth	Air dry, place them in clean and sterile container	No preservative
Scalp hairs with root	Air dry sample, place in clean and sterile container	No preservative
Bone	Air dry, wrap in clean paper	No preservative
Blood stained clothes/ scrapings	Air dry sample, pack in clean paper	No preservative
Semen stains	Air dry clothes and pack in clean paper	No preservative
Vaginal swabs	Air dry, place the swabs in dry, clean and sterile container	No preservative
Vaginal smear	On glass slide, place slides in clean paper packet	No preservative
Vaginal fluid/seminal fluid	Collect in clean and sterile container	Frozen solid[15]
Saliva	Collect in clean and sterile container	Frozen solid[15]
Saliva stain on fabric	Air dry and pack in clean paper	No preservative

REFERENCES

1. Jeffreys AJ, Brookfield JFY, Semenoff R. Positive identification of an immigration test case using human DNA fingerprints. Nature 1985; 317: 818 – 9.
2. Fierro MF. Identification of human remains. In: Spitz WU (ed) Spitz & Fisher's Medicolegal investigation of Death, 3rd edn. 1993. Charlas C Thomas Publisher, USA. 71 – 117.
3. Tirpude BH, Sutay SS, Sheikh N. Crime solving tool – the DNA (a review article). J Mediclegal Assoc Maharashtra 2003; 15: 1 – 7.
4. Bardale R, Dixit PG, Deokar S. Mistaken identity, unfolded: A case report. Milestone 2005; 4:20–22.
5. Haglund WD, Reay DT, Tepper SL. Identification of decomposed human remains by deoxyribonucleic acid (DNA) profiling. J Forensic Sci 1990; 35: 724 – 9.
6. Raina A, Dogra TD, Murty OP. Identification of embalmed tissues using DNA fingerprinting techniques. In: Ajmani ML (Ed) Embalming, Principles and Legal Aspects, 1st edn. 1998. Jaypee Brothers Medical Publishers, New Delhi.
7. Helminen P, Ehnholm C, Lokki ML, Jeffrey A, Peltonen L. Application of DNA fingerprinting to paternity determinations. Lancet 1988; 12: 574 – 6.
8. Pramanik P, Sharma SK, Murty OP. Effect of DNA sample collection, storage and transport on DNA fingerprinting: an overview. Int J Med Toxicol Legal Med 2006; 8: 11 – 3.
9. Vij K, Biswas R. In: Basis of DNA and evidentiary issues, 1st edn. 2004. Jaypee Brothers Medical Publishers (P) Ltd., New Delhi.
10. Lee HC, Ladd CA, Scherezinger CA, Bourke MT. Forensic application of DNA typing. Part 2: collection preservation of DNA evidence. Am J Forensic Med Pathol 1998; 19: 10 – 18.
11. Manual published by Directorate of Forensic Science Laboratories, Home Dept., State of Maharashtra-Mumbai, 2007.
12. Rao GV. Collection and forwarding of forensic samples for DNA fingerprinting. J Indian Acad Forensic Sci 1997; 36: 69 – 73.
13. Sweet D, Lorente M, Lorente JA, Valenzuela A, Villanueva E. An improved method to recover saliva from human skin: the double swab technique. J Forensic Sci 1997; 42: 320 – 2.
14. Ludes BP, Mangin PD, Malicier DJ, Chalumeau AN, Chaumont AJ. Parentage determination on aborted fetal material through deoxyribonucleic acid (DNA) profiling. J Forensic Sci 1991; 36: 1219 – 23.
15. Kagne RN, Ambade VN, Pathak AG. DNA fingerprinting: Collection, preservation and dispatch of biological sample. Souvenir of Formedicon 2004, XIIth Annual Conference of Medicolegal Association of Maharashtra, 2004. 39 – 42.

CHAPTER 6

Medicolegal Autopsy

I will bear in mind always that I am a truth seeker, not a case maker; that is more important to protect the innocent than to convict the guilty.

- Anonymous

Autopsy

Synonyms: Also called as necropsy or postmortem examination

Autopsy means (autos = self, opis = view) to see for oneself. Necropsy (necros = dead, opis = view) is most accurate term for the investigative dissection of the dead body, but the term autopsy is commonly used and is more popular. Postmortem (post = after, mortem = death) examination is an alternative term used but suffers from lack of precision about the extent of examination. In some countries, many bodies are disposed off after external examination without dissection, in such situation; the procedure is called as postmortem examination.[1]

Types of Autopsy

Autopsy may be (Fig. 6.1):

1. Clinical autopsy (pathological autopsy or academic autopsy)
2. Medicolegal autopsy (forensic autopsy)

Clinical Autopsy

- It is done by Medical Practitioner or treating doctor with the consent of relatives to know the diagnosis or to confirm the diagnosis.

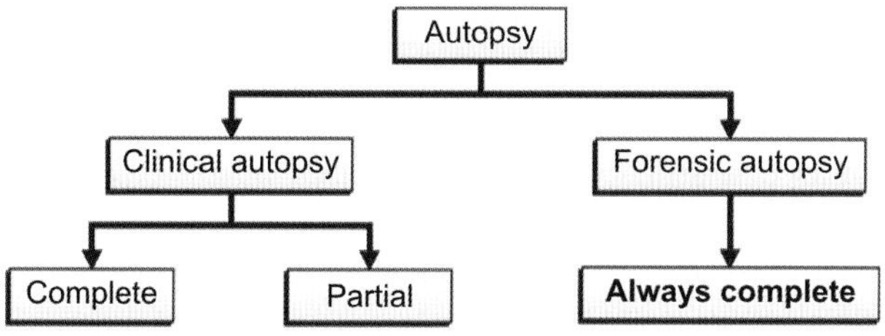

FIG. 6.1: Types of autopsy

- Here the autopsy may be complete or incomplete (partial) depending upon the consent obtained for that part of body.
- It is not done under legal obligation therefore no requisition from police is required.
- For doing clinical autopsy, consent of relatives is must. Without consent, a doctor cannot proceed for clinical autopsy.

Medicolegal Autopsy

- Medicolegal autopsy is a scientific examination of a dead body. It is carried out under the laws of State only on the requisition of a legal authority responsible for the investigation of sudden, suspicious or unnatural death. The legal authority is usually a police officer not below the rank of sub-inspector or an Executive Magistrate.[2, 3]
- Medicolegal autopsy is also called as forensic autopsy. But popular term for layperson remains postmortem examination.
- Differences between medicolegal and clinical autopsy are presented in Table 6.1.

Objectives for Medicolegal Autopsy

1. To determine the cause of death
2. To determine the manner of death
3. To estimate time since death
4. To establish identity of deceased when not known
5. To collect evidences to identify the object causing death and to identify criminal
6. To document injuries and to deduce how the injuries occurred
7. To retain relevant organs/viscera and tissues as evidence
8. In newborn infants – to determine the issues of live birth and viability

Table 6.1: Difference between forensic and clinical autopsy

Features	Forensic autopsy	Clinical autopsy
Synonyms	Also called as postmortem examination or medicolegal autopsy	Also called as pathological autopsy or academic autopsy
Consent	No consent is required	Consent of relatives is must
Conducted	Conducted under legal authority	Not so
Requisition	Requisition from legal authority is necessary	No such requisition is required
Procedure	Autopsy is always complete	The autopsy may be complete or incomplete (partial) depending upon the consent
Aim	- To know cause of death - To ascertain time since death - To know manner of death - To collect evidences etc.	Performed to confirm the clinical diagnosis or to arrive at diagnosis

Rules for Medicolegal Autopsy

- Medicolegal autopsy should be conducted by Registered Medical Practitioner only.
- Medicolegal autopsy should be conducted only on receiving official order (requisition) from the competent authority (i.e. police or magistrate) authorizing to conduct autopsy.
- The autopsy should be conducted at the earliest
- Whenever dead body is sent for medicolegal autopsy, it should be accompanied by a **dead body challan** and an **inquest report**. A dead body challan is a requisition submitted to doctor by investigating officer and contains name, age, sex, address along with probable date and time of death, date and time of examination of dead body. An inquest report is preliminary investigation to ascertain the matter of fact, the details of body, presence of any injury etc.
- The autopsy should be done at authorized center, preferably well-equipped mortuary.
- The doctor-conducting autopsy should carefully read the inquest report and requisition along with treatment record, if available.
- The body should be identified by police accompanying the body
- No unauthorized person should be allowed to be present at autopsy
- Autopsy should be done in daylight because colour changes such as jaundice, changes in contusion, postmortem artefacts, changes in postmortem lividity etc. cannot be appreciated in artificial light.[2, 4]
- Video recording – in case of death occurring in custody, video recording should be done and the video film/tape should be send to the Chairman, National Human Right Commission, New Delhi by doctor himself.
- Visit to scene of crime – if it is possible, visit to scene of crime by doctor should be practiced and is often beneficial and fruitful. Examination of scene of crime, though neglected aspect in India, is important and may provide evidence or clues to the nature and circumstances of crime.

Autopsy Report

Autopsy report consist of following parts

1. Introductory part or preamble – in this part name, age, sex, and residence of deceased is mentioned. The place from where the body was brought, date and time of examination of dead body, mention of authority ordering the examination are included.
2. Examination part – it consists of external examination and internal examination and findings recorded by doctor.
3. Opinion or conclusion – the opinion regarding the cause of death is given. The opinion is deduced from autopsy findings.

Requirements for Autopsy

For conducting autopsy along with well-equipped mortuary, instruments and chemicals are required. They are mentioned as below.

Instruments[5]

1. Scalpel of different size
2. Dissecting knife
3. Dissecting scissors
4. Large scissors
5. Enterotome
6. Saw – hack saw/ Councilman's saw/ Rachiotomy saw
7. Chisel
8. Hammer

9. Bone rongeur
10. Brain knife
11. Cartilage knife
12. Rib shears
13. Probe
14. Needle
15. Autopsy table/ Autopsy workstation.

Chemicals

1. Preservatives – common salt, rectified spirit
2. Fixative – formalin
3. Glycerine
4. Liquid paraffin
5. Sodium fluoride
6. Thymol
7. Potassium oxalate
8. Bottles of various sizes.

AUTOPSY PROCEDURE

It consists of external examination and internal examination.

External Examination

It consists of

1. Examination of clothes for any stains, soiling material, foreign material, any cut marks, tears, stab marks, loss of buttons etc.
2. Identity – in case of known body, police constable accompanying the body should identify body. If feasible, relatives can also be asked to identify the body. In unknown bodies, record identification marks like mole, tattoo, scars, deformity, fingerprint etc. The investigating officer may be requested to have photograph and fingerprints of body.
3. Preliminary particulars
   - Like height, weight, nutritional status, built, gross deformities, patterns of hair, colour of hair, any stains, presence of any foreign body, mud, grease, paint etc. should be noted.
   - Rigor mortis – presence or absence of rigor mortis, its distribution should be noted.
   - Postmortem lividity – regarding appearance, fixed, unfixed, site, colour, disintegrating etc. should be noted
   - Presence or absence of sign of decomposition, extent, presence of maggots, larvae, eggs etc should be recorded
   - Features – whether identifiable, distorted, bloated etc. should be noted
   - Skin and body surface should be search for any dermatological lesion, disease, any stains, foreign body, mud, grease etc. Dermal lesions may be in form of pustules, vesicles, any infections, boils, macular lesion, papule, purpura, bleeding spots, edema, cyanosis etc. should be sought for.
   - Perceive for any odour emitting from body, for example, insecticide like smell, fermentation like, kerosene like, garlicky etc.
   - State of natural orifices such as nose, mouth, ear, anus, vagina, urethra for any disease, injury, foreign body
   - Documentation of injuries – abrasion, contusion, laceration, incised, stab, chop, crush, burn, electrical injury etc. should be look for and properly recorded. The injuries should be described in a sequential manner for example starting from head to toe. The injuries should be noted in accordance with size, site, dimensions, and orientation to the axis of body and relations from the fixed anatomical landmarks. The dimensions should be recorded in metric system. The shape should be described whenever possible. The state of margins, angle and depth of wound along with direction should be recorded with reference to stab wounds.
   - External genitals – examine to know presence of any disease, injury, foreign body, stains, secretions, and any signs of sexual insult.

Internal Examination

Internal examination includes dissection and examination of

1. Cranial cavity
2. Thoracic cavity
3. Abdominal cavity
4. Dissection of spinal cord (when indicated)
5. Dissection of extremities (when indicated)

The question may arise, which cavity should be opened first? The answer is that depending on the requirement and convenience of autopsy surgeon, any cavity can be opened first. However, in fetus, usually abdominal cavity is opened first to record the position of diaphragm.

Incision

Following are the various types of incisions used for autopsy.

A) For Head

Coronal incision – is more preferable and easy type of incision. The incision begins from behind the ear and extends upwards on either side to meet coronally on head (Fig. 6.2).

B) For Trunk[6, 7]

Following are the various types of incisions described. Depending on the need, an autopsy surgeon can use the

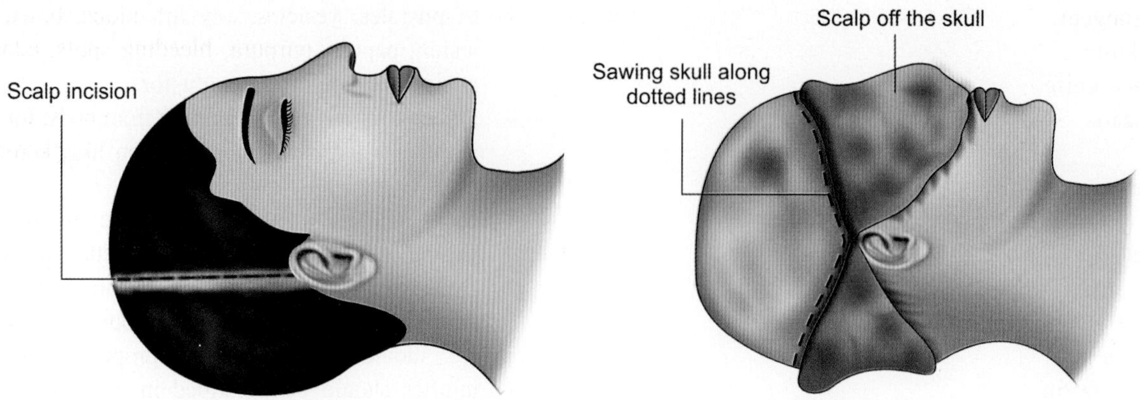

FIG. 6.2: Scalp incision and opening of skull

incision (Fig. 6.3). Table 6.2 describes the advantages and disadvantages of these incisions.

1. I-shaped incision – a straight incision is made from the chin (symphysis mentis) to pubis (symphysis pubis). It is commonest method used.
2. Y-shaped incision – it begins at a point close to acromial process and extends down below the breast and then medially across the xipiod process. A similar incision is made at opposite side of the body and from xipiod process the incision is carried downwards in a straight line to the pubis.
3. Modified Y-shaped incision – a straight incision from sternal notch to pubis is made. Now this incision is extended from suprasternal notch to the mid-point of clavicle and then upwards towards the neck behind ear. Similar incision is made on opposite side.

Autopsy Technique[8]

Following are the autopsy techniques

1. Technique of Virchow
   - In this technique, the organs are removed one by one
   - It is widely practiced and more popular method
   - It is considered as more convenient
2. Technique of Rokitansky
   In this technique, there is partial *in situ* dissection of organs with *en-bloc* removal.

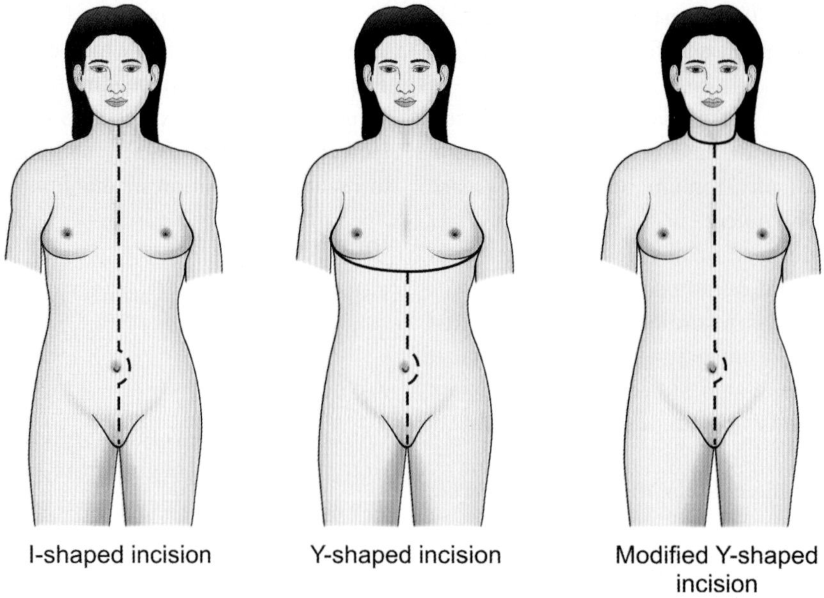

FIG. 6.3: Various types of incision for trunk

Table 6.2: Advantages and disadvantages of various incisions

	I-shaped incision	*Y-shaped incision*	*Modified Y-shaped incision*
Advantages	- Common method - Easy - Fast technique	- More cosmetic - Spares the skin at neck - Axillary and neck regions are easily accessible	- Better exposure of neck region - Faster than Y-shaped technique
Disadvantages	Do not give adequate exposure and access to axillary region and neck organs	- More tedious procedure - Require more time	- More tedious procedure - Require more time - Do not give adequate exposure and access to axillary region

3. Technique of Ghon
   In this technique, thoracic, cervical, abdominal and urogenital system organs are removed separately as organ blocks.
4. Technique to Letulle
   - In this technique, cervical, thoracic, abdominal and pelvic organs are removed *en-masse* and subsequently dissected into organ blocks.
   - This technique is considered as best technique.

Cranial Cavity

- After coronal incision, scalp is reflected
- The skullcap is removed by sawing through the bones. The line of cutting the bone extends horizontally on both sides from about the center of forehead to the base of mastoid process to external occipital protuberance backward.[7]
- The skull vault is examined for any fracture or hematoma
- Dura is examined for any collection of blood, any injury, any disease.
- The superior sagittal sinus is examined for presence of thrombosis
- Brain is examined *in situ* and then dissected out. Note for any injury, disease, or vascular malformation, or aneurysm. The ventricular system should be examined.

Chest and Abdominal Cavity

- The chest and abdominal cavity should be examined for presence of any injury, disease, pathological lesion or collection of blood/fluid
- The organs should be examined for presence of any injury, disease, and pathological lesion. The weight of organs, the size, shape, surface, consistency, cut surface, colour should be noted.

Opening of Spinal Cord

Spine is not routinely opened except for indications. Following are the indications:

1. Injury
2. Disease affecting spinal cord
3. Poisoning – strychnine.

Methods of opening spinal cord[8]

1. Posterior approach - Midline skin incision given over back over spinous process and bilateral laminectomies done with use of saw.
2. Anterior approach.

Preservation of Viscera and Other Articles

In suspected cases of poisoning, viscera has to be preserved. Similarly in violent crimes some evidences has to be preserved. Refer chapter 33 for medicolegal aspects of poisoning and for preservation of viscera and other articles.

LABORATORY INVESTIGATIONS

While conducting autopsy, the autopsy surgeon may need laboratory support for arriving at conclusion and opinion. Following are the usual type of laboratory support required

Toxicology

Refer chapter 33

Histopathology

- For histopathological examination, organ or pieces of organs are preserved in 10% formalin.
- Immunopathologic technique is also being applied to aid in diagnosis.[9]

Microbiology

- Autopsy samples for bacteriological, virological or mycological examination are taken
- Microbiological evaluation is more difficult in postmortem setting than clinical background. Within a postmortem interval of 4 to 6 hours, there is a body-wise redistribution of endogenous flora and becomes more pronounced with lengthening of postmortem interval.[10] However, in few deaths, microbiological evidence may be of immense help if samples are collected properly.
- Blood is taken in sterile syringe from large blood vessel before starting the autopsy. If culture from organ is required, the organ area should be seared to dryness with a flat-faced soldering iron and piece taken. Alternatively, modified print culture technique can be utilized. It consists of cutting the tissue/organ with sterile scalpel and print cultures are made on the agar.[11]
- The microbiological investigation is required in fungal infection, gastroenteritis, meningitis, septic abortion, toxic shock syndrome etc. The Table 6.3 outlines the procedure of collection of specimen for microbiological investigation.

Biochemical

- It is important that when biochemical analysis has to be done, the blood sample obtained at autopsy should be centrifuged and the serum separated as soon as possible. However, if red blood cells are required for analysis such as for investigation of hemoglobinopathies or for the determination of glycated hemoglobin, another sample preferably drawn from peripheral vein should be collected.[12]
- Along with blood, vitreous humor, cerebrospinal fluid, urine, pericardial fluid and synovial fluid can be utilized. Glucose, urea, creatinine, cholesterol, lipoprotein, catecholamine, magnesium, uric acid, proteins etc. can be determined.[13, 14]
- Biochemical tests are used to estimate time since death or to elucidate cause of death.[15, 16]

Enzyme Study

- Enzyme and isozyme are utilized in postmortem state to elucidate cause of death. CK isozymes were evaluated in the pericardial fluid for diagnosing myocardial infarction[17] and enzyme immunoassay for hCG determination in blood stains.[18]
- Enzymes studies are also utilized to estimate postmortem interval.[19]

Molecular Biology

- Certain condition can be diagnosed at postmortem period by utilizing molecular biology. A case report of diagnosis of sickle cell disease was reported by molecular analysis of the β globin gene.[20]

Immunological Study

- Immunological investigation has made inroads in forensic practice recently. The method is mainly used to explicate cause of death.
- Specific meningococcal polysaccharide (CPS) can be detected in postmortem blood by latex agglutination assay.[21]
- Specific IgE can be detected in postmortem sample in case of snakebite cases or wasp/bee envenomation.[22-24]

Table 6.3: Procedure of collection of specimen for microbiological investigation

Specimen	*Method of collection*	*Transportation*
Blood	Collect in bile broth/glucose broth/sterile bottle	Keep in incubator or refrigerator and transport to microbiology lab at the earliest
Pus	5 ml pus in sterile bottle	Keep in fridge or transport immediately to microbiology lab
Stool (feces) for Salmonella, Shigella, Cholera	Sterile bottle/ Carry Blair medium/rectal swab	Transport immediately to microbiology lab
Urogenital	Sterile container/ smear	Send to lab
Gas gangrene tissue specimen	Robertson media/smear on slide	Send to lab
Virological specimen	Collect in sterile container	Transported in vaccine bag with maintaining cold chain

DNA Profiling - Refer Chapter 5 (DNA Profiling)

Radiology

Radiology offers immense help at autopsy for deduction of subtle findings. More often X-rays are used as more sophisticated technique like CT scan, MRI, and Angiography has yet to be available in Indian setup for autopsy procedures. At autopsy, X-rays are used for following purpose:

1. For identification
2. To locate bony injury
3. Battered baby syndrome
4. Suspected fire arm and bomb blast cases
5. Suspected cases of Pneumothorax, barotraumas
6. Mutilated remains
7. For hyoid bone fracture/laryngeal skeleton fracture[25]
8. Air embolism.[26]

Forensic Photography[27]

Photography is important in forensic practice because they can act as evidence and may be produced in the court. The old Chinese saying "*one photograph is worth of thousand words*" hold true. Photography varies from conventional photography to superimposition to ultraviolet and infrared photography. The photograph should be taken from different angles for better understanding.

FETAL AUTOPSY

Objectives

1. To know cause of death
2. To determine whether fetus is live born, dead born or still-born
3. To ascertain viability of fetus
4. To ascertain intrauterine age of fetus
5. To know how long did it survive after birth?
6. To determine the manner of death
7. To estimate time since death
8. To collect material evidences
9. To establish identity of deceased when not known
10. To retain relevant organs/viscera and tissues as evidence.

In addition to adult autopsy, following things required attention while conducting fetal autopsy

- Note signs of maceration/mummification
- Note the state of umbilicus and umbilical cord
- Note the state of placenta, weight, disease,
- Note the length, weight and morphological features of fetus
- Note state of eyes, eyelids, eyelashes, papillary membrane
- Note state of scalp hairs, body hairs (lanugo), nails
- Note the colour of skin, wrinkling, presence of subcutaneous fat
- Note the sex of fetus
- Note for appearance of ossification centers.

Internal Examination

Examination of head
The scalp is reflected by coronal incision as in adults. For opening the skull cap, various methods are advocated such as[8, 28]

1. Beneke's technique (Fig. 6.4) – dotted line indicate incision
2. Baar's technique (Fig. 6.4) – dotted line indicate incision
3. Stowen's technique.

Examination of Chest and Abdomen

- Abdomen is open first to note the position of diaphragm and then chest is opened. Usually, in fetal autopsy, technique described by Letulle is more beneficial. Rest part of examination is same as that of adult.
- Another technique consists of application of technique outlined by MacPherson and Valdes-Dapera (1991) depending on gestational age of fetus. The technique is mentioned below:[29]
  - ⇨ If fetus is less than 12 weeks of gestation or less than 25 gm weight, the fetus may be examined by free-hand sectioning method. It consists of sectioning or cutting the trunk of fetus/embryo into slices of about 1 cm thickness. A dissection microscope may be used to examine the slices where necessary.
  - ⇨ For fetus between 12 to 22 week (or less than 400 gm), a mini-necropsy can be attempted and the organs are removed en bloc.
  - ⇨ For fetus above 22 weeks, full necropsy (routine autopsy) should be done.

Negative Autopsy

An autopsy that fails to reveal a cause of death with gross, microscopic, toxicological and other laboratory investigation is referred as negative autopsy.[30] About 3 to 5 percent autopsies are negative. The causes of negative autopsy are given below.

Causes

1. Inadequate history
2. Lapses in external or internal examination
3. Inadequate sample collection
4. Inadequate laboratory support.

Obscure Autopsy

In obscure type of autopsy, the findings do not lead to definite cause of death. There may be minimal, indefinite or obscure findings and causes confusion to medical examiner.[4]

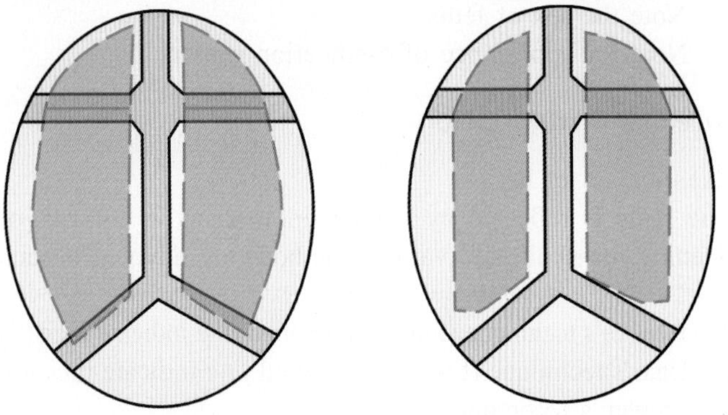

FIG. 6.4: Opening of fetal skull. Dotted lines indicate plane of incision

Causes of Obscure Autopsy

- Death due to endocrine dysfunction
- Vagal inhibition
- Concealed trauma such as concussion, reflex vagal inhibition
- Drug idiosyncrasy
- Biochemical disturbances such as Uraemic coma, hypoglycemia, hypokalemia, hyperkalemia etc.

Examination of Decomposed Bodies

- Autopsy should be done on same line as in other autopsies
- Record the injuries/ligature marks/fracture carefully
- Identify artefact produced by decomposition
- Note presence of any foreign body, mud, sand particles etc. in mouth/respiratory tract
- The necessary viscera and material evidence should be preserved for chemical analysis
- Pay attention to entomological aspects, if feasible
- If body is not identified, preserve appropriate samples *viz.* samples for DNA profiling, skull for superimposition, fingerprint etc.

Examination of Mutilated Bodies

Mutilation may be done:
- By criminals to destroy identity/evidences
- By criminals for convenient disposal of dead body
- May be due to postmortem artefact, e.g. body attacked by wild animals or birds.

Examination
- Ascertain that all parts are of human. Whether the parts belong to one individual or more than one individual?
- All separated parts should be organized together in proper fashion and the nature and character of parts should be recorded
- Manner of separation of parts should be elucidated. Whether injuries are antemortem or postmortem should be tried to make out.
- Identification – try to identify sex, age, race, stature, time since death, cause of death, place of disposal, samples for DNA profiling
- Appropriate viscera, material evidences should be preserved

Examination of Skeletal

Refer Chapter 4 Forensic Osteology.

EXHUMATION

- Exhumation means to dig out corpse from the ground. It is a lawful process of retrieval of previously buried body for postmortem examination.
- The term should be restricted to the removal of a body interred in a legitimate fashion in the graveyard.[1]

Purpose

Exhumation is carried out with following purpose
1. Identification
2. For second autopsy when first autopsy report is doubtful or ambiguous
3. In civil cases – such as for insurance purpose or negligence cases
4. Disputed cause of death
5. Suspected foul play

Authorization for Exhumation

The exhumation is carried out only on receipt of written order from the Executive Magistrate or Judicial Magistrate.

Time Limit for Exhumation

In India, there is no time limit for carrying out exhumation. However, the period of exhumation is restricted in other countries for example it is about 10 years in France and 30 years in Germany.

Procedure

- The procedure of digging out should be carried out under supervision of the Magistrate and in presence of medical examiner and police.
- The grave should be identified properly. The grave is then dig out carefully. The coffin should be identified. The body is lifted out and should be identified by relatives (Figs 6.5 to 6.7).
- The condition of clothes should be noted
- About 500 gm of soil from actual contact of body from above, lateral sides and below should be collected for chemical analysis in suspected poisoning. Similarly soil from control site should be collected.

FIG. 6.5: The exhumation site with grave (arrow)

FIG. 6.6: Body in grave

FIG. 6.7: The exhumed body

- Hairs from head and pubic region should be collected
- The body is shifted for postmortem examination. The autopsy procedure should be carried on same line as that of routine autopsy. Available viscera should be preserved for chemical analysis along with teeth, nails and bone.

POSTMORTEM ARTEFACTS

Postmortem artefact is any change or new feature introduced into the body after death and such feature or change posses' difficulty in interpreting the autopsy findings. The artefacts are physiologically unrelated to the natural state of the body or tissue, or the disease process, to which the body was subjected to before death. Therefore it is important to interpret these artefacts correctly otherwise misinterpretation may lead erroneous diagnosis.

Importance

Ignorance of artefacts or misinterpretation of such postmortem artefacts leads to.

1. Wrong cause of death
2. Wrong manner of death
3. Undue suspicion of criminal interference
4. A halt in the investigation of criminal investigation or unnecessary spending of time and effort as a result of misleading findings
5. Miscarriage of justice.

Classification

Postmortem artefacts are classified as:

1. Encountered during postmortem examination
2. Artefacts of decomposition
3. Third party artefacts
4. Artefacts of environment
5. Other artefacts.

Encountered During Postmortem Examination

- Pinpoint foci of extravasated blood from burst capillaries in areas of intense livor may simulate antemortem petechial hemorrhages
- Edema of conjunctiva, which is common finding after death from compression of the neck, also may occur as a postmortem artefact if the head is maintained in a dependent position
- Artefactual punctate hemorrhages may be misinterpreted that are found beneath the scalp when it is reflected from pericranium. The fine vessels passing from the subcutaneous layer of the scalp into pericranium are full of blood. When scalp is reflected, these vessels get torn and hemorrhages indistinguishable from antemortem ones may be produced.

- Regional or localized flattening of the cerebral convolutions may be a postmortem artefact and commonly found in occipital lobes. This artefact has to be distinguished from generalized flattening of convolutions caused due to cerebral oedema.
- Postmortem hypostasis of internal organs may simulate antemortem contusion
- Banding of esophagus may be seen especially when the tissues are congested. These bands are pale areas in mucosa caused by postmortem hypostasis being prevented from settling down due to regional anatomical architecture and curves of esophagus. These bands may be mistaken for injury.
- Rigor mortis of the heart may simulate concentric hypertrophy of the heart
- Rigor in pylorus of stomach causes it to be unduly firm and contracted.

Artefacts of Decomposition

- Postmortem bloating of body may create a misleading picture of obesity
- Bloody decomposition fluid oozing from mouth and nostrils may be misinterpreted as antemortem bleeding due to trauma
- Diffusion of hemolysed blood into tissues in areas of livor may be difficult to distinguish from genuine bruising in decomposed bodies (Fig. 6.8)
- Fissures or splits formed in the skin due to decomposition may simulate lacerated or incised wound
- Postmortem dilatations and flaccidity of vagina or anus may produce the appearance of sexual assault
- A deep groove may be seen around the neck, if deceased was wearing tight garment/dupatta/ cloth around the neck at the time of death. This groove simulates ligature mark
- Postmortem separation of child's skull suture by putrefaction gases may be misinterpreted as fracture (Figs 6.9 and 6.10)
- Internal hypostasis with hemolysis in meninges may resemble hemorrhage
- The presence of decomposed bloody fluid in chest may be misinterpreted as pleural effusion/hemothorax
- Gas bubbles in blood is an early sign of decomposition. Air in the right side of heart may be mistaken for air embolism
- Bursting of abdomen with protrusion of abdominal contents due to decomposition may be mistaken for abdominal trauma

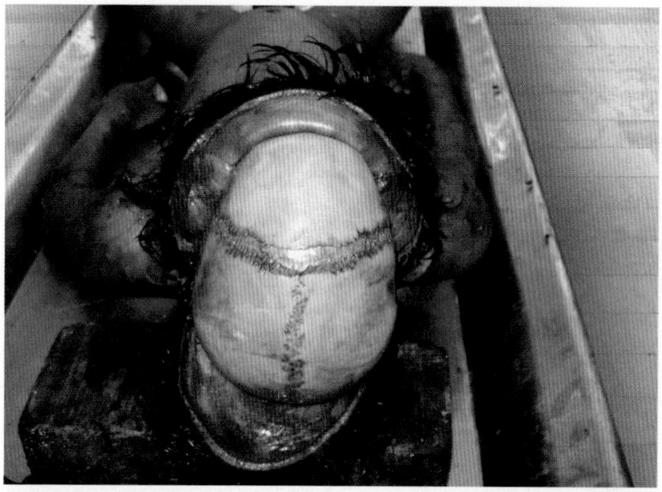

FIG. 6.9: Postmortem separation of skull in a child that may be mistaken for sutural fracture (note features of decomposition along with one fly sitting)

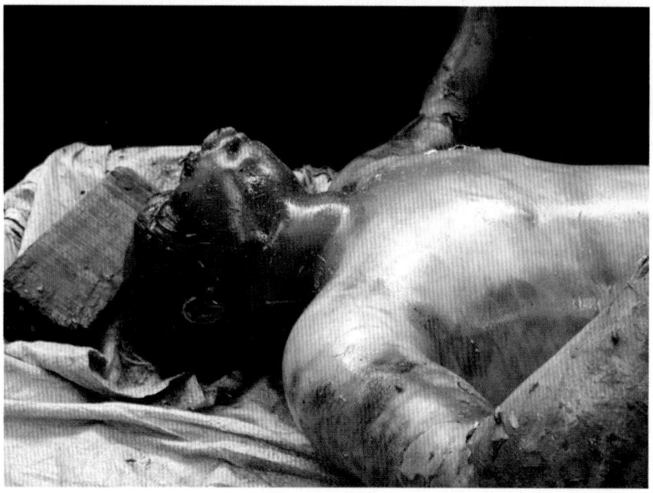

FIG. 6.8: Diffusion of hemolysed blood into tissues in areas of livor may be confused with contusion

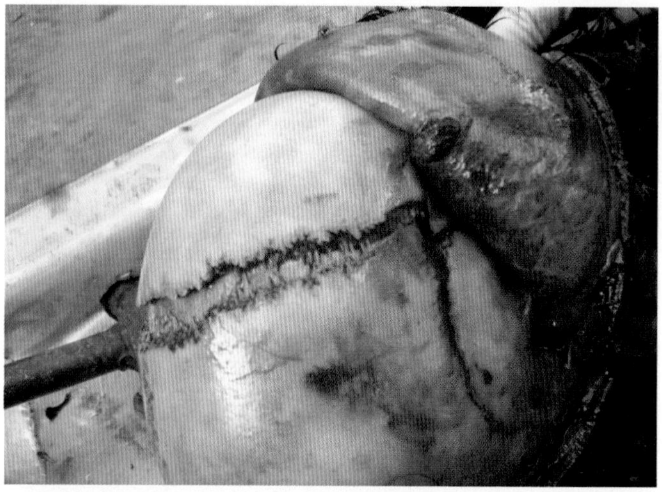

FIG. 6.10: Same case (as shown in Fig 6.9) with lateral view

- Due to postmortem autolysis, a perforation may be noted in stomach (gastromalacia) or in esophagus (esophago-malacia) and this perforation may be misinterpreted as antemortem perforation.
- Focal autolysis in pancreas may be mistaken for Pancreatitis
- Accumulation of blood in the tissues of neck in drowning may simulate antemortem hemorrhage due to strangulation
- Regurgitation and aspiration of gastric contents is a common agonal artefact. It may be mistaken for choking.
- Ethyl alcohol may be produced in decomposed body[31] and up to 0.15% of endogenous alcohol levels were recorded and considered as upper limit.[32] Postmortem production of alcohol has been attributed to bacterial action. Presence of such alcohol may be mistaken for alcohol intoxication.

Third Party Artefacts

A) Animals, birds, insect activity
   - Rodents gnaw away soft tissues of body especially ear, nose, lips etc. They produce shallow craters with irregular border nibbling with leave long grooves and lacks vital reaction (Fig. 6.11)
   - Dogs, cats, vultures bites may mimic puncture like injuries (Figs 6.12 and 6.13)
   - Insect's marks (ants, roaches etc.) resemble abrasion. These marks are dry, brown with irregular margins and are usually seen in moist areas of body such as groin, scrotum, anus, armpits etc. (Fig. 6.14).
   - Bodies recovered from water may show gnawing injuries by aquatic animals.

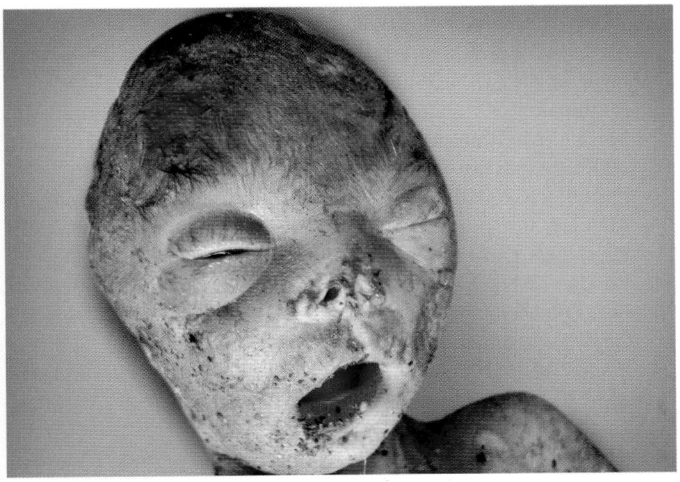

FIG. 6.11: Postmortem injury by rodents may be confused with antemortem injury. Note the location of injury - soft parts - lips and nose

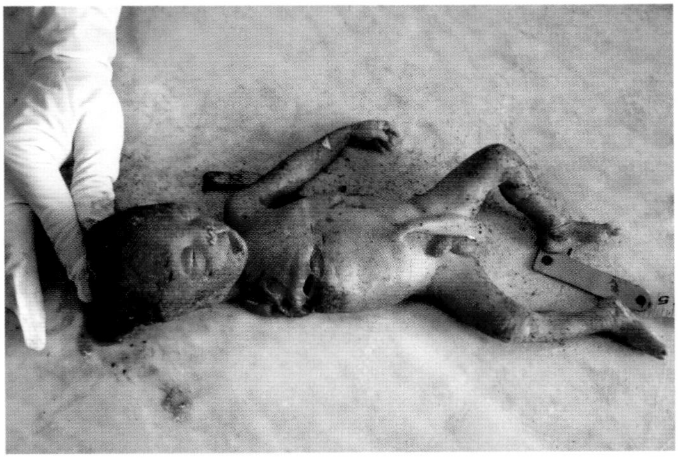

FIG. 6.12: Postmortem destruction by animals like dog, vultures etc. may resemble puncture or puncture lacerations

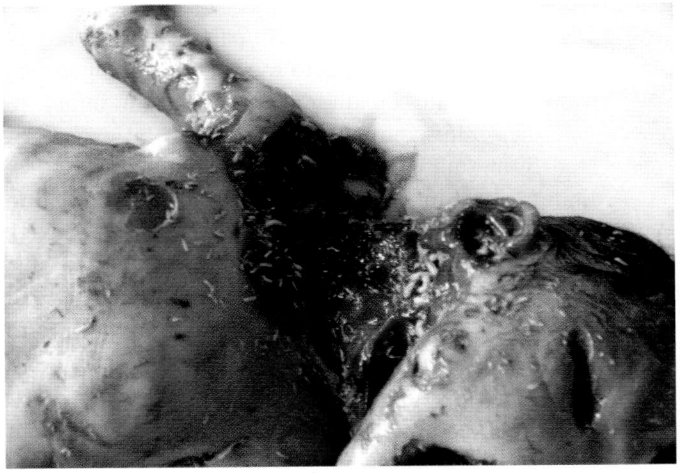

FIG. 6.13: Postmortem destruction by animals may resemble antemortem injuries

   - Flies or maggots may alter the appearance of wound.

B) Emergency medical treatment and surgical intervention
   - External cardiac massage may be associated with fracture of the ribs and rarely fracture of sternum.
   - Resuscitation procedure performed immediately after death may cause pneumothorax as an artefact and this should be differentiated[33]
   - Use of defibrillator may leave impression over chest that may be confused with contusion
   - Intra-cardiac injection given terminally may result in bruised heart and Hemopericardium
   - Investigative procedure like central venous line etc. may result in extravasation of blood in neck

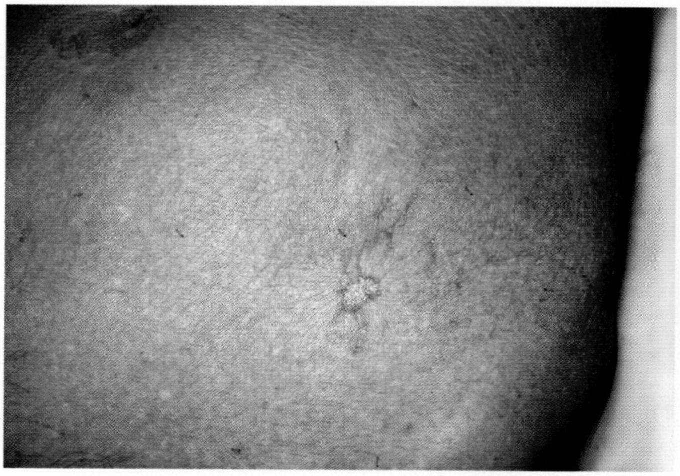

FIG. 6.14: Ant bites may resemble abrasion

muscles that may be confused with strangulation mark over neck
- Damage to mouth/lips/teeth/palate/pharynx/larynx may occur from attempts to introduce a laryngoscope
- Mouth-to-mouth breathing may result in injury to face, neck, lips, gums and that has to be differentiated from smothering
- Endotracheal intubation, positive pressure ventilation or artificial respiration may cause surgical emphysema and Pneumothorax

C) Deliberate mutilation or dismemberment
- A cadaver posses difficulties for disposal due to its size so mutilation or dismemberment may be attempted by criminals
- Sometimes, criminal may inflict injuries after death to mislead the investigations

D) Embalming artefact
- The embalmer may pass a trocar in any of the existing wound or may make a fresh wound for injecting embalming fluid
- Embalming provides chemical stiffening similar to rigor mortis, so difficulty may arise in estimating time since death.
- Embalming destroys cyanide, alcohol, opiates, carbon monoxide thus toxicological analysis becomes useless or difficult.[34]

E) Autopsy surgeon induced artefact
- During the opening of skull, an existing fracture of the skull may become extensive or a fresh fracture may be produced
- While giving incision over neck, the blood may accumulate in neck structures and resemble hemorrhages. These hemorrhages have to be differentiated from antemortem trauma.[35]
- Hyoid bone and thyroid cartilage, particularly in old people, may fracture while separating the neck structures forcefully and may resemble antemortem fracture
- Liver, if pulled apart, instead of being carefully dissected out, may cause tears in the diaphragm and very often causes denudation and laceration in the bare area of liver.

Artefacts by environment
- In burn cases, the subcutaneous fat becomes hard and ruptures. The ruptures may simulate an incised or lacerated wound
- Heat hematomas may simulate extradural hematoma.

Other artefacts
- Postmortem lividity is normally purplish or reddish blue. When body is kept in refrigerator or exposed to cold environment may have pinkish lividity
- Postmortem refrigeration of infant solidifies the subcutaneous fat and produces a prominent crease at neck. It may resemble strangulation mark
- Rough handling of body by undertaker may cause injury or fracture dislocation of C6C7. The fracture, called as undertaker's fracture, may resemble antemortem injury.
- Rigor mortis may be broken by attendants while shifting the body. Assessment of such broken rigor mortis may provide wrong time since death
- Digging tools may cause accidental injuries or fracture to body in exhumation cases.

REFERENCES

1. Pillay VV. Medicolegal autopsy. In: Textbook of Forensic Medicine and Toxicology, 14th edn. 2004. Paras Publishing, Hyderabad. 113 – 38.
2. Mathiharan K, Patnaik AK. Postmortem examination. In: Modi's Medical Jurisprudence and Toxicology, 23rd edn. 2005. LexisNexis Butterworths, New Delhi. 357 – 416.
3. Parikh CK. Medicolegal autopsy. In: Parikh's Textbook of Medical Jurisprudence and Toxicology, 5th edn. 1995. CBS Publishers and Distributors, Bombay. 83 – 116.
4. Reddy KSN. Medicolegal autopsy. In: The Essentials of Forensic Medicine and Toxicology, 22nd edn. 2003. K. Suguna Devi, Hyderabad. 82 – 107.
5. Pryce DM, Ross CF. General introduction. In: Ross's Postmortem appearances, 6th edn. 1963. Oxford University Press, London. 1 – 24.
6. Knight B. In: The coroner's autopsy, 1st edn. 1983. Churchill Livingstone, Edinburgh.
7. Saphir O. In: Autopsy diagnosis and technique, 3rd edn. 1951. Paul B Hoeber Inc., New York.

8. Ludwig J. In: Current methods of autopsy practice, 2nd edn. 1979. W B Saunders Company, Philadelphia.
9. Boonpucknavig V, Boonpucknavig S, Udomsangpetch R, Nitiyanant P. An immunofluorescence study of cerebral malaria. A correlation with histopathology. Arch Pathol Lab Med 1990; 114: 1028 – 34.
10. Rose GW, Hockett RN. The microbiologic evaluation and enumeration of postmortem specimens from human remains. HLS 1971; 8: 75 – 8.
11. Spencer RC. The microbiology of the autopsy. In: Cotton DWK, Cross SS (ed) Hospital Autopsy, 1st Indian edn. 1994. Jaypee Brothers, New Delhi. 144 – 57.
12. Forrest ARW. Toxicological and biochemical analysis. In: Cotton DWK, Cross SS (ed) Hospital autopsy, 1st Indian edn. 1994. Jaypee Brothers, New Delhi. 134 – 143.
13. More SD, Arroyo MC. Biochemical changes of the synovial liquid in corpses with regard to the cause of death. 1: calcium, inorganic phosphorus, glucose, cholesterol, urea nitrogen, uric acid, proteins and albumin. J Forensic Sci 1985; 30: 541 – 6.
14. Coutselinis A, Boukis D. The estimation of $Mg2^+$ concentration in cerebrospinal fluid (CSF) as a method of drowning diagnosis in sea water. Forensic Sci 1976; 7: 109 – 11.
15. Gurumukhi J, Sinha A, Murari A, Sharma GK. Role of pericardial fluid enzymes in estimation of time since death. J Forensic Med Toxicol 2001; 18: 22 – 7.
16. Robert V, Stewart MD. Postmortem diagnosis of myocardial disease by enzyme analysis of pericardial fluid. Am J Clin Pathol 1984; 82: 411 – 7.
17. Luna A, Carmona A, Villanueva E. The postmortem determination of CK isoenzymes in the pericardial fluid in various causes of death. Forensic Sci Int 1983; 22: 23 – 30.
18. Vallejo G. Human chorionic gonadotropin detection by means of enzyme immunoassay: A useful method in forensic pregnancy diagnosis in blood stains. J Forensic Sci 1990; 35: 293 – 300.
19. Gandhi R, Patnaik KA. A study of organ enzyme concentrations in relation to time of death. J Forensic Med Toxicol 1997; 14: 5 – 8.
20. Kutlar F, Mirmov D, Glendenning M, Holley L, Kutlar A. Postmortem molecular diagnosis of sickle β thalassaemia. J Clin Pathol 2005; 58: 548 – 9.
21. Challener RC, Morrissey AM, Jacobs MR. Postmortem diagnosis of meningococcemia by detection of capsular polysaccharides. J Forensic Sci 1988; 33: 336 – 46.
22. Pumphrey RSH, Roberts ISD. Postmortem findings after fatal anaphylactic reactions. J Clin Pathol 2000; 53: 273 – 6.
23. Selvanayagam ZE, Gnanavendhan SG, Ganesh KA, Rajagopal D, Rao PV. ELISA for the detection of venoms from four medically important snakes of India. Toxicon 1999; 37: 757 – 70.
24. Schwartz HJ, Squillace DL, Sher TH, Teigland JD, Yunginger JW. Studies in stinging insect hypersensitivity: postmortem demonstration of antivenom IgE antibody in possible sting-related sudden death. Am J Clin Pathol 1986; 85: 607 – 10.
25. Govindiah D. In: Forensic radiology, 1st edn, 2003. Paras Publishing, Hyderabad.
26. Saliba NA, Maya G. Air embolism during pneumoperitoneum refill. Am Rev Respir Dis 1965; 92: 810 – 12.
27. Murty OP. Forensic photography. Int J Med Toxicol Legal Med 2001; 3: 4 – 12.
28. Saukko P, Knight B. The forensic autopsy. In: Knight's Forensic Pathology, 3rd edn. 2004. Arnold, London. 1 – 51.
29. Variend. Fetal, perinatal and infant autopsies. In: Cotton DWK, Cross SS (ed) Hospital autopsy, 1st Indian edn. 1994. Jaypee Brothers, New Delhi. 99 – 115.
30. Rao NG. Postmortem examination. In: Textbook of Forensic Medicine & Toxicology, 1st edn. 2006. Jaypee Brothers Medical Publishers (P) Ltd., New Delhi. 137 – 56.
31. Gilliland MGF, Bost RO. Alcohol in decomposed bodies. Postmortem synthesis and distribution. J Forensic Sci 1993; 38: 1266 – 74.
32. Corry JEL. Possible sources of ethanol ante and postmortem: It's relationship to the biochemistry and microbiology of decomposition. J Applied Bacteriology 1978; 4: 1 – 56.
33. Leadbetter S, Knight B. Resuscitation artefact. Med Sci Law 1988; 28: 200 – 04.
34. Perper JA. Anatomical considerations. In: Spitz WU (ed) Spitz and Fisher's Medicolegal investigation of Death, 3rd edn. 1993. Charlas C Thomas Publisher, USA. 14 – 49.
35. Prinsloo I, Gordon I. Postmortem dissection artefacts of neck and their differentiation from antemortem bruises. S Afr Med J 1951; 25: 358 – 61.

CHAPTER 7

Death and Changes after Death

In this world nothing can be said to be certain except death.

- Benjamin Franklin

Definition

Death is inevitable! From ages it has been mourned. The process and agony of death has attracted many philosophers, scholars, saints, and literary people to put their views and each one had tried to define death in their own way. With evolution of scientific temperament and development of medical science, attempts were made to define death. **Thanatology** (Greek, thanatos = death, logus = science) *is branch of medical science that deals with the study of death.* Physician's concept of death is total stoppage of circulation of blood with consequent cessation of vital functions. Black's law dictionary (1968 edition) defined death as "the cessation of life, the ceasing to exist, defined by physicians as total stoppage of circulation of blood and cessation of the animal and vital functions consequent thereupon such as respiration, pulsation etc". Shapiro (1969) defines death as "the irreversible loss of the properties of living matter". Rentoul and Smith (1973) defined death as "complete and persistent cessation of respiration and circulation".

All these definitions lay emphasis on the cessation of respiratory and circulatory functions as a parameter to define death and declare a person dead. These definitions are challenged in recent times by two medical advances namely:[1]

1. Advanced resuscitation techniques – such as cardiopulmonary resuscitation (CPR), mouth-to-mouth respiration, cardiac massage, electro-conversion etc. These techniques are capable of effectively reviving many of the patients.
2. Advanced life-sustaining equipment – capable of maintaining blood pressure, circulation and respiration in individuals.

These developments necessitated, in many cases, the obvious revision of the definition of death from just cessation to irreversible cessation of respiration and heart activity. Therefore, in search, another definition of death was proposed, as "death is permanent and irreversible cessation of functions of the three interlinked vital systems of the body namely, the nervous, circulatory and respiratory system".[2] The definition holds that life is sustained on three interlinked vital systems namely - the nervous, circulatory and respiratory system – so called as "**Tripod of life**". It is obvious that all systems would fail if any one of the vital systems fails and that is why these systems are known as "**atria mortis**" i.e. the death's portals of entry.[3] However, this definition is also not considered as complete as it does not recognize the concept of brain death and utility of life-sustaining aid and equipment. Thus, in 1980, a model definition of death was put forth by representatives of the American Bar Association and the National Conference of Commissioners of Uniform State Laws as:[1, 4]

"An individual who has sustained either, (1) irreversible cessation of circulatory and respiratory functions or (2) irreversible cessation of all functions of the entire brain, including the brain stem, is dead".

Features of Model Definition

The features of the above-stated model definition are:

- The definition appears complete and elaborative
- It recognizes the concept of brain death and death by cardio-respiratory arrest
- It acknowledges the concept and utility of life-sustaining aid and equipment.

Statutory Definition

- Section 46 of IPC states that "death denotes the death of a human being unless the contrary appears from the context".
- Section 2 (b) of the Registration of Births and Death Act

1969 defines death as "permanent disappearance of all evidences of life at any time after live birth has taken place".

Medicolegal Implications of Death[5]

1. Declaration of death – declaration of death has importance because wrong declaration of death and shifting the body for cremation/ burial or at mortuary may land the doctor in trouble.
2. Certification of death – a doctor have to certify death of a person and death certificate cannot be issued unless death of the person is confirmed.
3. Disposal of the body – mistake in diagnosis and certification of death may cause difficulty for proper disposal of dead as per religious affiliation.
4. Organ transplantation – cadaveric organs or tissues for transplantation cannot be retrieved from a person unless the person is certified to be dead.
5. Presumption of death – *vide infra*

TYPES OF DEATH

There are two types of death as described below:
1. Somatic death
2. Molecular death

Somatic Death

- Also called as **clinical death** or **systemic death**
- Somatic death is characterized by complete loss of sensibility and the ability to move. There is complete and irreversible cessation of the functions of the circulatory, respiratory and central nervous system the so-called 'tripod of life' that maintains life and health. Thus, somatic death corresponds with physical stoppage of functions of heart, lung and brain. However, individual cells may not die and respond to chemical, thermal or electrical stimuli. For example pupils muscle may contract on application of myotic drug.
- Somatic death indicates demise of a person and it entitles Registered Medical Practitioner to certify that death has occurred.[6] Thus legal definition of death depends upon the diagnosis of somatic death.[7]

Molecular Death

- Also called as **cellular death**
- Molecular death means the death of individual cells of different tissues or organs.
- In absence of circulation and respiration, different cells die their molecular death at different time after somatic death depending upon the metabolic activity and availability of oxygen. Thus after somatic death, cells die in piecemeal process. The white blood cells are capable of movement in circulation up to 12 hours after death[8] and it takes about 1-2 hours for molecular death to occur in muscle.[9]
- In the series of molecular death, death of brain cells occurs earlier than other organs. As a general rule, organs that receive or need more blood supply during life will die early.
- This gap between the somatic and molecular death is important for two reasons as mentioned below:[10]
  1. Disposal of the body – in rare instances, the spontaneous movements of muscle may occur after somatic death and if such movements are witnessed or perceived by laypersons, the event may give rise to apprehension that the person was not actually dead but was prematurely disposed off.
  2. Transplantation purpose – after somatic death, molecular death occurs. In this period between somatic and molecular death, organs from dead body can be retrieved for the purpose of transplantation in other person. Thus this period is useful for cadaveric organ transplantation.

BRAIN DEATH

For applied purpose, brain death is classified into three types:
1. Cortical brain death
2. Brainstem death
3. Whole brain death

Cortical Brain Death

- Also called as **cerebral brain death** or **persistent vegetative state**
- In this condition, clinically patient is in irreversible coma and shows sign of severe brain dysfunction with loss of higher levels of cerebral activity resulted either from:
  1. Hypoxic insult
  2. Traumatic insult or
  3. Toxic insult
- In this condition the person will exist in a vegetative state because brain-stem is intact maintaining respiration and cardiac activity.
- Such vegetative people are not considered dead but because of irreversible loss of awareness, they are considered as "**living cadavers**".
- Disconnection of life support equipment is permissible

following a determination of brain-stem death whereas it is much more problematic in cases of persistent vegetative state.

Brainstem Death

- Practically brainstem death is considered, as death of a person because the vital centers that control respiration, cardiac activity and ascending reticular pathways that awakens are lost irreversibly and permanently. Here the cerebrum may be intact but functionally cut off from the brainstem.
- Diagnosis of brainstem death is based on brainstem death determination. With the advent of the Transplantation of Human Organs Act 1994, brain death is recognized in India. According to this Act, brainstem death is defined as "*brainstem death means the stage at which all functions of the brainstem have permanently and irreversibly ceased and is so certified*".

Whole Brain Death

- Also called as **mixed brain death**
- It consists of combination of both cortical and brainstem death.
- Brain death occurs in steps and the cells die because of anoxia. The first part of the brain to die is the cerebral cortex followed by midbrain and brainstem.

Importance of Determination of Brain Death

The practical medicolegal implications accorded to the determination of brain death are:

1. The earliest determination of brain death for prompt harvesting of organs for transplantation purpose.
2. The legality of discontinuation of life supporting equipment.
3. The determination of the time of death in criminal and civil litigation.

Determination of Brainstem Death

Brain death determination is done, in India, in accordance with the provisions laid down in the Transplantation of Human Organs Act 1994 and is certified by board of medical experts consisting of following:[11]

1. The Registered Medical Practitioner (RMP), in-charge of the hospital in which brainstem death has occurred.
2. An independent RMP, being a specialist, to be nominated by the RMP in-charge of the hospital from panel of names approved by the appropriate authority.
3. A neurologist or a neurosurgeon to be nominated by the RMP in-charge of the hospital from the panel of names approved by the appropriate authority.
4. The RMP treating the person whose brain-stem death has occurred.

Conditions

Diagnosis of brainstem death depends on the following conditions:

1. The patient must be in deep coma and the cause of coma is "irreversible structural brainstem damage" (i.e. prolonged hypoxia, trauma, illness or toxic insult) must be established.
2. Exclusion of the other causes of coma – *vide infra*
3. Demonstrating the absence of brainstem reflexes
4. No spontaneous respiration
5. The brain-dead person must be examined by board of medical experts twice at an interval of six hours
6. The brain-death certificate has to be signed by all the member of board

Following are the causes of coma that must be excluded:

- Hypothermia (core body temperature < 90° F or 32.2° C).
- Central nervous system depressant drugs such as barbiturates, benzodiazepines etc. overdose/poisoning
- Metabolic or endocrine disturbances[12]
- Intoxication (alcohol).

Brainstem Reflexes

Structural and functional damage of brain stem death should be assessed from the absence of following brainstem reflexes. Table 7.1 displays the reflexes and the cranial nerve.

1. Absence of pupillary response
2. Absence of corneal reflex

Table 7.1: Reflexes and the cranial nerves

Reflex	*Cranial nerve*	*In brainstem death*
Pupillary	Afferent - 2nd Efferent - 3rd	No response
Corneal	Afferent - 5th Efferent - 7th	No response
Vestibulo-ocular	Afferent - 8th Efferent - 3rd and 6th	No response
Grimace	Afferent - 5th Efferent - 7th	No response
Gag/cough	Afferent - 9th Efferent - 10th	No response

3. Absence of vestibulo-ocular reflex (caloric response)
4. Absence of grimace
5. Absence of cough/gag reflex
6. Absence of cranial motor nerve response to painful stimuli
7. Absence of spontaneous respiration.

Errors in Diagnosis of Death

Usually no difficulty arises in the diagnosis of somatic death but in certain cases error may occur due to feeble heart sounds or breathing movements. Similarly errors may arise if clinical examination is not done properly. Following are the conditions in which difficulty may arise or error may occur.

1. Case of apparent death
2. Hypothermia
3. CNS depressants, e.g. barbiturate poisoning
4. Metabolic and endocrine disturbances.

DEATH CERTIFICATE

For ensuring national and international comparability, it is necessary to have a uniform and standardized system of recording and certifying deaths. For the same purpose, we are using the death certificate recommended by WHO. The death certificate consists of two parts. **Part I** deals with the immediate cause and the underlying cause of death whereas **Part II** deals with other significant conditions or disease contributed to the process of death but did not lead to it.

- In part I of the death certificate, only one cause is to be entered on each line. Immediate cause of death is reported in line (a). The mode of death such as respiratory failure, heart failure etc. should not be mentioned.
- Line (b): If the condition on line (a) was the consequence of another condition then this condition is recorded in line (b).
- Line (c): Here antecedent cause of death should be recorded.

Cause of death – Refers to the disease or injury responsible for starting the chain of events, brief or prolonged, which produces death.

Cause of death may be divided into:

1. Immediate cause of death
2. Basic or antecedent or underlying cause of death
3. Contributory cause of death

Immediate cause of death – is the immediate or terminal event leading to death.

Basic cause of death/ antecedent cause of death/ underlying cause of death – refers to pathological process or injury responsible for the death. Thus it is a disease or injury that has initiated the train of morbid events leading directly to death or it is the circumstances of the accident or violence that produced the fatal injury.[13]

Contributory cause of death – refers to pathological process involved in or complicating or contributing to the death process but does not directly causes the death.

Mechanism of death – refers to the physiological or biochemical disturbance produced by the cause of death, which is incompatible with life.

Agonal period – is the time between a lethal occurrence and death.

Importance

1. Death of a person is certified
2. To know the cause of death
3. To know time of death
4. To know the manner of death
5. To know mode of death
6. Whether death is associated with pregnancy or pregnancy causes death
7. Was there delivery? Was it causes death?
8. Other significant conditions contributing to cause of death but not related to the disease or conditions causing it
9. Registration at local bodies – *viz.* Gram Panchyat/Municipality/ Municipal corporation.

Uses

1. For disposal of body – cremation/burial
2. For statistical purpose – mortality rate, age, sex etc.
3. For pension/insurance purpose
4. For inheritance/succession of property/legal heir
5. For service at place of father etc.

Salient Points

- According to the Registration of Birth and Death Act 1969 – it shall be duty of Registered Medical Practitioner or Medical officer, in-charge of the hospital to give information to the Registrar in respects of births and deaths occurring in a hospital [Section 8 (b)].[14]
- Certifying cause of death – the Registered Medical Practitioner shall, after the death of a person, issue death certificate without charging any fee [Section 10(3)].
- Any Registered Medical Practitioner who neglects or refuses to issue a certificate under subsection 3 of Section

10 of the Registration of Birth and Death Act 1969 shall be punished with fine which may extend to fifty rupees [Section 23(3)].

APPARENT DEATH

Apparent death is also called as suspended animation. It is defined as "*a state of body in which the vital functions are at such a low pitch that the body functions cannot be determined by ordinary methods of clinical examination*". In suspended animation, a person may last for few seconds to half an hour or more. In this condition, actually, the circulation, respiration etc. do not completely stop but is being maintained in their minimum. The causes of suspended death are mentioned in Table 7.2. Prompt resuscitation can revive the state. Apparent death is of two types as:

1. Voluntary suspended animation – here the person practiced it voluntarily for example yogis or 'sadhus' or 'sanyasi' may practice this method.
2. Involuntary suspended animation – here the person lands in apparent death spontaneously.

Presumption of Death

- Section 107 and 108 of IEA deals with presumption of death
- Presumption of death has importance in connection with inheritance or succession of property, divorce, re-marriage etc. in a missing person for a long period.
- Sec 107 of IEA – **Burden of proving death of person known to have been alive within thirty years** – when the question is whether a man is alive or dead, and it is shown that he was alive within thirty years, the burden of proving that he is dead is on the person who affirms it.

Table 7.2: Causes of suspended animation
Yogi
Trance
Cataplexy
Hysteria
Sunstroke
Concussion
Drowning
Electrocution
Frozen coma
Narcotics poisoning
Anesthesia

- Sec 108 of IEA – **Burden of proving that person is alive who has not been heard of for seven years** – provided that when the question is whether a man is alive or dead, and it is proved that he has not been heard of for seven years by those who would naturally have heard of him if he had been alive, the burden of proving that he is alive is shifted to the person who affirms it.
- In other words, section 107 of IEA presumes a person to be alive unless the contrary is proved by the person who claims him to be dead. Section 108 of IEA presumes, under certain conditions, that a person in question is dead; if it is proved that the said person has not been heard for 7 years by them who are expected to hear about him.

Presumption of Survivorship

- The question of presumption of survivorship may arise in connection with the inheritance or distribution of property when two or more persons, natural heirs of each other; loose their lives in a common disaster such as motor accident, aircraft crash, earthquake, shipwreck, battle etc. In such incidents, it has to be decided who died first (in other words who survived for longer time – presumption of survivorship).
- The law of India does not recognize any presumption regarding the probabilities of survivorship among the persons whose death was occasioned by one and the same cause and under such circumstances the Courts may decide in establishing the survivorship after examining the available facts and evidence.
- In absence of such evidence, following factors may be taken into consideration in determining the question of survivorship.
    1. Injury: What type of injury sustained and whether death by such injury may be instantaneous or may be prolonged etc.
    2. Age: What was the age of deceased who died in the same incident for example children may succumb to trauma earlier than adult etc.
    3. Sex: What was the sex of the deceased who died in the same incident for example female may succumb to trauma earlier than male etc.
    4. Built: What was the built of the deceased who died in the same incident for example thin built person may succumb to trauma earlier than strong built etc.

MODES OF DEATH

Synonym: Proximate cause of death.

Definition

The mode of death refers to "*an abnormal physiological state that pertained at the time of death*".

In all kinds of death, whether natural or unnatural, there are three modes of death and **Bichat** had classified them as (Fig. 7.1): (mnemonic – SAC – S = syncope, A = asphyxia, C = coma)

1. Coma
2. Asphyxia
3. Syncope

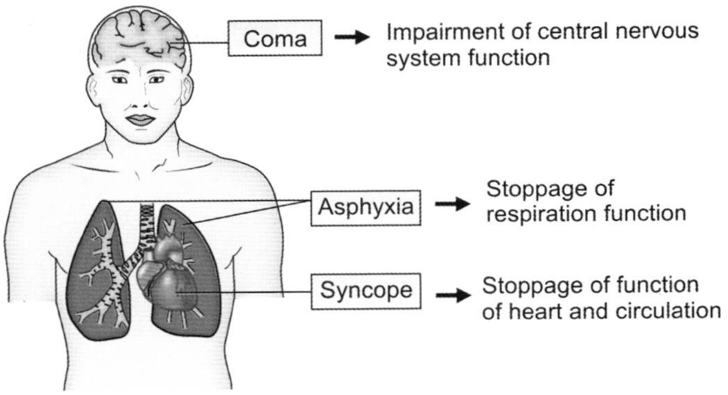

FIG. 7.1: Showing modes of death

Coma

- Coma refers to unconscious state of a person characterized by complete insensibility or unarousability. The unconsciousness is complete without any response to any sort of stimuli.
- When the patient is partially conscious and responds to deep and painful stimuli, it is termed as stupor.
- The causes of coma are presented in Table 7.3.

Syncope

- Syncope results from stoppage of functioning of heart with consequent cessation of circulation.
- In syncope there occurs loss of consciousness with postural collapse due to an acute decrease in cerebral blood flow.
- The causes of syncope are mentioned in Table 7.4.

Asphyxia

- Adelson[15] defined asphyxia, as "a state in living organism in which there is acute lack of oxygen available for cell metabolism associated with inability of body to eliminate excess of carbon dioxide".
- Causes of asphyxia are mentioned in Table 7.5

MANNER OF DEATH

Definition

Manner of death refers to *the way (or design/fashion) in which the cause of death comes into being.*

Accordingly manner of death is classified as (Fig. 7.2):

1. Natural
2. Unnatural – further classified as
   - Homicide
   - Suicide
   - Accident

Table 7.3: Causes of coma
Head injury
Intracranial hemorrhage
Encephalitis
Meningitis
Diabetic ketoacidosis
Uraemic coma
Hepatic encephalopathy
Apoplexy
Opium/barbiturate poisoning
Alcohol intoxication
Epilepsy
Heat stroke

Table 7.4: Causes of syncope
Vagal inhibition
Massive myocardial infarction
Aortic stenosis
Pulmonary stenosis
Pulmonary hypertension
Pulmonary embolism
Cardiac tamponade
Atrial myxoma
Anemia
Blow on epigastrium

Table 7.5: Causes of asphyxia
Mechanical causes
Hanging
Strangulation
Throttling
Smothering
Drowning
Choking
Compression over chest
Toxic causes
Opium poisoning
Carbon monoxide poisoning
Cyanide poisoning
Pathological causes
Acute oedema of glottis
Consolidation
Pleural effusion
Environmental causes
High altitude
Person trapped in well
Respiration in enclosed space

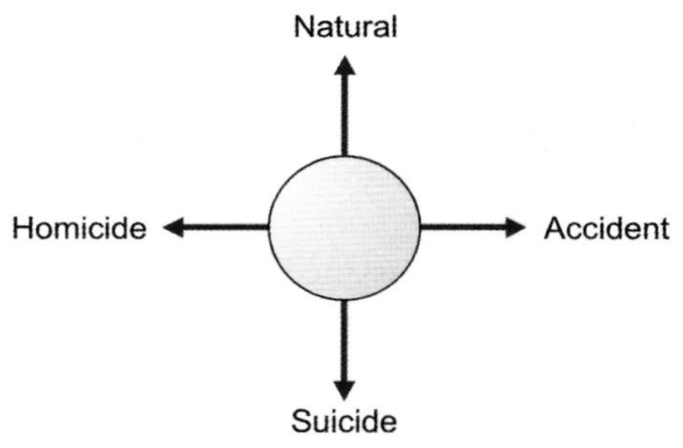

FIG. 7.2: Showing manner of death

(Mnemonic – SHAN – S = suicide, H = homicide, A = accident, N = natural)

CHANGES AFTER DEATH

Following death, numerous physical and chemical changes occur that ultimately leads to disintegration of body. The importance of these changes is related primarily to their sequential nature that can be utilized to estimate the time since death. Amongst these changes, some changes are related to somatic death and some are related with molecular death, therefore some changes appear immediately after death, some changes occur early whereas some changes appear late. The changes are as mentioned below. The correlation of these changes with type of death is mentioned in Table 7.6.

A. **Immediate changes after death**
   1. Stoppage of function of nervous system
   2. Stoppage of respiration
   3. Stoppage of circulation

B. **Early changes after death**
   1. Changes in eye
   2. Changes in skin
   3. Cooling of body
   4. Postmortem lividity
   5. Rigor mortis and changes in muscle
   6. Changes in body fluid

C. **Late changes after death**
   1. Putrefaction or decomposition
   2. Adipocere
   3. Mummification

IMMEDIATE CHANGES AFTER DEATH

Stoppage of Function of Nervous System

With somatic death all functions of nervous system ceases. The subject is insensible with loss of sensory and motor functions. There is loss of reflexes with flaccid muscle. The pupils are widely fixed and dilated and not reacting to the light. The diagnostic tests for confirmation of brain death are dealt above in section on brain death.

Stoppage of Respiration

With somatic death, there is entire and permanent cessation of respiration. The clinical examination and tests to establish cessation of respiration are mentioned below.

1. Inspection – no respiratory movements will be visible
2. Palpation – respiratory movements cannot be appreciated
3. Auscultation – no breath sound can be heard from any part of either lung
4. Tests – following are the tests (some tests are obsolete but briefed only for historical importance)

Table 7.6: Correlation between changes after death and type of death

Changes after death	*Type of death*
Immediate change after death	Somatic death
Early changes after death	Molecular death
Late changes after death	Molecular death

- Feather test – if feather is held in front of nose, no movement of feather will be noted if a person is dead.
- Mirror test – if the surface of mirror is held in front of mouth and nostrils, the surface gets dense due to condensation of warm and moist air exhaled from lungs. The phenomenon suggests on-going respiration and indicates person is alive.
- Winslow's test – a small bowl with water is placed over the chest of the person with arrangement of some light rays falling on the surface of water in the bowl. If the person is respiring then due to respiration his chest will move and slightest movement of chest wall will disturb the plain surface of water in bowl and that can be viewed as the rays of light reflected from the surface of water.

Stoppage of Circulation

With somatic death, the function of heart will cease with consequent cessation of circulation. The clinical examination and tests to establish cessation of cardiac activity are mentioned below.

1. Palpation – radial, brachial, femoral and carotid pulsation will be absent due to cessation of circulation
2. Auscultation – the whole pericardial area is ausculted for presence or absence of heart sounds. The auscultation should be done for at least one minute and repeated at short intervals if necessary. The conditions in which heart sounds are not easily audible are presented in Table 7.7.
3. Tests – following are the tests (some tests are obsolete but briefed only for historical purpose)
   - Diaphanous test – if in a dark room the outstretched hand is held against some bright light source then in presence of circulation, the hand will appear pinkish and translucent. If circulation has stopped then the hand will appear yellowish and opaque.
   - Magnus test – if a ligature is applied on a finger sufficiently to occlude superficial veins but not the deeper arteries then in case of continuing circulation, the finger distal to ligature will be swollen and appear bluish due to venous obstruction and accumulation of deoxygenated blood. If circulation has stopped then no such change will be evident.
   - Icard's test – in this test, 1 ml of 20% alkaline dye fluorescence solution is injected either in the dermis or subcutaneous tissue. In case of continuing circulation, the solution injected in the dermis spread locally at the site of injection whereas in case of subcutaneous tissue injection, the dye will travel to the farther part of body and even yellowish discolouration may appear in conjunctiva.
   - Pressure test – in case of continuing circulation, if pressure is applied over the nail of finger then the area of nail becomes pale but soon becomes red on relieving pressure. No such phenomenon is observed in dead persons.
   - Cut test – in case of continuing circulation, if small artery is cut, the blood will flow in jerky fashion under pressure. No such phenomenon is observed in dead person.
   - Heat test – in case of continuing circulation, if heat is applied to skin then there will be formation of blister and line of redness. No such phenomenon is observed in dead persons.
   - ECG tracing – in dead person, ECG tracing will reveal flat line i.e. suggestive of no cardiac activity

Table 7.7: Conditions where heart sounds are feeble

Causes
Feeble circulation
Excessive deposition of fat
Pericardial effusion

EARLY CHANGES AFTER DEATH

Early signs of death denotes onset of molecular death. The early changes of death are mentioned below.

Changes in the Eye

1. Loss of reflex – soon after death, eye loses its luster with loss of corneal and pupillary reflexes (Fig. 7.3).
2. Loss of muscle tone – after death due to loss of muscle tone, eyelids are usually closed.
3. Cornea – after death there occurs drying and desiccation of cornea with deposition of dust if eye remains open. With ongoing process, initially cornea becomes partially hazy and subsequently becomes hazy after 10 to 12 hours after death. Increase in atmospheric humidity and temperature are known to hasten the process but may be delayed if eye remains closed. The process of haziness may hasten in death due to uremia, narcotic poisoning and cholera whereas it is delayed in death due to apoplexy and poisoning by hydrocyanic acid or carbon monoxide poisoning. With the onset of decomposition, the cornea becomes opaque.

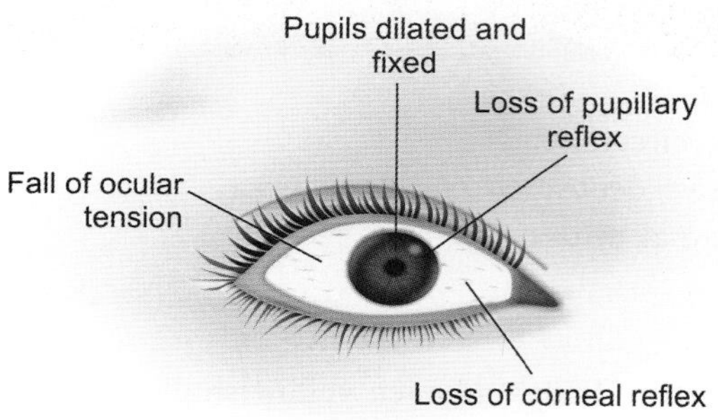

FIG. 7.3: Changes in eye after death

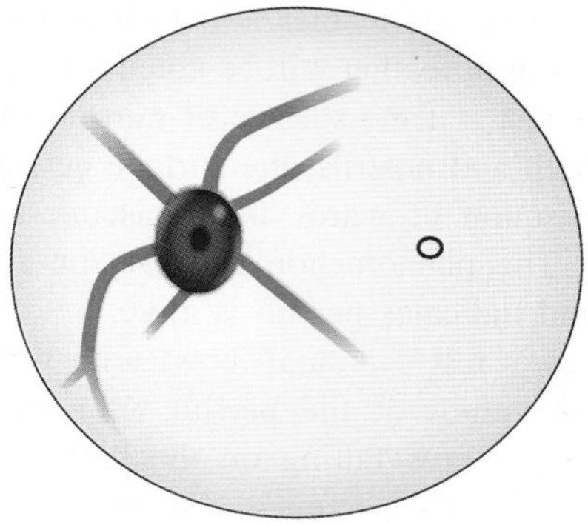

FIG. 7.5: Fundus showing phenomenon of trucking

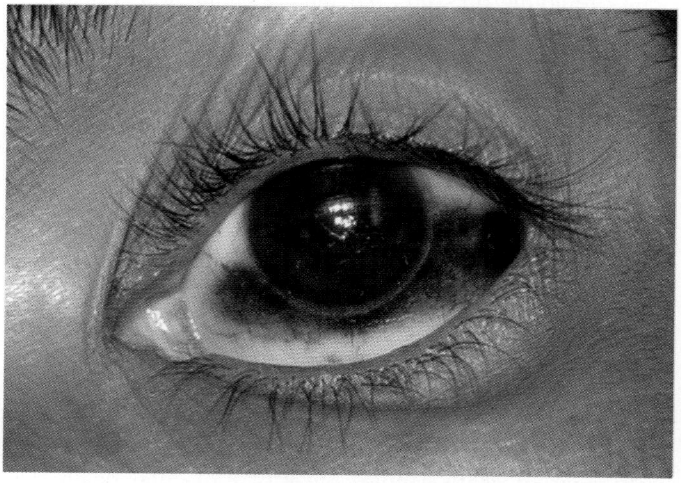

FIG. 7.4: Tache Norie sclerotiques

4. Tache Norie sclerotiques – this sort of change is seen in sclera when eye remains open. It developed because of drying and desiccation of the conjunctiva and sclera and appears as blackish brown discolouration. The phenomenon may be mistaken for contusion. These discoloured areas appear as a triangular patch with base on the limbus and the apex pointed towards medial or lateral canthus (Fig. 7.3). Two such triangular areas appear on both side of cornea. Within 2-3 hours, the exposed white part of eyeball becomes yellowish and within 8-10 hours it becomes blackish brown (Fig. 7.4).
5. Loss of ocular tension – ocular tension falls rapidly after death and within about two hours it becomes zero. Thus eye look sunken after death. The normal intra-ocular pressure[16] varies from 16 to 23 mm of Hg.
6. Pupil – the shape of pupil in life is circular but after death the shape may change due to loss of tone and elasticity of ciliary muscles. After death the pupils are fixed and widely dilated and do not react to light. However, in India, up to 4 hours after death, the pupils may react to myotic (4% pilocarpine) or mydriatic (1% tropicamide) drugs if installed in eyes.[17]
7. Retina and choroid plexus – the changes occurring are as follows:[18-20]
   - Immediately after death, on fundoscopic examination, there is evidence of arrest of capillary circulation with retinal veins appear segmented (blood in retinal vessel break up into segments – the phenomenon is known as '**trucking**') with settling of red blood cells in a rouleaux or boxcar pattern (Fig. 7.5).
   - For about 2 hours after death, retina appears pale and the area around the optic disc looks yellowish. The normal mottled appearance of choroidal plexus is retained till this period.
   - By about 3 hours, the mottled appearance of choroid plexus gradually becomes hazy
   - By about 5 hours, the mottled appearance of choroid disappears completely with homogenous appearance of the eye background.
   - By 6 hours after death, the optic disc outline becomes hazy and the smaller vessels are not recognized however larger vessels can be identified.
   - By 12 hours after death, the area of the optic disc can be known only by some convergent segmental vessels. After this duration, nothing in the retina can be recognized except a dark brown spot representing the macula.
8. Biochemical changes – following are biochemical changes observed in the vitreous humor of eye.
   - The normal antemortem concentration of potassium in vitreous humor in human eye is 2.6 to 4.2

mEq/L. There is linear rise in vitreous potassium with advancing time since death.[21]
- Vitreous transaminase (SGOT) estimation shows steady rise in the vitreous fluid as the postmortem interval increases.[17]

Changes in the Skin

- Skin becomes pale due to draining of blood from blood vessels of the skin.
- Skin looses its elasticity with loss of skin creases and the person may appear young
- Contact flattening and pallor – during the primary relaxation of muscle of the body, the areas that remain in contact with the ground become flat and due to contact pressure, the blood from the vessels under the skin surface is squeezed out resulting in flat and pale surface known as contact flattening and pallor.
- Cutis anserina may be observed.

COOLING OF BODY

Synonym: Algor mortis (algor = coldness, mortis = after death)

Normal oral temperature in living individual is 37°C (98.6°F) whereas rectal temperature is about 0.5°C higher than oral temperature[22]. After death, temperature of the body decreases progressively until it reaches the ambient temperature. The fall of temperature from the dead body is due to following two reasons:
- After death there is no heat generation due to loss of all physical, chemical and metabolic activity
- There is constant loss of body heat until it comes to the level of the environmental temperature, as the heat-regulating center gets inactive due to death.

Loss of body heat occurs from the surface by three mechanisms as:
1. Conduction – here transfer of heat occurs by direct contact with nearby object. Internal organs cool by conduction.
2. Convection – here transfer of heat occurs through moving air currents adjacent to the body
3. Radiation – here transfer of heat from body occurs to the surrounding by infrared rays.

Newton's Law and Explanation

Newton's law states that "*loss of heat from a body is directly proportional to the temperature difference between the surface of the body and the surrounding at a given time*". This Newton's hypothesis cannot be applied to cadaver because cadaver is composed of different material such as skin, fat, muscle, protein, fluid, mineral, bone etc. Thus there is qualitative difference between the surface of the cadaver and the inner core of the body. All these components may not cool in a same fashion. In contrast to cadaver, what Newton had suggested for the fall of temperature is with reference to an inert body with no such qualitative difference in its composition, especially between the surface and inner core. Therefore, Newton's law hold good for fall of temperature in an inert body but it cannot be applied to cadaver. This brings a different rate of fall of rate of temperature of different body parts (Fig. 7.6). Previously it was thought that, others factors remaining constant, the rate of fall of the cadaver body temperature is same all along after death starting from the moment of death. This would give a simple (exponential) curve for hourly fall of body temperature (Fig. 7.7). But practically, such thing does not happen. After death, the surface (outer core) temperature falls rapidly for some time but at the same period the loss of heat from the depth (inner core of cadaver) of the body is negligible. This is due to insulation provided by skin, fat and subcutaneous tissue. Some hours after death, when there is reasonable fall of surface temperature, a constant rate of flow of heat from the inner core of body establishes and then the fall of temperature of inner core of body achieves a regular and constant pattern. Thus, if we take into consideration of the rate of fall of the inner core temperature of the body, we get actually a simple (exponential) curve for this fall of temperature. But when we take into consideration the fall of surface temperature and inner core body temperature, we get a "sigmoid" or inverted "S" shaped curve with a plateau at the beginning and at the end of cooling process (Fig. 7.8). The initial plateau usually lasts for 3 to 4 hours and indicates loss of surface body temperature with practically no loss of heat or fall of inner core body temperature. Then after the initial plateau, there is sharp fall of temperature for about 9 to 12 hours and indicate loss of heat or fall of inner core body temperature. After this period, the rate of fall of inner core body temperature diminishes and by that time it becomes at the level of environmental temperature.

Recording of Temperature

Temperature in cadaver is recorded at following sites. The chemical thermometer is used to record the temperature. The thermometer is about 25 cm in length with graduation ranging from 0°C to 50°C.
- Rectum – 4 inches above the anus
- Sub-hepatic region

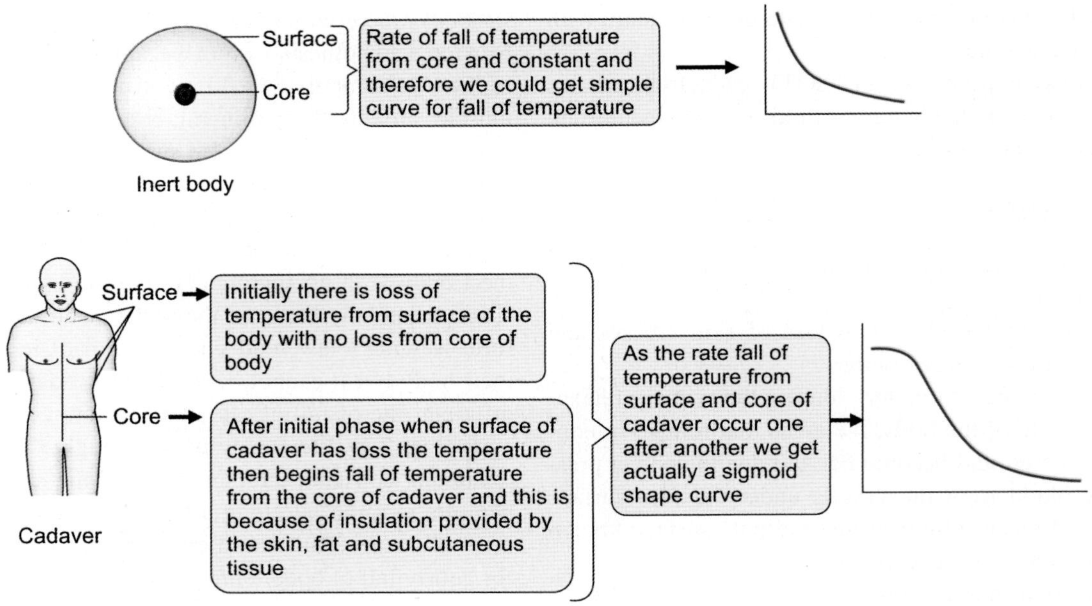

FIG. 7.6: Diagrammatic representation to show difference between rate of fall of temperature in an inert body and a cadaver

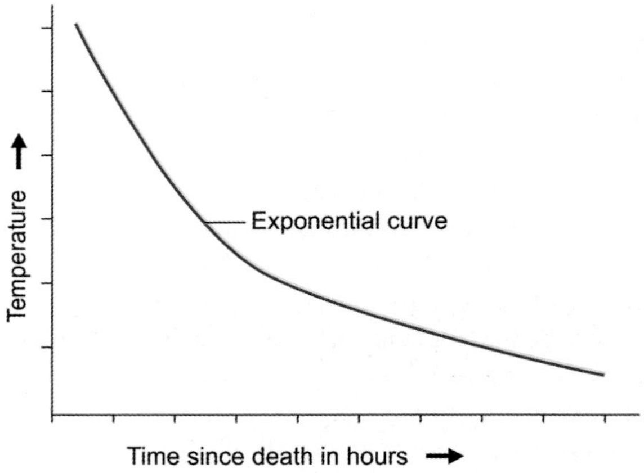

FIG. 7.7: Simple (exponential) curve for fall of body temperature

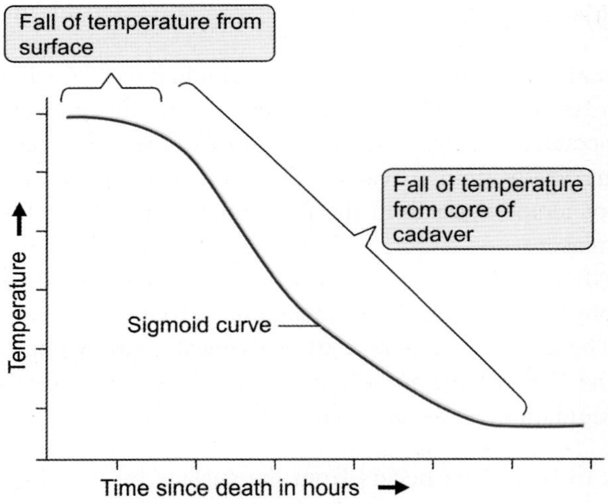

FIG. 7.8: Sigmoid shape curve

Practical Utility

Hourly recording of body temperature is more valuable for the purpose of determination of time since death. Estimation of postmortem interval by this means is more fruitful in cold or temperate countries where difference between the body temperature and environment is quite reasonable. In tropical countries like India such parameter is hardly of any utility where ambient environmental temperature exceeds that of body temperature especially in summer days; still can be practiced in other parts of season. While calculating death interval in temperate countries, Marshall and Hore formula is applicable with reasonable satisfaction but the same cannot be true with tropical countries like India except in some hilly region. For the rest part of India, the rate of fall of body temperature is taken on an average to be about 0.4°C to 0.7°C.

Factors Affecting the Cooling of Body

Various factors affect the cooling of dead body and may affect the reading and in turn the estimation of time since death may be affected. These factors are discussed as below.

1. Atmosphere temperature – if there is difference between the atmosphere and the body then cooling of body occurs in fashion as described above.
2. Media of disposal – the rate of cooling of dead body differs according to the media of disposal - whether disposed in water, air or buried in ground. Optimum cooling occurs in water media followed by disposal in air over ground and least in bodies buried in ground. Thus, the ratio of fall of body temperature in the three media i.e. water: air: grave is 4: 2: 1, popularly known as **Casper's dictum**.
3. Body built – thin built person loose heat rapidly in contrast to fatty because fat act as insulating cover and retains heat for longer duration.
4. Age – maximum heat loss occurs in infants and children in comparison to adults because of larger body surface area in the formers.
5. Clothing – clothing or protective gears like jacket, sweater etc. retains heat for longer duration so cooling of body is slower.
6. Air movement – environment with more air breeze movement will cause the faster cooling of body.
7. Position and posture of body – body with outstretched hand loses more heat because of greater surface of body is exposed.
8. Cause of death – if death is attributed to some infectious disease or septicemia or Bacteraemia then there may be high temperature of body at the time of death with postmortem production of heat by the action of infective organism so heat loss from the body will be slower.

Postmortem Caloricity

Postmortem caloricity is a term applied to a condition of a dead body where there is rise of body temperature observed in contrast to fall of body temperature.

This phenomenon is observed for the first two hours or so in bodies after death. The rise in body temperature can be credited to following conditions.

- Postmortem glycogenolysis – this is compulsory phenomenon observed nearly in all bodies and starts soon after death. In an average adult person, postmortem glycogenolysis produces up to 140 calories that has capacity to increase the body temperature at an instant time by 3.6°F or 2°C. Thus, considering the inner core body temperature, when the body is yet to loose heat there may be virtual rise of temperature of body.
- Cause of death – death caused by infective conditions or septicemia or Bacteraemia increases the body temperature by postmortem action of these organisms whereas in case of sunstroke or Pontine hemorrhages, there is loss of heat regulatory center. In case of strychnine or tetanus poisoning, the rise in body temperature is due to increase in muscular activity that causes to raise the body temperature. Table 7.8 displays the condition and mechanism of postmortem caloricity.

Medicolegal Importance

1. It is sign of death.
2. Time since death can be estimated.
3. Early cooling of body delays the process of rigor mortis and thus retards decomposition.

POSTMORTEM LIVIDITY

Synonyms: Livor mortis, postmortem hypostasis, vibices, Suggilation, postmortem staining.

Definition

Postmortem lividity is a purplish blue or reddish blue discolouration due to settling of blood by gravitational force within the dependent, dilated and toneless small veins and capillaries of rete mucosum.

Formation and Spread of Lividity

If body is left undisturbed without change of its position, then the postmortem staining starts appearing in small patches over

Table 7.8: Condition and mechanism of postmortem caloricity

Cause of death	*Mechanism*
Septicemia	Increased production of heat
Infectious disease	Increased production of heat
Sunstroke	Heat regulation center disturbed
Pontine hemorrhage	Heat regulation center disturbed
Tetanus	Heat production due to muscular activity
Strychnine	Heat production due to muscular activity

the dependent part of body by the end of first hour after death. Gradually the small patches increase in size and coalesce with each other to form uniformly stained areas. For this complete spreading of postmortem staining, it takes about 5-6 hours. Then the lividity gets fixed (when the livid area is pressed by thumb for a period of 30 seconds and if there is no evidence of blanching then it is said that lividity is fixed) until the onset of decomposition where it disappears by disintegrating (Figs 7.9 to 7.12). In early stages, postmortem hypostasis can be blanched by compressing the area say for example with thumb. Once the livor gets fixed, it cannot be blanched. Thus blanching of livor suggests non-fixed state of livor.

Fixation of Postmortem Lividity

If the body is undisturbed further (*vide supra*) then the staining over the areas gets fixed. If the position of the body is altered or disturbed after fixation of staining then the staining will remain more or less as such though the colour may slightly fade in intensity and no staining at newer area will reappear or even though it appear it will be very faint. However, if the position of body is changed before the fixation of lividity then

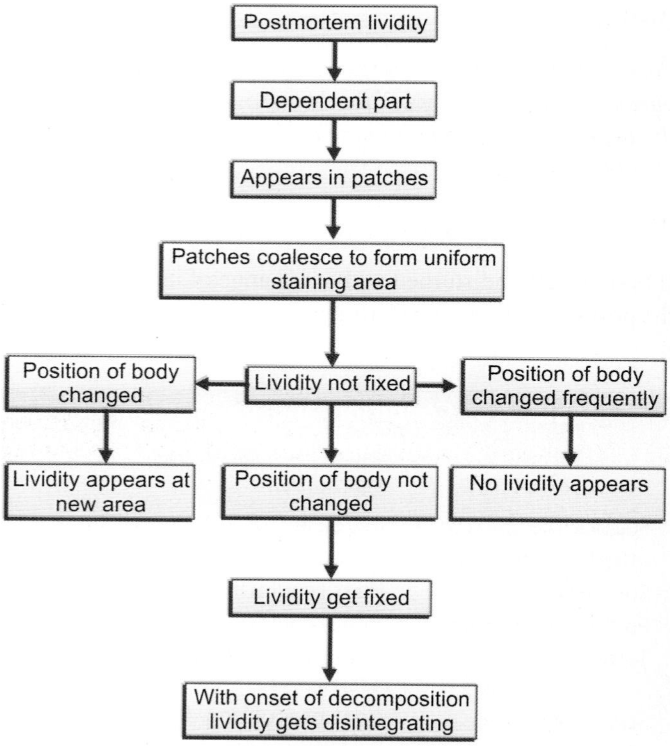

FIG. 7.9: Flowchart showing formation of postmortem lividity

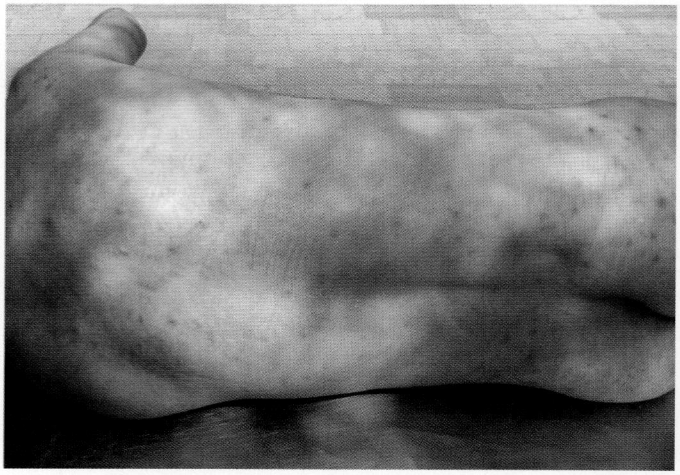

FIG. 7.10: Postmortem lividity

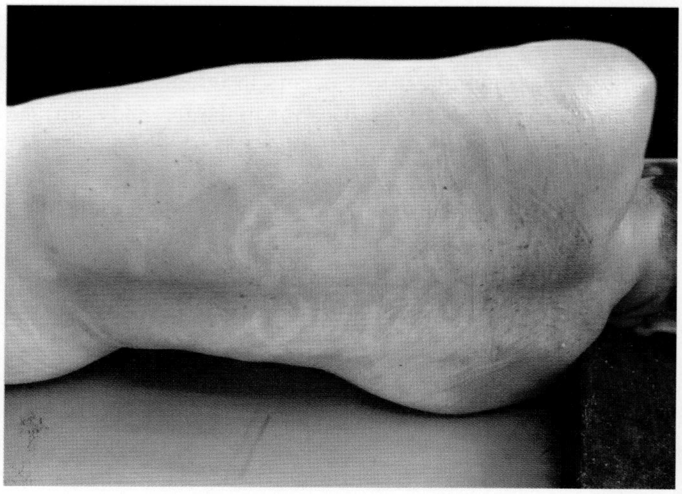

FIG. 7.11: Postmortem lividity

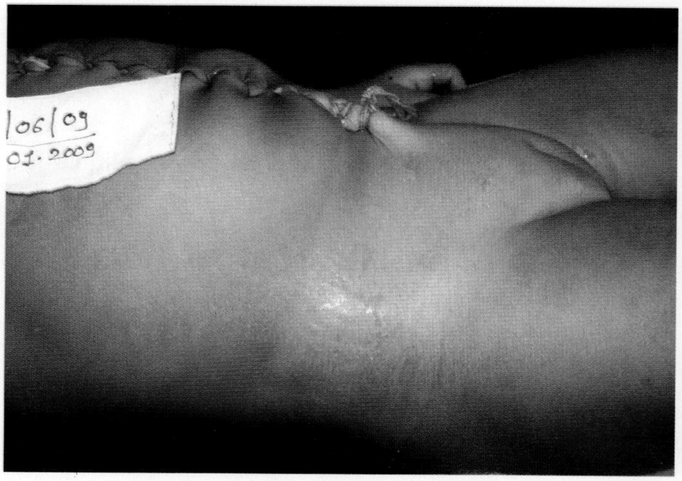

FIG. 7.12: Postmortem lividity

the lividity may reappear at newer area (Fig. 7.9). Fixation of lividity occurs mostly due to physical factors such as:

1. Firstly – after the formation of lividity, blood cannot be easily passed through out of vessels due to capillary action.
2. Secondly – by the time of complete appearance of lividity, rigor mortis is well established in the muscle. Due to rigor mortis vessels passing through the muscles are obliterated therefore it becomes difficult to pass blood through such vessels.
3. Thirdly – after establishment of rigor mortis, the vessels in the new areas are also compressed therefore these vessels cannot be distended to accommodate coming blood at the newer area.

Features

- Postmortem lividity is an intravascular phenomenon
- Postmortem lividity occurs in dependent part of body – for example if person is in supine position then lividity appears over back (Fig. 7.13)
- The normal colour of livor mortis changes from red to purple as oxygen gradually dissociates from the hemoglobin of red blood cells. This produces deoxyhemoglobin that is purple in colour and therefore postmortem lividity normally looks purplish.
- The areas of dependent part of body that remains in direct contact with the ground do not show evidence of any staining and rather these areas appear pale. The phenomenon is known as **contact pallor**. The phenomenon occurs due to – direct contact of body part will compress the vessels underlying the compressed areas and therefore they do not distended by the settling blood.
- Antemortem lividity may be formed in certain cases especially in persons with feeble circulation and the position of the lying person has not changed for certain hours.
- Postmortem staining also occurs on the dependent parts of all the internal organs. The lividity may be confused with the contusion of organs or congestion. The differences are mentioned in Table 7.9. The dependent part of intestine shows lividity and may be mistaken for intestinal infarction or intestinal strangulation. When the intestine is stretched, the hypostasis appears to be discontinuous with alternate bands of pale area and that of lividity (Fig. 7.14). Such pattern of lividity is called as vibices.
- Glove and stock lividity – it develops in the body that remains vertical after death, as for example in case of hanging if body remains suspended vertically for considerable time then the lividity will be more marked over dependent part of the body i.e. feet, legs, hands and distal part of arms. Such pattern of lividity appearing over hands (like gloves) and over feet (like stockings) is referred as glove and stock lividity (Figs 7.15 and 7.16).
- Postmortem lividity does not appear over scars or scarred areas as these areas are devoid of blood vessels.

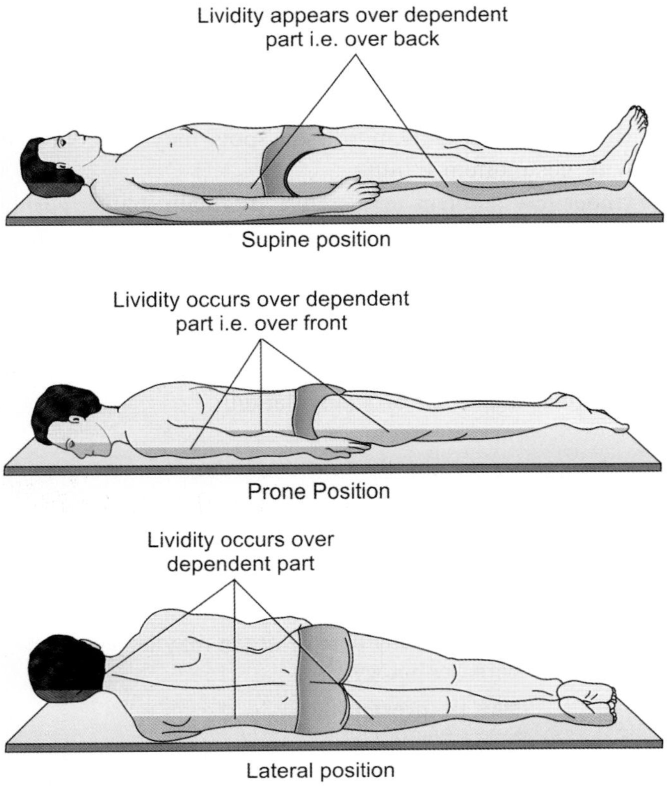

FIG. 7.13: Formation of lividity over dependent part of body

Factors Influencing

Following are the factors that influences the appearance of postmortem lividity

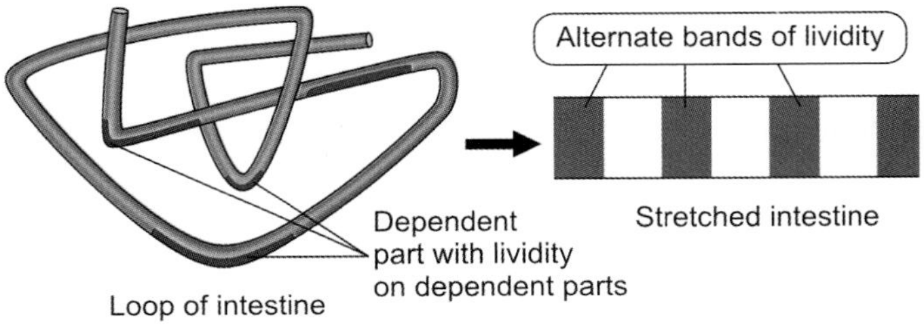

FIG. 7.14: Lividity in intestine

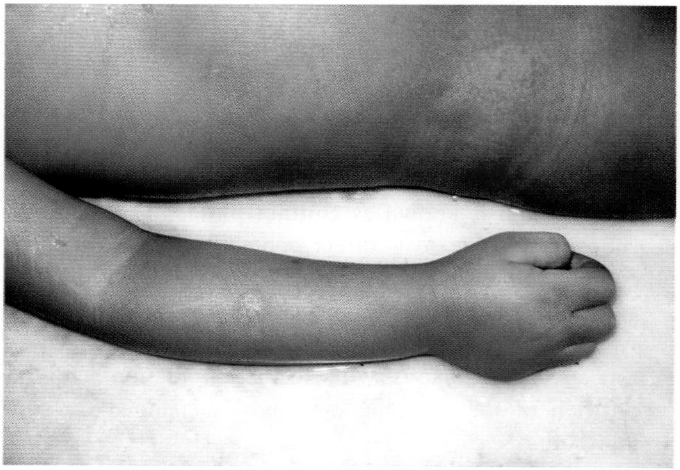

FIG. 7.15: Lividity on hand

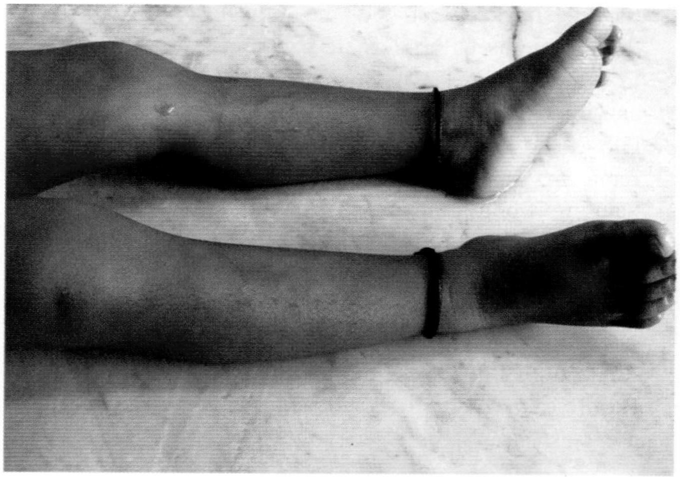

FIG. 7.16: Lividity on leg and feet

1. Position – fixed undisturbed position is essential for formation of lividity. Thus in a constant rotating body lividity usually does not appear.
2. Hemorrhage – if the person has excessive loss of blood or is in hemorrhagic shock, postmortem lividity may not be appreciated
3. Anemia – if the dead person is suffering from anemia then it becomes difficult to appreciate lividity
4. Complexion – postmortem lividity is more prominent in fair persons than darker complexion
5. Cold – if bodies are preserved in cold storage, then lividity may get fixed at later time and under such circumstances, it is not a good parameter to estimate death interval.[23]

Medicolegal Importance

1. Presence of postmortem lividity is sign of death.
2. Time since death can be estimated.
3. From the distribution of postmortem lividity, relative position of body can be identified.
4. Cause of death – from the colour of postmortem lividity, cause of death can be known in some cases. Table 7.10 presents the condition with color of lividity.
5. Postmortem lividity may appear in tissues under nails if hand remains in dependent position. In such condition, the lividity may be confused with cyanosis.
6. Postmortem lividity may be confused with contusion. The differences are mentioned in Table 9.5.
7. Blood dyscrasias/ hemorrhagic spots may be confused with postmortem lividity.
8. Under low ambient temperature, normally bluish purple postmortem lividity adopts a bright red or pink colour due to re-saturation of hemoglobin with oxygen. The important differential diagnosis of pink hypostasis is carbon monoxide poisoning (see Table 7.10).[24]
9. Postmortem lividity in intestine may be mistaken for intestinal infarction or strangulation.

Table 7.9: Difference between lividity and congestion

Features	*Postmortem lividity*	*Congestion*
Cause	Passive accumulation of blood in vessels	Stasis of vascular system due to presence of some pathology
Situation	Over dependent part of body	Whole or any part of organ may be affected with pathology
Swelling or oedema	Absent	May be present
Nature	Postmortem	Antemortem
Cut surface	Oozing of blood	Exudation of fluid mixed with blood from cut surface

Table 7.10: Color of lividity and cause of death

Cause	*Colour*	*Mechanism*
Carbon monoxide	Pink	Carboxyhemoglobin
Cyanide	Cherry-red	Excessive oxygenated blood
Fluoroacetate	Pink/cherry red	Excessive oxygenated blood
Refrigeration	Pinkish	Retention of oxygen in Cutaneous blood by cold
Hypothermia	Pinkish	Retention of oxygen in Cutaneous blood by cold
Sodium chlorate	Brown	Methemoglobin
Hydrogen sulfide	Green	Sulfhemoglobin
Aniline	Deep blue	Deoxygenated blood
Carbon dioxide	Bluish	Deoxygenated

CHANGES IN MUSCLE

After death, three sort of changes are identified in the muscles and these changes are as follows (Fig. 7.17):

1. Primary relaxation or primary flaccidity of muscles
2. Rigor mortis
3. Secondary relaxation or secondary flaccidity of muscles

Primary Relaxation

- This state of muscle begins with somatic death and in this phase molecular death does not occur.
- This stage lasts for 1-2 hours.
- All the muscles, voluntary and involuntary, are relaxed after death.
- Since the molecular death has not occurred, the muscles may respond to mechanical, electrical or chemical stimuli. In a recent study, muscular response to electrical stimulation had been elicited up to 8th hour after death.[25] Mechanical excitability of skeletal muscles can be identified up to 1.5 to 2.5 hours after death. If the quadriceps femoris muscle is stroked with hammer about 10 cm above the patella will cause upward movement of limb because of contraction of muscle. This sort of mechanical excitability is called as tendon reaction or **Zasko's phenomenon**. Peristalsis may occur in intestine with cilia movement of intestinal cells. Pupils react to atropine or physostigmine.
- In this stage, the muscle reaction is alkaline and the anaerobic activity in cells may continue.

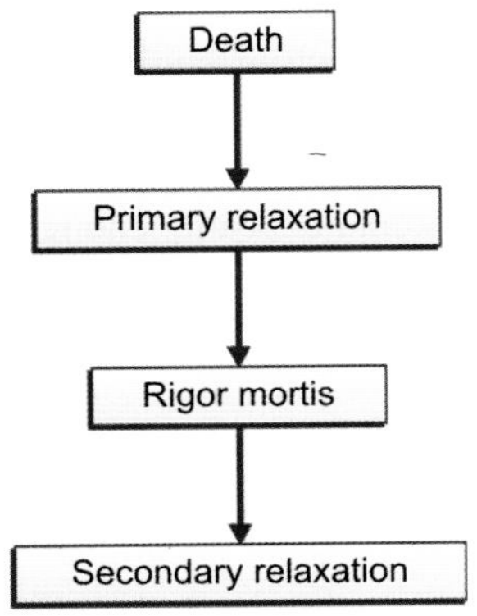

FIG. 7.17: Changes in muscles after death

Rigor Mortis

Synonyms: Cadaveric rigidity (rigor = rigidity, mortis = of death)

Definition

Rigor mortis is that state of muscles of dead body where they become stiff with some degree of shortening that follows the period of primary flaccidity.

Rigor mortis is the stiffening of muscle after death. Along with stiffening of muscle, shortening of muscle fibers, albeit small, have been noted. When rigor mortis is developed completely, the body and joints become stiff with flexion attitude of upper limb muscles (Fig. 7.18). Appearance of rigor mortis indicates death of individual cells (i.e. molecular death has occurred).

Forensic Anatomy and Physiology of Muscle

Before proceeding to mechanism, it is worth revising basic feature of muscle and its physiology. Skeletal muscle is composed of individual muscle fibers and each muscle fiber is a single cell that is multinucleated. The muscle fiber is long, cylindrical and is surrounded by sarcolemma. The muscle fibers are made up of myofibrils. Each myofibril is composed

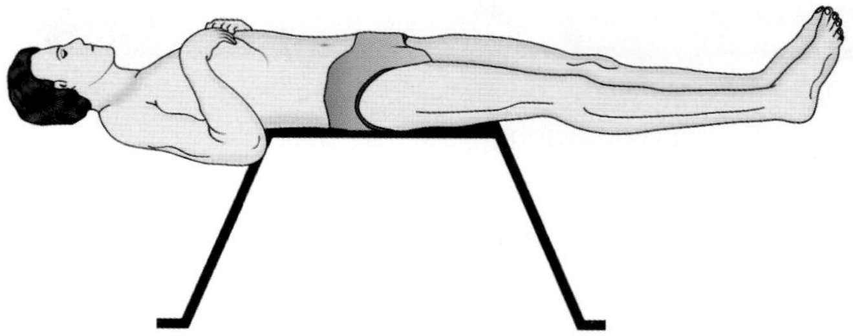

FIG. 7.18: Appearance of rigor mortis in body. Note the joints become stiff and the entire body can be placed over small top of table with maintaining the posture of trunk and lower limbs

of filaments. The filaments are of two types, the thinner one is called as actin and the thicker one is called as myosin. Each myofibril is surrounded by sarcoplasmic reticulum. The contractile mechanism in skeletal muscle depends on:

1. Myosin
2. Actin
3. Tropomyosin
4. Troponin – troponin I, troponin T, troponin C.

Sequence of Contraction and Relaxation in Life[26]

- For contraction – discharge of motor neuron → release of acetylcholine at motor end plate → binding of acetylcholine to receptor → Increased sodium and potassium conductance in end-plate membrane → generation of end-plate potential → generation of action potential in muscle fibers with inward spread of depolarization along T tubules → release of calcium from sarcoplasmic reticulum → calcium bind with troponin C and un-covers binding site on actin → formation of cross-linkages between actin and myosin and sliding of actin filaments over myosin causing shorting and thus contraction (Fig. 7.19 A).
- For relaxation – calcium pumped back into sarcoplasmic reticulum → release of calcium from troponin C → cessation of interaction between actin and myosin → relaxation of muscles (Fig. 7.19 B).
- Note that ATP provides the energy for both contraction and relaxation.

Mechanism of Rigor Mortis

- In life, for contraction and relaxation of muscles, ATP is required.[26] Thus the process is ATP dependent. The ATP is in high contraction in resting muscle and the balance between ATP consumption and re-synthesis is maintained. For synthesis of ATP, glycogen is required. After death, the failure of re-synthesis of ATP leads to a fall in its concentration within the muscle and accounts for the hardness and rigidity of muscle – the rigor mortis (stiffness after death).
- The extensibility of muscle begin to fall when its ATP levels drops to 95% and the muscles are least extensible when the ATP falls to the level of 15% of normal.
- At the time of somatic death, enough ATP is present in muscle to maintain the process of relaxation. For this process constantly ATP is breakdown to ADP and phosphate. For some time after somatic death, so long glycogen is available in the muscle, there is re-synthesis of ATP. With depletion of glycogen amidst anaerobic respiration and constant accumulation of lactate and phosphate in the muscle, no further ATP re-synthesis is possible and muscle begins to lose softness, elasticity and

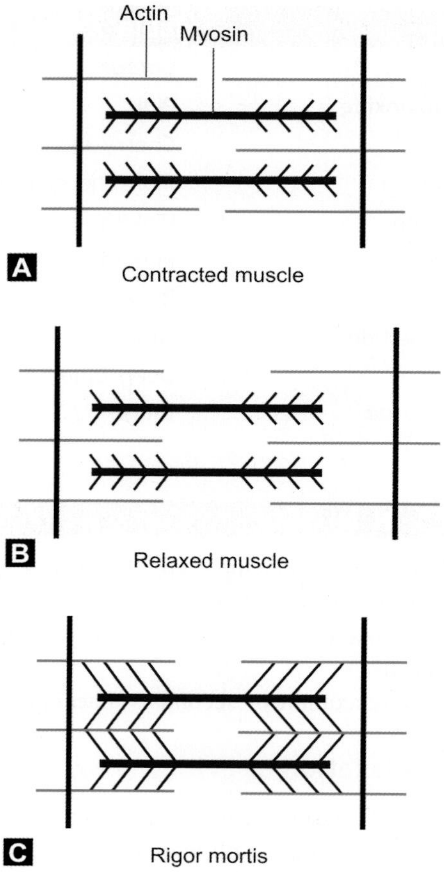

FIGS 7.19A to C: Diagram showing muscle during life and changes occurring after death

extensibility. Thus, gradually there is formation of viscid gel like acto-myosin complex that leads to stiffening and some shortening of muscles (Fig. 7.19 C).[27]

- The muscles remain in rigor until the muscle proteins are destroyed. The destruction of muscles is brought by autolysis caused due to release of enzyme lysosomes and heralds onset of decomposition.

Onset and Disappearance of Rigor Mortis

- Rigor mortis occurs in all sort of muscles i.e. striated, smooth and cardiac muscles
- It occurs earlier in involuntary muscle than voluntary muscle.
- In summer season, rigor mortis first appear in heart muscle at the end of first hour after death. In case of voluntary muscle, rigor mortis first appears in muscle of eye lids (orbicularis occuli).
- Rigidity spreads gradually within next few hours, chronologically, in the muscles of face, neck, jaw, trunk, upper limbs (from shoulder to hand), and lower limbs (from hip to foot). It appears lastly in the small muscles of hand and feet (Fig. 7.20). It disappears in the same fashion as followed in onset i.e. it disappears first in the muscles of face, neck, jaw, trunk, upper limbs (from shoulder to hand), and lower limbs (from hip to foot). It disappears lastly in the small muscles of hand and feet.[28]
- Rule of 12: It is generally considered that it takes about 12 hours after death to develop rigor mortis, remains for another 12 hours and takes about 12 hours to pass-off. This is also called as **March of rigor** (Fig. 7.21). This is only generalized categorization and the appearance and disappearance depends on number of factors. In India, even different states show considerable difference.
- The appearance and disappearance of rigor mortis as noted in the recent study conducted in India[28] is presented in Table 7.11.

Rigor in Internal Organs and Pupils

- Rigor may affect the pupil rendering them in unequal size.
- In heart, rigor causes ventricles to contract and may be mistaken for ventricular hypertrophy
- Rigor may affect dartos muscle of scrotum that compresses the testes and epididymis – causes postmortem emission of semen.[29]

Table 7.11: Stay of rigor mortis in India

Months	*Stay of rigor mortis*
April to June	11 hours 25 minutes to 28 hours 25 minutes
July to September	17 hours 15 minutes to 34 hours 20 minutes
October to December	16 hours 25 minutes to 61 hours 5 minutes
January to March	19 hours 5 minutes to 50 hours 15 minutes

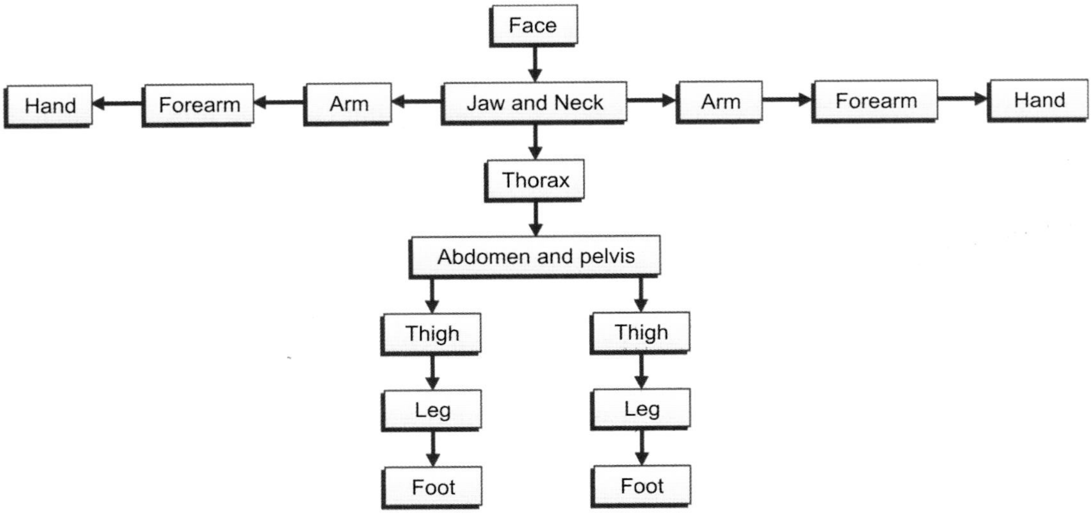

FIG. 7.20: Appearance of rigor mortis

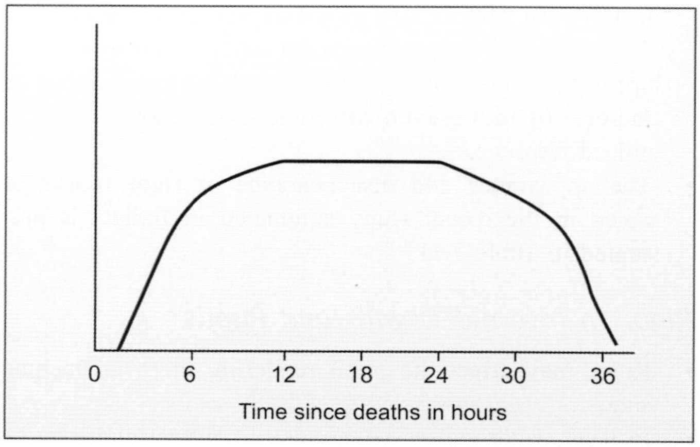

FIG. 7.21: March of rigor

Factors

Appearance of rigor mortis depends on many factors such as:

1. Age – it does not occur in fetus less than 7 months of intrauterine life, however, a case was reported in Modi's Textbook of Medical Jurisprudence that rigor mortis was recorded in 5 month fetus at Bombay famine hospital.
2. Physique of the person – rigor mortis appear early and passes off early in thin built subjects with weak musculature in comparison with well-built people.
3. Season – in summer season with high atmospheric temperature, rigor mortis appear early and passes off early in comparison with winter season with low environmental temperature.
4. Cause of death – rigor may appear early and passes off early in deaths preceded by high muscular activity causing considerable depletion of glycogen storage in muscle whereas in certain conditions the onset is delayed. In certain deaths, it appears early but stays longer. The conditions are presented in Table 7.12.
5. Condition of muscles before death – if the muscles are relaxed, then rigor sets late. If the muscles are exhausted then rigor mortis set early and passes-off early.

Medicolegal Importance

1. Presence of rigor mortis is sign of death
2. Time since death can be estimated
3. Indicates position of the body
4. Rigor mortis may be confused with cadaveric spasm, heat stiffening, cold stiffening
5. Breaking of rigor mortis – due to handling of the body or when force is used, the stiff joints may get loosened with breaking of rigor mortis. When breaking of rigor mortis occur in this fashion then the muscles do not resume rigor again. Such picture may cause difficulty in estimating time since death.
6. Rigor mortis is not functionally related with the nervous system, and therefore it is also developed in paralyzed limb.[31]

Table 7.12: Onset of rigor mortis and the conditions

Rigor mortis	*Cause*
Early onset and passes of early	Electrocution,[30] cancer, convulsions, hyperpyrexia, metabolic acidosis, uremia, hot environmental conditions
Delayed onset	Asphyxia, apoplexy, cold environmental conditions, hypothermia
Rapid onset but stays longer	Strychnine, hydrocyanic acid poisoning

Differential Diagnosis

Rigor mortis may be confused with

1. Cadaveric spasm
2. Heat stiffening
3. Cold stiffening
4. Gas stiffening

Cadaveric Spasm

Synonyms: Instantaneous rigor, instant rigor, cataleptic rigidity

- This is a rare condition
- *Cadaveric spasm is a state where muscles or group of muscle, instead of going under primary relaxation after death, go into a sudden state of stiffening.*
- The cause of this sudden stiffening is not known but is usually associated with violent deaths coupled with emotional disturbances at the time of death.
- Usually after death, the muscles undergo primary stage of relaxation. However, in certain deaths with cadaveric spasm, the muscles do not undergo primary stage of relaxation, rather they get stiffened at the moment of death.
- For example – in case of drowning deaths, the weeds/grass/mud/sand may be tightly grasped in hand or in case of suicide by shooting with firearm, the weapon may be firmly grasped in the hand.
- Cadaveric spasm continues through the stage of rigor mortis of the body and disappears with the onset of secondary relaxation.
- The condition commonly involves only a group of

muscles of hand or limb but rarely whole body may be involved.
- Differences between rigor mortis and cadaveric spasm are given in Table 7.13.

Medicolegal Importance

1. Presence of cadaveric spasm indicate that person was alive at the time of instantaneous rigor
2. If weeds/mud/grass particles are found grasped in hand in a drowned body, it indicates antemortem nature of drowning.
3. Presence of some object (like knife) or foreign body (like button, torn cloth, hairs etc.) may helpful in investigation to relate these things with crime.

Heat Stiffening

- When body is subjected to temperature above 65°C, rigidity develops in the body. This rigidity is due to coagulation of muscle proteins causing contraction of muscles.
- Such heat stiffening is associated with burns or high voltage electric burns.
- The stiffening remains until the muscles and ligaments get soften due to decomposition and in such state, the rigor mortis do not occur.
- Differences between rigor mortis and heat stiffening are given in Table 7.14.

Cold Stiffening

- When the body is subjected to freezing temperature, the tissue becomes frozen and gets stiff. Freezing causes solidification of body fluids and fat. Such cold stiffening simulates rigor mortis.
- If such body is re-warmed then the stiffness disappears and after that the rigor mortis sets in.

Gas Stiffening

- This sort of stiffening occurs in dead bodies showing signs of decomposition
- Due to decomposition, false rigidity is produced in the body due to accumulation of gases in the tissues.

Secondary Relaxation of Muscles

- It consists of secondary relaxation of muscles following rigor mortis and the changes are brought by the action of alkaline medium produced by putrefaction.
- Here the muscles become soft and flaccid. The muscle reaction is alkaline.
- No response to mechanical, electrical or chemical stimuli occur.
- Differences between primary relaxation and secondary relaxation of muscle are presented in Table 7.15.

DECOMPOSITION

Definition

It is disintegration of body tissues after death.

Decomposition is normal fate of an indisposed body. However, under certain specific environmental conditions, modified decomposition of the dead body occurs and in such cases instead of early and total destruction of dead body, it is preserved for considerable time. Such modified decomposition may occur in form of mummification or adipocere formation (Fig. 7.22).

Categories and stages of decomposition[32]

1. Early decomposition
2. Advanced decomposition
3. Partial skeletonization
4. Skeletonization

Table 7.13: Difference between rigor mortis and cadaveric spasm

Features	*Rigor mortis*	*Cadaveric spasm*
Time of onset	1-2 hours after death	Immediate
Muscles involved	All muscles of body are involved gradually	Usually group of muscles (like hand) are involved
Degree of stiffness	Comparatively moderate	Comparatively strong
Predisposing factors	None	Excitement, fear, emotional disturbance, etc.
Mechanism	Break down of ATP	Not known
Medicolegal importance	Helps to know time since death, position of body.	Help to suggest manner of death

Table 7.14: Difference between rigor mortis and heat stiffening

Features	*Rigor mortis*	*Heat stiffening*
Nature	Postmortem	May be antemortem or postmortem
Degree of stiffness	Comparatively moderate	Comparatively high
Mechanism	Break down of ATP	Due to coagulation of muscle
Associated features	Nothing specific	Signs of exposure to heat will be present for example burning, blisters, heat rupture etc

Table 7.15: Difference between primary and secondary relaxation of muscles

Features	*Primary relaxation*	*Secondary relaxation*
Time of onset	Immediately after death	After disappearance of rigor mortis and when decomposition occurs
Molecular death	No	Yes
Response to stimuli (Mechanical and electrical)	Present	Absent
Associated features	Nothing particular	Signs of decomposition present

Mechanism

Decomposition follows the arrest of biochemical process that develops, maintains and preserves the integrity of cellular element. During decomposition, the tissue components leak and break up releasing hydrolytic enzymes. The complex organic body tissues are break down into simpler compounds. The bacteria and other microorganism thrive on the unprotected organic components of the body. Thus, two parallel process of decomposition can be identified as follows (see Fig. 7.22). It should be noted that these process proceed simultaneously and for convenience it has been described separately.

1. Autolysis – Self dissolution of body tissues by the enzymes released from the disintegrating cells.
2. Putrefaction – These are the changes produced by the action of bacteria and other microorganism thriving on the body.
3. A third kind of postmortem destruction can be identified in some bodies that are not disposed. Such postmortem destruction is brought out due to attack of various types of animals such as insect, rodents, canines, fox, jackal, vulture, fish etc.

Autolytic Changes

- Autolysis is a process of self-destruction of body tissues by enzymes. The process may also occur in living person characterized by focal tissue injury and necrosis surrounded by inflammatory reaction. The same mechanism operates after death, however, in dead body, the process occurs on large scale and devoid of vital (inflammatory) reaction (as the living property is no more!). Autolysis is thought to be stimulated by the decrease in intracellular pH due to decreased oxygen level followed after death.
- This process occurs earlier and rapid in some tissues rich in hydrolytic enzymes such as pancreas and gastric mucosa; intermediate in tissues like heart, liver and kidneys and delayed in fibrous tissue like uterus or skeletal muscle.
- The process of autolysis is temperature dependent. Refrigeration of a body soon after death will retards the enzymatic self-digestion of cells whereas increase in temperature promotes degradation as seen in deaths preceded by fever, exertion or death in high ambient temperature.
- The phenomenon of autolysis is visible on gross and microscopic examination. For example grossly autolysis is observed as a skin slippage. In skin slippage, the release of hydrolytic enzymes releasing at dermo-epidermal junction causes loosening of epidermis from the underlying dermis as a result, the epidermis is easily peel-off the dermis (Fig. 7.23). Similarly hairs and nails are loosened. Microscopically, autolysis is identified by homogenous and eosinophilic cytoplasm with loss of cellular details with cell remains as debris.
- Internally autolysis can be noticed as a doughy consistency of the organs. Similarly the intima of large blood vessels appears stained by postmortem hemolysis. This hemolysis is nothing but autolysis of red blood cells.
- Gastromalacia is postmortem rupture of gastric wall due to the process of autolysis. It usually occurs in fundus area and is devoid of any vital reaction. Similarly oesophagomalacia is postmortem rupture of lower end of oesophagus due to autolysis and lacks vital reaction.

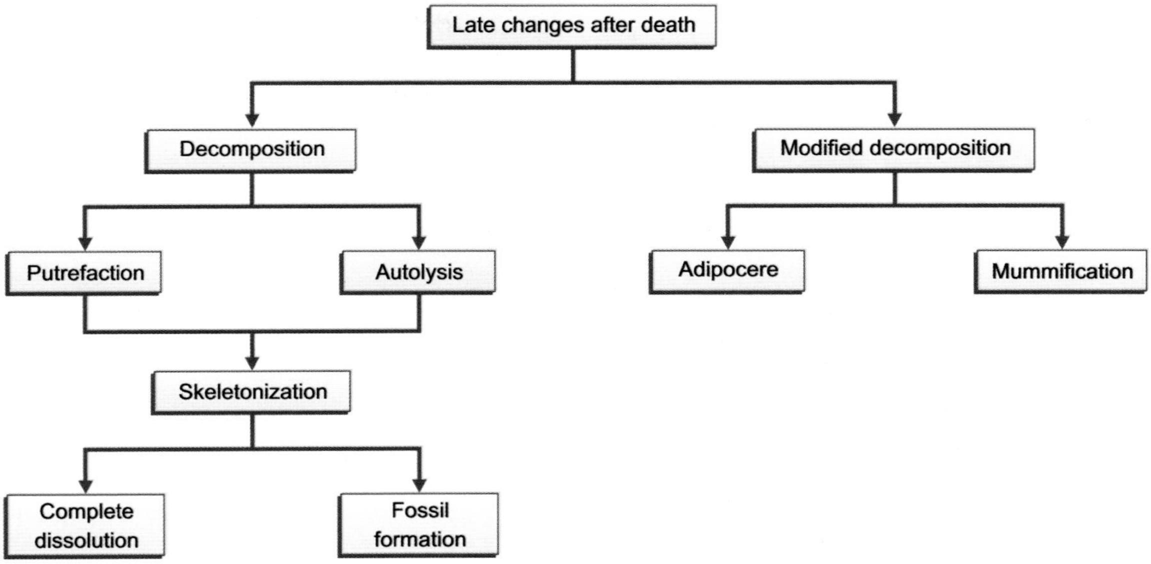

FIG. 7.22: Showing late changes after death

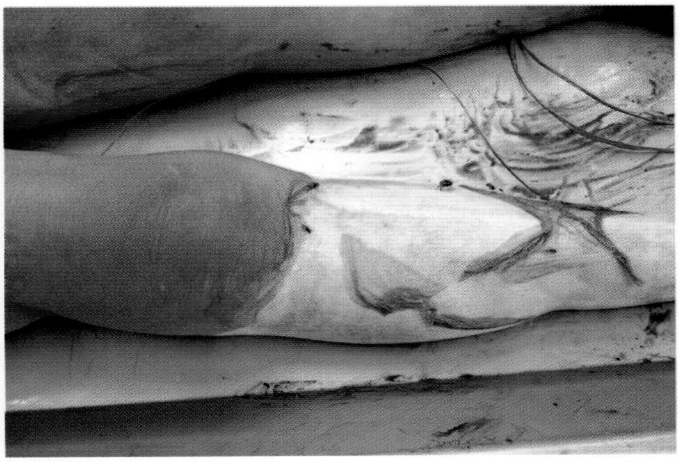

FIG. 7.23: Peeling of skin

- Disintegration of dead fetus in mother's womb is called as maceration and it is considered as aseptic autolysis.

Putrefaction

- Putrefaction changes depend on various factors as described below. Microorganisms responsible are – Clostridium welchii, B. coli, Staphylococci, non-hemolytic Streptococci, Dyptheroids, Proteous etc.
- As the process of putrefaction progresses, different gases are produced such as – hydrogen sulphide, carbon dioxide, mercaptans, methane, ammonia, etc. Methane burns readily when ignited. The rapid production and accumulation of gases causes both physical and chemical changes in the decomposing body as mentioned in Table 7.16.
- The physical changes consist of bloating the features with distension of abdomen by distending gases (Fig. 7.24). This causes obliteration of the identity of the deceased. In males, the gas is forced from the peritoneal cavity down the inguinal canal into the scrotum causing scrotal swelling.
- Different gases of decomposition induce the chemical changes. For example the hydrogen sulfide readily diffuses through the tissues. It reacts with hemoglobin to form sulfhemoglobin. This pigment initially outlines the superficial blood vessels and as decomposition progresses, a generalized green hue may be imparted to body (Fig. 7.25).
- Putrefaction occurs at different rate in various body tissues and depends up on their moisture content. Three main changes are noticed during putrefaction as:[33]

Table 7.16: Importance of gases of decomposition
- Causes bloating of features causing difficulty in identification
- Causes disintegrating and shifting of postmortem lividity causing difficulty in assessing the position of body
- Causes postmortem purging of feces, semen, decomposition fluid
- Causes expulsion of fetus from uterus

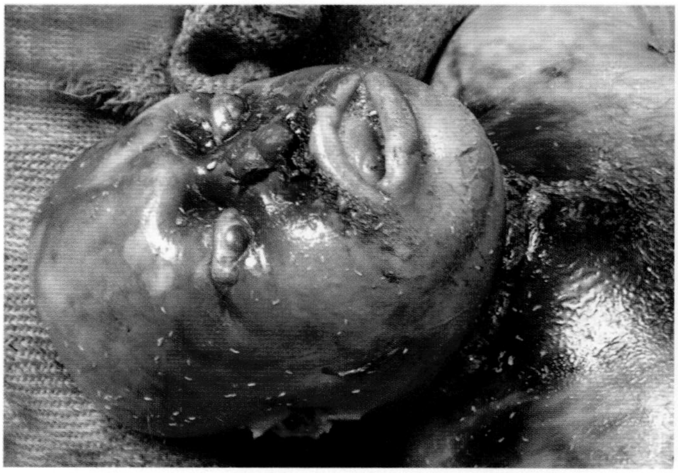

FIG. 7.24: Bloated features in decomposition

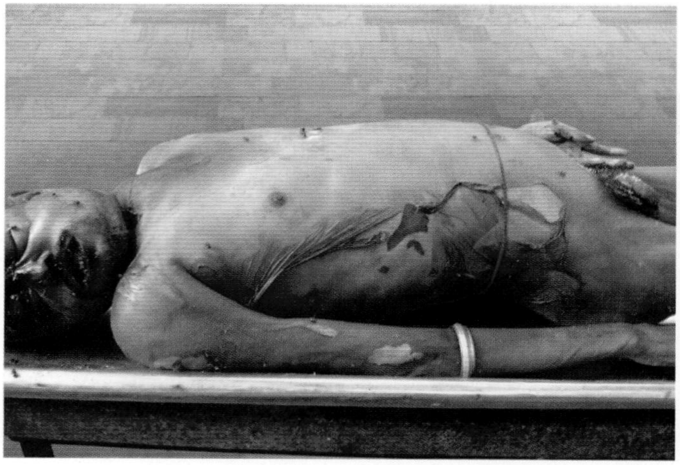

FIG. 7.25: Greenish discoloration of trunk

1. Change in color
2. Liberation of gases
3. Liquefaction of tissues

- Colour changes – colour changes is due to hemolysis of red blood cells. The liberated hemoglobin is converted into sulpmethemoglobin by hydrogen sulfide gas and imparts greenish discolouration.
- Liberation of gases – during the process of decomposition, the proteins and carbohydrates are split into simpler compounds. As a result, numbers of gases are liberated (*vide supra*). The offensive odour emitting from the dead body is due to formation of hydrogen sulfide gas and mercaptans. The gases are collected in the intestine within 12 to 18 hours in summer and 18 to 24 hours in winter.

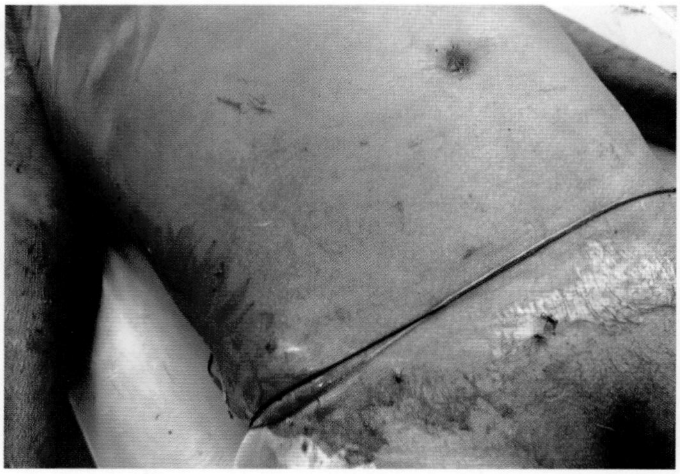

FIG. 7.26: Greenish discoloration of right iliac fossa

- Liquefaction of tissues – with advancement in decomposition, the organs are converted into thick semi-fluid matter.

Decomposition Changes External Signs

Putrefaction is the most absolute sign of death.[34] Externally, the first sign of putrefaction (decomposition) is a greenish discoloration of right side of abdomen over right caecal area (Fig. 7.26). Gradually the color spreads over the whole abdomen, thence on the chest (Fig. 7.27) and by this time a putrid odour becomes apparent.[35] The contents of caecum are more fluid and full of bacteria therefore putrefaction develops earlier. Since the caecum is close proximity with abdominal wall, the right lower abdomen stains first. Similarly, the surface of liver in contact with caecum also shows greenish discolouration. The greenish discolouration is due to formation of sulphmethemoglobin. In summer, the colour usually develops at about 12 to 18 hours and in winter it takes about 18-24 hours. There is formation of multiple blisters (Figs 7.28 and 7.29) containing air with denuded skin at places. The features puff up due to liberating gases and become unrecognizable; the whole body becomes bloated and the tissues sodden with fluid and eventually liquefy and disintegrate.[36] The marbling of skin becomes prominent by 24 hours in summer whereas it is manifested at about 36 to 48 hours in winter (Fig. 7.30). The blood vessels are invaded by microorganisms. The formation of sulphmethemoglobin causes greenish-brown staining of the inner walls of the blood vessels. The staining of blood vessel makes these vessels more prominent. The phenomenon gives rise to marbled appearance to the skin. Postmortem red coloration of teeth (pink teeth) – red coloration is due to hemolysis

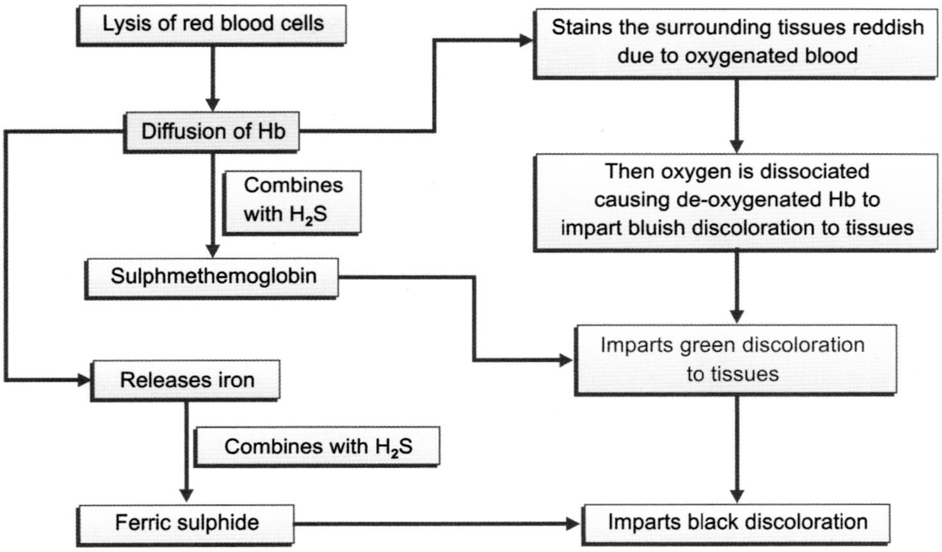

FIG. 7.27: Changes in decomposition

after exudation of hemoglobin derivatives through the dentine tubules.[37] Various products are formed during the process of decomposition and are mentioned in Table 7.17. As the decomposition process progresses, the peculiar odour emitted by body attracts flying insects, especially flies (*vide infra*). After invasion of the bodies by flies, they lay eggs in 18 to 36 hours depending on environmental conditions (Figs 7.31 and 7.32). They usually lay eggs near orifices. The eggs hatch within 12 to 24 hours to larvae. The larvae are also called as maggots (Fig. 7.33). Maggots are voracious eaters. Moreover, maggot secrets proteolytic enzymes that causes more destruction and may cause difficulty in interpreting the surface injury.

Internal signs

Decomposition of internal organs depends on multiple factors such as

1. Firmness of organ
2. Moisture content of organ
3. Density of organ
4. Quantity of blood in organ

Therefore, the order of tissue decomposition in internal organ is as follows:

1. Soft tissues
2. Firm tissues
3. Hard tissues

The sequences of early and late putrefaction occurring in internal organs[38] are presented in Table 7.18.

- Brain – with onset of decomposition, brain becomes discoloured, soft and pinkish-gray and then it becomes pasty. Finally brain liquefies.
- Larynx, trachea – mucosa becomes soft and changes its

Table 7.17: Products of decomposition

Products
Acids: acetic, palmitic, oxalic, succinic, lactic
Amines and amino acids: leucine, tyrosine, putrisine, cadaverine
Aromatic substances: indol, skatol
Mercaptans
Gases: Hydrogen sulfide, carbon dioxide, sulphur dioxide, ammonia etc
Enzymes: SGOT, LDH etc.

Table 7.18: Sequence of putrefaction in internal organs

Organs putrefying early	*Organs putrefying late*
Brain	Esophagus
Mucosa of trachea and larynx	Diaphragm
Stomach and intestine	Heart
Spleen	Lungs
Liver	Kidney
	Urinary bladder
	Uterus
	Prostate

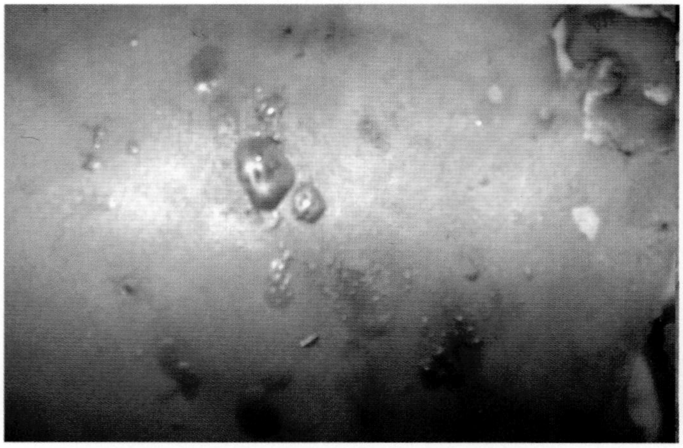

FIG. 7.28: Formation of multiple blisters

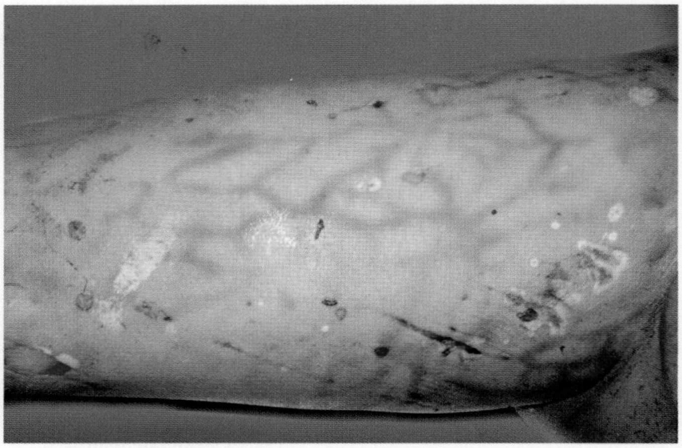

FIG. 7.30: Evidence of marbling

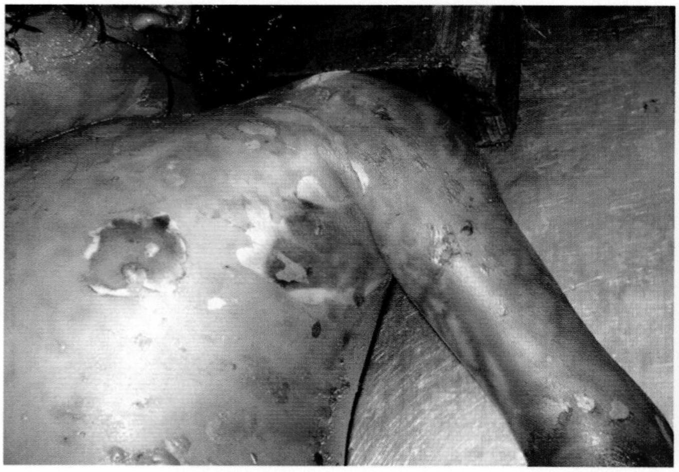

FIG. 7.29: Formation of multiple blisters and peeling of skin

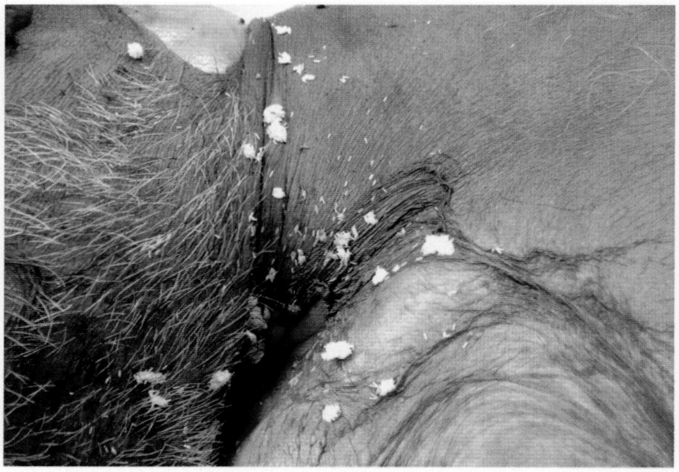

FIG. 7.31: Eggs

colour to brownish and later to green to black.

- Stomach and intestine – shows multiple dark red to brown patches initially on posterior wall and later on anterior wall. The mucosa appears macerated. Later, the intestine becomes dark, soft and pulpy.
- Liver – becomes soft and flabby in 12 to 24 hours in summer. Blister begins to appear on its surface. The liver appears foamy or honey-combed due to accumulation of decomposition gases. The liver takes greenish discolouration and later on changes to coal-black. The bile pigment diffuses from gallbladder and stains surrounding area (Figs 7.34 and 7.35).
- Heart – becomes soft and flabby. Later on blister filled with gases accumulate over the surface (Fig. 7.36). Finally it turns into pliable mass.
- Lung – multiple gas filled blisters develop under pleural surface. Later, the lung becomes soggy with oozing of blood-stained fluid.
- Kidneys – becomes brown then becomes soft and ultimately reduced into mass.
- Adrenal glands – medulla liquefies and cortex softens from within outwards and the gland appears like a cyst.
- Spleen – becomes soft, mushy, steel-gray in colour and ultimately reduced into diffluent mass.
- Urinary bladder – is quite resistant to decomposition
- Prostate – is the last organ to putrefy in male

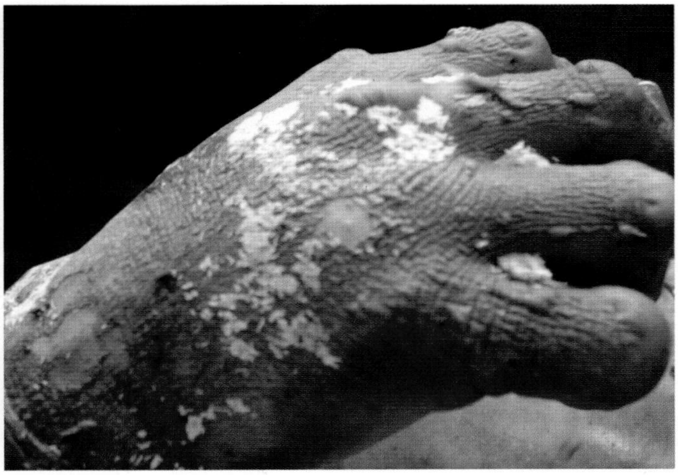

FIG. 7.32: Eggs

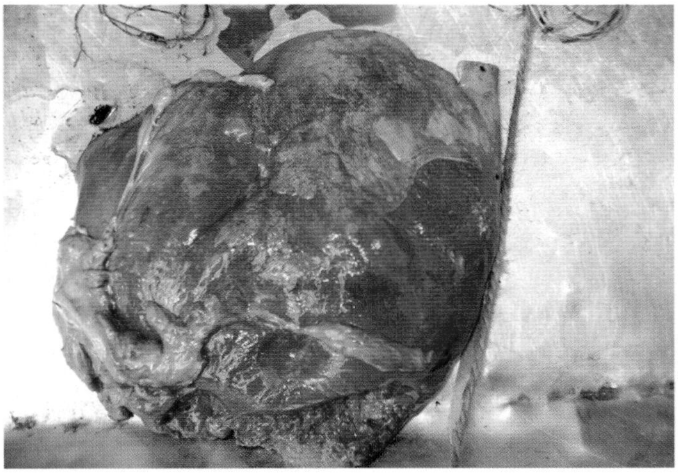

FIG. 7.34: Foamy liver

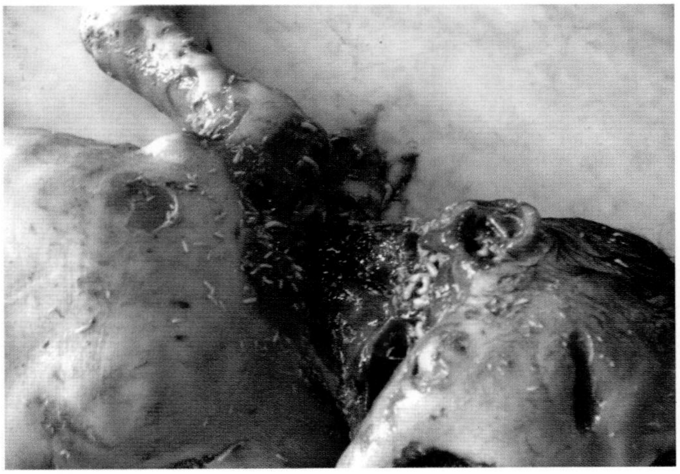

FIG. 7.33: Maggots

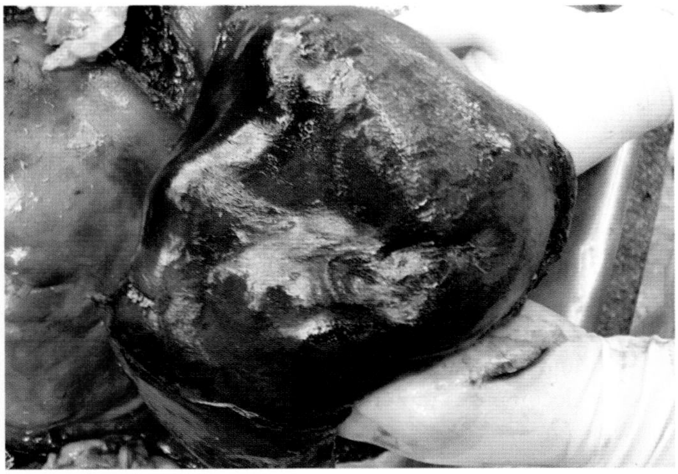

FIG. 7.35: Liver in decomposition

- Uterus – virgin (non-gravid) uterus is the last organ to putrefy in females. However, gravid or post-partum uterus putrefies early.

Colliquative putrefaction – here the soft tissues and organs become entirely liquefied. The wall of abdomen becomes soft and burst open due to which the abdominal content protrudes out. It takes place in India in 5 to 10 days.[34]

Factors

There are various external and internal factors affecting the process of decomposition. These factors are discussed below.

External Factors

1. Temperature – between 21°C to 43°C is favorable for decomposition. Decomposition is arrested below 0°C and above 50°C. Thus exposure to high temperature and low humidity accelerates the early decomposition.[39]
2. Moisture – moisture is essential for the process of decomposition because microorganism-causing decomposition requires moisture and optimum temperature for their growth. Therefore organs containing more water decompose earlier than dry ones.
3. Air – presence of air promotes decomposition by diminishing evaporation.

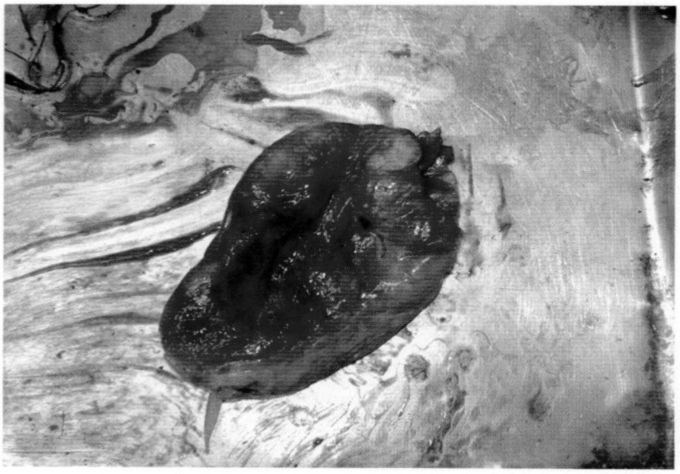

FIG. 7.36: Heart in decomposition

4. Manner of burial – decomposition begins early in bodies buried in shallow grave. Casper's dictum is useful for a rough assessment of the rate of decomposition. It is eight times slower under soil and two times slower under water compared to air (1:2:8).

Internal Factors

1. Age – bodies of children decomposes rapidly than adults. The bodies of old people do not decompose rapidly, probably owing to less amount of moisture.[40]
2. Sex – as such sex do not have any influence on decomposition however, a female in early postpartum period may decomposes rapidly if such death is associated with septicemia.
3. Condition of body – fat and flabby bodies decomposes earlier than thin and emaciated ones.
4. Cause of death – as mentioned in Table 7.19.
5. Scars – the rate of decomposition is retarded in scarred areas (at scars) as these areas are devoid of blood vessels.

Medicolegal Importance of Decomposition

1. It is sign of death
2. Time since death can be estimated
3. Bloating of features due to decomposition poses difficulty in identification
4. Advanced decomposition may obliterate the cause of death.

SKELETONIZATION

Skeletonization is the removal of tissues from the skeleton or bones. It may be (Figs 7.37 and 7.38):

Table 7.19: Conditions that accelerate or retards decomposition

Conditions
Accelerates decomposition
- Septicemia
- Rhabdomyolysis
- Cocaine overdose
- edematous area
Retards decomposition
- Dehydration
- Massive blood loss
- Cold environment
- Embalming

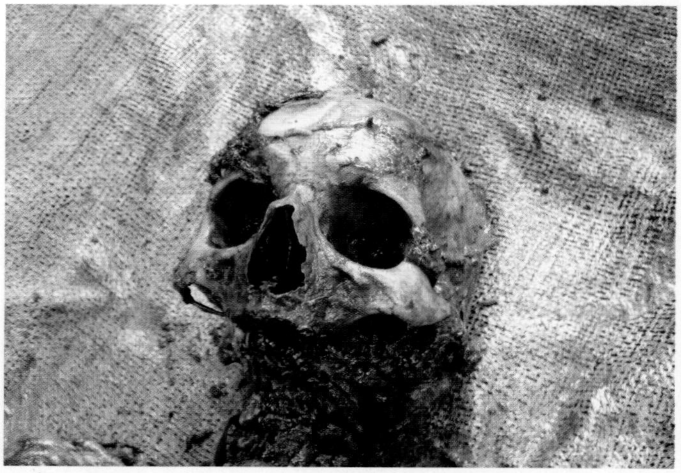

FIG. 7.37: Nearly complete skeletonization of face and head

FIG. 7.38: Partial skeletonization

1. Complete – here all soft tissues are removed
2. Partial – here only portions of bones are exposed

Skin, muscle, soft tissue and internal organs may lose before skeleton becomes disarticulated. According to Rodriguez & Bass (1985), the disarticulation usually proceeds from the head to downward (for e.g. mandible separates from the skull, skull separates from cervical spine). Similarly it also disarticulates from central to peripheral direction (for e.g. first there will be separation of spine then limbs).[41] Bones may either converted into fossil or may dissolute with time. There occurs decalcification and dissolution. Presence of acidic soil or water hastens the process. *For examination of individual bones, please refer chapter 4 on Forensic Osteology.*

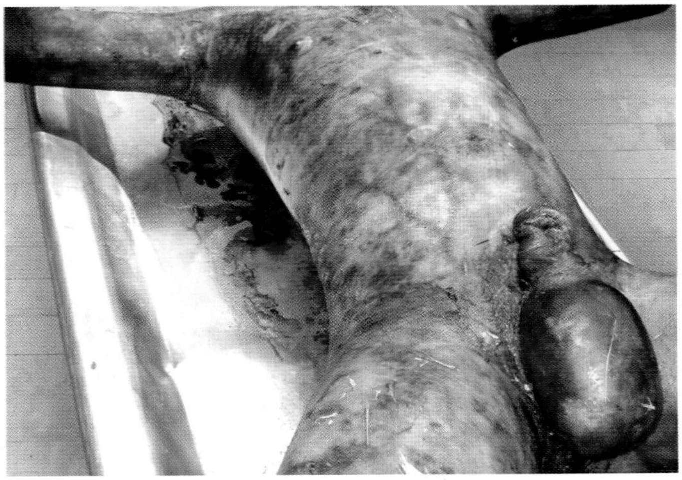

FIG. 7.39: Adipocere formation

ADIPOCERE

Synonym: Saponification, grave wax

Definition

Adipocere is modified form of decomposition characterized by formation of soft, waxy material in the dead body.

The name adipocere was given by Fourcroy (1789). Adipocere is derived from adipo (fat) and cire (wax) and indicates the properties of adipocere intermediate between fat and wax.

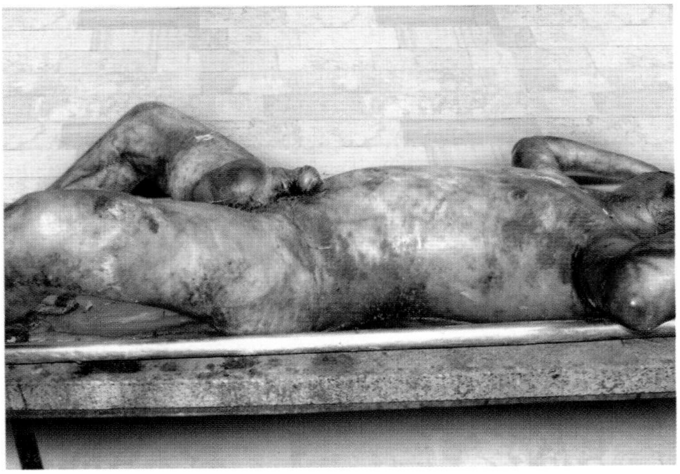

FIG. 7.40: Adipocere formation

Features (Figs 7.39 to 7.42)

- Adipocere, when fresh, is peculiar, hard, moist, whitish and translucent. It is inflammable and burns with a faint-yellow flame.
- Adipocere floats in water and dissolves in alcohol and ether.
- Adipocere has rancid smell. Some authorities describe the smell being 'earthy, cheesy and ammonical.[42]
- Adipocere, once formed, appears stable for considerable period
- Gram positive bacteria are able to degrade the adipocere[43]
- After some years, adipocere becomes brittle, cracked and chalky
- Adipocere is usually first seen in the subcutaneous fat of the cheeks, the breasts, the abdomen and then other organs and tissues.[44] It usually takes about three weeks for adipocere to develop completely however, in India, Dr Coull Mackenzie found it occurring within 3 to 15 days in bodies submerged in Hooghly river or buried in damp soil of lower Bengal. Dr Modi had also observed adipocere formation in 7 to 35 days.[40]

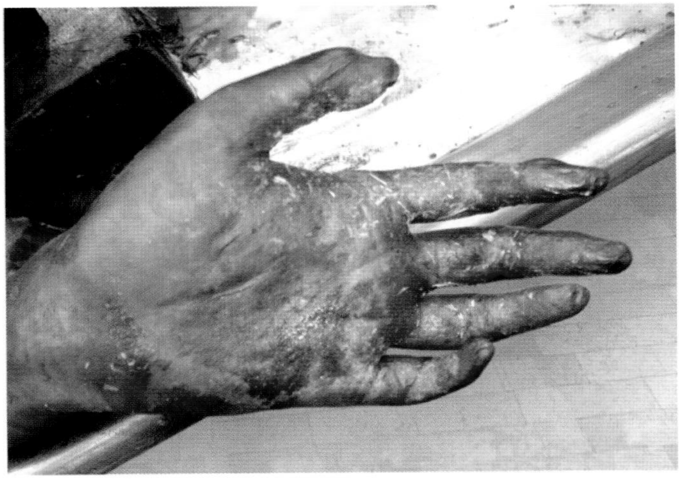

FIG. 7.41: Preserved hand in adipocere

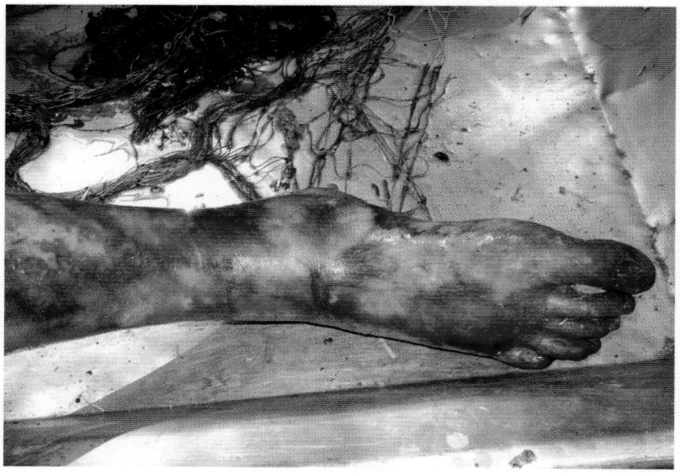

FIG. 7.42: Preserved foot and leg in adipocere

- Adipocere preserves the features therefore identity of the deceased can be made out. Similarly it preserves wounds, if present over body thus help in elucidating cause of death. According to Evans (1962) some diseases could be recognized on microscopic examination of adipocere tissue in a few instances.[45]

Mechanism (Fig. 7.43)

- Unsaturated fatty acids of body are converted into saturated fatty acids by the process of hydrolysis and hydrogenation.
- In adipocere, there is hydrogenation of unsaturated body fat into peculiar, hard, yellowish-white, waxy saturated fatty acids.[46] The process of adipocere formation begins in neutral fat (i.e. adipose) and is initiated by intrinsic lipases, which degrades the triglycerides into fatty acids. The fatty acids are hydrolyzed and hydrogenated into hydroxy-fatty acids. Thus adipocere consists mainly of saturated fatty acids like hydroxy-palmatic, oleic, hydroxy-stearic acid. The process is facilitated by degrading anaerobic bacteria such as *Clostridium welchii*. The *Clostridium welchii* secrets toxin containing lecithinase, proteases and phospholipases. The bacterial action creates ammonia-rich waste that contributes to forming an alkaline environment.[47]
- At the time of death, body contains about half percent fatty acids but as adipocere formation begins the body fat rose to 20% within a month and over 70% in three months.
- Initially the water required for the process is obtained from the body tissue (intrinsic water).

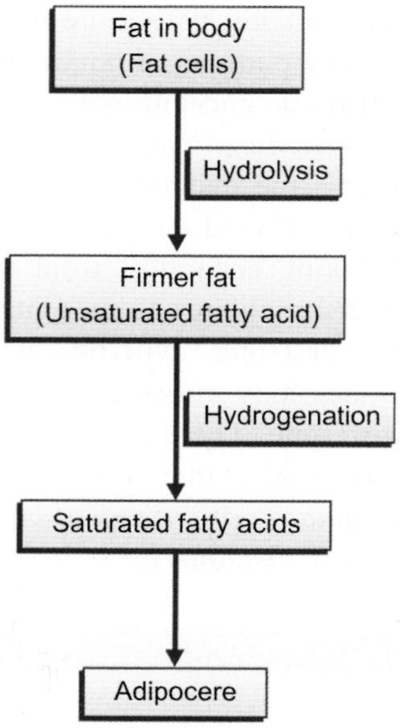

FIG. 7.43: Mechanism of adipocere formation

Requirements

Following are the requirements for formation of adipocere[48]

- Moist or aquatic environment
- Warm temperature
- Intrinsic bacterial enzymatic action
- Adipose tissue

Factors

The formation of adipocere depends on multiple factors such as:

1. Atmospheric condition – It is said that for formation of adipocere, the intermediate ambient conditions (**just right conditions** or **Goldilocks phenomenon**) are required. In other words, tissue will desiccate (mummified) if the conditions are too dry whereas if the conditions are too wet, the body may macerate or possibly liquefy.[49]
2. Temperature – when ambient temperature is too low or too high, no adipocere formation occurs, as the bacteria required for accelerating the process would not be proliferates at such temperature. Therefore, it is estimated that the optimum growth of adipocere occurs at an ambient temperature of 21-45°C.[49, 50]
3. Moisture – moisture or water is necessary for the process of adipocere formation. Initially body fluid is used for initiating the process but for completion of the adipocere, presence of moisture or water is necessary in the environment.

4. Air movement – retards the process because the air movements evaporates the body fluid and decreases the body temperature thus retarding the chemical process.
5. Place and media of disposal – more frequently occur in body submerged in water or buried in damp place. If buried, deep burial shows marked adipocere formation than shallow grave.
6. Humid climate favours adipocere formation.
7. Soil – in burial environment, the pH of soil, temperature, moisture and the oxygen content within the grave affects adipocere formation.[51]
8. Clothing – presence of clothing over the body appears to accelerate adipocere formation since it retains water.[52]
9. Coffin – if the body is buried within coffin, the coffin will retard the rate of adipocere formation.[53]
10. Water – adipocere forms well in warm water than cold water.[52]

Medicolegal Importance

1. Sign of death.
2. Time since death can be estimated.
3. Identification of the body can be possible as features are reasonably preserved.
4. Injuries can be make out thus helping in forming a cause of death.
5. Place of disposal can be known.

MUMMIFICATION

Definition

Mummification is modified form of decomposition characterized by drying desiccations of tissues under the conditions of high environmental temperature, low humidity and good ventilation in which the body tissues are converted into dark, hard and shriveled appearance.

Features

- The features of body are stay preserved (Fig. 7.44)
- The skin becomes dried due to dehydration of cells and displays brownish black discolouration and a parchment like appearance (Fig. 7.45). Mummification renders fingers and toes in dry, hard and shriveled state (Figs 7.46 and 7.47). The fingers under such conditions are unsuitable for fingerprinting.
- Drying of certain parts of the body may cause shrinkage of the skin and due to shrinking and consequent stretching, causes large splits especially these splits are common in

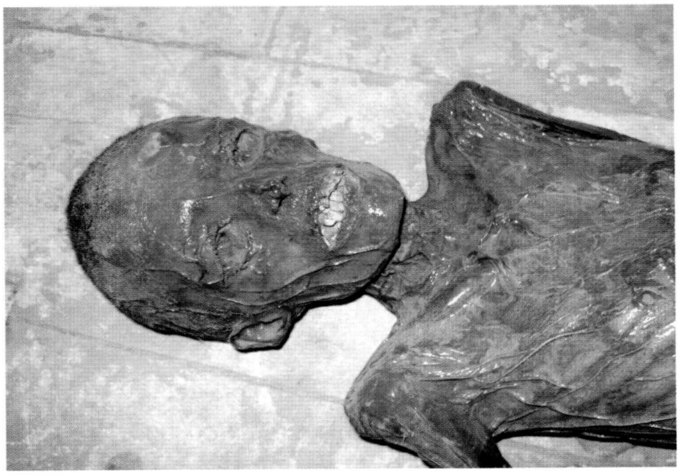

FIG. 7.44: Preserved features in mummification

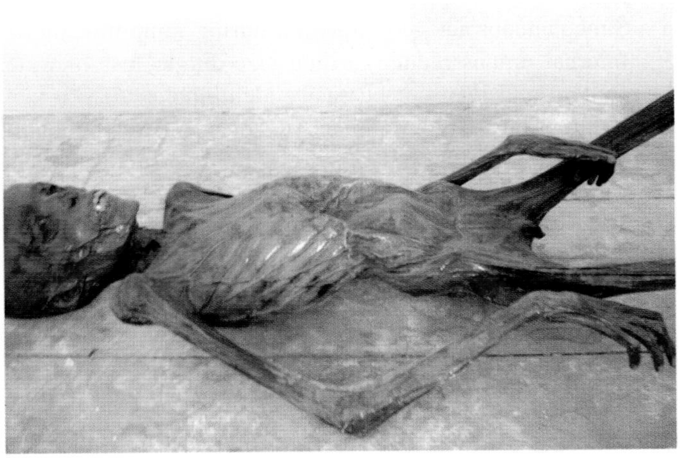

FIG. 7.45: Mummification

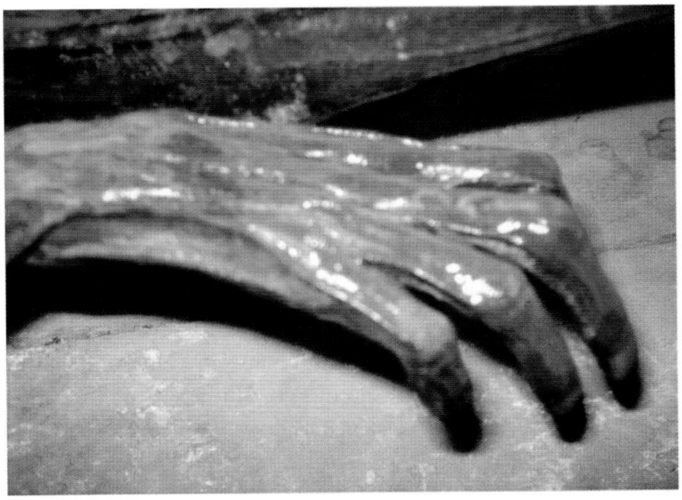

FIG. 7.46: Hand in mummified body

FIG. 7.47: Foot in mummified body

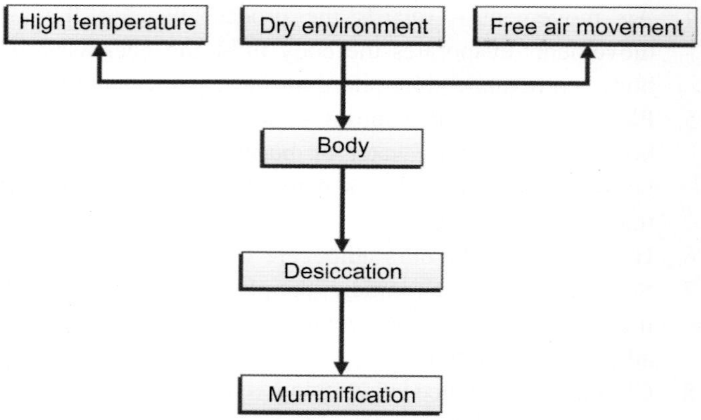

FIG. 7.48: Mechanism of mummification

the groin, neck and armpit. Such splits may resemble injury.

- Subcutaneous fat gets liquefied during mummification.
- Internal organs reduce in their size due to loss of water content and may not be easily identifiable.
- Destruction of mummified body occurs late. If remains exposed to environmental conditions for considerable period, the tissues are converted into dust.
- The time required for complete mummification of a body cannot be stated as it varies considerably and depends on multiple factors as discussed below. Peripheral mummification is fairly common phenomenon with distal extremities, especially the fingers and toes within 2 to 3 days.[46] In complimentary environmental conditions, the change may occur between 3 weeks to 3 months roughly.

Mechanism (Fig. 7.48)

- Mummification takes place where body loses fluid to environmental via evaporation.
- Due to absence of moisture and hot temperature, putrefactive bacteria cannot proliferate in such hostile environment.

Factors

The formation of mummification depends on multiple factors such as:

1. The size of body
2. Atmospheric conditions – hot temperature favours mummification formation. Similarly it requires dry environment i.e. it cannot occur in high humid conditions. Mummification results because one of the basic necessities for bacterial growth 'water' has been eliminated from the body.[54]
3. Air movement – free air movement promotes mummification formation.
4. Place of disposal – mummification occurs naturally when the air and/or soil are extremely dry.

Medicolegal Importance

1. It is sign of death.
2. Time since death can be estimated.
3. Identification can be possible as features are relatively preserved.
4. Place of disposal can be known.
5. Scrotal mummification may be confused or misinterpreted as a suspicious injury.[55]
6. It helps to identify cause of death if obvious injuries etc. are present.

FORENSIC ENTOMOLOGY

After death, if body is not disposed and left uncovered, the decomposition process and the peculiar odour of decomposition attracts flying insects, especially flies. *The study of these insects and their life cycle that are infesting the dead bodies is known as forensic entomology*. Forensic entomology is based on the analysis of insects and other invertebrates sequentially colonizing a corpse as decomposition progresses and on the developmental stages of their offspring. Various flying insects are attracted toward dead body and infest it but two groups are more common and they are:

1. Diptera (true flies)
2. Coleoptera (beetles)

Life Cycle of Fly

Flies are the first to attract toward corpse. Flies are of various types such as blue bottle flies, houseflies, and flesh flies. After invasion of the body, flies lay eggs in about 18 to 36 hours.

These eggs are usually laid down at mucocutaneous junctions such as lips, nostrils, anus, and vagina or even in open wounds. These eggs hatch within 12 to 24 hours, depending on type of fly and environmental conditions, to larvae. These larvae are called as maggots. Maggots are voracious eaters. Moreover, maggot secrets proteolytic enzymes that causes more destruction. These larvae grow in size and enclose themselves inside shell-like structures; the process is called as pupation to form pupa. The pupa may break out to release young flies capable of reproduction thus completing the life cycle (Figs. 7.49 to 7.52).

Collection and Preservation of Samples[56]

- Collect insects, both adults and immature, from the corpse and beneath the corpse
- In case of adult, collect two sort of samples, one sample consisting of killed insects and other sample consist of live ones for subsequent rearing
- Preserve adult insects in 70% ethanol or isopropyl alcohol
- Larvae should be preserved in larval fluid. If larval fluid is not available, place larvae in hot water (76.7°C) for 2-3 minutes and then transfer to 70% ethanol.

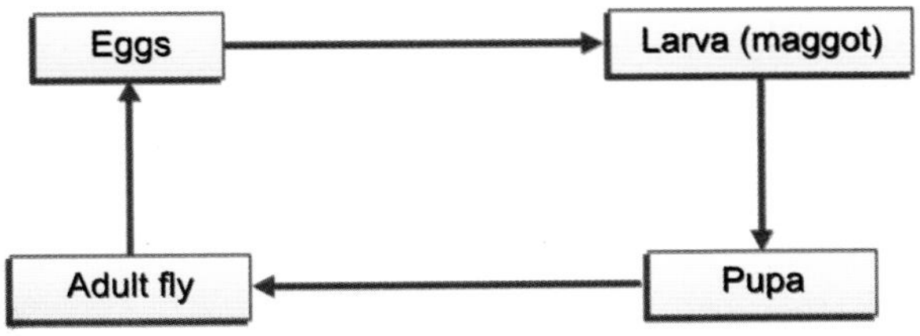

FIG. 7.49: Life cycle of fly

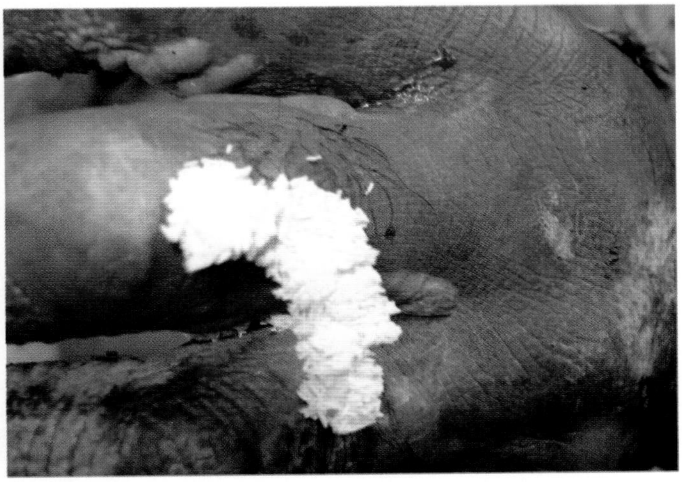

FIG. 7.50: Eggs

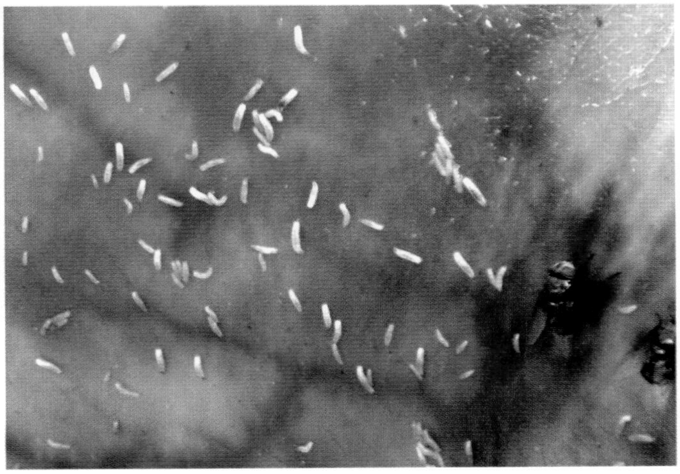

FIG. 7.51: Larvae (maggots)

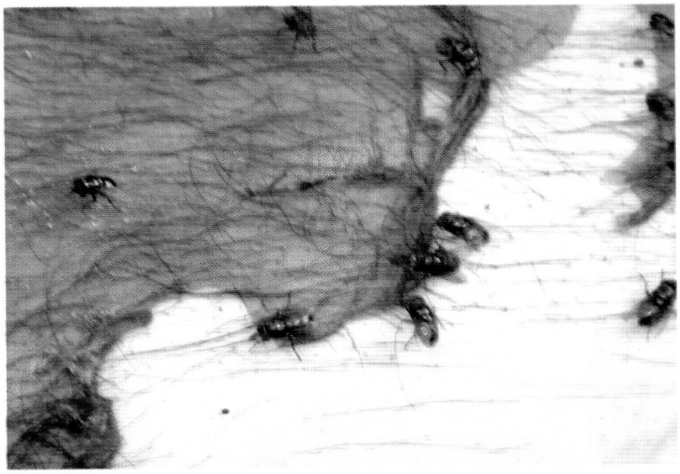

FIG. 7.52: Green-bottle flies

- Live specimens – place in carton with moist soil.
- Materials required for collection of specimens are described in Table 7.20.

Importance

Forensic entomology is important to establish:

1. Manner of death (up to some extent)
2. Cause of death (up to some extent) [57,58]
3. Movement of cadaver from one site to other
4. Postmortem interval[59]
5. Place of disposal.

Table 7.20: Material required for collection of entomological sample
Forceps
Glass vials
Ethyl alcohol
Ice cream cartons or equivalent
Vermiculite or other inert material
Insect net
Surgical gloves
Small artist brush
Plastic bags
Trowel

SUDDEN DEATH

The definition of sudden death varies according to the authority and convention. Accordingly, death occurring within 24 hour from the onset of symptom was considered as sudden death.[60] Many clinicians disagree with the definition as they feel that the period is too long, as many have witnessed death within minutes to hours after admission to hospital. Thus a comprehensive definition was proposed as "*a death which is not known to be caused by any trauma, poisoning or violent asphyxia and where death occurs all of sudden or within 24 hour of the onset of terminal symptoms*".

Etiopathology

The incidence of sudden death is about 10 percent of all causes of death. The causes of sudden natural death are given in Table 7.21.

Circumstances

The sudden deaths or many prefer to call it as unexpected deaths, have actual or potential medicolegal significance in respect to establish the cause and manner of death. The role of forensic expert is often vital in such deaths. The sudden or unexpected deaths usually fall under the following two categories:

1. Deaths occurring in persons who were being clinically examined for prolonged duration without adequate or satisfactory diagnosis or
2. Deaths occur due to any illness of brief duration and the treating doctor has little opportunity to analyze factors responsible for the causation of disease.

Whenever such body is referred to forensic expert, a complete autopsy should be done with relevant investigation to ascertain the cause of death.

Table 7.21: Causes of sudden natural death[61-65]
Cardiovascular system
- Ischemic heart disease
- Cardiomyopathies
- Myocarditis
- Valvular disorders
- Congenital heart disease
- Cardiac tamponade
- Aneurysm
- Aortic dissection
- Coarctation of aorta
Central nervous system
- Hemorrhage
- Ischemia/thrombosis
- Epilepsy
- Meningitis
- Astrocytoma
Respiratory system
- Pulmonary embolism
- Acute epiglottitis
- Fulminant tracheobronchitis
- Pneumonia
- Bronchial asthma
- Spontaneous Pneumothorax
Gastrointestinal system
- Rupture of esophagus
- Acute Pancreatitis
- Hematemesis
- Strangulated hernia
- Volvulus
- Perforation peritonitis
- Ruptured liver abscess
- Mesenteric thrombosis
Genito-urinary system
- Twisted ovarian cyst
- Toxemia of pregnancy
- Amniotic fluid embolism
- Uterine rupture
- Rupture of ectopic pregnancy
Miscellaneous
- Vagal inhibition
- Diabetic coma
- Status thymo-lymphaticus
- Anaphylaxis
- Amnoitic fluid embolism

REFERENCES

1. Perper JA. Time of death and changes after death: Part 1: anatomical considerations. In: Spitz WU (ed) Spitz and Fisher's Medicolegal investigation of Death, 3rd edn. 1993. Charlas C Thomas Publisher, USA. 14-50.
2. Nandy A. Death and postmortem changes. In: Principles of Forensic Medicine, 2nd edn. 2005. New Central Book Agency (P) Ltd., Calcutta. 133-73.
3. Vij K. Death and its medicolegal aspects. In: Textbook of Forensic Medicine and Toxicology, 3rd edn. 2005. Reed Elsevier India Pvt. Limited, New Delhi. 105-48.
4. The Editors. The practice of medicine. In: Fauci AS, Braunwald E, Isselbacher KJ, Wilson JD, Martin JB, Kasper DL, Hauser SL, Longo DL (eds) Harrison's Principles of Internal Medicine, Vol.1, 14th edn. 1998. McGraw-Hill, New York. 1-6.
5. Subrahmanyam BV. Death and Medicolegal aspects. In: Forensic medicine, Toxicology and Medical Jurisprudence, 1st edn. 2004. Modern Publishers, New Delhi. 28-54.
6. Gordon I, Shapiro HA. The diagnosis and the early signs of death: the phenomenon that occurs after death. In: Forensic Medicine-A Guide to Principles, 2nd edn. 1982. Churchill Livingstone, Edinburgh. 1-63.
7. Dikshit PC. Moment of death. In: Textbook of Forensic Medicine and Toxicology, 1st edn. 2007. Peepee Publishers and Distributors (P) Ltd., New Delhi. 35-46.
8. Shepherd R. The medical aspect of death. In: Simpson's Forensic medicine, 12th edn. 2003. Arnold, London. 27-36.
9. Reddy KSN. Death and its causes. In: The Essentials of Forensic Medicine & Toxicology, 22nd edn. 2003. K. Suguna Devi, Hyderabad. 108-21.
10. Parikh CK. Medicolegal aspects of death. In: Parikh's Textbook of Medical Jurisprudence and Toxicology, 5th edn. 1995. CBS Publishers and Distributors, Bombay. 130-79.
11. The Transplantation of Human Organs Act 1994 (42 of 1994).
12. Diagnosis of brain death. Statement issued by the honorary secretary of the conference of medical Royal Colleges and their Faculties in the United Kingdom on 11 October 1976. BMJ 1976; 2:1187-8.
13. Park K. Principles of epidemiology and epidemiologic methods. In: Park's Textbook of Preventive and Social Medicine, 14th edn. 1995. M/S Banarsidas Bhanot Publishers, Jabalpur. 45-106.
14. Arora K. The Registration of Birth and Death Act, 1969 (18 of 1969). Professional Book Publishers, New Delhi. 2007.
15. Adelson L. Homicide by cervical compression and by drowning, asphyxial deaths. In: The Pathology of Homicide, 1974. Charles C Thomas, USA. 521-75.
16. Roy IS. Intra ocular pressure and glaucoma. In: BM Chatterjee's Handbook of Ophthalmology, 4th edn. 1992. CBS Publishers and Distributors, Delhi. 162-201.
17. Behera A, Das S, Das GS. Eye is the spy of forensic medicine. Medicolegal Update 2005; 5:43-5.
18. Kevorkian J. The fundus oculi and the determination of death. Am J Pathol 1956; 32:1253-67.
19. Kevorkian J. The fundus oculi as postmortem clock. J Forensic Sci 1961; 6:231.
20. Wroblewski B, Ellis M. Eye changes after death. Br J Surg 1970; 57:69-71.
21. Singh D, Prashad R, Prakash C, Bansal YS, Sharma SK, Pandey AN. Determination of time since death from vitreous potassium concentration in subjects of Chandigarh Zone of North-West India. Int J Medical Toxicol Legal Med 2001; 4:12-7.
22. Gelfand JA, Dinarello CA. Fever and hyperthermia. In: Fauci AS, Braunwald E, Isselbacher KJ, Wilson JD, Martin JB, Kasper DL, Hauser SL, Longo DL (eds) Harrison's Principles of Internal Medicine, Vol.1, 14th edn. 1998. McGraw-Hill, New York. 84-9.
23. Bhat VJ, Palimar V, Kumar PG. Reliability of postmortem lividity as an indicator of time since death in cold stored bodies. Medicolegal Update 2006; 6:5-7.
24. Bohnert M, Weinmann W, Pollak S. Spectrophotometeric evaluation of postmortem lividity. Forensic Sci Int 1999; 99:149-58.
25. Suhani MN, Shahrom AW, Zarida H. Electrical excitation of skeletal muscle for the estimation of time since death in the early postmortem period. J Forensic Med Toxicol 2006; 23:1-6.
26. Ganong WF. Excitable tissue: Muscle. In: Review of Medical Physiology, 19th edn. 1999. Prentice-Hall International, London. 60-79.
27. Forster B. The contractile deformation of skeletal muscle in rigor mortis. J Forensic Med 1963; 10:133-47.
28. Dalal JS, Tejpal HR, Chanana A, Kaur N. Medicolegal study of rigor mortis to estimate postmortem interval. J Indian Acad Forensic Med 2006; 28:49-51.
29. Saukko P, Knight B. The Pathophysiology of death. In: Knight's Forensic Pathology, 3rd edn. 2004. Arnold, London. 52-97.
30. Krompecner T, Bergerioux C. Experimental evaluation of rigor mortis. VII. Effect of ante and postmortem electrocution on the evolution of rigor mortis. Forensic Sci Int 1988; 38:27-35.
31. Pillay VV. Thanatology. In: Textbook of Forensic Medicine & Toxicology, 14th edn. 2004. Paras Publishing, Hydrabad. 95-112.
32. Haglund WD, Sorg MH (ed). In: Forensic Taphonomy, 1st edn. 1997. CRC Press, Florida.
33. Dogra TD, Sinha A, Ajmani ML. Death and postmortem changes. In: Ajmani ML (ed) Embalming, Principles and Legal Aspects, 1st edn. 1998. Jaypee Brothers, New Delhi. 72-80.
34. Kamath MA. Examination of the living – examination of the dead. In: Medical Jurisprudence and Toxicology, 6th edn. 1960. The Madras Law Journal, Madras. 86-121.
35. Camps FE, Robinson AE, Lucas BGB. Changes after death. In: Gradwohl's Legal Medicine, 3rd edn. 1976. John Wright and sons Ltd Publications and distributed by Year Book Medical Publications, INC., Chicago. 78-100.
36. Simpson K. Changes after death. In: Forensic Medicine, 6th edn. 1972. The English Language Book Society and Edward Arnold (Publishers) Ltd, Great Britain. 7-17.
37. Brondum N, Simonsen J. Postmortem red colouration of teeth. A retrospective investigation of 26 cases. Am J Forensic Med Pathol 1987; 8:127-30.

38. Rentoul E, Smith H. The medicolegal aspects of death. In: Glaister's Medical Jurisprudence and Toxicology, 13th edn. 1973. Churchill Livingstone, Edinburgh. 113-39.
39. Galloway A, Brikby WH, Jones AM, Henry TE, Parks BO. Decay rates of human remains in an arid environment. J Forensic Sci 1989; 34:607-16.
40. Mathiharan K, Patnaik AK. Postmortem changes and time since death. In: Modi's Medical Jurisprudence and Toxicology, 23rd edn. 2005. LexisNexis Butterworths, New Delhi. 423-62.
41. Rodriguez WC, Bass WM. Decomposition of buried bodies and methods that may aid in their location. J Forensic Sci 1985; 30:836-52.
42. Evans WED. Adipocere formation in a relatively dry environment. Med Sci Law 1963 a; 3:145-8.
43. Pfeiffer S, Milne S, Stevenson RM. The natural decomposition of adipocere. J Forensic Sci 1998; 43:368-70.
44. Thurston G. Death. In: Mant AK (ed). Taylor's Principles and Practice of Medical Jurisprudence, 13th edn. 2000. B I Churchill Livingstone, New Delhi. 29-38.
45. Evans WED. Some histological findings in spontaneously preserved bodies. Med Sci Law 1962; 2:155-60.
46. Coe JI, Curran WJ, Hyg SM. Definition & time of death. In: Curren WJ, McGarry AL, Petty CS (edn.) Modern Legal Medicine, Psychiatry and Forensic Science, 1st edn. 1980. F.A. Davis Company, Philadelphia. 141-69.
47. Takatori T, Yamaoka A. The mechanism of adipocere formation 2. Separation and identification of oxo-fatty acids in adipocere. Forensic Sci 1977 b; 10:117-25.
48. Mant AK, Furbank R. Adipocere – a review. J Forensic Med 1957; 4:18-35.
49. O'Brien TG, Kuehner AC. Waxing grave about adipocere: soft tissue change in an aquatic context. J Forensic Sci 2007; 52:294-301.
50. Simonsen B. Early formation of adipocere in temperate climate. Med Sci Law 1977; 17:53-5.
51. Forbes SL, Stuart BH, Dent BB. The effect of the burial environment on adipocere formation. Forensic Sci Int 2005; 154:24-34.
52. Mellen PF, Lowry MA, Micozzi MS. Experimental observations on adipocere formation. J Forensic Sci 1993; 38:91-3.
53. Forbes SL, Stuart BH, Dent BB. The effect of the method of burial on adipocere formation. Forensic Sci Int 2005; 154:44-52.
54. Ajmani ML. Mummification. In: Embalming, principles and legal aspects, 1st edn. 1998. Jaypee Brothers, New Delhi. 81-5.
55. Patel F. Artefact in forensic medicine: Scrotal mummification. J Clin Forensic Med 2003; 10:263-6.
56. Lord WD, Burger JF. Collection and preservation of forensically important entomological materials. J Forensic Sci 1983; 28:936-44.
57. Introna F Jr., Lo Dico C, Caplan YH, Smialek JE. Opiate analysis in cadaveric blowfly larvae as an indicator of narcotic intoxication. J Forensic Sci 1990; 35:1-3.
58. Gunatilake K, Goff ML. Detection of organophosphate poisoning in a putrefying body by analyzing arthropod larvae. J Forensic Sci 1989; 34: 3-7.
59. Kashyap VK, Pillay VV. Cadaver insects of India and their use in estimation of postmortem interval. Indian J Forensic Sci 1988; 2:17-20.
60. Luke JL, Helpern M. Sudden unexpected death from natural causes in young adults. Arch Pathol 1968; 85:10-7.
61. Siboni A, Simonsen J. Sudden unexpected natural death in young persons. Forensic Sci Int 1986; 31:159-66.
62. Gormsen H. Sudden unexpected death due to myocarditis. Acta Pathol Microbiol Scand (suppl.) 1955; 105:30-48.
63. Sarkioja T, Hirvonen J. Causes of sudden unexpected death in young and middle aged persons. Forensic Sci Int 1984; 24:247-61.
64. Jay GW, Leestma JE. Sudden death in epilepsy. Acta Neurol Scand (suppl.) 1981; 82:1-66.
65. Balăzic J, Rott T, Jancigaj T, Popovic M, Zajfert-Slabe M, Svigelj V. Amnoitic fluid embolism with involvement of the brain, lungs, adrenal glands and heart. Int J Legal Med 2003; 117:165-9.

CHAPTER 8

Injury: General Considerations and Biophysics

Where there is injury let me sow pardon.

- St. Francis of Assisi (1181-1226)

Introduction

It is often said, injuries are never mute; they mostly express in form of pain and exist with their injured features. The only difficulty with them is their language and one who interpret them; they speak, else persist in scars indefinitely, revealing the past.

In medical jargon, injury is used synonyms with trauma or wound but their meaning is not same. An injury is any damage to any part of the body due to application of mechanical force. Wound is defined the forcible solution of the continuity of any tissue of body by mechanical force. Trauma is an insult to the state of well-being and the insult may be physical or mental.[1]

Perception of injury to medical man is different from a legal professional. The definition of injury given above is sufficient for medical man. However, legally injury will include "any lesion, external or internal caused by violence, with or without breach of continuity of skin". Thus, the legal conception of wound is more extensive than medical one. Wound has neither been defined nor been included in any of the statues of law in India. In place of ambiguous term wound, law uses the term 'hurt'. Hurt means, "*Whoever causes bodily pain, disease or infirmity to any person is said to cause hurt* (Section 319 of IPC).[2]

Definition and Features

Section 44 of IPC defines injury as "*any harm caused illegally to a person in body, mind, reputation or property*".
Salient features of this definition

1. This definition of injury has wider meaning. It has not only included bodily harm but also incorporated mental suffering and harm caused to reputation or property.
2. Use of term "illegal": here the word illegal is included in definition. The implications of this inclusion are that not all injuries caused are illegal. It means, there are some injuries, which are legal for example, if surgeon is doing operation; he inflicts surgical incision over patient with consent. Here, the surgical incision is not an illegal injury because it is caused for the benefit of patient.

Classification

Injuries are classified in many ways such as:

I) According to Causative Forces

A) Mechanical injuries

1. Blunt force injuries
   - Abrasion
   - Contusion
   - Laceration
   - Fracture and dislocations of teeth/bone
2. Sharp-edged weapon injuries
   - Incised wounds
   - Chop wounds
3. Piercing weapons – stab wounds
4. Firearm weapons – firearm wounds.

B) Thermal Injuries

1. Due to cold
   - Frost bite
   - Trench foot
   - Immersion foot
2. Due to heat
   - Burns
   - Scalds

C) Chemical injuries
1. Corrosion – corrosive acid/alkali/metal salts
2. Irritation – weak acids or alkali

D) Miscellaneous injuries
1. Electricity
2. Lightning
3. X-rays
4. Radioactive substances.

II) Medicolegal Classification

1. Suicidal injury or self-inflicted injury
2. Homicidal injury
3. Accidental injury
4. Defense wounds
5. Fabricated wounds.

III) Injuries in Relation to Death

1. Antemortem injury
2. Postmortem injury

IV) Legal Classification

1. Simple injury
2. Grievous injury.

PHYSICS OF WOUNDING (BIOPHYSICS OF INJURY)

Forensic Anatomy of Skin

The weight of skin is 4 kg and surface area in adult is 2 square meters. Skin is composed of
1. Epidermis
2. Dermis
3. Hypodermis

Epidermis is composed of:[3]
1. Basal layer or stratum basale or stratum germinativum
2. Prickle cell layer or stratum spinosum or malpighian layer
3. Granular cell layer or stratum granulosum
4. Stratum lucidum
5. Horny layer or stratum corneum.

Features

- Most superficial layer is the keratinized dead layer of cells, the stratum corneum that varies greatly in thickness from one part of body to another. On sole and palm, it is thickest while on protected areas such as scrotum and eyelids; it measures only a fraction of millimeter.
- The thickness has forensic relevance in the amount of injury that is needed to penetrate the skin and allow bleeding from the underlying tissues.[4]
- The living layer of skin combines with the horny layer to form the epidermis and has no blood vessels in its thickness.

Biophysics

- The human body is constantly subjected to mechanical force during the normal course of life. The body usually absorbs such forces either by
  1. Resilience and elasticity of its soft tissues or
  2. The rigid strength of its skeletal framework.
- Wound is produced only when the intensity of the applied force exceeds the capability of the tissues to adapt or resist.
- A wound is produced mechanically by physical contact between the weapon/object of offense and the body because of either:
  1. A moving weapon or object strikes the body or
  2. The moving body strikes against a stationary object or weapon.
- In first case, the inertia of body provides the counter force whereas in later case, it is the rigidity of some stationary object or weapon over which the body falls. Usually, a combination both forces are involved.
- Due to impact between the propelling force of weapon and the counter force offered by body, energy gets transferred to the body tissues that in turn produce changes in their state of rest or motion.
- Human body is composed of various complex tissues of varied physical properties such as
  1. State of solidity
  2. Fluidity
  3. Density
  4. Elasticity
- Because of these properties, a change in the state of rest or motion of the body produced by a forceful impact will not affect all tissues uniformly.

Forces Acting Over Body

There are three types of primary forces acting over body and are
1. Tensile force (traction-strain): It is a force that leads to pull a body apart and if sufficient, may cause separation of body into parts.
2. Compressive force (compression-strain): It is a force that tend to push body together and if sufficient, the body may break into pieces.

3. Shearing force (shear-strain): It is a force that tends to slide one part of body over an immediate adjacent part. This type of force produces alteration in body shape but do not change its volume.
- All body tissues except those contain gas will resist to compression i.e. they will resist to force to get reduced in volumes.
- Due to great variation in resistance of the various body tissues to the tensile force, rupture of tissue occurs when extensibility is exceeded. For example, bone is a rigid tissue; it will resist deformation but when its limit of elasticity is exceeded then fracture results.
- The soft tissues are soft, plastic and pliable. They will rupture when they are stretched beyond the limits of their tensile strength.

Force and Area

- The force acting over body varies directly with the mass of weapon and directly with the square of velocity of impact.

  Thus $F \alpha M$

  $F \alpha V^2$
- Applying with the formula Force = ½ × Mass × Velocity^2 (½ MV^2)
- It means that, for example, a one kg brick pressed against the scalp will cause no injury. However, the same brick of one kg if thrown against the head at a velocity of 10 feet per second may break the skull.
- Another factor of importance is the area over which the force acts. If the acting area is broad then the force will act over greater area and if acting area is small vice versa will occur. For example, if a plank of wood is used to strike against skin, the damage to skin will be greater if narrow edge is used than the impact from flat broad surface. Thus, it can be interpreted as "the force derived from same mass and velocity if applied over smaller area, it will cause greater harm than applying over broader surface".

Factors Influencing for Causation of Wounds

1. Nature of object/weapon[2]
   - If weapon used is sharp one for thrusting in body, the force is concentrated over the small area of strike. Hence a deep penetrating injury will result.
   - The force acting from blow by broad surface/blunt surface of weapon will be dissipated over larger area of body. Therefore the damage will be less than sharp weapon used.
   - A rigid weapon will produce more damage than a plastic or flexible weapon.
   - If the weapon breaks on striking the body, much of the kinetic energy is lost causing less damage.
2. Amount of energy discharged during impact
   - The kinetic energy is = ½ MV^2.
   - A mass of definite weight moving at a definite speed will gather definite amount of energy.
   - The amount of kinetic energy will be doubled when weight (i.e. mass) of weapon is doubled but it will be quadrupled (4 times) when velocity of the moving mass (i.e. weapon) is doubled. In other words, the relationship between energy and mass is linear while the relationship between energy and velocity is exponential.[5] Hence velocity of object/weapon is more important than its weight.
3. Conditions under which the energy is discharged
   - If the body is struck by an impact and due to the impact (i.e. momentum) if person is knocks down or falls, then the kinetic energy liberated will be small and local damage will be less. If the person do not falls i.e. he is standing and sustains the impact, then due to immobilization of person, more kinetic energy is liberated causing greater damage.
   - Similarly if time period of discharge of energy from blow/impact is increased, the destructive effect on the target tissues gets decreased.
4. Nature of tissue affected

   A) Skin
   - If impact is on skin, the skin being more pliable but little elastic, it gets readily affected when struck by weapon.
   - When skin surface gets rubbed, its superficial layer gets destroyed. However, skin is resistant to traction forces because of firm cohesion of keratinized cells.
   - Skin when struck with a blunt weapon, the cells affected will get flattened or elongated but not damaged that severely in comparison with the underlying subcutaneous tissue which gets more affected.
   - The skin will readily split when struck and crushed against rigid bone.
   - Except calcified cartilage or bone, skin offer more resistance to stab wound followed by muscle.[6-8]

   B) Subcutaneous tissue
   - The subcutaneous tissues are plastic and pliable due to deposition of fat amidst the supporting connective tissue fibers.
   - Due to such arrangement of subcutaneous layer, it acts as cushion for body. Therefore it will provide cushioning effect for ordinary blows. However, with severe blunt blows/impact, the subcutaneous vessels will get crushed and displaces fat droplets and tear

the connective tissue framework resulting in contusion or laceration.

C) Muscle

- Muscles are elastic and plastic
- Muscles can resist impact up to certain extent however, if its elasticity exceeds, the muscles will get avulsed, torn, rupture, stretch or crushed.

D) Bone

- The bones are rigid and elastic. They first bend against force without breaking and recoil back to its original shape after releasing the force.
- However, when the bone is bent beyond its limit of elasticity, it breaks at the point of maximum convexity of bending. Thus green stick fracture results.
- When applied force is acting over greater surface area, it causes extensive bending strains and bone breaks with multiple fracture fragments.
- A twisting strain produces spiral fracture.

E) Body fluid and gases

- Fluid can be easily displaced but cannot be compressed or reduced in size whereas gases can be compressed easily.
- Example – sudden compression of chest may cause rupture of capillaries and small venules in the face, neck and shoulder from the retrograde displacement of blood in these veins.
- Though gases are compressible, but violent compression may set up powerful pneumostatic force causing damage, e.g. blast injury.

REFERENCES

1. Pillay VV. Mechanical injuries. In: Textbook of Forensic Medicine and Toxicology, 14th edn. 2004. Paras Publishing, Hyderabad. 138–53.
2. Mukherjee JB. In: Forensic Medicine and Toxicology Vol. I, 2nd edn. 1994. Arnold Associates, New Delhi.
3. Singh IB. Skin and its appendages. In: Textbook of Human Histology, 5th edn. 2007. Jaypee Brothers Medical Publishers (P) Ltd., New Delhi. 199–212.
4. Saukko P, Knight B. Suffocation and asphyxia, fatal pressure on the neck, immersion deaths. In: Knight's Forensic Pathology, 3rd edn. 2004. Arnold, London. 352-411.
5. Eid HO, Abu-Zidan FM. Biomechanics of road traffic collision injuries: a clinician's perspective. Singapore Med J 2007; 48: 693–9.
6. Knight B. The dynamics of stab wounds. Forensic Sci 1975; 6: 249–55.
7. Jones S, Noks L, Leadbeatter S. The mechanics of stab wounding. Forensic Sci Int 1994; 67: 59–63.
8. O'Callaghan PT, Jones MD, James DS, Leadbeatler S, Holt CA, Nokes LD. Dynamics of stab wounds: force required for penetration of various cadaveric human tissues. Forensic Sci Int 1999; 104: 173–8.

CHAPTER 9

Mechanical Injury

Violence is the last refuge of the incompetent.

- Isaac Asimov

ABRASION

Definition

An abrasion is a type of mechanical injury characterized by loss of superficial layer of skin (i.e. epidermis) or mucous membrane due to application of mechanical force.

Features

- Pure abrasion involves only epidermis
- Abrasions do not ordinarily bleed because vessels are located in the dermis. However, due to corrugated nature of dermal papillae, quite often, dermis is also involved and thus abrasion exhibits bleeding.[1]
- An abrasion does not leave scar on healing.

Mechanism of Production

The mechanical force producing abrasion acts on the skin in one of the following way. However, combination of force may also act, at times, to produce abrasion (Fig. 9.1).

1. Sliding force (friction) or
2. Compression force

Sliding Force (Fig. 9.2)

- If causative force is narrow and sharp, linear abrasion is produced
- If causative force is wider or broad and rough, the abrasion caused will be wider and called as graze abrasion.

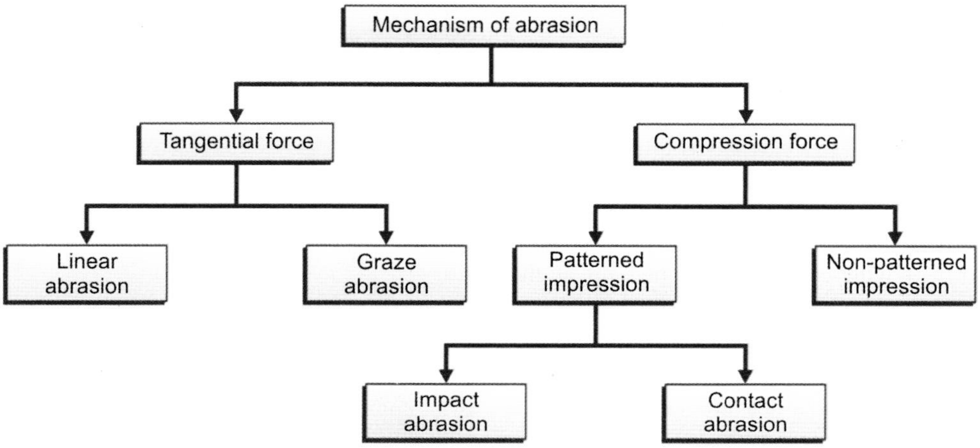

FIG. 9.1: Flow chart showing mechanism of abrasion

Compression Force (Figs 9.2A and B)

- Imprint abrasions are produced by perpendicular force acting on skin with imprint of acting object over superficial layer of skin. Such mechanism will imprint the design of object or weapon. Examples include – radiator mark of vehicle.
- Pressure abrasions are produced by relatively perpendicular force acting on skin with movement of object with crushing of superficial layer of epidermis. Such mechanism will imprint the design of object or weapon. Examples include – ligature mark in hanging or ligature strangulation.

Types

1. Linear abrasion
2. Graze abrasion
3. Pressure abrasion
4. Imprint abrasion

Linear Abrasion

- Also called as scratch abrasion.
- These abrasions are caused by sliding movement of sharp, narrow object such as pin, thorn, barb, prickle, pointed end of weapon etc. (Fig. 9.3).
- The feature of this abrasion is that it is wider at the starting point and shows heaping of epithelium (accumulation) at the end. This heaping up of epithelium indicates the direction of movement of causative weapon or object (also see Fig. 9.2).

Graze Abrasion

- Also called as sliding abrasion, gliding abrasion, brush abrasion, scrape abrasion (Fig. 9.4)
- These abrasions are produced by sliding movement of broad or wider surface against skin
- Graze abrasions are wider at the starting point and they get narrower at the end with heaping of epithelium at the end (Fig. 9.5).
- The abrasion shows, uneven, longitudinal, parallel lines (grooves or furrows) with epithelium heaped up at the ends. The heaping of epithelium gives indication regarding the direction of movement of causative object or surface.
- When the friction force is great, grazed area appears like burn injury. Such graze abrasions are called as brush burn.

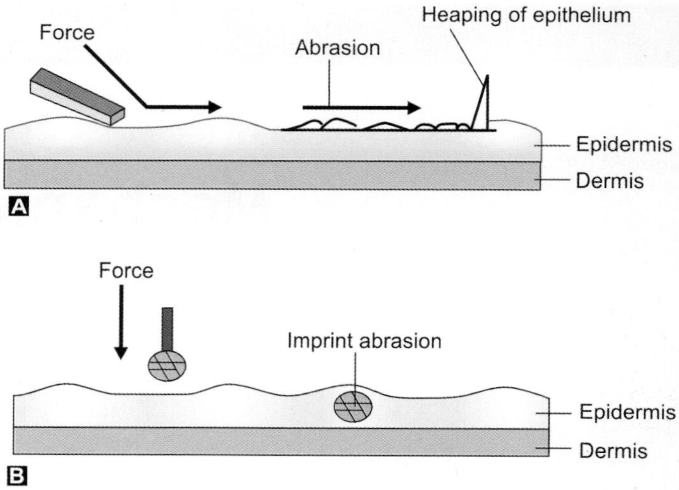

FIGS 9.2A and B: Mechanism of production of abrasion. **A:** Force acting tangentially producing linear or graze abrasion **B:** Force acting perpendicularly causing imprint abrasion

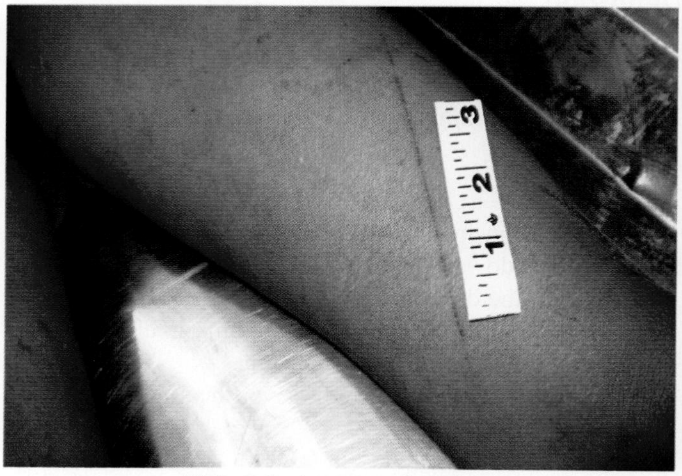

FIG. 9.3: Linear abrasion

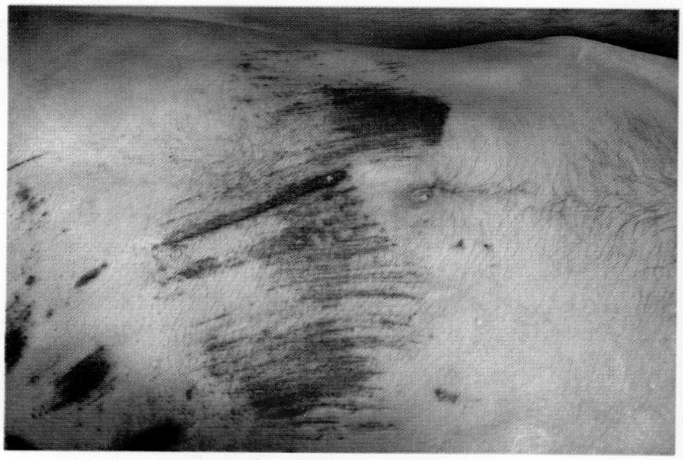

FIG. 9.4: Graze abrasion

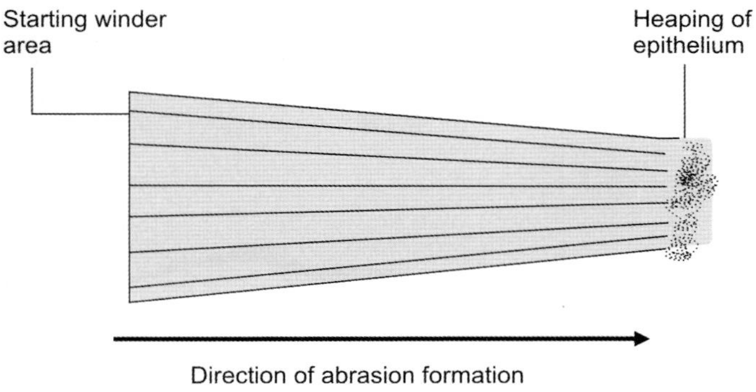

FIG 9.5: Showing graze abrasion formation

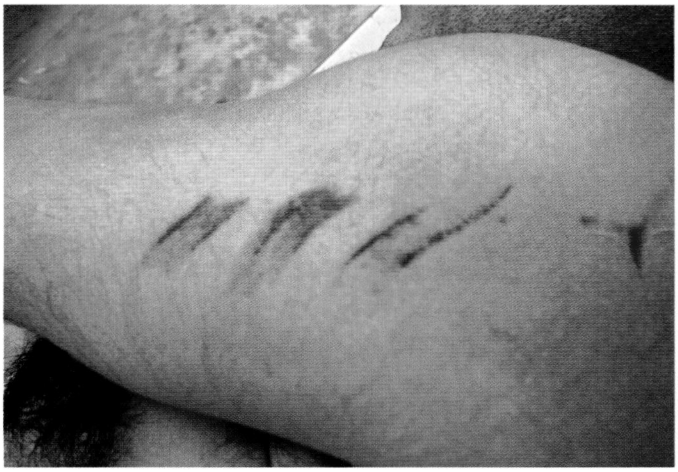

FIG. 9.6: Imprint abrasion

Imprint Abrasion

- Also called as patterned abrasion or impact abrasion or contact abrasion (Fig. 9.6)
- These abrasions are produced when; force is applied perpendicular to the skin i.e. at right angle.
- These abrasions are caused due to direct impact or imprint of the object or weapon to the skin at right angle. When object strikes the skin, the object stamped the skin; skin gets depressed or compressed as per the pattern of the object and reproduces the pattern of object.
- Examples – motor-tyre mark or radiator grill mark over skin in vehicular accident cases or whip marks on beating with whip.

Pressure Abrasion

- Also called as crushing abrasion (Fig. 9.7)
- Some authorities consider pressure abrasion as a type of imprint abrasion
- These abrasions are caused by direct impact or pressure of an object over the skin accompanied by slight movement resulting in crushing of superficial layer of skin. The pressure abrasion, due to crushing, on getting dried up resembles parchment like and appears brown to black.
- Example of pressure abrasion includes – ligature mark found in hanging or ligature strangulation.

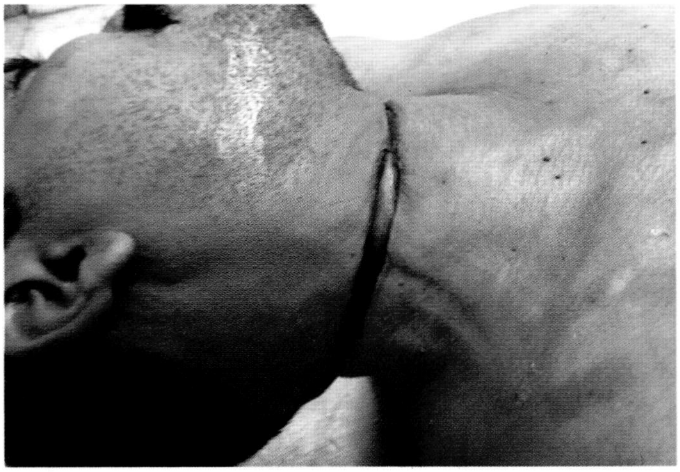

FIG. 9.7: Pressure abrasion

Other Types of Abrasions

1. Contused abrasion and abraded contusion (Figs 9.8 and 9.9): When the crushing force of the causative object is more, then the weapon or object fails to imprint the pattern or design. The crushing will cause damage of capillaries in the dermis with extravasation of blood (contusion) surrounding the abrasion. If the contused area is more marked than abrasion, it is called as **abraded contusion**. Alternatively, if abraded area is more prominent than contusion, it is called as **contused abrasion**.[2]
2. Postmortem abrasion (Fig. 9.10): These are the abrasions produced after death. These abrasions are pale white in colour and dry. Differentiation between postmortem and antemortem abrasion is given in Table 9.1. These abrasions may be caused by ant bites or by mechanical force for example dragging of body etc.

3. Ant bite marks in postmortem state may resemble abrasion. Ant bite marks are usually pale and are irregular in shape (map like). They are mostly located in moist regions of body such as axilla, groins, scrotum, nose, and mouth or around eyes (Fig. 9.11).
4. Fabricated abrasion: These are the abrasions inflicted by a person by oneself or with the help of others, with a motive to implicate another person for false allegation of injuries.
5. Nappy abrasions: These abrasions are seen in infants due to excoriation of skin at the nappy area i.e. groin and buttocks. Fecal matter or excreta cause excoriation.

Differential Diagnosis

Abrasions may be confused with

1. Postmortem abrasions
2. Excoriation of skin by excreta
3. Pressure sore/bed sore
4. Ant bites

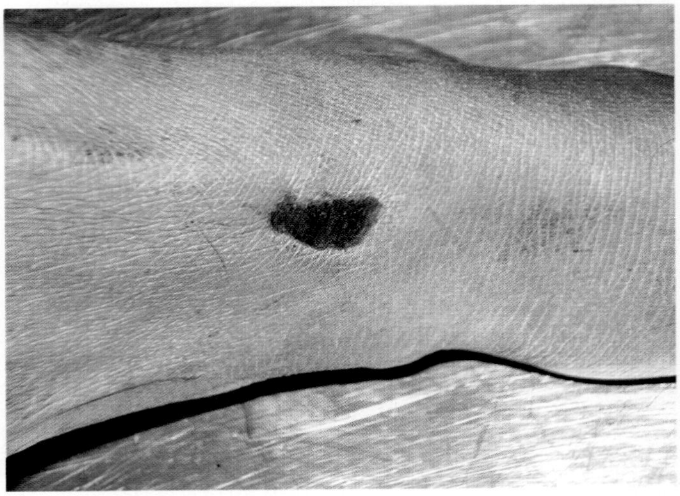

FIG. 9.9: Abraded contusion

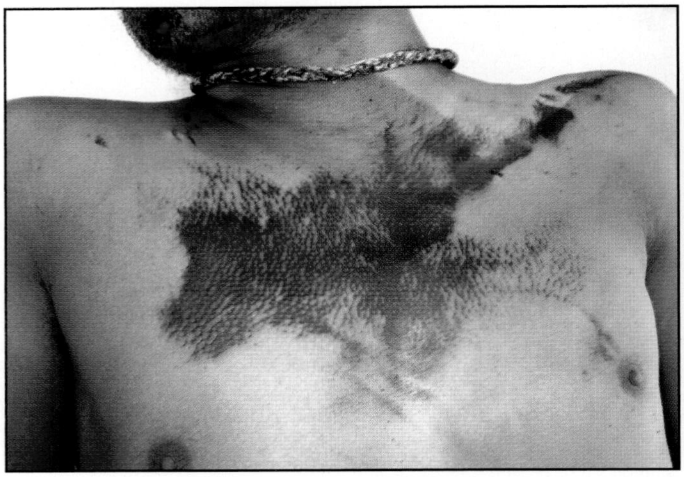

FIG. 9.8: Contused abrasion

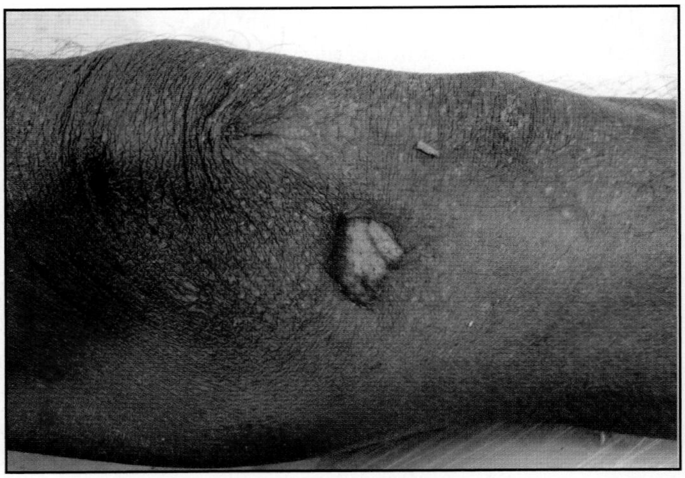

FIG .9.10: Postmortem abrasion

Table 9.1: Difference between antemortem and postmortem abrasion

Features	*Antemortem abrasion*	*Postmortem abrasion*
Site	At anywhere on body	Over bony prominences
Color	Bright red	Pale, dry and parchment like
Covering	Covered with scab composed of coagulation of blood and lymph	No such scab
Inflammation	Signs of inflammation present	No
Microscopy	Congestion and vital reaction present	No

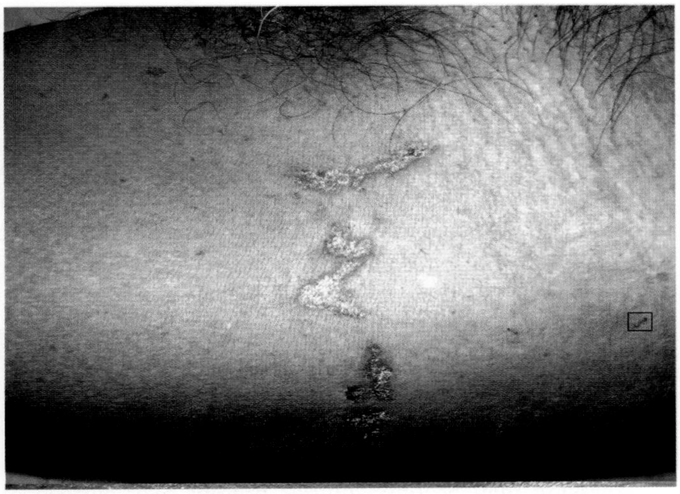

FIG. 9.11: Ant bite marks resembling abrasion. Note ant in black rectangle

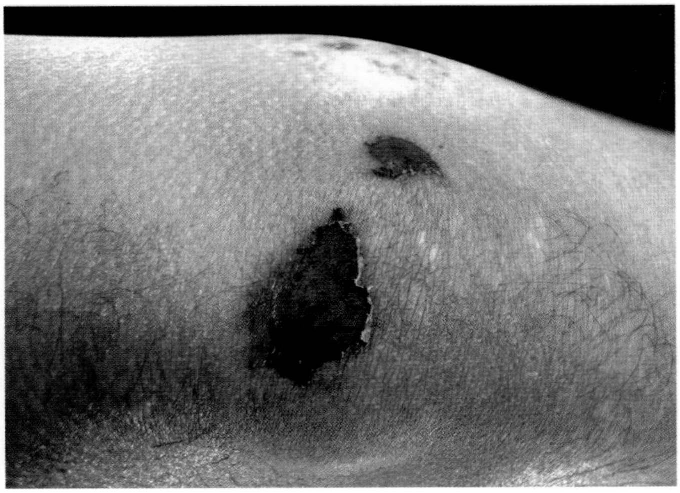

FIG. 9.12: Fresh abrasion

Healing of Abrasion

- Abrasion heals by undergoing contraction of wound and replacement of lost tissues. Initially the abrasion will be bright red in colour and it is covered by scab composed of blood and lymph.
- Microscopically, there is cellular infiltration seen at about 4 to 6 hour and about 12 hour three layers are identified consisting of surface zone of fibrin and red cells, a middle zone of polymorphnuclear cells and deeper layer of damaged and abnormally staining collagen. At about 48 hours, epithelial regeneration is evident at periphery with formation of granulation tissue at sub-epithelial area.
- Abrasions heal from periphery by new growth of epithelial cells. Usually, scab falls off by 7 to 10 days and leaves pale hypopigmented area.

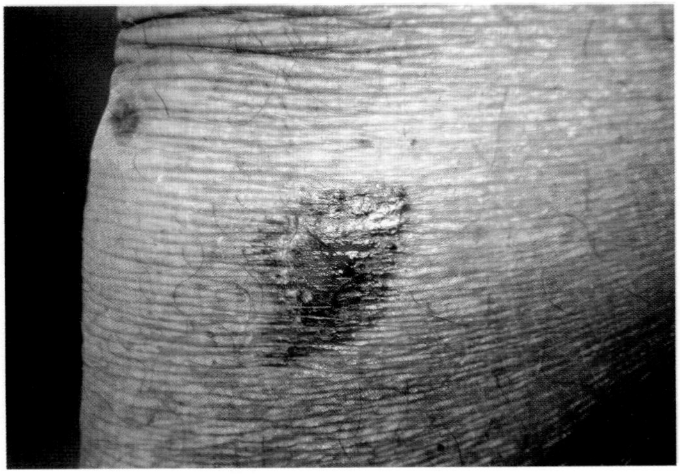

FIG. 9.13: Dark red scab

Age of Abrasion

Age of abrasion can be estimated. The features from which age is estimated are presented in Table 9.2 (Also see Figs 9.12 to 9.17).

Table 9.2: Age of abrasion

Age	*Features*
Fresh	Reddish, no scab
12 - 24 hour	Dark red scab
1-2 days	Reddish brown scab
3-5 days	Dark brown scab
5-7 days	Blackish scab shrinks and falling begins from margin
7-10 days	Scab falls off, leaving hypopigmented area

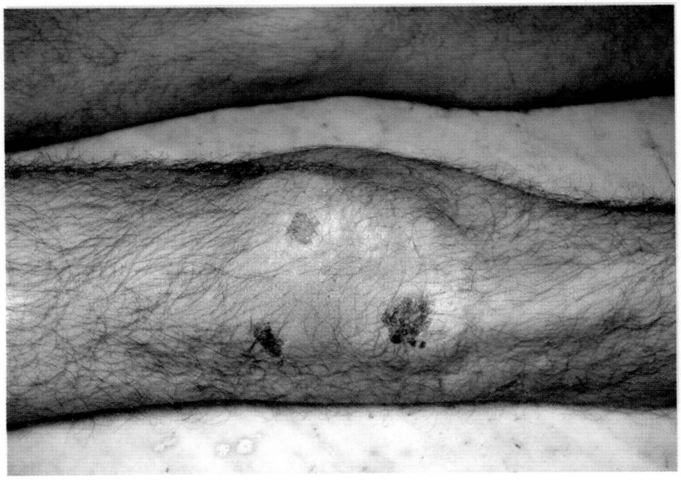

FIG. 9.14: Reddish brown scab

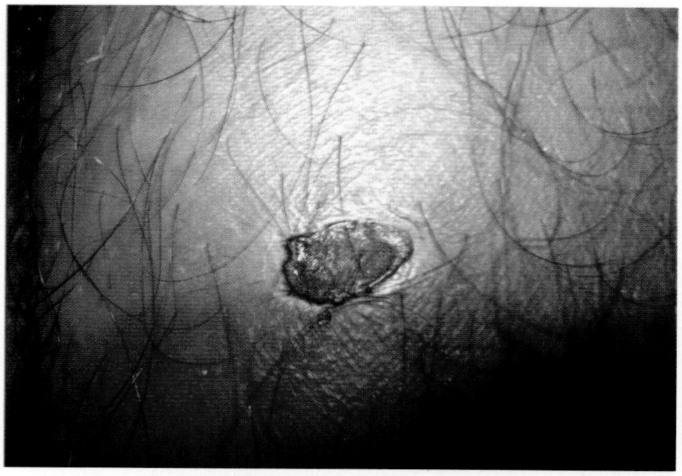

FIG. 9.15: Dark brown scab

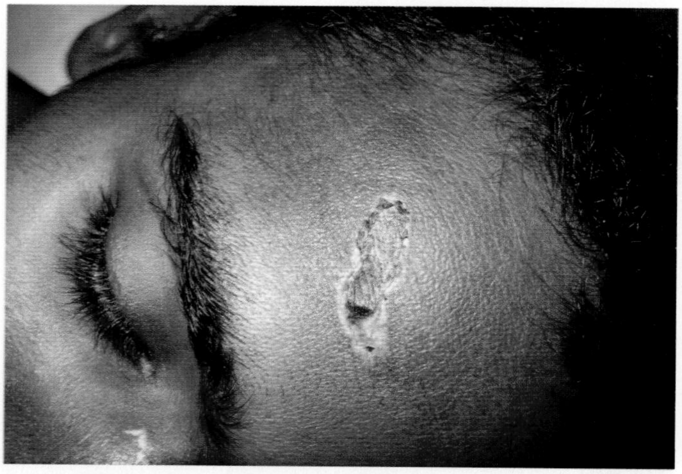

FIG. 9.16: Abrasion with falling of scab from periphery (margin)

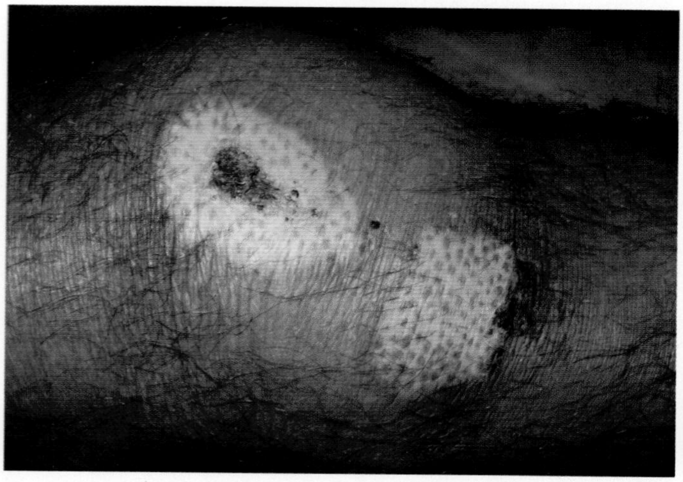

FIG. 9.17: Scab falls leaving hypopigmented area

Medicolegal Importance

1. Site of impact and direction of force used to inflict abrasion can be known
2. Type of weapon/object used can be identified
3. Time of assault can be determined from the age of abrasion
4. Abrasions are usually simple injuries. However, abrasion over cornea may produce corneal opacity and restrict vision of a person. Such hurt becomes grievous one.
5. Can give idea about some type of offenses committed. For example abrasion near private parts of female may be suggestive of sexual offense attempted or committed. Similarly abrasion at neck may be indicative of throttling. Abrasion around mouth and nose may be suggestive of smothering.
6. Abrasion may be only injuries present over surface of deep seated or internal injury.
7. Presence of foreign material along with abrasions, such as sand particles, mud, dirt, grease etc. may connect the injuries with scene of crime.

CONTUSION

Synonym: Bruise

Definition

A contusion is an extravasation or collection of blood due to rupture of blood vessels caused by application of mechanical force of blunt nature without loss of continuity of tissue.

Mechanism

Contusion is caused by blunt force impact causing crushing or tearing of subcutaneous tissue or dermis without breaking the overlying skin or mucous membrane. Due to rupture of blood vessels, there is extravasation of blood out of vessels and collected underneath the tissue. Collection of blood is accompanied by swelling and pain. A pure bruise lies beneath the intact epidermis (Fig. 9.18).

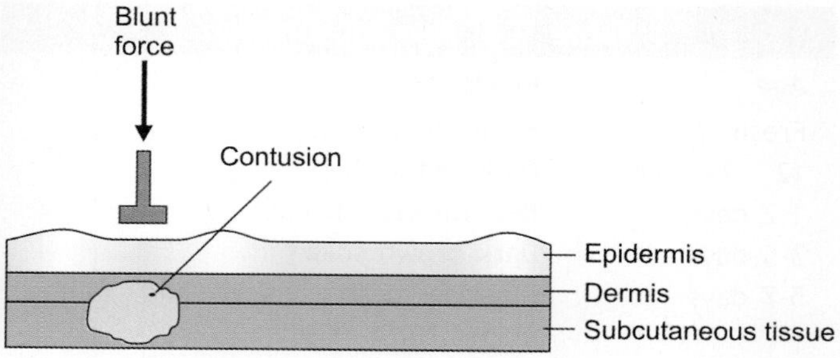

FIG. 9.18: Mechanism of contusion formation

Types

- Intradermal bruise
- Subcutaneous bruise
- Patterned contusion
- Deep bruise
- Tram-line contusion
- Six-penny bruises
- Horse-shoe-shaped contusion
- Contusion over organs
- Gravitating or shifting contusion
- Spectacle hematoma.

Intradermal Bruise

- In this type, the bruise is situated in the sub-epidermal layer of skin.
- Patterned bruises are often associated with intradermal bruise. Due to superficial position of these bruises and translucency of the skin that overlies these bruises, the patterned contusion becomes more prominent
- The bruises are usually occured at the point of application of force
- The margins in intradermal bruises are quite distinct
- Examples – motor tyre marks, impacts from whip, impact from rubber soles of shoes (Fig. 9.19).

Subcutaneous Bruise

- These bruises are the commoner types and are located in the subcutaneous tissue often in the fat layer above the deep fascia and therefore are fairly visible through the skin. Such bruise is called as **superficial bruise** (Fig. 9.20).

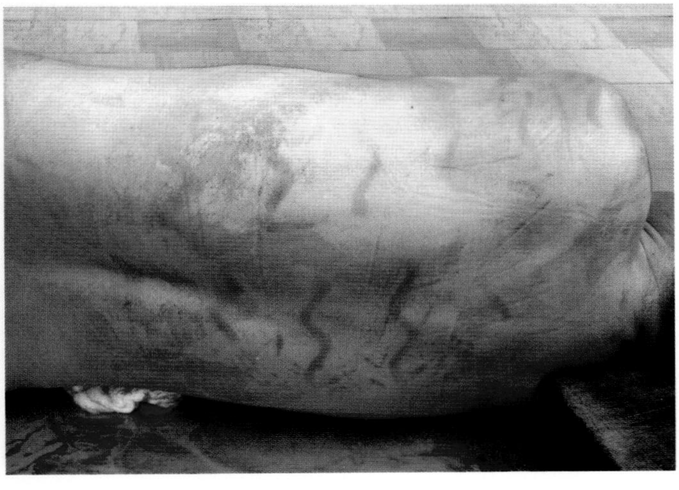

FIG. 9.19: Intradermal bruise

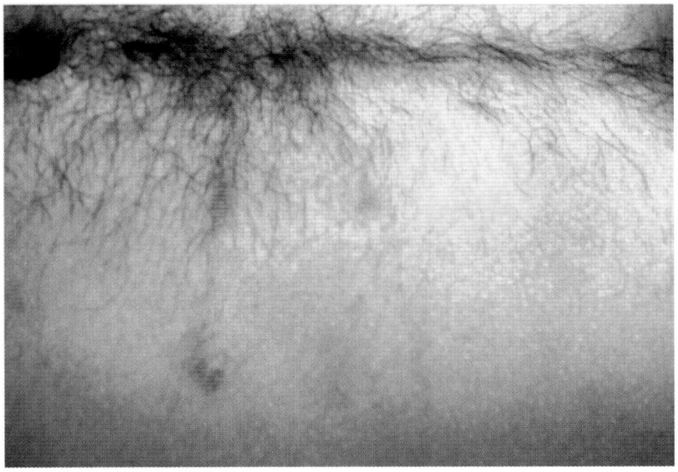

FIG. 9.20: Superficial contusion

- If such bruises are located below the deep fascia, such bruises are called as **deep contusions** and these bruise take time to appear over surface
- The features of these bruises are that the margins appear blurred especially at the edges.[3]

Patterned Contusion

- In certain cases, the surface may show patterned contusion. These contusions are called as patterned contusions because in such contusions, the imprint or design of the offending weapon or objected is imprinted over the skin.
- If such patterned contusions are present, they provide vital information regarding the nature of the offending object or weapon.
- Examples – discoid contusions produced over neck in manual strangulation by fingertips, impression of motor tyre, impression of rubber sole of shoe, tram-line contusion etc.

Shifting Bruise

- A bruise may appear at the site of application of mechanical force or may appear at different site from the initial point of contact. Such bruises that appear at different site from the actual site of application of mechanical force are called as shifting bruises.
- This sort of feature is frequently associated with deep-seated contusions.
- When the bruise is located in deep tissue then it takes time to appear at skin surface. The movement of bruise from deep-seated tissue to surface is governed by number of factors such as fascial planes, anatomical structure of that particular location and gravitational force acting.
- Example – let us take an example of contusion in forehead. If the victim survives for some period after sustaining

bruise than the contusion in forehead can slide downwards over the eyebrow and appear as black eye (Fig. 9.21). Similarly bruises situated at arm or thigh may gravitate downward to appear at lower surface at elbow or knee.

- Such shifting of bruises from the point of impact to newer area are also called as migratory contusions and if they appear at newer areas then such contusions are called as **ectopic contusions** or **percolated contusions**. Similarly the occurrence of bruises to come out from deep site to surface is also called as **come-out-bruise**. This phenomenon is due to hemolysis of blood. The freed hemoglobin stains the tissue more and more densely as time lapses.

Tram-Line Contusion

- Also called as rail-road contusion or tram-track contusion
- These contusions are caused by blow with rod, stick, whip or belt etc.
- The contusion is characterized by two-parallel tram-track like lines of hemorrhages with intermediary area of skin remains intact (Fig. 9.22).
- Mechanism – blow with object like stick or rod over skin causes the skin beneath the part of contact of weapon to get compressed. Due to compression of skin by the offending object or weapon, the blood in that part is displaced sideways causing tram-track like hemorrhages on the side of the skin.

Six-Penny Bruises

- These are the discoid shaped bruises of about a centimeter in diameter and resulted from fingertip pressure.
- These bruises are called as six-penny bruises because of the apparent resemblance with six penny
- These bruises are usually found in neck region in case of manual strangulation. They may also be noted over the arms, forearms or wrist of children in child abuse cases caused by holding a child.

Tissue and Organ Contusion[4]

- All organs can be contused. A contusion of the brain with bleeding into the substance of the brain, may initiate swelling with generalized accumulation of acid byproducts of metabolism that causes further swelling and impairment of brain functions. Contusion over brainstem often proves fatal.
- Heart is also vulnerable to contusion. A small contusion on the heart may cause serious disruption of the normal rhythm or cessation of cardiac actions by interfering with initiation and conduction of impulse responsible for heart beating. Similarly, large contusion, due to swelling and interference with muscle action, often prevent adequate cardiac emptying and lead to cardiac failure.
- Contusion of other organs may cause rupture of that organ's cellular covering with resulting bleeding, either slow or brisk into the body cavity containing that organ.

Factors

1. **Condition of tissue** – contusion results from extravasation of blood in the surrounding tissue. To accommodate this extravasated blood, space should be present in the tissue.

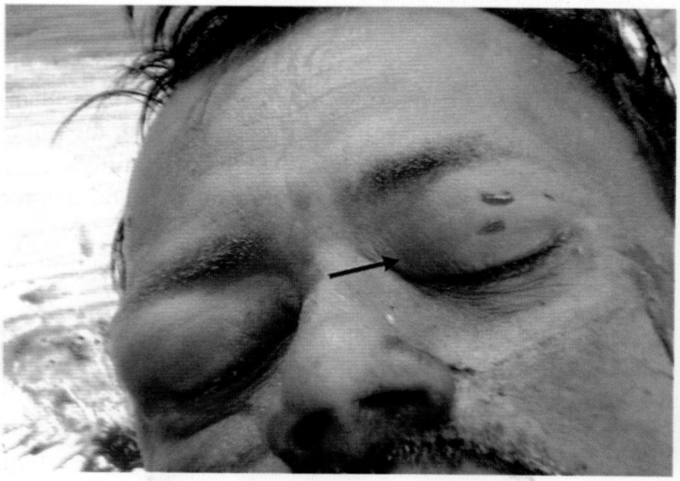

FIG. 9.21: Shifting bruise—black eye

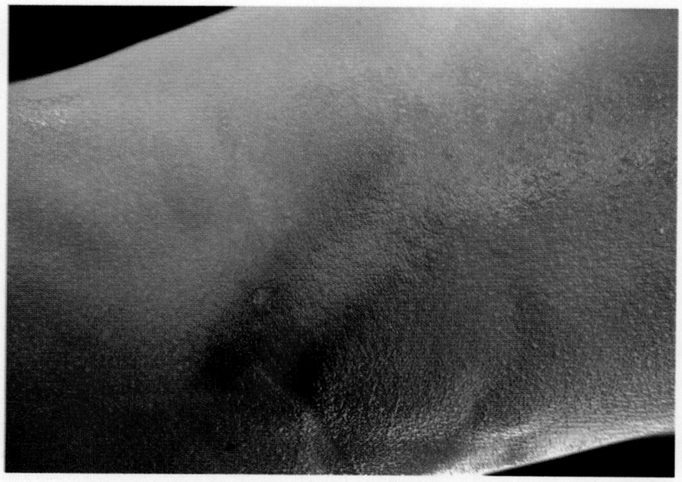

FIG. 9.22: Tram-line contusion

In lax tissue, comparatively more space is available and therefore bruising occurs with ease in lax tissue such as eye socket or scrotum, whereas it is rare in dense tissue such as sole of foot or palm of hand. Similarly, in fat people, there is greater volume of fat and therefore they are more susceptible for easy bruising than the thin people.

2. **Body part** – apparent prominence of contusion depends on the body part affected by the impact. Resilient areas or yielding areas such as abdominal wall or buttock will bruise lesser than unyielding or rigid surface such as head, chest or shin.
3. **Situation of bruise** – contusions located in dermis or in subcutaneous tissue above deep fascia are fairly visible whereas bruises situated in deeper tissues are visible on dissection.
4. **Condition of blood vessels** – the amount of blood extravasated in the surrounding area depends upon the state of blood vessels and coagulability of blood. In older individuals, the vessels being more fragile bruises easily and heavily even with trivial trauma.
5. **Presence of disease** – concomitant presence of any disease such as bleeding diathesis, scurvy, liver disorder, arteriosclerosis, purpura, leukemia, hemophilia, vitamin C and K deficiency, chronic alcoholic or certain medications such as aspirin will lead to bruising easily in comparison with normal people.
6. **Sex** – women will bruise easily in comparison with male counterparts because of presence of abundant subcutaneous fat and delicate tissues.
7. **Age** – older individuals' bruises easily – *vide supra*. Children tend to bruise more easily than adult because of softer tissue composition and less volume of protecting tissue.
8. **Colour of skin** – bruising is more apparent and easily visible in fair skin person than dark complexion persons.
9. **Optical character of skin** – bruises localized near the surface have more reddish appearance while bruises in deeper layer (subcutaneous) give a more bluish colour impression. This is because of optical characteristics of skin. Blood localized in the subcutaneous tissue appears blue on the surface due to scattering processes in the dermis (**Rayleigh scattering**) as the blue wavelengths of light are scattered (and thus reflected) to a greater extent than the red wavelengths.[5]

Repair and Healing

- With advancement in the age of bruise, the blood collected in contusion will begin to disintegrate causing hemolysis. The process of hemolysis liberates hemoglobin. The freed hemoglobin breakdown into hemosiderin → hematoidin → bilirubin by tissue enzymes and histiocytes. With breakdown of hemoglobin and formation of these pigments, certain colours changes are imparted to bruise that can be visualized by naked eye examination. These colour changes are utilized to estimate the age of bruises.
- The time taken for a bruise to disappear will depend on its size.[6] In larger extravasation – the changes usually begin at the margin and takes longer time to be absorbed than smaller contusions.[3]
- Microscopic examination – hemosiderin within macrophages may be seen as early as 24 hours after injury.[7] Hemotoidin is deposited as amorphous yellow granules. Neutrophils appear within one hour after injury and their count increases gradually. Lymphocytes make their appearance after 24-30 hours.[8]

Age of Contusion

There is temporal series of changes occurring in contusion in living person (Fig. 9.23). These changes are utilized to estimate age of contusions. The changes are enumerated[8--11] in Table 9.3 (Also see Figs 9.24 to 9.27).

Table 9.3: Age of contusion

Age	*Changes*	*Caused by*
Fresh	Red	Fresh extravasation of blood
1-3 days	Bluish	Deoxyhemoglobin
4 days	Bluish black to brown	Hemosiderin pigment
5-6 days	Greenish	Hematoidin pigments
7-12 days	Yellow	Bilirubin pigments
2 week	Complete disappearance of contusion	--

Stomping – kicking and jumping on a person is known as stomping.

Battle sign – here hemorrhage gravitates along the fascial planes from basilar fracture of skull and percolates behind and below the ear.

Postmortem contusion – it is stated that with greater degree of application of mechanical force in immediate postmortem period results in contusion. In such cases, the hemorrhage is little and scarce and these contusions are easily differentiated from antemortem bruises. The differentiating features are mentioned in Table 9.4.

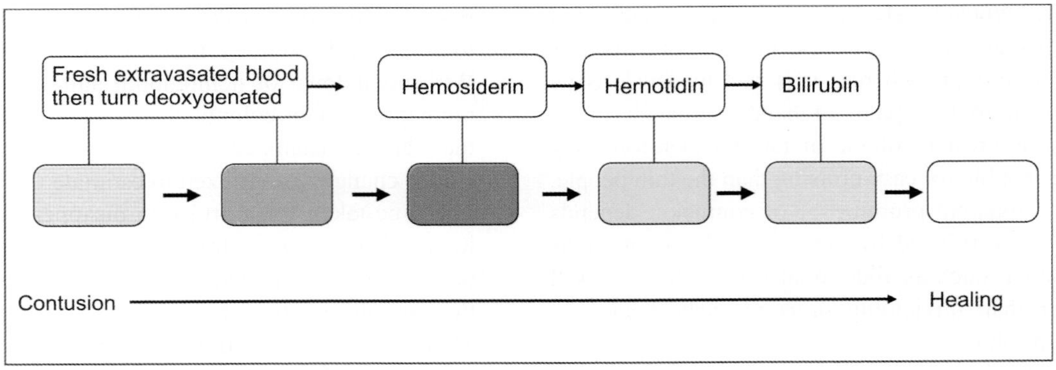

FIG. 9.23: Age of contusion – diagrammatic representation

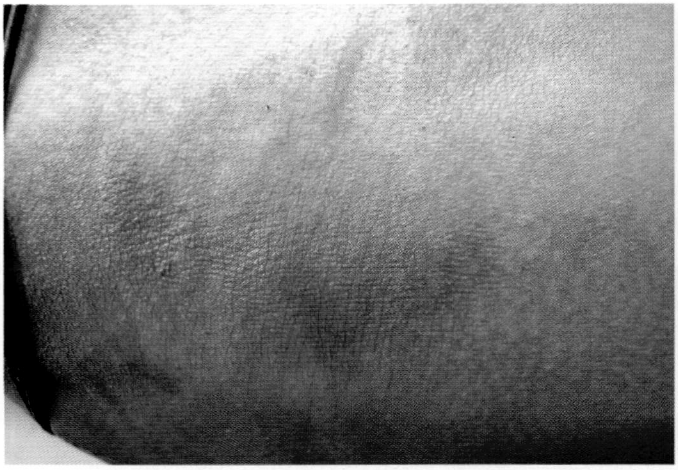

FIG. 9.24: Fresh contusion

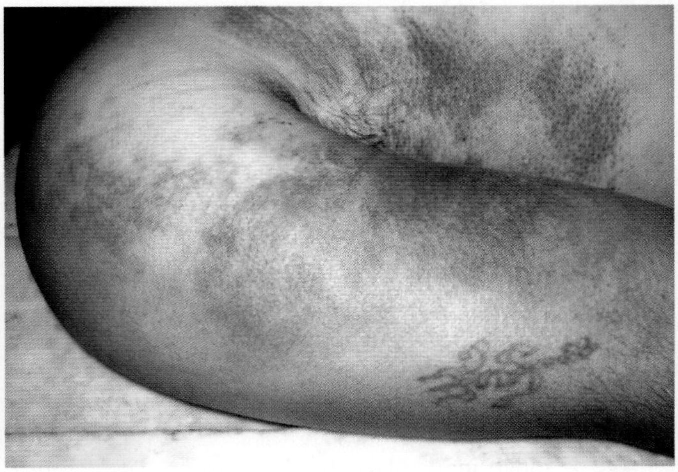

FIG. 9.26: Bluish black to brown contusion

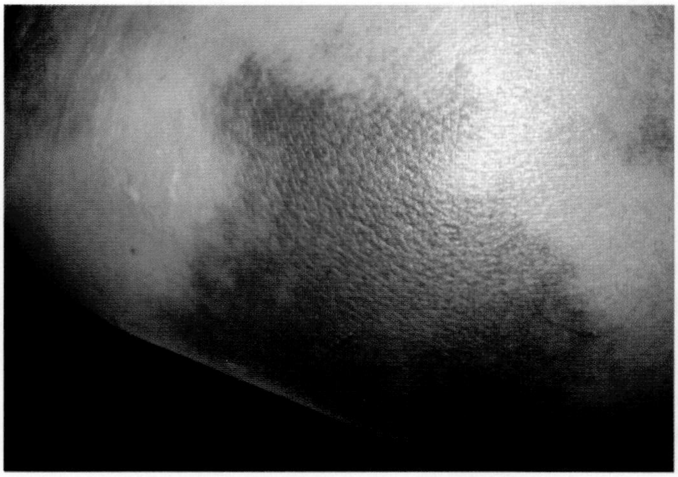

FIG. 9.25: Bluish contusion

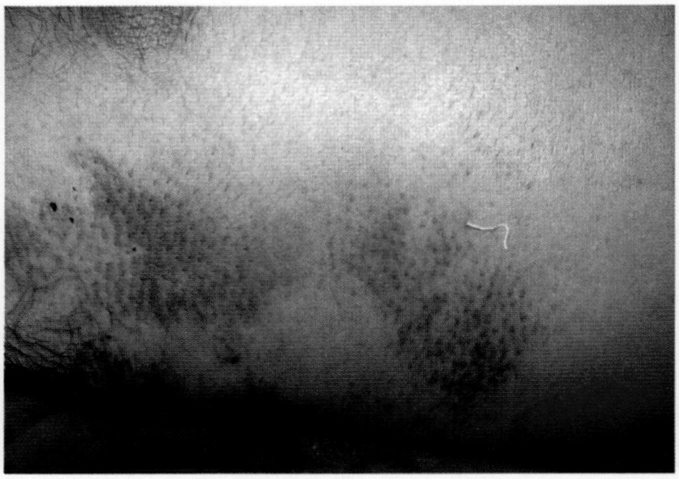

FIG. 9.27: Greenish contusion

Love bites (hickeys) – they are usually elliptical type of patterned bruises. They are caused due to mixture of suction and application of tongue pressure.[12] These bruises are usually found over neck, breast and thighs. These lover bite mark occurs, usually, during consensual lovemaking.

Table 9.4: Difference between antemortem and postmortem contusion

Features	*Antemortem contusion*	*Postmortem contusion*
Swelling	Present	Absent
Extravasation of blood	Present	Absent
Signs of inflammation	Present	Absent
Hemorrhage	Considerable	Insignificant

Value of Bruise

Bruises have less value than abrasion because

- The size may not correspond with the size of offending weapon
- The bruise may visible immediately or may be delayed in appearance
- The bruise may shift from the actual site of assault to other site as ectopic contusion
- The contusions do not indicate the direction of the force applied.

Complications[13]

- If inflicted on vital parts (e.g. neck, heart), the contusions may cause death
- Multiple contusions may cause death by shock and hemorrhage
- The contusions are painful lesions
- Multiple contusions of intestine may cause ischemia or gangrene
- The collected blood in contusion may act as a broth for proliferation and multiplication of bacteria
- Pulmonary fat embolism – due to fat expressed from fat cells and then liquid fat entering the injured and torn blood vessel may lead to pulmonary fat embolism.

Differential Diagnosis

The bruise may be confused with

1. Postmortem lividity (Table 9.5)
2. Congestion (Table 9.6)
3. Artificial bruise
4. Purpura – bruising need to be differentiated from purpura. Purpura develops spontaneously in those persons with a hemorrhagic tendency.

Artificial Bruises

Artificial bruises are produced due to application of some irritant substance or juice to the skin. Such irritant substance produces inflammation and vesication simulating bruises. These contusions are produced with malicious intention to make false allegations against somebody or to implicate someone else. Table 9.7 provides substances causing artificial bruises and Table 9.8 mentions differentiating features between contusion and artificial bruises.

Medicolegal Importance

1. Offending weapon can be known.
2. The age of injury can be determined.
3. Character and manner of injury can be known.
4. Application of degree of violence can be estimated.

Table 9.5: Difference between contusion and postmortem lividity

Features	*Contusion*	*Postmortem lividity*
Caused by	Rupture of vessels with extravasation of blood due to application of mechanical force	Due to stasis of blood in the vessels
Site	Any site	Only on dependent part
Surface	Elevated due to swelling	Not elevated
Swelling	Present	Absent
Colour	Variable, depends on the age of contusion	Usually purplish blue
Edges	Ill defined	Well defined
Incision	Show extravasation of blood in the surrounding tissue and cannot be washed off	Shows blood in vessels with oozing of blood from vessel and can be washed off
Microscopy	Signs of inflammation	No signs of inflammation

Table 9.6: Difference between contusion and congestion

Features	Contusion	Congestion
Caused by	Blunt mechanical force	Pathological condition
Colour	Variable, depends on the age of contusion	No change of colour
Margins	Diffuse and ill defined	Well defined
On dissection	Extravasation of blood	Engorged vessels with blood

Table 9.7: Causes of artificial bruises

Causes
Marking nut
Calatropis
Plumbago rosea
Plumbago zeylanica

5. A bruise is usually simple injury but if present on vital parts or organs may amount to grievous hurt or may cause death.
6. Injection of embalming fluid often enhances the appearance of a contusion on the body surface.[14]

Table 9.8: Difference between contusion and artificial bruise

Features	Contusion	Artificial bruise
Cause	Blunt mechanical force	Application of irritating substance/juice
Situation	Any where	On accessible part of body
Colour	Variable, depends on the age of contusion	Dark brown
Margin	Diffuse and ill defined	Well defined
Shape	May take shape of offending weapon	Irregular
Contents	Blood	Serum
Itching	Absent	Present
Vesication	Absent	Present
Chemical analysis	Negative	Positive for causative substance

LACERATED WOUNDS

Definition

Laceration wound is form of mechanical injury caused by hard and blunt force impact characterized by splitting or tearing of tissues.

Mechanism

When the skin or other structures are subjected to blunt forces, the tissue gets crushed or stretched beyond the limits of their elasticity leading to tearing of the skin or other tissue thus producing laceration. Laceration differs from the incised wounds because in laceration, the continuity of the tissues is disrupted by tearing rather than clean slicing (Fig. 9.28).

Types

Following are the types of lacerated wounds
1. Split laceration
2. Stretch laceration
3. Tear laceration
4. Avulsion laceration
5. Crush laceration
6. Cut laceration

Split Laceration

- Also called as incised looking laceration (Fig. 9.29)
- Split lacerations are caused by blunt force splitting the thickness of the skin most frequently when the skin and soft tissues are crushed between impacting force and underlying bone.
- These types of lacerations are usually found in body parts with underlying bones without much tissue in between.
- Common sites includes – scalp, face, shin etc.
- Due to splitting of skin these lacerations appear like incised wounds.

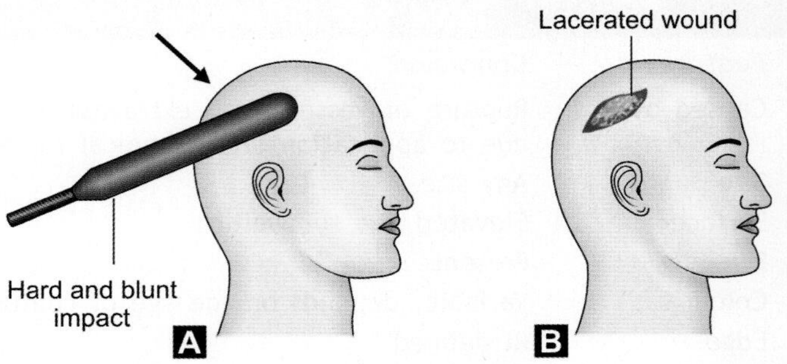

FIGS 9.28A and B: Mechanism of lacerated wound formation. **A:** The head is hit by hard and blunt object that results in lacerated wound as shown in **B**

Section A Forensic Medicine

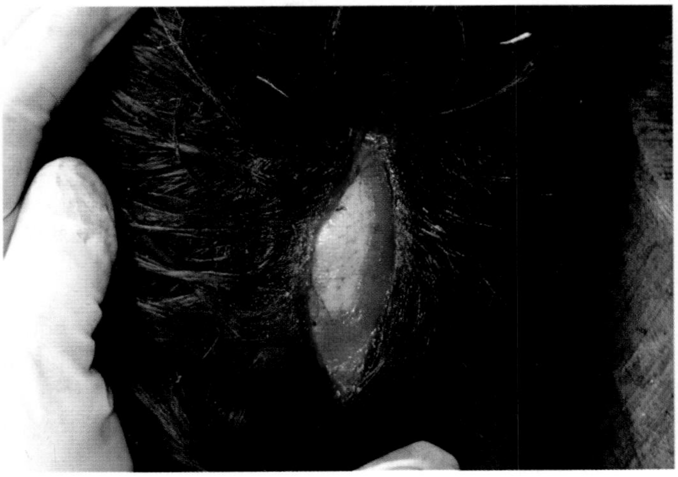

FIG. 9.29: Split laceration

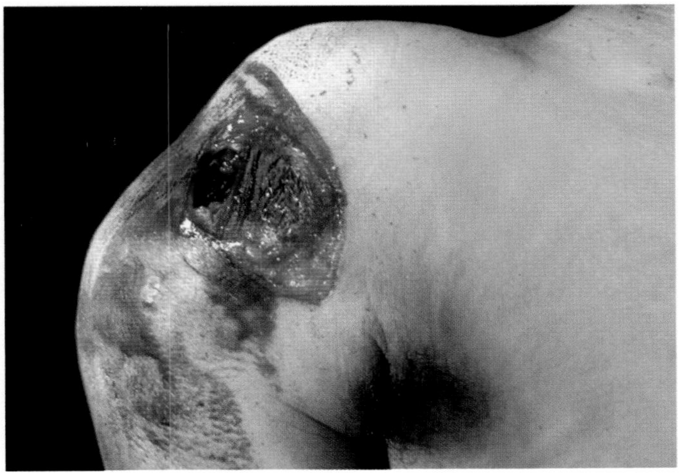

FIG. 9.30: Stretch laceration

Stretch Laceration

- Stretch laceration results due to over-stretching of the fixed skin till it ruptures. In such type of lacerated wound, there is localized pressure with pull that causes tearing of the skin. Thus a pulling force causes stretch laceration (Figs 9.30 and 9.31).
- Example – if pressure is applied over the thigh stretching the skin towards knee, then such force can cause laceration along the inguinal line.
- Striae-like lacerations or stretch mark-like lacerations are also considered as a variety of stretch laceration. These lacerations are superficial and multiple and mostly located at groins. They are usually present in road traffic accident victim when body part (usually thigh or abdomen) is run over. The crushing weight of the vehicle's wheel provides the pulling and stretching of the skin (Fig. 9.32).

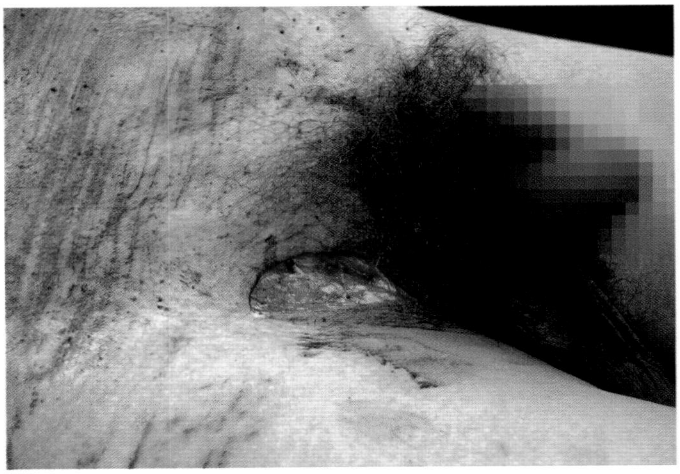

FIG. 9.31: Stretch laceration

Tear Laceration

- It is common form of laceration (Fig. 9.33)
- In this type, tearing of the skin and subcutaneous tissue occurs from localized impact by hard and blunt force
- The acting force from object or weapon rips the skin or tissues producing the laceration.

Avulsion Laceration

- Also called as flaying injury or grind laceration (Fig. 9.34)
- Avulsion laceration occurs due to grinding compression of the tissues to such an extent that the skin gets detached from the deeper tissues thus resulting in the de-gloving of the skin.
- Here, large area of the skin and subcutaneous tissue is rolled off from body part, almost always by the rotary action of the causative object such as rotating motor wheel or tyre.

Crush Laceration

- Here grinding and compression force causes crushing of tissues underneath. This form of injury may cause total or partial amputation of the affected body part for example limb (Figs 9.35 and 9.36).
- It may also be associated with avulsion and/or stretch laceration.

Cut Laceration

- Some textbook described this form of laceration and stated that it is caused by not-so-sharp edge of weapon.[8, 9] However, many authorities consider it as a sort of incised

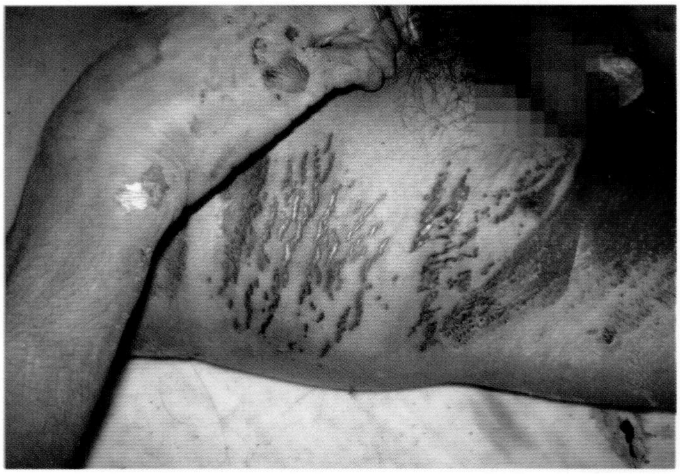

FIG. 9.32: Striae-like lacerations

wound and prefer not to group such injuries under the term - lacerated wound.[1, 15]

Patterned Laceration

- Up to some extent, some weapons may produce patterned laceration but the patterns are not prominent like patterned abrasion or bruises. From some injury pattern, some weapons shape may be recognizable. The examples are given below.
- Blow with hammer head with circular face may produce a circular or an arc of circle (crescentic) shaped laceration
- Long and thin objects may produce linear laceration
- Heavy focal blow may cause a linear or a stellate shaped laceration.

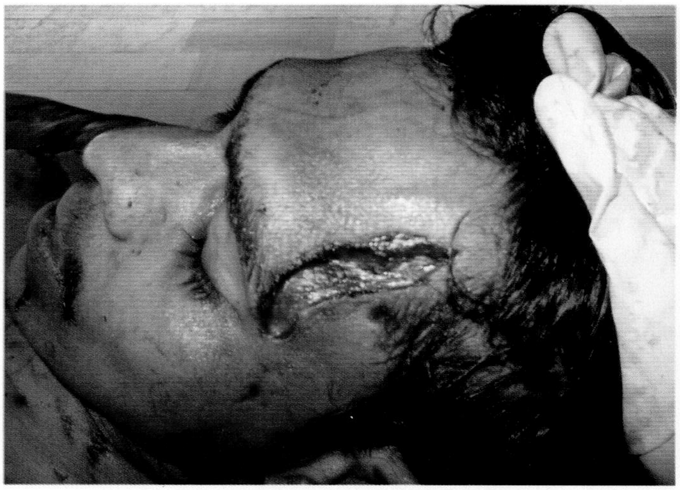

FIG. 9.33: Tear laceration

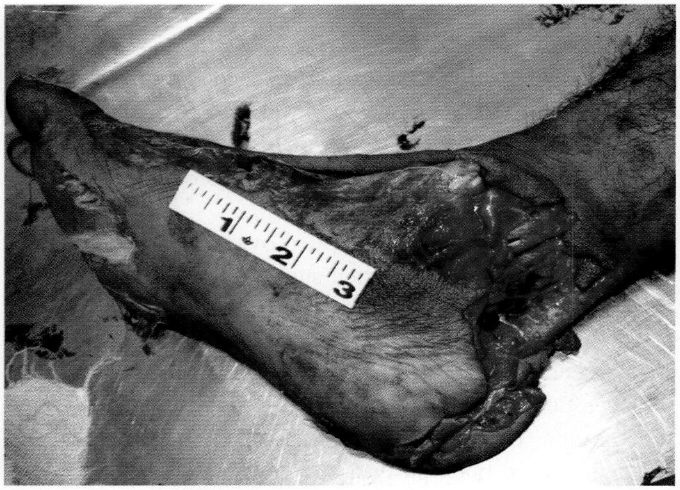

FIG. 9.35: Crush laceration

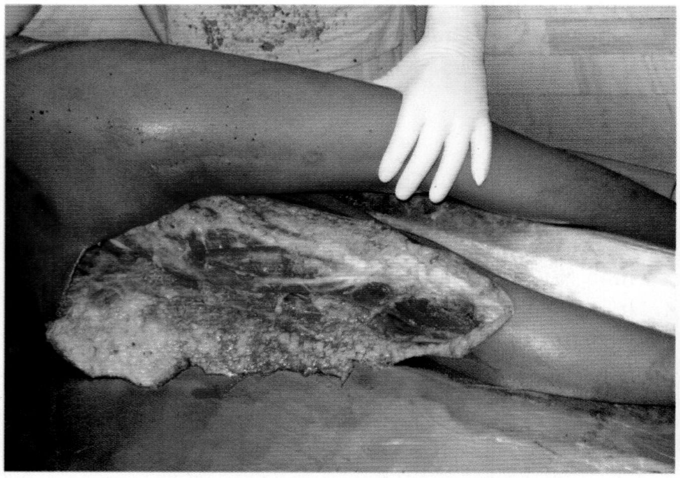

FIG. 9.34: Avulsion laceration

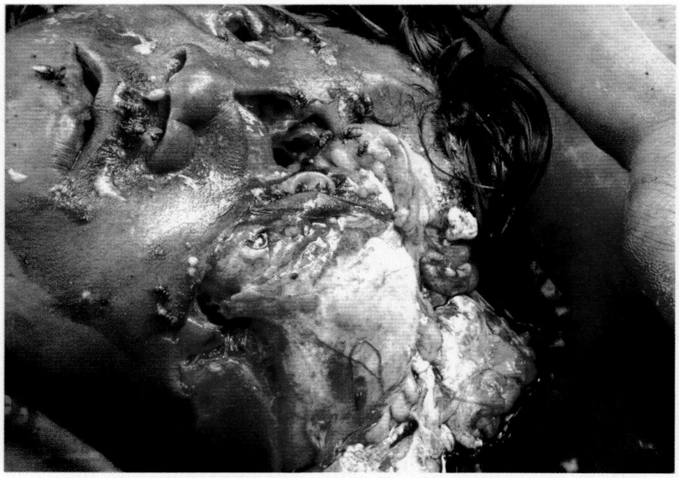

FIG. 9.36: Crush laceration

Boxer's Laceration

These are found in boxer's engaged in active boxing and develops when a boxing glance presses on the orbital margin.

Features (Fig. 9.37)

- In laceration wounds, continuity of the tissues or skin is disrupted by tearing or splitting rather than by clean slicing as observed in incised wound
- Lacerated wound is a three dimensional injury having length, breadth (width) and depth.
- Margins – the margins are irregular and ragged and may be slightly inverted.
- Lacerated wounds gape open
- There may be bruising and crushing of the edges often placed in a narrow zone and requires lens for viewing
- The underlying blood vessels, nerves and delicate tissue bridges may be observed in the depth of wound.
- Hairs bulbs are crushed
- There is absence of sharply linear injury in the underlying bone
- The ends of the lacerations at angles may show shallow tears, diverging from main laceration itself. Such small tears are known as shallow tails.
- Bleeding from lacerated wound is less in comparison to incised wound because the vessels are torn and crushed. The crushed vessels are capable of retracting and undergo thrombosis thus causing less hemorrhage.
- Foreign body or matter may be driven in the lacerated wound or may be soiled by grit, paints, fragments or glass etc.
- The shape and size of lacerated wound may not correspond to the causative weapon or object. However, sometimes peculiar weapon may leave patterned lacerated wound - *vide supra*.

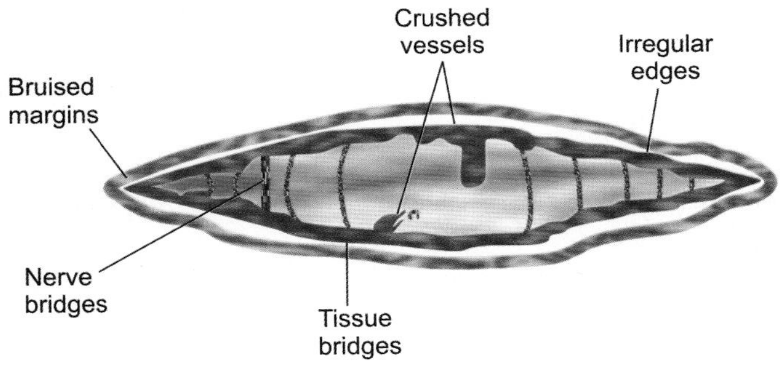

FIG. 9.37: Features of lacerated wound

- Examination of lacerated wound will reveal the direction of the application of the force or how the blow was applied to effect the laceration. The more undermined edge of the laceration is the side toward which the force of striking object was directed; the slopped side of the laceration is that side from which the blow was directed. Similarly the side of laceration with adjacent contusion is often the side from which the force was directed.[4]

Laceration of Organs

Lacerations of the internal organs are caused due to application of blunt mechanical trauma. It may possible that externally no injury may be evident but internal organs may suffer damage. For example, if kick is applied over yielding surface such as abdomen, externally there may be no evidence of injury but internally may cause injury to pancreas.[16]

Complication

1. Hemorrhage and shock
2. Death
3. Infection – act as portal of entry for bacteria
4. Pain and dysfunction of the affected body part

Medicolegal Importance

1. Cause of injury can be known
2. Type of lacerated wound may be known
3. Nature of injury can be ascertained – whether simple or grievous
4. Foreign bodies present in wound may help in identification of the offending weapon/place of incident etc.
5. Age of injury can be estimated
6. It can be known whether the injury is accidental or suicidal or homicidal
7. Direction of application of force can be known.
8. It may be confused with incised wound. The differentiating features are mentioned in Table 9.9.
9. Differences between antemortem and postmortem laceration are mentioned in Table 9.10.

INCISED WOUND

Synonyms: Slash, cut

Definition

An incised wound is form of mechanical injury characterized by orderly solution of skin and tissues by a sharp cutting force.

Table 9.9: Difference between lacerated wound and incised wound

Feature	Lacerated wound	Incised wound
Edges	Lacerated, irregular, ragged	Clean cut
Bruising of margins	Present	No bruising
Injury to blood vessels, nerves	Crushed	Clean cut
Hair bulbs	Crushed	Clean cut
Bleeding	Less	More
Underlying bone	No sharp injury	Sharp linear injury

Table 9.10: Difference between Antemortem and postmortem lacerated wound

Feature	Antemortem	Postmortem
Extravasation of blood	Present	Absent
Coagulation of blood	Present	Absent
Increase enzyme activity	Present	Absent
Signs of healing	Present	Absent
Pus/infection	Present	Absent

Mechanism

- Incised wound may be produced by light sharp cutting weapons like kitchen knife, razor, scalpel etc. Moderately heavy sharp cutting weapons like knife, kookri etc. or heavy sharp cutting weapons like sword, chopper, axe etc.
- The force is delivered over a very narrow area corresponding with the cutting edge of the blade of weapon.
- An incised wound may be produced by following mechanism (Fig. 9.38)
  1. By striking the body with sharp cutting edge.
  2. By drawing or swiping action of the weapon on the body
  3. By sawing – using the weapon saw-like. Sawing action of weapon results in production of more than one incised wounds on the skin at the beginning of the wound, which merges into one wound at the end (Fig. 9.39).

Features

- Incised wounds are always broader than the edge of the weapon causing it because of retraction of the divided tissues
- Often, it is somewhat spindle-shaped and gaping but may be zigzag if the skin is lax like skin of scrotum or axilla (Fig. 9.40).
- The length of incised wound is greater than the breadth or depth of wound.

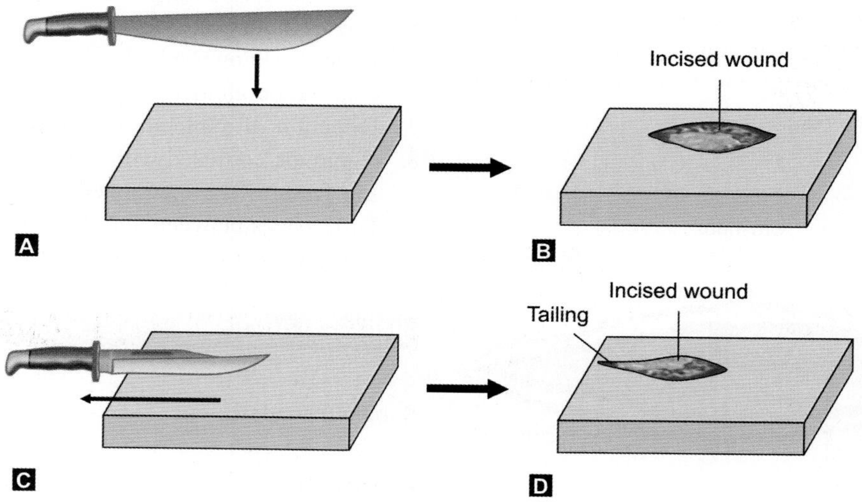

FIGS 9.38A to D: Mechanism of incised wound production. **A and B:** Incised wound produced by striking force **C and D:** Incised wound produced by drawing the weapon

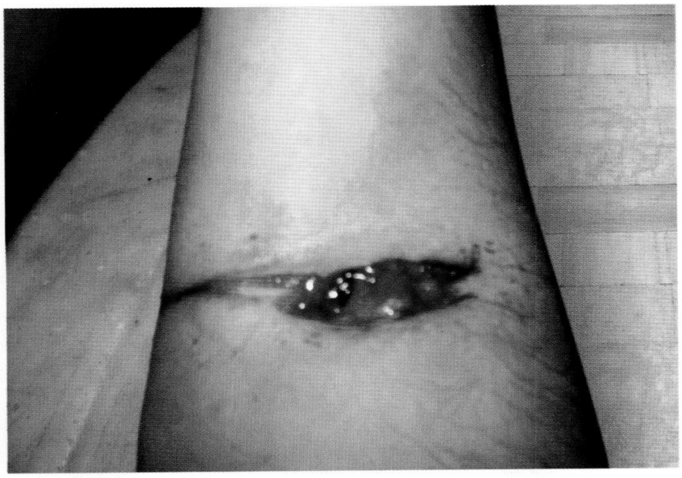

FIG. 9.39: Incised wound produced by sawing like mechanism. Note more than one wound merging into each other

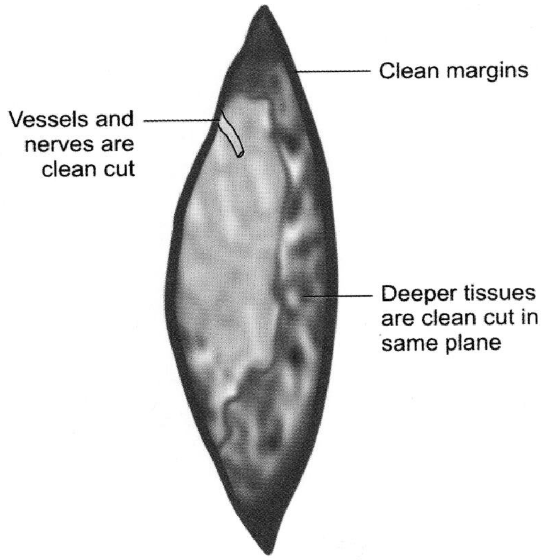
Clean margins
Vessels and nerves are clean cut
Deeper tissues are clean cut in same plane

FIG. 9.40: Features of incised wound

- Margins – margins of incised wounds are clean-cut, well defined (Fig. 9.41). Mostly the margins are everted but may be inverted in some, especially if thin layers of muscle fibers are closely attached to the skin as in scrotum.[15]
- Deeper tissues are all cut cleanly in the same plane.
- The length of incised wound has no relation to the length of the cutting edge of the weapon.
- If incised wounds are inflicted on body areas with loose skin, as in axilla, the wound appears irregular due to puckering of skin occurring at the time of cutting the tissue.

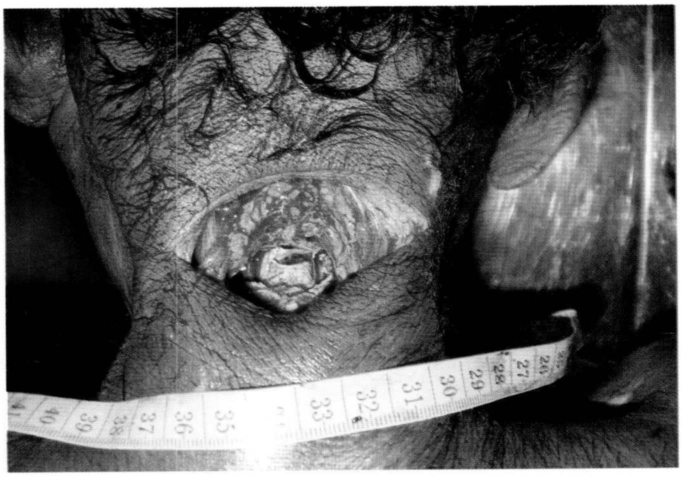

FIG. 9.41: Incised wound

- Usually, the starting end of incised wound is deeper than end part because the wound gradually becomes shallower and may ends in a "**tailing**" or scratch tailing. The tailing off of an incised wound indicates the direction in which the weapon was drawn off.
- Hemorrhage in case of incised wound is more in comparison with lacerated wound because the blood vessels are cleanly cut. The clean-cut ends are not effectively retracted and bleed considerably.
- If the weapon is struck obliquely on the body part, it will cause beveling of one edge and undermining of other edge. Undermined edge indicates the direction from which the slashing stroke was made (Fig. 9.42).

Glassing Injuries

These are the slash injuries caused by broken glass or broken glass bottle.

Self-Inflicted Wounds (Fig. 9.43)

- These injuries are on the accessible part of the body
- They are usually superficial or minor
- They are regular
- Similar in style or shape
- Multiple
- Parallel or grouped together
- Handedness – in right-handed person, injuries are predominantly on the left side and for left handed person; the injuries are inflicted on right part of body.
- Tentative cuts (also called as sympathy cuts) may be evident

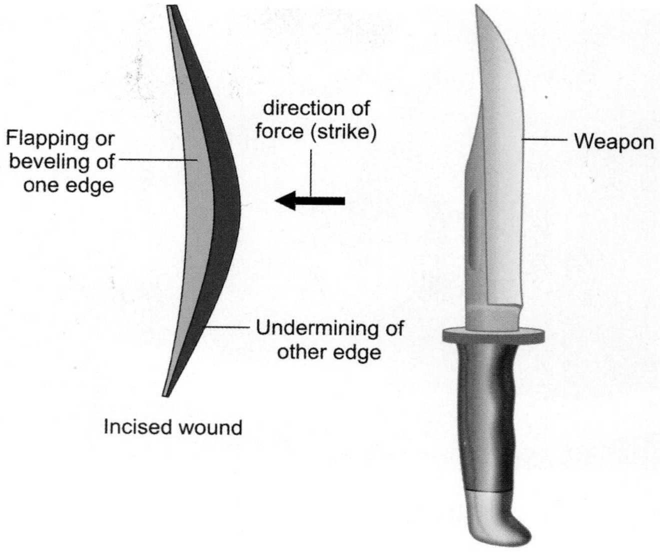

FIG. 9.42: Incised wound showing beveling of one edge and undermining of other edge

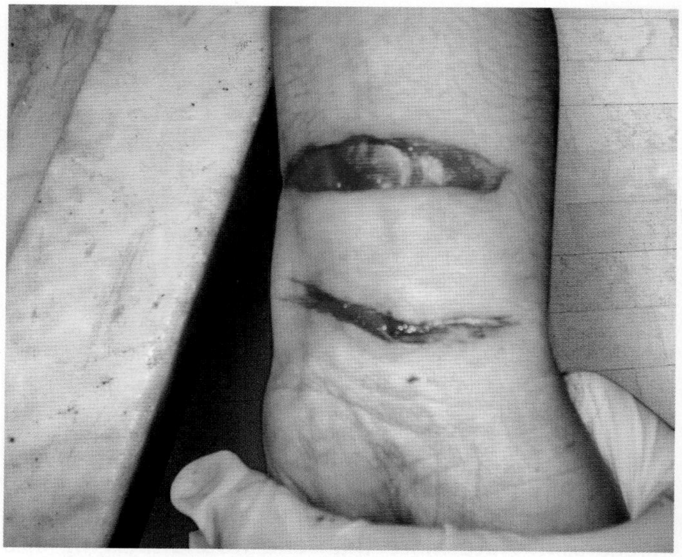

FIG. 9.43: Self-inflicted incised wounds

- Old scars of previous attempt of self-infliction may be noted
- There may be any underlying psychiatric disorder.

Defense Wounds

- Defense wounds are the injuries inflicted to a person when he tries to defend himself against an attack and are the result of instinctive reactions to assault (Fig. 9.44).
- The person may ward-off the weapon or trying to catch or grabbing the weapon – cuts the palm and ulnar aspect of hand.
- To protect the exposed surface of body, the upper limbs – extensor surface of forearms (ulnar side), the lateral/ posterior aspect of arm and dorsum of hand may receive injuries.
- Similarly the anterior and posterior aspects of lower limbs and back may be injured when an individual curls into a ball with flexion of spine, knees and hips to protect the anterior part of body.[17]

Medicolegal Importance

1. Cause of injury can be known
2. Nature of injury can be ascertained – whether simple or grievous
3. Age of injury can be estimated
4. It can be known whether the injury is accidental or suicidal or homicidal

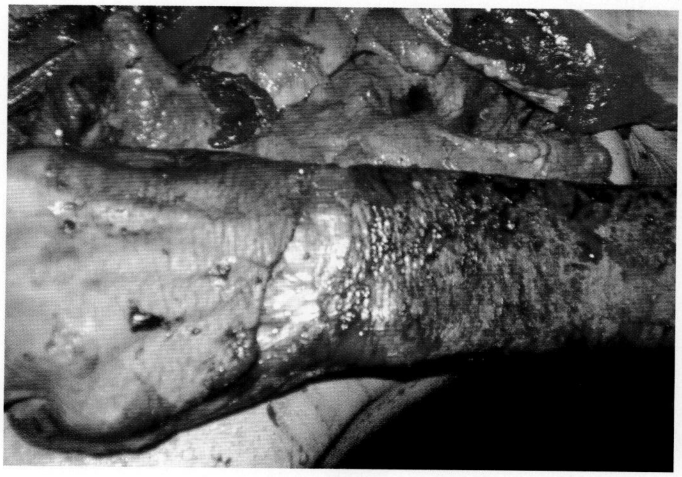

FIG. 9.44: Defense wound

5. Direction of application of force can be known.
6. It may be confused with lacerated wound. The differentiating features are mentioned in Table 9.9.
7. Self-inflicted injuries – *vide supra*
8. Defense injury – *vide supra*
9. Fabricated wounds – refer chapter 13.

CHOP WOUND

Definition

Chop wounds are type of incised wounds made by hacking or chopping motion with a fairly sharp and relatively heavy weapon.

Features

- Chop wounds are produced by relatively heavy sharp cutting weapons such as axe, chopper, sword (Figs 9.45 and 9.46)
- The edges of chop wounds are not so sharp akin to incised wound and often the margin shows bruising or abrasion.
- The weight of weapon act as crucial force to penetrate the weapon into tissues considerably
- The wound is comparatively wider and deeper than incised wound
- If the wound is inflicted obliquely, margin may show beveling
- Two parts in the chop wounds may be identified. The part of wound nearer to the assailant, known as heel end of the chop, is deeper than distal part from the assailant – known as toe end of the chop (Fig. 9.47). Thus identification of toe and heel end of the wound may offer help to know the relative position of the assailant and the victim.[8]

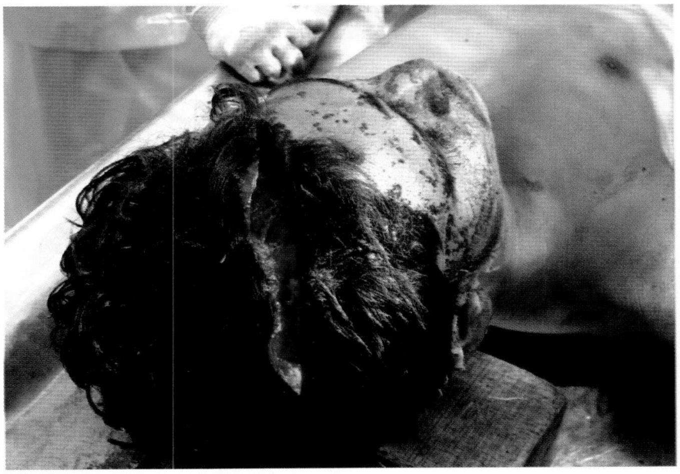

FIG. 9.45: Chop wounds

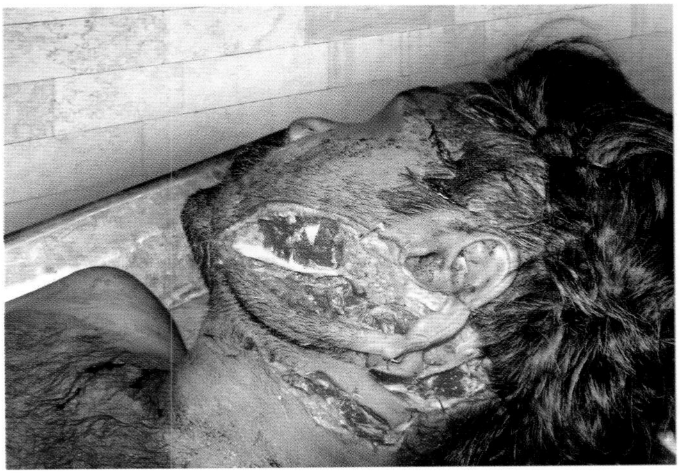

FIG. 9.46: Chop wounds

Medicolegal Importance

1. Chop wounds are usually homicidal in nature however, accidental injuries may be sustained by a person working in factories etc.
2. From the heel or toe end, the relative position of the assailant and the victim can be known.
3. The type of weapon used can be known.
4. Age of injury can be known.

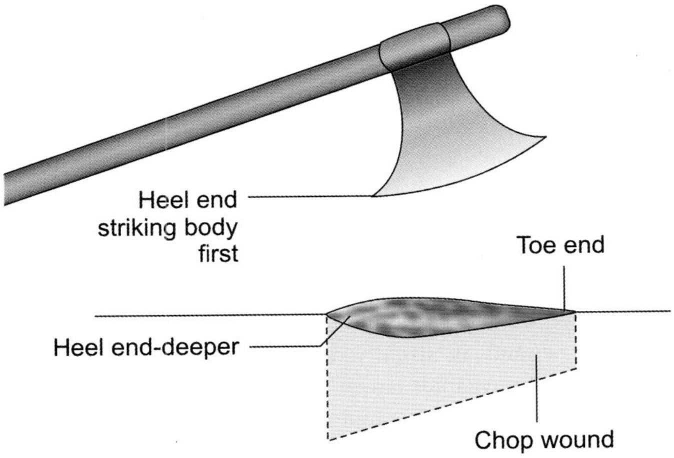

FIG. 9.47: Features of chop wound

STAB WOUNDS (PUNCTURE WOUNDS)

Definition

Stab wound is a piercing wound produced by application of mechanical force along the long axis of a narrow or pointed object.

Classification

Stab wounds are classified on following basis (Fig. 9.48):

A. Based on Depth of Penetration

1. Penetrating wounds
2. Perforating wounds

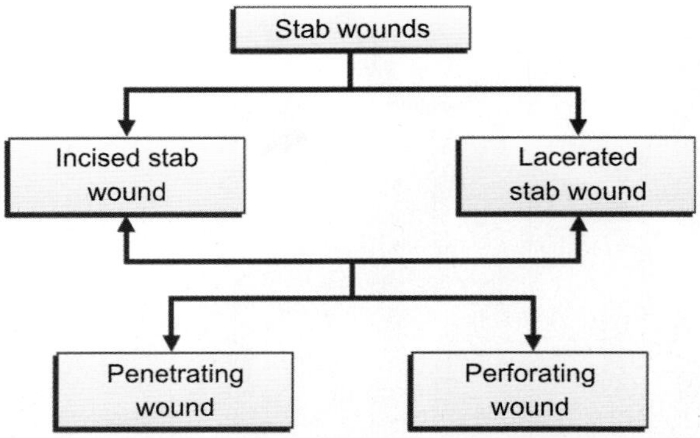

FIG. 9.48: Classification of stab injuries

B. Based on the Causative Weapon

1. Incised stab wounds – These wounds are caused by sharp edged, pointed weapons. They are further sub-classified as:
   - Penetrating wounds
   - Perforating wounds
2. Lacerated stab wounds – These wounds are caused by not so-sharp weapons or relatively blunt penetrating weapons. Such injuries can be caused by metal spike, wooden stake, garden fork, farm fork, screwdrivers, work-tool etc. They are further sub-classified as:
   – Penetrating wounds
   – Perforating wounds

Penetrating Wounds

- These are the stab wounds that terminate in the tissue/organ/cavity (Fig. 9.49A)
- In these wounds, only one surface wound is present on body due to entry of blade and no exit wound as the stab terminates in the tissues/organ/cavity.

Perforating Wounds

- These are the stab wounds that are passing the body through-and-through (Fig. 9.49B)
- In these wounds, two separate surface wounds will be observed over body; one caused by the entry of weapon and another caused by the exit of the weapon. The former is called as entry wound and later, the exit wound.
- Entry wound is usually larger than the exit wound because the weapon tapers towards the tip
- The edges of entry wound are usually inverted while in case of exit wounds, the edges are everted
- Foreign bodies such as cloth fabric/hairs etc. may be found in tract or near entry wound. The clothes may be pushed in the entry wound.

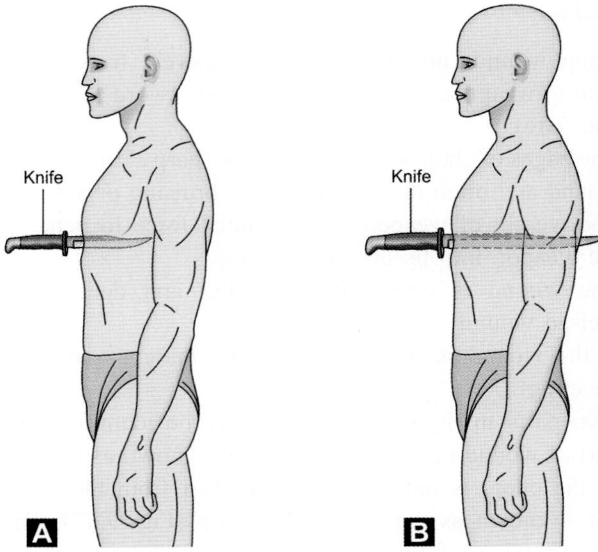

FIGS 9.49A and B: Stab wound. **A:** Penetrating wound. **B:** Perforating wound

- Joining the entry and exit wound gives direction of infliction of injury.

Features

Puncture wounds are popularly called as stab wounds. A stab wound by sharp, pointed and cutting edge weapon is a kind of incised wound that is deeper than its width.

1. Type of weapon used and wound caused (shape of wound)
   – The type of weapon usually means the type of blade and it includes whether it is sharp cutting or blunt edge? Whether it is single edged weapon or double-edged weapon? If single edged, what is the nature of the back edge? Whether it is serrated or squared-off? Whether the blade tapers from hilt to tip? (Fig 9.50).
   – Commonly knife is used to inflict stab wounds however, any weapon with pointed end or relatively pointed end can be used such as – knife, scissors, sword, sharp tools, modified tools, screw-drivers, shears, ice-picks, broken bottle, broken china etc.
   – Most of the knives have a single sharp edge and other edge being blunt or modified. Such weapon may produce wedge shaped stab wound with one end of the stab appear sharply cut like "V" point and other blunt (Fig. 9.50). The sharp angle represents injury caused by sharp edge of blade and blunt angle by blunt edge of weapon. However, it has to

be remember that such pattern is caused by weapons which have obvious differences between one sharp edge and other blunt edge (it may be modified as rounded or square-off).[3] If such pattern of injury is visible, a medical examiner can say that a single-edge weapon was used. Moreover, it is not necessary that it almost have such feature as discussed above. If the blunt edge is not obvious, the weapon may cause both angles sharp instead of one blunt and other sharp angle. In some weapons, one edge is sharp throughout and other edge is made sharp at distal part near the tip of blade with residual part of edge remaining blunt. When such weapon is used, the initial part of blade being sharp on both edges pierces the skin and as weapon advances in the body, the skin often splits behind the blunt edge to produce a symmetrical appearance.

- When one edge of weapon is sharp and other edge is made squared or flat, such weapon when used for stabbing may split back slightly from each corner of the angle, produced by non-sharp edge of weapon, forming the so called "**fish-tail appearance**"[18, 19] (Figs 9.50A to E).
- If one edge of a weapon is sharp and other edge is serrated, the angle produced by serrated edge may be torn or ragged in appearance and at times, when weapon is thrust obliquely, may leave serrated abrasions on the skin adjacent to the end of wound.
- If the weapon has a hilt and is propelled into full extent of the blade in the body, then there may be a hilt contusion or abrasion on the skin surrounding the wound. Presence of such hilt abrasion or contusion indicates that blade of weapon was pushed completely in the body and indicates force used for stabbing (Figs 9.51 and 9.52).
- External appearance of the wound may vary and resemble the cross-section of the weapon or blade of the weapon. Therefore, a stab wound may have spindle shape (Figs 9.53 to 9.56) or elliptical appearance or fish-tail appearance or ovoid or rounded or may be notched if accompanied by rocking.

2. Depth and thrust

If, for example knife is used for stabbing and the knife is withdrawn along the same track then it will form a track inside the body and the measurements of wound will indicate the dimensions of weapon. Thus the depth of stab wound is important parameter to assess the length of weapon used. However, as routine in forensic medicine, caution should be exercised while assessing the length of weapon blade

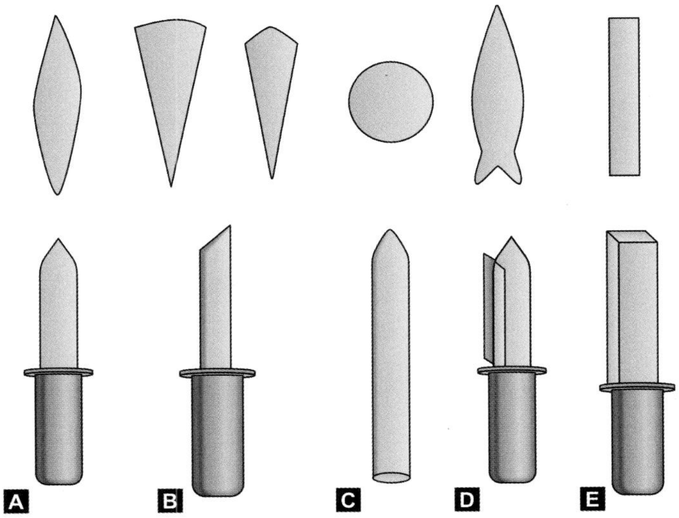

FIGS 9.50A to E: Stab wound. **A:** Stab wound caused by blade with both edges sharp resulting in spindle shaped. **B:** Wedge shaped wound or tear drop wound if one edge of blade is sharp and other is blunt. **C:** Round shape wound resulting from round object. **D:** Fishtail appearance of wound resulting from weapon with one edge sharp and other edge square-off. **E:** Rectangular shape or slit like wound that is caused due to rectangular object

from depth of the wound. Because, the depth measured at autopsy may be actually more than the length of blade of a weapon and this phenomenon is commonly encountered over body parts that are yielding or compressible such as abdomen, chest. Due to forceful thrust of weapon (for example with knife) over abdomen, the abdomen may be momentarily compressed or get indented at the impact site. Due to compression of body part, the tip of blade will penetrate more in depth than anticipated and apparently wounded that part that would have been out of reach. Now if same weapon is used to inflict on non-yielding part, say for example head then blade would not penetrate deeper than its length.

3. Movement of weapon in the wound
   - If, for example, knife is used for stabbing a person and the knife is withdrawn along the same track after inflicting the stab then the knife will form a injury inside the body called as tract of stab wound. Measurement of such track would indicate the dimension of the knife used to cause stab. However, caution should be exercised while opining the dimension of alleged weapon by mere track measurement. Now

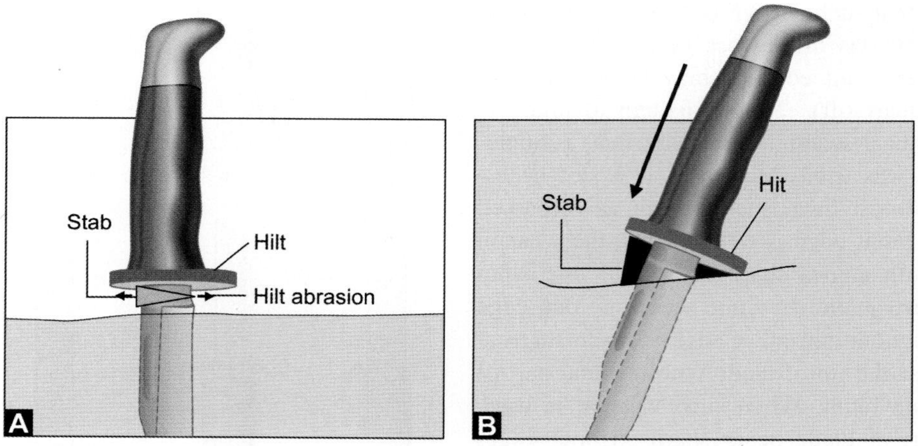

FIGS 9.51A and B: Stab wound with hilt abrasion. **A:** Weapon is penetrating skin perpendicularly and completely thus producing hilt abrasion around wound. **B:** Weapon is being thrust obliquely thus producing hilt impression on one side where hilt comes in contact (see text for details)

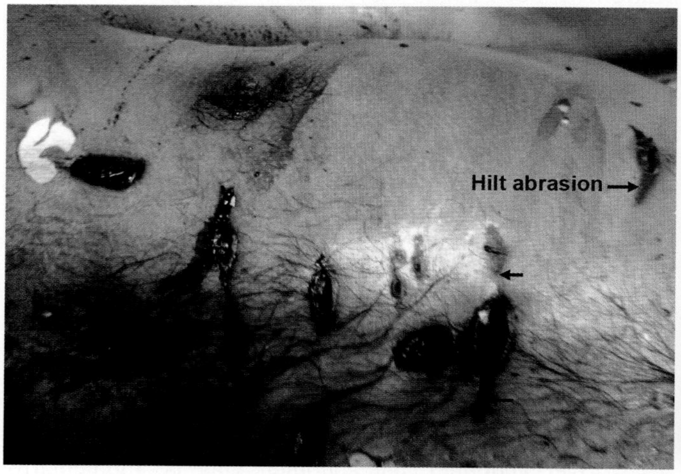

FIG. 9.52: Stab wound with hilt abrasion (black arrow indicates abrasion)

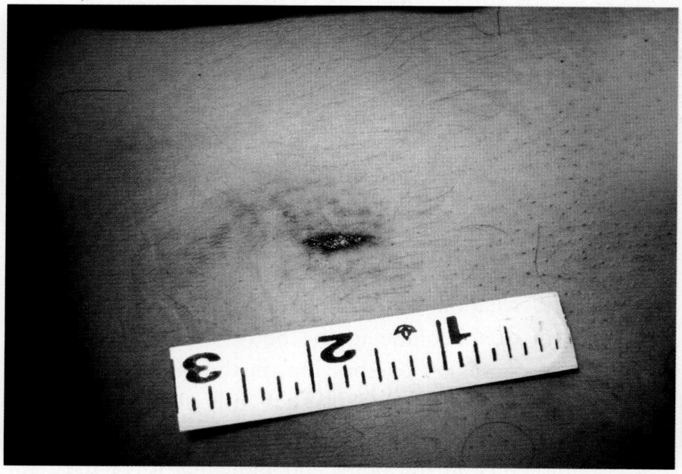

FIG. 9.53: Stab wound

suppose, if a person causes stab to another person with knife and he do not withdraw the knife along the same track but rotate the knife (rocking of weapon), then there will be greater wound defect. The term rocking is used when the weapon is moved inside the wound with leverage or angulation in the plane of wound. Due to rocking, the cutting edge of weapon extends the wound. The rocking can be done by the assailant with active movement of weapon inside the wound or may be done by the victim due to body movement in relation to knife (weapon). In some cases, both mechanisms may act.

4. Direction of stab wound
   – A medical examiner has to determine the direction of the wound in relation to the axis of the body. Direction depends upon the entry wound, the track and the exit wound if present. Careful dissection of the body in layers would reveal the track of the wound. With advancement in imaging techniques, attempts had been made to gauge the direction of wound by filling the wound defect with radio-opaque dye and X-ray films taken. However, these radio-opaque substances often exhibit leaks making more difficult to access the track. In similar pursuit, magnetic resonance imaging (MRI Scan) has been

FIG. 9.54: Stab wound

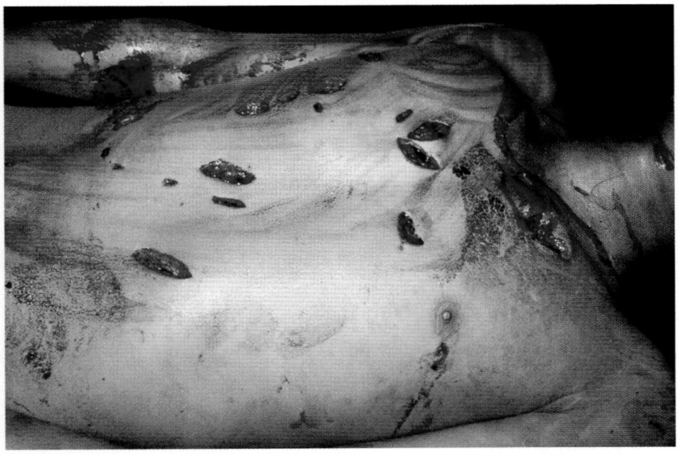

FIG. 9.55: Stab wound

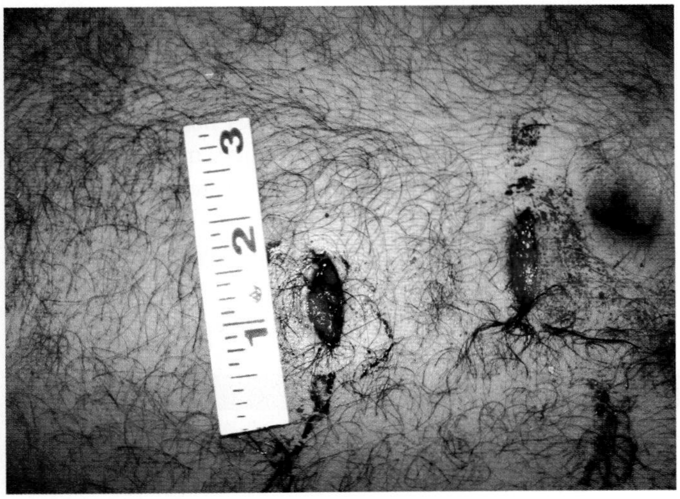

FIG. 9.56: Stab wound

attempted but these facilities are lacking in developing countries like India.

5. Pattern of stab injuries
   - If the weapon used for stabbing, enters the skin obliquely, the edge of the wound that first cut the skin becomes beveled while the other edge overhangs the wound.
6. Dimension of wound
   - Length of stab wound is usually corresponds with that of breadth of blade. However, the length of wound may be shorter in measurement than actual breadth of blade. This shortening of wound is due to elasticity of skin, gaping of wound and contraction or postmortem shortening of underlying muscles, especially when the muscle fibers are cut across.
   - The wound usually gaps across the centre to form a long ellipse. The extent of gaping depends upon the anatomical situation of wound over the body and whether the stab wound inflicted is in the line with or across the tension of Langer's lines or underlying muscle fibers. Therefore, a stab wound with the long axis at right angle to the elastic tissue of Langer's lines will gape open with the edges pulled apart by elastic tissues. Thus the wound appears wide and short (Fig. 9.57). If the wound is parallel to the elastic tissue lines, it will appear narrow and long and the gaping of wound will not be prominent.[4]
   - When the edges are apposed, the length of wound should be measured as it more accurately approximates to the breadth of blade when it was *in situ*.
   - Depth of stab wound is more than length and breadth.

Medicolegal Importance

1. Type of weapon used can be known.
2. Dimensions of weapon can be known.
3. Movement of knife in the wound can be known.
4. Depth of thrust can be known.
5. Direction of thrust can be known.
6. Amount of force used can be known.
7. Age of wounds can be known.
8. Manner of infliction – suicidal/homicidal/accidental can be known.

FRACTURES

Definition

Breach in the continuity of bone due to application of mechanical force or other traumatic agent is called as

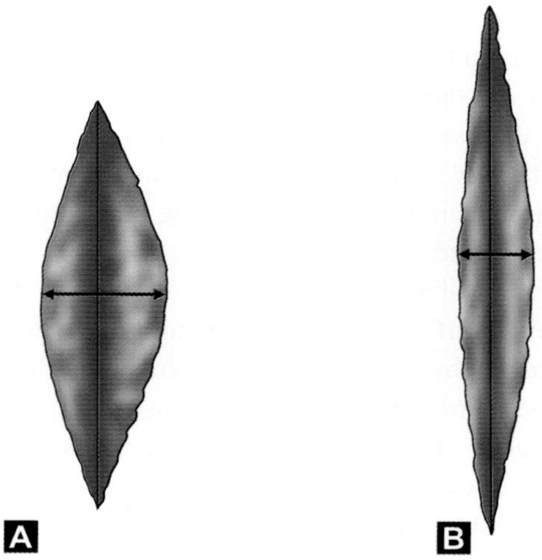

FIGS 9.57A and B: Stab wound. A: Stab wound appears short and wide because the long axis of wound is at across to muscle fibers or elastic tissue of skin. B: The wound is parallel to muscle or skin plane and thus it appears narrow and long

fracture. The force applied to bone may be direct or may be indirect.

Classification

Fracture are classified by various means such as

A. Based on etiology
   1. Traumatic fracture – fracture resulting from application of mechanical force
   2. Pathological fracture – due to some pathology or disease, the bone is weak and sustains fracture.

B. Based on displacements
   1. Un-displaced
   2. Displaced

C. With relation to skin and external environment
   1. Simple fracture – the overlying skin and tissues are intact
   2. Compound fracture or open fracture – here the overlying skin and tissues are torn and communicating with the exterior

D. Based on pattern of fracture
   1. Transverse fracture
   2. Spiral fracture
   3. Oblique fracture
   4. Segmental fracture
   5. Comminuted fracture

E. Direct fracture
   1. Focal fracture
   2. Crush fracture
   3. Penetrating fracture

F. Indirect fracture
   1. Traction fracture
   2. Angulation fracture
   3. Rotational fracture
   4. Vertical compression fracture
   5. Angulation-compression fracture

Complication of Fracture[20]

Early complications

- Shock
- Injury to vessels, muscles, tendons
- Injury to joints
- ARDS
- Fat embolism
- Deep vein thrombosis
- Pulmonary embolism
- Compartment syndrome
- Crush syndrome
- Aseptic traumatic fever

Delayed complications

- Septicemia
- Delayed union
- Non-union
- Mal-union
- Avascular necrosis
- Joint stiffness
- Sudeck's dystrophy
- Osteomyelitis
- Ischemic contracture
- Myositis ossificans

Medicolegal Importance

1. Fracture of bone constitute grievous hurt.
2. Fracture accompanied with vessel injury may endanger life.
3. Fracture associated with injury to nerve may cause deformity or loss of function.
4. Multiple fracture with hemorrhage may cause death of a person.
5. Age of injury can be known.

REFERENCES

1. Vij K. Injuries by blunt force, injuries by sharp force. In: Textbook of Forensic Medicine and Toxicology, 3rd edn. 2005. Reed Elsevier India Pvt. Limited, New Delhi. 325-54.

2. Pillay VV. Mechanical injuries. In: Textbook of Forensic Medicine and Toxicology, 14th edn. 2004. Paras Publishing, Hyderabad. 139-53.
3. Saukko P, Knight B. The pathology of wounds. In: Knight's Forensic Pathology, 3rd edn. 2004. Arnold, London. 136–73.
4. Petty CS. Death by trauma: Blunt and sharp instruments and firearms. In: Curran WJ, McGarry AL, Petty CS (ed) Modern Legal Medicine, Psychiatry and Forensic Science, 1st edn. 1980. F.A. Davis Company, Philadelphia. 363-490.
5. Bohnert M, Baumgartner R, Pollak S. Spectrophotometeric evaluation of the colour of intra- and subcutaneous bruises. Int J Legal Med 2000; 113:343-8.
6. Mant AK. Wounds and their interpretation. In: Mant AK (ed). Taylor's Principles and Practice of Medical Jurisprudence, 13th edn. 2000. B I Churchill Livingstone, New Delhi. 214-49.
7. Simpson CK. In: Forensic medicine, 8th edn. 1979. Edward Arnold, London.
8. Nandy A. Mechanical injuries. In: Principles of Forensic Medicine, 2nd edn. 2005. New Central Book Agency (P) Ltd., Calcutta. 209-62.
9. Dikshit PC. Mechanical injuries. In: Textbook of Forensic Medicine and Toxicology, 1st edn. 2007. Peepee Publishers and Distributors (P) Ltd., New Delhi. 155-72.
10. Rao NG. Trauma, injury and wound. In: Textbook of Forensic Medicine and Toxicology, 1st edn. 2006. Jaypee Brothers Medical Publishers (P) Ltd., New Delhi. 177-89.
11. Reddy KSN. Mechanical injuries In: The Essentials of Forensic Medicine and Toxicology, 22nd edn. 2003. K. Suguna Devi, Hydrabad. 195-234.
12. Parikh CK. Mechanical injuries – general aspects. In: Parikh's Textbook of medical Jurisprudence & Toxicology, 5th edn. 1995. CBS Publishers and Distributors, Mumbai. 235-57.
13. Petty CS. Soft tissue injuries: An overview. Am J Clin Pathol 1970; 10:201-19.
14. Spitz WU. Blunt force injury, sharp force injury. In: Spitz and Fisher's Medicolegal investigation of Death, 3rd edn. 1993. Charlas C Thomas Publisher, USA. 199-310.
15. Mathiharan K, Patnaik AK. Injuries by mechanical violence. In: Modi's Medical Jurisprudence and Toxicology, 23rd edn. 2005. LexisNexis Butterworths, New Delhi. 685-730.
16. Spitz WU. Hemorrhagic Pancreatitis following a kick in the abdomen. J Forensic Med 1965; 12:105.
17. Payne-James J, Crane J, Hinchliffe JA. Injury assessment, documentation and interpretation. In: Stark MM (ed) Clinical Forensic medicine – a Physicians Guide, 2nd edn. 127-58.
18. Rabinowitsch A. Medicolegal conclusions on the form of the knife used bare on the shape of the stab wounds received. J Forensic Med 1959; 6:160.
19. Watson AA. Stabbing and other incisional wounds. In: Mason JK (ed) The Pathology of Trauma.
20. Maheshwari J. Orthopedic trauma. In: Essential Orthopedics, 3rd edn. 2002. Mehta Publishers, New Delhi. 1-6.

CHAPTER 10

Firearm Injuries and Bomb Blast Injuries

There is nothing more exhilarating than to be shot at without result.

- Winston Churchill

FIREARM INJURIES

- *Firearm is any instrument or device designed to propel a projectile by means of explosion of gases generated by combustion of an explosive substance*
- Ammunition means the material used to cause the explosion i.e. the ingredients used such as bullet, pellet, powder etc.
- Ballistics is a science that deals with the investigation of firearms, ammunition and the effects arising from their use. Forensic ballistics is subdivided into three types[1] as (Fig. 10.1):

1. **Proximal (internal) ballistics:** It includes the study of firearms and projectiles used.
2. **Intermediate (external) ballistics:** It includes the study of movement or motion of the projectile after it exits from the firearm till the time it hits the target.
3. **Terminal (wound) ballistics:** It includes the study of injuries produced by firearm. The forensic doctors are concerned mainly with this terminal ballistics.

Classification of Firearms

Firearms are classified by various ways as:

A) According to condition of barrel
   1. Smooth bore firearm (shotgun)
   2. Rifled firearm
   3. Country made firearm

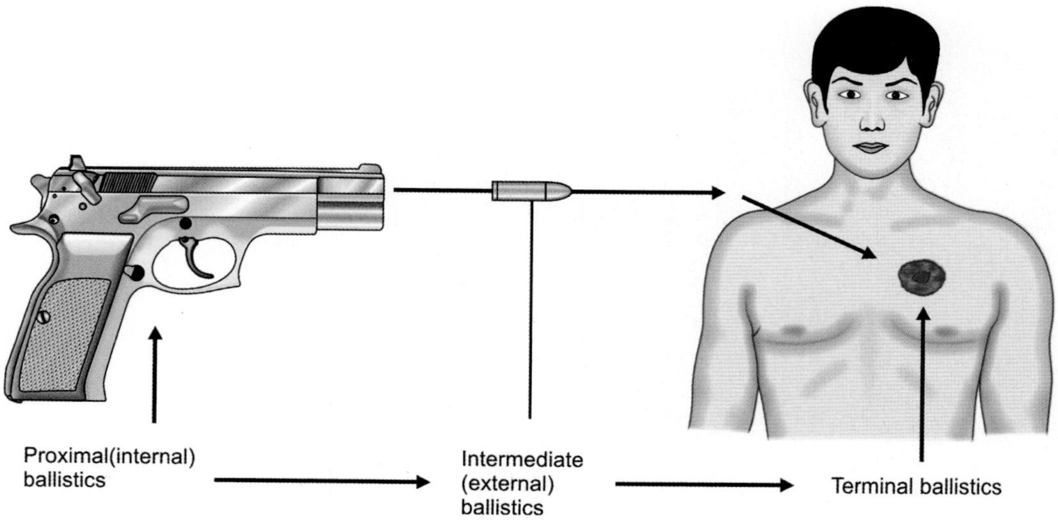

FIG. 10.1: Forensic ballistics

4. Air gun
5. Paradox gun

B) According to muzzle velocity[2]
1. Low velocity (up to 1200 ft/s)
for example revolver, pistol
2. Medium velocity (between 1200 – 2500 ft/s)
3. High velocity (> 3000 ft/s)
for example machine gun

Structure of Firearm

In general, firearm is composed of (Fig. 10.2):
1. Barrel
2. Grip or butt or stock
3. Action

Grip or Butt

This is the rear part of firearm and is held either in hand (for example in case of pistol or revolver) or can be supported by shoulder (for example in case of military rifle).

Barrel

- Barrel is a hollow steel tube or cylinder and the length varies according to type of gun. The lumen of tube or cylinder is known as **bore**.
- The front end of tube is known as muzzle end and the posterior end or rear end is known as breech end.
- **Chamber** is the posterior most (rear) part of the barrel and is wider than rest part of tube or cylinder and accommodates or houses the cartridge to be fired. The

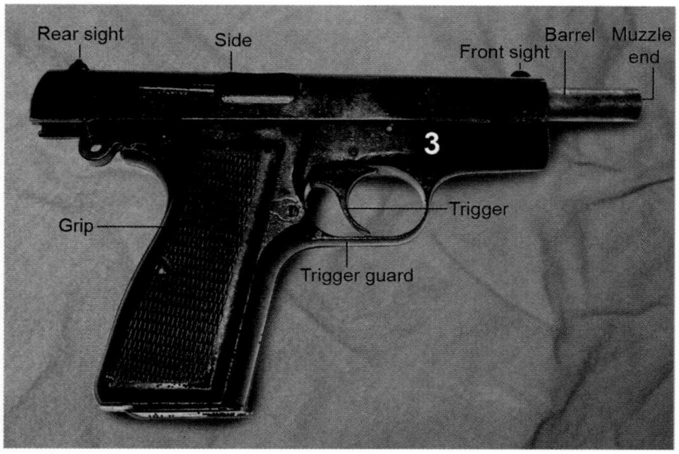

FIG. 10.2: Structure of firearm (photograph of 9 mm pistol)

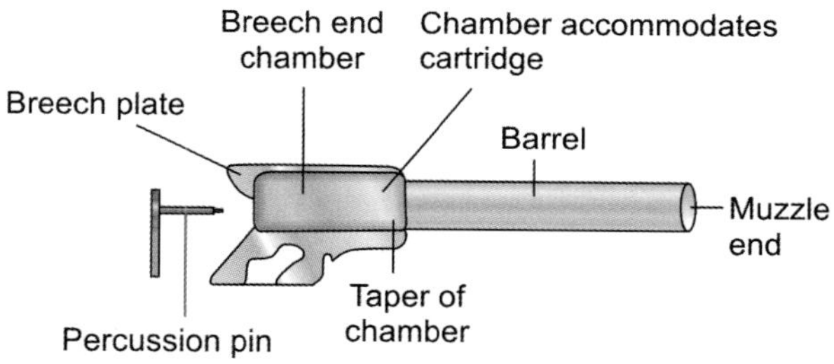

FIG. 10.3: Parts of firearm

backside of chamber has a metal plate called as **breech plate**. The breech plate has a central hole. Front part of a chamber tapers and this part is known as taper or lead. The lead then continuous anteriorly as barrel (Fig. 10.3).

Action

It consists of:
1. Trigger
2. Trigger guard
3. Bolt
4. Striker or hammer

Trigger: The lower part of firearm has a trigger. When trigger is pulled, it causes striker or hammer to strike on the posterior part of cartridge and causes bullet/pellet to eject from muzzle end of barrel.
Trigger guard: It is a metallic rim that surrounds trigger to prevent accidental firing.
Bolt: Also called as block and is present towards breech end of barrel. The part, which incorporates the firing pin, spring and trigger, is called as bolt.
Striker or hammer: At the posterior part of chamber, there is a hammer with a pointed pin (firing pin) and a spring.
Mechanism: When the trigger is pulled, the spring action causes to move the hammer and advance or protrude the firing pin to the chamber from the central hole of breech plate. As the firing pin moves forward, it strikes the base of cartridge. The striking of firing pin over cartridge produces heat and ignites the primer present in the cartridge. The action of pin is similar to matchstick which when rubbed or strike on surface of matchbox produces heat and then ignites (Fig. 10.4).

SMOOTH BORE FIREARM (SHOTGUN)

Smooth bore firearms are usually shoulder rest weapons (Fig. 10.5). The inner surface of barrel is uniformly smooth i.e. the bore of weapon is smooth (Fig. 10.6). The length of barrel varies from 52 to 72 cm.

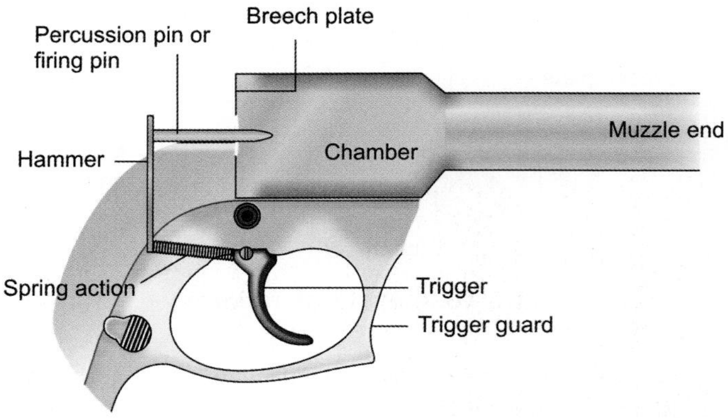

FIG. 10.4: Mechanism of firing

FIG. 10.5: Smooth bore firearm (*Courtesy*: Dr Manish Shrigiriwar, Associate Professor, Forensic Medicine, IGGMC, Nagpur)

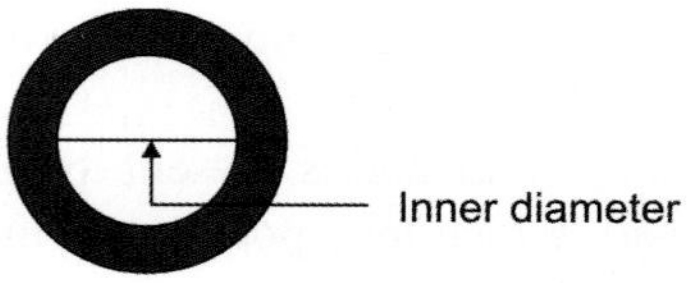

FIG. 10.6: Cross-section of barrel of smooth bore firearm

Types of Shotgun

A) Depending on length of barrel
- Long barrel
- Short barrel

B) Depending on loading of ammunition or cartridge
- Muzzle loading
- Breech loading

C) Depending on number of barrel
- Single barrel
- Double barrel
- Multi-barrel

D) Depending on choking of barrel
- Full choked
- Three-quarter choked
- Half choked
- Quarter choked
- Non-choked

Gauge or Bore

- Gauge or bore in smooth bore firearm means the inside diameter of barrel (see Fig. 10.6) (caliber is internal diameter of barrel in rifle firearm, *vide infra*).
- It is measured by two methods; direct and indirect method[3]

Direct method: In this method, the gauge is determined by measuring the inner diameter of barrel directly. The gauge is given in decimals of an inch or millimeters. For example 0.410 shotgun means, the internal diameter of barrel is 0.41 of an inch.

Indirect method: In this method, the gauge or bore of shotgun is indirectly determined by a known number of spherical balls of uniform size prepared from 1 lb (1 pound, 454 gm) of lead and each ball is fitting exactly in the barrel. For example 12 bore shot gun means, from 1 pound of lead 12 spherical balls are prepared of uniform size and the balls are exactly fitting in the barrel. Thus each ball would be of 1/12 pound of lead. Here the diameter would be 0.729 inch or 18.52 mm.

It is also noted that as the bore number increases, the inner diameter of barrel of shotgun decreases and vice versa.

Non-Choking

In non-choked shotgun, the barrel is of uniform size from muzzle end to chamber (i.e. breech end). Such type of barrel is called as cylindrical type barrel or cylinder bore. In other words, the barrel is not choked (Fig. 10.7).

Choking (Fig. 10.7)

- When the terminal part of muzzle end of shotgun becomes narrow and constricted, it is called choking of shotgun.
- The choke in a shotgun is the degree of constriction and expressed in thousands of an inch. Thus choking is the constriction or narrowing of the muzzle end of barrel by the fraction of an inch.
- Different degree of choking is given in Table 10.1.

Advantages of Choking

1. Choking keeps the pellets or shots compact together for long distance during the travel after exiting from muzzle end.

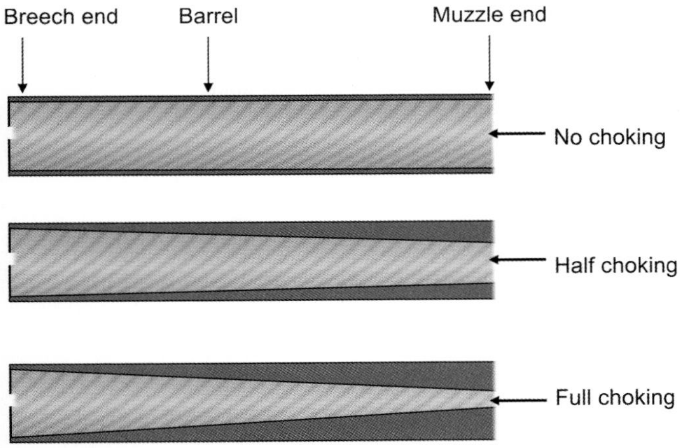

FIG. 10.7: Choking of smooth bore firearm

Table 10.1: Different degree of choking

Constriction of muzzle end		*Degree of choking*	*Degree of constriction*
In inch	*In mm*		
0.04	1	Full choke	40/1000th of an inch
0.03	0.75	Three-quarter choke	30/1000th of an inch
0.02	0.50	Half choke	20/1000th of an inch
0.01	0.25	Quarter choke	10/1000th of an inch
0	0	Improved cylinder	3 - 5/1000th of an inch

2. Choking reduces or prevents the dispersion of pellets and act like a single ball, thus exerting greater impact on victim.
3. Choking causes momentary obstruction to the pellets resulting in increased pressure behind the pellets and propels pellets with greater force.
4. Choking makes weapon more lethal.

Cartridge of Shotgun (Smooth Bore Firearm)

Cartridge is ammunition for firearms that is loaded into the chamber of firearm.

Cartridge of smooth bore firearm (shotgun) is composed of (Fig. 10.8):

1. Cartridge case
2. Projectile (missile)
3. Propellant (gun powder)
4. Detonator (primer)

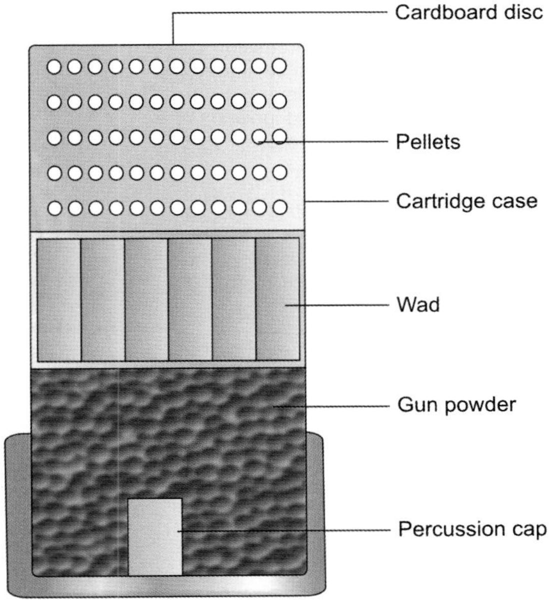

FIG. 10.8: Cartridge of smooth bore firearm

Cartridge Case

- It is the outer case or covering in which the explosive are stored together.
- It is cylindrical in shape and made up from special paper or cardboard or plastic material.
- The cartridge has two ends. One end is closed and is known as base. The base is made up of metal plate (usually brass) and has a central part called as percussion cap (primer cup). The primer cup contains detonator. The base may be rimmed or grooved.
- The anterior end is open and covered by cardboard.

Function of Cartridge Case

1. Holds the explosive agents together
2. Prevent backward escape of gases
3. Provide waterproof cover for gunpowder.

Detonator

- Also called as primer
- It is stored in primer cup (percussion cap).
- The purpose of primer is to ignite the gun powder
- When trigger is pulled, the hammer advances the percussion pin into the base of cartridge and ignites the primer. Then the flames/flashes of primer ignite the gunpowder (Fig. 10.9).
- Primer is composed of

1. Mercury fulminate or lead azide

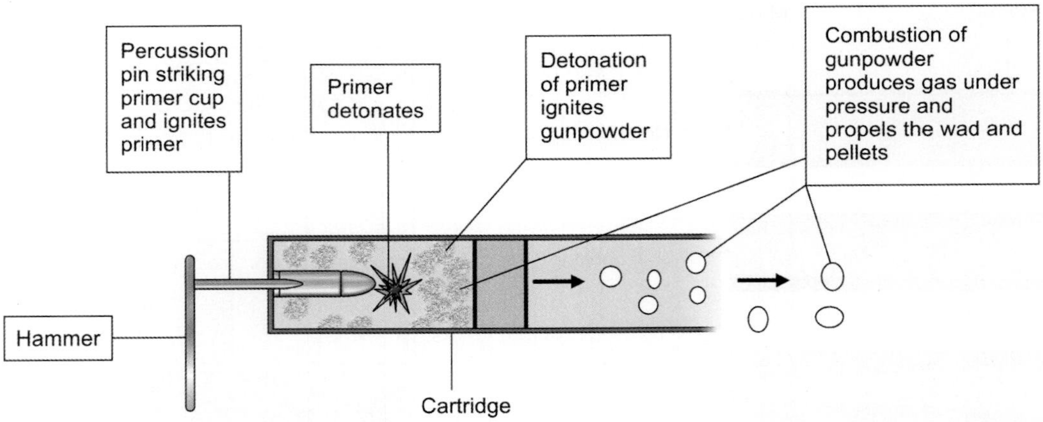

FIG. 10.9: Discharge of pellets from barrel

2. Potassium chlorate
3. Antimony sulphide

Propellant

- Also called as gunpowder
- It is placed next to the primer (detonator) in cartridge
- The ignited primer causes combustion of gunpowder (Fig. 10.9).
- The combustion of gunpowder produces hot gases under tremendous pressure and causes propelling out of pellets (or bullet) from firearm with velocity.
- There are three types of gunpowder available as mentioned below.
  1. Black powder
  2. Semi-smokeless powder
  3. Smokeless powder

Black Powder

- Black powder is a mixture of:
  - 75% potassium nitrite
  - 15% charcoal
  - 10% sulphur
  - Black powder is in granular form and designated as FG, FFG, FFFG etc. depending on the size of grains. More the number of 'F' more finer is the powder grains (F stands for fine and G for grain, thus FG means fine grain).
  - A single grain of black powder produces 200 to 250 cc of gas composed of carbon monoxide, carbon dioxide, nitrogen, hydrogen etc.

Smokeless Powder

Smokeless powder is of following type
1. Single base – consist of nitrocellulose
2. Double base – consist of combination of nitrocellulose and nitroglycerine
3. Triple base – consist of combination of nitrocellulose, nitroglycerine and nitroguanidine

Features

- Combustion of smokeless powder produces minimal smoke
- Most effective explosive and imparts higher velocity to projectile
- Single grain can generate 800 – 900 cc of gas
- Modern smokeless powder is mainly composed of nitrocellulose. Other explosive ingredients like nitroglycerine and stabilizers such as diphenylamite (DPA), ethyl centralite (EC), methyl entralite (MC), hydroquinone or resorcinol and flash supressors such as 2,4-dintrotoluene (2,4-DNT) are also usually present.[4]

Semi-Smokeless Powder

Semi-smokeless powder is composed of 20 percent smokeless powder and 80 percent black powder.

Projectile

- Smooth bore weapon have projectile in form of pellets (shot). Pellets comprises of multiple spherical balls of lead
- Shots or pellets are of two types[5]

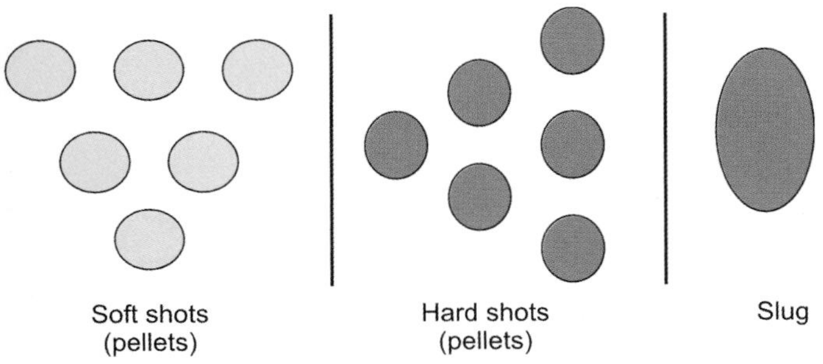

FIG. 10.10: Different types of pellets

1. Soft or drop shot – made up of soft lead (Fig. 10.10).
2. Hard or chilled shots – made from lead and hardened by antimony.

- In country-made or improvised firearms, the projectiles are in form of glass pieces, metal pieces, cork, wood, stones, nails, etc.
- In some shotguns, slugs are used instead of pellets. Slug is larger than pellet and is a single projectile. The slugs are similar to bullets. Shotgun slugs are of various types and are used for game hunting or for law enforcement applications.[6]

Wad

- Wad is a rounded, compressed disk (Fig. 10.11).
- The wad is placed between the pellets and gunpowder.
- It is made from compressed paper, felt, plastic, glazed-board, strawboard, cork etc.
- The diameter of wad is more so as to occlude the lumen of barrel. Here wad acts as a piston and seals off the bore completely.
- Often wad is impregnated with grease to lubricate bore.

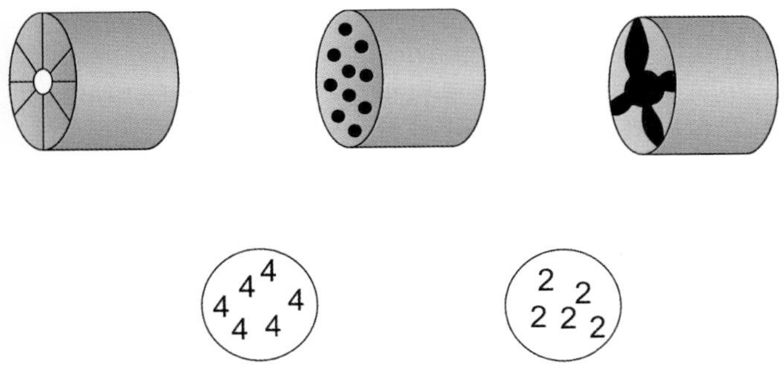

FIG. 10.11: Different types of wad

Function of Wad

1. Wad separates the pellets and gun powder apart.
2. Wad act as a piston and seals off the bore so as to prevent the escaping of expanding gases.
3. Wad lubricates the bore.

In summation, the cartridge case in smooth bore firearm is filled from below upwards i.e. from base as follows:

1. Percussion cap
2. Gun powder
3. Cardboard
4. Wad
5. Cardboard
6. Pellets or shot
7. Cardboard

RIFLED FIREARM

- Rifled firearms are powerful weapons.
- The term rifle refers to the rifling or grooving made on the inner surface of barrel.
- Unlike smooth bore firearm, where the internal surface of barrel is smooth, in rifled weapons, the internal surface of barrel has spiral grooves. The grooves run longitudinally from breech end to muzzle end and are twisted, spiral, multiple and parallel to each other. These grooves are called **rifling of a gun** (Fig. 10.12).
- Due to grooving on the internal surface of barrel, there are projecting areas accompanied. These projecting areas are called as '**lands**'.
- The number of grooves varies from two to more than 20, but most weapons have 6 spiral grooves. Similarly the grooving may varies in direction, depth and width with weapon. The direction of spinning may be clockwise or anti-clockwise. Magnitude of the rifling spins i.e. the distance covered for one complete turn of spin within barrel may also vary with weapon.
- Thus, pattern of rifling is not uniform in every gun. The grooving varies with make and manufacture of weapon.

Importance of Rifling

1. Rifling marks to particular weapon are unique like fingerprints.
2. Rifling marks imparted on bullet can help in identification of the weapon used in crime.

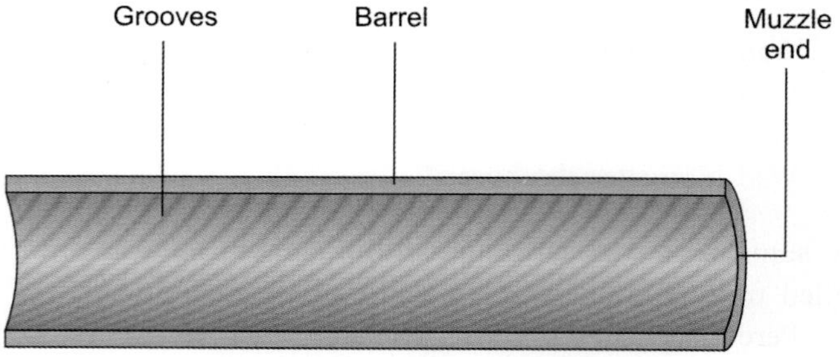

FIG. 10.12: Rifling of barrel in rifled firearm

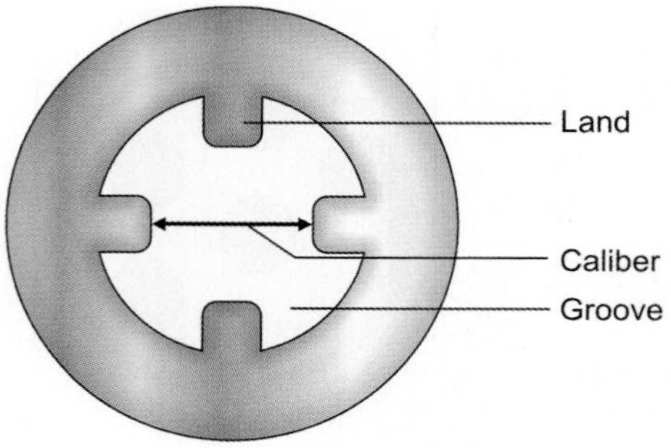

FIG. 10.13: Caliber of rifled firearm

Advantages of Rifling

1. Rifling gives spinning movement to bullet in its long axis. Spinning causes gyroscopic movement to bullet, which gives a steadiness, or stability to bullet while traveling in air.
2. Rifling increases the power of penetration by bullet.
3. Prevents wobbling (shaking) of bullet when travels in air.
4. Increases accuracy of target aimed.
5. Help to travel longer distance/range.

Caliber of Rifled Firearm

- Caliber of a rifled firearm is the inner diameter of the barrel. Here the inner surface of this type of weapon is rif-fled i.e. multiple grooves are present. Similarly along with grooves, lands are also present. Thus, caliber is the distance between two opposite lands of the riffling (Fig. 10.13).
- Caliber is expressed in fractions of an inch or millimeter for example if we have 0.303 rifle, it means a rifle weapon which has caliber of 0.303 of an inch.
- Example of rifles in inches – 0.22, 0.30, 0.303 etc. or may be expressed in millimeters for example 6.35, 7.62, 7.65 etc.

Classification of Rifled Firearm

A) Depending on length of barrel
   - Short barrel or hand rest or hand arm. Examples are
     1. Pistol (Fig. 10.14)
     2. Revolver
   - Long barrel or shoulder rest. Examples are
     1. Military rifle
     2. AK-47

B) Depending on muzzle velocity
   - Low velocity – up to 1200 feet/s
   - Medium velocity – up to 1200 to 2500 feet/s
   - High velocity – more than 3000 feet/s

C) Depending on the operative action i.e. installation of cartridge into chamber for firing

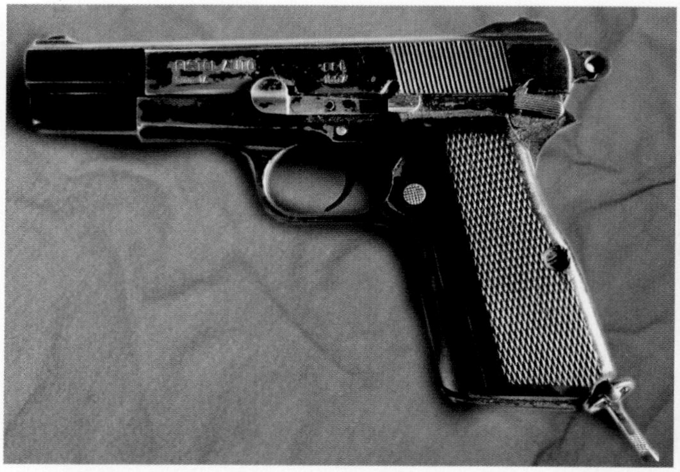

FIG. 10.14: Pistol (semi-automatic) (*Courtesy*: Dr Manish Shrigiriwar, Associate Professor, Forensic Medicine, IGGMC, Nagpur)

   - Slide action
   - Bolt action
   - Lever action
   - Semiautomatic
   - Automatic

Cartridge of Riffled Firearm

A cartridge is ammunition, which is loaded into the chamber of firearm and on firing, discharges the bullet. Cartridge of rifled firearm is composed of (Fig. 10.15):

1. Cartridge case
2. Detonator – same as for smooth bore firearm
3. Propellant – same as for smooth bore firearm
4. Projectile

Cartridge Case

- It is elongated cylindrical case made up of an alloy of copper and zinc
- The base frame has percussion cap similar to shotgun (smooth bore firearm)

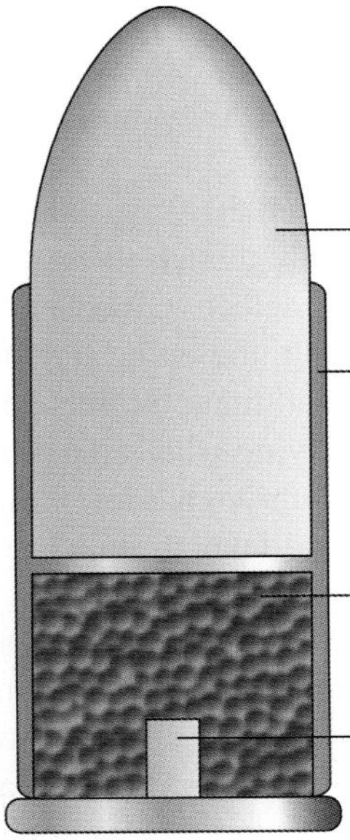

FIG. 10.15: Cartridge of rifled firearm

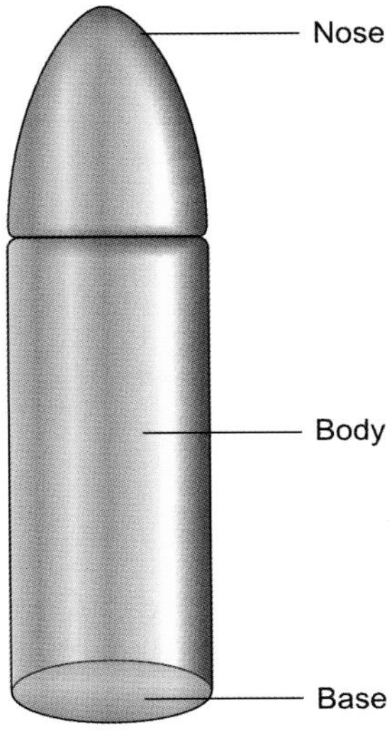

FIG. 10.16: Bullet

Projectile

- In riffled firearm, the projectile is in form of '**bullet**'
- The bullet is placed at the distant part of cartridge case. The anterior part of bullet remains exposed outside the cartridge case.
- The bullet is held in cartridge case either by a groove called **cannelure** or by an indentation of cartridge case.
- In summation, the arrangement of firearm cartridge in rifled weapon is from below upward in a fashion described below.
  1. Primer
  2. Gun powder
  3. Bullet

Bullet (Figs 10.16 and 10.17)

- Usually bullet is conical in shape and has following parts
  1. Base – is flat and held in cartridge case
  2. Body
  3. Nose – tip of bullet is called as nose
- Caliber of a bullet is its cross-sectional diameter
- Bullet may be short, medium or long depending on the size.
- Shape may be conical or oval
- Depending on pattern of nose, bullet is divided into following
  1. Round nose
  2. Square nose
  3. Pencil point nose
  4. Flat point
  5. Long round nose

FIG. 10.17: Bullet (*Courtesy*: Dr Manish Shrigiriwar, Associate Professor, Forensic Medicine, IGGMC, Nagpur)

Jacketed Bullet (Fig. 10.18)

Jacketed bullet has cover and two types of cover are available

1. Full metal jacket bullet: Tough metal jacket cover the bullet from all parts except at base. The jacket is made up of steel, copper, nickel and zinc.
2. Semi-jacket bullet: In this type, the bullet is covered by metal jacket from base and cylindrical part of body. The

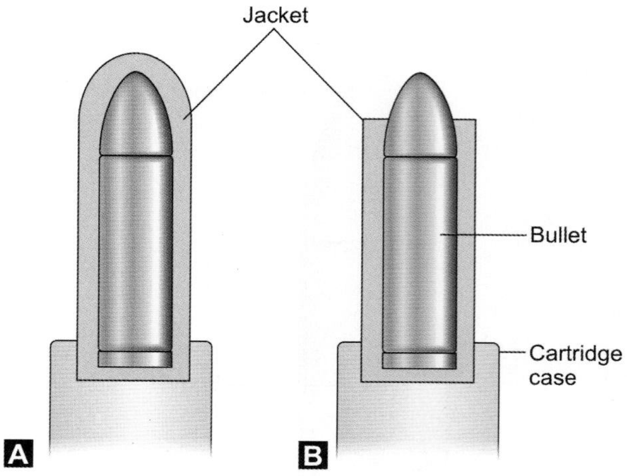

FIGS 10.18A and B: Jacketed bullets. **A:** Full jacket bullet, **B:** Semi-jacket bullet

nose is not covered. Advantage of this type of bullet is that it causes more damage.

Mushroom bullet – these are semi-jacketed bullets and they expand like mushroom when get impacted on target due to soft nose (the nose is not covered by jacket). This type of bullet causes more severe and extensive injuries.

Dumdum bullet – is a bullet, which is open at base, and the point (nose) is covered with jacket so as to form hollow at their nose. The purpose is that when bullet strikes body, it will expand and produces large hole.

Explosive bullet – these are the bullets containing explosive material and if such bullet explodes, it causes extensive damage.

Plastic bullet – the bullets are made up of solid cylinder of polyvinyl chloride. It is usually fired from smooth bored weapon and used for controlling the riots.

Rubber bullet – these bullets are made up of rubber and are yielding one. They are used by law enforcement agencies (police) to control the mob. They may cause abrasion or contusion.

Tandem bullet (Piggy back bullet) – at times, more than one bullet may be found in body though there is single entry wound. This occurs if there is defective mechanism of firing or faulty ammunition. On firing, the bullet fails to exit from muzzle end and on firing second time; the second bullet may eject from muzzle end but carrying with it the first one. Thus both bullets may be entered through same entry end one attached to other. This is called tandem bullet or piggyback bullet (Fig. 10.19).

Souvenir bullet – a bullet entered in body may lodge in tissue. If such bullet is not removed, the bullet may remain in body and gets covered by encapsulation of tissue. Thus it is a retained bullet inside the body. Such retained bullet inside body is called as souvenir bullet. Lead poisoning may occur from such bullet but is rare.

Frangible bullet – this is a type of bullet, which on striking the body breaks into multiple pieces.

Rifling Marks Over Bullet

Whenever bullet travels through barrel, the barrel and gun leaves it's marking over bullet. These markings are unique for that particular weapon. Such markings are of two types as:

- Primary markings – these are the marks produced by grooves and lands present in the barrel of a rifled firearm. The markings are parallel and spiral (Fig. 10.20).
- Secondary markings – these marks on bullet are caused due to certain individual features of inner surface of barrel like minor projections, or elevations or depressions.

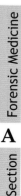

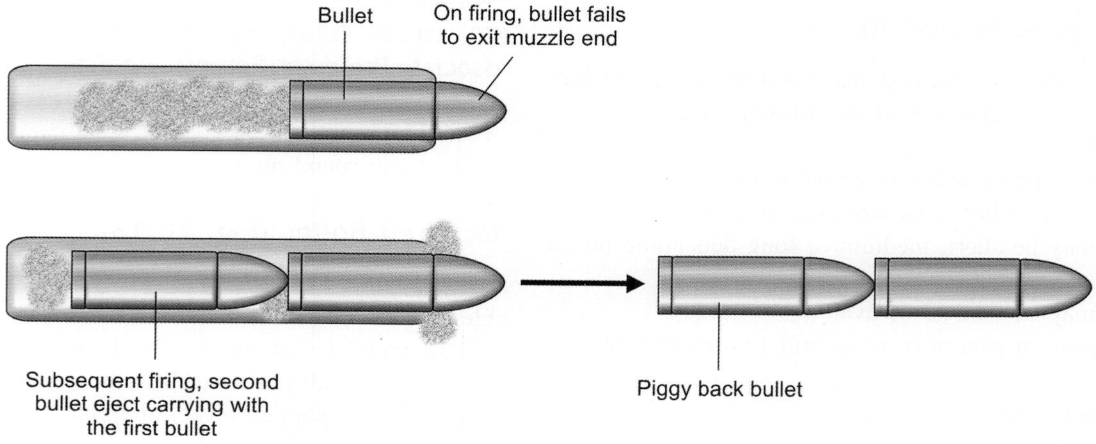

FIG. 10.19: Tandem bullet

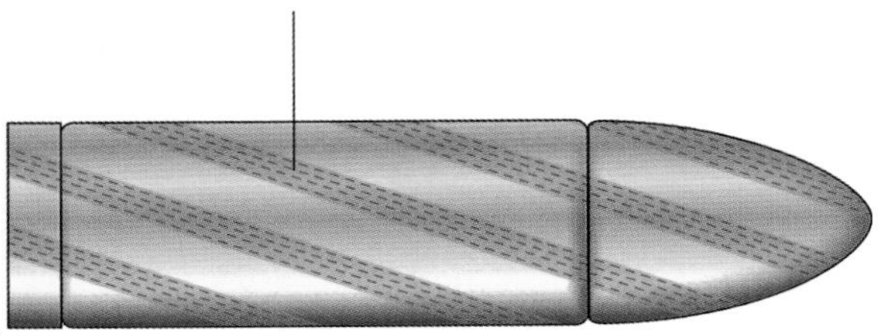

FIG. 10.20: Rifling marks over bullet

Table 10.2: Difference between smooth bore and rifled firearm		
Features	*Cartridge of smoothbore gun*	*Cartridge of rifle firearm*
Cartridge case	The posterior surface is made up of metal plate and anterior part is made up of cardboard disc	Made up of metal
Projectile	Pellets are used	Bullet is used
Wad	Present	Absent
Cardboard disc	Present	Absent

These marks are specific for a particular gun and not common to all guns.

Difference between smooth bore and rifled cartridge is mentioned in Table 10.2.

WOUND BALLISTICS (FIREARM WOUNDS)

Doctors doing autopsy of firearm cases are concerned with wound ballistics. The following issues need attention while conducting autopsy.

1. Whether the weapon is rifled or smooth bored?
2. The nature of projectile
3. The nature of propellant
4. The direction of firing
5. The range of firing

INJURIES CAUSED BY RIFLED FIREARMS (GUNSHOT WOUNDS)

- Wounds produced by rifled firearms are called as gunshot wounds.
- Penetrating wound produced by projectile (i.e. the bullet in rifled firearm) over body is called as **entry wound** (Fig. 10.21).
- The wound caused to body by projectile while leaving the body, after entering, is called as **exit wound** (Fig. 10.21).
- The path traveled by the projectile (i.e. the bullet in rifled firearm) between the entry wound and exit wound in body is called as **track of injury** (Fig. 10.21).
- The distance between the muzzle end of the firearm and the target (i.e. the victim) is called as **range of firing**[1](Fig. 10.21).

Features of Gunshot Wounds

- When rifled firearm is fired, along with bullet, many components will emerged from the muzzle end of gun and causes effects over target (i.e. the victim). The components and effects are mentioned in Table 10.3 (also see Figs 10.22 and 10.23)
- While entering the body, the bullet attempts to penetrate the skin against the elasticity of skin. The skin is stretched before penetration and with resultant perforation the margins become inverted. Similarly due to penetration, the bullet causes abrasion (*vide infra*). Due to elasticity of skin, the entry wound gets retracted and the wound appears small. While leaving the body, the bullet penetrates skin but here skin is unsupported unlike entry wound skin, therefore it gives-off causing more rent and everted margins (Fig. 10.24).
- Due to spinning movement of bullet, it causes friction of skin and produces the abrasion collar or areola (Fig. 10.25A). Normally, the abrasion collar measures about 0.3 cm. However, in some cases, the bullet may cause contusion instead of abrasion and this condition is referred as contusion collar.
- The barrel of firearm is usually lubricated. When such lubricated weapon is fired, the bullet carries the lubricant

Table 10.3: Showing different components emerging from muzzle end of firearm	
Components	Effects produced over body
Projectile in form of bullet	- Entry wound - Exit wound - Abrasion/contusion collar
Gun smoke and soot	Smudging/blackening
Gunpowder particles	Tattooing
Gases	Blast effect/ cherry red discoloration
Flame	Scorching/singeing
Metal particles	Metal ring
Grease or dirt	Grease collar

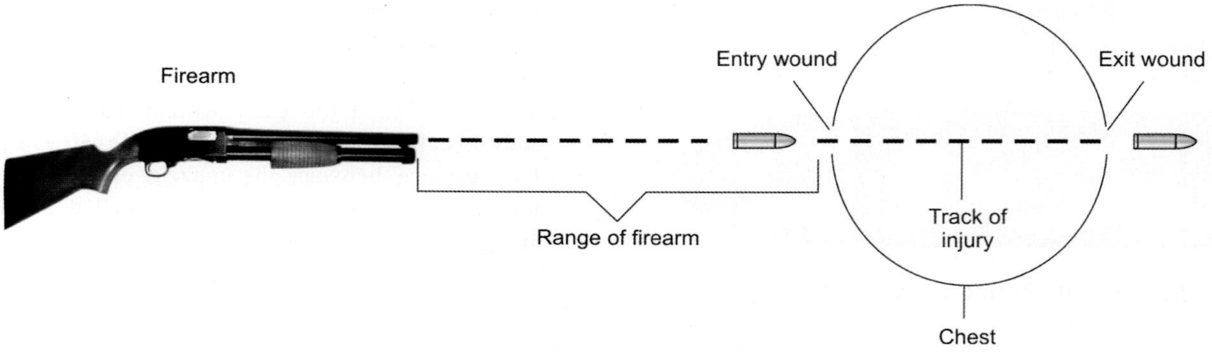

FIG. 10.21: Range of firing, entry, track and exit wound caused by firearm

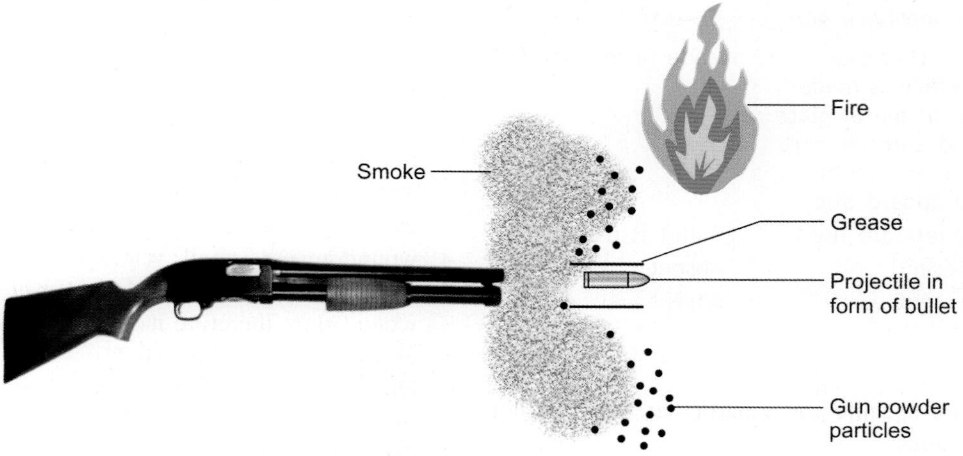

FIG. 10.22: Different components emerging from muzzle end of firearm

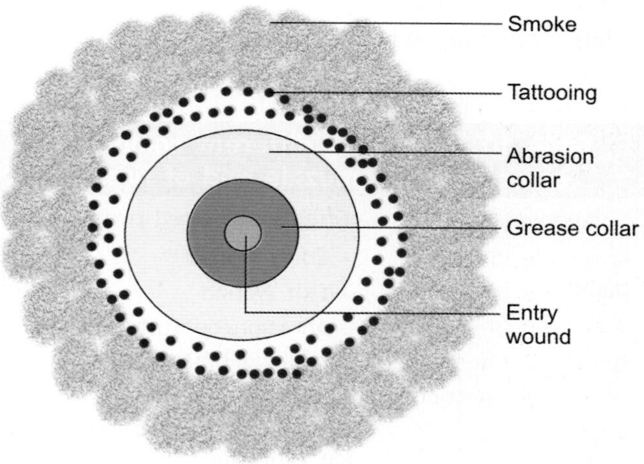

FIG. 10.23: Effects produced over body by the components emerged from muzzle end of firearm

while traveling through the barrel. While entering the body, the lubricant (grease) over the bullet gets deposited on the skin around the entry wound. The spinning movement of bullet while perforating the skin causes wiping of lubricant from its surface (Fig. 10.25B). The lubricant or dirt particles, that get deposited around the entry wound is called as grease collar or dirt collar.[1]

- When both collars i.e. abrasion and grease collars, are present, then the grease collar is seen in the inner zone and the abrasion collar at the outer zone (Fig. 10.25B).
- The flame emerging from the muzzle end of firearm may cause burning (scorching) of the skin and singeing of the hairs. The clothes may show evidence of burning and/or melting (Fig. 10.26).
- The grains of **un-burnt gunpowder** emerging from muzzle end of firearm causes **tattooing** on the skin. The tattooing is also called as **peppering** or **stippling**. Each

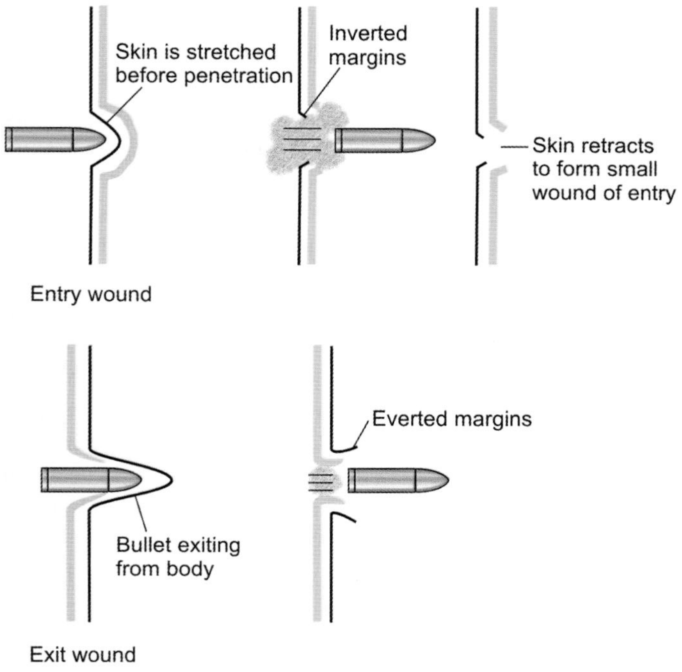

FIG. 10.24: Mechanism of entry and exit wound

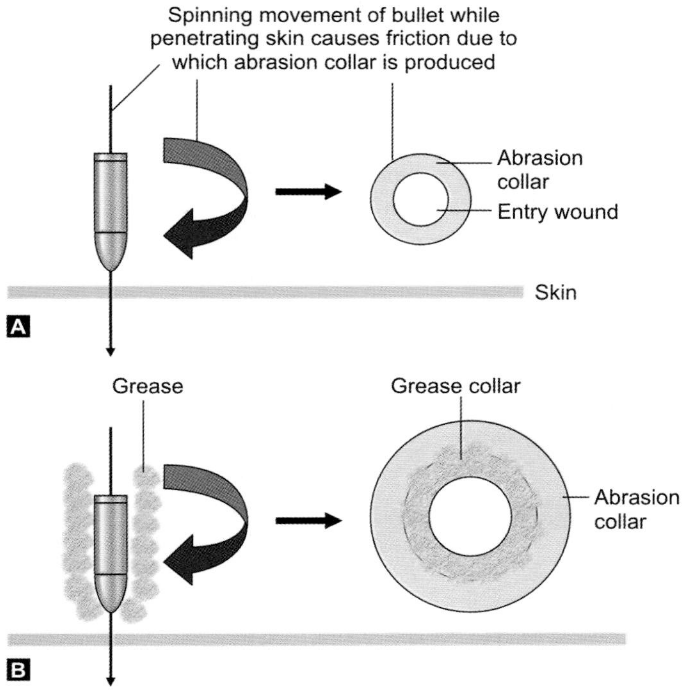

FIGS 10.25A and B: Abrasion and grease collar. **A:** Mechanism of production of abrasion collar **B:** Mechanism of production of grease collar

FIG. 10.26: T-shirt showing entry wound of firearm with evidence of burning and melting of clothes

grain of gunpowder acts as a minute missile and drives into the skin and imparts tattooing. This tattooing is seen on the skin as small, discrete, black specks, which cannot be, wiped off[7] (Fig. 10.23).

- Burning of gunpowder produces smoke. Blackening or smudging occurs due to superficial deposition of smoke particles on the skin (Fig. 10.23).
- The tissue around and beneath the wound of entry may be cherry red discoloured. The carbon monoxide emerging from the gases combines with hemoglobin and leads to formation of carboxyhemoglobin and imparts cherry red colour.
- A lead ring or metal ring may be present around the entry wound and it results from the deposition of lead or other metal particles. This ring can be appreciated on X-ray or by neutron activation analysis.
- Gases emerging from the weapon due to combustion of gunpowder may cause blast effect at the wound of entry in contact range firing. In contact shot, when the firing is done with muzzle end held against the skin, huge pressure is produced by the evolved gases. After emerging from muzzle end of gun, these gases gets accumulated between the skin and subcutaneous tissue and produces blast effect in form of tearing of skin, eversion of wound edges and extrusion of fat.[3]

Entry Wound in Rifled Firearm

- Rifled firearm produces two wounds, one, the wound of entry (entry wound) and other the wound of exit (exit wound).

- If there is only one wound i.e. the wound of entry, it means that either[8]:
  1. The bullet is in body.
  2. Exited or dropped from the same wound of entry.
  3. In exceptional circumstances, the bullet has been coughed out, lost in vomit or feces.
- The appearance of entry wound depends on:
  1. Type of weapon used and its caliber
  2. Type of projectile i.e. type of bullet used
  3. Type of propellant i.e. gunpowder used
  4. The striking velocity of bullet
  5. The site of body which is hit by bullet
  6. The range of firing
- The range of firing is considered as:
  1. Contact shot – here the muzzle end is in contact with body.
  2. Close shot – here the victim is within the distance traveled by flame.
  3. Near shot – here the victim is within the range of gunpowder deposition but outside the range of flame.
  4. Distant shot – here the victim is beyond the range of flame, smoke and gunpowder residue.

Contact Shot

- Also known as point blank shot.
- Here the muzzle end of weapon (i.e. gun) is in contact with skin.
- The wound of entry is large, shows cavitations and may be of triangular, stellate, cruciate or star shaped due to explosive effect of gas liberated. The gases get accumulated between skin and subcutaneous tissue and causes tearing of skin, thus imparting various shapes (Figs 10.27 and 10.28).
- Skin around the entry wound may also show imprint abrasion of muzzle end of gun (Fig. 10.29).
- The gases, flame, gunpowder, smoke and metal particles are driven into the track. Thus burning, soiling by smoke and tattooing are minimal or absent in the adjacent skin. The track is blackened by smoke with gunpowder residue and may show charring due to flame. Inner tissue may be cherry red due to carbon monoxide liberated in gases and conversion of hemoglobin to carboxyhemoglobin.
- If the wound is on head, blackening may be observed in pericranium area around the entry wound (Fig. 10.30). The fracture of skull may show typical features – the entrance wound shows a clean **punched-in hole** in the outer table while inner table (Fig. 10.31) shows beveled crater (Fig. 10.32) (also see Fig. 10.35). The reverse will occur at the exit wound i.e. the inner table at exit wound shows punched-out lesion (Fig. 10.33) while the outer table shows beveled opening (Fig. 10.34) (also see Fig. 10.35).
- The margins of entry wound may be everted with protrusion of fat because of gases coming out of the entrance wound under pressure.
- In contact shot, due to muzzle blast and negative pressure in the barrel, the barrel may suck blood, hair, fragments of tissue and clothe fibers inside. The phenomenon is called as '**back spatter**'.[5]

Close Shot (Figs 10.36 and 10.37)

- Flames travel about 7.5 cm in revolver or pistol and 15 cm in case of shoulder rifle
- Usually the entry wound appears to be circular when bullet strikes the body at right angle and may be of oval in shape if bullet strikes the skin at an acute angle. When bullet is entering perpendicularly, then the shape of wound would

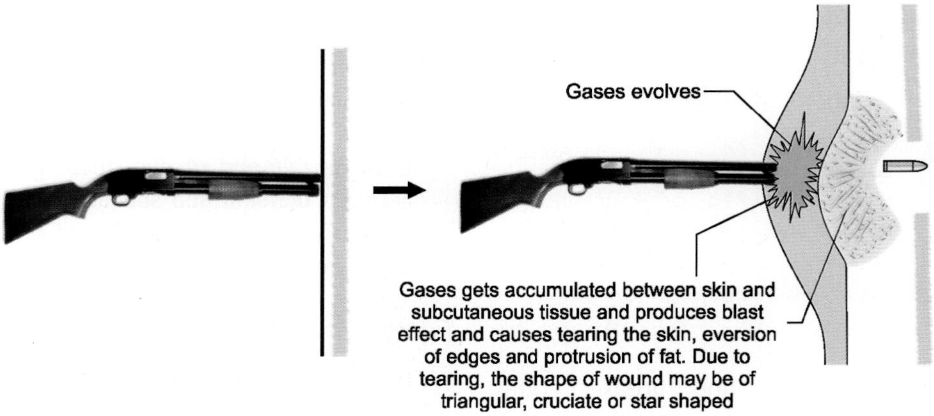
Gases evolves
Gases gets accumulated between skin and subcutaneous tissue and produces blast effect and causes tearing the skin, eversion of edges and protrusion of fat. Due to tearing, the shape of wound may be of triangular, cruciate or star shaped

FIG. 10.27: Shape of wound and effect of gases in contact shots

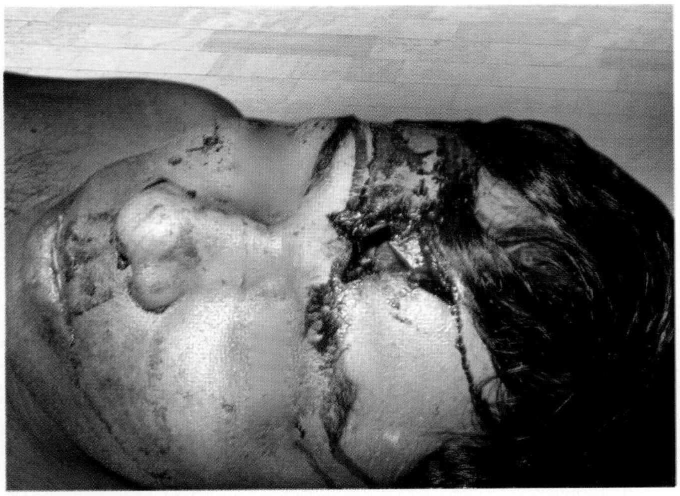

FIG. 10.28: Star shaped entry wound in contact shot

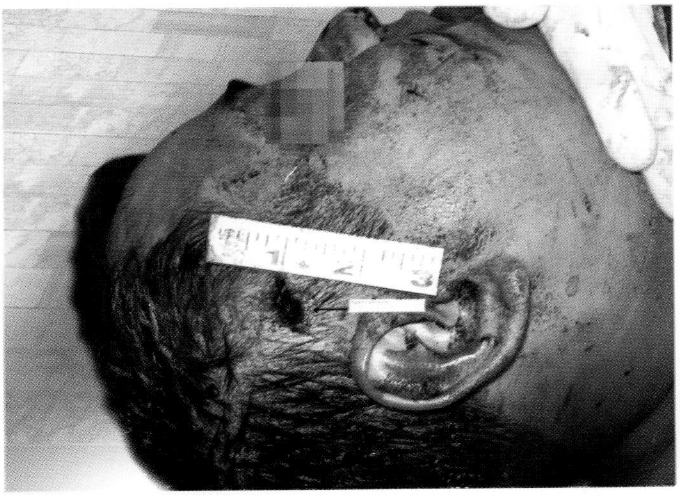

FIG. 10.29: Entry wound with muzzle impression (black arrow)

be circular with abrasion encircling the wound. In such wounds, the gunpowder residues are usually distributed circumferentially. In case of bullet entering the body at an angle then the entry wound may be of oval shape with abrasion margin more on the inclination side of bullet. In such entry wound, the gunpowder residues are distributed on one side from which the shot was fired (Fig. 10.38).

- The skin shows scorching, singeing, and blackening
- Abraded collar, grease or dirt collar may be present.
- The salient features of close shot in rifled firearm are summarized in Table 10.4.

Near Shot

- Here the victim is within the range of powder deposition but outside the range of flame i.e. within 60 cm.

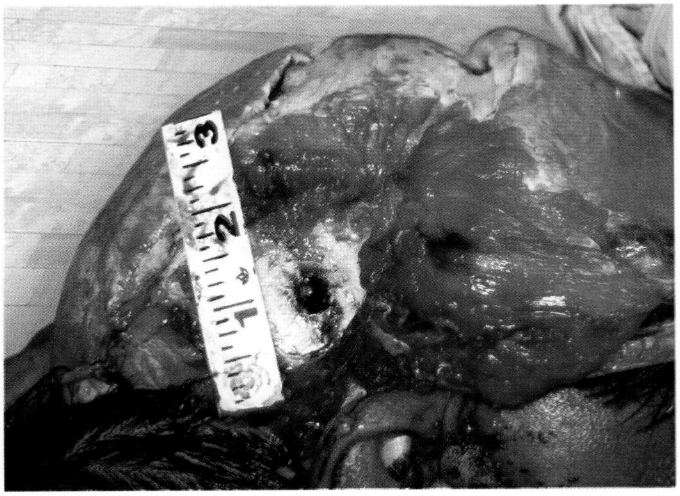

FIG. 10.30: Blackening around entry wound in pericranium area

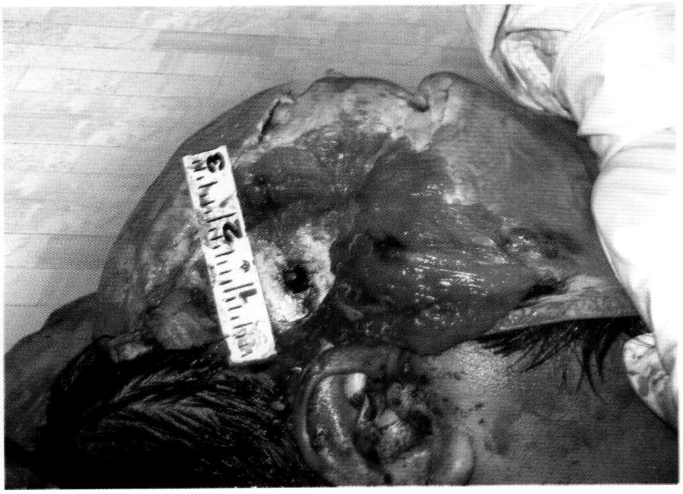

FIG. 10.31: Punched-in hole in outer table at entry wound

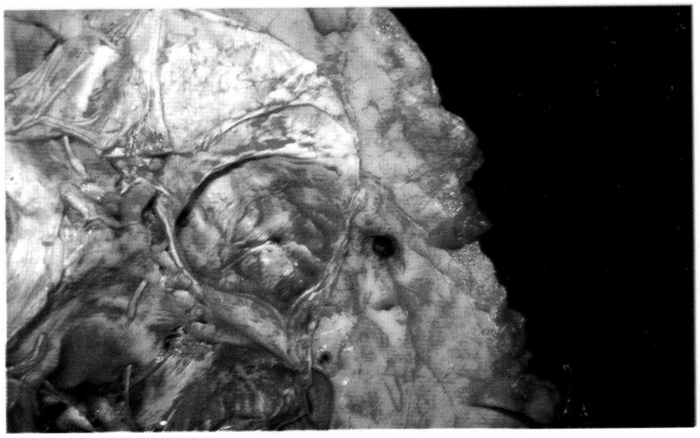

FIG. 10.32: Crater at inner table in entry wound

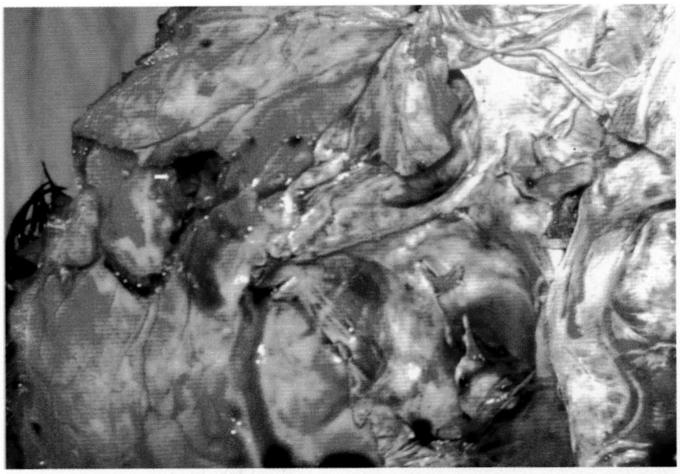

FIG. 10.33: Punched-out hole in inner table in exit wound (white arrow)

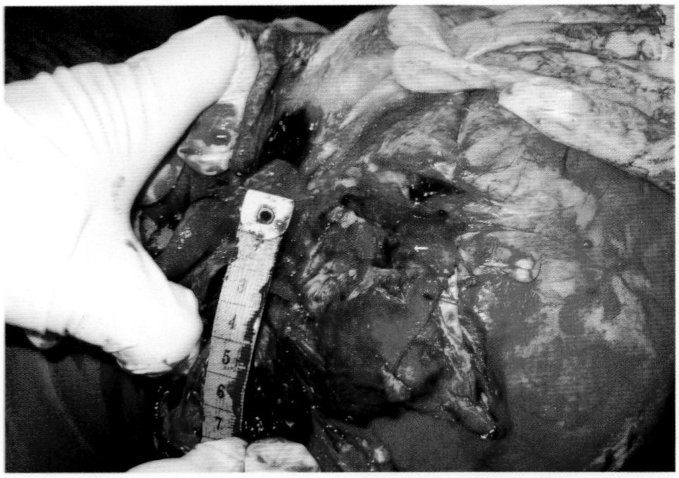

FIG. 10.34: Beveled margins at outer table in exit wound (white arrow)

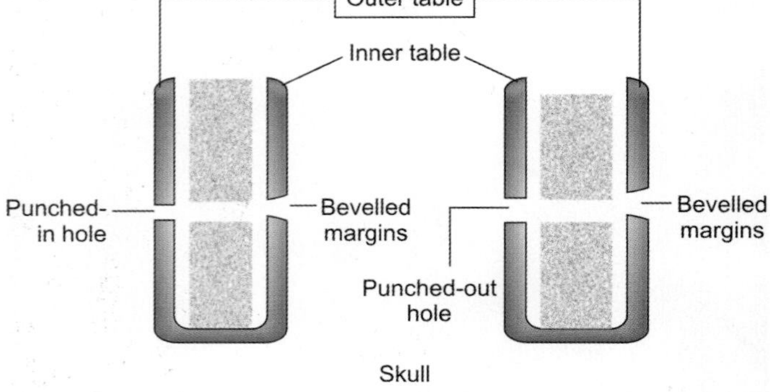

FIG. 10.35: Diagrammatic representation of entry wound and exit wound in skull

Table 10.4: Effects produced in close shot in rifled firearm

Components	*Distance traveled*	*Effects*
Flame	7.5 cm (revolver/pistol)	Scorching
	15 cm (shoulder rifle)	Singeing
Smoke	30 cm	Blackening
Gun powder	60-90 cm	Tattooing

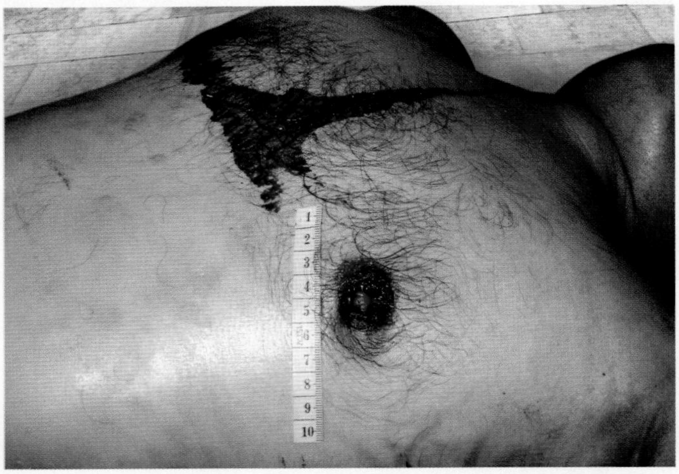

FIG. 10.36: Entry wound of rifled firearm—close shot

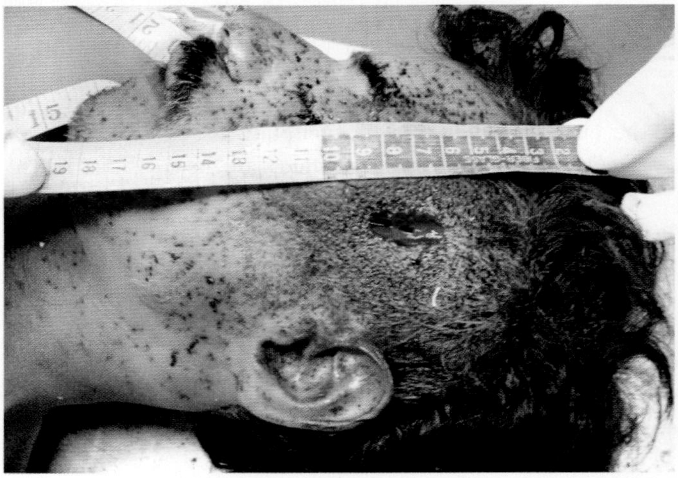

FIG. 10.37: Entry wound—close shot (*Courtesy*: Dr Manish Shrigiriwar, Associate Professor, Forensic Medicine, IGGMC, Nagpur)

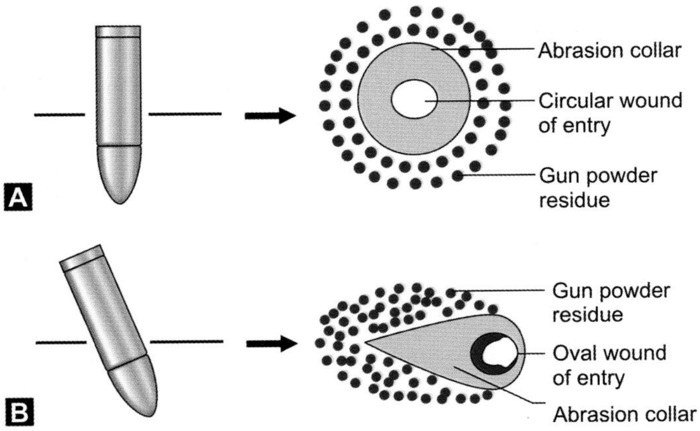

FIG. 10.38A and B: Shape of entry wound depending on bullet entry. **A:** Bullet enters perpendicularly while in **B:** Bullet enters obliquely

- If discharge of bullet occurs at a distance of about 15 cm or more, the effects of gases are usually lost due to dispersion and cooling of gases.[5]
- Singeing and scorching absent
- Abrasion collar present
- Grease collar present
- Blackening occurs up to 30 cm and beyond this range it is not seen.
- Tattooing present
- Edges of entry wound are inverted.

Distant Shot

- Here the victim is beyond the range of gunpowder
- Entry wound is circular
- Margins of entry wound are inverted
- Scorching, singeing, blackening, tattooing – absent.
- Grease collar may be present
- Abrasion collar may be present.

The salient features of contact, close, near and distant shots are summarized in Table 10.5.

Exit Wound (Fig. 10.39)

- Exit wound may be absent in some cases if bullet is lodged in body or lost in vomit/cough/feces or exit through same wound of entry.
- Similarly multiple exit wounds may be present due to:
  1. Breaking of bullet and fragment exit by different wounds.
  2. Fragment of bone along with bullet may cause two or more exit wounds.
- Exit wound may vary in size and shape. The variation is attributed to:
  1. Bullet tumbles in the body and exit by base end first rather than nose end or
  2. The bullet gets deformed or
  3. The bullet may break into pieces or
  4. Bullet may be accompanied by large bone fragment.
- Edges of exit wound may be everted or puckered or torn.
- Blackening, tattooing, singeing, abrasion collar, and grease collar are absent (Fig. 10.40)
- Differences between entry and exit wound are given in Table 10.6.

Importance of Exit Wound

Exit wound helps in:

1. Help in determining direction of firing.
2. Posture of victim at the time of firing can be ascertained.
3. Number of bullets in the body.

Unusual Effect of Rifled Firearm

Injuries caused by rifled firearm bullets are generally typical but at times may produce atypical lesion such as:

Table 10.5: Salient features of contact, close, near and distant shots of rifled firearm

Features	*Contact shot*	*Close shot*	*Near shot*	*Distant shot*
Range	In contact with skin	< 8 cm	30 - 60 cm	> 60 cm
Size of entry wound	Larger than bullet	Bullet size	Smaller than bullet size	Smaller than bullet size
Shape of entry wound	Varied	Circular	Circular	Circular
Muzzle imprint	Present	Absent	Absent	Absent
Edges of entry wound	Everted	Inverted	Inverted	Inverted
Scorching	Present	Present	Absent	Absent
Singeing	Present	Present	Absent	Absent
Blackening	Present	Present	Present up to 30 cm	Absent
Tattooing	Present	Present	Present	Absent
Abrasion collar	Present	Present	Present	Present
Grease collar	Present	Present	Present	Present

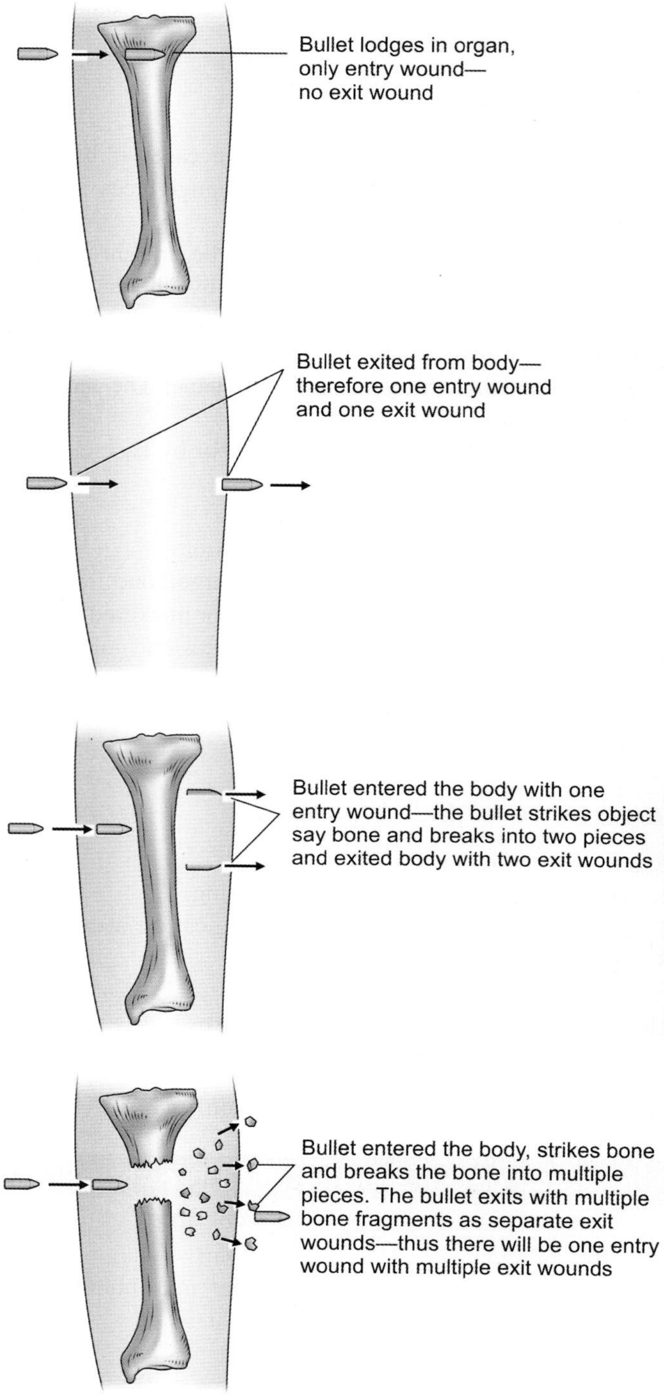

Bullet lodges in organ, only entry wound—no exit wound
Bullet exited from body—therefore one entry wound and one exit wound
Bullet entered the body with one entry wound—the bullet strikes object say bone and breaks into two pieces and exited body with two exit wounds
Bullet entered the body, strikes bone and breaks the bone into multiple pieces. The bullet exits with multiple bone fragments as separate exit wounds—thus there will be one entry wound with multiple exit wounds

FIG. 10.39: Different pattern of exit wound

- A bullet may produce atypical large entry wound
- Bullet graze – in this condition, the bullet hits the skin with an angle, it just licks the skin and goes off from the site without actually entering the body. Such bullet will produce only sliding abrasion or a laceration. Such lesions are called as bullet graze or bullet slap.
- A bullet may produce single entry wound with multiple exit wounds
- Ricochet bullet – a ricochet bullet is one, which gets deflected or deviated from its path by striking an intervening object in its way before striking the body (Fig. 10.41).
- It may possible to have multiple entry and exit wound with one bullet
- Tumbling of bullet – a bullet that tumbles (rotates end-on-end) during its motion is called tumbling bullet.
- Yawning of bullet – a bullet traveling in irregular fashion instead of traveling nose-on is called yawning bullet.
- Kennedy phenomenon – this is an artefact produced by surgical intervention. This name was derived from John F Kennedy, President of USA. The President was killed by bullet but the doctor who had first seen him had explored

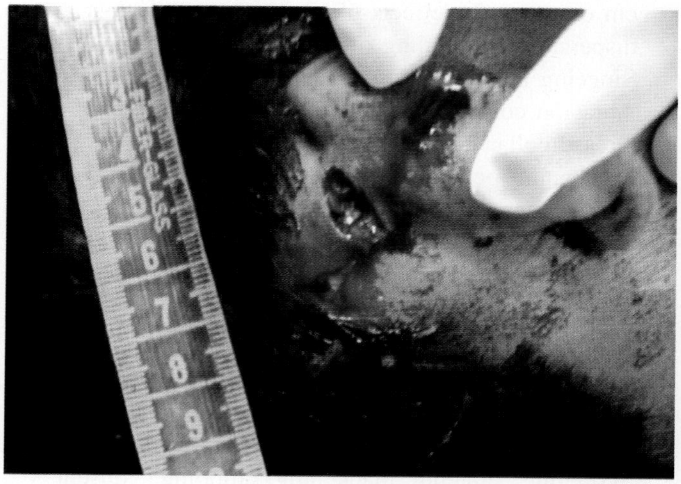

FIG. 10.40: Exit wound (*Courtesy*: Dr Manish Shrigiriwar, Associate Professor, Forensic Medicine, IGGMC, Nagpur)

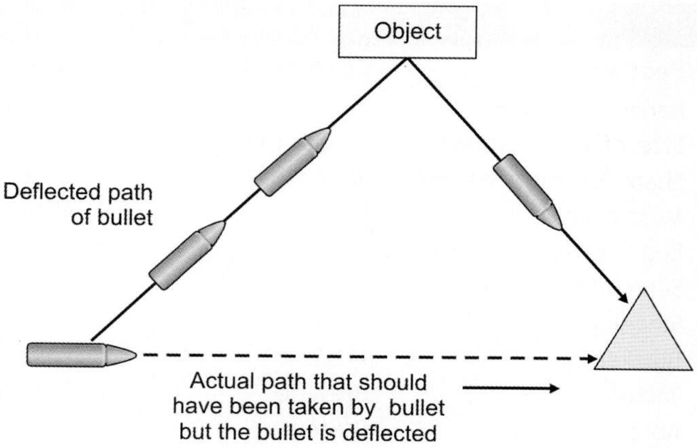

FIG. 10.41: Ricocheting of the bullet

Table 10.6: Difference between entry and exit wound

Features	Entry wound	Exit wound
Size	Smaller than the diameter of bullet, however in contact shot may be larger	Larger
Edges	Inverted	Everted
Abrasion collar	Present	Absent
Grease/dirt collar	Present	Absent
Tattooing	Present	Absent
Singeing of hairs	Present	Absent
Scorching/burning	Present	Absent
Bleeding	Less	More
Tissue around the wound	Cherry red due to carbon monoxide	No such change
Metal ring	May be present	Absent
Fat	No protrusion	May protrude

the wound surgically in a hope to remove the bullet and distorted the bullet wound. At autopsy, the wound of entry did not resemble with stated firearm. Later the first doctor revealed the fact and the ambiguity was made clear.

SMOOTH BORE FIREARM INJURY (SHOTGUN INJURIES)

Features

When shotgun is fired, it results in exit of following components from its muzzle end

1. Pellets
2. Wad
3. Cardboards
4. Gunpowder
5. Smoke
6. Flame
7. Gases

The characteristics of shotgun are[8]

1. Multiple pellets are used (unlike rifled firearm where single bullet is used)
2. Dispersion of pellets occurs i.e. shot disperses if distance traveled by them increases.

After firing the smoothbore weapon, the pellets travels in compact mass for certain distance and as the range (distance) increases, the pellet starts dispersing (i.e. spreading) from each other. As the distance increases more, the gained velocity by pellets will start decreasing so some pellets will fall on ground and some will travel further. When these pellets will hit the target i.e. the victim, the person will sustain multiple wounds caused by individual pellet (Fig. 10.42). Meanwhile, cardboard will fall so do wad. Flame will travel for small distance so does gases while smoke and gunpowder will travel some more distance (*vide infra*).

Table 10.7 summarizes the range of various components of smooth bore firearm.

Table 10.7: Range of various components of smooth bore firearm

Components	Distance travel
Flame	30 cm
Smoke	50 cm
Gunpowder	100 cm
Cardboard	2 meter
Wad	2 - 5 meter
Pellet	Compact mass up to 45 cm and then begins to disperse

Entry Wound

In smooth bore firearm, range is considered as

1. Contact range
2. Close range
3. Short range
4. Medium range
5. Distance range

Contact Shot[9]

- In contact range, muzzle end of smooth bore weapon is held firmly with skin
- The wound is single
- Burning or blackening is minimal or absent
- Muzzle impression of weapon present
- Cherry red colour present
- Shape of wound – usually it is circular. However, contact wound over bone i.e. wound over skin with underlying bone, e.g. scalp, sternum etc. may produce varied form of shape. The large volume of gas released from muzzle end gets accumulated under the skin but reflected back by underlying bone and thus momentarily raised skin and subcutaneous tissue like dome and causes laceration of skin and destruction of underlying subcutaneous tissue forming a split wound with cruciate or stellate or ragged wound with skin flaps (Figs 10.43 and 10.44).

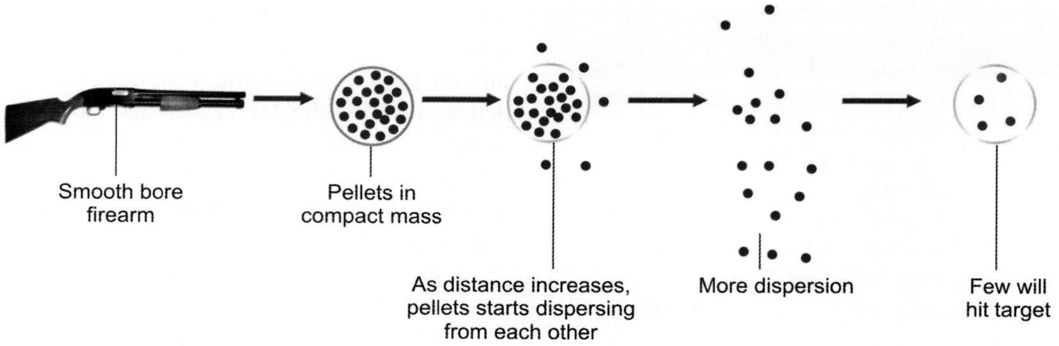

FIG. 10.42: Showing dispersion of pellets

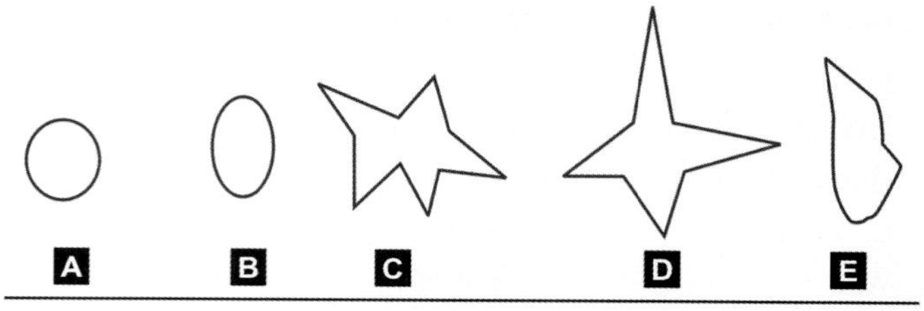

FIGS 10.43A to E: Different shapes in contact wound in shotgun. **A:** Circular, **B:** Oval, **C:** Star, **D:** Cruciate, **E:** Irregular shape

- When muzzle end is held in contact with skin, the pellets enter the body as a mass (en mass) and the accompanied gases produces explosive blast effect as mentioned above. Thus the entry wound is large and irregular. The edges may be charred or scorched by flame. The pellets are found en mass with wad and cardboards.

Close Range Wounds

- The close range is within 15 cm (6 inches)
- The wound of entry is circular if strike perpendicular to skin and the wound becomes elliptical if muzzle is held with an angle (Fig. 10.44).
- The edges are blackened and inverted.
- Blackening, due to smoke, of the skin round the wound is noted. Blackening spreads more widely than gunpowder tattooing.
- Tattooing by gunpowder
- Singeing of hairs
- Evidence of burning of skin in form of flare or zone of hyperaemia or even blister from flame exited from muzzle end.
- Tissue in and around the wound is cherry red
- Wad will be in depth of wound
- Pellet will be found en mass.

Short Range Wounds (See Figs 10.44A to F)

- Short range is within 15 cm to 1 meter
- Single hole persist for up to 1 meter (3 feet) and the edge of wound becomes crenated and scalloped. This is called "**rat hole**" or "**rat nibbling**" appearance from its resemblance to rodent teeth mark.
- Tattooing present
- Singeing of hairs present up to 30 cm (1 foot)
- Soot blackening present up to 20 inches (half-meter or 50 cm).

Medium Range Wounds

- Medium range is considered as distance of 1 meter to 4 meter
- More than 2 meter (> 2 m) - there is no burning, no smoke blackening, no tattooing
- Spreading (dispersion) of pellets increases progressively
- Satellite pellet holes begin to appear around the main entrance wound. As the spread of pellets increases progressively, the central wound (central hole) decreases (Fig. 10.44).
- Wad may be present. At times, wad may cause independent injury.

Distant Range Wounds

- Distant range is more than 4 meter
- The central wound (central hole) shrinks in size to nothing and no as distance increases, multiple pellet injuries are noted. The pellets spread widely and enter the body as individual missile producing separate injury and will produce its own track (Fig. 10.44). As the distance of firing increases progressively, the pellets will not be lethal and even if they penetrate the skin, they will lie in subcutaneous tissue.

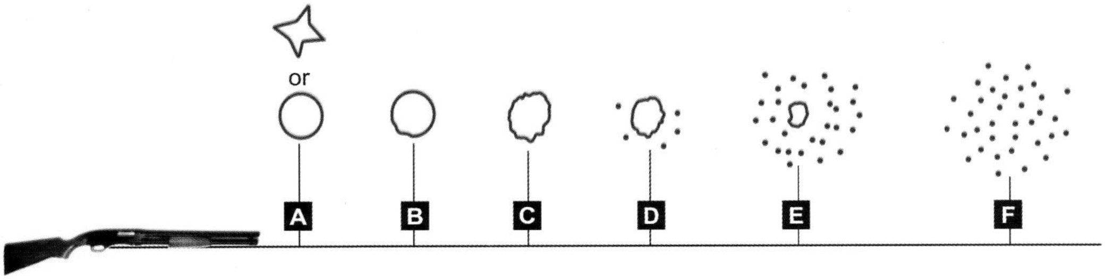

FIGS 10.44A to F: Appearance of entry wound in smoothbore firearms at increasing range of discharge. **A:** Contact wound may have circular or star/cruciate shaped wound. **B:** Close range. **C:** Short range with "rat-hole" appearance of wound. **D:** At medium range satellite pellet holes appears. **E:** As distance increases the central hole decreases in size. **F:** Distant range - no central hole with multiple pellets holes

- No wad injuries, no smoke, no flame, no tattooing will be noted.
- The salient features of smooth bore firearm are summarized in Table 10.8.

Exit Wound

- Exit wounds are uncommon in shotgun (smooth bore firearm) injuries because of small size of pellets and low muzzle velocity of the weapon. However, in following circumstances, exit wound may be present
  1. Contact wounds
  2. Tangential wounds
  3. Thin part of body such as neck or extremities.
- In case of exit wound, there is:
  1. No tattooing
  2. No scorching
  3. No singeing
  4. No blackening
- The margins of exit wounds are everted and ragged with gross tissue destruction.
- The internal track is diffusing than that of rifled weapon.

Unusual Ballistic Effects

Balling or welding effect: At times, due to defective or old ammunition, when shotgun is fired, the pellets exited the muzzle end in compact mass and move several meter without dispersion. This is because of welding of pellets amongst themselves and called as **balling effect**.

Billiard ball ricochet effect: In close range shots, when shotgun is fired, the pellets are bunched together and while striking the skin of victim, the pellets strike each other like billiard ball striking other balls and thus spreading out the pellets in wide pattern in body. Due to wide dispersion, it leads to confusion that firing would have been done from greater range.

Table 10.8: Features of smooth bore firearm

	Range				
Features	***Contact***	***Close (15 cm)***	***Short 15 cm - 1 m***	***Medium 1 m - 4 m***	***Distant > 4 m***
Number of wounds	Single	Single	Single	Multiple	Multiple
Shape of wound	Circular or varied if bone lies underlying	Circular	Rat hole	Satellite wounds around main wounds	Wider spread
Blackening	Present	Present	Present up to 50 cm	Absent	Absent
Tattooing	Present	Present	Present	Absent	Absent
Singeing	Present	Present	Present up to 30 cm	Absent	Absent
Scorching	Present	Present	Present up to 30 cm	Absent	Absent

AUTOPSY EXAMINATION

Autopsy examination consists of
1. Examination of clothes.
2. Radiological examination: X-ray examination/CT scan examination.
3. External and internal examination.
4. Collection, preservation and forwarding of exhibits/evidences.

Examination of clothes
- Presence of missile injury, any soiling, blood staining, tattooing, blackening needs detail attention
- Evidence of burning/singeing may be noted
- Examination of clothes gives idea regarding the range of firing and wound of entry and wound of exit.

Radiological examination
- Prior to autopsy, body is subjected for X-ray examination
- X-rays will help to identify number of missile (Figs 10.45 and 10.46)
- Help to locate the location/lodgment in body
- Help to provide track
- Help to know defect/fracture/injury of bone
- Help to know embolization of bullet in great blood vessels
- Act as evidence

Examination of body
- External examination – record the number of injuries, location, site, size, appearance, presence of tattooing, blackening, grease color, abrasion collar, etc.
- Internal examination – note the track of injury, the site of lodgment of missile.

Collection of evidences/exhibits
- Clothes
- Bullets/fragments/ pellets should be collected
- Skin around the entry wound for chemical identification of un-burnt powder.

Detection of Firearm Residue

Tests done to detect firearm residue are mentioned in Table 10.9.

Medicolegal Considerations

Medicolegal considerations related with firearm injuries are:
1. Type of firearm used
2. What is range of firing?
3. What is the direction of firing?
4. What is cause of death?
5. Whether, it is accidental, suicidal or homicidal injury?

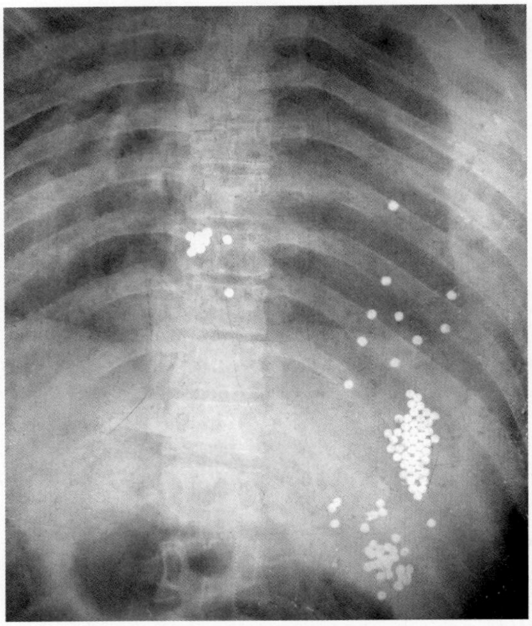

FIG. 10.45: X-ray chest showing multiple pellets (*Courtesy*: Dr Manish Shrigiriwar, Associate Professor, Forensic Medicine, IGGMC, Nagpur)

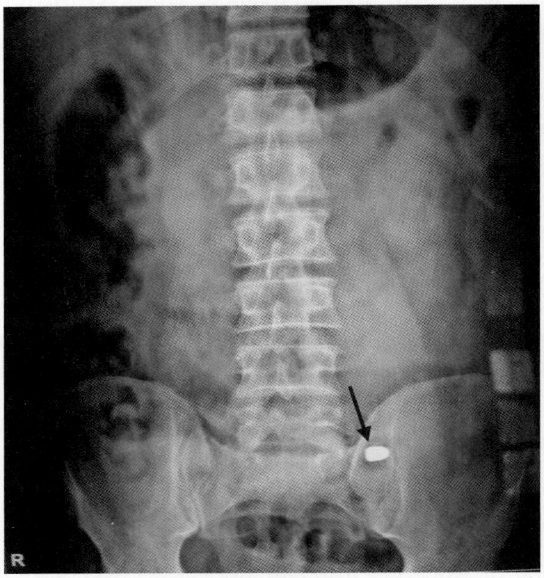

FIG. 10.46: X-ray abdomen showing bullet (arrow) (*Courtesy*: Dr Manish Shrigiriwar, Associate Professor, Forensic Medicine, IGGMC, Nagpur)

Accident, Suicide or Homicide

For suicide with shotgun – head appears to be common location followed by chest and abdomen. Most common location

Table 10.9: Tests done to detect firearm residue

Test	*Used for detection of*
Paraffin test	To detect presence of dermal nitrite
Harrison and Gilroy	To detect metal residues as lead, barium etc
Neutron activation analysis	To detect metal residues
Atomic absorption spectrophotometer	Lead

on the head happens to be intra-oral followed by under the chin, side of head and forehead. Contact wounds are the most common range of firing.[10] When gun is fired, the hands of dying person, holding the gun, receives particles of lead, antimony and barium from the discharge of firearm[11] (Fig. 10.47). The differences between accidental, suicidal and homicidal firearm injury are summarized in Table 10.10.

EXPLOSION AND BOMB BLAST INJURIES

Injuries

A person can be injured due to bomb blast injuries in many ways. Blast injuries are traditionally divided into four categories as:[12]

1. Primary blast injury – is caused solely by the direct effect of overpressure on tissue. Air is easily compressible, unlike water. As a result, a primary blast injury almost always affects air-filled structures such as the lungs, ear, and gastrointestinal tract. A tympanic membrane injury with hemorrhage in the middle ear is common findings in survived victims.[13]
2. Secondary blast injury – is caused by flying objects or missile generated or propelled by the explosion that strike people.
3. Tertiary blast injury – is a feature of high-energy explosions. This type of injury occurs when people fly through the air and strike other objects.
4. Miscellaneous blast related injuries – encompass all injuries caused by explosion for example collision, injuries by falling masonry, buildings, beams etc.

In addition, burns by flame or hot gases may be noted as person may sustain burn injuries with the explosion flame or hot gases.

Autopsy Findings

Objectives

The objectives of conducting autopsy of bomb blast victim's are:[14]

1. Identification
2. Documentation of injuries

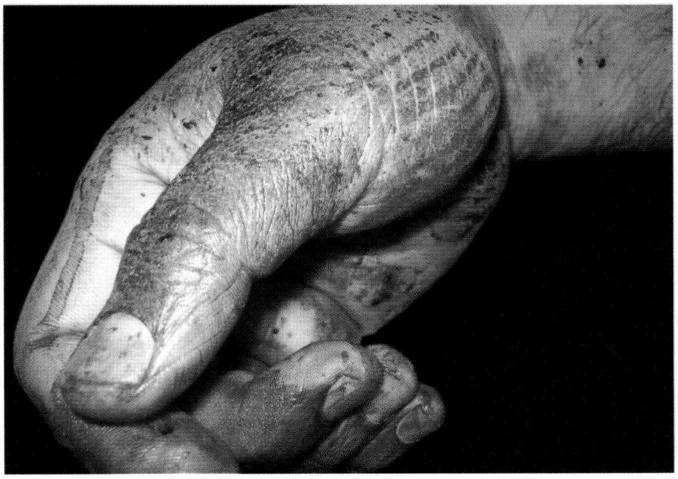

FIG. 10.47: Gunpowder residue over hand in case of suicide with pistol

Table 10.10: Difference between accidental, suicidal and homicidal firearm injury

Features	*Accidental injury*	*Suicidal injury*	*Homicidal injury*
Site of entry wound	Any part	Head or chest	Any part
Range	Close	Contact or close	Any
Direction	Any	Upward or backward	Any
Number of wounds	One	Usually one	One/multiple
Firearm residue on hand	Present	Present	Absent
Weapon at the scene	Present	Present	Absent or planted
Motive	Absent	Financial worry/depression etc	Present - revenge, robbery etc
Suicide note	Absent	May be present	Absent

3. Determination of cause of death
4. Reconstruction of the scene of crime and relative position of bomb and victim
5. Collection of evidences – recovering any fragments of bomb, detonating or timing apparatus, powder etc.

Steps

1. X-ray the body
   - To identify radio-opaque objects (missile) or metal objects of bomb devices such as spring or missile like nails, screws, glass etc.
   - For identification of individual
2. Identification of individual
3. Documentation of injuries
   - Characteristic feature of bomb blast is "**body stippling**" with injury triad of bruising, abrasions and lacerations.
   - Burn injuries are either flash burns or flame burns.
   - Due to disruptive effect of a bomb, the whole of the body or part of the body may be blown into pieces.
   - There may be alveolar hemorrhages due to tearing of alveolar septa.
4. Collection of samples/evidences: Samples to be collected are given in Table 10.11.

Table 10.11: Collection of sample

Test	*Samples*
For toxicology	Blood
	Urine
	Liver
	Bile
	Lung
	Stomach with contents
	Vitreous fluid
	Skin
For tissue matching /DNA	Hair
	Blood
	Muscle
For identification	Footwear
	Jewelry
	Pocket contents
	Clothes
For ballistic examination	Clothes
	Skin
	Powder traces
	Paint fragments
	Oil or grease stains
	Glass or other foreign material
	Metal fragments

REFERENCES

1. Pillay VV. Firearm and explosive injuries. In: Textbook of Forensic Medicine and Toxicology, 14th edn. 2004. Paras Publishing, Hyderabad. 154–72.
2. Dikshit PC. Firearm injuries. In: Textbook of Forensic Medicine and Toxicology, 1st edn. 2007. Peepee Publishers and Distributors (P) Ltd., New Delhi. 182–99.
3. Rao NG. Firearms and explosive injuries. In: Textbook of Forensic Medicine and Toxicology, 1st edn. 2006. Jaypee Brothers Medical Publishers (P) Ltd., New Delhi. 217–42.
4. Muller D, Levy A, Vinokurow A, Ravreby M, Shelef R, Wolf E, Eldar B, Glattstein B. A novel method for the analysis of discharged smokeless powder residues. J Forensic Sci 2007; 52: 75–8.
5. Reddy KSN. Mechanical injuries. In: The Essentials of Forensic Medicine and Toxicology, 22nd edn. 2003. K. Suguna Devi, Hyderabad. 143–94.
6. Nelson CL, Winston DC. A new type of shotgun ammunition produces unique wound characteristics. J Forensic Sci 2007; 52: 195–8.
7. Ramchandran A, Chandran MR. Forensic traumatology. In A Short Textbook of Forensic medicine and Toxicology, 1st reprint edn. 2006. All India Publishers & Distributors, Regd., New Delhi. 108–63.
8. Parikh CK. Firearm injuries. In: Parikh's Textbook of Medical Jurisprudence and Toxicology, 5th edn. 1995. CBS Publishers and Distributors, Bombay. 258–304.
9. Saukko P, Knight B. Gunshot & explosion deaths. In: Knight's Forensic Pathology, 3rd edn. 2004. Arnold, London. 245–80.
10. Molina DK, Wood LE, DiMaio VJM. Shotgun wounds. A review of range and location as pertaining to manner of death. Am J Forensic Med Pathol 2007; 28: 99–102.
11. Jaiswal AK, Moon DV, Moharana M, Gupta M. Determination of lead in forensic samples by atomic absorption spectrophotometer. Medicolegal Update 2006; 6: 23–5.
12. Lavonas E, Pennardt A. Blast injuries. E-medicine. Available from: http:/www.emedicine.com/emerg/topic63.html.
13. Wathore SD, Chikhalkar BG, Chavan GS, Tasgaonkar VN. Bomb blast injuries: nature and clinicopathological co-relation assists investigation. Souvenir of Formedicon 2004, XIIth Annual Conference of Medicolegal Association of Maharashtra, 2004. 37.
14. Agrawal VR, Pawale DA. Special considerations in postmortem examination of an explosion. J Medicolegal Assoc Maharashtra 2001; 13: 18–21.

CHAPTER 11

Regional Injuries

Conviction is worthless unless it is converted into conduct.

- Thomas Carlyle

Regional injuries consist of injuries sustained to various anatomical region of the body. Amongst regional injuries, injury sustained to head is more common.

HEAD INJURY

Definition

Head injury is defined by National Advisory Neurological Disorder and Stroke Council as "*a morbid state resulting from gross or subtle structural changes in the scalp, skull and/ or the contents of the skull, produced by mechanical force*".

Classification

A) Depending on the state of dura, head injuries are classified as[1]

1. Closed head injury: Here the dura remains intact, irrespective of whether skull is fractured or not.
2. Open head injury: Here the dura is open i.e. torn. The dura may be torn by
   - Penetrating injury
   - Bone fragment or
   - As a consequence of skull fracture

B) Depending on duration of unconsciousness and Glasgow coma scale,[2] head injury can also be classified as mentioned in Table 11.1.

SCALP INJURIES

Scalp is covering of head and extends from the eyebrow anteriorly to superior-nuchal line posteriorly and laterally from one temporal line to the other. Scalp is composed of:

1. S – skin
2. C – connective tissue
3. A – aponeurosis (galea aponeurotica)
4. L – loose areolar tissue
5. P – pericranium (periosteum)

Following sort of injuries may be present over scalp

1. Abrasion
2. Contusion
3. Laceration – may be confused with incised wound. Types of scalp laceration are:
   – Linear
   – Y-shaped
   – Stellate
   – Cruciate
   – Penetrating
   – Crescent etc.
4. Incised wounds
5. Avulsion
6. Puncture wounds

Table 11.1: Classification of head injury

Type	*Duration of unconsciousness*	*Glasgow coma scale*
Minor or mild head injury	< 30 minutes	13-15
Moderate head injury	> 30 min and < 6 hours	9-12
Severe head injury	> 6 hours	8 or less

Contusion of Scalp

- Bruise of scalp may be mobile
- A bruise in the anterior scalp may shift downward to appear around the eye, thus causing "**black eye**" or **spectacle hematoma**.
- A contusion in temporal scalp may shift downward and appear behind the ear – **similar to battle sign**.
- These shifting bruises are also called as **ectopic contusion, percolated bruises** or **migratory contusions**.
- Hematoma may occur beneath the galea aponeurotica and called as **under-scalp hematoma** or sub-galeal hemorrhage or sub-galeal hematoma (Fig. 11.1).

Injury to Face

Face may sustain:

1. Abrasion
2. Contusion
3. Laceration
4. Incised wound
5. Chop
6. Penetrating wound
7. Fracture of bone

Injury to Ear

External ear may sustain following sort of injuries

1. Abrasion
2. Contusion
3. Laceration
4. Cut/chop
5. Avulsion from root
6. Hematoma of external ear pinna
7. Tympanic membrane may be ruptured due to hard and blunt impact and causes deafness.

Injury to Eye

- Blunt force may cause injury to cornea, iris, lens, vitreous hemorrhage, and detachment of retina, or even traumatic cataract.
- Penetrating injury
- Black eye
- Subconjunctival hemorrhage

Black Eye (Fig. 11.2)

- Also called as **periorbital hematoma**
- It is bruising of the eye lid i.e. periorbital area
- It is caused in following ways (Fig. 11.3)
  1. By direct trauma
  2. Blood gravitating or shifting downwards from an injury on frontal area of scalp or
  3. Blood entering the orbit from behind or above due to fracture in the orbit – commonly fracture of floor of anterior fossa of skull.
- Spectacle hematoma: Hemorrhage in the soft tissue around the eyes in eyelids of both eyes is called spectacle hematoma or raccoon eyes i.e. in other words black eye on both side is a spectacle hematoma. It usually suggests fracture of base of skull.

Injury to Teeth

- Fracture/ fracture dislocation of tooth/teeth
- Contusion and laceration of gums
- Fracture of alveolar margin

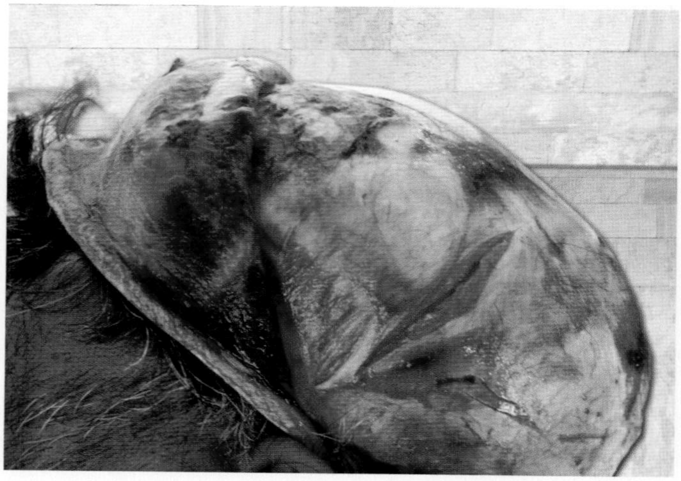

FIG. 11.1: Under scalp hematoma

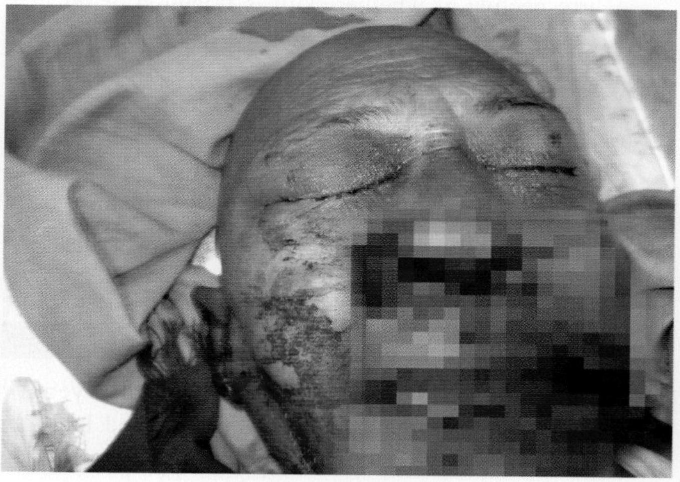

FIG. 11.2: Black eye

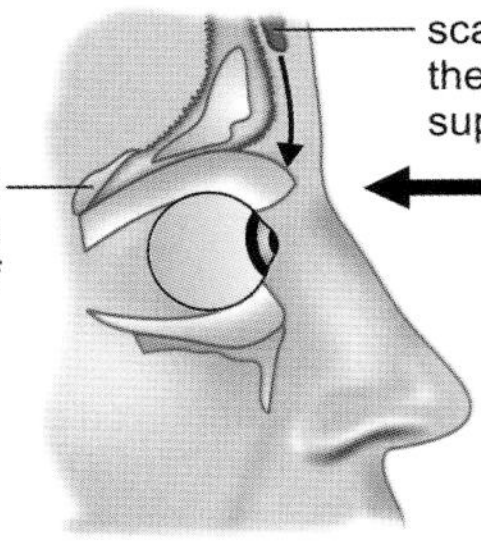

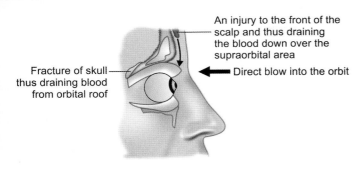

FIG. 11.3: Mechanism of production of black eye

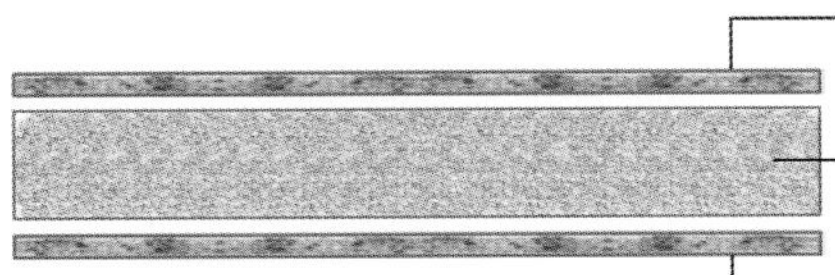

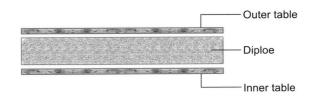

FIG. 11.4: Skull bone

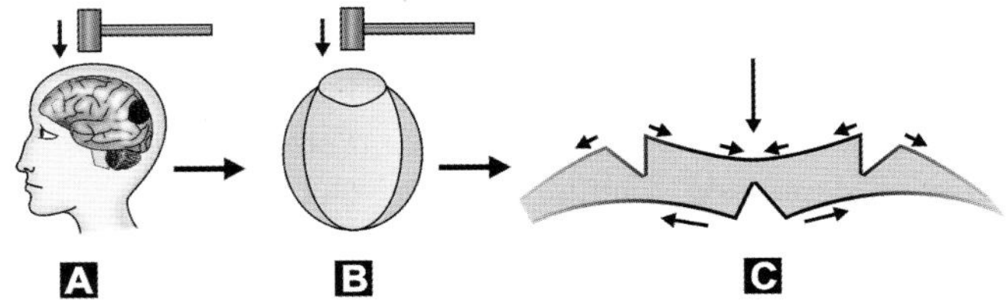

FIGS 11.5A to C: Mechanism of skull fracture

INJURY TO SKULL

Forensic Anatomy of Skull

- In broader sense, bones of head are collectively known as calvaria (cranium, skull). Thus, it can be considered as brainpan excluding the bones of face.[3, 4] Skullcap or calva is roof of skull often called as vault. Rest part is base of skull.
- In adult, skull consists of two parallel tables of compact bones. The outer table is twice in thickness that of inner table. Both, outer and inner, table of bones are separated by a soft cancellous bone - the diploe (Fig. 11.4). Skull varies in thickness, the average frontal and parietal thickness is 6-10 mm and temporal bone is 4 mm, and the occipital bone in midline is 15 mm or more.[5]

Mechanism of Skull Fracture

As per Rowbotham's hypothesis, fracture of skull is caused by:
1. Direct application of force to skull – for example blow over head with iron rod.
2. Indirect violence – for example fall from height on feet or buttock.

1. Direct Force Fracture

Direct force fracture results from following mechanism
1. Fracture due to local deformation
2. Fracture due to general deformation

A) Fracture due to local deformation[5, 6] (Figs 11.5A to C)

- If skull receives a focal force impact, then there is momentary distortion of the shape of skull. Due to continued force, the area under the point of impact tries to bend inward. The adult skull is incompressible. Due to incompressibility of skull and the inward bend caused by focal impact, the skull undergoes compensatory mechanism wherein there occurs bulging of other area. This is called as "**struck hoop analogy**".
- Now if the acting force over skull exceeds the limit of elasticity of skull, both the intruded (i.e. inward bend) and extruded (i.e. the bulging area) areas get fractured.
- The skull bones of infant are more elastic and may distort more than adult.
- When the focal impact is severe, depressed fracture may occur and may follow the actual shape of the impacting object.

B) Fracture due to general deformation[6]

- As per Rowbotham's hypothesis, skull behaves like an elastic sphere, thus:
  1. When skull is compressed in one plane, it bulges in other directions. For example if the skull is compressed laterally, the vertical and longitudinal diameters are increased and fracture may occur in these planes, if the bones are stretched beyond the limits of skull elasticity (Fig. 11.6).
  2. Similarly, fracture may occur if the head is compressed between two external objects say for example between wood plank and wall or between wood log and the spinal column.

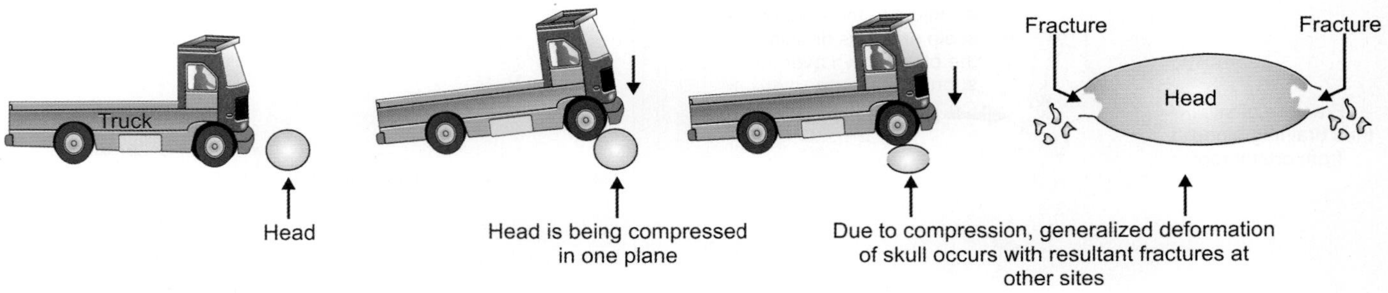

FIG. 11.6: Fracture of skull due to general deformation

- Fracture due to general deformation results in fissured type and occur in part of the skull distant from the site of application of force.
- When a severe local impact force causes focal and general deformation, a combination of depressed fracture and radial fracture may result resembling "spider web" pattern.

Puppe's Rule

- When two or more separate fracture occurs from successive impacts and meet each other, the later fracture (second fracture in Fig. 11.7) will terminate in the earlier fracture (first fracture in Fig. 11.7). The termination of second fracture will interrupt the cranial distortion, which precedes fracturing.[7]

2. Skull Fracture Due to Indirect Violence

- Vault or base of skull may be fractured by indirect violence. The causative force applied may be away from skull but is transmitted to skull. The force may be applied to:
  1. Force applied to chin: Blow on chin may cause fracture of glenoid fossa. Force applied below the mandible may be transmitted through the maxilla to the base of skull and fracture the cribriform plate.
  2. Force applied to feet or buttock: For example in fall from height, the force is transmitted upwards through the spinal column and may produces ring fracture around basiocciput.

Skull Fracture

Types of skull fractures are

A) Fracture of vault of skull
1. Linear or fissured
2. Depressed (signature)
3. Comminuted [Mosaic (spider web)]
4. Pond or indented
5. Gutter
6. Diastatic or sutural
7. Perforating
8. Cut fracture

B) Fracture of base of skull (basilar fracture)
1. Linear or fissured
2. Ring
3. Hinge
4. Longitudinal
5. Secondary

Linear Fracture (Fissured) (Figs 11.8 to 11.10)

- Linear fracture may involve outer or inner or both table of skull
- Common type
- Such fracture can be straight or curved
- In children or young person, the liner fracture may pass into a suture line and causes diastasis fracture.

Depressed Fracture (Figs 11.11 and 11.20)

With severe local force application say for example hammer; the fracture bone is driven inward into cranial cavity. Thus also called as **signature fracture** or **fracture a la signature**, as the pattern resembles that of causative weapon.

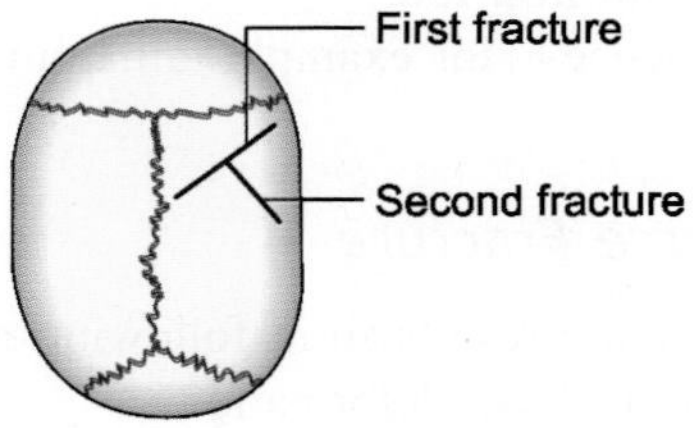

FIG. 11.7: Puppe's rule

Comminuted Fracture (Figs 11.12 and 11.20)

Here the bone is broken into pieces i.e. fragmentation of bones occurs. Non-displaced comminuted fracture resembles a spider web or mosaic pattern.

Pond Fracture

- Here there is dent (dimple like) formation over the skull and the dent resembles like that of concave pond (Fig. 11.13).
- This type occurs only in skull of infants
- Due to pliable bones of infant, the force applied produce depression without fracture. The depression of bone is comparable with distortion produced by squeezing a table-tennis ball or ping-pong ball.

Gutter Fracture[8] (Figs 11.14 and 11.15)

- Gutter fracture is formed when part of the thickness of skull bone is removed so as to form a gutter or furrow in the bone.
- They are caused when the weapon strikes the skull tangentially for example glancing bullet injury.

Diastatic Fracture (Sutural Fracture) (Fig. 11.16)

- Here the fracture occurs along the line of sutures of skull for example coronal suture fracture etc.
- Usually occurs in children and young adults because of non-fusion of sutures and results in separation of skull sutures.

Perforating Fracture (Fig. 11.17)

Here the skull is perforated by a sharp pointed object or bullet. The fracture involves injury to outer and inner table of

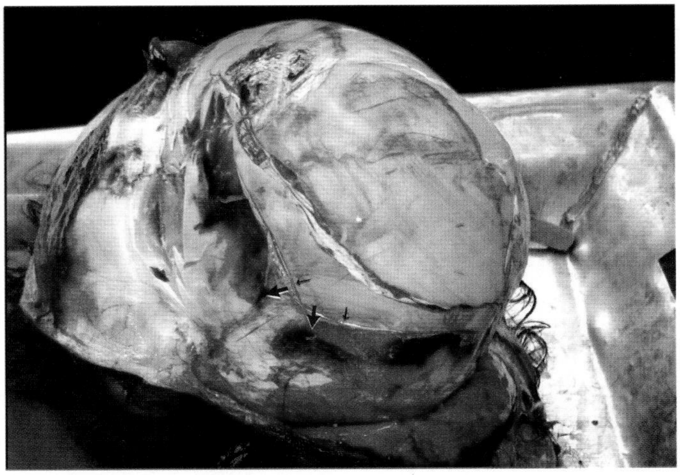

FIG. 11.9: Linear fracture (black arrows)

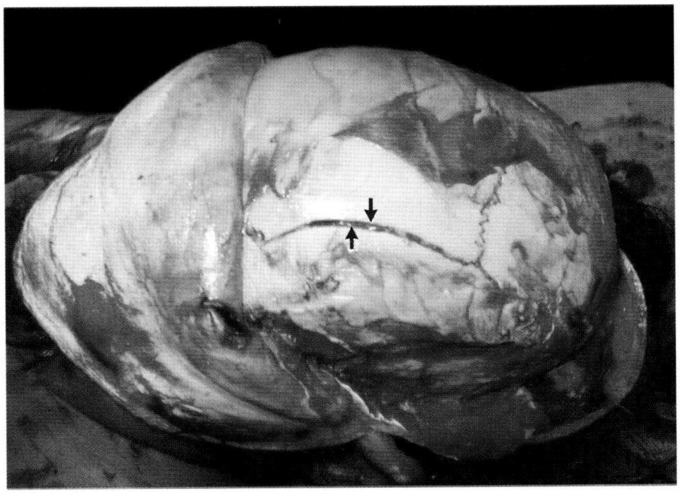

FIG. 11.10: Linear fracture (black arrows)

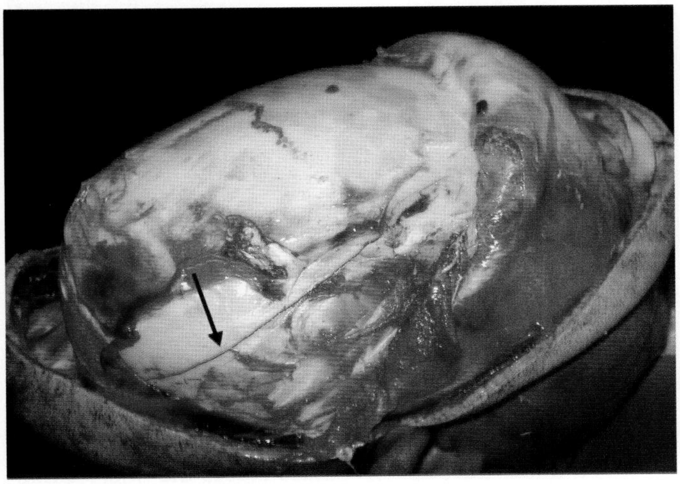

FIG. 11.8: Linear fracture (black arrow)

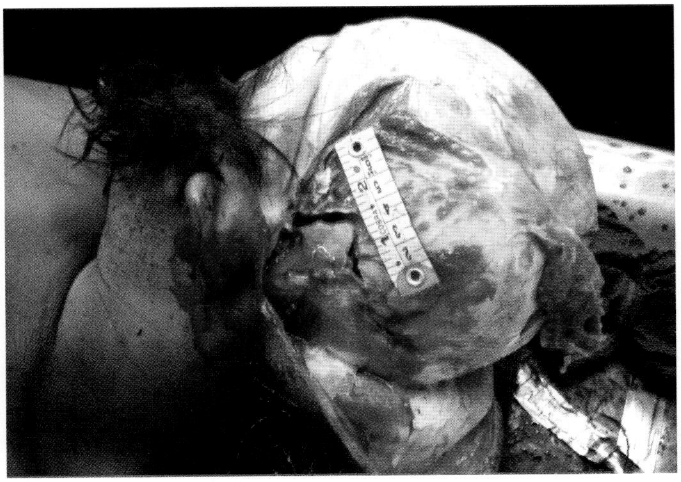

FIG. 11.11: Depressed fracture

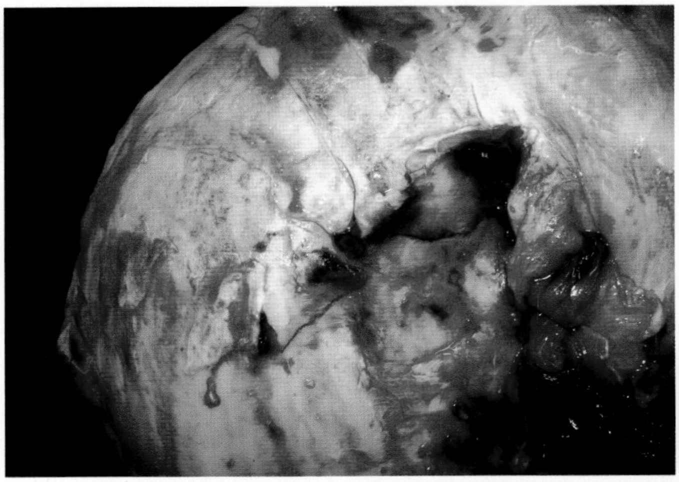

FIG. 11.12: Comminuted fracture

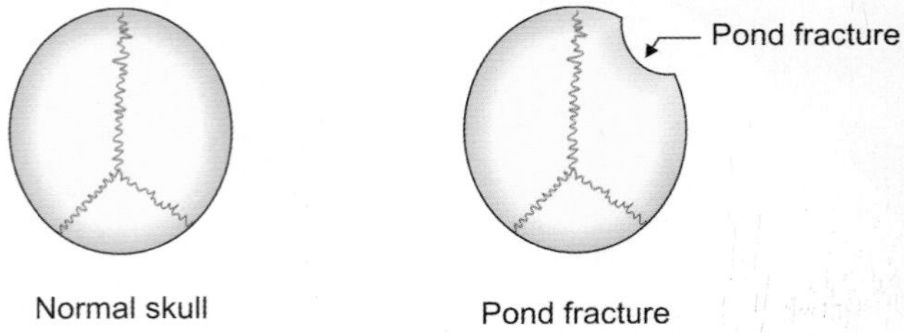

FIG. 11.13: Pond fracture

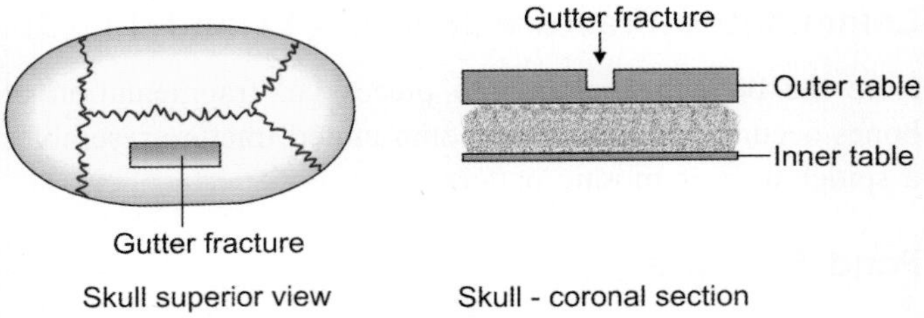

FIG. 11.14: Gutter fracture

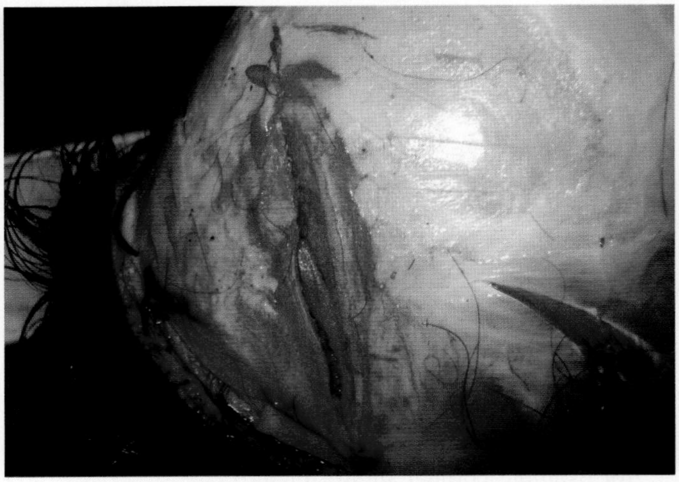

FIG. 11.15: Gutter fracture

skull and shape and size may correspond to the dimensions of offending agent.

Cut Fracture (Fig. 11.18)

- These fracture are accompanied with sharp weapons like sword or chopper
- Fracture involves either outer table or both tables. If involved both tables, it will cause clean-cut gap corresponding with the thickness of blade. If involved outer table, it is labeled as partial cut fracture.

Ring Fracture (Fig. 11.20)

- This is a fissured fracture that occurs round the foramen magnum in posterior cranial fossa.
- It occurs due to:
  - Fall from height and person landing on the feet or buttock or
  - Severe impact on the vertex that may drive the skull downwards on the spinal column.

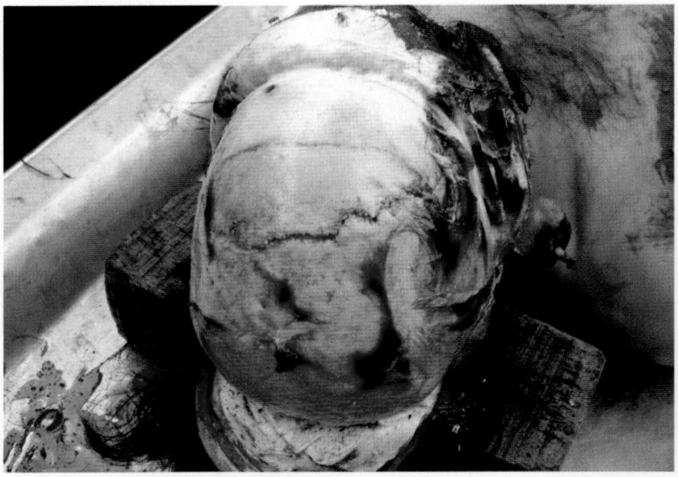

FIG. 11.16: Sutural fracture

Hinge Fracture[5] (Figs 11.19 and 11.20)

- It is a linear fracture that passes across the floor of middle cranial fossa, often following the petrous temporal

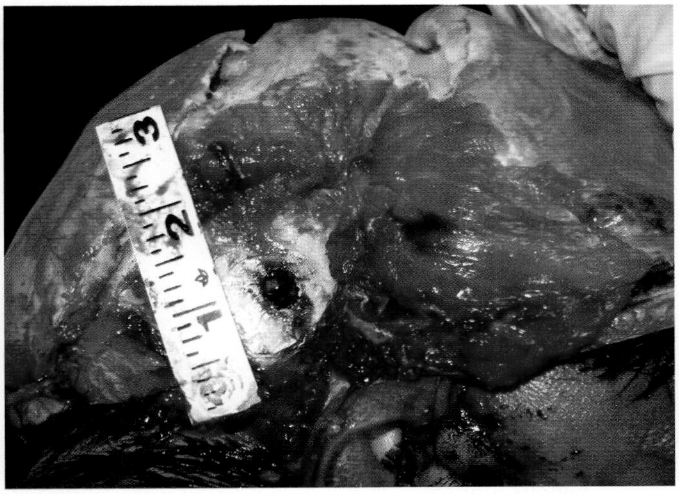

FIG. 11.17: Perforating fracture

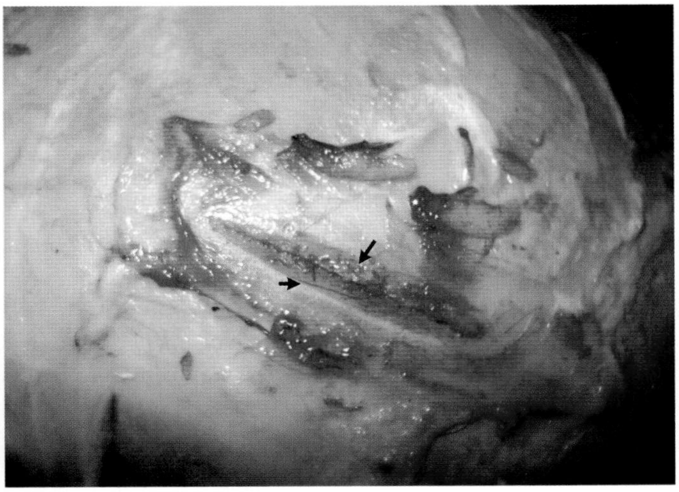

FIG. 11.18: Cut fracture of skull involving outer table (black arrow)

or greater wing of sphenoid bone into pituitary fossa on both sides thus separating the base of skull into two halves.
- Caused by heavy blow or impact on the side of the head.
- The fracture is also called as motorcyclist's fracture.

Complication of Skull Fracture

1. Injury to brain
2. Intracranial hemorrhage
3. Fracture of anterior cranial fossa may involve frontal, ethmoidal or sphenoidal air sinuses
4. Intracranial infections – meningitis/encephalitis
5. Cranial pneumatocele or pneumocranium
6. Cranial nerve injury
7. Traumatic epilepsy
8. CSF otorrhea
9. Coma
10. Cerebral edema
11. Increased intracranial pressure/tension
12. Death

INJURY TO MENINGES AND BRAIN

Forensic Anatomy of Meninges

The brain is covered by three layers and from outward to inward they are (Fig. 11.21A):
1. Dura mater
2. Arachnoid mater

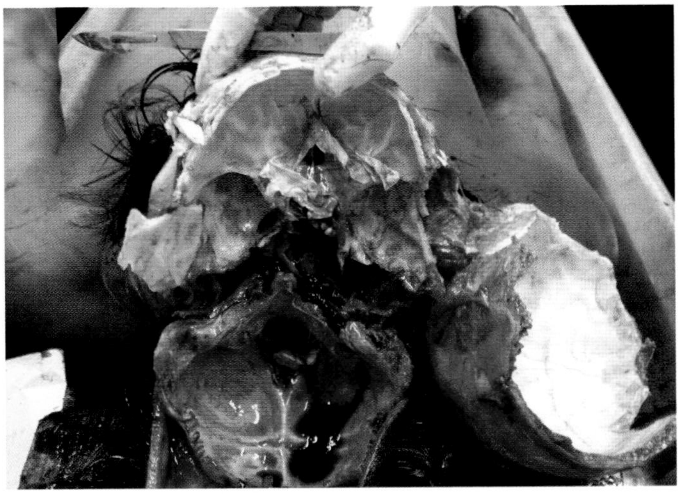

FIG. 11.19: Hinge fracture

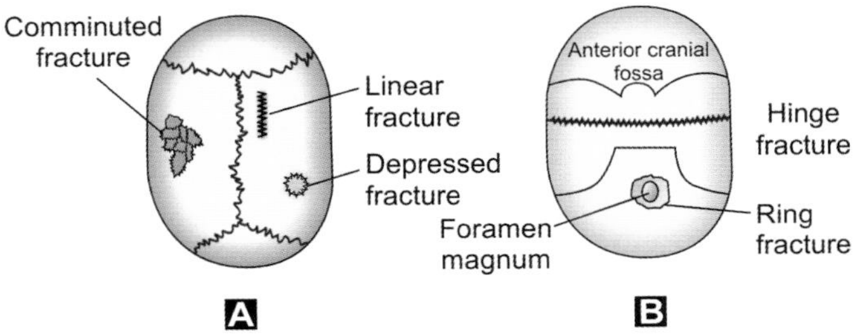

FIGS 11.20A and B: Different types of fracture

3. Pia mater

- Dura is composed of two layers; the outer layer is attached to the skull internally and acts as internal periosteum. The meningeal (dural) arteries are situated between outer layer of dura and skull.
- Arachnoid – is thin vascular membrane closely associated with pia.
- Pia mater – is an inseparable membrane covering the brain.
- Epidural space – or extradural space is a space between dura and skull and contains meningeal (dural) arteries.
- Subdural space – space between dura and arachnoid is called as subdural space. The cerebral veins cross this space to reach the sinuses. Thus the parts of veins in this subdural space are called as bridging veins. The largest bridging vein is the great vein of Galen.
- Subarachnoid space – is a space between arachnoid and pia. Subarachnoid space contains blood vessels that enter and exit the brain and cranial nerves. The space is filled with CSF.

Intracranial Hemorrhage

Intracranial hemorrhages are of following types:

1. Extradural or epidural
2. Subdural
3. Subarachnoid
4. Intracerebral
5. Intraventricular

Extradural Hematoma (EDH)

- Also called as epidural hematoma or subperiosteal hemorrhage (Figs 11.21C and 11.22)
- It is a hemorrhage that occurs in the epidural space between the skull and dura
- **Causes** are as follows[1]
  1. Mechanical trauma – most common cause
  2. Following surgery - rare
  3. Bone eroding process – rare cause
  4. Vascular malformation – rare
- **Sources** of extradural hemorrhage are as follows. EDH occurs due to rupture of:[9]
  1. Meningeal artery – most common
  2. Diploic veins – rare
  3. Venous sinuses – rare
- Thus, extradural hematoma is mostly arterial bleed and usually due to trauma
- **Mechanism**: In most cases, extradural hematoma occurs in presence of fracture that causes dura to get separated from skull bone and this fracture results in injury to meningeal artery or its branches (Fig. 11.23).

Sites are as follows:

1. Temporoparietal area – common site (rupture of middle meningeal artery – common)
2. Occipital and basal area – least common sites
3. Bilateral extradural hematomas are rare and if present, they are commonly found in parietotemporal area.[10]

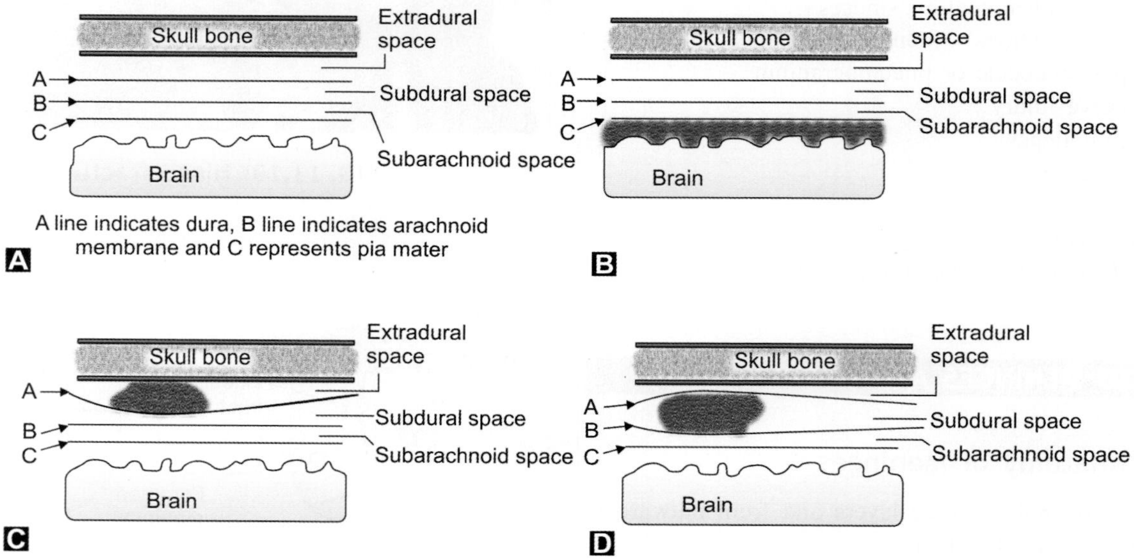

FIGS 11.21A to D: Normal anatomy and various intracranial hemorrhages

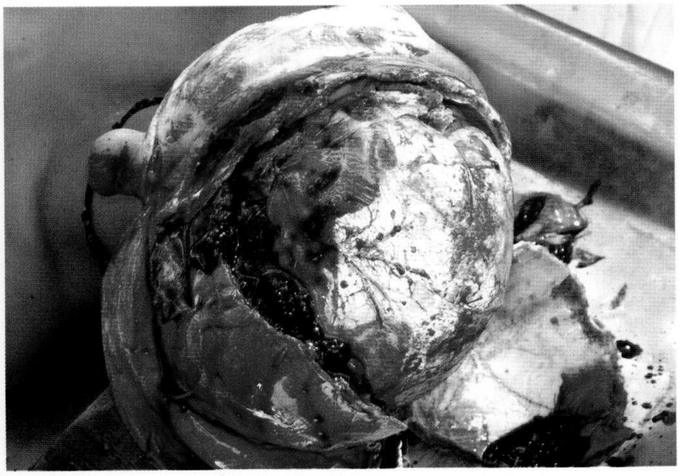

FIG. 11.22: Extradural hematoma

- **Fatality**: It is suggested that volume of 35 ml is needed for clinical signs to appear and a volume of 100 ml EDH is considered as fatal.[5]
- **Features** are as follows:[1]
  1. Presence of lucid interval
  2. Contralateral paresis
  3. As EDH enlarges, it exerts pressure on the brain due to which contusion may appear. The onset of contusion indicates pressure on brain and the brain is being displaced. Thus, the contusion simulates inebriation or alcohol intoxication.
  4. The pupils on the side of hematoma is usually dilated and not reactive to light indicating that medial part of temporal lobe - the uncus is exerting pressure on 3rd cranial nerve paralyzing its parasympathetic fibers responsible for papillary constriction.
  5. The continued added pressure on deep brain may induce coma. The pressure may displace the structures around the third ventricle and brainstem. Death may occur as a result of compression of brainstem and downward displacement of cerebellar tonsils.
- **Fate** of EDH: May follow one of the following course
  1. May shrink due to escape of blood into scalp through fracture vault
  2. Resorption
  3. Encapsulation and chronic epidural hematoma.

Medicolegal Importance of EDH

1. EDH is associated with lucid interval
2. They are not conter-coup injury
3. EDH may be confused with heat hematoma
4. EDH may be confused with alcohol intoxication.

Subdural Hematoma (SDH)

- It is collection of blood in the subdural space i.e. between dura and arachnoid membrane (Fig. 11.21D)
- Causes of SDH[1, 8] are mentioned in Table 11.2

Site as mentioned below
  1. Most common site – lateral aspect of cerebral hemisphere
  2. Least common site – posterior cranial fossa, around the brainstem and cerebellum

- **Mechanism**: In traumatic lesion, there is
  1. Gliding type movement between dura and skull causes tearing of one or several bridging veins causing subdural hemorrhage (Fig. 11.24). Thus in majority, SDH is venous bleed and bridging veins are major source.
  2. Sometime, SDH is arterial in origin and is caused by small rents in the arachnoid and adjacent cerebral arteries.

Classification

SDH are classified into three types[11]
1. Acute – patient presents within 48-72 hours of injury
2. Subacute – patient presents between 3 – 20 days
3. Chronic – patient presents from 3 weeks to several months.

Acute Subdural Hematoma (Figs 11.25 to 11.27)

- Trauma is common cause and may be associated with closed or open head injury
- Mechanism involved in causing acute SDH is – change in the velocity of the head, either acceleration or deceleration with rotational component.[5]
- SDH is quite mobile and may gravitate to lower side and thus do not depend on the site of application of force.

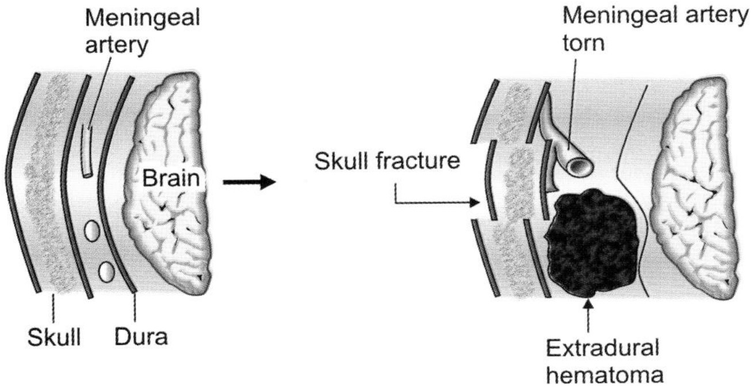

FIG. 11.23: Mechanism of EDH formation

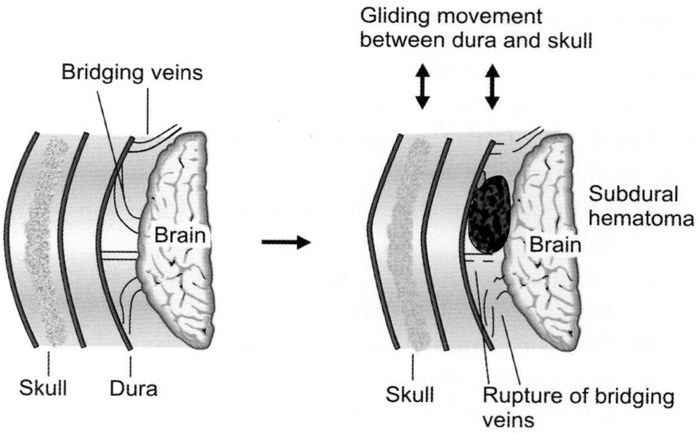

FIG. 11.24: Mechanism of formation of SDH

- It is common lesion than extradural hematoma and 35 – 100 ml is required to cause neurological signs.[5]

Clinical Features of Acute SDH

- The onsets of symptoms are delayed as the bleeding is of venous origin and take longer time to accumulate.
- Lucid interval may be present
- There is gradual decline in consciousness and may have speech defects
- Ipsilateral papillary disturbances – hemianopia and contralateral hemiparesis

Chronic Subdural Hematoma

- The lesion is found commonly in old people or chronic alcoholics
- In these people, there is usually atrophy of brain and due to which there is increase in subdural space. This increase in space permits more free movement of brain within the skull. Thus there are higher risks of rupturing bridging veins.

Table 11.2: Causes of subdural hematoma

1. Trauma: due to rupture of
   - Rupture of bridging veins
   - Rupture of dural venous sinuses
   - Laceration or contusion of brain and dura
2. Pathological: due to
   - Rupture of aneurysm
   - Malformed blood vessels
   - Hypertensive bleed within superficial part of brain that ruptured in subdural space

- SDH from natural causes is often bilateral while traumatic variety is usually unilateral.[9]
- With passage of time, SDH becomes organized and encapsulated. The gross appearance of SDH varies with age. Recent lesions (up to weeks) are red-brown with a gelatinous membrane covering the surface (Figs 11.28 and 11.29). The contents are thick with central part remaining fluid. Older hematoma up to months is firm with tough membrane on both surfaces. The contents may be liquid or firmer and variegated. Loculation is common with depressed underlying brain. Repeated trauma may cause repeated hemorrhage. Successive hemorrhage increases the volume of SDH and causes neurological

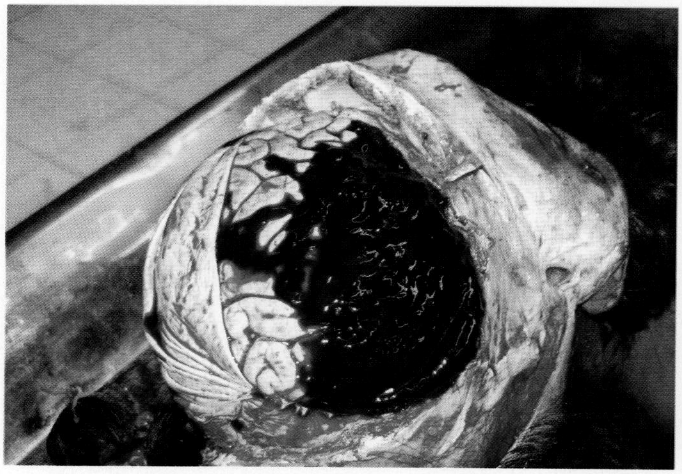

FIG. 11.25: Acute subdural hematoma (note it is below the dura and above arachnoid)

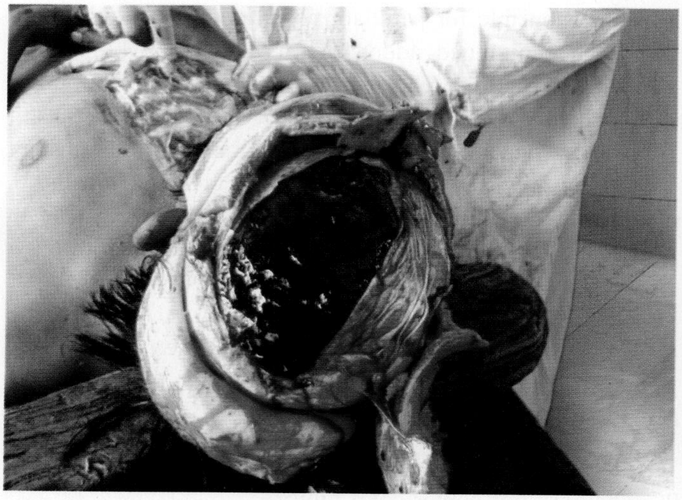

FIG. 11.26: Acute subdural hematoma (note it is below the dura and above arachnoid)

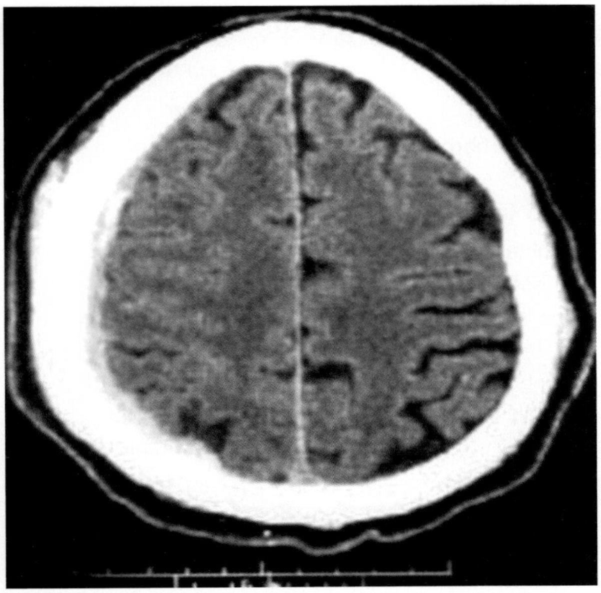

FIG. 11.27: CT scan of head showing subdural hematoma on right side

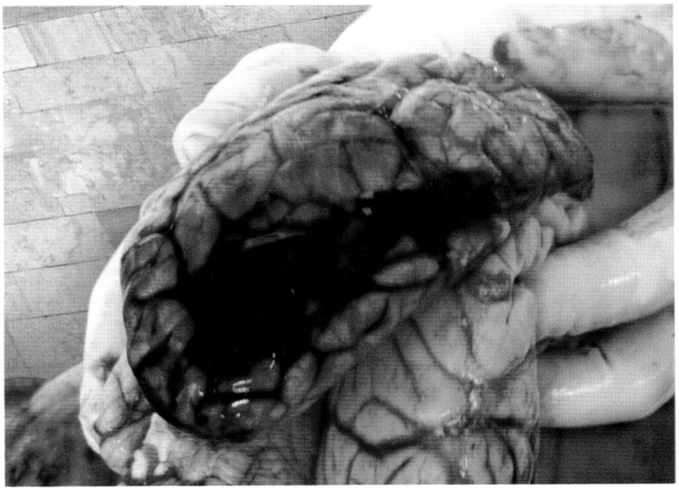

FIG. 11.28: Chronic subdural hematoma over left fronto-temporal region

symptoms. This type of hemorrhage is known as **pachymeningitis hemorrhagica**.[8]

- The gross and microscopic findings for dating of SDH are provided in Table 11.3.[12]

Medicolegal Importance

- Clinically symptoms may be mistaken for schizophrenia, pre-senile or senile dementia
- Lucid interval is present.

Subarachnoid Hemorrhage (SAH)

Subarachnoid hemorrhage occurs in the subarachnoid space i.e. between the arachnoid and pia mater (see Fig. 11.21B).

Causes

Subarachnoid hemorrhage may be caused due to trauma or may be due to pathological causes. The causes are given below:

A) **Traumatic causes**
1. Laceration of brain
2. Cortical contusion
3. Blunt impact
4. Penetrating injury
5. Blow on neck causing laceration of vertebral artery[13]
6. Severe hyperextension of head – as fall onto forehead
7. Prolonged hyperextension may cause tear in a basal or vertebral artery[14]
8. Traumatic rupture of basilar artery.[15]

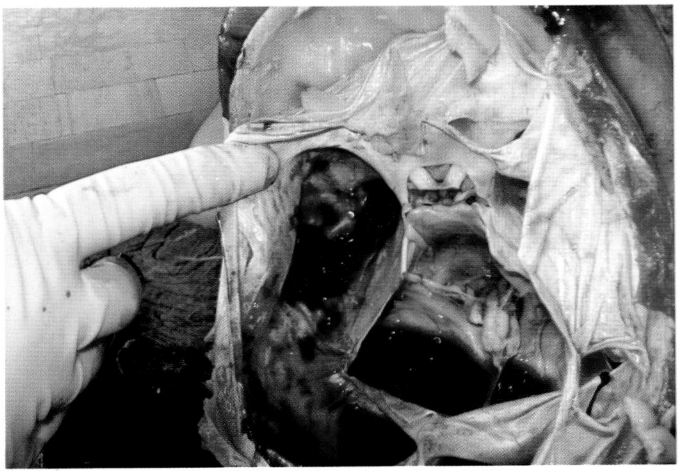

FIG. 11.29: Chronic subdural hematoma over left middle cranial fossa

B) **Pathological causes**
1. Saccular aneurysm
2. Arteriovenous malformation
3. Bleeding dyscarasias
4. Rupture of an intracerebral hemorrhage of non-traumatic origin into subarachnoid space.

Features

- SAH is considered as most common intracranial hemorrhage (Figs 11.30 and 11.31)

Table 11.3: Gross and microscopic findings for dating of SDH

Period	*Clot*	*Dural surface*	*Arachnoid surface*
24 hour	Fresh clot, intact RBCs	Thin fibrin layer	Thin fibrin layer
2-3 days	Intact RBCs	Thin fibrin layer, early fibroblastic activity	Thin fibrin layer
4-5 days	RBCs loose shape and contour	Neomembrane is 2-5 layers thick	Thin fibrin layer
5-8 days	Lysis of RBCs, clot liquefies, fibroblast enter the clot	12-14 layer of fibroblast; visible grossly when clot scrapped away	Thin fibrin layer
10-11 days	Clot broken into islands by growing capillaries and fibroblasts with thick fibrin strands	Fibroblast migrates towards clot	Siderophages are visible
15-17 days	Capillary formation obvious	Membrane one fourth to half in thickness of dura	Membrane covers the undersurface completely
18-26 days	Large vessels permeate	Membrane is of same thickness that of dura	Membrane half thickness to dura
1-3 months	Giant capillaries, secondary hemorrhage may occur	Hyalinization of membrane	Hyalinization of membrane
3-6 months	Fresh hemorrhage may be noted	Hyalinised, thick and fibrous like dura	Hyalinised, thick and fibrous like dura

- The SAH may be unilateral or bilateral or basal. It may be localized or diffuse.
- Basal SAH may prove rapidly fatal
- As SAH becomes older, yellowish discolouration of leptomeninges may be seen.

Clinical Features

- Transient loss of consciousness
- Headache
- Stiffness of neck
- Photophobia
- Deterioration of consciousness
- Focal neurological deficit may occur.

Medicolegal Importance

1. SAH may be due to trauma or due to pathological cause.
2. A trauma may precipitate the rupture of aneurysm.

Intracerebral Hemorrhage

Here the hemorrhage occurs in the cerebral tissue. It is also called as parenchymatous hemorrhage.

Causes: It may be traumatic or non-traumatic in origin

A) **Trauma**

1. Laceration of brain
2. Blunt trauma with or without fracture

B) **Non-traumatic cause** (pathological cause) [16]

1. Hypertension
2. Arteriovenous malformation
3. Spontaneous hemorrhage
4. Bleeding into cerebral neoplasm

Features (Figs 11.32 and 11.33)

- Traumatic intracerebral hemorrhages measures from 2 – 5 cm in diameter and are demarcated.[1]
- These hemorrhages results from shearing forces that tear blood vessel in parenchyma
- If persist, the hematoma get organized with encapsulation.
- Multiple punctate hemorrhages may be seen in bleeding diathesis, septicemia, fat embolism etc.[9]

Intraventricular Hemorrhage

Here the hemorrhage occurs in the ventricular system of the brain.

Causes: It may be due to trauma or due to pathological cause

A) Trauma

B) Non-traumatic causes (pathological causes)

1. Retrograde flow of subarachnoid hemorrhage into ventricles.
2. Rupture of arteriovenous malformation in the wall of ventricle.
3. Rupture of Berry's aneurysm of posterior communicating artery and bleeding into anterior portion of temporal horn of lateral ventricle.

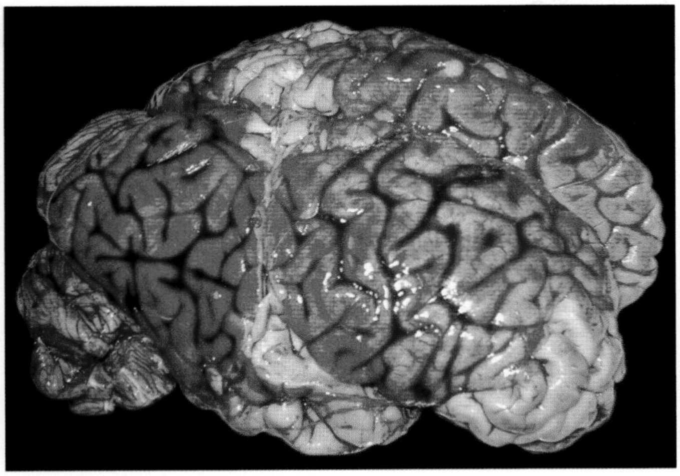

FIG. 11.30: Subarachnoid hemorrhage

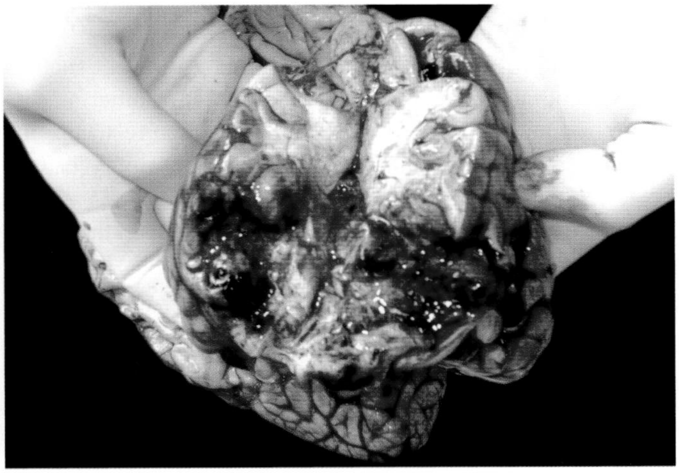

FIG. 11.32: Intracerebral hemorrhage

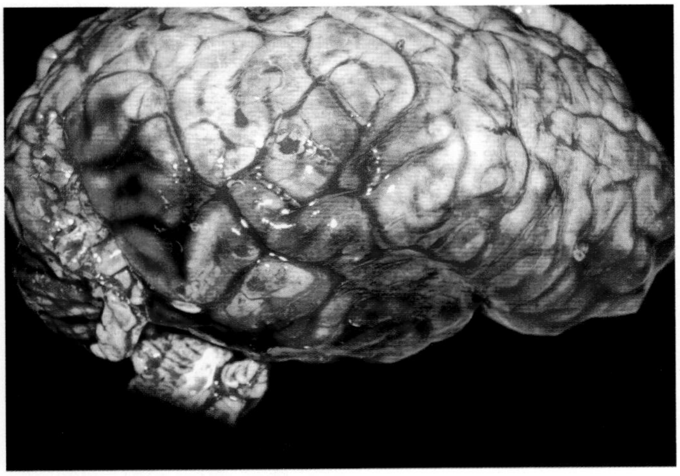

FIG. 11.31: Subarachnoid hemorrhage

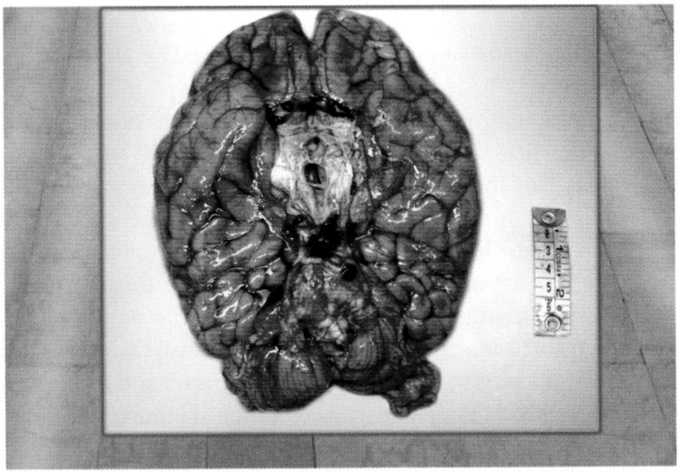

FIG. 11.33: Brainstem hemorrhage along with some basal SAH

4. Rupture of Berry's aneurysm of basilar artery through the floor of third ventricle.

Features

- Ventricular hemorrhage is usually arterial in origin.
- If intraventricular hemorrhage is sole finding, it is result of head striking a firm object as in a fall or fall-like injury.
- Brown or yellow discolouration of the ependyma, choriod plexus and leptomeninges are due to deposition of hemosiderin and hemotoidin and suggest the presence of old blood.

INJURY TO BRAIN

Brain injury may be classified, depending on state of dura, as:
1. Closed – dura intact
2. Open – dura ruptured

Brain injury can also be classified as primary brain injury or secondary brain injury.[17] It is mentioned in Table 11.4.
1. Primary brain injury – is the injury caused at the time of impact.
2. Secondary brain injury – is subsequent or progressive brain damage arising from events developing as a result of primary brain injury.

Brain can be Injured by[5,8] (Figs 11.34A to D)

1. Direct intrusion – either by foreign body/ object such as sharp pointed penetrating weapon, bullet or other missile or fragment of skull as in compound fracture where the skull is displaced (Fig. 11.34B). Thus the injury caused is an open type of injury.
2. By distortion or deformation of skull – here the localized part of skull undergoes deformation which produces shear strain in the brain under the deformed part of skull (Fig. 11.34C). The produced shear strains may cause contusion in the superficial area of the brain. If fracture results due to continued distortion of skull, the bone piece may penetrate the dura and enter the cranial cavity thus causing injury to brain by bone fragment as mentioned above (Fig. 11.34B).
3. Movements of brain in relation to the skull (Fig. 11.34D).

Mechanism of Brain Injury

The mechanism of injury to brain is explained by **Holbourn's hypothesis**[8, 9, 18]

1. Compression of the constituent units while being forced together
2. Tension of the units, which pulls them apart
3. Sliding or shear strains which moves adjacent strata of brain tissue laterally. The process can be equated with game of playing cards. The pack of playing cards being displaced so that such card slides upon its neighbour

- When force is applied to head, it will cause change in the linear velocity of the skull in the same axis and the forces involved are either linear acceleration or linear deceleration. In either, acceleration or deceleration, the initial sudden velocity applied to the scalp and skull is then transmitted to the brain. Thus these linear forces tend to produce compressional or rarefactional forces, but these forces do not cause damage to brain since the brain can be distorted but cannot be compressed. To cause damage to brain, along with change in velocity (i.e. either acceleration or deceleration) a rotational component is necessary.
- Thus, when force is applied to skull, the application of velocity would set the head in rotation (linear + rotational force) and this force is transmitted from skull to brain. The rotational and linear forces cause gliding or shear strain in brain and move adjacent strata of tissue laterally (like playing cards slide one another).
- In addition to the shearing forces damage, the brain may be forced against the sharp edge of the tentorial opening and the edges of falx, causing damage to the base of cerebrum, corpus callosum and the brainstem.

Table 11.4: Classification of brain injury

Brain injury
Primary brain injury
1. Diffuse axonal injury
2. Cerebral concussion
3. Cerebral contusions and lacerations
Secondary brain injury
1. Intracranial hematoma
2. Cerebral edema
3. Cerebral ischemia
4. Cerebral herniation
5. Infection
6. Epilepsy
7. Hydrocephalous

- Similarly, the interior of the skull i.e. the configuration of the base of skull is also responsible for additional brain damage. The rough floor of anterior cranial fossa, the sharp edges of wing of sphenoid and the bar of petrous temporal bone are also capable to cause damage due to their roughness.

Cerebral Concussion

Also called as commotio cerebri or stunning brain shock. Definition: It is defined by Trotter (1914) as *"a transient paralytic state due to head injury which is of instantaneous*

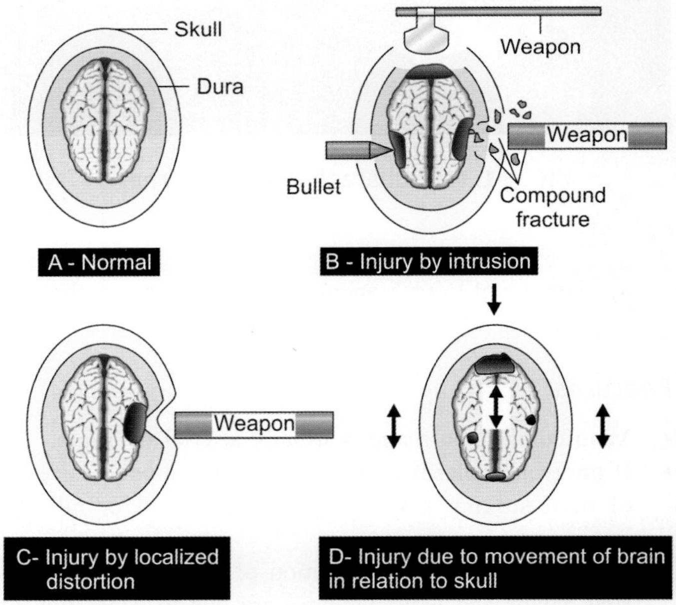

FIGS 11.34A to D: Diagrammatic representation of brain injury (black area represents brain injury)

onset, does not show any evidence of structural cerebral injury and is always followed by amnesia from the actual moment of the accident".

- Cause: It occurs due to acceleration/deceleration of head. At low levels of acceleration/deceleration, anatomic changes of neurons do not occur but physiologic functions are affected.

Classification[9]

Cerebral concussion are classified into three grades as

1. Grade I: No loss of consciousness
2. Grade II: Loss of consciousness but for less than 5 minutes
3. Grade III: Unconsciousness for more than 5 minutes associated with memory loss for more than 24 hours.

Features

- There may be no loss of consciousness or transient loss of consciousness. If unconsciousness persist for hours to days, then there is likely to be structural damage.
- Concussion is believed to be due to diffuse neuronal injury of submicroscopic dimensions.
- Occasionally concussion may prove fatal causing respiratory paralysis with no significant lesion demonstrated at autopsy.
- Post-traumatic and retrograde amnesia may be present
- At times, concussion may be followed by post-concussion state characterized by headache, unsteadiness, nausea, vomiting, anxiety and mental irritability.

Autopsy Findings

At autopsy no visible structural damages are noted in brain. Occasionally, punctate hemorrhages may be present.

Medicolegal Importance

1. Retrograde amnesia – here patient is unable to recollect the event that leads to accident or injury. The retrograde amnesia may be true or false (feigned) as in malingering act.
2. It may be confused with punch drunk or drunkenness.

Diffuse Axonal Injury (DAI)

It is classified into three grades by Adams et al (1989).[19] The grading is mentioned in Table 11.5. Microscopic examination – hallmark of DAI is axonal swelling (retraction balls) in the cerebral white matter, corpus callosum and upper brain stem. There is axonal swelling. It is caused by angular or rotational acceleration and deceleration effects.

Diffuse Neuronal Injury

In this condition, neurons and nerve fibers sustain diffuse traumatic damage. The condition may be partially or wholly reversible.

Table 11.5: Adams classification of diffuse axonal injury

Grades	*Features*
1	Histological evidence of axonal injury in the white matter of the cerebral hemisphere, corpus callosum, brainstem and less commonly in cerebellum
2	In addition to grade 1, there is focal lesion in corpus callosum
3	In addition to grade 1 and 2, there is focal lesion in the dorsolateral quadrant or quadrants of the rostral brainstem

Cerebral Edema

Traumatic cerebral edema is an accumulation of fluid in the extracellular space. It may be of following types:

1. Vasogenic cerebral edema
2. Cytotoxic cerebral edema
3. Mixed type

- Due to injury, there is breakdown of blood-brain-barrier (BBB) and exudation of fluid occurs
- Vasogenic edema: Due to vascular insult, there is increased permeability of endothelial cells to macromolecules as a result there is exudation of fluid. The extravasated fluid accumulates in extravascular space of the brain matter.
- Cytotoxic edema: It occurs due to metabolic dysfunction in cell causing intracellular accumulation of fluid.
- Ischemia is an important cause of cerebral edema because it alters the membrane permeability. It causes vasogenic oedema due to opening of tight junctions in the endothelial cells and causes cytotoxic edema because of cellular membrane damage causing abnormal fluid accumulation in cell. In this way, a mixed type of edema develops.

Cerebral Contusion

- *Cerebral contusions are the circumscribed areas resulting from extravasations of blood in traumatized area of brain*. The integrity of cortex is maintained.[9, 20]
- Contusions are produced as a result of shearing forces within the brain tissue at the moment of impact.[1]
- In almost all cases there is also some degree of subarachnoid hemorrhage.[21]

Classification

Cerebral contusions are divided into:
1. Contusion hemorrhages
2. Contusion necrosis
3. Contusion tears

Contusion Hemorrhages

- These are the blunt force injuries and are found in gray matter and then in white matter (Fig. 11.35)
- These hemorrhagic lesions occur at the crest of brain convolutions (gyri) facing the dura.[22] The pattern of contusion resembles a cone with the base at the dural surface and apex pointing inward i.e. toward the white matter.

Contusion Necrosis

They are present over crest of gyrus, usually conical in shape with base directed towards gyrus. The area shows necrosis, hemorrhage and oedema and overlying area may show subarachnoid hemorrhage (Fig. 11.36).

Contusion Tears

- Contusion tears are caused by stretching and shearing forces within brain produced by blunt trauma.
- Here there is greater degree of disruption of brain occurs sufficient to produce macroscopic tears referred as contusion tears.

Classification of Contusion According to Causative Mechanism

1. Coup and contrecoup contusion
2. Intermediary contusion*
3. Fracture contusion*
4. Gliding contusion*
5. Herniation contusion*

* Lindenberg and Freytag introduced terminology for these contusions based on their causative mechanism.[23, 24]

Coup and Contrecoup Contusion (See Figs 11.37 and 11.38)

- Coup injury or coup contusion refers to injury that occurs at the site of impact.
- While contrecoup contusion or injury refers to injury that occurs opposite to the point of impact (contre).
- Let us take an example, suppose a person XYZ is standing. If a person ABC hits the head of XYZ with iron rod over parieto-occipital area, then coup injury will be produced in XYZ. The XYZ is standing and his head is stationary while the rod, which is causing the injury, is moving. Here, an impact on stationary head causes the deformation of skull and the force is transmitted to brain but brain lags behind the skull for brief period thus leading to coup injury. Such type of injury is also called as acceleration injury (Fig. 11.38A).
- When a moving head strikes the stationary object, then moving skull is suddenly stopped by the stationary object. The skull stops, but brain within the skull moves for a brief period and hits the skull internally. Thus brain will suffer injury on opposite site. Such injury is called as contrecoup injury or contusion.[25] Abrupt deceleration of a moving head is characterized by a relatively injury at the site of impact (coup injury) and an extensive contusion of the brain, remote and usually opposite to the point of impact (contrecoup injury) (Fig. 11.38B).
- Let us take same example, suppose a person XYZ is standing and he falls on ground. The skull will strike the ground first and the moment of skull will be arrested by ground but brain in skull moves for a brief period thus causing contrecoup injury.

Cerebral Lacerations

- These are the traumatic lesions with loss of continuity of the brain substance
- Surface lacerations are accompanied with tear of pia mater and subarachnoid hemorrhage
- Penetrating injury can produce lacerations also seen underneath the skull fracture
- Severe hyperextension of head may cause laceration in the pyramidal tract at junction of medulla and pons

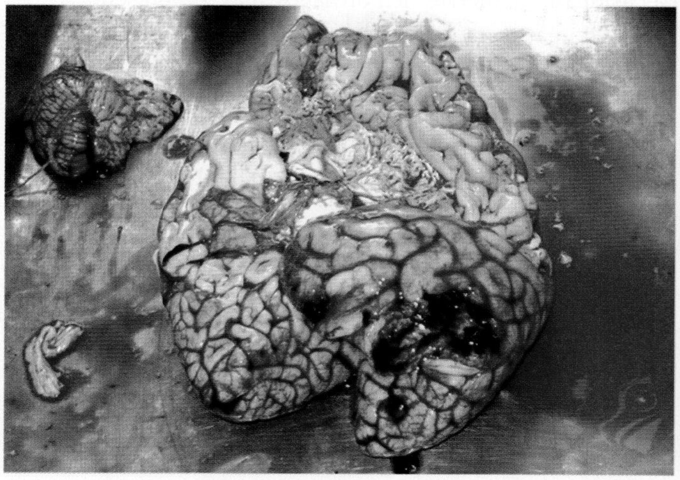

FIG. 11.35: Contusion hemorrhage

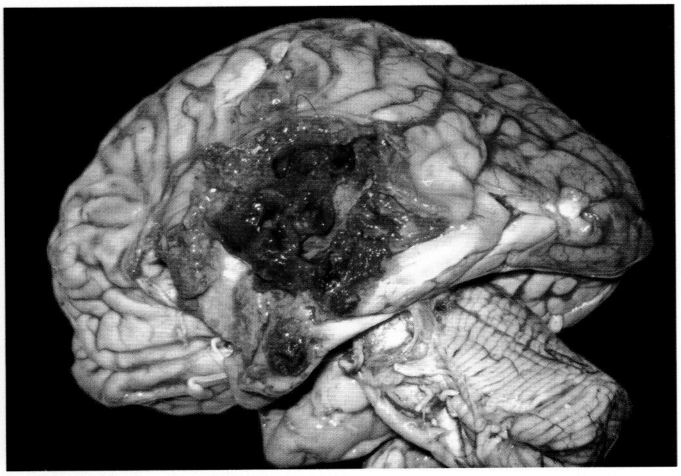

FIG. 11.36: Contusion necrosis

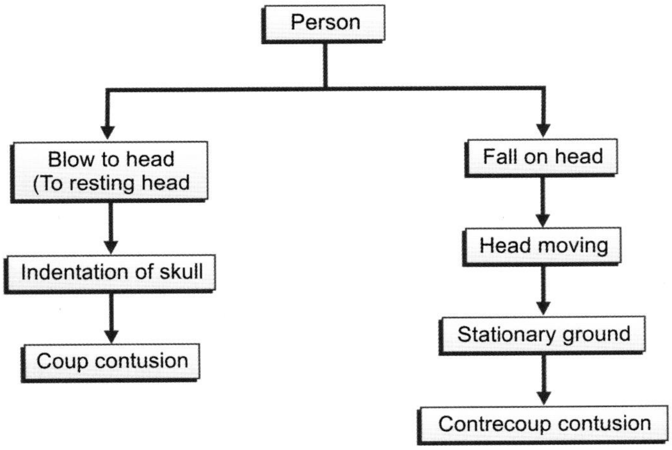

FIG. 11.37: Showing mechanism of coup and contrecoup contusion

- Healing of deep lacerations involving ventricles may produce large glial cyst filled with CSF – called as **traumatic proencephalic cysts**.

Boxer's Injury (Punch Drunk Syndrome)

- No sports are immune from injuries however; boxing appears more hazardous and fatal due to injuries sustained to brain. The acute injuries are less common but occur rarely and may prove fatal.[26] The death may occur in the ring (ground) or after removal to hospital. The most common lesion in acute episode appears to be subdural hematoma. Extradural bleed never occurs as boxing hardly causes skull fracture. Subarachnoid hemorrhage may occur in some cases due to rupture of berry's aneurysm.
- It is the chronic changes induced in the brain that concerns more. Repeated blowing in boxing over head induces traumatic encephalopathy known as "**punch-drunk syndrome**".[27] This syndrome is characterized by deterioration in speed and coordination, slurred speech, defective memory, slow thoughts, stiff-limbs, ataxia, unsteady gait, parkinsonian like dementia etc.
- Brain may show cortical atrophy, hydrocephalous, perforation of septum pellucidum, and loss of neurons from cerebellum and substantia nigra.

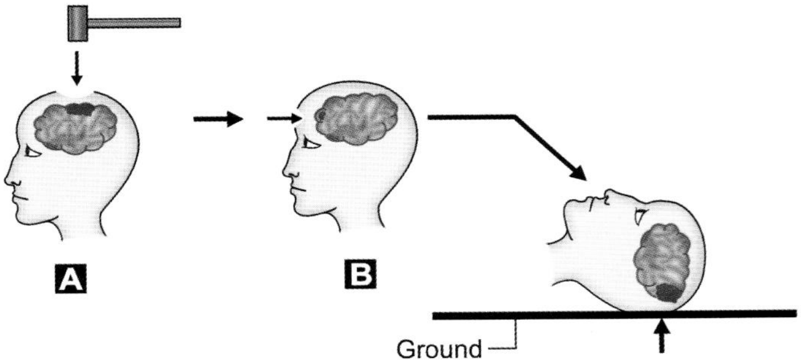

FIGS 11.38A and B: Coup and contrecoup injury. **A:** Coup injury while **B:** Contrecoup injury

INJURY TO SPINE AND SPINAL CORD

Fracture

The thoraco-lumbar segment is the commonest site of injury followed by lower cervical part of spine.[28] The spinal fractures are classified based on mechanism of infliction of injury to spine and are classified as:

1. Flexion injury – results in compression fracture of vertebral body with dislocation.
2. Flexion-rotation injury – fracture dislocation of vertebra occurs.
3. Vertical compression injury – vertebral body is crushed and breaks into pieces.
4. Extension type injury – here chip fracture of anterior rim of vertebra occurs.
5. Direct trauma – resulting in fracture/dislocation.
6. Indirect trauma – fracture resulting from transmitted force for example fall from height.

Spinal cord

Injuries produced to spinal cord are:

1. Concussion

2. Compression
3. Pithing
4. Penetrating injury
5. Laceration
6. Transection
7. Whiplash injury

Concussion of spinal cord causes temporary paralysis, affecting the upper and lower extremities or bladder and bowel. The paralysis is temporary and recovery occurs in about 48 hours. Such type of lesion occurs commonly in railway or motor collision and also called as railway spine.
Whiplash injury: Here there is contusion or laceration of spinal cord due to sudden hyperflexion and then hyperextension of spine without fracture of spinal column.
Pithing[29]: Pithing is killing by inserting or pushing fine needle into nape of neck between base of skull and upper cervical vertebra.

Injury to Neck

Common injuries sustained to neck are:
1. Contusion
2. Abrasion
3. Lacerated wound
4. Incised wound/chop/cut throat
5. Ligature injury

Cut-Throat Injury

- May be suicidal or homicidal
- Differences are mentioned in Table 11.6.

INJURY TO CHEST

Chest injuries are
1. Closed wounds – abrasion, contusion
2. Penetrating or open wounds – stab/puncture

Penetrating Injury to Chest Causes

- Hemothorax
- Pneumothorax

Injury to Lung/Heart

Injury to lungs
1. Contusion
2. Lacerations
3. Stab/penetrating
4. Blast injuries

Injury to Heart

1. Contusion[30]
2. Lacerations
3. Stab/penetrating injury
4. Blast injuries
5. Hemopericardium/cardiac tamponade

Injury to Diaphragm

- Traumatic diaphragmatic injury may be blunt or penetrating. Blunt injuries are rare and are often associated with a high mortality in the injured patients. Diaphragmatic injury rarely occurs alone in patients with blunt trauma; multiple rib fractures are of the most frequent findings. The pathophysiologic effects of a ruptured diaphragm on circulation and respiration are due to impaired functions of diaphragm, compression of lungs, and displacement of the mediastinum with impairment of venous return to the heart.[31, 32]
- Blunt trauma is commonly caused in motor vehicle accidents whereas penetrating trauma can result from gunshot and stab wounds or crushing type of trauma.
- Traumatic diaphragmatic rupture was first described by Sennertus in 1541. Ambroise Parè, in 1579, described the first case of diaphragmatic rupture diagnosed at autopsy.
- Traumatic diaphragmatic injury is more common on left side than right. The relative infrequency of right-sided injury is attributed to the buffering action of the liver in protecting the diaphragm. On left side, majority of tears occur in a radial direction in the posterolateral areas of the diaphragm.[33, 34] Bilateral diaphragmatic injury is exceedingly rare occurrences.[35]
- Chest radiographs – is important diagnostic tool – the presence of an opacity in the chest, large air-filled bubbles, an indefinable diaphragm or displacement of mediastinum should rose the suspicion of diaphragmatic injury.

INJURY TO ABDOMEN

Abdominal injury may be:
1. Closed injury
2. Open injury

Injury to Stomach

- Stomach may get bruised or lacerated following blunt trauma or may get injured with penetrating trauma
- The distend stomach is more liable for rupture than empty one. The distended stomach tends to rupture by absorbing the impact from blunt abdominal trauma. In other words, it works like an airbag and protects adjacent

Table 11.6: Difference between suicidal and homicidal cut-throat

Suicidal cut throat	*Homicidal cut throat*
Usually multiple injuries of varying length and depth preceded by hesitation cuts	Single or multiple but deep wounds
Tailing may be on right side in right handed person	Tailing may be on either side
The wounds are usually oblique in direction and sloped towards the floor of mouth	The wounds are usually horizontally and sloped away from the floor of mouth
Carotid arteries are usually preserved	Carotid arteries are frequently cut
No marks of resistance, no defense cuts	Marks of resistance may be noted, defense wounds may be present
Suicidal note may be left	No such note
The act may be done in secluded place, room may be closed from inside, the spot is undisturbed	May be done at any place, disturbance of scene of crime, no locking of room from inside

organs such as liver and pancreas.[36] The rupture usually occurs at the pyloric end along the lesser curvature due to reduced elasticity as a result of deficient muscular layer, paucity of mucosal folds and location of magenstrasse.[37]

Injury to Intestine

Intestinal injury ranged from bruising to laceration to perforation to avulsion. Intestinal injury may result due to:
- Crushing of bowel against spine or
- Shearing of the bowel and its mesentry at point of fixation.

Injury to Pancreas

- Isolated pancreatic injuries are rare and often associated with injuries of other abdominal organs. Two-thirds of pancreatic injuries are associated with penetrating abdominal trauma and one-third associated with blunt abdominal trauma.[38]
- Pancreas is relatively fixed in position in abdomen and is placed across the vertebral column. It may be involved in compression type of abdominal trauma or blunt abdominal trauma where it gets caught between vertebral column and offending force.[39]
- Injury to pancreas may evolve into pseudo-cyst.[40]

Liver

Injury to liver may be of following types:
- Contusion
- Laceration

Laceration of liver may be of different types and are:
1. Transcapsular
2. Subcapsular
3. Parenchymal
4. Coronal
5. Crush laceration
6. Contrecoup laceration

Injury to Spleen

The spleen has thin capsule and weak supportive tissue framework with friable pulp. Due to which, the spleen is susceptible to blunt trauma. Similarly it is prone for penetrating trauma due to relatively superficial position in abdomen. The blunt injury may vary from subcapsular tear/hematoma to parenchymal injury to fragmentation. The grade of injury to spleen is presented in Table 11.7.[41]

Injury to Kidney

Kidneys can be injured by
- Direct trauma – to flanks and lumbar region
- Indirect trauma – such as hyperextension or hyperflexion injury or fall.

The injuries range from contusion to subcapsular hematoma to laceration to penetrating injury to avulsion injury. The degrees of closed renal injuries are mentioned in Table 11.8.[42]

Injury to Bladder

- Bladder may be injured with blunt trauma or with penetrating force. The pattern of injury varies from contusion to laceration to rupture.
- Distended bladder is more susceptible for injury than empty one. Due to distension, the bladder wall becomes thin and can be easily ruptured
- Bladder rupture occurs either extra-peritoneally or intraperitoneally.

Table 11.7 Grades of spleen injury

Grades	Features
Grade 1	Minor subcapsular tear or hematoma
Grade 2	Parenchymal injury not extending to the hilum
Grade 3	Major parenchymal injury involving vessels & hilum
Grade 4	Shattered spleen

Table 11.8: Degree of closed renal injury

Degree	Features
1	Subcapsular hematoma
2	Laceration
3	Avulsion of one pole
4	Avulsion of renal pedicle

- Distended bladder may rupture intra-peritoneally with voiding of contents in peritoneal cavity causing chemical peritonitis
- Extra-peritoneal rupture is commonly associated with pelvic fracture. The urine escapes out extra-peritoneally into abdominal wall, inguinal region, scrotum and thigh.

REFERENCES

1. Lindenberg R. Mechanical injuries of brain and meninges. In: Spitz WU (Ed) Spitz and Fisher's Medicolegal investigation of Death, 3rd edn. 1993. Charlas C Thomas Publisher, USA. 585-636.
2. Mahapatra AK. Introduction. In: Mahapatra AK, Kamal R (eds) A Textbook of Head injury, 2nd edn. 2001. Modern Publishers, New Delhi. 1-4.
3. Sahana SN. Human anatomy, Vol. 1, Special edn. 1988. KK Publishers (P) Ltd., Howrah.
4. Mathiharan K, Patnaik AK. Regional injuries. In: Modi's Medical Jurisprudence and Toxicology, 23rd edn. 2005. LexisNexis Butterworths, New Delhi. 795-846.
5. Saukko P, Knight B. Head and spinal injuries. In: Knight's Forensic Pathology, 3rd edn. 2004. Arnold, London. 174-221.
6. Gordon I, Shapiro HA. Regional injuries of medicolegal importance. In: Forensic Medicine – a guide to principles, 2nd edn. 1982. Churchill Livingstone, Edinburgh. 250-339.
7. Dikshit PC. Regional injuries. In: Textbook of Forensic Medicine and Toxicology, 1st edn. 2007. Peepee Publishers and Distributors (P) Ltd., New Delhi. 200-23.
8. Reddy KSN. Regional injuries. In: The Essentials of Forensic Medicine and Toxicology, 22nd edn. 2003. K. Suguna Devi, Hyderabad. 195-233.
9. Pillay VV. Regional injuries. In: Textbook of Forensic Medicine and Toxicology, 14th edn. 2004. Paras Publishing, Hyderabad. 173-90.
10. Subrahmanian MV, Rajendraprasad GB. Bilateral extradural hematomas. Br J Surg 1975; 62: 397- 400.
11. Kamal R. Acute subdural hematomas. In: Mahapatra AK, Kamal R (eds) A textbook of head injury, 2nd edn. 2001. Modern Publishers, New Delhi. 128-35.
12. Munro D, Merritt HH. Surgical pathology of subdural hematoma. Based on a study of 105 cases. Arch Neurol Psychiatry 1936; 35: 64-78.
13. Cameron JM, Mant AK. Fatal subarachnoid hemorrhage associated with cervical trauma. Med Sci Law 1972; 12: 66-70.
14. Miyazaki T, Kojima T, Chikasue F, Yashiki M, Ito H. Traumatic rupture of intracranial vertebral artery due to hyperextension of the head: reports on three cases. Forensic Sci Int 1990; 47: 91-8.
15. Bunai Y, Nagai A, Nakamura I, Ohya I. Traumatic rupture of the basilar artery: report of two cases and review of literature. Am J Forensic Med Pathol 2000; 21: 343- 8.
16. Easton JD, Hauser SL, Martin JB. Cerebrovascular diseases. In: Fauci AS, Braunwald E, Isselbacher KJ, Wilson JD, Martin JB, Kasper DL, Hauser SL, Longo DL (eds) Harrison's Principles of Internal Medicine, Vol.2, 14th edn. 1998. McGraw-Hill, New York. 2325.
17. Kerr RCS, Maartens NF. Craniocerebral trauma. In: Russell RCG, Williams NS, Bulstrode CJK (eds) Bailey and Love's Short practice of surgery, 24th edn. 2004. Hodder Arnold, London. 594-605.
18. Holbourn AH. Mechanics of head injuries. Lancet 1943; 245: 438-41.
19. Adams JH, Doyle D, Ford I, Gennarelli TA, Graham DI, McLellan DR. Diffuse axonal injury in head injury: definition, diagnosis and grading. Histopathology 1989; 15: 49-59.
20. Vij K. Regional injuries. In: Textbook of Forensic Medicine and Toxicology, 3rd edn. 2005. Reed Elsevier India Pvt. Limited, New Delhi. 407-45.
21. Ropper A. Traumatic injuries of the head and spine. In: Fauci AS, Braunwald E, Isselbacher KJ, Wilson JD, Martin JB, Kasper DL, Hauser SL, Longo DL (eds) Harrison's Principles of Internal Medicine, Vol.2, 14th edn. 1998. McGraw-Hill, New York. 2391-2.
22. Adams JH, Graham DI, Scott G, Parker LS. Brain damage in fatal non-missile head injury. J Clin Pathol 1980; 33: 1132-45.
23. Lindenberg R, Freytag E. Morphology of cortical contusions. Arch Pathol 1957; 63: 23-6.
24. Lindenberg R, Freytag E. The mechanism of cerebral contusions: a pathologic-anatomic study. Arch Pathol 1960; 69: 440 -4.
25. Gurdjian ES. Cerebral contusion: re-evaluation of the mechanism of their development. J Trauma 1976; 16: 35-51.
26. Wase VV, Vable MS, Belsare S. An unexpected death due to boxing injury: a sports misadventure. J Medicolegal Assoc Maharashtra 2000; 12: 15-6.
27. Martland MS. Punch drunk. JAMA 1928; 91: 1003-5.
28. Maheshwari J. Spinal injuries. In: Essentials Orthopedics, 3rd edn. 2004. Mehta Publishers, New Delhi. 143-52.

29. Rao NG. Regional injuries. In: Textbook of Forensic Medicine and Toxicology, 1st edn. 2006. Jaypee Brothers Medical Publishers (P) Ltd., New Delhi. 189-207.
30. Holanda MJ, Dominguez MJ, Lopez-Espadas F, Lopez M, Diaz-Reganon J, Rodriguez-Borregan JC. Cardaic contusion following blunt chest trauma. Eur J Emerg Med 2006; 13: 373-6.
31. Beauchamp G, Khalfallah A, Girard R, Dube S, Laurendeau F, Legros G. Blunt diaphragmatic rupture. Am J Surg 1984; 148: 292-5.
32. Ward RE, Flynn TC, Clark WP. Diaphragmatic disruption secondary to blunt abdominal trauma. J Trauma 1981; 21: 35.
33. Hood RM. Traumatic diaphragmatic hernia. Ann Thorac Surg 1971; 12: 311-24.
34. McCune RP, Roda CP, Eckert C. Rupture of diaphragm due to blunt trauma. J Trauma 1976; 16: 531-7.
35. Sharma OP. Traumatic diaphragmatic rupture: Not an uncommon entity – personal experience with collective review of the 1980's. J Trauma 1989; 29: 678-82.
36. Shinkawa H, Yasuhara H, Naka S, Morikane K, Furuya Y, Niwa H, Kikuchi T. Characterstic features of abdominal organ injuries associated with gastric rupture in blunt abdominal trauma. Am J Surg 2004; 187: 394-7.
37. Yajko RD, Seydel F, Trimble C. Rupture of stomach from blunt abdominal trauma. J Trauma 1975; 15: 177-83.
38. Mahale A, Gupta A, Paudel K. A rare case of pancreatic injury: A case report. Indian J Radiol Imaging 2006; 16: 437-9.
39. Jain S, Telang P, Joshi MA, Prabhakar S. Isolated pancreatic injury following blunt abdominal trauma in a child. Indian J Crit Care Med 2007; 11: 96-8.
40. El Musharaf HA, Al Auriefi MA. Traumatic pancreatic pseudocyst. Saudi J Gastroenterol 1996; 2: 160-3.
41. Available from http:/www.surgical-tutor.org.uk/trauma/spleen
42. Fowler CG. The kidneys and ureters. In: Russell RCG, Williams NS, Bulstrode CJK (eds) Bailey and Love's Short practice of surgery, 24th edn. 2004. Hodder Arnold, London. 1311-2.

CHAPTER 12

Road Traffic Accidents

It is better to go slow than never.

- Anonymous

In road traffic accidents, injuries may be sustained to:
1. Pedestrian
2. Cyclist/motorcyclist
3. Occupants of a vehicle.

INJURIES TO PEDESTRIAN

A pedestrian may sustain following types of injuries (Fig. 12.1). (This mechanism of pedestrian injury is called as **Waddle's Triad**).
1. Primary impact injuries
2. Secondary impact injuries
3. Secondary injuries.

Primary Impact Injuries

- These are the injuries caused by vehicle when it first struck or hit the person (i.e. pedestrian) (Fig. 12.1).
- The importance of primary impact injury is that the body of victim may bear design/pattern of the part of vehicle in form of imprint abrasion or patterned bruise.
- Common parts of vehicle which may struck or hit a person includes:[1]
    1. Bumper
    2. Wing
    3. Grill
    4. Headlight
    5. Fender
    6. Radiator
    7. Door handle.
- The body part which bears the injury depends upon the position of person such as:
    1. Was the pedestrian struck by front of car/vehicle?
    2. Was the pedestrian struck by side of the car/vehicle?
    3. Was the pedestrian standing on road?
    4. Was the pedestrian walking on road?
    5. Was the pedestrian lying on road?
- If the victim is struck by front of the vehicle then the person may sustain bumper injuries on legs. The injury comprises of damage to skin and fracture of bone (known as **bumper fracture**). Bumper fracture usually involves tibia. The fracture is wedge shaped with base of triangular fragment indicating the site of impact and apex pointing the direction of vehicle (Fig. 12.2).
- Interpretation:

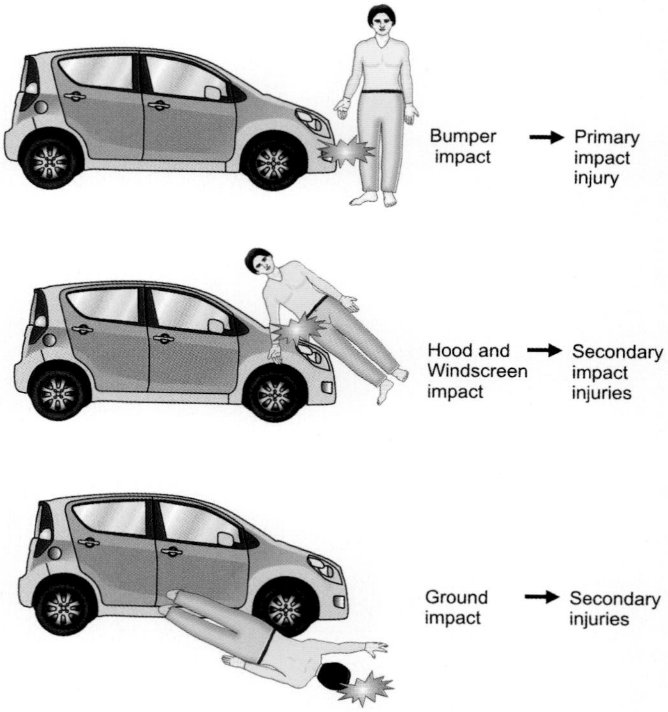

FIG. 12.1: Injuries sustained to pedestrian

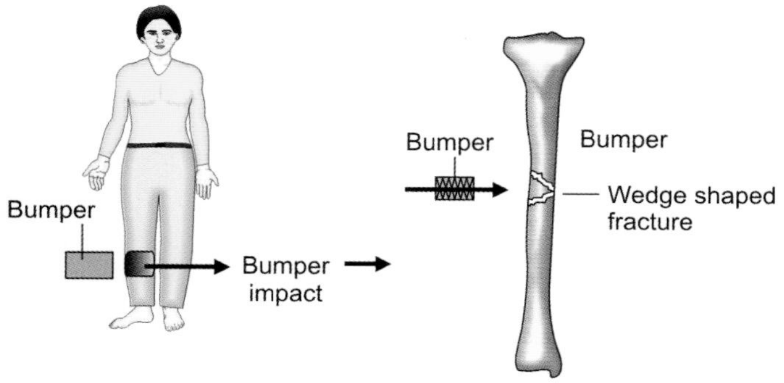

FIG. 12.2: Injuries sustained due to bumper

1. If bumper injuries are at different levels on the two legs or absent on one leg, it indicates that the person was walking or running when hit by car/vehicle
2. If bumper injuries are at the same level on both legs, it indicates that the person was standing.
3. The level of bumper injury (i.e. the height of injury from ground level) varies with the height of bumper of different vehicle. It means that the offending vehicle can be identified.

- Similarly grill and head light rims, radiator may produce pattern injuries
- The findings of primary impact injury are important to find out the relative position of pedestrian and vehicle and kind of vehicle involved in the incident.

Secondary Impact Injuries[2]

- After sustaining primary impact injury, the person may be lifted off the ground and thrown on the vehicle (Fig. 12.1). Thus these secondary impact injuries are resulted from the impact of body of a person and the vehicle for a second time.
- Here, the person may strike to windshield or bonnet or placed on top of a car/vehicle.
- After the second impact injuries, the victim will be thrown on the ground.

Secondary Injuries

- These are the injuries that occur after second impact injuries when the victim is thrown off the vehicle on the ground (Fig. 12.1). Thus, these are the injuries that are sustained by a person when falls on the ground.

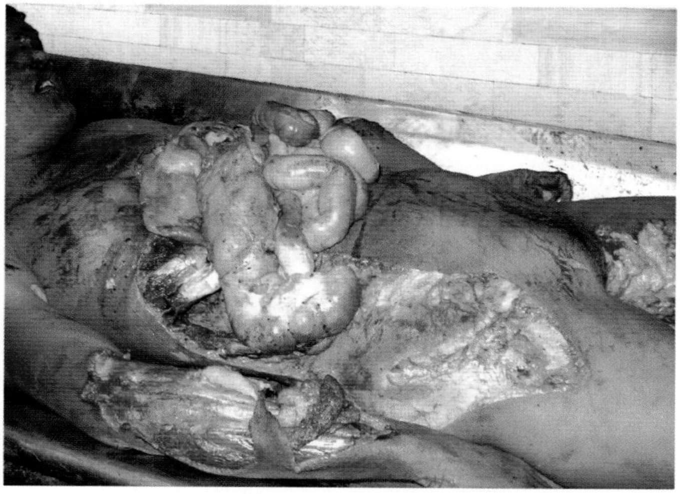

FIG. 12.3: Run over by vehicle

- Here, the victim sustains secondary injuries from the ground. Head injury is more common though injuries to other part may occur.
- Some time, the victim may be run over by the same vehicle or another vehicle (Fig. 12.3).

INJURIES SUSTAINED BY MOTORCYCLIST

Injuries sustained by motorcyclist are much more serious than car travelers because

1. Inherent instability of two-wheeler
2. Unprotected and lack of protective gear
3. Rash and negligent driving

Any part of body may sustain injury but two regions are more affected and are:

- **Head:**

1. Injury sustained to head is common in motorcyclist followed by thoracic and abdominal region.[3] Fall on road surface and sustaining injury to lateral part with fracture of temporo-parietal bone is more common.[4]
2. Fracture occurring in skull of motorcyclist can be summarized as:[5]
   - Fall on side with side impact to head causes basal skull fractures especially hinge type (also called as **motorcyclist fracture**) (Figs 12.4 and 12.5).
   - Impact on face causes fracture of facial skeleton.
   - Impact on forehead causes sagittal fracture of base of skull.
   - Impact on chin causes mandibular fracture.
   - Impact on crown of head by fall may cause ring fracture.

- Legs: are often injured in primary impact i.e. dash with other vehicle or fixed structure or the leg may be trapped

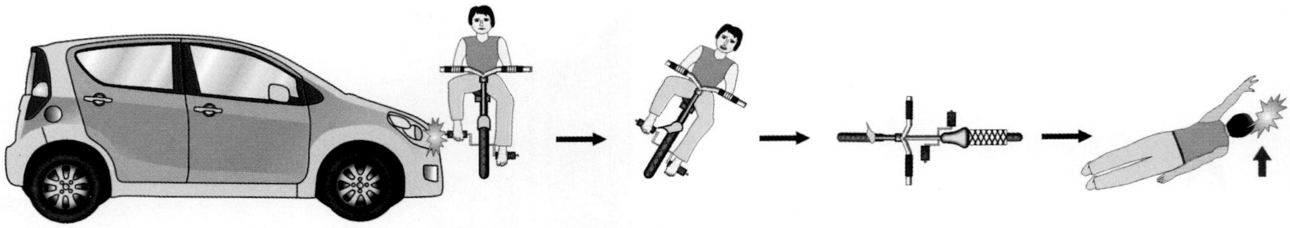

FIG. 12.4: Injuries sustained by motorcyclist

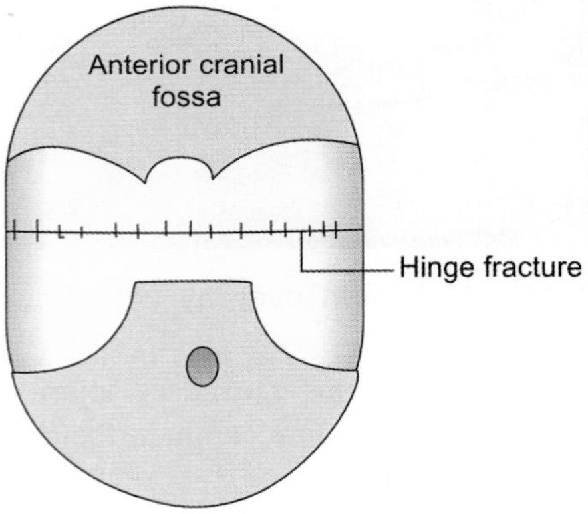

FIG. 12.5: Motorcyclist fracture

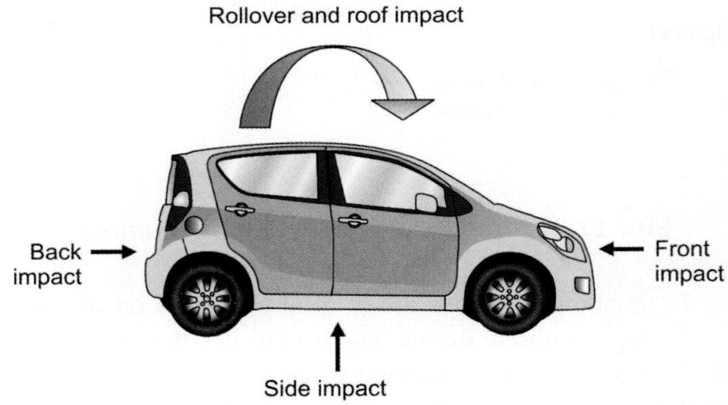

FIG. 12.6: Diagram showing various types of impacts sustained by a vehicle

in the motorcycle frame.[1] In non-fatal injuries, this is frequently injured part of body.[6]

- **Tail getting or under-running**: It is rarely seen in motorcyclist and in this condition motorcyclist drives his two-wheeler into the back of a truck or some other heavy vehicle. This occurs due to sudden and unexpected stoppage of the truck. In such accidents, head and shoulder of motorcycle rider are smashed against the tail-board of truck. In extreme cases, there may be decapitation.[7]

INJURIES SUSTAINED TO OCCUPANT OF VEHICLE

In vehicular accidents cases, the occupants of vehicle may sustain different patterns of injury according to the position of the occupant. The occupant of car can be divided as:

1. Driver
2. Front seat passenger
3. Rear seat passengers

In collisions, a vehicle may sustain following sort of impact (Fig. 12.6)

- Front impact
- Back impact
- Side impact
- Rollover and roof impact

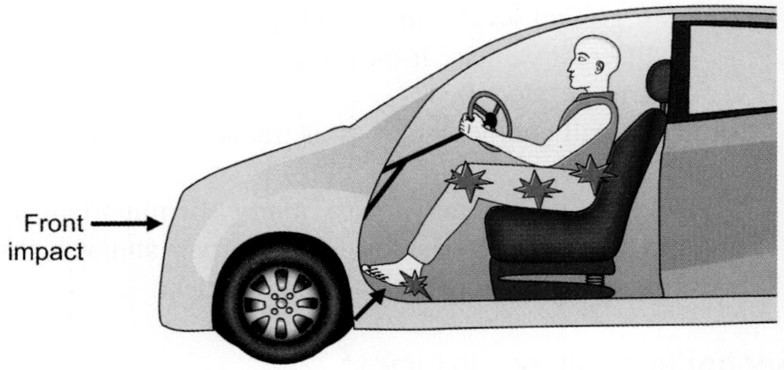

FIG. 12.7: Injuries sustained by driver in front impact. Black irregular spots indicate probable sites of injury

Injuries Sustained to Occupant Without Seat Belt or Protected Air Bags (Front Impact)

- When a car collides with other vehicle or stationary object, there is deceleration of car. Initially, the force is transmitted through the lower limbs of the driver from foot to hip (Fig. 12.7). Transmission of energy will strain the lower limb at its weakest point and that weak point could be ankle, knee, femur or hip. The hip is considered as weakest part of the lower limb. The flexed knee may also hit the dashboard and the energy can be transmitted through the femur upwards or through the tibia downwards.[8] After this, the unrestrained (i.e. without seat belt) driver may slide forwards and his legs strikes the fascia/parcel-shelf/dashboard area, his abdomen or lower chest strikes the steering wheel, then the body flexes across the steering wheel. The head flexes and strikes the windscreen or windscreen rim or side pillar (see Fig. 12.8 and Figs 12.9 to 12.11). At times, the windscreen may perforate or break and ejects out the driver from the car over the bonnet or on the ground. Also, it may happen, the door gets open and driver ejects out through open door.[1] The driver and passengers sustains polytrauma and injuries over head commonly.[9]

- Impact over leg causes abrasion, laceration and fracture
- Impact over abdomen or lower chest causes steering wheel and internal injury – rupture of liver, spleen, fracture sternum, ribs, cardiac contusion, hemothorax etc.
- Injury to spine: Spine shows fracture in cervical region so called whiplash injury.
- Face may sustain injuries due to windscreen. The glass used for windscreen is toughened one and non-laminated in some countries. So when injury occurs, the glass broke and shatters into small cubes. These glass cubes may cause "V" shaped lacerations. These are called as **dicing injuries** or **sparrow-foot** lacerations.[5, 10]
- The patterns of injuries are similar to front seat passenger except steering wheel impact and injuries over leg.
- The unrestrained passenger or person in the rear part of car are projected forwards and strikes the back part of front seat.

Injuries Sustained to Occupant (Back Impact)

If a car is hit from backside, the car accelerates and may lead to hyperextension of the head. If the driver is restrained, then the hyperextended head strikes the back of seat and causes rebound flexion of head (Figs 12.12 and 12.13). Such movement of head is called as whiplash that may cause whiplash injury. Such injuries are more common where seat do not have head restraint. Presence of head restraint prevents hyperextension hyperflexion of head (Fig. 12.10). Moreover, presence of head restraint also prevents collision between front and back seat passengers.

FIG. 12.8: Injuries sustained by unrestrained driver in front impact

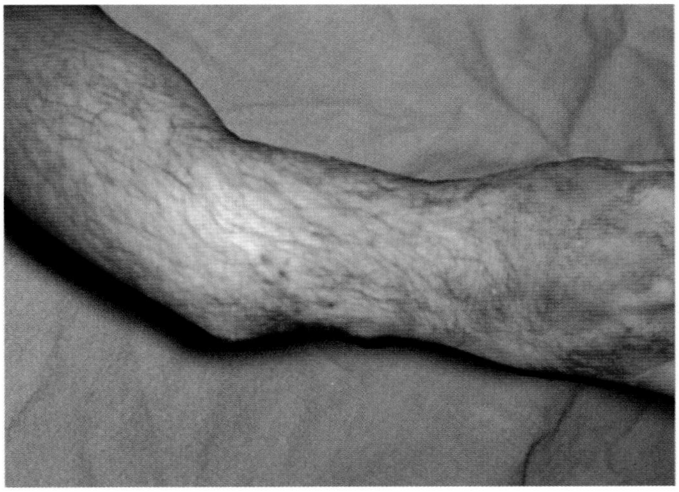

FIG. 12.9: Driver who had sustained injuries over right upper limb, note fractures at forearm

Seat Belt Injuries

- Though seat belts prevent injuries and reduced death rate, however, at times cause injuries.
- Following are types of seat belts (Fig. 12.14):
  1. Lap-strap type
  2. Shoulder diagonal type
  3. Diagonal plus lap-strap
  4. Shoulder harness

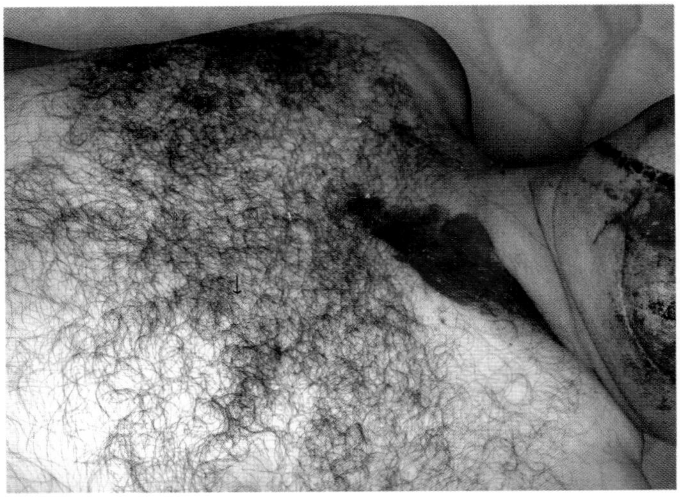

FIG. 12.10: Steering wheel impact (black arrow)

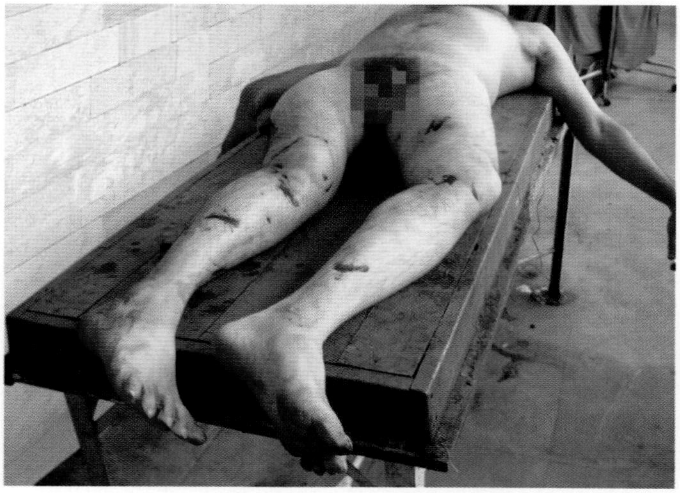

FIG. 12.11: Injuries sustained to unrestrained driver to lower limbs with fracture at right thigh, right leg and left knee

- Seat belt injuries may be simple or fatal
- Contusion due to seat belt is common and may occur over chest or abdomen
- If single lap-strap type seat belts are worn, may cause rupture of mesentery or intestine. Bladder can be ruptured.
- The aorta can be compressed due to active flexion over lap type strap or belt. Lumbar spine may show compression type fracture.

REFERENCES

1. Huelke DF, Gikas PW. Cause of death in automobile accidents. JAMA 1968; 203: 1000–07.
2. Mackay GM. Some features of traffic accidents. BMJ 1969; 4: 799–801.
3. Larson CF, Hardt-Madsen M. Fatal motorcycle accidents in the county of Funen (Denmark). Forensic Sci Int 1988; 38: 93–9.
4. Saukko P, Knight B. Transportation injuries. In: Knight's Forensic Pathology, 3rd edn. 2004. Arnold, London. 281–300.

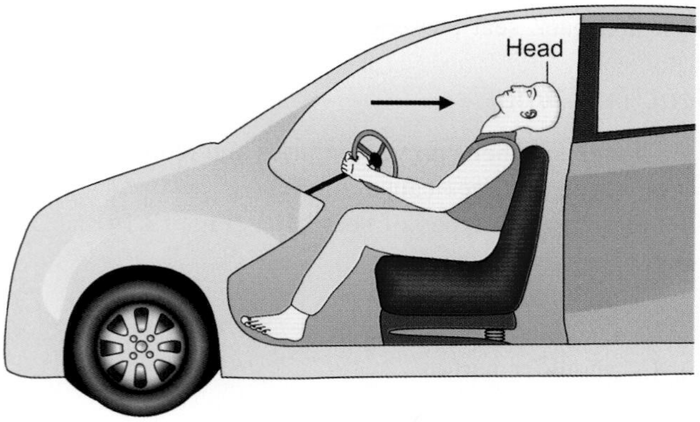

FIG. 12.12: Injuries sustained to driver in back impact

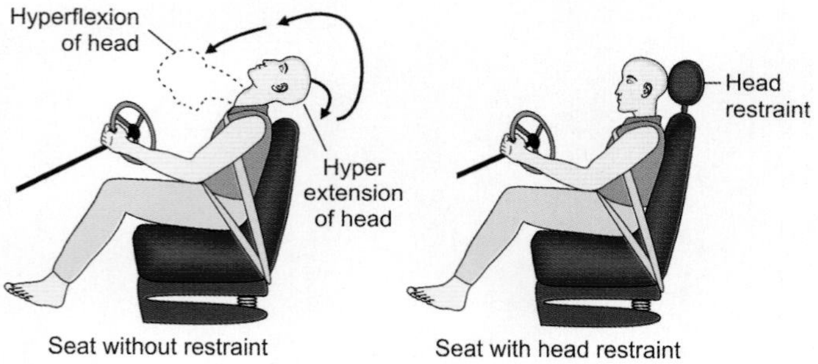

FIG. 12.13: Diagram showing mechanism of injury in back impact

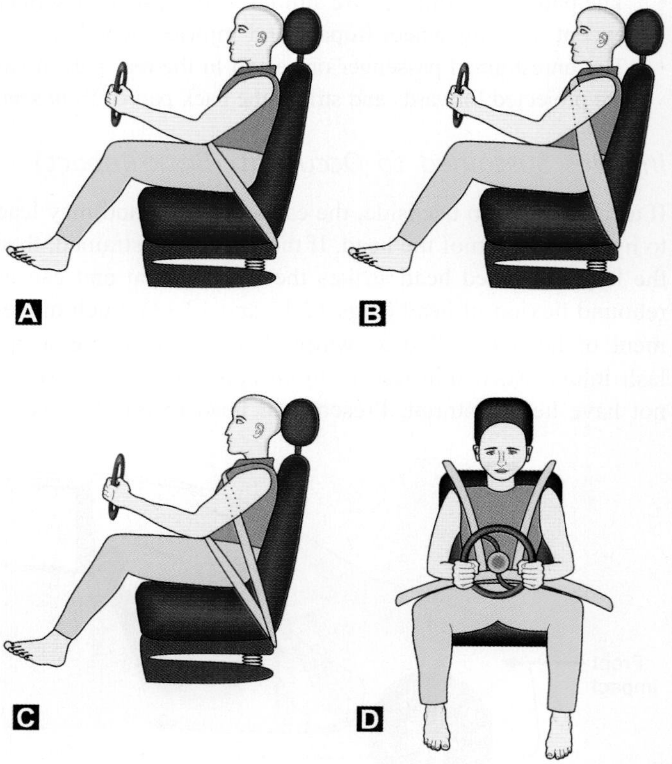

FIGS 12.14A to D: Different types of seatbelts. A: Lap strap, B: Shoulder diagonal type, C: Diagonal plus lap strap D: Shoulder harness

5. Spitz WU. The road traffic victim. In: Spitz and Fisher's Medicolegal investigation of Death, 3rd edn. 1993. Charlas C Thomas Publisher, USA. 528–66.
6. Sharma S, Singh S, Sinha US, Kapoor AK. Mode, type and distribution of injuries in non-fatal road traffic accidents-an Indian study. J Forensic Med Toxicol 2006; 23: 15–20.
7. Vij K. Transportation injuries. In: Textbook of Forensic Medicine and Toxicology, 3rd edn. 2005. Reed Elsevier India Pvt. Limited, New Delhi. 446–56.
8. Eid HO, Abu-Zidan FM. Biomechanics of road traffic collision injuries: a clinician's perspective. Singapore Med J 2007; 48: 693–9.
9. Murty OP, Rahman SNA, Mydin JBK, Husain NK, Ilias SR. Pattern of injuries in driver and other occupants of four wheel vehicles in fatal accidents – a Malaysian study. J Forensic Med Toxicol 2006; 23: 33–43.
10. Reddy KSN. Regional injuries. In: The Essentials of Forensic Medicine and Toxicology, 22nd edn. 2003. K. Suguna Devi, Hyderabad. 195–233.

CHAPTER 13

Injury: Medicolegal Considerations

As physicians are preservers of the sick, so are the laws of injured.

- Epictetus

Responsibilities of RMP

- Every doctor is bonded by law to give information about certain offenses to police (Sec 39 CrPC). A doctor can be prosecuted under Sec 201 IPC for destruction of evidence if doctor fails to inform the police
- It is duty of doctor to preserve the trace evidences
- While examining an injured person, the injuries should be recorded in detail and documented in form of injury certificate. The type of injury, location, direction, dimensions, shape, presence of foreign bodies, age of injuries, probable weapon causing the injury, nature of injury etc. should be recorded.
- After receiving a requisite requisition from the Investigating officer or court, the RMP should issue the injury certificate
- While examining a person for medicolegal purpose, a doctor-patient relationship is not established.

Examination of Injured Person

While examining an injured, following details should be noted. The proforma of injury certificate is provided in Table 13.1.

History

- How was the injury caused or sustained
- With what weapon/agent the said injury was caused
- What time was the injury sustained
- Pre-existing illness or diseases affecting the injured person
- Regular physical activity (for example contact sports etc.) and occupation
- Regular medications, e.g. anticoagulants, steroids
- Handedness of the injured person and suspected person i.e. left, right or both hands
- Use of drug and alcohol

Preliminary Particulars

1. Name
2. Age/sex
3. Resident of
4. Place of incident
5. Date and time of incident
6. Presence of pain/tenderness/stiffness
7. The person/police constable who brings him

Examination Proper and Opinion

1. Nature of injury – includes abrasion, contusion, and laceration, incised, stab etc.
2. Size of injury
3. Situation on the body
4. Whether simple, grievous or dangerous hurt
5. What kind of weapon could cause the said injury/injuries
6. Age of injury
7. Remarks – such as whether further investigations such as X-rays, USG/CT scan etc. are required or whether referred to higher center for further evaluation and management.

Simple Injury

- *A simple injury is one which is neither extensive nor serious and which heals rapidly without leaving any permanent deformity or disfiguration.*
- Law does not define simple hurt. Any injury that is non-grievous one is considered as simple.[1]

Table 13.1: Proforma of injury certificate

1	2	3	4	5	6	7	8
Sr. no	Nature of injury	Size of injury	Situation over body part	Simple/grievous	Kind of weapon causing it	Age of injury	Remarks

Grievous Hurt

According to Section 320 of IPC, the following kinds of hurt only are designated as "grievous hurt".

- Firstly – emasculation
- Secondly – permanent privation of the sight of either eye
- Thirdly – permanent privation of the hearing of either ear
- Fourthly – privation of member or joint
- Fifthly – destruction or permanent impairing of the powers of any member or joint
- Sixthly – Permanent disfiguration of the head or face
- Seventhly – fracture or dislocation of a bone or tooth
- Eighthly – any hurt which endangers life or which causes the sufferer to be during the space of twenty days in severe bodily pain or unable to follow his ordinary pursuits.

Dangerous Injury

- Is a part of grievous hurt and refers to any injury, which poses imminent danger to life by its direct or imminent effect. It is either extensive or serious in relation to organs or part wounded. The injury is likely to prove fatal in absence of surgical aid.[2]
- The concept of dangerous injury is not a precise one.
- There is a fine distinction in the degree of body injury between that is "dangerous to life" and that is "likely to cause death".

Injury Likely to Cause Death

- It is one, which poses imminent danger to life or constitutes great threat to life on account of its great severity and involvement of body structures/important organs or extensive body surface – death in such causes is not merely possible but is likely.
- The word 'imminent' indicates a danger, which is impending. The dangerous injury may prove fatal in absence treatment or surgical aid.

Injury sufficient to cause death in ordinary course of nature

- It is injury/injuries, which by virtue of its own direct effect can bring about a fatal result. Here, as a result of the injury, death is highly probable.
- Causing death by intentionally inflicting such wounds, as it is sufficient to cause death in ordinary course of nature, will constitute murder as per Section 300 of IPC.

Assault

- Section 351 of IPC deals with an assault as "*whoever makes any gesture or any preparation, intending or knowing it to be likely that such gesture or preparation will cause any person present to apprehend that he who makes that gesture or preparation is about to use criminal force to that person, is said to commit an assault*".
- Explanation – mere words do not amount to an assault. But the words, which a person uses, may give to his gestures or preparations such as meaning as may make those gesture or preparation amount to an assault.
- In other words we can put it into, as "every attack or threat or attempt to apply force on another person in a hostile manner is an assault".
- Example – even showing a fist or finger or shaking of head in a hostile manner will technically constitute an assault.

Battery

- Concept of battery is not recognized in India. In India, the word assault includes both the assault and battery.
- Battery is beating or wounding a person. Hence it can be said that assault brought into execution is a battery.

Manner of Causation of Injury

Manner refers the way in which an injury is caused or inflicted. An injury can be caused by suicidal infliction or may be homicidal or accidental in nature. The medical examiner should be cautious while opining regarding the manner of causation of injury. Following points may help for differentiation.

1. Situation and character of injury
   - Suicidal injuries are usually inflicted on accessible or approachable part of body. They are generally inflicted on the front or side of the body (Fig. 13.1).

- Presence of defense wounds on hand and forearm suggest an attempt made by injuring individual to ward-off the attack. Presence of defense wounds suggests homicidal nature of injury causation (Fig. 13.2).

2. The number, direction and extent of injury
   - Presence of multiple, deep injuries distributed extensively over body favors homicidal infliction (Fig. 13.3)
   - Presence of many, superficial injuries, grouped together especially over one side of body over accessible part suggests self-inflicted injuries.
   - Presence of hesitation cuts favors suicidal manner of injuries (Fig. 13.4).
3. Circumstances and scene of crime
   - Evidence of struggle, torn clothes, loss of buttons, disarranged room furniture etc. favors homicidal nature of injuries
   - Presence of suicide note may be of value as corroborative evidence of suicidal attempt.

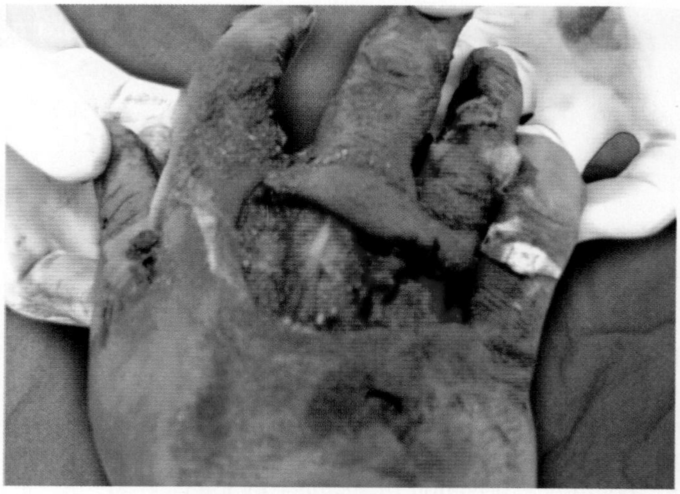

FIG. 13.2: Defense wounds

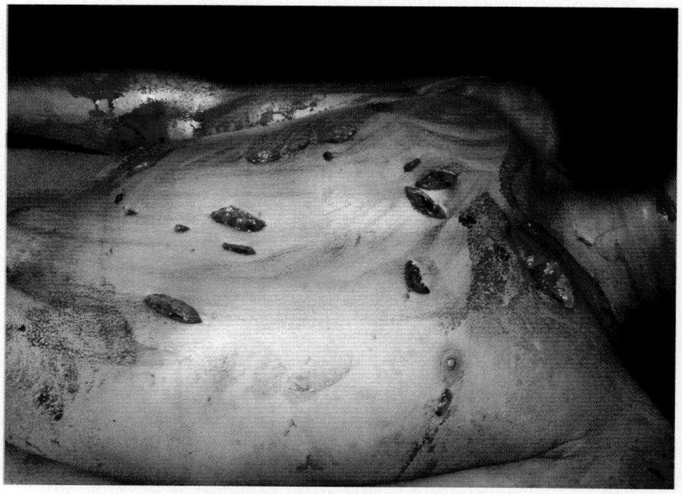

FIG. 13.3: Multiple stab wounds

Fabricated Injury

- Also known as fictitious or forged wounds
- The fabricated wounds are produced by a person on his own body (i.e. self inflicted) or occasionally caused by other on him (i.e. self suffered) with an intention to impose false charge or false accusation on others.
- The injuries are produced as per story prepared by a fabricator person to involve other. In this attempt he may inflict multiple superficial injuries according to his story.

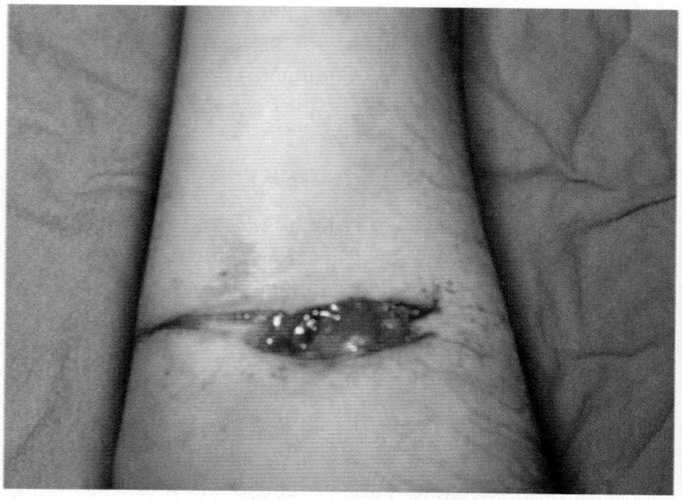

FIG. 13.1: Suicidal cut injuries over left cubital fossa

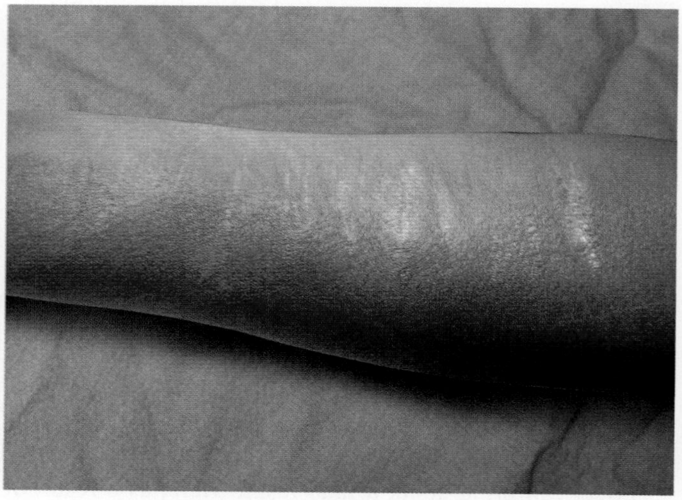

FIG. 13.4: Hesitation cuts (healed)

Antemortem and Postmortem Injuries

At times, it becomes difficult to opine whether the said injury is antemortem or postmortem. The injuries has to be carefully looked for feature such as:

- Hemorrhage – if injury is inflicted during life (i.e. antemortem injury) there may be copious hemorrhage and the wounds exhibit extravasation of blood in the surrounding structures. Similarly blood accumulates in wound and an antemortem clot may be formed.
- Spurting of blood from bleeding vessels is another cardinal feature. The spurting or spraying of blood may be identified over clothes/body or at the scene of crime
- Retraction of edges of wound
- Signs of inflammation
- Signs of repair
- Presence of infection
- Leukotriene B4 (LTB4) in skin samples can be detected by HPLC to distinguish antemortem and postmortem injury. LTB4 is found in antemortem wounds where as it will be absent in postmortem wounds.[3]
- D-dimer (DD) is an intermediate product of fibrin metabolism. DD measurements are done by ELISA D-dimer test. DD is useful marker to distinguish between antemortem and postmortem wounds.[4]
- The difference between antemortem and postmortem injuries are enlisted in Table 13.2

Table 13.2: Difference between antemortem and postmortem injury

Features	Antemortem injury	Postmortem injury
Hemorrhage	Copious	Slight
Extravasation of blood	Present	Absent
Clotting	Present	Absent
Retraction of wound edges	Present	Absent
Vital reaction	Present	Absent
Repair process	Present	Absent
Infection	Present	Absent
Microscopic exam	RBC/WBC/platelet infiltration present	Absent
Fibrin	Present	Absent
Enzyme histochemistry		
Adenosine triphosphatase	Present	Absent
Aminopeptidase	Present	Absent
Acid phosphatase	Present	Absent
Alkaline phosphatase	Present	Absent
Serotonin	Present	Absent
Histamine	Present	Absent

Age of Injury

Age of injury can be assessed by clinical examination, microscopic examination and by histochemical methods. Healing and age of individual injury has been dealt in chapter 9. Here only microscopic and histochemical methods are discussed.

Microscopic Method

It is based on conventional histological appearance[5] and presented in Table 13.3.

Histochemical Methods

1. Activity of adenosine tripohosphatase (ATPs), aminopeptidase, acid phosphatase, alkaline phosphatase and esterase increases in antemortem wounds. At the end of one hour, adenosine tripohosphatase and esterase activity increases and at about two hours, aminopeptidase activity increases. At about four hours, acid phosphatase increases and about eight hours, the alkaline phosphatase activity increases.[6] The timing of their appearance is presented in Figure 13.5.
2. In antemortem wounds – two zones can be identified. The central zone is in immediate vicinity of injury, 0.2-0.5 mm wide. The zone becomes necrotic due to which the cell loses enzyme activity and becomes negative zone for enzymes. This phenomenon is called as 'negative vital reaction'. Immediately beyond this zone, lies a peripheral zone of 0.1-0.3 mm width. Due to infliction of injury and reparative process, enzymatic activity in this zone is markedly increased compared to normal tissue beyond the injury site. The phenomenon of increase in enzyme activity is referred as 'positive vital reaction' (See Fig. 13.6.). In other words, two zones can be demonstrated in antemortem wounds. No such zone develops in postmortem wound.[7]
3. Histamine and serotonin are vasoactive amines and are known to increase in the earliest phase of injury. To

Table 13.3: Dating of wound by histological appearances

Duration	*Features*
30 minutes - 4 hours	- Polymorphnuclear cell appears - Fibrin appears
4- 12 hours	- Polymorphnuclear cell population prominent - Mononuclear cell arrears - Tissue edema and swelling of vascular endothelium noted
12-24 hours	- Polymorponuclear cell population decreases - Mononuclear population increases - Removal of necrosed tissue begins - Basophilic tinge to ground substance - Mitosis visible in fibroblasts
24-72 hours	- Leucocytes reache at peak - Fibroblasts begin to appear - New capillaries begin to bud from vessels - Stroma becoming granulation tissue
3-6 days	- Collagen begins to form - Giant cells visible - Epidermis grows actively
10-15 days	- Fibroblasts are more active - Collagen laid down - Cellular reaction subsides - Vascularity decreases - Epidermis become thin and flat but without papillae (rete pegs).

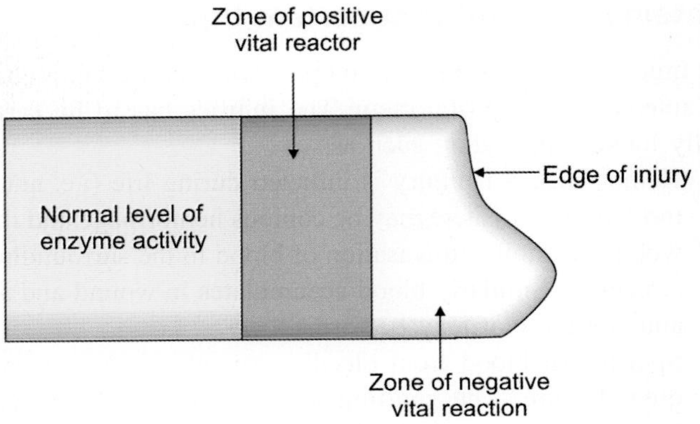

FIG. 13.6: Showing difference in enzyme activity in antemortem wound

establish that the said injury is antemortem, the level of histamine must be at least 50 percent greater than the control sample whereas for serotonin, at least twice the concentration than control sample.[8, 9]

4. It is said that tissue cathespins increased due to injury and can be demonstrated within 5-10 minutes.

Complications of Injury/Injuries

A wound may heal completely or may get complicated. Following are the complications of injuries:

1. Infection (Fig. 13.7)
2. Cicatrisation
3. Keloid formation (Fig. 13.8)
4. Disfigurement
5. Deformity (Fig. 13.9)
6. Malunion/non-union of bone

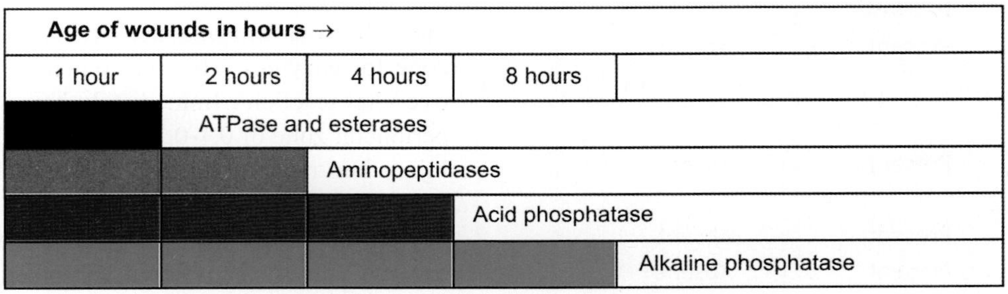

Age of wounds in hours →
1 hour
2 hours
4 hours
8 hours
ATPase and esterases
Aminopeptidases
Acid phosphatase
Alkaline phosphatase

FIG. 13.5: Showing histochemical method to estimate age of wounds

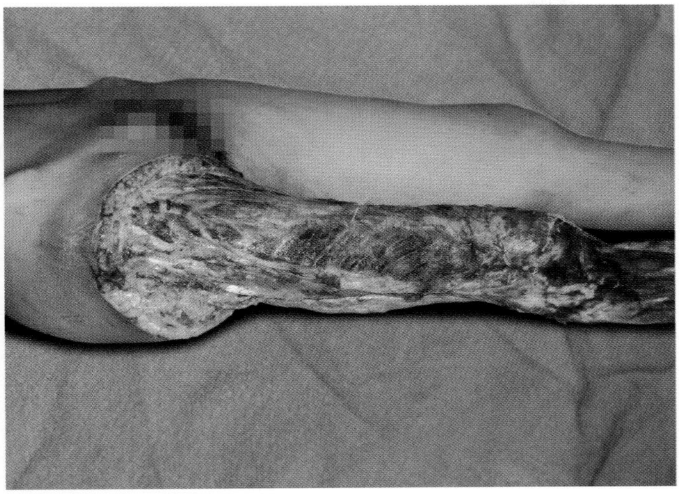

FIG. 13.7: Infected wound

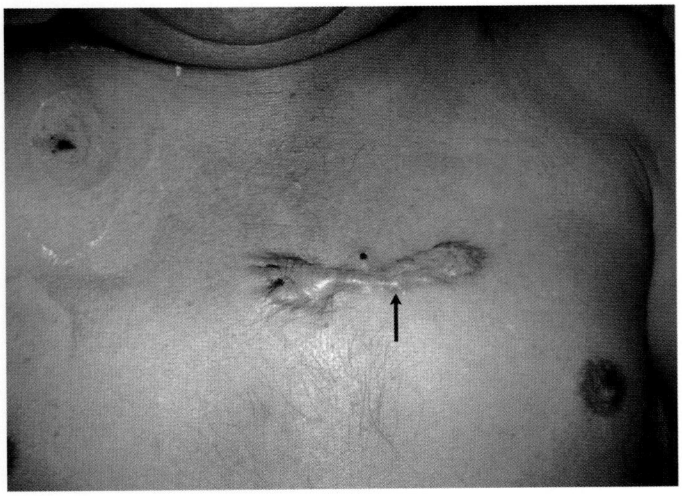

FIG. 13.8: Keloid formation

7. Impairment of vision/hearing/locomotion
8. Disability
9. Death

Cause of Death from Injuries

Immediate Cause of Death

1. Hemorrhage
2. Injury to vital organs
3. Neurogenic shock
4. Air embolism
5. Vagal inhibition
6. Injury to head

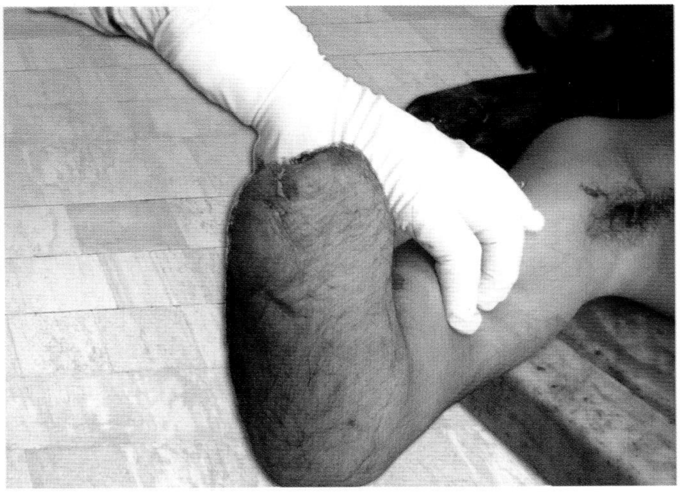

FIG. 13.9: Deformity

Delayed Cause of Death

1. Infection and septicemia
2. Crush syndrome
3. Disseminated intravascular coagulation
4. Thrombo-embolism
5. Fat embolism
6. ARDS
7. Renal failure
8. Secondary shock
9. Gangrene and necrosis

Volitional Act

- Sometimes it is possible that a person may be able to speak, walk or perform volitional act even after receiving mortal injury involving a vital organ such as brain, lung or heart.
- Such performance of act by a person after receiving an injury is called volitional act of a person.

Ewing's Postulate[10,11]

It is suggested that trauma may occasionally be cause of new growth or cancer. Therefore, in accepting trauma as a cause of new growth/cancer, Ewing's postulate should be satisfied. The postulate states that:

1. There must be evidence of previous site normal prior to trauma.
2. The application of adequate trauma must be proved.
3. There must be proof of reasonable time interval between injury and appearance of the tumor.
4. The disease must develop in the exact locality of the injury.
5. The nature of the tumor must be proved by microscopy.

WEAPONS

Definition

Weapons are the means or mechanical devises which when applied in a hostile manner, will produce injury.

Types of Weapons

Weapons may be dangerous or deadly

1. Dangerous weapon – Section 324 and 326 of IPC defines danger weapon as " *any instrument used for shooting, stabbing or cutting, or any instrument which, if used as a weapon of offense is likely to cause death; or by means of fire or any heated substance, or by means of any poison or any corrosive substance, or by means of any explosive substance or by means of any substance which is deleterious to human body to inhale, to swallow or to receive into blood or by means of any animal.*"
2. Deadly weapon – Section 148 of IPC deals with deadly weapon as "*whoever is guilty of rioting, being armed with deadly weapon, which when used as a weapon of offense is likely to cause death, shall be punished with imprisonment of either description for a term which may extend to three years, or with fine, or with both*".[12]

Kinds of Weapon

The weapons of offense can be grouped into:

1. Hard and blunt weapons
2. Sharp cutting weapons
3. Pointed weapons
4. Mixed variety
5. Firearms

These weapons are further subdivided as:

I. **Hard and blunt weapons**
   A) Depending on weight
      1. Light (Fig. 13.10)
      2. Moderately heavy (Figs 13.11 to 13.13)
      3. Heavy (Fig. 13.14)
   B) Depending on surface
      1. Smooth surface (Fig. 13.15)
      2. Irregular surface (Fig. 13.16)
   C) Depending on property
      1. Flexible – example cane, whip etc. (Fig. 13.17)
      2. Non-flexible – example lathi, iron rod (Fig. 13.18)

II. **Sharp cutting weapons** (fig 13.19)
   A) Depending on weight
      1. Light (Fig. 13.20)
      2. Moderately heavy (Fig. 13.21)
      3. Heavy (Fig. 13.22 and 13.23)
   B) Depending on edge
      1. Single cutting edge (Fig. 13.24)
      2. Double (both) cutting edge (Fig. 13.25)
   C) Depending on point may be
      1. Sharp cutting edge with pointed ends (Fig. 13.26)
      2. Sharp cutting edge with non-pointed (blunt) ends (Fig. 13.27)

III. **Firearms**
   A) Depending on barrel surface (Fig. 13.28)
      1. Smooth bore
      2. Rifled weapon
   B) Depending on length, may be
      1. Shoulder rest – example musket, AK-47 etc.
      2. Hand rest – example revolver, pistol

FIG. 13.10: Hard and blunt—light weapon

FIG. 13.11: Hard and blunt—moderately heavy (e.g. brick)

FIG. 13.12: Hard and blunt—moderately heavy

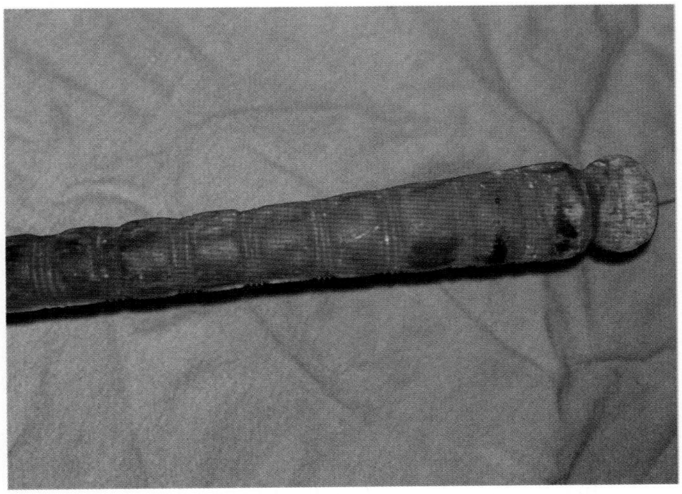

FIG. 13.13: Hard and blunt—moderately heavy

FIG. 13.14: Hard and blunt weapon—heavy (e.g. stone)

FIG. 13.15: Hard and blunt—smooth surface

FIG. 13.16: Hard and blunt—irregular surface

FIG. 13.17: Hard and blunt—flexible (e.g. rope)

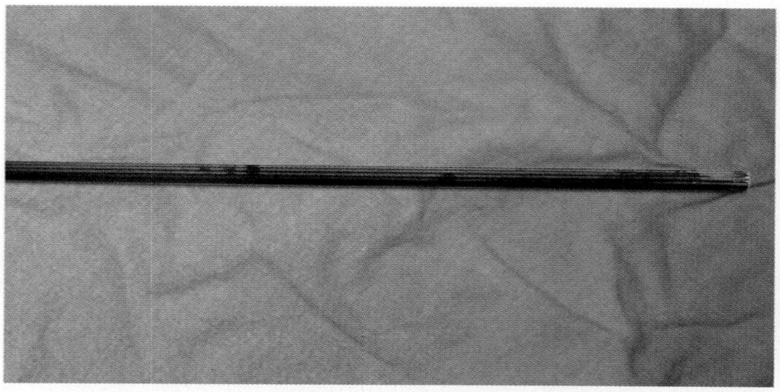

FIG. 13.18: Hard and blunt-non-flexible (e.g. rod)

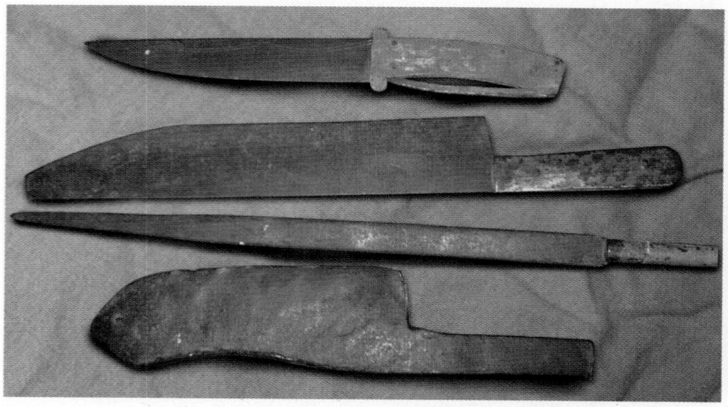

FIG. 13.19: Various types of sharp cutting weapons

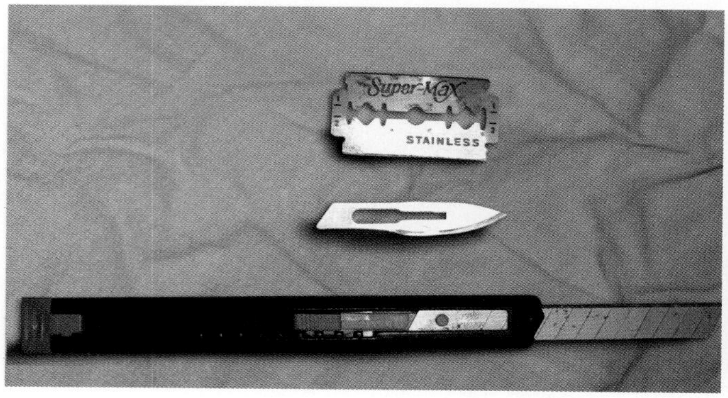

FIG. 13.20: Sharp cutting weapons—lightweight

FIG. 13.21: Sharp cutting weapons—moderately heavy

FIG. 13.22: Sharp cutting—heavy weapon

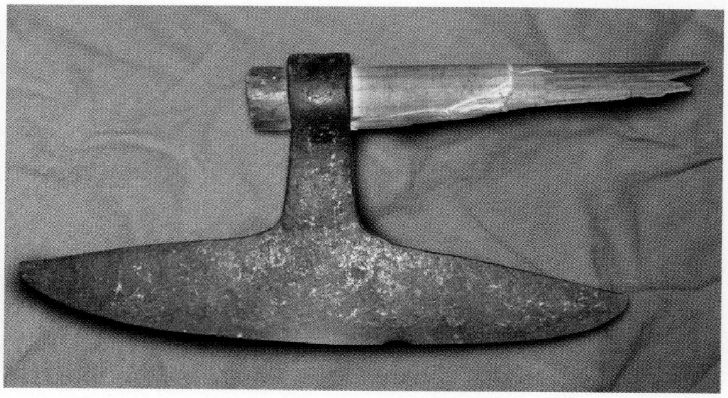

FIG. 13.23: Cutting weapon—moderately to heavy weapon

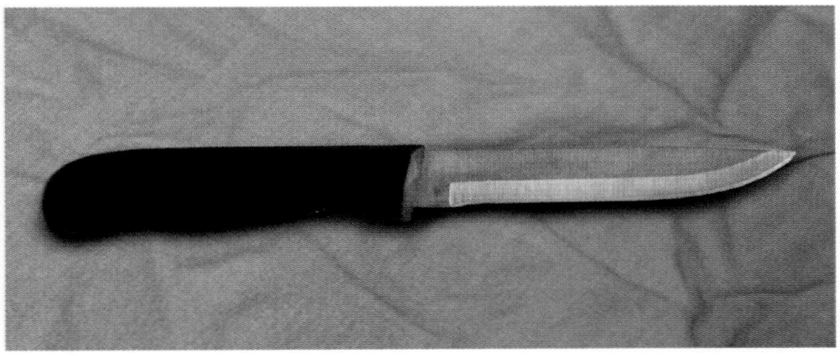

FIG. 13.24: Sharp cutting edge (single) with pointed weapon

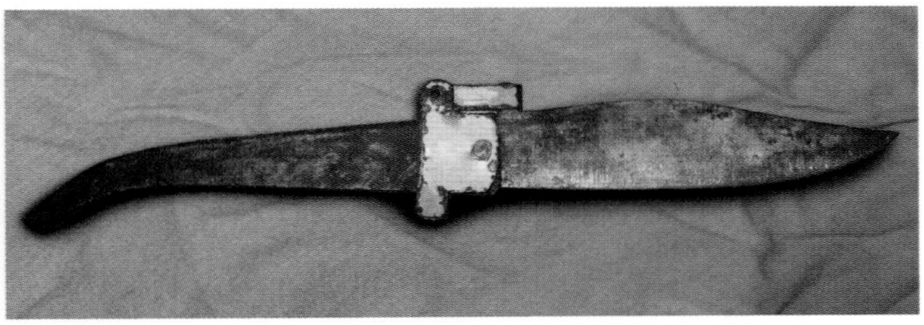

FIG. 13.25: Sharp cutting edges (double edged) with pointed weapon

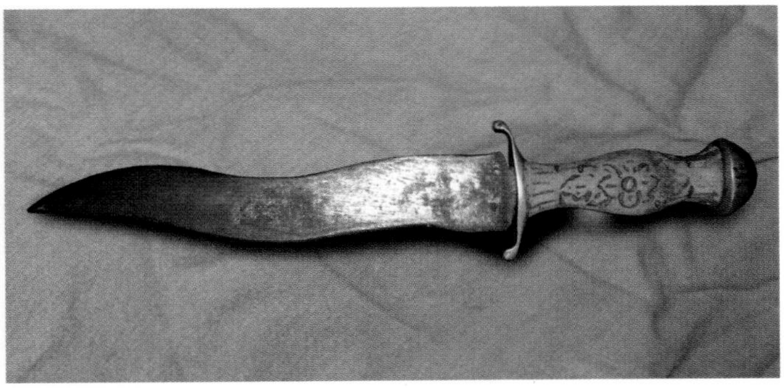

FIG. 13.26: Sharp cutting edge with pointed weapon

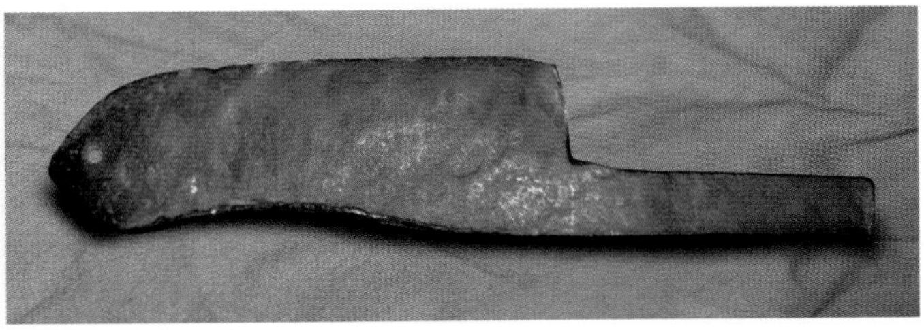

FIG. 13.27: Cutting edge with blunt end

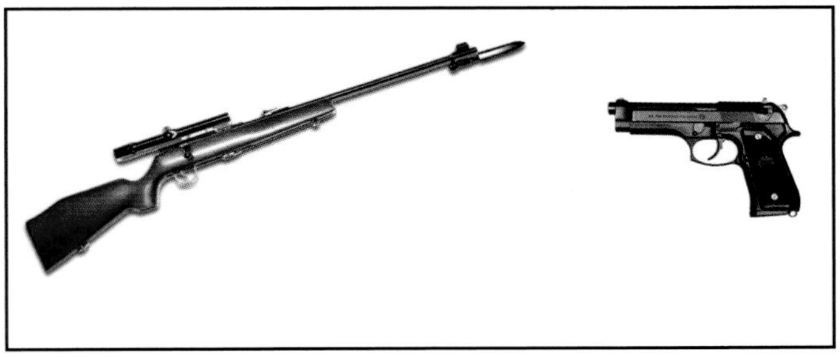

FIG. 13.28: Firearms (*Courtesy*: Dr Manish Shrigiriwar, Associate Professor, Dept. of Forensic Medicine, IGGMC, Nagpur)

INJURIES AND LAW

1. Section 299 of IPC – deals with culpable homicide.
2. Section 300 of IPC – deals with murder.
3. Section 301 of IPC – deals with culpable homicide by causing death of person other than person whose death was intended.
4. Section 302 of IPC – deals with punishment of murder.
5. Section 304 of IPC – deals with punishment for culpable homicide not amounting to murder.
6. Section 304 A of IPC – deals with causing death by negligence – whoever causes the death of any person by doing any rash or negligent act not amounting to culpable homicide, shall be punished with imprisonment of either description for a term which may extend to two years, or with fine, or with both.
7. Section 304 B of IPC – deals with dowry death.
8. Section 305 of IPC – deals with abetment of suicide of child or insane person.
9. Section 306 of IPC – deals with abetment of suicide.
10. Section 307 of IPC – deals with attempt to murder.
11. Section 308 of IPC – deals with attempt to commit culpable homicide.
12. Section 309 of IPC – deals with attempt to commit suicide.
13. Section 321 of IPC – deals with voluntarily causing hurt – whoever does any act with the intention of thereby causing hurt to any person, or with the knowledge that he is likely thereby to cause hurt to any person and does thereby cause hurt to any person, is said voluntarily to cause hurt.
14. Section 322 of IPC – deals with voluntarily causing grievous hurt – whoever voluntarily causes hurt, if the hurt, which he intends to cause or knows himself, to be likely to cause is grievous hurt, and if the hurt, which

he causes if grievous hurt is said voluntarily to cause grievous, hurt.
15. Section 323 of IPC – deals with punishment for causing hurt.
16. Section 325 of IPC – deals with punishment for voluntarily causing grievous hurt.

HOMICIDE

The word 'homicide' is derived from Latin word homo = man and cide = I cut. Thus homicide is the causing of death of a human being by a human being.[13] The WHO defines homicide as "any death resulting from injury purposefully inflicted by another person".[14] In India, homicide is the killing of a human being. It is usually murder as defined under Section 300 of IPC or may be culpable homicide not amounting to murder (Section 299 of IPC) or even justifiable homicide (exception 1 of Section 300 of IPC).[15] Thus the homicide can be classified as follows.

Classification (Fig. 13.29)

A) Lawful homicide
   1. Excusable homicide
   2. Justifiable homicide
B) Unlawful (culpable) homicide
   1. Murder (culpable homicide amounting to murder)
   2. Culpable homicide not amounting to murder

Excusable homicide – here the homicide is committed with no criminal intention and knowledge or caused unintentionally by an act done in good faith or in self defense.

Justifiable homicide – here the homicide is caused that is permissible by law for example judicial hanging.

Culpable Homicide

- Section 299 of IPC – deals with culpable homicide – whoever causes death by doing an act with the intention of causing death, or with the intention of causing such bodily injury as is likely to cause death, or with the knowledge that he is likely by such act to cause death, commits the offenses of culpable homicide.
- Explanation 1 – a person who causes bodily injury to another who is labouring under a disorder, disease or bodily infirmity, and thereby accelerates the death of that other, shall be deemed to have caused his death
- Explanation 2 – where death is caused by bodily injury, the person who causes such bodily injury shall be deemed to have caused the death, although by resorting to proper remedies and skilful treatment the death might have been prevented.

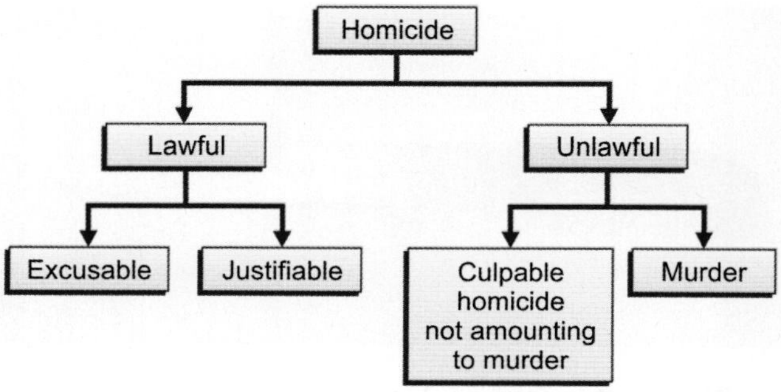

FIG. 13.29: Classification of homicide

- Explanation 3 – the causing of the death of child in the mother's womb is not homicide. But it may amount to culpable homicide to cause the death of a living child, if any part of that child has been brought forth, though the child may not have breathed or been completely born.

Murder

- Section 300 of IPC – deals with murder – except in the cases hereinafter except, culpable homicide is murder, if the act by which the death is caused is done with the intention of causing death, or –
- Secondly – if it is done with the intention of causing such bodily injury as the offender knows to be likely to cause the death of the person to whom the harm is caused or –
- Thirdly – if it is done with the intention of causing bodily injury to any person and the bodily injury intended to be inflicted is sufficient in the ordinary course of nature to cause death, or –
- Fourthly – if the person committing the act knows that it is so imminently dangerous that it must, in all probability, cause death or such bodily injury as is likely to cause death, and commits such act without any excuse for incurring the risk of causing death or such injury as aforesaid.
- Exception 1 – when culpable homicide is not murder – culpable homicide is not murder if the offender, whilst deprived of the power of self-control by grave and sudden provocation, causes the death of the person who gave the provocation or causes the death of any other person by mistake or accident. The above exception is subject to the following provisions:
  – First – that the provocation is not sought or voluntarily provoked by the offender as an excuse killing or doing harm to any person

- Secondly – that the provocation is not given by anything done in obedience to the law, or by a public servant in the lawful exercise of the powers of such public servant
- Thirdly – that the provocation is not given by anything done in the lawful exercise of the right of private defense
- Explanation – whether the provocation was grave and sudden enough to prevent the offense from amounting to murder is a question of fact.

- Exception 2 – culpable homicide is not murder if the offender, in the exercise in good faith of the right of private defense of a person or property, exceeds the power given to him by law and causes the death of the person against whom he is exercising such right of defense without premeditation, and without any intention of doing more harm than is necessary for the purpose of such defense.
- Exception 3 – culpable homicide is not murder if the offender, being a public servant or aiding a public servant acting for the advancement of public justice, exceeds the powers given to him by, and causes death by doing an act which he, in good faith, believes to be lawful and necessary for the due discharge of his duty as public servant and without ill-will towards the person whose death is caused.
- Exception 4 – culpable homicide is not murder if it is committed without premeditation in a sudden fight in the heat of passion upon a sudden quarrel and without the offenders having taken undue advantage or acted in cruel or unsafe manner. Explanation – it is immaterial in such cases which party offers the provocation or commits the first assault.
- Exception 5 – Culpable homicide is not murder when the person whose death is caused, being above the age of eighteen years, suffers death or takes the risk of death with his own consent.

REFERENCES

1. Ramchandran A, Chandran MR. Forensic traumatology. In A Short Textbook of Forensic medicine and Toxicology, 1st reprint edn. 2006. All India Publishers and Distributors, Regd., New Delhi. 108–63.
2. Mukherjee JB. In: Forensic Medicine and Toxicology Vol. I, 2nd edn. 1994. Arnold Associates, New Delhi.
3. He L, Zhu J. Distinguishing antemortem from postmortem injuries by LTB4 quantification. Forensic Sci Int 1996; 81: 11–6.
4. Hernandez-Cueto C, Vieira DN, Girela E, Marques E, Villanueva E, Sa FO. Diagnostic ability of D-dimer in the establishment of the vitality of wounds. Forensic Sci Int 1995; 76: 141–9.
5. Saukko P, Knight B. The pathology of wounds. In: Knight's Forensic Pathology, 3rd edn. 2004. Arnold, London. 136–73.
6. Fatteh A. Histochemical distinction between antemortem and postmortem skin wounds. J Forensic Sci 1966; 11: 17–27.
7. Raekallio J. Enzyme histochemistry of vital and postmortem skin wounds. J Forensic Med 1966; 13: 85–90.
8. Raekallio J. Determination of the age of wounds by histochemical and biochemical methods. Forensic Sci 1972; 1: 3–16.
9. Zhong FC, Zhen ZJ. Localization and quantification of histamine in injured skin as parameters for the timing of wounds. Forensic Sci Int 1991; 51: 163–71.
10. Mathiharan K, Patnaik AK. Medicolegal aspects of wounds. In: Modi's Medical Jurisprudence and Toxicology, 23rd edn. 2005. LexisNexis Butterworths, New Delhi. 743–82.
11. Parikh CK. Injuries – medicolegal aspects. In: Parikh's Textbook of medical Jurisprudence and Toxicology, 5th edn. 1995. CBS Publishers and Distributors, Mumbai. 305–35.
12. Pillay VV. Medicolegal aspects of injuries and death. In: Textbook of Forensic Medicine and Toxicology, 14th edn. 2004. Paras Publishing, Hyderabad. 203–17.
13. Dikshit PC. Medicolegal aspects of injuries. In: Textbook of Forensic Medicine and Toxicology, 1st edn. 2007. Peepee Publishers and Distributors (P) Ltd., New Delhi. 263-79.
14. Ambade VN, Godbole HV, Keoliya AN. Types of trauma in homicides. Milestone 2004; 3: 99–103.
15. Rudra A. Medicolegal aspects of injuries. In: Dogra TD, Rudra A (eds) Lyon's Medical Jurisprudence and Toxicology, 11th edn. 2007. Delhi Law House, Delhi. 463–90.

CHAPTER 14

Thermal Injuries

One of the disappointing things about taking care of burns seems to be that with every thousand more that I take care of it, I get less good at predicting burn depth. I don't know if this happens to others or not.

- Dr Andrew M Munster

Introduction

Thermal injuries are caused either due to exposure to cold or exposure to heat. The effect of heat or cold over body may be in generalized form or may have localized effect to a particular body part. Thus the thermal injuries are classified as follows:

Due to Exposure to Cold

1. General effects: Hypothermia
2. Local effects: Such as
   - Frost bite
   - Trench foot
   - Pernio (chilblains).

Due to Exposure to Heat

1. General effects
   - Heat stroke
   - Heat cramps
   - Heat exhaustion.
2. Local effects: Such as
   - Burns
   - Scalds.

EXPOSURE TO COLD

Hypothermia

Definition

Hypothermia is state where an individual's core body temperature is below 35°C (95°F).

Classification

It is classified as[1]

1. Mild hypothermia – core body temperature is 35 to 32°C
2. Moderate hypothermia – core body temperature is < 32 to 28°C
3. Severe hypothermia – core body temperature < 28°C

Causes

It is caused by

1. Exposure to severe cold with exhaustion – called as environmental hypothermia
2. Immersion hypothermia
3. Excessive heat loss due to increases cutaneous blood flow – burns, psoriasis, toxic epidermal necrolysis.
4. Inadequate heat production due to decreased metabolism in conditions such as malnutrition, hypothyroidism, hepatic failure etc.
5. Inadequate heat production due to drugs such as phenothiazines, barbiturates, ethanol, opiates etc.

Causes of Death

1. Ventricular fibrillation
2. Disseminated intravascular coagulation
3. Acid-base imbalance
4. Bronchospasm
5. Pulmonary edema.

Autopsy Findings

- Postmortem lividity is pinkish – due to persistent oxyhemoglobin in the capillaries. Due to cold, there is low metabolic activity and cold tissues fail to take up the delivered oxygen.

- **Rarely** skin is pale (white) and thus hypothermic deaths are also called as "**white deaths**".[2]
- Skin may show erythematous patches or irregular red or violet patches on exposed parts of body. They are often present over extensor surfaces of large joints, such as the outer side of hips, the elbows and knees and at flank and face.[3]
- Lungs are oedematous with fresh hemorrhages
- Trachea contains froth with evidence of bronchspasm.
- Gastric mucosa may show small hemorrhages and ulceration (**Wischnewski ulcers**)
- Organs are congested
- Kidneys may show signs of acute tubular necrosis
- Urinary catecholamine levels are elevated in hypothermic deaths. The increased level of catecholamine indicates prolonged agonal stress.[4, 5]
- There is hyperglycemia with glucose in urine.[6]

Pernio (Chilblains)

It is a vasculitic disorder associated with exposure to cold. When exposed to cold, patient develops raised erythematous lesion on lower part of legs and feet. These lesions are associated with Pruritis and burning sensation.[7]

Immersion Foot

- Also called as trench foot
- It occurs when foot or hand is exposed to a low temperature of 5 to 6°C if the limbs are wet.[8]
- **Wetness** is an important contributory factor because when limbs are wet, cold is more penetrating. Necrosis of fingers, toes or hand and feet may occur. Obliterating angiitis causes severe gangrene and loss of tissue.

Frostbite

- Frostbite occurs from exposure to severe environmental cold exposure or dry cold or from direct contact with cold object (below 0°C).
- It is commonly seen in mountaineering and polar expeditions.
- Tissue injury results from freezing and vasoconstriction.[7]
- It usually affects the distal aspects of extremities or exposed parts of face such as ears, nose, chin and cheeks.
- Degrees of frostbite and the pathological features are described in Table 14.1.

EXPOSURE TO HEAT

Hyperthermia

Definition

The normal temperature in human is said to be 37°C (98.6°F). *Hyperthermia is an elevation of body temperature above the hypothalamic set point.*

Causes

Causes are as follows

1. Heat stroke
2. Drug induced – such as amphetamines, monoamine oxidase inhibitors, tricyclic antidepressants
3. Neuroleptic malignant syndrome – due to phenothiazines, haloperidol, fluoxetine etc.
4. Malignant hyperthermia – due to inhalational anesthetic agents, succinyl choline
5. Endocrine disorder – such as thyrotoxicosis, pheochromoctoma

Heat Syncope

Synonyms: Heat collapse, heat exhaustion, heat prostration

It is due to effect of heat on the circulatory system and has following features[8, 9]

- Prostration
- Peripheral circulatory failure
- Pallor
- Hypotension
- Flushing of face
- Headache
- Giddiness
- Collapse
- Oliguria
- Irritability.

Table 14.1: Degrees of frostbite and their features

Degree	*Pathological features*
1	Redness and edema of skin
2	Only epidermis is affected, there is blister formation
3	Skin and subcutaneous tissue is necrosed
4	Total loss of tissue in the exposed area including muscle and bone

Heat Cramps

Synonyms: Miners cramps, Stoker's cramps, Boiler's room cramps.

- Heat cramps occur due to exposure to high temperature
- Here the patient complains of painful spasm of voluntary muscles of body due to excessive perspiration and loss of body fluid and electrolytes.
- Treatment consist of administration of fluid and correction of electrolyte imbalance.

Heat Stroke

Synonyms: Sunstroke, heat hyperpyrexia, thermic fever, systemic hyperthermia

In heat stroke, there is impairment of heat regulation mechanism in the body with body temperature raised to 106°F (41°C) with sudden unconsciousness hence the name stroke.[10] *It is defined as core body temperature above 106°F (41°C)*. The features of heat stroke are:

- Hot and dry skin
- Increased depth of respiration
- Tachycardia
- Headache
- Nausea
- Vomiting
- Weakness
- Dizziness
- Convulsions
- Delirium
- Stupor
- Coma
- Hypotension
- Death is due to paralysis of heat regulatory center.

Autopsy Findings

- Postmortem caloricity
- Rigor mortis – sets in early and passes off early
- Putrefaction is rapid
- Congestion of abdominal organs
- Brain – edematous and congested with petechial hemorrhages in white matter
- Lungs – congested with evidence of fresh hemorrhages
- Autopsy findings of heatstroke victims depend on the time that has elapsed since the onset of event and actual death. Petechial hemorrhages and ecchymoses of serosal membrane in the thoracic and abdominal organs might be the only findings in early phase. In those who survive more than 12 to 24 hours, widespread cellular degeneration, organ hemorrhages and fibrin thrombi can be detected. The changes include focal necrosis of the myocardium, reno-tubular, adrenal and centrilobular hepatic necrosis along with neuronal degeneration and microglial reaction in the CNS with peripheral rhabdomyolysis, pancreatitis and disseminated intravascular coagulopathy.[11]

BURNS

Burns are not uncommon injuries and vary from minor and insignificant injuries to severe forms. A burn injury is defined as "*tissue injury due to application of heat in any form to the external or internal body surface*". The application of heat may be in the form of:[12]

1. Dry heat – burns
2. Moist heat – scalds
3. Mechanical injuries causing friction – brush burns or friction burns
4. Chemical burns or corrosive burns or caustic burns – due to application of acids, alkalis and corrosive metal salts
5. Burns due to lightning/electricity
6. Burns due to radiation, X-rays, UV rays, radium, laser, infrared rays, explosion injuries etc.

Causation of Burns

- Young infants – sustain burns from liquid being spilled and scalds are common in this age
- Toddlers – in an attempt to explore their environment may injure themselves and again scalds are common in this age group
- Children – burn injuries common for example playing with match box, bonfire games etc.
- Battered baby syndrome – here children are sustained purposeful burn injuries/scalds or burns from cigarette, metal fork etc.
- Epileptics, intoxicated, senile persons are prone for burn injuries
- Dowry death/ bride burns – heinous but common practice in India
- Explosion injuries to workers in factories/furnaces, mines
- Transportation accidents – burns are less common but common in aviation accidents.

Pathophysiology

Burn injury causes coagulative necrosis of the epidermis and underlying tissues. Burns bring cellular damage primarily by transfer of energy inducing coagulative necrosis. Chemicals and electricity causes direct injury to cell membrane in addition to transfer of heat. The burn injury of skin has been divided into three zones of coagulative necrosis as (Fig. 14.1):

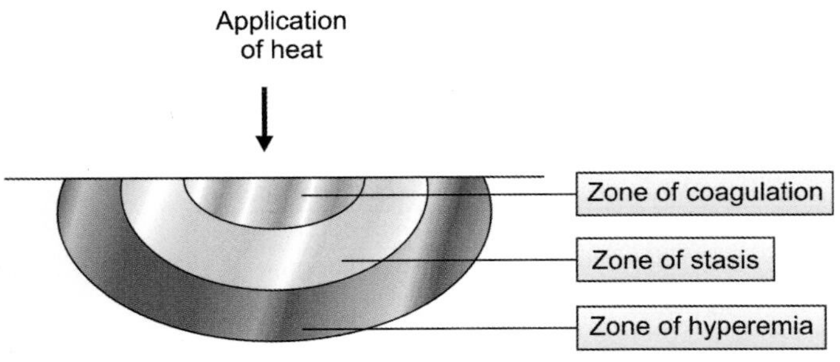

FIG. 14.1: Different zones identified in burns

- Zone of coagulation – this is the necrotic area of burn. The cells in this zone are irreversibly damaged by the injury.
- Zone of stasis – this zone has moderate degree of cellular insult with decreased tissue perfusion. The cells in this zone may survive or go on to coagulative necrosis depending on the severity of causative agent and body environment. This zone is also associated with vascular damage and vessel leakage.
- Zone of hyperemia – this zone is characterized by vasodilatation from the inflammation. This zone contains viable tissue from which healing process begins.

DRY HEAT BURNS

Classification of Burns

Burns have been classified by the American Burn Association and the American College of Surgeon's committee on trauma as.[13]

1. Minor – superficial burns of less than 15 percent total body surface area (TBSA).
2. Moderate – are defined as
   - Superficial burns of 15 to 25 percent TBSA in adults or
   - 10 to 20 percent TBSA in children or
   - Full thickness burns of less than 10 percent TBSA and burns not involving eyes, ears, face, hands, feet or perineum.
3. Major burns – above plus most full thickness burns in infants and elderly patient.

Estimation of Depth of Burn

Estimation of depth of burn constitutes degree of burns and denotes the depth and extent of injury caused to skin and underlying structures. When heat is applied to skin, the depth of injury depends on:

1. Temperature applied
2. Duration of contact
3. Thickness of skin
4. Heat-dissipating capacity of the skin (blood flow).

Burn depth estimation is done by various means such as:

1. Clinical assessment – it is naked eye examination
2. Biopsy and microscopy[14]
3. Vital dyes[15]
4. Ultrasound
5. Fluorescent fluorometry[16]
6. Laser Doppler flowmetry
7. Thermography[17, 18]
8. Light reflectance method[19]
9. MRI scan
10. Radioactive isotopes.[20]

Clinical Assessment

Burn depth estimation (degrees of burn) is done by naked eye examination and evaluation of burn depth area. Following are the different classification used to assess the depth of burns.

Dupytren's Classification[10]

Dupytren had classified burns into six degrees as (Fig. 14.2):

- First degree – it is superficial burn involving only epidermis with low degree of heat for small or short period of time. It is characterized by appearance of erythema over area of contact and reddening of skin.
- Second degree – burns are limited to epidermis. There may be blister formation with hyperemia and singeing of hairs. The lesion is painful.
- Third degree – burns limited to part of thickness of dermis (epidermis is destroyed completely). There is blister formation with hyperemia and singeing of hairs. The lesion is painful and heal by scar formation.
- Fourth degree – burns involves dermis (it is whole skin thickness burn). The lesion is painful and heal by scar formation.
- Fifth degree – burn depth extend to subcutaneous (hypodermis) tissue. The lesion is less painful due to destruction of nerves and heals with deep scarring and may cause contracture.
- Sixth degree – burn lesion extends deeper to involve muscles and bones. The lesion heals by deep scarring and causes contracture.

Advantage of Dupytren's Classification

- It is more precise
- Give details of the injury.

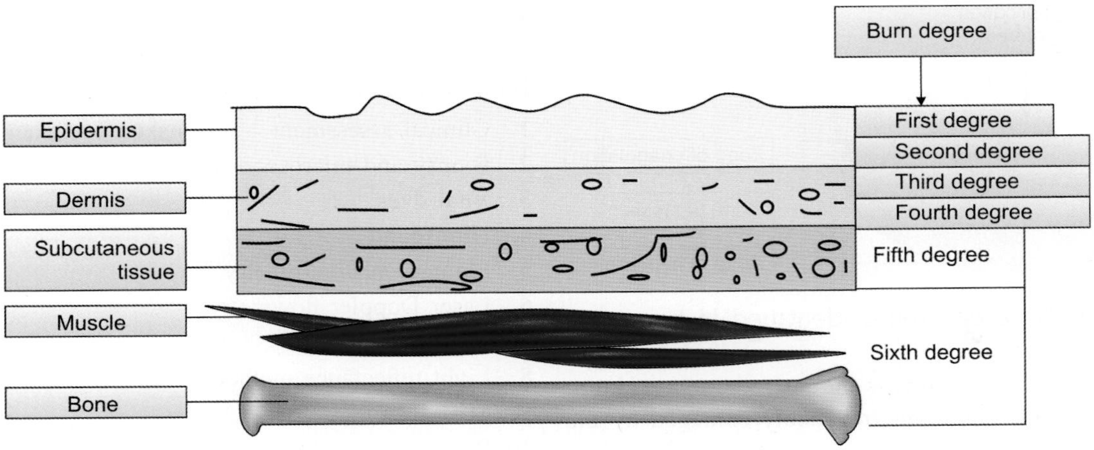

FIG. 14.2: Dupytren's classification of burns

Disadvantage of Dupytren's Classification

- Limited value in practice due to exhaustive details
- Subjective variation.

Wilson's Classification

To overcome the tedious Dupytren's classification, a more practical classification was proposed by Wilson. Wilson had divided the burns into three degree. Wilson had merged every two-degree of Dupytren into one (Fig. 14.3).

- First degree—epidermal burns—it includes first and second degree of Dupytren's classification. There is reddening of skin and erythema. Blisters may form and lesion may be painful. It heals without scar formation.
- Second degree—dermo-epidermal burns—it includes third and fourth degree of Dupytren's classification. The lesion is painful and characterized by blister formation or charring and destruction of full thickness of skin. The burns are painful and heal by permanent scar.
- Third degree—deep burns—it includes fifth and sixth degree of Dupytren's classification. The burns are less painful due to nerve destruction. There is charring and destruction of tissues beneath the skin as fat, muscle or bone. These burns heal by deep scar formation, contracture, disfigurement and leads to impairment or loss of function of affected part.

Advantages of Wilson's Classification

- More convenient
- Practical
- Easy to apply.

Modern Classification

This is easier and gross classification, dividing the burns into two degrees namely superficial and deep burns (Fig. 14.4)

- Superficial burns – it is dermo-epidermal burn injuries and here burns do not extend the full thickness of skin.

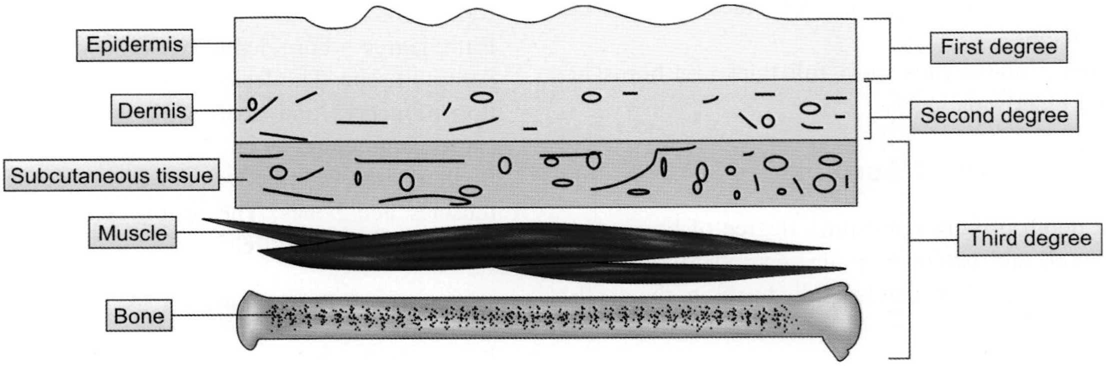

FIG. 14.3: Wilson's classification of burns

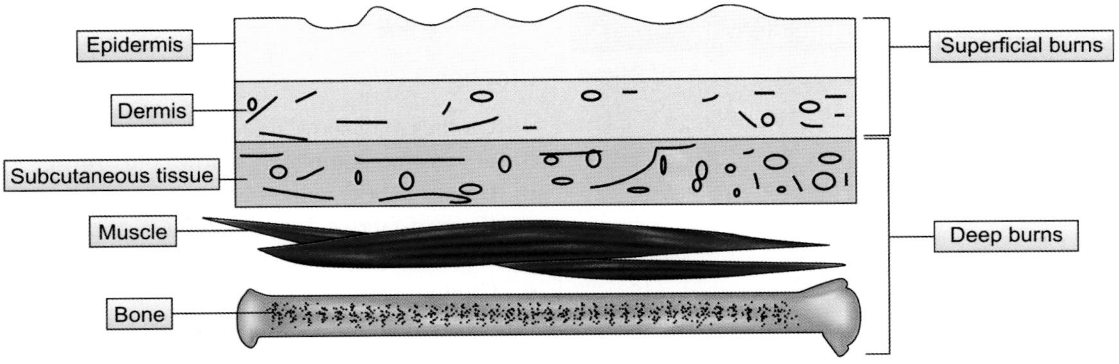

FIG. 14.4: Modern classification

- Deep burns – here the burn lesion involves deeper structures beneath the skin. Any burns involving more than true skin are grouped in this category.

Estimation of Extent of Burn (Surface Area)

The estimation of extent of burns is done to note the involvement of total body surface area (TBSA). For estimating the surface area or assessing the percentage of burns following methods are used.

1. Wallace rule of nine – the estimation of burn surface area in adult is usually carried out by "Wallace Rule of Nine". Table 14.2 summarizes the calculation of involved body surface area (Fig. 14.5).
2. Lund and Browder charting[21] – this charting is usually used in children because children under 4 years of age have much larger heads and smaller lower limbs in proportion to body size than do adults. In infants, the head accounts for nearly 20% of TBSA than adults (Fig. 14.6). Table 14.3 summarizes the calculation of involved body surface area by Lund and Browder method.
3. Clinical method – this is clinical method used to access the small burn areas. For estimation of small burns, the patient's hand can be used as a parameter. The palm of patient account for 1 percent of burn surface.

Cause of Death

Immediate

1. Neurogenic shock
2. Hypovolemic shock

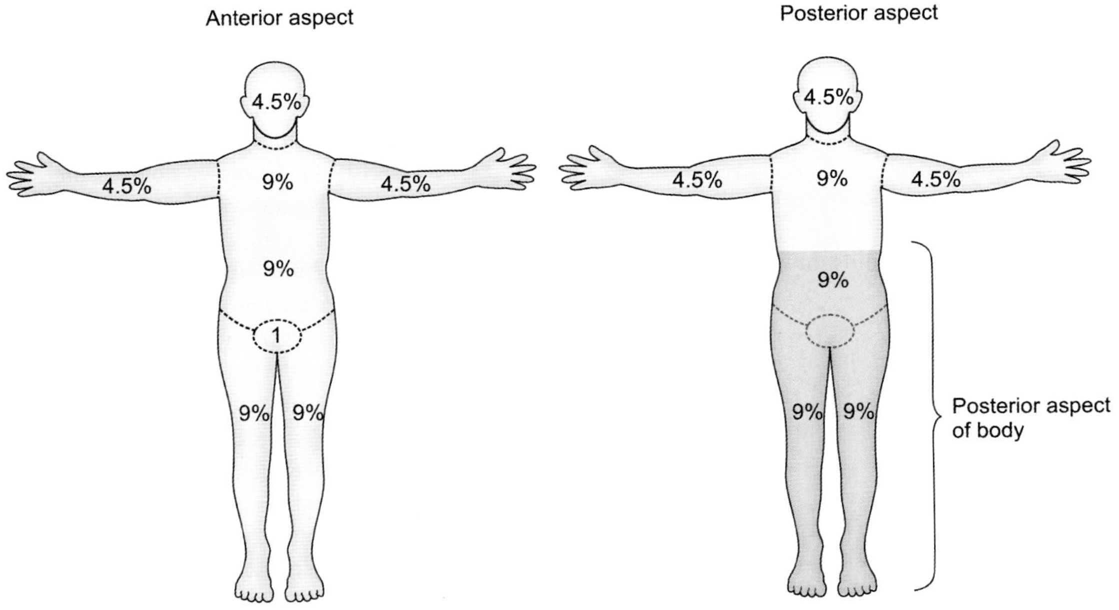

FIG. 14.5: Estimation of burn surface area in adult by Wallace Rule of Nine

Table 14.2: Wallace rule of nine

Body part	*% of burns*
Head, neck and face - Face and neck – 4.5% - Scalp – 4.5%	9
Anterior trunk - Chest – 9% - Abdomen – 9%	18
Posterior trunk - Upper back – 9% - Lower back* – 9%	18
Right upper limb# - Anterior arm, forearm and hand – 4.5% - Posterior arm, forearm and hand – 4.5%	9
Left upper limb# - Anterior arm, forearm and hand – 4.5% - Posterior arm, forearm and hand – 4.5%	9
Right lower limb† - Anterior thigh, leg and foot – 9% - Posterior thigh, leg and foot – 9%	18
Left lower limb† - Anterior thigh, leg and foot – 9% - Posterior thigh, leg and foot – 9%	18
Genitals	1

* Includes buttock
# Includes deltoid
† Includes inferior gluteal fold

3. Inhalation of smoke
4. Inhalation of carbon monoxide
5. Laryngeal edema/edema of glottis due to inhalational burns
6. Injuries sustained while escaping or falling of masonry/ buildings etc.

Delayed

1. Septicaemic shock
2. Toxemia
3. Renal failure
4. Pulmonary embolism (rare)
5. Fat embolism (rare)
6. ARDS.

Autopsy Findings

Clothes

- Clothes may show singeing of fibers or melting of clothes or may be completely burnt (Fig. 14.7).
- Cotton fabric ignites easily and burns faster than other types of fabrics. However, nylon or polyester fabric melts and sticks to body.
- Clothes should examined for presence of any inflammable material such as kerosene, petrol etc.

External Examination

- There may be the blackening of body due to deposition of soot. If inflammable material like kerosene is used, then burns area may show more deposition of soot.
- Due to application of heat, muscles may get contracted and stiffened (**heat stiffening or heat rigor**). It is due to coagulation and denaturation of muscle proteins. Due to this, the body occupies a peculiar posture with generalized flexion of the trunk, upper limbs and lower limbs. The upper limbs are flexed in such a pattern with the fingers appear curled inwards similar to the attitude or pose of a boxer (**pugilist**). Thus such appearance of body is called as **boxer's attitude or fencer's attitude or pugilistic attitude** (Figs 14.8 and 14.9). Such posture may be seen in antemortem as well as in postmortem burns (in other words, presence of pugilistic attitude do not differentiate whether the burns are antemortem or postmortem in nature). Contraction of the paraspinal muscles often causes a marked **opisthotonos**.
- The postmortem staining may be bright if carbon monoxide has been inhaled. Presence of such feature suggests antemortem nature of burn.
- Hairs are either singed or completely burnt away (Figs 14.10 and 14.11). In lesser degree, the singeing pattern may be obvious and ends appear to be clubbed. The keratin at hair end melts with the heat and solidifies on cooling. Scalp hairs, eyebrows, eyelashes, body hairs, axillary hairs and even pubic hairs may be affected.
- Burns may vary from mere reddening to charring. However usually, dermo-epidermal burns are much commoner. These burns present with formation of multiple blisters. These blisters contain serous fluid rich in protein and chloride. When denuded, these blisters have red base with an erythematous areola (Figs 14.12 and 14.13).
- When skin is ignited, the subcutaneous fat acts as a fuel and produce damage to deeper part. In depth, the muscle beneath will appear partly cooked or cooked and coagulated (Figs 14.14 and 14.15).

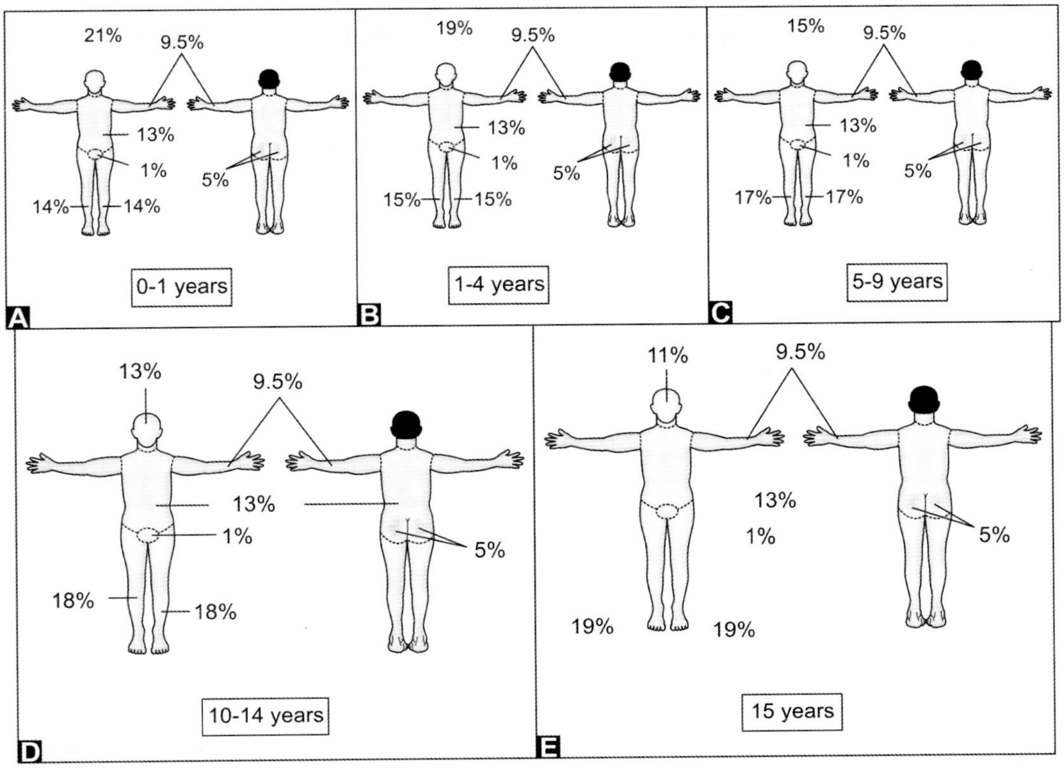

FIGS 14.6A to E: Estimation of burn surface area in children. **A:** 0 to 1 year, **B:** 1 to 4 years, **C:** 5 to 9 years, **D:** 10 to 14 years, **E:** 15 years

- In severe burns or sustained application of heat, the muscle or even bone may be charred (Figs 14.16 to 14.18).
- Heat ruptures may be evident over body and may be confused with antemortem incised wounds. Due to continued application of heat, the skin gets contracted and splits. Such splitting of skin appears as lacerated or incised wounds (Figs 14.19 and 14.20). The splits may occur anywhere but more commonly occurs over extensor surface or elbows or knees joint or other joints or head. These splits should not be confused with incised or lacerated wounds. Presence of these splits on particular location will differentiate from mechanical injuries. In such heat ruptures or splits, no bleeding or formation of blood clot will be noted. There will be no extravasation of blood in the space or in surrounding tissues. There will be presence of intact blood vessel or nerve stretching across the floor of the split. Seeking such difference will eliminate the confusion between splits and lacerated or incised wound. Similarly presence of such splits wound does not indicate antemortem or postmortem nature of burns.
- If death occurs some days after the incident, there will be presence of pus and necrosis in the burn areas. There may be ulceration and sloughing of tissue (Figs 14.21 to 14.23).

Internal Findings

- Blood may be bright if death is associated with carbon monoxide inhalation. Presence of carbon monoxide in blood (> 5% saturation of the blood with carboxyhemoglobin) is valuable indicator that person was alive when the fire began and suggests antemortem nature of burns.
- It was also noted that if substances such as lacquered wood have been burnt (containing cyanide) or plastic (contains thiocyanate), the fire victims could have high levels of cyanide in their blood. In estimating cyanide, it is important that fresh blood sample should be analyzed (with fluoride as preservative) because cyanide may be produce in blood if stored for prolonged period.[10] Similarly cyanide may be produced in postmortem period in body due to decomposition.[22, 23] Therefore caution should be employed while interpreting cyanide in blood but levels > 0.3 percent can be attributed to active inhalation by victim when he caught fire.[24]

Table 14.3: Lund and Browder charting

Area	Birth – 1 year (%)	1 – 4 year(%)	5 – 9 year(%)	10 – 14 year (%)	15 year (%)	Adult (%)
Head and Face	19	17	13	11	9	7
Neck	2	2	2	2	2	2
Anterior trunk	13	13	13	13	13	13
Posterior trunk	13	13	13	13	13	13
Right buttock	2.5	2.5	2.5	2.5	2.5	2.5
Left buttock	2.5	2.5	2.5	2.5	2.5	2.5
Genitals	1	1	1	1	1	1
Right upper limb	9.5	9.5	9.5	9.5	9.5	9.5
Left upper limb	9.5	9.5	9.5	9.5	9.5	9.5
Right lower limb	14	15	17	18	19	20
Left lower limb	14	15	17	18	19	20

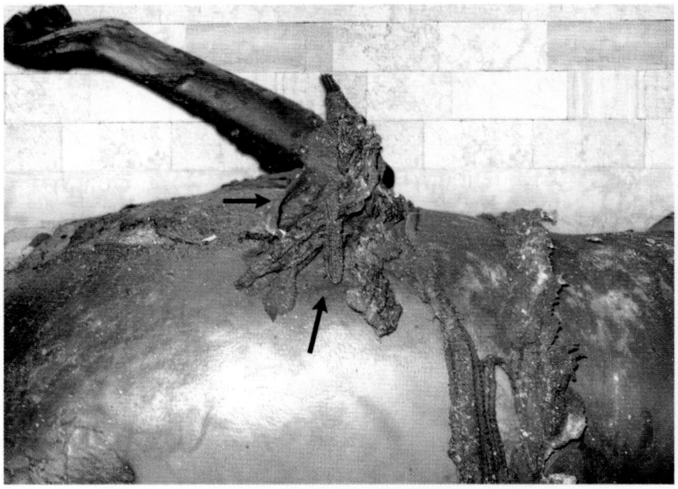

FIG. 14.7: Burnt clothes (black arrow)

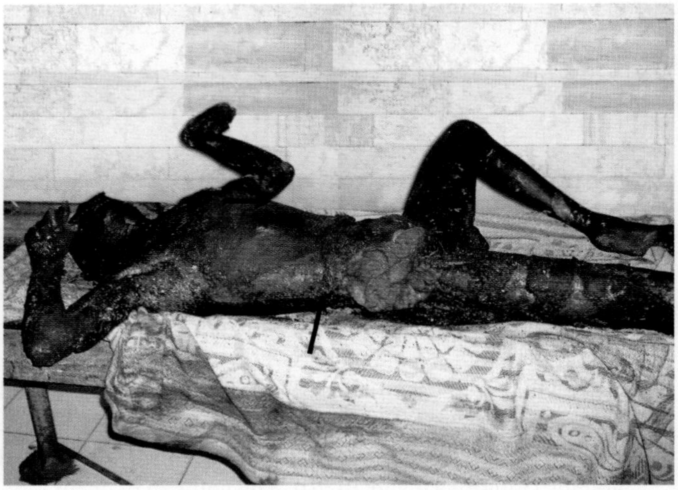

FIG. 14.8: Pugilistic attitude

- Internal organs are congested or may show partly cooked or cooked appearance, or coagulated, firm and pallid (Fig. 14.24).
- Soot particles or carbon particles may be seen in the respiratory passage due to smoke inhalation. Presence of such soot particles in the lower respiratory tract (below the vocal cords) indicates person was breathing during the fire and suggests antemortem nature of burns (Fig. 14.25). Histological demonstration of soot in the more peripheral bronchi far as terminal bronchioles is an absolute proof of respiratory effort during fire.[3] The carbon or soot is usually mixed with mucus of respiratory tract and adherent to the tracheal and bronchial mucosa. Similarly there may be evidence of swallowed soot with soot particles in oesophagus and stomach and at times the stomach contents may be soot stained or mixed. Again such finding is of importance because it suggests the act of swallowing that in turn proposes antemortem state of burns.
- Evidence of inhalational burns may be evident with burns and edema of oral cavity, tongue or glottis, or larynx.
- Bones may show **heat fracture** or **thermal fracture**. The heat fracture may be of following types as:
  - Bursting type – here the increased intracranial pressure due to steam pressure in skull causes separation of ununited sutures or bursts the skull causing gaping defect and widely separated margins (Figs 14.26 and 14.27).

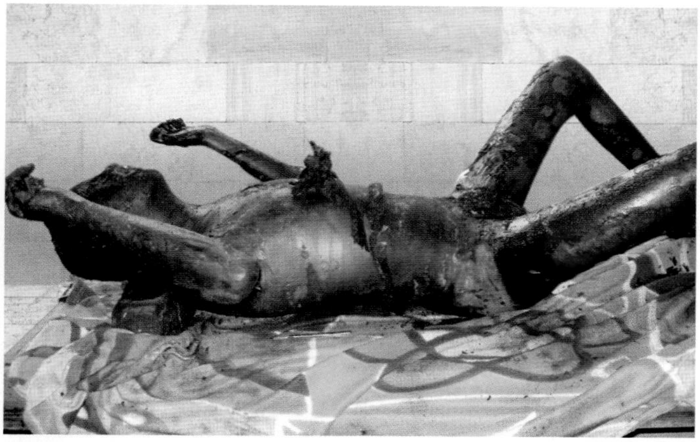

FIG. 14.9: Pugilistic attitude

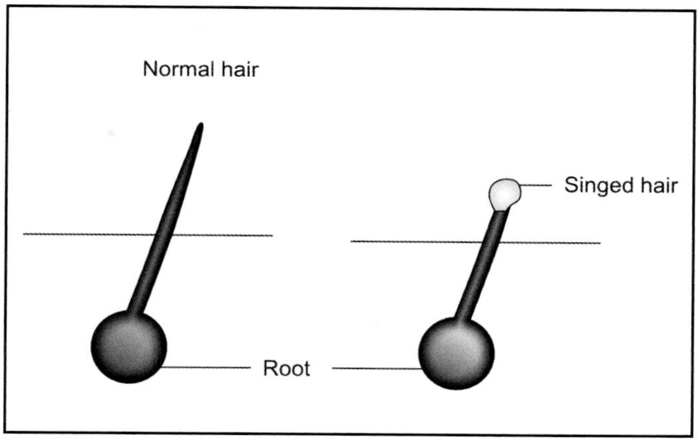

FIG. 14.10: Showing normal and singed hair

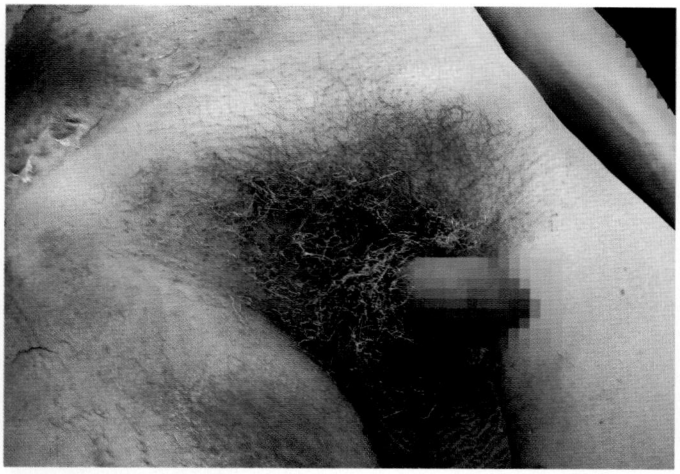

FIG. 14.11: Singeing of pubic hairs

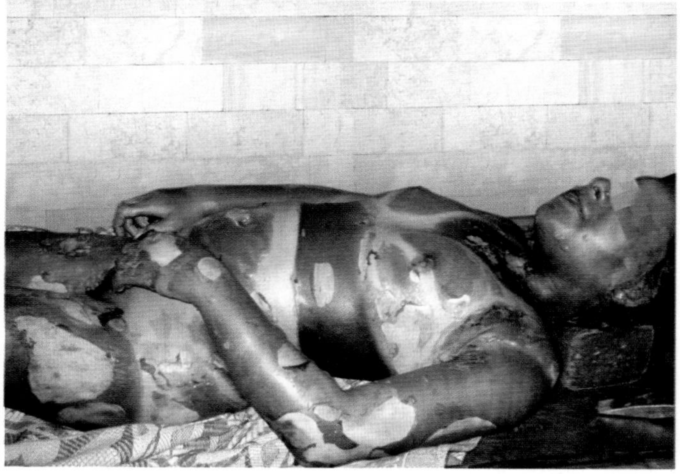

FIG. 14.12: Fresh burns

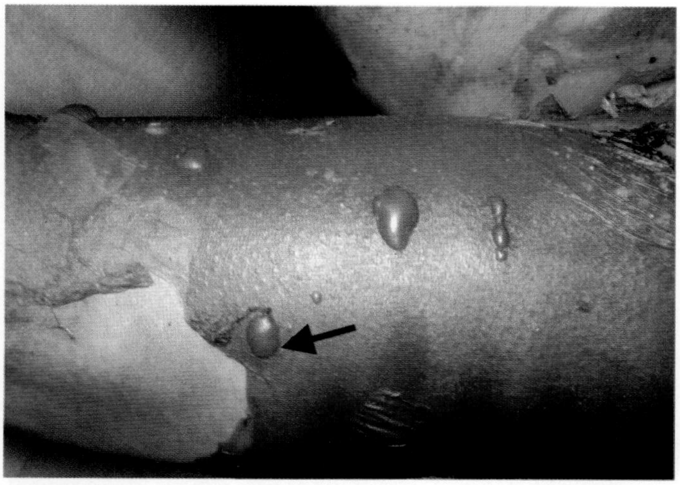

FIG. 14.13: Showing blister formation (black arrow) and peeling of skin

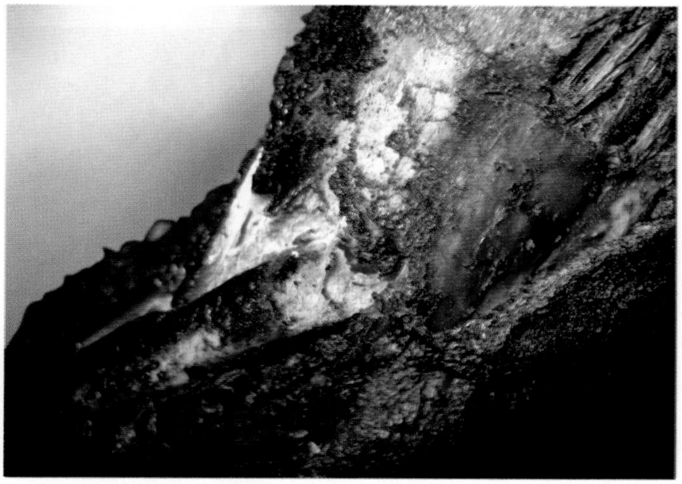

FIG. 14.14: Burns of deeper tissue

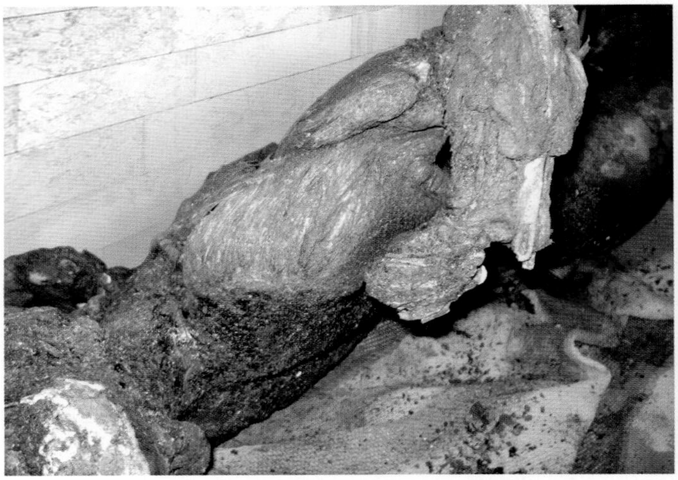

FIG. 14.15: Cooked muscles

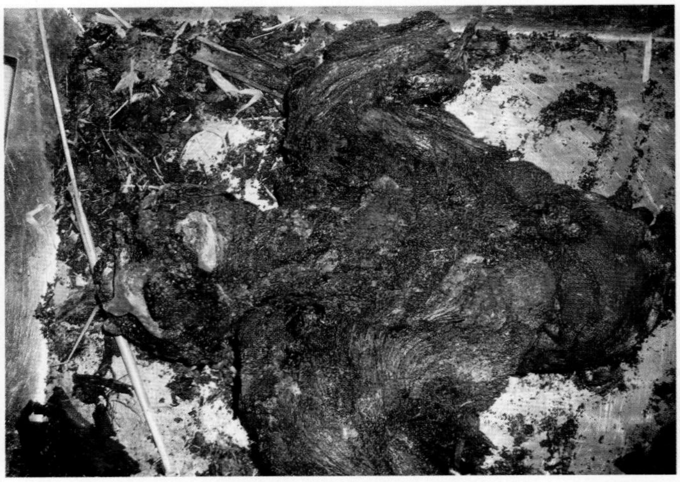

FIG. 14.16: Charring due to burns

FIG. 14.17: Charring due to burns

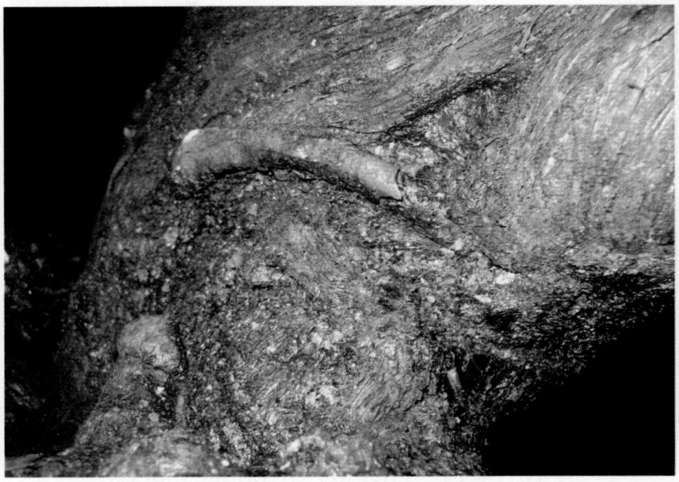

FIG 14.18: Charring of bone (note clavicle)

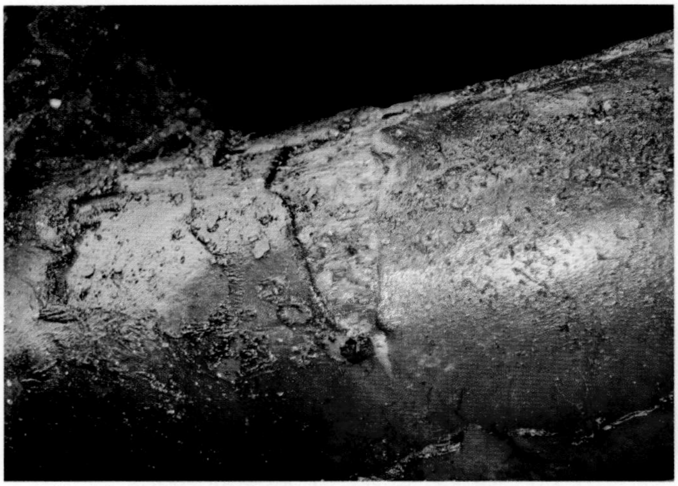

FIG. 14.19: Split due to burn

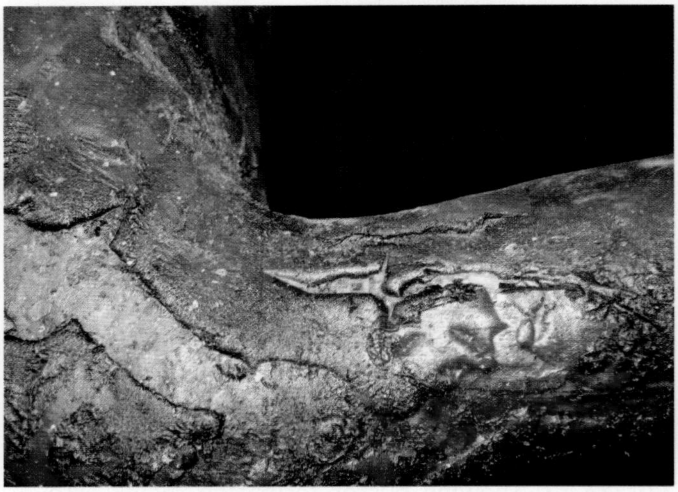

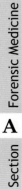

FIG. 14.20: Split due to burn

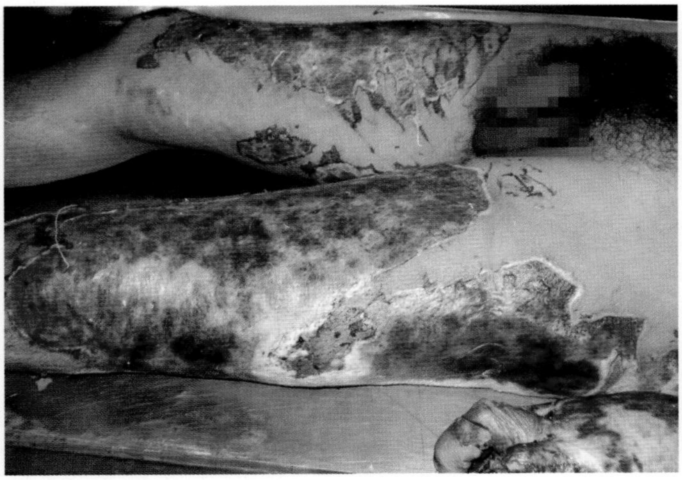

FIG. 14.21: Burns with infection

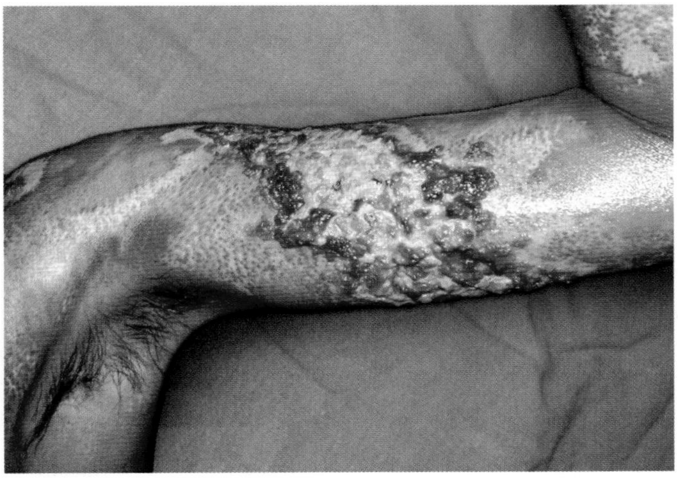

FIG. 14.22: Burns with infection

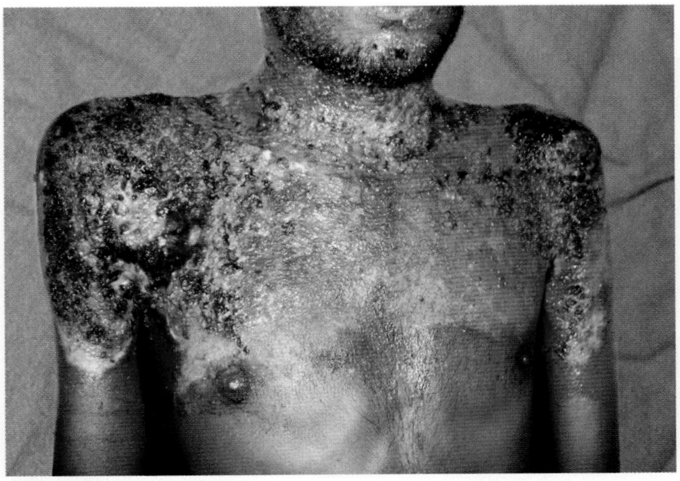

FIG. 14.23: Burns with infection

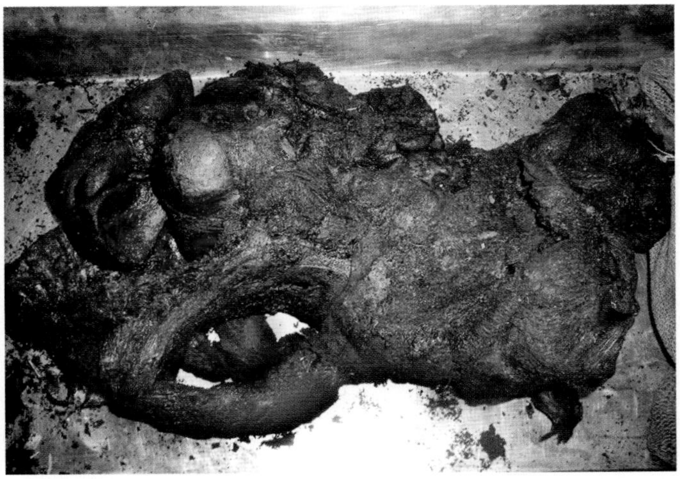

FIG. 14.24: Cooked internal organs

  - Surface fracture — here the fracture occurs due to drying of the bone with contraction and involves only outer table of the skull. Since it involves only outer table, no displacement of fracture occurs and fracture lines are frequently stellate.
  - Curved fractures — these are peculiar curved fractures often seen in bones of extremities exposed to high temperature (Figs 14.28 and 14.29).
- Heat hematoma
  - This occurs in head if the victim has been sustained to intense heat for longer duration.
  - This heat hematoma appears in extradural space and has resemblance with true extradural hematoma. True extradural hematoma is usually caused due to mechanical trauma and fracture where as this heat hematoma is not accompanied by mechanical trauma.
  - This heat hematoma may arise either from venous sinuses or may be emitted out of the Diploic space of the skull through emissary venous channels (Fig. 14.30).
  - The clot is soft, spongy from gas bubbles, friable and has honeycomb appearance. The heat hematoma is usually tawny or chocolate brown in colour. If carbon monoxide is present then it may be of bright color.
  - Presence of carbon monoxide in the heat hematoma serves to confirm the conclusion that the hemorrhage is a heat artefact and not a fatal injury occurring before the fire.[10]
  - The exterior of skull overlying the heat hematoma is frequently charred with burnt scalp.
  - The parieto-temporal region is common site of occurrence of heat hematoma.

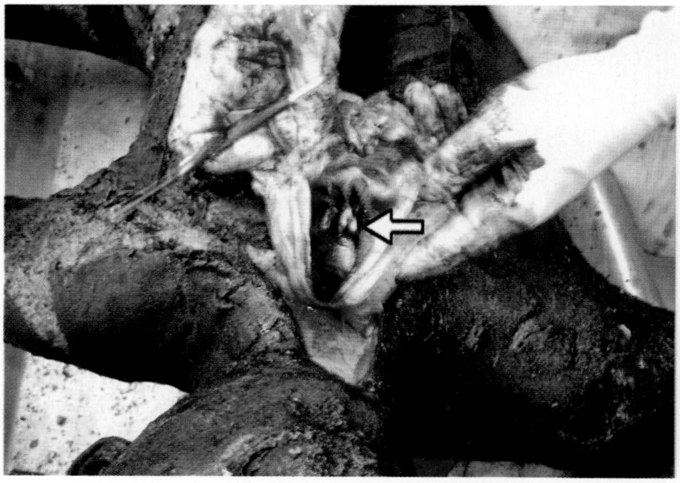

FIG. 14.25: Soot particles in respiratory passage (white arrow)

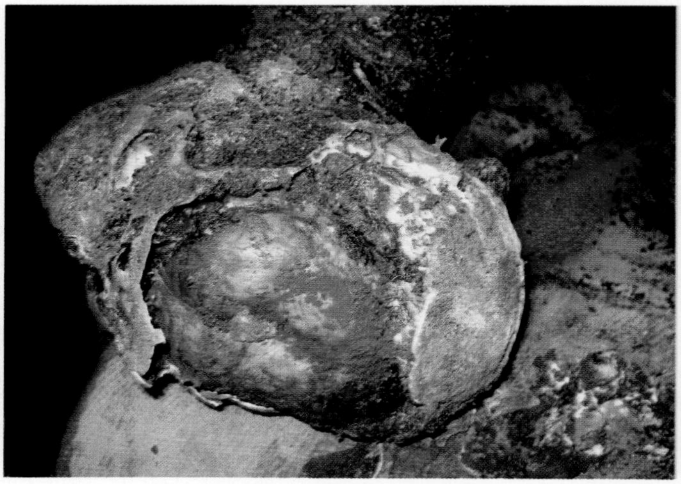

FIG. 14.26: Burst fracture

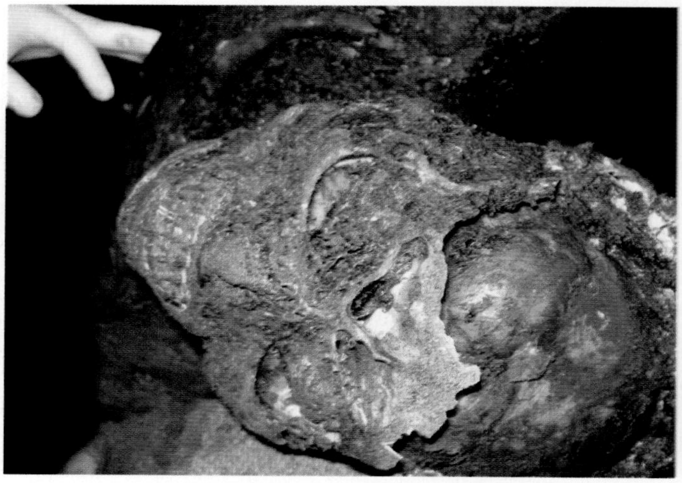

FIG. 14.27: Burst fracture (Note frontal sinuses are also exposed)

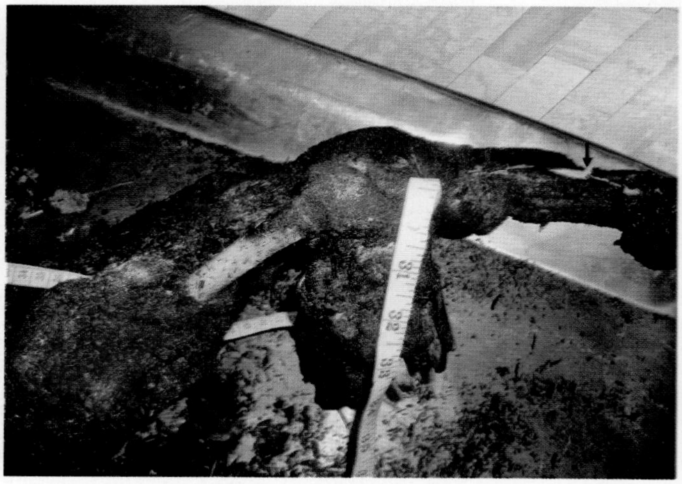

FIG. 14.28: Heat fracture (black arrow)

- Curling's ulcer may be noted in the stomach and/or duodenum.

Medicolegal Importance

1. Identity of deceased – if burns involve face with charring, may create problem in identity of victim
2. Whether the burns are antemortem or postmortem?
3. What is the time of sustaining burn injuries?
4. What is cause of death?
5. Whether the antemortem burns were sufficient to cause death?
6. Whether the burns are suicidal, homicidal or accidental?
7. Bride burns and dowry death.

Antemortem and Postmortem Burns

The features differentiating antemortem burns from postmortem burns are presented in Table 14.4.

Age of Burns

The aging of burns depends on the extent and depth of burns and causative agent, period of application, presence of infection, age, associated debility and heat dissipating capacity of skin. The rough guide for age estimation of burns is presented in Table 14.5.

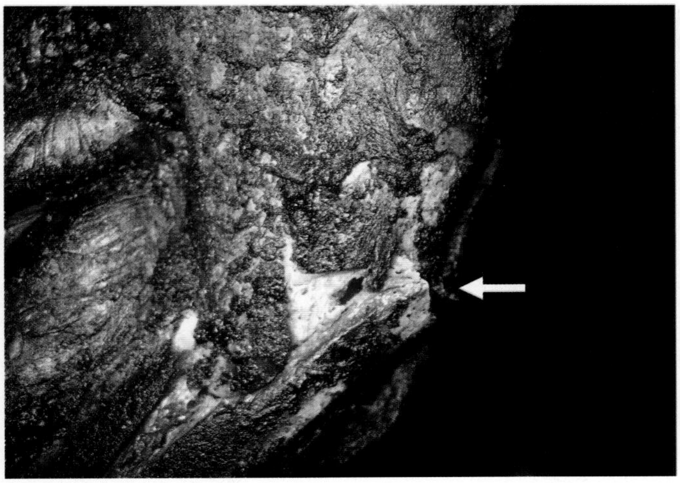

FIG. 14.29: Heat fracture (white arrow)

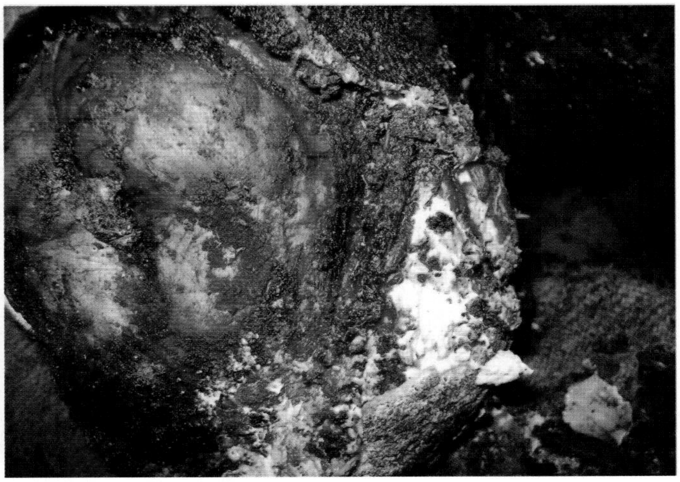

FIG. 14.30: Heat hematoma

Bride Burns and Dowry Deaths

Bride burns and dowry deaths are not uncommon in India. A daughter-in-law is subjected to burns by her husband or in-laws at the stake of dowry or else forced to commit suicide. It was estimated that about 30.92% homicidal burnings of married women in the in-laws house occurred whereas 21.05% victims committed suicide by burning themselves.[25,26] The figures are the testament of the growing menace of the problem. Following are the legal provisions that dealt with these incidents. The new "the protection of women from Domestic Violence Act 2005" has extended the definition of domestic violence and includes dowry demands.[27]

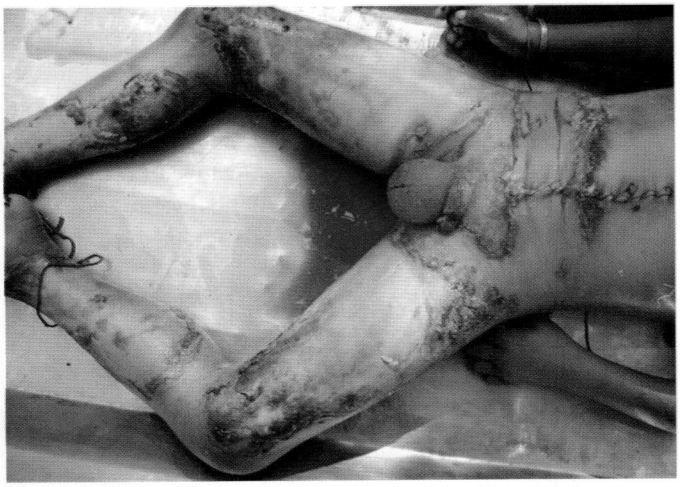

FIG 14.31: Scalds (*Courtesy*: Dr Manish Shrigiriwar, Associate Professor, Dept. of Forensic Medicine, IGGMC, Nagpur)

Section 304-B of IPC

1. Dowry death – where death of a woman is caused by any burn or bodily injury or occurs otherwise than under normal circumstances within seven years of her marriage, and it is shown that soon before her death she was subjected to cruelty or harassment by her husband or any relative of her husband for, or in connection with, any demand for dowry, such death shall be called 'dowry death' and such husband or relative shall be deemed to have cause her death.
2. Whoever commits dowry death shall be punished with imprisonment for a term, which shall not be less, then seven years but which may extend to imprisonment for life.

Section 498-A of IPC

Whoever, being the husband or the relative of the husband of a woman subjects her to cruelty, shall be punished with imprisonment for a term, which may extend to three years, and shall be liable to fine.

Explanation: for the purposes of this section, 'cruelty' means

1. Any willful conduct which is of such a nature as is likely to drive a woman to commit suicide or to cause grave injury or danger to her life, limb or health (whether mental or physical) or
2. Harassment of a woman where such harassment is with a view to coercing her or any person related to her, to meet any unlawful demand for any property or valuable security or on account of failure by her or any person related to her to meet such demand.

Table 14.4: Difference between antemortem and postmortem burns		
Features	***Antemortem burns***	***Postmortem burns***
Line of redness	Present around burn area	Absent
Blisters	Present and contains serous fluid rich in protein and chlorides. The base is red, inflamed with raised papilla	Usually absent and if present contains air and clear fluid. The base is dry, pale or yellow, hard and horny
Vital reaction	Present	Absent
Reparative process	Present	Absent
Infection	Present	Absent
Carbon/soot particles in respiratory passage	Present	Absent
Carboxyhemoglobin in blood	Present	Absent or low level
Cyanide in blood	Present	Absent or low level
Enzyme activity (Histochemistry)	Present and is time related - Cathepsin – immediate - Serotonin – 10 min - Histamine – 20 min - Esterase – 1 hour - ATPase – 1 hour - Acid phosphatase – 3 hr - Alkaline phosphatase – 4 hr	Absent

Table 14.5: Age of burn wounds	
Period	***Features***
Immediately to 1 hour	- Redness occurs - Vesication appears - Signs of inflammation - Blood vessels are dilated with oozing of fluid
6 – 12 hour	- Inflammatory reaction intensifies - Polymorphnuclear cell infiltration - Epidermis coagulated
12 – 24 hour	- Exudates begins to dry
24 – 72 hours	- Exudates forms dry, brown crust - Inflammatory zone begins to disappear - Slough and Pus formation begins
4 – 6 days	- Superficial slough fall off
Fortnight	- Deep slough separates out - Granulation tissue covers the surface
Weeks to months	Formation of cicatrix and deformity

Section 113-A of IEA: Presumption as to Abetment of Suicide by a Married Woman

When the question is whether the commission of suicide by a woman had been abetted by her husband or any relative of her husband and it is shown that she had committed suicide within a period of seven years from the date of her marriage and that her husband or such relative of her husband had subjected her to cruelty, the court may presume, having regard to all the other circumstances of the case, that such suicide had been abetted by her husband or by any relative of her husband.

Explanation: For the purposes of this section, 'cruelty' shall have the same meaning as in Section 498-A of the IPC.

Section 113-B of IEA: Presumption as to Dowry Death

When the question is whether a person has committed the dowry death of a woman and it is shown that soon before her death, such woman had been subjected by such person to cruelty or harassment for, or in connection with, any demand for dowry, the court shall presume that such person had caused the dowry death.

Explanation: For the purposes of this section, 'dowry death' shall have the same meaning as in Section 304-B of the IPC.

SCALDS

Scald injuries are the tissue damage caused from application of moist heat. Usually water is common causative agent however, other culprits being oil, molten rubber, liquid chemicals, tar, molten metals etc. Application of liquid to the body at or near its boiling point or in its gaseous form (steam) will cause the scalds. Application of water of 50°C at vulnerable part will cause scald.[28, 29]

Classification

Scalds are classified into three degrees as:[30]

- First degree – characterized by erythema formation of affected part
- Second degree – characterized by blister formation with increased vascular permeability
- Third degree – characterized by drying and desiccation of underlying tissue with necrosis.

Features (Figs 14.31 to 14.33)

- Scalds do not cause charring, carbonization or singeing of surface hairs.
- Shape of scalds may vary but have sharply demarcating edge, corresponding to the limits of contact of the fluid or water.
- When hot water is splashed, the water or fluid runs under due to gravity causing **trickle pattern**. If hands are immersed in hot water such as bucket, a horizontal level may be made by hot water (Fig 14.34). When water is poured or splashed over body, the area of initial contact will suffer greater damage but decreases in severity as the cooling of water or liquid runs away over lower body parts.
- Occasionally the steam may be inhaled and causes scalding of oral cavity, nasal mucosa, epiglottis and larynx.
- The wearing apparel or clothes may either minimize the damage caused due to spurting of water or may cause more damage if it holds water or liquid as may causes contact with skin for a longer period. Thus the clothes may act as double edge sword.

Differential Diagnosis

The scald has to be differentiated from

1. Dry burns (Table 14.6)
2. Toxic epidermal necrolysis[10]
3. Drug eruptions.

Cause of Death

- Shock
- Hypovolemic shock
- Electrolyte disturbances
- Secondary infection
- Asphyxia due to inhalation of moist steam.

Medicolegal Importance

1. Scalds are usually accidental injury often involved infants, toddlers or children.
2. Scalding may be intentional when someone with malicious intention throws hot water or liquid over someone else's body to cause injury/hurt and/or disfigurement.
3. It may be one pattern of battered baby syndrome.
4. Suicide is very rare; one case of suicidal scalding (cited in Polson et al in Essentials of Forensic Medicine Textbook) was reported by Donalies G (1942) where a person immersed himself in a soup cauldron after attempted suicide by hatchet blows.

INJURIES DUE TO ELECTRICITY

Electrical energy is obtained from chemical energy, mechanical energy or light energy. Electric burns constitute a unique type of thermal injuries. The tissue damage associated with an electric injury occurs when an electric energy is converted to thermal energy or heat.[31] Although the commercial use of electricity as a source of power began in 1849, accidental death from this origin was not reported[32] until 1879.

Sources

1. Domestic
2, Industrial/commercial/transport
3, Electricity distribution system
4. Lightning.

Elementary Physics

- When an electric charge is passing through a wire, we can say that an electric current is flowing through the wire
- An electric level is called as electric potential
- The unit of electric charge is called as coulomb (C)
- The unit of potential difference is called as volt (V)
- The unit of electric current is called as ampere (A)
- There is mathematical relationship between potential difference, current and resistance – the well-known

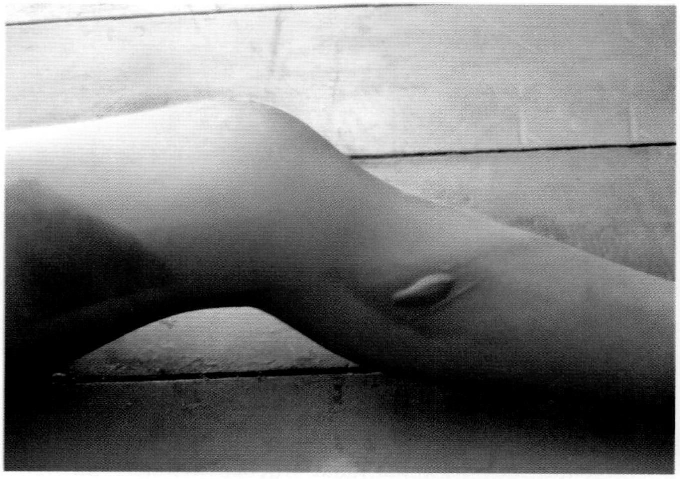

FIG. 14.32: Scald

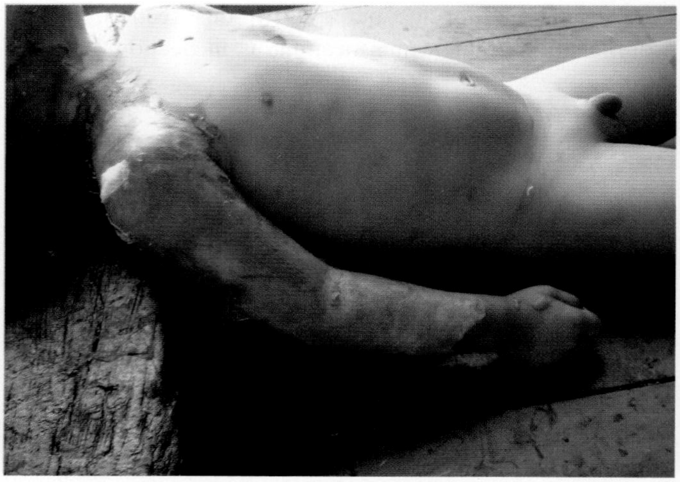

FIG. 14.33: Scalds

Table 14.6: Difference between scalds and burns

Features	*Scalds*	*Burns*
Cause	Moist heat	Dry heat
Clothes	Not burnt but may be wet	May show evidence of burns, singeing, melting of fibers
Site	Injury occurs at and below the site of application of causative agent	Injury occurs at and above the site of application of causative agent|
Skin	Erythema, blister, may be sodden and bleached	Reddening to Superficial burns to charring
Splashing	Present	Absent
Charring of skin	Absent	Present
Singeing of hairs	Absent	Present
Scar	Thin and less contracted	May be thick and contracted

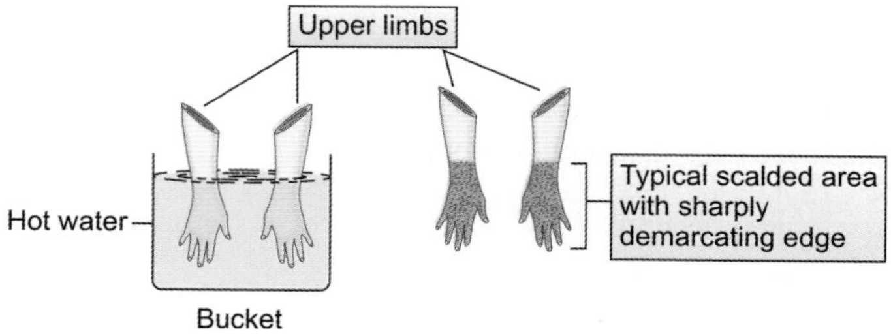

FIG. 14.34: Typical scalds in upper limbs

Ohm's law – in which the current varies directly with the voltage and inversely with the resistance. This law has considerable relevance to biological electrical damage.

Type of Current

There are two types of current namely:

1. Alternating current (AC)
2. Direct current (DC)
   - The direct current (DC) is less dangerous than alternate current (AC). A current of 50 to 80 mA of AC can be fatal in seconds whereas 250 mA DC for the same time is often appears non-fatal.
   - In DC the electricity flows constantly in the same direction whereas in AC, the flow occurs alternatively in the opposite direction
   - The usual frequency of AC is 50 cycles/sec (CPS). The AC between 40 to 150 cps is most dangerous. Ordinary household supply of current is around 50 cps and that of commercial supply is between 25 to 50 cps.

Very low or very high frequency of cycles, e.g. less than 10 cps or more than 100 cps, is harmless for body.

Mechanism of Electrocution

- In low or medium voltage current: The precise mechanism of electrocution is not known. It appears that ventricular fibrillation is an important factor in electrocution deaths by low or medium tension (voltage) current. Usually, deaths occur by ventricular fibrillation however, in some cases the death may be attributed to asphyxia or respiratory paralysis. The current passing through the chest may induce tetanic contraction of extrinsic muscles of respiration and thus causes mechanical asphyxia. If the head is in the circuit, then there may be paralysis of respiratory center or cardiac arrest due to inhibition of centers in brainstem. Prolonged ventricular fibrillation may cause ischemic brain insult and death.
- In high voltage current: Here the death is due to arching (flash-over) of electric current or due to ignition of clothes. Due to ignition of clothes, person may sustain burn injuries. Some victims may be thrown off from the site and sustains secondary injuries due to fall.

Cause of Death in Electrocution

1. Ventricular fibrillation
2. Tetanic asphyxia
3. Respiratory arrest
4. Cardiac arrest
5. Cerebral anoxia
6. Burns
7. Secondary injuries sustained.

Electrical Injuries

There are three types of electrical injuries noted depending on the nature of contact and strength of electric current as (Fig. 14.35):

1. Contact injury
2. Spark burns/injury
3. Flash burns.

Contact Injury

Contact injury is due to close contact with an electrically live object such as wire with domestic voltage (Fig. 14.35). The damage varies from a small and superficial injury or burn to charring depending up on the time of contact that is maintained with the object. A characteristic electrical injury may be present at the point of entry (**entry wound**) and may be at the point of exit (**exit wound**).

Spark Burn/Injury

Spark burn/injury is due to poor or intermittent contact with live electrical object/appliance/wire. Here resistance offered by tissue/skin is also important. The lesion caused by such intermittent contact may be a dry pitted area (often very tiny) or nodule due to arching of current from the conductor (wire/appliance/object) to the skin. A yellowish parchment like scab (keratin nodule) may be noted with a pale halo round the lesion. It is due to melted keratin that fuses on cooling (*vide infra*) (Fig. 14.35).

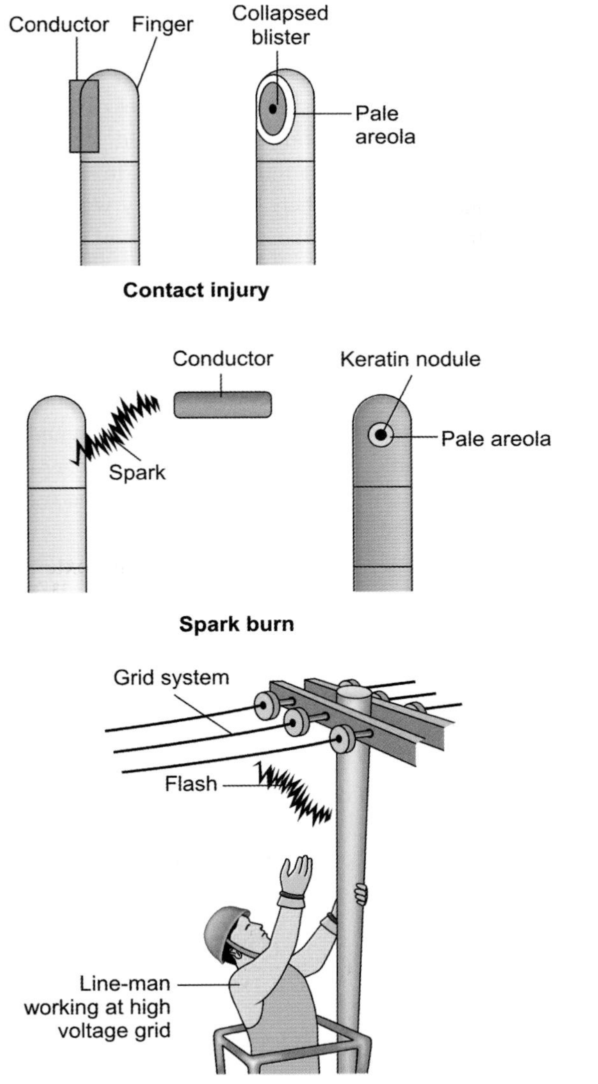

FIG. 14.35: Mechanism of causation of electrical injuries

Flash Burns

Flash burns are due to contact with very high voltage (high-tension wires) and usually seen in lines-man working on the grid system and not frequently in thieves stealing wires from these overhead lines. Here, there may be actual arching of the current occur on the man approaching towards wire without actual contact (Fig. 14.35). Sometimes, the heat may cause ignition of clothes and person sustains burn injuries.

Production of Cutaneous Electric Marks

- Contact of body part with electric device or wire may leave cutaneous lesion and are called as electrical marks (electrocution mark) or electrical burns. The point of contact acts as entry sites for current to travel in the body. In some persons, another mark may be observed. It is called as exit wound from which the current leaves. The exit point is the site where the body was 'earthed' or 'grounded' (Fig. 14.36). However, it must be borne in mind that not in each and every case there will be entry wound and exit wound. In some cases, the entry wound of electrocution may not be observed for example if person's hand is wet with water or electrocution occurring to a person in bath-tub. In such cases, no electrical marks may be observed because larger acting surface area and low resistance exhibited by skin due to getting wet. An electrical burn is self-limiting, once the current ceases no further skin and muscle damage is possible because amperage falls to zero. Tissue temperature is critical factor in determining the magnitude of tissue injury before the current ceases.[31]

An electrical mark may not be visible externally if applied at concealed part such as oral cavity,[33] anus or vagina.

When a current passes through body, the appearance of electric lesion depends on

1. The density of current passage in terms of skin area
2. The conductivity of skin and it usually varies according to moisture content of tissue

The skin lesion is a thermal burn resulting from heating of the epidermis and dermis as the current passes. Theoretically, the heat generated can be determined from the formula

$$GC = \frac{C2R}{4.187}$$

Where GC = heat in gram calories per second
C = current in ampere
R = resistance in ohms

If current passes through a wide area of body then the resistance per unit area is small and thus the heating effect

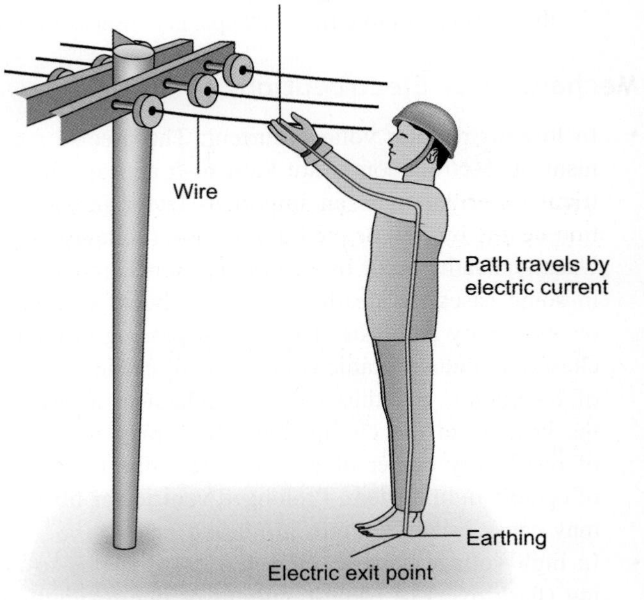

FIG. 14.36: Entry and exit of electric current

of current is proportionately less. The temperature in the tissues directly under the contact point of current can easily reach 95°C. Tissue damage can occur within 0.25 seconds when the temperature reaches a mere 50°C.

Lesion Produced by Electrocution

The various lesion produced by electrocution are as follows

1. **Collapsed blister**: When the skin is in firm contact with an electrical conductor (appliance/wire etc.), the passage of current through the skin causes production of heat due to resistance offered by the skin. Due to this the tissue fluid heats up and produce steam. The steam splits the layers of epidermis or the epidermo-dermal junction and produces a raised blister. The blister may rupture if current continues or may not rupture if contact is for short duration. When the current ceases, the blister cools and collapses giving the appearance of collapsed blister at autopsy. The collapsed blister is usually circular, producing a raised gray or white ring or margin with an umbilicated center (Figs 14.37 and 14.38).
2. **Spark lesion**: When the contact of skin and the electric conductor is not firm so that an air gap, albeit small, exists between skin and conductor, the current jumps the gap as a **spark**. In dry air, 1000 V will jump several millimeters and 100 KV about 35 cm. The high temperature

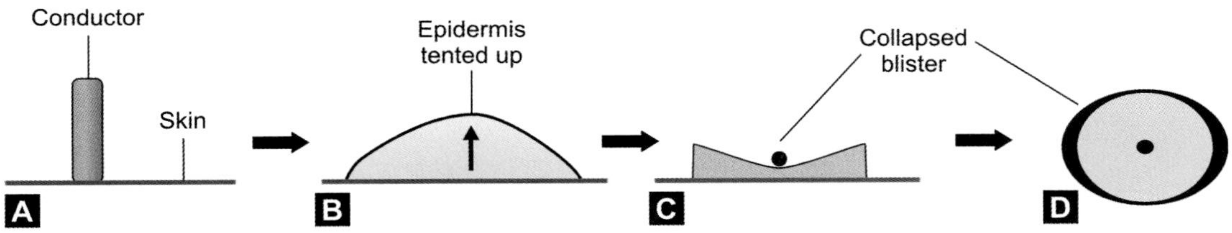

FIGS 14.37A to D: Mechanism of blister formation. **A:** Conductor is applied to skin, **B:** Passing current causes raised blister, **C:** After cooling, the blister collapse (profile view), **D:** Collapsed blister (superior view) with raised margin with umbilicated center

causes the outer skin keratin to melt over small area. On cooling, the keratin fuses into a hard brownish nodule, raised above the surrounding surface and usually surrounded by pale halo or areola. Such lesions are called as spark lesion (also see Fig. 14.35).

3. **Crater lesion**: In low or medium voltage current fatalities, the skin may exhibit a crater rather than blister. The crater is an electric mark, round or oval, shallow, bordered by a ridge of skin of about 1 to 3 mm high, around part or whole of the circumference of crater. It is tough on palpation. The crater floor is lined by pale flattened skin; the ridge pattern is usually preserved, but because of flattening, the ridges are broad and barely above the general level (Figs 14.39 and 14.40). If the skin is dry and hard like sole or palm then due to greater resistance offered by skin, there may be some cracking of skin evident. The skin of mark is usually pale but if heat produced is considerable, then floor may exhibit blackening. The crater may be surrounded by pale areola.
4. When the domestic current flows through skin for considerable time, there may be charring, blistering and peeling of skin (Figs 14.41 and 14.42).
5. **Crocodile skin**: In high-voltage current, sparking may occur over many millimeters or centimeters. The sparking may cause multiple focal burns or spark lesion resembling crocodile skin (Figs 14.43 and 14.44).

Features

- Appearance of an areola or pale halo around the electric mark is considered as more useful indicator for electrocution. It occurs at the periphery of electric lesion in form of blanched area. This halo occurs due to arteriolar spasm from direct effect of current on vessel wall musculature. The pallor survives death and can be noted at autopsy. It is considered as pathognomic of electrical damage.
- **Patterned electrical marks** – An electric conductor may leave its impression or pattern or shape on the skin. From the pattern of electrical injury, the causative appliance can be identified.
- **Exit marks** – These are noticed as grayish white circular spots, firm to touch and free from inflammatory reaction. The wound of exit may show splitting of skin in form of puncture or lacerated wounds instead of formation of craters or blisters as in entry wound. If the exit wound is on feet, the shoe may get torn and the sole of feet lacerated.
- Exogenous burns – These are flash burns.
- **Endogenous burns (Joule burns)** – The joule burns occur in contact injuries. When the contact with an electric conductor is for prolonged period, the skin acquires a biscuit or brownish colour and with further continued contact there may be even charring of skin. These burns are produced at the site of entry of current and are due to production of heat because of resistance offered by the skin – popularly called as Joule effect.[34] This burn is different from exogenous burns.
- Metallic traces in electrical marks (**metallization**) – When current is passing from a metal conductor, there occurs electrolysis due to which the metal ions are deposited in the skin and subcutaneous tissue at the point of entry. These metal ions combine with tissue anions and forms metal salts. The metallization, when gross may be visible to naked eye such as bright green imprint seen due to copper wire. They can also be detected by chemical, histological, histochemical or spectroscopic examinations.

Factors Influencing the Appearance of Electric Marks

The factors are:[35]

1. Nature of current – whether alternating or direct current (*vide supra*)
2. Voltage
3. Ampere
4. Resistance – Skin offers the maximum resistance to the flow of current than internal organs. The resistance offered by skin varies with its thickness and condition. Skin

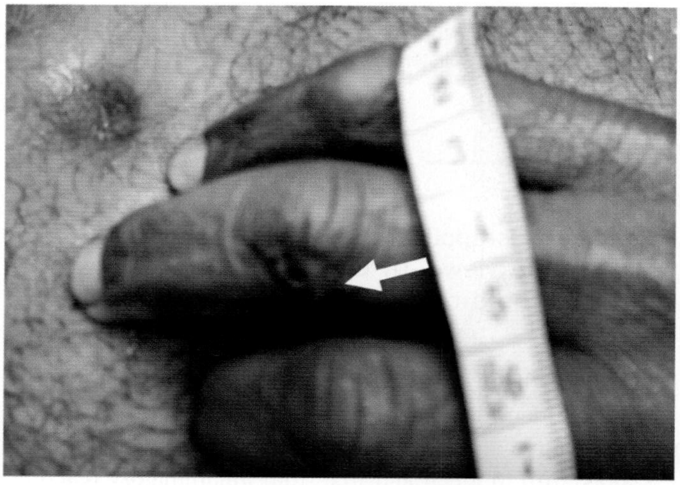

FIG. 14.38: Collapsed blister in electrocution (white arrow)

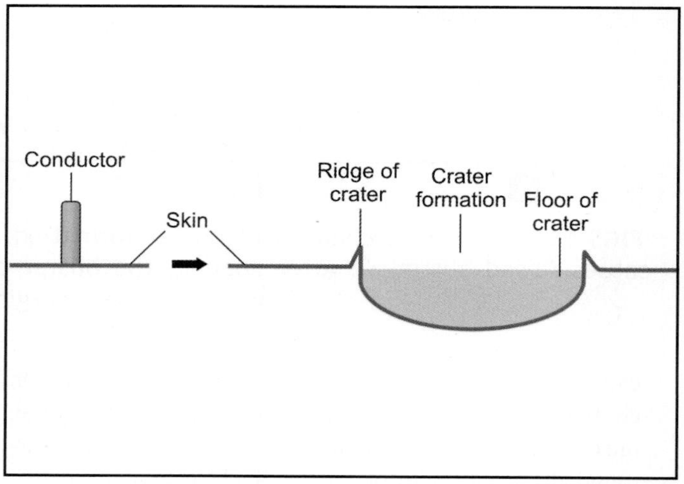

FIG. 14.39: Mechanism of crater formation

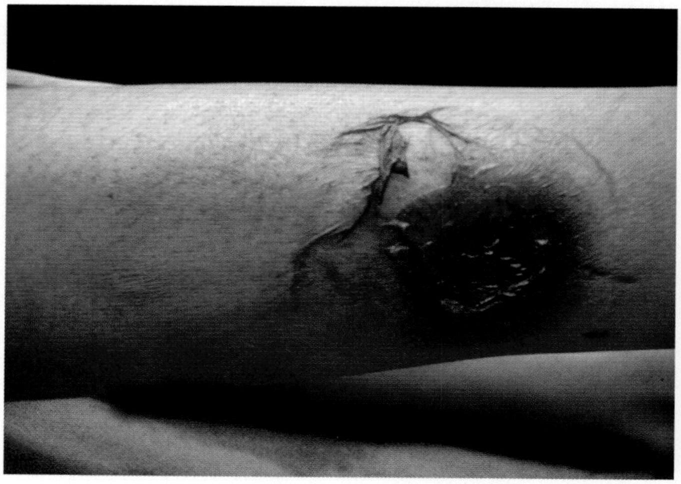

FIG. 14.40: Crater formation in contact electric injury (*Courtesy*: Dr Manish Shrigiriwar, Associate Professor, Dept. of Forensic Medicine, IGGMC, Nagpur)

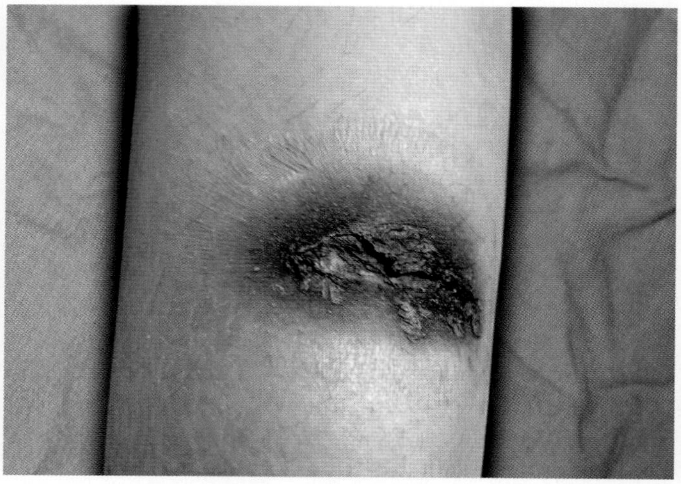

FIG. 14.41: Charring due to domestic supply

resistance is normally around 5000 ohms but is altered by the degree of moisture.[36] If wet with water, practically it offers no resistance whereas dry skin offers resistance. The resistance offered by keratin thick skin of sole and palm is more than thin skin elsewhere. Once inside the dermis, the semi-fluid cytoplasm and vascular system provide easy access to current without much resistance.
5. Earthing
6. Duration of current
7. Alertness of person
8. Area of contact
9. Point of entry.

Autopsy Findings

- Circumstances will reveal the live wire, the appliances, broken circuit etc. corroborative with electrocution
- External examination will reveal the electric marks discussed. If the death is associated in bathtub, no marks may be evident.
- There may be metallization of electrocution mark.
- Internal examination will reveal congested organs, pulmonary edema, and petechial hemorrhages over pericardium, pleura or brain.
- Laboratory findings:

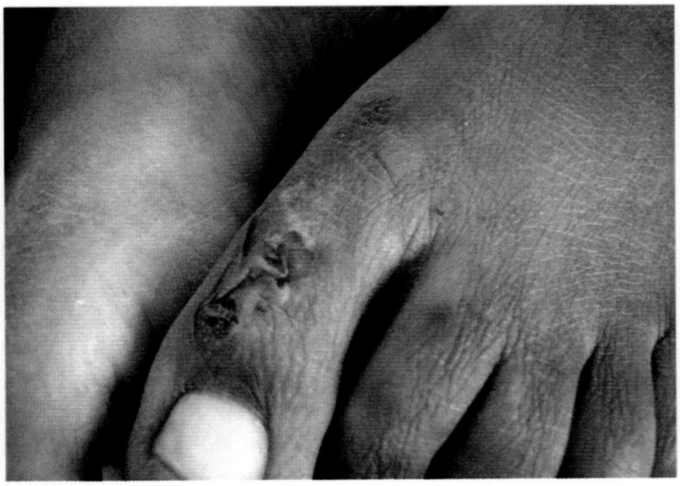

FIG. 14.42: Blistering and peeling at domestic supply

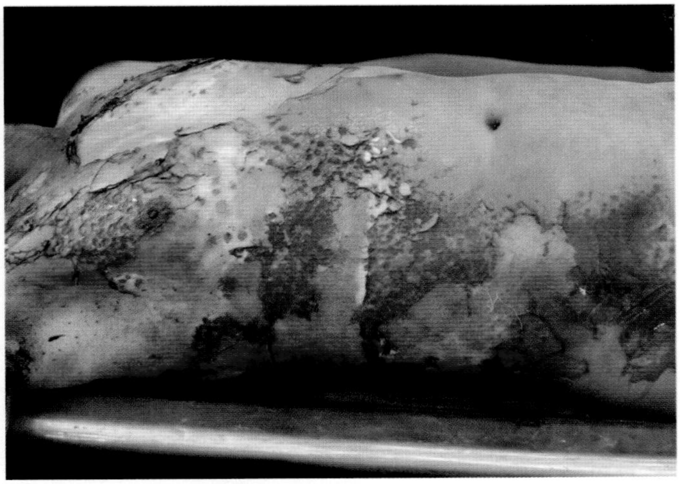

FIG. 14.43: Crocodile burns

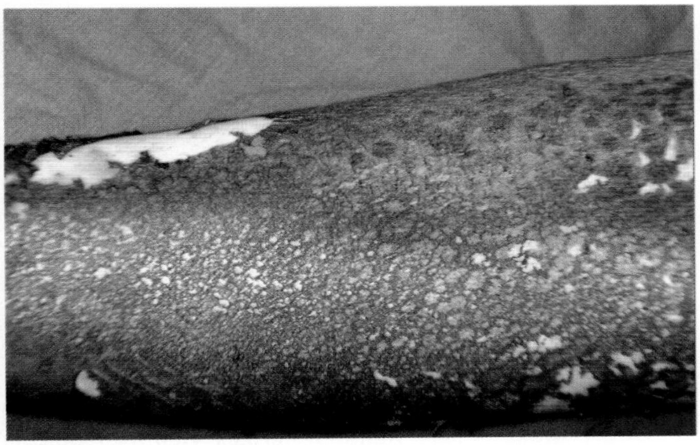

FIG. 14.44: Crocodile burns

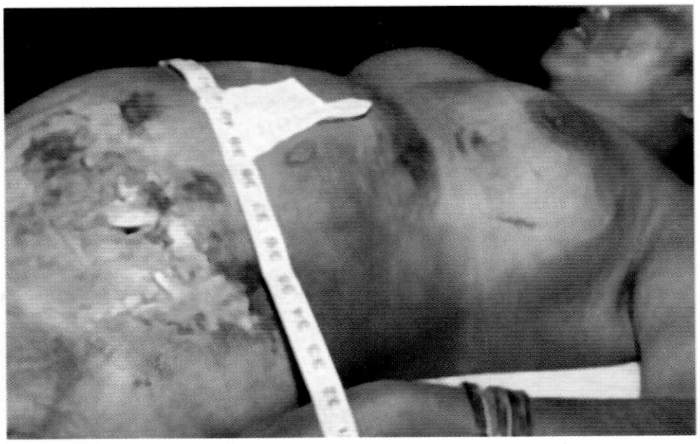

FIG. 14.45: Surface burns due to lightning (*Courtesy*: Dr Manish Shrigiriwar, Associate Professor, Dept. of Forensic Medicine, IGGMC, Nagpur)

1. Chemical analysis: Metal residue can be detected as discussed above.
2. **Acroreaction** test can be done to detect metal ions. It is a microchemical test devised by Skalos.[37] This test is not routinely done.
3. Histopathological examination may reveal supportive findings of electrocution. The major findings occurring in electric marks[38] are summarized in Table 14.7.
4. Electron microscopy.[39]
5. Histochemical.

Medicolegal Importance

1. Accidental deaths[40] – these are common and most of fatalities occur while working
2. Suicide[41] – with electric current has been reported
3. Homicide[33] – with electric current has been reported
4. Judicial electrocution[42]
5. Custodial torture – low voltage current may be employed as method to torture a person in custody
6. Child abuse
7. Auto-erotic electrocution.[43]

Table 14.7: Histological findings of skin in electrocution

Histology
- Vacuolation in epidermis and dermis
- Dermo-epidermal separation
- Degenerative changes in keratin layer
- Hyperkeratosis
- Nucleus streaming
- Pyknoses of nuclei
- Degeneration of collagen in dermis with coagulative necrosis

LIGHTNING

In India, deaths from lightning are not uncommon and occasional tragedies occur where number of people are killed or injured in a single episode.

Sources

Lightning occur during[44]

1. Thunderstorms
2. Snow storm
3. Dust storm
4. Sand storm
5. Volcanic eruptions
6. Nuclear explosion

Elementary Physics[8, 45-47]

Turbulence in cloud causes development and charge separation and as a result, the upper surface of the cloud becomes positively charged and the lower surface gets negatively charged. From the cloud sources, three verities of lightning strokes may occur as:

1. Intra-clouding lightning: Here the lightning occurs due to stream of the negative charge from lower surface of cloud to positive charge of upper surface of same cloud. These lightning are visible only as glow of cloud.
2. Inter-clouding lightning: Here lightning occurs due to streamlining of negative charge from one cloud to positive charge of another cloud. The phenomenon can be visible as a spark of light moving from one part of sky to the other.
3. Cloud to earth lightning: Here the lightning occurs due to flow of negative charge from cloud to positive charge of earth. Usually the atmosphere surrounding the earth act as insulator for lightning but when the potential difference between the charges becomes great, the current will arc between the cloud and earth creating a lightning stroke. In such an electric arc, current flows through high-temperature ionized air, which forms a pathway, composed of positive and negative ions. Thunder is simply the sound of air that has been explosively expanded by the lightning stroke. The flow is usually not visible due to low luminosity. The speed of this flow is sometimes more than 100 km/sec. The charge descends in steps and the initial part of the descent is known as "leader stroke". When the stepped leader is within 30 to 40 feet from the surface of earth, it creates an electrical field, sufficient to cause electrical discharge of positive charge from the surface of earth or any tall structures (for example building, tree, tower etc.). This positive discharge from earth or tall structure is called as "streamers" or "pilot". When the pilot stroke meets the leader stroke, it causes tremendous generation of electric current and then this wave of current moves towards the earth. This movement is known as return stroke. Lightning is very high voltage direct current (DC) between 10 million and 100 million volts.

Morphology of Lightning Stroke

The various morphologies of lightning are

1. Forked lightning – has many branches.
2. Streak lightning – travels with no branches.
3. Ribbon lightning – appears as side-by-side strokes.
4. Sheet lightning – appear in interrupted balls.
5. Ball lightning.

Lightning can strike a victim in following ways:

1. Direct stroke – here lightning strikes victim or objects immediately overhead such as umbrella or tree.
2. Splash strike – here the lightning strikes an object nearby like building and then jumps to a nearby person.
3. Ground current.
4. Individuals can be struck indoors by lightning while using the telephone or electrical appliances.

Effects of Lightning

Spencer had described four patterns of lightning effects as:[48]

1. Due to direct effect of high voltage electric current.
2. Burning by superheated air.
3. Due to successive expansion and regression of heated air surrounding the spark.
4. The sledge-hammer blow – due to compression of air occurring constantly throughout the path, ahead of the high-speed return stroke.

Due to Electric Current

Lightning is very high voltage direct current (DC) between 10 million and 100 million volts. A person may die instantaneous due to electrocution or may remain unconscious. Rapid resuscitation of such person may have chances of survival.

Due to Heat Effect

Any degrees of burn may be sustained in lightning depending on the proximity of the flash. The burn injury varies from singeing to superficial burns to deep burns. Usually the exposure of lightning stroke is extremely short, less than one ten-thousandth of a second. Because of victim's exposure is so brief, no burns or only minor singeing of hair is seen.[49]

Due to Successive Expansion and Regression of Heated Air

Due to successive expansion and regression of heated air, there will be blast effect. This causes extensive mechanical injuries like lacerations and contusions with tearing of clothes and shoes. Occasionally there may be gross distortion and mutilation of the body.

Autopsy Findings

Circumstances

- History of recent lightning or occurrence of storm is important.
- At the scene of a lightning strike, there may be damage to nearby trees such as splitting or removal of bark. Charred arc marks may be present on the walls of nearby buildings.
- The ground may display a fern pattern in the grass resembling the cutaneous discolouration seen on some victims.[45]

Clothes

- The clothes may show singeing of fibers or melting or may catch fire and burn.[45]
- At times, the clothes may be completely torn off the body and tear ends may be scorched
- The boots or shoes and the waist belts may also burst open.

Examination

- It is said that rigor mortis appears soon after death and pass off quickly.
- The pattern of injuries may vary from case to case. There may be injuries of disruptive kind in one body and there may be no external mark in another.
- In most cases, it is usual to find areas of burning and the burns may be restricted to areas of collar stud or other metal objects, e.g. metal support of a corset to steel hairpins.
- The skin may show clusters of punctate burns caused by electrical arcing or may show singeing of hairs.
- Rupture of ear drums may occur due to explosive effects or by electricity induced muscular contractions.[50]
- Petechial hemorrhages may be noted in brain. There may be chromatolysis and fragmentation of axons.
- There is congestion of internal organs and pulmonary edema.
- The heat produced by the flash may be sufficient to fuse or magnetize the metal or metallic objects or metallic objects worn or carried by victim such as metal button, or tooth fillings, hair pins, pendent, key, key-chain etc.
- Spencer (1932) [29] grouped the external marks of lightning into three classes as
  1. Surface burns
  2. Linear burns
  3. Arborescent or filigree burns.

Surface Burns (Fig. 14.45)

- These are tissue burns and are usually related to metallic objects worn or carried by the victim
- Sometimes secondary burns from ignition of clothing are noted
- There may be blisters, fissures or charring of deeper tissues and bones depending upon the intensity and extent of burn.

Linear Burns

- Linear burns are of size 1 to 12 inches long and 1/8 to 1 inches wide may be found on body area where the skin of that part offers less resistance.
- The usual sites are moist creases and folds of skin.

Arborescent Marks

- These are also called as filigree burns or feathering or Lichtenberg figures or fern-leaf pattern (Fig. 14.46)
- Arborescent markings are characteristics of lightning
- Arborescent markings are multiple, superficial, irregular, tortuous markings on the skin resembling branches of tree. This fern-like pattern of erythema in the skin is commonly found over shoulder or chest.

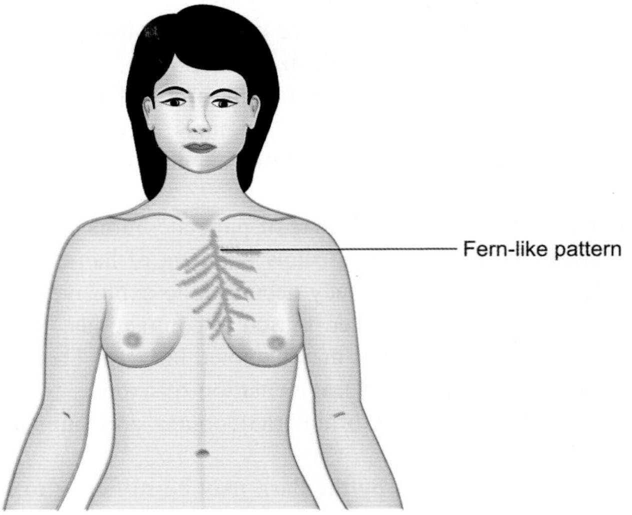

FIG. 14.46: Arborescent marks in lightning

- The precise mechanism of their formation is not known but it was hold that they may be due to minute deposition of copper on the skin. Another view was that it might be caused due to staining of the tissues by hemoglobin from lysed RBCs along the path of electric current.
- These injuries fade over time. It was reported that the mark completely disappears by 2 to 3 days.[51]

REFERENCES

1. Petty KJ. Hypothermia. In: Fauci AS, Braunwald E, Isselbacher KJ, Wilson JD, Martin JB, Kasper DL, Hauser SL, Longo DL (eds) Harrison's Principles of Internal Medicine, Vol.2, 14th edn. 1998. McGraw-Hill, New York. 97-9.
2. Dikshit PC. Thermal injuries. In: Textbook of Forensic Medicine and Toxicology, 1st edn. 2007. Peepee Publishers and Distributors (P) Ltd., New Delhi. 237-54.
3. Saukko P, Knight B. In: Knight's Forensic Pathology, 3rd edn. 2004. Arnold, London.
4. Sudler DW, Pounder DJ. Urinary catecholamines as markers of hypothermia. Forensic Sci Int 1995;76:227-9.
5. Hirvonen J, Huttunen P. Increased urinary concentration of catecholamine in hypothermic deaths. J Forensic Sci 1982; 27:264-71.
6. Hirvonen J. Necropsy findings in fatal hypothermia cases. Forensic Sci 1976;8:155-64.
7. Creager MA, Dzau VJ. Vascular diseases of the extremities. In: Fauci AS, Braunwald E, Isselbacher KJ, Wilson JD, Martin JB, Kasper DL, Hauser SL, Longo DL (eds) Harrison's Principles of Internal Medicine, Vol.2, 14th edn. 1998. McGraw-Hill, New York.1398-406.
8. Nandy A. Thermal injuries. In: Principles of Forensic Medicine, 2nd edn. 2005. New Central Book Agency (P) Ltd., Calcutta. 263-77.
9. Rao NG. Effects of cold and heat. In: Textbook of Forensic Medicine & Toxicology, 1st edn. 2006. Jaypee Brothers Medical Publishers (P) Ltd., New Delhi. 243-53.
10. Mant AK. Wounds and their interpretation. In: Mant AK (ed). Taylor's Principles and Practice of Medical Jurisprudence, 13th edn. 2000. B I Churchill Livingstone, New Delhi. 214-49.
11. Hiss J, Kahana T, Kugel C, Epstein Y. Fatal classic and exertional heat stroke-report of four cases. Med Sci Law 1994;34: 339-43.
12. Brown RF. Injury by burning. In: Mason JK (ed) The Pathology of Trauma, 2nd edn. 1993. Edward Arnold, London. 178-91.
13. Curreri PW, Luterman A. Burns. In: Schwartz SI, Shires GT, Spencer FC (eds) Principles of Surgery, 5th edn. 1989. McGraw-Hill Book Company, Singapore. 285-306.
14. Hinshaw JR, Pearse HE. Histologic techniques for the differential staining of burned and normal tissue. Surg Gynecol Obstet 1956;103:726.
15. Goulian D. Early differentiation between necrotic and viable tissue in burns. Plast Reconstr Surg 1961;27:359-65.
16. Dingwall AR. A clinical test for differentiating second from third degree burns. Ann Surg 1943;149:68-75.
17. Lawson RN, Wlodek G, Webster DR. Thermographic assessment of burns and frostbite. Canad Med Assoc J 1961;84: 1129.
18. Maldick R, Georgiade N, Throne F. A clinical evaluation of the use of the thermography in determining degree of burn injury. Plast Reconstr Surg 1966;38:512-8.
19. Heimbach DM, Afromowitz MA, Engrav LH, Marvin JA, Bernice Parry RN. Burn depth estimation – man or machine. J Trauma 1984;24:373-7.
20. Bennett JE, Dingman RO. Evaluation of burn depth by the use of radioactive isotopes. Plast Reconstr Surg 1957;20:261-7.
21. Pruitt BA Jr., Goodwin CW Jr., Pruitt SK. Burns: Including cold, chemical and electric injuries. In: Sabiston DC, Lyerly HK (eds) Textbook of Surgery, Vol. 1, 15th edn. 1997. Prism Books (Pvt.) Ltd., Bangalore. 221-52.
22. Lokan RJ, James RA, Dymock RB. Apparent postmortem production of high levels of cyanide in blood. J Forensic Sci Soc 1987;27:253-9.
23. Noguchi TT, Eng JJ, Klatt EC. Significance of cyanide in medicolegal investigations involving fires. Am J Forensic Med Pathol 1988;9:304-9.
24. Reddy KSN. Thermal deaths In: The Essentials of Forensic Medicine and Toxicology, 22nd edn. 2003. K. Suguna Devi, Hyderabad. 260-76.
25. Kumar V, Tripathi CB, Kanth S. Burnt wives – a circumstantial approach. J Forensic Med Toxicol 2001;18:14-9.
26. Murty OP, Paul G. Bride burning and burns – certain differentiating aspects of injuries thereof. J Forensic Med Toxicol 1995;12:13-27.
27. Millo T, Murty OP. Female victims of violent crimes and abuses: An overall view of Indian scenario. Int J Med Toxicol Legal Med 2006;8:18-24.
28. Bull JP. Burns. Postgrad Med J 1963;39:717-25.
29. Polson CJ, Gee DS, Knight B. The Essentials of Forensic Medicine, 4th edn. 1985. Pergamon Press, UK. 271-350.

30. Pillay VV. Thermal injuries. In: Textbook of Forensic Medicine and Toxicology, 14th edn. 2004. Paras Publishing, Hyderabad. 191-203.
31. Hunt JL, Mason AD Jr., Masterson TS, Pruitt BA. The Pathophysiology of acute electric injuries. J Trauma 1976; 16:335-40.
32. Robinson DW, Masters FW, Forrest WJ. Electrical burns: A review and analysis of 33 cases. Surgery 1965;57:385-90.
33. Shrigiriwar MB, Bardale RV, Dixit PG. Importance of examination of oral cavity. Medicolegal Update 2006;6:77-8.
34. Dale RH. Electrical accident. Br J Plast Surg 1954; 7: 44-50.
35. Zhang P, Cai S. Study on electrocution death by low-voltage. Forensic Sci Int 1995;76:115-9.
36. Davis MR. Burns caused by electricity: A review of seventy cases. Br J Plast Surg 1958;11:288-300.
37. Adjutantis G, Skalos S. The identification of the electrical burn in cases of electrocution by the acro-reaction test. J Forensic med 1962;9:101-4.
38. Shrigiriwar M, Bardale R, Dixit PG. Electrocution: a six-year study of electrical fatalities. J Indian Acad Forensic Med 2007; 29:50-3.
39. Torre C, Varetto L. Dermal surface in electric and thermal injuries. Observations by scanning electron microscope. Am J Forensic Med Pathol 1986;7:151-8.
40. Odesanmi WO. Things are not always what they seem! Joule burns in electrocution – a report of four cases. Med Sci Law 1987;27:63-7.
41. Marc B, Baudry F, Douceron H, Ghaith A, Wepierre JL, Garnier M. Suicide by electrocution with low-voltage current. J Forensic Sci 2000;45:216-22.
42. Jones GRN. Judicial electrocution and the prison doctor. Lancet 1990;335:713-4.
43. Klintschar M, Grabuschnigg P, Beham A. Death from electrocution during auto-erotic practice: case report and review of the literature. Am J Forensic Med Pathol 1998;19:190-3.
44. Cwinn AA, Cantrill SV. Lightening injuries. J Emerg Med 1985;2:379-88.
45. Lifschultz BD, Donoghue ER. Deaths caused by lightning. J Forensic Sci 1993;38:353-8.
46. Cooper MA. Lightning injuries: Prognostic signs for death. Ann Emerg Med 1980;9:134-8.
47. Kobernick M. Electrical injuries: Pathophysiology and emergency management. Ann Emerg Med 1982;11:633-8.
48. Subrahmanyam BV. Injuries from burns, scalds, lightning and electricity. In: Modi's Medical Jurisprudence and Toxicology, 22nd edn. 2001. Butterworths India, New Delhi. 309-32.
49. Lifschultz BD, Donoghue ER.. Electrical and lightning injuries. In: Spitz WU (ed) Spitz and Fisher's Medicolegal investigation of Death, 3rd edn. 1993. Charlas C Thomas Publisher, USA. 516-27.
50. Masselo W. Lightning deaths. Medicolegal Bullet 1988;37: 1-9.
51. Domart Y, Garet E. Images in clinical medicine. Lichtenberg figures due to lightning strike. N Engl J Med 2000;343:1536.

CHAPTER 15

Violent Asphyxia

Assassination on the scaffold is the worst form of assassination, because there it is invested with the approval of society.

- George Bernard Shaw

Asphyxia is derived from Greek word and literally means pulselessness. However, in forensic practice, the term asphyxia is used to describe a condition in which the supply of oxygen to the blood and body tissues is reduced appreciably below the normal working level by any interference with respiration.

The purpose of breathing is to convey oxygen from atmosphere into the lungs and removes carbon dioxide from the lungs to the atmosphere. When the process is arrested, there will be interference with the passage of oxygen and carbon dioxide. Thus asphyxia is considered as a sate in which these two elements are combined and includes:[1]

1. Hypoxia of the tissue i.e. lack of oxygen supply to the body and
2. Hypercapnea where there is an increase in carbon dioxide retention in the blood and tissues.

Definition: Adelson defined asphyxia, as "*a state in living organism in which there is acute lack of oxygen available for cell metabolism associated with inability of body to eliminate excess of carbon dioxide.*"[2]

Along with term asphyxia, other terms such as anoxia or hypoxia are used. These terms are defined as follows:

- **Anoxia**: It is a state characterized by lack of oxygen supply to body and tissues.
- **Hypoxia**: It is a condition in which there is an inadequate or reduced supply of oxygen to tissues.

ANOXIA

Gordon had classified the anoxia as follows (mnemonic **ASHA** = A – anoxic anoxia, S – stagnant anoxia, H – histotoxic anoxia, A – anoxia)

1. Anoxic anoxia
2. Stagnant anoxia
3. Anemic anoxia
4. Histotoxic anoxia.

Anoxic Anoxia

This results from either:

- Prevention of oxygen entering to lungs or
- Inability of lungs to oxygenate the blood.

It includes:

A. Due to lack of available oxygen in the air for inspiration, e.g. at high altitude, staying near by fire
B. Due to inspiration of an inert gas like methane, sewer gas etc.
C. Due to breathing in a vitiated atmosphere deficient in oxygen like bottom of unused well or interior of a granary.
D. Due to interference with respiration by any mechanical obstruction in air passage, e.g. smothering, hanging, strangulation, choking etc.
E. Due to low oxygen content in anesthetic mixture of gases.
F. Due to interference with respiratory movements or function as seen in traumatic asphyxia, penetrating chest injury, paralysis of respiratory muscles etc.
G. Due to congenital defect of heart or lung or blood vessel.

Stagnant Anoxia

This is a condition where there is slowing down of circulation with impaired oxygen delivery to tissues. This may be seen in:

A. Congestive cardiac failure
B. Peripheral circulatory failure/shock
C. Acute corrosive/irritant poisoning
D. Heat stroke

Anemic Anoxia

It indicates reduced oxygen carrying capacity of blood. Here there is oxygenation of blood in the lungs but blood has reduced capacity to transfer the oxygen to tissues. It may be seen in:

A. Anemia
B. Carbon monoxide poisoning
C. Hemorrhage
D. Formation of stable components of hemoglobin like sulphemoglobin, methemoglobin etc.

Histotoxic Anoxia

In this condition, there is interference with tissue oxygenation. Here cells are not in a position to utilize the oxygen delivered to them.

Histotoxic anoxia is subdivided into following:

A. Extra-cellular Histotoxic anoxia: Here tissue oxygenation is interfered because oxygen cannot be taken up by cell. For example inhibition of cytochrome oxidase system by cyanide poisoning.
B. Pericellular histotoxic anoxia: Oxygen cannot be taken up by cell due to reduced permeability of cell membrane. For example barbiturate poisoning, halothane, chloroform, ether etc.
C. Substrate histotoxic anoxia: The oxygen cannot be utilized due to insufficient cell metabolism. For example hypoglycemia.
D. Metabolite histotoxic anoxia: The oxygen cannot be utilized by cell due to toxic effect of accumulated end products of cell metabolism. Here the toxic end products of cell are not removed due to which there is interference in cell respiration.

TYPES AND CAUSES OF ASPHYXIA

Following are types of asphyxia (Fig. 15.1):

1. Mechanical asphyxia
2. Traumatic asphyxia
3. Environmental asphyxia
4. Toxic asphyxia
5. Pathological asphyxia

Mechanical Asphyxia

In this type of asphyxia, flow of air into the body is interfered by mechanical means.

Mechanical causes are:

- Closure of external respiratory orifice viz. mouth and nose – smothering
- Occlusion of oral cavity and oropharynx – gagging

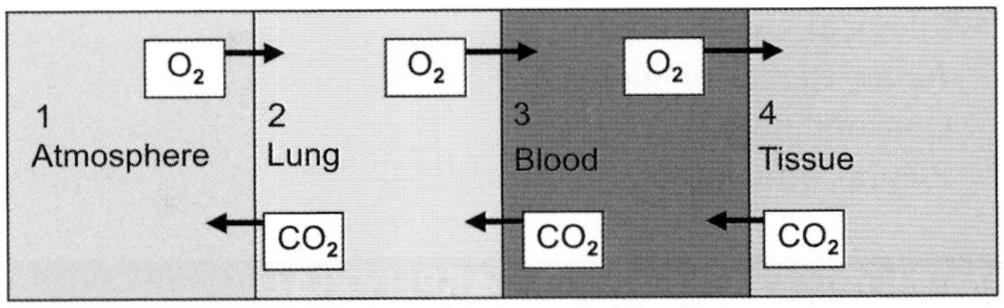

FIG. 15.1 Showing passage of oxygen (from site 1 to 4) and carbon dioxide (from site 4 to 1). Interference for respiration at site 1 causes suffocation. Mechanical obstruction at site 1 and 2 prevents transfer of oxygen and carbon dioxide. Pathology and drowning prevents transfer of oxygen from site 2 to 3. Carboxyhemoglobin, anemia etc. prevents transfer of oxygen from site 3. A Cyanide etc. poison prevents utilization of oxygen at site 4.

- Occlusion of airway by pressure on neck –hanging, strangulation
- Obstruction of air passage internally - choking.

Traumatic Asphyxia

The asphyxia is caused by pressure and fixation of the chest and abdomen.

Traumatic causes are:

- Stampede
- Pneumothorax due to penetrating injury to chest
- Person crushed under vehicle
- Person crushed by fall of wall/collapse of house/earthquake.

Environmental Asphyxia

Non-availability of oxygen in the air causes asphyxia

Environmental causes are:

- High altitude
- Person trapped in well or granary
- Respiration in enclosed space.

Toxic Asphyxia

This form of asphyxia results from poisonous substances.

Toxic causes are:

- Opium poisoning
- Carbon monoxide poisoning
- Cyanide poisoning
- Gelsemium poisoning.

Pathological Asphyxia

Presence of disease in respiratory passage or in lung prevents oxygenation and causes asphyxia.

Pathological causes are:
- Acute edema of glottis
- Consolidation
- Pleural effusion etc.

PATHOPHYSIOLOGY OF ASPHYXIA

The normal O_2 content of arterial blood PO_2 with 95 percent saturation of Hb ranged from 90 to 100 mmHg (12-13.5 kPa) in young to middle aged person. In persons above 60 year of age, it may drop to 60 to 85 mmHg (8-10 kPa). Reduction to 60 mmHg (8 kPa) results in hypoxia even though the hemoglobin is 90 percent saturated. 40 mmHg (5 kPa) represents severe hypoxia and death might be expected when the level falls to 20 mmHg (3 kPa).[1, 3]

Once asphyxia sets in, it causes further anoxia i.e. asphyxia begets asphyxia. Thus a vicious cycle of asphyxia sets in. Due to decreased oxygenation of blood there is asphyxia that leads to capillary dilatation, engorgement and stasis of blood. This result decreases venous return to heart. Diminished venous blood flow causes reduction in pulmonary flow of blood, which leads to deficient oxygenation of blood in lungs thus causing asphyxia (Figs 15.2 and 15.3).

STAGES OF ASPHYXIA

The clinical features produced by asphyxia are divided into three stages and they are:[4, 5]

1) Stage of dyspnea
   - Breathlessness,
   - Feeling of oppression in the chest
   - Heaviness in head,

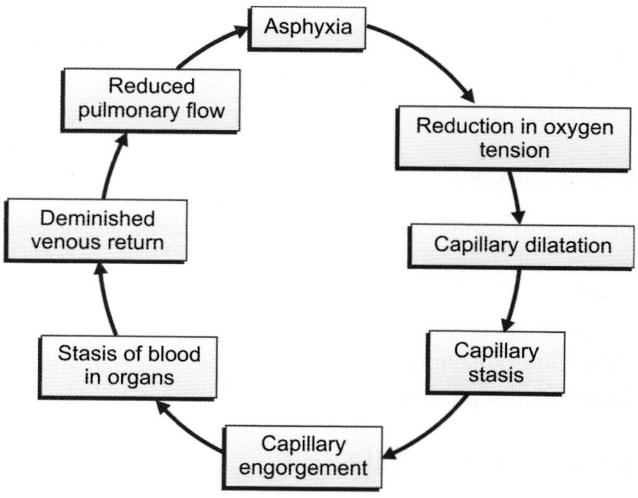

FIG. 15.2: Vicious cycle of asphyxia

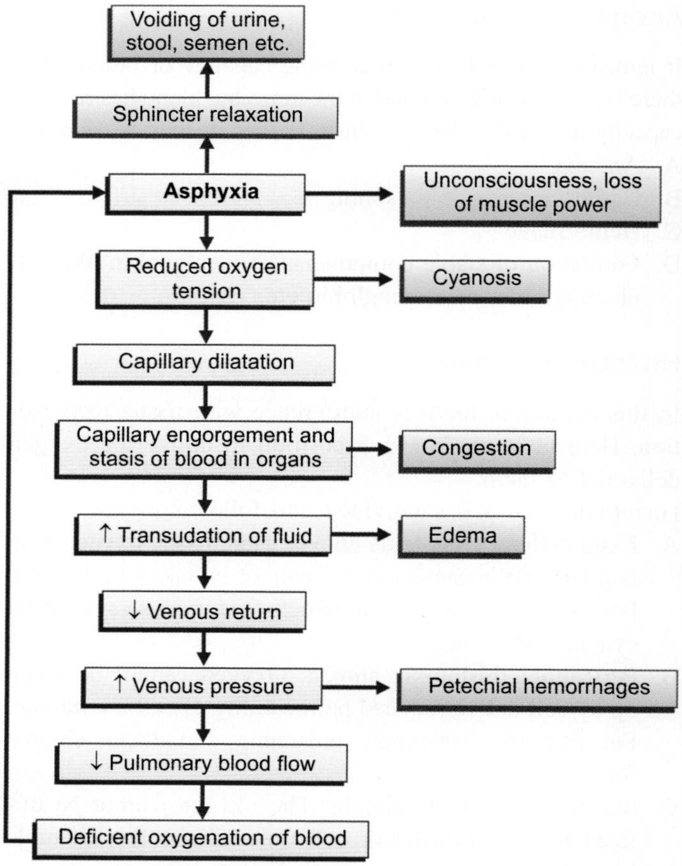

FIG. 15.3: Mechanism of appearance of classical signs of asphyxia

   - Ringing in the ears
   - Tachycardia
   - Raised blood pressure
   - Stage last for a minute.
2) Stage of convulsion
   - Retention of carbon dioxide
   - Increase blood lactate
   - Respiration becomes labored and spasmodic
   - Sympathetic and parasympathetic effects are prominent with increased secretion of saliva; increase heart rate, and increase gastrointestinal motility, incontinence of bowel and bladder with relaxation of sphincters and voiding of urine, feces and semen.
   - Clouding of consciousness and convulsions
   - Stage last for 1 to 2 minute.
3) Stage of exhaustion and respiratory failure

- Anoxic brain damage with paralysis of respiratory centers
- Complete insensibility,
- Flaccidity of muscle
- Reflexes are lost
- Pupils are widely dilated
- Prolonged sighing respiration occurs at longer and longer intervals until they cease altogether and death ensues.
- Heart may continue to beat for few more minutes
- Stage last for 2 to 3 minute.

SIGNS OF ASPHYXIA

Following signs are considered as **classical signs** of asphyxia:

1) Cyanosis
2) Congestion of organs
3) Petechial hemorrhages
4) Pulmonary edema
5) Fluidity of blood
6) Dilatation of right chamber of heart

Cyanosis (Fig. 15.4)

- The word cyanosis is derived from Greek means "dark blue"
- Indicates bluish colouration of skin or mucous membrane. It is more pronounced in parts having abundant capillary and venous circulation like lip, tip of nose, nail-beds, ear lobes, tip of tongue etc.
- Normally well-oxygenated blood is bright red but with increase in quantity of reduced hemoglobin, it assumes dark colour. This imparts bluish purple colour to skin and thus cyanosis is evident. There must be at least 5 gm of reduced hemoglobin per 100 ml blood before cyanosis becomes evident. Thus diminished oxygen tension in the blood with consequent rise in proportion of reduced hemoglobin is necessary for cyanosis.
- Cyanosis may not be evident in:
  - Marked anemia
  - When dermis is thick
- Cyanosis may be confused with postmortem lividity.

Petechial Hemorrhages[3,6,7]

- These are small-point collections of blood and vary in size from a tenth of a millimeter to about two millimeter. If larger than two millimeter, they are called as ecchymoses.
- Petechial hemorrhages are also called as "Tardieu's spot". But Tardieu spots specifically refer to Petechial hemorrhages occurring in the visceral pleura.
- These hemorrhages are caused by an acute rise in venous pressure. The rise in venous pressure causes over-distention and rupture of thin-walled venules, especially in lax tissue such as eyelid, pleura, epicardium (Fig. 15.5) etc.
- Stasis hemorrhages are fine pin-head hemorrhages seen beneath the mucosa of larynx, especially in subglottic space. They are seen in strangulation cases above the level of ligature mark. These hemorrhages are due to venous stasis and subsequent venous rupture.

Pulmonary Edema

Pulmonary edema is a condition where there is excess of fluid present in lung alveoli. The fluid accumulates due

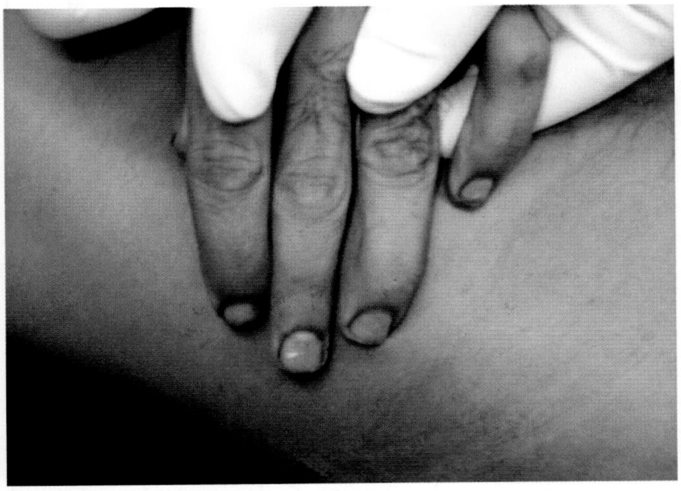

FIG. 15.4: Cyanosis of nails

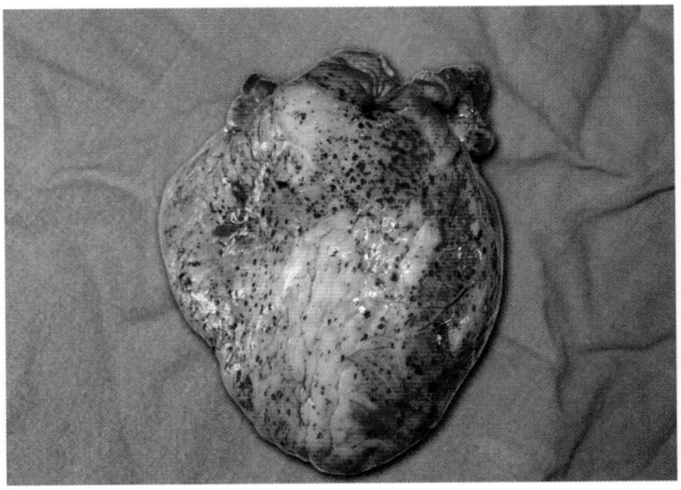

FIG. 15.5: Petechial hemorrhages over epicardium

to raised pulmonary vessel pressure and associated anoxia (Fig. 15.6).

Congestion of Organs

Hypoxia causes decrease oxygen tension in blood with increased reduced hemoglobin with capillary dilatation, engorgement and stasis of blood. The stasis of blood in capillaries causes congestion of organs.

Fluidity of Blood

In past fluidity was considered as a marker of asphyxia. It was thought that anoxia/hypoxia causes release of fibronolysin enzymes from vessel wall. These enzyme causes fluidity of blood. However, fluidity of blood in postmortem state is a non-specific and erratic procedure.

Mechanical Asphyxia (Violent Asphyxia)

In violent asphyxial deaths, there is evidence on the body of some mechanical interference with the process of breathing.

HANGING

Definition: *Hanging is a form of violent death produced by suspending the body with a ligature round the neck, the constricting force being the weight of the body or a part of body weight.*

Types

Types of hanging are given in Table 15.1 (also see Figs 15.7 and 15.8)

- Typical Hanging: When the body is suspended by ligature with a point of suspension at center of occiput i.e. when the knot is at the nape of neck, the type of hanging is called as typical hanging.
- Atypical hanging: In this type of hanging, the point of suspension is not at occiput i.e. the knot is not at nape of neck. Thus when knot in hanging is at other than nape of neck, it is called as atypical hanging. The common

Table 15.1: Displays types of hanging

Types of hanging
A) On the basis of knot position:
1) Typical hanging
2) Atypical hanging
B) On the basis of degree of suspension:
1) Complete hanging
2) Partial or incomplete hanging
C) On the basis of manner of death:
1) Suicidal hanging
2) Homicidal hanging
3) Accidental hanging
D) In relation to death:
1) Antemortem hanging
2) Postmortem hanging
E) Others:
1) Judicial hanging
2) Autoerotic hanging
3) Lynching
4) Rescue hanging

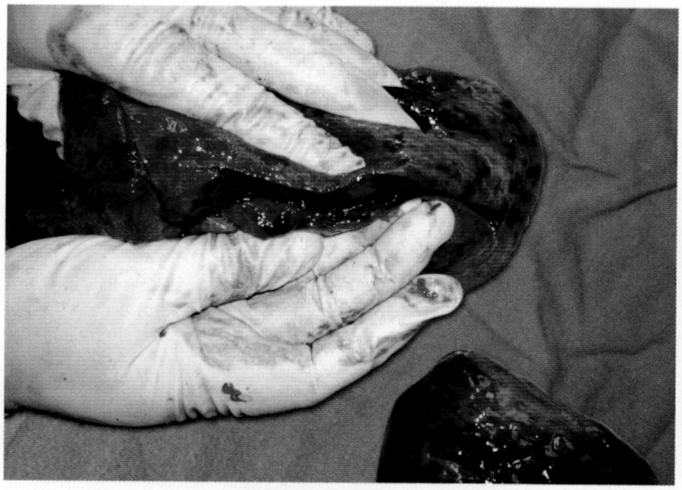

FIG. 15.6: Pulmonary edema

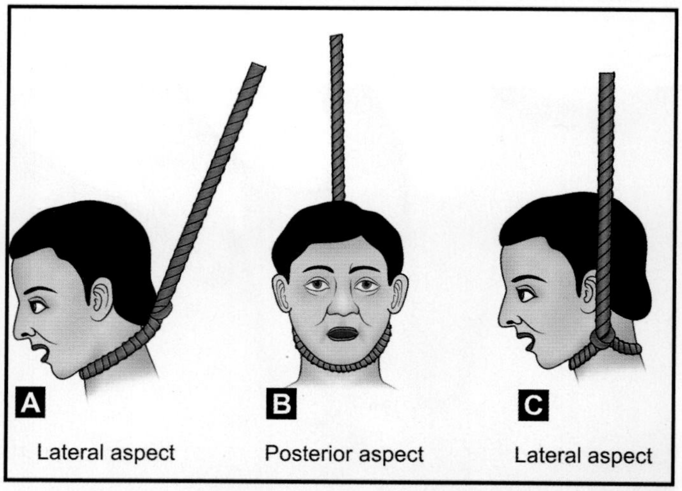

FIGS 15.7A to C: Typical and atypical hanging. **A** and **B** display typical hanging - note here that the knot is at the nape of neck whereas **C** demonstrates atypical hanging—note the position of knot

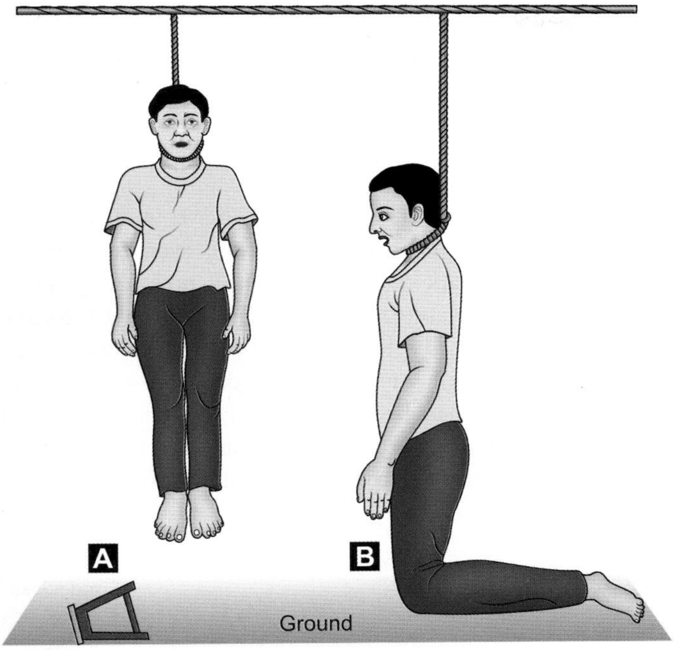

FIGS 15.8A and B: Complete and partial hanging. **A** shows complete hanging - note the body is completely suspending in air whereas **B** demonstrates partial hanging - note the knees are touching the ground

position for knot in atypical hanging is at mastoid process or at angle of mandible.

- Complete hanging: In this type, the body is suspended on the ligature in air without touching the ground or any other article such as table, chair etc. **The constricting force here is the entire weight of body**.
- Incomplete or partial hanging: When body is suspended on the ligature with some body parts touching the ground or other articles, the hanging is called as partial hanging. For example, hanging in sitting position, kneeling or lying position. Here the **constricting force is the part of body weight**.

Mechanism of Hanging

- In hanging the constricting force may be-
  1) Weight of entire body as in complete hanging or
  2) Part of body weight as in partial hanging.
- A constriction pressure of 2 kg is sufficient to occlude jugular venous system causing cerebral venous congestion.
- A constricting pressure of 5 kg can compress the carotid arteries causing cessation of blood supply to brain.
- A constricting force of 15 kg can compress the trachea causing obstruction to respiration.
- A constricting force of 30 kg can obstruct the vertebral arteries.
- Thus it is not necessary that body should be suspended by ligature completely as in complete hanging. Even though, body is touching the ground as in partial hanging, the person may succumb to death.

Cause of Death

A) Immediate causes
   1) Asphyxia: Obstruction of air way.
   2) Venous congestion: Obstruction of jugular venous system.
   3) Cerebral anemia: Compression of carotid arteries causing cerebral ischemia.
   4) Vagal inhibition: Vagus nerve or carotid bodies when compressed may cause vagal inhibition with cessation of heart.
   5) Combination of asphyxia and venous congestion.
   6) Fracture dislocation of cervical vertebrae.

B) Delayed causes
   1) Aspiration pneumonia.
   2) Infection and septicemia.
   3) Pulmonary edema.
   4) Hypoxic encephalopathy.
   5) Laryngeal edema.
   6) Abscess of brain/encephalitis.

Sequelae of Rescue Hanging

If a person survives in attempted hanging, he may have following secondary effects:

1) Hemiplegia
2) Epileptiform convulsions
3) Amnesia
4) Dementia
5) Cervical cellulites/retropharyngeal abscess
6) Parotitis.

Symptoms in Hanging

1) Loss of power
2) Subjective sensation such as flashes of lights
3) Ringing in ears
4) Blurring of vision
5) Mental confusion
6) Loss of consciousness
7) Convulsions.

Fatal Period

- Death occurs immediately if cervical vertebrae are fracture-dislocated or due to Vagal inhibition
- Asphyxia and others: usual period is 3 to 5 minute.

Ligature Material

Ligature material are any material used that is readily available for the purpose. It may be rope, metallic chains, wire, electric cord, packing twice,[8] cable, belt, bed-sheet, sari, scarf, oodhani, dupatta, trouser, underwear, dhoti etc. The ligature material should be removed and preserved properly. The noose should be preserved and this is done by cutting the noose away from the knot and then securing the ends with thread. The knot is also secured by tying with thread (Fig. 15.9).

Knot

Knots are of following types (Fig. 15.10):
1) Simple slip knot- most commonly used
2) Fixed knot/granny knot.

Knot may be present at following site:
1) Mastoid or mandibular angle
2) Below chin
3) Occiput.

Noose

The noose may be (Fig. 15.10):
1) Fixed noose
2) Running noose.

Autopsy Findings

Clothes: Clothes may bear saliva stains.

External Examination:

A) Findings in neck
- **Ligature mark** (Figs 15.11 to 15.19) is most important finding in neck. The ligature used for hanging causes a mark over neck. It is a pressure abrasion made by ligature. The mark is in form of furrow or groove in the tissue and is pale in colour, which may turn yellowish-brown to dark brown later on. The mark may be accompanied by reddish abraded edges caused due to constriction. The mark is hard and parchment like due to drying and desiccation of abraded skin.

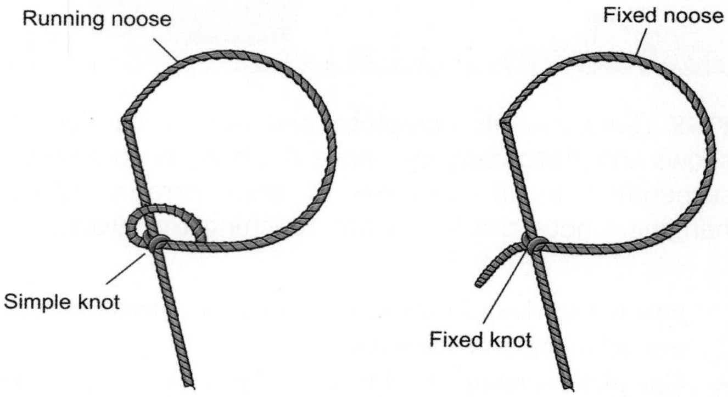

FIG. 15.10: Showing simple slip knot and fixed knot. Similarly note the noose—fixed and running

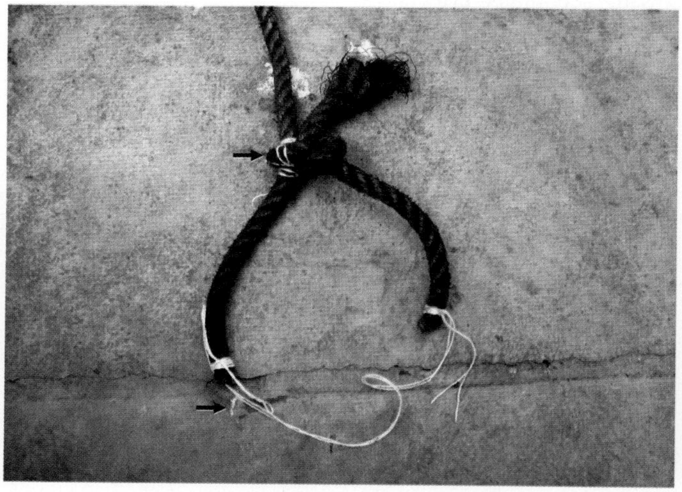

FIG. 15.9: Way to preserve noose and knot of ligature material (black arrow)

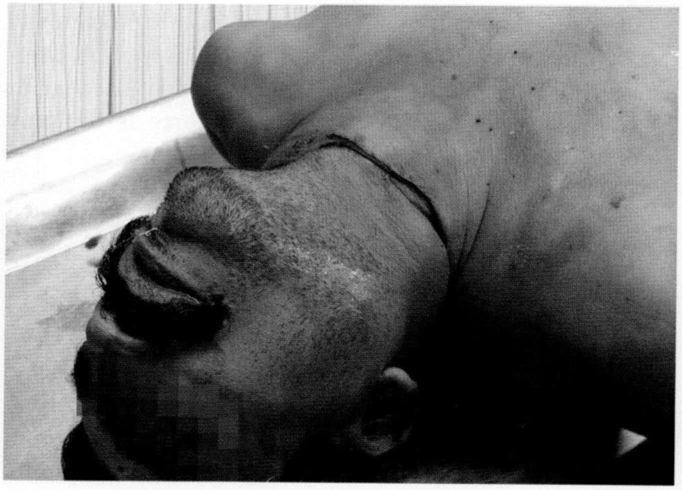

FIG. 15.11: Ligature mark in hanging

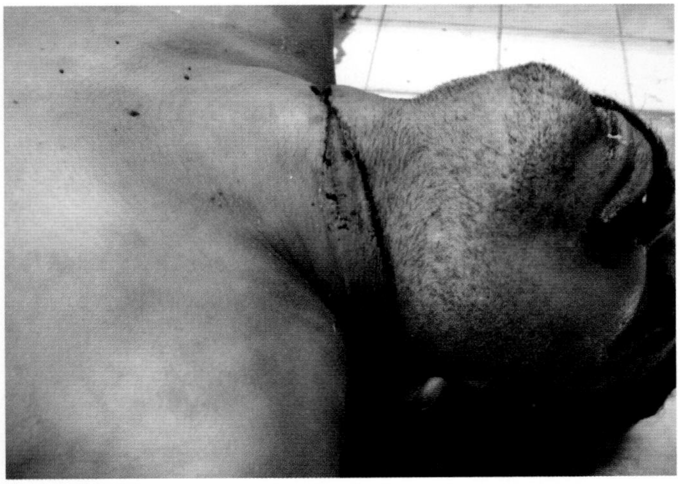

FIG. 15.12: Ligature mark in hanging

FIG. 15.14: Hanging to tree (*Courtesy*: Dr Mohd. Ali, Dept. of Forensic Medicine, GMCH, Nagpur)

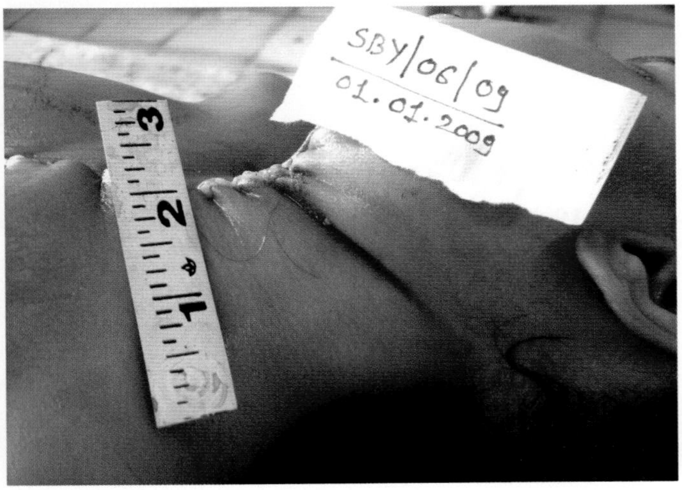

FIG. 15.13: Ligature mark—note traversing obliquely and backwards

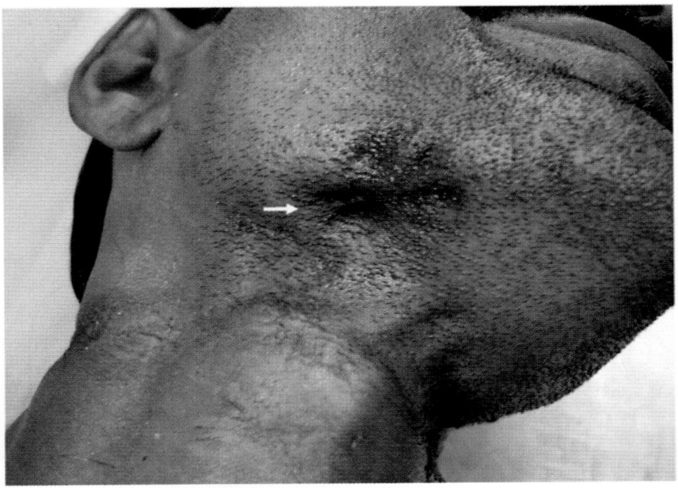

FIG. 15.15: Ligature mark with knot impression at right submandibular region (arrow)

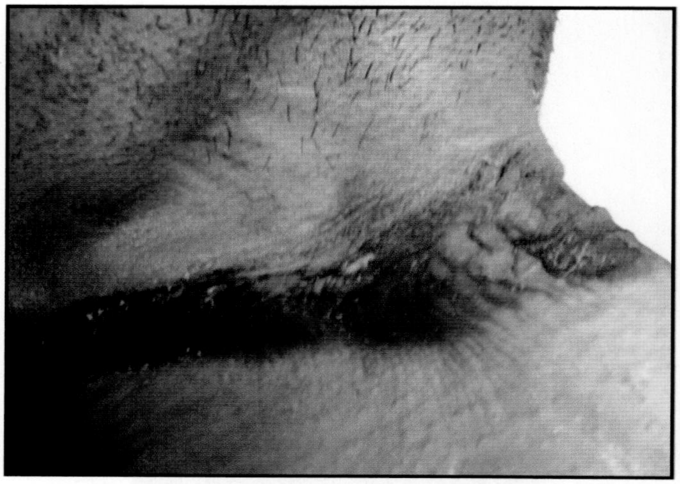

FIG. 15.16: Ligature mark—note abraded base with line of congestion above the mark

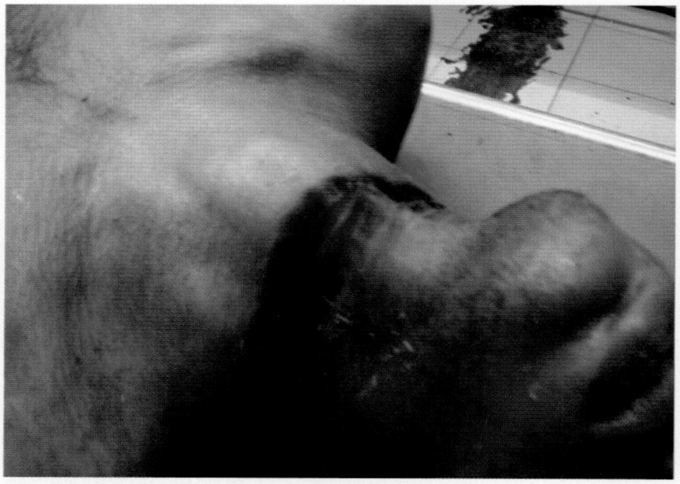

FIG. 15.18: Ligature mark—note breadth caused by broad ligature material

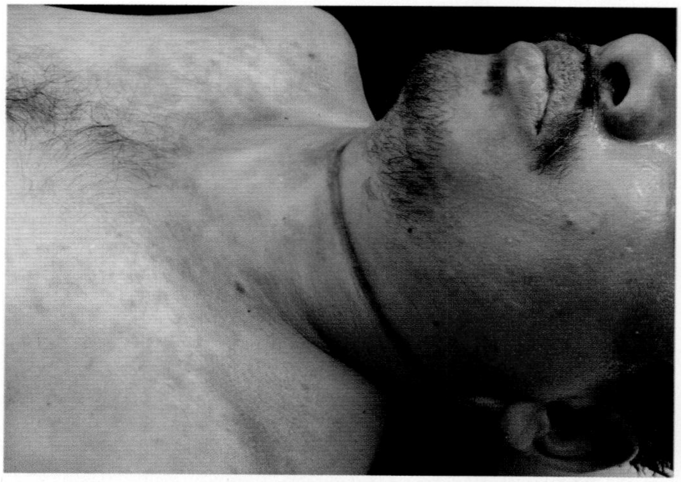

FIG. 15.17: Ligature mark in typical hanging

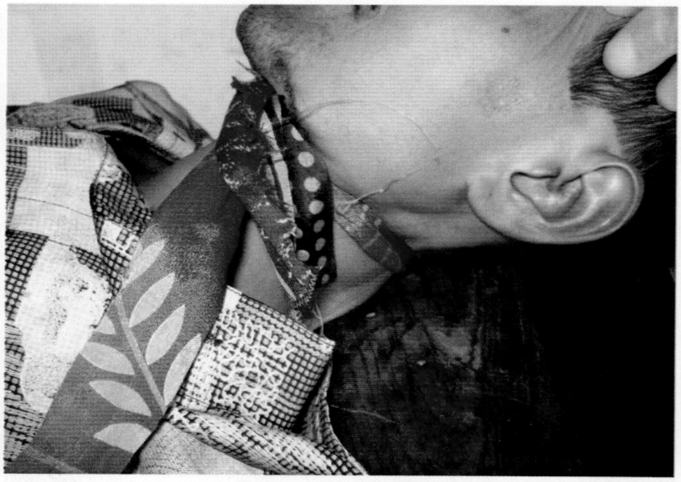

FIG. 15.19: Ligature mark with ligature material *in situ*

- The ligature mark is usually situated above the thyroid cartilage and is running obliquely passing backward and upwards on either side of the neck. The percentage of situation of ligature mark is given in Table 15.2.
- In case of fixed knot, the ligature mark is produced as inverted "V" shaped impression with apex of V corresponding with the site of knot.
- In case of slip knot, the noose may tighten around the neck producing mark over neck except at knot.
- The ligature mark may be horizontal to oblique if:
  1. Hanging is from low point of suspension.
  2. In partial hanging when body leans forward.
  3. If ligature is winded twice or more times round the neck.
- A line of congestion along the ligature mark may be seen. The base of groove may be abraded or contused or may show ecchymoses. At times, the ligature may imprint the pattern of ligature for example rope imprint or metal chain imprint.
- Neck may be stretched and elongated (Fig. 15.20)
- Associated injuries around the ligature mark (Periligature injury/injuries) such as rope burns can be seen. Rope burns are caused by friction of rope against the skin. Such friction generates heat that causes second-degree burn injuries resulting in

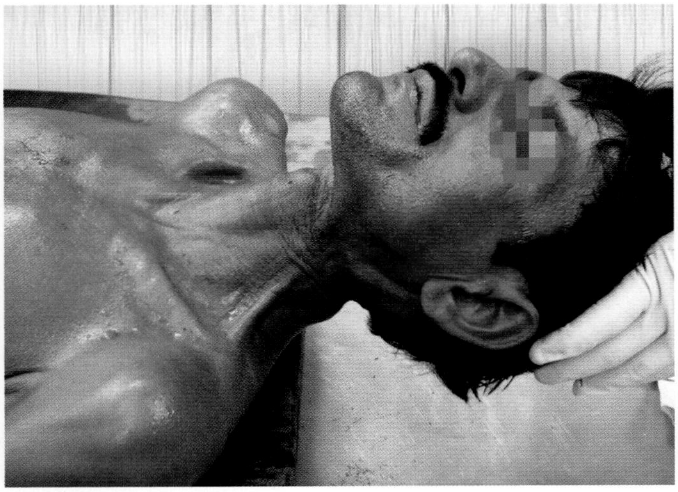

FIG. 15.20: Neck is stretched and elongated

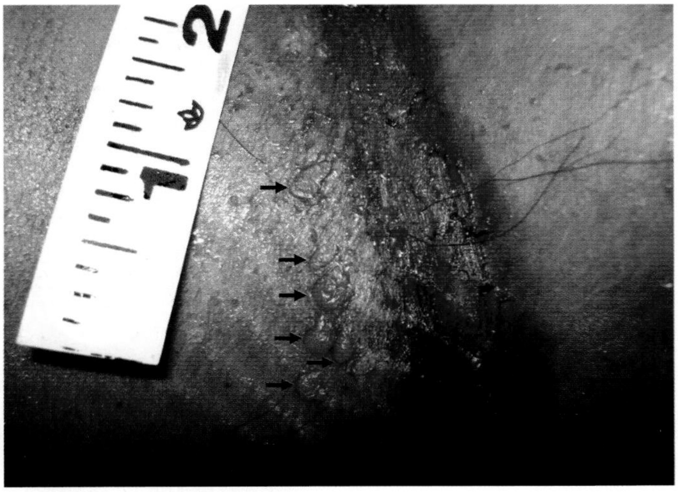

FIG. 15.21: Blisters around ligature mark (see black arrows)

Table 15.2: Showing position of ligature mark

Position of ligature	*% of cases*
Above thyroid cartilage	80%
At level of thyroid cartilage	15%
Below the level of thyroid cartilage (especially in partial hanging)	05%

production of blisters in the upper layer of skin. Thus presence of rope burns (and/or blisters) is suggestive of an antemortem nature of hanging (Fig. 15.21).[9,10]

- Ligature mark may be faintly visible or not so prominent if:
  1. Beard or portion of cloth intervenes between ligature and skin.
  2. Soft material such as towel etc. are used.

Factors Affecting Ligature Mark

1. Composition of ligature: If hard or thick and rough ligature is used, the mark may be pronounced. If soft material is used, it may leave barely visible mark.
2. Width of material: Broad ligature material may leave broad mark with less grooving whereas thin ligature material may have deep, narrow grooved impression (Figs 15.18 and 15.19).
3. Weight of body: Heavier the body, greater will be the prominence of mark.
4. Rescue hanging: If person survives then ligature mark becomes less prominent and heals with turning into pale scar like mark (Fig. 15.22).

Pseudo ligature mark

A pseudo mark may be mistaken for ligature mark.

1. In obese individuals or infants, the skin folds of neck may appear as ligature mark.
2. In decomposed bodies, the pattern of necklace or neck jewelry or neck clothing such as scarf, dupatta, chunni, oodhni etc. may be mistaken for ligature mark.

B) Findings in face
- Face may be congested, puffed up and shows petechial hemorrhages over skin or conjunctiva.[12]
- Blood tinged froth may be seen oozing from nostrils due to pulmonary oedema
- Sign of salivary dribbling from the corners of mouth with stains of saliva over chin or chest or neck. It is vital feature (Fig. 15.23).
- In some cases, the knot of ligature may press the cervical sympathetic ganglia on that side. Due to this, the eye on that side may remain open and pupil is dilated. This is considered as vital feature and referred as **Le facie sympathique** (Fig. 15.24).

C) Other findings
- Glove and stock pattern of postmortem lividity may be seen if body remains suspended for long time (Fig. 15.25).
- Cyanosis
- Voiding of urine/stool/semen.

Internal Examination

A) Neck
- The tissues underneath the mark are dry, white and glistening with occasional ecchymoses in the adjacent muscles.[11]

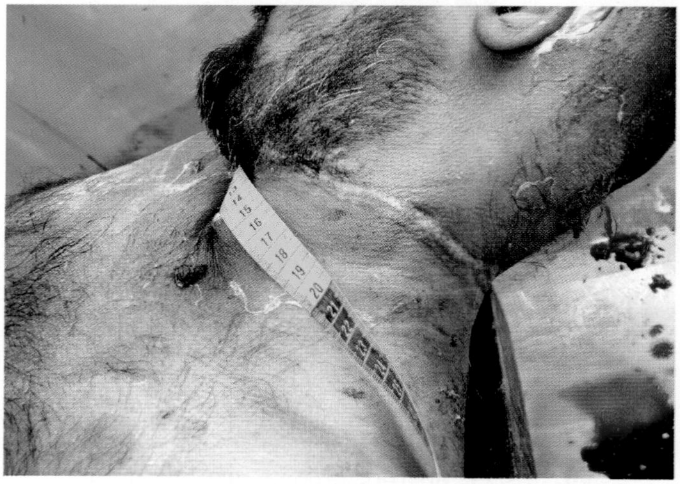

FIG. 15.22: Ligature mark in rescue hanging

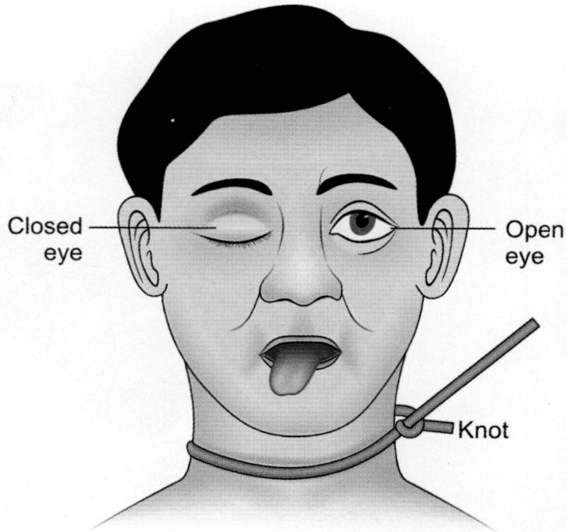

FIG. 15.24: Le facie sympathique

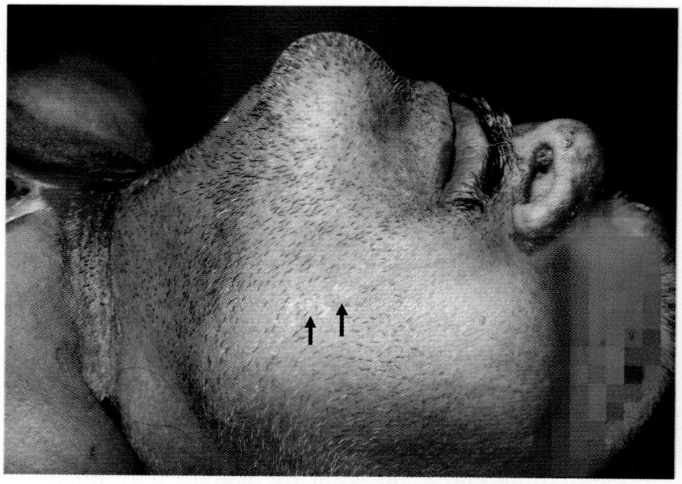

FIG. 15.23: Dribbling of saliva from left angle of mouth (black arrows)

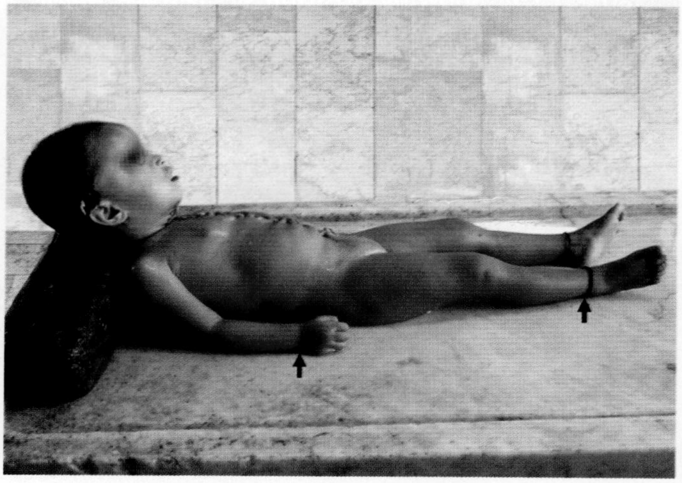

FIG. 15.25: Glove and stock type of lividity

- Muscles of neck: Platysma and sternocleidomastoid may show contusion in some cases if violence is considerable
- Carotid arteries: May be injured by the ligature whereby there is slight bleeding into their walls or a horizontal breach of the intima at the level of the ligature.[7]
- Hyoid bone: Occasionally, hyoid bone may be fractured and is more common in individuals above 40 years of age. The fracture involves the greater horn of hyoid bone. It is also called as **anteroposterior compression fracture** or **abduction fracture**. It is suggested that as the hyoid bone is pressed backward against the vertebral column, it results in anteroposterior compression of hyoid bone with diverging of greater cornu (Fig. 15.26). The periosteum is torn on the **inner aspect** of hyoid bone.[6]
- The superior horn of thyroid cartilage may get fractured due to pressure on the thyrohyoid membrane.
- If hanging is associated with long drop, there may be injury to larynx and/or fracture-dislocation of upper cervical vertebrae.
- Microscopic examination of thyroid gland and salivary gland shows focal interstitial hemorrhages whereas lymph gland shows congestion. These findings support the antemortem nature of hanging.[13]

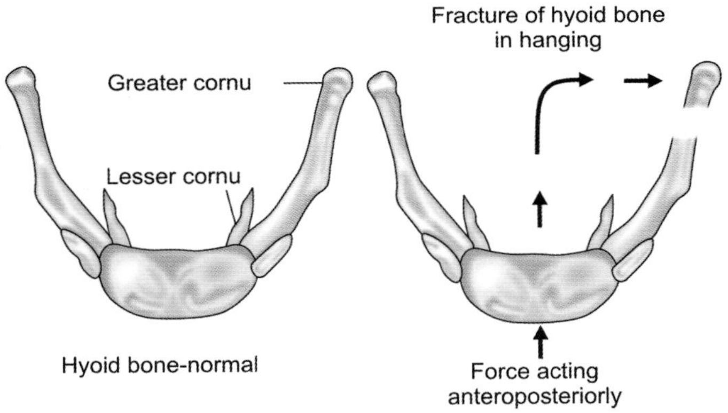

FIG. 15.26: Fracture of hyoid bone in hanging

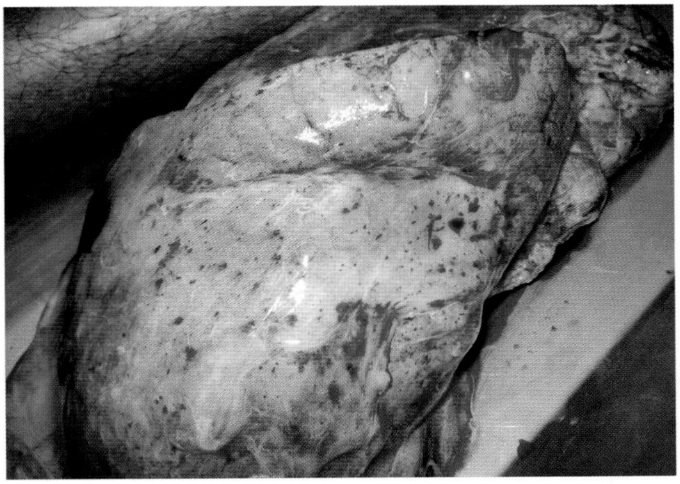

FIG. 15.27: Petechial hemorrhages

– Typical hanging are related to fracture of neck structures and to lesser extent to congestion of face while atypical hangings show a high frequency of congestion of face and a low frequency of fracture neck structure.[8]

B) Brain
  – May be congested if there is compression of jugular venous system
  – May be pale if there is compression of carotid and vertebral arteries.

C) Lungs: Lungs are congested and edematous with Tardieu spots over pleura (Fig. 15.27)

D) Abdominal viscera congested.

Judicial Hanging

- In India, hanging is the way of legal execution of death sentence
- The face of the condemned person is covered with black mask then he is asked to stand on a platform. Then noose is adjusted around his neck with knot under the angle of jaw i.e. submental position. With the help of lever, the platform is pulled back and the person drops down to 5 to 7 meters. The sudden stoppage of moving body associated with position of knot causes the head to be jerked violently.[11] This causes fracture-dislocation of cervical vertebrae at the level of C_2C_3 or C_3C_4. Rarely dislocation of atlanto-occipital joint may occur.

Lynching

It is a homicidal hanging. In this type, a suspected person or criminal guilty of crime is hanged by crowd. Mob of people catch the offender and hanged him forcibly to tree or lamppost.

Autoerotic Hanging

- Also called as sexual asphyxia, asphyxiophilia, hypoxiphilia, kotzwainism, autoerotic asphyxia, hypoxyphilic behavior.
- It is a form of sexual paraphilia where a person is often dressed in female attire and asphyxiates himself with a ligature with some form of mechanism. The person voluntarily induces and controls cerebral hypoxia to obtain sexual fulfillment. It is thought that the resulting hypoxia enhances sexual pleasure and gratification by masturbation.[6, 14]
- Accidental fatalities during autoerotic sexual activity usually result from failure of the escape mechanism.
- In such fatalities, often body is found in a secluded area with room locked from inside. The pornographic ligature may be present at the scene of crime. There may be a protective pad between skin of neck and ligature to prevent ligature injury.
- Majority of fatalities are accidental and mostly in males. However, in rare instances, females have been involved in such practice.[15]

Medicolegal Importance

1. Hanging may be suicidal, homicidal or accidental. Suicidal manner is more common than homicidal or accidental.
2. Accidental hanging may occur:
   – Accidentally at work place for example in factories, entrapment in belt.[16]

- Playing and mimicking hanging by children
- Sexual deviation-auto-erotic hanging
- During professional performance, e.g. circus, magic show etc.
- Infants and toddlers may get accidentally hanged in restraining belt of bed or crib.

3. Hanging may be Antemortem or postmortem. Differences are given in Table 15.3.
4. Whether it is a hanging or strangulation? Differences are given in Table 15.4.

Table 15.3: Enlist antemortem and postmortem differences in hanging

Features	*Antemortem*	*Postmortem*
Ligature mark	Produces imprint mark, may be grooved, brownish, parchment like	No such features
Salivary dribble	Present	Absent
Le facie sympathique	Present (rare)	Absent
Blisters	Present	Absent
Asphyxial signs	Present	Absent
Drag marks over body	Absent	May be present

STRANGULATION

Definition: *Strangulation is a form of violent asphyxial death caused by constricting the neck by means of ligature or by any other means without suspending the body.*

In strangulation the constriction force is other than the weight of victim's body. There is application of external force such as compression of neck by hands, by rope, by belt, by stick etc.

Types

A) Strangulation deaths are classified on the basis of means used to constrict the neck and are of following types.
   1. Ligature strangulation
   2. Manual strangulation or throttling
   3. Mugging
   4. Bansdola
   5. Garroting
   6. Palmar strangulation

B) Depending on manner of death, strangulation is classified as:
   1. Homicidal strangulation
   2. Accidental strangulation

Cause of Death

1. Asphyxia
2. Cerebral hypoxia
3. Cerebral congestion
4. Combined- asphyxia and venous congestion
5. Vagal inhibition
6. Fracture dislocation of cervical vertebrae

LIGATURE STRANGULATION

Definition: *Ligature strangulation is a violent form of death caused by constricting the neck by means of a ligature without suspending the body.*

Table 15.4: Difference between hanging and strangulation

Features	Hanging	Strangulation
Manner	Usually suicidal	Usually homicidal
Saliva	Dribbling from mouth over chin or chest	No such dribbling
Ligature mark	Oblique, non-continuous, usually above the level of thyroid cartilage	Horizontal, continuous, usually at or below the level of thyroid cartilage
Tissue underneath mark	Dry, pale, hard and glistening	Bruised
Neck muscle	Injury to neck muscle rare	Injury to neck muscle common
Neck	Stretched and elongated	Not so
Larynx and trachea	Injury/fracture rare	Injury/fracture more common
Bleeding	From nose, mouth or ear is less common	From nose, mouth or ear is common
Signs of asphyxia	Less prominent	More prominent

Ligature may be in form of rope, belt, wire, cable, dhoti, dupatta etc.

Autopsy findings

External Examination

1) Findings in neck: The appearance of neck and findings produced may vary according to the means used viz. rope, wire, cable etc.
   A) Ligature mark
      - The ligature mark is usually well defined and grooved. The mark is present over neck at any level but commonly it is placed at the level or below the thyroid cartilage. The mark completely encircles the neck horizontally (transversely) and may be prominent on front and at sides (Fig. 15.28).
      - The mark may be multiple, if ligature is twisted many times round the neck.
      - If knot is applied, there may be a wider area of contusion at the site of the knot
      - The mark may be oblique as in hanging if the victim has been dragged by a cord after he has been strangled in a recumbent posture or if the victim was sitting and the assailant applied ligature on the neck while standing behind him, thus using the force backward and upward.[17]
      - Initially the base of mark is pale with reddish margin however, later on, it becomes dry, dark, hard and parchment like.
      - If breadth of ligature is wide, the mark impression will be wider and superficial. If ligature used is narrow one for example metal wire, it may leave narrow but deeper impression on neck skin. At times the mark is such deep that it appears that neck has been pierced by wire, so called **cheese-cutter** method or phenomenon.[3]
      - The ligature mark of strangulation is not obliterated by putrefaction, but is preserved. Even though the mark gets obscured due to on going decomposition, subcutaneous hemorrhages in relation to mark may be found.[11]
   B) Other signs (Fig. 15.29):
      - Signs of asphyxia are more prominent
      - The face is puffy, edematous and congested
      - The eyes are prominent, open, bulging and suffused with scleral hemorrhages. Conjunctiva shows congestion and petechial hemorrhages. Occasionally with more violence, there may be subconjunctival hemorrhage (Fig. 15.30).
      - Petechial hemorrhages may also be noted on eyelids, face and forehead
      - Sphincters may be relaxed with voiding of urine, feces or semen.

Internal Examination

A) Findings in neck:
   - Neck structures should be examined at the end of autopsy after examining the cranial cavity and chest and abdomen. The purpose being, the neck will be relatively bloodless, as blood will be drained out from neck vessels.
   - Superficial hemorrhages may be present underneath the ligature mark with evidence of hemorrhages in muscle and soft tissue in and above the area

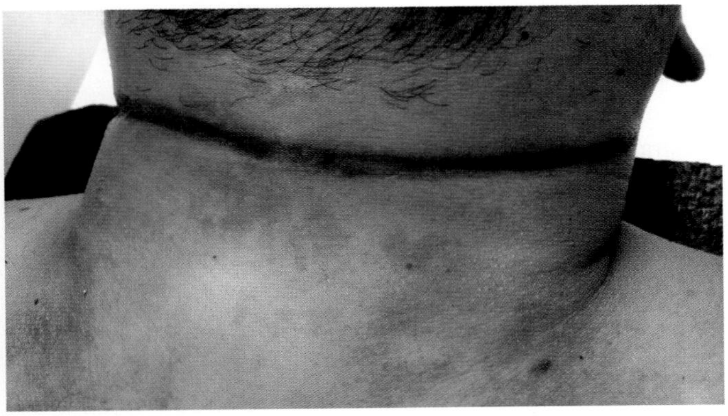

FIG. 15.28: Ligature mark in ligature strangulation

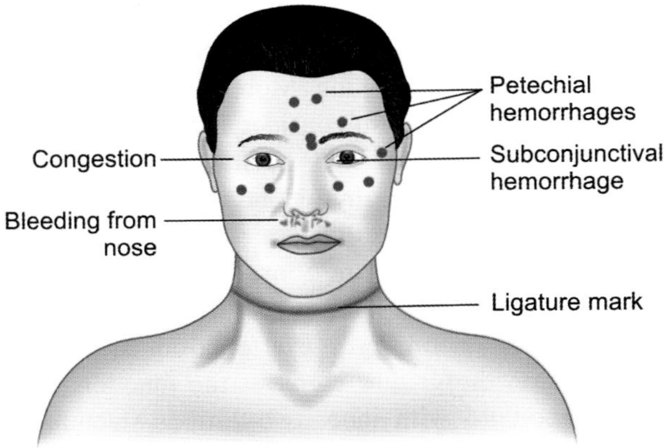

FIG. 15.29: Strangulation mark with different manifestation seen over face

Section A Forensic Medicine

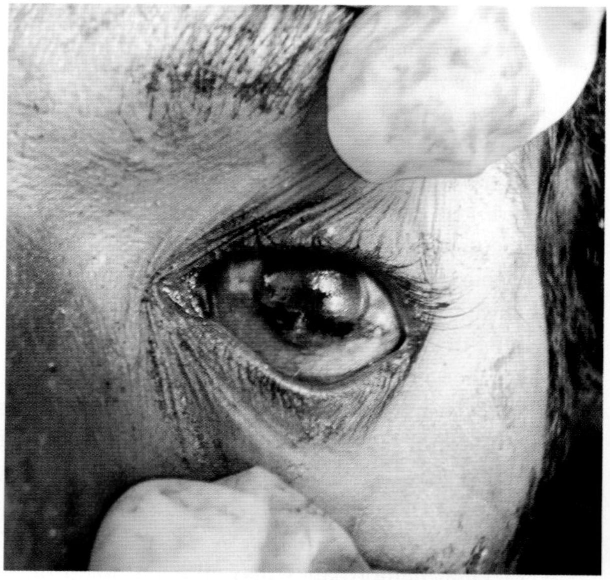

FIG. 15.30: Suffused conjunctiva

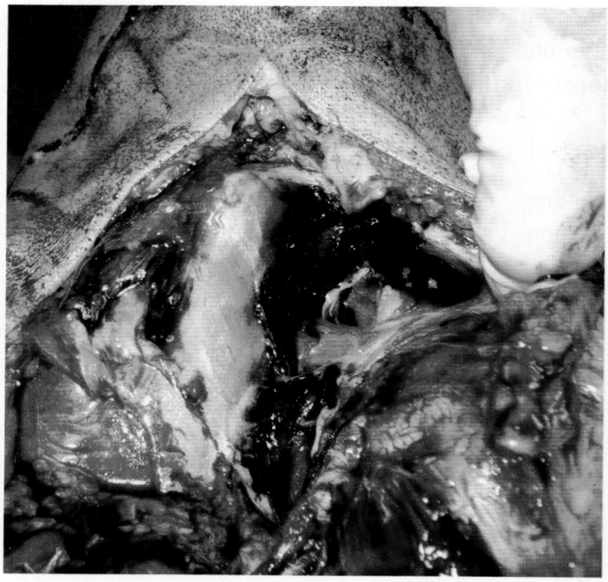

FIG. 15.31: Internal findings in neck in strangulation

compressed. The neck muscles may show hematoma or even lacerations (Fig. 15.31).

- If violence applied is more, there may be extensive bruising of the deeper structures and tissues of the neck.
- Subcapsular and interstitial hemorrhages may also be noted in thyroid.[11]
- There may be extravasations or laceration of carotid sheath. The intima of carotid may show hemorrhagic infiltration or may show transverse intimal tears.[6]
- The base of tongue may show deep lingual hemorrhages.[9, 18]
- Fracture of hyoid bone and thyroid cartilage may be seen in some cases. However, hyoid fractures are not common because the level of ligature is below the hyoid bone and traction on the thyrohyoid ligament is not much acting. Moreover, if broad ligature material is used with considerable force, hyoid bone or thyroid cartilage may be fractured.[7, 19] Similarly the hyoid bone or thyroid horns may be fractured, especially where the ligature rides at the level of the thyrohyoid ligament or above.[3] Hyoid may be fractured by: [11,20,21]
  1. Direct lateral force exerted from side of neck. Here, the greater cornu at the junction of outer one-third with inner two-third is fractured with broken fragment displaced outward.
  2. Indirect violence where hyoid is drawn upward and traction is applied through thyrohyoid membrane called as traction fracture or tug fracture.
- In some cases one or both superior horns of thyroid may be fractured. However, fracture of thyroid lamina or cricoid cartilage is uncommon and occurs only when considerable force is used.
- The cartilage of larynx or tracheal rings may be fractured if considerable force is used.[17]

B) Other findings:

- Lungs may be congested and edematous and may show fresh hemorrhages in parenchyma
- Pleura show petechial hemorrhages. There may be emphysematous bullas on lung surface due to overdistension and rupture of interalveolar septa.
- Abdominal viscera- congested.

Medicolegal Importance

1) Homicidal strangulation is more common than accidental strangulation. Moreover, in forensic practice, it is said that strangulation is always homicidal unless proved otherwise. Suicidal strangulation is a rare phenomenon and occurs only if suicide employs special method and instrumentation.
2) Accidental strangulation may occur if some material like scarf, dupatta, machine belt etc. is suddenly wrapped around the neck and constricting the neck causing death.[16]
3) The strangulation may be mistaken for hanging or vice versa. It is important to distinguish between strangulation

and hanging. The salient differentiating features are summarized in Table 15.4.

THROTTLING (MANUAL STRANGULATION)

Definition: *It is violent asphyxial death produced by compression of neck manually i.e. by using human hands.*

The neck is compressed by using hands. Either one hand or both hands may be used to throttle a person.

Autopsy Findings

In addition to signs of asphyxia, injuries may be seen in neck. The injuries are in form of contusion and/or abrasion and depend on:

1) The relative position of victim and the assailant.
2) The number of assailant.
3) The manner of grasping the neck, either with one hand or both hands.
4) Degree of pressure exerted on the neck.

The following patterns of injuries are present:

1) Cutaneous contusions
2) Cutaneous abrasions
3) Hemorrhages/contusions into the deep structure of the neck
4) Injury to hyoid bone and laryngeal complex.

Contusions over Neck

- Contusions are produced as a result of grasping the neck of victim by assailant's fingers. Contusions produced by tips and pads of fingers are oval or round in shape and are of size of digits measuring about 1.5 to 2 cm. However, the size may alter due to bleeding underneath the skin.
- If one hand is used, it may be possible to have one prominent contusion on one side of neck (due to thumb) and three to four contusions on the other side (due to fingers) (Fig. 15.32A).
- When both hands are used the thumb mark of one hand and finger marks of other hand on either side of neck may be found (Fig. 15.32B).
- However, caution should be exercised while interpreting these bruises as many factors influences for their appearance.

Abrasions on Neck

- Scratch abrasions may be present over neck and are caused by fingernails of either hands of assailant or that of victim in attempt to ward off the assailant (Fig. 15.32).

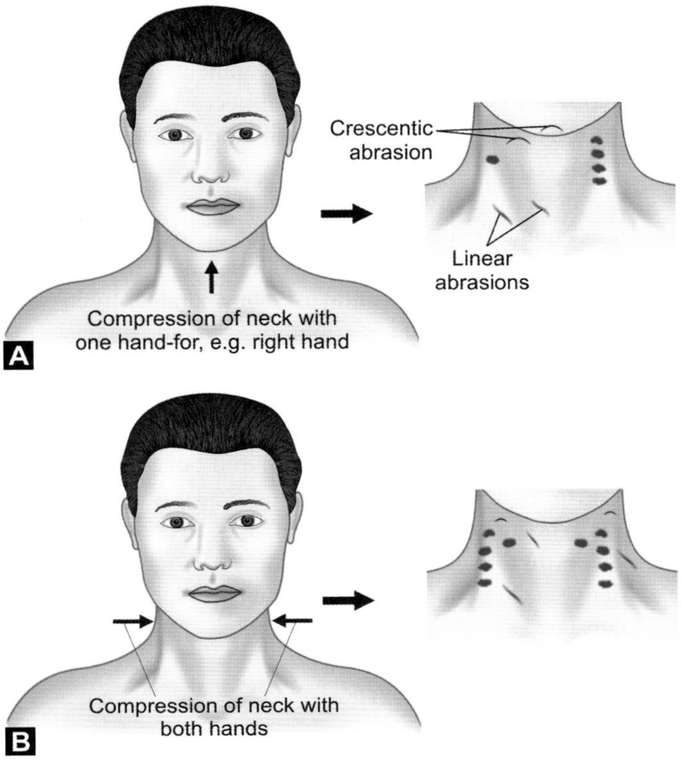

FIGS 15.32A and B: Findings on neck in throttling

- There may be crescentic or semi-lunar abrasions over neck and are caused due to nails embedded in the neck (Figs 15.32A and B).

Hemorrhages/Contusions into the Deep Structure of the Neck

- On internal examination bruising of neck muscles may be present as a direct result of force applied. At times, laceration of deeper structure of neck involving muscle and soft tissue may be noted.
- Hemorrhages are common in strap muscles and platysma.
- The pharynx, tonsils, base of tongue and upper part of larynx may show extensive bleeding if duration and degree of compression is more.[7]
- Hemorrhages may appear beneath the capsule of thyroid, submaxillary and carotid lymphatic glands. Hemorrhages may also appear in the lymphatic glands of the anterior triangle of the neck.[3, 7]

Injury to Hyoid Bone and Laryngeal Complex

- Thyroid fractures are common as maximum pressure is likely to be effected at this site and involves more commonly the upper horns. Fracture of body of thyroid is rare.[1] Microscopy from fracture site and surrounding tissue reveals hemorrhage, development of coagulative myocytolysis or contraction band necrosis, deposition of fibrin and occurrence of inflammatory reaction if death is delayed.[22]

- The body of thyroid can be broken by a "karate blow" or "commando punch" to the front of neck.[11]
- The cricoid is rarely injured. If cricoid is injured, it is associated with application of considerable force with antero-posterior compression of cricoid against the spine.[1]
- Hyoid bone fracture: Fracture of hyoid bone is common in manual strangulation than ligature strangulation.[23, 24] Inward compression fracture of hyoid bone may be seen by grip high up in the neck (Fig. 15.33). Similarly avulsion type of fracture may be noted as a result of traction on the thyrohyoid membrane.[7, 25]
- Many of the victims of mechanical asphyxia showed high level of plasma thyroglobulin.[26]

HYOID BONE FRACTURE

There are three types of hyoid bone fracture:
1) Antero-posterior type fracture or outward type fracture
2) Inward compression fracture
3) Avulsion or traction or tug fracture
   - **Antero-posterior type fracture**: It is commonly seen in hanging or ligature strangulation.[21] In this type of fracture, the hyoid bone is forced backward due to which divergence of greater horns are increased resulting in fracture of greater horn with outward displacement of the fractured fragment. In this type, the periosteum is torn or disrupted on the inner side of hyoid bone and due to which the fractured fragment can be easily moved outward (Fig. 15.26).
   - **Inward compression fracture**:[11] It is seen in case of throttling (Fig. 15.33). In throttling cases, the force of compression is directed inward and act over hyoid bone. The fingers of grasping hand squeeze the greater horns toward each other due to which the distal fragment of hyoid bone (greater horn) get fractured and the bone fragment is displaced inwards. The periosteum is broken or torn on the outer side of the hyoid bone and due to which the bone fragment can be easily moved inwards but cannot move easily outward.
   - **Avulsion fracture**:[19, 27] This is indirect type of fracture. The hyoid bone is drawn upward and held by muscle and thyrohyoid membrane attached to its upper and anterior surface. Violent lateral or downward movements of thyroid cartilage or direct pressure applied between the cartilage and the hyoid bone will exercise traction force through the thyrohyoid membrane due to which there is avulsion fracture of hyoid bone.

Bansdola

It is form of strangulation. In bansdola, a wooden poles or sticks or rods or bamboos are used. One bamboo or stick is placed over front of neck and another is placed behind the neck. One end of these sticks or bamboos are tied together by a rope and other ends are brought forcefully together so as to squeeze or compress the neck in between two sticks to cause death (Fig. 15.34).

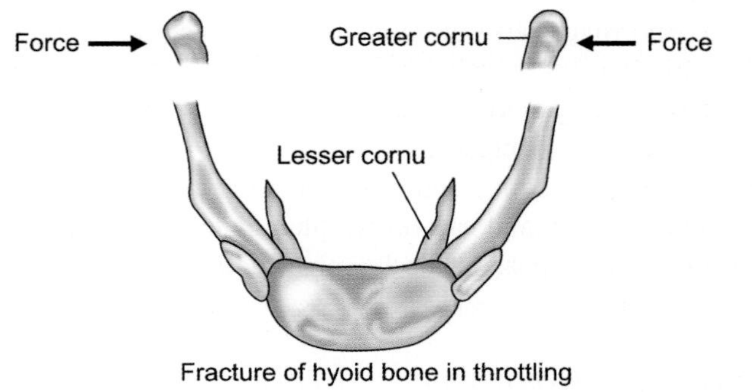

FIG. 15.33: Fracture of hyoid bone in throttling

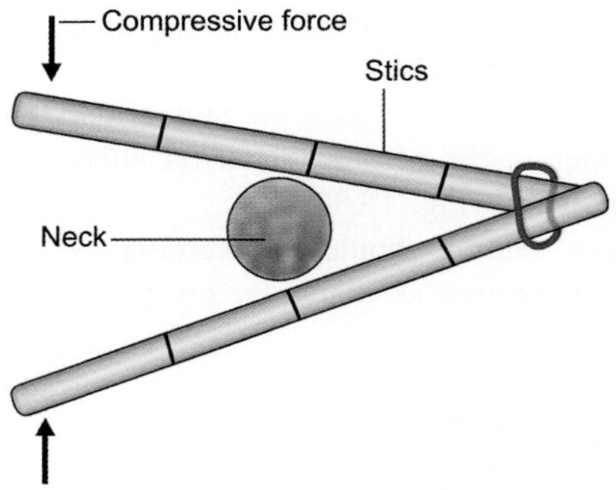

FIG. 15.34: Bansdola

Garroting

- Garroting is a type of strangulation. Thugs used this method around 1867 in India. The robbers used this method in lonely places to kill travelers and rob them.
- There are various methods such as Indian method, Spanish method etc.
- In Indian method, the victim is attacked from behind without warning. The neck is grasped by a ligature thrown from behind and is quickly fastened or tightened by twisting it with lever or two sticks tied at the end of ligature (Fig. 15.35). Asphyxiation of the unaware victim causes rapid loss of consciousness and death.
- Spanish method: In Spain it is method of judicial execution. Here, a twisting device known as Spanish windlass is used. It consists of iron color that is placed around the neck and tightened by screw for strangulating the victim.

Mugging

- Also known as arm lock
- This is a type of strangulation. It is caused by holding the neck of person in the bend of the elbow (or bend of knee). Here pressure is exerted over larynx or side of neck by the forearm and arm (Fig. 15.36).

Palmar Strangulation

In this type, the palm of one hand is placed horizontally across the mouth and nostrils and then reinforced the pressure by placing the other hand on the top of first hand at right angle to the other. Here the heel of palm of upper hand presses the front of neck.

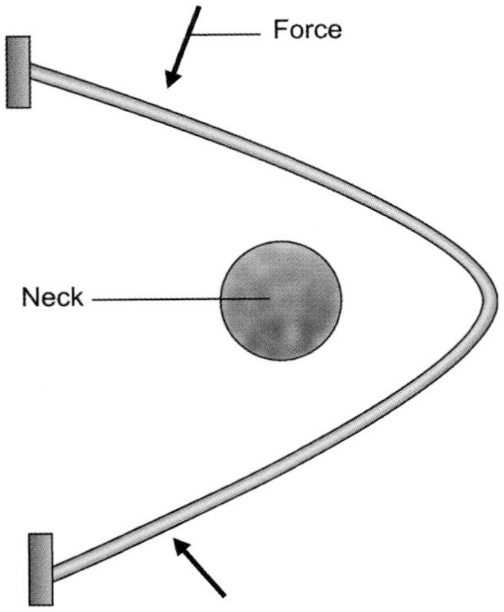

FIG. 15.35: Garroting

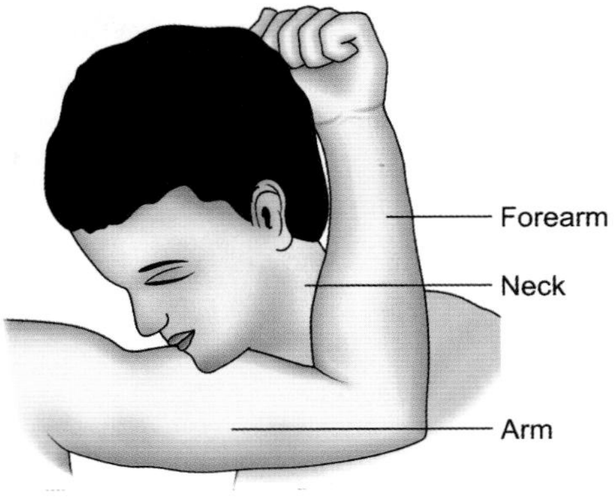

FIG. 15.36: Mugging

SUFFOCATION

Definition: *Suffocation is a type of mechanical asphyxia caused-*

1. *Either due to lack of oxygen in the environment or*
2. *By mechanical obstruction to the air passage by means other than constriction of neck and drowning.*

Causes

Causes are mentioned in Table 15.5

Types of Suffocation

1) Smothering
2) Choking
3) Gagging
4) Traumatic asphyxia
5) Burking
6) Overlying
7) Inhalation of irrespirable gases

SMOTHERING

Definition: *It is form of asphyxia caused by mechanical occlusion of the external respiratory orifices i.e. the nose and mouth.*

Death is caused by obstructing the air passage i.e. mouth and nostril by means of hand, cloth, pillow, towel etc. (see Fig. 15.37)

Autopsy Findings

- There may be pale area around the mouth and nose (circumoral and circumnasal pallor) due to pressure of

Table 15.5: Displaying causes of suffocation
Causes of suffocation
1. Deprivation of oxygen in air (environmental suffocation) such as: • Presence of toxic gases in air such as CO, CO_2, SO_2 etc • Decompression • High altitude
2. Plastic bag suffocation
3. Obstruction to air passage by means (other than compression of neck and drowning): A) External means • Smothering • Overlying • Traumatic asphyxia B) Internal means • Gagging • Choking

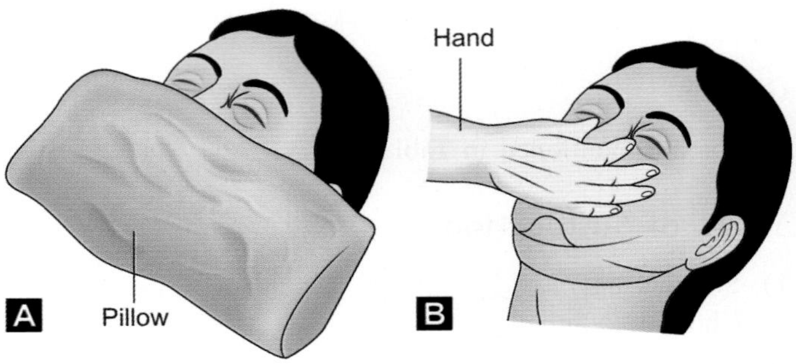

FIGS 15.37A and B: Smothering **A:** By pillow, **B:** By hand

the object say for example pillow with cyanosis of face. Nose may be flattened and its septum may be fractured.

- Face may also show congestion and/or petechial hemorrhages. In some cases, abrasions, scratches or contusions may be noted.
- If soft material is used to close mouth and nostrils, no obvious injuries may present externally. However, the object used may be stained with saliva, blood and mucosal cells.
- There may be contusions at lips, gums and tongue. The inner surface of lips may be lacerated due to pressure on teeth.
- Foreign bodies in form of fibers or piece of cloth etc. may be found in oral cavity if such objects are used to compress mouth and nose.

Medicolegal Importance

1) Homicidal smothering are common
2) Accidental smothering is rare
3) Sexually perverted person may cover the head with plastic bag during autoerotic activity and get suffocated.
4) A newborn baby may die due to suffocation if the baby is born with membrane (amniotic sac) covered with (**cul-de-sac birth** or caul birth).

GAGGING

Definition: *Gagging is a type of asphyxia caused by preventing the air entry into the respiratory tract by stuffing gag material into the mouth.* The gag material may be rolled cloth, cotton, rug, paper etc. (Fig. 15.38).

Mechanism

A gag is pushed into the mouth to occlude the pharynx. Initially the airway remains patent through nostrils but due to constant foreign body irritation, there is pooling of saliva and mucous secretions. These secretions soak the gag material and swells up. Thus due to increase in size of gag, it obstruct the air passage.

Autopsy Findings

Autopsy findings consist of congestion and abrasion of hard and soft palate with edema of pharynx. Gag may be present in the oral cavity.

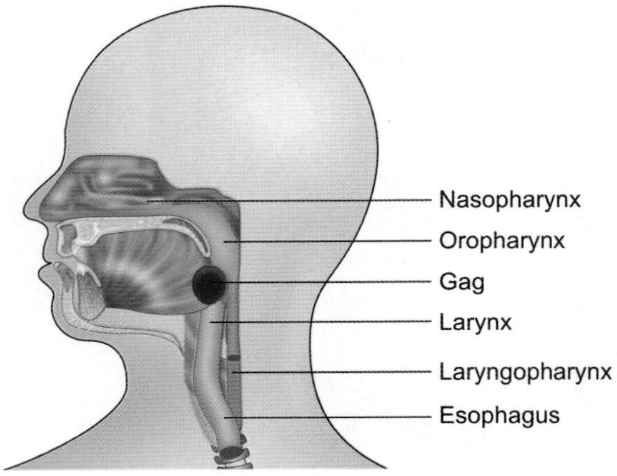

FIG. 15.38: Gagging

Medicolegal Importance

1) Homicidal death: Gags are inserted into mouth of infants or incapacitated person with an intention to kill them.
2) Some times accidental death may occur when a gag is inserted into the mouth of a victim to prevent from shouting.

Overlying

- Overlying is also called as **compression suffocation**
- It results when mother or other person sharing a bed with infant. During sleep, the mother or person may compress the infant by overlying over it. Death occurs due to compression of chest and these deaths are accidental in nature.

Burking

- Burking is a form of mechanical asphyxia where death is caused by a combination of smothering and traumatic asphyxia.
- In early part of 19th century in England, William Burke and William Hare had invented this procedure.
- William Burke and Hare kill people and sold their bodies to Dr Robert Knox for medical school. The modus operandi consisted of inviting a person to their house and offer alcohol to the guest. As soon as their guest was drunk enough, the victim was put to ground and Burke used to sit on chest and closes the mouth and nose of victim by his hands and Hare used to pull the victim round the room by the feet.
- Medicolegal importance: This method combines smothering and traumatic asphyxia.

CHOKING

Definition: *Choking is a form of asphyxial death caused by mechanical obstruction of the air passage from within.*

- Thus in choking, there is blockage of airway internally.
- Choking may be caused by objects like-coins, dentures, fish or animal bone, piece of meat, seed, food bolus, button, round worm, mud, cotton, edible fruit seeds, toffee, candies etc. (Fig. 15.39)

Mechanism

- Large foreign body may be obstructed in the pharynx or larynx and occlude the lumen completely thus causing asphyxia.

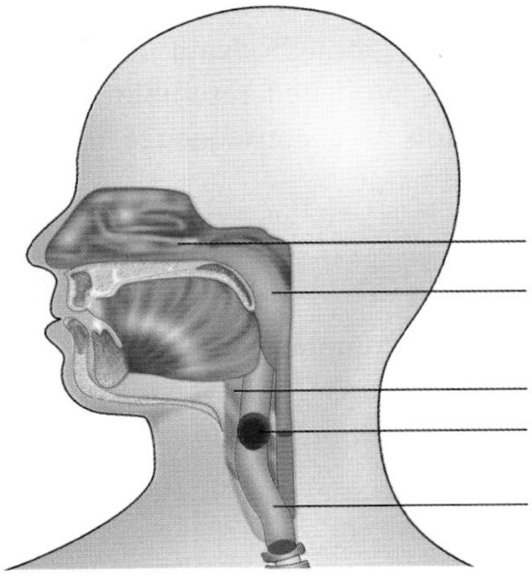

FIG. 15.39: Choking

- Small foreign body may partially block the lumen of airway and irritates the respiratory tract. Irritation causes increase in secretions and may induce laryngeal spasm.
- An object may also induce reflex cardiac inhibition and causes death.

Cause of Death

1) Asphyxia
2) Vagal inhibition
3) Laryngeal spasm

Autopsy findings: In addition to signs of asphyxia, following additional findings may be noted:

- Foreign body that causes obstruction will be found in the respiratory passage.
- Respiratory passage is congested and at the site of foreign body may show edema and inflammation.

Medicolegal Importance

1. Choking is usually accidental. In children, choking may occur while playing with small objects or while eating may inhale solid particle or food bolus. In elderly or mentally ill patient, may swallow the food without chewing and may inhale the food bolus.
2. Suicidal or homicidal choking is rare phenomenon. A case of homicidal choking is reported in literature where an adult was killed by choking using large amount of tissue paper.[28]
3. Café coronary: A person under the influence of alcohol may some time inhale food bolus or piece of bone or meat as intoxication causes depression of gag reflex. The foreign body in larynx or trachea causes parasympathetic

stimulation from laryngeal nerve that result in cardiac arrest and death.[6] Here, though death occurs due to choking, the symptoms produced resemble that of due to myocardial infarction as a consequence of coronary blockage and thus the name.

TRAUMATIC ASPHYXIA

Synonyms: Crush asphyxia, compression asphyxia

Definition: *Traumatic asphyxia is form of violent asphyxia caused due to mechanical fixation of the chest preventing respiratory movements.*

Causes

1. The chest and usually abdomen are compressed by an unyielding object so that chest expansion and diaphragmatic movements are prevented.[3] This may occur in:
   - Person buried under rubble of collapsed building (Fig. 15.40)
   - Person buried under sand, grains, coal etc. or by falling of timber or masonry in industrial accidents.
   - Person trapped under automobile or vehicle.
2. Crushing in crowds as occurs in stampede. Chest is compressed and respiratory movements are prevented by stampeding people piling on the top of each other. Such deaths are called as **Riot crush** or **human pile death**.[21]

Fall of wall with person trapped under wall material

FIG. 15.40: Diagrammatic representation of traumatic asphyxia

Autopsy Findings

- Intense congestion, petechial hemorrhages and cyanosis over head, neck and over chest above the site of compression are cardinal features. Petechial hemorrhages are also noted over conjunctiva and periorbital skin. Hemorrhage may be seen in the tissue around the site of compression. There may be injuries over the chest resulting from object felled over chest.
- Internally there are hemorrhages over pleura. Injuries to chest may be present with fracture of ribs. Lungs and heart may show contusions and/or laceration.

Medicolegal Importance

1. Deaths are usually accidental.
2. Death may be homicidal as in burking.

DROWNING

Definition: *Drowning is a form of asphyxial death where air entry into lungs is prevented due to submersion of mouth and nostrils into water or any fluid medium.*

Thus drowning constitutes impairment of tissue oxygenation consequent to submersion in the fluid medium. Complete submersion is not necessary because the process will be complete even if the nose and mouth are submerged.

Causes of Drowning

- Inability to utilize the buoyancy of body
- Exhaustion
- Hypothermia
- Entrapment in whirlpool/tidal waves.

Types of Drowning

Drowning is classified as:

- Typical drowning (wet drowning)
- Atypical drowning (dry drowning)

Classification of drowning is presented in Table 15.6.

Typical Drowning

The term typical drowning indicates obstruction of air passage and lungs by fluid. It is also known as wet drowning.

Atypical Drowning

Indicates condition in which there is very little or no inhalation of water in air passage and includes dry drowning, immersion syndrome, and submersion of an unconscious and secondary drowning.

Table 15.6 Classification of drowning

Types
1. Dry drowning
2. Wet drowning • Fresh water • Salt water
3. Shallow water drowning
4. Immersion syndrome
5. Secondary drowning

Wet Drowning

This is a classical form of drowning either in fresh water or salt water. Here water is inhaled and swallowed and lungs get water lodged.

Dry Drowning

In some cases, no or little water is inhaled in respiratory tract. Death occurs from asphyxia caused due to laryngeal spasm. In such cases, death is more or less instantaneous with lung fields are left dry. This is best type of case for resuscitation (see Fig. 15.41).

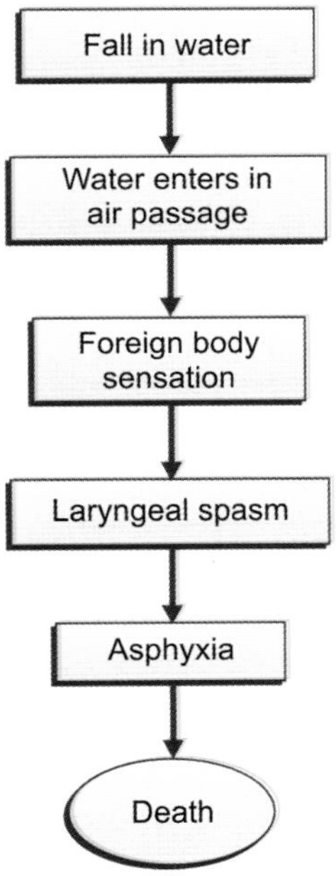

FIG. 15.41: Mechanism of death in dry drowning

Shallow Water Drowning:

- In this condition, drowning occurs in small puddle of water when depth of water is only few inches but sufficient to submerge the mouth and nostrils (Fig. 15.42).
- It occurs mostly accidental in those persons who are disabled or incapacitated such as small children, epileptics, drunkards, comatosed persons following head injury etc.

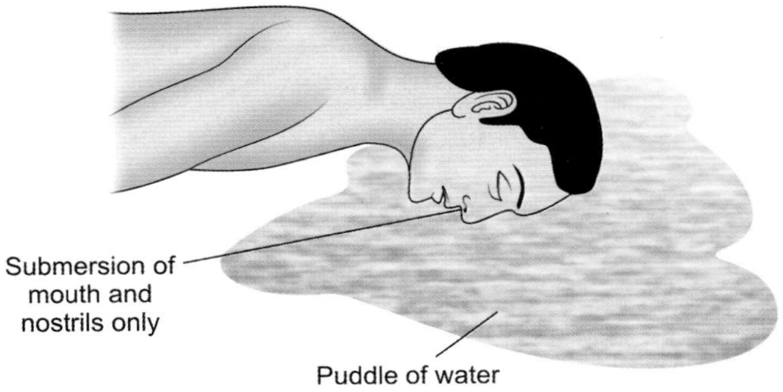

FIG. 15.42: Shallow water drowning

Immersion Syndrome

- Also called as hydrocution
- In this condition death is not due to drowning but results from cardiac arrest due to vagal inhibition. Sudden contact of cold water with body surface especially epigastrium, ears, nostrils, larynx or pharynx stimulates nerve endings and causes vagal inhibition (Fig. 15.43).

Secondary Drowning

- Also called as near drowning
- It refers to a condition where there is survival of a person following an immersion episode. The victim may die subsequently as a result of pathophysiological consequences.
- This is not drowning in truest sense but a complication or Sequelae of drowning.
- A victim when rescued from water may appear alert and breathing or apparently responds to initial resuscitative measures. However, his condition may deteriorate and succumb to death. Death occurs as a sole or combine effect of pulmonary edema, aspiration pneumonia and/or electrolyte imbalance (Fig. 15.44). Therefore, it is aptly said "a person may die in a fluid medium without drowning and if drowned, without necessarily inhaling fluid".

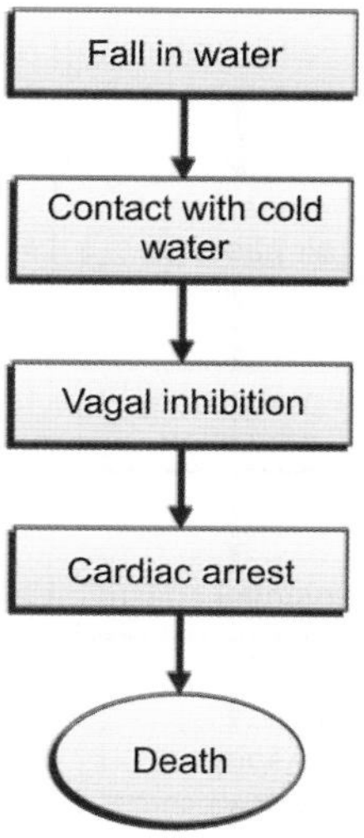

FIG. 15.43: Mechanism of death in immersion syndrome

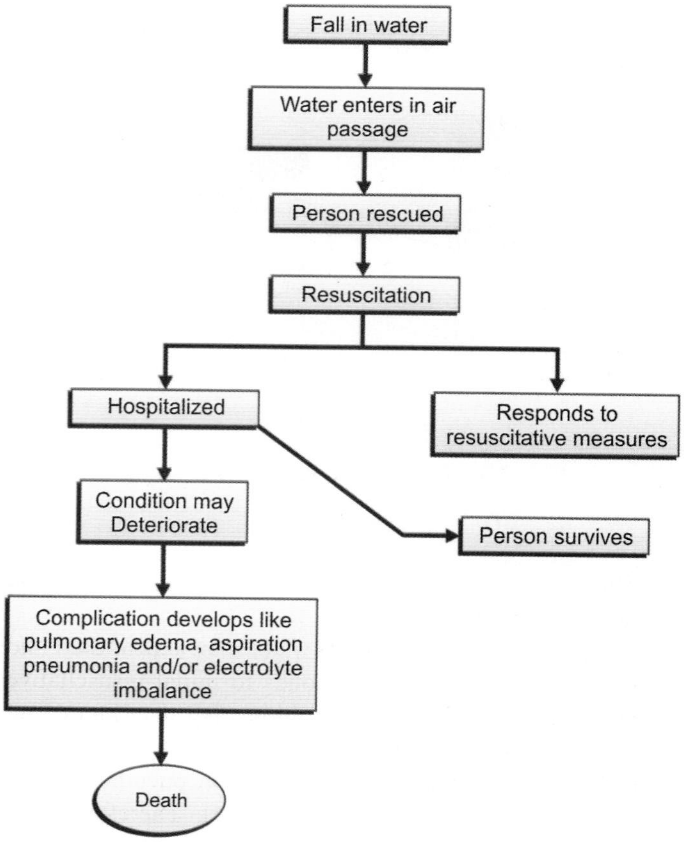

FIG. 15.44: Mechanism of secondary drowning

Mechanism of Drowning

- The specific gravity of a human body as a whole is 1.08. The specific gravity of other parts is: fat-0.9, bone-2.01, muscle-1.08, brain-1.04, soft organs-1.05 and inflated lungs-0.94. Thus, the major portion of the body has a tendency to float and this is known as natural buoyancy.
- When a person falls in water, he immediately sinks to the depth of water proportionate to momentum accrued during fall, weight and specific gravity of body. The person at this stage may die at once, either from head injury or from coronary artery insufficiency or from sudden cardiac arrest due to vagal inhibition.
- Usually the person rises up again to water surface due to natural buoyancy of body and air locked in the body associated with struggling movements of limbs. On reaching the surface of water, person tries to breathe and cries for help. In this attempt, the person inhales and swallows water that causes violent coughing thus diminishing the air reserve in the lungs. The forceful expiratory effort will churn the water already inhaled with air and mucus present in the respiratory tract into froth, which will block the air entry but not the water entry (Fig. 15.45).[1]
- Similarly, rising level of CO_2 in blood will initiate inspiration; causing inhalation of water leading to repeated coughing and churning of air into froth.

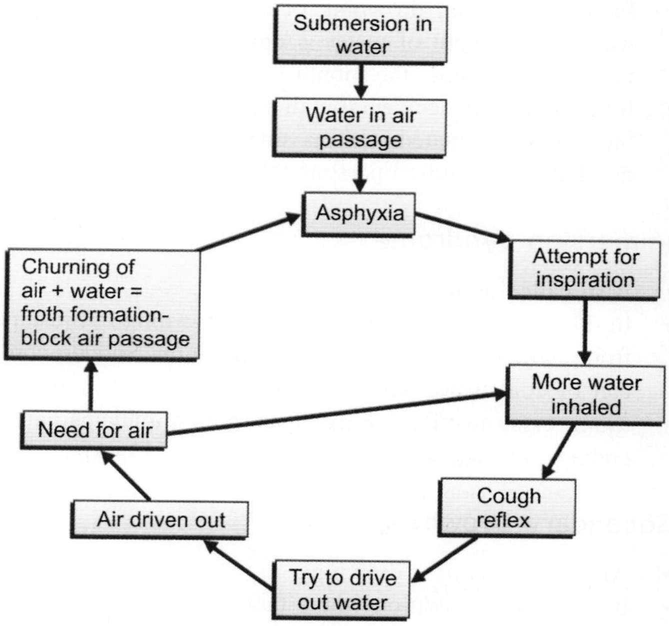

FIG. 15.45: Mechanism of drowning

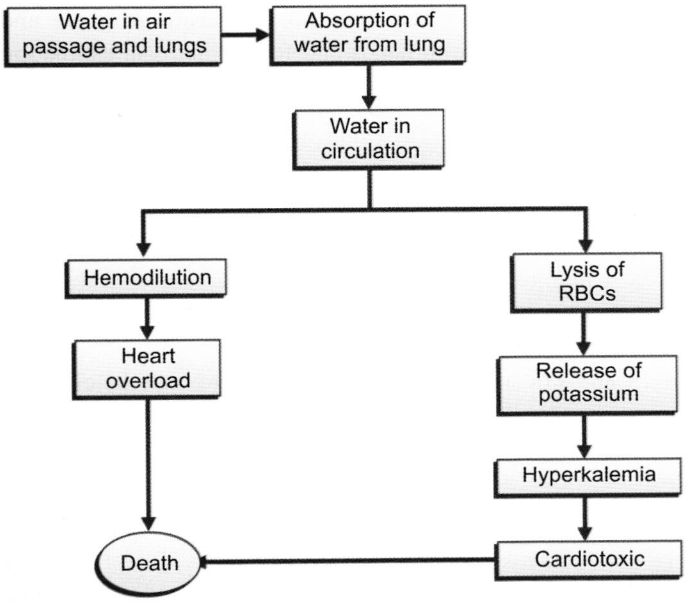

FIG. 15.46: Pathophysiology of fresh water drowning

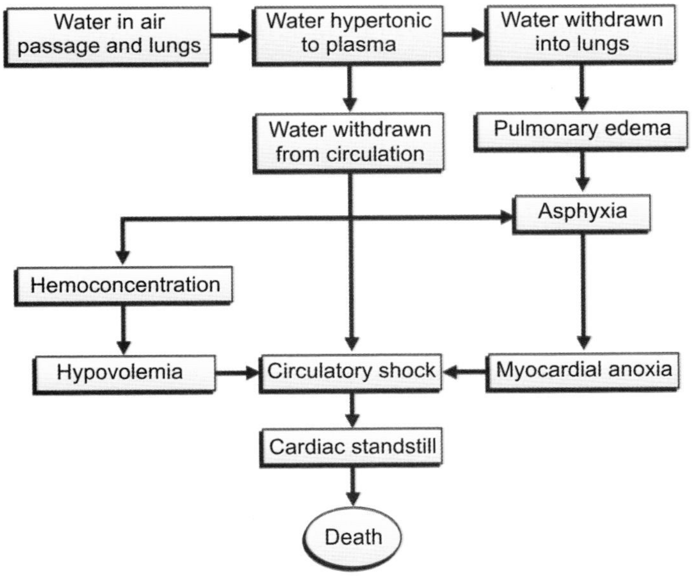

FIG. 15.47: Pathophysiology of salt water drowning

- Due to movements of limbs, the person raises again inhales water again. In struggle for life, the process of rising and sinking goes on for some time and eventually exhaustion and insensibility sets in and finally body sinks at the bottom.
- Convulsions may precede death. Similarly there may be spasm of group of muscle especially hands will be clinched, tightly grasping mud, sand, aquatic vegetations etc. as a sign of cadaveric spasm. The dead body will remain at bottom until it floats up due to decomposition.

Pathophysiology

- Immersion in fluid medium causes death by variety of mechanism, asphyxia due to inhalation of water being more common. However, small number of persons may die due to vagal inhibition as in dry drowning or secondary drowning.
- Inhalation of fluid in lung causes number of changes. Reflex vasoconstriction → pulmonary hypertension → broncoconstriction →increased airway resistance → denaturation of lung surfactant → lung compliance falls → decrease lung tissue for ventilation → abnormal ventilation/perfusion ratio → hypoxia → hypercapnia → respiratory acidosis → asphyxia.

Fresh Water Drowning (Fig. 15.46)

- Aspirated fresh water rapidly traverses the alveolar septum and capillary wall and leaves the lung causing hemodilution.
- Fresh water is hypotonic to pulmonary circulation. About 3 to 5 liters of water is absorbed from alveolar bed within 3 minute of initial period of struggle and apnea thus causing hemodilution and abrupt increase in blood volume up to 72 percent with hemolysis. As a result, there is excess of K^+ with reduction in Na^+, Ca^{++} and Cl^-concentration. There is electrolyte imbalance together with O_2 deprivation and accumulation of CO_2.
- The heart is subjected to anoxic insult, fluid overload and hyperkalemia. Myocardial anoxia and hyperkalemia leads to ventricular fibrillation and death occurs within 4 to 5 minutes.

Salt Water Drowning (Fig. 15.47)

- Seawater is osmotically hypertonic to plasma – contains about 3.5% of dissolved salt.
- Since the water is hypertonic, drowning with seawater results in withdrawal of water from pulmonary circulation. About 42 percent of water may be withdrawn from circulation into the lung field resulting in pulmonary edema, hemoconcentration and hypovolemia.
- Due to hemoconcentration, viscosity of blood increases and there will be increase in hematocrit and plasma Mg^+ & Na^+ level. Red blood cells will shrink.
- Appearance of fulminating pulmonary edema with progressive hypovolemia causes circulatory collapse and myocardial anoxia. Death in seawater drowning is delayed and takes about 8 to 12 minutes.

- The differences between fresh water and sea water drowning are displayed in Table 15.7.

Causes of Death

1) Asphyxia
2) Vagal inhibition
3) Ventricular fibrillation
4) Myocardial anoxia
5) Laryngeal spasm
6) Exhaustion
7) Hypothermia
8) Concussion/head injury
9) Apoplexy.

Autopsy Findings

External examination:

1. Clothes are wet
2. Skin is cold, wet and pale. Skin may show **cutis anserina** i.e. appearance of gooseflesh or goose skin. It is a state of puckered and granular appearance of skin with hairs standing on end due to contraction of erector pilorum muscle (Fig. 15.48).
3. Washerwoman's hand: Prolonged immersion in water leads to maceration of skin due to imbibitions of water. There is whitening, soddening, bleaching and wrinkling of skin particularly on palmar surface of hands and soles of feet (Figs 15.49 and 15.50). Subsequently the epidermis gets separated from the dermis in glove and stock fashion from hands and feet. It helps in estimation of approximate duration of immersion as:[29]
   - Wrinkling: if water is cold, skin gets wrinkled soon after immersion
   - Bleaching of cuticle: become evident after 12 hours of immersion
   - Bleaching, corrugation and soddening becomes pronounced within 24 hours
   - Cuticle begins to separate from palm and sole by 48 hours.
4. Cadaveric spasm: Grass, mud, sand etc. may be clinched in hands. Presence of cadaveric spasm indicates person was alive when he was drowned.

Table 15.7: Difference between fresh and sea water drowning

Features	*Fresh water drowning*	*Sea water drowning*
Water	Hypotonic	Hypertonic
Changes in blood	Hemodilution Hyponatremia Hyperkalemia Hypocalcaemia Decrease in chlorides	Hemoconcentration Hypernatremia Increase magnesium
Time required for death	4-5 minute	8-12 minute
Changes in lung	-Retains shape after removal -edematous, voluminous, doughy	-Do not retain shape -Marked edema, soft, jelly like

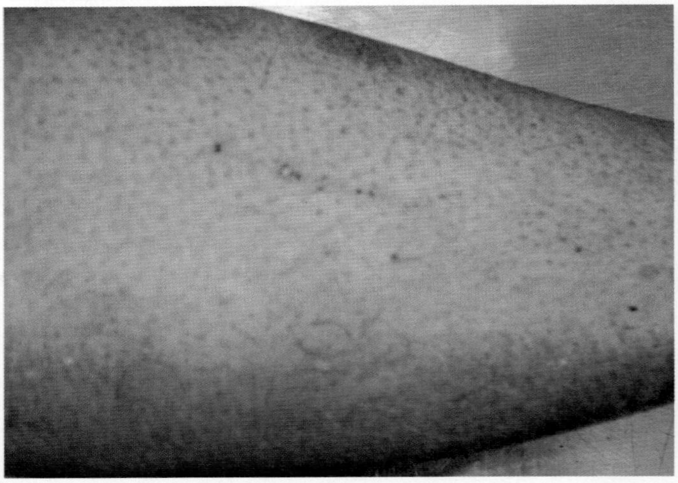

FIG. 15.48: Cutis anserina

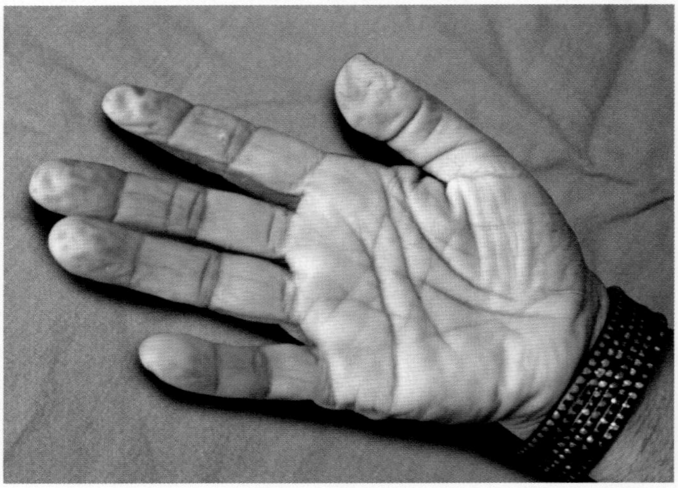

FIG. 15.49: Washerwoman's hand

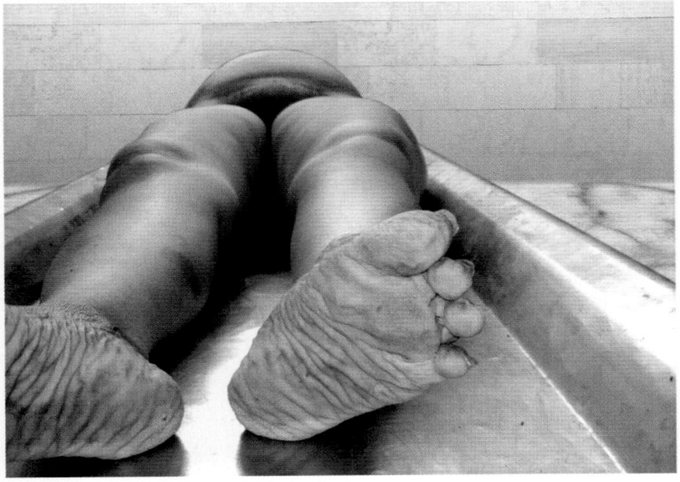

FIG. 15.50: Washerwoman's feet

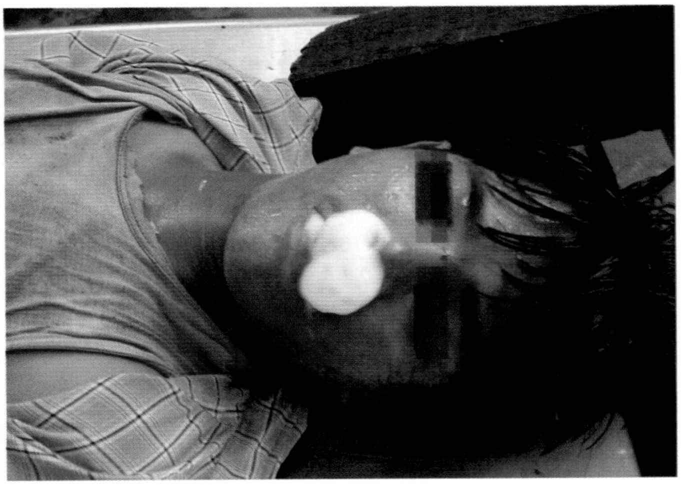

FIG. 15.51: Typical froth seen in drowning (note mushroom like froth)

5. Rigor mortis appear and passes early due to exhaustion and/or violent struggle for life.
6. Postmortem lividity: Dependent lividity may be pronounced in the face, head, neck and anterior chest because the body floats partly head-down in water. The colour of lividity may be bright pink due to cold preservation of oxyhemoglobin. If water is turbulent or flowing and turning the body constantly, lividity may not appear.
7. Eyes: Conjunctiva is suffused and congested. Few subconjunctival hemorrhages may be noted.
8. Froth (foam cone, champigon de mousse): fine, whitish, leathery, tenacious, copious froth is seen oozing from mouth and nostrils. The froth extends vertically in cone shape when the body is undisturbed (Figs 15.51 to 15.53). At time, the mass of foam may look like balloon or mushroom. The mass of foam consisting of fine bubbles does not readily collapse when touched with point of knife. This type of froth is produced by the process of churning of air, mucus and water in the respiratory tract. Presence of such peculiar foam is essentially vital phenomenon.

Internal Examination

1) Changes in lungs
   - Appearance: The lungs are voluminous, oedematous, ballooned, water lodged, bulging. The distended lung surface shows indentions of ribs. Lung feels heavy, doughy in consistency and pits on pressure by fingers. On cut section, oozes fine, copious leathery froth. In fresh water drowning, lungs retained the shape (Figs 15.54 and 15.55). In salt water drowning, lungs are heavy, saggy, ballooned and cut section exudes copious frothy fluid and the cut section does not retain shape.
   - Paltauff's hemorrhages: These are subpleural hemorrhages mostly noted over anterior surface and margins of lungs. They are caused due rupture of interalveolar partitions beneath the pleura (Fig. 15.56).
   - Emphysema aquosum: The lungs feel heavy, doughy, spongy and water lodged. This state is referred as emphysema aquosam. This condition indicates that the person was conscious and struggles for life.

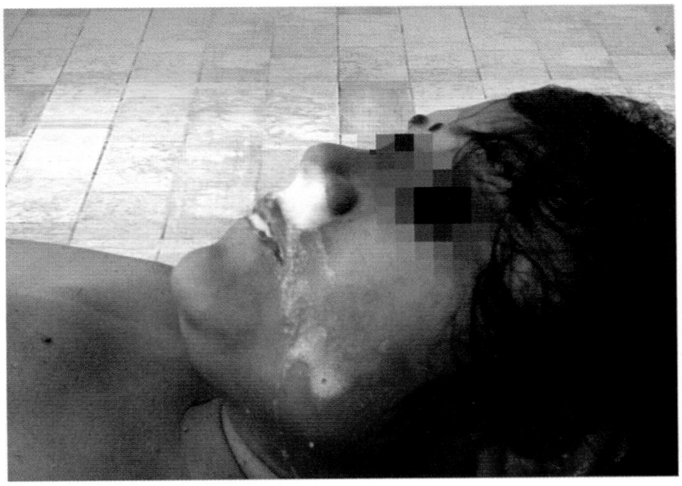

FIG. 15.52: Froth in drowning

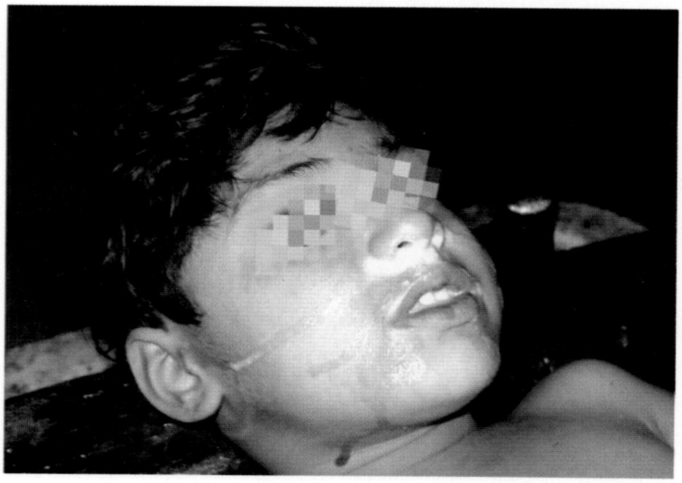

FIG. 15.53: Froth in drowning

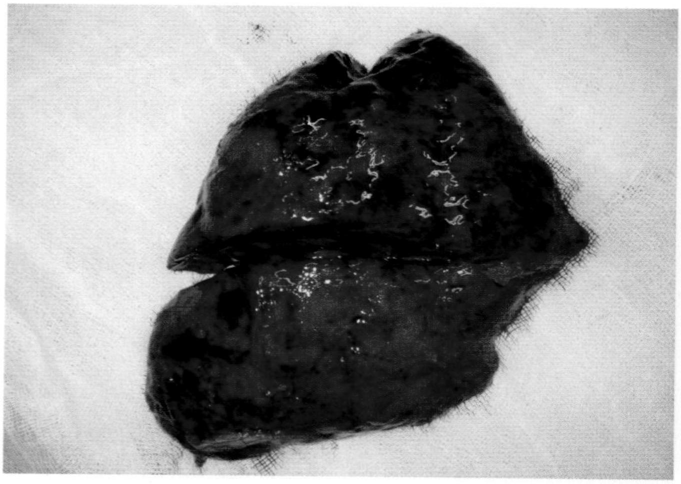

FIG. 15.54: Lungs in drowning

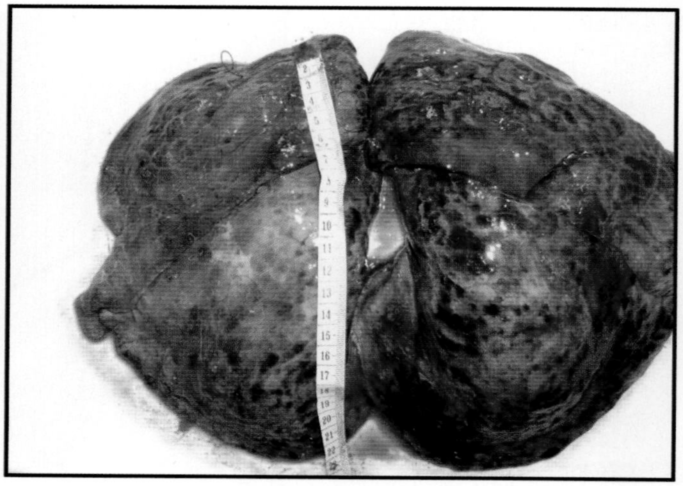

FIG. 15.55: Lungs in drowning

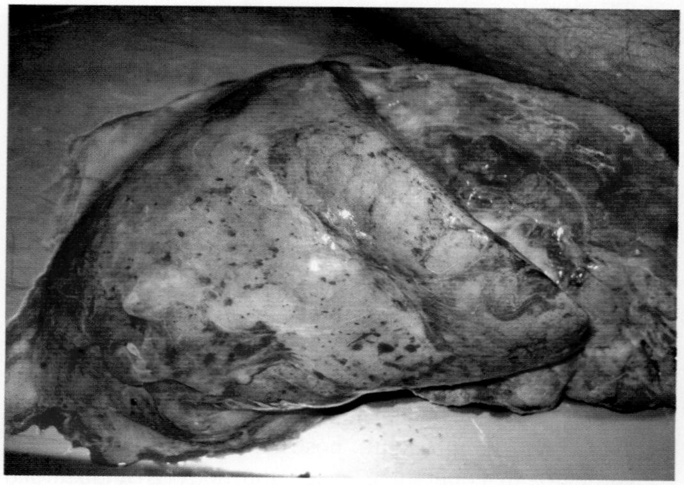

FIG. 15.56: Paltauff's hemorrhages

- Edema aquosum: This condition develops when person is passively immersed with no violent effort of respiration in water or when person is unconscious. It is a state of mere flooding of lungs with the water with no formation of column of froth.
- Weight of lungs: Weights of lungs in drowning are around 600 to 700 gm whilst non-drowning lung weighs about 370 to 540 gm.[30]

2) Other findings
   - Respiratory passage shows whitish, fine froth and may show sand, mud, silt, grit, vegetations etc.
   - Blood is usually dark and fluid.
   - Stomach and proximal intestine may contain swallowed water or in addition may show sand, mud, grit, silt etc.
   - Water may be found in middle ear and claimed to be positive proof of antemortem drowning. Water is forced into middle ear during violent respiratory effort.
   - Hemorrhage in middle ear and mastoid air cells are considered as vital sign. These hemorrhages are produced due to barotraumas due to pressure difference between middle ear and surrounding water.[31, 32]

Laboratory Findings

Microscopy

- Lung: Pulmonary alveoli are distended and contain fluid with foreign material such as aquatic vegetation. The alveolar septal wall appears stretched and thinned with compression of capillaries along with some ruptured alveoli (Fig. 15.57).[3, 9]
- Blood: Fresh water drowning- shows low RBC count with hemolysis. In seawater drowning- relative increase in RBC count with RBCs appear crenated and shrunken (Figs 15.58A and B).[5]

Biochemical

- **Gettler test**: This test is of historical importance and do not have practical importance. According to Gettler, hemodilution due to fresh water drowning reduces plasma concentration of chloride content of blood on left side of heart. A difference of 25 mg/100 ml of chloride between right and left side of heart is considered as significant.[33]
- **Strontium test**: Difference of 75 µg/L of strontium concentration between right and left side of heart is considered as significant in seawater drowning.[34]

Diatoms (Fig. 15.59)

- Diatoms are unicellular algae found whenever there is water and sufficient sunlight for photosynthesis
- Diatoms belong to a class of plants known as Diatomaceae. More than 10,000 species have been described. They are generally 40 to 200 µm in diameter or length.
- Diatoms are classified as:
  - Oligohalophilic diatoms: living in fresh water
  - Mesohalophilic diatoms: live in sea or brackish water
  - Polyhalophilic diatoms: live in sea or brackish water.

Features

Diatoms are made up of box or frustule (shell of silica) composed of two valves fit together to enclose the cytoplasm. They have either radial symmetry (centric diatoms) or elongated (pinnate diatoms).

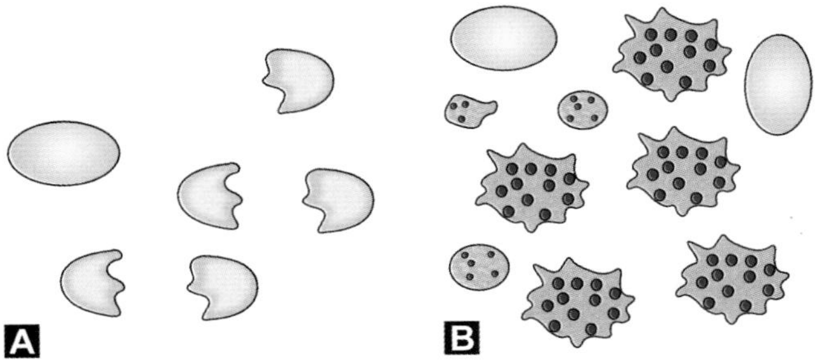

FIGS 15.58A and B: Blood film showing RBCs. **A:** Fresh water drowning showing lysis of RBCs with low count. **B:** Salt water drowning with RBCs appear crenated and shrunken and relative increase in count

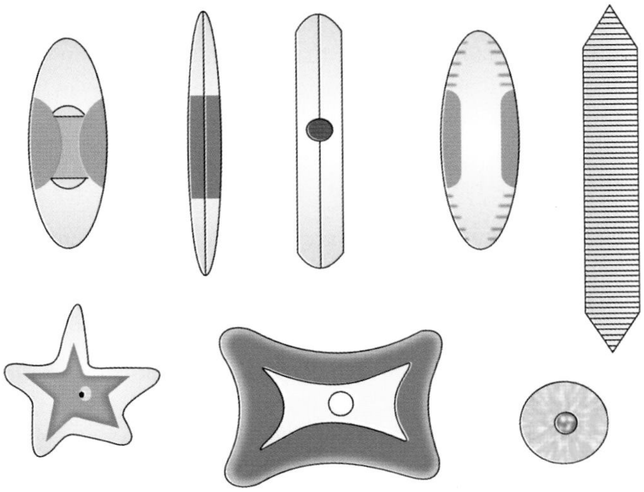

FIG. 15.59: Diatoms

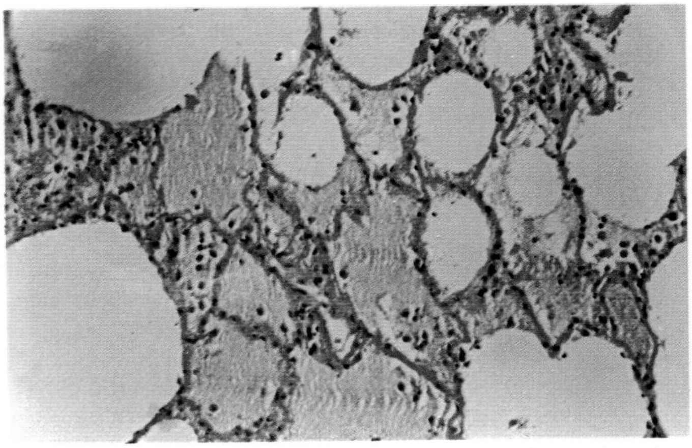

FIG. 15.57: Microphotograph of drowning lung showing distended pulmonary alveoli, (H & E X 45) (*Courtesy* Dr Manish Shrigiriwar, Associate Professor, Forensic Medicine, IGGMC, Nagpur)

Principle of Diatom Test

The diatom test is based on principle that when a living person is drowned in water containing diatoms, many diatoms will penetrate the alveolar wall and be carried to distant organs such as brain, kidney, liver, bone marrow etc.

Procedure of Diatoms Demonstration

2 to 5 gm of tissue or bone marrow is taken in a flask and concentrated nitric acid is added. The preparation is heated for 15 to 20 minutes. This yields a transparent yellow fluid. The fluid is centrifuged and the centrifuged deposit is examined by placing a cover slip.

Importance of Diatoms

Demonstration of significant quantities of diatoms indicate:
- Death was due to drowning
- Person was alive when he was submerged in water
- Site of drowning can be known by comparing diatom species in body and the source/site where body was found.

Advantage

Diatoms resist decomposition and can be demonstrated even in highly decomposed body.

Drawback

- Caution should be exercised while interpreting result solely on basis of positive diatom test since diatoms are ubiquitous and present in soil, water, laboratory apparatus etc. so contamination may occur.[17]
- Similarly diatoms can be demonstrated even in non-drowning deaths.[6]

Medicolegal Importance

1. Most drowning deaths are suicidal or accidental in nature.
2. Accidental drowning can occur in toddlers and children by fall in bath tub,[35] bucket, swimming pool etc.
3. Accidental deaths can also occur in recreational activities such as boating, diving, hypoxic lap etc.
4. Accidental deaths can be related with fishing or occupational activity. Mass fatality may occur in boat sinking, floods etc.
5. Homicidal drowning are rare.
6. Question may be raised whether drowning is antemortem or postmortem. Differences are given in Table 15.8.

Table 15.8: Difference between antemortem and postmortem drowning

Features	*Antemortem drowning*	*Postmortem drowning*
Cadaveric spasm	May be seen	Absent
Froth	Fine, whitish, copious, leathery, tenacious, increases on compression of chest	No froth
Stomach and intestine	Water may be present. May also present sand, mud, grit, silt etc	Absent
Respiratory tract	Contains fine froth. May contain mud, sand, vegetations etc	Absent
Middle ear and mastoid air cell	Hemorrhage present	No hemorrhage

REFERENCES

1. Puller P. Mechanical asphyxia. In: Mant AK (ed). Taylor's Principles and Practice of Medical Jurisprudence, 13th edn. 2000. B I Churchill Livingstone, New Delhi. 282-321.
2. Adelson L. Homicide by cervical compression and by drowning, asphyxial deaths. In: The Pathology of Homicide, 1974. Charles C Thomas, USA. 521-575.
3. Saukko P, Knight B. Suffocation and asphyxia, fatal pressure on the neck, immersion deaths. In: Knight's Forensic Pathology, 3rd edn. 2004. Arnold, London. 352-411.
4. Subrahmanyam BV. Deaths from asphyxia. In: Modi's Medical Jurisprudence and Toxicology, 22nd edn. 2001. Butterworths India, New Delhi. 251-94.
5. Nandy A. Violent asphyxial deaths. In: Principles of Forensic Medicine, 2nd edn. 2005. New Central Book Agency (P) Ltd., Calcutta. 315-43.
6. Pillay VV. Asphyxial deaths. In: Textbook of Forensic Medicine and Toxicology, 14th edn. 2004. Paras Publishing, Hyderabad. 218-41.
7. Polson CJ, Gee DS, Knight B. The Essentials of Forensic Medicine, 4th edn. 1985. Pergamon Press, UK. 351-479.
8. Simonsen J. Patho-anatomic findings in neck structures in asphyxiation due to hanging: a survey of 80 cases. Forensic Sci Int 1988; 38: 83-91.
9. Spitz WU. Asphyxia, drowning. In: Spitz and Fisher's Medicolegal investigation of Death, 3rd edn. 1993. Charlas C Thomas Publisher, USA. 444-515.

10. Mohanty MK, Rastogi P, Kumar PG, Kumar V, Manipady S. Periligature injuries in hanging. J Clinical Forensic Med 2003; 10: 255-58.
11. Reddy KSN. Mechanical asphyxia. In: The Essentials of Forensic Medicine and Toxicology, 22nd edn. 2003. K. Suguna Devi, Hyderabad. 278-310.
12. Elfawal MA. Deaths from hanging in the Eastern Province of Saudi Arabia. Med Sci Law 1999; 34:307-12.
13. Dixit PG, Mohite PM, Ambade VN. Study of histopathological changes in thyroid, salivary gland and lymph nodes in hanging. J Forensic Med Toxicol 2001; 18: 1-4.
14. Alberto-Garza-Leal J, Landron F. J. Autoerotic asphyxial death initially misinterpreted as suicide and a review of the literature. J Forensic Sci 1991; 36: 1753-59.
15. Sass FA. Sexual asphyxia in the female. J Forensic Sci 1975; 20: 181-85.
16. Vyawahare MS, Dixit PG, Bardale RV. Unusual case of accidental strangulation- a case report. J Medicolegal Assoc Maharashtra 2006; 18: 19-21.
17. Mathiharan K, Patnaik AK. Deaths from asphyxia. In: Modi's Medical Jurisprudence and Toxicology, 23rd edn. 2005. LexisNexis Butterworths, New Delhi. 565-614.
18. Sperry K. An unusual, deep lingual hemorrhage as a consequence of ligature strangulation. J Forensic Sci 1988; 33: 806-11.
19. Vij K. Asphyxial deaths. In: Textbook of Forensic Medicine and Toxicology, 3rd edn. 2005. Reed Elsevier India Pvt. Limited, New Delhi. 165-221.
20. Rao NG. Asphyxial death. In: Textbook of Forensic Medicine and Toxicology, 1st edn. 2006. Jaypee Brothers Medical Publishers (P) Ltd., New Delhi. 157-76.
21. Dikshit PC. Asphyxial deaths. In: Textbook of Forensic Medicine and Toxicology, 1st edn. 2007. Peepee Publishers and Distributors (P) Ltd., New Delhi. 286-316.
22. Rajs J, Thiblin I. Histologic appearance of fractured thyroid cartilage and surrounding tissue. Forensic Sci Int 2000; 114:155-66.
23. Pollanen MS, Chiasson DA. Fracture of the hyoid bone in strangulation: comparison of fractured and unfractured hyoids from victims of strangulation. J Forensic Sci 1996; 41: 110-13.
24. Ubelaker DH. Hyoid fracture and strangulation. J Forensic Sci 1992; 37:1216-22.
25. Camps FE, Hunt AC. Pressure on the neck. J Forensic Med 1959; 6: 116-36.
26. Tamuki K, Scito K, Katsvmata Y. Enzyme-linked immunosorbent assay for determination of plasma thyroglobulin and its application to postmortem diagnosis of mechanical asphyxia. Forensic Sci Int 1987; 33: 259-265.
27. Gordon I, Shapiro HA. In: Forensic Medicine-A Guide to Principles, 2nd edn. 1982. Churchill Livingstone, Edinburgh. 81-131.
28. Kurihara K, Kuroda N, Murai T, Shihozuka, Yanagida J, Matsuo, Nakamura T. A case of homicidal choking mistaken for suicide. Med Sci Law 1992; 32: 65-67.
29. Mukherjee JB. Violent asphyxial deaths. In: Forensic Medicine and Toxicology Vol. I, 2nd edn. 1994. Arnold Associates, New Delhi. 475-539.
30. Copeland AR. An assessment of lung weights in drowning cases- the Metro Dade County experience from 1978 to 1982. Am J Forensic Med Pathol 1985; 6: 301-4.
31. Mueller WF. Pathology of temporal bone hemorrhages in drowning. J Forensic Sci 1969; 14: 327-36.
32. Niles NR. Hemorrhage in the middle ear and mastoid in drowning. Am J Clin Pathol 1963; 40: 281-84.
33. Gettler AO. A method for the determination of death by drowning. JAMA 1921; 77: 1650-52.
34. Azparren J, De La Rosa I, Sancho M. Biventricular measurements of blood strontium in real cases of drowning. Forensic Sci Int 1994; 69: 139-48.
35. Schmidt P, Madea B. Death in the bathtub involving children. Forensic Sci Int 1995; 72: 147-55.

CHAPTER 16

Virginity, Sexual Offenses and Perversions

The trauma of pregnancy resulting from rape is not merely physical. We must consider sympathetically the damage it can wreak on a sensitive mind

- Dr Alec Bourne (1938)

VIRGINITY

Definition

Virginity is defined as the state of being ***Virgo intacta*** *i.e. one who has never had sexual intercourse.*
Defloration means loss of virginity i.e. a female who has had sexual intercourse.

Medicolegal Importance

A. Civil cases
   1. Nullity of marriage: Presence of virginity after marriage indicates non-consummation of marriage by the act of sexual intercourse and in such cases the marriage can be declared null and void.
   2. Divorce: Non-virgin state before marriage may be cited as ground for divorce.
   3. Defamation: A woman may sue a person for damage of her reputation that she is not virgin.

B. Criminal cases
   In rape cases, loss of virginity indicated commission of crime.

SIGNS OF VIRGINITY

For convenience, the signs of virginity are described as those found in the genital and extra-genital organs.

Extragenital Signs—Breast

- Breasts are firm, elastic and hemispherical with small-undeveloped nipple surrounded by pinkish areola in fair skin woman.
- With frequent handling, the breast becomes larger and flabby.

Genital Signs

- Labia majora – are thick, firm, elastic and rounded. They lie in contact with each other completely hiding the labia minora and vaginal orifice.
- Labia minora – are soft, small and pinkish in color. They always lie behind the labia majora. However, in habituated females, they become dark, enlarge and peep out from labia majora.
- Anterior commissure, posterior commissure and fourchette are intact
- Usually the hymen is intact
- Vaginal orifice is small and admits tip of little finger only.
- Vagina – is narrow and tight. The mucosa is rugose, pinkish in color, sensitive to touch and walls are in close apposition.
- The differences between virgin and deflorated female are mentioned in Table 16.1.

Table 16.1: Difference between virgin and deflorated

Features	*Virgin*	*Deflorated*
Definition	One who has never had sexual intercourse	Means loss of virginity
Breast	Hemispherical and firm, areola pinkish, nipple small	Pendulous, enlarged
Labia majora	Firm, lie in apposition	Separated and flabby
Labia minora	Pink, soft	Enlarged, pigmented, separated, peep out
Fourchette	Intact	May be intact/torn or may show healed scar
Fossa navicularis	Less conspicuous	Disappears
Hymen	Intact, edges are distinct and regular with narrow opening	Usually torn (in false virgin, it may remain intact)
Vagina	Narrow, apposed, mucosa rugose, sensitive	Wide, capacious, rugosity may partially lost

Hymen

Hymen is a thin but firm fold of connective tissue lined on both sides by stratified squamous epithelium. It is about 1 mm in thickness and situated at the vaginal orifice. However, in certain cases, it may be thick, tough and fleshy. Developmentally it is remnant of the vaginal plates that develops between Mullerian duct and the cloaca and has no useful function.[1]

Types (Fig. 16.1)

Hymen is classified as follows:

1. Annular – the opening is in the center
2. Crescentic or semilunar – the opening is placed anteriorly
3. Cribriform – in this type, the hymen has multiple opening
4. Septate – a thin strip of tissue is present in between two lateral openings
5. Fimbriated – opening of hymen is in the center but the margins are wavy or undulating (i.e. fimbriae) and shows multiple notches
6. Infantile – the hymen have small and linear opening in the center
7. Imperforate – hymen with no opening
8. Absent – in some cases hymen may be congenitally absent[2]
9. Marginal – the hymen is in form of thin rim with larger opening in the central part.

Importance of Hymen

- The marginal type of hymen may appear intact even when sexual intercourse has taken place whereas the fimbriated type of hymen may appear torn even in the intact state.

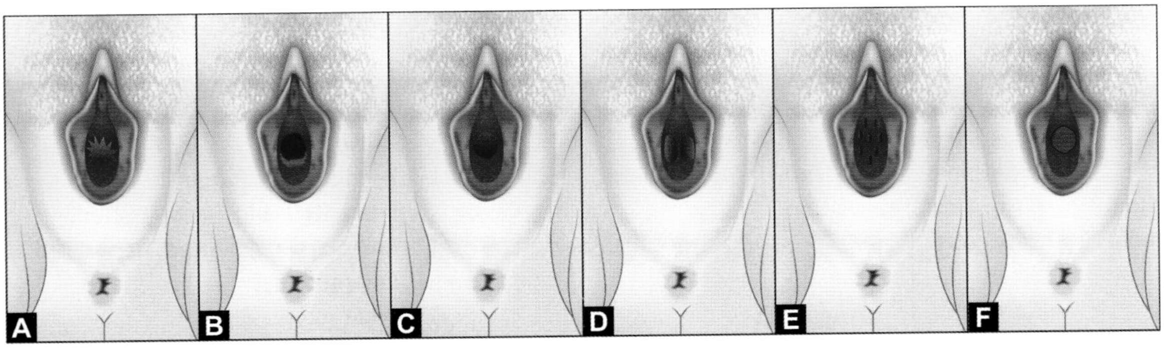

FIGS 16.1A to F: Different types of hymen. **A:** Fimbriated; **B:** Crescentic; **C:** Annular; **D:** Septate; **E:** Cribriform; **F:** Imperforate

- The hymen may remain intact even after sexual intercourse. In such cases, the hymen is elastic, fleshy and yielding type. Such female who had sexual intercourse and even have intact hymen are called as **false virgins**. The differences between true and false virgin are given in Table 16.2.
- Hymenoplasty – is surgical repair to form a hymen. The hymen is usually taut, has narrow aperture and reveal fine surgical scars at the site of repair of previous tears.

Rupture of Hymen

- Rupture of hymen occurs by an act of sexual intercourse or may be due to other reasons
- Usually it is assumed that hymen is ruptured at the time of first coitus. As a result of sexual intercourse, the hymen is usually torn posteriorly at 6 O'clock position or may tear at postero-lateral sites (5 O'clock and/or 7 O'clock position) as bilateral tears (Fig. 16.2).
- The tear extends from hymenal orifice to the point of their attachment to the vaginal wall (i.e. the tears are usually complete).
- A habituated female (i.e. female who had frequent sexual intercourse) shows torn hymen known as **carunculae hymenalis**.
- A female who had given birth to child exhibits only remnants of hymen known as **carunculae myrtiformes**.
- Other causes of rupture are as follows:
  A) In true virgins, the hymen may be ruptured by:
    1. Surgical operations for imperforate hymen/per vaginal examination.
    2. Instrumental masturbation.
    3. Accidental fall on protruding object (not usually possible without associated injuries).
    4. Insertion of foreign bodies, e.g. solapith into vagina.
    5. Careless insertion of sanitary tampon.

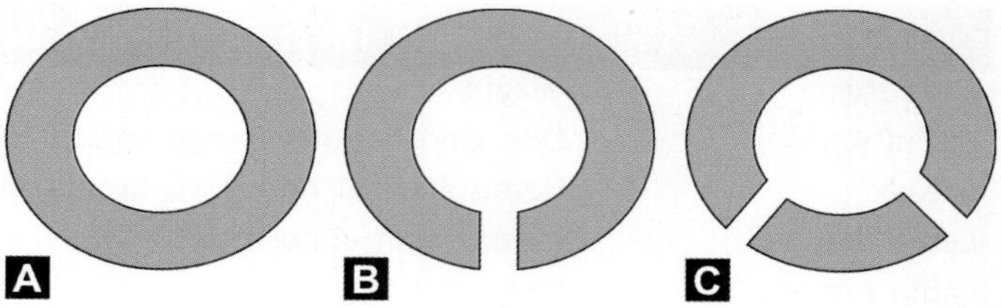

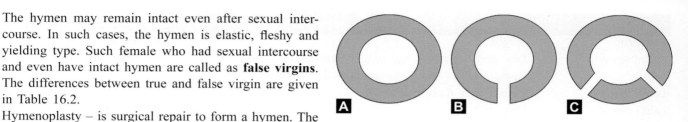

FIGS 16.2A to C: Diagrammatic representation of hymen and rupture. **A:** Normal hymen, **B:** Rupture of hymen in posterior aspect (6 O'clock position) and **C:** Rupture of hymen in posterolateral aspect bilaterally (5 O' and 7 O'clock position)

  B) Ulceration – disease like diphtheria destroys the entire hymen.

Sexual Offenses

Sexual offences are classified as:

1. Natural sexual offenses
   - Rape
   - Adultery
   - Incest
2. Unnatural sexual offenses
   - Sodomy
   - Lesbianism
   - Bestiality
   - Buccal coitus
3. Sexual deviations/perversions/paraphilias
   - Fetishism
   - Transvestism
   - Sadism
   - Pedophilia etc.
4. Sex-linked offenses
   - Indecent assault
   - Offenses under Immoral Traffic Act

Table 16.2: Difference between true and false virgin

Features	*True virgin*	*False virgin*
Breast	Hemispherical and firm, areola pinkish, nipple small	Pendulous, enlarged
Labia majora	Firm, lie in apposition	Separated and flabby
Labia minora	Pink, soft	Enlarged, pigmented, separated, peep out
Clitoris	Small	Enlarged
Vestibule	Narrow	Wide
Vagina	Narrow, apposed, mucosa rugose	Roomy, rugosity of mucosa may partially lost
Hymen	Intact, hardly admits tip of little finger	Intact, thick, fleshy, loose/folded/elastic, easily admits two fingers through

Natural Sexual Offenses

RAPE

Definition

Section 375 of IPC defines rape as unlawful sexual intercourse by a man with a woman:

1. Against her will;
2. Without her consent;
3. With her consent, when her consent has been obtained by putting her or any other person in whom she is interested in fear of death or hurt;
4. With her consent, when the man knows that he is not her husband and that her consent is given because she believes that he is another man to whom she is or believes herself to be lawfully married;
5. With her consent, when at time of giving such consent, by reason of unsoundness of mind or intoxication or the administration by him personally or through another of any stupefying or unwholesome substance, she is unable to understand the nature and consequences of that to which she gives consent;
6. With or without her consent, when she is under 16 years of age.

Explanation: Penetration is sufficient to constitute the sexual intercourse necessary to the offense of rape.

Exception: Sexual intercourse by a man with his own wife, the wife not being less than 15 years of age, is not rape.

Punishment

Punishment for the offense of rape is prescribed under Sec 376 of IPC (Fig. 16.3)

1. Under Sec 376 **subsection 1**:
   - This clause provides punishment for rape as defined under Sec 375 of IPC
   - The minimum punishment prescribed for rape is 7 years (which may be extended to 10 years) and shall also liable to fine.
   - In case of a person who was charged with rape of his own wife, the wife being not under 12 years old, he shall be punished with imprisonment for a period of two years or fine or both.
2. Under Sec 376 **subsection 2**: Whoever, –
   - 2 (a): Being police officer commits rape within the limits of the police station, or in the premises of any station or on a woman in his custody or in a custody of a police officer subordinate to him; or

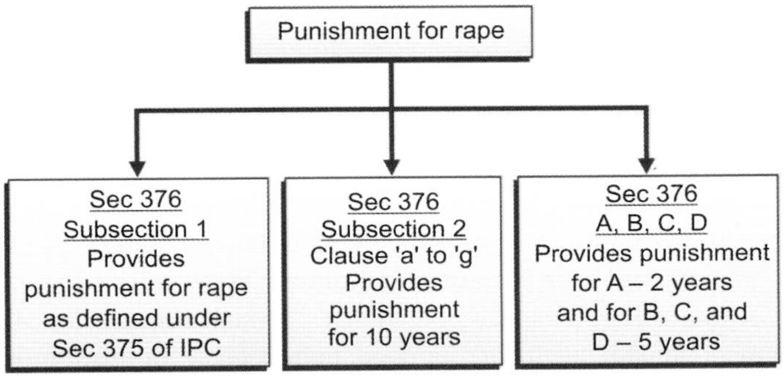

FIG. 16.3: Flow chart exhibiting punishment prescribed for rape

   - 2 (b): Being a public servant, take advantage of his official position and commits rape on a woman in his custody as such public servant or in the custody of a public servant subordinate to him; or
   - 2 (c): Being on the management or on the staff of a jail, remand home or other place of custody established by or under any law for the time being in force or of a woman's or children institution takes advantage of his official position and commits rape on any inmate of such jail, remand home, place or institution; or
   - 2 (d): Being on the management or on the staff of a hospital, takes advantage of his official position and commits rape on a woman in that hospital; or
   - 2 (e): Commits rape on a woman knowing her to be pregnant; or
   - 2 (f): Commits rape on a woman when she is under 12 years of age; or
   - 2 (g): Commits gang rape,
   - Shall be punished with rigorous imprisonment for a term which shall not be less than ten years but which may be for life and shall also be liable to fine.
3. Under Sec 376 A
   A husband who has sexual intercourse with his own wife, who is living separately, shall be punished with imprisonment of either description for a term, which may extend to two years and shall also be liable to fine.
4. Under Sec 376 B
   Intercourse by public servant with woman in his custody – whoever, being a public servant, takes advantage of his official position and **induces or seduces**, any woman, who is in his custody as such public servant or in the custody of a public servant subordinate to him, to have sexual intercourse with him, such **sexual intercourse not amounting to the offense of rape**, shall be punished with imprisonment of either description for a

term which may extend to five years and shall also be liable to fine.

5. Under Sec 376 C
   Intercourse by superintendent of jail, remand home etc. – whoever, being the superintendent or manager of a jail, remand home or other place of custody established by or under any law for the time being in force or of a woman's or children institution, takes advantage of his official position and induces or seduces any female inmate of such jail, remand home, place or institution to have sexual intercourse with him, such **sexual intercourse not amounting to the offense of rape**, shall be punished with imprisonment of either description for a term which may extend to five years and shall also be liable to fine.
6. Under Sec 376 D
   Intercourse by any member of the management or staff of a hospital with any woman in that hospital – whoever, being on the management of a hospital or being on staff of a hospital takes advantage of his official position and has sexual intercourse with any woman in that hospital, such **sexual intercourse not amounting to the offense of rape**, shall be punished with imprisonment of either description for a term which may extend to five years and shall also be liable to fine.

Types of Rape

Statutory Rape

It is a forcible sexual intercourse by a man with a woman, who is less than 16 years of age.

Marital Rape

- Also called as spousal rape
- Under sec 376 A of IPC, it is a forcible sexual intercourse by a man with his wife without her consent if:
  - Wife is living separately from him under a decree of separation OR
  - Wife is living separately from him under any custom or usage
- It is punishable with imprisonment of either description for a term, which may extend to two years or with fine or with both.

Custodial Rape (Custody Rape)

- It is done by persons taking advantage of their custodial positions and has forceful sexual intercourse with woman in their custody.
- The provisions of Section 376 2(a to d) recognize this condition and prescribe punishment (*vide supra*).

Gang Rape

- Also called as group rape or pack rape
- When rape is committed on a female by more than one person acting in furtherance of their common intention, it is called as gang rape.
- It is punishable under Section 376 {clause 2 (g)} of IPC.

Date Rape

- Also called as acquaintance rape
- It is a forcible sexual intercourse by a boyfriend with girlfriend when they are on date (for stay or vacation).
- In such cases, the girl may allege that her boyfriend had given her some intoxicant and proceed with the act.
- Adolescent and young girls are more likely to be victims of sexual assault.[3]
- The concept of date rape is not recognized in India.

Stranger Rape

It is the rape committed by a male on a female who had no previous contact with the victim.

Medical Examination of Rape Victim

- Doctors, examining a victim of rape are shouldered with dual responsibilities, firstly they have to treat the patient and provide support and secondly they have to examine the victim and collect material evidences to facilitate and aid the justice.[4]
- A female nurse or attendant should be present while examining victim. Section 53 (2) of CrPC states that whenever female has to be examined it should be done by (or under supervision) of a lady doctor.
- The medical examination consists of:
  1. Recording history
  2. Examination of clothes
  3. Physical examination
  4. Collection of material evidence

Consent

Written informed consent of a victim is a must without which a doctor cannot proceed with medical examination. A victim of and over 12 years of age can give consent. If she is child under 12 years of age or of unsound mind, then consent of parent or guardian should be taken.

History

The history includes
- Whether the victim had attended menarche? If yes, whether she was menstruating at the time of alleged incident?
- Her marital status and history
- Obstetric history, if relevant
- History of any venereal disease
- History about the incident, the time, the location, date, nature of assault, whether penetration was vaginal/anal/ oral. Number of assailants.
- Whether there was any ejaculation/discharge?
- Whether resistance offered?
- Whether bath taken or local washing done?

Clothes

- Clothes should be examined for presence of blood stains, semen stains, secretions, mud particles, any hair or foreign material etc.
- Note for any damage to clothes in form of torn marks cut, tear, rip, wear and tear, loss of buttons etc. Damage to clothes can be interpreted as indicating a struggle or that force was used.
- Microscopy can identify blood on the cut thread ends of a cut.[5]

Physical Examination

General examination
- A good light is essential
- Record two identification marks
- Record general built, height and weight
- Record vital parameters
- Examine mental maturity in relation to age
- Mental status – confused/clear/apprehensive
- Request the victim to stand on a large clean, white sheet of paper and undress herself. The purpose is to collect any material evidence that falls on the paper
- Examine the presence of any fresh or dried blood stains/ semen stain/saliva stains etc. on the body. These should be scrapped/swabbed and collected
- Note presence of injuries over body. The injuries may be found over face, neck, breast, inner aspect of thigh etc. Look for recent physical assault injuries like grip marks, bite marks, ligature impressions etc.

Local Examination (Fig. 16.4)

- A good light is essential and the lithotomy position is preferable
- Pubic hairs – Note whether shaved/unshaved/matted with semen/blood. Search for presence of any foreign hair. Take clippings of pubic hair from victim for comparison
- Thigh – Note presence of contusions and/or abrasions or any stains
- Look for any vaginal bleeding
- Labia majora and minora – Note presence of any swelling/injury/stains/soiling
- Hymen –
  - » The hymen may be conveniently examined by inserting a specially designed glass globe on a stem, which is then partially withdrawn so that the hymen is spread around its circumference. However, in most instances, a conventional examination using a speculum is carried out.[6]
  - » Note the state of hymen whether torn or intact. If torn, its extent, position, fresh or old (Table 16.3).
  - » It is said that tears of the hymen due to rupture with fingers are usually lateral, whilst rupture with the penis are usually posterior.[6]
  - » In children hymen may not be ruptured but becomes red and congested because hymen is deeply situated. Adult penis may not penetrate without causing gross damage. There may be bruising of labia.[7]
- Vagina –
  - » Look at vaginal mucosa for presence of any injury/ foreign body.
  - » Rugae of vaginal wall – distinct/not distinct
  - » Look for vaginal canal and fornix for collection of any fluid/semen

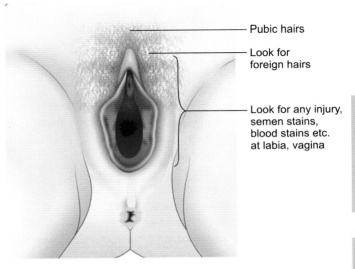

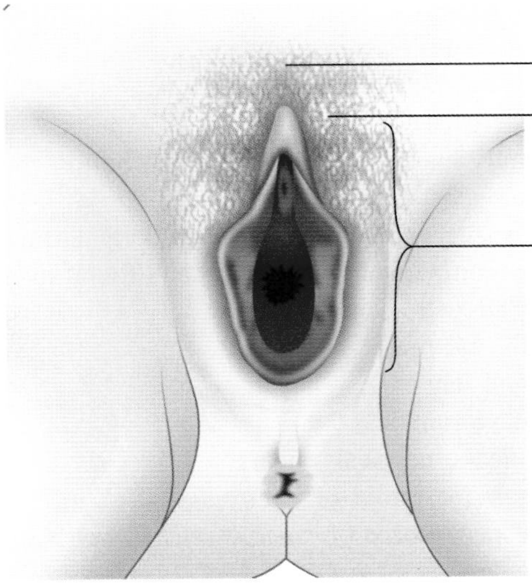
Pubic hairs
Look for foreign hairs
Look for any injury, semen stains, blood stains etc. at labia, vagina

FIG. 16.4: Genital examination

Table 16.3: State of hymen

Hymen
Fresh • Bleeding • Margins swollen • Reddish • Tender • Inflamed
2-3 days • Swollen margins • Congestion • Margins shows healing by week but do not unite

» The examination should include deep vaginal examination, as occasionally, high vaginal tears occur, especially in violent assaults on children
» Colposcopy – provides magnification in a range of 5 to 30 times and greater illumination and thus help in detection of minor trauma. Many authorities recommend use of colposcopy examination in sexual assault victims.
» Toluidine blue – Toluidine blue stains nuclei and is used on the posterior fourchette to identify lacerations of the keratinized squamous epithelium that are not apparent on gross visualization.

- Anus – look for any discharge/hemorrhage/injury.

Hymen may not be ruptured if:
- If penetration was not full
- If victim happens to be female child as hymen is deeply situated
- If hymen if tough, fleshy, elastic (false virgin)
- If female is deflorated.

Samples to be collected in victim
1. Clothes and undergarments
2. Foreign evidentiary material – like hair, fiber, button etc.
3. Fingernail scrapings
4. Scrapings from suspected stain marks from body surface
5. Scalp hairs – for comparison with scalp hairs found over body/clothes of alleged accused
6. Swab from teeth bite mark
7. Combing of pubic hairs
8. Hair clipping of victim
9. Vaginal swab/smears, cervical smears
10. Washings of posterior fornix of vagina for
    - Detection of spermatozoa (*for details refer Chapter 30: Trace Evidences*)
    - Presence of mycobacterium smegmatis (smegma bacilli)
    - Presence of sexually transmitted disease
11. Blood for
    - Serology
    - Pregnancy test
    - For presence of drug/intoxicant
    - DNA profiling
    - For venereal disease
12. Urine for
    - Pregnancy test
    - Detection of alcohol
13. Condom if found at scene of crime – laboratory examination of condom may reveal presence of blood/vaginal epithelial cells on one side and semen on the other. Pubic hairs may also be present. DNA profiling of semen may be of help.[8]

Medical Examination of Accused

The medical examination consists of:
1. Recording history
2. Examination of clothes
3. Physical examination
4. Collection of material evidence

Consent

Consent of the accused should be taken prior to examination. In case of minor, the consent from his parents or legal guardian is taken. If the accused is in police custody and refuse to consent for medical examination, then the examination can be carried out without the consent of accused as per provisions of Section 53 (1) of CrPC.

Clothes

Clothes should be examined for presence of blood stains, semen stains, stains of vaginal secretions, mud soiling, for presence of any foreign body such as scalp hair, pubic hair etc. Note any cut marks or tear marks over cloth.

General Physical Examination

- Record two identification marks
- Record height, weight, built
- Record vital parameters
- Note for presence of any stains or soiling over body
- Note for presence of any foreign body
- Note for presence of any injury over body
- Foreign material such as blood, vegetable matter or mud stains on the knees, buttocks and pubic hairs should be looked for.[6]
- Systemic medical examination should be done.

Genital Examination (Fig. 16.5)

- Examine the genital organs with reference to development and for potency
- Note for presence or absence of smegma under the prepuce. The smegma is thick, cheesy whitish secretion with disagreeable odour comprising of desquamated epithelium and smegma bacilli (Mycobacterium smegmatis). It takes about 24 hours to collect the smegma on corona glandis. The smegma is wiped out during the act of sexual intercourse. Therefore presence of smegma indicates non-participation of a male in recent sexual intercourse act. However, caution should be exercised because the smegma may be removed by a person during daily bath as a part of maintaining local hygiene.
- Examine penis for swelling, tenderness and injury especially to the rim of the glans and the frenulum.[6]
- Examine the shaft of penis for presence of vaginal epithelial cells and/or for presence of bloodstains. Glycogen rich vaginal epithelial cells may be detected from penis in sexual assault case.[9] Wipe the shaft of penis with moist filter paper and exposed to vapors of Lugol's iodine. Development of brown colour indicates presence of glycogen rich vaginal epithelial cells. Similarly microscopic examination may also show vaginal epithelial cells (Fig. 16.6).

Samples to be Collected in Accused

1. Clothes and undergarments
2. Foreign evidentiary material – like hair, fiber, button etc.
3. Fingernail scrapings
4. Scrapings from suspected stain marks from body surface
5. Scalp hairs – for comparison with scalp hairs found over body/clothes of victim
6. Swab from teeth bite mark
7. Combing of pubic hairs
8. Pubic hair clipping of accused
9. Urethral swab
10. Swab from glans
11. Blood for
    - Serology
    - For presence of drug/intoxicant
    - DNA profiling
    - For venereal disease.

Complications or Dangers of Rape

1. Hemorrhage and shock due to injuries sustained to genitals or perineum
2. Death may occur due to:
    - Assault to obtain consent or put her in fear

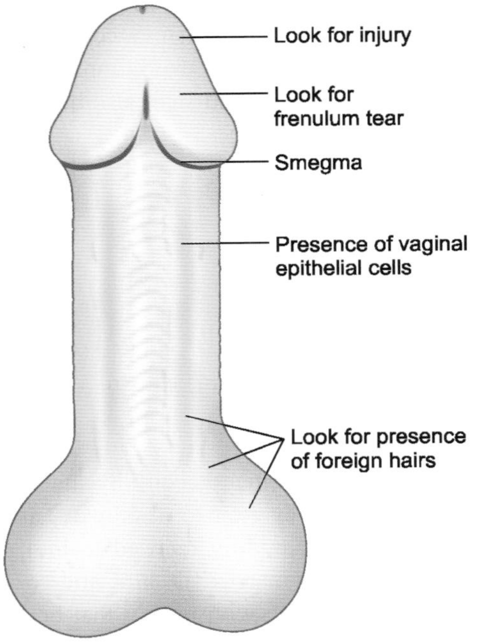

FIG. 16.5: Genital examination in male

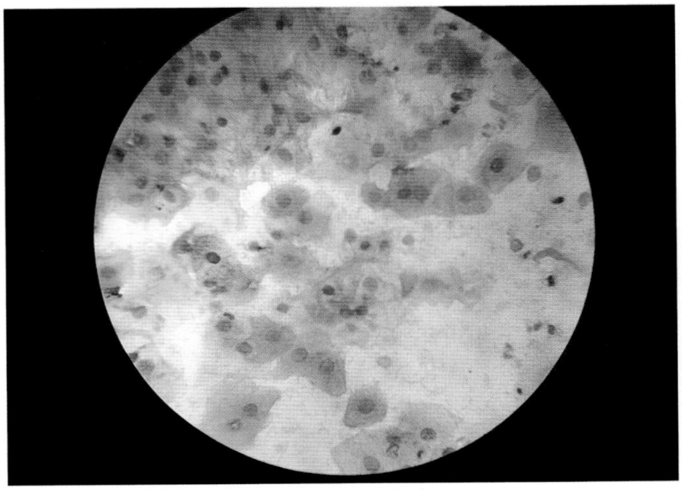

FIG. 16.6: Microphotograph showing vaginal epithelial cells (H & E X 45)

- By suffocation – to prevent shouting
- Strangulation – to hide the crime
- Suicide – due to depression or frustration of being raped
- Intoxicants – overdose or adulteration

3. Mental agony, which disrupts the victim's physical, social, mental and sexual life.
4. **Rape trauma syndrome**: The syndrome includes behavioral, somatic or psychosocial reaction to the act of forceful sexual intercourse. It is regarded as post-traumatic stress disorder. The syndrome has been defined in two stages:[10]
   - Immediate – the phase of disorganization characterized by feeling of guilt and humiliation.
   - Delayed – or phase of reorganization characterized by protracted response in form of recurrent and intrusive recollection of stressful event either in flashbacks or in dreams.

Medicolegal Aspects

1. Rape is a legal term and not medical diagnosis. Whether the rape has taken place or not is a legal conclusion drawn by judicial officer and not by medical doctor.
2. Mere penetration by penis up to vulva is sufficient to constitute the sexual intercourse necessary to the offense of rape.
3. Under existing provisions of law, in India, a female cannot be accused of raping a male. However, she can be guilty of an indecent assault.
4. Consent: According to the existing provisions of law, a female above 16 years is capable of giving valid consent for sexual intercourse. However, the consent should be free, voluntary, without any fear/fraud or under pressure, given prior to the act of sexual intercourse when the female is full possession of her senses (mental faculty).
5. Presumption as to absence of consent: In certain prosecution cases of rape – under subsection 2, clause 'a' to 'd' – i.e. custodial rape where sexual intercourse is proved and question is whether it was without the consent of the woman alleged to have been raped and the woman states in her evidence that she did not consent for the act then there is presumption in favour of absence of consent (Section 114A of IEA). In other words, it can be said that if in custodial rape cases if female says that she had not consented for the act then it can be assumed by the Court that she had not given the consent.
6. Age of accused: In Indian law, no minimum or maximum age under or over which a male is incapable of committing rape is prescribed. In English law, a boy under 14 years of age is incapable of committing a rape. However, if Section 82 and 83 of IPC are applied, a boy of less than 7 years cannot be held guilty (Section 82 of IPC) or a boy above 7 years of age but below 12 years cannot be held guilty if the boy has not attained sufficient maturity of understanding to judge the nature and consequences of his act (Section 83 of IPC).
7. There is no minimum or maximum age of female under or over which she cannot be raped.
8. Prostitutes have the same security of law as for others. A prostitute can also complain to the court of law in case if the act of sexual intercourse was performed against her consent.[11] Similarly, consent for act of sexual intercourse provided by a prostitute under the age of 16 years becomes invalid.[12]
9. Section 366 of IPC deals with kidnapping, abducting or inducing woman to compel for marriage.
10. Section 366-A of IPC deals with procuration of minor girl – whoever, by any means whatsoever, induces a minor girl under the age of 18 years to go from any place or to do any act with intent that such girl may be, or knowing that it is likely that she will be, forced or seduced to illicit intercourse with another person, shall be punishable with imprisonment which may extend to ten years, and shall also be liable for fine.
11. Section 366-B of IPC deals with importation of girl from foreign country – whoever, imports into India from any country outside India or from the State of Jammu & Kashmir any girl under the age of 21 years with intent that she may be or knowing it to be likely that she will be forced or seduced to illicit intercourse with another person, shall be punishable with imprisonment which may extend to ten years, and shall also be liable for fine.

Natural Sex Offenses not Amounting to Rape in India

Following are the offenses:

1. Intercourse by a man with his wife during separation (Sec **376 A** of IPC)
2. Intercourse by public servant or others who seduces or induces the woman subordinate to him (Sec **376 B, C and D** of IPC)
3. Adultery (Sec **497** of IPC)
4. Cohabitation cause by man deceitfully inducing a belief of lawful marriage – every man who by deceit causes any woman who is not lawfully married to him, to believe that she is lawfully married to him and to cohabit or have sexual intercourse with him in that belief, shall be punished with imprisonment of either description for a term which may extend to ten years, and shall also liable to fine (Sec **493** of IPC).[13]

INCEST

- *It is defined as a sexual intercourse by a man with a woman who is closely related to him by blood or by marriage* i.e. within the forbidden degrees of relationship.[14]
- Examples are sexual intercourse between father and daughter, son and mother, siblings[15], brother and step-sister, nice and uncle etc.
- In India, as such, incest is not an offense, unless it is brought into any of the sections of 376 or 497 of IPC (rape or adultery).
- It usually occurs between family members and recognized as:[2]
  1. Between father and daughter – the Electra Complex
  2. Between mother and son – the Edipus Complex
  3. Between brother and sister – the Pharaonic incest.

ADULTERY

- *Adultery means voluntarily sexual intercourse between one spouse and a person of the opposite sex, not his or her partner, during the continuation of marriage.*
- In other words, it is voluntary natural sexual intercourse by a married man with another married woman or between a married woman and some other man who is not her husband.
- Section 497 of IPC states that – whoever has sexual intercourse with a person whom he knows or has reason to believe to be wife of another man, without the consent or connivance of that man, such sexual intercourse not amounting to rape is guilty of offence of adultery, and the guilty shall be punished with imprisonment of either description for a term which may extend to five years, or with fine or with both.
- A criminal suit can be filed only against the male adulterer since adultery is an invasion on the right of husband over his wife. In such cases, the wife shall not be held guilty and cannot be punishable as an abettor. However, the distressed husband can file for divorce.
- The scope of this section is limited to adultery committed with a married woman. Having sexual intercourse with an unmarried girl, or prostitute or a widow or even with a married woman whose husband consents for the act or with his connivance, are not covered by this section.[16]

UNNATURAL SEXUAL OFFENSES

Law of India permits only natural sexual intercourse between man and woman and any practice of sexual intercourse against the order of nature is punishable under Section 377 of IPC. **Section 377 of IPC** states that – *whoever voluntarily has carnal intercourse against the order of nature with any man, woman, or animal shall be punished with imprisonment for life, or with imprisonment of either description for a term which may extend to ten years and shall also be liable to fine.*

Explanation – penetration is sufficient to constitute the carnal intercourse necessary to the offence described in this section.

SODOMY

- It is anal intercourse between man and man or between man and woman i.e. it is penile-anal intercourse.
- The name sodomy is derived from town Sodom where it was practiced. In ancient Greek, people used to practice it thus it is also called as "Greek Love".
- It is also known as **buggery**. Buggery is a lay term used to refer to penile penetration of the anus of man or woman.
- The person who is doing anal intercourse (i.e. the offender) is called as active agent and other partner is called as passive agent. It is called as pederasty when the passive agent is a child and child is known as catamite.
- Rarely, sodomy may be practiced by two men who alternatively act as active and passive agent.

Medical Examination

Examination of passive agent

- Examination of clothes should done for presence of stains, soiling matter or foreign body
- General physical examination should be done
- Knee-elbow position is preferable
- Genital examinations findings in person not habituated and habituated person are described below.

Anal findings in fresh/recent in non-habituated agent (Fig. 16.7)

- Pain and tenderness during examination
- Foreign hair or loose hair may be noted
- Evidence of used lubricant traces can be found
- Bleeding
- Bruising or perianal abrasions may be evident
- Semen
- Tear or anal laceration may be noted. The anal lacerations are usually triangular in shape with base at external sphincter and apex inward. The lacerations are rarely 2 to 3 cm in length.
- The only proof of sodomy is presence of spermatozoa in the anal canal.

Anal Findings in Habitual[17,18] (Figs 16.8 and 16.9)

- Blood stains or fresh injury is rarely observed
- Perianal hairs are usually shaved and local hygiene is maintained
- Generalized reddening and thickening of perianal tissue
- External venous congestion
- Condylomata, warts, chancre etc.
- Funneled anus
- Scars or tags (either single or multiple). The scar may extend to the perianal region.
- Fissures
- Dilatation of anus
- Reflex anal dilatation may be noted and the person do not experience pain or tenderness
- Loss of sphincter tone
- Shortening and eversion of anal canal
- There may be evidence of prolapsed rectum.

Samples to be Preserved

- Swab from perianal region
- Swab from anal canal
- Any foreign pubic hair
- Undergarments.

Examination of Active Agent

- Examination of clothes should be done for presence of stains, soiling matter or foreign body
- General physical examination should be done
- Feces may be identified from penis in active partner.[9]
- Injury in form of abrasion may be noted over glans penis or tearing of frenulum may be evident.

Medicolegal Aspects

1. To punish the offender under Sec 377 of IPC, it is necessary that penetration, though little, should be proved strictly. If no penetration is there and only attempt is made to thrust the penis into anus, the offense is tried under Sec 511 of IPC.[19]
2. Consent of passive partner is not a defense and both partners' i.e. active and passive partners will be prosecuted.
3. In a married couple, if the sodomy act is done with consent of wife then also it is an offense and wife would also be held guilty along with husband. Legally, marriage gives implied consent for normal sexual intercourse (i.e. sexual intercourse between penis and vagina) and not for anal intercourse.
4. In a married couple, if wife do not give consent for anal intercourse then the husband alone would be held guilty of the offense.
5. Under Sec 13 of Hindu Marriage Act, the wife can apply for divorce if the husband is doing anal intercourse or guilty of sodomy.
6. Accidental death was reported during the act of sodomy. The author reported that during the act, manual strangulation resulted from application of forearm on the neck in "choke holding" manner.[20]

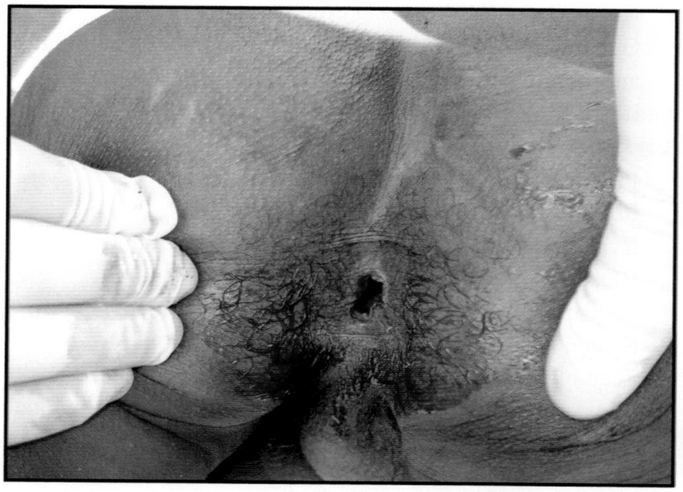

FIG. 16.7: Anal findings in non-habitual agent

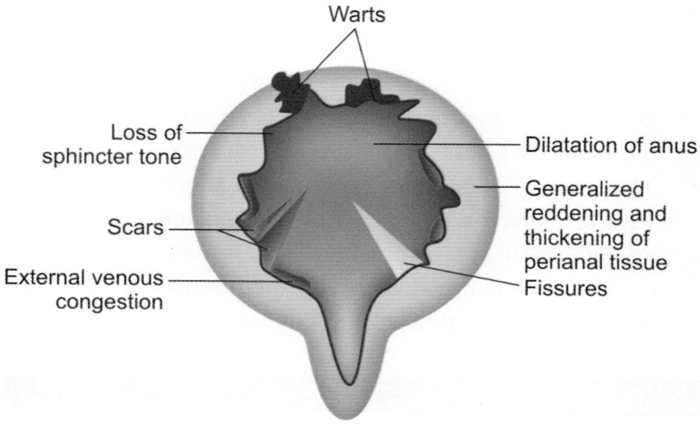

FIG. 16.8: Diagrammatic representation of anal findings in habitual passive agent

Section A Forensic Medicine

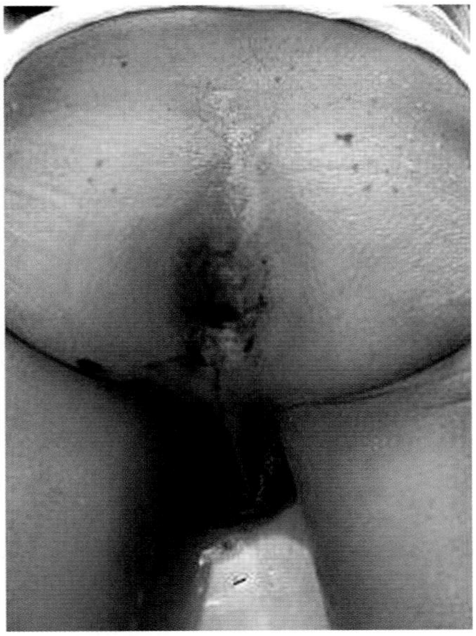

FIG. 16.9: Anal findings in habitual passive agent (*Courtesy*: Dr Manish Shrigiriwar, Associate Professor, Forensic Medicine, IGGMC, Nagpur)

LESBIANISM

- Also called as tribadism, sappism or female homo-sexuals
- It is a female homosexuality wherein woman derives sexual pleasure and gratification by mutual friction of genitals (it is female counterpart of sodomy).
- The term lesbianism is derived from an island, the Isle of Lesbos in the Aegean Sea (off the coast of Greece) where it was practiced by females. The word sappism is originated from the fact that the island was ruled by Queen Sappho.
- The active partner is known as "**butch**" or "**dyke**" and the passive agent is called as "**femme**".[2]

Medicolegal Aspects

1. Continued lesbianism can be a valid ground for divorce or annulment of marriage under Hindu Marriage Act.
2. Lesbian female may be morbidly jealous and commit homicide or suicide or both.

BUCCAL COITUS

- Also called as **oral coitus** or "**Sin of Gomorrah**"
- It is said that this practice was prevalent in town Gomorrah that was twin city of Sodom.
- It can be performed and practiced by both sexes i.e. male and female
- When the intercourse is between oral cavity and penis (i.e. Buccal-penile), the act is called as "**fellatio**". The partner who performs (i.e. the male) is called as "**fellator**" and the other person on whom it is performed (i.e. female or male who is sucking penis) is called as "**fellatee**". Fellatio is also referred as irrumation.
- When the female genital organs including clitoris is sucked (or stimulated by mouth) by male or female partner, then the act is called as "**cunnilingus**" (i.e. the practice is Buccal-vaginal act).
- **Anilingus** is the sexual activity in which the anus is licked, sucked or rubbed by the lips and/or tongue.

Dangers of Buccal Coitus

1. Injury may occur to penis in form of abrasion or puncture lacerations
2. Sudden accidental death of another partner may occur due to aspiration of semen or impacting penis in lower part of pharynx.

Medical Examination

Active partner:

- There may be evidence of abrasion on penis or puncture lacerations. There may be fresh or dried saliva and/or buccal mucosal cells present over penis.
- Amylase may be detected from penile swabs suggestive of oral sexual intercourse.[9]

Other partner: Spermatozoa may be present in the oral cavity.

Medicolegal Aspects

1. It is unnatural sexual act and punishable under Sec 377 of IPC
2. As per Hindu Marriage Act, a female can seek divorce if her husband is insisting and repeatedly demanding for Buccal coitus
3. In some countries, penetration of the vagina or anus with tongue during non-consensual cunnilingus or anilingus is considered to be legally analogous to non-consensual penile penetration of the vagina and anus. The British Parliament has created a new offense of "assault by penetration" which is defined as non-consensual penetration of the anus or vagina by an object or a body part.

BESTIALITY

- It means sexual intercourse by a human being with a lower animal
- Animals usually preferred are:
  1. By males: cows, female sheep, goat, calves, mare, she-ass, cat[21]
  2. By females: dogs, horses etc.
- The intercourse may be vaginal or anal with animal
- The act is done by a person having mental aberration. At times, the act is done in mistaken belief that gonorrhea is cured by intercourse with she-ass.

Medical Examination

In Accused

- Stains over clothes may be present of – dung, mud, secretions
- Signs of injuries over penis. Similarly injuries over body may be seen due to kicking or biting by animal
- Stains over penis – in form animal feces, secretions, blood
- Animal hairs may be present
- Infection transmitted from animal such as genital lesions may be present.[21]

In Animal

- Injuries to genital region
- Presence of human spermatozoa in vaginal or anal canal of animal.

Medicolegal Aspects

1. It is criminal offense in India.
2. It is valid ground for divorce.
3. It is cruel to animal and violates the right of animal of sexual independence.

SEXUAL PARAPHILIAS

- Sexual paraphilias are disorder of sexual preferences in which sexual arousal occurs persistently and significantly in response to objects, which are not a part of normal sexual arousal.[22]
- In other terms, it is the achievement of sexual gratification by means other than natural sexual intercourse.

Sadism

- The term is derived from Marquis de Sade, who wrote novels regarding the practice of sadism
- In sadism, the person gets sexual gratification (sexual arousal and orgasm) by inflicting pain, torture and humiliation to other partner.
- It is commonly found in male partners and he may bite, whip, beat or ill-treat the partner to achieve sexual arousal.
- Lust murder – in extreme case of sadism a person may kill his partner and killing of partner acts as stimulus to sadist for achieving sexual gratification. **Prof. V.V. Pillay** had quoted a sentence of Ted Bundy – a serial rapist and murderer in Textbook of Forensic Medicine and Toxicology which reads as "sometimes when I am doing it with a woman, I get this urge to hurt her, to draw her blood. I just can't help it ...." This sentence aptly reflects the mental make-up of these persons.

Masochism

- It is opposite to sadism
- Here the person gets sexual gratification from being bitten, tortured or humiliated by partner. He often asks his partner to beat him or inflict pain.
- It was first described by an Austrian novelist, Leopold Von Sacher Masoch (1836–1895), hence the name "masochism".

Bondage

This is a condition where both sadism and masochism are present.[23]

Fetishism

- It is usually found in males
- In this sexual deviation, the male experiences sexual gratification by seeing some part of body of a female or some article belonging to her for example sandal, scalp hairs, inner garments etc.
- The fetish person contravenes law at times while stealing these objects. He may commit violence and criminal act while taking that object.

Transvestism (Eonism)

- In this deviation, there is desire to wear the clothes of opposite sex. For example a male may have desire to wear female dress.
- In some obsessed persons, they may even change their sex, by surgery, to be part of opposite sex.

Exhibitionism

- In exhibitionism, the sexual pleasure is obtained by indecent exposure of the genital organ in public place.

- It may be a willful and intentional act, mostly found in males. These persons expose their penis to women or girls.
- It is a criminal act and is included as an obscene act and is punishable under Sec 294 of IPC. Imprisonment up to 3 months or fine or both may be awarded.

Voyeurism (Scoptophilia)

- In this deviation, sexual pleasure is obtained by repeatedly seeing (or looking or peeping) the other person while undressing, bathing or doing sexual intercourse.
- **Peeping Tom** is the name given to male voyeurs who repeatedly do such activities.

Troilism

It is extreme form of voyeurism where husband get sexual gratification by watching or seeing his wife doing sexual intercourse with another person. At times, the husband forces or induces his wife to do sexual intercourse with another man to achieve satisfaction.

Frotteurism

- In this deviation, sexual satisfaction is obtained by touching the body or body parts of other person. For example in a crowded city bus, a male may rub his genital organ with buttocks of female standing with him or a person may touch private parts of female.
- This act is punishable under Sec 290 of IPC.

Necrophagia

- Sexual pleasure is obtained by eating flesh of a dead person.
- It is extreme degree of sadism.

Necrophilia

- In this condition, sexual pleasure is obtained by doing sexual intercourse with dead bodies.
- Apart from other sections, the act is punishable under Sec 297 of IPC for causing indignity to human corpse.

Masturbation

- In this condition, sexual gratification is obtained by deliberate self-stimulation of own genital organ.
- It is offense when practiced in public place.

Myxoscopia

Sexual pleasure obtained by watching sexual intercourse of other person or couple. It is a type of voyeurism.

Satyriasis

Excessive sexual desire and drive in males.

Nymphomania

Excessive sexual desire and drive in females.

Pornographomania

Sexual pleasure obtained by watching or referring pornographic material or literature.

Erotographomania

Sexual pleasure is obtained by obscene and vulgar writings in public places. For example, writing vulgar things in public urinals, train toilets etc.

Coprolalia

Sexual pleasure obtained by using obscene and vulgar language in public.

Undism

Sexual satisfaction obtained by watching the act of urination of another person.

Coprophilia

Sexual gratification achieved by smelling or touching fecal matter (stool) of opposite sex.

Ecoutage

Sexual pleasure obtained by hearing sounds of love-making or sexual intercourse.

Pygmalionism[24]

Sexual gratification achieved by watching or handling nude statues of opposite sex.

Gerontophilia or Gerontosexuality[25]

The term gerontophilia is used to denote a specific sexual inclination towards the elderly.

Bobbit Syndrome

In this type of perversion, the female partner amputes the penis of her male partner with a sharp cutting weapon.[13]

Pedophilia

A pedophile is an adult who repeatedly engages in sexual activities with pre-pubescent children. It may be heterosexual pedophile or homosexual pedophile.[26]

SEX-LINKED OFFENSES

Sexual Harassment

- Working women are the victims of sexual harassment by male counterparts or seniors
- Sexual harassment includes such unwelcome sexually determined behavior, whether directly or by implication, as:[27]
  1. Physical contact or advances;
  2. Demand or request for sexual favors
  3. Sexually colored remarks
  4. Showing pornography
  5. Any other unwelcome physical, verbal or non-verbal conduct of sex nature.

Indecent Assault

- It is an offense committed on a female with intent or knowledge to outrage her modesty. For example slapping over buttock or pressing thigh etc.
- The offense is punishable under Sec 354 of IPC.

Trafficking

Trafficking means the moving, selling or buying of women and children for prostitution within and outside a country for monetary or other considerations with or without consent of person subjected to trafficking.[28]

REFERENCES

1. Sadler TW. Urogenital system. In: Langman's Medical Embryology, 8th edn. 2000. Lippincott Williams and Wilkins, Philadelphia. 304 – 44.
2. Pillay VV. Sexual offences and paraphilias. In: Textbook of Forensic Medicine and Toxicology, 14th edn. 2004. Paras Publishing, Hyderabad. 286 – 305.
3. Rickert VI, Wiemann CM. Date rape among adolescent and young adults. J Pediat Adolesc Gynecol 1998; 11: 167 – 75.
4. Hazelwood and Burgess (eds). In: Practical aspects of rape investigation: a multi-disciplinary approach, 1st edn. 1990. Jaypee Brothers, New Delhi.
5. Boland CA, McDermott SD. Clothing damage analysis in alleged sexual assaults – the need for a systematic approach. Forensic Sci Int 2007; 167: 110 – 15.
6. Knight B. Sexual offenses. In: Legal aspects of medical practice, 5th edn. 1992. Churchill Livingstone, Edinburgh. 225 – 38.
7. Mathur PN, Gehlot RK, Suman A, Saini OP. Need to preserve vaginal swab in victims of sex assault. Indian Internet J Forensic Med Toxicol 2004; 3: available at www.icfmt.org
8. Brauner P, Gallili N. A condom – the critical link in a rape. J Forensic Sci 1993; 38: 1233 – 6.
9. Keating SM. Information from penile swabs in sexual assault cases. Forensic Sci Int 1989; 43: 63 – 81.
10. Burgess AW, Holmstrom IL. Rape trauma syndrome. Am J Psychiatry 1974; 131: 981 – 6.
11. Chadha PV. Sexual offences. In: Handbook of Forensic Medicine and Toxicology, 5th edn. 2004. Jaypee Brothers Medical Publishers (P) Ltd., New Delhi. 146 – 56.
12. Rautji R. Sexual offences-I: Rape. In: Dogra TD, Rudra A (eds) Lyon's Medical Jurisprudence and Toxicology, 11th edn. 2007. Delhi Law House, Delhi. 491 – 516.
13. Nandy A. Sexual offences and sex perversions. In: Principles of Forensic Medicine, 2nd edn. 2005. New Central Book Agency (P) Ltd., Calcutta. 419 – 37.
14. Mathiharan K, Patnaik AK. Sexual offences. In: Modi's Medical Jurisprudence and Toxicology, 23rd edn. 2005. LexisNexis Butterworths, New Delhi. 895 – 964.
15. Carison BE, Maciol K, Schneider J. Sibling incest: reports from forty-one survivors. J Child Sex Abus 2006; 15: 19 – 34.
16. Vij K. Medicolegal examination of the living. In: Textbook of Forensic Medicine and Toxicology, 3rd edn. 2005. Reed Elsevier India Pvt. Limited, New Delhi. 457 – 500.
17. Hobbs CS, Wynne JM. Buggery in childhood – a common syndrome of child abuse. Lancet 1986; 2: 792 – 6.
18. Bruni M. Anal findings in sexual abuse of children. J Forensic Sci 2003; 48: 1343 – 6.
19. Franklin CA. Sexual offenses. In: Modi's Medical Jurisprudence and Toxicology, 21st edn. 1988. Tripathi Private Ltd., Bombay. 387.
20. Michalodimitrakis M, Frangoulis M, Koutselinis A. Accidental sexual strangulation. Am J Forensic Med Pathol 1986; 7: 74 – 5.
21. Mittal A, Shenoi SD, Kumar KB. Genital lesions following bestiality. Indian J Dermatol Venereol Leprol 2000; 66:95 – 6.
22. Ahuja N. In: A short textbook of Psychiatry, 5th edn. 2004. Jaypee Brothers Medical Publishers (P) Ltd., New Delhi.
23. Subrahmanyam BV. Sexual offences. In: Forensic Medicine, Toxicology and Medical Jurisprudence, 1st edn. 2004. Modern Publishers, New Delhi. 123 – 31.
24. Basu R. Sexual offences. In: Fundamentals of Forensic medicine and Toxicology, revised reprint 2004. Books and Allied (P) Ltd., Kolkata. 195 – 203.
25. Kaul A, Duffy S. Gerontophilia – a case report. Med Sci Law 1991; 31: 110 – 4.
26. Tasto DL. Pedophilia. In: Curren WJ, McGarry AL, Petty CS (ed) Modern Legal Medicine, Psychiatry and Forensic Science, 1st edn. 1980. F.A. Davis Company, Philadelphia. 815-26.
27. Sharma RK. Sexual offences. In: Concise Textbook of Forensic medicine and Toxicology, 1st edn. 2005. Reed Elsevier India Pvt. Limited, New Delhi. 109 – 18.
28. Murty OP. Manual for medical officers dealing with medicolegal cases of victims of trafficking for commercial sexual exploitation and child sexual abuse. An initiative of Department of Women and Child Development, Government of India and UNICEF. 2005.

CHAPTER 17

Impotence, Sterility and Sterilization

The possession of virility and procreative power neither requires to be, nor can be, proved to exist by any physician, but is rather, like every other normal function, to be supposed to exist within the usual limits of age.

- Casper

In sexual act, normally males are active partners and females are relatively passive. Therefore, impotence is a term generally applied to the incapacity of male partner to perform sexual intercourse. In females, word impotence is not used; instead term 'frigidity' is used.

IMPOTENCE

Definition

Impotence, in male, is defined as "*persistent inability to develop or maintain a penile erection sufficient to conclude coitus to orgasm and ejaculation*".

Types of Impotence

Impotence may be:

1. Temporary
2. Permanent

Causes of Impotence

Causes are mentioned in Table 17.1. Other causes are discussed below.

1. Age – impotence is generally observed at the extreme of age.
2. Malformations and local acquired causes – presence of malformations or congenital anomaly or local acquired causes renders a person impotent. The malformations are:
   - Absence of male genital organ[1]
   - Klinefelter's syndrome
   - Cryptorchidism
   - Phimosis
   - Epispadias
   - Partial or total amputation of penis
   - Pre-pubertal castration
   - Inflammatory hydrocele
   - Filareasis of scrotum
   - Carcinoma of penis
   - Lesion of CNS or spinal cord including injury to spinal cord
   - Chronic disease – diabetes mellitus, autonomic neuropathy
3. Functional or psychological cause
   - This is the most common cause of temporary impotence
   - Fear, timidity, anxiety, guilt sense, hypochondrias, sexual over indulgence etc. may be the reasons
   - Excessive passion may leads to pre-mature ejaculation and thus causing flaccidity of penis renders a man temporary impotent. This phenomenon is quite common in newly wedded person referred as **bride-groom impotence**.[2]
   - Aversion to sexual intercourse with a particular female. It means that a person is potent with other female but becomes impotent with particular female. This condition is referred as **impotence quod hanc**.
   - Aversion to sexual practice in general i.e. with all females. This condition is called as **sexual aversion disorder**. It is defined as "persistent or recurrent aversion to, and avoidance of, all or almost all, genital sexual contact with a sexual partner.[2]
   - A homosexual person may be impotent with a female partner for natural and complete sexual intercourse.

Medicolegal Importance

Impotence has medicolegal importance in civil and criminal matters.

In Civil Cases

1. Nullity of marriage and divorce
   - Legally, marriage is a contract between male and female and it is presupposed that it will be consummated by act of sexual intercourse. Thus, marriage gives implied consent for natural and complete sexual intercourse.
   - Under Section 12 of Hindu Marriage Act 1955 or Section 24 of Special Marriage Act 1954, a wife may seek divorce on the ground that her husband was impotent at the time of marriage and continues to be impotent therefore he is incapable of fulfilling the rights of consummation of marriage by an act of sexual intercourse.
2. In cases of disputed paternity – a man may claim that, he being impotent has not fathered the child.
3. Compensation cases – a man may claim higher compensation for an injury that has caused him impotent.

In Criminal Cases

1. Impotence may be taken as plea for rape cases, unnatural sexual offenses.
2. Impotence may be stated as plea for adultery.

Table 17.1: Causes of impotence
Endocrine causes
– Testicular failure (primary or secondary)
– Hyperprolactinemia
Disease of penis
– Peyronie's disease
– Previous priapism
– Penile trauma
Disorders of CNS and spine
– Anterior temporal lobe lesions
– Disease of spinal cord
– Tabes dorsalis
– Disease of dorsal root ganglia
Vascular disorders
– Leriche syndrome
– Atherosclerotic occlusion or stenosis of the pudendal and/or cavernosa arteries
– Arterial damage from pelvic radiation
– Venous leak
– Disease of sinusoidal spaces
Drug induced
– Histamine (H_2) blockers e.g. cimetidine
– Spironolactone
– Ketoconazole
– Clonidine
– Beta blockers
– Monoamine oxidase inhibitors
– Tricyclic antidepressants
– Barbiturates
– Diazepam
– Alcohol
– Heroin
– Tobacco
– Methadone

FRIGIDITY

Definition

Frigidity is *a psychological defect in female having an abnormal aversion to sexual intercourse.*

Types

Frigidity may be:
1. Temporary
2. Permanent

Causes

1. Age – since female is relative passive agent, age as such has no effect however, sexual desire is low in old age.
2. Malformations – such as
   - Total occlusion or absent vagina
   - Imperforate hymen
   - Intersex state – such as Turner's syndrome.
3. Local or general disease – such as
   - Presence of local inflammatory lesion in genital tract makes sexual intercourse painful. The condition is called as **dyspareunia**. Due to which, the act may be deferred temporally.
   - Vaginal stenosis.
4. Functional or psychological causes
   - This is most common cause of frigidity
   - Hatred, fear, timidity, shyness, passion, anxiety, neurotic temperament may cause temporary difficulty in sexual intercourse

- **Vaginismus** is a psychosomatic condition, which causes copulation difficult. Whenever, sexual intercourse is attempted, there is painful spasm of sphincter vaginae and levator ani with simultaneous spasmodic contraction of the adductor muscles of thighs and erector spinee, thus making penetration impossible.
- The Vaginismus may either be:
  - Primary – when organic lesion is present
  - Secondary – due to painful local inflammatory lesion
  - Psychogenic – due to fear, timidity or anxiety.
- Sexual aversion disorder or sexual arousal disorder – in this disorder, there is persistent or recurrent lack of subjective sense of sexual excitement and pleasure during sexual activity.[2]

Medicolegal Importance

1. Nullity of marriage
2. Divorce cases

STERILITY

Definition

- Sterility means *inability of a person to procreate*
- In male, sterility is defined as "*inability to beget children or inability to fertilize the ovum*"
- In female, sterility is defined as " *inability to conceive*"
- In present days, the term **infertility** is used rather than sterility
- A person may be impotent and sterile or impotent and non-sterile (i.e. fertile) or potent and sterile.

Types

Sterility may be:
1. Relative
2. Absolute

It may also be classified as:
1. Physiological
2. Pathological

- Absolute sterility – refers to incapacity to reproduce child and the disease is irremediable
- Relative sterility – refers to diminished capacity to procreate children and the malady can be corrected
- Physiological sterility – refers to sterility that occurs at extreme age. For example, a male child of 2 years is sterile but at puberty he will be able to secrete semen and gains power of procreation.
- Pathological sterility – refers to presence of any disease or condition by virtue of which the person is incapable to procreate.

Causes

In Male

1. Age – at extreme age, a male may be sterile
2. Malformation
   - Hypospadias
   - Epispadias
   - Congenital absence of testis.
3. Local or general disease
   - Azoospermia
   - Oligospermia
   - Exposure to X-rays
   - Orchitis
   - Inflammatory affection of testis or epididymis, prostate gland or seminal vesicle of gonorrheal origin
   - Varicocele.

In Females

1. Age – at extreme age, a female may be sterile.
2. Malformations
   - Absence of uterus
   - Bifid uterus
   - Absence of ovaries
   - Total occlusion of vagina
3. Local or general disease
   - Tuberculosis endometriotis
   - Gonorrhea
   - Polycystic ovary

Medicolegal Importance

1. Disputed paternity – the putative father may take plea that he being sterile, has not fathered the child.
2. Compensation cases – for loss of reproductive capability as a result of injury or occupation or surgical operation.
3. In adoption cases – sterility can be taken as a plea for adoption purposes.
4. Absolute sterility in male may be one of indication for artificial insemination.

STERILIZATION

Definition

Sterilization is a procedure to make a male or female sterile (infertile) without affecting the potency of that person.

Types

It may be:

1. Voluntary
2. Compulsory

Voluntary

Voluntary sterilization procedure is performed on a married person with the consent of both partners (i.e. husband and wife). It is performed for following purpose:

- Contraceptive sterilization – it is done to limit the size of family, i.e. for the purpose of family planning
- Therapeutic sterilization – is performed to prevent danger to the health or life of a woman who will bear pregnancy
- Eugenic sterilization – the procedure is done to prevent the conception and birth of children who is likely to be physically or mentally defective. The objective of such sterilization is to improve the race by preventing the transmission of disease.

Compulsory

It is performed compulsory on person by an order of State (Government). It is not done in India.

Methods

The sterilization may be done by temporary or permanent methods.

Permanent Methods

- In male – by doing vasectomy
- In female – by doing tubectomy

Temporary Methods[3]

Following are the temporary methods:

1. Barrier methods
   - Physical methods – such as condoms, vaginal diaphragms, vaginal sponge
   - Chemical methods – such as foams, jellies, paste, suppositories
   - Combined – i.e. physical + chemical
2. Intrauterine devices – like copper-T, Lippes loop
3. Hormonal methods
   - Oral pills
   - Depot formulations
4. Miscellaneous methods – such as:
   - Coitus interrupts
   - Rhythm method
   - Breastfeeding

Guiding Principles

With increasing education, awareness and rapid urbanization, the request for temporary or voluntary sterilization is increasing. The doctors performing these procedures are not immune and an action can be initiated against them in civil court or consumer forum due to failure of operation that resulted in unwanted pregnancy. To avoid legal actions or charge of negligence, doctors should take precautions. The guiding principles are presented below.

1. For permanent method, informed written consent of both partners i.e. husband and wife, should be obtained.
2. The couple should be told that the said methods, i.e. tubectomy or vasectomy are permanent in nature. However, there is small but real chance of failure of the procedure and that may result in unintended pregnancy. In other words, the procedure is not 100 percent sure.
3. After vasectomy, the male partner should be asked to use barrier method or alternative contraception for about three months or until the seminal examination shows absence of spermatozoa on two successive occasions.
4. While prescribing contraceptive pills, medical examination of the female should be carried out. The complications or adverse effects, if any, should be explained to the patients.

Medicolegal Implications

1. In failure of sterilization operation, doctors are held responsible for the unwanted pregnancy by the concerned couple. Therefore, it is necessary that doctor should explain the couple before sterilization operation that the procedure is not 100 percent sure and in case if couple suspects pregnancy, they should contact the concerned doctor immediately. While giving judgment in one such failed sterilization case, honorable Court quoted – medical negligence plays its game in strange ways. Sometimes it plays with life; sometimes it gifts an unwanted child.[4]
2. Adultery – failure of vasectomy in male causes considerable anxiety to female. The male may suspect his wife to have sexual relationship with other person.
3. Disputed paternity
4. Legitimacy of child
5. Divorce

REFERENCES

1. Rose EF. Congenital absence of adult male external genitalia associated with sudden death: case report. J Forensic Sci 1969; 14: 227-34.
2. Pillay VV. Impotence, frigidity and sterility. In: Textbook of Forensic Medicine and Toxicology, 14th edn. 2004. Paras Publishing, Hyderabad. 252-61.
3. Park K. Demography and family planning. In: Park's Textbook of Preventive & Social Medicine, 14th edn. 1995. M/S Banarsidas Bhanot Publishers, Jabalpur. 282-312.
4. Yadav M, Kushwaha V. Issue of failed sterilization, medical negligence and compensation: a global review. J Indian Acad Forensic Med 2007; 29:23-7.

CHAPTER 18

Pregnancy and Delivery

The true index of a man's character is the health of his wife.

- Cyril Connolly

PREGNANCY

Pregnancy is a physiological state in female where she conceives and carries developing product of conception in her womb until birth of a child.

Medicolegal Importance

A) **Civil cases**
   1. Nullity of marriage: If a female is pregnant before marriage from another person and she concealed the pregnancy at the time of marriage with other man to whom she get married then the marriage can be declared as null and void.
   2. Divorce: Pregnancy resulted in a female who had no access (i.e. she had not done sexual intercourse with her husband) to her husband within the reasonable period matching with the duration of pregnancy then a decree of divorce may be allowed to the husband.
   3. In case of breach of promise of marriage
   4. In alimony: In divorce cases, pregnant women are allowed higher maintenance allowance.
   5. Inheritance of property
   6. Blackmailing
   7. Defamation
   8. Compensation cases: If a husband of pregnant woman dies due to negligence of another person, higher compensation is paid.
   9. Pregnancy may be taken as a plea to avoid court.

B) **Criminal cases**
   1. Pregnancy is a positive proof of sexual intercourse in rape cases.
   2. Pregnancy may be cause for suicide in unmarried female.
   3. Pregnancy may be motive for murder if that pregnancy is due
      - To sexual intercourse by man with woman (illicit sexual intercourse)
      - Murder may be done by husband when husband suspects that his wife is pregnant by another person (infidelity of wife).
   4. Execution of death sentence: under Section 416 of CrPC, there can be postponement of capital sentence of pregnant woman – if woman sentenced to death is found to be pregnant, the High Court shall order the execution of the sentence to be postponed and may, if it thinks fit, commute the sentence to imprisonment for life.[1]
   5. Pregnancy related with criminal abortion or concealment of birth.

DIAGNOSIS OF PREGNANCY IN LIVING

Diagnosis of pregnancy in living is done on presence of signs and symptoms in that female. These signs and symptoms are divided into three groups (Table 18.1):

1. Presumptive evidence of pregnancy
2. Probable evidence of pregnancy
3. Positive evidence of pregnancy

Presumptive Evidence of Pregnancy

1. **Secondary Amenorrhea**
   - Cessation of menses in a female, who is in reproductive age and have previous regular menses, is suggestive of pregnancy.
   - However, amenorrhea may be due to other causes such as ovarian dysgenesis, polycystic ovarian disorder etc.

Table 18.1: Summarizing the evidences of pregnancy in living

Signs and symptoms
Presumptive evidence
a. Symptoms
1. Amenorrhea
2. Morning sickness
3. Increased salivation
4. Perverted appetite
5. Irritable temper
6. Fatigability
7. Frequency of micturation
b. Signs
1. Breast changes
2. Jacquemir's sign
3. Barne's sign
4. Pigmentation of skin
5. Linea nigra
6. Striae gravidrum
Probable evidence
Symptom
Quickening
Signs
1. Enlargement of abdomen
2. Goodell's sign
3. Hegar's sign
4. Braxton-Hick's sign
5. Ballotment
6. Uterine soufflé
7. Laboratory tests
Positive evidence
Signs
1. Fetal parts and movements
2. Fetal heart sound
3. X-ray examination
4. Sonography

2. **Breast Changes**

They are more pronounced and prominent in primigravida (i.e. pregnant for first time) female. The changes imparted by pregnancy are:

- Breast becomes full, tender and increase in size
- Superficial veins become prominent
- By 8th week, hyperpigmentation of the areola and nipple occurs with appearance of Montgomery's tubercles (Fig. 18.1).

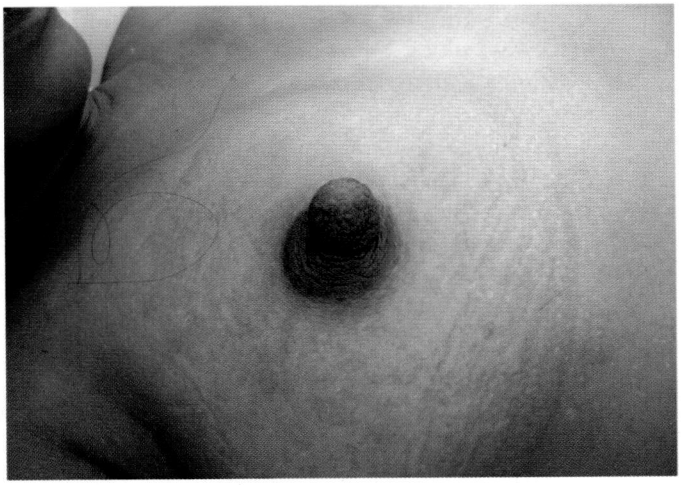

FIG. 18.1: Hyperpigmentation of areola and nipple

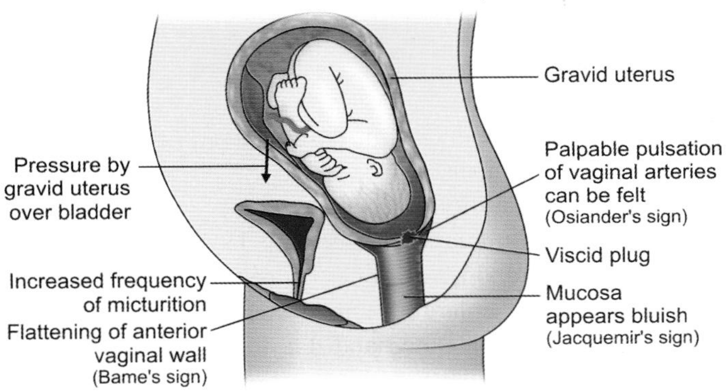

FIG. 18.2: Gravid uterus with various signs of pregnancy

- By 12th week, colostrum can be squeezed out of nipple and later milk can be extracted as pregnancy advances
- However, these breast changes can also be seen in other conditions as:
  - » Ovarian tumors secreting prolactin
  - » Women taking contraceptive pills or tranquilizers.[2, 3]

3. Changes in Vagina (Fig. 18.2)
   - **Jacquemir's sign** (or **Chadwick's sign**): The normal pinkish mucosa of vagina changes to bluish by 4th week of pregnancy. The change in vaginal mucosa colour is due to venous congestion due to venous obstruction by pressure of gravid uterus. However, it can be observed in other conditions such as pelvic tumor (uterine fibroid).

- **Barne's sign**: Flattening of anterior vaginal wall due to upward tilting of cervix
- **Osiander's sign**: Palpable pulsation of the vaginal arteries felt through the lateral fornics at 8th week due to high arterial tension of pelvic arteries. This is called as Osiander's sign. However, similar pulsation may be felt in acute pelvic inflammation.
- The secretion of mucous from vagina is increased.

4. Pigmentation of skin
   - Pigmentation may occur on forehead and cheeks in form of dark brown patches.
   - A linear pigmentation present over abdomen from ensiform cartilage to the symphysis pubis and is known as **linea nigra** (Fig. 18.3).
   - The skin over abdomen shows depressed lines, pinkish or slightly bluish in appearance. These lines are called as striae gravidarum (Fig. 18.4).
5. Morning sickness
   - Morning sickness refers to nausea and at times followed by vomiting soon after waking.
6. Sympathetic disturbances
   - Increased salivation
   - Perverted appetite with desire for unusual food
   - Irritable temper
   - Easy fatigability
7. Frequency of micturation (see Fig. 18.2)
   - In early and late trimester of pregnancy, due to pressure of enlarging gravid uterus over bladder, the bladder gets irritated and due to which female have increase frequency of micturation.

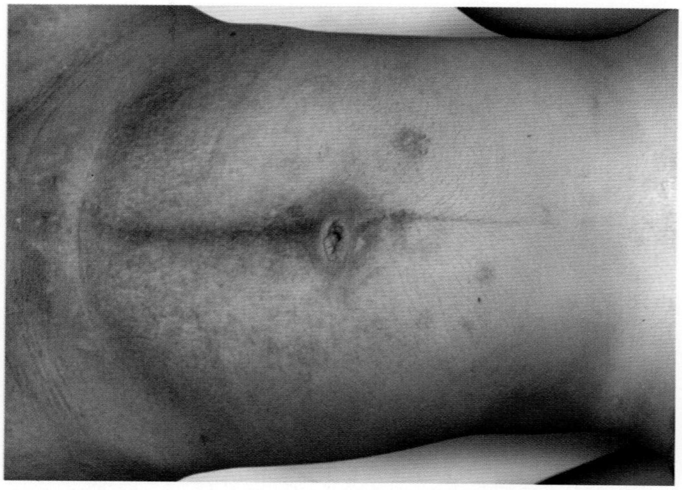

FIG. 18.3: Abdomen showing linea nigra (*Courtesy*: Dr Vaibhav Sonar, Lecturer, Dept. of Forensic Medicine, GMC, Miraj)

Probable Evidence of Pregnancy

1. Enlargement of abdomen
   - The abdomen begins to enlarge as pregnancy advances. Enlargement of abdomen is due to progressive and uniform enlargement of gravid uterus. The uterine enlargement is proportionate to the period of pregnancy.
   - By 12th week, uterus can be palpated just above symphysis pubis; it is half way between the symphysis and umbilicus at 16th week and at the level of umbilicus at 24th week. Then the fundus raises one third of the way to the xiphisternum. At 28th week, fundus of uterus is 1/3rd between umbilicus and xiphisternum; it is 2/3rd between umbilicus and xiphisternum at 32 week. At 36 week, the uterus reaches at the xiphisternum (Fig. 18.5).

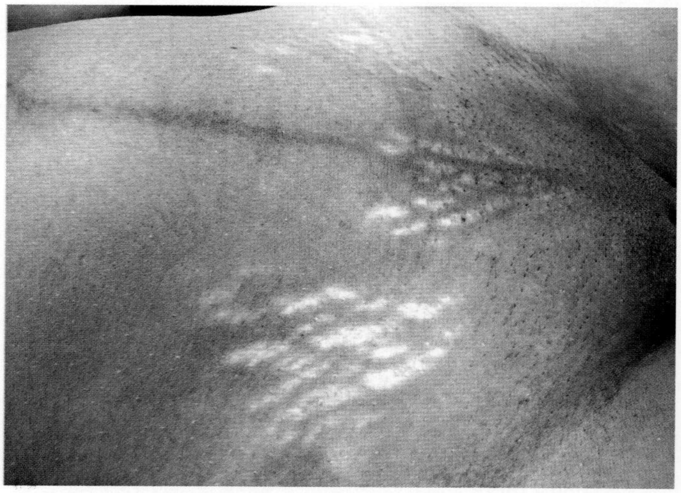

FIG. 18.4: Striae gravidarum

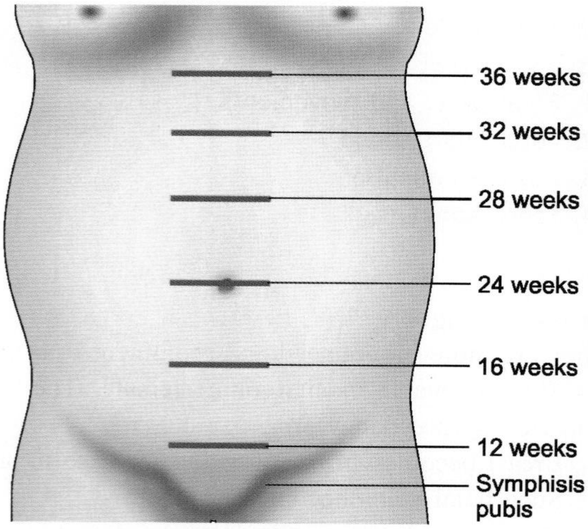

FIG. 18.5: Abdomen showing enlargement with level of fundus at different weeks of gestation

2. Changes in cervix
   - Goodell's sign: the cervix normally is hard as tip of nose. However, due to pregnancy, it begins to soften from below upwards and is felt soft as lips. The softening of cervix is known as **Goodell's sign** and can be identified by 16th week (Fig. 18.6).
   - Mucous becomes thick and viscid plug blocks the cervical canal.
3. Hegar's sign
   - Lower segment of uterus becomes soft and is easily compressible. This is known as **Hegar's sign**. It becomes positive at 8 to 10 weeks (Fig. 18.6).
4. Braxton-Hick's sign
   - These are the intermittent contractions occurring in uterus. These contractions can be palpable as early as 16th week (Fig. 18.6).
   - These contractions can also be felt in other conditions such as
     » Hematometra
     » Soft myomas
     » Cystic distension of uterus
5. Ballottement
   - These are objective signs of pregnancies and can be elicited on external and/or internal examination
   - External ballottement – in this procedure the patient is asked to lie in supine position. One hand is placed on one flank and other hand displaces the fetus. The other hand perceives the movement of fetus (Fig. 18.7).
   - Internal ballottement – here the test is performed with patient is in lithotomy position. Two fingers are inserted into the vaginal fornix. With the tips of fingers, the head is gently pushed upwards. Here due to tossing, the fetus moves upward and returns back to its original position and the movement is felt by the fingers.
   - The test is positive by 16 to 20 weeks
   - Ballottement test can be negative if the amount of amniotic fluid is scanty (i.e. oligohydrimnois) or fetus is not in vertical lie.
6. Uterine soufflé
   - It is a soft blowing murmur, caused due to passage of maternal blood into the dilated arteries of uterus. The murmur is synchronized with the pulse of mother. It can be heard with a stethoscope applied on either side of uterus (Fig. 18.6). It is usually audible from 16th week onwards.
   - The test can also be positive in rapidly growing vascular uterine fibromyoma.
   - The test to be not confused with fetal heart sound because fetal heart sound are more rapid in its rate and are not synchronized with mother's pulse.
7. Quickening
   - Quickening is appreciation of fetal movements by mother in her womb (Fig. 18.6)
   - A mother is said to be "quick with child" when mother perceives the fetal movement or quickening in her womb. This occurs at about 18 to 20 weeks of pregnancy.
8. Laboratory investigations
   The laboratory test for pregnancy are classified as:
   1. Bio-assay or biological tests
   2. Immunoassay or immunological tests

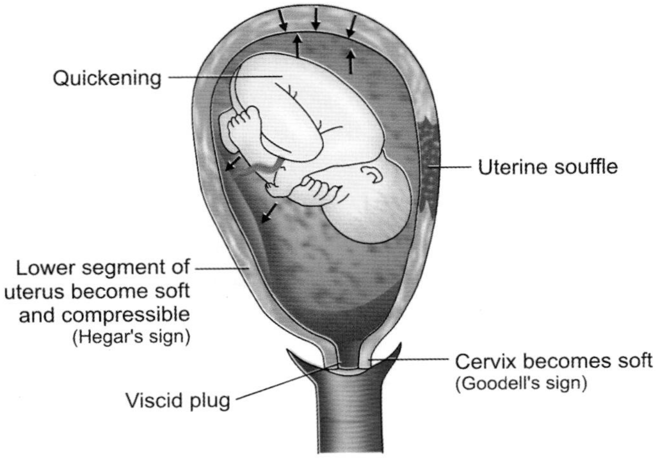

FIG. 18.6: Pregnancy showing probable evidences

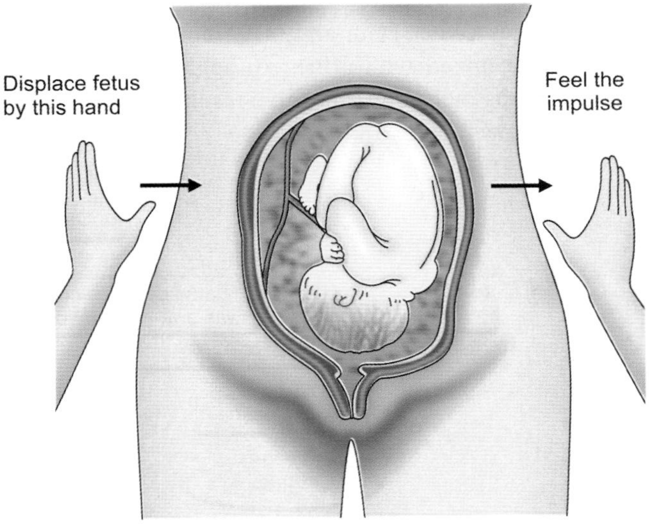

FIG. 18.7: Showing procedure how to do external ballottement

3. ELISA test
4. Radio-immunoassay

Biological Tests

- In past, these methods were employed and now are of historical importance. These methods are based on principle that pregnant females have increased level of human chorionic gonadotropin (hCG) in urine (or blood) and when the urine is injected in animal, the animal gives reaction.
- These tests are as given in Table 18.2
- Disadvantages of biological tests are:
  – Tests are time consuming
  – Animals have to be sacrificed (killed)

Immunological Tests

The tests are summarized in Table 18.3. Immunological tests are based on principle that – antigen present in urine or serum (hCG) reacts with antibody. There are two types of test available

1. Agglutination inhibition test
2. Direct agglutination test
   – **Agglutination inhibition test**: In this type of test, one drop of urine is mixed with one drop of solution that contains hCG antibody. If no hCG is present in urine, the antibodies added will remain free. Now a drop of another solution is added which contains latex particles coated with hCG (as antigen). Agglutination of latex particles suggests that female is not pregnant (agglutination inhibition).
   – **Direct agglutination test**: In this type of test, latex particles coated with anti-hCG monoclonal antibodies are mixed with urine. An agglutination reaction develops indicating a positive result. It means female is pregnant (Fig. 18.8).

Fallacies of Tests

Tests are based on presence of hCG and therefore can also be positive in other conditions such as:
1. Hydatidiform mole
2. Chorinoepithelioma

Table 18.2: Biological test for pregnancy

Name of test	*Test animal*	*Result*	*Period for test*
Ascheim-Zondek	Female mice	Corpus luteum	5 days
Friedman	Female rabbit	Corpus luteum	2 days
Hogben (Xenopus)	Female toad/frog	Extrusion of eggs	24 hours
Galli-Mainini	Male toad	Extrusion of sperms	2 - 5 hours

Table 18.3: Showing immunological test of pregnancy

Test	*Result*	*Positive on days after LMP*
Agglutination inhibition	Absence of agglutination	2 days after missed period
Direct agglutination	Presence of agglutination	2-3 days after missed period
Two-site sandwich immunoassay	Colour bands in control and test window	1st day after missed period
ELISA	--	27th day of cycle
Radio immunoassay	--	25th day of cycle

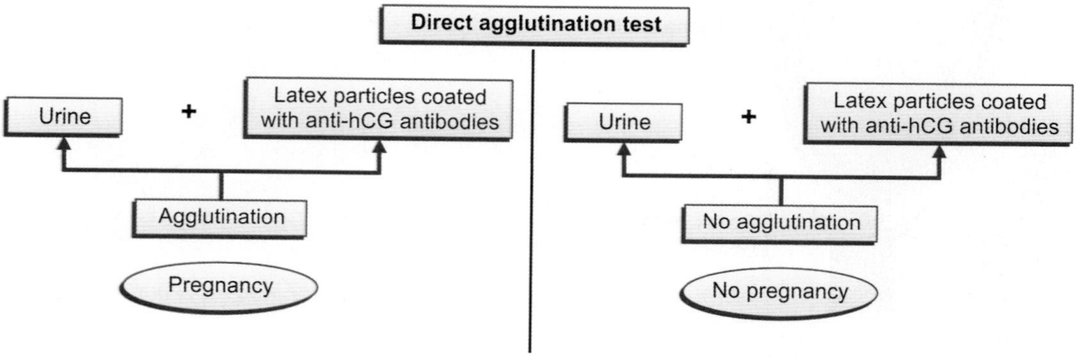

FIG. 18.8: Flow chart showing direct agglutination test

Positive Evidence

1. Fetal parts and fetal movements
   - The test can be done by palpation of fetal parts and movements by placing hands over abdomen. Fetal movements are appreciated by 16 to 20 weeks.
   - Fetal parts or movements cannot be palpated/appreciated in a female having fatty abdominal wall or if there is hydramnios.
2. Fetal heart sounds
   - It is absolute sign of pregnancy and usually heard at about 18 to 20 week
   - Fetal heart sounds (FHS) are like muffled tickling of a watch and can be heard by fetoscope.
   - The fetal heart sound rate is about 160/minute at 5th month and 120/minute at 9th month of pregnancy.
   - FHS can be detected much earlier by using advanced techniques like Doppler at about 10 to 12 week. Echocardiography can detect the FHS at about 7th week and real-time sonography detects at about 8th week.
   - FHS are not synchronous with mother's pulse
   - FHS are not heard in:
     - When fetus is dead
     - Hydramnios – excessive quantity of liquor amnii
     - When abdominal wall is very thick.
3. X-ray examination (Fig. 18.9)
   - By X-ray, the diagnosis of pregnancy can be certain after 16th week.
   - X-ray will reveal fetal skeleton in form of
     - Circular shadow of skull outline
     - Ladder-like shadow of ribs
     - Beaded shadow of spine
     - Linear shadows of limbs
   - X-rays are contraindicated in first trimester of pregnancy due to radiation hazards
   - X-ray sign of fetal death are:
     - Presence of gas in heart and great vessels like aorta (**Robert's sign**)
     - Collapse of spinal column due to loss of muscle tone – usually hyperflexion of spine
     - **Spalding's sign** – overlapping of skull bones caused by liquefaction of brain.
4. Sonography
   - By this method, gestational sac (ring) is determined by 5th week and distinct echos of embryo within gestational sac by 8th week. The USG features observed are – fetal pole by 6th week, yolk sac at 6th week and cardiac pulsation appreciated at 7th week (Fig. 18.10).

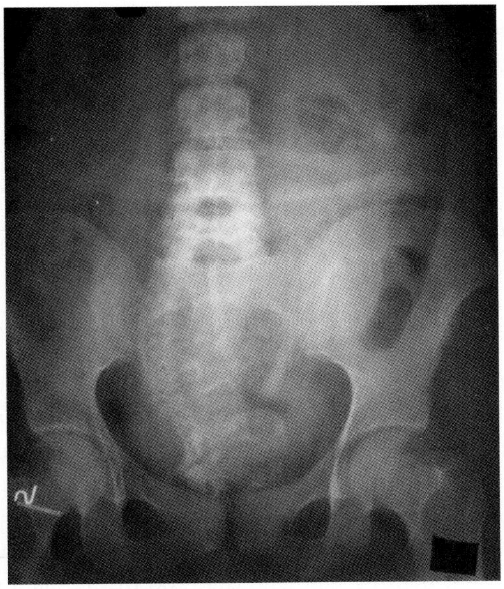

FIG. 18.9: X-ray abdomen showing fetus

Diagnosis of Pregnancy in Dead

In addition to signs found in living persons, following are important signs of pregnancy found in dead female.

1. Presence of product of conception
   - Product of conception is found in uterus in form of fertilized ovum, embryo or fetus (Fig. 18.11).
   - Presence of placenta
2. Changes in uterus
   - Uterus is enlarged, thickened and increase in size (Fig. 18.12).

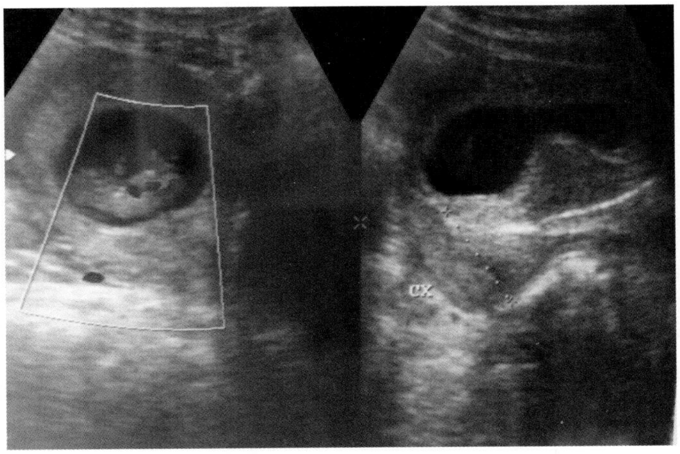

FIG. 18.10: USG appearance—gestational age about 9 weeks

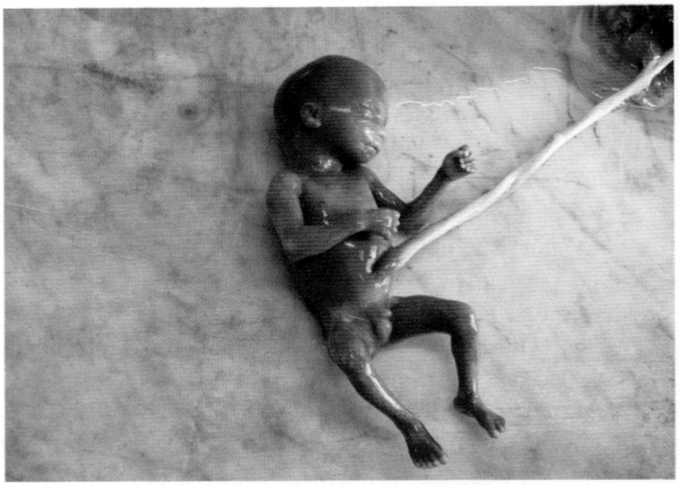

FIG. 18.11: Product of conception

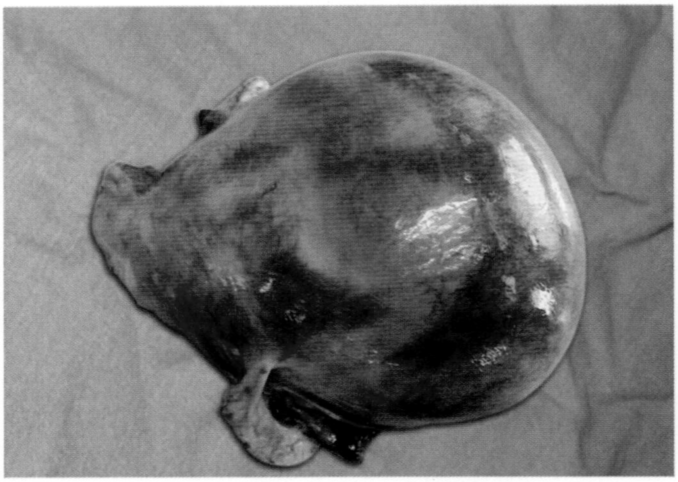

FIG. 18.12: Gravid uterus

- Marks of attachment of placenta
- Microscopic examination of uterus reveals hypertrophy and hyperplasia of myometrium.

3. Changes in ovary
   - Corpus luteum is present in ovary. If fertilization occurs, the corpus luteum do not degenerate but rather continue to develop and attains largest size at about 16th week of pregnancy. It secretes progesterone
4. Laboratory investigation
   - hCG can be detected in blood/urine.

PERIOD OF GESTATION

Average Duration of Pregnancy

- The average duration of pregnancy is 266 days (38 lunar weeks) from conception or it is **280 days (40 lunar weeks, 10 lunar months or 9 calendar months and 7 days)** from the first day of the last menstrual period in woman with regular menstrual cycles. The former is called as **ovulatory age** or fertilization age and later is called as **gestational age** or menstrual age.
- The ovulatory or fertilization age is usually used by histologist or embryologist
- The gestational or menstrual age is used by Obstetricians and legal professionals.

Minimum Duration of Pregnancy

- The child born on or after 210 days or 7 months is considered as viable. However, cases have been reported where children born even less than 210 days have also survived.[4]

Maximum Duration of Pregnancy

- In India, the law does not lay down any fixed limit of gestation. Each case is decided on its own merits.
- Cases have been reported where females have given birth even after 352 days from last day of menstruation.[4]

Calculation of Expected Date of Delivery

Expected date of delivery (EDD) is calculated by:

1. Nagele's rule – in this traditional method, EDD is calculated by adding 7 days to the first day of the last menstrual period (LMP) and count back three months (90 days). If a leap year intervenes, add 6 days instead of 7 days.[5]
2. Sonography method – by measuring crown rump length, biparietal diameter etc.

Calculation of Duration of Pregnancy

Following are the methods to estimate duration of pregnancy

1. Clinical method – here height of fundus is measured with reference to anatomical landmark and period of pregnancy is calculated for example if fundus is at umbilicus, then period of pregnancy is 24 weeks etc. (*vide supra*).
2. McDonald's rule – in this rule, height of fundus is measured by a flexible tape and duration of pregnancy is calculated from one of the following formulae:[6]

- Height of fundus (in cm) × 2/7 = duration of pregnancy in lunar months or
- Height of fundus (in cm) × 8/7 = duration of pregnancy in weeks.

Pseudocyesis

- Synonyms: false or spurious pregnancy, phantom pregnancy, imaginary pregnancy
- In this condition, the woman believes or imagines that she is pregnant. The fact is that, she is not pregnant.
- The woman has subjective symptoms of pregnancy in form of enlarged abdomen, breast changes with amenorrhea.
- The woman have imaginary thoughts that fetus is growing inside her womb.
- X-ray or sonography will resolve the issue.

Fetus Papyraseous

- It is also known as fetus compressus
- In twin pregnancy, one fetus may grow and develop more than other fetus. The second under-developed fetus may get compressed and flattened. Such fetus is termed as fetus papyraseous or compressus.[8]

DELIVERY

Introduction

- Delivery is the expulsion or extraction of a viable fetus out of womb at term.
- It is not synonymous with labor; delivery can take place without labor as in elective Caesarean section. Thus, delivery may be vaginal either spontaneous or assisted or it may be abdominal (as in Caesarean section).
- Labour: Series of events that take place in the genital organs in an effort to expel the products of conception out of the womb through vagina into the outer world is called labour.
- Parturition is the process of giving birth. Parturient is a patient in labour.
- Delivery occurring at full term i.e. 280 days or 40 weeks is called as full-term delivery.
- Delivery occurring prior to 37 completed weeks of pregnancy is called as pre-term labour.
- Puerperium is a period that begins soon after placenta is expelled and lasts for about 6 weeks.

MEDICOLEGAL IMPORTANCE

Questions arise in civil or criminal cases, when doctor has to determine whether the female has delivered or not. Following are the medicolegal importance.

Civil Cases

1. Feigned (pretended) delivery and suppositious child
2. Affiliation and adoption cases
3. Contested paternity
4. Legitimacy of child
5. Nullity of marriage
6. Divorce
7. Inheritance of property
8. Higher maintenance allowance (alimony) in divorce cases
9. Higher compensation in compensation cases

Criminal Cases

1. Abortion
2. Infanticide
3. Concealment of birth
4. Blackmail
5. Delay in execution of judicial death sentence up to 6 months after delivery
6. Delivery of child as a evidence of rape
7. Homicide and suicide

Evidence of Delivery in Living

Recent Evidences

Symptoms

1. Fatigue
2. Lassitude
3. Loss of weight
4. Diuresis
5. After pain
6. Rise in temperature

Signs

1. Breast: Full, enlarged, firm, contains colostrum or milk. Hyperpigmentation of the areola and nipple.
2. Abdomen: Abdomen becomes lax and flabby. Skin is wrinkled and shows striae gravidrum. If cesarean section is done, then operative mark may be identified.
3. Perineum may shows:
   - Rupture of fourchette and posterior commissure

- Perineum may be lacerated
- Perineum may show episiotomy wound, scar or sutured and healing wound.

4. Labia: May be swollen, tender, bruised or lacerated and inflamed.
5. Vagina may be:
   - Dilated widely, roomy
   - Walls are smooth and relaxed.
   - Mucosa shows ironed-out rugae
   - May be bruised or lacerated
   - Caruncula myrtiformis of the hymen.
6. Lochia: It is an alkaline discharge from the uterus having a peculiar, sour, disagreeable smell. It is composed of red blood cells, white blood cells, debris of deciduas, epithelial cells and bacteria. If infected, lochia is foul smelling. As duration of puerperium progress, the lochia changes as:
   - Lochia rubra – for first 4 to 5 days, it is red and contains blood clots
   - Lochia serosa – 5 to 10th day, it is watery, serous and pale
   - Lochia alba – after 10th day onward, it becomes yellowish-white, thicker and scantier.
   - At about 2 to 3 weeks it disappears.
7. Changes in cervix
   - Soon after delivery, cervix is soft, thin, flabby and collapsed.
   - The external os may show lacerations and admits two fingers. It contracts slowly and by the end of 1st week, it admits one finger with difficulty.
   - The internal os begins to close in the first 24 hour.
8. Changes in uterus
   - Intermittent uterine contractions can be appreciated for first 4 to 5 days.
   - After delivery, uterus shows signs of involution.
   - By 1 to 3 day – fundus of uterus is midway between umbilicus and symphysis pubis.
   - By 2nd week – fundus descends into true pelvis
   - By 5 to 6 weeks – uterus attains normal size.

Laboratory Findings

Blood or urine gives positive result for pregnancy up to seven to 10 days after delivery.

Evidences of Remote Delivery in Living

1. Breast: Lax, flabby, pendulous, with dark pigmented nipple and areola.
2. Abdomen: Wall is lax, and shows striae gravidrum.
3. Labia: Labia majora are dark and are partially open. Labia minora are darkly pigmented and protrude through the gap.
4. Perineum: Shows scar of old tear or episiotomy wound or that of perineal laceration. Posterior commissure may show healed areas.
5. Vagina: Capacious, walls are not approximated with loss of rugosity of vaginal mucosa.
6. Hymen: Represented by tags called carunculae myrtiformes.
7. Cervix: External os appears transverse slit like opening.

EVIDENCES OF DELIVERY IN DEAD

Evidences of Recent Delivery in Dead

In addition to above signs, following features are noted:
1. Uterus – features are mentioned in Table 18.4.
2. Ovaries and fallopian tubes are congested.
3. Broad and round ligaments are lax.
4. Peritoneum – covering over lower part of uterus is folded and wrinkled (Fig. 18.13).
5. Bladder mucosa – shows congestion and edema.

Evidences of Remote Delivery in Dead

In addition to above signs, following features are noted
1. Uterus – size enlarged than nulliparous state. The walls are concave from inside forming a round or pear shaped uterine cavity (Table 18.5 and Fig. 18.14).

Table 18.4: Showing features of involuting uterus

Features	Size of uterus (Length × breadth × thickness in cm)	Weight	Diameter of site of placental attachment
Fresh delivered	20 × 15 × 5	1000 gm	10 cm
3 days postpartum	17 × 10 × 4	700 gm	7 cm
End of 1st week	14 × 8 × 4	500 gm	4 cm
End of 2nd week	12 × 7 × 3	300 gm	2.5 cm
End of 6th week	10 × 6 × 2.5	80 gm	1.5 cm

2. Cervix
   - External os shows transverse slit like opening (Fig. 18.14)
   - Cervical canal is cylindrical in shape
   - Internal os ill defined
   - Cervix may show areas of healed scars

Precipitate Labor

- It usually occurs in multigravida having wider pelvis and strong contractions
- Precipitate labour is a labour that occurs suddenly and the three stages of labour are not well defined.

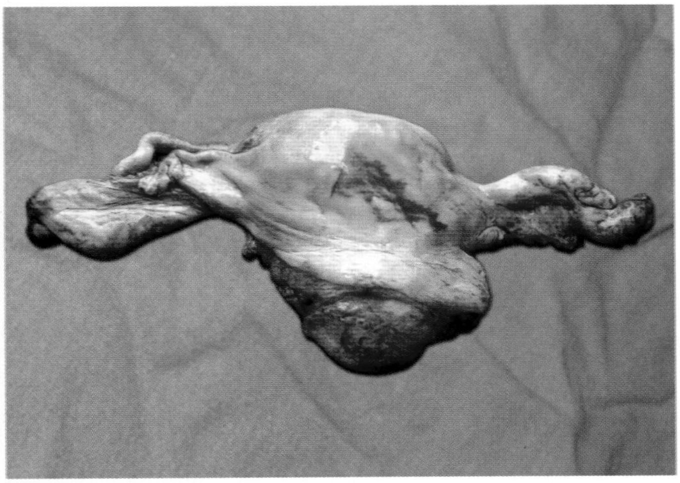

FIG. 18.13: Uterus with peritoneum. Peritoneum is folded and wrinkled

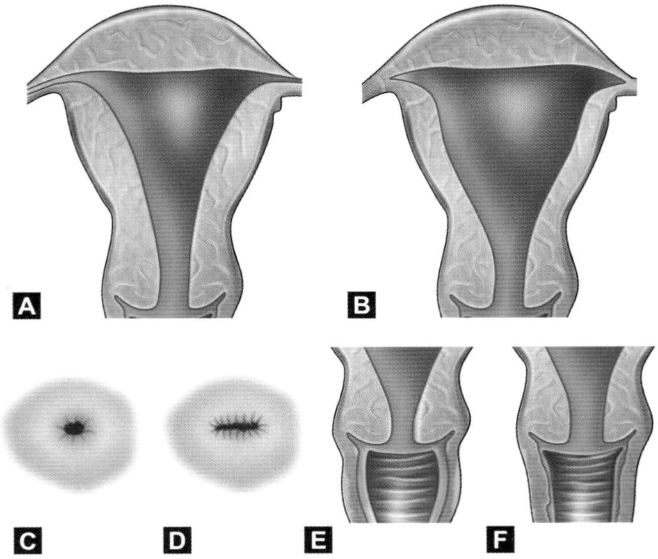

FIGS 18.14A to F: Diagram showing difference between nulliparous and gravid uterus and cervix. **A:** Nulliparous uterus with convex walls and triangular cavity. **B:** Parous uterus with concave wall and pear shaped cavity. **C:** Nulliparous cervix with circular external os. **D:** Parous cervix with slit like external os. **E:** Nulliparous cervix with conical cervical canal. **F:** Parous cervix with cylindrical cervical canal

Table 18.5: Difference between nulliparous and parous uterus

Features	*Nulliparous*	*Parous*
Size	7 cm x 5cm x 2 cm	10 cm x 6 cm x 2.5 cm
Weight	40 gm	80 gm
Ratio between body and cervix	1:1	2:1
Fundus	- Less convex	- More concave
	- lie at same line of broad ligament	- Lie at higher level than line of broad ligament
Uterine cavity	Walls are convex from inside forming triangular cavity	Walls are concave from inside forming a round or pear shaped cavity
Cervix - external os	Circular	Transverse slit
Cervix - internal os	Circular, well defined	Ill-defined
Cervix - canal	Conical	Cylindrical

- Medicolegal importance:
  – Mother may be charged with infanticide
  – Injury to fetus may occur

Birth in Caul

- In such labour, the child may be born with intact membranes surrounding him or her (Fig. 18.15).
- Medicolegal importance – death of child may occur due to suffocation.

Posthumous child – child born after death of a father in a legally married couple

Suppositious child – it is a child presented by a woman and the woman pretends that she has delivered the child. Actually, the child is not her child i.e. suppositious child.

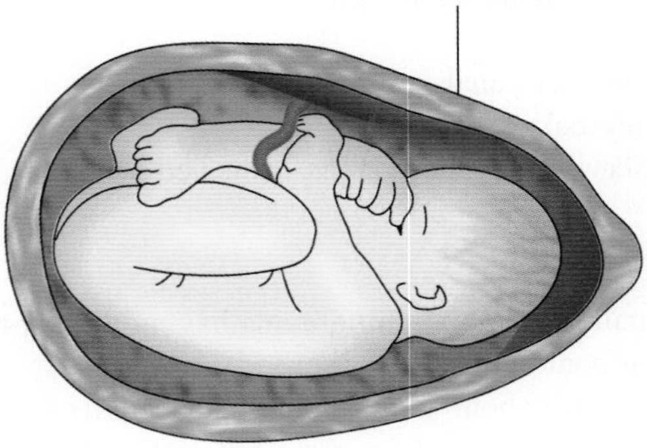

FIG. 18.15: Birth in caul. Here the fetus born with intact membranes

Disputed Maternity

Maternity is motherhood of child. The question of disputed maternity may arise in:

- In hospital birth case where newborn babies are mixed up.
- In alleged suppositious child
- Medical examination and DNA typing will settle the issue.

REFERENCES

1. Satyanarayana, Krishna Rao. In: The Law relating to medical profession in India, 1st edn. 1962. Bestseller Publications, Hyderabad.
2. Konar H, Dutta DC. In: Textbook of Obstetrics, 6th edn. 2004. New Central Book Agency (P) Ltd., Calcutta.
3. Dawn CS. Undergraduate and postgraduate textbook of obstetrics and neonatology, 14th edn. 2000. Dawn Books, Calcutta.
4. Sharma RK. Virginity, pregnancy and delivery. In: Concise Textbook of Forensic Medicine and Toxicology, 1st edn. 2005. Reed Elsevier India Pvt. Limited, New Delhi. 103-9.
5. Mathiharan K, Patnaik AK. Virginity, pregnancy and delivery. In: Modi's Medical Jurisprudence and Toxicology, 23rd edn. 2005. LexisNexis Butterworths, New Delhi. 875-94.
6. Vij K. Medicolegal examination of the living. In: Textbook of Forensic Medicine and Toxicology, 3rd edn. 2005. Reed Elsevier India Pvt. Limited, New Delhi. 457-500.
7. Pillay VV. Virginity, pregnancy and delivery. In: Textbook of Forensic Medicine and Toxicology, 14th edn. 2004. Paras Publishing, Hyderabad. 262-72.
8. Nandy A. Pregnancy and delivery. In: Principles of Forensic Medicine, 2nd edn. 2005. New Central Book Agency (P) Ltd., Calcutta. 390-400.

CHAPTER 19

Abortion and Medical Termination of Pregnancy

The vilest abortionist is he who attempts to mould a child's character.

- George Bernard Shaw

ABORTION

- *Abortion is premature expulsion of products of conception from womb, either spontaneous or induced at any time before the period of gestation is completed.*
- The word abortion is derived from the Latin word 'arboriri' that means, "to get detached from the proper site".[1]
- Legally there is no difference between abortion, miscarriage or premature delivery.[2] However, medical jargon carries different meaning. Medical terminology is given below. In medical terminology (Fig. 19.1):
  - » Abortion means expulsion of products of conception in the first trimester of pregnancy.
  - » Miscarriage means expulsion of product of conception in second trimester.
  - » Premature delivery refers to expulsion of fetus after 7 months of pregnancy but before term.

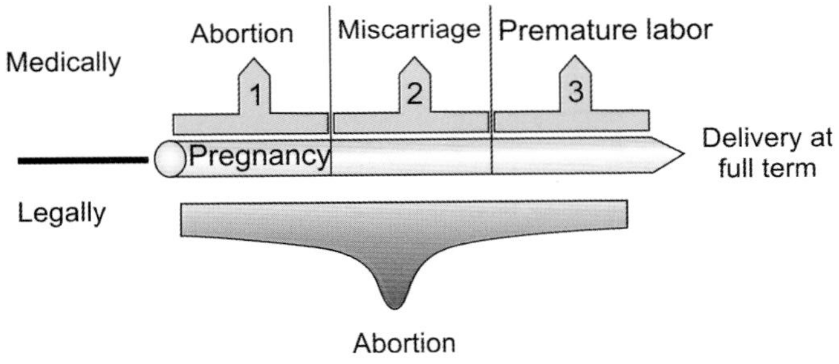

FIG. 19.1: Diagram representing difference between legal and medical concept on abortion.

Classification

Abortion is classified into following two major groups (Fig. 19.2):

1. Natural (spontaneous)
2. Artificial (Induced)

Induced abortion may be:

Justifiable abortion (therapeutic)

Criminal abortion

Natural abortion may be:

Isolated abortion

Recurrent abortion

Natural Abortion

Spontaneous or natural abortion occurs usually in first or second trimester of pregnancy and the causes[3] are as mentioned in Table 19.1.

Unsafe Abortion

- This term has been proposed by WHO
- It means abortion not provided through approved facilities and/or persons.[4]

Fabricated Abortion

- This is false sort of abortion with malicious intention to accuse someone
- A female may allege a person that due to assault by that person, she has aborted. In her support, she may produce false things such as menstrual pads or killed animal fetus pertaining that it is abortus material.

Table 19.1: Causes of spontaneous abortion

Causes of abortion
1. Chromosomal abnormalities
- Trisomy
- Triploidy
- Turner's syndrome
- Blighted ova
2. Abnormalities of placenta
- Acute hydramnios
- Multiple pregnancy
- Hydatidiform mole
- Placenta praevi
3. Infection of mother
- Acute infections like malaria
- Toxoplasmosis
- Syphilis
- Listeria monocytogens
4. Disease of mother
- Hypertension
- Chronic nephritis
5. Drugs/radiation
- Inhalation of nitrous oxide
- X-rays
6. Local abnormalities
- Retroverted uterus
- Fibromyoma
- Cervical incompetence

Induced Abortion

- It is a type of abortion which is deliberately induced
- It may be justifiable (therapeutic) or criminal.

CRIMINAL ABORTION

- Any abortion, which does not come under the rules of the Medical Termination of Pregnancy (MTP) Act 1971, is considered as criminal abortion.[5]
- Thus, in other words, it is an unlawful expulsion of product of conception at any stage of gestation by any unqualified person or a qualified doctor and is punishable under the law.[6, 7]

Motives for Criminal Abortion

1. Unmarried girls and widows may, at times, resort to criminal abortion when child is product of illicit sexual intercourse. This is done to get rid of the developing life or in some cases to save the honor and pride of self or family.
2. A poor family may procure criminal abortion to avoid the addition of a member to family. These families seek the services of an unskilled person since he may take fewer fees in comparison with a qualified one.
3. Female feticide i.e. killing of female fetus. In India, some societies are keen to have male child. When female is pregnant, these people do sex determination test (at present unlawful act) and if the sex of baby is found to be female, they persuade the pregnant lady to abort the product of conception.

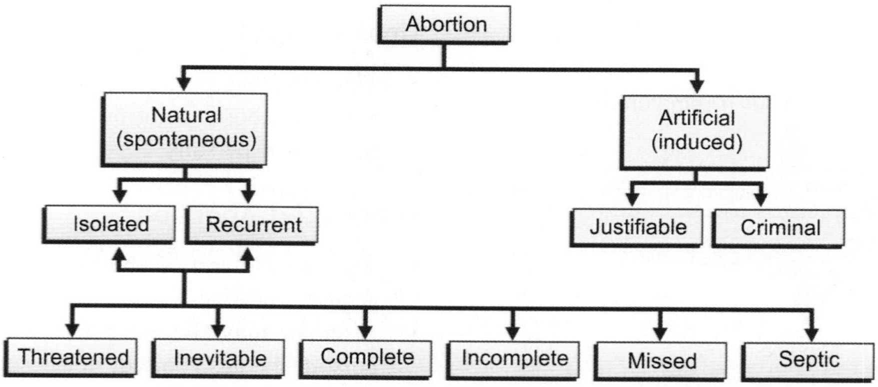

FIG. 19.2: Classification of abortion

Legal Aspects of Criminal Abortion

The IPC 312, 313, 314, 315 and 316 deals with offenses of criminal abortion or attempted criminal abortion and punishments for these offenses.

1. 312 IPC – **causing miscarriage** – whoever voluntarily causes a woman with child to miscarry, shall, if such miscarriage be not caused in good faith for the purpose of saving the life of the woman, be punished with imprisonment of either description for a term which may extend to three years, or with fine, or with both; and, if the woman be quick with child, shall be punished with imprisonment of either description for a term which may extend to seven years, and shall also be liable to fine.
   Explanation: A woman, who causes herself to miscarry, is within the meaning of this section.
2. 313 IPC – **causing miscarriage without woman's consent** – whoever commits an offense defined in the section 312 of IPC without the consent of the woman, whether the woman is quick with child or not, shall be punished with imprisonment for life, or with imprisonment of either description for a term which may extend to ten years, and shall also be liable to fine.
3. 314 IPC – **death caused by act done with intent to cause miscarriage, if act done without woman's consent** – whoever, with intent to cause miscarriage of a woman with child, does any act which causes the death of such woman, shall be punished with imprisonment of either description for a term which may extend to ten years, and shall also be liable to fine. If the act is done without woman's consent – shall be punished either with imprisonment for life or with the punishment above mentioned.
   Explanation: It is not essential to this offense that the offender should know that the act is likely to cause death.
4. 315 IPC – act done with intent to prevent child being born alive or to cause it to die after birth – whoever, before the birth of any child, does any act with the intention of thereby preventing that child from being born alive or causing it to die after its birth, and does by such act prevent that child from being born alive, or causes it to die after its birth, shall, if such act be not caused in good faith for the purpose of saving the life of the mother, be punished with imprisonment of either description for a term which may extend to ten years, or with fine, or with both.
5. 316 IPC – causing death of quick unborn child by act amounting to culpable homicide – whoever, does any act under such circumstances that if he thereby caused death he would be guilty of culpable homicide, and does by such act cause the death of quick unborn child, shall be punished with imprisonment of either description for a term which may extend to ten years, and shall also be liable to fine.

Methods to Induce Criminal Abortion are Grouped as (Fig. 19.3):

1. Use of abortifacient drugs
2. Application of mechanical violence (Table 19.2)

Abortifacient Drugs

These drugs are classified as:

1. Ecbolics: These drugs initiate uterine contraction and causes abortion. Examples are:
   - Ergot preparations
   - Synthetic estrogen
   - Pituitary extract
   - Quinine
   - Gossypium (cotton root bark)
2. Emmenagogues: These drugs promote uterine congestion and induce bleeding thus expelling product of conception. Examples are:
   - Borax
   - Sanguinarine
   - Oil of savin
3. Irritants: These are of following types
   - Genitourinary tract irritants – these agents produce inflammation of genitorurinary tract and reflexly irritate the uterus and induce uterine contraction – example Cantharides, turpentine oil.
   - Gastrointestinal tract irritants – these agents cause reflex contraction of uterine muscles – example: croton oil, colocynth etc.
   - Systemic poisons – For example: arsenic, mercury, calatropis, copper, unripe fruit of papaya, Plumbago etc.
   - Abortion pills – these pills are made up of lead diphenylephylene etc.

Table 19.2: Means used to induce criminal abortion

Methods used
A. *Abortifacient drugs*
1. Ecbolics
2. Emmenogogues
3. Irritant poisons
4. Systemic poisons
5. Abortion pills
6. Abortion stick
B. *Mechanical violence*
1. General violence
2. Local violence

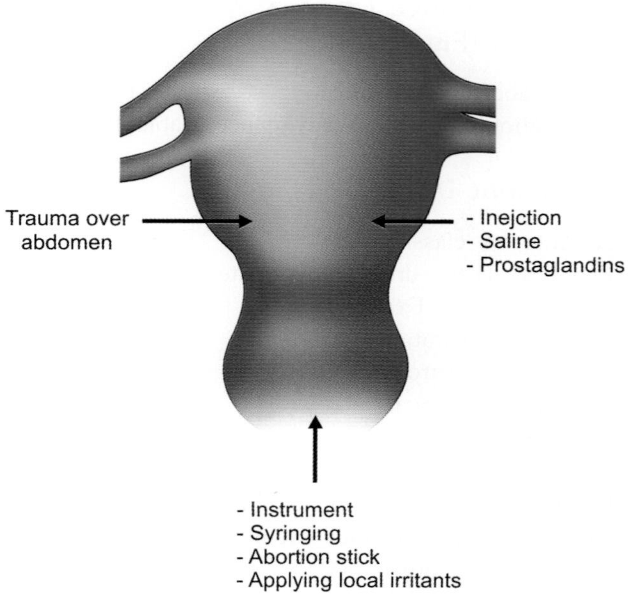

FIG. 19.3: Various means used to induce criminal abortion

Violence

1. General violence – may act directly or indirectly on uterus. Following are examples of general violence
   - Severe form of exercise like excessive cycling, riding, jumping etc.
   - Application of blows or kicks over abdomen or pressure on abdomen by kneading or firmly massaging the abdomen
   - Cupping: a flame light (diya) is placed on abdomen and a metal mug (lota) is placed over the flaming light (diya) (Fig. 19.4).
2. Local method
   A) By unskilled or semiskilled person (Fig. 19.5)
   - Rupture of membrane by abortion stick, metal rod, knitting needle, hair pin etc.
   - Application of abortion paste
   - Use of root of plant as Abortifacient agent
   - Syringing: either for aspiration of fluid or forced filling of uterine cavity with fluid and air.

   B) By skilled person
   - Low rupture of membrane
   - Vacuum aspiration
   - Dilatation and evacuation
   - Use of laminaria tent
   - Use of prostaglandins.

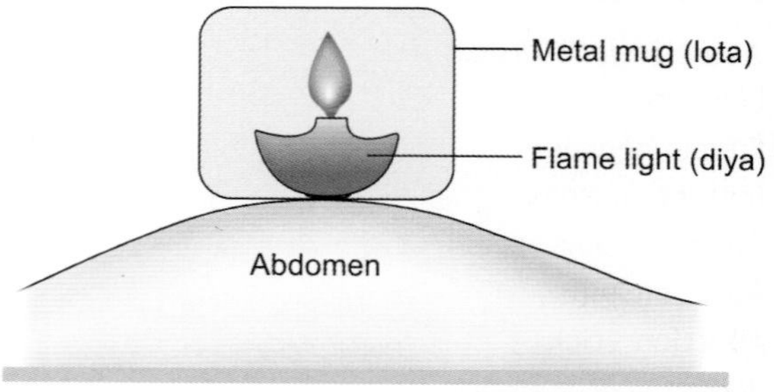

FIG. 19.4: Diagram showing the procedure of cupping

Abortion Stick

- This is a thin wooden or bamboo stick about 15 to 20 cm in length and 0.5 to 1 cm in diameter. One end of stick is wrapped with cloth or cotton wool and is soaked in or smeared with irritant abortifacient substances (Fig. 19.6).
- The substances consist of juice of marking nut, calatropis, oleander, abrus, plumbago or paste made up of arsenic oxide, arsenic sulphide, lead etc.
- The stick is then passed into the uterus per vaginally resulting in rupture of membrane and expulsion of product of conception.
- Complications of abortion sticks are:
  1. Local injury
  2. Hemorrhage and shock
  3. Perforation of uterus
  4. Perforation peritonitis
  5. Incomplete abortion

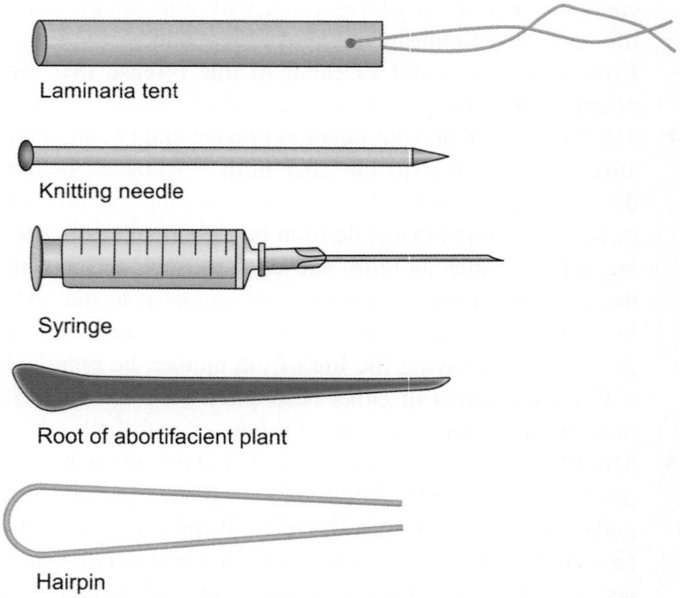

FIG. 19.5: Different material used to procure criminal abortion

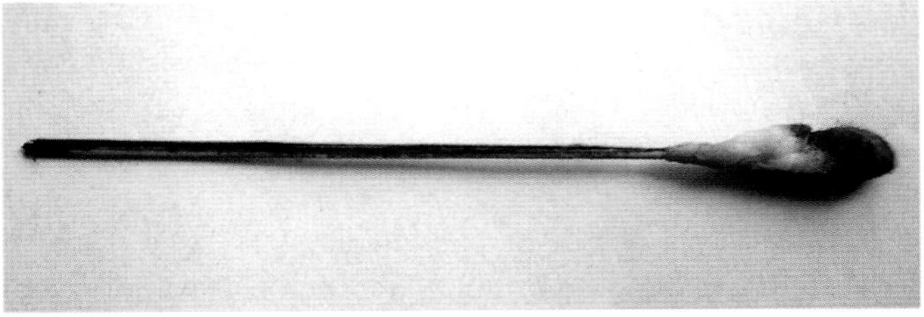

FIG. 19.6: Abortion stick

6. Embolism
7. Septicemia

Complication of Criminal Abortion

Immediate

1. Hemorrhage
2. Perforation of uterus
3. Shock due to vagal inhibition resulting from instrumentation
4. Fat embolism
5. Air embolism
6. Amniotic fluid embolism
7. Incomplete abortion
8. Local injury

Delayed

1. Septicemia
2. Tetanus
3. Endometritis
4. Renal failure
5. Peritonitis
6. Sterility
7. Recurrent abortion

Causes of Death in Criminal Abortion

1. Vaso-vagal shock
2. Hemorrhagic shock
3. Perforation of uterus
4. Septicemia
5. Embolism
6. Disseminated intravascular coagulation

Duties of Registered Medical Practitioner in Criminal Abortion

Despite the enactment of MTP Act, the number of illegal and unsafe abortion in India continues to be very high with large number of abortions being performed every year by untrained persons in totally unhygienic conditions.[8] Unsafe abortion today, constitutes the single largest cause of pregnancy-related deaths.[9] When a female comes to RMP with history of criminal abortion or attempted criminal abortion, then:

1. Doctor should record history of the incident, the method adopted to procure abortion.
2. If death is imminent, doctor must arrange for dying declaration.
3. If female dies, he should report matter to the police.

Medical Evidence of Abortion

It consists of
1. Examination of female.
2. Examination of aborted material.

Examination of Female (During life)

1. General: Female will have exhaust look, increase temperature, increase pulse.
2. Breasts: Are heavy, enlarged, areola and nipples are pigmented, clostrum/milk may ooze on squeezing the breasts (Fig. 19.7).
3. Abdomen: Is lax and wrinkled. Striae may be present along with linea nigra (Fig. 19.8). Involuting uterus may be palpable.
4. Perineum: Laceration or bruises may be noted, inflammation is evident
5. Labia: majora and minora will be inflamed and bruised (Fig. 19.9)
6. Vagina: Tags of membrane, partial aborted material, blood, foreign body, abortion stick etc. may be found. The vaginal wall is contused, abraded or lacerated. The wall is lax, dilated.
7. Cervix: The external os would be patulous, ulceration or erosions may be present. Cervical canal may be dilated with abrasions or lacerations.
8. Uterus: May be enlarged on bimanual examination or may be showing signs of involution.
9. Swab from cervical canal will reveal chemical used for procuring abortion and can be used for bacteriological examination.
10. Urine examination: hCG may be detected up to 7 days.

Examination of Female (After Death)

In addition to above, following findings may be noted at autopsy

- Clothes: Undergarments may show blood, clots, pieces of product of conception, stains of chemicals used etc.

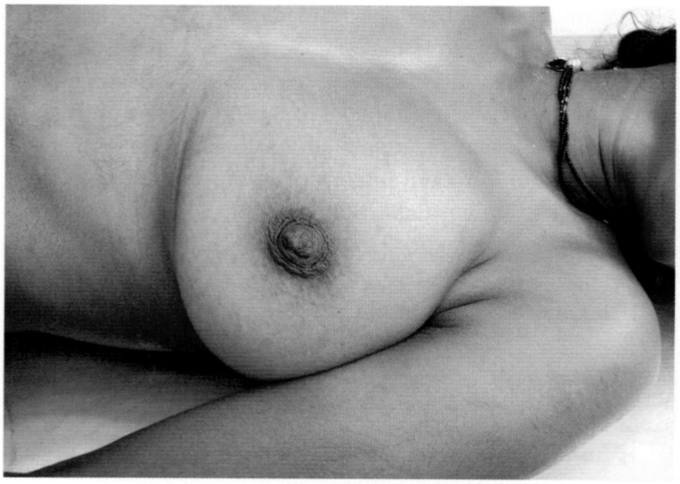

FIG. 19.7: Changes in breast

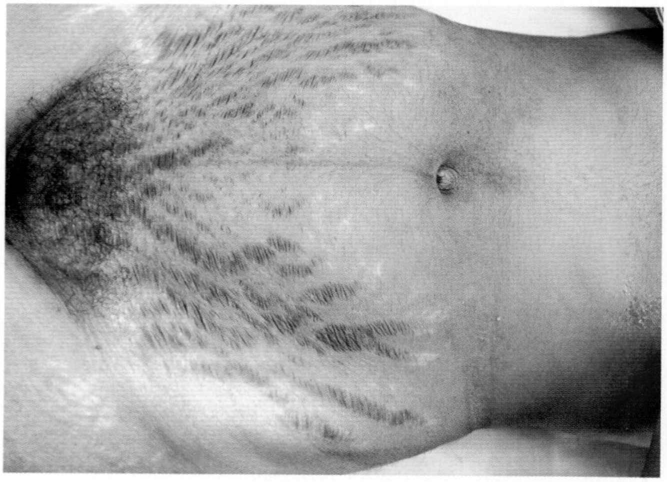

FIG. 19.8: Abdomen with striae marks

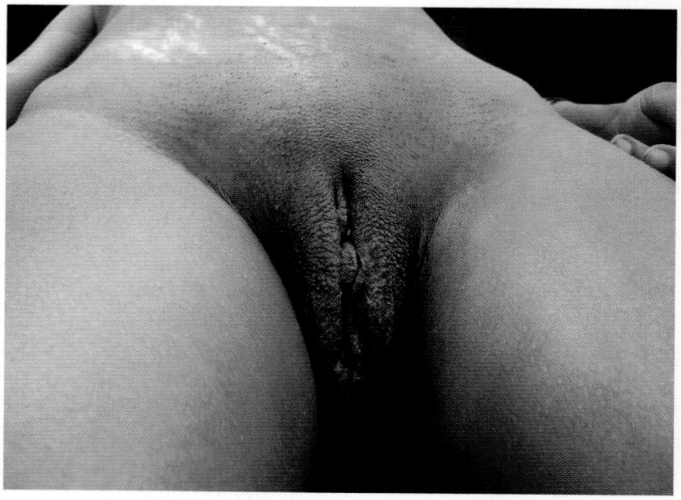

FIG. 19.9: External genitals in abortion

- Uterus: Enlarged, cavity may show presence of partially separated product of conception, foreign body, blood clots, presence of any paste or chemical, evidence of injury or perforation etc.
- Evidence of infection
- Ovaries: Presence of corpus luteum
- Differences between criminal abortion and natural abortion are given in Table 19.3.

Examination of Aborted Material

- Police may request medical examiner to examine a substance alleged to have been expelled from uterus as product of conception. Doctor should examine the substance carefully.
- The alleged product of conception should be washed. If it happens to be product of conception, it may be suggestive of criminal abortion.
- Difficulty arises in early months of pregnancy when embryo is small or not found. In such cases presence of chorionic villi on microscopic examination will confirm that it is product of conception.
- During first three months of pregnancy, the fetus is expelled with its membrane en mass but after this period, the fetus is born first and then after that placenta is detached and expelled. If only placenta is sent for medical examination then it should also be examined to ascertain injuries or tears and any degenerative changes in its surface.[5]
- The fetus should be examined to determine its:
  1. Probable intrauterine age.
  2. Presence or absence of injuries on body.
  3. Viability of child.

Table 19.3: Showing difference between natural and criminal abortion

Features	*Natural abortion*	*Criminal abortion*
Reason	Predisposing disease	History of pregnancy in unmarried girl or widow
Infection	Rare	Frequent
Injuries to genitals	Absent	Frequently present
Signs of violence	Absent	Present
Application of chemical or drugs	Absent	Present
Foreign body	Absent	Present

Medicolegal importance of placenta

1. At term placenta is about 500 gm in weight.
2. Period of gestation can be estimated.
3. Some poisons may be detected in placenta.
4. Retained placenta or pieces of placenta may be found in criminal abortion and may be the cause of death due to hemorrhage.
5. Disease can be ascertained.
6. Transfer of poisons, drugs, bacteria or antibodies across placenta (placental barrier) may result in fetal death, fetal infections or fetal malformations.

JUSTIFIABLE ABORTION (THERAPEUTIC)

- It is also called as therapeutic abortion or legal abortion
- In 1970, the World Medical Association (WMA) adopted a resolution on therapeutic abortion, known as "**Declaration of Oslo**".
- It is performed either in accordance with the legal provisions under the Medical Termination of Pregnancy (MTP) Act 1971 (i.e. legal abortion) or caused in good faith to save the life of the pregnant woman.[10]

Medical Termination of Pregnancy[11]

With enactment of Medical Termination of Pregnancy (MTP) Act 1971, abortion is liberalized in India, under the provisions of Act, but it is not legalized.

Indications

As per MTP Act 1971, pregnancy can be terminated on the following grounds (mnemonic "SETH" - S = social, E = eugenic, T = therapeutic, H = humanitarian).

1. Therapeutic

When continuation of pregnancy may cause risk to the life of the pregnant woman or may cause grave injury to her physical or mental health, it can be terminated on therapeutic ground.

2. Eugenic

If there is possibility that child born would be suffering from physical or mental abnormalities that lead the child to be handicapped, then such pregnancy can be terminated on eugenic grounds.

3. Humanitarian

When the pregnancy is caused by rape then it can be terminated on humanitarian ground.

4. Social

When pregnancy has resulted due to failure of contraceptive method adopted by married woman or her husband for the purpose of limiting the number of children, then such pregnancy can be terminated on social grounds.

Important: In an emergency, a Registered Medical Practitioner can terminate pregnancy at any place, irrespective of duration of pregnancy. Abortion done in good faith to save the life of a woman, if it appears that continuance of pregnancy would endanger maternal health is not considered as criminal abortion.[12]

Rules for Doing MTP

1. Qualification Required

- Only qualified Registered Medical Practitioner, having following required experience can terminate the pregnancy.
- A RMP who has assisted in at least 25 cases of MTP in a recognized hospital
- A Doctor with MD in Gynecology and Obstetrics or DGO qualification or has 6 months of experience in house-surgeonship in obstetrics in a recognized hospital.

2. Place - MTP can be Carried Out at

- A hospital maintained or established by government
- Non-government hospital approved by government (license to be obtained from the Chief Medical Officer/ Civil surgeon of the district).

3. Consent

- A female above 18 years of age with sound mind can give consent for MTP
- In minor females (i.e. age less than 18 years) or mentally ill (lunatic), consent of parents or guardian is necessary.

4. Duration of Pregnancy

- When duration of pregnancy is below 12 weeks of gestation, one Registered Medical Practitioner (RMP) can terminate the pregnancy.
- When duration of pregnancy is above 12 weeks but less than 20 weeks (i.e. 12–20 weeks), then two RMP are required to terminate the pregnancy.

5. Documentation and Record[13]

- According to regulation 5 of MTP Regulations, all approved centers are required to maintain an admission register in the format prescribed in form III.

- A fresh register should be started in each calendar year with new serial number generated by mentioning the year against the serial number
- The admission register is a secret document. It should be maintained for at least 5 years from the last entry.

Methods of Inducing MTP[14]

Up to 12 Weeks

1. Manual vacuum aspiration
2. Suction evacuation and/or curettage
3. Dilatation and curettage
4. Mifepristone
5. Mifepristone and misoprostol (PgE_1)
6. Methotrexate and misoprostol
7. Tamoxifen and misoprostol

Between 13 to 20 Weeks

1. Dilatation and evacuation
2. Oxytocin infusion
3. Induction by prostaglandins E_1 (misoprostol) 15 methyl $PGF_{2α}$ (carboprost), PGE_2 (dinprostone) and their analogues. (Used as intravaginally, intramuscularly or intra-amniotically)
4. Hysterotomy – less common method

Complications of MTP

Immediate

1. Hemorrhage and shock
2. Perforation of uterus, intestine
3. Laceration of cervix or vagina
4. Incomplete abortion
5. Endometritis
6. Embolism

Delayed

1. Menstrual disturbances
2. Sterility
3. Pelvic inflammatory disease
4. Recurrent abortion or premature labor
5. Rh isoimmunization
6. Psychological sequelae

Medicolegal Importance of Abortion

1. When abortion is induced without proper indication or in contravention to the provisions of MTP Act, it is considered as criminal abortion and is punishable by law.
2. When Doctor violates the provisions of MTP Act, he is liable to be punished by the law and similarly his act amount to **misconduct** in professional sense.
3. To bring a false charge of assault against any person, a female may plead that she has been assaulted and due to assault, abortion was induced.
4. A female may be falsely charged or implicated for inducing criminal abortion.

REFERENCES

1. Pillay VV. Abortion. In: Textbook of Forensic Medicine and Toxicology, 14th edn. Paras Publishing, Hyderabad. 2004;273–8.
2. Ramchandran A, Chandran MR. Human sexual function – medicolegal considerations. In A Short Textbook of Forensic medicine and Toxicology, 1st reprint edn. All India Publishers and Distributors, Regd., New Delhi. 2006;63–99.
3. Padubidri V, Daftary SN. Abortion. In: Howkins and Bourne Shaw's Textbook of Gynaecology, 10th edn. B I Churchill Livingstone, New Delhi. 1989;244–55.
4. Vij K. Abortion and delivery. In: Textbook of Forensic Medicine and Toxicology, 3rd edn. Reed Elsevier India Pvt. Limited, New Delhi. 2005;545–62.
5. Mathiharan K, Patnaik AK. Abortion, medical termination of pregnancy and female feticide. In: Modi's Medical Jurisprudence and Toxicology, 23rd edn. LexisNexis Butterworths, New Delhi. 2005;1013–46.
6. Sharma RK. Abortion and medical termination of pregnancy. In: Concise Textbook of Forensic medicine and Toxicology, 1st edn. Reed Elsevier India Pvt. Limited, New Delhi. 2005;126–31.
7. Rao NG. Sexual jurisprudence. In: Textbook of Forensic Medicine and Toxicology, 1st edn. Jaypee Brothers Medical Publishers (P) Ltd., New Delhi. 2006;281–320.
8. Kumar S. Medical abortion in purview of MTP Act, India (1971). Consortium on national consensus for medical abortion in India. Available from http:/www.aiims.edu/aims/events/gynaewebsite.
9. Kabra SG. Reproductive health care for women: a saga of excess, exploitation and violation. Indian J Med Ethics 1997; 5: available from www.ijme.in/052mi047.html.
10. Subrahmanyam BV. Abortion and medical termination of pregnancy. In: Modi's Medical Jurisprudence and Toxicology, 22nd edn. Butterworths India, New Delhi. 2001;581–603.
11. The Medical Termination of Pregnancy Act 1971 (Act No. 34 of 1971).
12. Reddy KSN. Abortion. In: The Essentials of Forensic Medicine and Toxicology, 22nd edn. K. Suguna Devi, Hyderabad. 2003;345–54.
13. Sherier N. Medicolegal aspects – medical methods for early abortion. Consortium on national consensus for medical abortion in India. Available from http:/www.aiims.edu/aims/events/gynaewebsite.
14. Konar H, Dutta DC. Hemorrhage in early pregnancy. In: Textbook of Obstetrics, 6th edn. New Central Book Agency (P) Ltd., Calcutta. 2004;174.

CHAPTER 20

Infant Deaths and Female Feticide

One cot death is a tragedy, two cot deaths is suspicious and, until the contrary is proved, three cot death is murder.

- Prof. Meadow (British Pediatrician)

Introduction

All infants are susceptible, like adults to natural disease from which they could die. They may also die as a result of congenital anomalies[1] or by application of violence or may present as case of sudden death. The causes of death in infant are summarized in Table 20.1.

Table 20.1: Showing causes of death in infants

Causes of death in infants
Natural causes
– Immaturity
– Debility
– Congenital malformation
– Hemorrhage
– Erythroblastosis fetalis
– Neonatal jaundice
Accidental causes
– Prolonged labour
– Prolapsed of cord
– Injuries sustained during labour
– Suffocation
– Precipitated labour
Criminal causes (homicidal)
– Acts of commission
– Acts of omission
Other causes
– Sudden infant death syndrome
– Battered baby syndrome

INFANTICIDE

Definitions

1. Infanticide: It means unlawful destruction of a newly born child and is regarded as murder in law. It is punishable under Sec 302 of IPC.
2. Feticide: It means killing of fetus prior to birth.
3. Neonaticide: It means killing of neonate.
4. Filicide: It is defined as killing of a child or a step-child, aged between 0 and 18 years, by his or her parents.[2] Filicide is broad term and includes neonaticide, infanticide and pedicide.

Causes

Death due to application of violence and may be caused either by:
1. Acts of commission or
2. Acts of omission

Acts of Commission

These are the willful acts done to cause the death of infant. It includes:
1. Suffocation
2. Strangulation
3. Drowning
4. Head injury
5. Fracture-dislocation of cervical spine
6. Concealed puncture marks (pithing)
7. Poisoning

Acts of Omission

Acts of omission refer to failure to take care of child or negligent towards the child during or after birth. It includes:
1. Failure to provide assistance during labor.
2. Failure to clear the air passage after birth.
3. Failure to cut and ligate the umbilical cord.
4. Failure to feed the child.
5. Failure to protect the child from heat or cold.

Medicolegal Questions

Following questions are raised while doing autopsy in infanticide case:
1. Was the child still-born or dead born?
2. Was the child born alive (i.e. live born)?
3. If born alive, how long did the child survive the birth?
4. What was the cause of death?

Status of Infant: was the Child Still-born, Dead-born or Live-born?

An infant may be live born, dead born or still born. The terms are defined as below.

Still-Born (Still Birth) Child

- Definition: "*The child which has issued forth from the mother after the 28th week of pregnancy and did not any time, after being completely expelled, breathes, or shows any other signs of life*".
- Thus, a still-born child is alive in uterus up to the initiation of birth process and died during the process (i.e. delivery) but did not show any sign of life after being completely born. In other words, after birth, the child was still (immobile) and therefore the term still born child.
- Causes of still-birth are mentioned in Table 20.2.

Table 20.2: Showing causes of still-birth

Causes of still-birth
Fetal causes
– Malposition of fetus
– Congenital anomaly
Maternal causes
– Tuberculosis
– Diabetes mellitus
– Eclampsia
– Placental abnormalities
Combined causes
– Pre-maturity
– Birth hypoxia
– Birth trauma
– Malnutrition

Dead-born Child (Dead Birth)

- Definition: *A dead-born child is one, which had died in uterus before the birth process begins and may show rigor mortis, maceration or mummification at birth.*
- Fetal death has been defined by World Health Organization (WHO) as "death before complete expulsion or extraction from its mother of a product of conception, irrespective of the duration of pregnancy".[3]

Rigor Mortis

- Rigor mortis may set in early stages of death.
- Presence of rigor mortis may cause difficulty in delivery.

Maceration

- Definition: *It is a process of aseptic autolysis occurring in fetus that remains dead in the uterus surrounded by liquor amnii.*
- Maceration in fetus is sign of death.
- Mechanism: The cells of fetus break down after death and due to enzymatic action (autolysis) body becomes soft and flaccid. Unlike putrefaction or decomposition, there is no bacterial action in maceration.
- Duration required: If fetus remains in uterus after death, then the earliest sign of maceration is seen at about 6 to 12 hours in form of areas of desquamation and appearance of brown-red discolouration of umbilical cord stump[4].
- Features (Fig. 20.1):
  - The macerated fetus is soft and flabby and flattens when kept on table.
  - Emits sweetish disagreeable smell
  - The earliest sign of maceration is skin slippage (seen at 6-12 hours).
  - Skin is sodden and shows red or purple colouration with large blebs (or blisters) containing serous or sero-sanguineous fluid. The epidermis is easily peeled off leaving moist, greasy areas underneath. Abdomen is distended.
  - Joints become abnormally mobile or flexible with bones get flexible and are easily detached from the soft parts.
  - Skull bones show loss of alignment and they override over each other due to shrinkage of brain after death, known as **Spalding sign**. Brain becomes pulpy and grayish-red in colour.

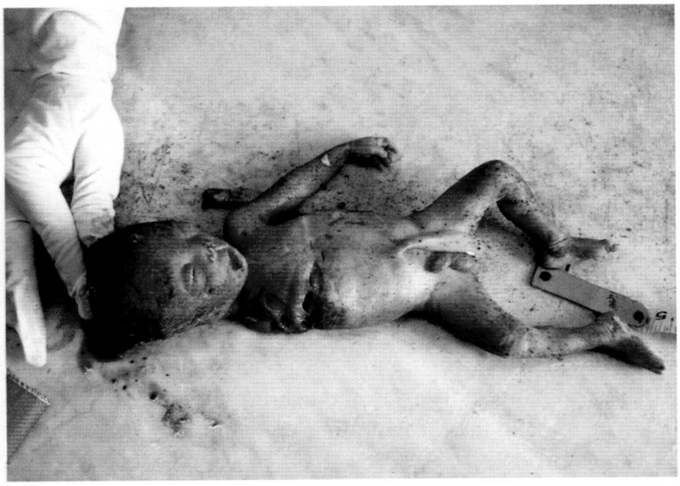

FIG. 20.1: Macerated fetus

- Body cavities contain reddish serous fluid.
- Internal organs become soft and edematous
- Umbilical cord is red, smooth, softened and thickened.

Mummification

- It is drying and shriveling of fetus occurring in uterus after death
- It results when liquor amnii is scanty and no air enters the uterus.

Putrefaction

If the membranes are ruptured early and air enters the uterus, then the dead fetus shows signs of putrefaction instead of maceration.

Live-born Child (Live-birth)

- *A child showing a sign of life, even when only part of the child is out of mother, though the child has not breathed or completely born, is considered as live-born child.*
- Causing death of such child is treated in the same manner as homicide.

Viability of Child

- Viability means the ability of fetus to lead a separate existence after birth by virtue of certain degree of development.
- A child is viable after 210 days or 7 months or 30 weeks of intrauterine life.

Evidence of Live Birth (Signs of Live Birth)

The law in India presumes that every child found dead was born dead unless the contrary is proved. Proof of live birth is required in civil or criminal cases.

In Civil Cases

Following are considered as signs of live birth.

1. Crying of baby
2. Movement of body or hand or foot
3. Muscle twitching or twitching of eyelid
    - These signs are sufficient to establish the proof of live birth in civil cases. Crying of a child is considered as strong proof of live birth but, at times, it is possible that (after rupture of membrane) fetus may cry even when it is in uterus or in vagina. Following two conditions are considered:

1. **Vagitus uterinus**: Crying of a child even when it is in uterus
2. **Vagitus vaginalis**: Crying of a child even when it is in vagina
    - Thus, it may possible that child may didn't show any sign when it comes out although cry of child is heard by people. So crying of child is not conclusive proof of live birth.

In Criminal Cases

In criminal cases, signs of live birth have to be demonstrated by autopsy examination of the child. Following are the external and internal autopsy findings in live birth.

External changes

1. Changes in chest
2. Changes in skin
3. Changes in umbilicus

Internal changes

1. Changes in lung
2. Position of diaphragm
3. Changes in heart and circulation
4. Changes in gastrointestinal tract
5. Changes in middle ear
6. Changes in kidneys
7. Changes in blood

External Findings at Autopsy

1. Changes in Chest:

A live birth child will respire and due to act of respiration, certain changes are induced and are mentioned in Table 20.3.

2. Changes in Skin

- After live birth, color of skin is pinkish red and darkens after 2 to 3 days. The permanent complexion of skin comes by seven days after birth.
- Desquamation of skin is seen by 2nd day onwards
- Physiologic jaundice manifests by 2nd day.

3. Changes in Umbilicus and Umbilical Cord[8]

The changes occurring in umbilicus and umbilical cord are summarized in Table 20.4.

Internal Changes

Signs of live birth observed in internal examination are as follows

Table 20.3: Chest difference between live birth and still-born child

Features	*Respired (live)*	*Unrespired (dead/still birth)*
Diameter	Increase in antero-posterior diameter (Fig. 20.2)	None
Circumference	Circumference of chest is 1-2 cm more than that of abdomen at the level of umbilicus	Circumference of chest is about 1-2 cm less than that of abdomen at the level of umbilicus
Intercostal space	Increases	Narrow
Shape of chest	Arched or drum shaped	Flat

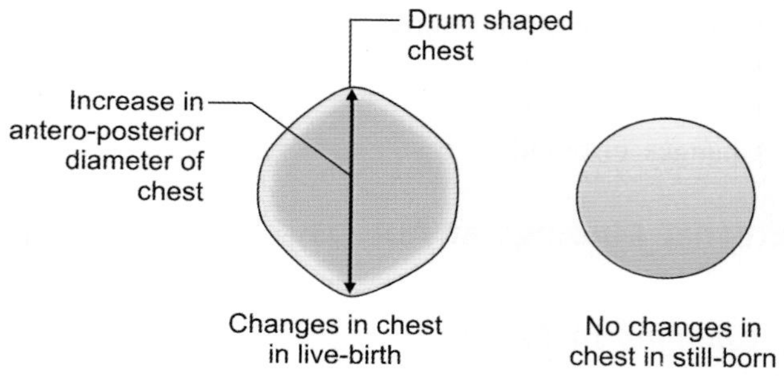

FIG. 20.2: Shape of chest in respired and unrespired fetus

I. Changes in Lungs

Due to respiration, following changes occur in lungs of live birth child. Differences between respired and unrespired lungs are summarized in Table 20.5.

A) Gross and microscopic examination

1. Volume: non-respired lungs appear small, collapsed, lie in the back part of chest on side of vertebral column whereas respired lungs appear voluminous; filling the whole pleural cavities and medial margin overlaps the mediastinum and pericardium.
2. Colour, consistency and appearance: Before respiration, the lungs are uniformly reddish-brown and hard in consistency like that of liver, non-crepitant. The pleurae over lungs are loose and wrinkled. After respiration, air cells (alveoli) are distended with respired air. The distended alveoli are raised above the surface. With initiation of respiration, the blood in lungs become oxygenated and imparts bright red or pinkish colour to lungs with mottled appearance. The respired lungs are spongy, elastic and crepitant. However, lungs may be crepitant in dead fetus if the fetus is showing:
   - Signs of decomposition (putrefaction) or
   - If fetus is given artificial respiration.
3. On cut section: In non-respired lungs, the cut surfaces are uniform, hard and exude little froth-less fluid. In respired lungs, the cut surfaces are spongy and exude frothy blood.
4. Margins: In non-respired lungs, margins of lungs are sharp. After respiration, the lung margins become rounded.

Table 20.4: Changes occurring in umbilicus and cord

Features	*Time*
Shrinkage of lumen of blood vessels	Just born
Cut margin of cord dries up with blood clot	2 hour
Contraction of umbilical arteries	10 hour
Drying of cord	24 hour (1 day)
Inflammatory line (red ring) at base of umbilical cord stump	48 hour (2 day)
Shriveled and mummified cord	2-3 day
Obliteration in umbilical vein	4-5 day
Cord shriveled, dry and falls-off	5-6 day
Complete healing of umbilicus	7-10 day

Table 20.5: Differences between respired and unrespired lungs

Features	*Unrespired lung*	*Respired lung*
Gross and microscopy		
Color and Appearance	Uniformly reddish brown	Light red or pink, mottled
Volume	Lung small, lies in the chest cavity posteriorly	Volume increased, fills the chest cavity completely
Pleura	Loose and wrinkled	Taut and stretched
Surface and consistency	Smooth surface, hard liver like constituency, non-crepitant	Uneven surface, spongy, crepitant
Margins	Sharp	Smooth and rounded
Cut section	Do not oozes frothy blood	Oozes frothy blood
Microscopy	Alveolar lining epithelium is cuboidal to columnar with less vascularization	Alveoli appear expanded with flattening of epithelium and increased vascularization
Tests		
Fodere's test	Average weight of lung (both) varies from 30-40 gm	Average weight of both lungs increases and varies from 60-70 gm
Ploucquet's test	Weight of both lungs is about 1/70th of the weight of whole fetus	Weight of both lungs is about 1/35th of the weight of whole fetus
Specific gravity	1040-1050	0.940-0.950
Hydrostatic test	Lung pieces sink	Lung pieces floats

5. Blood in lung bed: The amount of blood in lung bed in respired lungs are about twice that of blood found in stillborn child.
6. Microscopy: Respired lung alveoli appear expanded with flattening of epithelium and increased vascularization. In non-respired lungs, the alveolar lining epithelium is cuboidal to columnar with less vascularization.

B) Tests

1. Static test or Fodere's test
   - Before respiration – average weight of lung (both) varies from 30 to 40 gm
   - After respiration – the average weight of both lungs increases and varies from 60 to 70 gm. The increase in weight is due to increase in circulation.
2. Ploucquet's test
   - Before respiration – the weight of both lungs is about 1/70th of the weight of whole fetus.
   - After respiration – the weight of both lungs is about 1/35th of the weight of whole fetus.
3. Specific gravity
   - Non-respired lung – specific gravity is 1040 to 1050
   - Respired lung – specific gravity is 0.940 to 0.950
4. Hydrostatic test
   - Also called as floatation test
   - The test is used to differentiate between respired and non-respired lungs and is based on following principle:
   - *Principle*: If an infant breaths after birth, air will enter in lungs and makes them lighter and floats in water.
   - *Procedure*: Ligate the bronchi at hilum and placed individual lung in water. If the lung floats in water, remove lung and cut into many pieces and then squeeze or press the pieces between sponges and again place the individual pieces into water. A piece of liver may be used that will serve as control.
   - *Inference*: Depending on floatation or sinking of lung/ pieces following inference can be drawn
     - If lung pieces floats – respired lung
     - If lung pieces sinks – unrespired lung
     - If liver piece floats – inconclusive
   - Reason: Floating of lung and pieces can be explained as
     - In first part – lung floats because – after respiration is established, air will expand the collapsed alveoli. The specific gravity of lung before respiration varies from 1040 to 1050. However, after respiration, the specific gravity is about 0.940-0.950, which is less than that of water. Thus the floatation of lung in water indicates the act of respiration and lung is respired one.

- In second part – the pieces of lungs float because – after respiration, residual air is present in respired lung. The residual air cannot be squeezed out by pressing. Thus due to presence of air in lung pieces, the pieces will float. It indicates that child has respired after birth.

Drawbacks or fallacies of hydrostatic test

1. Respired lung may sink in following conditions:
   - Pulmonary edema
   - Pneumonia
   - Atelectasis – non-expansion of lung
   - Obstruction by alveolar duct membrane
   - Due to feeble respiration.
2. Non-respired lung may float in following conditions:
   - Putrefaction – presence of gases of decomposition may cause floatation of unrespired lung
   - Artificial respiration.

Hydrostatic Test is Not Necessary or Indicated in:

1. Fetus is dead born with signs of maceration/mummification.
2. Born before 180 days of gestation (non-viable).
3. The stomach contains milk.
4. Umbilical cord separated and scar formed at umbilicus.
5. When fetus has gross congenital anomalies incompatible with life, for example, anencephaly, monster etc.

II. Position of Diaphragm

- In fetal autopsy, abdomen is opened first to note the position of diaphragm. The features of diaphragm in respired infant are mentioned in Table 20.6.
- The position of diaphragm may be affected by presence of gases of decomposition developing within the chest and abdominal cavity.

III. Changes in Heart and Circulation

The changes occurring in heart and circulation of live birth child are mentioned in Table 20.7.

IV. Changes in Gastrointestinal Tract

1. **Radiological evidence:** Presence of air, demonstrated on X-ray, in gastrointestinal tract is a strong evidence of respiration. It is suggested that during the act of respiration, some air is swallowed in stomach and due to peristaltic movement; the air gradually descends in small and large intestine that can be demonstrated on X-rays. The sequence of appearance of air is mentioned in Table 20.8. The presence of air in GIT may be confused with

Table 20.6: Showing shape and position of diaphragm

Features	*Unrespired*	*Respired*
Position of diaphragm	Lies at the level of 4-5th rib	Descends and lies at the level of 6-7th rib
Shape of diaphragm	Concave arch	Flattened and depressed

Table 20.7: Changes in heart and circulation

Changes	*Duration*
Ductus arteriosus obliteration	10th day
Foramen ovale closure	Second month
Closure of ductus venosus	4-5 day

Table 20.8: Showing duration of appearance of air in GIT

Features	*Duration*
Air in stomach	Minutes after birth
Air in small intestine	1-2 hours after birth
Air in large intestine	5-6 hours after birth

   - Putrefaction gases in gastrointestinal tract
   - Artificial respiration.
2. **Breslau's second life test** or stomach-bowel test
   - The test is based on following principle
     Principle: Air is swallowed in stomach during respiration. Stomach and intestine will float in water if air is present.
     Procedure: Stomach and intestine are removed after tying ligature at each end. Then they are placed in water.
     Result and interpretation: The results and inferences are as follows:
     - If stomach and intestine floats – it indicates presence of air in GIT and suggest child has respired after birth.
     - If stomach and intestine sinks in water – it indicates absence of air and suggest non-establishment of respiration in a child after birth.
   - The test has less utility and act as corroborative evidence rather than conclusive evidence
   - Drawbacks: The test may be positive (i.e. float in water):
     - If air or gases is present in GIT due to decomposition

- If air or gases is present in GIT due to artificial respiration

Advantages: The test is useful when air is prevented from entering into lungs by:

- Foreign body or
- Due to occlusion of bronchi or
- Due to presence of tracheo-bronchial fistula

3. **Demonstration of air under water:** if stomach is dissected under water, air bubbles will be released from stomach if the child has respired.
4. **Presence of milk or liquid food in stomach** is a definitive evidence of live birth of child and establishes that child had lived for some time.

V. Changes in Middle Ear (Wredin's Test)

Middle ear contains gelatinous material before birth. If child respires after birth, with act of respiration, the sphincter at pharyngeal end of Eustachian tube relaxes and air enters in middle air replacing the gelatinous substance within few hours.

VI. Changes in Kidneys

Deposition of uric acid, in form of brownish yellow crystalline streaks, in pelvis of the kidneys has been regarded as a proof of live birth. But this is not reliable evidence of live birth.

VII. Miscellaneous Evidences of Live Birth

1. Blood: Following changes are noted
   - Nucleated RBCs disappear from blood within 24 hours after birth
   - Fetal hemoglobin, which is 80 percent at birth, decreases to 7 to 8 percent at 3rd month.
2. Caput succedaneum:
   - Caput succedaneum is an edematous swelling occurring in the scalp at the presenting part of head in vertex presentation of fetus. This swelling occurs due to compression of head during delivery and causes extravasation of fluid in the subcutaneous tissue. The swelling is diffuse, boggy and is not limited by the suture line. It disappears spontaneously within 24 hours after birth.
   - Presence of caput succedaneum indicates fetus being alive during delivery.
   - This swelling has to be differentiated from cephalhematoma. Differences are given in Table 20.9.

Abandonment of a Child

Section 317 of IPC deals with abandonment of a child, and as per this section exposure and abandonment of child under 12 years by parent or person having care of it is punishable offense. *Whoever being the father or mother of a child under the age of 12 years or having care of such child, shall expose or leave such child in any place with the intention of wholly abandoning such child, shall be punished with imprisonment of either description for a term, which may extend to seven years or with fine or with both.*

Concealment of Birth

- Intentional concealment of birth is a punishable crime in India
- Section 318 of IPC deals with it
- The section states that "*whoever, by secretly burying or otherwise disposing of the dead body of a child, whether such child die before or after or during its birth, intentionally conceals or endeavours to conceal the birth of such child, shall be punished with imprisonment of either description for a term, which may extend to two years or with fine or with both*".

SUDDEN INFANT DEATH SYNDROME (SIDS)

Also Called as Cot Death, Crib Death or SIDS

In international conference held in 1969, Beckwith proposed following definition "*the sudden death of any infant or young child which is unexpected by history and in whom a thorough necropsy fails to demonstrate an adequate cause of death*". A more comprehensive definition was proposed in 1989 by the National Institute of Child Health and Human Development stressing the need of examination of scene of death. It defines infant deaths to be classified as SIDS if:[5]

1. The death of infant occurs up to the age of 1 year of age
2. A thorough postmortem examination fails to demonstrate an adequate cause of death.
3. A death scene investigation is conducted and yields no evidence of unnatural cause of death and
4. A review of the infant and the mother's medical records reveal no history of medical condition that might have caused death.

Factors Influencing the Risk of SIDS

1. Age: Death is common between 2 weeks to 2 years with peak incidence occurs at around three month.
2. Sex: The incidence is more with male baby and most surveys show the ratio of 1:1.3.

Table 20.9: Difference between caput succedaneum and cephalhematoma

Caput succedaneum	*Cephalhematoma*
It is an edematous swelling occurring in the scalp due to stagnation of fluid in the layers of scalp at the presenting part of head	It is collection of blood between the pericranium and bones of skull. It is due to rupture of small emissary veins from the skull and may be associated with fracture of skull bone
The swelling is diffuse and boggy	The swelling is usually unilateral and over a parietal bone. It is circumscribed, soft, fluctuant and incompressible swelling
It is not limited by the suture line	The swelling is limited by the suture line of the skull as the pericranium is fixed to the margin of the bone.
It develops during the process of birth	It is never present at birth but gradually develops after 12-24 hours.

3. Twins: The incidence is more in a member of a twin pair as opposed to singletons.

Etiology and Theories of Causation of SIDS

Many theories are proposed for the causation of SIDS but all remain speculative. Following are the proposed theories:

1. Allergy to cow's milk
2. Allergy to house-mite
3. Spinal hemorrhages
4. Calcium deficiency
5. Selenium deficiency
6. Biotin deficiency
7. Magnesium deficiency[6]
8. Vitamin C deficiency
9. Vitamin D deficiency
10. Vitamin E deficiency
11. Overlying
12. Metabolic enzymes defect
13. Prone sleeping position[7]
14. Hypoxic conduction defect in heart[8] etc.

Autopsy Findings

- External findings are almost none with occasionally inconstant froth at mouth and nostrils. Stomach contents may be present in mouth, nostrils or on the face. The hands of child are found to be clenched around fibers from the bedclothes.
- Internal examination may show petechial hemorrhages in visceral pleura and thymus gland. There may be some petechial hemorrhages or larger ecchymoses on the epicardial surface of heart
- There may be evidence of laryngitis, tracheitis, tracheobronchitis or congenital heart disease in some cases.

Medicolegal Importance

1. The SIDS may be mistaken for infanticide.
2. May be perplexed with battered baby syndrome.

BATTERED BABY SYNDROME

- Also called as Caffey's syndrome, child abuse syndrome, maltreatment syndrome, non-accidental injury of childhood
- Definition: *A battered child is one that suffers repetitive physical injuries inflicted by parent or guardian, which are non-accidental in nature.*
- **Caffey** (1946) first reported the unusual combination of recurrent subdural hematoma with fracture of long bones but thought that the phenomenon could be due to metabolic abnormality. **Silverman** (1953) was the first to point out that both, subdural hematoma and bone fracture were the result of severe recurrent trauma. **Kempe** et al (1962) coined the term "**battered child syndrome**" now frequently called the "battered baby syndrome".[9]

Features of Battered Baby Syndrome[10]

- Age is usually less than 2 years
- Seen slightly more in male sexes
- There is general condition of neglect in child
- Disproportionate amount of soft tissue injury and history is inconsistent with pattern of injury
- Occurrence of injuries at different times
- History given by parents are incompatible with clinical findings
- There may be history of multiple admission to hospital
- Such children usually belong to broken families, low socioeconomic strata or the child may be result of unwanted pregnancy or as a result of illegitimate sexual relationship.

- Battering of child is result of sudden loss of temper by parents or may be due to psychiatric problems associated with parents.

Examination

- The child may be scared and under fear.
- Multiple surface injuries may be present over body with different age of injuries suggesting physical abuse of child. History provided by parents regarding the accidental nature of injuries sustained to child do not corroborate with the physical findings or injuries.
- Multiple contusions may be seen at cheeks, mouth, neck, and wrist, forearms, at chest, abdomen or thigh. Buttocks and back may shows multiple superficial burn injuries or whip injuries.
- Skeletal injuries in form of periosteal hematoma are common. Limb fracture may be present in the region of metaphysis and epiphysial part of growing bones or may have multiple rib fractures. The X-ray detects old fractures, healing fractures or fresh fractures of different age.
- There may be injury to eyelid, posterior subcapsular cataract, choroidoretinal atrophy, pre-retinal and retinal hemorrhages, optic atrophy, retinal detachment, and papilledema.[9-12]

Diagnosis

- Nature of injuries inconsistent with history provided by parents
- Recurrent injuries and injuries of different age with different stage of healing
- Purposeful delay in seeking medical aid by parents.

Medicolegal Implications

1. In India, the incidence of battered baby syndrome is less.
2. If death of child occurs, a charge of homicide may be labeled against offending parent.

CINDERELLA SYNDROME

- This syndrome was first described by Peter Lewin[13] in 1976.
- In some family, a single child, particularly female child, is chosen for battering. The child is usually the youngest or eldest child in the family. The child is repeatedly abused while other children (i.e. brother or sisters) of same family are spared.
- The child may develop inattention disorder, temper tantrums, failing grades and may leave the home.[13]
- In other variety of syndrome, few adopted female child accuse their step-parents of maltreatment.[14]

SHAKEN BABY SYNDROME

- Shaken baby syndrome was first described by Guthkelch[15] in 1971.
- Shaken baby syndrome is violent act of abuse that can cause myriad neurological, cognitive and other functional deficits. In the most serious cases, deaths can result.[16]
- It is a form of child abuse characterized by retinal, subdural and/or subarachnoid hemorrhage caused by severe shaking.

Mechanism

In this syndrome, the infant is generally held by thorax and shaken, causing repetitive acceleration-deceleration trauma, which leads to typical paravertebral rib fracture, intracranial hemorrhage and eye injuries. Intracranial hemorrhages are produced without obvious external injuries and are due to whiplash action. In children, head is relatively heavy and skull bones are immature and partially membranous. Brain is soft and immature and has relatively a larger subarachnoid space. The neck muscles are weak. When baby is held, the heavy head moves due to weak neck muscles. Thus, shaking of baby produces indirect acceleration-deceleration traction stress due to movement of head in to and fro manner.[17]

Features

- Involves young children, usually less than 2 years
- The shaking injury may be induced by parent or child caretaker who may get irritated with child's cry or due to psychiatric disorder
- Retinal hemorrhages may be noted and may be unilateral or bilateral.[18]
- There may be bilateral vitreous hemorrhage.[19]
- CT scan or MRI may be of great value in evaluation of brain injuries.

Autopsy findings

- Intracranial hemorrhage may be in form of subdural hematoma, commonly located in the interhemispheric fissure, or cerebral edema with subarachnoid hemorrhage.
- There may be brain stem damage.[17]
- Optic nerve sheath and optic nerve intradural hemorrhages are also noted.[20]

MUNCHAUSEN'S SYNDROME BY PROXY

- Roy Meadow first described the Munchausen's syndrome by Proxy in 1977 in England[21, 22] with reference to the persistent help-seeking behavior exhibited by parents particularly mother.
- It is also called as factitious illness by Proxy
- It is a form of child abuse where parent brought the child to Doctor for false or induced signs and symptoms of illness with a fictitious (fabricated) history.
- Usually mothers are involved for inducing the illness in child
- The child is admitted in many hospitals for non-existing disease or illness and parent causes their children needless hospital investigations and operations.[21]
- The syndrome involves three forms of abnormal illness behavior as:[23]
  1. False accounts of symptoms
  2. Fabricated symptoms
  3. Induction of symptoms
- Some examples of induced illness are as follows
  - A mother may give insulin to child and then take the child to doctor for hypoglycemic symptoms
  - A mother may give laxative to child to induce or produce diarrhea in child and then take to doctor for treatment of diarrhea.

FEMALE FETICIDE

Female feticide is *killing of female fetus*. In India, there is constant decline in female births and problem is compounded by female feticide. There is continuous decline in the sex ratio from 972 female per 1000 men in 1901 to 927 female per 1000 male according to 2001 census and these figures testifies the fact. Unfortunately, in many cases of feticide, qualified doctors are involved.[24, 25] The practice of sex-determination is widely prevalent in India and with increased availability of ultrasound machines; a corresponding decline in female birth rate was observed.[26] To curb the growing menace of female feticide, the Pre-natal Diagnostic Techniques (Regulation & Prevention of misuse) Act 1994 (PNDT Act 1994) was enacted. Subsequently it was amended and now it is called as The Pre-conception & Pre-natal Diagnostic Techniques (Prohibition of sex selection) Act 2003 (PCPNDT Act 2003).

Reasons for Female Feticide

- There are many reasons for female feticide and some of them are given below:
- For want of male child, female fetus are killed in conception period
- Traditional gender bias in India and male child are preferred over female child
- Due to rampant practice of dowry, birth of daughter in family is considered as an economic liability
- Due to typical mentality, in India son is considered as honor and pride of family and the son is entitled to use father name.

PCPNDT ACT 2003[27]

Preconception and prenatal Diagnostic Techniques Act 2003 (PCPNDT) prohibits sex selection before or after conception and the use of pre-natal diagnostic techniques to determine sex of fetus.

Sex can be Determined By:

1. Amniocentesis
2. Chorionic villous biopsy
3. Ultrasonography scan and imaging techniques

Features of PCPNDT Act

- Act prohibits sex selection before or after conception
- Regulates the use of prenatal diagnostic techniques
- Gynecologist or RMP have to conduct pre-natal diagnostic techniques at recognized place
- Nursing home or RMP or hospital where ultrasonography is used have to display the board stating "hospital does not do sex determination test".
- Prenatal diagnostic techniques can be conducted for purpose of determination of chromosomal or genetic or congenital abnormalities.
- Written consent of pregnant woman is must to undergo PC and PND technique
- Doctor contravening the provisions of Act shall be punished for 3 years imprisonment and fine of Rs. 10,000.
- Any person seeking help for sex selection shall also be held guilty and a provision of punishment for 3 years and fine of Rs. 50,000 is made under the Act.
- Doing sex determination test amounts to misconduct by Medical Council of India.[28]

Pre-Requisite for Doing PCPNDT

PCPNDT should not be carried out unless any one or more conditions, mentioned below, are fulfilled:
1. History of two or more spontaneous abortion.
2. Age of two pregnant female is above 35 years.

3. History of exposure to teratogenic drug, radiation or infections.
4. History of mental or physical deformities or genetic disease in family.

Indications

PCPNDT is carried out only to detect:
1. Chromosomal abnormalities
2. Genetic or metabolic abnormalities
3. Hemoglobinopathies
4. Sex-linked genetic diseases
5. Congenital anomalies

Rights of an Unborn Child

Law recognizes the fetus as special aggregates of cell with potential for independent life and thus protects the right of an unborn child. However, the concept of personhood has not been extended to include fetus. The process of birth is essential before the Constitutional guarantee to life becomes operational. Assuming that a fetus is not a person, yet it is a potential person and therefore entitled for some moral right to:
1. Be preserved from period of conception to birth.
2. Not to be harmed by drugs.
3. Not to be aborted.

REFERENCES

1. Cameron JM. Infant deaths. In: Mant AK (Ed). Taylor's Principles and Practice of Medical Jurisprudence, 13th edn. B I Churchill Livingstone, New Delhi. 2000; 334–72.
2. Karakus M, Ince H, Ince N, Arican N, Sozen S. Filicide cases in Turkey, 1995-2000. Croat Med J 2003; 44: 592–5.
3. Sims MA, Collins KA. Fetal death. A 10-year retrospective study. Am J Forensic Med Pathol 2001; 22: 261–5.
4. Genest DR, Singer DB. Estimating the time of death in stillborn fetuses: III. External examination; a study of 86 stillborns. Obstet Gynecol 1992; 80: 593–600.
5. Sharma BR. Sudden Infant death syndrome – a subject of medicolegal research. Am J Forensic Med Pathol 2007; 28: 69–72.
6. Peterson DR, Beckwith JB. Magnesium deprivation in sudden unexpected infant death. Lancet 1973; 2: 330.
7. Taylor BJ. A review of epidemiological studies of sudden infant death syndrome in Southern New Zealand. J Pead Child Health 1991; 27: 344–8.
8. Ferris JA. Hypoxic changes in conducting tissue of the heart in sudden death in infancy syndrome. BMJ 1973; 2: 25–5.
9. Mushin AS. Ocular damage in the battered-baby syndrome. BMJ 1971; 3: 402–4.
10. Harcourt B, Hopkins D. Ophthalmic manifestations of the battered-baby syndrome. BMJ 1971; 3: 398–401.
11. Mushin A, Morgan G. Ocular injury in the battered baby syndrome. Report of two cases. Br J Ophthalmol 1971; 55: 343–7.
12. Cameron SM. What's in a name? Cinderella revisited. BMJ 2005; 331: 1543–4.
13. Lewin PK. Letter: Cinderella syndrome. Can Med Assoc J 1976; 115: 109.
14. Goodwin J, Cauthorne CG, Rada RT. Cinderella syndrome: children who simulate neglect. Am J Psychiatry 1980; 137: 1223–5.
15. Guthkelch AN. Infantile subdural hematoma in relationship to whiplash injuries. BMJ 1971; 2: 430–1.
16. Miehl NJ. Shaken baby syndrome. J Forensic Nuris 2005; 1: 111–7.
17. Ray M, Ghosh D, Malhi P, Khandelwal N, Singhi PD. Shaken baby syndrome masquerading as apparent life threatening event. Indian J Pediatr 2005; 72: 85–6.
18. Pitetti RD, Maffei F, Chang K, Hickey E, Berger R, Pierce MC. Prevalence of retinal hemorrhages and child abuse in children who presents with an apparent life-threatening event. Pediatrics 2002; 110: 557–62.
19. Spirn MJ, Lynn MJ, Hubbard GB. Vitreous hemorrhage in children. Ophthalmology 2006; 113: 848–52.
20. Wygnanski-Jaffe T, Levin AV, Shafiq A, Smith C, Enzenduer RW, Elder JE, Morin JD, Stephens D, Aterafu E. Postmortem orbital findings in shaken baby syndrome. Am J Ophthalmol 2006; 142: 233–40.
21. Meadow R. Munchausen's syndrome by proxy. The hinterland of child abuse. Lancet 1977; 2: 343–5.
22. Schreier H. Munchausen by proxy defined. Pediatrics 2002; 110: 985–8.
23. Adshead G, Bluglass. Attachment representation in mothers with illness behaviour by proxy. Br J Psychiatry 2005; 187: 238–33.
24. Chaturvedi S, Chhabra P, Bhardwaj S, Smanla S, Kannan AT. Fetal sex-determination in Delhi – a population based investigation. Trop Doct 2007; 37: 98–100.
25. Sharma BR. Female feticide in India: issues and concerns. J Indian Acad Forensic Med 2008; 30:157-60.
26. Bardia A, Paul E, Kapoor SK, Anand K. Declining sex ratio: role of society, technology and government regulation in Faridabad district, Haryana. Natl Med J India 2004; 17: 181–3.
27. Pre-Conception and pre-Natal Diagnostic Techniques Act 2003 (Prohibition of sex selection).
28. Indian Medical Council (Professional conduct, etiquette and ethics) Regulations, 2002. Gazette of India dated 06.04.2002, part III, section 4.

CHAPTER 21

Legitimacy, Paternity and Medicolegal Aspects of Marriage Annulment

Keep your eyes wide open before marriage and half-shut afterwards.

- Benjamin Franklin

This chapter deals with legitimacy, paternity and medicolegal aspects of marriage annulment.

LEGITIMACY

As per section 112 of IEA, a child born during the continuance of a valid marriage between his mother and any man or within 280 days after its dissolution, the mother remaining unmarried is presumed to be legitimate.

The child becomes illegitimate or bastard, if:
1. The child is born out of wedlock OR
2. Birth of child is not within a competent period after the cessation of the relationship of a man and wife OR
3. Born within wedlock when procreation by the husband is not possible because of congenital or acquired malformation or disease.

Medicolegal considerations:

Question of legitimacy of child arises in following conditions:
1. Inheritance: A legitimate child is entitled to inherit the property of his father.
2. Affiliation cases: If a woman had made charges against a man that he is father of that child, in such cases, the court can sanction a monthly allowance for maintenance of child.
3. Suppositious child: A suppositious child means fictitious child. A woman may produce a child (which is not her child) and pretend that she was pregnant and delivered this child by the particular man. Such cases occur for succession of estate.[1]
4. Paternity cases.

PATERNITY

- Paternity means fatherhood.
- Paternity can be determined by:
  1. Resemblance of features with parents
  2. Hereditary disease or deformities
  3. Blood group tests
  4. DNA profiling (DNA fingerprinting)
- A child may resemble his father in features, complexion, color of iris, gestures and other personal peculiarities. Even though, such evidences are present, they have only corroborative value.
- At times, the child may not resemble the parents but resembles with grandparents (**Atavism**)
- Thus, ***atavism is a state where a child does not resemble his or her parents but resembles with grandparents*** (Atavus = grandfather).

MEDICOLEGAL ASPECTS OF MARRIAGE ANNULMENT

Annulment of marriage means nullification or invalidation or cancellation of marriage. A marriage can be declared null and void (invalid) if a petition to a court is made by either husband or wife on following grounds:[2]
1. Bigamy: If either party has a spouse living at the time of marriage
2. Impotence
3. Underage: If either party is underage i.e. if male is below 21 years or female is below 18 years.

4. Mental unsoundness: If either party was mentally unsound at the time of marriage.
5. Consent to marriage was obtained by coercion or fraud.
6. There was pregnancy by some person other than the petitioner (i.e. husband) at the time of marriage and the petitioner was ignorant of the fact at the time of marriage.
7. Consanguinity: If the parities are within prohibited degree of relationship to each other.

The wife can apply for divorce of marriage on following grounds:

1. Adultery
2. Cruelty
3. Desertion
4. Conversion to another religion
5. Mental unsoundness developing after marriage
6. Veneral disease in form of communicable form
7. Renunciation (turning "Sanyasi" or "Sadhu")
8. Husband found guilty of:
    a) Rape
    b) Sodomy or
    c) Bestiality
9. Mutual consent
10. Either spouse not being heard of for 7 years or more (Sec 107 & 108 of Indian Evidence Act)
11. Undergone a sentence of imprisonment for seven years.

Definitions of Some Terms

Cruelty: It is defined as danger to life, limb or bodily pain or mental health or giving rise to a reasonable apprehension of such danger.

Desertion: Willful neglect continuously for two years implies deliberate voluntary withdrawal from cohabitation and abandonment of one spouse by the other without other's consent.

REFERENCES

1. Vij K. Legitimacy and medicolegal aspects of marriage annulment. In: Textbook of Forensic Medicine and Toxicology, 3rd edn. 2005. Reed Elsevier India Pvt. Limited, New Delhi. 573–5.
2. Kumar V, Vrinda. Nullity and dissolution of marriage and its medicolegal aspects. Int J Med Tixicol Legal Med 2001; 4:27-37.

CHAPTER 22

Assisted Reproduction

All happy families resemble one another, each unhappy family is unhappy in its own.

- Leo Tolstoy

Assisted Reproductive Technique

Assisted reproductive technique (ART) is being increasingly used in infertile couples to beget children. However, at times, these procedures raised ethical, social, medical and legal issues. This chapter deals with the medicolegal issues related with assisted reproduction.

Definition of ART

It encompasses all techniques that attempt to obtain a pregnancy by manipulating the sperm or/and oocyte outside the body and transferring the gametes or embryo into the uterus.[1]

ART Procedures

They are as follows:

1) Artificial insemination
2) Intrauterine insemination with either husband's or donor semen (IUI-H or IUI-D)
3) *In vitro* fertilization and embryo transfer (IVF-ET).
4) IVF- associated techniques:
   a) Gamete intrafallopian tube transfer (GIFT)
   b) Tubal embryo transfer (TET)
5) Intracytoplasmic sperm injection (ICSI)
6) Oocyte donation (OD) or embryo donation (ED).

ARTIFICIAL INSEMINATION

Definition

Artificial insemination is a procedure of transferring semen into the reproductive system of a woman other than coitus.[1]

Types: It is of following types

1. Artificial insemination husband (AIH): Here semen of husband is used.
2. Artificial insemination donor (AID): Here semen of donor is used.

Indications

AIH

1. When husband is impotent but fertile.
2. When husband is unable to deposit semen in vagina due to defect or malformation, for example, hypospedias, epispedias etc.

AID

1. Husband has non-obstructive azoospermia i.e. sterile.
2. Husband has a hereditary genetic defect.
3. The couple has Rh incompatibility.
4. When woman is iso-immunized and has lost previous pregnancies and intrauterine transfer is not possible.
5. Husband has severe oligospermia and couple does not wish to undergo any of the sophisticated ART such as ICSI.

Guiding Principles

AIH do not raise significant ethical or medicolegal problems but due care should be taken while doing AID.

1) Consent: Written informed consent of both parties (i.e. the husband and wife of recipient and husband and wife of donor) should be obtained.
2) Confidentiality should be maintained. Identity of donor or the recipient should not be revealed to any one.
3) Regarding donor:
   a) Be less than 40 years
   b) Should have no relation with recipient couple
   c) Should have children of his own

d) Should be potent and fertile
e) Should be in sound mind and health and free from any hereditary or sexually transmitted disease (STD).

Medicolegal Aspects

AIH does not raise much questions but certainly AID raises many issues such as:

1) Legitimacy of child
   - The question raised is whether child born with Artificial insemination (AID) would be legitimate? As the husband is not the father of child, law considers such child as illegitimate.
   - If the person who is not father of that child and mentions his name in the column of legal documents, for example school certificate, birth certificate etc. then whether it would be not an offense for furnishing false information?
   - If the person who is not father of that child then how property should be inherited by child?
   - The general opinion is that the parents should adopt the child legally so that:
     - Child becomes legitimate
     - Child can inherit property
     - False declaration or furnishing false information is prevented.
2) Adultery:
   The question raised is that does artificial insemination (donor) amount to adultery? In India, question of adultery does not arise, as under section 497 of IPC sexual intercourse is necessary to constitute the offense.
3) Nullity of marriage and divorce:
   - Artificial insemination could not be a reason for nullity of marriage or divorce because sterility is not ground for it. If artificial insemination is due to impotence of husband then it can be a ground on account of non-consummation of marriage (by sexual intercourse).
   - Does artificial insemination is valid ground for adultery? The answer would be "no" as the procedure of artificial insemination does not constitute sexual intercourse.
4) Incest:
   Risk of incest between children of donor and children of recipient is postulated.

THE DELHI ARTIFICIAL INSEMINATION (HUMAN) ACT 1995[2]

The Act is applicable to the National Capital Territory of Delhi. It regulates the donation, sale and supply of human semen and ovum for purpose of artificial insemination. It requires the medical practitioners (RMP) to observe following things:

1) Requires written consent of husband and wife seeking artificial insemination.
2) Test recipient for HIV 1 and 2 and other sexually transmitted diseases before performing artificial insemination.
3) Not to segregate XY/XX chromosome for artificial insemination.

SEMEN BANKING

Human sperm are preserved in semen banks. As per the guidelines[1], following things are to be observed:

Requirement for sperm donor:

- Donor must be free from HIV, hepatitis B and C infection, hypertension, diabetes mellitus, sexually transmitted diseases and identifiable and common genetic disorders.
- Age should not be less than 21 years and not above 45 years.
- Semen analysis of donor should meet WHO criteria
- Blood group and Rh status should be determined and placed on record.

Regarding the bank:

- Record of all donors must be kept for 10 years
- The bank may advertise suitably
- Record of semen received, stored and supplied should be maintained
- Semen sample must be cryopreserved for at least 6 months before first use at which time the donor must be tested for HIV and hepatitis B and C.

POSTHUMOUS REPRODUCTION

- Posthumous child is a child born after the death of his father.
- With advent of semen banking, a man may preserve his semen for later use.
- If after the death of husband, a female wants to use that semen for reproduction many ethical, social, medical and legal issues arises due to such posthumous reproduction.[3]
- A female can utilize sperm retrieved from husband, when he was alive and that has been stored, after death of her husband. She can also demand to retrieve the sperm from dead body of husband.
- Rothman first reported viable postmortem retrieval of sperm in 1980 from a 30-year-old man who became brain dead after a car accident.[4]
- The first pregnancy after postmortem retrieval was reported in 1998 and the subsequent birth was reported[5] in March 1999.

SURROGATE BIRTH AND SURROGATE MOTHERHOOD

1. Surrogacy is an arrangement in which a woman agrees to carry a pregnancy that is genetically unrelated to her and her husband with an intention to carry it to term and hand over the child to the genetic parents for whom she is acting as a surrogate.[1]
2. Surrogacy with oocyte donation: It is a process in which a woman allows insemination by sperm/semen of the male partner of a couple with a view to carry the pregnancy to term and hand over the child to the couple.
   - In first type, the ovum and sperm of a couple is utilized and fertilized *in vitro* and then implant the embryo in the womb of a surrogate female.
   - In second type the sperm of the husband is utilized and the surrogate female donates her oocyte.

Medicolegal Issues

1. Legitimacy of child: Whether child born through surrogate method would be legitimate? Law says "no". However, if the parents adopt the child then the child becomes legitimate.
2. Name of mother: In some legal documents, name of mother has to be entered. The question arises whose name should be entered as mother of child? The name of genetic mother should be entered.
3. Commercial transaction: There is no specific law in India; however, in general law prohibits the use of body for commercial purpose.[6]
4. Revoking of contract: Surrogate mother may revoke the contract and refuse to hand over the child to the couple.

STEM CELL RESEARCH

There is growing interest in embryonic stem cell research for their potential use in developing spare organs or replacing defective tissue. Stem cells are the tissue precursor cells that have the ability to self-renew and differentiate into more specific adult cells required in the body.[7] The promise of human embryonic stem cells and their importance to the fledgling field of regenerative medicine is obvious.[8]

Sources of Stem Cells

Stem cells are derived from three main sources as:[9]
1. Embryonic stem cells
2. Adult stem cells
3. Umbilical cord stem cells

Uses of Stem Cells

There are two distinct uses of stem cells[10]
1. Use of stem cells to create genetically identical person i.e. Reproductive cloning.
2. Use of stem cells to develop genetically compatible biomaterial for replacement of diseased tissue in patients with devastating medical conditions – popularly called as therapeutic cloning.

Indian Perspective

- Research on embryos is restricted to the first 14 days and should be conducted only with the permission of the owner of embryos i.e. with the informed consent of donor.[11]
- No commercial transaction will be allowed for the use of embryos for research.
- Sale or transfer of human embryo to any party outside the country is prohibited.

CLONING

Cloning is defined as *creation of an organism that is exact genetic copy of that person*. In other words, it means a precise genetic copy of a life form.[7]

Types of Cloning

1. Reproductive cloning – it is creation of copy of genetically identical human being.
2. Therapeutic cloning – in this type, stem cells are used for therapeutic purpose.

Techniques for Cloning

1. Artificial embryo twinning
2. Somatic cell nuclear transfer
3. Embryo cloning

Risk of Cloning

1. It is said that immunity level will be low in cloned organism and would more prone for infection.
2. May have high chances of carcinoma.
3. Congenital abnormalities would be more if there were defect or error while doing the procedure of cloning or programming cloning.

Issues Related with Cloning and Stem Cell Research

1. Ethical issues: Society seems divided over the issue of stem cells and cloning for biomedical research. Supporters uphold the technique because it has a promising potential

to treat and cure many diseases and might be boon for regenerative medicine. However, opponents held that it is an intentional exploitation and destruction of nascent human life created for research, thereby undermining human dignity. The important question that is commonly raised, is it ethical to create embryo for research?

2. In law, destruction of an embryo is not murder because embryo is not regarded as person. Widely detained philosophical and moral views hold that the status of person requires further development, such as nervous system capable of sentience. By day 14, the primitive streak, the first sign of development of the nervous system, may be observed. Based on this principle, some countries, including India, permit research for a specified purpose on embryos of less than 14-day limit.
3. The United Nations Organization has banned reproductive cloning.
4. It is feared that exploitation of women may occur. For cloning or stem cell research purpose, ova from female donors are required. The increasing demand for ova may lead to exploitation of women by repeated hormonal treatment for stimulation of ovaries.
5. In India, informed consent from donors is required for research on their embryo.
6. Social issues: It is argued that stem cell research and cloning involves tremendous cost and investment. Therefore, the procedure may be restricted to limited centers and cannot be afforded by poor people. Thus, the very purpose of such research may be defeated.

REFERENCES

1. Indian Council of Medical Research and National Academy of Medical Sciences. National guidelines for accreditation, supervision and regulation of ART clinics (draft). New Delhi: ICMR/NAMS; 2002.
2. The Delhi Artificial Insemination (Human) Act 1995.
3. Bardale R, Dixit PG. Birth after death: questions about posthumous sperm retrieval. Indian J Med Ethics 2006; 3: 122-3.
4. Rothman CP. A method for obtaining viable sperm in the post-mortem state. Fertil Steri 1980; 34: 512.
5. Strong C, Gingrich JR, Kutteh WH. Ethics of postmortem sperm retrieval. Hum Reprod 2000; 15: 739-45.
6. Mathiharan K, Patnaik AK. Impotence, sterility and artificial insemination. In: Modi's Medical Jurisprudence & Toxicology, 23rd edn. LexisNexis Butterworths, New Delhi. 2005; 847-74.
7. Dhai A, Moodley J, McQuoid-Mason DJ, Rodeck C. Ethical and legal controversies in cloning for biomedical research – a South African perspective. S Afr Med J 2004; 94: 906-9.
8. Daley GQ. Cloning and stem cells – handicapping the political and scientific debates. N Engl J Med 2003; 349: 211-2.
9. Bagaria V, Patil N, Sapre V, Chadda A, Singrakia M. Stem cells in orthopedics: Current concepts and possible future applications. India J Med Sci 2006; 60: 162-9.
10. Drazen JM. Legislative myopia on stem cells. Editorials. N Engl J Med 2003; 349: 300.
11. Mudur G. India to tighten rules on human embryonic stem cells research. BMJ 2001; 323: 530.

CHAPTER 23

Starvation

History gets thicker as it approaches recent time.

- A J P Taylor

Definitions

- Starvation results from deprivation of regular and constant supply of food that is required to maintain life and health. It includes the term malnutrition.
- Malnutrition is a state that results from taking inadequate food (in sufficient quantity and quality) for some period.
- Cachexia means severe inanition.
- Emaciation means loss of body weight.

MALNUTRITION

Nutritional Marasmus and Kwashiorkor are two extreme forms of malnutrition.

- Marasmus: The subject is emaciated and body weight is less than 60% of the expected weight for age. The skin appears dry and inelastic. Hairs are hypopigmented. Abdomen is distended due to wasting and hypotonia of abdominal muscles.[1]
- Kwashiorkor: It is characterized by growth retardation, psychomotor changes, and edema of dependent parts. The edema starts initially at lower extremities and later involves upper limbs and face. The face is puffy and appears moon-shaped.

STARVATION

Starvation may be:

1. Acute
2. Chronic

Acute starvation – here the water and food necessary for body are suddenly and completely withheld.

Chronic starvation – here there is gradual deficiency in the supply of food.

- The minimum food requirement for an adult is about 2000 calories, if the person is not performing any activity.[2]
- Life is threatened when more than 40% of the original body weight has been lost.

Fatal Period

- Total deprivation of water and food results death in about 10 to 12 days.[3, 4]
- If food alone is withdrawn, death may occur in 6 to 8 weeks or even more.

Factors Affecting Death Due to Starvation[5]

1. Age: Old person bears the deprivation of better than adults due to low requirement. Similarly, adult bear the starvation better than children.
2. Condition of body: Fatty and healthy people bear starvation better than ill and thin.
3. Sex: Female bear starvation better than male due to higher fat store in body.
4. Exposure to cold: Person exposed to cold cannot withstand starvation because it increases the basal metabolic rate of body.

Clinical Features

Chronic starvation results in malnutrition with manifestation of Marasmus or Kwashiorkor. Two main types of starvation are seen; one is dry type and another is wet type.

- Wet type: This type is manifested by marked edema of face, trunk and limbs. There is ascites and pleural effusion. The edema is due to hypoproteinemia.
- Dry type is manifested by emaciation with leg edema. There is loss of body weight to half the normal. These people show marked hypotension and feeble pulse.
- Loss of well-being, hunger, apathy, fatigue, loss of flesh, polyuria, pigmentation, cachexia, hypothermia, extreme

lethargy, mental retardation, edema, first there is constipation then diarrhea, and reduced resistance to infection.

Autopsy Findings[6]

External Findings

- Emaciation
- In infants and children, crown-rump, head diameter, mid-arm circumference, weight should be recorded so as to make comparison with standard pediatric percentile growth charts.
- Skin: Skin of face is stretched tightly across the cheek bones. Skin appears pale, lustrous and semi-translucent with loss of subcutaneous fat. In adults, it is dry brittle, coarse, rough with flaking hyperkeratosis and fissured. Skin infections are common. There may be infected bed/pressure sores over dependent parts.
- Head appears deceptively large than trunk
- Eyes are deeply sunken due to loss of orbital fat. Cheek bones appear prominent, cheeks are sunken with loss of fat and the lines of jaw are obvious.
- The limbs are almost skeletal due to loss of fat and muscles.
- Ribs are prominent with concavities of intercostal spaces and sunken supracalvicular fossae. The abdomen is scaphoid (Fig. 23.1).
- Hairs are dry, lusterless and brittle. May be hypopigmented.
- Nails are brittle and ridged
- Tongue is dry and thickly coated
- There may be edema of feet.

Internal Findings

- Loss of adipose tissue from omentum, mesentry and perirenal fat stores.
- There is atrophy of organs (except brain) with reduction in size
- Gut is empty and filled with gas. The wall is contracted and translucent from stomach to colon. Faecoliths are usually present and may ulcerate the intestinal linings.
- Gall bladder is distended (Fig. 23.2)
- Bones may show features of demineralization.

Medicolegal Importance

1. Starvation may be the manifestation of self-neglect or may be a criminal act
2. The infant, children and older people are the unfortunate victims of intentional starvation.
3. Starvation may be homicidal. During Second World War many people (helpless Jews) suffer deliberate starvation in Nazi concentration camps in Belsen and other places in Germany.
4. Starvation may be accidental if person is caught/entombment in mines, earthquakes or landslides. Accidental starvation may be seen in famine and flood.
5. Suicidal starvation occurs when someone deliberately withhold food as seen among prisoner who go on hunger strike as a form of protest. Mahatma Gandhi was also known to have done hunger strike as a part of non-violence movement against British rule. Many political leaders do the hunger strike for the demands or in protest of injustice. Voluntary starvation is also practiced by some people as a part of religious ceremony or for purpose of achieving salvation.
6. Article 21 of Indian Constitution guarantees the citizen of India for "Right to life and liberty" and food is basic human need to live life. Thus in broader sense, it is responsibility of State to provide food for the inhabitants.
7. Hunger striker is a mentally competent person, who has indicated that he has decided to embark on a hunger strike and has refused to take food and/or fluids for a significant interval.[7]
8. Forcible feeding of person on hunger strike – in India, if the hunger striker causes the imminent danger to life as a result of deliberate starvation, such person can be taken into custody by State for force-feeding and to save the life. Provision of Sec 309 of IPC – attempt to commit suicide may be applied in such cases.
9. Medical profession and hunger strikers – the doctor treating the hunger striker is faced with duel facts. On one hand, it is his moral duty to exercise his skills to save the life and act in the best interest of the patient. On the other hand, it is his duty to respect the patient's autonomy. The problem arises when a hunger striker has issued a clear instruction not to treat him against his wishes. Under such circumstances, the moral obligation urges doctor to save the life but the duty urges to respect the patient's autonomy. The World Medical Association (WMA) declaration on hunger strikers (1991) states that the ultimate decision on intervention or non-intervention should be left with the individual doctor.[7]
10. In view of law, forcible feeding of prisoner, against their wishes, is not an assault but quite lawful because the prisoners are under the care of State and State must take adequate measures to prevent the prisoner from injuring himself or taking his own life.[8]
11. Homicidal starvation may occur in illegitimate children as a part of neglect. The Bombay Children Act 1948 provides

special provision to discourage the neglect of children. It states that whoever having the actual charge of, or control over, a child willfully assaults, ill-treats, neglects, abandons or exposes him or causes or procures him to be assaulted, ill-treated, neglected, abandoned or exposed or negligently fails to provide adequate food, clothes or medical aid or lodging for a child in a manner likely to cause such child unnecessary mental and physical suffering shall, on convection, be punished with imprisonment of either description for a term not exceeding two years or with fine or both. For the purpose of this Act, a child means a boy or girl who has not attained the age of 16 years.[9]

12. Section 317 of IPC deals with exposure and abandonment of child under 12 years by parent or person having care of it.

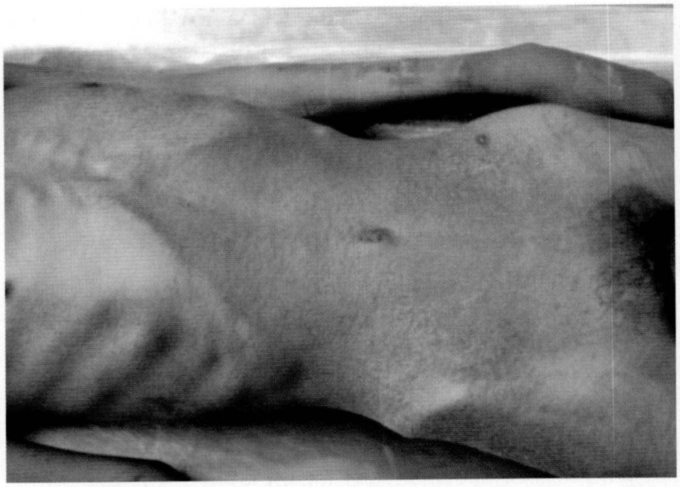

FIG. 23.1: Showing scaphoid abdomen in starvation

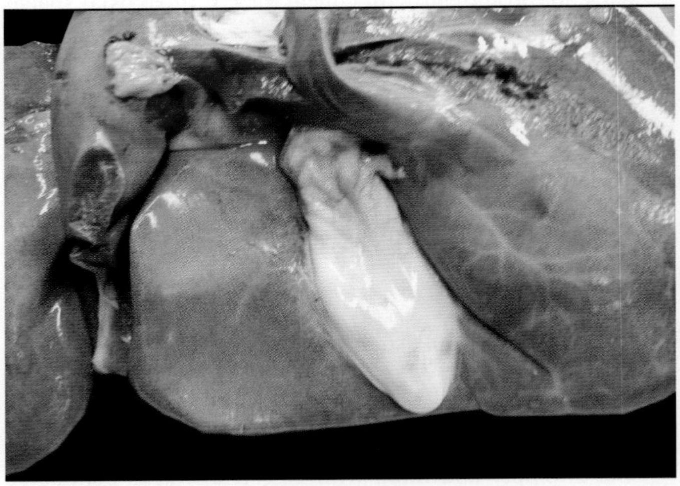

FIG. 23.2: Distended gallbladder

REFERENCES

1. Ghai OP. Nutrition and nutritional disorders. In Essential of Pediatrics, 4th edn. 1996. Interprint, New Delhi. 40-54.
2. Gee D. Deaths from physical and chemical injury, starvation and neglect. In: Mant AK (Ed). Taylor's Principles and Practice of Medical Jurisprudence, 13th edn. 2000. B I Churchill Livingstone, New Delhi. 249-81.
3. Vij K. Starvation and neglect. In: Textbook of Forensic Medicine and Toxicology, 3rd edn. 2005. Reed Elsevier India Pvt. Limited, New Delhi. 267-9.
4. Pillay VV. Starvation. In: Textbook of Forensic Medicine and Toxicology, 14th edn. 2004. Paras Publishing, Hyderabad. 249 -51.
5. Rudra A. Starvation. In: Dogra TD, Rudra A (eds) Lyon's Medical Jurisprudence and Toxicology, 11th edn. 2007. Delhi Law House, Delhi. 1029-35.
6. Saukko P, Knight B. Neglect, starvation and hypothermia. In: Knight's Forensic Pathology, 3rd edn. 2004. Arnold, London. 412-20.
7. Subrahmanyam BV. Law in relation to medical men. In: Modi's Medical Jurisprudence and Toxicology, 22nd edn. 2001. Butterworths India, New Delhi. 683-740.
8. Mathiharan K, Patnaik AK. Deaths from starvation, cold and heat. In: Modi's Medical Jurisprudence and Toxicology, 23rd edn. 2005. LexisNexis Butterworths, New Delhi. 615-28.
9. Parikh CK. Starvation. In: Parikh's Textbook of medical Jurisprudence and Toxicology, 5th edn. 1995. CBS Publishers and Distributors, Mumbai. 223-6.

CHAPTER 24

Euthanasia

Life consists of more than just a desire to stay alive.

- C R Flint

Introduction

Euthanasia means *infliction of a painless death of a person who is suffering from severe, incurable pain or disease.*
Synonyms: Mercy killing, physician assisted suicide
Euthanasia is classified into various types as:[1]

1. Voluntary – when the dying person voluntarily gives consent for the act and request for mercy killing.
2. Non-voluntary – in this type the dying person is unable or incapable to give consent or unable to refuse consent because of unconsciousness or due to coma.
3. Compulsory – here the society/state takes decision to terminate the life of person.
4. Active – in this type of euthanasia, doctor causes painless death of a person by an active act i.e. by an act of commission, for example, giving lethal dose of barbiturate or morphine injection to a person so as to cause death.
5. Passive – here doctor causes death of a person by doing nothing to save the life i.e. by an act of omission, for example, withdrawal of life support/ventilation support.
6. Pediatric – here euthanasia is administered to children
7. Geriatric – here euthanasia is administered to old individuals.

Whether euthanasia should be administered to a person or not is still debatable topic and, as usual, society is divided over the issue. Some favors euthanasia and gives arguments whereas other opposes the concept at the outset and proposes their propositions. Moreover, the role of Physician appears in such practices to be crucial and alas! This community is again divided over the same issue. Following paragraphs highlights the views expressed by both parties.

VIEWS IN FAVOR OF EUTHANASIA

Campaigners for euthanasia put forth the following reasons in favour of euthanasia:

- Patients who are suffering from an agonizing incurable disease or suffering from severe pain, euthanasia will help these patients to die with dignity.[2]
- If a person is suffering from intractable pain or suffering or debility then he has the right to terminate the life. A conscious dying person can take his own decision and can deny the terminal care provided by the doctor. Acting against the patient's wishes or without consent may attract legal liabilities and technically speaking it is an assault. The right to refuse treatment is recognized concept in some countries such as Britain and United States. Adults are presumed to be competent to make decisions unless there are reasons to suppose otherwise and therefore can make their decision.[3]
- Many activists thought that there is no moral obligation on the part of doctor to preserve the life at the expense of suffering. Now in some countries, the advanced medical directives or so-called living wills have been recognized which entitles the patient to refuse treatment any time in future.[4]
- Palliative drugs may help in relief from pain and suffering but only to limited degree. Moreover, most drugs used for the purpose are not safe and may produce unintended harm to the patient in addition to his suffering.[3]
- Many families are emotionally unable to handle the prolonged suffering of their loved ones. Patients and families are clear that it is not death that they are afraid of – it is the process of dying that terrifies them.[5]
- Doctors have been using aggressive measures in an attempt to prolog life. In an unconscious patient, how it is wise to continue the body functions by artificial means over a period of months or years? Physicians equate beneficence with saving life at any cost, even when patient's material resources have been exhausted. This commitment can lead to patient being kept alive

with little regard to the quality of living as well as dying. Promoters of concept of death with dignity have questioned this 'medicalised dying'. Therefore, prolonging the life with intensive medical care and life support system for indefinite period makes dying difficult and cruel.[6, 7]

VIEWS AGAINST EUTHANASIA

- It is considered that no person has right to take away the life of another person. Traditional medical ethical codes never sanctioned euthanasia, even on request. The Hippocratic Oath states "I will give no deadly medicine to anyone if asked, nor suggest such counsel......" The International Code of Medical Ethics declares, "A doctor must always bear in mind the obligation of preserving the human life from the time of conception until death". World Medical Association confirmed that assisted suicide, like euthanasia, is unethical and must be condemned by medical profession.
- Many people are sick of experiencing uncontrollable pain in their final days. However, with adequate palliative care, the pain can be controlled. New researches into pain control methods are leading to possibility of total pain control.[8]
- A patient with terminal illness often suffers from depression or a sense of worthlessness, which may affect their judgment. Elderly individuals who don't want to be financial or care-taking burden on their family may succumb. Loosing the opportunity of caring of people denies us an essential part of our humanity.
- Medical research is essential if medicine is to advance further and if focus changes from curing to killing the individual then the whole process is threatened. If euthanasia is legalized, we can expect advances in the science of killing.[8]
- Voluntary euthanasia legislation makes doctors less accountable and gives them more power that can be easily abused. Patients generally decide in favour of euthanasia on the basis of information given to them by doctor about their diagnosis, prognosis, treatment available and anticipated degree of future suffering. At times, diagnosis or prognosis may be mistaken or misjudged.[9]

EUTHANASIA: STATUS IN INDIA

- Euthanasia is not legalized in India. On request of a patient, any act done by doctor to assist the patient to end his life can be considered as an offense. The patient will commit an offense of suicide covered under Sec 309 of IPC and person (Doctor) who causes death of such person are abetting the act and is covered under Sec 306 of IPC (abetment of suicide). If doctor provides medical treatment intended to cause death without that of patient's consent, may be charged with murder or culpable homicide.
- In Article 21 of Constitution of India, there is a provision guaranteeing protection of life and personal liberty and cannot imply extinction of life. It is difficult to construe Article 21 to include within the right to die as a part of fundamental right guaranteed therein. 'Right to life' is a natural right embodied in Article 21 and therefore unnatural termination or extermination of life is incompatible and inconsistent with the concept of right to life.[1]
- As per Indian Medical Council (Professional conduct, etiquette and ethics) regulations, practicing voluntary euthanasia shall constitute unethical conduct.[10]
- At present euthanasia is not legalized therefore no question arises about its practice in India. However, most of medical men thought that it should not be legalized and practiced. At concluding note, it will be useful to remember the words of Lord Edmund Davis – "killing both pain and patient may be good morals but is far from certain that it is good law".[11]

REFERENCES

1. Murkey PN, Singh KS. Euthanasia (mercy killing). J Indian Acad Forensic Med 2008; 30:92-5.
2. Prakash A. Puzzle over mercy killing. The Hitvada newspaper, Sunday July 29, 2007.
3. Jindal SK. Issues in the care of the dying. Indian J Med Ethics 2005; 2: 79-80.
4. Samuels AJP. The advance directive (or living will). Med Sci Law 1996; 36: 2-8.
5. Mamdani B. Options at the end of life. Indian J Med Ethics 2004; 1: 130-1.
6. Chopra-Chatterjee S, Mohanty S. Socio-ethical issues in the deployment of life-extending technologies. Indian J Med Ethics 2005; 2: 81-2.
7. Rastogi AK. End-of-life issues neglected in India. Indian J Med Ethics 2005; 2: 83-4.
8. Dongre AP, Bardale RV, Dingre NS. Euthanasia. J Medicolegal Assoc Maharashtra 2002; 14: 5-7.
9. Ventafride V. Euthanasia: more palliative care is needed (letter). BMJ 1994; 309: 472.
10. Indian Medical Council (Professional conduct, etiquette and ethics) Regulations, 2002.
11. Gupta BD. Euthanasia: personal viewpoint. J Punjab Acad Forensic Med Toxicol 2004; 4:17-20.

CHAPTER 25

Human Rights, Torture and Medical Ethics

The worst form of inequality is to try to make unequal things equal.

- Aristotle

INTRODUCTION

- Article 3 of Universal Declaration of Human Rights states "everyone has the right to life, liberty and security of a person".
- Article 21 of the Constitution of India guarantees "no person shall be deprived of his life or personal liberty except according to the procedure established by law".
- Thus right to life, liberty and security of a person are recognized as a fundamental right by the Universal Declaration of Human Right (article 3) of 1948 and article 21 of the Indian Constitution.

TORTURE

Definition

The World Medical Association adopted a declaration called as "Declaration of Tokyo (1975)", which defines torture as "*a deliberate, systematic or wanton infliction of physical or mental suffering by one or more persons acting alone or on the orders of any authority, to force another person to yield information, to make a confession, or for other reason*".

Reasons for Torture

1. To obtain information
2. To force confession
3. To obtain statement incriminating others
4. To spread terror in society
5. To destroy personality

Types of Torture

1. Physical torture
2. Psychological torture
3. Sexual torture

Physical torture: Here the method of torture involves infliction of pain, suffering, discomfort or dysfunction of body. The methods are:

1. Beating
2. Application of heat/cold
3. Electrical torture
4. Pulling and/or twisting of nails/hairs/tongue/teeth/breast/genitals
5. Suspension
6. Mutilation
7. Forced labour

Psychological torture: The methods are:

1. Deprivation techniques and involves
   - Social deprivation
   - Perceptual deprivation
   - Sensory deprivation
   - Sleep deprivation
   - Nutritional deprivation
   - Hygienic deprivation
   - Health services deprivation
2. Coercion techniques
3. Communication techniques

Sexual torture: The torture may be in form of:

1. Undressing
2. Rape
3. Infliction of injuries to private parts
4. Introduction of foreign body

5. Mutilation of genital organs/breast
6. Unnatural sexual intercourse

Consequences or Complications of Torture

Physical Complications

Early

1. Injuries
2. Hemorrhage
3. Infections

Delayed

1. Scars
2. Mutilations
3. Malunion of bones
4. Disfiguration
5. Impairment of vision/hearing/joint

Psychological Complications

1. Depression
2. Sleep disturbances
3. Low self esteem
4. Stress disorder

Torture and Medical Ethics

- Freedom from torture is among the human rights contained in the United Nations' Universal Declaration of Human Rights.
- Violation of human rights by Registered Medical Practitioner (RMP) is an unethical act. The Physician shall not aid or abet torture nor shall he be a party to either infliction of mental or physical trauma or concealment of torture inflicted by some other person or agency and doing such thing is clear violation of human rights.[1]
- Doctors are obliged by Hippocratic Oath not to use their professional knowledge in order to harm their patients.
- Geneva Declaration of the WMA binds the doctor with the words "the health of my patient will be my first consideration".
- Tokyo Declaration adopted by World Medical Association (WMA) in 1975 states that[2]
  1. A doctor shall not countenance, condone or participate in the practice of torture or other forms of cruel, inhuman or degrading procedures.
  2. A doctor shall not provide any premises, instruments, substances, or knowledge to facilitate the practice of torture.
  3. The World Medical Association will support and encourage the international community, the national medical associations and fellow professional colleagues, to support a doctor and his family, in the face of threats or reprisal resulting from refusal to condone the use of torture or other forms of cruel, inhuman, or degrading treatment.
- The declaration of Hamburg of WMA prohibited the medical doctors throughout the world from countenancing, condoning or participating in practice of torture or other forms of cruel, inhuman or degrading procedures for any reason.

Legal Aspects

- Section 330 and 331 of IPC deals with the crime and punishment of voluntarily causing hurt or grievous hurt for the purpose of extorting confession or any information.
- In India, the protection of Human Rights Act 1993 was enacted for protection of human rights. The Act provides for the constitution of a National Human Rights Commission, State Human Rights Commission in states and Human Rights Courts for protection of human rights and for matters connected therewith or incidental thereto.

Involvement of Doctors in Torture

Doctors may some time be involved in infliction of torture by the State or authorities. Doctor may help torture in following ways (Doctor should not help in such procedure)

1. Assessing torture technique
2. Training others in technique
3. Assessing detainees' fitness
4. Provide methods for torture

REFERENCES

1. Indian Medical Council (Professional conduct, etiquette and ethics) regulations, 2002.
2. World Medical Association, Declaration of Tokyo. World Medical Journal 1975; 22.

CHAPTER 26

Medicolegal Aspects of AIDS

Prophylaxis is preferable to therapy.

- J Leahy Taylor

The acquired immunodeficiency syndrome (AIDS) was first recognized in United States in the summer of 1981. In 1983, human deficiency virus (HIV) was isolated from a patient with lymphadenopathy and by 1984; it was documented clearly to be causative agent of AIDS.[1]

AIDS and Law

- Article 21 of the Constitution of India guarantees right to life and personal liberty. It is fundamental right of HIV positive individuals to have access to adequate treatment provided by government.
- A writ of habeas corpus can be filled in the High Court or in the Supreme Court if a person is unjustly or illegally isolated alleging him to be HIV positive.
- A civil suit under the law of tort may be filled to claim compensation for violation of fundamental right to personal liberty.
- A legal action can be initiated against a person who is infected with HIV if:
  1. A person **unlawfully or negligently** do the act to spread infection of disease dangerous to life, shall be punished with imprisonment of either description for a term which may extend to 6 months or with fine or with both (Under section 269 of IPC).
  2. A person **willfully or malignantly** does any act to spread the infection of disease dangerous to life shall be punished with imprisonment of either description for a term which may extend to 2 years or with fine or with both (Under section 270 of IPC).
- Action against blood bank can be initiated supplying infected blood to a person resulting in death of that person due to HIV infection (Under section 304 A of IPC).

AIDS and Medical Practice

- It is unethical on part of doctor to refuse treatment or investigation to a person infected with HIV.
- A doctor may be held guilty for professional misconduct for this unethical behavior.[2]

AIDS and Autopsy

- Forensic persons working in mortuary are considered to be at high risk owing to the fact that HIV has been isolated from blood and body fluids. In India, data are lacking regarding the risk of HIV transmission from mortuary. Viable HIV could be isolated from blood at autopsy up to 21 hours after patient's death and viable HIV was isolated up to 14 days from spleen specimen.[3] Similarly, HIV antibodies had been detected from postmortem vitreous humor specimens up to 34 hours.[4] However, for detection of antibodies, serum is considered as more reliable specimen.[5]
- To prevent the transmission it was suggested that patients should be screened before doing autopsy. However, it is not possible to screen each and every individual for HIV in a mortuary setup due to various factors. Ethical considerations, lack of laboratory facility, financial constraints, window period of patient etc. are some factors. In addition, the test is time consuming taking approximately four hours to perform.[6] Therefore a "**Universal Precautions**" should be adopted for every case.

Universal Precautions[7,8]

- HIV has been isolated from number of body fluid and tissues. Therefore, all persons performing or assisting autopsies may have contact with blood, semen, vaginal secretions, cerebrospinal fluid, synovial fluid, pleural fluid, pericardial fluid, peritoneal fluid, amniotic fluid and tissues should follow universal precautions to prevent themselves from contacting the infection. There are now several well-documented cases of HIV infection occurring in health care workers who had been exposed to HIV infected blood, although the rate of infection appears to be less than 1% even with a needle prick.[6]

- The staff members transporting the body to mortuary should wear protective clothing.
- During autopsy, the persons should wear AIDS suit which comprises of disposable type of scrub suit, a plastic apron, double rubber gloves, cap, face-mask, goggles and shoe-covering. Sharp weapons cut should be avoided. Production of aerosol of biological material during sawing bone etc. may pose special problem. A vacuum dust exhaust and filter should be used.
- Autopsy samples and specimens required for further analysis should be collected in leak proof containers.
- After completion of autopsy, the body should be wrapped in polythene sheet. First fold of sheet should be overhead, second fold over legs and third and fourth folds are placed from the side of the body so as to overlap and should be sealed with waterproof tape. Then the body is placed in another plastic bag. While handing over the body to the relatives, proper instruction should be given.
- Disposable and used sharp instruments like scalpel blades etc. should be placed in puncture proof container.
- Usable instruments should be placed in two percent aqueous glutaraldehyde solution for four hours and then washed with clean water and autoclaved before using again.
- The biological material left should be disposed as per the guidelines issued by Hospital Waste Management and Bio-medical Waste (management and handling) rules.
- Autopsy table, wall and floor should be disinfected with sodium hypochlorite solution.

REFERENCES

1. Fauci AS, Lane HC. Human immunodeficiency virus (HIV) disease: AIDS and related disorders. In: Fauci AS, Braunwald E, Isselbacher KJ, Wilson JD, Martin JB, Kasper DL, Hauser SL, Longo DL (eds) Harrison's Principles of Internal Medicine, Vol.2, 14th edn. 1998. McGraw-Hill, New York. 1791.
2. Indian Medical Council (Professional conduct, etiquette and ethics) regulations, 2002.
3. Karhunen PJ, Brummer-Korvenkontio H, Leinikki P, Nyberg M. Stability of human immunodeficiency virus (HIV) antibodies in postmortem samples. J Forensic Sci 1994; 39: 129-35.
4. Klatt EC, Noguchi T. AIDS and infection control in forensic investigation. Am J Forensic med Pathol 1990; 11: 44-9.
5. Pepose JS, Pardo FS, Donegan E, Quinn TC. HTLV-III ELISA testing of cadaveric sera to screen potential organ transplant donors. JAMA 1986; 256: 864.
6. Little D, Ferris AJ. Determination of human immunodeficiency virus antibody status in forensic autopsy cases in Vancouver using a recombinant immunoblot assay. J Forensic Sci 1990; 35: 1029-34.
7. Kumar A. AIDS and autopsy – an abstraction of medico-legal, socio-legal and ethico-legal implications. J Forensic Med Toxicol 2001; 18: 20-6.
8. Dhanvijay AG. Biosafety guidelines for autopsies in AIDS. Souvenir of Formedicon 2004, XIIth Annual Conference of Medicolegal Association of Maharashtra, 2004. 43.

CHAPTER 27

Anesthetic and Operative Deaths

It is a good remedy sometimes to use nothing.

-Hippocrates (460 - 355 BC)

Anesthesia means absence of all sensation. Without anesthesia, it is impossible to imagine any operative procedure.

Types of Anesthesia

1. General anesthesia
2. Local anesthesia
   - Regional
   - Spinal anesthesia

Regional anesthesia may be produced by three was:

1. Surface application
2. Infiltration
3. Nerve block.

Anesthetics

Anesthetics are the drugs or agents producing anesthesia. The anesthetics are classified as:

A. General anesthetics
   1. Inhalational agents
      - Gas – nitrous oxide
      - Liquids – ether, halothane, enflurane, isoflurane, sevoflurane.
   2. Intravenous agents
      - Inducing agents – thiopentine sodium, profol, etomidate
      - Slower acting drugs – benzodiazepines, ketamine, fentanyl.

B. Local anesthetics
   1. Injectable
      - Low potency, short duration – procaine, chloroprocaine
      - Intermediate potency and duration – lidocaine, prilocaine.
      - High potency, long duration – tetracaine, bupivacaine, ropivacaine.
   2. Surface acting
      - Soluble – cocaine, lidocaine
      - Insoluble – benzocaine.

Skeletal muscle relaxants are classified as:

A. Peripherally acting

1. Neuromuscular blocking agents
   a) Non-depolarizing blockers
      - Long acting – d-tubocurarine, gallamine
      - Intermediate acting – vecuronium, atacurium
      - Short acting – mivacurium.
   b) Depolarizing blockers
      - Succinylcholine
      - Decamethonium.
2. Directly acting agents – dantrolene sodium

B. Centrally acting
   - Mephensin group – mephensin, chlorzoxazone
   - Benzodiazepines
   - GABA derivatives – baclofen.

CLASSIFICATION OF ANESTHETIC PATIENTS

For assessing physical fitness to undergo anesthetic procedure and surgery, the American Society of Anesthesiologists (ASA) classifies the patients[1,2] into six categories as described in Table 27.1

Anesthetic Deaths

Death may be

- During anesthesia
- Post-anesthetic death

A. Death occurring during administration of anesthesia but not due to anesthesia

The causes may be various such as:

1. Death due to injury or disease for which the operation is being done. The injury or disease may be serious and caused death.
2. Death may be due to disease or disorder other than that for which operation is being done.
3. Death may be due to surgical procedure or surgical complications, for example
   - Accidental cutting of large blood vessel
   - Shock
   - Incompatible blood transfusion.

B. Deaths as a direct result of administration of anesthesia. The causes are

1. Death due to respiratory failure/respiratory depression
2. Airway obstruction
3. Pneumothorax
4. Aspiration of gastric contents
5. Hypovolemia
6. Cardiac arrhythmias
7. Equipment failure
8. Overdose of anesthetic agent
9. Anesthetic misadventure
10. Inexperience
11. Monitoring and vigilance failure
12. Malignant hyperthermia
13. Drug induced reactions to anesthetics[3] (Table 27.2)
14. Adverse drug reaction.

DEATH DUE TO SURGICAL PROCEDURE

Death due to surgical procedures are grouped as:

A. Death occurring during operation
   1. Death due to anesthetic agents
   2. Death due to injury or disease for which the operation is being done.
   3. Death may be due to disease or disorder other than that for which operation is being undertaken
   4. Death due to surgical procedure or occurring complication
   5. Technical mishaps, e.g. explosion from electrocautry.

B. Post-operative deaths
   1. Delayed hemorrhage
   2. Pulmonary embolism
   3. Nosocomal infections
   4. Surgical complication
   5. Failure of artificial devices kept in body.

AUTOPSY AND INVESTIGATION

Autopsy

- Obtain detail history and information of anesthetic procedure, operative technique
- Odour of anesthetic agent may be detected
- Examine surgical site
- Resuscitation measures and intubation may induce artificial artefacts. Interpret findings carefully
- Position of endotracheal tube must be checked by pre-autopsy radiograph. A ring of edematous esophageal mucosa at the level of tube and distention of stomach and intestine indicates esophageal intubation.
- Examine for presence of emphysema, pneumothorax or air embolism
- Examine all body cavities *in situ*
- Specimens and samples for histopathological, toxicological, bacteriological examination and those required to

Table 27.1: Displaying ASA classification

Category	*Status of patient*
ASA I	Normal healthy individual
ASA II	Patient with mild systemic disease
ASA III	Patient with severe systemic disease that is not incapacitating
ASA IV	Patient with incapacitating systemic disease that is constant threat to life
ASA V	Moribund patient who is not expected to survive 24 hours without operation
E	Emergency operation

Table 27.2: Possible drug induced reaction to anesthetics

Drug	*Untoward reactions*
Phenothiazines	Arterial hypotension, tachycardia
Adrenocorticoids	Circulatory collapse
Mono-amine oxidase (MAO) inhibitors	Potentiation of vasopresor drugs
Antihypertensive compounds	Circulatory depression
Vasopressin	Coronary vasoconstrictions
Insulin	Intra-operative hypoglycemia
Oxytocin	Potentiation of vasopressor drugs

exclude hazards associated with blood transfusion must be collected.

Samples to be Preserved at Autopsy

1. Alveolar air should be collected with a needle and syringe under water by pulmonary puncture before chest is opened
2. Blood should be collected in syringe under oil before opening body cavity
3. Both lungs – placed in a nylon bag and sealed immediately
4. Brain
5. Cerebrospinal fluid (CSF) in spinal anesthesia
6. Two grams of fat from mesentry
7. Ten gram of skeletal muscle
8. Liver
9. Kidneys
10. Urine
11. Blood for culture
12. Blood for serology
13. Exudates for bacteriological examination
14. Tissue sample for histopathology
15. Skin from injection site

Medicolegal Aspects

1. Informed consent of patient should be obtained with reference to the physical status of the patient. Legally separate consent for anesthesia apart from surgery has to be taken.
2. Documentation is important regarding
   - Pre-anesthetic evaluation and assessment of patient
   - Pre-operative record of events
   - Record regarding operative and anesthetic procedure
   - Falsification of record or scratching out the record should be avoided
3. Death occurring during anesthetic or surgical procedure should be reported to police (Sec 39 CrPC).

Important Points

1. Develop patient-doctor relationship
2. Explain the procedure to patient/relatives
3. Establishment of identity is important in surgical practice such as
   - Type of surgery to be performed
   - The side – left or right
   - Self-identification i.e. the patient must feel the presence of doctor during surgery
   - Re-identification – patient could see the familiar face of the doctor on awakening.

Hospital Investigation

Apart from medicolegal investigation, the hospital investigation offers an opportunity to investigate the causes for such deaths. The surgical-anesthesiology review meetings have advantage that problems of particular relevance to that system may be identified. Predisposing factors can be identified. Alternative approaches which might have used be discussed and possible ways of preventing such an outcome in future may be proposed.[4] The algorithm of the anesthetic/surgical death investigation process[5] is presented in Figure 27.1.

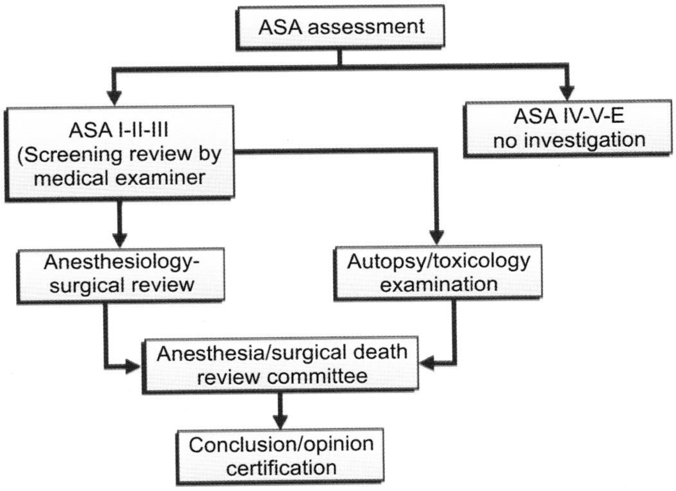

Fig. 27.1 Showing algorithm of anesthetic/surgical death investigation

REFERENCES

1. American Society of Anesthesiology classification of physical status. Anesthesiology 1963; 24: 111.
2. Tinker JH, Roberts SL. Anesthesia Risk. In: Miller RD (Ed) Anesthesia, Vol. I, 2nd edn. 1986. Churchill Livingstone, New York. 359-80.
3. Gupta PK. In: Practice of Anaesthesia and Resuscitation, 2nd edn. 1989. Current Books International, Calcutta.
4. Runciman WB. Audit and quality assurance. In: Aitkenhead AR, Jones RM (Eds) Clinical Anaesthesia, 1st edn. 1996. Churchill Livingstone, New York. 729-48.
5. Reay DT, Eisele JW, Ward R, Horton W, Bonnel HJ. A procedure for the investigation of anesthetic/surgical deaths. J Forensic Sci 1985; 30: 822-7.

CHAPTER 28

Medicolegal Aspects of Embalming

When all is said and done, more is said than done.

- Lou Holtz

- Embalming is a procedure by which a dead body is treated with preservatives to prevent putrefaction.
- There are many artificial means by which dead body can be preserved and includes:
  1. By freezing the body below 0° centigrade
  2. By embalming
  3. By mummification—an ancient Egyptian method of preserving dead bodies.
- Embalming is done in:
  1. Medical schools to preserve dead bodies for the purpose of education and dissection.
  2. When the dead body has to be taken from one country to another or in same state for last rituals when transit time required would be more so that decomposition does not occur.
- Embalming is done by injecting embalming fluid in the body.

COMPOSITION OF EMBALMING FLUID[1]

1. Preservative: Formalin/methanol/phenol
2. Germicides: Phenol and its derivatives, glutaraldehyde
3. Buffers: Sodium borate, sodium bicarbonate, sodium carbonate, magnesium carbonate
4. Wetting agents: Glycerin, glycols, sorbitol, sodium lauryl sulphate
5. Anticoagulants: Sodium citrate, sodium oxalate
6. Dyes: Eosin, ponceau
7. Vehicles (diluents): Water, glycerin, sorbitol, alcohol
8. Perfuming agents (deodorants): Methyl salicylates, oil of clove

Method of Embalming

1. Arterial embalming: In this method, embalming fluid is injected into selected artery.
2. Cavity embalming: In this procedure, organs of thoracic and abdominal cavities are treated with embalming fluid.

Legal Aspects of Practice of Embalming[2]

- Identification of body by near relative is done before the procedure
- Consent for the procedure should be obtained
- Death certificate should be referred before embalming
- In medicolegal cases, it should be done after autopsy.

MEDICOLEGAL ASPECTS OF EMBALMING

Embalming should never be allowed before medicolegal autopsy as it may induce artefact and poses difficulty in interpreting the findings.

1. Embalming provides chemical stiffening similar to rigor mortis, so difficulty may arise in estimating time since death.
2. Embalming altar the appearance of body so interpretation of injuries becomes difficult
3. Embalming destroys cyanide, alcohol, opiates, carbon monoxide thus toxicological analysis becomes useless or difficult.[3]
4. Embalming procedure kills bacteria so bacteriologic evaluation becomes useless.
5. Due to embalming blood group cannot be made out.
6. The dimensions of wounds may be modified by the embalmer while introducing embalming fluid through them or new wounds may be produced due to use of trocher for injecting embalming fluid.

REFERENCES

1. Ajmani ML. Embalming chemicals and fluids. In: Embalming, principles and legal aspects, 1st edn. 1998. Jaypee Brothers Medical Publishers, New Delhi. 111-8.
2. Dev PK, Rao NG. In: Practical Forensic Medicine, 3rd edn. 2007. Jaypee Brothers Medical Publishers, New Delhi. 217-21.
3. Perper JA. Anatomical considerations. In: Spitz WU (Ed) Spitz and Fisher's Medicolegal investigation of Death, 3rd edn. 1993. Charlas C Thomas Publisher, USA. 14-49.

CHAPTER 29

Forensic Psychiatry

When you live in the shadow of insanity, the appearance of another mind that thinks and talks as yours does is something close to a blessed event.

- Robert M Pirsig

Introduction

- Forensic Psychiatry deals with the application of knowledge of psychiatry in the administration of law and justice.
- Insanity (lunacy or mental unsoundness or mental derangement or mental disorder) is defined as *a disease of mind or the personality in which there is derangement or impairment of mental or emotional processes*.
- The Indian Lunacy Act 1912 defined lunatic *as an idiot or a person of unsound mind*. However, The Mental Health Act 1987 has replaced the Indian Lunacy Act 1912. The Mental Health Act 1987 uses the term "**mentally ill person**" instead of lunatic. The Mental Health Act defines mentally ill person as "*a person who is in need of treatment by reason of any mental disorder other than mental retardation*".[1]
- Insanity is an old term used loosely to denote any mental disorder or mental illness. The Indian Penal Code employs the term unsoundness of mind while referring to insanity.
- It is better to use term mentally ill person (as defined under Mental Health Act 1987) rather than using term such as insane or lunatic.
- Psychiatric disorders – is a disturbance of cognition or conation or affect. Cognition denotes the thought, conation means action and affect refers to feeling of a person. Thus, in psychiatric disorder there is disequilibrium between thought, action or feeling.

Classification

ICD-10 (International Classification of Diseases – 10th Revision 1992) is prepared by WHO. Chapter F of ICD-10 classifies psychiatric disorders as follows:[2, 3]

1. Organic mental disorder – in this disorder, there is demonstrable organic cause or lesion related to brain. The organic disorders may be primary (primary brain pathology) or secondary (brain dysfunction due to systemic disease). The organic disorders are sub-classified as:
   - Delirium
   - Dementia
   - Organic amnestic syndrome
   - Other organic mental disorder
2. Mental and behavioral disorders due to psychoactive substance use – these are the disorders related with use or abuse of psychoactive substances or drugs such as alcohol, cannabis, amphetamine, cocaine, LSD etc. Psychoactive substances are the drugs that are capable of altering the mental functioning. Following are the patterns of the drug use disorders
   - Acute intoxication
   - Withdrawal state
   - Dependence syndrome
   - Harmful use
3. Schizophrenia, schizotypal and delusional disorders – these disorders result from disturbances of thought, perception, affect and behaviour. Following disorders are included under this group:
   - Schizophrenia
   - Schizotypal disorder
   - Persistent delusional disorder
   - Acute and transient psychotic disorder
   - Induced delusional disorder
   - Schizo-affective disorders
4. Mood (affective) disorders – these disorders are characterized by disturbances of mood and includes:
   - Mania (manic depression)

- Depression (depressive disorder)
- Bipolar mood disorder
- Persistent mood disorder
- Recurrent depressive disorder
- Other mood disorders.

5. Neurotic, stress-related and somatoform disorders – these disorders are characterized by disturbances of emotion. They are previously called as neurotic disorders (neurosis) and includes
   - Anxiety (anxiety disorder)
   - Phobia (phobic anxiety disorders)
   - Obsessive-compulsive disorder
   - Dissociative disorder (conversion)
   - Somatoform disorder
   - Stress and adjustment disorders.
6. Behavioral syndromes associated with physiological and physical disturbances – these disorders were previously called as "psychosomatic disorders". These disorders includes
   - Eating disorders, e.g. anorexia nervosa, bulimia
   - Sleep disorders
   - Sexual dysfunctions
   - Puerperal psychiatric disorders.
7. Disorders of adult personality and behavior – it includes
   - Personality disorders
   - Impulse disorders
   - Gender identity disorders
   - Disorders of sexual preference
   - Disorders associated with sexual development and orientation
8. Mental retardation
9. Disorders of psychological development – it includes
   - Speech and language disorders
   - Pervasive developmental disorders.
10. Behavioural and emotional disorders of childhood and adolescence – includes
    - Hyperkinetic disorders
    - Conduct disorders
    - Tic disorders
11. Unspecified mental disorders

DISORDERS

A patient may present to Psychiatrist in variety of way, he may present with speech disorder, or with disorder of perception or with disorder of thought or in combination. The following discussion provides disorders with which a patient may present.

DISORDERS OF PERCEPTION

Hyperesthesia: In this condition, there is increased intensity of sensations.
Hypoesthesia: In this condition, there is decreased intensity of sensation.
Micropsia: In this disorder, a person sees objects smaller than they really are.
Macropsia: In this disorder, person sees objects larger than the original one.
Porropsia: In this disorder, a person may see object farther away from him (actually the object is not away).

Hallucination

Definition: *Hallucination is defined as a false perception without any external object or sensory stimulus.*
Hallucinations may occur in:
- Schizophrenia
- Affective disorders
- Organic mental disorders

Types

1. Auditory hallucinations: These hallucinations are more common and consist of hearing of noises or voices when no other person is present, i.e. the noise is perceived without any stimulus. Auditory hallucinations may be of following types:[4]
   - Elementary type: Person hear only noises
   - Partly organized: Person hears music
   - Completely organized: Person hears hallucinatory voices.
2. Visual hallucinations: It consists of seeing images, flash of light, etc. Visual hallucinations may be of:
   - Elementary type: Person sees only flashes of light
   - Partly organized: Person sees as patterns or unformed images
   - Completely organized: Person sees as images, figures or image of people, animal or objects.
3. Olfactory hallucinations: Here the person perceives non-existent smell/odour.
4. Gustatory hallucinations: Here patient perceives good or bad taste without eating actual food.
5. Tectile hallucinations: Here person senses or perceives abnormal touch. For example, a person may feel that bugs or insects are crawling over his skin (Formication). Some patient experiences feeling of cold winds blowing on them or sensation of heat present over skin; actually things are not present.

6. Command hallucinations: Here person feels that he is being ordered by hallucinating voices to do things or act.
7. Synesthesia: A stimulus perceived by a sensory organ other than the one that should actually perceive it. For example visualizing music, hearing different colors, etc .
8. Kinesthetic or psychomotor hallucinations: here the person feels that some part of body, say for example, right upper limb is moving; actually the limb is stationary.

Medicolegal Importance of Hallucination

1. A person may commit crime or violent act under hallucinations.
2. Person committing crime, under hallucinations, is not held responsible or guilty for the unlawful act.

Illusion

- Illusion is defined as *false interpretation of an external object or stimulus, which has real existence*. For example a person may mistake rope as a snake or tree as ghost or self-shadow as ghost.
- In illusion stimuli from a perceived object are combined with a mental image to produce a false perception.
- Pareidolia is a type of illusion in which vivid illusions occur without making any effort for example, formation of different images, such as human face, lion, dog, monkey etc. in the cloud or in fire.[4]

DISORDERS OF THOUGHT, THINKING AND SPEECH

Retarded thinking: In this condition, the process of thinking gets slowed down.

Thought blocking: In this condition, the process of thinking gets blocked i.e. person is unable to express.

Thought withdrawal: In this condition a person thinks that his thoughts are ceased and feels that thoughts are removed by external force.

Thought broadcasting: Here a person feels that his thoughts are broadcasting or escaping from his mind and are followed by or experienced by others.

Thought insertion: In this condition, a person feels that thoughts are being inserted into him by some external force.

Verbigeration: Senselessly or uselessly repeating some words or phrase over and over again.

Perseveration: It means persistent repetition of words or a sentence or phrase beyond the point of relevance.

Echolalia: Repetition or echoing or mimicking of words or phrase that has been heard.

Mutism: Complete absence of speech

Circumstantiality: Person goes into unnecessary details of the circumstances and the conversation wanders off the point or central theme. However, the person returns to central theme after expressing too many unnecessary details.

Tangentiality: Here the person suddenly digresses or divert into unnecessary details of the speech or fact that is completely distracted from the central theme and the person never returns back to the original theme after digression (unlike in circumstantility).

Metonymy: Here person uses imprecise word in place of proper word.

Neologism: Means formation of new words and the meaning of words could not be understood or found in dictionary.

Obsessive-Compulsive Disorder

Obsession: It is a disorder of thought and is defined as *an idea or thought that is constantly entertained by the patient, which is irrational but persists in spite of all efforts to drive it from patient's mind.*

Compulsion: It is a behaviour that follows the obsession. Example – washing hands frequently as person feels that his hands are dirty.

Delusion

- It is a disturbance of thought.
- Definition: *It is a false but firm belief in something that is not a fact.* It persists even after its falsity has been clearly proved or demonstrated.

Types

1. Delusion of grandeur: Here the person feels that he is rich or famous but actually he may be poor.
2. Delusion of poverty: Here the person feels that he is poor but actually he may be rich.
3. Delusion of persecution: Here the person thinks that some persons are persecuting against him.
4. Delusion of reference: Here the person imagines that other persons are referring him in a special way, for example, people are talking about him, newspaper are writing about him etc.
5. Delusion of influence (or control): Here the person feels that his thoughts are being controlled by some external force.
6. Nihilistic delusion: Here the person feels that nothing exists around him or that there is no world.
7. Delusion of infidelity: Here the person imagines or thinks that his wife is unfaithful to him. It is also called as "**Othello Syndrome**" or **conjugal paranoia**.

8. Hypochondrial delusions: A person believes that he is ill or is convinced that something wrong is happening with his body. Actually the person is healthy.
9. Delusional dysmorphophobia: Here the person thinks that he is ugly.
10. Erotomania delusion: It usually occurs in woman. A female thinks that a person is in love with her. The thoughts are erotic. It is also called as **Cerambault's syndrome**.
11. Delusion of self-accusation (or self-reproach): Here the person blames himself for the trivial things that happened in past.

Medicolegal Importance of Delusion

1. Delusional ideas or thoughts may affect the conduct of a person.
2. When labouring under delusional ideas, a person may commit suicide or homicide or other crime.
3. A person doing the unlawful act under delusional thought cannot be held responsible for the act.

Disorders of Consciousness and Higher Functions

Consciousness: It is awareness of the self and the environment.
Confusion: here the thinking process lacks clarity and coherence.
Clouding of consciousness: Here there is mild impairment of intellectual cognitive functions along with decreased awareness of environment.
Delirium: It is characterized by clouding of consciousness and disorientation associated with decreased attention span and distractibility.
Twilight state: Here the field of consciousness is narrowed with decreased interest in environment followed by amnesia. The person may do some automatic act and may suffer from visual hallucinations.
Fugue: It is a state of altered awareness during which an individual forgets part or whole of his life and wanders away.
Confabulation: It is a false memory that the patient believes to be true.

Amnesia

- Amnesia means loss of memory
- Amnesia may be retrograde or antegrade amnesia
- Retrograde amnesia means loss of memory for an event that has occurred in past
- Antegrade amnesia means inability of a patient to remember or record new things or memory.

Mental Retardation

- Synonyms: Mental subnormality, ologophrenia.
- Definition: Mental retardation is defined as *significantly subaverage general intellectual functioning, associated with significant deficit or impairment in adaptive functioning which manifests during the developmental period.*[3]
- Mental retardation is classified on the basis of intelligence quotient (IQ). IQ is calculated as: IQ = **Mental age × 100 ÷ Chronological age**
- The World Health Organization's (WHO) classification of mental retardation is given in Table 29.1
- Causes of mental retardation are given in Table 29.2
- Previously mental retardation were categorized as
  1. Idiot – IQ less than 20.
  2. Imbecile – IQ between 20 to 50.
  3. Moron (also called as feeblemindedness) – IQ from 50 to 75.

Medicolegal Importance

1. These persons/patients need legal guardians.
2. May be dangerous to self or others.
3. May be involved in repeated antisocial acts as IQ is low to realize the things.

Disorders of Emotions

Anxiety: It is an unpleasant affective state and is defined as "*a fear for no adequate reason*".
Panic: It is a severe state of anxiety characterized by catatonic motor behavior.

Phobia

Phobia means *an irrational fear of an object, situation or activity often leading to persistent avoidance of the feared object, situation or activity.*

Types

Agoraphobia – fear of situations
Social phobia – fears of social activities or interaction

Table 29.1: Classification of mental retardation

Classification	*Intelligence quotient*
Mild mental retardation	50 - 70
Moderate mental retardation	35 - 49
Severe mental retardation	20 - 34
Profound mental retardation	< 20

Table 29.2: Causes of mental retardation

Causes of mental retardation
Genetic causes
Down's syndrome
Fragile X-syndrome
Turner's syndrome
Klinefelter's syndrome
Pneylketonuria
Homocystinuria
Microcephaly
Antenatal causes
Neural tube defects
Rh Incompatibility
TORCH infection
Intrauterine growth retardation (IUGR)
Perinatal causes
Birth injuries
Birth hypoxia
Kernicterus
Prematurity
Postnatal causes
Head injury
Encephalitis
Cretinism
Cerebral palsy
Lead poisoning
Miscellaneous causes
Maternal malnutrition
Protein energy malnutrition (PEM)
Iodine deficiency
Consanguineous marriage

Simple phobia – fear of object. Examples of simple phobias are:

- Aerophobia – fear of high places
- Zoophobia – fear of animals
- Xenophobia – fear of strangers
- Algophobia – fear of pain
- Claustrophobia – fear of closed places

Disorders of Body Functions

Somnambulism: It is a condition in which a person walks about in his sleep. This is also called as sleep walking.

Somnolentia or semi-somnolence: This condition is midway between sleep and wakefulness. This condition is also called as sleep drunkenness.

Impulse

It is sudden and irresistible force or desire compelling a person to do an act without motive or thought.

Types

1. Kleptomania – irresistible desire or impulse to steal objects or articles of small value.
2. Pyromania – irresistible desire or impulse to set fire or objects on fire.
3. Dipsomania – irresistible desire or impulse to drink alcohol.
4. Mutilomania – irresistible desire or impulse to maim or hurt or torture animals.
5. Trichotillomania – irresistible desire or impulse to pull out one's own hair.

Schizophrenia

- Eugen Bleuler introduced the term schizophrenia and it means split minded
- Bleuler had proposed fundamental symptoms, which were thought to be diagnostic of schizophrenia and are summarized as follows: (also called as 4 A's of Bleuler).
  1. Ambivalence – inability to decide for or against.
  2. Autism – withdrawal into self.
  3. Affect disturbances – disturbances of feeling.
  4. Association disturbances – loosening of association, thought disorder.

Clinical Features

1. Thought and speech disorder consist of
   - Autistic thinking
   - Thought blocking
   - Neologism
   - Mutism
   - Echolalia
   - Verbigeration
   - Delusion.
2. Disorders of perception and consist of auditory or visual hallucinations.
3. Disorder of affect.
4. Disorder of motor behavior.

Types of Schizophrenia

1. Paranoid
2. Hebephrenic
3. Catatonic
4. Residual

5. Simple
6. Undifferentiated.

Medicolegal Importance

- Under influence of delusion, schizophrenic person may do unlawful act or criminal act.
- A person doing the unlawful act under delusional ideas cannot be held responsible for the unlawful act.

PSYCHOSIS AND NEUROSIS

The term psychosis and neurosis were used in past to differentiate the mental disorders into two groups.

Psychosis

In psychosis following things are noted:
- There is gross impairment of reality with loss of contact with surrounding. There is impairment in social, interpersonal and occupational functioning.
- There is disturbance in personality
- There is loss of insight
- There is presence of delusion and hallucinations
- Example include – schizophrenia, mood disorders.

Neurosis

In neurosis following things are noted
- There is presence of insight and presence of symptoms causes distress to the patient
- Personality is relatively preserved.
- Contact with surrounding is preserved
- Example include – anxiety disorders, phobias, obsessive compulsive disorder
- Differences between psychosis and neurosis are provided in Table 29.3.

Personality Disorder

International Classification of Disease (ICD) 9th edition classifies personality disorder as:[5]

Table 29.3: Difference between psychosis and neurosis

Features	*Psychosis*	*Neurosis*
Severity	Major	Minor
Contact with reality	Loss of contact	Contact preserved
Insight	Absent	Present
Personality	Impaired	Preserved

1. Paranoid personality disorder
2. Affective personality disorder
3. Schizoid personality disorder
4. Explosive personality disorder
5. Anankastic personality disorder
6. Hysterical personality disorder
7. Asthenic personality disorder
8. Sociopathic personality disorder or psychopath
9. Other or unspecified personality disorder.

Psychotic Murderer

- Psychotic murderer is a person who kills people because either:
  1. He has lost contact with reality and he is unaware of the nature of his act or
  2. He has impaired judgment or the justification for his act is faulty.
- These psychotic killers kill person either in the state of depression where they feel hopelessness or in a state of schizophrenia under the delusional ideas.

Sexual Killer

The sexual killer is a person who kills another person of opposite sex to derive sexual gratification by an act of killing or by inflicting pain and suffering that result in death.

Psychopathic Killer

- Also called as sociopath killer
- It is a personality disorder characterized by recurrent episodes of impulsive behaviour, which is against the social structure. These persons often indulge in antisocial acts and do not learn from their past experiences. Thus repetitive antisocial behaviour of these people is characteristic feature.

Jealous Killer

Jealous killer is a person who, under the delusion of jealousy (mostly delusion of infidelity) of spouse, kills the partner.

Oneiroid State

- Also called as onerophrenia
- It is a dream-like state that may last for days or weeks. The person suffers from mental confusion, amnesia, illusions, hallucinations, disorientation, agitation and anxiety.
- It occurs in delirium and early schizophrenia.

Lucid Interval

- This is a period occurring in the cases of mental illness during which there is complete cessation of the symptoms of mental illness, so that person can judge his acts normally.
- This is temporary period of resolution of symptoms in a mentally ill person.

Medicolegal Importance

1. In lucid interval, a person can judge his acts.
2. During this period a person is held responsible for his criminal act.
3. A person can make valid will.
4. A person can give evidence.
5. A person can make contract.

Causes of Mental Illness

1. Hereditary
2. Environmental factors
3. Psychogenic cause
4. Organic cause
5. Unknown.

Rights of Mentally Ill Person

1. Right to treatment
2. Right to refuse treatment
3. Visitation right
4. Communication right
5. Right to privacy
6. Economic rights
7. Right to habeas corpus.

Diagnosis of Mentally Ill Person

History

- Interview of patient/relatives
- Personal history
- Antenatal/perinatal/postnatal history
- Past psychiatric and treatment history
- Family history
- Social history.

Examination

- Symptoms
- Mental status
- General appearance and behavior
- Speech
- Thought
- Mood and emotion
- Perception
- Cognition
- Insight
- Judgment.

Laboratory Examination

- Toxicological/drug level examination
- CT scan/MRI scan
- Endocrine tests.

Feigned Insanity

- Also called as false insanity, fabricated insanity, artificial insanity
- In this condition, a person fabricates the sign and symptoms of insanity
- A person may feigned insanity to escape from punishment or with some other aim
- In most of the cases, it is easy to detect feigned insanity from true insanity but small number of cases may poses difficulty. Differences between true and feigned insanity are given in Table 29.4.

MENTAL HEALTH ACT 1987[1]

The Mental Health Act (MHA) 1987 was enacted for better treatment and care of mentally ill persons. The Act made provisions with respect to management of property and affairs of mentally ill persons. The Act also provides protection of human rights of mentally ill persons. The MHA 1987 contains 10 chapters and 98 sections.

1. Chapter 1 deals with various definitions. **Here the term mentally ill person is used instead of insane or lunatic.** Similarly instead of lunatic prisoner, the term mentally ill prisoner is used and instead of mental hospital, the term psychiatric hospital or psychiatric nursing home is used.
2. Chapter 2 provides procedure for establishing mental health authorities at Center and State levels.
3. Chapter 3 deals with the procedure for establishment and maintenance of psychiatric hospitals or psychiatric nursing homes.
4. Chapter 4 provides provisions for admission and detention of mentally ill person in psychiatric hospital or psychiatric nursing home.
5. Chapter 5 deals with the inspection, discharge, leave of absence and removal of mentally ill person.

Features	True insanity	Feigned insanity
Onset	Usually gradual	Sudden/abrupt
Predisposing cause	Present	Absent
Motive	Absent	Present
Symptoms	Usually uniform and suggest a particular type of disorder	Symptoms are often exaggerated and do not confined to particular disorder
Facial expression	Vacant, fixed, listless	Frequent change, exaggerated grimaces
Observation	Features continued	Features exaggerated under observation and absent when patient is not observed
Insomnia	Often persist for prolong period	Cannot withstand sleep for more period
Exertion	Can withstand fatigue and hunger for prolonged period	Cannot withstand fatigue and hunger for prolonged period
Personal hygiene	Do not pay attention, habits are dirty and filthy	Pretend but pay attention
Frequent examination by psychiatrist	Does not mind examinations	Resents because fear of detection

Table 29.4: Difference between true and feigned insanity

6. Chapter 6 deals with judicial inquisition regarding alleged mentally ill person possessing property, custody of his person and management of his property.
7. Chapter 7 deals with liability to meet cost of maintenance of mentally ill persons detained in psychiatric hospitals or psychiatric nursing homes.
8. Chapter 8 deals with protection of human rights of mentally ill persons.
9. Chapter 9 deals with penal (punishments) ties and procedures.
10. Chapter 10 deals with miscellaneous particulars.

Procedure of Admission and Detention (Restraint of the Insane)

Procedures for admission and detention of mentally persons, in psychiatric hospitals or psychiatric nursing homes, are prescribed in chapter 4 of MHA 1987. The procedures are as follows

1. **Admission on voluntary basis**
   - Any major person, who considers himself to be a mentally ill and desires to be admitted to any psychiatric hospitals or psychiatric nursing home for treatment, may request the medical officer-in-charge of that hospital for voluntary admission as a voluntary patient (Section 15 of MHA 1987).
   - If the mentally person is minor, the parents or guardian of that person may request the medical officer-in-charge of that hospital for voluntary admission as a voluntary patient (Section 16 of MHA 1987).
2. **Admission under special circumstances**
   - If the mentally person is incapable of expressing his willingness for treatment and admission in hospital as a voluntary patient, an application on that behalf by a relative or friend of mentally ill person can be made to the medical officer-in-charge of that hospital. If the medical officer is satisfied that it is necessary to admit the patient as inpatient in hospital, he can admit the patient.
   - However, no such person admitted as inpatient be kept for a period exceeding 90 days except in accordance with the other provisions of the Act.
3. **Admission under reception order**
   - Reception order on application – an application for a reception order may be made, to the Magistrate within the jurisdiction, by the medical officer-in-charge of psychiatric hospital or psychiatric nursing home or by the husband, wife or any other relative of mentally ill person. If the Magistrate considers that it is necessary to treat the mentally person, in the interest of his health and personal safety or for the protection of others, a reception order may be passed

by the Magistrate for that purpose. The Magistrate may also dismiss the application.
- Reception orders on production of mentally ill persons before Magistrate.

4. **Admission as inpatient after judicial inquisition** (inquiry).
5. **Admission as a mentally ill prisoner.**

Discharge of Mentally Ill Person

1. Voluntary patients should be discharged within 24 hours of the receipt of request for discharge made by patient or if minor, made by the guardian.
2. Mentally ill person received in psychiatric hospital on application made by his relatives or friends in this condition the friends or relatives may apply to the Magistrate for his discharge.
3. The medical officer-in-charge of psychiatric hospital can order the discharge of any patient, on recommendation of two medical practitioners one of whom should be a psychiatrist.
4. A person detained on reception order can be discharged, if judicial inquisition finds him of sound mind.
5. Any relative or friend of mentally ill person can make an application to the medical officer-in-charge of the psychiatric hospital for discharge. The medical officer-in-charge forwards the request application to the appropriate authority (Magistrate) under whose order the mentally ill person was detained. Such authority can pass an order of discharge if the relatives or friend executes a bond to take proper care of such mentally ill person.

Responsibilities of Mentally Ill Person

CIVIL RESPONSIBILITIES

1. Management of property and custody of his person
   - Chapter 6 of MHA 1987 deals with management of property of mentally ill person.
   - If a mentally ill person is incapable of taking care of himself, the District Court or the Collector of the district may appoint any suitable person to be his guardian (Section 53 of MHA 1987).
   - The district Court may appoint any suitable person to be manager for the property belonging to mentally ill person and to supervise the same. The Court may grant the manager the necessary power and may order the sale of property for the payment of his debts and expenses.
2. Consent
   - According to section 90 of IPC, consent given by a person suffering from mental illness or of unsound mind, becomes invalid. It is because the person, by reason of unsoundness of mind, is unable to understand the nature and consequences of the act to which he gives consent.
   - Similarly consent given by mentally ill female to the act of sexual intercourse becomes invalid and the act amounts to rape (Section 375 of IPC).
3. Business contract[6]
   - As per Indian Contract Act 1872, a contract becomes invalid, if at the time of doing such contract or making such contract, one of the parties was mentally ill. It is stated that by reason of unsoundness of mind, the person is incapable of understanding the nature and consequences of the contract. The mentally ill person is unable to form a rational judgment as to its effect up on his interests.
   - Mental illness developing after contract does not make it invalid unless performance of service becomes impossible.
   - Mentally ill person when in lucid interval may make a contract.
4. Evidence[7]
   - According to Section 118 of IEA, a mentally ill person is not considered as incompetent to give evidence, unless he is prevented by his mental illness from understanding the questions put to him and giving rational answers to them.
   - In other words, a person suffering from mental illness can testify however, he should be able to understand the questions properly and answers them reasonably and accordingly. If the said mentally ill person is unable to understand the questions asked and answer them properly, the Court can consider him incompetent for evidence.
   - A person suffering from mental illness but is in lucid interval is competent to give evidence.
5. Tort liabilities
   - Tort, to put in simple terms, is a failure to respect the general rights of others, independent of a contract. Thus it is a civil wrong. It is related with the actions of trespass, conversion or defamation etc.
   - A mentally ill person is liable for tort unless the disease of his mind is so great that he cannot understand the nature and consequences of his act. It is to the defendant to prove that the disease of his mind is so great as to entitle him to exemption from the rule of general liability.

6. Guardianship
   - A mentally ill person cannot be act as a legal guardian of a minor.
7. Testamentary capacity
   - Testamentary capacity of a person means capacity of a person to make a valid Will. To make a valid Will, it should have following components:
     1. The person should be of sound mind.
     2. The person making Will should understand the nature of Will.
     3. The person should have knowledge of his property that has to be disposed off.
     4. The person should recognize the individuals who have moral claims to heir his property.
   - A civil court may invalidate the Will if the person making such Will is of unsound mind at the time of making Will
   - A Will made under the influence of somebody else is also invalid
   - A person suffering from mental illness but during the period of lucid interval can make valid Will
   - Holograph will is a Will written by testator in his own handwriting.
8. Marriage
   - According to the Hindu Marriage Act 1955, the marriage solemnized becomes null and void if at the time of marriage:
     1. Due to unsoundness of mind, if either party is incapable of giving a valid consent to a marriage; or
     2. Though capable of giving valid consent, has been suffering from mental disorder of such a kind or to such an extent as to be unfit for marriage and the procreation of children; or
     3. Has been subject to recurrent attacks of insanity.
   - According to section 13 of Hindu Marriage Act, a divorce can be granted on a petition presented by either spouse on the ground that the other party has been incurably of unsound mind or has been suffering continuously or intermittently from mental disorder of such kind and to such an extent that the petitioner cannot reasonably expected to live with the respondent (i.e. with the patient).
9. Transfer of property
   - According to the Transfer of Property Act 1882 (section 7), only persons competent to contract are authorized to transfer property. In other words, person suffering from mental illness is not competent to transfer the property.
10. Adoption
   - According to the Hindu Adoptions and Maintenance Act 1956, any Hindu male, who is of sound mind and is not minor, can adopt a child with consent of his wife provided that his wife is of sound mind
   - Any Hindu female, who is of sound mind and is not minor and is not married, can adopt a child.

CRIMINAL RESPONSIBILITIES

McNaughten Rule

Responsibility means liability of the person for his acts or omissions and the person is liable for punishment for any illegal action. The law presumes every individual to be sane (i.e. of sound mind) and responsible for his criminal act, unless the contrary is proved.

The criminal responsibility of an insane got public attention in 1843. Daniel McNaughten, a 29 year Scotsman, labouring under delusion, shot dead Edward Drummond, the secretary to the British Prime Minister Sir Robert Peel. McNaughten was paranoid schizophrenic and had delusion that Sir Robert Peel was conspiring against him. He had intended to kill Sir Robert Pell but mistakenly killed Drummond. The Jury, after hearing medical evidence of 9 physicians, found McNaughten not guilty by reasons of unsoundness of mind. The Queen Victoria, Sir Robert Peel and other well-known persons were outraged by the verdict. They invited 15 eminent judges to the House of Lords and were requested to respond to series of questions on criminal responsibility of insane. The answers given by the learned judges were immortalized in the history and have come to be known as '**McNaughten rule**' or '**the legal test**' or "**Right - wrong test**".

The McNaughten rule states that "*to establish a defense on the ground of insanity, it must be clearly proved that at the time of committing the act, the party accused was labouring under such a defect of reason from the disease of the mind, as not to know the nature and quality of the act he was doing or, if he did know it, that he did not know he was doing what was wrong*".

Therefore, according to McNaughten rule, to plead not to be guilty, the accused has to prove that:
1. He was suffering from mental illness and
2. The mental illness was of such degree that he is unable to understand the nature or quality of his act or was unable to understand what he was doing was wrong.

Criticism of McNaughten Rule

- It is argued that for deciding insanity of a person, only cognitive (intellectual) factors or reasons are taken into consideration but other factors also influence the conduct and behaviour of a person such as

1. Emotional factors
2. Ability of individual to control the impulse
3. Loss of self-control.

- It was held that McNaughten rule is old and obsolete and needs correction. Subsequent to McNaughten rule, new rules were provided and debated such as Curren's rule, Durham's rule, ALI test, etc. A brief account is presented regarding these rules.

Durham Rule (1954)

The Durham's rule states, "*an accused is not criminally responsible if his unlawful act was the product of mental disease or mental defect*".

- It was held that the rule was broader then McNaughten rule. However, the rule had created problems.
- The rule states that the unlawful act of a person was product of **mental disease** or **mental defect**. The ambiguity was with reference to these words because what constitute mental disease or mental defect was not made clear or defined. Next thing was that the Judges would have to rely on the psychiatrists to decide whether the act was product of mental defect or disease; it means giving blank cheque to medical evidence. Thus the judicial authorities would have little to do while rendering the independent and impartial judgment.

Curren's Rule (1961)

The Curren's rule states that "an *accused person will not be criminally responsible, if at the time of committing the act, he did not have the capacity to regulate his conduct to the requirements of law, as a result of mental disease or defect*".

As per Curren's rule, it was contested that, at the time of committing the criminal act, a person may have knowledge that what he was doing was wrong but he neither had the capacity nor the will to control (adjust) his act. Therefore such person should not be held responsible.

American Law Institute (ALI test, 1970)

The ALI test held that "*a person is not responsible for criminal conduct if at the time of such criminal conduct as a result of a mental disease or defect, he lacks substantial capacity, either to appreciate the wrongfulness of his conduct or to adjust his conduct to the requirements of law*".

- It was considered as a significant affair with reference to criminal responsibility and moves forward from McNaughten rule and Durham's rule. Instead of knowing the difference between right and wrong, the defendant is now subjected to appreciate it.
- Similarly, it was not assumed merely the criminal act to be product of mental disease or mental defect. The defendant has to prove that due to mental disease the accused person lacks the substantial capacity to appreciate his behaviour or obey the law.

Indian Perspective

The law in India presumes every individual to be sane and responsible for his criminal act, unless the contrary is proved. Similarly the law also presumes that for every criminal act there must be a **mensrea** (mens = mind, rea = criminal) i.e. criminal intent of mind. The prayer of mental unsoundness is usually brought forward in criminal cases in order to escape punishment because if it is proved that a person is mentally ill then the accused is not held guilty. If such statement is raised then, the burden of proving mental unsoundness lies on the defense. The plea of insanity is taken:

1. In bar of trail – when the accused is insane and cannot plead.
2. In bar of conviction – here the accused who was insane when the crime was committed.
3. In bar of infliction of capital punishment – when a condemned prisoner is insane.

The present law on the defense of insanity is an adoption of McNaughten's rule and is contained in **Section 84 of IPC**. Section 84 of IPC states that "*nothing is an offense which is done by a person who, at the time of doing it, is, by reason of unsoundness of mind, incapable of knowing the nature of the act, or that he is doing what is either wrong or contrary to law*".[8]

Reviewing this section, it reveals that if a mentally ill person has to be exempted from criminal responsibility, it must be shown that:

1. Unsoundness of mind existed at the time of committing the crime.
2. The unsoundness of mind is of such degree that the accused person is unable to know the nature of the act or
3. If he knows the nature of act, he is unable to understand what he is doing is either wrong or contrary to the law.
   - Thus, a person can be exempted from criminal responsibility if his intellectual (cognitive) functions have been affected by unsoundness of mind.
   - The idiots, imbeciles and persons who are deprived of all understanding are not responsible for criminal offenses and do not present any difficulty in the Court of law. Difficulty, however, arises in those

cases where person labors under a partial delusion and are otherwise quite normal or sane.[9]

Doctrine of Diminished Responsibility or Partial Responsibility

- It provides that though a person may not be insane, in the common meaning of the word, his responsibility for his criminal actions may have been reduced by some mental impairment, albeit temporary.[10] It is argued that McNaughten rule has offered right-wrong test. If a person wants exemption from his criminal act on grounds of insanity, it must be clearly proved that his cognitive faculties have been affected by unsoundness of mind. Moreover, the unsoundness of mind is of such degree or nature that he is unable to understand the nature or quality of his act or was unable to understand what he was doing was wrong.
- The McNaughten rule has been criticized with an argument that some forms of mental illness affect person's volition or power to act, or there are other disorders such as impulse, neurosis or personality disorder without impairing his cognitive functioning. The McNaughten rule laid stress only on the cognitive faculties of a person and did not take notice of impairment of emotional or volitional factors. It was suggested that though such persons are quite responsible for their acts but should be considered partially responsible for their acts owing to such form of mental illness and these persons should receive less punishment.

Other Conditions[11]

Criminal responsibilities of an insane in some special circumstances are considered below. There are certain conditions, which are ambiguous and cause difficulty to medical person or the investigating officer. These conditions deserve greater attention and the doctors should be cautious while dealing with such cases.

1. Somnambulism – is a condition in which a person walks about in his sleep and therefore also called as sleepwalking. The person is not held responsible for any unlawful act committed during sleepwalking state.
2. Somnolentia (semi-somnolence) – is a condition midway between sleep and wakefulness. The person is not held responsible for any unlawful act committed during Somnolentia state.
3. Hypnotism (mesmerism) – is a condition where a trance or sleep like state is induced by a process of suggestion. A hypnotized person may do acts as per orders given by hypnotizer. After wearing of hypnotism, the person does not remember the acts done by him. Hypnotism cannot be pleaded as defense in criminal acts. Both parties i.e. the hypnotizer and hypnotic person are held guilty.
4. Drunkenness – If a person voluntarily consumes alcohol or an intoxicating drink with knowledge or intent and commits crime under the influence of drink then the person is held responsible for his act (Section 86 of IPC). However, if any intoxicant was administered to a person without his knowledge or against his will then the person is not held responsible for his act (Section 85 of IPC).

REFERENCES

1. The Mental Health Act, 1987. Vide S.O. 43(E), dated 11th January 1993, published in Gazette of India.
2. World Health Organization International Classification of Diseases, 10th edn. revised (mental disorders), Geneva.
3. Ahuja N. In: A Short Textbook of Psychiatry, 5th edn. 2004. Jaypee Brothers Medical Publishers (P) Ltd., New Delhi.
4. Hamilton M. In: Fish's Clinical Psychopathology, 2nd edn. 1994. Varghese Publishing House, Bombay.
5. World Health Organization International Classification of Diseases, 9th edn. (Mental Disorders), Geneva.
6. Tirpude BH, Nishat SA, Chaudhary BL. Psychiatry and Civil law. Medicolegal Update 2006; 6: 99-104.
7. Rastogi P. Civil responsibilities of mentally ill. J Indian Acad Forensic Med 2007; 29:7-9.
8. Chandrachud YV, Manohar VR (Ed), Ratanlal Dhirajlal, The Indian Penal Code, 28th edn. 2002. Wadhwa Company, Nagpur.
9. Franklin CA. Insanity and its medicolegal aspects. In Modi's Medical Jurisprudence and Toxicology, 21st edn. 1988. Tripathi Private Ltd., Bombay. 448-500.
10. Knight B. Legal Aspects of Mental Disorders. In: Legal Aspects of Medical Practice, 5th edn. 1992. Churchill Livingstone, Edinburgh. 339-46.
11. Pillay VV. Forensic Psychiatry. In: Textbook of Forensic Medicine and Toxicology, 14th edn. 2004. Paras Publishing, Hyderabad. 306-19.

CHAPTER 30

Trace Evidences

Getting caught is the mother of invention.

- Robert Byrne

BLOOD AND BLOODSTAINS

The normal total circulating blood volume is about 8 percent of the body weight (5600 ml in a 70 kg man) and about 55 percent of this volume is plasma.[1]

Medicolegal Importance

Civil Cases

1. Disputed paternity/maternity
2. Divorce and nullity of marriage

Criminal Cases

1. Identification of victim
2. Identification of offender, offending site, offending weapon, etc.

Examination of Blood/Bloodstains

Examination of blood/bloodstains consist of following steps:

1. Is it bloodstain?
2. If blood, whether human or animal? (What is species?)
3. If human, then:
   - Age of stain
   - Sex
   - Source
   - Antemortem/postmortem
   - Blood group
   - Distribution of pattern of bloodstains

A. Blood/BloodStain or Not

Bloodstains may resemble rust stains or pan stains. Therefore it is essential to determine whether the given sample is blood or not. Identification of blood in stain is based on presence of

1. Blood cells — RBCs, WBCs, platelets
2. Hemoglobin and its derivatives
3. Serum proteins

It is done by screening and confirmatory tests

Screening Tests

Screening tests are based upon the principle of presence of enzyme peroxidase in red blood cells. Such reagents are used in these tests so that action of peroxidase is demonstrated with change in the color of reagents, so that it could be said whether given sample is blood or not. Following are chemical screening tests. These tests are summarized in Table 30.1.

1. Benzedine test
2. Phenophthalein test (Kastle-Meyer test)
3. Leucomalachite green test
4. Orthotolidine test (Kohn & O'Kelly test)
5. Luminal test

Advantages of Screening Test

1. Screening tests are sensitive tests
2. Less time is required and are economical
3. If screening tests are negative, then no need to proceed for confirmatory tests.

Table 30.1: Screening test for blood

Test	*Reagent used*	*Result*
Benzedine	- Benzedine solution - Hydrogen peroxide	Blue color
Phenophthalein	- Alkaline phenophthalein - Hydrogen peroxide	Pink color
Leucomalachite green	- Stock solution of Leucomalachite green + glacial acetic acid + distilled water	Bright green
Orthotolidine	- Hydrogen peroxide - 4% Orthotolidine in ethyl alcohol + glacial acetic acid + distilled water - Hydrogen peroxide	Blue color

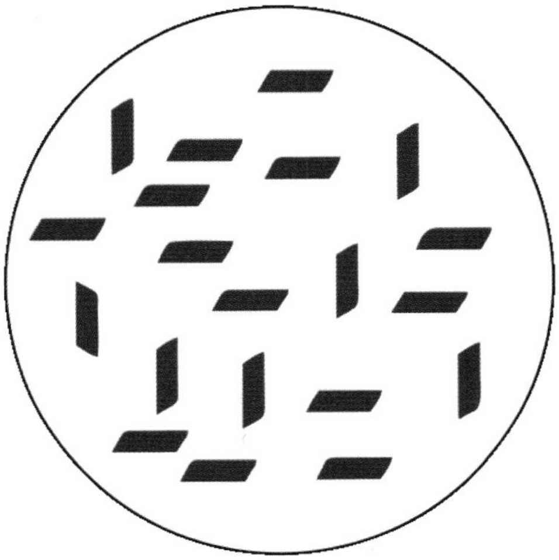

FIG. 30.1: Microphotograph showing hemin crystals

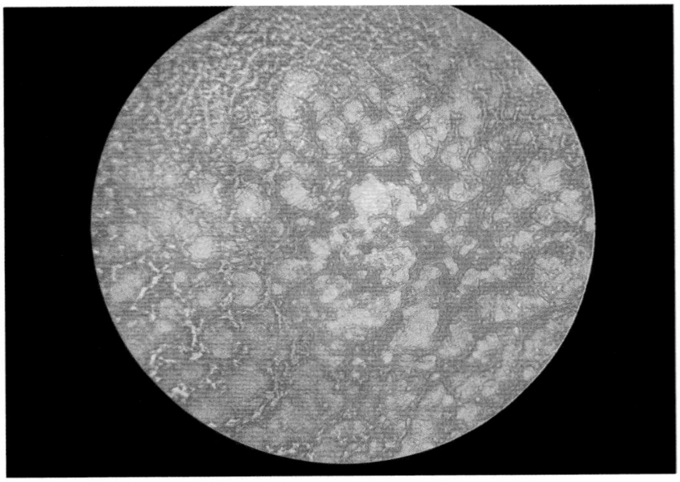

FIG. 30.2: Microphotograph showing hemochromagen crystals

Disadvantages

1. These are only screening tests and are not confirmatory
2. Tests can be positive with any organic substance, which contains peroxidase enzyme example sputum, pus, body fluid, green vegetable, apple, potato, onion, pan etc. So false positive results may be obtained.
3. Benzedine is known carcinogen agent.

Confirmatory Tests

These are:

1. Crystal tests, e.g. Teichmann test, Takayama test
2. Microscopic examination
3. Spectroscopic examination
4. Electrophoresis
5. Chromatography

Crystal Tests

- Teichmann test (Hemin crystal test): stain extract and few crystals of sodium chloride are taken and heated with glacial acetic acid. If stain happened to be blood, dark brown rhomboid shaped crystals will be formed as visible under microscope (Fig. 30.1).
- Takayama test (Hemochromogen crystal test): when blood-stain extract is heated with Takayama reagent (Pyridin + NaOH + glucose & distilled water), pink feathery crystals will be visible under microscope (Fig. 30.2).

Microscopic Examination

Microscopic examination can be done by wet film or stained smears with Leishman's stain. Presence of intact red blood cells confirmed presence of blood (Fig. 30.3). The morphology of RBCs are noted as follows:

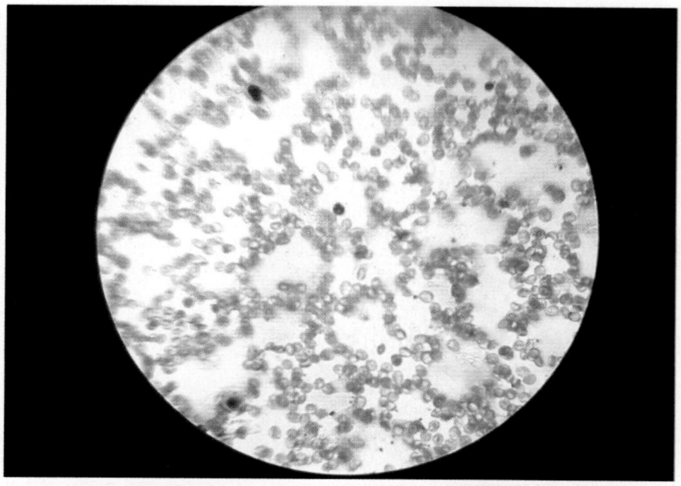

FIG. 30.3: Microphotograph showing blood film with human RBCs (Leishman's stain X45)

Human — RBCs are circular, biconcave, non-nucleated cells with a diameter of 7.2 μ.

All mammalians RBCs are circular, biconcave and non-nucleated cells except that of camels. In camel, the RBCs are oval, biconvex and non-nucleated.

In birds, fish, amphibians and reptiles, RBCs are oval, biconvex and nucleated cells.

Spectroscopic Examination

Hemoglobin and its derivatives show characteristic bands of absorption at specific wavelength. Presence of two or more bands in the Spectroscopic examination confirms the presence of blood in the given stain (Fig. 30.4).

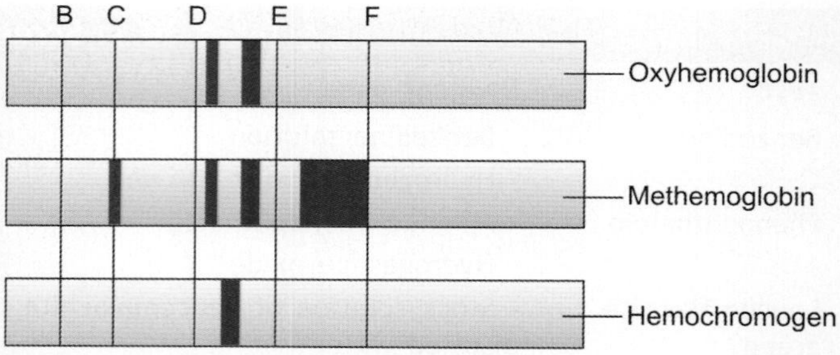

FIG. 30.4: Spectroscopic examination of hemoglobin and its derivatives

B. Identification of Species Origin

Identification of species origin can be done by:

1. Microscopic examination
2. Iso-enzyme method
3. Serological examination: consist of:
   - Precipitation test
   - Gel diffusion
   - Double diffusion in agar gel
   - Precipitation – electrophoresis

C. Identification of Blood Group

Various types of blood groups are noted and are:

1. ABO group system
2. Rh system
3. MNSs system
4. Kell system
5. Duffy system
6. Lutheran system
7. P system
8. Bombay blood group

Blood group from blood/stains can be determined by following methods:[2]

1. Absorption-elution technique
2. Absorption-inhibition method
3. Mixed agglutination test

D. Age of Bloodstain

Age of a bloodstain can be known by:

1. Change in color, i.e. gross examination: fresh stains appear red and sticky. As age advances, it turns brown due to oxidation of hemoglobin to methemoglobin.
2. Color changes measured on colorimeter or spectrophotometer
3. Immunoelectrophoressis can be used to determine the age of bloodstains. There is gradual disappearance of beta-globulins and gamma-globulins with increase in the age of blood stains.[3]

E. Identification of Sex

Sex from bloodstains can be identified by

1. Leishman stained blood films — for presence of Davidson body (Fig. 30.5)
2. Demonstration of Y chromosome on fluorescence microscopy
3. DNA analysis

F. Source of Blood

Source of blood refers to the origin of blood from body part/parts. The various source of blood are mentioned in Table 30.2.

G. Antemortem or Postmortem Blood/Stain

- Antemortem bleed causes coagulation where blood is partly solidified with separation of serum. The clot can be taken *en masse* from the spot and stained area after removal of the clot usually retains the impression of fibrinous network owing to the process of clot formation.[7]
- Rapid assay for D-dimer using monoclonal antibody coated-latex particles is useful for discriminating between postmortem and antemortem blood in bloodstains.[8]

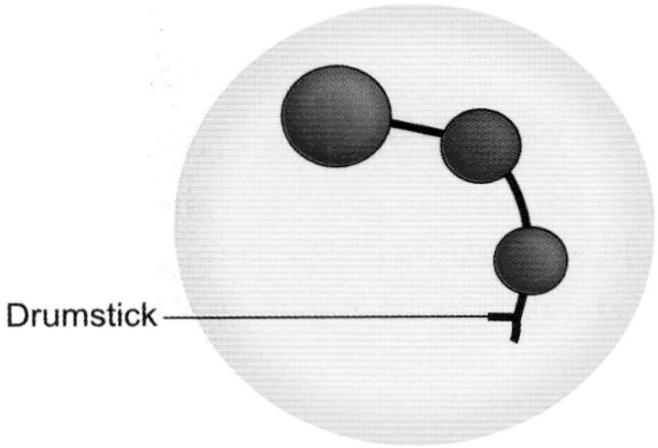

FIG. 30.5: Davidson body

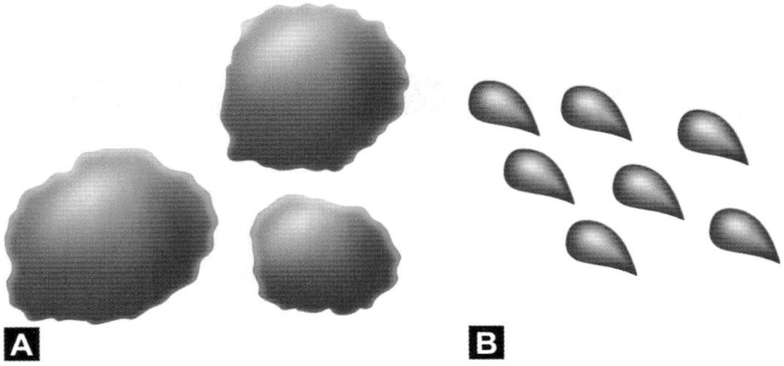

FIGS 30.6A and B: Source of blood. **A:** Venous blood; **B:** Arterial blood, jet like

Table 30.2: Source of blood and their features

Source of blood	*Features*
Fetal blood	- Presence of fetal hemoglobin. - Electrophoresis - demonstration of HbF or α-fetoprotein - ELISA for determination of α-fetoprotein[4]
Arterial blood	- Bright red - Copious loss - Shows spurting or jet like ejection due to high pressure and velocity (Fig. 30.6)
Venous blood	- Dark red - Oozes gradually with no evidence of spurting (Fig. 30.6)
Gastric bleed or hematemesis	- Altered color blood (chocolate) due to conversion of blood into acid hematin by gastric hydrochloric acid - Acidic in reaction
Nasal bleed	Blood mixed with nasal mucosal cells, mucus or hairs
Hemoptysis	- Bright red color blood (due to oxygenation of blood in lung) and frothy (due to churning effect with the inspired and expired air) - Alkaline in reaction
Menstrual blood	- Do not clot (absence of fibrin) - Acidic in reaction (lactic acid of vagina) - Dark colored fluid blood with foul smell - Microscopic examination reveals presence of vaginal epithelial cells, endometrial debris and at times monilia parasite
Abortion/pregnancy/delivery[5,6]	- Dark colored - Endometrial and placental debris with at times fetal remains - Detection of human chorionic gonadotropin by enzyme immunoassay. - Heat stable alkaline phosphatase (in later stage) - Presence of placental lactogen (15th week onwards)

H. Direction and Distribution Pattern of Blood Stains

The pattern or distribution of blood or stains at the scene of crime is often helpful regarding the idea about the height and direction of blood fall (Fig. 30.7). The pattern and distribution is given in Table 30.3

SEMEN

Semen contains sperms and the secretions of seminal vesicles, prostate, Cowper's glands and urethral glands. About 2.5 to 3.5 ml of semen is ejaculated and normally contains 100 million sperms per milliliter of semen. Human sperm move at a speed of about 3 mm/minute through the female genital tract and reach the uterine tube in about 30 to 60 minutes after sexual intercourse.

Composition: Mentioned in Table 30.4

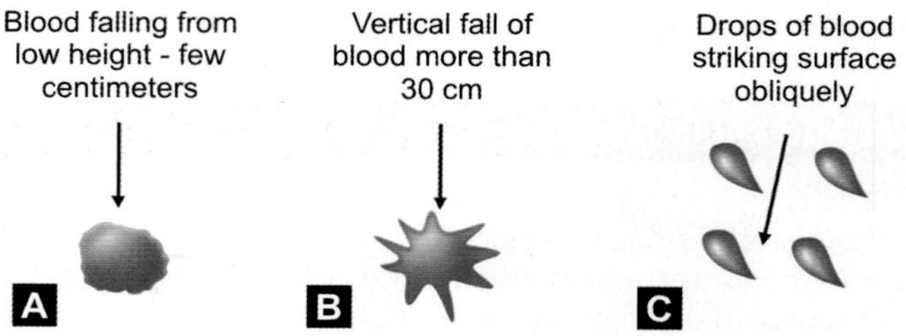

FIGS 30.7A to C: Pattern of bloodstains. **A:** Round bloodstain suggestive of falling from low height, **B:** Stain with prickly edges and **C:** Drops striking surface obliquely producing spear like shape with pointed ends indicate direction

Table 30.3: Pattern of bloodstains at scene of crime

Pattern of fall	*Features*
Blood falling vertically from low height (few centimeters)	Round or circular drops with sharply delineated margin
Vertical fall above 30 cm	Circular blood drop with irregular margin (prickly edges), the projections become finer with increase in height of fall
Fall from an angle	Drops striking surface obliquely may produce spear like shape or exclamation mark like appearance. The pointed end indicates the direction of motion.

Examination of Semen/Seminal Stains

Identification of seminal stains is useful in investigation of sex-related crimes.

Naked Eye Examination

- A dry seminal stain is grayish-white in color with irregular map like appearance. The stain area appears stiffened.
- Seminal stains may be mistaken for starch stains.

Ultraviolet Light Examination

- Seminal stains fluorescence bluish-white in color. Fluorescence is not specific for seminal stains because other stains like body fluid, saliva, pus cell, milk, some fiber whitener stains etc may also give fluorescence.
- Invisible or old stains can be visible under ultraviolet light.

Table 30.4: Composition of semen

Composition
Color - white, opalescent
pH - 7.35-7.50
Sperm - 100 million/ml
Components
- Fructose
- Phosphorylcholine
- Ergothioneine
- Ascorbic acid
- Flavins
- Prostaglandins
- Spermine
- Citric acid
- Phospholipids
- Fibrinolysin
- Zinc
- Acid phosphatase
- Phosphate
- Bicarbonate
- Hyaluronidase

Chemical Methods

Following are the chemical methods. These tests are summarized in Table 30.5

1. Acid phosphatase test
2. Zinc test
3. Florence test
4. Barberio's test

Other Tests

1. ELISA – for human semen identification and is based on biotinylated monoclonal antibody to seminal vesicle specific antigen.[9]
2. Prostate specific antigen (P 30) has been utilized to identify semen as a marker.[10]

Confirmatory Methods

Following are the confirmatory methods for semen:

1. Microscopic examination
2. Electrophoresis
3. Immunological methods

Microscopy

- The presence of at least one unbroken spermatozoon on microscopy is an absolute proof of semen. Sperms can be viewed on microscopy by
    1. Wet films (Fig. 30.10)

Table 30.5: Chemical methods for detection of semen

Test	Features
Barberio's test	Spermine present in semen reacts with picric acid to form yellowish needle shaped crystals of spermine picrate (fig 30.8)
Florence's test	Choline from semen reacts with Florence solution (potassium iodide + iodine + distilled water) to form brownish rhomboid shaped crystals of choline iodide (fig 30.9)
Zinc test	Presence high concentration of zinc (140 mg/ml) is used as marker for semen
Acid phosphatase	Acid phosphatase is found in high concentration in semen compared to other body fluids. Demonstration of acid phosphatase suggest stain/ secretions as semen[11]

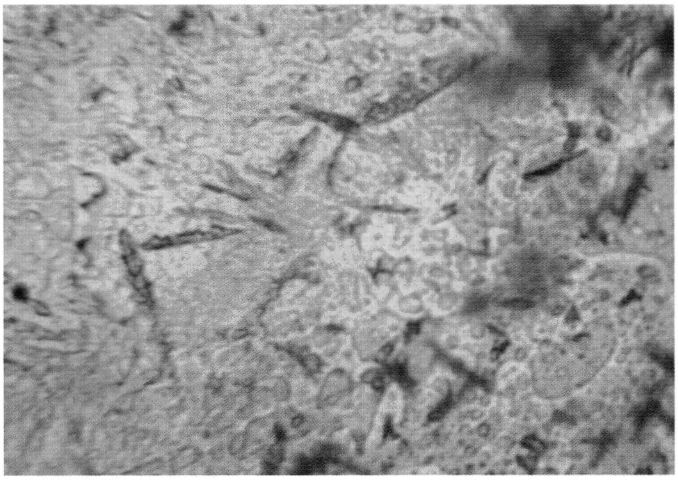

FIG. 30.8: Microphotograph showing spermine picrate crystals (Barberio's test)

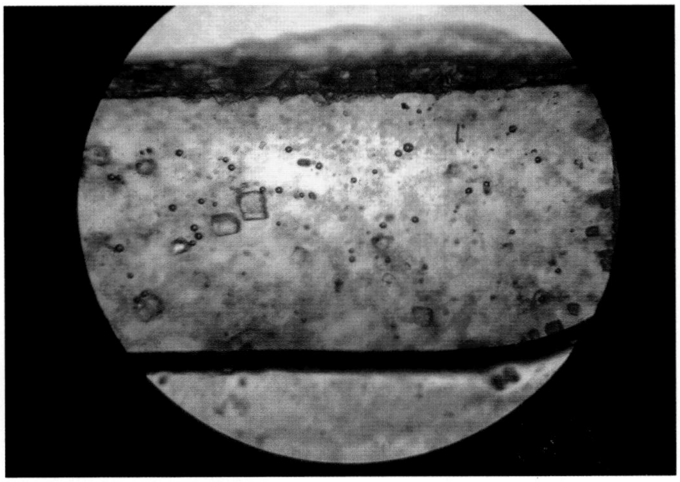

FIG. 30.9: Microphotograph showing choline iodide crystals (Florence's test)

    2. Smears stained with hematoxylin or Ziehl-Neelsen's stain (Fig. 30.11)
- Human spermatozoon is about 50 μ in length. The head is flat oval shaped and is approximately 4-6 μ in length, 2-6 μ in width and 1.5 μ in thickness (Fig. 30.12).
- Spermatozoon consist of head, neck and tail
- Morphology of spermatozoon is different even among closely related species in terms of form, size, and structure and thus species identification of seminal stains can be possible.[12]
- Spermatozoa may not be seen in semen in following conditions:

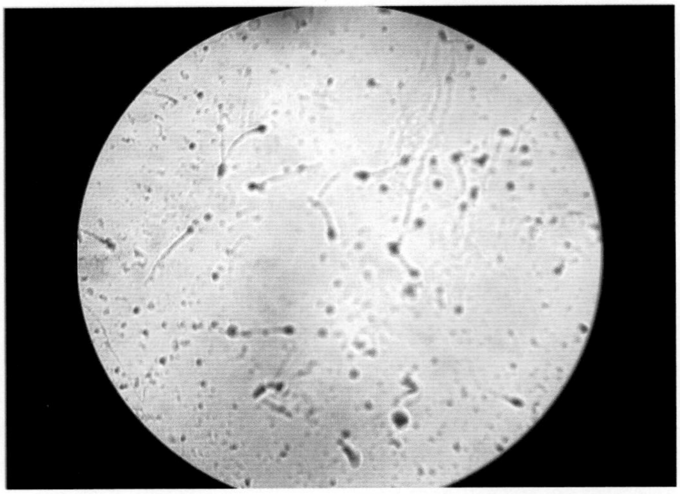

FIG. 30.10: Microphotograph showing sperms in wet films (X45)

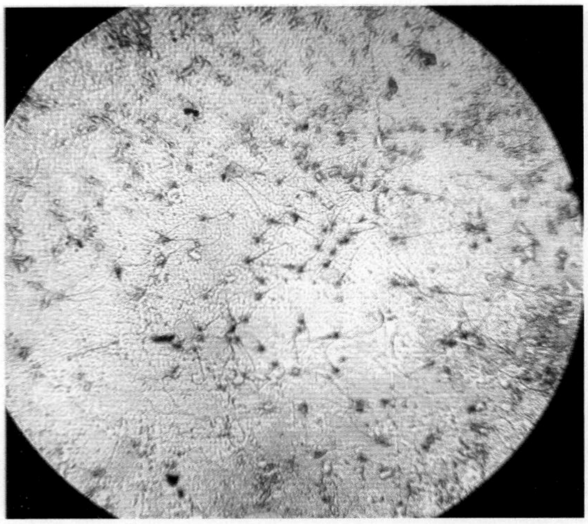

FIG. 30.11: Microphotograph showing sperms (H and E, X45)

1. Azoospermia
2. Vasectomy
3. Old age

Determination of species

Determination of species can be done by:

1. Microscopy
2. Precipitation reaction

Determination of blood group

ABO group, PGM, AK, HLA, LDH etc can be demonstrated in the semen of secretors

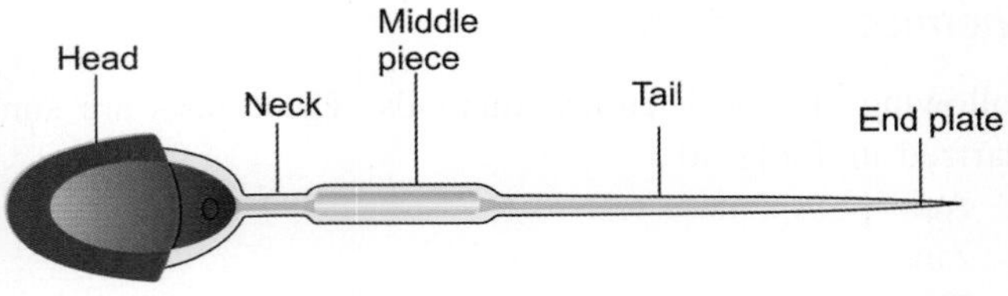

FIG. 30.12: Morphology of spermatozoon

Identification

Each sperm is an intricate motile cell, rich in DNA with a head that is made up mostly of chromosomal material.[1] DNA profiling (fingerprinting) can be done to identify the offender.

Sperms[13]

- At room temperature – full motility persist for about 3 hour, 50 percent are motile by 8 hour and 10 percent by 24 hour.
- In living persons – intact sperms may be found in vaginal washings up to 12 hours after coitus, while sperm heads can be detected up to 24 hours.[11]
- In dead persons
  1. Vagina – sperm head found up to 9 days in vagina
  2. Cervix – sperm head found up to 12 days in cervix
  3. Uterus – sperm head found up to 15 days
  4. Anus – sperms found up to 2 days
  5. Mouth/oral cavity – up to 9 hours

SALIVA

Saliva is a fluid secreted by salivary glands and contains:

- Digestive enzymes – lingual lipase, α-amylase
- Mucins
- Glycoprotein
- IgA
- Lysozyme
- Lactoferrin

Circumstances

Saliva stains may be found over:

1. Clothes
2. Unburnt portion of cigar, cigarettes or beedis
3. Body or private parts such as breast, face etc in sexual offenses.

Importance

1. Saliva is important evidential type of material in many cases such as sexual offenses — allegations of rape, oral sex, licking or biting.

2. Drugs of abuse can be tested from saliva
3. Blood groups can be determined in secretors
4. Sex of a person can be demonstrated from the buccal cells present in saliva
5. Invisible dried stains of saliva over skin can be detected by fluorescence spectroscopy. It is rapid, sensitive and non-destructive technique.[14]

Saliva Stains are Confirmed by

1. Presence of buccal squamous cell and/or
2. Amylase — detection of saliva is dependent on the presence of high level of enzyme amylase. However, other body fluids such as blood, nasal secretions, breast milk may contain amylase but in lower amounts.[15]

HAIRS AND FIBERS

Hairs resist decomposition for a longer period. Important information can be obtained from hairs.

A. Whether it is Hair or Fiber?

- At times hair may be confused with fibers. To differentiate between hair and fibers, the morphology of hair should be known. Hair is an appendage of skin and is composed of (Fig. 30.13):
  1. Root (or hair bulb) – lies in subcutaneous part and from root hair grows
  2. Shaft
  3. Tip
- Hair consists of three layers namely (Fig. 30.14):
  1. Cuticle – the outermost layer
  2. Cortex – lie between cuticle and medulla
  3. Medulla – innermost layer

B. Whether Hair is Human or Animal?

Differences are given in Table 30.6. Also see Figs 30.15 and 30.16

C. Hair Derived from What Body Part - Presented in Table 30.7

D. Sex from Hair

- Distribution of hair over body of an individual and features is helpful in identifying sex
- Length of hair – long in female, short in males
- Presence of Barr bodies in root sheath

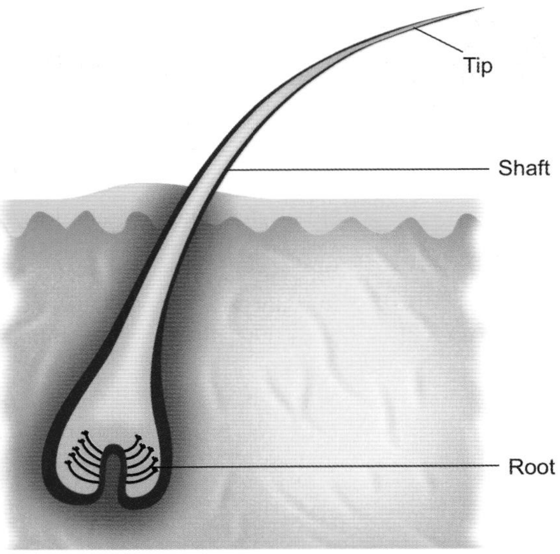

FIG. 30.13: Morphology of human hair

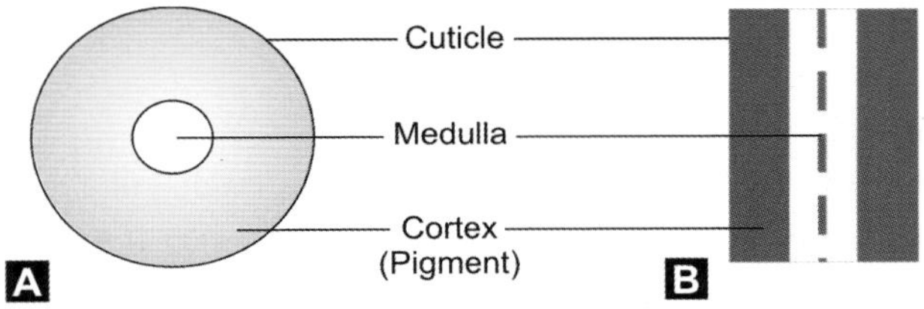

FIGS 30.14A and B: Human hair. **A:** Cross section, **B:** Vertical section

E. Age from Hair

Estimation of age can be done by:

- Knowing the type of hair viz. primordial, lanugo hair etc
- Loss of hair from scalp (baldness) with advancing age
- Graying of hairs
- Appearance of body hairs such as:
  1. Lanugo hairs suggest — hairs are from newborn infants
  2. Presence of pubic hair suggest — appearance of puberty
  3. Presence of axillary hairs suggest — appearance of puberty

F. Blood Group

Blood group from hair can be determined

G. Race

Race – refer chapter identification

Table 30.6: Difference between human and animal hair

Characteristics	*Human hair*	*Animal hair*
Feature	Fine and thin	Coarse and thick
Cuticle	Scales are small, flattened (Mortize type VII), serrated margin and surrounds the shaft	Scales are large, projecting, wavy or step-like and in various patterns
Cortex	Thick, 4-10 times as broad as medulla	Thin, rarely more than twice the breadth of medulla
Medulla	Varies considerably, may be narrow, absent or fragmented or discontinuous	Broad, always present, continuous and wider
Pigment distribution[5,16]	Towards periphery	Around the medulla
Medullary index	Below 0.3	Above 0.5
Shaft	Diameter ranges 50-150 μ	Diameter either less than 25 μ or more than 300 μ
Precipitation test	Specific for human	Specific for animal

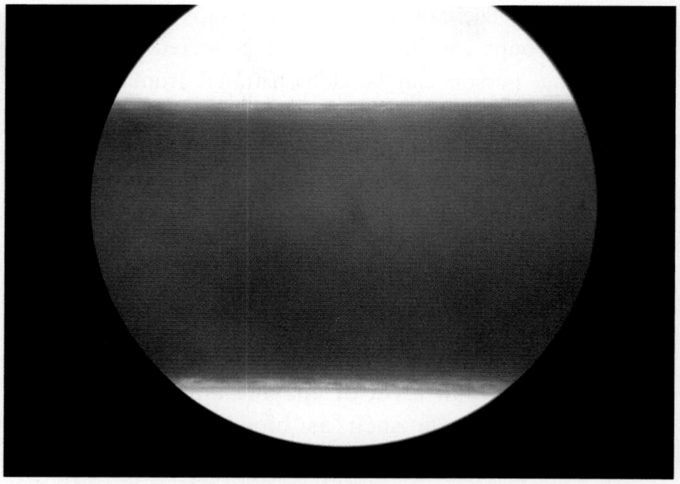

FIG. 30.15: Microphotograph showing human hair

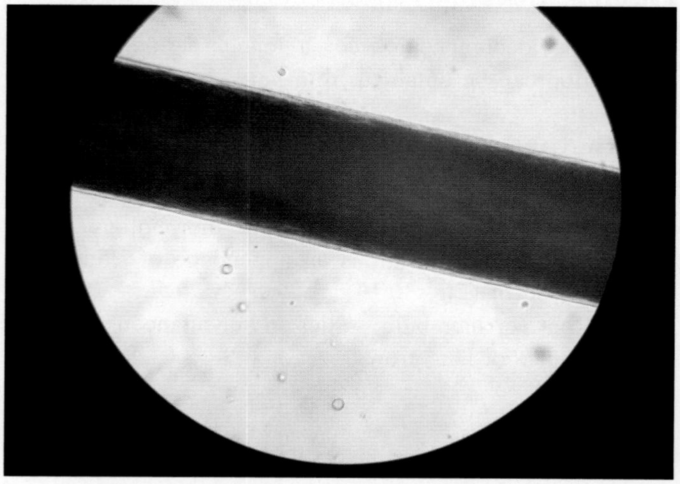

FIG. 30.16: Microphotograph showing animal (dog) hair

Table 30.7: Origin of hair from body part

Origin of hair	*Features*	*Tip*	*Cross-section*
Scalp	Long, slender	- Tapered tip in females - Cut or chopped in males	Circular/oval
Beard	Short, thick	Blunt or sharply cut	Triangular
Eyebrow/eyelash	Short, thick and sharp	Pointed	Circular
Chest	Short, stout	Fine	Circular
Axillary	Short, stout and curly	Round or frayed	Circular
Leg/arm	Fine, short and flexible	Fine	Circular
Pubic	Thick and curly	Round or frayed	Irregular
Nose	Stiff and thick	Pointed	Circular

H. Hair and Poisoning

Hair & poisoning – certain metallic poisons such as arsenic etc are deposited in hair. Chemical analysis of hair may reveals presence of poison

I. Hair and Dyeing

- Bleached hairs are brittle, dry and straw coloured
- If dyeing is done to hairs, dyeing is not uniform and roots are of different colour than the rest part of hair.

J. Hairs and Stains

Hairs and stains – vital information can be obtained from hair soiling or stains as

- Mud stains – place of incident, struggle
- Semen stains – sexual offense
- Blood stains – injury, etc
- Saliva stains – hanging, etc

K. Injury from Hairs

- Blunt force injury – crush injury to shaft with flattening and splitting
- Sharp weapon injury – clean cut surface
- Burns or firearms – singed hairs

L. Did Hair Fall Naturally or was it Forcibly Removed?

- In naturally fallen hairs, the root is distorted, atrophied and smooth. Root sheath is absent.
- In pulled hairs – hair bulbs are larger, irregular and root sheaths are ruptured

M. Morphology of Fibers

- Cotton – flattened and twisted fibers with long tubular cells (Fig. 30.17)
- Jute – smooth fibers
- Silk – long, clear threads without any cells
- Wool – outer layer of flattened cells and overlapping margins (Fig. 30.18)

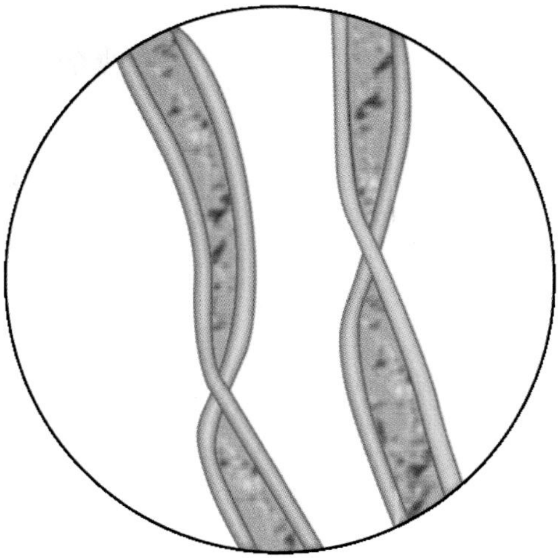

FIG. 30.17: Microphotograph showing cotton fibers

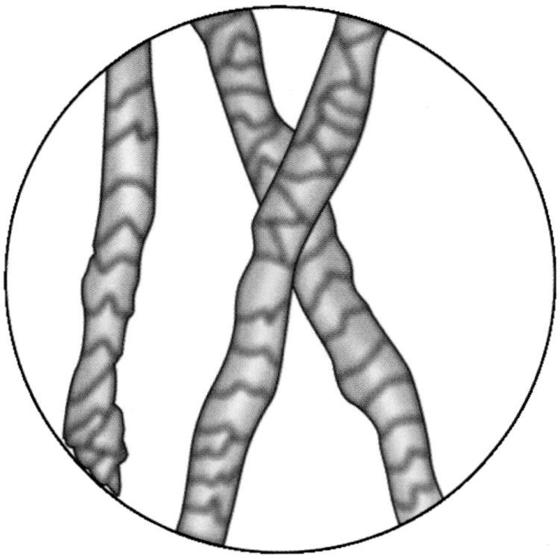

FIG. 30.18: Microphotograph showing wool fiber

REFERENCES

1. Ganong WF. In: Review of Medical Physiology, 19th edn. 1999. Prentice-Hall International, London.
2. Nandy A. Identification from trace substances and their other evidential values. In: Principles of Forensic Medicine, 2nd edn. 2005. New Central Book Agency (P) Ltd., Calcutta. 112 – 32.
3. Rajamannar K. Determination of the age of blood stains using Immunoelectrophoressis. J Forensic Sci 1977; 22: 159 – 64.
4. Katsumata Y, Sato M, Tamaki K, Tsutsumi H, Yada S, Oya M. Identification of fetal blood stains by ELISA for human alpha-fetoprotein. J Forensic Sci 1985; 30: 1210 – 5.
5. Pillay VV. In: Textbook of Forensic Medicine and Toxicology, 14th edn. 2004. Paras Publishing, Hyderabad.
6. Vallejo G. Human chorionic gonadotropin detection by means of enzyme immunoassay: A useful method in forensic pregnancy diagnosis in blood stains. J Forensic Sci 1990; 35: 293 – 300.
7. Vij K. Identification. In: Textbook of Forensic Medicine and Toxicology, 3rd edn. 2005. Reed Elsevier India Pvt. Limited, New Delhi. 54 – 104.
8. Sakurada K, Sakai I, Sekiguchi K, Shiraishi T, Ikegaye H, Yoshida K. Usefulness of a latex agglutination assay for FDP D-dimer to demonstrate the presence of postmortem blood. Int J Legal Med 2005; 119: 167 – 71.

9. Herr JC, Woodward MP. An enzyme-linked immunosorbent assay (ELISA) for human semen identification based on a biotinylated monoclonal antibody to a seminal vesicle-specific antigen. J Forensic Sci 1987; 32: 346 – 56.
10. Sensabaugh GF. Isolation & characterization of a semen specific protein from human seminal plasma: a potential marker for semen identification. J Forensic Sci 1978; 23: 106 – 15.
11. Dongre AP, Shrigiriwar MB. Detection of spermatozoa and acid phosphatase level in vaginal fluid. J Forensic Med Toxicol 2000; 17: 1 – 5.
12. Mathiharan K, Patnaik AK. Examination of biological stains and hairs. In: Modi's Medical Jurisprudence and Toxicology, 23rd edn. 2005. LexisNexis Butterworths, New Delhi. 471 – 560.
13. Reddy KSN. Sexual offences. In: The Essentials of Forensic Medicine and Toxicology, 22nd edn. 2003. K. Suguna Devi, Hyderabad. 326 – 44.
14. Soukos NS, Crowley K, Bamberg MP, Gillies R, Doukas AG, Evans R, Kollias N. A rapid method to detect dried saliva stains swabbed from human skin using fluorescence spectroscopy. Forensic Sci Int 2000; 114: 133 – 8.
15. Martin NC, Clayson NJ, Scrimger DG. The sensitivity and specificity of red-starch paper for the detection of saliva. J Forensic Sci Soc 2006; 46: 97 – 105.
16. Rao NG. Forensic identity. In: Textbook of Forensic Medicine and Toxicology, 1st edn. 2006. Jaypee Brothers Medical Publishers (P) Ltd., New Delhi. 77 – 114.

CHAPTER 31

Forensic Science Laboratory

If Justice goes astray, the people will stand about in helpless confusion.

- Confucius (Chinese Philosopher)

Forensic Science Laboratory

Forensic science laboratory (FSL) provides services for scientific examination and evaluation of evidences. Doctors providing medicolegal services have to submit the exhibits/evidences collected during medical examination to forensic science laboratory for analysis and evaluation of the exhibits. Therefore, it is necessary for the doctors that they should have some idea regarding the set-up, functioning and services provided by these laboratories.

Functions of FSL

1. To examine evidence material.
2. To help the investigating officer for scientific guidance in crime detection.
3. To help the investigation officer to collect evidences by visiting scene of crime.
4. To train the investigating officer for use of modern and sophisticated techniques in crime detection.

Set-up of FSL

FSL have following main divisions:[1]

1. Analytical toxicology division
2. Serology/Biology division
3. General analytical and Instrumentation division
4. Physics division
5. Ballistics division
6. Fingerprinting division
7. Document analysis division
8. Photography division
9. DNA profiling division
10. Polygraphy (lie-detector) division
11. Prohibition (Alcohol/narcotics analysis) division
12. Trace evidence division
13. Narcoanalysis division
14. Brain fingerprinting
15. Forensic acoustic-speaker identification
16. Cyber forensics

POLYGRAPHY

- Also called as mechanical lie detector
- It is a process by which a study of functioning of different body systems is studied to detect lies.

Principle

It is based on principle that if a person is telling lie, and if there is fear that the lie will be detected, the emotional fear results in stimulation of sympathetic nervous system that causes physiological changes and some of these changes can be recorded.

Polygraphy Process Uses and Record Following Parameters

1. Blood pressure
2. Pulse
3. Respiration
4. Galvanic skin reaction

Procedure

- Consent of person is taken prior to the procedure and the process is explained to the concerned person. The person has to answer the questions in "**Yes**" or "**No**" as answers. The questions will be of suggestive in nature.

- The person, on whom the test is to be performed, is asked to sit in a chair and instruments are attached to him. Arm cuff is placed for recording blood pressure and pulse. A belt is placed around the chest to record respiration and an electrode connection is attached to the tip of one side of index finger to record galvanic skin reaction. The response of person to question is recorded graphically on a single paper.
- Usually not more than 10 questions are asked to a person at any single setting. Three types of questions are asked as:
  1. Irrelevant questions: Having no relation with the incident.
  2. Relevant questions: Having relation with the incident
  3. Control questions.
- Amongst all responses, the response to change in respiration and galvanic skin reaction are assumed to be more reliable.

Following Persons are Unsuitable for the Test

1. Mentally ill person/unsound.
2. Over-reactive personality.
3. Drug addicts.
4. Persons suffering from and diseases of the respiratory and cardiovascular system.
5. Restless and non-cooperative.

Medicolegal Aspects of Polygraphy

1. It is established that classification of guilty can be made with 75 percent to 97 percent accuracy, but the rate of false positive is sufficiently high.[2] Thus, controversy continues regarding the accuracy of polygraph testing in detecting deception.[3]
2. Results of such tests are inadmissible in courts.
3. Due to high false-positive results, questions are raised regarding the efficacy of this test to use as the sole arbiter of guilt or innocence.

NARCOANALYSIS

- Narcoanalysis is a procedure of investigation of mental content of a person done after application of a light general anesthetic drugs.
- This investigative technique is based on the principle that at a point very close to unconsciousness, the subject would be mentally incapable of resistance to questioning, and incapable of inventing falsehood that he has used to conceal his guilt.
- It involves administration of light anesthetic agents or drugs intravenously
- Drugs commonly used are
  1. Thiopentone sodium (Sodium pentothal)
  2. Scopolamine hydrobromide
  3. Sodium secnol
  4. Benzodiazepines
- Adverse effects of Thiopentone sodium include laryngospasm; shivering and delirium may occur during recovery. It can precipitate acute intermittent porphyria in susceptible individuals.

Medicolegal Aspects of Narcoanalysis

- It is also known that if the subject has used/abused intoxicants and other narcotics, a degree of "cross-tolerance" could occur. Therefore in an attempt for analysis, wrong dose may be given to subject and put the subject in coma or may even cause death.[4]
- The procedure of narco-analysis and subsequent interrogation has raised serious ethical issues for involvement of medical professionals in the procedure. Many think that narco-analysis is a form of torture. Involvement of physicians in such procedure is nothing but abetting the torture and using the medical knowledge for inflicting torture. Therefore, the procedure of narco-analysis suffers from problem of torture. In addition to violating the laws related to torture, narco-analysis also violates the dignity of a person.[5]
- A doctor participating in narco-analysis is participating in torture. Code of medical ethics prescribed by Medical Council of India clearly mentions that the Physician shall not aid or abet torture nor shall he/she be a party to either infliction of mental or physical trauma.[6]
- It is said that doing Narcoanalysis violates the established principles of Article 20(3) of the Constitution of India. However, the Bombay High Court recently ruled that, subjecting six of the accused in multicrore rupee fake stamp paper case, to "certain physical tests involving minimal bodily harm" such as narco-analysis, lie detector tests and brain mapping, did not violate their constitutional rights specifically the protection against self-incrimination guaranteed by Article 20(3) of Constitution of India. The judicial sanction for these methods rest on the argument that protection of Article 20(3) does not apply at the investigative stage.[7]
- It is also stated that narco-analysis violates section 161(2) of CrPC which say that no person accused of any offense shall be compelled to be witness against himself.

BRAIN FINGERPRINTING

- Dr Lawrence A. Farwell has invented, developed, proven and patented the technique of Farwell brain fingerprinting.[8]
- Brain fingerprinting determines if specific information is present in the brain of criminal regarding the criminal act. It is like seeking fingerprints at the crime scene and thus the name brain fingerprinting.[9]
- Brain fingerprinting is an investigative technique to measure recognition of familiar stimuli by measuring electrical brain wave response to words, phrases or pictures that are presented on a computer screen.[10]
- Brain fingerprinting technology is based on the principle that there are brain wave responses. Brain fingerprinting measures brainwaves functioning to detect awareness of crime-relevant information in order to distinguish between guilty and innocent suspects.[11]
- It was discovered that P300, a larger and specific brain wave response, is elicited when the brain processes noteworthy information it recognizes. Dr Farwell named and patented it as MERMER® (memory and encoding related multifaceted electroencephalographic response).

REFERENCES

1. Manual published by Directorate of Forensic Science Laboratories, Home Dept., State of Maharashtra-Mumbai, 2007.
2. The American Medical Association Council on Scientific Affairs. Polygraph. Council on Scientific Affairs. JAMA 1986; 256: 1172-5.
3. McMahon M. Polygraph testing for deception in Australia: effective aid to crime investigation and adjudication? J Law Med 2003; 11: 24-47.
4. Jagadeesh N. Narcoanalysis leads to more questions than answers. Indian J Med Ethics 2007; 4: 9.
5. Jesani A. Medical professionals and interrogation: lies about finding the truth. Indian J Med Ethics 2006; 3: available from www.ijme.in/issue144.html.
6. Indian Medical Council (Professional conduct, etiquette and ethics) Regulations, 2002. Gazette of India dated 06.04.2002, part III, section 4.
7. Kala AK. Of ethically compromising positions and blatant lies about 'truth serum'. Indian J Psychiatry 2007; 49: 6–9.
8. Available from http:/www.forensic-evidence.com
9. Farwell LA. Available from http:/www.brainwavescience.com
10. Available from http:/www.en.wikipedia.org/wiki/brain_fingerprinting
11. Dikson K, McMahon M. Will the law comes running? The potential role of "brain fingerprinting" in crime investigation and adjudication in Australia. J Law Med 2005; 136: 204-22.

Section B
Toxicology

CHAPTER 32

Toxicology: General Considerations

All substances are poison; there is none, which is not a poison. The right dose differentiates a poison and a remedy.

— Paracelsus (1493-1545)

Toxicology

- The word toxicology is derived from Greek and means "an arrow" which indicates its primitive use for smearing tips of arrows for slaying purpose.[1]
- Toxicology is defined as *a branch of medical science, which deals with poison in relation to their sources, properties, action, the symptoms which they produce, fatal dose, toxicity, diagnosis, treatment and autopsy features*.

Classification

Toxicology is divided into four main categories:
1. Forensic toxicology
2. Clinical toxicology
3. Industrial toxicology
4. Environmental toxicology

- Forensic toxicology: It is that *branch of toxicology, which deals with the medical and legal aspects of the harmful effects of chemicals on humans*.[2] It combines fundamental toxicological principles with analytical toxicology.
- Clinical toxicology: *It deals with causation, diagnosis and management of poisoning in humans*.

Poison

- Definition: *Any substance if, taken in any account, by any route, produces harmful effect (i.e. disease, deformity or death, the 3 D's) over the body then it will be called as poison*.
- The word poison is derived from the Latin *potus* means to drink. The term *potus* became *potio* and then poison in old French, a drink that could harm or kill.[3]

Drug

Drug is any substance or product that is used or is intended to be used to modify or explore physiological systems or pathological states for the benefit of the recipient (WHO).

Routes of Administration

A. *Local*

1. Dermal
2. Ocular
3. Nasal
4. Vaginal
5. Rectal
6. Urethral

B. *Systemic*

1. Oral
2. Sublingual
3. Rectal
4. Cutaneous
5. Inhalational
6. Nasal
7. Parenteral

Routes of Elimination

1. Urine
2. Faces
3. Exhaled air
4. Saliva
5. Sweat
6. Milk
7. Bile

Action of Poison

A poison may have:

1. Local action: A poison may act at the site of application, for example, application of concentrated sulfuric acid to face produces chemical burns.
2. Systemic action: A poison may act over a given system when taken, for example, ingestion of aconite causes cardiac toxicity and death.
3. Combined action: Some poison have local action and similarly they act as a systemic poison, for example, carbolic acid when applied to skin it act locally as corrosive and when ingested acts as systemic poison.

Factors Affecting the Action of Poison

1. Route of administration
2. Age
3. Idiosyncrasy
4. Dose
5. Concentration of poison
6. Chemical state of poison
7. Physical state of poison
8. Area of application
9. Tolerance

Toxicity Rating of Poison

The **toxicity rating** has been evolved to appraise the nature of poison to the physician treating the patients. The higher the toxicity rating for a given poison the greater would be its potency. The toxicity rating is based on the mortality and is applicable for acute exposure of a single substance. The toxicity rating is given in Table 32.1.

CLASSIFICATION

A. Based on Nature of Poison

I. Corrosive
   a. Strong acids
      – Mineral or inorganic acids, e.g. H_2SO_4, HCL
      – Organic acids, e.g. carbolic, acetic, oxalic acid
   b. Strong alkalis, e.g. sodium hydroxide
   c. Metals, e.g. mercuric chloride, ferric chloride.

II. Irritants
   a. Inorganic
      – Non-metal, e.g. phosphorus, iodine
      – Metal, e.g. arsenic, lead etc.
   b. Organic
      – Animal, e.g. snake, scorpion
      – Plant or vegetable, e.g. castor, calatropis etc.
   c. Mechanical, e.g. chopped hair, metal pieces etc.

III. Systemic
   a. Cerebral poisons
      – Somniferous
      – Inebriants
      – Stimulants
      – Deliriant
      – Depressant
      – Psychotropics
   b. Spinal poisons, e.g. strychnine
   c. Peripheral nerve poison, e.g. curare
   d. Cardiac poison or cardio-toxic, e.g. aconite
   e. Asphyxiants, e.g. carbon monoxide
   f. Nephrotoxic, e.g. mercury
   g. Hepatotoxic, e.g. phosphorus

IV. Miscellaneous, e.g. food poisoning

Table 32.1: Toxicity rating

Fatal dose	*Rating*
Less than 5 mg/kg	6 - super toxic
5 to 50 mg/kg	5 - extremely toxic
51 to 500 mg/kg	4 - very toxic
501 mg/kg to 5 gm/kg	3 - moderately toxic
5.1 gm/kg to 15 gm/kg	2 - slightly toxic
More than 15 gm/kg	1 - practically non-toxic

B. Based on Manner of Use

1. Homicidal poisons
2. Suicidal poisons
3. Accidental poisons
4. Abortifaciant poisons
5. Stupefying poisons
6. Cattle poisons
7. Arrow poisons
8. Use to fabricate injury or malingering
9. Use to cause injury
10. Use for torture

C. Based on Source of Poison

1. Domestic or house-hold poisons
2. Agricultural poisons
3. Environmental poisons
4. Industrial poisons
5. Food and drinks poisons
6. Drugs and medicines

DIAGNOSIS OF POISONING

A patient with consumption of poison may present as:
1. Fulminant poisoning
2. Acute poisoning
3. Subacute poisoning
4. Chronic poisoning

Diagnosis in Living

1. History
2. Symptoms
3. Signs
4. Laboratory examination.

History and Symptoms

- Sudden onset of vomiting/diarrhea/pain in abdomen
- Onset of symptoms to many persons who had taken food together
- History of consumption of poison or suspicious material
  1. Persistent vomiting and/or diarrhea with or without dehydration
  2. Pain in abdomen
  3. Altered sensorium/drowsiness/unconsciousness/coma
  4. Breathlessness, constriction in chest, choking sensation
  5. Convulsions
  6. Palpitations, arrhythmias, chest pain
  7. Hypothermia
  8. Paralysis

Table 32.2: Poisons having typical odour

Poison	*Smell*
Cyanide	Bitter almond like
Phosphorus	Garlicky
Arsenic	Garlicky
Selenium	Garlicky
Thallium	Garlicky
Aluminum phosphide	Garlicky
Phenol	Phenolic
Organophosphorus	Kerosene like/garlicky
Conium	Mousy
Marijuana/Ganja	Burnt rope like
Hydrogen sulfide	Rotten egg like
Zinc phosphide	Fishy
Carbon monoxide	Coal gas
Nitrobenzene	Shoe polish
Chloroform	Acetone like
Camphor	Moth balls
Acetic acid	Vinegar

Clinical Examination

General Examination

- Peculiar odour (causes given in Table 32.2)
- Taste (causes given in Table 32.3)
- Temperature-hypothermia (Table 32.4)/hyperthermia (Table 32.5)
- Ocular changes (causes given in Table 32.6)
- Oral manifestations (causes given in Table 32.7)

Central Nervous System

- Grading of coma (given in Table 32.8)
- Patient may be drowsy, deliriant or in coma (Causes given in Table 32.9)
- Convulsions (causes given in Table 32.10)
- Tremors (Table 32.11)
- Neuropathy (Table 32.12)
- Movement disorder (Table 32.13)
- Paralysis (Table 32.14)
- Headache (Table 32.15)
- Paresthesia (Table 32.16)
- Gait (Table 32.17)
- Delirium (Table 32.18)
- Encephalopathy (Table 32.19)
- Tingling (Table 32.20)
- Ataxia (Table 32.21)
- Psychosis (Table 32.22)

Table 32.3: Taste of poisons

Taste	*Poison*
Bitter	Datura, strychnine
Burning	Acids
Acrid	Calotropis
Sweet	Aconite
Sour	Oxalic acid
Metallic	Copper, Iodine
Sweet burning	Carbolic acid
Caustic	Alkali

Table 32.4: Poisons producing hypothermia

Poison
Opiates
Alcohol
Carbon monoxide
Barbiturate

Table 32.5: Poisons producing hyperthermia

Poison
Strychnine
Cocaine
Datura
Curare

Table 32.6: Poisons producing ocular changes

Ocular change	*Poison*
Miosis	Opium
	Morphine
	Organophosphorus
	Barbiturates
Mydriasis	Alcohol
	Datura
	Carbon monoxide
	Cocaine
Nystagmus	Alcohol
	Thallium
Strabismus	Botulinus toxin
	Thallium
Hippus	Aconite
Diplopia	Opium
	Cannabis
	Alcohol
Photophobia	Mercury
	Quinine
Blurred vision	Alcohol
	Datura
	Aconite
	Nicotine
Lacrimation	Ammonia
	Chili powder
	Irritant gases
Ophthalmoplegia	Thallium
Altered colour perception	Carbon monoxide
	Cannabis
	LSD
	Digitalis
Corneal deposit	Amodiaquine
Xanthopsia	Aconite
Ptosis	Thallium
	Gelsemium
	Botulinus toxin
Optic neuritis/retrobulbar neuritis	Methanol
	Quinine
	Thallium
Conjunctivitis	Copper dust
	Acid fumes
	Marijuana
Deposition in lens	Mercury
Icterus/jaundice	Phosphorus
	Arsenic
	Bismuth
	Carbon tetrachloride
	Copper
Corneal edema	Chloroquine
	Irritant poisons
	Metal/acid fumes
Pitting of optic disc	Lead
Retinopathy	Chloroquine
	Phenothiazines
Fixation of pupils	Anesthetic agents
	Reserpine
	Rauwolfa alkaloids
Complete or partial blindness	Methyl alcohol
	Arsenic
	Chloroquine
	Ergot
	Lead
	Mercury
	Tobacco
Corneal stippling	Chloroquine
Retinal stippling	Lead
	Chloroquine
	Phenothiazines
	Tranquilizers
Papilledema	Lead
	Vitamin A toxicity
Retinal hemorrhage	Carbon monoxide
	Lead

Cont...........

Table 32.7: Poisons producing oral changes

Oral change	*Poison*
Salivation (Sialorrhea)	Organophosphates
	Mineral acids
	Alcohol
	Aconite
	Croton
	Chili seeds
	Tobacco
	Copper
	Scorpion
Dryness of mouth	Datura
	Ephedrine
	Scopolamine
	Antihistaminics
	Antidepressants
Xerostomia	Narcotics
	Tricyclic antidepressants
Gingival hyperplasia	Phenytoin
	Sodium valporate
Stomatitis	Cyanide
	Calatropis
	Iodine
Parotitis	Iodine
Glossitis	Cyanide
Discoloration of teeth	Fluoride
	Tetracycline

Table 32.8: Glasgow coma scale

Features observed	*Score*
Eye opening	
a. Spontaneous	4
b. To speech	3
c. To pain	2
d. Nil	1
Best motor response	
a. Obeys	6
b. Localizes	5
c. Flexes (withdrawal)	4
d. Flexes abnormally (decorticate rigidity)	3
e. Extends (decerebrate rigidity)	2
f. Nil	1
Best verbal response	
a. Oriented	5
b. Confused conversation	4
c. Inappropriate words	3
d. Incomprehensible sounds	2
e. Nil	1

Table 32.9: Causes of coma

Poison
Alcohol
Carbon monoxide
Opium
Organophosphates

Table 32.10: Causes of convulsions

Poison
Cocaine
Strychnine
Opium
Alcohol
Calotropis

Table 32.11: Causes of tremors

Poison
Alcohol
Mercury
Manganese
Cocaine
Arsenic

Table 32.12: Causes of neuropathy/neuritis

Poison
Alcohol
Lead
Organophosphate
Methanol

Table 32.13: Causes of movement disorder

Poison	*Disorder*
Strychnine	Rigidity
	Opsithonus
	Trismus
Carbon monoxide	Parkinsonsism
Organophosphates	Fasciculation

Table 32.14: Causes of paralysis
Poison
Arsenic
Poison hemlock
Curare
Lead
Manganese

Table 32.15: Toxic causes of headache
Poison
Alcohol
Aniline
Cyanide
Tobacco
Nitrite

Table 32.16: Causes of paresthesia
Poison
Aconite
Alcohol
Arsenic
Cannabis
Poison hemlock
Ergot
Lead
Thallium

Table 32.17: Poisons causing various types of gait

Gait	***Poison***
Staggering or rolling	Alcohol
	Barbiturate
	CNS depressants
	Phenothiazines
Stiff gait	Tranquilizers
	Reserpine

Table 32.18: Causes of delirium
Poison
Calotropis
Datura
Cannabis
Cocaine

Table 32.19: Toxic causes of encephalopathy
Poison
Arsenic
Lead
Thallium

Table 32.20: Toxic causes of tingling
Poison
Aconite
Yellow oleander
Cyanide
Phenol

Table 32.21: Toxic causes of ataxia
Poison
Alcohol
Carbon monoxide
Lead
Lithium
Narcotics
Thallium

Table 32.22: Causes of psychosis
Poison
Cannabis
Datura
Cocaine
Alcohol

Table 32.23: Toxic causes of tachycardia
Poison
Carbon monoxide
Cannabis
Amphetamine
Atropine (Datura)
Poison hemlock
Nitrites

Cardiovascular System

- Pulse-tachycardia/bradycardia (causes given in Tables 32.23 and 32.24)
- Blood pressure: hypotension/hypertension (causes given in Tables 32.25 and 32.26)
- Arrhythmias (causes given in Table 32.27)
- Circulatory collapse (Table 32.28)
- Vasoconstriction (Table 32.29)

Table 32.24: Toxic causes of bradycardia
Poison
Organophosphates
Aconite
Barium
Digitalis
Neostigmine
Pilocarpine

Table 32.25: Causes of hypotension and shock
Poison
Aconite
Arsenic
Nitrites
Organophosphates
Snake bite
Iron

Table 32.26: Toxic causes of hypertension
Poison
Amphetamine
Zinc phosphide
Ephedrine
Chlorthiazides

Table 32.27: Toxic causes of arrhythmia/cardiac irregularities
Poison
Carbamates
Aconite
Oleander
Digitalis
Zinc phosphide
Lithium

Table 32.28: Causes of circulatory collapse
Poison
Aconite
Barbiturate
Carbon monoxide
Cocaine
Corrosive poison
Lead
Mercury
Nicotine
Nitrites

Respiratory System

Dyspnoea (causes given in Table 32.30)
Pulmonary edema (causes given in Table 32.31)
Respiratory distress (causes given in Table 32.32)
Cough (Table 32.33)
Laryngospasm (Table 32.34)
Bronchitis (Table 32.35)
Emphysema (Table 32.36)

Table 32.29: Causes of vasoconstriction and/or gangrene
Poison
Ergot
Lead
Tobacco
Cocaine
Amphetamine

Table 32.30: Causes of dyspnea
Poison
Carbon monoxide
Strychnine
Phosphine
Arsine

Table 30.31: Toxic causes of pulmonary edema
Poison
Organophosphates
Chlorine
Digitalis
Snake bite
Opium

Table 32.32: Causes of respiratory distress
Poison
Alcohol
Opium
Organophosphates
Snake bite
Aconite
Barbiturate

Table 32.33: Toxic causes of cough

Poison
Acid fumes
Metal fumes
Formalin
Chlorine
Sulfur dioxide
Copper
Ammonia

Table 32.34: Toxic causes of laryngospasm

Poison
Irritant poisons
Metal/acid fumes
Strychnine
Thiopental
Ammonia

Table 32.35: Toxic causes of bronchitis

Poison
Chromium dust
Nitrogen oxide
Osmium
Phosgene
Tobacco smoke
Aluminum chloride

Table 32.36: Toxic causes of emphysema

Poison
Tobacco smoke
Silica exposure

Gastrointestinal System

- Vomiting (Table 32.37)
- Diarrhea (Table 32.38)
- Constipation (Table 32.39)
- Gastroenteritis (Table 32.40)
- Melena (Table 32.41)
- Abdominal pain (Table 32.42)
- Abdominal distension (Table 32.43)
- Ileus (Table 32.44)
- Thirst (Table 32.45)
- Dysphagia (Table 32.46)
- Odynophagia (Table 32.47)
- Pancreatitis (Table 32.48)

Table 32.37: Color of vomitus in different poisons

Color of Vomitus	Poison
Blue	Iodine
Green	Paris green,
	Cannabis
	Copper sulfate
Brown	Acid
	Alkali
	Zinc phosphide
Blood	Chronic alcoholism
(Hematemesis)	Manganese
	Carbon tetrachloride
	Thallium

Table 32.38: Poisons producing diarrhea

Poison
Arsenic
Boric acid
Cyanide
Food poisoning
Iron

Table 32.39: Poisons producing constipation

Poison
Ergot
Calcium salts
Lead
Opium
Arsenic

Table 32.40: Toxic causes of gastroenteritis

Poison
Arsenic
Thallium
Croton

Table 32.41: Poisons producing melena

Poison
Alcohols
Anticoagulants
Corrosive
Iron

Table 32.42: Poisons producing abdominal pain
Poison
Caustics
Cholinergic agents
Cocaine
Iron
Salicylates

Table 32.43: Poisons producing distension of abdomen
Poison
Anticholinergics
Caustics

Table 32.44: Poisons producing ileus
Poison
Anticholinergics
Barium
Botulinus toxin
Lead
Thallium

Table 32.45: Poisons producing thirst
Poison
Arsenic
Atropine
Chloral hydrate
Lead

Table 32.46: Poisons producing dysphagia
Poison
Camphor
Corrosives
Hydrogen sulfide
Marine animal bites

Table 32.47: Poisons producing odynophagia
Poison
Camphor
Corrosives
Hydrogen sulfide
Scorpion sting

Table 32.48: Causes of toxic pancreatitis
Poison
Copper
Zinc
Organophosphate
Methanol

Table 32.49: Poisons imparting color to urine

Poison	***Color***
Green	Phenol Cresol
Orange	Rifampicin Phenothiazines Santonin
Yellow	Dinitrophenol Arsine
Pink	Aniline Eosin Mercury
Purple	Porphyrins
Brown to black	Thymol Naphthalene
Red	Phenolphthalein Mephensin
Blue	Methylene blue

Table 32.50: Poisons producing albuminuria
Poison
Arsenic
Mercury
Chromate
Phenol
Thallium

Genitourinary System

- Color of urine (Table 32.49)
- Albuminuria (Table 32.50)
- Hemoglobinuria (Table 32.51)
- Glycosuria (Table 32.52)
- Hematuria (Table 32.53)
- Porphyrinuria (Table 32.54)
- Oliguria (Table 32.55)
- Polyuria (Table 32.56)
- Dysuria (Table 32.57).

Table 32.51: Poisons producing hemoglobinuria

Poison
Acetic acid
Arsine
Copper
Nitrites
Snake bite

Table 32.52: Poisons producing glycosuria

Poison
Morphine
Anesthetic agents

Table 32.53: Poisons producing hematuria

Poison
Allopurinol
Arsenic
Mercury
Phenols

Table 32.54: Poisons producing porphyrinuria

Poison
Lead
Mercury
Benzene
Carbon tetrachloride

Table 32.55: Poisons producing oliguria

Poison
Arsenic
Phenol
Chromate
Carbon tetrachloride

Table 32.56: Poisons producing polyuria

Poison
Alcohol
Mercury
Nitrites
Bismuth
Digitalis

Table 32.57: Poisons producing dysuria

Poison
Arsenic
Anticholinergics
Mushrooms

Table 32.58: Poisons producing myopathy

Poison
Sea snake
Pentazocine
Meperdine
Heroin
Alcohol
Iodide

Table 32.59: Poisons producing myalgia

Poison
Copper
Arsenic
Lead
Sea snake

Table 32.60: Poisons producing rhabdomyolysis

Poison
Bee stings
Barbiturates
Cocaine
Heroin
Paraquat
Snake bite

Table 32.61: Poisons producing fasciculation

Poison
Lead
Organophosphate
Strychnine
Mercury
Scorpion bite

Musculoskeletal System

- Myopathy (causes given in Table 32.58)
- Myalgia (Table 32.59)
- Rhabdomyolysis (Table 32.60)
- Fasciculation (Table 32.61)
- Smooth muscle depressant/stimulant (Table 32.62)

Blood Manifestations

- Anemia (Table 32.63)
- Blood dyscrasia (Table 32.64)
- Thrombocytopenia (Table 32.65)
- Leukocytosis (Table 32.66)
- Leukopenia (Table 32.67)
- Pancytopenia (Table 32.68)
- Polycythemia (Table 32.69)
- Stippling (Table 32.70)
- Bone marrow depression (Table 32.71)
- Hemolysis (Table 32.72)
- Methemoglobin formation (Table 32.73)
- Sulfhemoglobinemia (Table 32.74)

Table 32.62: Smooth muscle Depressants/Stimulant

Feature	*Poison*
Depressant	Barbiturates
	Nitrites
	Papaverine
Stimulant	Barium salts

Table 32.63: Poisons producing anemia

Poison
Chronic alcohol
Arsenic
Lead
Opium

Table 32.64: Poisons producing blood dyscrasia

Poison
Aniline
Benzene
Cadmium
Lead
Naphthalene
Zinc
Iron
Acetic acid

Table 32.65: Poisons producing thrombocytopenia

Poison
Promazine
Sulfonamide
Chloramphenicol

Table 32.66: Poisons producing leukocytosis

Poison
Snake poisoning
Pilocarpine
Titanium tetrachloride
Thallium

Table 32.67: Poisons producing leukopenia

Poison
Aniline
Arsenic
Antimony
Lead
Chloromphenicol
Sulfonamides
Promazine

Table 32.68: Poisons producing pancytopenia

Poison
Chloromphenicol
Sulfonamides
Erythromycin

Table 32.69: Poisons producing polycythemia

Poison
Arsenic
Carbon monoxide
Aniline
Cobalt

Table 32.70: Poisons producing stippling

Poison
Lead
Antimony
Bismuth
Barbiturate

Table 32.71: Poisons producing bone marrow depression

Poison
Beryllium
Cadmium
Fluoride
Phosphorus
Selenium

Table 32.72: Poisons producing hemolysis

Poison
Sea snake
Arsine
Castor
Copper sulfate
Nitrofurantion
Lead

Table 32.73: Poisons causing methemoglobin formation

Poison
Aniline
Nitrobenzene
Nitrites
Methylene blue
Toluidine
Copper

Table 32.74: Poisons causing sulfhemoglobinemia

Poison
Poisons producing methemoglobin
Aniline derivatives

Table 32.75: Dermal features in poisoning

Poison	Feature
Color	Pink - carbon monoxide Cherry red - cyanide Cyanosis - organophosphate, strychnine
Dry hot	Datura
Sweating/moist	Organophosphate Arsenic Opium Pilocarpine
Flushing	Alcohol Arsenic Cyanide Datura
Blisters/ bullae	Barbiturate Carbon monoxide Viper snake bite Marking nut juice Methaqualone Meprobamate Tricyclic antidepressants Mustard Calatropis Plumbago
Petechiae, purpura or hemorrhagic lesion	Phosphorus Arsenic Benzene Dicumarol Heparin
Dermatitis	Arsenic
Skin lesion	Acne - bromide, thallium Pigmentation - arsenic Erythema - iodide Papule - antimony dust Pustule - croton oil Rash - thallium, mercury
Hair loss/ alopecia	Thallium Arsenic
Pruritis	Ergot Chloroquine
Exfoliation	Arsenic Chloroquine
Hirsutism	Barbiturate
Corrosion	Acid/alkali Chromic acid Iodine Mercuric chloride Phenol
Edema	Arsenic Mercury Oxalate Phenol
Pallor	Arsenic Barbiturate Cocaine Lead
Ulcers	Acids/alkali Chromate Fluoride Iodine
Urticaria	Bromide Phenobarbitone Sulfonamide Thiouracil Iodine

Cont..........

Dermal Manifestation

- Given in Table 32.75.

Ear Manifestations

- Rhinorrhea (Table 32.76)
- Deafness (Table 32.77)
- Vertigo (Table 32.78)
- Tinnitus (Table 32.79).

Others

- Poisons causing fever (Table 32.80)
- Poisons acting on enzyme system (Table 32.81)
- Excretion of poison (Table 32.82).

Table 32.76: Poisons producing rhinorrhoea

Poison
Iodine
Arsenic

Table 32.77: Toxic causes of deafness

Poison
Methyl alcohol
Ergot
Quinine
Tobacco
Streptomycin

Table 32.78: Causes of vertigo

Poison
Alcohol
Cannabis
Carbon monoxide
Cyanide
Ergot
Tobacco

Table 32.79: Causes of tinnitus

Poison
Aminoglycosides
Furosemide
Indomethacin
Quinine

Table 32.80: Toxic causes of fever

Poison
Arsenic
Datura
Barbiturates
Cocaine
Metal fumes

Table 32.81: Poisons acting on enzyme system

Poison
Phosphorus
Cyanide
Organophosphate
Mercury
Lead

Table 32.82: Excretion of poisons

Excretion	*Poison*
Bile	- Narcotic drugs - Cocaine - Paracetamol
CSF	Alcohol
Vitreous humor	Alcohol
Fatty tissue	Pesticides

MANAGEMENT

Principles of management consist of

1. Stabilization and evaluation
2. Decontamination
   - Eye
   - Skin
   - Gut
     - Emesis
     - Gastric lavage
     - Catharsis
     - Activated charcoal
     - Bowel irrigation
3. Poison elimination
4. Antidote administration
5. Nursing care
6. Psychiatric care

Stabilization and Evaluation: Consist of

1. A- maintenance of **airway**
2. B- maintenance of **breathing**

3. C- maintenance of **circulation**
4. D- disability (neurologic status) management: assess level of consciousness.

Decontamination

1. Eye: If ocular exposure occurs due to poisons, eye should be irrigated with copious water for 15 to 20 minutes.
2. Skin: Absorption of poison is possible by dermal route. In case of dermal exposure, the affected area should be washed thoroughly with plain water. Remove the clothes and irrigate the area copiously with water.
3. Gut.

A. Emesis[4]

- **Agents used**
  - Syrup of ipecacuanha
  - Apomorphine
  - Stimulation of posterior pharyngeal wall.
- **Indications**
  - Conscious patient
  - Ingestion of poison within 4 to 6 hour.
- **Contraindications**
  - Coma/convulsion/unconscious patient
  - Impaired gag reflex
  - Corrosive/volatile poison ingestion
  - Pregnancy.
- **Complications**
  - Aspiration pneumonia
  - Mallory Weiss tears
  - Laryngospasm.

B. Gastric Lavage

- **Indications**
  - Conscious patient
  - Ingestion of poison within 1 to 2 hour.
- **Contraindications**
  - Coma/convulsion/unconscious patient
  - Impaired gag reflex
  - Corrosive/volatile poison ingestion
  - Marked hypothermia
  - esophageal varices
  - Significant electrolyte imbalance.
- **Complications**
  - Aspiration pneumonia
  - Mallory Weiss tears
  - Perforation of esophagus/stomach
  - Laryngospasm
  - Hypothermia
  - Electrolyte imbalance.
- **Procedure**
  - Protect airway
  - Place patient on lateral position
  - Tube should be passed orally
  - Lubricate the inserting end of tube
  - Use mouth gag
  - The position of tube in stomach should be confirmed
  - Lavage is carried out with saline or water.
- **Precautions**
  - Never embark on procedure as routine
  - Do not do in non-toxic agent ingestion
  - Obtain consent and explain procedure
- **Agents used**
  - Ewald tube (Fig. 32.1)
  - Lavacuator
  - Ryle's tube (in children)
  - Boas tube

C. Activated Charcoal

- Activated charcoal is tasteless, black, fine powder. It adsorbs the poisons in stomach and hence decreases the systemic absorption of poison.
- Dose is given as 1 gm/kg body weight
- Required quantity of activated charcoal is mixed with water and this mixture is administered to patient.

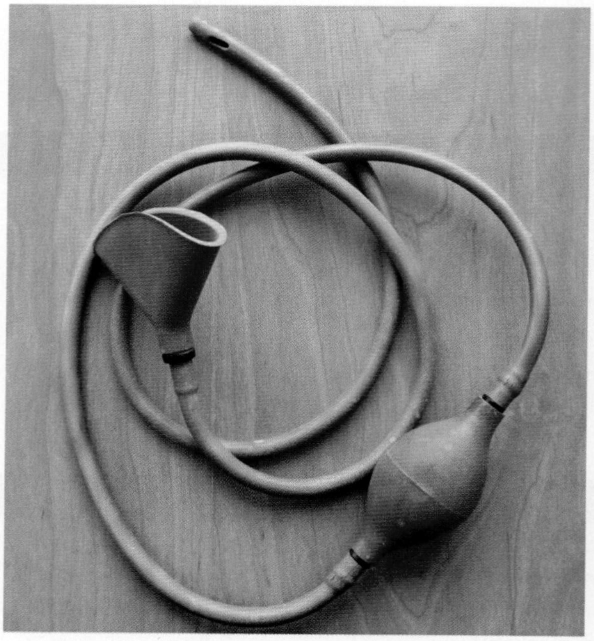

FIG. 32.1: gastric lavage tube (*Courtesy* Dr P G Dixit, Professor and Head, Forensic Medicine, GMC, Nagpur)

- Disadvantages
  - Unpleasant taste
  - Provokes vomiting
  - May cause diarrhea/constipation
- Contraindications
  - Paralytic ileus
  - Intestinal obstruction
  - Perforation of stomach

Poison Elimination

Poison can be eliminated by
1. Hemodialysis
2. Hemoperfusion
3. Peritoneal dialysis
4. Plasma perfusion

Antidote Administration

ANTIDOTES

Definition

Antidotes are the substances used to counteract or neutralize the effects of poison.
Table 32.83 provides antidotes that should be available in emergency room.[5] Table 32.84 presents poisons and their antidotes.

Classification

Antidotes are classified as:

1. Physical or Mechanical or Non-Specific Antidotes

- These antidotes retard the absorption of poison by mechanical action.
- Examples – activated charcoal, demulcents such as – milk, starch, egg-white (egg albumin)
- Activated charcoal acts mechanically by adsorbing the poison and retaining it within its pores
- Demulcents are the substances that form a protective coating on the gastric mucosa and thus retard absorption.

2. Chemical Antidote

- These compounds counteract the action of poison by neutralizing the poison or forming harmless or insoluble components
- Example – in corrosive alkali poisons weak vegetable acids like citric acid, lemon juice may be used.

Table 32.83: Recommended emergency antidotes

Antidotes
Activated charcoal
Amyl nitrate
Antivenin
Calcium chloride
Calcium gluconate gel
Desferrioxamine
Digoxin immune Fab
Ethanol
Folic acid
Fomepizole
Flumazenil
Glucagons
Leucovorin
Methylene blue 1%
A-Actyl cysteine
Naloxone
Physostigmine
Polyethylene glycol electrolyte
Pralidoxine
Sodium bicarbonate
Sodium nitrite 3%
Sodium thiosulfate
Succimer
Thiamine hydrochloride
Vitamin K_1

Table 32.84: Recommended antidotes for poisons

Antidote	*Poison*
Acetylcysteine	Paracetamol
Amyl nitrite	Cyanide
Atropine	Organophosphate
Desferrioxamine	Iron
Ethanol	Methanol
Flumazenil	Benzodiazepines
Glucose	Insulin
Naloxone	Opiates
d-penicillamine	Copper
Physostigmine	Central anticholinergics

3. Physiological or Pharmacological Antidote[6]

- These agents act on the tissue of the body. These substances work either in one of the following ways:
  - Reduces the toxic conversion of poison – for example, ethanol is used as antidote in methyl alcohol poisoning because ethanol inhibits the metabolism of

methanol to toxic metabolites by competing for the same enzyme (alcohol dehydrogenase)
– Competition at receptor site – some antidotes are capable to compete with the poison and displace the poison from the specific receptor site thereby antagonizing the poisonous effects completely. For example, in opiate poisoning naloxone is used. Naloxone antagonizes the effect of opiate by acting at opioid receptors.
– Blocking the receptor site – some antidotes are capable of blocking the receptor site acted by poisonous substance thereby blocking the poisonous effect of substance. For example, in organophosphorus poisoning atropine is used. Organophosphorus acts at muscarinic receptors producing toxic effects. Administration of atropine will block the effects of organophosphate.

4. Universal Antidote

- It is an obsolete antidote and had only historical importance.
- The composition of universal antidote is provided in Table 32.85.

5. Chelating Agents

- These agents interact with poison to form an inert complex, which is then excreted from the body.
- These agents are primarily used in heavy metal poisoning
- These agents with metal ions forms ring structure within their molecule. The name chelating is derived from Greek, *chele* = crab – the compound holds the metal like a crab's claw.
- Examples – BAL, Succimer, Disodium edetate, penicillamine, desferrioxamine, calcium disodium edetate.

British Anti-Lewisite (BAL)

Synonyms: dimercaprol, dimercaptopropanol.

Table 32.85: Composition of Universal Antidote

Components	*Quantity*	*Mechanism*
Charcoal	2 parts	Adsorbs poisons
Magnesium oxide	1 part	Neutralizes acids
Tannic acid	1 part	Precipitates alkaloids, certain glycosides and metals

Features

It is an oily, pungent smelling liquid, developed during Second World War by British as an antidote to the arsenic war gas lewisite.

Mechanism of Action

BAL has two SH (thiol) groups. The two SH group binds to those metals that produce toxicity by interacting with sulfhydryl containing enzymes in the body. BAL will combine with these metals forming BAL-metal complex thus dislodge the metal from acting site.

Indications

BAL is useful against metals that interfere with sulfhydryl enzymes in the body such as arsenic, mercury, bismuth, copper, antimony, and nickel.

Contraindications

BAL is contraindicated in iron and cadmium poisoning because BAL-iron and BAL-cadmium complex are toxic.

Dose[7]

BAL is administered intramuscularly as 5 mg/kg stat followed by 2 to 3 mg/kg every 4 to 8 hours for two days and then once a day for 10 days.

Adverse Effects

- Tachycardia
- Vomiting
- Tingling and burning sensation
- Cramps
- Sweating

Succimer

Synonyms: dimercaptosuccinic acid.

- The agent is similar to BAL in chelating properties
- It is less toxic than BAL and orally effective
- It is used against arsenic, mercury and lead poisoning.

Calcium Disodium Edetate

Features

It is not absorbed from gastrointestinal tract. It should be used as intravenous route because intramuscular injection is painful. It is distributed extracellularly.

Mechanism of Action

It chelates metal extracellularly and removes metals from the body by exchanging with calcium. It is rapidly excreted in urine by glomerular filtration carrying the toxic metal along with it. The compound is not metabolized in the body.

Indications

Useful in lead, zinc, cadmium, copper, manganese.

Contraindications

In cases with raised intracranial pressure where fluids are restricted.

Dose[7]

One gram is diluted in 200 to 300 ml in saline or glucose solution and infused intravenously over one hour twice daily for 3 to 5 days.

Adverse Effects

- Renal damage
- Acute febrile reaction
- Anaphylaxis may occur
- Thrombophlebitis.

Penicillamine (D-penicillamine)

Synonyms: Cuprimine.

Features

It is dimethyl cysteine, obtained as a degradation product of penicillin and available in d-isomer and l-isomer form. The d-isomer is used because l-isomer is more toxic and produces optic neuritis. It is absorbed after oral administration, metabolized in the body and excreted in urine and feces.

Mechanism of Action

Exact mechanism is not known.

Indications

1. Copper poisoning – drug of choice
2. Mercury poisoning – alternative to BAL
3. Chronic lead poisoning
4. Wilson's disease
5. Cystinuria and cystine stones

Dose

- For copper and mercury poisoning – 1 to 1.5 gm/day in divided doses
- For Wilson's disease – 0.5 to 1 gm/day in divided doses, one hour before meals or two hour after the meals to avoid the chelation of dietary metals.

Adverse Effects

- Cutaneous reaction
- Febrile illness
- Nephrotoxicity
- Bone marrow depression
- Anorexia
- Nausea
- Loss of taste

Desferrioxamine

Features

Ferrioxamine is a long chain iron-containing complex obtained from an actinomycete. Chemical removal of iron from it yields desferrioxamine that has great affinity for iron.[7] If administered orally, little amount is absorbed. It binds with iron present in GIT and prevents its absorption. If administered parenterally, desferrioxamine is partially metabolized and rapidly excreted in urine.

Mechanism of Action

Desferrioxamine molecule turns round the ferric ion and forms a stable non-toxic complex that is excreted in urine. One gram of desferrioxamine is capable of removing 85 mg of elemental iron. It removes loosely bound iron and iron from hemosiderin and ferritin but do not remove iron from hemoglobin or cytochrome.

Indications

- Acute iron poisoning
- Transfusion siderosis.

Dose

- It is drug of choice in iron poisoning. It should be given intramuscularly – 0.5 to 1 gm repeatedly 4 to 12 hourly.
- In severe life threatening poisoning or patient with shock should receive intravenous desferrioxamine – 15 mg/kg/hour with a maximum daily dose up to 360 mg/kg or up to 6 gm total.[8]

Adverse Effects

- Fall in blood pressure
- Itching, urticaria, rashes
- Abdominal pain
- Diarrhea
- Muscle cramps

DIAGNOSIS IN DEAD (AUTOPSY FINDINGS)

Diagnosis of poisoning in dead is done by:

1. Autopsy findings
2. Laboratory examination

Autopsy Examination

External Examination

- Evidence of soiling of clothes
- Presence of bottle/container/label in pocket
- Presence of suicide note
- Vitriolage
- Trickling of poison/stigmata of poison over skin
- Presence of injuries
- Smell from body
- Rigor mortis: in some condition rigor may appear early or in some delayed (given in Table 32.86).
- Postmortem lividity: poisons may impart peculiar colour (given in Table 32.87)
- Some poisons resist decomposition or some may hasten (given in Table 32.88).

Table 32.86: Poisons causing early appearance of rigor mortis

Poison
Strychnine
Hydrocyanic acid

Table 32.87: Color of postmortem lividity

Poison	*Color*
Cyanide	Cherry red
Carbon monoxide	Pink
Opium	Blackish
Hydrogen sulphide	Bluish green
Phosphorus	Dark brown
Potassium chlorate	Chocolate brown
Nitrites	Reddish brown

Internal Examination

- Cranial cavity: Presence of odour/cerebral edema/hemorrhages. Causes of cerebral edema are given in Table 32.89.
- Chest cavity: Note for presence of pleural effusion, pericardial effusion, state of lungs and heart, hemorrhages, pulmonary edema
- Abdominal cavity: Stomach contains gastric contents of various colours. Mucosa may show erosions, ulcers, hemorrhagic gastritis or perforation (causes given in Table 32.90). Gastric mucosa may be stained with the colour of poison (given in Tables 32.91 and 32.92).
- Examine the state of intestine, liver, spleen, kidneys, pancreas, bladder, esophagus, lip, and oral cavity (see Tables 32.93 to 32.96).

Table 32.88: Poisons resisting decomposition

Poison
Arsenic
Datura
Alcohol
Formalin

Table 32.89: Causes of cerebral edema

Poison
Alcohol
Organophosphate
Aluminium phosphide

Table 32.90: Perforation of stomach

Poison
Sulfuric acid
Hydrochloric acid

Table 32.91: Color of gastric mucosa

Poison	*Color*
Sulfuric acid	Blackish
Nitric acid	
Tobacco	Yellow
Arsenic	Red velvety
Copper sulfate	Bluish green
Iodine	Mucosa brown, gastric contents blue if starch is present
Alkali	Bleached, sodden
Mercury	Slate color
Ferrous sulphate	Green

Table 32.92: Appearance of stomach

Poison	*Appearance*
Sulfuric acid	Soft
Alkali	Bleached, sodden
Phenol	Leather like
Oxalic acid	Scalded

Table 32.93: Hepatic necrosis (acute central necrosis)

Poison
Arsenic
Carbon tetrachloride
Chloral hydrate
Chloroform
Chromium salts

Table 32.94: Cloudy degeneration of liver

Poison
Bismuth
Mercury

Table 32.95: Chronic liver degeneration and cirrhosis

Poison
Alcohol
Carbon tetrachloride
Gold
Manganese

Table 32.96: Tubular necrosis/degeneration

Poison
Arsenic
Bismuth
Mercury
Lead

Laboratory Examination

It consists of analysis of viscera, body fluids and blood for poisons. The laboratory method consist of:

1. Qualitative assays – type of poison is known.
2. Quantitative assays – type of poison as well as quantitation can be known.

Qualitative Assays

Thin layer chromatography is a simple and inexpensive technique for qualitative estimation of poison.

Quantitative Assays

- Gas chromatography
- High performance liquid chromatography
- Mass spectrometry
- Radio-immuno-assay
- Atomic absorption spectrophotometry
- Neutron activation analysis.

REFERENCES

1. Kamath MA. In: Medical Jurisprudence and Toxicology, 6th edn. 1960. The Madras Law Journal, Madras.
2. Loomis TA. Introduction and scope. In: Essentials of Toxicology, 2nd edn. 1974, Lea and Febiger, Philadelphia. 1-12.
3. Boyd EM. History and general information. In: Predictive Toxicometrics 1st edn. 1972, Scientechnica (Publishers) Ltd. Bristol 1-15.
4. Pillay VV. General toxicology. In: Textbook of Forensic Medicine, 14th edn. 2004. Paras Publishing, Hyderabad. 350-74.
5. Brent J l. In: Critical care toxicology: diagnosis and management of the critically poisoned patient, 1st edn. 2005. Elsevier Division.
6. Pillay VV. Principles of diagnosis and management. In: Comprehensive Medical Toxicolgy, 1st edn. 2003. Paras Publishing, Hyderabad. 8-40.
7. Tripathi KD. Chelating agents. In Essentials of Medical Pharmacology, 4th edn. 1999. Jaypee Brothers Medical Publishers (P) Ltd. New Delhi. 872-5.
8. Schiavone FM. Metals: iron intoxication. In Viccellio P (ed) Handbook of Medical Toxicology, 1st edn. 1993. Little, Brown and Company, Boston. 294-302.

CHAPTER 33

Toxicology: Medicolegal Considerations

Be so true to thyself, as thou be not false to others.

- Francis Bacon

Duties of Medical Practitioner

A poisoning case may present to Medical Practitioner as a case of:

1. Suicidal ingestion of poison
2. Homicidal poisoning
3. Accidental exposure
   - Irrespective of manner of poisoning, it is duty of doctor to treat the patient to the best possible way. If adequate facilities are not available in a hospital, the patient should be given first-aid measures and then referred to higher medical center.
   - Doctors working in a government set-up are required to report every case of poisoning to the Police.
   - Doctors working in private set-up are not under legal obligation to inform Police of accidental or suicidal poisoning cases. However, if death of patient occurs, then police has to be informed. Doctor is bound under S 39 of CrPC to inform police regarding all cases of homicidal poisoning. Failure to inform may be culpable under Sec 176 of IPC.
   - If Police requires information regarding poisoning cases (irrespective of manner of exposure) and doctor is summoned by Investigating Officer, then the doctor is under obligation to give all information regarding the case (under sec 175 CrPC). If Doctor conceals the fact or information, then doctor may be prosecuted under Sec 202 of IPC. Similarly providing false information by doctor to Police is culpable under Sec 193 of IPC.
   - The attending doctor should collect and preserve evidences suggestive of poisoning such as empty bottle/container of poison brought by patient/relatives, soiled clothes, remaining food, vomitus, feces or gastric lavage, etc (Fig. 33.1). Deliberate omission to collect or preserve evidences is punishable under Sec 201 of IPC. All collected exhibits (evidences) should be handed over to Investigating Officer in properly sealed condition.
   - If the condition of poisoned patient is serious and is conscious, the doctor should arrange for dying declaration or should record if circumstance warrants.
   - If patient dies and exact diagnosis or cause of death could not be made out or the patient is brought dead, the doctor should inform the Police regarding the matter and should not issue a death certificate.[1]
   - If it occurs to be a case of food poisoning case or death, the Public Health Authorities must be notified.
   - Preservation of record: the indoor patient's record should be made and preserved for up to 3 years. If relative of patient seek record, it should be provided within 72 hours.[2]

Poisons and the Indian Penal Code

1. Sec 272 IPC – adulteration of food or drink intended for sale.
2. Sec 273 IPC – sale of noxious food or drink.
3. Sec 274 IPC – adulteration of drugs.
4. Sec 275 IPC – sale of adulterated drugs.
5. Sec 276 IPC – sale of drug as a different drug or prescription.
6. Sec 277 IPC – punishment for fouling water of public spring or reservoir.
7. Sec 278 IPC – punishment for voluntarily making atmosphere noxious to health.
8. Sec 284 IPC – negligent conduct with respect to poisonous substance.

9. Sec 299 IPC – deals with culpable homicide.
10. Sec 300 IPC – deals with murder.
11. Sec 304-A IPC – causing death by negligence.
12. Sec 320 IPC – deals with grievous hurt.
13. Sec 324 IPC – voluntarily causing hurt by dangerous weapons or means.
14. Sec 326 IPC – voluntarily causing grievous hurt by dangerous weapons or means.
15. Sec 328 IPC – causing hurt by means of poison etc. with intent to commit an offense.
16. Sec 336 IPC – act endangering life or personal safety of others
17. Sec 337 IPC – causing hurt by act endangering life or personal safety of others.
18. Sec 338 IPC – causing grievous hurt by act endanger ing life or personal safety of others.

Poisons and Relevant Act and Rules

- The Poison Act 1919
- The Drugs and Cosmetics Act 1940
- The Drugs and Cosmetics Rules 1945
- The Drugs (Control) Act 1950
- The Drugs and Magic Remedies (Objectionable advertisements) Act 1954
- The Prevention of Food Adulteration Act 1954
- The Prevention of Food Adulteration Rules 1955
- The Insecticides Act 1968
- The Insecticides Rules 1971
- The Water (Prevention and control of pollution) Act 1974
- The Water (Prevention and control of pollution) Rules 1975
- The Narcotic drugs and psychoactive substances Act 1985
- The Narcotic drugs and psychoactive substances Rules 1985
- The Narcotic drugs and psychoactive substances (Amendment) Act 2001.

The Poison Act 1919

This Act was amended in 1958 and repealed in 1960. The Act deals with import of poisonous substances into India and regulates the grant of license for possession of certain poisonous substances and sale.

The Drugs and Cosmetics Act 1940

The Act was amended in the year 1964 to include Ayurvedic and Unani drugs. Under this Act, the Central Government has constituted:

- The Drugs Technical Advisory board – the function is to advise the Central Government and the State Government on technical matters arising out of the administration of the Act.
- Ayurvedic and Unani Drugs Technical Advisory Board
- The Drugs Consultative Committee – the function is to advise the Central Government, the State Government and Drugs Technical Advisory Board on matters tending to secure uniformity throughout India in the administration of the Act.

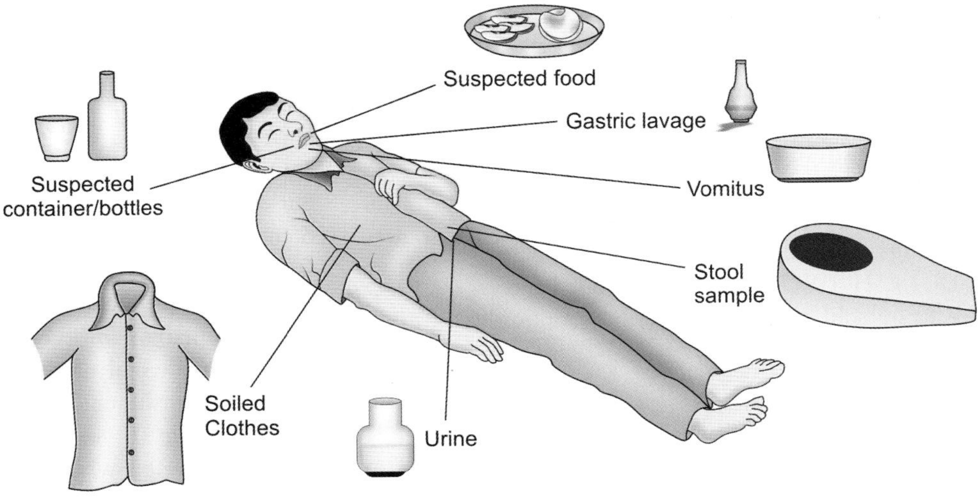

FIG. 33.1: Diagrammatic representation regarding samples and exhibits to be preserved by doctor

- Establishment of Central Drugs Laboratory – the function is to analyze or test samples of drug imported into India and picked up by the Assistant Drug Controllers.
- According to this Act, no person shall import or manufacture for sale or stock or exhibit for sale or distribute any patent or proprietary medicine unless it is displayed on its label or container, either the true formula or a list of ingredients contained in it, in a manner readily intelligible to the members of the medical profession.
- When taking the sample of a drug or cosmetics for analysis, the drug inspector should pay the fair price of the sample and divide the samples into four portions as:
  1. One portion will be resorted to the shopkeeper or vendor.
  2. The second portion should be sent to the government analyzer for analysis.
  3. Third portion should be retained for production in the Court when required.
  4. Fourth portion should be sent to the person from whom the shopkeeper or vendor had made the purchase.
- Offenses punishable under this Act shall be tried only by the Magistrate of the First Class.

The Drugs and Cosmetics Rules 1945

The Rules are meant for regulation of manufacture, distribution and sale of the drugs and cosmetics. It classified drugs into various Schedules as:

- Schedule C – biological and other products
- Schedule E – list of poisonous substances under Ayurvedic, Siddha and Unani system
- Schedule F – vaccines and sera
- Schedule G – hormonal preparations, antihistamines, anti-cancer drugs
- Schedule H – barbiturates, amphetamines, reserpine, ergot and sulphonamides
- Schedule J – drugs claimed to prevent or cure aliments such as appendicitis, blindness, cancer, cataract, epilepsy, hydrocele etc. which must not be advertised or imported
- Schedule L – list of prescription drugs (which includes drugs from Schedule H also).

Schedule H and L drugs are required to be labeled with the words "SCHEDULE H DRUG" and "SCHEDULE L DRUG". Warning – to be sold by retail on the prescription of a Registered Medical Practitioner only.

The Drugs (Control) Act 1950

The Act regulates the sale, supply and distribution of drugs. It also guides the manufacture or dealer in fixing the maximum price for every drug.

The Drugs and Magic Remedies (Objectionable Advertisements) Act 1954

The Act bans advertisements that offend decency or morality. It also intended to prevent self-medication and treatment that may cause harmful effects. Under this Act, advertisements of magic remedies in relation to treatment of certain diseases, e.g. venereal disease, increase sexual potency etc. are forbidden.

The Narcotic Drugs and Psychoactive Substances Act 1985 (NDPS)

This Act repeals and renders obsolete three Acts namely –

1. The Opium Act 1857
2. The Opium Act 1878
3. The Dangerous Drugs Act 1930

- According to this Act, a narcotic drug refers to the cocoa leaf, cannabis (hemp), opium, poppy straw and includes all manufactured drugs. A manufactured drug means all the cocoa derivatives, medicinal cannabis, opium derivatives and poppy straw concentrate and any other narcotic substance preparation, which the Central Government may by notification, declare to be manufactured drug.
- The Act defines psychotropic substance as any substance, natural or synthetic, included in the list of psychotropic substances specified in a Schedule to the Act. The Schedule lists 77 psychotropic substances.
- Under section 27 of the Act, if a person possess in a small quantity, any narcotic drug or psychotropic substance intended for personal use and not for sale or distribution, or consumes any narcotic or psychotropic substance, he shall be punished with imprisonment for a term, which may extend to one year or with fine or with both. The small quantity as quoted in the definition means:
  1. 5 gm of hashish
  2. 250 mg of heroin, smack and brown sugar
  3. 5 gm of opium
  4. 125 mg of cocaine
  5. 500 gm of ganja
- NDPS Act prohibits the cultivation of poppy, cannabis and coca plants, however restricted cultivation is allowed for medicinal or scientific purpose.
- The minimum punishment for any offense committed under the Act is 10 years rigorous imprisonment and fine of Rs. 1 lakh while maximum punishment is 20 years rigorous imprisonment and fine of Rs. 2 lakh.

Collection and Preservation of Viscera for Chemical Analysis

For chemical analysis, it is duty of doctor to collect and preserve viscera and other exhibits properly.

Collection

Table 33.1 outlines the guidelines for collection of routine viscera (Fig. 33.2). Table 33.2 states the additional viscera and body fluids that have to be preserved in some circumstances.[3]

Table 33.1: Collection of routine viscera and blood

Specimen	*Quantity*
Stomach	Entire stomach
Stomach contents	Entire (preferably)
Small intestine (jejunum)	- 30 cm in adults - Entire length in infants
Small intestinal contents	Up to 100 gm
Liver (portion containing gall bladder)	- 500 gm in adults - Entire in infants
Kidney	- One half of each kidney in adults - Both kidneys in infant
Urine	30-50 ml
Blood	10-20 ml

Preservatives

After collection of viscera, it is important to preserve them properly with proper preservative. Following account provides guidelines for preservation of viscera and body fluids.

Viscera

Rectified spirit is used as a preservative for viscera in all cases of poisoning except following poisons.

- Phosphorus
- Alcohol
- Phenol (carbolic acid)
- Paraldehyde
- Acetic acid

It can be remembered by a mnemonic " **PAPPA** is not preserved in rectified spirit".

The viscera are also preserved in saturated solution of common salt (sodium chloride). Preserving viscera in saturated solution of common salt is routinely practiced in India because it is economical. Saturated solution of common salt is also used to preserve viscera in all poisoning cases except following:

- Inorganic acid (mineral acid) poisoning
- Vegetable poisoning

Thus, the viscera can be preserved in rectified spirit or saturated solution of common salt for analysis of poisons. In suspected cases of rabies, the brain has to be preserved for demonstration of Negri bodies. For this purpose, 1 to 2 cm cube of brain is collected and preserved in 50 percent glycerol solution (Table 33.3).

Body fluids

Urine[5]

- For alcohol – 30 mg phenyl mercuric nitrate for 10 ml or thymol (Table 33.4)

Table 33.2: Additional viscera and body fluids collected at autopsy

Specimen	*Quantity*	*Toxicant sought*
Adipose tissue	200 gm	Insecticides, thiopental
Bile	All available	Opiate, paracetamol[4]
Brain	500 gm	Volatile poisons, alcohol, anesthetics, barbiturates, CO
Brain	1-2 cm cubes	For rabies
Lung	One whole	Methadone, gases, inhalants
Vitreous humor	All available	Digoxin, electrolytes, glucose
CSF	10 ml	Alcohol
Spinal cord	Entire length	Gelsemine, strychnine
Skin (with underlying tissue)	Affected portion	Corrosive, injected poison, snake bite
Bone (preferably femur)	10 cm length	Heavy metals
Scalp hairs (plucked)	15 to 20 strands	Heavy metals
Uterus	Whole	Abortifacient drugs
Heart	Whole	Cardiac poisons

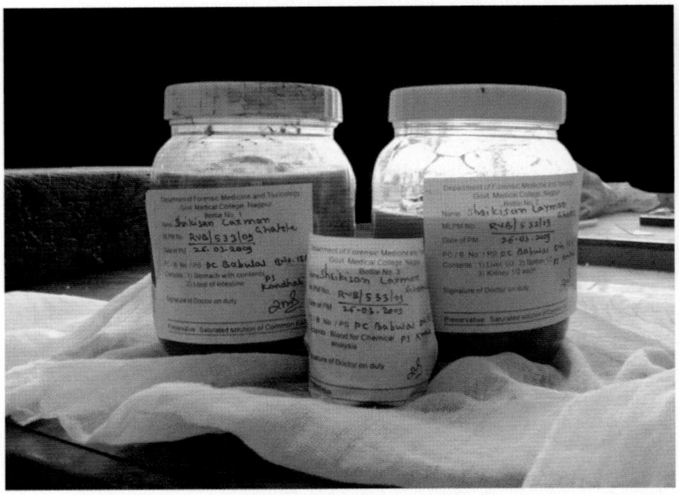

FIG. 33.2: Collection of routine viscera at autopsy, bottle 1 contains - stomach with loop of intestine with their contents, bottle 2 contains pieces of liver, spleen and kidneys and bottle 3 contains blood.

- For catecholamines in hypothermia – urine preserved by hydrochloric acid
- For routine toxicology – saturated solution of common salt or equal amount of rectified spirit.

Blood[6]

1. For volatile poisons – alcohol, ether, chloroform, hydrocyanic acid etc. – airtight container under frozen condition without any preservative (for immediate process).
2. For alcohol in postmortem blood sample – fluoride.
3. For alcohol in living – 10 mg of sodium fluoride (acting as enzyme inhibitor) and 30 mg of potassium oxalate (acting as anticoagulant) for 10 ml of blood.
4. For blood grouping – blood in equal quantity with 5 percent (w/v) solution of sodium citrate in water containing 0.25 percent v/v formalin.
5. For carbon monoxide – blood in bottle with 1 to 2 cm layer of paraffin.
6. For oxalic acid and ethylene glycol – 30 mg of sodium citrate for 10 ml of blood.

Table 33.3: Preservative for preservation of viscera

Specimen	*Preservative*
Viscera	Rectified spirit or saturated solution of common salt
Brain for rabies	50% glycerol

Table 33.4: Preservative for urine

Preservative	*Quantity to be added*
Boric acid	0.5 gm/60 ml
Formaldehyde	2-4 drops/30 ml
Thymol	0.1 gm/100 ml
Toluene	Enough to cover the surface so that no bacteria can invade the barrier and multiply

7. For fluoride poisoning – 10 mg of sodium nitrate.
8. For DNA typing – 0.5 percent w/v of EDTA.
9. For biochemical and immunological analysis – sent in frozen condition.

Note: Heparin and EDTA should not be used as anticoagulant in alcohol as they interfere with alcohol detection. Vitreous humor should be sent in frozen condition.

Non-Detection of Poison

Poison may not be detected on chemical analysis and the reasons may be:

1. Poison is completely metabolized
2. Poison is neutralized
3. Obscure poison
4. Delayed death after poison ingestion
5. Decomposed body (some poisons may not be detected)
6. Defective preservation
7. Defective analysis
8. Poison analyzed late

REFERENCES

1. Gargi J, Rai H, Chanana A, Rai G, Singh K, Garg S. Role of doctor in poisoning: a review. J Punjab Acad Forensic Med Toxicol 2008; 8:32-4.
2. The Indian Medical Council (professional conduct, etiquette and ethics) Regulations, 2002. Published in Part III, Section 4 of the Gazette of India, dated 6th April, 2002.
3. Poklis A. Forensic Toxicology. In: Eckert WG (ed) Introduction to Forensic Sciences, 2nd edn. 1997. CRC Press, Florida. 107-32.
4. Millo T, Jaiswal AK, Behera C. Collection, preservation and forwarding of biological samples for toxicological analysis in medicolegal autopsy cases: a review. J Indian Acad Forensic Med 2008; 30:96-100.
5. Rao NG, Kurien A. In: Practical Forensic Medicine, 3rd edn. 2007. Jaypee Brothers Medical Publishers (P) Ltd. New Delhi.
6. Laboratory procedure manual, forensic toxicology 2005. Directorate of Forensic Sciences, Ministry of Home Affairs, Govt. of India. Selective and Scientific Books Publishers, New Delhi. 2nd edn. 2005.

CHAPTER 34

Corrosive Poisons

It hurts to be on the cutting edge.

- Proverb

Corrosive poisons *are the substances which are caustic i.e. capable of burning the tissue when applied.* The local injury inflicted may be of varying degree and severity ranging from superficial burns to charring. Corrosive substances include acids, alkalis and some metallic salts and non-metallic compounds. They are mentioned in Table 34.1.

INORGANIC ACIDS

Mechanism of Action

- In concentrated form, inorganic acids acts as corrosive and in dilute form, they act as irritant poison.
- These acids act mainly at local site of application with minimal remote or systemic action
- Inorganic acids are powerful desiccants. When these agents come in contact with body, they extract water from the tissue and liberate heat. The acid precipitates the protein and causes coagulation necrosis of the tissue in contact. They fix, destroy and erode the tissue.

Table 34.1 Showing corrosive substances

Compound	*Examples*
Inorganic acids	Sulfuric acid, hydrochloric acid etc
Organic acids	Acetic acid, carbolic acid etc
Alkali	Sodium hydroxide, potassium hydroxide etc
Metal salts	Ferric chloride, zinc chloride, chromate etc
Non-metal compound	Iodine, potassium permanganate, hydrogen peroxide etc

- Converts hemoglobin to hematin
- There is formation of eschar, which has self-limiting effect, and formation of eschar minimizes the further damage of tissue. Thus, due to precipitation of proteins and formation of eschar, the acids do not penetrate tissue much deeper and causes less damage than alkalis.
- Acids cause more damage to the stomach than that of esophagus.[1] It is thought that squamous epithelium of esophagus is more resistant to acids but vulnerable for alkalis. Columnar epithelium of stomach is susceptible for acids and causes gastric outlet obstruction. The pyloric spasm induced by the presence of acid in stomach results in maximum damage to pylorus and pyloric antrum.[2] In rare cases duodenal obstruction may be seen.[3] However, in rare cases, acids may also produce esophageal injury.[4]

Pathophysiology

Following phases have been identified after ingestion of corrosive agent:[5]

1. Inflammatory stage: It occurs during the first 4 days. edema and erythema develops first followed by thrombosis of vessels and tissue necrosis.
2. Granulation stage: It starts at about day 4 and ends approximately 7 days after ingestion. Fibroplasia results in the formation of granulation tissue with the laying down of collagen over the denuded areas of mucosal sloughing.
3. Perforation: Most often occur between day 7 and 21. During this period the tissues are week and the risk of perforation is high.
4. Cicatrization stage: Starts at 3 weeks and may persist for years. Dense fibrous tissue formation occurs at variable rates. Overproduction of scar tissue results in stricture formation and obstruction.

Clinical Features

Local application: produces chemical burns.

Ingestion:

- Pain in mouth, throat and abdomen
- Dribbling of saliva
- Eructation
- Retching
- Vomiting
- Hematemesis
- Dysphagia
- Dysarthria
- Dyspnea and dysphonia due to regurgitation or fumes.

Management

- Dilution of acid by milk or water
- Demulcent – starch, egg white, milk
- Supportive measures
- Contraindication.
  1. Gastric lavage
  2. Emesis
  3. Neutralization with alkali as it may cause exothermic reaction and increases the risk of perforation
  4. Carbonated alkali – may react with acid and produces carbon dioxide gas that may distend the stomach and increases risk of perforation.

Complication of Inorganic Acid Poisoning

A) Acute:[6, 7]
1. Massive gastric hemorrhage
2. Bronchopneumonia
3. Perforation of stomach
4. Perforation peritonitis
5. Transient laryngeal edema
6. Infection/sepsis
7. Renal failure
8. Shock.

B) Delayed (Chronic)
1. Gastric outlet obstruction/pyloric stenosis
2. Malnutrition.

Cause of Death

A) Early
1. Shock
2. Spasm or edema of larynx
3. Perforation peritonitis
4. Toxemia

B) Delayed
1. Aspiration pneumonia
2. Secondary infection
3. Renal failure
4. Malnutrition

Preservation of Viscera

In case of inorganic acid poisoning deaths, viscera should be preserved in rectified spirit.

Medicolegal Importance

1. Accidental poisoning – common (mistaken for medicine, industrial, etc).[8]
2. May be thrown over face or body with malicious intention (vitriolage).
3. Suicide – rare.[8]

SULFURIC ACID H_2SO_4

Synonyms: Oil of Vitriol

Properties

- Heavy, oily, colourless, odourless and non-fuming liquid
- Hygroscopic
- Carbonizes organic substances.

Fatal dose: 5 to 10 ml
Fatal period: 12 to 18 hours.

Autopsy Findings

- Corrosion of chin, angle of mouth, lips, oral mucosa, tongue, throat.
- Corrosion over hands may be noted
- Teeth chalky white
- The corroded area of skin or mucous membrane appear brownish or blackish (due to chemical charring of the affected tissue)
- Perforation of stomach may be seen.

NITRIC ACID

Synonyms: Aqua Fortis, Red Spirit of Nitre

Properties

- Clear, colourless, fuming liquid
- Pungent odour
- With organic substances, it causes yellowish discolouration due to **xanthoproteic** reaction.

Fatal dose: 10 to 15 ml
Fatal period: 12 to 24 hours.

Autopsy Findings

- Corrosion of skin, angle of mouth, lips, mucosa with yellowish discolouration
- Stomach wall is soft and friable, ulcerated.
- Perforation is less common.

HYDROCHLORIC ACID

Synonyms: Muriatic Acid, Spirit of Salts

Properties

- Colorless, odourless, volatile, fuming liquid
- May acquire yellowish tinge when exposed to air.

Fatal dose: 15 to 20 ml
Fatal period: 18 to 30 hours.

Autopsy Findings

- The skin or mucous membrane shows corrosion. However, corrosion is less severe.
- The skin may be brownish discolored and parchment like
- Coagulation of the surface of the tongue and the mucosa of pharynx and esophagus is seen[9]
- Stomach is soft, edematous, congested, and desquamated or may be ulcerated
- Perforations is less common
- Stomach contents – mixed altered blood with mucus
- Inflammation and edema of respiratory passage.

VITRIOLAGE

- Vitriolage means throwing of acid on the face or body of a person with a malicious intention to cause bodily harm or disfigurement or to cause blindness.
- The term is derived from the practice of throwing sulfuric acid (oil of vitriol). However, it is broadly used to denote injury caused by throwing any corrosive substance such as acid or alkali.

Organic Acid

Examples are:

1. Acetic acid
2. Carbolic acid
3. Oxalic acid
4. Formic acid
5. Citric acid
6. Picric acid.

ACETIC ACID

Synonyms: Ethanoic Acid, Ethylic Acid

Properties

- Colourless, volatile liquid with pungent odour
- Pure acetic acid is an ice-like solid below 16°C, hence it often described as **glacial acetic acid**. Above this temperature, it is colourless liquid.
- The dilute form of acid is called as **vinegar** (vinegar is about 4-5% solution).[10]

Fatal dose: 50 to 100 ml (concentrated)
Fatal period: about 48 hours.

Mechanism of Action

- In concentrated form it acts as corrosive
- In dilute form it acts as an irritant
- Systemic absorption causes hemolysis, hemoglobinuria, renal failure, disseminated intravascular coagulation, metabolic acidosis and liver dysfunction.[11]

Autopsy Findings[11]

- Massive geographic liver necrosis
- Degeneration and swelling of renal tubular epithelium.

CARBOLIC ACID

Synonyms: Phenol, Hydroxy-Benzene

Properties

- Colourless, prismatic, needle-like crystals that turns pink and liquefies when exposed to air (Fig. 34.1)
- Has sweetish burning taste and phenol like smell
- Concentrated phenol is a dark brown liquid and contains impurities like cresol (Fig. 34.2).
- Lysol is 50% solution of cresol in saponified vegetable oil. However, phenol is 8 times more toxic than Lysol
- Dettol is chlorinated phenol with turpineol
- Household phenol (sold as phenyle) contains five percent phenol in water.
- Derivatives of phenol
  1. Cresol
  2. Thymol
  3. Creosate (coal tar)

4. Menthol
5. Tannic acid
6. Napthol
7. Resorcinol.

Uses

1. Antiseptic and disinfectant
2. Manufacture of plastic

Absorption, Metabolism and Excretion

- Phenol is absorbed from skin, gastric mucosa, per rectum, per vagina and respiratory tract
- Phenol is converted into hydroquinone and pyrocatechol and excreted in urine. Traces are excreted by lungs, salivary glands, and skin.

Fatal dose:
- 2 gm crystals
- 25 to 50 ml of household phenol

Fatal period: 3 to 4 hours.

Mechanism of Action[12,13]

- Phenol has local as well as systemic action
- Locally it acts as corrosive agent and when absorbed, it causes CNS depression, metabolic acidosis and renal failure.
- Carbolic acid has great penetrating power and it coagulates protein.
- Phenols have a powerful antipyretic effect similar to that of salicylates.
- Phenols and derivatives of phenols cause methemoglobinemia.

FIG. 34.1: Carbolic acid crystals

FIG. 34.2: Carbolic acid in liquid form

Clinical Features

Local: When applied to skin or mucosa, it causes burning pain, numbness, tingling and anesthesia. It causes corrosion and produce white eschar (scar), which falls off in few days leaving brown stained area.

Systemic:
1. GIT: Burning pain followed by tingling numbness and anesthesia. Nausea and vomiting.
2. RS: Respiration is slow and labored.
3. CNS: Headache, giddiness, unconsciousness, convulsions, coma.
4. Oliguria and hepatic failure.
5. Urine: May be colorless but on exposure to air turns green due to oxidation of phenol metabolites (hydroquinone and pyrocatechol). It is known as **carboluria**.
6. The hydroquinone and pyrocatechol may cause pigmentation in the cornea and various cartilages, a condition known as **oochronosis**.

Management[13]

- Skin: Wash with undiluted polyethylene glycol.
- Oxygen/ventilatory support
- Intravenous fluids and vasopressors to support blood pressure
- Ingestion: Cautious stomach wash with sodium or magnesium sulfate solution
- Lidocaine for ventricular arrhythmias
- Benzodiazepines for seizures
- Treat methemoglobinemia – if methemoglobinemia is > 30%, ingest Methylene blue (1-2 mg/kg). Exchange transfusion may be needed if methemoglobinemia is > 70%.

Autopsy Findings

- Phenol smell
- Corrosion of skin, at angle of mouth, chin. Corrosions are initially white but turns brown in colour
- Splashing may be noted
- Tongue – white and swollen
- Mucosa of stomach is tough, white or gray, corrugated and arranged in longitudinal folds and looks leathery.
- Mucous membrane of mouth, throat, lips are sodden whitened or ash gray
- Urine on exposure to air turns green.

Medicolegal Importance

1. Accidental poisoning.
2. Suicidal ingestion.
3. Homicide – not possible.

OXALIC ACID

Synonyms: Salts of Sorrel, Acid of Sugar

Properties (Fig. 34.3)

- Colourless, transparent, odourless, prismatic crystals resembling the crystals of magnesium sulphate and zinc sulphate (differences are mentioned in Table 34.2).
- It has sour and slightly bitter acidic taste
- It is present in rhubarb leaves, beets and many other vegetables.
- Potassium oxalate, sodium oxalate and ammonium oxalate are toxic salts of oxalic acid.

Uses

1. Bleaching and cleansing agent
2. Ink remover
3. Rust remover
4. Metal polishing

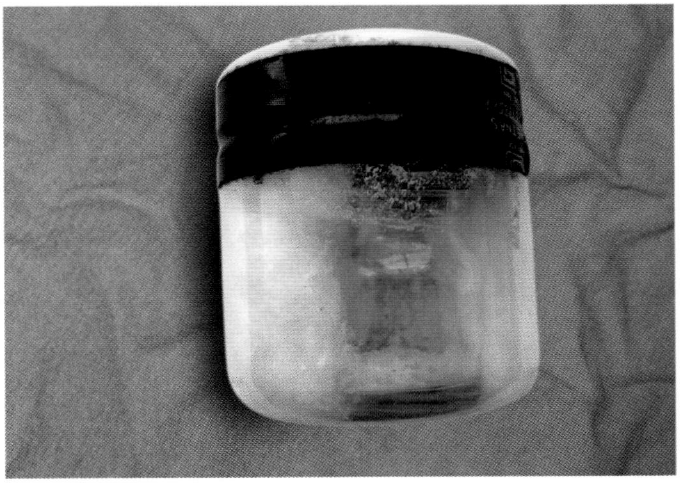

FIG. 34.3: Oxalic acid

5. Cleaning brass and copper articles

Fatal dose: 15 to 20 gm

Fatal period: 1 to 2 hours

Mechanism of Action

- Local: It acts as corrosive when used in concentrated form and act as irritants when used in dilute form
- Systemic: After absorption, oxalic acid combines with calcium ion and causes **hypocalcemia**. It also causes tubular necrosis and renal failure.

Clinical Features

Local: Corrosion of mucosa with underlying congestion. The corroded area is referred as "**scalded**" in appearance.

Systemic

- Vomiting and diarrhea
- Hypocalcemia (**tetany**)
- Muscle irritability, tenderness, cramps
- Convulsions

Table 34.2 Showing difference between oxalic acid, magnesium sulphate and zinc sulphate

Features	*Oxalic acid*	*Magnesium sulphate*	*Zinc sulphate*
Taste	Sour and acid	Bitter	Metallic
Reaction	Strongly acid	Neutral	Slightly acid
Heat	Sublimes	Fixed	Fixed
Sodium carbonate	Effervescence and no precipitate	No effervescence and white precipitate	No effervescence and white precipitate
Stains (ink)	Disappears	No action	No action

- **Accoucher's hand** due to carpopedal spasm
- Chavostek's sign positive. When tapping is done over facial nerve area, there is spasm of facial muscles.
- Metabolic acidosis
- Renal failure
- Uremia.

Management

- Local exposure: Wash the affected skin with copious water
- Gastric lavage with calcium gluconate or calcium lactate
- Calcium gluconate intravenously
- Symptomatic.

Autopsy Findings

- Scalded mucosa of GIT
- Mucous membrane of mouth, tongue, pharynx, esophagus may be bleached and has scalded appearance
- Kidneys show edema, congestion with oxalate crystals in renal tubules with necrosis of proximal convoluted tubule.

Medicolegal Importance

1. Accidental poisoning – common
2. Suicidal ingestion – rare
3. Homicide – not possible.

CORROSIVE ALKALIS

Properties (Figs 34.4 and 34.5)

- Common corrosive alkalis are given in Table 34.3
- Ammonia is a colourless gas with pungent odour. It condenses to a liquid at –33.4°C. The chemical formula is NH_3.
- Ammonium hydroxide is a liquid containing about 30 percent ammonia
- Other corrosive alkalis occur as white powder or colourless solution.

Mechanism of Action

- In concentrated form, alkali acts as corrosive and in dilute form they act as irritant
- Strong alkali produces liquefaction necrosis and causes saponification of fats and dissolves proteins thus causing deep penetration in the tissue resulting in extensive tissue destruction.[5]

Table 34.3 Showing corrosive alkalis

Alkali	*Common name*	*Uses*
Ammonium hydroxide	Ammonia, Hartshorn	Fertilizer, refrigerant, pant remover, oil remover
Ammonium carbonate	Sal volatile	Top job
Sodium carbonate	Washing soda	Household cleaning agent, detergent
Potassium carbonate	Pearl ash, salt of tartar	Household cleaning agent, detergent
Sodium hydroxide	Caustic soda	Drain cleaner
Potassium hydroxide	Caustic potash	Drain cleaner
Calcium hydroxide	Slaked lime	Paint, industrial

- Production of ulcers are more common
- Esophagus is more commonly affected than stomach resulting in stricture formation or perforation.
- Type of material ingested may result in varying degree and location of injury, details are mentioned in Table 34.4.

Fatal Dose

- Sodium carbonate – 30 gm
- Potassium carbonate – 15 gm
- Sodium hydroxide – 5 gm
- Potassium hydroxide – 5 gm
- Ammonia – 30 ml

Fatal period: 24 hours.

Clinical Features

Local: Application causes chemical burns of the skin with skin showing grayish, soapy, necrotic areas without charring.

Inhalation

- Irritation of eyes and watering
- Cough, breathlessness
- Respiratory tract – edematous and inflamed
- Laryngeal edema or spasm may occur causing death.

FIG. 34.4: Washing soda

FIG. 34.5: Potassium carbonate

Ingestion

- Caustic taste and burning pain
- Abdominal pain
- Vomiting and vomitus is alkaline in reaction
- Diarrhea and tenesmus
- The lips, mucous membrane of oral cavity, and the tongue appears soft, swollen, bleached and bogy.
- The mucosa of GIT is swollen, soft, grayish or bleached and sloughs easily
- Esophagus is affected commonly than stomach and results in dysphagia, drooling and hematemesis.
- Alkali induced injury of esophagus is classified by Hawkins et al.[14] It is determined at esophagoscopy. Alkali induced injury of esophagus is mentioned in Table 34.5.

Management

Local: Wash the affected area with copious water.

Ingestion

- Milk or water may be given to dilute the alkali
- Contraindications:
  1. Gastric lavage
  2. Emesis
  3. Neutralization with acid as it may cause exothermic reaction and increases the risk of perforation.
- Assess the injury of esophagus by esophagoscopy
- Symptomatic.

Autopsy Findings

- Ammonia like odour may be perceived
- Mucosa of mouth, tongue, esophagus and stomach is bleached and sodden with areas of necrosis
- Esophagus may show esophagitis or perforation
- Pulmonary edema
- Inhalation – laryngeal edema
- Skin application – chemical burns

Table 34.4 Showing type alkali ingested and lesion produced

Type of alkali preparation	*Ingestion*	*Location of injury*	*Degree of injury*
Powder/solid/granules	Not swallowed, spit out	Mouth, pharynx, upper esophagus	Injury localized, less severe, penetrating
Liquid	Swallowed	Distal esophagus, stomach, duodenum	Injury generalized, deep, circumferential, more severe

Table 34.5 Displays esophageal injury (on esophagoscopy)

Grade of esophageal injury	Features
0	No visible lesion
1	Burns limited to mucosa characterized by the presence of edema and/or erythema
2	Burns penetrating beyond the mucosa characterized by presence of ulceration and/or whitish membrane
3	Presence of perforation

Medicolegal Importance

1. Accidental poisoning – common (mistaken for medicine, industrial etc.)
2. May be thrown over face or body with malicious intention (vitriolage)
3. Suicide – rare.

REFERENCES

1. Mills SW, Okoye MI. Sulfuric acid poisoning. Am J Forensic Med Pathol 1987; 8: 252-5.
2. Sharma J, Debnath PR, Agrawal LD, Gupta V. Gastric outlet obstruction without esophageal involvement: A late sequlae of acid ingestion in children. J Indian Assoc Pediatr Surg 2007; 12: 47-9.
3. Tamisanis AM, Di Noto C, Di Rovasenda E. A rare complication due to sulfuric acid ingestion. Eur J Pediatr Surg 1992; 2: 162-4.
4. Gaudreault P, Parent M, McGuigan MA, Chicoine L, Lovejoy FH Jr. Predictability of esophageal injury from signs and symptoms: A study of caustic ingestion in 378 children. Pediatrics 1983; 71: 767-70.
5. Homan CS. Acids and alkalis. In: Viccellio P (ed) Handbook of Medical Toxicology, 1st edn. 1993. Little, Brown and Company, Boston. 249-63.
6. Eamir O, Hod G, Lernau OZ, Mogle P, Nissan J. Corrosive injury to the stomach due to acid ingestion. Am Surg 1985; 51: 170-2.
7. Dilawari JB, Singh S, Rao PN, Anand BS. Corrosive acid ingestion in man – a clinical and endoscopic study. Gut 1984; 25: 183-7.
8. Arevalo –silva C, Eliashar R, Woblqeternter J, Elidan J, Gross M. Ingestion of caustic substances: a 15 year experience. Laryngoscope 2006; 116: 1422-6.
9. Yoshitome K, Miyaishi S, Ishikawa T, Yamamoto Y, Ishizu H. Distribution of orally ingested hydrochloric acid in thoracoabdominal cavity after death. J Anal Toxicol 2006; 30: 278-80.
10. Rentoul E, Smith H. Toxic materials. In: Glaister's Medical Jurisprudence and Toxicology, 13th edn. 1973. Churchill Livingstone, Edinburgh. 517-709.
11. Yashito K, Kazui S, Keiichi I, Takashi O. Massive non-inflammatory periportal liver necrosis following concentrated acetic acid ingestion. Arch Pathol Lab Med 2000; 124: 127-9.
12. Lo Dico C, Caplan YH, Levine B, Smyth DE, Smialek JE. Phenol: tissue distribution in a fatality. J Forensic Sci 1989; 34: 1013-5.
13. Barclay PJ. Phenols. In: Viccellio P (ed) Handbook of Medical Toxicology, 1st edn. 1993. Little, Brown and Company, Boston. 264-70.
14. Hawkins DB, Demeter MJ, Barnett TE. Caustic ingestion: Controversies in management: A review of 264 cases. Laryngoscope 1980; 90: 98-109.

CHAPTER 35

Inorganic Irritants: Non-metallic Poisons

All people have the right to stupidity but some abuse the privilege.

- Anonymous

Examples are:
1. Phosphorus
2. Iodine
3. Chlorine
4. Bromine
5. Fluorine

IODINE

Features

- Bluish-black, soft and scaly crystals with metallic luster (Fig. 35.1)
- It has unpleasant taste
- It gives off violet colored vapour with iodine like odour

FIG. 35.1: Iodine Crystals

Uses

- Used in antiseptic preparations such as Lugol's iodine, tincture of iodine etc.
- Therapeutic purpose – radioactive iodine is used in treatment of goiter.

Mechanism of Action

- It is a protoplasmic poison fixing proteins and causing necrosis.
- Locally, strong iodine solution may cause an intense irritation.
- Systemic toxicity is due to combination of free iodine with serum bicarbonate causing metabolic acidosis. It is also associated with hyperchloremia, hypernatremia, hyperosmolarity and renal failure.
- Iodine vapours are irritant to respiratory passage.

Absorption, Metabolism and Excretion

- Elemental iodine is absorbed quickly from gastrointestinal tract.
- Small doses of iodine are usually changed to iodide and iodate in the bowel. Large doses are absorbed unchanged and reacts with body proteins. They are changed largely to iodide and iodate before being excreted by all glands of the body.

Fatal dose
- 2 to 4 gm of iodine
- 30 to 60 ml of tincture

Fatal period: 24 hours.

Clinical Features

Iodine may cause acute or chronic poisoning.

Acute Poisoning

1. Inhalation: Vapors of iodine causes irritation of respiratory tract, rhinorrhea and produces cough, pulmonary edema and glottic edema.
2. Local: Application may cause irritation, inflammation, and necrosis with yellowish-brown staining of skin.
3. Ingestion: When ingested, iodine act as corrosive with pain extending from mouth to abdomen, increased salivation, metallic taste, vomiting and diarrhea. The vomitus may be dark brown or blue in colour with iodine odour. Iodine may cause nephritis, renal failure with suppressed urine or scanty urine. **Urine is red-brown in color** and contains albumin.
4. Iodine induced acute sialadenitis (**iodide mumps**), consisting of diffuse submandibular and parotid gland enlargement. It has been identified as a complication of using iodide in contrast radiography.[1,2]

Chronic Poisoning

- Also called as **iodism**
- It causes metallic taste, anorexia, insomnia, lymphadenopathy, and emaciation.
- Parotid swelling (**iodine mumps**)
- Stomatitis
- Conjunctivitis
- Rhinorrhea
- Skin manifestations in form of erythema, urticaria and acne together referred as "**ioderma**".

Management

Acute Poisoning

- Decontamination
  - Skin exposure: Wash with copious water or 20 percent alcohol
  - Eye exposure: copious irrigation with running water
  - GIT: Gastric lavage can be attempted if no esophageal injury is present or suspected. Gastric lavage can be done with
    1. Starch solution or
    2. Five percent solution of sodium thiosulfate (thiosulfate converts iodine to iodide)
    3. Administer activated charcoal
- Sodium bicarbonate for metabolic acidosis
- Hemodialysis followed by continuous venovenous hemodiafiltration[3]
- Supportive measures.

Chronic Poisoning

- Stop iodine intake
- Increase intake of sodium chloride. Sodium chloride will compete with iodide at the level of renal tubules and thus promotes excretion of iodides.

Autopsy Findings

- Clothes will have yellow stains
- The skin, lips, angle of mouth and mucosa will be stained yellowish brown
- Gastric mucosa may be yellowish-brown stained. However, it may appear blue if starch is present in stomach or starch solution is used to treat the patient.
- Iodine like odour
- Congestion of organs.

Medicolegal Importance

1. Accidental poisoning may occur due to therapeutic exposure
2. Iodinated radiologic contrast media or agents are known to produce anaphylactic reactions.

PHOSPHORUS

There are two verities of phosphorus
1. White or yellow phosphorus
2. Red phosphorus

Differences are mentioned in Table 35.1.

Table 35.1: Showing difference between yellow and red phosphorus

Features	*Yellow phosphorus*	*Red phosphorus*
Colour and appearance	White, waxy, crystalline translucent soft cylinders. On exposure to air becomes yellow	Violet-red, amorphous mass
Taste and odour	Garlicky odour and taste	Odourless and tasteless
Luminosity in dark	Luminous	Not luminous
Exposure to air	Phosphorescence	Not Phosphorescence
Toxicity	Highly toxic	Non-toxic

Uses

1. Matches
2. Fire works
3. Military use (incendiary bombs, gun powders etc.)
4. Insecticide and rodenticide
5. Fertilizers.

Fatal dose: 60 to 120 mg (roughly 1 mg/kg body weight)
Fatal period: 4 to 10 hours.

Mechanism of Action

- Yellow phosphorus is a protoplasmic poison and affects cellular oxidation.
- It is also hepatotoxic and cardiotoxic
- It causes fatty infiltration and necrosis of liver and kidney
- Locally it produces severe irritation or burn injuries of skin and mucosa.

Absorption, Metabolism and Excretion

- Phosphorus is absorbed quickly when stomach contains fatty food.
- After absorption, it is distributed to all organs where it is retained and metabolized to hypophosphate. The hypophosphate is excreted through urine and small part is excreted unchanged through feces and expired air.

Clinical Features

A. Acute poisoning[4]

Three stages are usually recognized in acute phosphorus poisoning extending over a period of 8 to 10 days.

1. First stage: It is one of acute irritation of GIT with vomiting, diarrhea and abdominal pain. There is garlicky odour. Vomitus and stool may be luminous in the dark. Fumes may evolve from the stools and called as **smoky stool syndrome**.
2. Second stage: If patient survives, the acuteness of symptoms may subside and condition appears to improve.
3. Third stage: The symptoms of first stage re-appear with increased severity. Manifestation of hepatic failure in form of tender and enlarged liver, jaundice, pruritis and encephalopathy. There are purpuric hemorrhagic areas and cramps. Convulsions may appear at later stage. Renal failure develops with oliguria, hematuria, and albuminuria.
   - Decrease in granulocyte count noted[5]
   - Bone marrow depression. Biopsy reveals decreased cellular mass with degenerative changes[5]
   - Local application causes corrosive burns.

B. Chronic poisoning

- Occurs due to long term exposure
- Nausea, vomiting, diarrhea, eructation and abdominal discomfort
- Wasting and weakness of muscle
- Anemia,
- Jaundice
- **Phossy jaw** or **glass jaw** develops. It is osteomyelitis of jawbone (lower jaw) due to chronic phosphorus poisoning. Initially there is toothache in caries tooth with swelling of gums. There is loosening of teeth, sloughing of gums followed by necrosis, sequestration and osteomyelitis of mandible.
- The epiphysis of children become compact and in adults, the Haversian canals and marrow spaces are filled with dense bone.

Management

- Do not give milk or oily or fatty food/drink because it will enhance the absorption of phosphorus.
- Gastric lavage with potassium permanganate (1:5000). Potassium permanganate oxidizes phosphorus into less toxic phosphoric acid and phosphate.
- Intravenous fluid support
- Vitamin K for hypoprothrombinemia
- Blood/products for correction of coagulation cascade
- Glucose for hypoglycemia
- Calcium gluconate for hypocalcemia
- Benzodiazepines for convulsions.

Autopsy Findings[6]

- Petechial hemorrhages may be noted over skin
- Jaundice
- Garlicky odour
- Gastric mucosa is yellowish or greenish-white in colour and is softened
- Gastric contents emits garlicky odour and luminous in dark
- Liver shows necrobiosis. Liver is enlarged, doughy in consistency, uniformly yellow and contains many hemorrhagic areas in parenchyma
- Heart, kidneys and voluntary muscle fibers shows fatty degeneration
- On microscopy, hepatocellular necrosis and cholestasis are seen.

Medicolegal Importance

- Accidental poisoning – few
- Suicidal or homicidal poisoning – rare

- Yellow phosphorus rolled up in wet cloth was employed to set fire to postal letterboxes during the Indian civil disobedience movement[7] in 1932.

REFERENCES

1. Nakadar AS, Harris-Jones JN. Sialadenitis after intravenous pyelography. BMJ 1971; 3: 351-2.
2. Kalaria VG, Porsche R, Ong LS. Iodide mumps: acute sialadenitis after contrast administration for angiography. Circulation 2001; 104: 2384.
3. Kanakiriya S, De Chazal I, Nath KA, Haugen EN, Albright RC, Juncos LA. Iodine toxicity treated with Hemodialysis and continuous venovenous hemodiafiltration. Am J Kidney Dis 2003; 41: 702-8.
4. McCarron MM, Gaddis GP, Trotter AT. Acute yellow phosphorus poisoning from pesticide pastes. Clin Toxicol 1981; 18: 693-711.
5. Tafur AJ, Zapatier JA, Idrovo LA, Oliveros JW, Garces JC. Bone marrow toxicity after yellow phosphorus ingestion. Emerg Med J 2004; 21: 259-60.
6. Fernandez OU, Conizares LL. Acute hepatotoxicity from ingestion of yellow phosphorus containing fire works. J Clin Gastroenterol 1995; 21: 139-42.
7. Pande TK, Pandey S. White phosphorus poisoning – explosive encounter. J Assoc Phys Ind 2004; 52: 249-50.

CHAPTER 36

Inorganic Irritants: Metallic Poisons

The only medicine for suffering, crime and all other woes of mankind, is wisdom.

- Thomas Huxley

Even at present times, many metals and their salts causes morbidity and mortality. This chapter deals with poisoning of arsenic, mercury, lead, copper, zinc, iron, thallium and antimony compounds.

COPPER

Pure metallic copper is not poisonous but many salts of copper are poisonous (Fig. 36.1). The copper salts are presented in Table 36.1.

Uses

1. Insecticide
2. Fungicide
3. Algaecide (to kill algae in water)

FIG. 36.1: Copper metal

Table 36.1: Showing salts of copper

Chemical name	*Common name*	*Features*
Copper sulphate (See Fig. 36.2)	Blue vitriol, *Nila tutia* (Hindi)	Crystalline blue powder
Copper subacetate	Verdigris *Zangal*	Crystalline green powder
Copper acetoarsenite	Paris green Emerald green	Crystalline green powder
Copper arsenite	*Scheele's green*	Crystalline green powder
Copper carbonate	Mountain green	Crystalline green powder

4. Used in alloys
5. Used as pigments.

Absorption, Metabolism and Excretion

- Copper is normal constituent of body and normal content is 150 mg. It is present in two forms – bound with albumin and other form bound with copper enzyme ceruloplsmin.
- Copper is absorbed through skin, GIT, lungs and mucous membrane
- It is excreted through bile and traces are found in saliva and milk.

Clinical Features

Acute Poisoning

Ingestion:

- Metallic taste

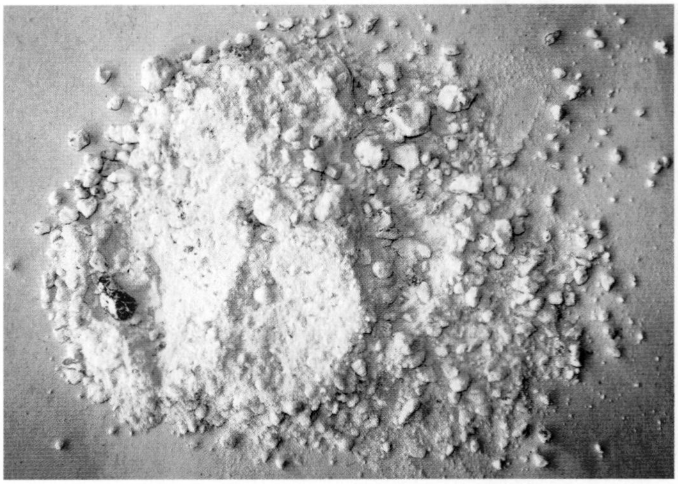

FIG. 36.2: Copper sulphate

- Increased salivation
- Colicky abdominal pain
- Nausea and vomiting. Vomitus is bluish or greenish in color
- Diarrhea
- Myalgia
- Pancreatitis
- Methemoglobinemia
- Hemolysis
- Jaundice
- Oliguria and renal failure
- Convulsions
- Delirium
- Coma.

Inhalation of Copper Fumes or Dust Causes

- Respiratory tract irritation
- Cough
- Conjunctivitis
- Metal fume fever.

Chronic Poisoning

- Abdominal pain
- Greenish line on dental margins of gum (**Clapton's line**) [1]
- **Vineyard Sprayer's lung disease**: Copper sulphate is used as an insecticide spray in vineyards. During spraying, chronic inhalation of copper sulphate causes this disease.
- Greenish hair discolouration
- Wilson's disease.

Management

- Gastric lavage with potassium ferrocyanide. Ferrocyanide converts copper salts into insoluble cupric ferrocyanide.
- Chelation – initially with dimercaprol 2.5 mg/kg four hourly IM followed by oral penicillamine 2 g/day
- Symptomatic.

Fatal Dose

- Copper sulphate – 30 gm
- Copper subacetate – 15 gm

Fatal period: 1 to 3 days

Autopsy Findings

- Jaundice
- Greenish-blue froth at mouth
- Bluish line on gums
- Greenish or bluish stomach contents and gastric mucosa (Fig. 36.3)
- Hemolysis
- Kidneys – tubular necrosis, edema of medulla and appearance of eosinophilic cast[2]
- Muscle atrophy
- Liver – soft and fatty. Microscopy shows centrilobular necrosis.[2]

Medicolegal Importance

1. Suicidal poisoning – common

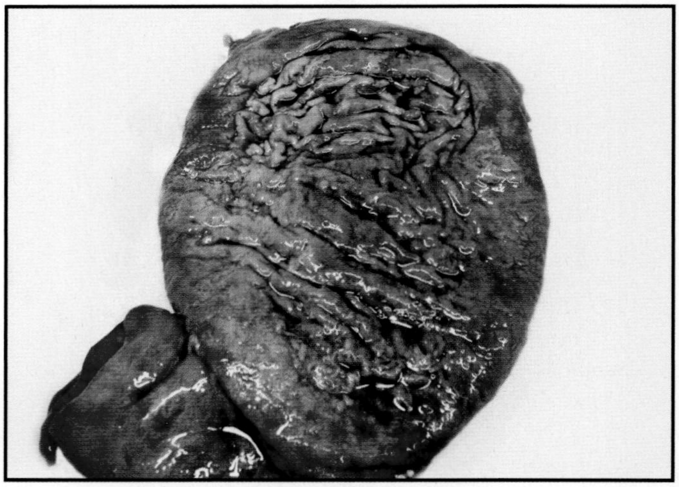

FIG. 36.3: Gastric mucosa in copper sulphate poisoning

2. Accidental poisoning may occur in children.
3. Chronic poisoning – industrial hazard.
4. Use to procure criminal abortion.
5. Cattle poison.

THALLIUM

Properties

- Thallium is soft and pliable metal
- Have tin-white colour but tarnishes the surface on exposure to air due to formation of black thallous oxide
- Thallium sulfate is odourless and tasteless.

Toxic Compounds of Thallium

1. Thallium sulfate
2. Thallium acetate
3. Thallium iodide
4. Thallium nitrate
5. Thallium carbonate.

Uses

1. Dye industry
2. Optical glass
3. Imitation jewelry
4. Rodenticide
5. Depilatory agent
6. Fire works.

Mechanism[3]

- Exact mechanism is unclear but postulated that thallium results in ligand formation with protein sulphydryl group of enzymes and inhibits cellular respiration.
- It disrupts calcium homeostasis
- Interaction with riboflavin and riboflavin based cofactors.

Clinical Features

Acute Poisoning[4]

- Pain in abdomen
- Features of gastroenteritis
- Hematemesis
- Hematochezia
- Headache
- Confusion
- Disorientation
- Paraesthesia
- Hallucinations
- Convulsions
- Retrobulbar neuritis
- Ophthalmoplegia
- Peripheral neuropathy.

Chronic Poisoning

- Alopecia - falling of hairs from head, eyebrows and axilla are common
- Skin rash
- Acneform eruptions
- Dystrophy of nails
- Ascending sensorimotor neuropathy
- Ataxia
- Optic neuropathy
- Encephalopathy
- Ptosis
- Nystagmus
- Combination of alopecia and skin rash, painful peripheral neuropathy and mental confusion with lethargy is called as **thallium triad.**[1]

Management[5]

- Gastric lavage with ferric ferrocyanide (Prussian blue). Prussian blue binds thallium in the intestine and enhances its fecal excretion.
- Hemodialysis
- Forced diuresis
- Supportive measures.

Autopsy Findings

- There may be alopecia
- Stomatitis
- Fatty degeneration of liver and heart
- Tubular necrosis
- Pulmonary edema
- Cerebral edema

Fatal dose: 12 mg/kg body weight[6]
Fatal period: 24 to 30 hours

Medicolegal Importance

1. Popular as ideal homicidal agent.
2. Also consumed as suicidal agent.

ARSENIC

Arsenic is a metalloid and per se is not very toxic, however, arsenic salts are toxic.[7] The arsenic has inorganic and organic compounds. Inorganic compounds are mentioned in Table 36.2.

Table 36.2: Showing inorganic compounds of arsenic

Compound	Common name	Properties
Arsenious oxide (Arsenic trioxide)	Sankhya Somakhar White arsenic	White crystalline powder
Arsenic disulphide	Manseel Red arsenic	Red powder
Arsenic trisulphide	Hartal Yellow arsenic Orpiment	Yellow powder (Fig. 36.4)
Sodium arsenates	-	White or grayish powder
Potassium arsenates	-	
Arsenic acid	Arsenic pentoxide Arsenic anhydride	White crystalline powder
Arsenic trichloride	-	Colourless fuming liquid
Arsenic triodide	Arsenious iodide	Orange colour crystals (Fig. 36.5)
Arsine	Arseniuretted hydrogen Arsenic hydride	Colourless and inflammable gas, Garlicky odour
Sodium arsenite	-	White powder
Potassium arsenite	-	White powder
Copper arsenite (Fig. 36.6)	Scheele's green	Greenish crystalline powder
Copper acetoarsenite	Paris green	Greenish crystalline powder

Organic compounds of arsenic are:
1. Cacodylic acid
2. Sodium cacodylate
3. Atoxyl
4. Stovarsol

Uses

1. Rodenticide
2. Weed killer
3. In alloys
4. Depletory
5. Coloring agent

FIG. 36.4: Arsenic trisulphide (*Courtesy*: Dr Vaibhav Sonar Lecturer, Forensic Medicine, GMS, Miraj)

Sources

1. Rocks and soil
2. Hot spring mineral water
3. Drinking water
4. Sea water
5. Vegetable, fruits and grains
6. Sea food
7. Industrial sources

Absorption, Excretion and Metabolism

- Arsenic is absorbed through all routes *viz.* through skin, inhalation, and GIT mucosa. However, cutaneous absorption is low except in cases of damaged skin. The inorganic pentavalent forms are absorbed at higher rate than bivalent forms.[8]
- The absorbed inorganic arsenic undergoes methylation mainly in liver to monomethylarsonic acid and dimethylarsinic acid and excreted in urine.[9]
- After absorption, arsenic is redistributed to the liver, lungs, intestinal wall, spleen, and kidneys. It has minimal penetration in blood-brain-barrier.

Mechanism of Action

- Arsenic reversibly combines with sulphydrl enzymes. It blocks Krebs cycle and interrupts oxidative phosphorylation causing depletion of ATP and death of cell.

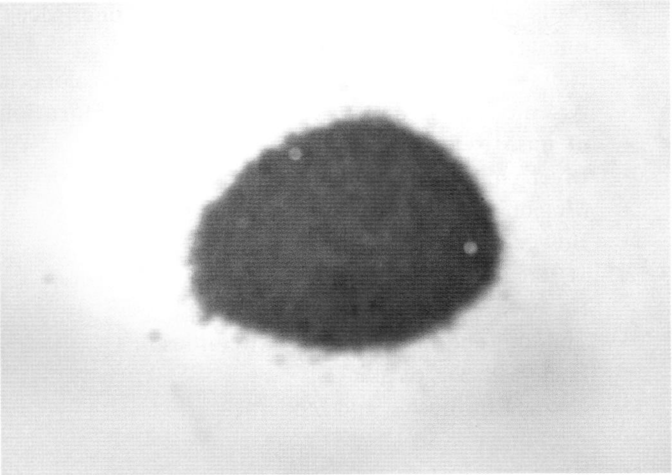

FIG. 36.5: Arsenic triodide

FIG. 36.6: Copper arsenite

- It also inhibits transformation of thiamine into acetyl CoA and Succinyl –CoA resulting in thiamine deficiency.
- It replaces the phosphorus in the bones
- Arsenic is incorporated into hair, nails and skin.
- It causes increased permeability of small blood vessels with inflammation and necrosis of intestinal mucosa thus causing manifestation of hemorrhagic gastroenteritis.

Clinical Features

Acute poisoning

A patient with acute arsenic consumption may present in

1. Fulminant type: collapse and circulatory failure
2. Gastroenteritis type
3. Narcotic form
   - Metallic taste
   - Garlicky odour
   - Nausea and vomiting
   - Colicky abdominal pain
   - Profuse diarrhea resembling rice water stool of cholera. Difference between arsenic poisoning and cholera is summarized in Table 36.3
   - Circulatory failure
   - Intense thirst
   - Oliguria
   - Uremia
   - Ventricular tachycardia
   - Headache
   - Vertigo
   - Tremors
   - Convulsions

Table 36.3: Showing difference between arsenic poisoning and cholera

Features	*Arsenic poisoning*	*Cholera*
Pain in throat	Before vomiting	After vomiting
Conjunctiva	Inflamed	Not inflamed
Vomitus	Contains mucus, bile and streaks of blood	It is watery or whey like
Purging	Follows vomiting	Usually precedes vomiting
Stools	Rice watery in early stages, later becomes bloody, discharged with straining and tenesmus	Rice water liquid, involuntary jet
Laboratory examination	1. Radio-opaque shadow on X-ray of abdomen in arsenic trioxide poisoning 2. Coproporphyrin in urine 3. Arsenic detected in chemical analysis	Vibrio cholera detected on microscopic examination

- Formication
- Delirium
- Tenderness in muscle
- Paralysis
- Hyperpyrexia
- QT prolongation, tachyarrhythmia including torsades de pointes may develop within first 24 hours after ingestion.[10]

Subacute Poisoning

This results when arsenic is given in small doses at frequent intervals. The features are:

- Dyspepsia
- Cough
- Tingling in throat followed by vomiting
- Diarrhea with tenesmus and abdominal pain
- Cramps in muscle
- Restlessness.

Chronic Poisoning

The features are exhibited in four stages[6]

1. First stage
   - GIT symptoms dominate
   - Malaise
   - Loss of appetite
   - Salivation
   - Colicky abdominal pain
   - Constipation (sometimes diarrhea)
   - Vomiting
   - Gums – red and soft
   - Circumscribed edema of ankle
   - Periorbital edema
2. Second stage
   - Cutaneous eruptions
   - Voice – hoarse and husky
   - Rhinorrhea
   - Skin – generalized or localized fine mottled pigmentation of skin (**Rain drop pigmentation**, see Table 36.4)
   - Epithelial hyperplasia with keratosis – mostly on sole and palms
   - Nails – become brittle and show **Mees' line**. Mees' line are white transverse lines over nails
   - Hairs – dry and may fall off; patchy or diffuse alopecia
   - Arsenic dust – flexor eczema, painless **perforation of nasal septum**.
   - Liver enlarged (hepatomegaly) and cirrhotic
   - Melanosis of neck, eyelids and nipples
   - Bowen's disease.
3. Third stage
   - Headache
   - Tingling and numbness of extremities
   - Hyperasthesia of skin
   - Cramps in muscle and tenderness
   - Arthralgia
   - Knee jerk lost
   - Impotence
   - Bone marrow depression with aplstic anemia
   - Interference with folic acid metabolism with deficiency
   - Hematological abnormalities (Table 36.5).
4. Fourth stage
   - Peripheral neuropathy
   - Neuropathy is hallmark of arsenic poisoning. It is usually symmetrical sensorimotor polyneuropathy resembling Guillain-Barre syndrome
   - Weakness of muscle and atrophy – extensor muscles more commonly affected resulting in **wrist drop** and **foot drop**
   - Ataxia
   - Tremors
   - Emaciation
   - Anemia
   - Dysuria
   - Delusion
   - Encephalopathy
   - Death.

Table 36.4: Displaying differential diagnosis of raindrop pigmentation of arsenic

Rain drop pigmentation may be mistaken for
1. Addison's disease
2. Secondary syphilis

Table 36.5: Showing hematological abnormalities in arsenic poisoning

Hematological abnormalities
• Leukopenia
• Thrombocytopenia
• Mild eosinophilia
• Karyorrhexis - manifested by bizarre nuclear forms
• Megaloblastic anemia
• Basophilic stippling

Differential Diagnosis

1. Acute poisoning resembles cholera
2. Alcoholic neuritis
3. Guillain-Barre syndrome.

Management[10,11]

Acute poisoning
- Gastric lavage
- Administer activated charcoal
- Aggressive fluid resuscitation and cardiovascular support remains the mainstay of initial management.
- Chelation – BAL, Succimer (DMSA), or DMPS. Every 50 mg BAL binds 30 mg of arsenic.
- Exchange transfusion
- Continuous venovenous hemodiafiltration.

Disadvantage of BAL

- Have to give as an intramuscular injection
- Unpredictable bioavailability.

BAL is Contraindicated in:

Patients with glucose-6-phosphate dehydrogenase deficiency because BAL may cause hemolysis.

Chemical Test for Arsenic Detection

1. Reinsch's test
2. Marsh's test
3. Gutzeit test.

Fatal dose: Arsenious oxide – 180 mg
Fatal period: 12 to 48 hours.

Autopsy Findings

- Rigor mortis last for longer duration
- Jaundice
- GIT – mucosa is congested and edematous. The mucosa may be reddened or show hemorrhagic gastroenteritis. The focal hemorrhages give rise to flea bitten appearance and this appearance is considered as characteristic. The mucosal appearance is described as red velvet like[12]
- Subendocardial hemorrhages in heart with fatty degeneration
- Liver – fatty degeneration.

Preserved for Chemical Analysis

1. Routine viscera
2. Long bone – femur
3. Scalp hairs
4. Muscle
5. Skin
6. Nails.

Medicolegal Importance

1. Homicidal poison – in past it is considered as ideal homicidal poison. The arsenic is administered in chronic way to a person and the clinical features is manifested for natural disease
2. Used as cattle poison[13]
3. Accidental poisoning: due to
   - Used in indigenous medicine – chronic poisoning
   - Well water (tube well water)[7]
   - Adulteration with alcohol drink
   - Mistaken for medicine
   - Arsenophagist – some people take arsenic daily as an aphrodisiac and are habituated for arsenic.

MERCURY

Synonyms: Quick silver. Para

Features

- Only metal, which is liquid at room temperature
- Metallic mercury is having bright silvery luster and is volatile at room temperature. The fumes are odourless and invisible (Fig. 36.7).
- It is 13.5 denser than water
- Metallic mercury is not poisonous if taken by mouth, as it is not absorbed. However, if vapours are inhaled, may exert toxic effects.
- Mercury exists in three forms:[14]
  1. Elemental mercury – Hg^o – vapours are toxic
  2. Inorganic mercury
  3. Organic mercury.
- Inorganic salts are of two types as:
  4. Mercuric (bivalent Hg^{++}) – more poisonous
  5. Mercurous (monovalent Hg^{+}) – less poisonous.

Toxic Compounds

Inorganic compounds are mentioned in Table 36.6.

Organic Compounds

Organic compounds of mercury are more toxic than inorganic compounds and are:
1. Ethyl mercury
2. Methyl mercury
3. Mercurochrome.

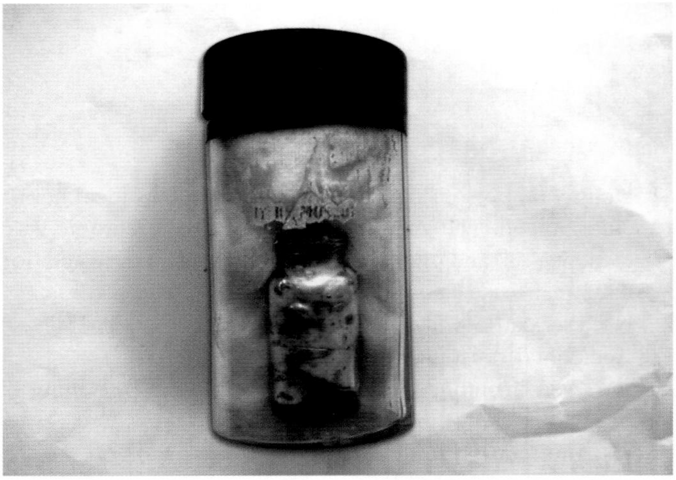

FIG. 36.7: Mercury (*Courtesy*: Dr PG Dixit, Prof and Head, Forensic Medicine, GMCH, Nagpur)

Table 36.6: Displaying inorganic compounds of mercury

Compound	*Common name*	*Features*
Mercuric oxide	Sipichand	Brick-red crystalline powder (Fig. 36.8)
Mercuric chloride	Perchloride of mercury Corrosive sublimate	Heavy colourless prismatic crystals
Mercuric iodide	Red iodide	Scarlet red powder (Fig. 36.9)
Mercuric cyanide	-	White prismatic crystals
Mercuric nitrate	-	Deliquescent crystalline
Mercuric sulphide	Cinnabar, Hingul Ras sindoor, Cheena sindoor Pigment vermillion	Red crystalline powder (Fig. 36.10)
Mercuric sulphate	-	White crystalline powder
Mercurous chloride	Calmol, raskapoor Subchloride of mercury	Fibrous, heavy, dirty white mass (Fig. 36.11)
Mercurous nitrate	-	Colorless crystalline powder

Uses

1. Barometers, thermometers
2. Ceramics
3. Dry cell batteries
4. Felt hat
5. Antiseptic and disinfectant
6. Embalming
7. Fingerprint powder
8. Grain preservative
9. Pesticide
10. Paints

Absorption, Metabolism and Excretion

- Elemental mercury is readily absorbed through alveolar membrane and enters the blood. Mercury slats are absorbed through skin, GIT mucosa, vaginal mucosa and bladder. Organic compounds can pass placental barrier and cause fetal toxicity.
- In blood mercury is converted into mercuric ions and causes tubular damage during excretion. In CNS, mercury acts on cerebellum, temporal lobe, basal ganglia and corpus callosum.[1] Mercury gets deposited in liver, kidneys, spleen and bone.
- Mercury is excreted in urine, feces and bile with enetero-hepatic circulation.[14]

Mechanism of Action

- Mercury compounds act by inactivating sulphydril enzymes causing interference with cellular metabolism.[15]

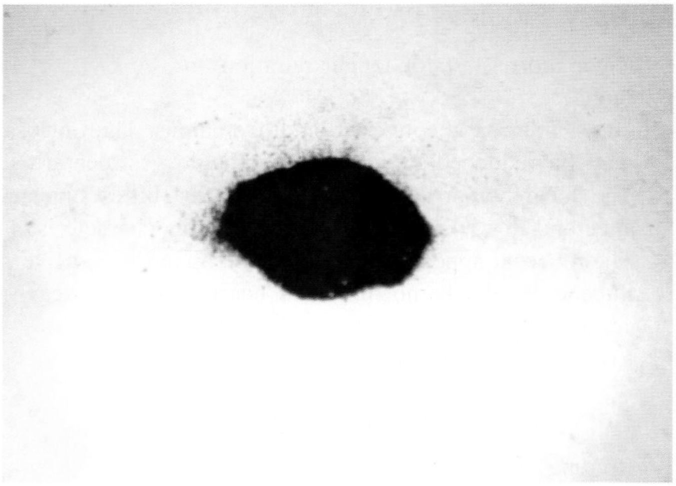

FIG. 36.8: Mercuric oxide

FIG. 36.9: Mercuric iodide

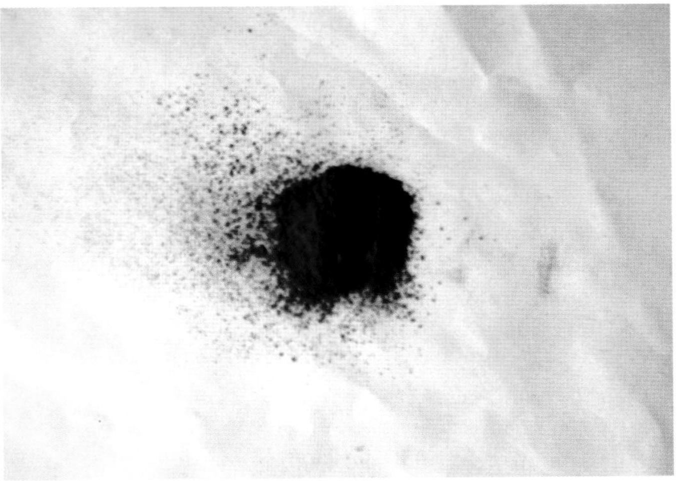

FIG. 36.10: Mercuric sulphide

Fatal Dose

- Mercuric chloride – 1 gm
- Mercuric cyanide – 0.6 to 1.3 gm
- Mercuric nitrate – 4 gm
- Mercurous chloride (calomel) – 1.5 to 2 gm

Fatal period: 3 to 5 days.

Clinical Features

A. Acute poisoning with inorganic compounds
Inhalation:

- Breathlessness
- Cough

FIG. 36.11: Mercurous chloride

- Fever, chills (metal fume fever)
- Headache
- Blurring of vision
- Non-cardiogenic pulmonary edema
- Convulsions
- Ataxia
- Delirium.

Injection

- Subcutaneous or intramuscular injection of mercury causes abscess formation with ulceration
- Intravenous administration results in thrombophlebitis, granuloma formation and pulmonary embolism
- Intra-arterial administration results in peripheral embolism with ischemia and gangrene.

Ingestion

- Metallic taste
- Abdominal pain
- Vomiting
- Shock
- Corrosion of mouth and tongue
- Hematemesis
- Renal failure
- Pulmonary edema
- Urine – pinkish in colour
- Glossitis and ulcerative gingivitis
- Loosening of teeth
- Necrosis of jaw
- Membranous colitis

Management

- Gastric lavage with egg white or albumin or milk to bind the mercury
- Demulcents
- Laxative
- X-ray follow up
- Chelation with BAL, DMPS
- Supportive

B. Poisoning by organic compounds
  - Dysarthria
  - Ataxia
  - Paraesthesia
  - Neuropathy
  - Diminished visual and auditory activity
  - Mental deterioration
  - Chorea
  - Minimata disease

C. Chronic poisoning
  - Also called as hydrargyrism, mercurialism
  - Excessive salivation (Ptyalism, Sialorrhea)
  - Metallic taste
  - Anorexia
  - Insomnia
  - Headache
  - Gingivitis
  - Halitosis
  - Blue line on gums
  - Lassitude
  - Visual blurring
  - Concentric constriction of visual field (**tunnel vision**)
  - **Mercuria lentis** – opacities of the anterior capsule of the lens of eye due to deposition of mercury
  - Ataxia – reeling gait
  - Tremors – classical manifestation of chronic mercury poisoning and is referred as "**Danbury tremor**". The tremors are coarse, intentional type, interspersed with jerky movements, initially involving hands. Later it involves lip, tongue, arms and legs. The advanced condition of tremors is called as "**Hatter's shakes**" (because the condition was first described among felt hat workers). In Hatter's shakes, the tremor becomes so severe that daily activities of person are grossly impaired such as shaving, writing, holding cup etc. As the disease progresses, the most severe form of tremor are called as "**Concussio mercurialis**" which means no activity is possible (Fig. 36.12).
  - Mercurial erethism – a classical manifestation of chronic mercury poisoning characterized by cluster of psychiatric symptoms including disturbance in personality, abnormal shyness, timidity, loss of self confidence, insomnia, excitability, progressing later into delirium with hallucinations (**Mad as hatter**).
  - Colitis
  - Melanosis coli
  - Mercury dermatitis – from mercuric sulphide (cinnabar) as red areas of tattoo has been reported. Also contact dermatitis as occupational hazard had been noted.[16]
  - Dementia
  - Renal failure
  - Acrodynia (Pink disease):
    - Seen mostly in children and caused by chronic mercury exposure. It causes anorexia, insomnia, profuse sweating, skin rash, redness, vesication and desquamation (peeling) of palm, finger, sole and photophobia.
    - The hands and feet becomes – **p**uffy, **p**inkish, **p**ainful, **p**araesthetic, **p**erspiring and **p**eeling (remember 6 P's)[1]
    - Shedding of teeth and ulceration of gums.

Autopsy Findings

- Emaciated body
- Mouth, throat, stomach appear grayish with softening and corrosion with hemorrhagic areas
- Colitis[12]
- Liver and heart – fatty degeneration
- Kidneys – pale, swollen with edema of renal cortex with necrosis of renal tubules.

Medicolegal Importance

1. Poisoning occur due to accidental consumption of mercury as
   - Folk medicine/indigenous medicine
   - Toothpaste
   - Industrial exposure

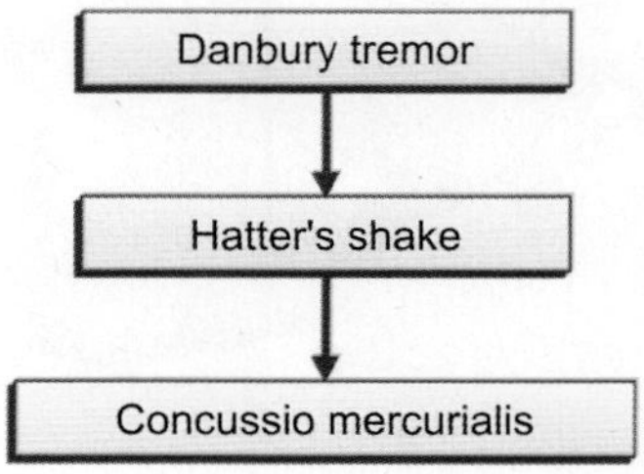

FIG 36.12: Flow chart displaying progression of tremors caused by mercury poisoning

- Dental amalgam
- Food poisoning – consumption of contaminated fish with methyl mercury
- Dry cell battery

2. Homicide and suicide – rare
3. Use to procure criminal abortion.

LEAD (SISHA)

Properties

- Lead is heavy, soft, steel-gray metal which gives off toxic fumes when it is melted (Fig. 36.13)
- Lead and its compounds are toxic. The toxic compounds are mentioned in Table 36.7.

FIG. 36.13: Lead metal granules

Sources

1. Automobile exhaust
2. Battery making
3. Glass manufacture
4. Plastic manufacture
5. House paints
6. Steel welding and cutting.

Table 36.7: Displaying toxic compounds of lead

Compound	*Common name*	*Features*
Lead acetate	Sugar of lead Salt of Saturn	White acicular crystals (Fig. 36.14)
Lead carbonate	White lead Safeeda	White powder (Fig. 36.15)
Lead nitrate	-	Crystalline powder
Lead sulphate	-	White powder
Lead chromate	Chrome yellow	Bright yellow powder (Fig. 36.16)
Lead chlorate	-	White needle shaped crystals
Lead iodide	-	Bright yellow powder
Lead sulphide	Surma	Cubic crystals (Fig. 36.17)
Lead monoxide	Mudrasang Litharge	Brick-red scaly mass
Lead tetraoxide	Sindur Metia sindur Red lead	Scarlet crystalline powder (Fig. 36.18)
Lead tetra-ethyl	-	Heavy, oily, volatile liquid

Uses

1. Paint
2. Glazing of pottery and enamel ware
3. Anti-knock for petrol
4. Lead-acid batteries
5. Projectiles for firearms
6. Glass.

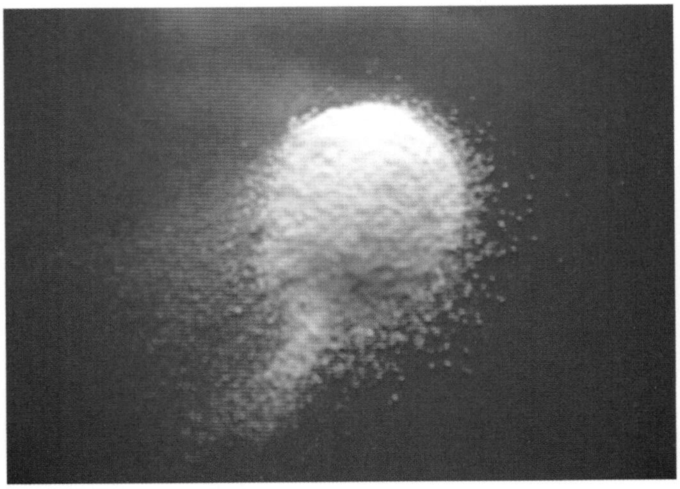

FIG. 36.14: Lead acetate

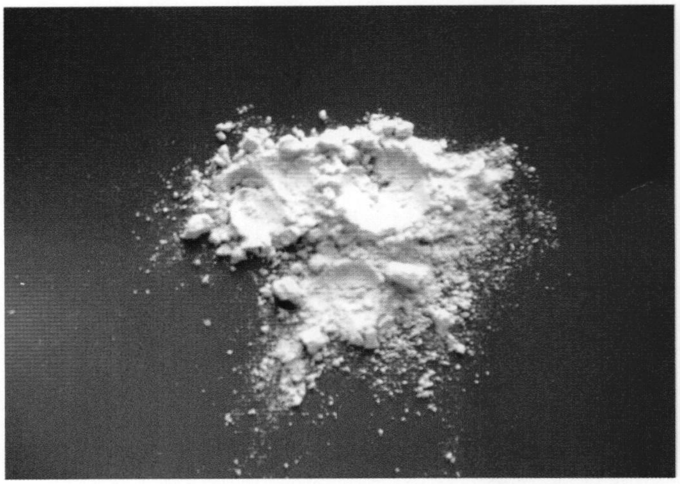

FIG. 36.15: Lead carbonate

FIG. 36.16: Lead chromate

Mechanism of Action (Fig. 36.19)

- Combines with sulphhydryl enzymes and inhibit cell metabolism[15]
- It also inhibits following enzymes required for heme synthesis and causes anemia[1]
  1. Aminolaevulinic acid dehydratase
  2. Aminolaevulinic acid synthetase
  3. Coproporphyrinogen oxidase
  4. Ferrchelatase
- It causes hemolysis.

Absorption, Metabolism and Excretion[17]

- Absorbed from all routes *viz*. skin, GIT mucosa, inhalation
- After absorption, it is stored in bones as phosphate and carbonate. It is also deposited in liver and kidney
- Lead is a cumulative poison and its rate of excretion is less than absorption. It is excreted in urine and bile.

Fatal Dose

- Lead acetate – 20 gm
- Lead carbonate – 40 gm
- Lead tetra-ethyl – 100 mg/kg

Fatal period: 2 to 3 days.

Clinical Features

Acute poisoning

- Metallic taste

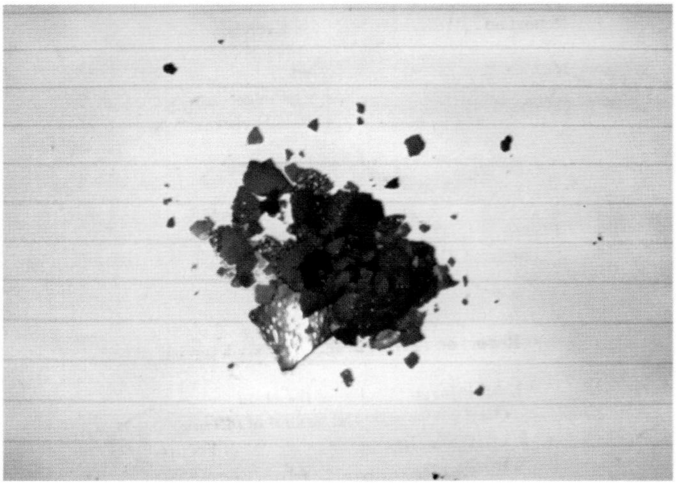

FIG. 36.17: Lead sulphide

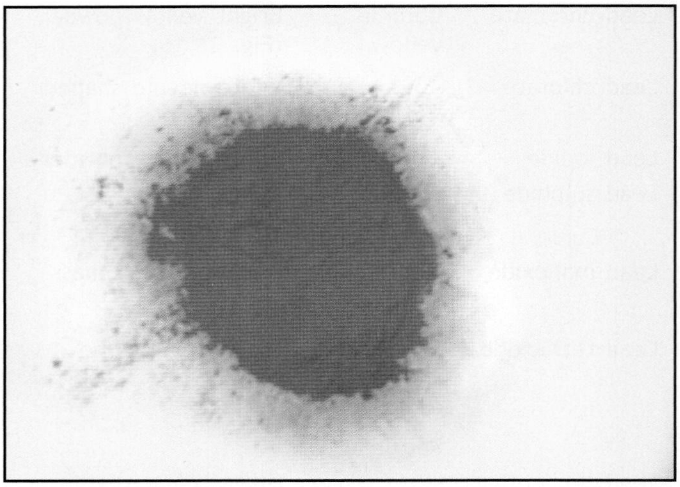

FIG. 36.18: Lead tetraoxide

Succinyl CoA + Glycine
↓ *δ-Aminolevulinate synthase* (Pb X)
δ- Aminolevulinate
↓ *δ- Aminolevulinate dehydratase* (Pb X)
Porphobilinogen
↓ *Porphobilinogen deaminase*
Uroporphyrinogen III cosynthase
Uroporphyrinogen III
↓ *Uroporphyrinogen decarboxylase*
Coproporphyrinogen III
↓ *Coproporphyrinogen oxidase* (Pb X)
Protoporphyrin IX
↓ *Ferrchelatase* + Fe^{2+} (Pb X)
Heme

FIG. 36.19: Showing biosynthesis of heme with interference by lead. (Pb X) indicates step inhibited by lead

- Vomiting
- Colicky abdominal pain
- Constipation
- Ataxia
- Apathy
- Headache
- Insomnia
- Paraesthesia
- Lethargy
- Drowsiness
- Acute lead encephalopathy
- Convulsions
- Coma.

Chronic Poisoning

- Called as **plumbisim**, **saturnism**
- Myalgia
- Paraesthesia
- Fatigue
- Irritability
- Abdominal discomfort/pain
- Arthralgia
- Tremor
- Headache
- Anorexia
- Vomiting
- Weight loss
- Facial pallor – especially around the mouth (**circum-oral pallor**) is considered as consistent sign of chronic lead poisoning. It is due to vasospasm in addition to anemia.
- Anemia – is due to impairment in heme synthesis and is hypochromic and microcytic type anemia. There is reduced erythrocyte life span[18]
- Blood – there are immature red cells in circulation such as reticulocytes and basophilic stippled cells. Basophilic stippling or punctate basophilia means presence of many dark coloured pinhead sized spots in the cytoplasm of red blood cells. The spots are aggregation of ribonucleic acid (RNA) due to inhibition of the enzyme pyrimidine-5' nucleotidase that normally eliminates degraded RNA.
- Lead line (Burtonian line) – a bluish line is present on gums. The line formation is due to lead sulphide. Lead sulphide is formed due to action of hydrogen sulphide gas, liberated from the decomposed food in the mouth, with lead.[18]
- Colic and constipation (dry belly ache) - Colic affects intestine, ureter or uterus. The attack of colic lasts for few minutes and is in form of severe, intermittent cramps. During colic, the abdominal wall is rigid and contracted. Constipation is associated with the colic.
- Lead palsy – is a late phenomenon. The extensor muscles are paralyzed causing wrist drop or foot drop. It is **motor** type of paralysis. The motor paralysis is due to:
  1. Interference with phosphocreatine metabolism
  2. Peripheral neuropathy.
- Lead encephalopathy – it is more common in children and presents with sudden onset of vomiting, irritability, headache, ataxia, vertigo, convulsions and coma.
- Hypertension
- Arteriosclerotic nephritis
- Amenorrhea
- Sterility
- Abortion.

Management

- Chelation: The use of calcium chelate of disodium EDTA act as an ion exchanger in which the Ca^{++} is exchanged for the heavy metal ion and a soluble and stable chelate of lead is formed. This lead chelate is excreted by kidneys as a ring complex[15]
- Diazepam for convulsions
- Thiamine
- Calcium gluconate.

Autopsy Findings

- Pale skin
- Blue line on gums
- Emaciation
- Lead line on X-ray

- GIT – ulceration, hemorrhage with contracted wall
- Renal tubular degeneration
- Bone marrow hyperplasia
- Segmental demyelination of peripheral nerves
- Paralyzed muscles are flaccid and show fatty infiltration
- Elevated delta-Aminolaevulinic (ALA) levels in post-mortem blood.[19]

Medicolegal Importance

1. Accidental poisoning may occur in children (**pica**)
2. Plumbisim – industrial hazard
3. Use to procure criminal abortion
4. Cattle poison
5. Lead bullet/ missile embedded in person in firearm injury may cause chronic poisoning (plumbisim), however, reported cases are few.[20, 21]
6. Suicide or homicide – rare.

IRON

Poisonous iron slats are:
1. Iron sulphate (ferrous sulphate)
   - Also known as green vitriol (Fig. 36.20)
   - Green monosymmetric crystals
2. Ferric chloride (perchloride of iron)
   - It is water soluble and irritant
   - When water is evaporated, yellow crystals are formed.

Mechanism of Action

- In concentrated form it acts as corrosive and in dilute form act as irritant.

FIG. 36.20: Ferrous sulphate (*Courtesy*: Dr PG Dixit, Prof. and Head, Forensic Medicine, GMCH, Nagpur)

- It increases capillary permeability
- After absorption, when serum iron level exceeds the body's binding capacity, the free iron produces an increase in reactive oxygen species (ROS) or free radicals. This causes cellular damage.[22]
- It inhibits mitochondrial functions.
- It also causes hepatic damage, hypoglycemia and hypoprothrombinemia.

Clinical Features

Four stages are identified and are:

Stage I: Stage of Gastrointestinal Toxicity

- Metallic taste
- Vomiting and diarrhea
- Abdominal pain
- Pallor
- Shock
- Lethargy
- Acidosis
- Hematemesis
- Black stool.

Stage II: Stage of Apparent Stabilization or Quiescent Phase

- Headache
- Confusion
- Delirium

Stage III: Stage of Mitochondrial Toxicity and Hepatic Necrosis

- Hepatic failure
- Hypovolaemia
- Hypotension
- Multiorgan failure
- Coagulopathy
- Hypoglycemia
- Jaundice
- Convulsions
- Coma
- Death

Stage IV: Stage of Recovery and/or Gastric Scarring

- Recovery may occur and patient presents with:
  - Gastric scarring or
  - Pyloric obstruction.

Management[23-27]

- Gastric lavage with normal saline
- Activated charcoal
- Whole bowel irrigation may be of benefit because it will rapidly and effectively clean the gut. For bowel irrigation, polyethylene glycol lavage solution given at the rate of 30 to 40 ml/kg/hour for 4 to 8 hours.
- Chelation – desferrioxamine is used as specific antidote. Desferrioxamine is given when there are serious clinical symptoms or when serums iron level > 500 µg/dL is measured within 8 hours of ingestion. Desferrioxamine is given as continuous intravenous infusion in normal saline at 15 mg/kg/hour. Each 100 mg of desferrioxamine binds to 9 mg of elemental iron producing ferrio-xamine complex, which gets excreted by kidney.

Fatal dose: ferrous sulphate – 20 to 40 gm
Fatal period: variable.

Autopsy Findings

- Hemorrhagic necrosis or corrosion of gastrointestinal mucosa
- In ferrous sulfate – greenish-blue colour of mucosa (Fig. 36.21)
- Hepatic and renal necrosis
- Jaundice
- Pyloric stenosis.

Medicolegal Importance

1. Accidental poisoning
2. Homicide/suicide – rare
3. Use to procure criminal abortion.

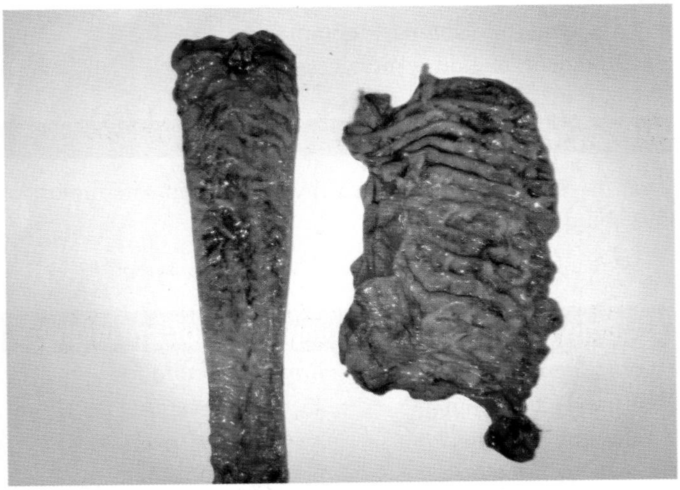

FIG. 36.21: Gastric and intestinal mucosa in ferrous sulphate poisoning

ZINC (JASAT)

Zinc is soft, bluish white, lustrous metal. The poisonous compounds are listed in Table 36.8.

Clinical Features

- Metallic taste
- Salivation
- Vomiting
- Substernal pain
- Abdominal pain
- Diarrhea
- Convulsions
- Shock
- Metal fume fever
- Pneumonitis
- Acute pancreatitis with raised serum amylase level
- Hepatic damage
- Renal failure
- Coagulation failure.

Fatal Dose

- Zinc phosphide – 5 gm
- Zinc sulphate – 10 to 20 gm
- Zinc chloride – 5 gm

Fatal Period: Variable

Table 36.8: Showing poisonous compounds of zinc

Compound	*Common name*	*Properties*
Zinc sulphate (Fig. 36.22)	White vitriol Safed tutia	• Colourless crystalline salt • Resembles magnesium sulphate and oxalic acid (also see Table 34.2)
Zinc chloride	Butter of zinc	Colourless opaque mass
Zinc oxide	Jasat, Bhasham White zinc	White odourless powder
Zinc phosphide (Fig. 36.23)	-	Steel gray powder with garlicky odour
Zinc stearate	-	White bulky powder

FIG. 36.22: Zinc sulphate (*Courtesy*: Dr PG Dixit, Prof and Head, Forensic Medicine, GMCH, Nagpur)

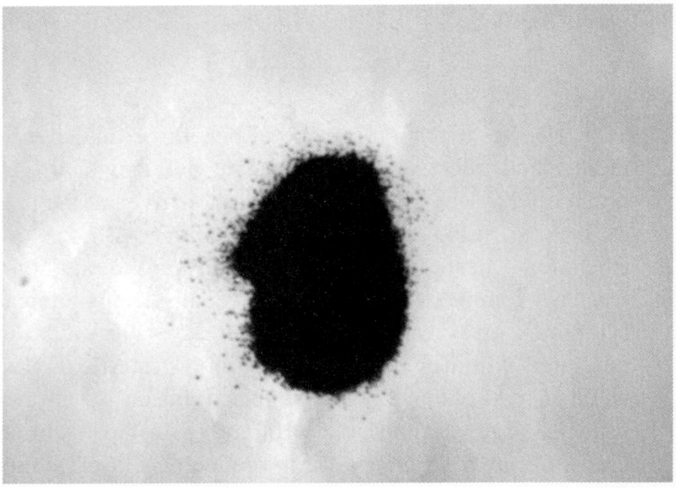

FIG. 36.23: Zinc phosphide

Management

- Gastric lavage
- Chelation
- Supportive.

Autopsy Findings[1]

- Acute hemorrhagic gastritis, esophagitis
- Pancreatitis
- Liver necrosis
- Acute tubular necrosis
- Pulmonary edema

Medicolegal Importance

1. Accidental poisoning – common
2. Suicide/homicide – rare
3. Metal fume fever.

ANTIMONY

Poisonous antimony compounds are given in Table 36.9.

Clinical Features

- Vomiting
- Abdominal pain
- Diarrhea
- Hematemesis
- Dermatitis
- Renal failure and oliguria
- Hepatic failure

Management

- Gastric lavage
- Chelation with BAL
- Hemodialysis
- Supportive

Fatal Dose

- Antimony tartarum – 90 to 180 mg
- Antimony trichloride – 8 to 12 ml

Fatal period: 24 hours.

Medicolegal Importance

1. Accidental poisoning – common
2. Suicide/homicide – rare

METAL FUME FEVER

This is a syndrome caused by inhalation of fumes of following metals

Table 36.9: Showing compounds of antimony

Compound	*Common name*
Antimony tartarum	Tarter emetic
Antimony trioxide	Antimonious oxide
Antimony trichloride	Butter of antimony
Antimony trisulphide (Fig. 36.24)	Black antimony Surma

FIG. 36.24: Antimony trisulphide

1. Antimony
2. Cobalt
3. Cadmium
4. Chromium
5. Copper
6. Iron
7. Lead
8. Manganese
9. Magnesium
10. Mercury
11. Nickel
12. Selenium
13. Zinc
    - Persons involved in welding, galvanizing, smelting, metal refining, electroplating, alloy making etc. are affected
    - The syndrome resembles flu-like illness and begins after four to six hours after exposure to metal fumes.
    - It is characterized by fever, chills, myalgia, cough, dyspnea, fatigue, metallic taste, salivation, sweating and cyanosis.

REFERENCES

1. Pillay VV. Heavy metals. In: Comprehensive Medical Toxicology, 1st edn. 2003. Paras Publishing, Hyderabad. 97-140.
2. Kurisaki E, Kuroda Y., Sato M. Copper-binding protein in acute copper poisoning. Forensic Sci Int 1988; 38: 3-11.
3. Jha S, Kumar R, Kumar R. Thallium poisoning presenting as paresthesia, paresis, psychosis and pain in abdomen. J Assoc Phys Ind 2006; 54: 53-5.
4. Tsai YT, Huang CC, Kuo HC, Wang HM, Shen WS, Shih TS, Chu NS. Central nervous system effects in acute thallium poisoning. Neurotoxicology 2006; 27: 291-5.
5. Klaassen CD. Pesticides. In: Gilman AG, Rall TW, Nies AS, Taylor P (eds) Goodman and Gilman's the Pharmacological basis of Therapeutics, Vol. II, 8th edn. 1991. Pregamon Press, New York. 1626-39.
6. Mathiharan K, Patnaik AK. Inorganic Irritant Poisons (II). In: Modi's Medical Jurisprudence and Toxicology, 23rd edn. 2005. LexisNexis Butterworths, New Delhi. 107-216.
7. Pillay VV. Heavy metals. In: Textbook of Forensic Medicine and Toxicology, 14th edn. 2004. Paras Publishing, Hyderabad. 395-441.
8. Quatrehomme G, Ricq O, Lapalus P, Jacomet Y, Ollier A. Acute arsenic intoxication: forensic and toxicologic aspects (an observation). J Forensic Sci 1992; 37: 1163-71.
9. Dikshit PC. Metallic poisons. In: Textbook of Forensic Medicine and Toxicology, 1st edn. 2007. Peepee Publishers and Distributors (P) Ltd., New Delhi. 469-87.
10. Lai MW, Boyer EW, Kleinman ME, Rodig NM, Ewald MB. Acute arsenic poisoning in two siblings. Pediatrics 2005; 116: 249-57.
11. Hu H. Heavy metal poisoning. In: Fauci AS, Braunwald E, Isselbacher KJ, Wilson JD, Martin JB, Kasper DL, Hauser SL, Longo DL (eds) Harrison's Principles of Internal Medicine, Vol.2, 14th edn. 1998. McGraw-Hill, New York. 2564-9.
12. Vij K. Irritant poisons. In: Textbook of Forensic Medicine and Toxicology, 3rd edn. 2005. Reed Elsevier India Pvt. Limited, New Delhi. 642-61.
13. Rudra A. Metallic irritant poisons. In: Dogra TD, Rudra A (eds) Lyon's Medical Jurisprudence and Toxicology, 11th edn. 2007. Delhi Law House, Delhi. 1132-72.
14. Hammond PB, Beliles RP. In: Doull J, Klaassen CD, Amdur MO (eds) Casarett and Doull's Toxicology, 2nd edn. 1980. MaCmillan Publishing Co. New York.
15. Loomis TA. The basis of antidotal therapy. In: Essentials of Toxicology, 2nd edn. 1974. Lea and Febiger, Philadelphia. 129–44.
16. Bidstrup PL. The comparative toxicity of mercury compounds. In: Forensic Toxicology – Proceedings of a symposium held at the chemical defense establishment Porton Down 29-30 June 1972. John Wright and Sons Limited, Bristol 1974. 143–48.
17. Nandy A. Metallic chemical irritants. In: Principles of Forensic Medicine, 2nd edn. 2005. New Central Book Agency (P) Ltd., Calcutta. 475–90.
18. Beattie AD. Clinical and biochemical effects of lead. In: Forensic Toxicology – Proceedings of a symposium held at the chemical defense establishment Porton Down 29-30 June 1972. John Wright and Sons Limited, Bristol 1974. 121–34.
19. Hugelmeyer CD, Moorhead JC, Horenblas L, Bayer MJ. Fatal lead encephalopathy following foreign body ingestion: case report. J Emerg Med 1988; 5: 397–400.
20. DiMaio VJ, DiMaio SM, Garriott JC, Simpson P. A fatal case of lead poisoning due to a retained bullet. Am J Forensic Med Pathol 1983; 4: 165–9.
21. Linden MA, Manton WI, Stewart RM, Thal ER, Feit H. Lead poisoning from retained bullets: Pathogenesis, diagnosis and management. Ann Surg 1982; 195: 305–13.

22. Ercal N, Gurer-Orban, Aykin-Burns N. Toxic metals and oxidative stress part I: Mechanisms involved in metal induced oxidative damage. Curr Top Med Chem 2001; 1: 539–39.
23. Baranwal AK, Singhi SC. Acute iron poisoning: Management guidelines. Indian Pediatrics 2003; 40: 534–40.
24. Chyka PA, Butler AY, Herman MI. ferrous sulfate adsorption by activated charcoal. Vet Hum Toxicol 2001; 43: 11–3.
25. Whitten CF, Gibson GW, Good BS, Goodwin JF, Brough AJ. Studies in acute iron poisoning-I. Desferrioxamine in the treatment of acute iron poisoning: clinical observations, experimental studies and theoretical considerations. Pediatrics 1965; 36: 322–35.
26. Whitten CF, Gibson GW, Good BS, Goodwin JF, Brough AJ. Studies in acute iron poisoning-II. Further observations on desferrioxamine in the treatment of acute experimental iron poisoning. Pediatrics 1966; 38: 102–10.
27. McGuigan MA. Acute iron poisoning. Pediatr Ann 1996; 25: 33–8.

CHAPTER 37

Organic Irritants: Plants and Vegetables

Like tree, like fruit

- Proverb

These are organic irritants derived from poisonous plants. Phytotoxicology is term used to denote the study of plants that produce or evoke specific deleterious effects on human. The organic irritants are classified as:

1. Gastrointestinal irritants: e.g. castor, abrus, capsicum
2. Cardiotoxic poisons: e.g. aconite, oleander, tobacco, etc.
3. Neurotoxic poisons: Datura, cannabis, opium
4. Hepatotoxic poisons: e.g. neem, akee (Blighia sapida)
5. Dermal irritants: e.g. mango, St. John's wort.

POISONOUS PARTS OF PLANT

1. All parts of plant are poisonous, e.g.
   - Nerium odorum
   - Cerbera thevetia
   - Calatropis
2. Leaves, e.g.
   - Tobacco
   - Conium maculatum (hemlock)
   - Curare
   - Digitalis
3. Fruits, e.g.
   - Capsicum annum
   - Strychnous nux vomica
   - Colocynth
4. Seed, e.g.
   - Abrus
   - Castor
   - Croton
   - Datura
   - Semicarpus anacardium
5. Stem/bark, e.g.
   - Cinchona bark
   - Plumbago rosea
6. Root, e.g.
   - Aconite
   - Plumbago
   - Colocynth

TOXIC PRINCIPLE IN PLANT

Toxic substances in plant may present in form of:

- Toxalbumin (phytotoxin)
- Alkaloids
- Glycosides
- Resins
- Irritant juices
- Acrid oils
- Amino acid
- Plant acids

Examples are given in Table 37.1

ABRUS

Botanical name: Abrus precatorius
Common name: Rati, gunja, jequirity

Features

- Abrus is green, slender, climbing vine bearing compound leaves. Flowers are pinkish and seeds are present in seed pots.
- Each seed pot contains 3 to 5 seeds. Seeds are egg shaped with 5 mm in diameter and having weight of 105 mg. Seed has an attractive hard glossy outer shell. The seeds are of three types:
  1. Scarlet red seeds with a black spot at one end (Fig. 37.1).
  2. Black seeds with a white spot at one end (Fig. 37.2).
  3. White seeds with a black spot at one end (Fig. 37.3).

Table 37.1: Showing toxic substance and active principles in plants

Toxic substance	*Active principle*
Toxalbumin	Abrin
	Ricin
	Crotin
Alkaloids	Atropine
	Strychnine
	Aconitine
	Nicotine
	Curarine
	Ergotamine
Glycosides	Nerin
	Thevetin
	Cerebrin
	Digoxin
	Calotropin
Resins	Cannabinol
Juice/oils	Semicarpol
Plant acids	Oxalic acid
	Malic acid

Toxic Part of Plant

- Seed
- Root
- Leaves

Toxic Principle

- Abrin

FIG. 37.1: Abrus seeds—red variety

- Present in seed and is toxalbumin
- Abrin is similar to viper snake venom

Mechanism of Action[1, 2, 3]

- Abrin is composed of two polypeptide chains (A and B). These chains are connected by a disulfide bond
- Chewing or crushing of seed releases abrin. The "B" polypeptide chain (called as heptomer) binds to the intestinal cell membrane while "A" polypeptide chain (called as effectomer) enters the cytoplasm. In cytoplasm, "A" polypeptide chain act on 60S ribosomal subunit and prevents binding of elongation factor EF-2 thus inhibiting protein syntheses, thereby causing cell death.

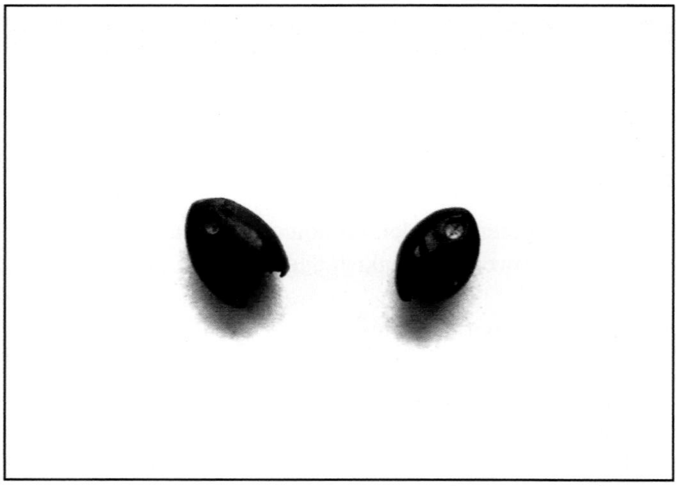

FIG. 37.2: Abrus seed—black variety

FIG. 37.3: Abrus seeds—white variety

Clinical Features

1. Dermal manifestations: When abrin is injected in skin, there will be inflammation, swelling, ecchymoses and necrosis at the site. Similarly there will be faintness, vertigo, vomiting, dyspnoea and convulsion occurs before death. The symptoms resemble those of viper snakebite.
2. Ocular exposure: Causes redness, chemosis, swelling and conjunctivitis.
3. Oral ingestion: Causes pain in abdomen, vomiting, diarrhoea, bleeding per rectum, cardiac arrhythmias, convulsions and CNS depression.

Management

- Gastric lavage
- Supportive measures
- Convulsions can be controlled by diazepam/lorazepam
- Local exposure should be treated with copious irrigation with plain water

Fatal Dose

- 1 to 2 crushed seeds
- 90 to 120 mg of abrin

Fatal period: 3 to 5 days

Autopsy Findings

- Local-fragments of needle or sui may be found in the skin along with oedema, inflammation, local necrosis and ecchymoses
- GIT-shows edematous bowel with hemorrhage[4]
- Cerebral edema
- Liver, spleen, kidneys — congested

Medicolegal Importance

1. Accidental poisoning may occur in children while exploring the seeds.
2. Homicide by sui prepared with abrin (sui is needle or spike made with crushed seed alone or mixed with onion paste. Then the needle is dried under sun. The sui is kept between two fingers and is pushed into skin of other person).
3. Cattle poison.
4. Malingerers use powder of abrus seed to produce conjunctivitis.
5. When intact seeds are swallowed or when seeds are boiled or cooked, they are not poisonous.

CASTOR

Botanical name: Ricinus communis
Common name: Castor, arandi

Features

- Castor plants are tall plants and grow all over India. The plant bears lobate leaves with toothed margins (Fig. 37.4). The fruits are globular and clustered with spiny projections over capsule (Fig. 37.5). The fruit contains castor seeds (Fig. 37.6).
- Seeds are flattened-oval in shape and are available in two sizes. Large variety seeds are mottled, dark brown in color with shiny hard seed coat. Small variety seeds

FIG. 37.4: Castor plant

FIG. 37.5: Castor fruit

FIG. 37.6: Castor seeds

are a about 1 to 2 cm X 0.8 cm in size and resembles croton seeds (Fig. 37.7).

Toxic part of plants: All parts of plant but seeds are more toxic

Toxic Principle

- Ricin (toxalbumin)

Mechanism of Action

- Ricin is composed of two polypeptide chains (A and B). These chains are connected by a disulfide bond.
- In GIT, chain "B" binds the cell surface and chain "A" enters into cytoplasm. Chain "A" acts on 60S ribosomal unit of cell and disrupt protein synthesis.

Clinical Features[5]

- Abdominal pain
- Vomiting and diarrhea
- Dehydration
- Convulsions
- Drowsiness
- Delirium
- Hepatic failure
- Oliguria
- Uremia
- Death may be due to multiorgan failure or cardiovascular collapse
- The pulp of seed contains allergenic glycoprotein, which may cause dermatitis, rhinitis, asthma, and conjunctivitis in allergic individuals.[1, 6]

Management

- Gastric lavage and administer activated charcoal
- The urine should be alkalinized with sodium bicarbonate. This is to prevent precipitation of hemoglobin in the renal tubules.[7]
- Supportive treatment

Fatal dose
- 5 to 10 seeds
- 1 mg/kg body weight for Ricin

Fatal period: 2 to few days

Autopsy Findings

- Mucosa of GIT may be inflamed with hemorrhages
- Crushed seeds with pericarp may be found in stomach
- Hemorrhages in organs.

Medicolegal Importance

1. Accidental poisoning
2. Seeds are used for homicidal purpose
3. Used to procure criminal abortion
4. Cattle poison
5. Seed powder may be used to induce conjunctivitis for malingering
6. Small variety seeds may be confused with croton seeds, differences are mentioned in Table 37.2
7. Can cause anaphylactic type of hypersensitivity in humans.[8]

CROTON

Botanical name: Croton tiglium
Common name: Nepala, Jamalgota, croton

Features

- Croton plant has elliptical leaves with metallic green in color.

Table 37.2: Showing difference between castor and croton seeds

Features	*Castor seed*	*Croton seed*
Appearance	Grayish brown, mottled, glossy	Dark brown, non-glossy, not mottled
Shape	Flattened-oval in shape	Oval
Cross section at tip	Lumen is almost circular	The lumen is slit like with radiating creases

- Croton seeds are oval, non-glossy, and 1 to 2 cm long, dark brown or brownish-gray in color (Fig. 37.7). The seed contains toxic principle.

Toxic Part of Plants

- Seed
- Stem
- Leaves

Toxic Principle

- Crotin (toxalbumin)
- Crotonoside (glycoside)

Clinical Features

- Pain in abdomen
- Salivation
- Vomiting
- Diarrhoea (watery)
- Vertigo
- Circulatory failure/shock

Management

- Gastric lavage
- Symptomatic

Fatal dose: 4 seeds have cause death
Fatal dose: 4 to 6 hours

Autopsy Findings

- Signs of inflammation in GIT
- Abdominal viscera congested

Medicolegal Importance

1. Accidental poisoning
2. Used to procure abortion
3. Seeds may be used for homicidal purpose
4. Used in quack medicine
5. Arrow poison

CAPSICUM

Two varieties are noted as:
1. Capsicum annum — less hotter
2. Capsicum frutescenes — hotter than C. annum

Common name: Chili, red pepper, mirch

Features

- This small shrub bears tapering fruits which become red when ripe (Fig. 37.8)
- The fruit contains small and flat yellowish seeds (Fig. 37.9). The seeds resemble to Datura seeds. Differentiating points are given in Table 44.2 (Chapter 44).

Toxic part of plant: Fruit and seed

Toxic Principle

- Capsaicin
- Capsicin

Mechanism of action: The vanillyl acid present in capsicum causes depletion of substance P at nerve terminals. This results in local swelling and pain due to dilatation of blood vessels and intense excitation of sensory nerve endings.[1]

FIG. 37.7: Croton seeds

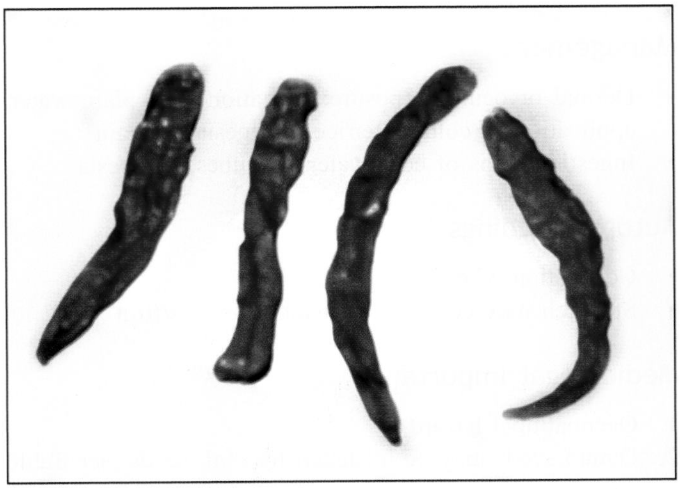

FIG. 37.8: Red chili fruit

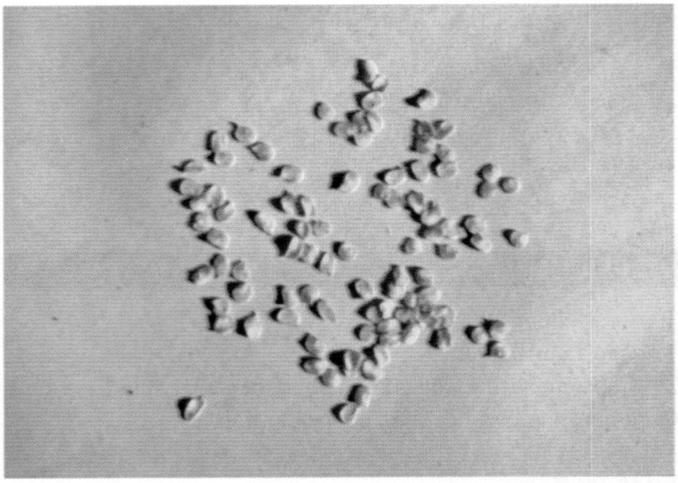

FIG. 37.9: Chili seeds

Clinical Features

1. Dermal exposure: Burning sensation, pain
   - Chili burns: Person occupationally exposed to chili powder may have pain, irritation and erythema
   - Hunan hand: Contact dermatitis caused due to chili
2. Ocular exposure: Causes pain, lacrimation, conjunctivitis, blephrospasm
3. Inhalation: Cough, irritation. Chili worker's cough – occupational exposure results in coughing.
4. Ingestion:
   - Burning pain in mouth
   - Salivation
   - Vomiting
   - Abdominal pain
   - Diarrhoea (burning)

Management

- Dermal or ocular exposure: Irrigation with plain water, application of cold water/ice, analgesia for pain
- Ingestion: Sips of cold water/ice cubes, analgesia

Autopsy Findings

- Congestion of organs
- Stomach may contains remnants of seeds/fruit

Medicolegal Importance

1. Occupational hazard
2. Datura seeds may be mistaken for chili seeds (see Table 44.2 for differentiation)
3. Chili powder used for
   - Torture
   - Extortion
   - Forced confession
   - Child abuse
   - Robbery
   - Rape

CALOTROPIS

Calotropis plants are of two varieties:

1. Calotropis gigantea — has purple color flowers (Fig. 37.10)
2. Calotropis procera — has white colour flowers (Fig. 37.11)

Common name: Madar, Akdo

Features

- The plant grows wildly with thick green oblong leaves.
- The stem or leaves, when break or incised, yields thick, acrid, milky juice.

Toxic part of plant: All parts are toxic

Toxic Principle

- Calotoxin
- Calotropin (glycoside)
- Calactin
- Uscharin

Clinical Features

1. Dermal exposure: Application to skin causes irritation, redness and vesication
2. Ocular exposure: Irritation, lacrimation, conjunctivitis
3. Ingestion: Causes
   - Acrid bitter taste
   - Burning pain in mouth
   - Vomiting
   - Diarrhoea
   - Stomatitis
   - Tetanic convulsions
   - Delirium
   - Circulatory failure/shock

Management

- Gastric lavage
- Demulcents
- Supportive measures
- Diazepam/lorazepam for convulsions
- Dermal or ocular exposure: Wash the affected area with water

FIG. 37.10: Calotropis gigantea

FIG. 37.11: Calotropis procera

Fatal dose: Uncertain
Fatal period: Varies from half hour to eight hours

Autopsy Findings

- Froth at mouth and nostrils
- Stomatitis
- Inflammation of GIT
- Abdominal viscera — congested
- Vesication, inflammation and redness at the site of contact

Medicolegal Importance

1. Accidental poisoning
2. Used in folk medicine
3. Used to fabricate wounds — malingers may apply juice to produce artificial bruise or conjunctivitis
4. Used in abortion stick to procure criminal abortion
5. Infanticide
6. Cattle poison
7. Root of C. procera is poisonous to cobra snakes. Snake charmers use root to scare away snake or to subdue them.

MARKING NUT

Botanical name: Semicarpus anacardium
Common name: Marking nut, bhilawa, biba

Features

Marking nuts are generally heart-shaped blackish nuts with rough projection at base. The nut bears thick pericarp and contains brownish-black, acrid, oily juice (Fig. 37.12).

Toxic part of plant: Nut

Toxic Principle

- Semecarpol
- Bhilawanol

Clinical Features

1. Dermal exposure: When applied to skin, it causes irritation, inflammation, vesication formation, pain and itching. The blister contains acrid serum. The skin lesion resembles contusion. Later on the lesion turned into ulcer with sloughing of skin.
2. Ingestion: Causes

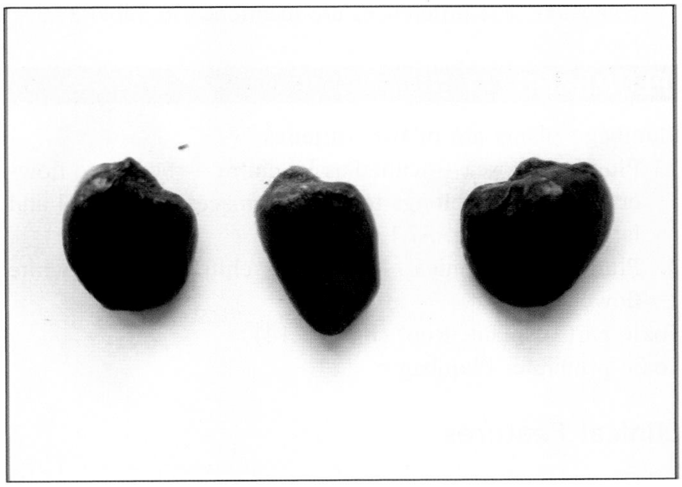

FIG. 37.12: Marking nut

- Blister formation in and around oral cavity
- Vomiting
- Diarrhea
- Abdominal pain
- Hypotension/shock
- Delirium
- Coma

Management

- Gastric lavage
- Activated charcoal
- Supportive measures

Fatal Dose

- 5 to 8 seeds (nut)
- 10 gm of marking nut juice

Fatal period: 12 to 24 hours

Autopsy Findings

- Blister formation in and around oral cavity and throat
- GIT inflammation
- Fatty degeneration of liver has been reported

Medicolegal Importance

1. Accidental poisoning — quack medicine
2. Juice is applied to external genitalia of female as punishment for infidelity
3. Used to fabricate bruise/wound
4. Juice is thrown over other person to cause harm/injury
5. Juice is applied to cervical os to procure criminal abortion
6. Skin lesion produced by marking nut may be confused with contusion. The differences are mentioned in Table 37.3.

Table 37.3: Displaying difference between contusions and marking nut lesion

Features	*Contusion*	*Marking nut lesion*
Shape	Regular	Irregular
Margin	Diffused	Sharp and clear
Color changes	Occurs	Does not occur
Itching	Absent	Present
Extravasation of blood	Present	Absent
Blisters	Absent	Present
Nail beds	Not significant	Similar lesions due to itching
Caused by	Rupture of capillaries	Chemical damage to skin

PLUMBAGO

Plumbago plants are of two varieties:

1. Plumbago rosea — called as lal chitra — bears red flowers. The plant belongs to Plumbaginaceae with oval and large leaves (Fig. 37.13).
2. Plumbago zeylanica — called as chitra — bears white flowers

Toxic part of plant: Root (Fig. 37.14)

Toxic principle: Plumbagin

Clinical Features

1. Dermal exposure: Application of root to skin causes irritation, inflammation and vesication
2. Ingestion: Causes pain in abdomen, vomiting, diarrhoea, shock, CNS depression

Management

- Gastric lavage
- Demulcents
- Symptomatic

Fatal dose: Uncertain

Fatal period: Uncertain

Autopsy Findings

- Skin may show vesication and inflammation
- GIT irritation
- Viscera congested

FIG. 37.13: Plumbago rosea

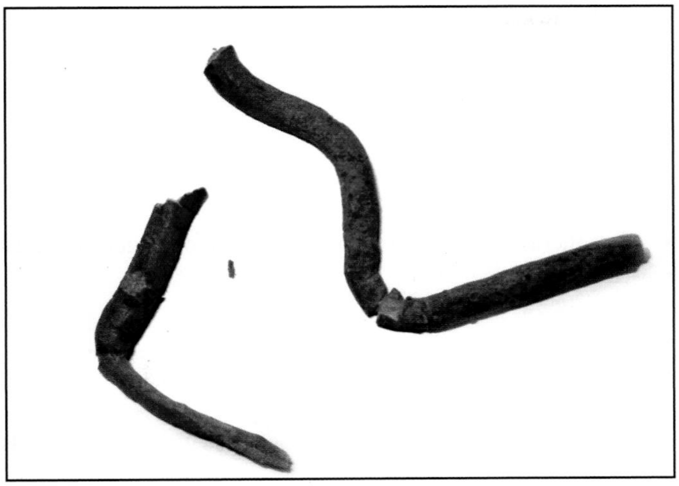

FIG. 37.14: Root of Plumbago

FIG. 37.15: Colocynth plant with fruits

Medicolegal Importance

1. Root paste is applied to cervical os to procure criminal abortion.
2. Root paste is used to fabricate bruises (false bruise).
3. Rarely used for homicide.

COLOCYNTH

Botanical name: Citrullus colocynthus
Common name: Colocynth, Indrayani, Bitter apple

Features

- It is a creeping plant with triangular leaves
- The plant bears globular fruit, 3 to 4 inches in diameter with greenish-yellow appearance and dry spongy pulp (Fig. 37.15). Fruit contains oval-flattened, brownish color about 5 mm long seeds (Fig. 37.16).

Toxic Part of Plant

- Fruit
- Root
- Leaves

Toxic principle: Colocynthin (glycoside)

Clinical Features

- Pain in abdomen
- Vomiting
- Watery diarrhoea
- Shock

Management: Symptomatic

Fatal dose: 1 to 3 gm
Fatal period: 24 hours

Autopsy Findings

- Inflammation of gastrointestinal tract
- Abdominal organs congested

Medicolegal Importance

1. Accidental poisoning
2. Used to procure criminal abortion
3. Suicide

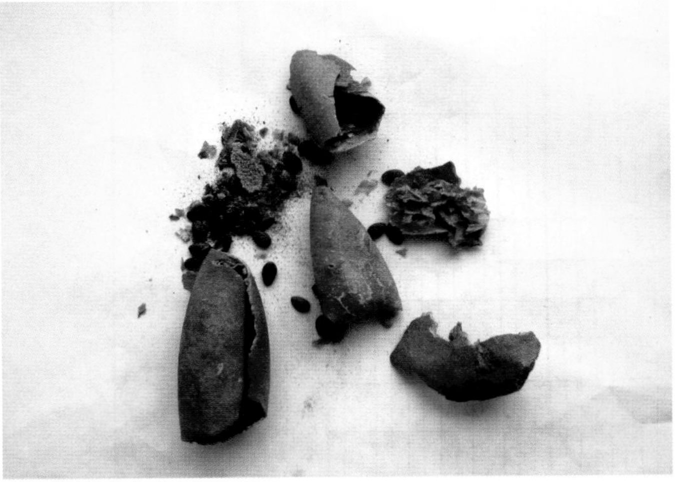

FIG. 37.16: Colocynth fruit with seeds

ERGOT

Ergot is dried sclerotia of the fungus Clavices purpurea.[9] The fungus infests certain grains such as rye, maize, barley, wheat, oats, etc. (Fig. 37.17). The fungus at grains germinates into hyphae and these hyphae penetrate deep into the grains and hardened into a purplish structure called sclerotium, which elaborates number of ergot alkaloids.

Alkaloids of Ergot

- Ergotamine
- Ergotoxin
- Ergometrine
- Dihydroergotamine

Clinical Features

Acute Poisoning

- Nausea
- Vomiting
- Diarrhoea
- Giddiness
- Breathlessness
- Muscular weakness
- Tingling and numbness in hand and feet
- Paraesthesia
- Cramps in muscle
- Bleeding from nose and other mucosal surface

Chronic Poisoning (Ergotism)

Prolonged use of ergot leads to a condition called ergotism characterized by:

FIG. 37.17: Ergot

- Burning of extremities
- Hemorrhagic vesication
- Pruritis
- Formication
- Nausea
- Vomiting
- Bradycardia
- Peripheral ischemia leading to gangrene of fingers and toes
- Headache
- Miosis
- Delirium
- Hallucinations
- Convulsions
- Ischemia of cerebral, mesenteric, coronary and renal vessels

Management[1]

- Gastric lavage with activated charcoal
- Hypertension or cerebral/mesentric/cardiac ischemia — IV nitroglycerine or nitroprusside
- Peripheral ischemia — oral prazocin, captopril or nifedipine
- Convulsions and hallucinations — diazepam or lorazepam
- Hypercoagulable state — heparin or dextran.

Medicolegal Importance

- Accidental poisoning occurs with consumption of contaminated grains
- Ergots preparations are used to induce abortion.

REFERENCES

1. Pillay VV. Poisonous plants. In: Comprehensive Medical Toxicology, 1st edn. 2003. Paras Publishing, Hyderabad. 473–508.
2. Dickers KJ, Bradberry SM, Rice P, Griffiths GD, Vale JA. Abrin poisoning. Toxicol Rev 2003; 22: 137–42.
3. Frohne D, Pfander HJ. In: A colour atlas of poisonous plants. Translated by Bisset NG, 2nd edn. 1984. Wolfe Publishing Ltd. London.
4. Henry JA, Wiseman HM. In: Management of poisoning. WHO handbook for health care workers, 1st Indian edition 1998.
5. Audi J, Belson M, Patel M, Schier J, Osterloh J. Ricin poisoning: a comprehensive review. JAMA 2005; 294: 2342–51.
6. Brugsch HG. Toxic hazards: the castor bean. New Eng J Med 1960; 262: 1039–40.
7. DeManuelle MS. Systemic poisonous plant intoxication. In: Viccellio P (ed) Handbook of Medical Toxicology, 1st edn. 1993. Little, Brown and Company, Boston. 639–47.
8. Lockey SD Jr. Anaphylaxis from an Indian Necklace. JAMA 1968; 206: 2900–1.
9. Lillehoj EB, Ciegler A, Detroy RW. Fungal toxins. In: Blood FR (Ed) Essays in Toxicology, Vol. 2, 1st edn. 1970. Academic Press, New York. 40.

CHAPTER 38

Organic Irritants: Animal Bites and Stings

Deceitfulness is more dangerous than venomous bite

— Anonymous

Examples of animal irritants include snake, scorpion, bee, wasp, ant, spiders, centipedes, etc. This chapter deals with commonly encountered animal bites and stings. Snake have venomous bites that inject venom through specialized oral structure called as fangs whereas scorpions, bees and wasps have stings. The stings of these animals are painful and at times prove fatal.

SNAKE

Snakes are cylindrical, long, limbless, cold-blooded reptiles. The body of snake is divided into:

1. Head
2. Trunk
3. Tail
   - There are about 3500 species of snakes known amongst which about 350 species are venomous. In India, about 216 species are found and amongst them, about 52 are poisonous
   - Differences between poisonous and non-poisonous snakes are mentioned in Table 38.1.

Poisonous Snakes

Poisonous snakes are divided into 5 families

1. Colubridae: e.g. African boomslanag snake, twig snakes.
2. Alractaspididae: e.g. mole vipers or adders.
3. Elapidae: e.g. cobra, krait, coral snake.
4. Viperidae: e.g. Russell's viper, saw-scaled viper.
5. Hydrophidae: e.g. Sea snakes.

Common Poisonous Snakes in India

1. Cobras: Common cobra, King cobra.
2. Kraits: Common krait, banded krait.
3. Vipers: Russell's viper, Saw-scaled viper.
4. Sea-snakes: Banded sea snake, amphibian sea snake.

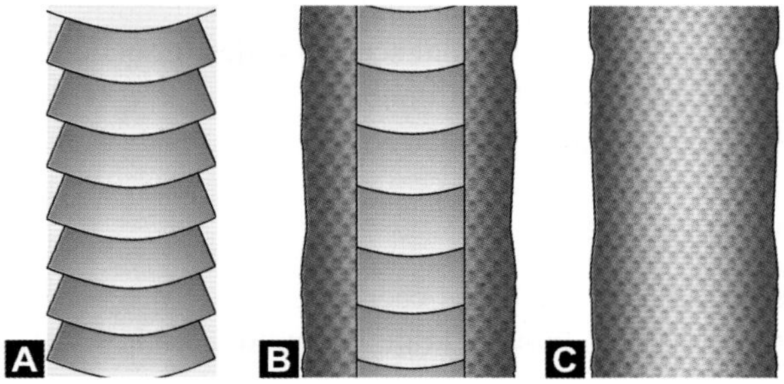

FIGS 38.1A to C: Belly scales of snake. **A:** Shows belly scales of poisonous snake – note that the scales are broad and complete whereas B and C show belly scale of non-poisonous snake

Table 38.1: Difference between poisonous and non-poisonous snakes

Features	*Poisonous snake*	*Non-poisonous snake*
Physical features	Stout, dull color	Slender, brightly colored
Tail	Rounded or flattened or abruptly tapering tail	Gradually tapering
Belly scales	Broad and complete (Figs 38.1A to C)	Small and do not extend across the entire width
Teeth	At least one pair of teeth in the upper jaw are modified to form fangs	All teeth are uniformly small in size, no fangs

Common Non-Poisonous Snakes in India

1. Rat snake (Dhaman)
2. Vine snake
3. Bronze back tree snake
4. Banded kukri
5. Sand boa

Non-poisonous snakes, at times, may resemble poisonous snakes and create confusion. These non-poisonous snakes resembling poisonous snakes[1] are given in Table 38.2.

FEATURES OF COMMON POISONOUS SNAKES

Common Cobra

Zoological name: Naja naja
Common names: Common cobra, nag
Features (Fig. 38.2):

- Common cobras are usually brown or black in color
- Head is covered with shields. The third supra-labial shield touches the eye and nose
- A small wedge shaped scale called as cuneate is present between 4th and 5th infra-labials
- Pupils are round
- Hood is present. Dorsal aspect of hood may have monocellate (monocele) or binocellate (spectacle) mark (Fig. 38.3). Ventral surface of hood have two dark spots
- Fangs are short, grooved and situated anteriorly
- Tail is cylindrical. Caudal scales (scales on undersurface of tail) are divided and double
- Venom — neurotoxic.

FIG. 38.2: Common cobra (*Courtesy*: Shrikant Bhimrao Uke, "Sarp Mitra" Nagpur)

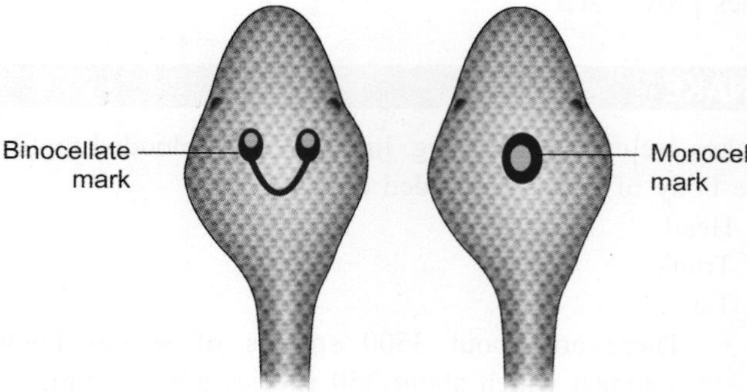

FIG. 38.3: Dorsal aspect of cobra with marks

Common Krait

Zoological name: Bungarus caeruleus
Common name: Indian krait, common krait, Maniyar, Kawadya
Features (Figs 38.4, 38.5 and 38.6):

- Usually steel blue or black in color with single or paired white bands on back. The bands are more distinct towards the tail
- Pupils are round
- Large hexagonal scale presents over back
- The 4th infra-labial scale is the largest scale of other infra-labial scales
- The subcaudal (ventral scales distal to vent) are undivided and entire
- Fangs are short, grooved and situated anteriorly
- Venom — neurotoxic.

Table 38.2: Non-poisonous snakes resembling poisonous snakes

Non-poisonous snake	*Poisonous snake*
Rat snake	Common cobra
Common cat snake	Saw-scaled viper
Banded kukri	Banded krait
Sand boa	Russell's viper
Common wolf snake	Common krait

FIG. 38.4: Common krait head

FIG. 38.5: Common krait

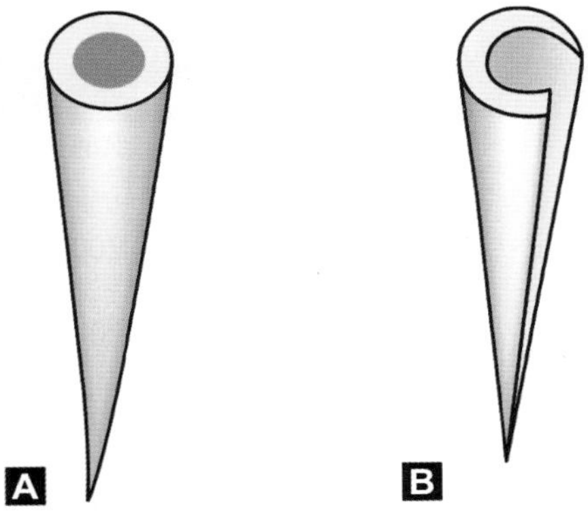

FIGS 38.6A and B: Fangs in poisonous snake. **A:** Canalized fang whereas **B:** is grooved fang

Banded Krait

Zoological name: Bungarus fasciatus
Common name: Banded krait
Features (Fig. 38.7):

- Inverted "V" shaped mark on head
- Broad black and yellow glistening bands encircle the body. On cross-section, the bands are triangular in shape
- As per habitat, the snake is shy in nature often seen basking near water bodies usually in morning hours
- Venom — neurotoxic.

Saw Scaled Viper

Zoological name: Echis carinatus
Common name: Carpet viper, phoorsa, afai
Features (Fig. 38.8):

- Aggressive snake
- Viviparous
- Usually brown in color and grows up to 1.5 to 2 feet
- Head triangular with small scale. White "arrow mark" or "spear mark" may present on head
- Pupils are vertical
- Wavy white line (zig-zag pattern) may present on each flank
- Diamond shaped markings over back
- Belly scales are broad and cover entire width
- The scales of viper are serrated, saw like thus name saw-scale viper
- Fangs are long, curved, hollow, channelised and hinged (Fig. 38.6A)
- Venom — vasculotoxic and hemotoxic.

FIG. 38.7: Banded krait (*Courtesy*: Shrikant Bhimarao UKe, "Sarp Mitra" Nagpur)

FIG. 38.8: Saw scaled viper (*Courtesy*: Shrikant Bhimrao Uke, "Sarp Mitra" Nagpur)

FIG. 38.9: Russell's viper

- (Can also be remembered as 5 V's; V= viper, V=viviparous, V=vertical pupil, V=v shaped head (triangular), V=vasculotoxic venom).

Russell's Viper

Zoological name: Vipera russelli
Common name: Kander, ghonas
Features (Fig. 38.9):

- Head is large, flat and triangular with small scales. White V shaped mark present on head
- Pupils are vertical
- Large nostrils
- Body is stout and fatty with brown or yellowish color.
- Body scales are semi-elliptical
- Three rows of chained dark spots present on back
- Tail is narrow and short. Scales are divided into two rows
- Fang are long, curved, hollow, channelised and hinged
- When disturbed, makes a loud and hissing sound
- Venom — Vasculotoxic and hemotoxic.

Sea Snakes

- Sea snakes are usually bluish, grayish or greenish in color. They have prominent nostrils and are situated on the top of snout
- Body is flat and belly scales are not broad
- Tail is flattened and paddle shaped
- Venom — myotoxic.

VENOM COMPOSITION

Snake venom is the toxic saliva secreted by modified parotid salivary gland. The features of snake venom are as follows:

1. Physical appearance — clear, amber colored when fresh
2. Chemical composition — consists of
   - Toxins — low molecular weight polypeptide and proteins, glycoproteins
   - Enzymes — proteinases, hydrolases, transaminase, hyaluronidase, cholinesterase, phospholipase, ATPase, ribonuclease, deoxyribonuclease.
3. Types of venom — may be
   - Neurotoxic — cobra, krait
   - Hemotoxic — vipers
   - Myotoxic — sea snake
4. Fatal dose and amount of venom injected is mentioned in Table 38.3.

Table 38.3: Fatal dose and amount of venom injected per bite

Snake	*Fatal dose*	*Amount of venom injected per bite*
Cobra	12 mg of dried venom	200–350 mg
Krait	6 mg of dried venom	20–22 mg
Russell's viper	15 mg of dried venom	150–200 mg
Saw scaled viper	8 mg of dried venom	25 mg

CLINICAL FEATURES

Non-Poisonous Snake

- Fear and apprehension
- Sweating
- Patient may be in state of shock with feeble pulse, hypotension, syncope, rapid and shallow breathing
- Bite area — may show multiple teeth marks (Figs 38.10A and B).

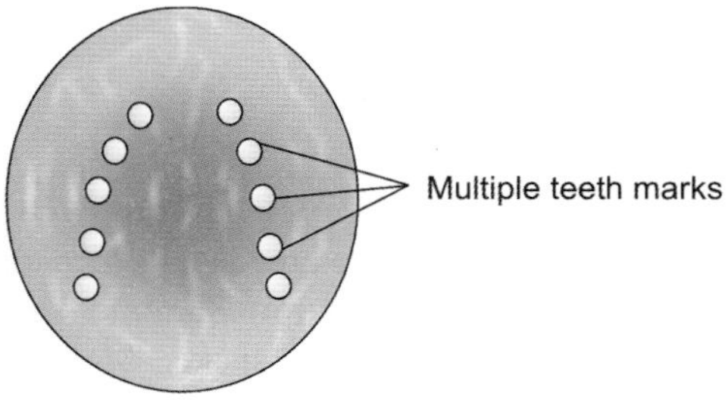

FIG. 38.10A: Bite mark in non-poisonous snake

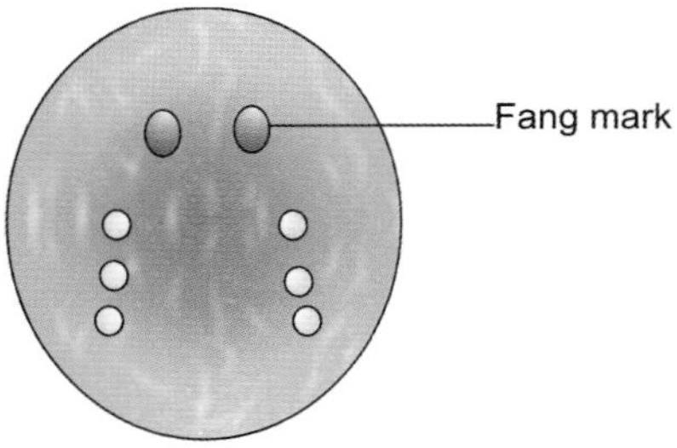

FIG. 38.10B: Bite mark in poisonous snake

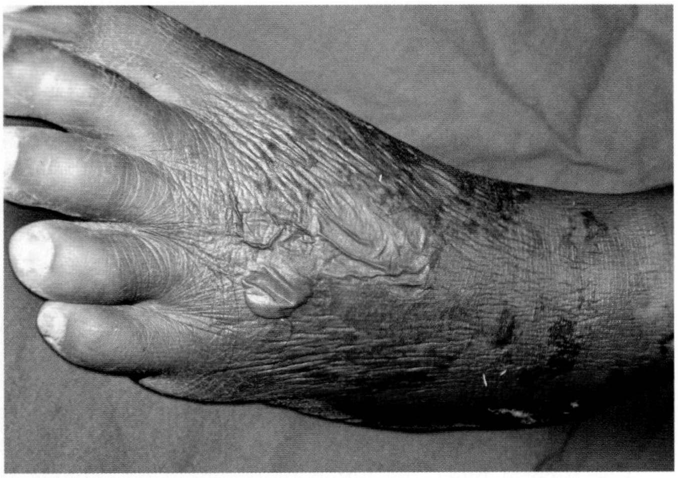

FIG 38.11A: Bite area in elapid bite

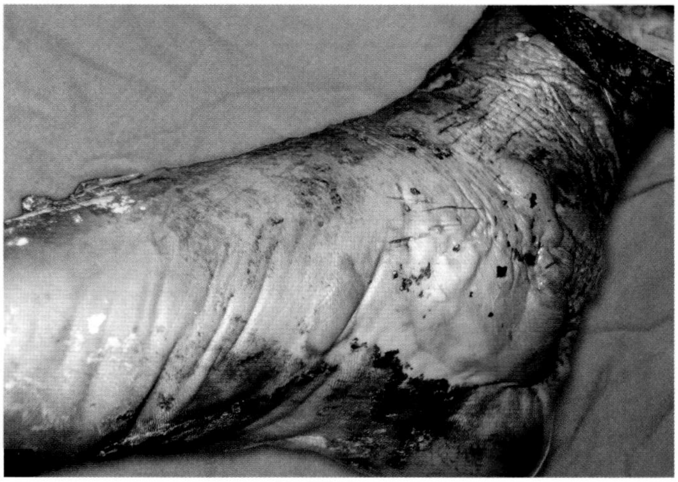

FIG. 38.11B: Local features in Viperid bite

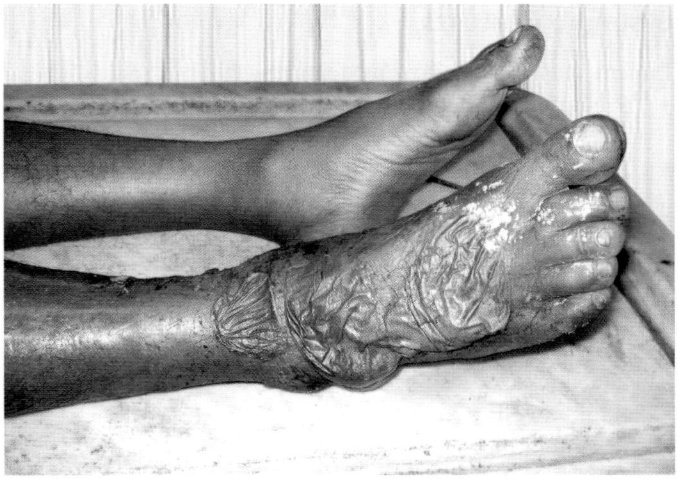

FIG. 38.11C: Local features in Viperid bite

Poisonous Snake

Elapid Bite

Local Features

- Fang marks (Figs 38.11A to C)
- Burning pain
- Swelling and discoloration sometimes associated with some blisters (Fig. 38.11A)
- Serosanguinous discharge from bite site
- In comparison with viper bite, local manifestations are milder in elapid bite.

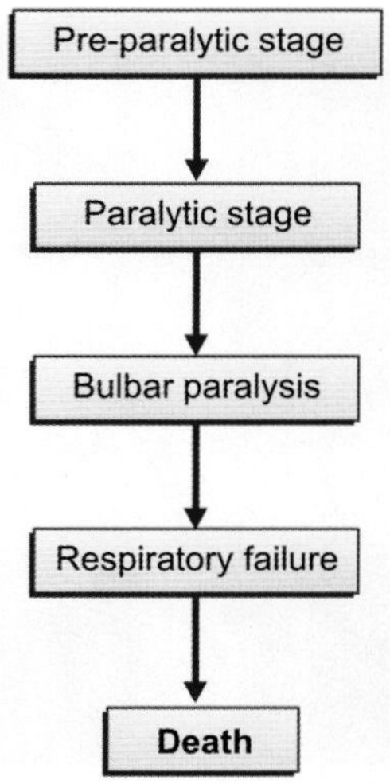

FIG. 38.12: Flow chart showing clinical features in elapid bite

Systemic Features

Patient may have following features
- Pre-paralytic stage — characterized by vomiting, headache, giddiness, weakness, lethargy
- Paralytic stage — characterized by spreading paralytic features with ptosis, ophthalmoplegia, drowsiness, dysartheria, convulsions, bulbar paralysis, respiratory failure and death (Fig. 38.12).

Viperid Bite

Local features
- Rapid swelling of the bitted site
- Discoloration
- Blister formation — may extend to entire limb and even spread to trunk (Figs 38.11B and C)
- Bleeding from bite site
- Pain

Systemic Features

- Generalized bleeding—epistaxis, hemoptysis, hemetemesis, bleeding gums, hematuria, malena, hemorrhagic areas over skin and mucosa
- Shock
- Renal failure

Hydrophid Bite

Local features
- Local swelling
- Pain

Systemic Features

- Myalgia
- Muscle stiffness
- Myoglobinuria
- Renal failure

Diagnosis

Diagnosis depends on:
1. Identification of fang marks
2. Identification of snake—vide supra
3. Laboratory methods

Fang Marks

Usually, two fang marks in form of puncture wound can be noticed. The puncture wounds are usually separated from each other by a distance varying from 8 mm to 4 cm depending up on the type of poisonous snake. At times, due to sideswipe, a single mark may be produced or if the area is bitten at multiple times, it may result in more fang marks (Figs 38.10 and 38.11).

Laboratory Methods

- Complete blood count—leucocytosis may be evident with thrombocytopenia
- Smear — hemolysed and fragmented RBCs
- Increased prothrombin time and increased partial thromboplastin time
- Immunodiagnosis — consist of:[2-4]
  1. Immunodiffusion
  2. Counter-current immunoelectrophoresis
  3. ELISA
  4. Radioimmunoassay

Management

Non-poisonous snakebite
- Allay the anxiety and fear
- Reassure the patients that all snakes are not poisonous

Poisonous Snakebite

First Aid and Field Management (Figs 38.13A to D)

- Reassurance
- Limit systemic spread of venom by immobilizing the affected part (e.g. limb)
- For Viperid bites, the bitten limb should be splinted if possible and kept at approximately heart level

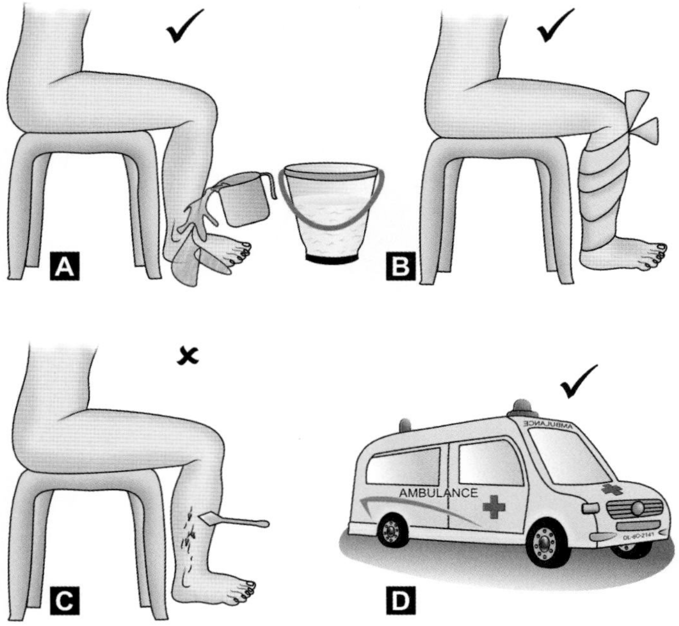

FIGS 38.13A to D: First aid in snakebite

- For elapid or sea snakebites, the Australian pressure-immobilization technique is beneficial. In this method, the entire bitten limb is wrapped with an elastic or crepe bandage and then splinted
- Tourniquet—a proximal lymphatic-occlusion constriction band or torniquet may limit the spread of venom if applied within 30 minutes. The tourniquet should be applied such that it does not prevent arterial flow of blood and the distal pulsation should be appreciated.

Hospital Management

- Monitor vital signs, cardiac rhythm, oxygen saturation and urine output
- The level of local edema/swelling/erythema in the bitten limb should be marked and the circumference should be measured every 15 minutes until swelling has stabilized
- Intravenous access with fluid resuscitation. If needed, vasopressors (e.g. dopamine) should be administered
- Blood and urine should be collected for laboratory evaluation — see Table 38.4
- Care of bite site — apply dry sterile dressings. Splint may be applied
- Tetanus immunization should be updated as appropriate
- If the swelling in the affected limb continues and impending tissue perfusion causing muscle compartment syndrome, intracompartmental pressure should be checked. If pressure is elevated prompt surgical consultation should be obtained while antivenin continues
- Antivenin therapy—antivenin should be administered only when indicated. Table 38.5 displays indication for administration of antivenin. Antivenins are available as monovalent (i.e. species specific) or polyvalent. In India, polyvalent antivenin is available that is effective against common cobra, common krait, Russell's viper and saw-scaled viper. The antivenin should be administered with caution. Usually the antivenins are of equine origin and carry risk of anaphylaxis or delayed-hypersensitivity type of reactions. Prior to administration of antivenin infusion, the patient should receive appropriate loading doses of intravenous antihistamines. The antivenin should be administered as intravenous infusion. It should be dissolved in 500 ml of normal saline or Ringer's lactate or 5% dextrose for adults and 20 ml/kg for children. The adverse reactions of antivenin are mentioned in Table 38.6
- Severe hemorrhage or bleeding may require blood or fresh frozen plasma

Table 38.4: Laboratory tests in snakebite cases

Laboratory investigations
Blood
- Complete blood count
- Blood group and cross-matching
- Liver function test
- Kidney function test
- Coagulation studies
Urine
- For blood
- For myoglobin
ECG
Arterial blood gas analysis
Chest X-ray

Table 38.5: Indications for antivenin therapy

Indications
- Deranged coagulation profile
- Spontaneous bleeding
- Rapidly progressive and severe local swelling
- Persistent hypotension
- Neurotoxic or myotoxic features
- Depressed consciousness
- Laboratories abnormalities

Table 38.6: Adverse reactions to antivenin
Adverse reactions
- Anaphylaxis
- Delayed type of hypersensitivity reaction

- If there are features of neurotoxicity, neostigmine may be required. Every injection of neostigmine should be preceded with atropine
- Oxygen, ventilatory support
- Management of renal failure on usual line.

Autopsy Findings

- Evidence of fang marks, local swelling, discoloration, blister formation, bleeding
- Bleeding diathesis
- Froth at mouth and nostrils
- Pulmonary edema
- Congested organs.

Medicolegal Importance

1. Most of the deaths are accidental in nature.
2. Due to snakebite permanent functional loss may occur in the bitten limb. Though the exact incidence is not known but such loss may be due to injury to muscle, nerve or vessels or due to scar contracture.

SCORPION

Features (Fig. 38.14)

- Scorpions belongs to family arachnida
- The scorpions grow up to 3 inches and the body composed of 18 segments divided into following parts
    1. Cephalothorax i.e. fused head and chest, placed anteriorly
    2. Abdomen
    3. Tail: tail has 6 segments and terminates in a bulbous enlargement called telson. The telson contains sting and venom apparatus.
    4. Two claws
- Common species found in India is Mesobuthus tamulus (Indian red scorpion). These scorpions are found abundantly in Western Maharashtra, parts of Karnataka, Andhra Pradesh, Saurashtra, Pondicherry and Tamil Nadu.[5]
- An agitated scorpion presses its sting into victim's body and leaves the venom

FIG. 38.14: Indian red scorpion

- Nocturnal in habit
- Usually found under rocks, vegetation, wall cervices, etc.

Venom

Scorpion venom is clear, colorless fluid and contains following toxic components

- Phospholipase
- Acetyl cholinesterase
- Hyaluronidase
- Serotonin
- Neurotoxin

Mechanism of Action[6,7]

- Scorpion venom delays the inactivation of sodium channels of autonomic nervous system resulting in autonomic storm (Fig. 38.15)
- α-Receptor stimulation plays an important role in the pathogenesis of pulmonary edema
- Scorpion venom is powerful arrhythmogenic agent.

Clinical Features[6-12]

1. Local
    - Increasing local pain. The pain is typically described as burning and excruciating
    - Swelling
    - Redness

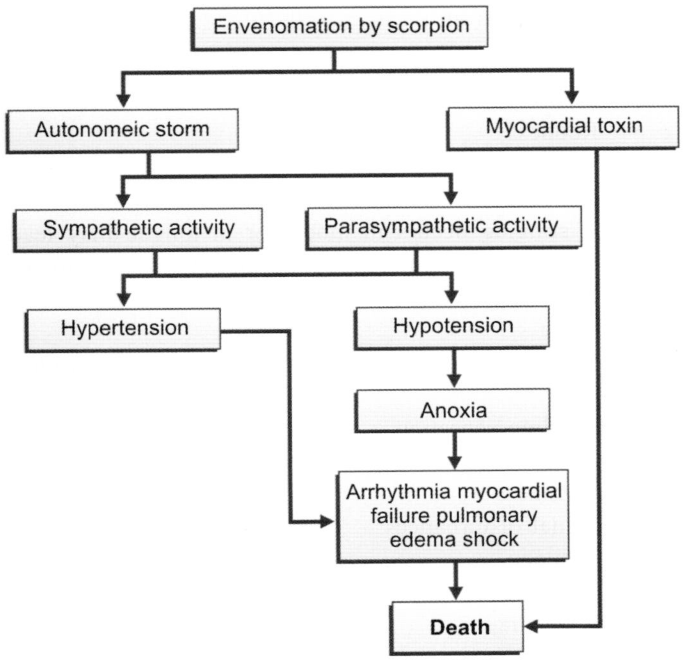

FIG. 38.15: Mechanism of scorpion envenomation

- Itching
- Ecchymoses

2. Systemic
    - Sweating
    - Urticaria
    - Salivation
    - Vomiting
    - Breathlessness and cough
    - Hemoptysis
    - Priapism
    - Hypertension
    - Bradyarrhythmias
    - Pulmonary edema
    - Myocarditis
    - Myocardial ischemia
    - Restlessness
    - Giddiness
    - Convulsions
    - Intracerebral hemorrhage leading to paralysis

Laboratory Findings

- ECG—ST segment depression or elevation, acute myocardial infarction like pattern, inverted T waves, left anterior hemiblock, Q waves
- Elevated creatine phosphokinase (CPK).

Management[7,13,14]

- Immobilized affected limb
- Oxygen administration
- Prazosin—a postsynaptic alpha-blocker, reverses both inotropic and hypokinetic phases and reverses the metabolic effects caused by depressed insulin secretion
- Inotropic support (e.g. Dobutamine) for patients presenting with hypotension and marked tachycardia
- Sodium nitroprusside for massive pulmonary edema
- Antivenom therapy should be reserved for potentially life threatening complications.

Autopsy Findings

- Local part swollen, inflamed, sting may be present, surrounding tissue may show hemorrhagic infiltration
- The sting sites are usually at peripheral sites or part of body such as toes, fingers, palms, soles, etc. However, occasionally, other part may be involved such as back, shoulder, etc.
- Systemic examination reveals pulmonary edema, pulmonary hemorrhages, gastrointestinal tract hemorrhage, intracerebral hemorrhage, signs of consumption coagulopathy, myocarditis.

Medicolegal Importance

Accidental envenomation occurs and fatality is more in children.

BEES AND WASPS

- The order Hymenoptera includes the bee, wasp and ant (Figs 38.16 and 38.17)
- Honeybees are two-winged flies and have barbed sting
- Wasps and hornets stings are smooth and capable of repeated stinging

FIG. 38.16: Honeybee

FIG. 38.17: Wasp

BEES

Bee Venom

Bees inflict painful stings. A sting is delivered by a posterior, tapered, needle-like structure designed to inject venom. The stings are strongly barbed and are designed to remain embedded in skin. Bees inject approximately 50 μg of venom. The contents of venom are as follows:

1. Biogenic amines
   - Histamine
   - 5-hydroxy tryptamine
   - Acetylcholine
   - Apamin
2. Enzymes
   - Phospholipase A
   - Hyaluronidase
   - Acid phosphatase
   - Minimine
3. Toxic peptides
   - Mellitin
   - Apamin
   - Mast cell degranulating peptide

Mechanism of Action[15]

- Melittin is the main pain-inducing compound that functions by altering membrane integrity
- Melittin in association with phospholipase A_2 causes red-cell hemolysis. Once Melittin disrupts the membrane, phospholipase A_2 cleaves bonds in the fatty acid portion of bilipid layer.

Clinical Features

1. Local
   - Pain
   - Redness
   - Swelling
   - Pruritis
   - If stinging occurs in mouth or in tongue may lead to airway obstruction by developing edema and/or dysphagia.[16] Uvulitis may occur.[17]
2. Systemic
   - Person allergic to bee venom may develop anaphylaxis
   - Tingling sensation
   - Flushing
   - Dizziness
   - Visual disturbances
   - Syncope
   - Vomiting and diarrhea
   - Wheezing
   - Urticaria
   - Angiedema
   - Glotic edema
   - Coma
   - Renal failure[18]
   - Hemolysis with hematoglobinuria
   - Rhabdomyolysis[18]

Management

- The stings of honeybees should be removed quickly. Removal of bee stings that have been embedded for more than one minute will have little or no effect in reducing envenomation since most of the venom empties from detached honeybee stings within 10 to 20 seconds.[15,19]
- Patient with systemic reaction (shock, bronchospasm, generalized urticaria or angioedema) should be treated with parental epinephrine.[20]
- Patient should be observed for delayed manifestations
- Serum levels of hemoglobin and myoglobin should be observed
- Renal failure should be treated on conventional line with intravenous fluid and diuretics.[18] Dialysis may be required.
- Antihistamines.

WASP

Venom

Wasp venom is composed of following:

1. Biogenic amines

- Histamine
- 5-hydroxy tryptamine
- Acetylcholine

2. Enzymes
   - Phospholipase A and B
   - Hyaluronidase
3. Toxic peptides
   - Kinin
4. Others
   - Antigen-5
   - Acid phosphatase

Clinical Features

1. Local
   - Pain
   - Redness
   - Swelling
2. Systemic
   - Person allergic to venom may develop anaphylaxis
   - Tingling sensation
   - Flushing
   - Dizziness
   - Syncope
   - Vomiting and diarrhea
   - Wheezing
   - Urticaria
   - Angioedema
   - Renal failure
   - Hemolysis with hematoglobinuria
   - Rhabdomyolysis
   - Hallucinations[21]

Management

- Patient with systemic reaction (shock, bronchospasm, generalized urticaria or angioedema) should be treated with parental epinephrine.[20]
- Patient should be observed for delayed manifestations
- Serum levels of hemoglobin and myoglobin should be observed
- Antihistamines
- Analgesics for pain.

REFERENCES

1. Govindiah G. Poisonous snakes. In: Handbook of Poisonous Snakes & Plants, 1st edn. 2004. Paras Publishing, Hyderabad. 2-33.
2. Dhaliwal JS, Lim TW, Sukumaran KD. A double antibody sandwich micro-ELISA kit for the rapid diagnosis of snakebite. Southeast Asian J Trop Med Public Health 1983;14:367-73.
3. Selvanyagam ZE, Gananvendhan SG, Ganesh KA, Rajagopal D, Rao PV. ELISA for the detection of venoms from four medically important snakes of India. Toxicon 1999;37:757-70.
4. Greenwood BM, Warrell DA, Davidson NM, Ormerod LD, Reid HA. Immunodiagnosis of snake bite. BMJ 1974;4:743-5.
5. Mahadevan S. Scorpion sting. Indian Pediatrics 2000;37:504-13.
6. Garg AK, Pimparkar AB, Abraham PP, Chikhalikar AA. Myocarditis and pulmonary oedema following scorpion bite (a case report). J Postgrad Med 1983;29:46-8.
7. Bawaskar HS, Bawaskar PH. Clinical profile of severe scorpion envenomation in children at rural setting. Indian Pediatrics 2003;40:1072-81.
8. Bawaskar HS, Bawaskar PH. Cardiovascular manifestations of severe scorpion sting in India (Review of 34 children). Ann Trop Pediatr 1991;11:381-7.
9. Mundle PM. Pulmonary oedema following scorpion stings. BMJ 1961;1:1042.
10. Bisarya BN, Vasavada JP, Bhat A, Nair PNR, Sharma VK. Hemplegia and myocarditis following scorpion bite. Indian Heart J 1977;29:97-100.
11. Margulis G, Sofer S, Zalstein E, Zunker N, Ilia R, Gueron M. Abnormal coronary perfusion in experimental scorpion envenomation. Toxicon 1994;32:1675-8.
12. Poon-King T. Myocarditis from scorpion stings. BMJ 1963; 1:374-7.
13. Bawaskar HS, Bawaskar PH. Vasodilators: Scorpion envenoming and the heart (An Indian experience). Toxicon 1994; 32:1031-40.
14. Bawaskar HS, Bawaskar PH. Prazosin for vasodilator treatment of acute pulmonary oedema due to scorpion sting. Ann Trop Med Parasitol 1987;1:719-23.
15. Vetter RS, Visscher PK, Camazine S. Mass envenomations by honeybees and wasps. West J Med 1999;170:223-7.
16. Shah D, Tsang T. Bee sting dysphagia (letter). Ann Intern Med 1998;129:253.
17. Butterton JR, Clawson-Simons J. Hymenopetra uvulitis (letter). N Engl J Med 1987;317:1291.
18. Vikrant S, Patial RK. Renal failure following multiple bee stings. Indian J Med Sci 2006; 60: available at www.indianjmedsci.org
19. Schumacher MJ, Tveten MS, Egen NB. Rate and quantity of delivery of venom from honeybee stings. J Allergy Clin Immunol 1994;93:831-5.
20. Sporer KA. Arthropod envenomation. In Viccellio P (ed) Handbook of Medical Toxicology, 1st edn. 1993. Little, Brown and Company, Boston. 677-84.
21. Levick N, Braitberg G. Massive European wasp envenomation of a child. Emerg Med 1996; 8:239-45.

CHAPTER 39

Mechanical Irritants

Take calculated risks. That is quite different from being rash

- George S Patton

Mechanical irritants, *per se*, are not poisons and do not cause toxic effects but cause local irritation at the site of application. For example, glass powder can cause irritation of gastrointestinal mucosa if ingested. These agents are considered as "unwholesome drugs" or other drugs of the section 328 of IPC.

Examples are:

1. Powdered glass/glass particles (Fig. 39.1)
2. Diamond powder
3. Needles/metal pins (Fig. 39.2)
4. Chopped animal hairs
5. Vegetable hairs
6. Stone pieces
7. Nails

Clinical Features

- Powdered glass, diamond powder, needles, etc. may cause pain in abdomen, nausea and vomiting, may injure tissue and causes bleeding. If bleeding is considerable and acute, death may occur due to hemorrhagic shock. If bleeding is gradual and concealed, e.g. malena may induce anemia, weakness, general debility, etc.
- Similarly death may occur if the agents cause perforation of stomach or intestine
- Pieces of chopped hairs cause nausea, vomiting and irritation. GIT mucosa may be inflamed.

Fatal dose and fatal period: Uncertain

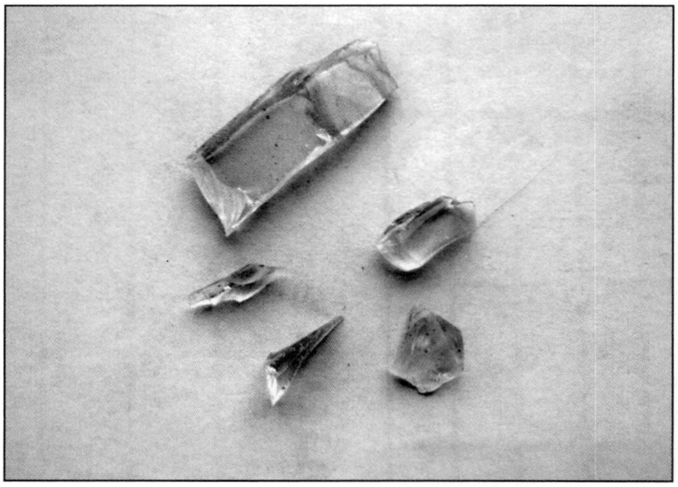

FIG. 39.1: Glass particles

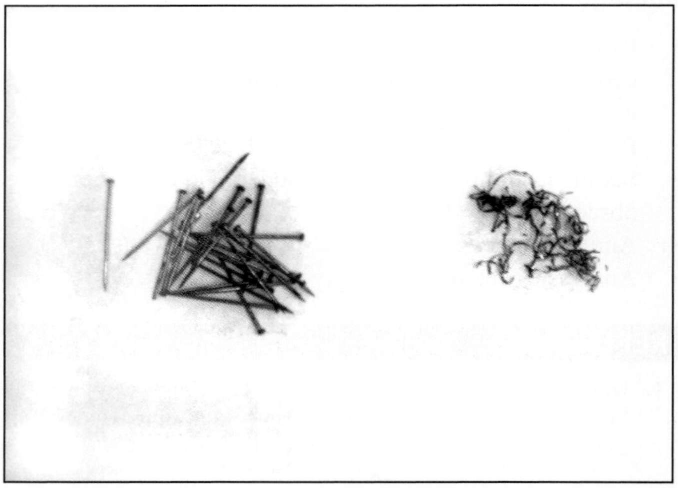

FIG. 39.2: Metal pins

Complication[1]

- Bowel/esophagus perforation
- Mechanical intestinal obstruction
- GIT hemorrhage
- Perforation peritonitis.

Management

- Bulky food and then purgatives to pass the irritants in stools
- Ice pieces to reduce thirst
- Analgesics to relieve pain.

Autopsy Findings

- Erosions may be noted in mouth, pharynx, esophagus, stomach and intestine
- Fragments of glass, stone, hairs, etc. may be found in GIT adhered to mucosa
- Mucosa of GIT may be inflamed.

Medicolegal Importance

1. Accidental ingestion may occur with jam, jelly or food, etc.
2. Show-men may swallow glass particles while showing the show
3. These agents may be used with an evil intention to cause ill health and death
4. Occasionally used as cattle poisons
5. These agents are considered as "unwholesome drugs" under section 328 of IPC
6. Children having access to these substances may accidentally ingest them or may inhale in respiratory tract causing respiratory obstruction.[2]

REFERENCES

1. Uyemura MC. Foreign body ingestion in children. Am Fam Physician 2005;72:287-91.
2. Joshi SV. Foreign bodies in both main bronchi–a unique experience. Milestone 2003;2:157-8.

CHAPTER 40

Pesticides

Sure, it is going to kill a lot of people, but they may be dying of something else anyway

- Othal Brand, member of Texas pesticide review board, on chlordane

Pesticides are the compounds used to kill pests. Pests may include insect, rodent, fungi etc. Pesticides are classified as:[1]

1. Insecticides: these are the compounds used to kill or repel insects and related species. Examples are — organophosphates, carbamate, organochlorine, pyrethroids.
2. Rodenticide: these are the compound used to kill rodent like rat, mice, mole etc. Examples are — zinc phosphide, barium carbonate, strychnine, warfarin etc.
3. Herbicide: these are the compounds used to kill weed. Examples are — acrolein, glyphosate, paraquat etc.
4. Fungicide: these are the compounds used to kill fungi and moulds. Examples are — thiocarbamate, sodium azide.
5. Miscellaneous compounds include lead, copper, mercury, nicotine etc.

ORGANOPHOSPHORUS COMPOUNDS

Organophosphate poisoning is the most common poisoning in India followed by aluminium phosphide.[2] Organophosphorus compounds are available as dust powder or liquid. Organophosphorus compounds are classified as (Fig. 40.1):

1. Alkyl compounds — such as tetraethyl pyrophosphate (TEPP), hexa ethyl tetraphosphate (HETP), octa methyl pyrophosphate (OMPA), malathion etc.
2. Aryl compounds — such as parathion, chlorothion, diazinon (Tik-20), paraoxon etc.

Absorption, Metabolism and Excretion

- Organophosphorus compounds are absorbed by any route — skin, conjunctiva, inhalation, oral or by direct injection.
- Some compounds such as parathion are stored in body fat and are released slowly in the circulation thus prolonging the duration of toxic action.
- Parathion is first metabolized to paraoxon, which is the active toxic agent and then to paranitrophenol that is excreted into urine. Malathion is metabolized in liver by esterases and part of this metabolized product is excreted in urine as phosphate.

Mechanism of Action

Organophosphorus compounds are inhibitors of acetylcholinesterase. Acetyl cholinesterase is required to hydrolyse acetylcholine to choline and acetic acid (Fig. 40.2). As a result, there is accumulation of acetylcholine with continued stimulation of local receptors and eventual paralysis of nerve or muscle (Fig. 40.3). Organophosphate intoxication leads to characteristic end-plate abnormalities that reflect the degree of AchE inhibition and increase in Ach concentration at the neuromuscular junction.[3]

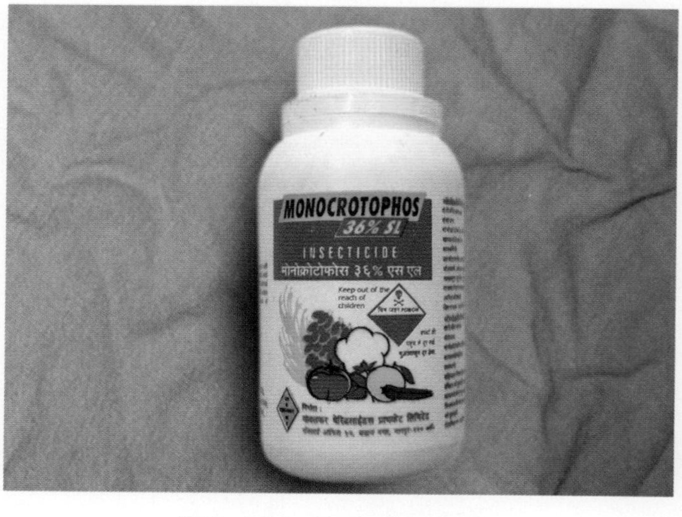

FIG. 40.1: Monocrotophos

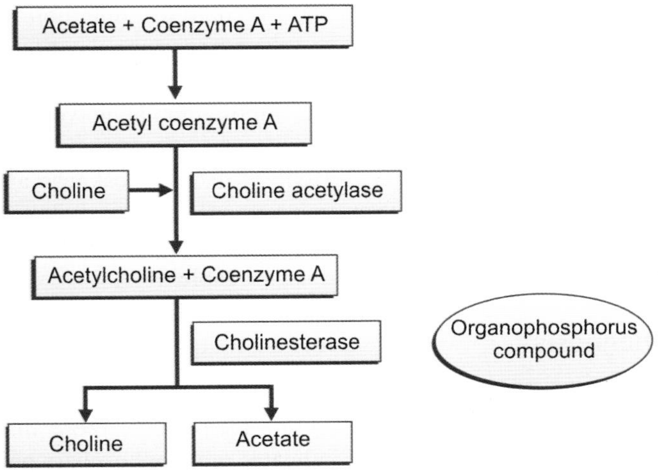

FIG. 40.2: Flow chart showing mechanism of formation of acetylcholine and inhibition of cholinesterase enzyme by mark "X"

Fatal Dose

- Malathion about 60 gm[4]
- TEPP 100 mg
- OMPA 175 mg
- Parathion 175 mg
- HETP 350 mg
- Diazinon 1 gm

Fatal period
24 hours

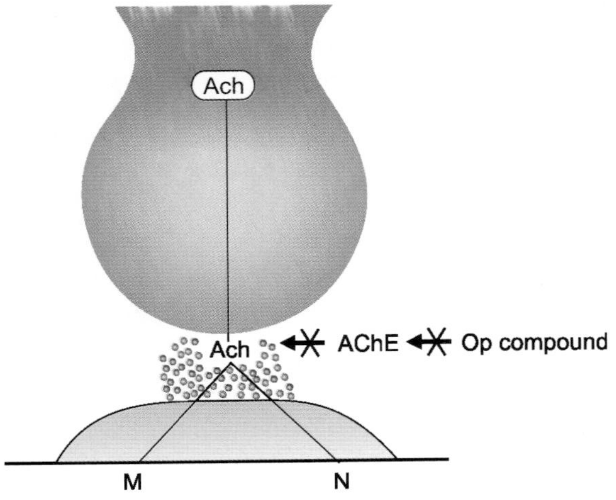

FIG. 40.3: Diagram showing action of acetylcholine on receptors due to inhibition of cholinesterase by organophosphorus compound. M indicates muscarinic receptor and N indicates nicotinic receptor

Clinical Features

Organophosphate insecticide poisoning in human can produce:[5]

- Acute poisoning — due to acute peripheral and central cholinergic block
- An intermediate syndrome with weakness
- A delayed distal polyneuropathy

Acute Poisoning

A. Muscarinic effects

Due to muscarinic like action, following clinical features are observed

1. Bronchial tree — cough, increased secretions, bronchoconstriction, wheezing, dyspnea, pulmonary edema.
2. Gastrointestinal — nausea, vomiting, abdominal cramp, diarrhea.
3. Sweat glands — increased sweating.
4. Salivary glands — increased salivation.
5. Lacrimal glands — increased lacrimation. **Chromodacryorrhea** (shedding of red tears) due to accumulation of porphyrin in the lachrymal glands is seen very rarely.[6]
6. Eyes — miosis, blurring of vision or dimness of vision. Miosis develops due to the inhibition of cholinesterase and marked parasympathomimetic stimulation of iris. However, dilatation of pupil in organophosphate intoxication have been recorded, therefore, it is essential not to rely only on pupillary size as diagnostic criteria for organophosphate compound poisoning.[7]
7. Heart — slow pulse, hypotension.
8. Urinary bladder — frequency of micturation, urinary incontinence.

{Muscarinic manifestation can be remembered with the mnemonic **"DUMBELS"** D = diarrhea, U = urination, M = miosis, B = Bronchospasm, bradycardia, E = emesis (vomiting), L = lacrimation, S = salivation}

B. Nicotinic effects

The nicotinic effects are as follows:

1. Striated muscles — easy fatigue, weakness, muscular twitching, fasciculation, cramps
2. Sympathetic ganglia — pallor, occasional elevation of blood pressure (hypertension), tachycardia
3. Increased adrenal medulla activity

(Nicotinic manifestation can be remembered with the mnemonic "**MATCH**" M = muscle weakness and fasciculation, A = adrenal medulla activity increase, T = tachycardia, C = cramps in muscle, H = hypertension).

C. CNS effects

The CNS effects are:

1. Irritability
2. Apprehension
3. Restlessness
4. Fine fibrillary tremors of hands, eyelids, face or tongue
5. Muscular weakness
6. Convulsions — the convulsions may be tonic (limbs stretched and rigid) or may be clonic (rapid repetitive movement). Clonic convulsions are more common.[8]
7. Mental confusion progressing to stupor to coma
8. Depression of respiratory and circulatory centers.

D. Other features

- Toxic myocarditis had been reported.[9]
- Pancreatitis may be noted. The parasympathetic stimulation of the pancreas with Ach, pilocarpine or vagal stimulation causes augmentation of the secretory flow and increased intraductal pressure. However, the exact cause of Pancreatitis is unknown.[10]
- Organophosphorus compound produce metabolic acidosis by respiratory depression, bronchoconstriction, pulmonary edema, CNS depression and lactacidosis.[11]

Causes of Death

1. Respiratory failure
2. Cerebral hypoxia
3. Hyperthermia
4. Hepatic failure
5. Renal failure

Intermediate Syndrome[12]

- Intermediate syndrome is a neurotoxic effect that appears after acute cholinergic crisis but before the expected onset of delayed neuropathy.
- The cardinal feature of the syndrome is muscular weakness, affecting predominantly the proximal limb muscles and the neck flexors. Cranial nerve palsies are common. (The intermediate syndrome predominantly affect muscles innervated by the cranial nerves — neck flexors, proximal muscles of the limb and the muscles of respiration).
- This syndrome carries a risk of death because of the associated respiratory depression.
- The muscle weakness had an acute onset, noticed within 24 to 96 hours after poisoning.

Delayed Polyneuropathy[12-15]

- Delayed polyneuropathy appears 2 to 3 weeks after poisoning
- The delayed polyneuropathy is due to inhibition of enzyme neurotoxic esterase with nerve demyelination.
- In delayed polyneuropathy, the paralysis is usually limited to the distal muscles of the limbs; cranial nerves and respiratory muscles are spared.
- The disorder is characterized by flaccid weakness and atrophy of distal limb muscles or spasticity and ataxia.
- Difference between intermediate syndrome and delayed polyneuropathy are mentioned in Table 40.1.

Diagnosis

1. Cholinesterase level
   - Depression of RBC cholinesterase level more than 50 percent of normal indicates organophosphate poisoning. The decrease is due to binding by phosphate group of pesticide. It is better parameter than plasma cholinesterase.[16]
   - Depression of plasma (serum) cholinesterase activity more than 50 percent of normal indicates Organophosphate poisoning. This test is not specific as plasma cholinesterase activity is also depressed in cirrhosis of liver, neoplasia, malnutrition, septicemia due to burns, obstructive jaundice.
2. Colorimetric method
   - 1 ml sample urine is taken and 1 ml of NBB {45% in acetone 4-(nitrobenzyl) pyridine} added and mixed for 30 seconds in vortex mixer. The mixture is heated

Table 40.1: Difference between intermediate syndrome and delayed polyneuropathy

Variable	*Intermediate syndrome*	*Delayed polyneuropathy*
Time of onset after poisoning	1 to 4 days	2 to 3 weeks
Site of weakness		
- Limb muscles	Proximal	Distal
- Neck muscles	Present	Absent
- Cranial nerves	Present	Absent
- Respiratory muscles	Present	Absent
Electromyogram	Tetanic fade	Denervation
Recovery, from time of onset	4 to 18 days	6 to 12 months
Organophosphate compound commonly involved	Fenthion, dimethoate, monocrotophos	Methamidophos, trichlorphos, leptophos

at 100° C for 20 minutes. Organophosphate insecticide shows a characteristic purplish blue color that can be read using spectrophotometer.[17]
3. P-nitrophenol test
4. Paper chromatography
5. Thin layer chromatography (TLC) [18]
6. Gas chromatography (GC) [19]
7. Gas chromatography-mass spectrometry (GC-MS)
8. High performance liquid chromatography (HPLC) [20]
9. ECG may show right axis deviation, ST segment depression and T wave inversion.[21]

Management

Principles of treatment consist of:
- Stabilization of patient
- Decontamination
- Antidote administration
- Supportive measures
- Nursing care

Decontamination

- Skin — the affected part should be washed thoroughly with copious water
- Ocular — copious eye irrigation with normal saline or tap water
- Ingestion — gastric lavage and administration of activated charcoal.

Antidote Administration

- Atropine is competitive antagonist of acetylcholine and blocks muscarinic manifestations of Organophosphate. It does not reverse peripheral muscular paralysis, which is nicotinic action. The atropine should be given 2 mg intravenous promptly with dose repeated every 10 minutes till pupil dilates (up to 200 mg has been administered in a day).[22] Some authorities recommend administration of atropine until bronchial and other secretions have dried. According to them pupil size and heart rate cannot be used as end-points.[23] Continued treatment with maintenance doses may be required for 1 to 2 weeks.
- Oximes are used as they helps to regenerate acetylcholinesterase at muscarinic, nicotinic and CNS sites. Pralidoxime (2-PAM) is given intravenously as 500-mg/20 ml infusion in a dose of 1 to 2 gm (children 20 to 40 mg/kg).

Supportive Measures

- Oxygen administration, ventilator assistance
- Maintain vital parameters, hydration, urine output
- Convulsions should be controlled with judicious use of diazepam.

Avoid Giving

- Other acetylcholinesterase inhibitors such as Physostigmine, endorphonium
- Succinylcholine for rapid intubation.

Autopsy Findings

- Insecticide like smell (sometimes garlicky or kerosene like)
- Froth at mouth and nostrils
- Cyanosis
- Constricted pupils
- Stomach contents have insecticide like smell. Mucosa stained with compound color, congested and eroded (Figs 40.4 and 40.5)
- Congestion of organs
- Pulmonary edema
- Cerebral edema
- Features of toxic myocarditis had also been reported. Microscopic examination of heart reveals dilatation of pericardial blood vessels with hemorrhages in the surrounding tissues, interstitial edema of myocardium, inflammatory cells, hemosiderin-laden macrophages and fatty infiltration of the myocardium.[21]

Medicolegal Importance

1. Accidental poisoning may occur in farmers while spraying in the fields or opening the lid of the containers.[24]
2. Suicidal poisoning is common with this insecticide.
3. Homicidal is rare as it is difficult to mask the smell of insecticide.

ORGANOCHLORINES

Organochlorine insecticides are chlorinated hydrocarbons and are divided into four types as:
- DDT (dichlorodiphenyl-trichloroethane) and analogues
- Benzene hexachloride group — e.g. BHC, lindane (Fig. 40.6)
- Cyclodines and related compounds — e.g. endrin, aldrin, dieldrin, endosulfan, sobenzan
- Toxaphene and related compounds — e.g. toxaphene.

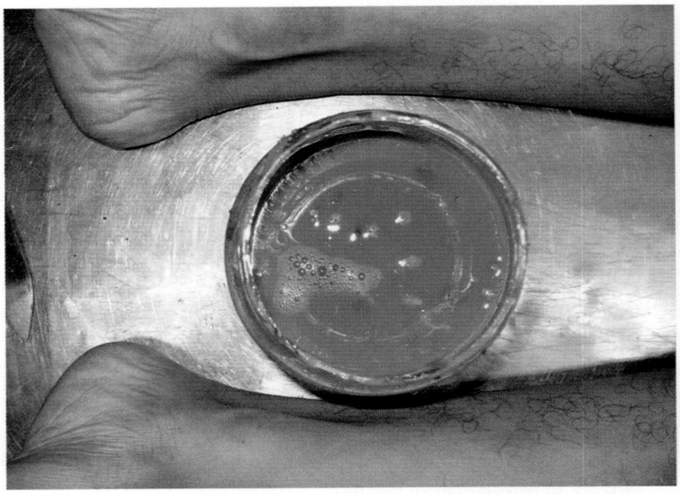

FIG. 40.4: Organophosphate compound found in stomach

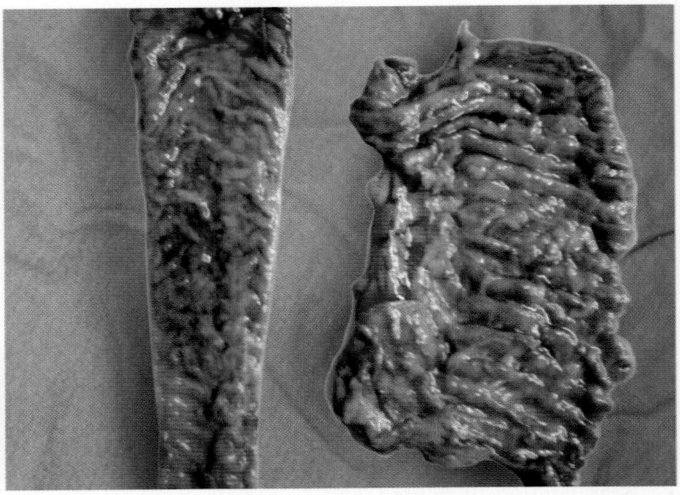

FIG. 40.5: Gastric mucosa stained with compound color and showing congestion

Availability

These compounds are available as
- Dusting powder
- Emulsion
- Granules
- Solutions.

Fatal dose
- DDT 15 to 30 gm
- Lindane 15-30 gm
- Aldrin, endrin, dieldrin 2 to 6 gm.

Absorption, Metabolism and Excretion

Organochloride compounds are absorbed through skin, inhalation and through gastrointestinal tract. Most of the compounds are metabolized slowly in the body and remains in tissues, especially in fatty tissues for prolonged duration. These compounds are metabolized in liver and are excreted in urine, feces and milk.

Mechanism of Action[25]

- Organochlorines affect nerve impulse transmission by altering membrane Na^+ and K^+ flux, resulting in CNS hyperexcitability.
- Organochlorines produces myocardial irritability thus predisposing to cardiac arrhythmias
- DDT and related compounds affect the sodium channel and sodium conductance across the neuronal membrane, especially of axons
- Cyclodine and lindane appear to inhibit the GABA-mediated chloride channels in the CNS.

Clinical Features

Acute poisoning
- GIT — nausea, vomiting, diarrhea hyperaesthesia or paresthesia of mouth and face
- CNS — headache, vertigo, myoclonus, mydriasis, weakness, agitation, confusion, convulsions, coma.
- Respiratory system — cough, wheezing, if aspiration or inhalation occurs
- Renal failure
- Hepatitis
- Dermatitis.

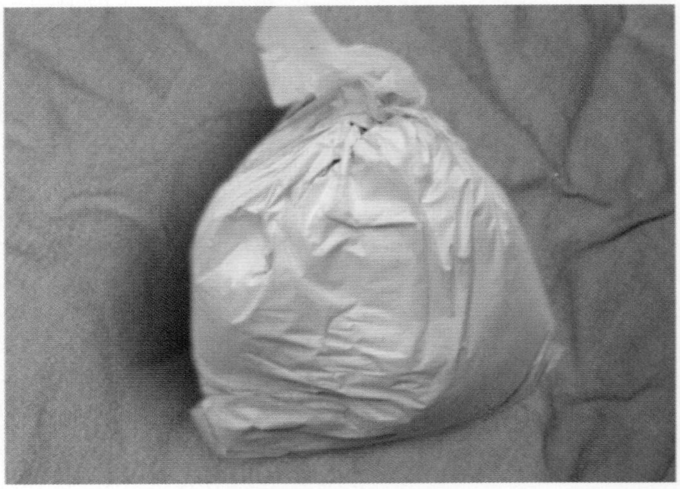

FIG. 40.6: Lindane

Chronic Poisoning

Exposure of these compounds for prolonged duration may result in cumulative toxicity characterized by anorexia, weight loss, weakness, tremors, opsoclonus, ataxia, pseudotumor cerebri, abnormal mental changes, oligospermia, thrombocytopenic purpura. Lindane and BHC have been linked to aplastic anemia.

Management

- Skin — the affected part should be washed thoroughly with copious water
- Ocular — copious eye irrigation with normal saline or tap water
- Ingestion — gastric lavage and administration of activated charcoal
- Oxygen administration, ventilator assistance
- Maintain vital parameters, hydration, urine output
- Convulsions should be controlled with judicious use of diazepam or lorazepam.
- Hyperthermia should be managed in usual way
- Arrhythmias can be managed with lidocaine.

Avoid Giving

- Epinephrine — may exacerbate ventricular arrhythmias
- Atropine
- Oil based fluid/food/cathartics

Autopsy Findings

- Insecticide like smell
- Froth at mouth and nostrils
- Cyanosis
- Congestion of organs
- Pulmonary edema
- Cerebral edema.

Medicolegal Importance

1. Accidental poisoning may occur in farmers while spraying in the fields or opening the lid of the containers.
2. Suicidal poisoning is also common with this insecticide.
3. Homicidal is rare as it is difficult to mask the smell of insecticide.

CARBAMATE

Carbamates are popular insecticides and include aldicarb, propoxur (Baygon), carbaryl, carbofuran, methomyl, triallate, bendiocarb etc.

Mechanism of Action

Carbamate causes reversible inhibition of acetylcholinesterase due to which there is accumulation of acetylcholine at muscarinic and nicotinic receptors and in the CNS.

Fatal Dose

- Extremely toxic or highly toxic — carbaryl, carbfuran, methomyl, propoxur
- Moderately toxic or slightly toxic — aldicarb, triallate.

Clinical Features

Clinical features of Carbamate poisoning are same that of Organophosphate poisoning with following difference:
- Carbamate causes reversible inhibition of acetylcholinesterase, therefore the signs and symptoms are less severe than Organophosphate poisoning
- Carbamate toxicity is short lived and it hydrolyse spontaneously from the site
- It does not penetrate effectively in CNS so it produce little or no CNS toxicity.

Management

Decontamination

- Skin — the affected part should be washed thoroughly with copious water
- Ocular — copious eye irrigation with normal saline or tap water
- Ingestion — gastric lavage and administration of activated charcoal.

Antidote Administration

- Atropine is competitive antagonist of acetylcholine and blocks muscarinic manifestations. The atropine should be given 2 mg intravenous promptly with dose repeated every 10 minutes till signs of atropinization are evident.
- Oximes are ineffective in Carbamate poisoning and are not recommended.[25]

Supportive Measures

- Oxygen administration, ventilator assistance
- Maintain vital parameters, hydration, urine output.

Autopsy Findings

- Insecticide like smell
- Froth at mouth and nostrils

- Cyanosis
- Constricted pupils
- Congestion of organs
- Pulmonary edema
- Cerebral edema.

Medicolegal Importance

1. Accidental poisoning may occur.
2. Suicidal poisoning is also common with this insecticide.
3. Homicidal is rare as it is difficult to mask the smell of insecticide.

PYRETHRUM, PYRETHRINS AND PYRETHROIDS

- Pyrethrum is extract of the chrysanthemum flower. Pyrethrum contains six active components labeled pyrethrins.
- Pyrethroids are synthetic derivatives of pyrethrins.
- These compounds are commonly used as insect and mosquito repellants.
- Examples — allethrin, D-allethrin, cypermethrin, permethrin etc (Fig. 40.7).

Mechanism of Action

- Pyrethroids prolong the inactivation of the sodium channel by binding to it in the open state.[1]
- These compounds quickly inactivate insects but mammals are relatively resistant to them. However, in most of the cases, toxicity with these agents occurs because of the allergic reactions to these compounds.[26]

FIG. 40.7: Pyrethrum derivatives

Fatal Dose

Pyrethrum 1 gm/kg

Clinical Features

- Dermal exposure causes erythema, dermatitis, blister formation
- Ocular exposure causes irritation, lacrimation
- Inhalation causes rhinorrhea, sore throat, wheezing, cough, dyspnea
- Ingestion causes nausea, vomiting, paresthesia, vertigo, fasciculation, hyperthermia, altered mental status, convulsions, pulmonary edema and coma.

Management

Decontamination

- Skin — the affected part should be washed thoroughly with copious water
- Ocular — copious eye irrigation with normal saline or tap water.

Systemic Poisoning

- Ingestion — gastric lavage and administration of activated charcoal
- Fatty substance should be avoided as they promotes the absorption through GIT
- Allergic reaction should be treated with epinephrine and antihistamines
- Bronchospasm should be treated with appropriate bronchodilators
- Convulsions should be controlled with judicious use of diazepam
- Oxygen administration, ventilator assistance.

Autopsy Findings

- Insect repellant like smell
- Froth at mouth and nostrils
- Cyanosis
- Congestion of organs
- Pulmonary edema
- Cerebral edema.

Medicolegal Importance

1. Accidental poisoning may occur.
2. Suicidal poisoning is rare.

PARAQUAT

These are popular herbicides. They are spread on unwanted weeds and other vegetations. Paraquat and diquat belongs to dipyridyl group.

Fatal Dose

4 mg/kg

Clinical Features

Paraquat causes corrosion to mucosa of mouth, esophagus and gastrointestinal tract. It causes pain in mouth and in abdomen. There is diarrhea, vomiting, dysphagia and aphonia. Patient develops hepatic failure and renal failure. There may be metabolic acidosis with hyperglycemia.[27] Lungs show pulmonary edema and after 4 to 5 days may show pulmonary fibrosis with progressive respiratory failure.

Management

- Gastric lavage with activated charcoal[28] may be beneficial if performed within one hour of ingestion of poison
- Pain should be controlled by giving ice-cold fluid and parental analgesics
- Hemodialysis or Hemoperfusion is said to be beneficial
- Supportive measures include maintenance of airway, circulation, hydration, urine output and vital parameters.

Autopsy Findings

- Corrosion around lips, mouth, esophagus and erosion in GIT
- Lungs may be edematous or may appear stiffened with evidence of hemorrhage and pulmonary fibrosis
- Liver — signs of hepatic failure and kidneys show acute tubular necrosis
- Other organs congested.

Medicolegal Importance

1. Accidental poisoning may occur.
2. Suicidal poisoning may occur.

ALUMINIUM PHOSPHIDE

Aluminium phosphide is used as a grain preservative. In northern part of India, it is the leading cause for death due to poisoning.[29]

Availability

Aluminium phosphide is available in grayish green tablets of 3 gm each. Each tablet release 1 gm of phosphine (Fig. 40.8). The tablets are available in market with various trade names such as — celphos, alphos, sulphas etc.

Fatal Dose

3 gm

Fatal Period

12 to 36 hours

Mechanism of Action

Aluminium phosphide liberates phosphine when it comes in contact with air and moisture. It reacts with acidic media (HCL) of stomach and release phosphine gas, which is rapidly absorbed from gastrointestinal tract by simple diffusion. Phosphine is a protoplasmic poison interfering with enzymes and protein synthesis. In animal studies, phosphine has been shown to cause non-competitive inhibition of cytochrome oxidase of myocardial mitochondria.[16]

Clinical Features[30-32]

- Metallic taste
- Vomiting
- Thirst
- Burning sensation
- Pain in abdomen
- Diarrhea

FIG. 40.8: Aluminium phosphide tablets

- Persistent hypotension with shock
- Dyspnea
- Cough
- Tachycardia
- Tachpnea
- Bleeding diathesis
- Restlessness
- Altered sensorium
- Coma
- Respiratory distress.

Diagnosis

- Garlicky smell
- Altered liver function tests with raised transaminase levels
- Increased PT and PTT
- ABG shows metabolic acidosis
- ECG — sinus tachycardia, ST depression in leads II and III.
- Silver nitrate test – the patient is asked to breathe through a piece of filter paper impregnated with 0.1 N silver nitrate solution for 5 to 10 minutes. If filter paper becomes black, it suggests presence of phosphine. The blackening is imparted because phosphine reduces silver nitrate to silver.

Management

- Secure airway, oxygen, ventilator assistance
- Manage shock with intravenous fluid and inotropic support
- Manage metabolic acidosis with sodium bicarbonate
- Magnesium sulfate administration remains controversial. It is said that administration of magnesium sulfate is beneficial for management of cardiac arrhythmias
- Gastric lavage is contraindicated since administration of water will release phosphine from the available aluminium phosphide in the stomach.

Autopsy Findings[30,33]

- Typical garlicky odor
- Congested organs
- Bright fluid blood
- Pleural effusion
- Pulmonary edema
- Toxic myocarditis
- Bleeding diathesis
- Gastric mucosa shows shedding
- Kidney shows acute tubular necrosis
- Liver shows fatty change, congestion, edema, inflammatory infiltrate in portal tract and centrizonal necrosis.

Medicolegal Importance

1. Suicidal poisoning is common with this agent, especially in the northern part of India.
2. Rarely accidental poisoning may occur to workers working in grain elevators, wear houses and grain freighter etc.[33]

REFERENCES

1. Pillay VV. Pesticides. In: Textbook of Forensic Medicine and Toxicology, 14th edn. 2004. Paras Publishing, Hyderabad. 478-96.
2. Bhatkule PR, Wahab SN, Pathak AA. Some epidemiological factors related to poisoning cases. Milestone 2003; 2: 193-7.
3. Besser R, Gutmann L, Dillmann U, Weilemann LS, Hopf HC. End-plate dysfunction in acute organophosphate intoxication. Neurology 1989; 39: 561-6.
4. Jadhav RK, Sharma VK, Rao GJ, Saraf AK, Chandra H. Distribution of malathion in body tissues and fluids. Forensic Sci Int 1992; 52:223-9.
5. Wadia RS, Sadagopan C, Amin RB, Sardesai HV. Neurological manifestations of organophosphorus insecticide poisoning. J Neurol Neurosurg Psychiatry 1974; 37:841-7.
6. Reddy KSN. Agricultural poisons. In: The Essentials of Forensic Medicine and Toxicology, 22nd edn. 2003. K. Suguna Devi, Hyderabad. 428-35.
7. Dixon EM. Dilatation of the pupils in parathion poisoning. JAMA 1957; 163:444-5.
8. Thompson TS, Treble RG, Magliocco JC. Case study: fatal poisoning by malathion. Forensic Sci Int 1998; 95:89-98.
9. Limaye MR. Acute organophosphorus compound poisoning. J Indian Med Assoc 1965; 47:492.
10. Dressel TD, Goodale RL, Arneson MA, Booner JW. Pancreatitis as a complication of anticholinesterase insecticide intoxication. Ann Surg 1979; 189:199-204.
11. Yadav R, Shukla PS, Yadav S. Acid-base disturbances in patients of poisoning. Indian Med Gazette 1993; June: 197-9.
12. Senanayake N, Karalliedde L. Neurotoxic effects of organophosphorus insecticides – an intermediate syndrome. N Engl J Med 1987; 316:761-3.
13. Senanayake N, Johonson MK. Acute polyneuropathy after poisoning by a new organophosphate insecticide. N Engl Med 1982; 306:155-7.
14. Lotti M, Becker CE, Aminoff MJ. Organophosphate polyneuropathy: pathogenesis and prevention. Neurology 1984; 34:658-62.
15. Driskell WJ, Groce DF, Hill RH Jr. Methomyl in the blood of a pilot who crashed during aerial spraying. J Anal Toxicol 1991; 15:339-40.
16. Kumar R, Singh B, Singh N, Singh J. Review of management of common poisoning in India. Medicolegal Update 2005; 5:31-8.
17. Namera A, Utsumi Y, Yashiki M, Ohtani M, Imamura T, Kojima T. Direct colorimetric method for determination of organophosphates in human urine. Clinica Chimica Acta 2000; 291:9-18.

18. Erdmann F, Brose C, Schutz H. A TLC screening programme for 170 commonly used pesticides using the corrected R-value. Int J Leg Med 1990; 104:25-31.
19. Miyazaki T, Yashiki M, Chikasue F, Kojima T, Hibino H. A case of death from prothiophos poisoning. Forensic Sci Int 1988; 30:13-9.
20. Sharma VK, Jadhav RK, Rao GJ, Saraf AK, Chandra H. High performance liquid chromatographic method for the analysis of organophosphorus and carbamate pesticides. Forensic Sci Int 1990; 48:21-5.
21. Chhabra ML, Sepaha GC, Jain SR, Bhagwat RR, Khandekar JD. ECG and necropsy changes in organophosphorus compound (malathion) poisoning. Indian J Med Sci 1969; 424-9.
22. Tripathi KD. Cholinergic system and drugs. In Essentials of Medical Pharmacology, 4th edn. 1999. Jaypee Brothers Medical Publishers (P) Ltd. New Delhi. 83-102.
23. Linden CH, Lovejoy FH Jr. Poisoning and drug overdosage In: Fauci AS, Braunwald E, Isselbacher KJ, Wilson JD, Martin JB, Kasper DL, Hauser SL, Longo DL (eds) Harrison's Principles of Internal Medicine, Vol.2, 14th edn. 1998. McGraw-Hill, New York. 2523-44.
24. Chavan KD, Kachare RV, Goli SK. A retrospective study of acute poisoning in adults – in rural region of Beed district of Maharashtra. J Medicolegal Assoc Maharashtra 2002; 14:7-9.
25. Ford M. Insecticides and pesticides. In Viccellio P (ed) Handbook of Medical Toxicology, 1st edn. 1993. Little, Brown and Company, Boston.303-14.
26. Ghai OP. Poisoning and accidents. In Essential Pediatrics, 4th edn. 1996. Interprint, New Delhi. 440-5.
27. Barale F, Singer P, Xicluna A, Arbez-Gindre F. Deliberate poisoning with Paraquat death in less than 24 hours. Toxicol Eur Res 1983; 5:123-6.
28. Huang NC, Hung YM, Lin SL, Wann SR, Hsu CW, Ger LP, Hung SY, Chung HM, Yeh JH. Further evidence of the usefulness of acute physiology and chronic health evaluation II scoring system in acute paraquat poisoning. Clin Toxicol 2006; 44:99-102.
29. Bajaj R, Wasir HS. Epidemic aluminium phosphide poisoning in Northern India. Lancet 1988; 1:820-21.
30. Bardale R. Clinical profile and autopsy findings in aluminium phosphide poisoning. J Indian Soc Toxicol 2006; 2: 28.
31. Puranium CM, Raman PG, Sarmar P, Kulkarni CV, Verma M. Aluminium phosphide poisoning – a clinical, biochemical and histopathological study. J Assoc Phys Ind 1989; 37:29.
32. Singh S, Dilawari JB, Vashist R, Malhotra HS, Sharma BK. Aluminium phosphide ingestion. BMJ 1985; 290; 1110-11.
33. Wilson R, Lovejoy FH, Jaeger RJ, Landrigan PL. Acute aluminium phosphide poisoning abroad a grain freighter. JAMA 1980; 244:148-50.

CHAPTER 41

Cardiac Poisons

Laughter, bubbling from within, is the heart's own medicines.

- W B Nesbit

Examples are:
1. Tobacco
2. Digitalis
3. Oleander
4. Quinine
5. Aconite
6. Hydrocyanic acid

TOBACCO

Tobacco (tambakhu) is prepared from cured leaves of Nicotina tabacum.

Active Principles

- Nicotine
- Nornicotine
- Dried leaves contain 1 to 8 percent of nicotine. Nicotine is colorless, volatile, bitter and hygroscopic liquid.

Toxic part: tobacco leaves (Fig. 41.1).

Uses

- Smoking tobacco
- Chewing
- Snuff
- Insecticide

Mechanism of Action

Nicotine acts on nicotine receptors present in autonomic ganglia, adrenal medulla, central nervous system, spinal cord, neuromuscular junction and chemoreceptors of carotid and aortic bodies.

FIG. 41.1: Tobacco

Absorption, Metabolism and Excretion

Tobacco or nicotine is absorbed from skin, mucous membrane and lungs. It is metabolized in liver and excreted in urine. Small amounts are also excreted in milk.

Fatal Dose

40 to 60 mg of nicotine
15 to 30 gm of crude tobacco
Fatal period: 5 to 15 minutes

Clinical Features

Acute Poisoning

- Nausea and vomiting

- Diarrhea
- Pain in abdomen
- Salivation
- Tachycardia followed by bradycardia
- Anxiety
- Headache
- Blurred vision
- Confusion
- Fasciculation
- Convulsions
- Paralysis
- Coma

Chronic Poisoning

- Also known as nicotine addiction
- Common among smokers, tobacco chewers
- Develops physical dependence, manifested by recurrent craving for tobacco, tolerance, cough, impaired memory and amblyopia.
- Tobacco withdrawal is manifested by change in mood, insomnia, restlessness, constipation, headache and anxiety.

Complications

- Carcinoma of lung, esophagus, mouth, larynx
- Smokers cough
- Bronchitis
- Thromboangiitis obliterans
- Tobacco amblyopia

Maternal Smoking Leads to:[1]

- Increased risk of spontaneous abortion
- Fetal death
- Increased frequency of abruptio placentae or placenta previa
- Low birth weight baby

Cause of Death[1]

- Respiratory failure — due to paralysis of CNS or paralysis of the endings of the respiratory nerves (myoneural junctions).
- Early death — due to stimulation of vagal cardiac ganglia with stand still of heart.

Management

- Gastric lavage with activated charcoal
- Benzodiazepines for convulsions
- Symptomatic treatment.

Autopsy Findings

- Brownish stains may present over skin
- Brownish froth at mouth and nostrils
- Signs of asphyxia
- Tobacco smell may present
- Brownish discoloration of esophagus and gastric mucosa
- Stomach may contains fragments of tobacco leaves
- Pulmonary edema

Medicolegal Importance

1. Accidental poisoning may occur due to overdose
2. Occupational hazard
3. Malingering to induce illness
4. Suicide or homicide is rare

COMMON OLEANDER

Botanical name: Nerium odorum
Common names: Common oleander, white oleander, Kaner.

Features

- Shrub grows all over India and bears lanceolate leaves with white or pink flowers (Figs 41.2 and 41.3).
- The leaves give clear thick juice.

Toxic part of plant: all parts

Toxic Principles

- Oleandrin (glycoside)
- Nerin
- Folinerin

Mechanism of Action

The glycosides have digoxin like action and inhibit sodium-potassium ATPase

Fatal Dose

- 15 to 20 gm root
- 5 to 15 leaves.

Fatal period: 20 to 36 hours

Clinical Features

- Nausea and vomiting
- Diarrhea
- Tachycardia
- Breathlessness

FIG. 41.2: White oleander

FIG. 41.3: Pink oleander

- Ventricular fibrillation
- Delirium
- Drowsiness.

Management

- Gastric lavage with activated charcoal
- Atropine for AV block and sinus tachycardia
- Symptomatic treatment.

Autopsy Findings

- Congestion of organs
- Petechial hemorrhages over heart.

Medicolegal Importance

1. Root used for causing abortion
2. Accidental death occurs due to consumption of folk medicine containing oleander
3. Cattle poison
4. Suicide
5. Homicide is rare
6. Common oleander resist decomposition and burning, thus can be detected from decomposed bodies or ash.

YELLOW OLEANDER

Botanical name: Cerbera thevetia
Common name: Yellow oleander, pila Kaner, exile.

Features

- This shrub resembles common oleander but have large bell-shaped yellow color flowers (Fig. 41.4).
- The plant bears fruits, which are diamond to globular in shape and 4 to 5 cm in length. The fruits are initially greenish in colour but turns yellow and then black when becomes ripe. The fruit contains a single nut, which is elongated triangular with deep groove along the edge.[2] Each nut contains 5 pale yellow seeds (Figs 41.5 to 41.7).
- Milky juice (sap) exudes from all parts of plant.

Toxic part of plant: all parts but seed and root are more toxic.

Toxic Principles

- Thevetin
- Thevetoxin
- Cerberin

Fatal Dose

- 8 to 10 seeds
- 15 to 20 gm of root
- 5 to 10 leaves

Fatal period: 2 to 3 hours if powdered root taken.

Clinical Features

- The milky juice (sap) if applied to skin may cause inflammation in sensitive individuals
- Numbness in mouth and tongue
- Vomiting
- Diarrhea
- Headache
- Giddiness
- Loss of muscle power
- Tachycardia

FIG. 41.4: Yellow oleander

- Cardiogenic shock[3]
- Jaundice[4]
- Renal failure[4]

ECG Changes[2,5]

- Sinus bradycardia
- A-V block I and II°
- Flattening or inversion of T wave
- ST depression
- Ventricular and atrial ectopics.

Management[6,7]

- Gastric lavage with multiple dose activated charcoal is said to be effective since charcoal binds glycoside in the gut lumen and promotes their elimination

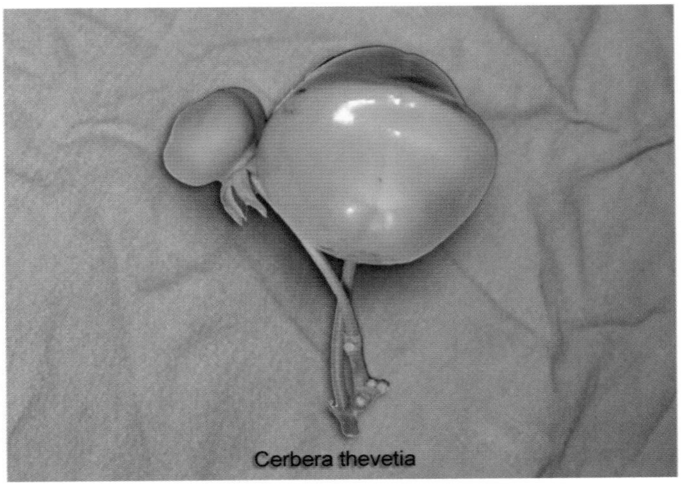

FIG. 41.5: Fruit of yellow oleander

- Bradyarrhythmias are treated with intravenous boluses of atropine and intravenous infusion of isoprenaline.
- Temporary cardiac pacing
- Administration of antidigoxin Fab fragment is consider as effective but expensive and not widely available.

Autopsy Findings

- Congestion of organs
- Subendocardial and perivascular hemorrhage with focal myocardial edema[5]

Medicolegal importance: Same as for common oleander.

ACONITE

Common name: mitha zahar, bish, bikh, monk's hood

Botanical name

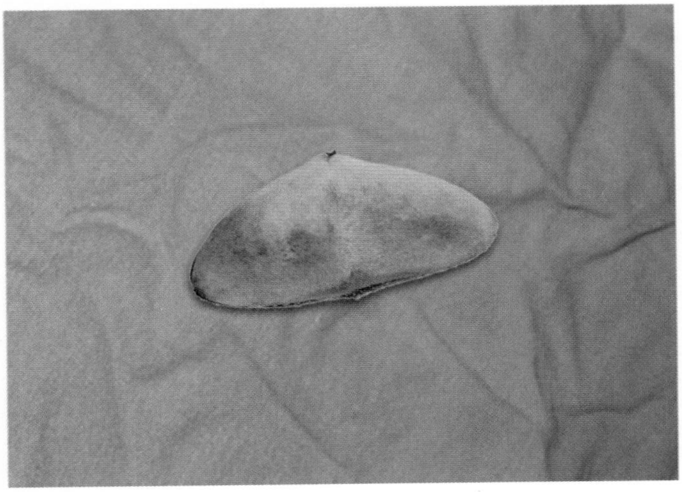

FIG. 41.6: Nut of yellow oleander

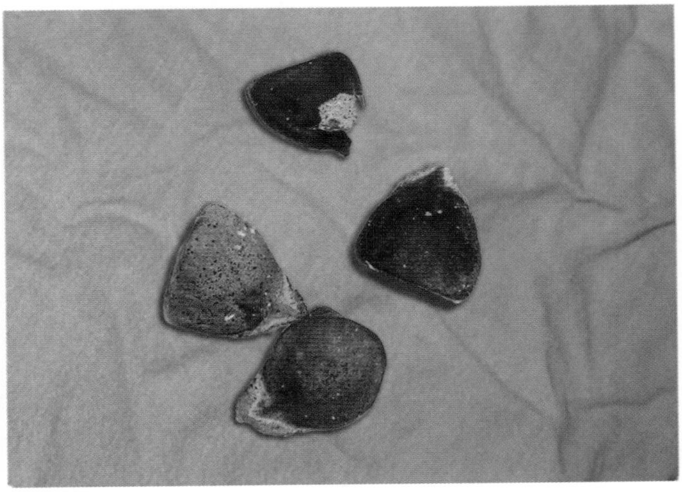

FIG. 41.7: Seeds of yellow oleander

- Aconitum napellus — European variety
- Aconitum columbianum — American variety
- Aconitum ferox — Indian variety.

Features

- Perennial plant with deeply cut leaves and long spikes of deep blue color flowers, with on upright downy stalks (Fig. 41.8). The upper sepal of flower resembles a hood or helmet or cowl, hence the common name monkshood.[8]
- Aconitum ferox variety found in India and grows in Himalayas.
- The root is stout and dark, conical and shows scars of broken rootlets, shriveled with longitudinal wrinkles (Fig. 41.9). The root is about 5 to 10 cm long and 1.5 to 2 cm thick at upper end. The root may resemble horseradish root. However, horseradish root is cylindrical and pungent.

Toxic Parts

- Root (more toxic)
- Seeds and Foliage.

Toxic Principles

- Aconitine
- Mesoaconitine
- Hypoaconitine
- Pseudoaconitine
- Ind-aconitine
- Bikh-aconitine
- Aconine.

Mechanism of Action

- Aconitine acts on nerve axons by opening sodium-channels. It also inhibits complete repolarization of the membrane of myocardial tissue causing repetitive firing.
- It stimulates vagal medullary center.

Metabolism

Metabolism of aconitum alkaloids is mainly carried out by the enzyme esterase. Aconitine is converted into benzoyaconine through hydrolysis in C-8 position and into aconine.

Fatal Dose

- 1 to 2 gm of root
- 3 to 5 mg of aconitine

Fatal period: 2 to 6 hours.

Clinical Features

- Nausea and vomiting
- Salivation
- Tingling and numbness in mouth and lips
- Diarrhea
- Palpitation
- Weakness
- Hypotension
- Ventricular ectopics

FIG. 41.8: Aconite plant

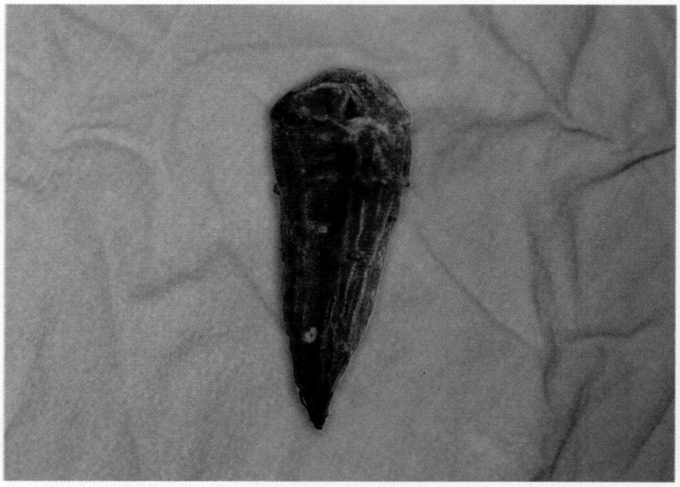

FIG. 41.9: Root of aconite

- Arrhythmias
- Vertigo
- Blurring of vision, hippus, mydriasis, xanthopsia
- Convulsions.

Management

- Gastric lavage with activated charcoal
- Benzodiazepines for convulsions
- Symptomatic treatment.

Autopsy Findings

- No specific findings
- Organs are congested.

Medicolegal Importance

1. Aconite is considered as near ideal homicidal poison, as it is sweet in taste and can easily be given with pan or other foodstuff.
2. Suicide
3. Accidental poisoning may occur due to mistaken with horseradish. On cut section, aconite appears pink whereas horseradish appears white
4. Root used to procure abortion
5. Arrow poison
6. Cattle poison
7. Aconite gets easily destroyed by decomposition and may not be detected in chemical analysis.

HYDROCYANIC ACID

Cyanide occurs as solid, liquid or in gaseous state as:

- Gas form — Hydrogen cyanide (HCN)
- Liquid form — Hydrocyanic acid (Prussic acid)
- Solid form — occurs as salts such as potassium cyanide/ sodium cyanide.

Source

1. Plants: cyanide is present in form of cyanogenic glycoside in wide variety of plants such as:
   - Bitter almond (Figs 41.10, 41.11)
   - Sorghum
   - Johnson grass
   - Bamboo
   - Apricot
   - Peach.
2. Combustion: such as
   - Burning of plastic furniture
   - Burning of silk or wool
   - Cigarette smoking.

Absorption, Metabolism and Excretion

- Ingestion: Salts of cyanide releases hydrogen cyanide in stomach due to action of hydrochloric acid and then absorbed as cyanide ion (CN^-). It is concentrated in RBCs. Enzyme rhodanase (present in mitochondria of liver and kidney) converts them to thiocyanate. This reaction needs sodium thiosulfate. Some cyanide is converted into cyanocobalamin (vitamin B12) in presence of hydroxocobalamin (vitamin B12a). Small amounts of cyanide are excreted in breath and sweat.
- Inhalation: Cyanide gas is rapidly absorbed from respiratory system.
- Dermal: Hydrocyanic acid is also absorbed through the skin.

FIG. 41.10: Bitter almond

FIG. 41.11: Bitter almond

Mechanism of Action

Cyanide reversibly inhibits ferric iron containing enzymes. Cyanide attaches to the iron of the prosthetic group of cytochrome oxidase resulting in disturbance of the transport and utilization of oxygen in cells and causing a cytotoxic anoxia.[9]

Fatal Dose

- 50 to 100 mg for hydrocyanic acid
- 200 to 300 mg for sodium/potassium cyanide
- 50 to 80 bitter almonds
- Inhalation of 1 part in 2000 — hydrogen cyanide

Fatal period: 2 to 10 minutes.

Clinical Features

Inhalation

- Constriction about throat
- Dizziness
- Loss of consciousness
- Coma
- Death

Ingestion

- CNS: Headache, anxiety, agitation, dizziness, confusion, convulsions, coma
- CVS: Initially bradycardia and hypertension and latter tachycardia and hypotension, arrhythmias
- RS: Tachypnea followed by bradypnea
- GIT: Nausea, vomiting, abdominal pain, numbness.

Skin

- Perspiration
- Cherry red color
- Bullae.

Chronic poisoning: Chronic low level of exposure leads to:

- Headache
- Amblyopia
- Optic atrophy
- Peripheral neuropathy
- Ataxia
- Deafness
- Glossitis
- Stomatitis.

Management

- Ingestion: gastric lavage with 5 percent sodium thiosulfate solution
- Antidote- amyl nitrate — inhaled
- Sodium nitrate slowly I.V.
- Sodium thiosulfate 25 percent solution I.V.
- Mechanism of action of nitrites: nitrates induce methemoglobinemia, which causes detachment of cyanide from the heme group of cytochrome oxidase since methemoglobin has a higher binding affinity for cyanide. Cyanide combines with methemoglobin and form non-toxic cynmethemoglobin.
- Mechanism of action of sodium thiosulfate: sodium thiosulfate serves as a substrate for the enzyme rhodanese to catabolise cyanide to non-toxic thiocyanate, which is excreted in the urine.

Autopsy Findings

- Bitter almond like smell
- Cherry red color of postmortem lividity
- Cyanosis
- Froth at mouth and nose
- Bright red color blood[9]
- Pulmonary edema
- Serosal surface may show hemorrhages
- Stomach mucosa may be eroded and blackened due to formation of alkaline hematin.

Samples to be preserved for chemical analysis

- Blood
- Routine viscera
- Lung
- Brain
- Heart
- Spleen is considered as best specimen due to presence of more RBCs.

Medicolegal Importance

1. Suicidal use of cyanide is not common and is usually limited to specific occupational groups. Suicide with this agent is more common in those persons who are employed in electroplating, chemistry, mining and metal heat treatment and have ready access to this chemical.[10]
2. Homicide — rare
3. Accident — industrial/laboratory mishaps
4. Embalming interferes with cyanide detection, therefore interpretation in postmortem period becomes difficult.

REFERENCES

1. Kintz P, Kieffer I, Messer J, Mangin P. Nicotine analysis in neonates' hair for measuring gestational exposure to tobacco. J Forensic Sci 1993; 38: 119-23.

2. Saravanapavananthan N, Ganeshamoorthy J. Yellow oleander poisoning— a study of 170 cases. Forensic Sci Int 1988; 36: 247-50.
3. Saraswat DK, Garg PK, Saraswat M. Rare poisoning with Cerebra thevetia (yellow oleander). Review of 13 cases of suicidal attempt. J Assoc Physicians India 1992; 40: 628-9.
4. Samal KK, Sahu HK, Kar MK, Palit SK, Kar BC, Sahu CS. Yellow oleander (Cerbera thevetia) poisoning with jaundice and renal failure. J Assoc Physicians India 1989; 37: 232-3.
5. Bose TK, Basu RK, Biswas B, De JN, Majumdar BC, Datta S. Cardiovascular effects of yellow oleander ingestion. J Indian Med Assoc 1999; 97: 407-10.
6. De Silva HA, Fonseka MM, Pathmeswaran A, Alahakone DG, Ratnatilake GA, Gunatilake SB, Ranasinha CD, Lalloo DG, Aronson JK, de Silva HJ. Multiple –dose activated charcoal for treatment of yellow oleander poisoning: a single-blind, randomized, placebo-controlled trial. Lancet 2003; 361: 1935-8.
7. Fonseka MM, Seneviratne SL, de Silva CE, Gunatilake SB, de Silva HJ. Yellow oleander poisoning in Sri Lanka: Outcome in a secondary care hospital. Hum Exp Toxicol 2002; 21: 293-5.
8. Long HC. In: The poisonous plants, reprint edition 1994. Asiatic Publishing House, Delhi. 13-14.
9. Ballantyne B. The forensic diagnosis of acute cyanide poisoning. In: Forensic Toxicology – Proceedings of a symposium held at the chemical defense establishment Porton Down 29-30 June 1972. John Wright and Sons Limited, Bristol 1974. 99-113.
10. Cina SJ, Raso DS. Suicidal cyanide ingestion as detailed in final exit. J Forensic Sci 1994; 39: 1568-70.

CHAPTER 42

Somniferous Poisons

Among the remedies which it has pleased Almighty God to give man to relieve his sufferings; none is so universal and so efficacious as opium.

— Thomas Sydenham(1680)

Narcosis means to induce sleep. Somniferous poisons refer to agent capable of inducing sleep. Narcotic drugs were the term employed to categorize these agents. Examples are:

1. Opium
2. Morphine
3. Heroin
4. Codeine

OPIUM

Common name: Afim

Opium (afim) is the dried extract of the poppy plant (Papaver somniferum). The word "opium" is Greek for "Juice".

Features

- Opium plant grows up to 0.3 to 1.5 meter in height. The plant bears whitish color flowers with 5 to 8 capsules.
- The unripe opium capsules are incised to obtain the extract, which is milky fluid (Figs 42.1 and 42.2).
- The milky fluid on drying yields opium. Crude opium is irregular mass of brownish in color with a characteristic smell and bitter taste.
- Poppy seed (khaskhas) are white seeds used as condiment in India for cooking (Fig. 42.3).
- Opium plants are cultivated under license in India in state of Rajasthan, UP and MP.

Active Principles

Opium contains alkaloids, which are divided into two groups:

1. Phenanthrene group: have narcotic properties
   - Morphine
   - Codeine
   - Thebaine (non-analgesic).

FIG 42.1: Unripe poppy capsule

2. Benzoisoquinoline group: have mild analgesic but no narcotic properties
   - Papaverine
   - Noscapine (narcotine).

Classification

Opium and Its Derivatives are Classified as:

1. Natural: e.g. morphine, codeine
2. Semi-synthetic: e.g. heroin, hydromorphine, oxymorphine
3. Synthetic: e.g. meperidine, methadone, fentanyl etc.

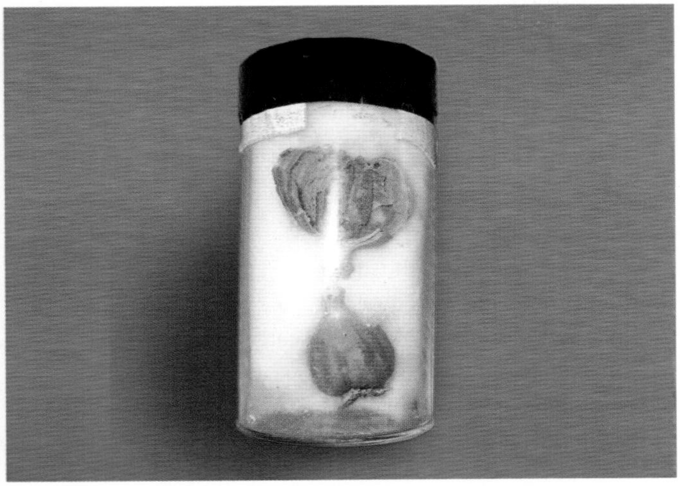

FIG. 42.2: Ripe poppy capsule

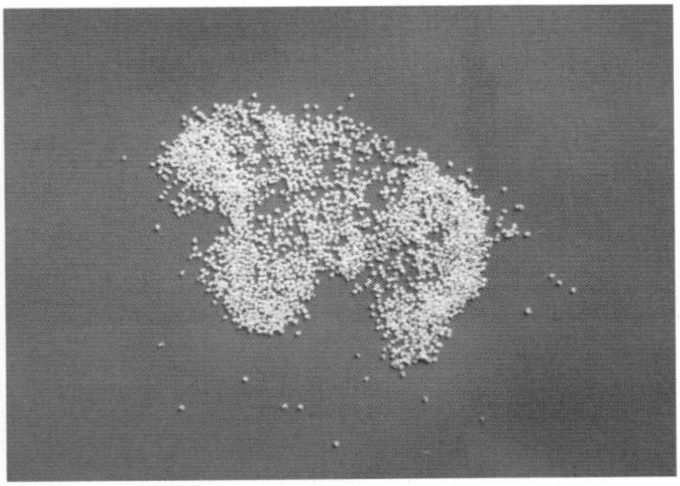

FIG. 42.3: Khaskhas

Absorption, Metabolism and Excretion

- Morphine is N-demethylated and O-demethylated along with unchanged drug are conjugated with glucuronic acid. The unchanged and unconjugated morphine are excreted by the colon and by the kidneys. A small amount is excreted into the milk.
- Heroin is reduced to morphine by the liver.

Mechanism of Action

- Opioids act by acting on specific opioid receptors. Opioid receptors are μ (MU), δ (DELTA) or κ (KAPPA) located at spinal and supraspinal sites in CNS.
- Opioid receptors are part of family of G-protein-coupled receptors and act to open potassium channels and prevent the opening of voltage-gated calcium channels, which reduces neuronal excitability and inhibits the release of pain neurotransmitters.
- The μ receptors are important and two subtypes are recognized. The μ1 receptors are associated with analgesia, euphoria and dependence whereas μ2 receptors are associated with respiratory depression and inhibition of gut motility.
- The κ receptors are responsible for analgesia at the level of spinal cord. The role of δ receptors in humans is not clear.

Clinical Features

The Effects Occur in Three Stages[1]

1. Stage of excitement:
   - The stage is short
   - The person feel better with increased sense of well-being
   - Talkativeness
   - Restless or hallucinations
   - Flushing of face.
2. Stage of stupor
   - Headache
   - Nausea and vomiting
   - Giddiness
   - Drowsiness
   - Miosis
   - Stupor.
3. Stage of narcosis
   - Patient passes into deep coma
   - Muscles becomes flaccid
   - Diminished or absent reflexes
   - Hypothermia
   - Hypotension
   - Bradycardia
   - Bradypnea
   - Non-cardiogenic pulmonary edema
   - Convulsions
   - Respiratory depression
   - Death.

- The **classic triad** for opioid poisoning is **miosis, coma and respiratory depression**. Miosis is due to parasympathetic stimulation (of Edinger-Westphal nucleus). However, once brain develops anoxic insult, there may be mydriasis.
- There may be abdominal distention
- Opium contract smooth muscle. The tone of pylorus is increase, colon is made spastic and small intestine

becomes more tonic with increase in rhythmic activity but decrease in propulsive rate. This results in constipation.
- Retention of urine occurs because bladder sphincter is made tonic preventing micturation.

Management

- Oxygen/assisted ventilation
- Fluid and vasopressors
- Gastric lavage is effective since the opium is slowly absorbed from gastrointestinal tract[2]
- Ventricular tachyarrhythmia can be managed by lidocaine
- Naloxone is a potent antagonist and does not cause respiratory or circulatory depressant action.[3] The aim of naloxone administration is to reverse the respiratory and central nervous system depression. Caution should be exercised while giving naloxone because it can precipitate acute withdrawal syndrome in chronic opioids users.[4]
- A recently introduced antidote is nalmefene. Nalmefene has pure opiate antagonistic effects and could prove superior to naloxone.

Differential Diagnosis

1. Alcohol intoxication
2. Barbiturate poisoning
3. Carbolic acid poisoning
4. Carbon monoxide poisoning
5. Uremic coma
6. Diabetic coma
7. Hysteria
8. Cerebral hemorrhage
9. Head injury
10. Cerebral malaria
11. Meningitis/encephalitis
12. Heat hyperpyrexia.

Fatal Dose

- Crude opium — 500 mg
- Morphine — 200 mg
- Heroin — 50 mg
- Pethidine — 1 gm
- Fatal period: 6 — 12 hours.

Autopsy Findings

- Signs of asphyxia
- Froth at mouth and nostrils
- Smell of opiate may present
- Injection marks/skin abscess/scarring in addicts
- Emaciation
- Pulmonary edema
- Cerebral edema.

Medicolegal Importance

- Drug abuse
- Accidental death due to drug overdose
- Suicide may be attempted for painless and peaceful death
- Cattle poison
- Doping for horse race
- Homicide — rare
- Infanticide
- Used in euthanasia.

REFERENCES

1. Patnaik VP. Vegetable alkaloid poisons. In: MKR Krishnan's Handbook of Forensic Medicine 11th edn. 1999. Paras Publishing Hyderabad. 266-72.
2. Bordbar A, Mesry S, Yousofic A. Acute opium poisoning: a report of two hundred cases in Iran. Anaesthesia 1975; 30: 223-7.
3. Evans LE. Use of naloxone in opiate poisoning. BMJ 1973; 2: 717.
4. Kumar R, Singh B, Singh N, Singh J. Review of management of common poisoning in India. Medicolegal Update 2005; 5: 31-8.

CHAPTER 43

Inebriant Poisons

Drink drives out the man and brings out the beast.

— **Albert Camus**

Inebriant are the substances capable of causing intoxication. Examples of inebriant compounds are:

- Alcohol
- Barbiturates
- Chloral hydrate
- Ether
- Ethyl chloride
- Chloroform
- Tetrachlorethane
- Paraldehyde

ALCOHOL

The word 'alcohol' is derived from the Arabic word "*Al kohl*" which means "something subtle". The term whiskey is derived from USQUEBAVGH, Gaelic for "water of life". Alcohols are hydroxy derivatives of aliphatic hydrocarbons. When unqualified, 'alcohol' refers to ethyl alcohol or ethanol (C_2H_5OH).

There are three categories of alcohols:

1. Monohydroxy alcohols — these alcohols have only one hydroxyl (OH) group. For example, ethanol, methanol, isopropanol.
2. Dihydroxy alcohols — these alcohols have two hydroxyl (OH) groups and are known as glycols. For example, ethylene glycol, propylene glycol.
3. Trihydroxy alcohols — they are not really alcohols, but are only derivatives. For example, propane derivative glycerol or glycerine.

Ethyl Alcohol

Synonyms: ethanol, grain alcohol

Features

- Alcohol is clear, colorless liquid with typical fruity odor and having burning taste.
- Ethanol is both — water and lipid soluble. The hydroxyl and ethyl moieties confer both hydrophilic and lipophilic properties. Thus ethanol is an "amphophyle".
- The aliphatic alcohol forms a homologous series beginning with methanol, ethanol, n-propanol, isopropanol etc. The first three are readily soluble in water in all proportions but as the carbon chain length increases, water solubility decreases and octanol (8 carbons) is almost insoluble in water.
- All alcohols have general formula R-OH.
- The specific gravity of ethanol is 0.79, i.e. 1 ml of alcohol weighs 0.79 gm.
- Alcohol beverages are primarily a mixture of water and ethyl alcohol with small amounts of other substances, which impart the characteristic odor and taste to the beverage. These substances are referred as **congeners** because they are simultaneously produced during the fermentation process. Congeners consist of organic acids and esters.[1]

Sources and Preparations

Alcohol is produced by fermentation of sugar by yeast. The process halts at a concentration of alcohol, by volume, of approximately 15 percent because of the death of yeast above this level. The sugar from cereal, vegetable or fruit is used. If cereal is used as raw material for alcohol preparation then it has to be malted first to convert the starch into maltose because yeast cannot ferment starch. Malt is produced by moistening the barley and allowing it to sprout, which is then dried, ground and added to the cereal in water resulting in the formation of mash. Beer is brewed by filtering mash and treating the filtered liquid with yeast. Whiskey is prepared by adding the yeast directly to the mash. Strong alcoholic beverages are distilled after fermentation. Distillation further increases the alcohol concentration.

Types of Alcohol Beverages

Alcohol beverages are of various types as described below

A. Malted liquors — they are fermented product but are undistilled liquids so alcohol concentration is low. Examples are beer, stout.

B. Wines — prepared by fermentation of natural sugars such grape or fruits. These drinks are also un-distilled. Wines are called "dry wine" when all sugar present has been fermented and "sweet wine" when some sugar is left. They are of following varieties:
   - Light wines — such as claret, cider. Alcohol content did not exceed 15 percent
   - Fortified wines — such as port, sherry. Here distilled beverages are added from outside. Alcohol content varies from 16 to 22 percent.
   - Effervescent wines — such as champagne. These drinks are bottled before fermentation is complete. The alcohol content varies from 12 to 16 percent.

C. Spirits — these are distilled drinks and alcohol content varies from 40 to 55 percent. Example includes —rum, whiskey, gin, brandy, vodka etc (Fig. 43.1).

Types of Alcohol

1. Absolute alcohol — contains 99 percent w/w ethanol (dehydrated alcohol)
2. Rectified spirit — contains 90 percent w/w ethanol (distilled)
3. Proof spirit — it is an old term and refers to a standard mixture of alcohol and water of relative density 12/13 at 51°F, i.e. 49.28 percent of alcohol by weight or 57.10 percent by volume. Proof strength of alcoholic beverages is expressed in degrees. The ethanol content of various alcoholic beverages is expressed by volume percent or by proof. The proof being twice the percentage of alcohol by volume. Nowadays, alcohol is referred by percentage alcohol by volume (% v/v). This is equivalent to the number of milliliter of pure alcohol per 100 ml of the drink (Fig. 43.2 label of beverage bottle).

Glossary

- Denatured means the alcohol is processed in a prescribed manner so as to make it unfit for human consumption.
- Liquor includes spirits, denatured spirits, wine, beer, toddy and all liquids consisting of or containing alcohol.
- Country liquor includes all liquors produced or manufactured in India as per specifications for country liquor
- Indian made foreign liquor is liquor produced in India as per specifications. Examples — rum, gin, whiskey, brandy etc.
- Foreign liquor means potable duty-paid foreign liquor
- Rectification includes every process whereby liquor is purified or refined for making it potable

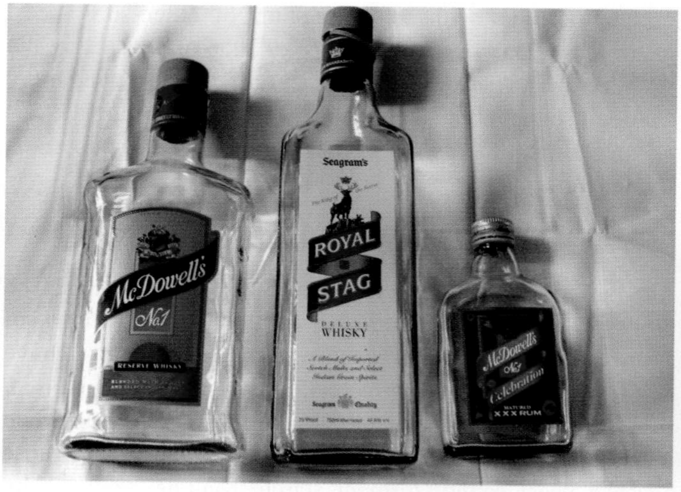

FIG. 43.1: alcohol beverages

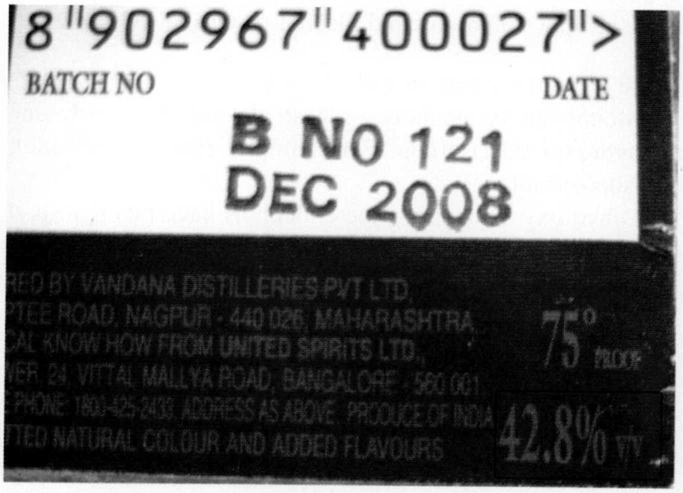

FIG. 43.2: label of alcoholic beverage showing percentage of alcohol by volume (% v/v) (in black rectangle)

- Spirit means any liquor containing alcohol and obtained by distillation
- Toddy means fermented or unfermented juice drawn from a coconut, brab, date or any kind of palm tree and includes sweet toddy
- Sweet toddy or nira or neera means unfermented juice drawn from a coconut, brab, date or any kind of palm tree into receptacles treated in the prescribed manner so as to prevent fermentation.

Uses of Alcohol

1. Beverage
2. Solvent
3. Medicinal and therapeutic
4. Antidote in methanol poisoning
5. Preservative
6. Fuel.

Absorption, Metabolism and Excretion

Alcohol is rapidly absorbed from the stomach (20%) and small intestine (80%). Due to thinner mucosa, better blood supply and a larger surface area, the upper small intestine — the duodenum and jejunum has maximum capacity for absorption of alcohol than gastric mucosa. As alcohol is lipid soluble, it diffuses from stomach and intestine by simple diffusion. However, alcoholic beverages more than 20 percent are absorbed slowly because higher concentration of alcohol inhibits gastric peristalsis and thus delays gastric emptying. Alcohol is subjected to gastric "first pass metabolism" due to presence of gastric dehydrogenases but they are not present in intestine. The female has less alcohol dehydrogenase than male. When alcohol is absorbed, a substantial fraction is removed from the portal vein blood by first pass hepatic metabolism. Hepatic metabolism of alcohol shows saturation kinetics at low alcohol concentrations, so the fraction of alcohol removed decreases as the concentration of alcohol reaching liver increases. Thus, if alcohol absorption is rapid and portal vein concentration is high, most of the alcohol escapes into the systemic circulation whereas with slow absorption, more alcohol is removed by first pass metabolism. This is one reason why drinking alcohol on an empty stomach produces a much greater effect. Vaporized ethanol may be rapidly absorbed by inhalation.

There are various factors that affect absorption of alcohol and these factors are discussed below.

- Food — presence of food in the stomach prolongs the absorption of alcohol.[2] Presence of starch, proteins and fatty food retards the absorption. It is stated that with presence of food in stomach, as much as 17 to 20 percent of alcohol ingested escapes absorption and never appears in the blood.
- Concentration — diluted alcohol or alcohol with high concentration are absorbed slowly whereas alcohol in the concentration of 10 to 20 percent are absorbed rapidly.
- Habit and tolerance — in habituated person alcohol is absorbed rapidly.
- Drugs may interfere with absorption and these drugs are given in Table 43.1.
- Gastrectomy may cause rapid absorption of alcohol. Similarly alcohol is absorbed rapidly in persons who had truncal vagotomy and drainage operation due to increased gastric emptying.

More than 90 percent of ethanol consumed is metabolized in the body and only 5 to 10 percent is excreted unchanged by kidneys (urine), lungs (breath), feces and skin (sweat). Alcohol in the systemic circulation is metabolized through three pathways:

1. Alcohol dehydrogenase (ADH) pathway — in the cell cytosol
2. Microsomal Ethanol Oxidizing System (MEOS) — located on the endoplasmic reticulum
3. Peroxidase-Catalase system — in hepatic peroxisomes.

ADH pathway is the principal pathway metabolizing more than 90 percent of the systemic ethanol. Ethyl alcohol is first oxidized to acetaldehyde by alcohol dehydrogenase and then this gets converted into acetic acid by aldehyde dehydrogenase which in turn is converted to acetyl coenzyme A and enters the Krebs (Citric acid) cycle where it is metabolized to carbon dioxide and water (Fig. 43.3). Alcohol metabolism by alcohol dehydrogenase follows first order kinetics after the smallest dose. Once the blood concentration exceeds about 10-mg/100 ml, the enzymatic processes are saturated and elimination rate no longer increases with increasing

Table 43.1: Drugs affecting gastric emptying

Drugs affecting gastric emptying
Drugs slowing gastric emptying
- Drug with anticholinergic action like – atropine, chlorpromazine, Tricyclic antidepressants
- Drugs with an adrenergic actions like – amphetamine
- Drugs with opioid action like – codeine, heroin, methadone
Drugs hastening emptying of gastric contents
- Metoclopramide
- Cisapride
- Erythromycin

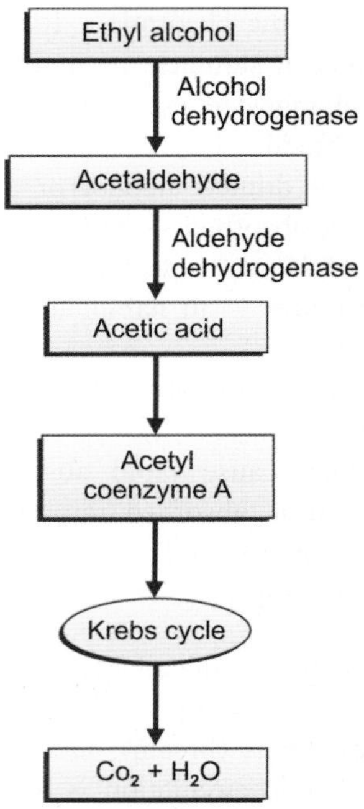

FIG. 43.3: Metabolism of alcohol

concentration but becomes steady at 10 to 15 ml/hour. Thus, alcohol is subject to dose dependent kinetics, i.e. saturation or zero-order kinetics.

Mechanism of Action

- Alcohol is a central nervous system depressant that decreases activity of neurons with behavioral stimulation at low blood level.
- Alcohol produces simultaneous changes in many neurotransmitters and increases the fluidity of neuronal cell membranes.
- Alcohol in small doses interferes with cortical function like conduct, judgment, self-criticism and release of inhibitory tone but in larger doses depresses the medullary processes.

ALCOHOL INTOXICATION

Alcohol intoxication is a state associated with behavioral, psychomotor and cognitive changes in an individual. Acute alcohol intoxication is also called as **acute alcohol poisoning** or **inebriation**. The clinical features are described below. Consumption of alcohol produces following stages. The features of intoxication and blood level are presented in Table 43.2.

- **Stage of excitement** characterized by a sense of well-being, sober, euphoria, increased confidence and excitement. There is depression of inhibitory controlling capacity of higher centers. The person is free in action, speech and emotions. But as the consumption of alcohol goes on, the person may land in the stage of in-coordination.
- **Stage of in-coordination** is characterized by muscle in-coordination; sense perception and skilled movements are affected. The individual becomes irritable, quarrelsome with slurring of speech and unsteady gait. The face will be flushed and breath smells of alcohol. There is increase in reaction time.
- **Stage of coma** as the consumption of alcohol continues, the person becomes drowsy and lands into coma.
- Alcohol causes mydriasis (dilatation of pupil) in the initial stages but as person lands in stage of coma, the pupil becomes constricted (meiosis). The so-called **McEwan** sign (described in the most of the textbook on forensic medicine) is positive in coma. Pinching of the skin or light slapping of a person causes the constricted pupil of person to be dilated.
- Diagnostic criteria for alcohol intoxication — as per DSM IV developed by American Psychiatric Association are provided in Table 43.3.
- Clinically, distinction between ethanol and methanol poisoning is presented in Table 43.4.

Alcohol Intoxication and Brain Functioning

Impairment of frontal lobe
- Impaired judgment
- Awkward motor coordination
- Decreased concentration
- Impaired abstraction
- Language is incoherent and disconnected

Impairment of parietal lobe
- Depersonalization
- Abnormalities in orientation

Impairment of temporal lobe
- Defect in recent memory
- Blackouts — lack of formation of new memory
- Defect in language reception
- Difficulty in understanding or listening

Impairment of occipital lobe
- Impaired visual acuity
- Reduced ability to discern object and motion (blurred vision)

Table 43.2: Features of intoxication and blood level

Blood alcohol Concentration (mg/100 ml)	Level of Intoxication	Clinical features
0–50	Sobriety	Sober behavior
50–100	Euphoria	Feeling of well-being, increased self-confidence, decreased inhibition
100–150	Excitement	Free in action and emotion, talkativeness, fine movements affected, impairment in memory and comprehension
150–200	Confusion/in-coordination	In-coordination of muscle, skilled movements and perception affected, increased reaction time, slurred speech, staggering gait, confusion, disorientation, visual disturbances
200–300	Stupor	Diminished response to stimuli, inability to stand or walk, vomiting
300–500	Coma/death	Unconsciousness, abolished or diminished reflexes, subnormal temperature, incontinence of urine & feces, respiratory distress, death.

Table 43.3: Diagnostic criteria for alcohol intoxication as per DSM IV

Diagnostic criteria

- Recent ingestion of alcohol
- Clinically significant maladaptive behavioral or psychological changes (for example, inappropriate sexual aggressive behavior, mood labiality, impaired judgment, impaired social or occupational functioning) that developed during or shortly after alcohol ingestion
- One (or more) of the following signs, developing during or shortly after alcohol use:
  - Slurred speech
  - Incoordination
  - Unsteady gait
  - Nystagmus
  - Impairment in attention or memory
  - Stupor or coma
- The symptoms are not due to a general medical condition or are not better accounted for by another mental disorder.

Table 43.4: Clinical differentiation between ethanol and methanol poisoning

Alcohol	Odor	Acidosis	Visual changes
Ethanol	Present	+	-
Methanol	Absent	++	+

Differential Diagnosis of Alcohol Intoxication

- Barbiturate poisoning
- Diabetic coma
- Carbon monoxide poisoning
- Hypoglycemia
- Head injury
- Cerebro-vascular episode

Death from Alcohol Intoxication

1. Respiratory failure
2. Circulatory failure
3. Aspiration of gastric contents
4. Hypoglycemia

Fatal Dose

- Levels of blood alcohol above 500mg/100 ml are considered to be probably fatal.[3]
- The fatal dose in adult is 6 gm of ethanol/kg body weight and in children it is 3-gm/kg body weight.

Management[4]

Principles of management of alcohol intoxication are:

- Secure airway

- Maintain adequate blood pressure and circulation
- Rule out head and spine injury
- Administer thiamine 100 mg intravenously followed by glucose 25 to 50 gm intravenously to protect against development of Wernicke-Korsakoff syndrome
- Manage hypothermia in usual way
- Nasogastric intubation and gastric lavage, may be helpful if patient presents within one hour after incident
- Access status of acidosis. A worsening acidosis after thiamine, glucose and fluid therapy should raise the possibility of ethylene glycol or other ingestion.

DRUNKENNESS

A medical practitioner is frequently asked by law enforcing authorities to examine a person for causing nuisance in public places or driving vehicle under the influence of alcohol or had committed an offence under its influence. Under such circumstances, a doctor is expected to examine the person and opine regarding following points:

- Whether the examined person had consumed alcohol? And
- If he had consumed alcohol, whether he is under its influence?

The medical practitioner engaged for such job should always exercise caution while furnishing an opinion. The RMP should know what is drunkenness? How to examine such person? How to collect exhibits which might be used as evidence in court of law. The following account provides guidelines for such procedure and practice.

Definition

Drunkenness is a condition produced in a person who has taken alcohol in a quantity sufficient to cause him to lose control of his faculties to such an extent that he is unable to execute the occupation in which he is engaged at the material time.

Examination

Aims of examination

- Whether the person had consumed alcohol?
- If he had consumed alcohol, whether he is under its influence?
- Whether the state is due to alcohol intoxication or some other natural illness or due to other intoxicants or due to head injury?
- Whether it is safe for him to be detained in police custody or whether he should be admitted in the hospital for treatment?

Consent

Like other examinations, the consent should be obtained from the person before proceeding for examination. Where a person is too drunk or otherwise unconscious so that no consent could be obtained, then the doctor should make examination as possible but the result of his examination should not be given to police until retrospective consent has been obtained from the person when he has recovered completely. However, if the person had been arrested for a criminal offence and is under the custody of police, then as per CrPC Sec. 53(1), the medical practitioner can proceed with the examination of accused without his consent.

Preliminary Particulars

Preliminary particulars such as name, age, sex, address, identification marks, time and date of medical examination, name of accompanying person and brief history should be recorded.

Physical Examination (Figs 43.4 to 43.7)

1. General appearance — state of clothing (whether soiled by vomitus or feces), behaviour, disposition.
2. Record vital data such as — temperature, pulse, respiratory rate and blood pressure. In alcohol intoxication there is tachycardia and vasodilatation of cutaneous vessels that results in warm and flushed skin. Respiratory rate may be increased. Low doses of alcohol causes a mild drop in blood pressure but more consumption results in dose-dependent increase in blood pressure.
3. Speech — **normal, thick, slurred or over-precise**. Speech production is a complex motor activity and requires coordination and is considered as sensitive index of alcohol intoxication. Slight distortion of certain consonants is one of the early signs of in-coordination of muscles of tongue and lips. Certain test phrases may be used to bring out this difficulty in speech such as "***British constitution***", "***truly rural***" etc. A sober person may say that he is not good at such phrases; the drunken person often embarks to get them correctly.[5]
4. Breath — smell of alcohol present or absent. The congeners present in alcoholic beverages impart peculiar odor that could be appreciated in the breath of drunken person. However, certain other preparations may also impart such odor and the substances are given below:
   - Ayurvedic preparations — contains alcohol up to 14 percent.
   - Wincarnis — contains alcohol up to 20 percent.
5. Stance — does he stand properly or sway when standing erect with his feet together and eyes closed? A drunken

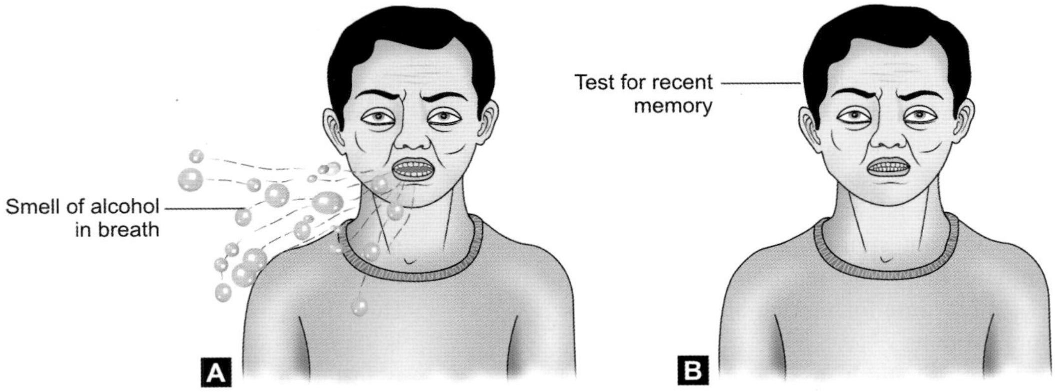

FIGS 43.4A and B: **A:** In drunken person, there is alcohol smell in breath **B:** Shows that recent memory is affected in drunken person

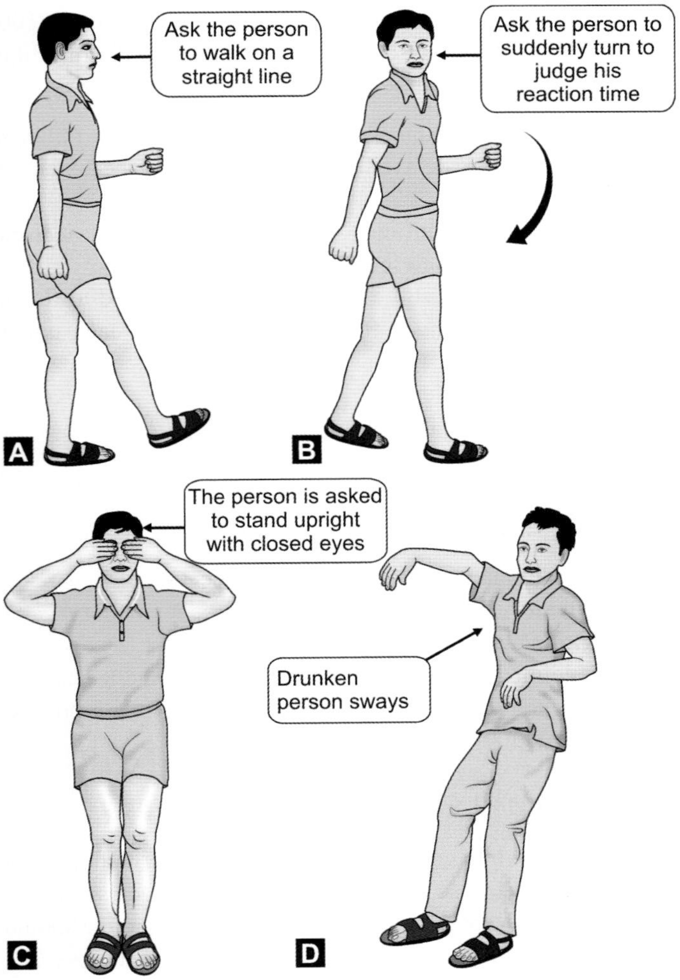

FIGS 43.5A to D: **A:** Shows how to test gait, **B:** Shows how to judge reaction time and **C:** Shows how to do Romberg test

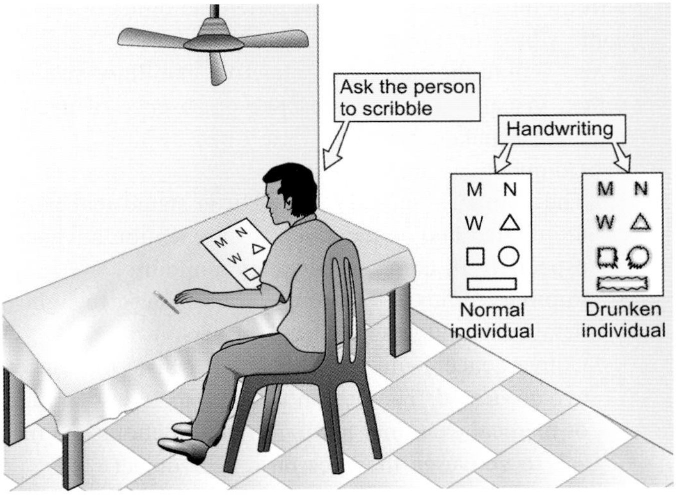

FIG. 43.6: Shows results of handwriting in normal and drunken person

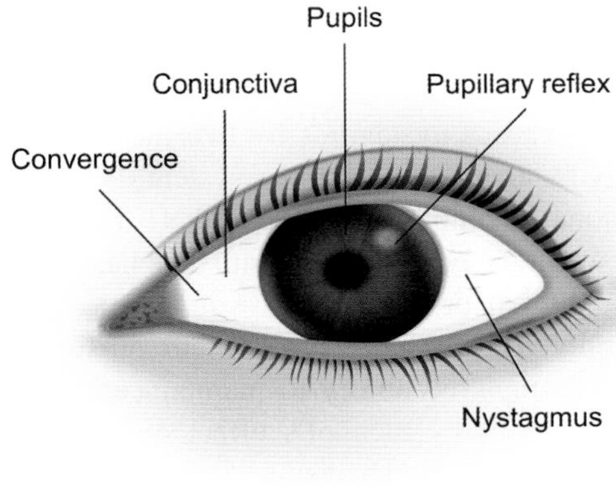

FIG. 43.7: Shows what to see in eyes of drunken person

person sways while doing such exercise. This is a – positive **Romberg sign.** (In Romberg's test, the person is asked to stand with his feet closely approximated, first with his eyes open and then with his eyes closed).

6. Gait — observe whether the gait is normal or staggering? A drunken person has staggering gate. The person is asked to walk on a straight line. His gait should be observed. While walking straight, the person is asked suddenly to turn to judge the reaction time. Drunken person will take more time for turning and takes one or two steps before turning.
7. Writing — the person should be asked to write few lines in a language familiar to him. Note the time taken to write, repetition or omission of words, ability to read his own handwriting. The drunken person often takes more time to copy a sentence and may have difficulty in writing the letters N, M or W. Often; he omits or repeats some words or alphabets.
8. Eyes — note the state of conjunctiva, pupillary size and reflex, visual acuity and presence or absence of nystagmus. In drunken person:
   - Conjunctivas are congested
   - The pupils — in early stages, it is stated that pupils are dilated and as the level of intoxication advances, especially in coma, it becomes pinpoint.
   - Pupillary reflex — the pupillary response to light is delayed or sluggish in drunken person.
   - Convergence — in this test, the extrinsic muscles of eye are tested. The person is asked to follow a finger of medical examiner in all normal directions and then ask to converge the eyes on a near object.
   - Nystagmus — nystagmus is noted in alcohol intoxication. The presence of fine lateral nystagmus (alcohol gaze nystagmus AGN) indicates alcohol intoxication. Due to reduced visual acuity and dilated pupils, drunken person stares and tries to steady his gaze leading to alcoholic gaze nystagmus.[6]
   - Alcohol causes nystagmus by two mechanisms:
   1. Firstly by acting on vestibular system — it can cause positional alcohol nystagmus (PAN) detected when the patient is lying supine with the head turned to either the left or right side.
   2. Secondly by inhibiting the smooth pursuit system. There is impaired ability to maintain eccentric gaze brought about by alcohol's effect on ocular movements via neural mechanisms — results in horizontal gaze nystagmus (HGN).
      – PAN occurs in two stages — PAN-I and PAN-II
      – PAN-I is associated with acute elevation of blood alcohol tending to occur approximately 30 minutes after alcohol ingestion. In PAN-I, the first phase of nystagmus is in the direction toward which the head is turned.
      – PAN-II — normally occurs at approximately 5 to 6 hours after drinking and is characterized by nystagmus in the opposite direction to that seen in PAN-I.
      – HGN is a jerky eye movements noted when gaze is directed to one side. The first phase of HGN is in the direction of gaze and it becomes intensified at a more eccentric gaze position. It may be seen in normal individuals at extreme lateral gaze, when detected at lesser deviations, it is considered as pathological. An angle of onset of 40° or less from the midline is a sensitive indicator of a blood alcohol level in excess of 100 mg/100 ml. HGN is also noted in other conditions like ingestion of sedative and tranquilizing drugs.
9. Reflexes — in drunken person, knee and ankle reflexes are sluggish or delayed. Planter reflex may be extensor or flexor.
10. Muscular coordination — following are some test used to determine muscle coordination
    - Finger nose test — here the person is asked to touch nose by his index finger alternately with each upper limb
    - Finger to finger test
    - Unbuttoning and buttoning the shirt
    - Picking objects from floor.

Systemic Examination

CNS — examination is carried out to access:
- Memory — test the ability for recent memory
- Orientation to time and place.

Other systemic examination should be done in the usual way. Note presence or absence of injuries or any pathological condition resembling alcohol intoxication.

Collection and Preservation of Samples

- Blood — while collecting blood sample, spirit should not be used to cleanse the surface rather the surface should be washed with soap and water. Five ml blood sample should be collected in screw-capped bottle of universal size. The cap should be properly secured after adding appropriate preservative. five mg of sodium fluoride (acting as enzyme inhibitor) and 15 mg of potassium oxalate (acting as anticoagulant) for 5 ml of blood.

- Urine — for proper analysis, two samples of urine are required. The first sample should be collected and after 20 to 30 minutes later second sample should be collected. The concentration of alcohol in second sample reflects the blood alcohol during the inter-specimen interval. The difference in the alcohol concentrations in the two samples indicate whether the person was in absorptive phase, or at its peak or in the elimination phase. Multiplication of alcohol concentration in the second sample by 0.75 will give an approximate value of blood alcohol level at the time when the urine is being secreted. Phenyl mercuric nitrate or thymol is used as preservative.

Opinion

After examination of the person, the medical examiner should furnish opinion in one of the following ways:

1. The individual has not consumed alcohol.
2. The examined individual has consumed alcohol but he is not under its influence.
3. The examined individual has consumed alcohol and he is under its influence.

Interpretation of Blood Alcohol Result

- The proof strength of a liquid is obtained by dividing the alcohol percent (volume strength) by 0.571. For example, if we want to calculate proof strength of a wine containing 10 percent alcohol, therefore $10 \div 0.571 = 17.5^{\circ}$ proof. Similarly the percentage of alcohol in a liquid is obtained by multiplying the proof strength by 0.571. For example – whisky is 75° proof will contain - - 75 X 0.571 = 42.8 percent by volume of alcohol[7] (Fig. 43.2).
- Concentration of alcohol in blood is expressed as mg%, i.e. (w/v) or as percentage. For example – 60 mg% (w/v) = 0.06% (w/v), i.e. 60 mg of alcohol per 100 ml blood (weight/volume).
- Concentration of alcohol in solid tissue like viscera is expressed as mg of alcohol per 100 grams of tissue (w/w).
- The amount of alcohol consumed can be determined from the blood alcohol level.
- For calculating blood levels, various methods are used and amongst them method advocated by Widmark is popular. The Widmark formula is provided in equation is – **a = cpr**. Where a = amount of alcohol in grams absorbed in body, c = concentration of alcohol in blood in grams/kg, p = weight of person in kilogram and r = constant. In men, the constant is 0.68 and in women it is 0.55.
- For urine analysis, the formula is – **a = ¾ qpr**. The other factors are same and q = concentration of alcohol in urine in grams/liter.

Breathe Analyzer

- Also called as alcometer, intoximeter or drunkometer
- Breath analyzer serve as on-spot test for police
- Legally admissible as per sec 185 of Motor Vehicle Act 1988
- In contemporary period, more sophisticated versions are available.

Principle

The concentration of alcohol in lung air is dependent on arterial blood. It is established that there is correlation between breath and blood alcohol and the ratio is assumed to be 2100:1, i.e. amount of alcohol in 2100 ml of alveolar air = amount of alcohol in one ml of blood. This is based on Henry's law. The law state that when a volatile substance (alcohol) is dissolved in liquid (blood) and is brought to equilibrium with air (alveolar air), there is fixed ratio between the concentration of the volatile substance (alcohol) in air (alveolar air) and its concentration in liquid (blood) and ratio remains constant at given temperature.

Sources of Errors in Breathe Analyzer

1. Variation in ratio between different individuals
2. Use of ethanol containing products
3. Belching or regurgitation of gastric alcohol contents
4. Inadequate expiration (in unconscious or un-cooperative subject)
5. COPD disease
6. Use of metered dose inhalers
7. Poor technique.

Alcohol and Traffic Accidents (Figs 43.8 to 43.11)

It is established that driving vehicle under influence of alcohol causes more accidents leading to increase in morbidity and mortality. Driving a vehicle under the influence of alcohol is an offense in India under the Motor vehicle Act 1988. A fine up to Rs. 2000 can be imposed or imprisonment can be awarded that can be extended up to 6 months or both. The statutory limit of blood alcohol is **30 mg%** in India (as per Sec 185 of Motor vehicle Act 1988). The increase in accidents are attributed to following factors:[8]

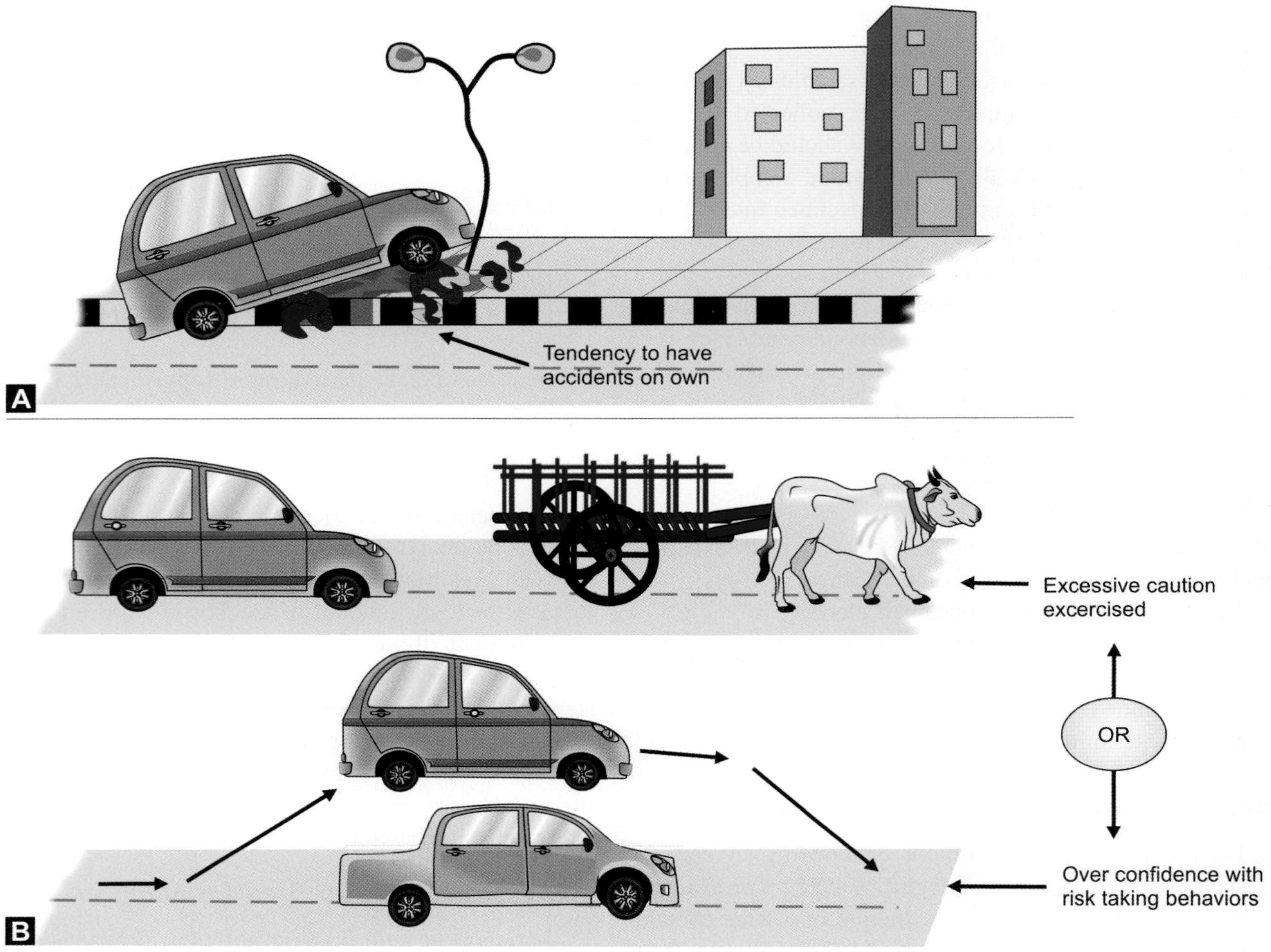

FIGS 43.8A and B: Drinking and accidents: **A:** Drunken person has tendency to have accidents. **B:** Some persons may exercise excessive caution while driving while others are overconfident and risk taking

1. Risk taking behavior
2. Impaired performance
3. Increased reaction time
4. Tracking
5. Poor mental coordination
6. Information processing
7. Visual — blurring of vision, decrease visual acuity, strong lights are needed to distinguish objects and dim objects are not distinguished at all. There is also lack of color discrimination.
8. Psycho-motor performance
9. Altered time and space perception
10. Impairment of judgment
11. Skilled movements affected
12. Tendency to drive vehicle in the middle of road
13. Inaccurate cornering and poor judgment.

ALCOHOLISM

Also called as chronic poisoning, ethanolism, alcohol abuse, alcohol dependence

Definition

Alcoholism is a disorder characterized by excessive drinking that results in injury to person's health or inadequate social functioning or both.

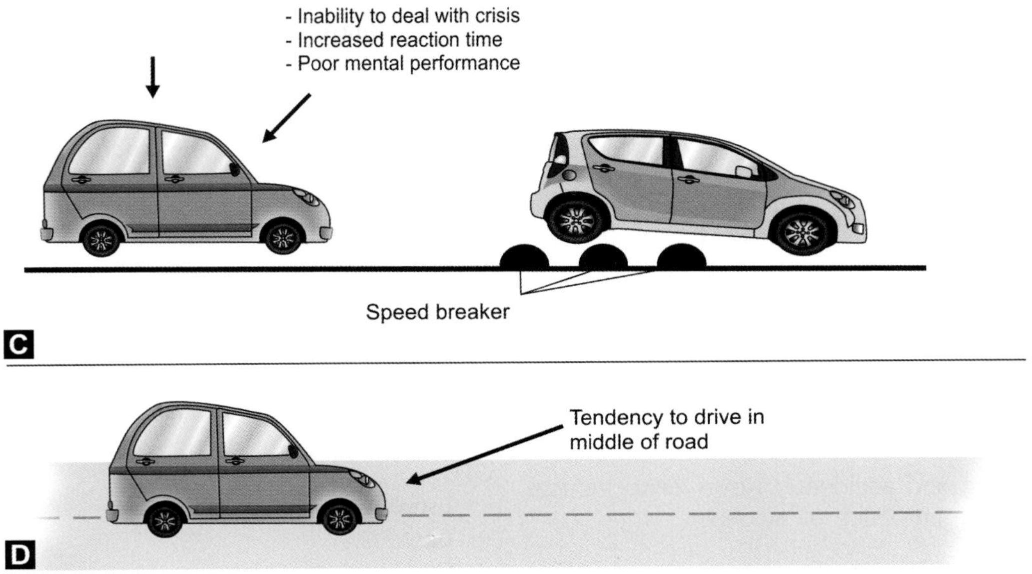

Figs 43.8C and D: Drinking and accidents: **C:** The drunken persons are unable to deal with crisis, they have increased reaction time. **D:** Some individuals have tendency to drive vehicle in the middle of road leaving one's lane

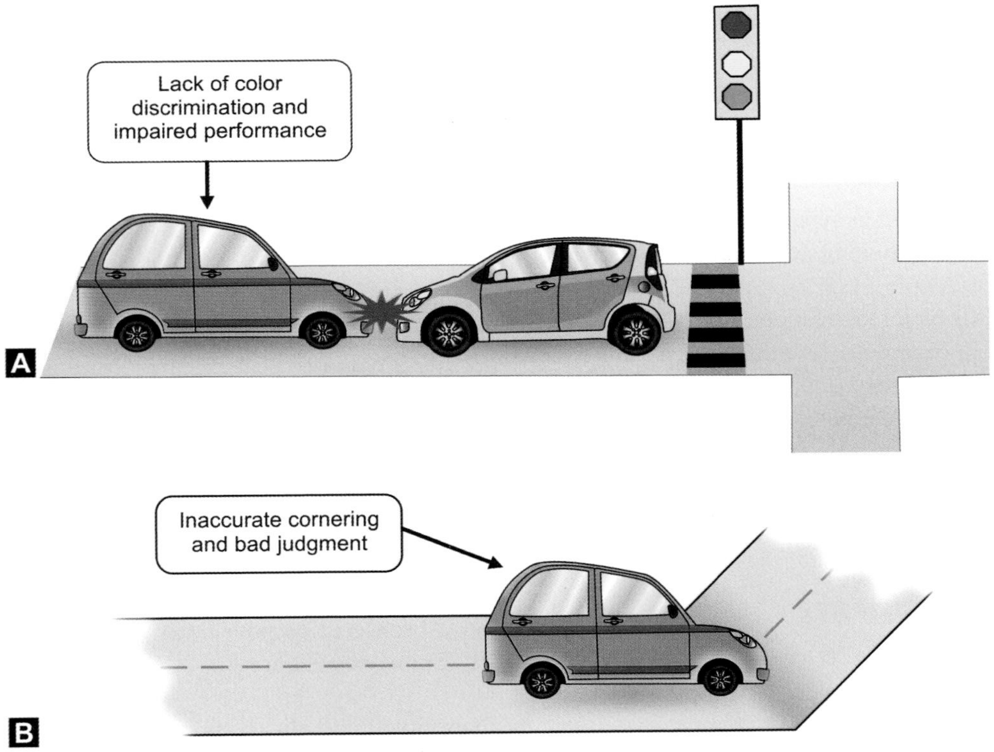

FIGS 43.9A and B: Drinking and accidents: **A:** The drunken person have decrease visual acuity; strong lights are needed to distinguish objects and dim objects are not distinguished at all. There is also lack of color discrimination. **B:** These people have bad judgment and inaccurate cornering while driving a vehicle

FIG. 43.10: Drinking and accidents: Never drive vehicle under influence of alcohol

DSM-IV defines alcoholism as repeated alcohol-related difficulties in at least three of following seven areas of functioning:

1. Tolerance
2. Withdrawal
3. Taking larger amounts of alcohol over longer period than intended
4. Inability to control use
5. Spending great deal of time associated with alcohol use
6. Giving up important activities to drink
7. Continued use of alcohol despite physical or psychological consequences.

Alcohol abuse is considered as repetitive problem with alcohol in any one of the following four areas of life without alcohol dependence:

1. Inability to fulfill major obligations
2. Use of alcohol in hazardous situation such as driving etc
3. Incurring legal problems
4. Use despite social or interpersonal difficulties.

Dipsomania is an irresistible desire to take large amounts of alcohol until the person become almost unconscious from its effect.

Complication of Alcoholism

CNS

- Alcoholic blackouts
- Fragmented sleep (restless sleep)
- Peripheral neuropathy
- Wrenicke's and Korsakoff's syndrome
- Cerebellar degeneration
- Cognitive problems
- Permanent CNS impairment
- Marchiafava-Bignami syndrome — it is rare idiopathic syndrome of dementia and seizures with degeneration of the corpus callosum. The syndrome is primarily reported in male Italian drinkers of red wine.

CVS

- Mild to moderate hypertension with heavy drinking
- Alcohol cardiomyopathy
- Holiday heart — atrial or ventricular arrhythmias, especially paroxysmal tachycardia can occur after a binge in individuals with no evidence of heart disease.[9]

GIT

- Esophagitis
- Gastritis
- Duodenal ulcerations
- Upper GIT bleeding
- Mallory-Weiss syndrome
- Anorexia
- Abdominal pain
- Esophageal varices
- Atrophy of gastric cells
- Pancreatitis
- Mal-absorption
- Diarrhea secondary to increased small-bowel motility and decrease water and electrolyte absorption
- Fatty liver
- Alcoholic cirrhosis
- Alcoholic hepatitis.

Genitourinary system

- Increase sexual desire in men but decrease erectile capacity (William Shakespeare wrote very aptly regarding alcohol and sexual function – " alcohol provokes the desire, but it takes away the performance")
- Testicular atrophy
- Shrinkage of seminiferous tubules
- Decrease sperm count
- Amenorrhea
- Decrease in ovarian size
- Absence of corpora lutea with infertility
- Spontaneous abortion.

Nutritional complications

- Folic acid deficiency
- Pyridoxine deficiency
- Thiamine deficiency

- Iron deficiency
- Zinc deficiency
- Vitamin A, D, K deficiency

Hematopoietic system
- Increase in RBC size
- With folic acid deficiency — hypersegmented neutrophils, reticulocytopenia and hyperplastic bone marrow
- With malnutrition — sideroblastic changes
- Decrease granulocyte mobility and adherence
- Delayed hypersensitivity response to new antigen
- Toxic granulocytosis
- Mild thrombocytopenia
- Hypersplenism

Others
- Alcoholic myopathy

Fetal Effects of Alcohol[10]

Alcohol crosses the placental barrier and reaches fetus. The fetal abnormalities may range from selected fetal alcohol effect (FAE) to full-blown fetal alcohol syndrome (FAS). The FAS are classified as follows:
1. Facial dysmorphology
2. Prenatal and antenatal growth deficiency
3. CNS involvement, including mental retardation

Similarly still births and spontaneous abortions are more common.

Cause of Death

Following are the causes of alcohol related deaths[11,12]
- Cirrhosis
- Fatty liver
- Hepatic failure
- Ruptured esophageal varices
- Alcoholic cardiomyopathy
- Pancreatitis

Withdrawal

Sudden cessation of alcohol by such person results in withdrawal reaction. The withdrawal reaction may manifest as:
- Abstinence syndrome develops 6 to 8 hours after cessation of alcohol and is characterized by tremors, agitation, sweating, nausea, headache and insomnia
- Alcohol hallucinations appear 24 to 36 hours after cessation of alcohol
- Seizures (also called as rum fits) occur 7 to 48 hours after cessation of alcohol. The seizures are clonic-tonic in nature with or without loss of consciousness
- Alcohol ketoacidosis
- Delirium tremens
- Wernicke's and Korsakoff's syndrome.

Delirium Tremens

- The disorder appears after 3 to 5 days after cessation of alcohol and the onset is sudden
- The disorder is characterized by clouding of consciousness, disorientation with loss of recent memory.
- The disorder may be associated with vivid hallucinations — mostly visual or sometimes auditory in nature
- There is agitation, restlessness, shouting, tremor, ataxia and insomnia
- Autonomic disturbances are common and includes — sweating, fever, tachycardia, hypertension and dilated pupils
- When person is suffering from delirium tremens, he is not held responsible for any act because the he is considered to be of unsound mind during the state.

Wernicke's and Korsakoff's Syndrome

It is alcohol-induced persisting amnestic disorder and occurs due to thiamine deficiency. Korsakoff's syndrome presents with:
- Profound anterograde amnesia (inability to learn new things)
- Milder retrograde amnesia
- Impairment in visuo-spatial, abstract and conceptual reasoning
- Most of the patient demonstrates an acute onset of Korsakoff's syndrome in association with Wernicke's syndrome whereas rest person shows gradual onset.

Wernicke's Syndrome

Wernicke's syndrome or encephalopathy is an acute form of syndrome characterized by drowsiness, disorientation, amnesia, ataxia, peripheral neuropathy, horizontal nystagmus, and diplopia due to ophthalmoplegia.

Saturday Night Paralysis

An intoxicated person, while sitting in a chair, may hang his arm over a chair and sleep. The resultant hanging of arm over chair compresses brachial plexus causing paralysis of the muscles. The phenomenon is frequent on the weekends where a person may have binge drinking on Saturday evening with subsequent paralysis.

Alcohol Palimpsest (Alcoholic Blackouts)

The patchy amnesia, which is not associated with unconsciousness, has been called as alcoholic palimpsest.

Management

- Adequate nutrition and rest
- Vitamin B supplementation
- Judicious use of benzodiazepines to combat withdrawal reaction
- Aversion therapy is meant for gradual weaning away the person from habit of alcohol consumption. The therapy is instituted after taking care of withdrawal reaction. **Disulfiram** has been used as an aversion technique. It is assumed that disulfiram interferes with the oxidative metabolism of alcohol (inhibits enzyme aldehyde dehydrogenase) with accumulation of aldehyde. Accumulation of aldehyde produces unpleasant symptoms (also called as **aldehyde syndrome**) whenever person consumes alcohol therefore person prefer not to drink. The unpleasant symptoms are given in table 43.5. The adverse effects of disulfiram therapy are given in Table 43.6.
- Counseling and psychotherapy
- Rehabilitation.

Autopsy Findings

- Smell of alcohol
- Congested conjunctiva
- Rigor mortis may be delayed
- Decomposition may be retarded
- Organs are congested
- Dark fluid blood
- In chronic alcoholics — fatty or cirrhotic liver, cardiomyopathy, pancreatitis, cerebellar degeneration, cerebellar atrophy, atrophy of gastric cells, testicular atrophy, degeneration of seminiferous tubules.

Medicolegal Importance

1. As per Sec 85 of IPC, a person is not held responsible for his criminal act if at the time of doing the act the person happens to be intoxicated and provided that the alcohol or intoxication was given to him without his knowledge or against his will. According to this section, voluntarily drunkenness is no excuse for commission of crime.
2. As per Sec 86 of IPC, an act done is not an offence unless done with a particular knowledge or intent, a person who does the act in a state of intoxication shall be liable to be dealt with as if he had the same knowledge as he would have had if he had not been intoxicated unless the thing which intoxicated him was administered to him without his knowledge or against his will.
3. According to Sec 510 of IPC — misconduct by a drunken person in public place is punishable with imprisonment up to 24 hours.
4. When person is suffering from delirium tremens, he is not held responsible for any act because the he is considered to be of unsound mind during the state.[13]
5. Consent for examination of drunken person — vide supra
6. According to Sec 129-A, under Bombay Prohibition Act 1949 (BPA) — the prohibition officer or police officer, who has reasonable grounds for believing that

Table 43.5: Aldehyde syndrome

Symptoms
CVS
Uneasiness
Tightness in chest
Syncope
Hypotension
Tachycardia
Arrhythmias
RS
Tachpnea
CNS
Blurred vision
Confusion
Vertigo
Throbbing headache
Weakness
GIT
Abdominal pain
Nausea
Vomiting
Others
Sweating
Flushing

Table 43.6: Adverse effects of disulfiram

Adverse effects
Metallic taste
Malaise
Abdominal discomfort
Rashes

Section B Toxicology

the person has consumed alcohol, may produce such person for medical examination of drunkenness and/or collection of blood. The medical examiner examines the person and issues a certificate in the prescribed form "A" containing the details of clinical examination. The blood samples collected by medical examiner forwards the same to Chemical examiner (Regional Forensic Science Laboratory) vide form "B". The chemical analyzer, after analyzing the sample, forwards his report as prescribed in format "C".

7. In State of Bombay Vs Balwant Ganpati, the Bombay High Court held that Article 20 (3) of the Constitution of India was not violated when blood for chemical analysis was taken under Sec 129-A of the Bombay Prohibition Act.
8. Sec 84 of the Bombay Prohibition Act 1949 provides that any person, who is found drunk or drinking in a common drinking house or is found there present for the purpose of drinking, shall, on conviction, be punished with a fine which may extend to five hundred rupees.
9. Sec 85 of the Bombay Prohibition Act 1949 provides that any person found drunk and incapable of controlling himself or behaves in a disorderly manner under the influence of a drink in any street or thorough fare or public place or in any place to which the public have or are permitted to have access, shall, on conviction, be punished with imprisonment for a term which may extend to one to three months and with fine which may be extend to two hundred to five hundred rupees.
10. Sec 65 and 66 (1) of the Bombay Prohibition Act 1949 provides penalty for illegal import, export, manufacture, sale, purchase or transport of an intoxicant without proper license, permit or authorization.
11. A medical practitioner may be sued for damages caused while treating a patient under intoxicated state or a surgeon may be held negligent for death of patient if the surgeon performs operation under the influence of alcohol. The surgeon can be prosecuted under Sec 304-A of IPC.
12. Treating the patient under the influence of alcohol is considered as infamous conduct (professional misconduct).
13. Many homicides are triggered by the aggressive behaviour engendered by alcohol[14].
14. Studies have shown that alcohol can be generated in putrefying bodies. Postmortem production of alcohol in decomposing bodies has been attributed to bacterial action.[15] Such production of alcohol in bodies is referred as endogenous alcohol. It is stated that the upper limit of endogenous production of alcohol[16] is 0.15%.
15. Alcohol is highly hydrophilic, so once it enters the systemic circulation; it is distributed evenly throughout total body water. Because women have more body fat compared with men and fat contains no water, higher peak alcohol levels are achieved in women than in men of the same weight.

METHYL ALCOHOL

Synonyms: Methanol, wood spirit, wood alcohol, wood naphtha

Features

- Methanol is colorless and volatile liquid
- Peculiar nauseating odor
- Burning taste
- It is obtained from the distillation of wood.

Absorption and Metabolism

- Methanol is rapidly absorbed from the gastrointestinal tract, through lungs and skin
- It is metabolized in liver. It is first metabolized to formaldehyde by the enzyme alcohol dehydrogenase and then the formaldehyde is further metabolized into formic acid by the enzyme aldehyde dehydrogenase (Fig. 43.12). Methanol follows zero order kinetics and the half-life is about 20 to 60 hours.

Mechanism of Action

Methanol itself is not toxic but two metabolites formed — formaldehyde and formic acid are highly toxic. These compounds are responsible for causing profound metabolic acidosis and visual defect and blindness.

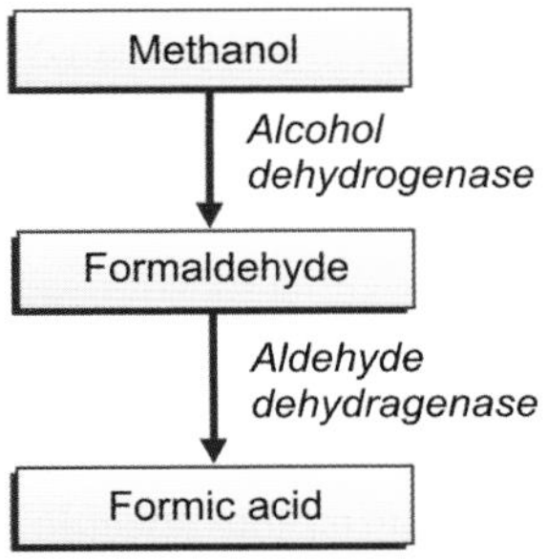

FIG. 43.11: Metabolism of methanol

Fatal Dose

60 to 100 ml.

Fatal Period

24 to 36 hours.

Clinical Features

The clinical features may be delayed for 12 to 24 hours. Patient may present with:

- Nausea
- Vomiting
- Abdominal pain
- Headache
- Breathlessness
- Dizziness
- Vertigo
- Tachycardia
- Hypotension
- Profound metabolic acidosis
- Convulsions
- Delirium
- Coma
- Visual disturbances are common and are attributed to the toxic effects of formic acid. There may be blurring of vision, or frank blindness. There is retrobulbar degeneration in the form of necrosis of myelinated portion of optic nerve and supposed to be cause for visual loss.[17]
- Photophobia
- Constriction of visual fields
- Fundoscopic examination reveals – hyperemia of optic disk, papilledema, decrease pupillary light reflex, retinal edema.

Diagnosis

- High anion gap acidosis
- Fundoscopic examination — vide supra
- Blood methanol level — more than 50 mg/100 ml indicates severe poisoning.

Management

- Protect eyes from light
- Maintain respiration, circulation and blood pressure
- Gastric lavage with sodium bicarbonate
- Antidote — ethanol is the specific antidote. Ethanol competes with the alcohol dehydrogenase enzyme and prevents metabolism of methanol, which is then excreted unchanged in urine. Ten percent ethanol is administered through a Nasogastric tube; loading dose of 0.7 ml/kg is followed by 0.15-ml/kg/hour drip.[18] Alternatively, 10% ethanol is administered at a dose of 10 ml/kg intravenously over 30 minutes, followed by 1.5 ml/kg/hour, so as to produce and maintain a blood ethanol level of 100 mg/100 ml.[19]
- Sodium bicarbonate for acidosis and it also prevents retinal damage.
- Folinic acid (folate therapy) intravenously — it enhances the removal of formic acid
- Hemodialysis
- Potassium chloride may be required if hypokalemia develops due to alkali therapy
- 4-methyl pyrazole is a specific inhibitor of alcohol dehydrogenase and retards methanol metabolism. Slow intravenous infusion of 100 mg has been found to effective.

Autopsy Findings

- Cyanosis
- Stomach and intestine may be hyperemic and inflamed. Patchy submucosal hemorrhages may be noted.
- Pulmonary edema
- Cerebral edema
- Retinal edema
- Necrosis of myelinated portion of optic nerve.

Medicolegal Importance

Most of deaths are due accidental consumption of methanol due to non-available of regular alcohol or due to adulteration of regular alcohol with methanol.

REFERENCES

1. Ferimuth HC, Spitz WU. Forensic aspects of alcohol. In: Spitz WU (Ed) Spitz and Fisher's Medicolegal investigation of Death, 3rd edn. 1993. Charles C Thomas Publisher, USA. 767-76.
2. Watkins RL, Adler EV. The effect of food on alcohol absorption and elimination pattern. J Forensic Sci 1993; 38:285-91.
3. Kaye S, Haag HB. Terminal blood alcohol concentrations in 94 fatal cases of alcoholism. JAMA 1957; 165:451-2.
4. Avila JA, Schmidt EW, Nichols CG. Alcohols. In: Viccellio P (ed) Handbook of Medical Toxicology, 1st edn. 1993. Little, Brown and Company, Boston.616-22.
5. Reddy KSN. CNS depressants. In: The Essentials of Forensic Medicine and Toxicology, 22nd edn. 2003. K. Suguna Devi, Hyderabad. 470-93.
6. Subrahmanyam BV. Common irritants and poisons. In: Forensic medicine, Toxicology and Medical Jurisprudence, 1st edn. 2004. Modern Publishers, New Delhi. 204-12.
7. Mattoo BN, Kawale GB, Parikh CK. Inebriant poisons In: Parikh's Textbook of Medical Jurisprudence and Toxicology, 5th edn. 1995. CBS Publishers and Distributors, Bombay. 847-76.

8. Stark MM, Norfolk G. Substance misuse. P 285-326. In: Stark MM (ed) Clinical Forensic Medicine – a Physicians Guide.
9. Schuckit MA. Alcohol and alcoholism In: Fauci AS, Braunwald E, Isselbacher KJ, Wilson JD, Martin JB, Kasper DL, Hauser SL, Longo DL (eds) Harrison's Principles of Internal Medicine, Vol.2, 14th edn. 1998. McGraw-Hill, New York. 2503-8.
10. Miller NS, Gold MS. In: Alcohol (drug of abuse) Vol. 2, 1st edn. 1991. Plenum Medical Book Company, New York.
11. Clark JC. Sudden death in the chronic alcoholic. Forensic Sci Int 1988; 36:105-11.
12. Tan TTC. The sudden fatty liver death: a case report and overview. Med Sci Law 1983; 23:108-11.
13. Rao NG. Neurotoxics. In: Textbook of Forensic Medicine and Toxicology, 1st edn. 2006. Jaypee Brothers Medical Publishers (P) Ltd., New Delhi. 395-425.
14. Saukko P, Knight B. Forensic aspects of alcohol. In: Knight's Forensic Pathology, 3rd edn. 2004. Arnold, London. 552-9.
15. Gilliland MGF, Bost PO. Alcohol in decomposed bodies. Postmortem synthesis and distribution. J Forensic Sci 1993; 38:1266-74.
16. Corry JEL. Possible sources of ethanol ante and postmortem: It's relationship to the biochemistry and microbiology of decomposition. J Applied Bacteriol 1978; 4:1-56.
17. Dode CR, Mohanty AC. Predictive toxicity of methyl alcohol. J Medicolegal Assoc Maharashtra 2001; 13:9-13.
18. Tripathi KD. Ethyl and methyl alcohol. In Essentials of Medical Pharmacology, 4th edn. 1999. Jaypee Brothers Medical Publishers (P) Ltd. New Delhi. 358-66.
19. Pillay VV. Inebriant poisons. In: Textbook of Forensic Medicine and Toxicology, 14th edn. 2004. Paras Publishing, Hyderabad. 452-78.

CHAPTER 44

Deliriant Poisons

Belladonna: In Italian, a beautiful lady; in English, a deadly poison.

- Ambrose Bierce

Deliriant are the poisons acting on the brain and inducing altered consciousness with confusion, delusions, hallucinations and agitation. Examples are given below:

1. Datura
2. Deadly night shade (Atropa belladonna)
3. Henbane (Hyoscamus)
4. Indian hemp (Cannabis sativa)
5. Cocaine

DATURA

Common name: Thorn apple, Jimson seed

Features

- Datura is a wild shrub up to 3 to 5 feet and grows at waste places (Fig. 44.1)
- Plant bears dark green oval leaves with trumpet or bell shaped flowers. Two varieties of Datura fastuosa are found in India:[1]
  - Datura niger — deep purple color flowers
  - Datura alba — white color flowers
- The plant bears fruits which are spherical and have multiple spikes, thus called as "thorn apple" (Fig. 44.2). The fruit contains brownish kidney shaped seeds (Fig. 44.3).

Toxic part: all parts are toxic but seeds are more toxic.

Active Principle

- Hyoscine (scopolamine)
- Hyoscyamine
- Atropine

} Together referred as beladonna alkaloids

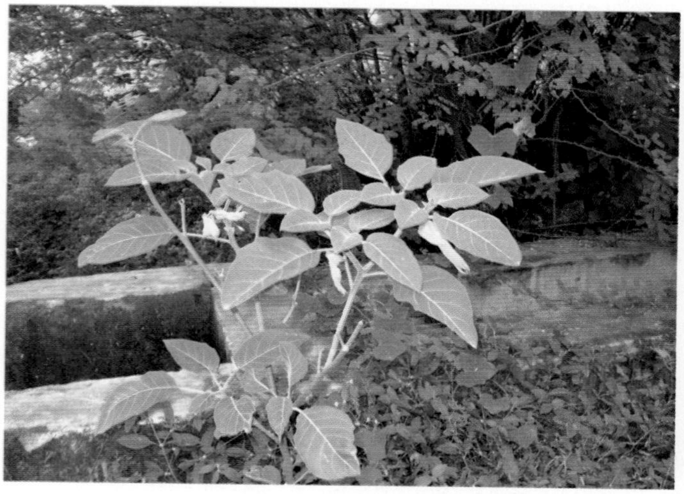

FIG. 44.1: Datura plant

FIG. 44.2: Datura fruit

FIG. 44.3: Datura seeds

Table 44.1: Dose related progression of symptoms

Dose of atropine	*Symptoms*
0.5 mg	Dry mouth
1 mg	Dilatation of pupils Blurring of vision or Diplopia
2–4 mg	Increases cardiac and respiratory activity Elevate blood pressure
5 mg	Temperature elevation Inability to swallow Urine retention
10 mg or more	Restlessness Hyperactivity Agitation Clouded sensorium Disorientation Hallucinations Delirium Coma

Mechanism of Action

- The alkaloids competitively inhibit the muscarinic effects of acetylcholine.
- Site of action are at all postganglionic parasympathetic and few postganglionic sympathetic (sweat glands, smooth muscles) innervations.
- Majority of the CNS actions are due to blockage of muscarinic receptors in the brain viz. vagal stimulation, decrease in heart rate. High doses cause cortical excitation, restlessness, disorientation, hallucinations and delirium followed by respiratory depression and coma.

Absorption, Metabolism and Excretion

- The alkaloids are quickly absorbed from all mucus membrane and skin.
- The alkaloids are excreted by the kidneys.

Clinical Features

The clinical features are best summarized in classical phrase quoted by Morton Still "**blind as bat, hot as hare, dry as bone, red as beet and mad as hen**". It can also remember as **D**s. The progression of symptoms with loss of cholinergic function is dose related to atropine[2] and is summarized in Table 44.1

- **D**ryness of mouth (dry as bone)
- Bitter taste
- **D**ifficulty in talking
- **D**ysphagia
- **D**ilated pupils
- **D**iplopia
- **D**ifficulty in vision (blurring of vision, blind as bat)
- **D**ry hot skin with flushing (red as beet)
- Hyperpyrexia (hot as hare)
- **D**runken gait (ataxia)
- Hyperreflexia
- Convulsions
- **D**elirium, hallucinations, agitation, amnesia, incoherence, visual or auditory hallucinations (mad as a hen)
- **D**eficit of recent memory. Remote memory undisturbed
- **D**ysuria
- **D**istention of bladder (retention of urine)
- **D**eath.

Management

- Treat the patient in quiet and dark environment
- Gastric lavage with activated charcoal
- Catheterize bladder
- Cathartic is given, even if patient is treated 24 hours after ingestion because intestinal motility is decreased
- Monitor and regulate patient's temperature
- Hyperpyrexia — hydration, cold sponging
- Agitation can be controlled with judicious use of diazepam/lorazepam

- Antidote is physostigmine. Intravenous physostigmine is given slowly over 5–10 minutes if hyperthermia, delirium, convulsions, hypertension and arrhythmias occurred.

Drug Contraindicated

1. Phenothiazines
2. Antihistamines
3. Morphine
4. Tricyclics
5. Quinidine
6. Disopyramide
7. Procainamide

Autopsy Findings

- Signs of asphyxia
- Gastrointestinal tract shows inflammation
- Seeds or fragments may be found in stomach
- Pulmonary edema

Medicolegal Importance

1. Accidental death may occur since datura seeds may be mistaken for chilly seeds. The differences are given in Table 44.2
2. Suicide – rare
3. Homicide
4. Datura seeds are used as stupefying agent to rob people.[3] Robbers usually mix the datura seeds with food or drinks and offer to travelers in train. Once the passengers are stupefied, they robbed them. Thus datura gains popularity as **railroad poison**.

Table 44.2: Difference between datura and chili seeds

Features	*Datura seeds*	*Chili seeds*
Color	Brownish	Yellowish
Size	Bigger	Smaller
Shape	Kidney shaped	Round
Surface	Pitted	Smooth
Smell	Odorless	Pungent
Taste	Bitter	Pungent
On section	Embryo curves outward	Embryo curve inward towards hilum

5. Used as love philter or potions. In Anthony and Cleopatra, it was mentioned that Cleopatra employed the datura extract in her famous wooing of Caesar.[4]
6. Datura seeds are abused. The seeds are mixed with cigarette and belladonna and smoked as hallucinogen.[5]
7. Datura seed resist putrefaction of body
8. Criminal responsibility: Datura produces temporary insanity. Usually, the poison is administered without the victim's knowledge. Hence the individual is not held responsible for his acts under the influence of Datura.
9. Scopolamine is used as truth serum.

Fatal Dose

- 50 to 100 seeds
- 10 to 100 mg of atropine

Fatal period: 24 hours

CANNABIS

Botanical name: Cannabis sativa or Cannabis indica
Common name: Indian hemp

Features

- Cannabis sativa plant grows all over India however; the cultivation is restricted by government.
- The plant is dioecious, i.e. the sexes are separate. The female plant is taller and grows about 4 to 6 meter and bears luxurious foliage than male counterpart (Fig. 44.4).
- Nabilone is a synthetic cannabinoid and possess antiemetic properties. It is found to be useful in patients receiving cancer chemotherapy.[6]

Preparations of Cannabis

The various preparations of Cannabis sativa, which is used, are as follows:

1. Bhang: also called as sidhi, patti, sabji. Bhang is made from dried leaves of plant pressed into cakes (Fig. 44.5).
2. Ganja: is derived from flowering tops (Fig. 44.6).
3. Charas: also known as hashish or hash and is derived from resinous exudates of plant
4. Majun: a sweet prepared with any of the above preparation added (Fig. 44.7).
5. Marijuana: this term is used in America and many texts considered it as synonymous with ganja. It is prepared from the leaves and flowering tops of the plant.

Active Principle

Three active preparations are abundantly found and include:

FIG. 44.4: Cannabis plant

FIG. 44.5: Bhang

- Cannabinol
- Cannabidiol
- Several isomers of tetrahydrocannabional. The isomer responsible for most of the characteristic effect of cannabis is l-Δ^9- tetrahydrocannabional (Δ^9- THC).

Fatal Dose

- Charas — 2 gm/kg body weight
- Ganja — 8 gm/kg body weight
- Bhang — 10 gm/kg body weight

Fatal period: about 12 hours

Mechanism of Action[7]

- Cannabis act at cannabinoid receptors. Two types of cannabinoid receptors have been identified and are CB_1 and CB_2.
- CB_1 — widely distributed with highest concentration in brain neurons
- CB_2 — found in cells of immune system, spleen, tonsils and immune cells.

Absorption, Metabolism and Excretion

- Cannabis (Δ^9- THC) is absorbed from the gastrointestinal tract and as smoke or vapor from the respiratory tract. It is slowly absorbed from subcutaneous or intramuscular injection.

FIG. 44.6: Ganja

FIG. 44.7: Majun

- Δ^9- THC is rapidly converted by liver microsomes into an active metabolite 11-hydroxy- Δ^9- THC. 11-hydroxy-Δ^9- THC is converted into an inactive metabolite and excreted in urine, feces and bile.

Clinical Features

- Subjective perception of relaxation and euphoria
- Some impairment in thinking, concentration and perceptual and psychomotor functions occur
- Higher doses causes hallucinations, sedation and at times dysphoria with unpleasant sensation
- Excitement
- Impulsive ideas/stray ideas
- Size of objects and distance is distorted[7]
- Recent memory and selective attention is impaired[7]
- Changes in perception of color, shape and time[8]
- Increase in appetite
- Nausea
- Dry mouth
- Tachycardia
- Palpitations
- Hypotension
- Angina may be precipitated by ganja smoking in persons with coronary insufficiency.

Differential Diagnosis

1. Cocaine intoxication
2. Amphetamine intoxication
3. Sedative
4. Tricyclic antidepressants
5. Panic attacks

Management

- Gut decontamination
- Benzodiazepines for paranoia
- Haloperidol for acute psychotic state
- Supportive measures.

Autopsy Findings

- Signs of asphyxia
- Unabsorbed bhang may be identified in the stomach.

Medicolegal Importance

1. Drug of abuse
2. Acute intoxication causes impairment in motor skills and judgment, affects vision and perception of time and space. Therefore, it may be dangerous to drive a vehicle under the influence of cannabis.
3. A case is reported where a young adult male died after consuming bhang, who was suffering from heart ailment.[9]
4. Cannabis is known to induce suicidal ideation
5. Run amok: under the influence of the substance, a person get frenzy and goes on killing other persons who comes in his way until the homicidal tendency last. Thereafter, the person commits suicide or surrender.

COCAINE

Features

- Cocaine is an alkaloid derived from plant Erythroxylon coca.
- It is produced as a salt (cocaine hydrochloride) or as an alkaloid known as freebase or crack.
- The free base (crack) is a colorless, odorless, transparent, crystalline substance. It makes cracking sound when heated, thus known as crack.
- Cocaine hydrochloride is a white powder. It is usually adulterated with other substances such as caffeine, amphetamine, strychnine etc. When it is adulterated with heroin, it is called as speed ball.

Routes of Administration

1. Chewing – coca leaves
2. Pyrolysis (smoking)
3. Snorting
4. Intravenous injection
5. Ingestion

Mechanism of Action

- Cocaine is CNS stimulant. CNS stimulant effects and euphoria are mediated through inhibition of dopamine reuptake in the nucleus accumbens. However, in chronic cocaine user, it causes dopamine depletion and impairment of dopaminergic function in the brain.
- Cocaine potentates' nor-epinephrine and epinephrine. Cocaine blocks the reuptake of neurotransmitters at the synapse due to which there is increase in the concentration of nor-epinephrine and epinephrine. The increase in concentration of nor-epinephrine and epinephrine causes sympathomimetic effects such as tachycardia, hypertension, hyperthermia, diaphoresis, mydriasis and vasoconstriction.

Absorption, Metabolism and Excretion

- Cocaine is well absorbed from oral, nasal and respiratory site.
- With intravenous injection or inhalation, the onset effects are rapid with peak level achieved in 3 to 5 minutes. The half-life is approximately 1 hour.
- It is metabolized by liver and plasma cholinesterase to benzoylecgonine, ecgonine methyl ester and ecgonine.
- The metabolites are excreted through urine.

Fatal Dose

- Oral — 50 mg
- Mucosal — 100 mg

Fatal period: few minutes — few hours

Clinical Features

Acute poisoning

- Anxiety
- Agitation
- Restlessness
- Tremors
- Hyperthermia
- Tachycardia
- Hypertension
- Convulsions
- Hyperreflexia
- Psychosis
- Auditory or visual hallucinations
- Altered tactile sensation: the person feel that some small insects are crawling on his skin. This is known as **Magnan's symptom** or **cocaine bugs** (formication).
- Mydriasis
- Pulmonary edema
- Rhabdomyolysis[10]
- Intestinal ischemia/abdominal pain/colitis[11]
- Blindness due to occlusion of retinal artery as a consequence of vasoconstriction.
- Myocardial ischemia/infarction due to coronary artery vasospasm[12-14]
- Intracranial hemorrhage such as subarachnoid hemorrhage or intracerebral hemorrhage or infarction may occur.[15]

Management

- Hyperthermia managed by cooling blanket/ ice water sponging/ice water bath
- Convulsions — diazepam/lorazepam
- Tachycardia — beta-blockers
- Chest pain — calcium channel blockers, nitrates
- Ventricular arrhythmias — lidocaine
- Supportive measures.

Autopsy Findings

- Signs of asphyxia
- Nasal septum ulceration and perforation may be noted in chronic snorting abuser.[16]
- There may be multiple scar marks at injection site in chronic abuser
- There may be infective endocarditis as sequelae to septic injection site and practice.
- Hepatic necrosis may be present especially in coca paste smokers.
- Heart may show evidence of myocardial infarction. Microscopy shows lymphocytic infiltrate, coagulative necrosis of myocardial fibers and intimal proliferation.[17]

Samples to be Preserved

1. Blood
2. Brain
3. Skin from injection site
4. Swab from nasal mucosa

Medicolegal Importance

1. Drug of abuse
2. Body may get decompose rapidly
3. Accidental deaths are common due to overdose or adulteration
4. Provoke the users for violent behaviour. Acute intoxication may cause person to be aggressive and paranoid.
5. Prostitutes may place cocaine solution into vagina to produce local constriction and causes intoxication.
6. **Body packer syndrome**: persons engaged in smuggling of cocaine fill the drug in balloon or condom or polythene bag and swallowed to conceal the contraband. This act is called as body packing. The packets may cause intestinal obstruction.[18, 19] Sometime, sudden death may be caused due to rupture of the bag or condom within gastrointestinal tract.[20-22]
7. **Body stuffer syndrome**: in this syndrome, the person who smuggled the cocaine, on the verge of being arrested for possessing cocaine, swallows the drug to conceal the evidence. This act causes cocaine poisoning.[23]

REFERENCES

1. Guharaj PV. Poisonous plants. In: Forensic Medicine, 1st edn. 1982. Orient Longman Hyderabad. 359-77.

2. Mikolich JR, Paulson GW, Cross CJ. Acute anticholinergic syndrome due to jimson seed ingestion. Ann Intern Med 1978; 83: 321-5.
3. Frohne D, Pfander HJ. Datura stramonium In: A colour atlas of poisonous plants. Translated by Bisset NG, 2nd edn. 1984. Wolfe Publishing Ltd. London. 206-7.
4. Goldsmith SR, Frank I, Ungerleider JT. Poisoning from ingestion of a stramonium-belladonna mixture. JAMA 1968; 204: 169-70.
5. Cummins BM, Obetz SW, Wilson MR Jr. Belladonna poisoning as a facet of psychodelia (letter). JAMA 1968; 204: 153.
6. Satoskar RS, Bhandarkar SD, Rege NN. Psychotogenic drugs. In: Pharmacology and Pharmacotherapeutics, 9th edn. 2005. Popular Prakashan Private Limited, Mumbai. 217-20.
7. Bennett PN, Brown MJ. Cannabis. In: Clinical Pharmacology, 9th edn. 2003. Churchill Livingstone, New Delhi. 189-92.
8. Matthew H, Lawson AAH. Drug addiction. In: Treatment of common acute poisoning, 3rd edn. 1975. Churchill Livingstone, Edinburgh. 184-91.
9. Gupta BD, Jani CB, Shah PH. Fatal Bhang Poisoning. Med Sci Law 2001; 41: 349-52.
10. Roth D, Alarcon FJ, Fernandez JA, Preston RA, Bourgoignie JJ. Acute Rhabdomyolysis associated with cocaine intoxication. N Engl J Med 1988; 319: 673-7.
11. Nalbandian H, Sheth N, Dietrich R, Georgious J. Intestinal ischemia caused by cocaine ingestion. Surgery 1985; 3: 374-6.
12. Hollander JE. Management of cocaine associated myocardial ischemia. N Eng J Med 1995; 333: 1267-72.
13. Coleman DL, Ross TF, Naughton JL. Myocardial ischemia and infarction related to recreational cocaine use. West J Med 1982; 136: 444-6.
14. Mathias DW. Cocaine-associated myocardial ischemia. Review of clinical and angiographic findings. Am J Med 1986; 81: 675-8.
15. Lichtenfeld PJ, Rubin DB, Feldman RS. Subarachnoid hemorrhage precipitated by cocaine snorting. Arch Neurol 1984; 41: 223-4.
16. Vilensky W. Illicit and licit drugs causing perforation of the nasal septum. J Forensic Sci 1982; 27: 958-62.
17. Simpson RW, Edwards WD. Pathogenesis of cocaine induced ischemic heart disease. Arch Path Lab Med 1986; 110: 479-84.
18. McCarron MM, Wood JD. The cocaine 'body packer' syndrome: Diagnosis and treatment. JAMA 1983; 250: 1417-20.
19. Sinner WN. The gastrointestinal tract as a vehicle for drug smuggling. Gastrointest Radiol 1981; 6: 319-23.
20. Welti CV, Wight RK. Death caused by recreational cocaine use. JAMA 1979; 241: 2519-22.
21. Introna F Jr, Smialek JE. The mini-packer syndrome: fatal ingestion of drug containers in Baltimore, Maryland. Am J Forensic Med Pathol 1989; 10: 21-4.
22. Price KR. Fatal cocaine poisoning. J Forensic Sci Soc 1974; 14: 329-33.
23. Roberts J, Price D, Goldfrank LR. The body stuffer syndrome: A clandestine form of drug overdose. Am J Emerg Med 1986; 4: 21-7.

CHAPTER 45

Spinal Poisons

Some seeds fell by the wayside.

— The Bible

Examples of spinal poisons are:
- Strychnos nux vomica
- Physostigmatis semina or calabar bean
- Physostigmine (eserine)
- Gelsemium sempervirens or jasmine

STRYCHNINE

Botanical name: Strychnos nux vomica
Common name: Kuchila, dog buttons

Physical Features[1]

- Belongs to family Loganiaceae
- A vine found in South India
- Plant bears oval dark green leaves
- Fruits are globular and contain disk-shaped seeds. The seeds are round, disk shaped, concave on one side and convex on the other side. Seeds are ash gray in color and covered with silky fibers. The seeds are about 2.5 cm in diameter and 5 mm in thickness. The pericarp of seed is tough (Fig. 45.1).

FIG. 45.1: Nux vomica seeds

Uses

- Rodenticide
- For killing stray dogs
- As folk medicine
- Arrow poison for hunting

Toxic Parts of Plant

- Leaves
- Fruits and seed
- Root and stem
- Bark.

Toxic Principles

- Seed contains two active principle namely:
  - Strychnine
  - Brucine
- Root, stem, bark and leaves contains:
  - Brucine as toxic principle
  - Lagonin as glycoside
- Strychnine is an odorless white crystalline prism that melts at 275 to 285°C with decomposition. It is very bitter in taste and more powerful than brucine.

Mechanism of Action[2]

- Strychnine antagonizes the inhibitory neurotransmitter amino-acid glycine at postsynaptic receptors.
- Inhibitory glycine receptors are abundant in the spinal cord and brain stem where they are mainly involved in regulation of motor functions. When inhibitors are

blocked, ongoing neuronal excitability is increased and sensory stimuli produce exaggerated reflex effects thus producing powerful muscle contractions.
- Glycine receptors in higher brain centers such as substantia nigra, neostriatum and hippocampus are commonly insensitive to strychnine, explaining why strychnine symptoms are largely spinal in origin.

Absorption, Metabolism and Excretion

Strychnine is well absorbed from gastrointestinal mucosa and nasal mucosa but not through the skin. It is metabolized in liver. In non-fatal human poisoning, strychnine disappearance followed first order kinetics with a half-life of 10 hours to 16 hours. It is excreted mainly by kidneys with traces in bile, milk and saliva.[2,3]

Clinical Features

- If seeds are swallowed uncrushed, the hard pericarp resist digestion and seeds are passed in feces without any poisonous symptoms.
- With crushed seeds, symptoms begin to appear within 15 to 30 minutes.
- Bitter taste in mouth
- Sense of uneasiness, restlessness, fear and anxiety
- Increase difficulty in breathing and swallowing
- Muscle twitching and spasm of muscle followed by convulsions. The convulsions last for 30 seconds to 2 minute and are precipitated by slightest stimuli such as sudden noise, a current of air or gentle touching of patient. The convulsions are first clonic but eventually becomes tonic. In between the convulsions, the muscles are completely relaxed and it is an important diagnostic feature.
- The convulsions are more marked in anti-gravity muscles and body arches in hyperextension position and lies on heel and head. This position of body is known as **opisthotonos**. It is most common position. However, at time, the body may bend forward and the condition is called as **emprosthotonos**. If body bends side wise (i.e. lateral bending), the condition is called as **pleurothotonos**.
- Contraction of the muscles of face causes widening of the angle of mouth with creases appearing around eyelids. This condition is known as **risus sardonicus**. Also called as **sardonic smile** due to grimacing that occurred due to muscle contraction of face.
- There is difficulty in breathing during convulsions due to contraction of chest muscles and diaphragm.
- Patient remains conscious and maintains clear sensorium during and between convulsions.[4]
- There may be frothing at mouth and pupils are dilated.

- Prognosis is good if interval for appearance of convulsions increases and period of convulsion decreases. Prognosis is bad if reverse occurs, i.e. when convulsions appear rapidly and last longer.

Complications

- Hypoxia
- Hyperthermia
- Rhabdomyolysis
- Metabolic acidosis/ lactic acidosis

Causes of Death

- Medullary paralysis due to hypoxia
- Respiratory failure due to spasm of respiratory muscles

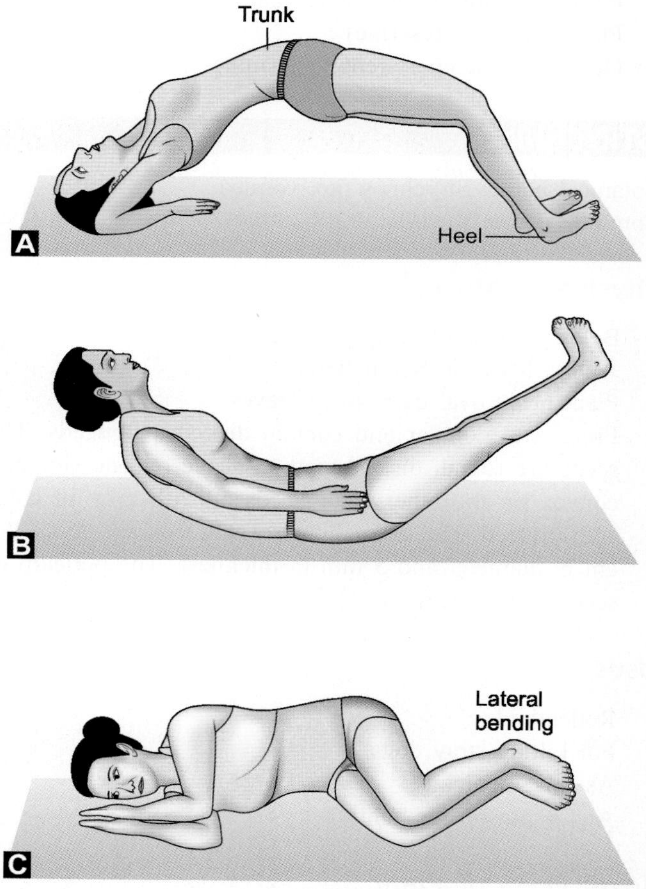

FIGS 45.2A to C: Showing various positions in strychnine poisoning. **A:** Indicates opisthotonos, **B:** Indicates emprosthotonos and **C:** Indicates pleurothotonos position

Differential Diagnosis

1. Tetanus — difference between tetanus and strychnine poisoning is given in Table 45.1
2. Rabies
3. Meningitis
4. Cocaine intoxication
5. Phenothiazine poisoning
6. Phencyclidine
7. Hysteria

Fatal Dose

- Seeds — 1 to 2 crushed seeds
- Strychnine — 50 to 100 mg

Fatal Period

- 1 to 2 hour

Management

- Patient should be managed in calm environment.
- Emesis is contraindicated as the procedure may precipitate convulsions. However, cautiously gastric lavage may be carried out after protecting air way. Activated charcoal should be administered and is considered as effective.
- Management of convulsions is important and can be treated by lorazepam or diazepam. If benzodiazepines are ineffective, short acting barbiturate can be administered. Intractable convulsions may need muscle relaxants such as pancuronium.
- Rest symptomatic measures.

Autopsy Findings

- Rigor mortis— appear and disappear early
- Postmortem caloricity
- Signs of asphyxia
- Froth at mouth
- Serosal surface may show hemorrhagic areas
- Occasionally muscle may show hemorrhages or evidence of rupture
- Spinal cord is congested. Microscopy shows multiple hemorrhages in anterior and posterior horns with ring hemorrhages around the capillaries. Neurons may show chromatolysis.[3]
- Organs are congested.

Samples to be Preserved

- Routine viscera
- Blood
- Spinal cord

Medicolegal Importance

1. Accidental poisoning may occur in children who may chew the seeds out of curiosity.
2. Accidental poisoning may occur in adults due to consumption of folk/indigenous medicinal preparation.
3. Accidental poisoning in adults may occur due to strychnine consumption as it is considered as aphrodisiac.
4. Homicide rare due to bitter taste and dramatic appearance of symptoms, however cases have been reported.[5]
5. Used to kill cattle.

Table 45.1: Showing difference between strychnine and tetanus

Features	*Strychnine*	*Tetanus*
History of	Poisoning	Injury
Onset	Sudden	Gradual
Fever	Not usual	Usual
Convulsions	All muscles are involved at the time of convulsions	All muscles are not affected at same time
Lock jaw	Absent	Present
Muscle	Relaxed in between convulsions	Are stiff and not fully relaxed
Fatal period	1–2 hour	> 24 hour
Laboratory findings	Chemical test for strychnine positive	No poison Bacteria present on microbiological investigation

REFERENCES

1. Govindiah G. Strychnos nux vomica. In: Handbook of Poisonous Snakes and Plants, 1st edn. 2004. Paras Publishing, Hyderabad. 48-49.
2. Krieger R. In: Handbook of Pesticide Toxicology – principles Vol. 1, 1st edn. 2000. Academic Press San Diego, California.
3. Perper JA. Fatal strychnine poisoning- a case report and review of the literature. J Forensic Sci 1985; 30: 1248-55.
4. Smith BA. Strychnine poisoning. J Emerg Med 1990; 8:321-5.
5. Benomran FA, Henry JD. Homicide by strychnine poisoning. Med Sci Law 1996; 36: 271-3.

CHAPTER 46

Peripheral Nerve Poisons

Plant the crab tree where you will, it will never bear pippins.

- Proverb

Examples are:
1. Curare
2. Conium maculatum

CURARE

Curare is found in various species of strychnous plants and chondrodendron tomentosum plants.
Uses: Skeletal muscle relaxant

Active Principles

Curarine

Mechanism of Action[1]

- The action is on peripheral muscles. Curarine blocks the postsynaptic nicotinic acetylcholine receptors at myoneural junction and thus causes paralysis of skeletal muscle without affecting consciousness.
- Initially the small muscles of the eye, fingers and toes are affected followed by paralysis of neck, upper and lower limbs and finally diaphragm and intercostal muscles are paralyzed causing respiratory failure.

Absorption, Metabolism and Excretion

Curare is slowly absorbed from GIT. Absorption is rapid when given by subcutaneous or intramuscular route. Curarine is metabolized by liver and excreted into urine.[2]

Clinical Features

- Flaccidity of muscle
- Headache
- Hypotension
- Vertigo
- Mydriasis
- Blurring of vision
- Hyperthermia
- Convulsions
- Death is due to paralysis of respiratory muscle.

Complications

- Malignant hyperthermia
- Rhabdomyolysis

Fatal dose: 30 to 60 mg
Fatal period: 1 to 2 hours

FIG. 46.1: Curare plant

Management

- Air way maintenance and respiration
- Atropine
- Neostigmine (antagonizes block).

Autopsy Findings

- Signs of asphyxia
- Organs are congested.

Medicolegal Importance

1. Arrow poison
2. Rarely used for homicide
3. Anesthetic deaths due to overdose
4. Derivative of curare in combination with barbiturate is used for euthanasia.[3]

CONIUM MACULATUM

Botanical name: Conium maculatum
Common names: Poison hemlock, Socrates poison, common hemlock, spotted hemlock
Toxic parts of plant: all parts of plant

Toxic Principles[4]

- Coniine (alkaloid)
- Gamma-coniceine (alkaloid)

Mechanism of Action

Mechanism of action is two fold and the alkaloid act at:[5]

1. Neuromuscular junction as a non-depolarising blockers (similar to curare) and causes flaccid paralysis
2. Autonomic ganglia producing nicotinic effects such as salivation, mydriasis, tachycardia followed by bradycardia.

Fatal dose: 60 mg of coniine
Fatal period: 1 to 3 hours

Clinical Features[6]

- Nausea, vomiting
- Abdominal pain
- Salivation
- Tremors
- Sweating
- Convulsions
- Mydriasis
- Tachycardia followed by bradycardia
- Motor paralysis

FIG. 46.2: Conium maculatum plant

- Hypotension
- Coma
- Respiratory failure.

Complications[5]

- Rhabdomyolysis
- Acute renal failure
- Respiratory failure.

Management

- Air way maintenance and respiratory support
- GIT decontamination with activated charcoal
- Benzodiazepines for convulsions.

Autopsy Findings

- Signs of asphyxia
- Mousy odor (due to free coniine in plant)
- Organs are congested.

Medicolegal Importance

1. In ancient times, poison hemlock was used for execution. Socrates was executed by giving poison hemlock.
2. Poisoning is rare in India.
3. Not popular suicidal agent
4. Accidental poisoning may occur.

REFERENCES

1. Lee MR. Curare: the South American arrow poison. J R Coll Physicians Edinb 2005; 35: 83-92.
2. Thienes CH, Haley TJ. Poisoning of nerve ends and myoneural junctions of somatic nerves. In: Clinical Toxicology 5th edn. 1972. Lea and Febiger Philadelphia. 104-6.
3. Willems DL, Groenwoud JH, van der Wal G. Drugs used in physician-assisted death. Drugs Aging 1999; 15: 335-40.
4. Cromwell BT. The separation, micro-estimation and distribution of the alkaloids of hemlock (Conium maculatum L.). Biochem J 1956; 64: 259-66.
5. Frank BS, Michelson WB, Panter KE, Gardner DR. Ingestion of poison hemlock (Conium maculatum). West J Med 1995; 163: 573-4.
6. Vetter J. Poison hemlock (Conium maculatum L.). Food Chem Toxicol 2004; 42: 1373-82.

CHAPTER 47

Asphyxiants

Do not get into a mud fight with a pig. You will get mud all over you, and the pig will like it.

— **Anonymous**

These are the agents which cause asphyxia.

Classification

Asphyxiants are classified as:

1. Simple asphyxiants
2. Respiratory irritants
3. Systemic asphyxiants
4. Volatile compounds

Simple Asphyxiants

These are the inert gases and when these gases are breathed in high concentration, they act mechanically by displacing or excluding oxygen.

Examples are:

- Carbon monoxide
- Nitrogen
- Butane
- Ethane
- Methane.

Respiratory Irritants

These agents, when inhaled cause destruction of the respiratory tract or lung or both and cause inflammatory changes.

Examples are:

- Ammonia
- Chlorine
- Formaldehyde
- Hydrogen sulphide
- Smoke
- Methyl isocyanate.

Systemic Asphyxiants

These agents cause systemic toxicity.

Examples are:

- Carbon monoxide
- Hydrogen cyanide gas
- Smoke.

Volatile Compounds

These agents act as anesthetic agents.

Examples are:

- Aliphatic hydrocarbons
- Halogenated hydrocarbons
- Aromatic hydrocarbons.

CARBON MONOXIDE

Properties

- It is colorless, odorless, tasteless, non-irritant gas
- It is lighter than air
- Soluble in water
- Burns with blue flame.

Sources

1. Fire
2. Produced whenever there is incomplete combustion of carbon/fuel such as wood, charcoal, kerosene etc.
3. Automobile exhaust
4. Tobacco smoke
5. Generates in gun-powder, mines and detonation of explosive.

Mechanism of Action

- Carbon monoxide (CO) has 230 to 270 times greater affinity for hemoglobin than that of oxygen. Thus, it displaces oxygen from its combination with hemoglobin and forms a relatively stable compound known as **carboxyhemoglobin**. Formation of carboxyhemoglobin results in reduced arterial oxygen content and causes tissue anoxia.[1]
- Furthermore, CO causes a leftward shift of the oxyhemoglobin dissociation curve affecting the offloading of oxygen from hemoglobin to the tissue.
- The resultant effect is decreased ability of blood to carry oxygen and deliver to the tissues.

Clinical Features

Acute Poisoning

- The clinical features progresses as the percentage of saturation of CO increases in the blood. Initial symptoms are breathlessness, mild headache and as percentage increases, there is impairment of higher intellectual functions.[2] The clinical features are summarized in Table 47.1
- Several types of skin lesions may be produced in carbon monoxide poisoning. The lesions vary in degree from areas of erythema and edema to marked blister and bulla formation. The bullae are geographic in shape and may be few or more in number and are not necessarily located at pressure sites.[3]
- There may be development of metabolic acidosis and rhabdomyolysis.[4]
- Eye: There may be venous engorgement, tortuosity, disk edema and flame-shaped retinal hemorrhages.[5]
- Carbon monoxide has direct cardiac toxicity and induces atrial and ventricular arrhythmias. Angina or myocardial infarction may be induced or precipitated.[6]

Table 47.1: Showing percentage of carboxyhemoglobin and signs and symptoms produced in carbon monoxide poisoning

% of CoHb	*Clinical features*
0 - 10	No symptoms
10 - 20	Tightness across forehead Slight headache Dilatation of cutaneous blood vessels
20 - 30	Headache Throbbing in temples
30 - 40	Severe headache Weakness Dizziness Dimness of vision Nausea and vomiting Collapse
40 - 50	Same as above plus greater possibility of collapse or syncope Increased respiration and pulse
50 - 60	Syncope Coma with intermittent convulsions Cheyne-strokes respiration
60 - 70	Depressed cardiac function and respiration Possible death
70 - 80	Weak pulse and slowed respiration Respiratory failure and death

Chronic Poisoning

- Headache
- Confusion
- Dizziness
- Weakness
- Paresthesia
- Visual disturbances
- Hypertension
- Hyperthermia
- Palpitation
- Aggravation of angina
- Parkinsonism
- Incontinence
- Ataxia
- Polycythemia

Differential Diagnosis

1. Alcohol intoxication
2. Cerebrovascular episode (CVE)
3. Meningitis/encephalitis
4. Epilepsy

Complication After Acute Exposure

1. Dementia
2. Blindness
3. Amnesia

Management

- Remove patient from vitiated environment
- Oxygen administration. Hyperbaric oxygen is considered to be beneficial
- Convulsions should be treated with benzodiazepines
- Physical activity curtailed — to minimize the incidence of cerebral demyelination
- Mannitol for cerebral edema.

Autopsy Findings

- Pinkish coloration of skin and mucosa
- Pinkish color postmortem lividity
- Blisters may present on dependent parts such as calves, buttocks, wrist, knee
- Froth at mouth and nostrils
- Features of asphyxia
- Blood — pinkish red and fluid
- Internal organs — pinkish red
- Pulmonary edema
- Petechial hemorrhages in white matter and putamen
- Necrosis of basal ganglia especially globus pallidus.

Medicolegal Importance

1. Accidental death
2. Suicide — it is popular agent in western countries to commit suicide. The victim usually uses motor vehicle exhaust for the act of self-destruction.

CARBON DIOXIDE

Properties

- Atmosphere contains about 0.4 percent
- Heavy, odorless, colorless gas
- In solid form called as "dry snow"

Sources

1. Combustion: produced by complete combustion of carbon containing compounds
2. Respiration
3. Decomposition of organic matter
4. Mine explosions
5. Manholes, wells, soil or cellar

Clinical Features

The clinical features vary with concentration of carbon dioxide gas inhalation. The features are described in Table 47.2.

Table 47.2: Showing percentage of carbon dioxide and clinical features produced

CO_2 concentration	Clinical features
Up to 2%	No physical uneasiness
2 - 5 %	Respiratory rate increases and deep
5 - 10%	Headache, dizziness, confusion, nausea, vomiting, dyspnea, disturbances of vision
> 10%	Tachycardia, increase heart rate, blood pressure raised, vasoconstriction
20 - 30 %	Fall of respiratory minute volume, convulsions
40 - 50%	Paralysis of respiratory center

Management

- Administer oxygen
- Supportive measures.

Autopsy Findings

- Cyanosis
- Froth at mouth and nostrils
- Congestion
- Petechial hemorrhages
- Dark fluid blood
- Venous engorgement

Medicolegal Importance

Accidental deaths — worker working in deep well, dampen pit, overcrowding in ill-ventilated room etc.

HYDROGEN SULFIDE

Properties

- Colorless, heavy, inflammable gas
- Rotten egg like smell
- Hydrogen sulfide, carbon dioxide and methane gases are formed in severs and called **sever gas**.

Sources

1. Formed during decomposition of organic substances containing sulfur
2. Found in sewer, cesspool, privy vaults.

Mechanism of Action

It acts as a cytochrome oxidase poison, blocking the electron transport chain that catalyzes the reduction of molecular oxygen to water.

Fatal Dose

1000 to 3000 p.p.m.

Clinical Features

- Breathlessness
- Cough
- Giddiness
- Nausea
- Lacrimation
- Photophobia
- Keratoconjunctivitis
- Muscular weakness
- CNS depression
- Delirium
- Convulsions
- Coma
- Death.

Management

- Shift the patient from vitiated environment
- Protect airway
- Oxygen administration
- Intravenous fluid and vasopressors
- Treat pulmonary edema with furosemide
- Supportive measures.

Autopsy Findings

- Signs of asphyxia
- Rotten egg like odor
- Postmortem lividity is greenish blue due to partial formation of sulfhemoglobin.
- Blood and viscera — greenish —purple.
- Petechial hemorrhage.
- Evidence of respiratory irritation in form of erosion of mucosa.[7]
- Lungs are congested and edematous.
- Liver — shows greenish-gray or ashen tint due to postmortem combination of hydrogen sulfide and methemoglobin.
- Urine thiosulfate and serum sulfhemoglobin levels can be determined.[8]

Medicolegal Importance

1. Accidental deaths
2. Occupational hazard for workers working in sewer tanks etc.
3. Putrefaction is rapid.

METHYL ISOCYANATE (MIC)

Properties

- Colorless liquid with pungent sweetish smell below 27°C
- Becomes gas at 39°C
- Highly volatile and inflammable

Uses

1. Manufacture of carbamate pesticide — carbaryl
2. Manufacture of adhesive
3. Manufacture of plastics

Mechanism of Action

Causes carbamylation at biochemical level

Clinical Features

Inhalation

- Lacrimation
- Irritation of eyes
- Blurring of vision
- Photophobia
- Corneal ulceration
- Cough
- Dyspnea
- Chest pain
- Hemoptysis
- Pulmonary edema
- Convulsions
- Coma
- Death.

Dermal

- Erythema
- Vesication.

Management

- Decontamination of skin and eyes
- Oxygen administration
- Bronchodilators and steroids
- Supportive

Autopsy Findings

- Signs of asphyxia
- Pulmonary edema
- Cerebral edema
- Visceral congestion
- In delayed death — degeneration of brain, heart, lung, liver and kidneys.

Medicolegal Importance

1. Accidental death
2. MIC was involved in Bhopal tragedy that occurred in 1984 causing more than 2000 deaths.[9]

REFERENCES

1. Matthew H, Lawson AAH. Poisoning by toxic inhalants. In: Treatment of common acute poisoning, 3rd edn. 1975. Churchill Livingstone, Edinburgh. 56-68.
2. Klassen CD. Nonmetallic environmental toxicants, air pollutants, solvents and vapors and pesticides. In: Gilman AG, Rall TW, Nies AS, Taylor P (eds) Goodman and Gilman's the Pharmacological basis of Therapeutics, Vol. II, 8th edn. 1991. Pregamon Press, New York. 1615-21.
3. Long PI. Dermal changes associated with carbon monoxide intoxication. JAMA 1968; 205: 50-1.
4. Henry JA, Wiseman HM. In: Management of poisoning. WHO handbook for health care workers, 1st Indian edn. 1998. 167-9.
5. Ferguson LS, Burke MI, Choromokos ER. Carbon monoxide retinopathy. Arch Ophthalmol 1985; 10: 66-8.
6. Chale SN. Carbon monoxide poisoning. In: Viccellio P (ed) Handbook of Medical Toxicology, 1st edn. 1993. Little, Brown and Company, Boston. 639-47.
7. Ago M, Ago K, Ogata M. Two fatalities by hydrogen sulfide poisoning: variation of pathological and toxicological findings. Leg Med 2008; 10:148-52.
8. Singh A, Sharma BR. Hydrogen sulphide poisoning: a case report of quadruple fatalities. J Punjab Acad Forensic Med Toxicol 2008; 8:38-40.
9. Mehta PS, Mehta AS, Mehta SJ, Makjijani AB. Bhopal tragedy's health effects: a review of methyl isocyanate toxicity. JAMA 1990;264:2781-7.

CHAPTER 48

Food Poisoning

One of the most striking changes in public health during the past decades has been the increase in the incidence of food poisoning and, at the same time, in our knowledge of the multiple factors responsible for it.

— Sir Graham Wilson

- *Food poisoning means illness resulting from ingestion of food with microbial or non-microbial contamination.* In other words, it is an acute gastroenteritis caused by ingestion of food or drink contaminated with either living bacteria or their toxins or chemical substances and poisons derived from plants and animals.[1]
- Food poisoning infections range from trivial intestinal disorders to life-endangering bacterial invasions of the bloodstream.[2]

Causes

- Poisoning by microbial contamination
- Poisoning by non-microbial contamination

Microbial Contamination

I. Bacteria

- Bacillus cereus
- Staphylococcus aureus
- Salmonella group (except *S. typhi*)
- Shigella
- Vibrio
- Escherichia coli
- Campylobacter
- Yersinia enterocolitics
- Listeria monocytogenes
- Clostridium.

II. Viruses

- Rotavirus
- Adenovirus
- Parvovirus.

III. Protozoa

- Giardia lamblia.

IV. Fungi

- Aspergillus flavus
- Fusarium roseum.

Non-microbial Contamination

I. Vegetable origin

- Lathyrus sativus
- Mushrooms
- Aggemone mexicana

II. Animal sources

- Poisonous fish like shellfish, scombroid fish etc.
- Mussel.

III. Chemicals

- Flavouring agents
- Coloring agents
- Preservatives.

1. Mycotoxins are toxic metabolites produced by molds. The disease caused by these metabolites, either by contact or by inadverant ingestion of the toxin when present in food or feeds, is called mycotoxicoses. Mycotoxicoses differ from mycoses. Mycoses means generalized invasion of living tissue by an actively growing fungus.[3]
2. Food additive: Food and Agriculture Organization of United Nations (FAO) defines food additive as "a non-nutritive substance added intentionally to food, generally in small quantities to improve its appearance, texture or storage properties".

3. Food poisoning outbreaks are associated with meat, sweat-marts (custards, cream confectionery, puddings, cakes etc), fish, egg and egg products, milk and milk products, vegetables and fruits.[4]

FOOD POISONING BY BACTERIA

- Food-borne bacterial toxins causes illness by two way:[5]
  1. Ingestion of food contaminated with microbial toxins or
  2. Ingestion of bacteria in contaminated food, which leads to intestinal colonization of bacteria and endogenous production of toxins.
- Some bacteria act through both mechanisms (described above) for example, B. cereus, C. botulinum, V. cholerae etc.
- Food poisoning due to C. perfringens has a slightly longer incubation period (8 – 14 hours) and results from the survival of heat resistant spores in an inadequately cooked food.[6]
- The clinical features and bacteria involved are summarized[7] in Table 48.1

Differential Diagnosis

1. Ulcerative colitis
2. Amebiasis
3. Heavy metal poisoning
4. Irritable bowel syndrome

Autopsy Findings

- In most of the cases (except botulism) there is gastrointestinal congestion, in some cases; there may be ulceration of mucosa or findings of gastro-enteritis.
- Abdominal organs are congested.

Samples to be Preserved

1. Stool (Table 48.2)
2. Vomitus
3. Remnants of food

Table 48.1: Summarizing bacteria and the symptoms produced by them

Bacteria	*Symptoms*	*Food sources*
A. Incubation period: 1-6 hours		
S. aureus	Nausea, vomiting, diarrhea	Poultry, salads, cream, pastries
B. cereus	Nausea, vomiting, diarrhea	Meat, fried rice
B. Incubation period: 8-16 hours		
C. perfrigens	Abdominal cramps, diarrhea	Beef, poultry, legume, gravies
C. Incubation period: > 16 hours		
V. cholerae		
E. coli	Watery diarrhea	Shell fish, water, salad, cheese, meats
Salmonella sapps.	Inflammatory diarrhea	Beef, poultry, egg, dairy products
Shigella sapps.	Dysentery	Egg, salad, lettuce, raw vegetables
V. Parahemolyticus	Dysentery	Molluscs, crustaceans

Table 48.2: Providing guidelines for stool collection and preservation

Causative agent	*How to collect*	*How to preserve*
Virus	Stool sample collected within 48-72 hours	Put stool sample in clean container. Refrigerate at 4°C (not to freeze)
Bacteria	Sample collected during active diarrhea with two rectal or stool sample. Place the swabs in Cary-Blair medium	- Transfer to lab quickly - If there is delay for analysis, freeze the sample at -70°C
Parasite	- Stool sample collected in clean container. - Place some stool sample into 10% formalin and polyvinyl alcohol preservative in a ratio of one part of stool to three parts preservative and mix well	Store at room temperature

Medicolegal Importance

1. Mass food poisoning may occur while having food at common eatery/function.
2. Public health authorities have to be informed.

REFERENCES

1. Park K. Food poisoning. In: Park's Textbook of Preventive and Social Medicine, 14th edn. 1995. M/S Banarsidas Bhanot Publishers, Jabalpur. 164-6.
2. Sir Howie J. Introduction. In: Taylor J (ed) Bacterial food poisoning, 1st edn. 1969. The Royal Society of Health, United Kingdom.
3. Lillehoj EB, Ciegler A, Detroy RW. Introduction. In: Blood FR (Ed): Essays in Toxicology, Vol. 2, 1st ed 1970. Academic Press, New York. 2-4.
4. Cockburn C. Reporting and incidence of food poisoning. In: Taylor J (Ed): Bacterial food poisoning, 1st edn. 1969. The Royal Society of Health, United Kingdom.
5. London MH. Food-borne toxins. In: Viccellio P (ed) Handbook of Medical Toxicology, 1st edn. 1993. Little, Brown and Company, Boston. 648-60.
6. Butterton JR, Calderwood SB. Acute infectious diarrheal diseases and bacterial food poisoning. In: Fauci AS, Braunwald E, Isselbacher KJ, Wilson JD, Martin JB, Kasper DL, Hauser SL, Longo DL (Eds) Harrison's Principles of Internal Medicine, Vol.2, 14th edn. 1998. McGraw-Hill, New York. 796-801.
7. Chowdhury AA, Nagar VS, Desai S. Food poisoning. Milestone 2004; 3: 49-51.

CHAPTER 49

Drug Dependence and Abuse

There is nothing makes a man suspect much, more than to know little.

- Francis Bacon

Psychoactive drugs are agents capable of altering the mental functioning of a person

There are four patterns of drug abuse.
1. Acute intoxication
2. Substance dependence
3. Harmful use
4. Withdrawal state

Acute Intoxication

Acute intoxication is a transient condition following the administration of alcohol or other psychoactive substances, resulting in disturbances in the level of consciousness, cognition, perception, affect or behavior or other psycho-physiological functions and responses.

Substance Dependence

Substance dependence is a cluster of physiological, behavioral and cognitive phenomenon in which the use of a substance or a class of substances taken on a much higher priority for a given individuals than other behaviors that once had greater value.

Harmful Use

Harmful use is characterized by:
1. Continued drug use despite awareness of harmful medical and/or social effects of drug being used and/or
2. A pattern of physical hazardous use of drug.

Substance Withdrawal

Substance withdrawal is a condition where symptoms results from the cessation of substance of abuse accompanied by a maladaptive behavior change.

Addiction

Addiction denotes a chronic disorder characterized by compulsive use of drugs resulting in physical, psychological and social harm and continued use despite evidence of that harm.

Classification

Psychoactive substances or drugs of dependence and abuse are classified as:
1. Ethanol
2. Tobacco
3. Opioids
4. Cannabis
5. Cocaine
6. Amphetamines and others
7. Hallucinogens — LSD, phencyclidine
8. Tranquillizers, sedatives and hypnotics — barbiturates, benzodiazepines etc.
9. Inhalants — solvents, ethers etc.
10. Miscellaneous: caffeine, Datura, analgesics etc.

Alcohol remains the preferred agent over the years, however many newer psychoactive drugs have joined it. These drugs are called as recreational drugs and includes marijuana (ganja), LSD, amphetamine etc. The recent trend identifies club drugs as new sojourn. These are referred as club drugs because of their prevalence at dance parties, rave parties and nightclubs. The most prominent club drugs[1] are given in Table 49.1.

Mechanism of Drugs of Misuse

1. Mimicking or substituting for natural transmitters as:
   - Opioids — endorphin/encephalin
   - Alcohol — GABA-A/endorphin

Table 49.1: Club drugs and their street names

Drugs	*Street names*
MDMA (3,4-methylenedioxymethamphetamine)	Ecstasy, X, M, rolls
GHB (gamma-hydroxybutyrate)	G, liquid ecstasy, soap
Flunitrazepam (Rohypnol)	Mexican valium, circles
Ketamine (Ketalar)	K, Special K, jet

- Benzodiazepines — GABA-A
- Cannabis — Anandamide ('ananda' is a Sanskrit word and it means bliss)
- LSD — 5-HT.

2. Increasing endogenous transmitter release
   - Cocaine — dopamine
   - Amphetamine — dopamine
   - Ecstasy — 5-HT/dopamine
   - Solvents — noradrenalin (?)
3. Blocking natural transmitters
   - Alcohol — glutamate
   - Barbiturates — glutamate.

Complications of Drug Abuse

A. Medical complications
- Malnutrition
- Self-neglect
- Dental decay
- Thrombophlebitis
- Pulmonary embolism
- Cellulites/abscess/septicemia
- Transmission of HIV/hepatitis B and C
- Psychiatric complications
- Death.

B. Social complications
- Social aloofness/isolation
- Antisocial behavior
- Theft/violence/crime.

Examination of a Person with Substance Abuse

- Record Blood pressure
- Pulse rate
- Temperature
- Pupil size
- Pupillary reaction to light
- Conscious level – lethargy, stupor/coma
- Restlessness/agitation
- Glasgow coma scale
- Orientation in time/place/person
- Speech
- Pallor
- Flushing
- Tremors at rest
- Yawning
- Lacrimation
- Rhinorrhea
- Gooseflesh
- Bowel sounds
- Presence of needle tracks
- Disordered perception
- Coordination
- Gait
- Romberg's test
- Auscultation of the chest
- Other systemic examination.

Autopsy Findings

- Clothes may contain drug, packets/chilam (Fig. 49.1)/ needle-syringe/tourniquet etc.
- Emaciation
- Injection marks in intravenous drug abuser, there may be multiple fresh injection marks and/or old linear track scars with fibrosis of veins often on the antecubital fossae, forearms, and dorsa of hands. Phlebitis of veins may be noted.
- Punctate areas of black discoloration (soot tattooing) may be noted and are caused by deposition of carbonaceous materials along the tract of needle. Such tattooing is called "**turkey skin**" as it resembles the plucked bird.

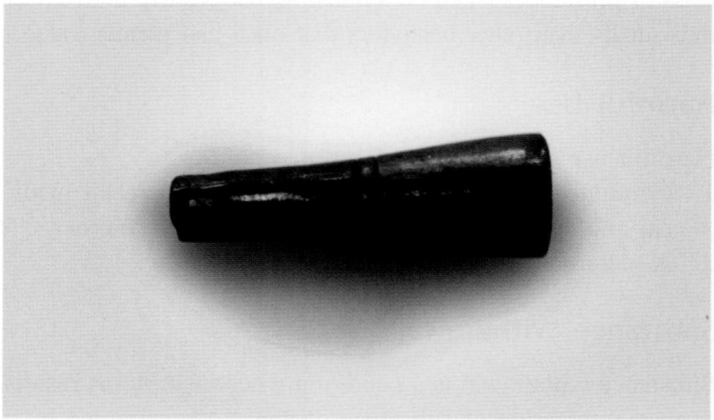

FIG. 49.1: Showing chilum for drug smoking

- Injection marks in subcutaneous drug user are in form of multiple circumscribed scars and are known as **skin poppers**.
- Multiple abscesses may be present. Regional lymph nodes are enlarged.
- Nasal septum ulceration and perforation may be noted in chronic cocaine snorting abuser.[2]
- Gastrointestinal tract may contain pills or capsules. There may be packets or containers as in the body packers and body stuffers.[3-5]
- There may be bowel ischemia or gangrene as in cocaine intoxication.[6]
- Rhabdomyolysis.[7]
- Pulmonary edema, tuberculosis may be present. There may be focal bleeding in lung, hemosiderin containing histiocytes, focal fibrosis and angiothrombosis.[8]
- There may be multiple spleen infarctions with secondary mixed bacterial infection and abscesses in chronic cocaine abuser.[9]
- There may be infective endocarditis as sequelae to septic injection site and practice.

REFERENCES

1. Gahlinger PM. Club drugs: MDMA, Gamma-hydroxybutyrate (GHB), rohypnol and ketamine. Am Fam Physician 2004; 69:2619-26.
2. Vilensky W. Illicit and licit drugs causing perforation of the nasal septum. J Forensic Sci 1982; 27: 958-62.
3. McCarron MM, Wood JD. The cocaine 'body packer' syndrome: Diagnosis and treatment. JAMA 1983; 250: 1417-20.
4. Sinner WN. The gastrointestinal tract as a vehicle for drug smuggling. Gastrointest Radiol 1981; 6: 319-23.
5. Roberts J, Price D, Goldfrank LR. The body stuffer syndrome: A clandestine form of drug overdose. Am J Emerg Med 1986; 4: 21-7.
6. Nalbandian H, Sheth N, Dietrich R, Georgious J. Intestinal ischemia caused by cocaine ingestion. Surgery 1985; 3: 374-6.
7. Merigian KS, Roberts JR. Cocaine intoxication: hyperpyrexia, rhabdomyolysis and acute renal failure. J Toxicol Clin Toxicol 1987; 25: 135-48.
8. Kringsholm B, Christoffersen P. Lung and heart pathology in fatal drug addiction. A consecutive autopsy study. Forensic Sci Int 1987; 34: 39-51.
9. Dettmeyer R, Schlamann M, Madea B. Cocaine-associated abscess with lethal sepsis after splenic infarction in a 17-year-old woman. Forensic Sci Int 2004; 140: 21-3.

CHAPTER 50

War Gases

Social justice cannot be attained by violence. Violence kills what it intends to create.

— Pope John Paul II

Introduction

War gases are the agents used to kill, injure or incapacitate the enemies. In civil conditions, these gases are used to disperse the unruly mob. The history of war gases begins with First World War where more than 100,000 people died and about 1.2 million affected due to use of chlorine, phosgene, and nitrogen mustard. In Second World War, the Germans developed and used number of nerve agents (tabun, sarin and soman together referred as "G" military agents) whereas English developed VX in 1952.[1]

Classification

1. Lacrimators: These are tear gases and causes tearing of eyes.
   Examples are:
   - Chloracetophenon (CAP)
   - Bromobenzyl cyanide (BBC)
   - Ethyl-iodo-acetate (KSK).
2. Lung irritants: These are asphyxiants or choking agents
   Examples are:
   - Chlorine
   - Phosgene
   - Diphosgene
   - Chloropicrin.
3. Vesicants: These are the agents that cause blisters
   Examples are:
   - Mustard gas
   - Lewisite.
4. Sternutators: These are nasal irritants
   Examples are:
   - Diphenylamine chlorarsine (DM)
   - Diphenyl chlorarsine (DA)
   - Diphenyl cyanarsine (DC).
5. Paralysants:
   Examples are:
   - Carbon monoxide
   - Hydrogen sulfide.
6. Nerve gases: These agents have acetylcholine like action.
   Examples are:
   - Tabun
   - Sarin
   - Soman
   - VX.

LACHRYMATORS (TEAR GASES)

The gases are fired in artillery shells or pen guns to disperse the rowdy mob.

Clinical Features

- The vapor of gas causes intense irritation of eye and lacrimation
- Spasm of eyelid
- Nausea and vomiting
- Irritation of air passage and sore throat
- Rhinorrhea
- Bronchorrhea
- Cough
- Prolonged exposure leads to blistering of skin, conjunctivitis, corneal ulceration, keratitis, and pneumonitis
- In rare case, they may cause acute laryngotracheobronchitis or death.[2]

Management

- Remove patient from exposure site
- Irrigation of eye
- Weak sodium carbonate solution may be applied to the affected skin.

REFERENCES

1. Eckert WG. Mass deaths by gas or chemical poisoning: a historical perspective. Am J Forensic Med Pathol 1991; 12:119-25.
2. Chapman AJ, White C. Death resulting from lacrimating agents. J Forensic Sci 1978; 23: 527-30.

Index

Page numbers followed by *f* refer to figures, and those followed by *t* refer to tables.

R